Also by Henry Kissinger

Years of Upheaval

HENRY KISSINGER

Years of Upheaval

LITTLE, BROWN AND COMPANY · BOSTON · TORONTO

LIBRARY OF CONGRESS CATALOG CARD NO. 81-86320

FIRST EDITION

The author is grateful to the following companies for permission to quote from selected material;
  CBS Inc. for excerpts from "A Conversation with Henry Kissinger" © CBS Inc. 1973/74. All
rights reserved. Originally broadcast February 1, 1973, over the CBS Television Network as part of the
CBS News Special Report: "A Conversation with Henry Kissinger"/*The CBS Evening News with
Walter Cronkite*/over the CBS Radio Network on *First Line Report* on June 4, 1974.
  Foreign Service Journal for excerpts from "U.S. Covert Actions in Chile, 1971–1973," December
1978.
  NBC News for excerpts from *Meet the Press* aired on January 28, 1973, and April 1, 1973.
  Newsweek for excerpts from "A Prisoner of Rhetoric" March 26, 1973, Copyright 1973, by
Newsweek, Inc. All rights reserved. Reprinted by permission.
  The *New York Times* for excerpts © 1972, 1973, 1974, by The New York Times Company.
Reprinted by permission.
  United Feature Syndicate, Inc. for excerpts from columns by Jack Anderson © 1972 United Feature
Syndicate, Inc.
  Universal Press Syndicate for excerpts from "The Price of Change" by William F. Buckley, Jr.
Copyright, 1980, Universal Press Syndicate. Reprinted with permission. All rights reserved.
  Excerpts from *White House Years* by Henry Kissinger (1979) courtesy of Little, Brown and
Company.
  The author is also grateful to the *Daily Telegraph,* the *Chicago Tribune, The Times* (London), and
the *Washington Post.*
  The maps on pages 456, 457, 505, and 533 are based on maps by Carta, Jerusalem, used in Chaim
Herzog, *The War of Atonement: October 1973* (London: George Weidenfeld & Nicolson Ltd., 1975;
Boston: Little, Brown and Company, 1975).

MV
*Published simultaneously in Canada
by Little, Brown & Company (Canada) Limited*

PRINTED IN THE UNITED STATES OF AMERICA

To Nancy

Contents

List of Illustrations

List of Maps

Foreword

A STRANGE combination of circumstances caused me to be entrusted with the day-to-day conduct of our nation's foreign policy during Richard Nixon's second term — a time of upheaval without precedent in this century. A President fresh from the second largest electoral victory in our history was unseated in a revolution that his own actions had triggered and his conduct could not quell. And amid the disintegration of the Nixon Presidency there occurred an explosion in the Middle East, disputes with our allies, an energy crisis, the unraveling of the Vietnam settlement, and a bitter domestic controversy over US–Soviet relations. We had begun Nixon's second term imagining that we were on the threshold of a creative new era in international affairs; seldom, if ever, had so many elements of foreign policy appeared malleable simultaneously. Within months we confronted a nightmarish collapse of authority at home and a desperate struggle to keep foreign adversaries from transforming it into an assault on our nation's security and that of other free peoples.

Nixon's first term (1969–1973) — the subject of my earlier volume, *White House Years* — was in a sense an adolescence. Amid turmoil over Indochina, the Administration was able to dominate events and help shape a new international structure of relations among the superpowers. Diplomacy in the second term, which ended abruptly in the late summer of 1974, was a rude accession of maturity. A weakened executive authority magnified the difficulty of every challenge even while the world afforded no respite from America's responsibilities as the leader and protector of the democracies.

Watergate had a severe impact on the conduct of diplomacy in almost all its dimensions, providing an object lesson, if one was needed, in how crucial a strong President is for the design and execution of a creative foreign policy. Yet through it all we managed to preserve the basic design of our foreign policy and even scored some important successes. American diplomacy in the Middle East during and following the October 1973 war contributed to a peace process that has continued, with great advances and some setbacks, to this day. And we laid the basis for mastering the energy crisis. It was an extraordinary period of testing, but statesmen do not have the right to ask to serve only in simple times.

During the years covered in this volume, my own perspective changed, and not only because of our domestic upheaval. On September 22, 1973,

I became Secretary of State, having served for Nixon's first four and a half years in the White House as Assistant to the President for National Security Affairs. As Secretary of State I was responsible for a much broader range of problems than as the national security adviser, who has the luxury of selecting those issues that seem of paramount importance. Most important, it fell to me to attempt to insulate foreign policy as much as possible from the domestic catastrophe. This role, imposed by necessity and by a seeming national instinct for survival, was buttressed in many fields by a bipartisan consensus that created almost a separate protected political process for the international conduct of the American government.

In describing the foreign policy of the period of Nixon's fall, the task of the memorialist is even more complex than usual. Intangibles of motivation and mood are more elusive still than with respect to the previous period. Inevitably what I have set down reflects my own vantage point; it is an account of my perceptions and convictions, which will have to be assessed in relation to what others thought and felt and what light documents unavailable to my researchers and me — many of them in foreign archives — will in time throw on the subjects discussed here. I intend to leave an annotated copy of this volume with my papers for the use of scholars who may someday wish to pursue the period in greater detail. This memoir is a description of how the issues appeared to one of the participants shaping the decisions. I have made a major and I hope conscientious effort to document my assertions.

I am grateful to the Secretary of State, the Director of the Central Intelligence Agency, the Under Secretary of Defense for Policy, and the Assistant to the President for National Security Affairs and their staffs for their cooperation in reviewing and clearing classified materials, including quotations. Changes they requested were made. President Nixon has kindly given his permission to cite some materials in his Presidential files.

I owe a deep debt of gratitude to associates who have sustained me since we served together in government and without whose skill and dedication this work would never have been completed. Peter W. Rodman, friend, confidant, and associate for over a decade, made a major contribution as editor, did a substantial part of the research, and was invaluable in his wise advice. William G. Hyland made a key contribution with his research and insight on Western European and Soviet affairs. Rosemary Neaher Niehuss did a superb job of research on the Middle East and the energy crisis, which occupy such a substantial part of this book; she was skillful, thoughtful, and indefatigable in organizing the voluminous material into manageable form. Mary E. Brownell applied her knowledge, judgment, and patience in dedicated research on a range of topics, from Chile to Watergate and the Washington Energy Conference.

William D. Rogers and Winston Lord permitted me to impose on a cherished friendship and read the entire manuscript; it owes a great deal to their counsel. Harold Evans was a great editor. He made an invaluable contribution with his fine eye for structure and his implacable assault on the redundant. Others who have read part of the manuscript and made helpful suggestions are Brent Scowcroft, Leonard Garment, David Ginsburg, John Freeman, Alan Greenspan, Peter Glenville, and Diane Sawyer.

Christine Vick, my personal assistant, was the manager and coordinator of all these simultaneous efforts. Not the least of her talents being the ability to read my handwriting, she was responsible for the typing of the manuscript. Chris kept track of the production of the book through its many stages, juggled the various prima donnas involved, kept everything on schedule, was always cheerful, in short, indispensable. Diane Tinker, Moira Dawson, Cathy Buchanan, Linda Komornik, and Christie Best did yeoman service assisting with the typing.

No author can receive better support from his publisher than Little, Brown extended to me. I am grateful to Genevieve Young for her perceptive (and persistent) editorial advice and to Betsy Pitha for her copyediting genius. Dick Sanderson produced excellent maps and Melissa Clemence expertly made the index.

At the Library of Congress, which houses my classified papers, my staff and I are grateful for the courtesy and assistance of Daniel J. Boorstin, the Librarian of Congress, and the dedicated staff of the Manuscript Division: Dr. Paul T. Heffron, chief; John Knowlton, Richard Bickel, Joseph Sullivan, Grover Batts, Mary Margaret Wolfskill, and Michael J. McElderry.

I owe a belated thanks also to Harry Zubkoff, whose news clipping and analysis service based in the Department of the Air Force has been of enormous value to US government personnel for years and has been an invaluable research aid for my staff in the preparation of *White House Years* and this volume.

I have dedicated this book to my wife, Nancy, who has given a new dimension to my life.

I alone am responsible for the contents of this book as I am for the actions it describes.

Washington, D.C.
November 1981

Note to the Reader

IN THIS volume I am yielding to the *Pinyin* phonetic spelling system officially adopted by the People's Republic of China on January 1, 1979, for the standardized transliteration of Chinese characters into languages using the Roman alphabet. Thus Mao Tse-tung becomes Mao Zedong, Chou En-lai becomes Zhou Enlai, and so forth. The old spelling is given in parentheses in the index. In accordance with American journalistic practice, some of the most familiar names — geographic names such as China, Peking, for example — are in the old form.

Years
of Upheaval

I

A Moment of Hope

Decision at the Swimming Pool

AUGUST of 1973 in California was glorious. Each morning, seduced from official papers, I sat outside on the veranda behind my office at the Western White House in San Clemente and watched as the sun burned the fog off the ocean. Occasionally I saw a slight, stoop-shouldered figure amble along the edge of the cliff beyond which lay only the beach and the Pacific. In that tranquil setting Richard Nixon was enduring the long final torment of his political career. Outside of the seclusion of his San Clemente retreat, the country buzzed with heated speculation about whether he would survive as President. He himself seemed calm. He rarely talked about Watergate — never illuminatingly. One had to know Nixon well to recognize his inner turmoil in the faraway look and the frozen melancholy of his features.

On the afternoon of August 21, Julie Nixon Eisenhower telephoned me to ask if my children, Elizabeth and David, wanted to come swim in the pool of the Nixon residence. Indeed they would. Later she called again and invited me to join them. I got my swimming trunks and walked over from my office, past the helicopter pad, to the Nixon family quarters, La Casa Pacifica, a quiet Spanish-style villa set off from the staff compound by large cypress trees and a high white wall. Manolo Sanchez, whose unstinting admiration of his master disproved the adage that no man is a hero to his valet, greeted me. Soon Nixon appeared and joined me and my children in the water. After a minute he suggested we go to the shallow end of the pool and chat about his news conference scheduled for the next morning. It was not the first time that my chief had discussed weighty matters with me in aquatic surroundings. At Camp David in April 1970, swimming in the pool while I walked along the edge, he had communicated his final decision to order American troops into the Cambodian sanctuaries.

I sat on the steps of the pool; the President of the United States floated on his back in the water. Matter-of-factly we reviewed some answers he proposed to give to foreign policy questions. Suddenly, without warmth or enthusiasm, he said: "I shall open the press conference by announcing your appointment as Secretary of State.'' It was the first time he had mentioned the subject to me.

It was not, of course, the first I had heard of it. Watergate had made the hitherto preeminent position of White House assistants untenable. My influence in the rest of the government depended on Presidential authority, and this was palpably draining away in endless revelations of tawdry acts, some puerile, some illegal. Alexander Haig, recalled as Presidential chief of staff in May, had volunteered to me earlier in the summer that he saw no other solution than to appoint me Secretary of State. The then Secretary, William P. Rogers, was expected to leave by the end of the summer in any event. Haig kept me informed of his tortuous discussions with Nixon on the subject; they could not have been easy. It was a painful decision for Nixon because it symbolized — perhaps more than any of the Watergate headlines — how wounded he was. He had never wanted a strong Secretary of State; foreign policy, he had asserted in his 1968 campaign, would be run from the White House. And so it had been. If Nixon was ready to bend this principle it showed how weak he had become.

I replied lamely that I hoped to justify his confidence. It was a platitude to maintain the fiction that he was conferring a great boon on me. In fact, both Nixon and I knew there was no other choice.

The next morning I received a phone call from Kenneth Rush, the Deputy Secretary of State. He congratulated me and pledged the full support of the Department. This was a generous gesture, especially as Rush undoubtedly knew that but for Watergate he, not I, would have been Bill Rogers's successor.[1] Rogers also called with his congratulations; we chatted politely but briefly. Then I settled back to watch the press conference on television.

Just as Nixon began to speak, my good friend the talented and beautiful Norwegian actress Liv Ullmann telephoned from Oslo on a matter I have since forgotten. I took the call to explain why I could not talk just then. I said that the President was making an important announcement on television. Since I coyly did not tell her what it was, I needed to add yet another sentence of explanation and by the time that was over, so was Nixon's brief reference to me. After announcing Rogers's resignation with warm and generous comments, Nixon named me as his replacement with these terse words: ''Dr. Kissinger's qualifications for this post, I think, are well known by all of you ladies and gentlemen, as well as those looking to us [sic] and listening to us on television and radio.'' He did not elaborate what they were. So it happened that by the time I hung up the phone I had missed hearing myself named as the next Secretary of State.

Congratulatory phone calls flooded into my office, while the remainder of Nixon's news conference was consumed by an interrogation on

Watergate. I took the calls with mixed feelings. What might have been a simple moment of gratification was beset with deep anxiety, for the news conference dramatized how much the Administration was under siege. We were straining all our efforts to prevent the unraveling of the nation's foreign policy as Nixon's Presidency, and with it all executive authority, slowly disintegrated. I had achieved an office I had never imagined within my reach; yet I did not feel like celebrating. I could not erase from my mind the poignant thought of Richard Nixon so alone and beleaguered and, beneath the frozen surface, fearful just a few yards away while I was reaching the zenith of acclaim.

Opportunity Lost

IT was all so utterly different from what we had hoped for in 1973. The year had begun with glittering promise; rarely had a Presidential term started with such bright foreign policy prospects.

In January 1973, a decade of bitter domestic divisions seemed to be ending with the Vietnam war. An overwhelming electoral mandate the previous November had given Nixon an extraordinary opportunity to reach out to all men and women of goodwill and to heal the nation's wounds. The suspicions of the debate over Vietnam lingered, but its protagonists were partly exhausted by the ordeal, partly confused by a new world in which the slogans of a decade had lost their relevance. Sooner or later, we hoped, antiwar critics would take solace in the end of the war even if they continued to question the tactics used. And those who had supported us could take pride in the fact that the nation's sacrifices had preserved its honor. Nixon himself might be haunted by his eternal premonition that all success was ephemeral; he was stronger and safer than a lifetime of surviving disaster permitted him to accept. In reality he faced no significant opposition; he had, after all, carried every state in the Union except one. It was possible to hope that the anguish of the past decade might teach all sides the fundamental lesson that a society becomes great not by the victories of its factions over each other but by its reconciliations.

Perhaps we were too euphoric but we were convinced that the United States had before it a rare opportunity for creativity in its foreign policy. At last we could turn as a united people to tasks from which the preoccupation with Indochina had deflected us. The usual fate of leaders is to inherit some intractable problem or commitment that has its own momentum — as indeed the war in Vietnam had blighted Nixon's first term. Now suddenly many factors in international relations seemed amenable to creative diplomacy at the same time:

• With our allies, the industrial democracies of the Atlantic Alliance and Japan, Nixon had in his first term ended the brutish quarrel with

France, safeguarded our troop commitment to Europe from Congressional assault, and preserved the ties of alliance through the superficial "shocks" of America's new initiatives with its Communist adversaries. The political and economic strength of Europe and Japan invited new initiatives to reaffirm the common future and common values of the democracies.

• In Nixon's first term we had improved relations with both Communist giants, the Soviet Union and the People's Republic of China. Their mutual distrust and fear would complicate giving concrete form to their ideological hostility to us; neither could go too far in challenging us without driving us toward its mortal enemy. Freed of the Vietnam war, the United States could resist aggressive acts that threatened international order. Backed by an overwhelming mandate, Nixon had the possibility to undertake negotiations of fundamental scope.

• In the Middle East, Egypt was beginning to turn away from the Soviet Union. America's tenacious diplomatic strategy had contributed to this development, which offered unprecedented prospects for peace diplomacy.

• With the prestige of the Vietnam settlement and the improved relations among the superpowers, the Nixon Administration could turn confidently to the Third World. We planned a new approach to Latin America and intended to use that as a point of departure for a new pattern of cooperative relations between industrial and developing nations.

As for me, at the beginning of 1973 I felt especially detached from the battles of the first term. The bureaucratic pressures and personal rivalries that are such an integral part of life in Washington had lost much of their meaning for me. For I had decided to resign by the end of the year.

I felt at liberty to do so because the vision of a new period of foreign policy, no longer overshadowed by a divisive war, was coupled with the conviction that an end had to be put to the Byzantine administrative procedures of Nixon's first term. No longer should power be centralized in the hands of Presidential assistants acting in secret from the rest of the government. My friend the venerable and wise David Bruce argued that if I was serious about making our achievements permanent, I should be prepared to entrust their elaboration to others. If we had built well and true, the nation's foreign policy would have to be institutionalized. To leave a legacy, rather than a tour de force, we would have to entrust greater responsibility to the permanent officials of the Department of State and the Foreign Service. This, Bruce suggested not too delicately, could not happen while I dominated all decisions from my White House office.

Reluctantly, I had come to agree with him. There were, to be sure, less elevated reasons that reinforced the argument from principle. My secret trip to China in 1971 had destroyed my previous anonymity, making it possible for Nixon's critics to diminish his achievements by exalting my own. And while I did not consciously encourage the process, there was no consistent record of my resisting it, either. Thereafter, the White House missed few opportunities to cut me down to size: during the India-Pakistan crisis, in the run-up to the 1972 Moscow summit, during the final phase of the Vietnam peace negotiations.[2]

Nixon was not wrong; I had become too public a figure for the post of national security adviser. The intangible bond between President and Assistant had become too frayed for me to be able to function much longer at the hub of the complex system of Presidential policymaking that circumvented the regular bureaucracy — if indeed such a system would have been sustainable for another four years in any circumstances, which I doubt.

Moreover, the national security team had been revamped and I had no stomach for going through another round of jockeying as new members sought to establish their relative positions. Secretary of Defense Melvin R. Laird, the great survivor, had indicated his desire to leave well before the 1972 election. He was replaced in the new year by the thoughtful Elliot Richardson, with whom I worked well when he was Under Secretary of State in 1969–1970. After his electoral victory Nixon fulfilled his long-standing plan to move out CIA Director Richard Helms by appointing him Ambassador to Iran. Helms's successor was James R. Schlesinger, who had come to Nixon's attention for his managerial expertise at the Bureau of the Budget and his courageous handling of a nuclear testing controversy as head of the Atomic Energy Commission. Secretary of State Rogers was spared in the general housecleaning, only because he had asked for a separate departure date to make clear that his leaving was his choice and not part of a wholesale realignment. His request was granted, but Nixon intended to replace him during the summer with his new deputy, Kenneth Rush.

A few years earlier, at the height of some bureaucratic struggle or other, I had told William Safire, then a Presidential speechwriter, that my victories were bound to be both temporary and fragile. To continue my influence, I had to win every bureaucratic battle; to destroy my authority, a Cabinet member needed only one success. Such odds were not survivable over the long run.[3] I had in fact avoided them for a full Presidential term, but there was no sense in courting fate with a new, able, and psychologically fresh group.

For all these reasons I intended to stay long enough in 1973 to see the peace in Indochina established; to launch the new initiative toward the industrial democracies that came to be known as the Year of Europe; and to consolidate the new Moscow–Washington–Peking triangle. I had spoken tentatively about a post-Washington career with some close friends: perhaps a fellowship at All Souls College at Oxford. Nancy Maginnes had just consented to become my wife, though our plans were to be delayed repeatedly by the crises soon to descend on us.

I shall never know whether I would in fact have carried out my intention, or would have become so absorbed in the conduct of affairs as to defer my departure. Nor can I prove that our vision of a hopeful future was attainable. It is futile to speculate on "might-have-beens." All our calculations were soon to be overwhelmed by the elemental catastrophe of Watergate.

But it was still in this mood compounded of elation and relief that on January 24, 1973, four days after Nixon's second Inauguration, I crossed the narrow street between the White House and the Old Executive Office Building to brief journalists on the newly concluded Vietnam agreement. After going through the agreement section by section I closed my remarks with a deeply felt appeal for national reconciliation:

The President said yesterday that we have to remain vigilant, and so we shall, but we shall also dedicate ourselves to positive efforts. And as for us at home, it should be clear by now that no one in this war has had a monopoly of anguish and that no one in these debates has had a monopoly of moral insight. And now that at last we have achieved an agreement in which the United States did not prescribe the political future to its allies, an agreement which should preserve the dignity and the self-respect of all the parties, together with healing the wounds in Indochina we can begin to heal the wounds in America.

A Spanish poet once wrote: "Traveler, there is no path; paths are made by walking." In that fleeting moment of innocence — so uncharacteristic of the Nixon Administration — we were confident that in the second term we would travel the road of our hopes and that we would walk a path leading to a better future.

II

A Visit to Hanoi

ONE of the first tasks before us in 1973 was to consolidate the Vietnam peace agreement that had been signed in Paris on January 27. This was the objective that took me on one of the most unusual diplomatic trips of my career: my first visit to Hanoi. In the capital of our ferocious antagonists who had brought war to Indochina and upheaval to America, I intended to discuss with the North Vietnamese leaders the strict observance of the Paris Agreement that I had negotiated with Le Duc Tho and on that basis the possibility of a more positive relationship between our two countries.

The Paris Agreement

THE Agreement on Ending the War and Restoring Peace in Vietnam had become possible when after ten years of bitter war and four years of negotiating stalemate, North Vietnam accepted what it had heretofore adamantly rejected: the continued existence of the Saigon government. The Agreement called for an immediate cease-fire in place throughout Vietnam; for the withdrawal of all remaining American troops (about 27,000); and for the release of prisoners of war throughout Indochina. Hanoi's infiltration of troops and matériel into South Vietnam was prohibited. International supervisory machinery was to police the cease-fire and regulate the entry of replacement equipment through designated checkpoints. Another provision restored the seventeenth parallel as the Provisional Military Demarcation Line between North and South Vietnam, prohibited all military movement across it, and permitted civilian movement only by agreement between the Vietnamese parties. Hanoi further agreed to withdraw its forces from Laos and Cambodia and not to use these countries' territory for military action against South Vietnam. The political settlement in South Vietnam was left to future negotiations between the Vietnamese parties.

The United States had made a determined effort to end the war in Laos and Cambodia as well as in Vietnam. North Vietnam had consistently refused, on the excuse that such matters were within the jurisdiction of the peoples of Laos and Cambodia. This solicitude for the sovereignty of North Vietnam's neighbors would have been touching had it not been so unprecedented; it seemed to apply only to the withdrawal of Hanoi's forces, not to their introduction, since tens of thousands of North Vietnamese troops had been systematically violating the peace and sovereignty of Laos and Cambodia for two decades and were, of course, still there.

In the end, Le Duc Tho agreed to arrange a cease-fire in Laos. After "consultations" with the Communist forces in Laos (the Pathet Lao, who were in fact totally subordinate to Hanoi), Le Duc Tho pledged in October 1972 that Hanoi would bring about a cease-fire in Laos within thirty days of the cease-fire in Vietnam. By early January Le Duc Tho shortened the interval to fifteen days.

On Cambodia, he flatly refused to be specific, claiming — truthfully, as it turned out — that Hanoi had less influence over its Cambodian Communist ally, the Khmer Rouge. In our talks from September 1972 through January of 1973, Le Duc Tho assured me again and again that when the war was settled in Vietnam, there was "no reason" for the war to continue in Cambodia.[1] But Hanoi would make no formal commitment other than a private understanding that it would "contribute actively" to restoring peace in Cambodia after the Vietnam war was settled. After we pressed in vain for months, Nixon reluctantly concluded that we could obtain more only by continuing the war in Vietnam. It was obvious we had no support at home for holding up an otherwise acceptable Vietnam agreement because of Cambodia, where Congress had sought for several years to reduce our involvement and our aid to the absolute minimum. If we did not proceed, Congress was certain to cut off all funds for Cambodia *and* Vietnam. Moreover, in the view of our Embassy in Phnom Penh as well as of our military experts, the Cambodian Communists would not be able to prevail without North Vietnamese combat support, which in turn was precluded by the terms of the Paris Agreement.

We sought to protect our position by two further steps. First, we persuaded the Cambodian President, Lon Nol, to call once again (for at least the fifth time in three years) for a cease-fire in Cambodia and to declare a unilateral cessation of offensive military operations. Second, before initialing the Paris Agreement, I handed Le Duc Tho a statement to the effect that

if, pending a settlement in Cambodia, offensive military activities are undertaken there which would jeopardize the existing situation, such operations would be contrary to the spirit of Article 20 (b) of the Agreement and to the assumptions on which the Agreement is based.

In plain English, this meant that if the Khmer Rouge rejected Lon Nol's proclamation of a cease-fire the United States would continue military support for the Cambodian government. Le Duc Tho indicated that he understood.

The Paris accords with all their ambiguities reflected the balance of forces in Vietnam in the wake of the climactic battles of 1972. As with any peace settlement, it depended on the maintenance of that balance of forces. We had no illusions about Hanoi's long-range goal of subjugating all of Indochina. In the final phase of the negotiations in November and December 1972, I repeatedly warned Nixon to that effect.[2] But I was also persuaded that our people would not sustain the prolongation of the war for a period of time that would make a military difference. In August 1972 President Nguyen Van Thieu of South Vietnam had expressed to me his estimate that if the war continued, by December 1973 North Vietnam would be weaker than it was in March 1972 — a marginal improvement over where we were. And all our political experts were convinced that the newly elected Congress would cut off funds for the war, starting in January 1973, using as a first target the Administration's request for supplementary appropriations to finance the cost of resisting Hanoi's spring offensive of 1972.

We were, in short, not just getting out under the cynical cover of a "decent interval" before the final collapse. We hoped for a decent settlement. The Agreement's risks were etched painfully in the minds of all the negotiators on our side. But we had achieved far better terms than most had thought possible. By 1972 our critics had reached the conclusion that Hanoi would never settle for anything less than the overthrow of our ally, the Thieu government in Saigon. This we had successfully resisted. A non-Communist South Vietnam had been given the chance to survive. With the proper mixture of rewards and punishments for Hanoi, we thought we had a reasonable chance to maintain the uneasy equilibrium in Indochina; certainly a better chance *with* an agreement than by continuing an inconclusive war in the face of mounting hostility at home and the near-certainty of a Congressional cutoff of funds.

I shall deal in Chapter VIII with whether it was realistic to expect that we could assemble the proper mix of rewards and punishments. We thought so and we had reason for our belief. For present purposes it is enough to stress that our intention was to make the Paris Agreement work. This was my attitude when I left Washington on February 7, 1973, on an eleven-day Asian journey that was to take me to the capital of our recent enemy, North Vietnam, as well as to those of two old friends, Thailand and Laos, and of a new friend, the People's Republic of China.

My feelings as I prepared for the trip to Hanoi had none of the exultation at a patiently prepared breakthrough that had marked my secret trip to China. Nor was there the inherent drama of superpower diplomacy that had characterized my first trip to Moscow. Lacking, too, was the prospect of the easy camaraderie of my many visits to European capitals or the sense of shared purpose that transcended the courteous formality of consultations in Tokyo. For four years I had read every scrap of information about the North Vietnamese, at once so self-absorbed and so bellicose, so brave and so overbearing. What is the blend of qualities that lifts a people to dominion over neighbors of roughly comparable endowments? What had given Rome preeminence in the world of city-states or Prussia in Germany or Britain in Europe? No doubt many physical factors were involved. But material elements needed the impetus of intangibles of faith and dedication. These — unfortunately for us — Hanoi had in obsessive abundance.

The Vietnamese had lived through centuries of Chinese rule without losing their cultural identity, a nearly unheard-of feat. They had outlasted French occupation, all the time nurturing the conviction that it was their mission to inherit the French empire in Indochina. Lacking the humanity of their Laotian neighbors and the grace of their Cambodian neighbors, they strove for dominance by being not attractive but single-minded. So all-encompassing was their absorption with themselves that they became oblivious to the physical odds, indifferent to the probabilities by which the calculus of power is normally reckoned. And because there were always more Vietnamese prepared to die for their country than foreigners, their nationalism became the scourge of invaders and neighbors alike.

More than passion the Vietnamese had an invincible self-confidence and a contempt for things foreign. This disdain enabled them to manipulate other peoples — even their foreign supporters — with a cool sense of superiority, by an act of will turning their capital for over a decade into a center of international concern. What we considered insolent deception was another definition of truth; whatever served Hanoi's purposes represented historical necessity. Like a surgeon wielding a scalpel, Hanoi dissected the American psyche and probed our weaknesses, our national sense of guilt, our quest for final answers, our idealism, and, yes, even the values of its sympathizers, whom it duped no less cold-bloodedly than its adversaries. Our misfortune had been to get between these leaders and their obsessions.

Our Indochinese nightmare would be over; Hanoi's neighbors were not as fortunate. Propinquity condemned them to permanent terror. Our relief that the war had ended was matched by their foreboding that their freedom would end if we equated peace with withdrawal. The exultation of Washington was replaced by the uneasiness of those who depended on us the closer we approached the borders of that implacable country conducting its aggressions in the guise of victim.

A Visit to Bangkok

I N the arc stretching from the Mediterranean around the rim of the Indian Ocean, including the Middle East, the Indian subcontinent, and all of Southeast Asia, Thailand alone escaped colonial occupation in the nineteenth century and did it by a careful, unobtrusive manipulation of the contending powers. To be sure, its geographic location at the junction of the French and British colonial spheres made it a natural buffer between European empires. But such a location had more often led to partition than to independence.

In any event, opportunity never translates itself into reality automatically. Thailand had maintained its independence because its leaders skillfully exploited its geographic position to rescue a margin of independence from the rivalry of physically stronger states; because it had a cultural identity relatively immune to subversion from neighboring countries; and above all because its policy had the resilience of a bamboo reed but also its toughness.

During World War II, Thailand supported Japan when the latter's conquests made it predominant in Southeast Asia; it switched to the Allies when Japan's defeat became inevitable. It accomplished these gyrations with such matter-of-fact grace that they appeared not as treachery but as the natural conclusions drawn by a self-confident nationalism. Thailand seemed to have an inexhaustible supply of leaders to embody the exact nuance of policy needed for a given circumstance. When conditions changed, the leader was discarded (though never deprived of honor). There was a personality for each situation, all sharing the commitment to Thai independence. My friend Lee Kuan Yew, the brilliant Prime Minister of Singapore, used to say that we needed to watch carefully when the Thai leaders associated with us would be replaced; it would herald a sea change, whatever the formal protestations.

But while Thailand could be adaptable in its dealings with distant empires, it perceived less margin for maneuver in the face of aggressors located on its borders. It never wavered in its conviction that Hanoi's conquest of Indochina must be resisted because it would be a mortal threat to Thailand's survival. Zealots in faraway lands might consider the rulers of Hanoi as the innocent victims of foreign aggression who would conduct themselves peaceably toward their neighbors once the conflict in Vietnam was settled. The leaders of Thailand had no such illusions; their country had not survived by wishful thinking. In their minds a victory for Hanoi in South Vietnam would lead automatically to Communist domination of Cambodia and Laos; this in turn would increase the pressure on Thailand, especially on the northeast province, acquired only during the past century and culturally close to Laos. Thailand did not propose to face North Vietnam's strength, discipline, and determination alone. Not noted for exposing itself to unnecessary risks, it nevertheless had permitted President John F. Kennedy to send marines there in 1962 as a counterweight to North Vietnamese pressures on Laos. Thai troops fought alongside ours in Vietnam; Thailand provided air bases for the war in Vietnam from 1966 onward. It sent volunteers (and occasionally even regular forces) to assist the neutralist government of Laos whenever the North Vietnamese and Pathet Lao approached too close to the Mekong River, which formed the boundary between Laos and Thailand.

No doubt the leaders in Bangkok acted as they did — in the Thai tradition of relying on a distant strong country to balance a nearby danger — because they could not imagine that the United States would permit itself to lose a war. They were baffled by our increasingly shrill domestic divisions over what seemed to them a clear-cut menace. At first they wrote them off as the inexplicable maneuvers of immature foreigners. But when the Pentagon Papers disclosed to the whole world the extent of their carefully calibrated participation in the Indochina war, the cautious policymakers in Bangkok developed serious doubts, which bubbled just below the level of action.

It cannot be said that the Thai leaders greeted the Paris Agreement with jubilation. They could not really understand why a superpower should compromise with a smaller regional bully. They favored anything that seemed to assure the continued independence of South Vietnam and a neutral Laos and Cambodia on Thailand's borders. But they had too much experience with North Vietnam and were too skeptical of man's perfectibility to confuse a temporary — one hoped, prolonged — weakness of Hanoi with a change of heart. Sooner or later the Thai believed Hanoi would resume a hegemonic course, and they wanted to deflect it from the borders of their kingdom. Everything for them therefore depended on whether the United States would help maintain the balance of power in Indochina, whose disturbance had triggered our intervention in the first place.

I was not surprised to find Bangkok full of premonitions. The Prime Minister was Field Marshal Thanom Kittikachorn, who in the best Thai style hid a calculating intelligence behind a bland and seemingly ponderous exterior (thereby gaining additional time for reflection and warding off the impetuous pressures for which Americans were notorious). He embodied Thai reliance on the United States. After the Congress in June 1973 passed the law prohibiting any further American military operations in or over Indochina, Thanom disappeared in one of those nearly anonymous moves by which the Thai signal adaptation to new circumstances.

On February 9, 1973, when I saw him, Thanom did not act as if this outcome was foreordained. Still committed to the strategy of the previous decade, he essentially wanted to know the answer to two questions: How would we react to North Vietnamese violations of the Agreement? And how many forces would we keep in Southeast Asia, particularly in Thailand, to help preserve the balance of power in the area? I made clear that we had the most cold-blooded assessment of Hanoi's ambitions and we would not stand idly by if it engaged in massive violations of the Agreement. On the other hand, I hoped on my visit to Hanoi to encourage tendencies toward peaceful construction.

With respect to the American military presence in Southeast Asia, the fact was that I was not certain because so much depended on our domestic politics. So I waffled. Some troops would be withdrawn, given the fact of a Vietnam cease-fire and our domestic realities. But substantial forces would be left or else Hanoi would be practically invited to attack. There is, I suppose, no alternative to such generalities when one is faced with a theoretical quandary that eventually only experience can resolve. And to the horror of the peoples of Southeast Asia, Thai fears proved more well-founded than my reassurances.

The Dilemmas of Cambodia

THERE is no doubt that Cambodia was the orphan of the Vietnam settlement. The engagements regarding it were the least binding; its indigenous Communists were the most ferocious. The non-Communist Cambodians, despite their reputation for passivity, fought perhaps the most heroically of all the peoples of Indochina, with the least outside help.

In 1973 I still hoped that we could end the war without abandoning those who had relied on us. I was determined to try once again to negotiate a cease-fire for Cambodia. To arm myself for my talks in Hanoi and in Peking, I met in Bangkok with our Ambassador to Cambodia, Emory C. (Coby) Swank. Phnom Penh was not on my itinerary because Spiro T. Agnew was visiting there as well as Saigon; staking the Vice President's prestige to the South Vietnamese government was one of the minor inducements for President Thieu to sign the Paris Agreement. Thieu's venomous hatred of me would have made a visit by me to Saigon unproductive in any event. On the other hand, I could not visit the other two capitals of Indochina while omitting Saigon. Thus I was forced to miss Phnom Penh and discuss the future of Cambodia in Bangkok — an omen of things to come.

Ambassador Swank was anything but a hawk on Indochina. He observed the restrictions imposed by the Congress with conviction and efficiency — without the sense of frustration that seized me as I watched the slow throttling of a courageous people. We differed as is normal among serious individuals; but I respected his professionalism, his hon-

esty, and his ability. Though Swank did not believe a military solution
was possible, he also did not delude himself about the character of our
adversaries. He was convinced that the Khmer Rouge were determined
on total victory regardless of the Paris Agreement or the unilateral cease-
fire declared by Lon Nol. And they were being aided by Hanoi. Forty-
two thousand North Vietnamese troops remained in Cambodia, he told
us, now in clear violation of Article 20 of the Paris Agreement.[3] The
overwhelming majority (35,000) were servicing Hanoi's supply system
for South Vietnam — violating the clauses against maintaining base areas
and infiltration in the countries of Indochina. There were 7,000 combat
troops, of which half were supporting and assisting the Khmer Rouge.[4]
All this compared to the fewer than 200 American personnel in Cambodia, military *and* civilian, all under severe legislative restrictions
(which will be discussed in Chapter VIII). There were no signs of any
North Vietnamese withdrawals; perhaps it was too early, but if the situation persisted this would be a most serious betrayal of Hanoi's undertakings.

As for Cambodia's former neutralist leader, Prince Norodom Sihanouk, who was in exile in Peking, it was Swank's judgment that he had
become irrelevant; he no longer had a following in Phnom Penh; he was
distrusted by Communists and government leaders alike. Swank expressed the hope that he would be permitted to tell Lon Nol that on my
forthcoming visit to Peking neither I nor any of my associates would
have any dealings with Sihanouk.

As will be seen, Swank thus took a somewhat harder line on Sihanouk than I did. It made sense in terms of Swank's necessities in Phnom
Penh and the passions that had seized the Cambodian parties. Swank
told me that Lon Nol was prepared to negotiate with anybody except
Sihanouk: with Hanoi, with the Khmer Rouge, or with Peking. And
Sihanouk took the same position with respect to Lon Nol. Both parties
were willing to court oblivion if they could only take their hated enemy
with them into it.

The monumental ruins of Angkor Wat in northwestern Cambodia have
long puzzled historians. What happened to the magnificent civilization
that produced them? Why did it disappear without a trace when it once
dwarfed all surrounding countries? No convincing explanation has ever
been advanced. I wonder whether it is possible that Cambodians are
occasionally seized by a suicidal madness. Here were Sihanouk and Lon
Nol, who had worked in close harmony all of their lives, fighting to
mutual destruction rather than settling for a compromise of their relatively trivial differences. They found it easier to turn over their country
to Cambodia's traditional enemies or to a maniacal indigenous group
whom both feared and despised. Lon Nol's government was in fact Sihanouk's without the Prince; before Sihanouk was deposed, Lon Nol

had been his Prime Minister and Defense Minister, corruptly profiting from the North Vietnamese supply routes into the sanctuaries. Sihanouk in turn had invited our bombing of the sanctuaries and sentenced the Khmer Rouge leaders to death *in absentia*. Yet by 1973 both these aristocrats were courting the Khmer Rouge, who hated them, and the North Vietnamese, who sought to dominate them. Rarely can there have been a more striking example of personal animosity fatally overriding rational calculation. Both leaders could have survived their conflict, played a role of dignity, and spared their people a holocaust had they been prepared to subordinate their personal feud and their egos to the necessities of their nation. Unable to do so, they doomed themselves and Cambodia.

And it was this blind hatred that in 1973 was the key obstacle to our dealing with Sihanouk. The previous November I had told Chinese Vice Foreign Minister Qiao Guanhua that we were prepared to work with the Chinese to end the war in Cambodia in a manner that would give Sihanouk a significant role.[5] But for Sihanouk to resume his traditional balancing act among the various contenders for power in Cambodia, I insisted there had to be some contenders left to balance. So long as he was nominal head of one faction — the Khmer Rouge — that was implacably determined on total victory, Sihanouk was dooming himself to irrelevance if the war continued or total subservience if the Khmer Rouge won. Though we did not insist on Lon Nol's remaining in office, it was in Sihanouk's own interest that the non-Communist forces represented by Lon Nol should survive in some form. Otherwise Sihanouk would become a dispensable figurehead, useful only to legitimize a Communist-dominated Cambodia, after which he would surely be discarded. (This, of course, is precisely what happened.)

Swank and I differed marginally also on the utility of military operations to bring about the cease-fire we both considered essential. Swank thought a cease-fire was more probable if there was only a minimum of American military pressure. I was willing to test that hypothesis. But if it failed, I believed that military pressure would be necessary. Experience had taught me that a deadlock with the Indochinese Communists would be broken only if the alternative was more painful to them. As yet this was a theoretical point. Lon Nol's unilateral cease-fire declaration had just been put on the table. The Khmer Rouge had rejected it but Swank as well as I still hoped that perhaps they had not yet shown their hand completely. In our optimistic view the possibilities of a negotiated outcome in Cambodia had not yet been exhausted.

Like Lon Nol, Swank preferred negotiations through Hanoi. I had my doubts; I thought Peking the better intermediary. Lon Nol's preference might be more convenient in the short run; strategically, it was the less productive. Hanoi wanted Cambodia as a satellite. Its aim was to dom-

inate Cambodia, reopen its southern supply route, and demoralize South
Vietnam by creating the impression that its ultimate overlordship of In-
dochina was inevitable. China, on the other hand, was above all interested in an independent Cambodia. Peking did not wish to see Phnom
Penh as a satellite of Hanoi. It preferred independent states in Southeast
Asia, not a region dominated by North Vietnam with its historic enmity
of China and dependence on Moscow. This interest happened to coincide with ours; it was also imperative for the survival of South Vietnam.
I thus sought to negotiate through Peking (which implied a role for
Sihanouk, who was based there). But no decision needed to be made
right away. My forthcoming visits to Hanoi and Peking would shed light
on what was possible.

A Visit to Vientiane

FOR years I had been reading battle reports from Vientiane, and, as
often happens, the mind's eye had fashioned a relationship between
the magnitude of the events and the scene of their occurrence: the dateline "Vientiane" evoked images of an intense metropolis under siege.
In reality Vientiane is a quiet, dusty, hot provincial city inhabited by a
gentle, peaceable people. Its pace is slow, its manners conciliatory; all
Laos wanted was to be left alone. And this is precisely what its relentless North Vietnamese neighbor would not grant it.

Vientiane, the capital of Laos, nestles on the banks of the Mekong
River, which constitutes the boundary with Thailand. Rare indeed is the
capital located at the edge of the national territory, its city limit coincident with the frontier of another country. It was as if the Laotians,
terrified of their North Vietnamese neighbors, had fled as far away from
their threatening shadow as possible; as if the tactile presence of Thailand was an assurance of Laotian survival.

Since the late 1950s Laos had been the victim of its geographic circumstance. The Demilitarized Zone (DMZ) along Vietnam's seventeenth parallel barred massive, direct infiltration from North Vietnam
into South Vietnam without a flagrant violation of the 1954 Geneva
Accords. By some convoluted North Vietnamese logic, bypassing the
DMZ through the territory of another sovereign country seemed more
legitimate even though Laotian neutrality had also been solemnly guaranteed by the same accords. The Ho Chi Minh Trail (actually a whole
network of routes) was hacked through jungles covering the southern
half of Laos. As in Cambodia, Hanoi simply appropriated the territory
of a neighbor and expelled the local population. And as in Cambodia,
those Americans who favored helping Laos retain its independence found
themselves accused of "expanding" to a peaceful country a war that
had been implanted there by an illegal North Vietnamese occupation.

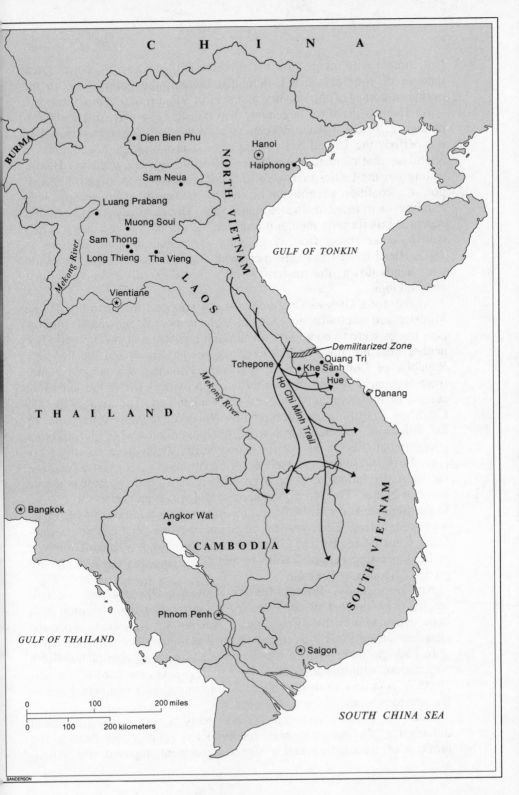

Southeast Asia, 1973

Not content with taking over the southern half of Laos, the North Vietnamese in 1961 armed a Communist faction, the Pathet Lao, in the northeast corner of the country and sent in some 6,000 combat troops.

As Hanoi's drive for hegemony was constant, so was America's ambivalence. In the 1950s, in keeping with the anti-Communist mood of the period, the United States supported a pro-Western government in Vientiane that claimed control over all of the national territory. Hanoi, testing out the tactics that were to become stereotyped, urged the creation of a coalition government headed by the neutralist Prince Souvanna Phouma — in fact a dedicated nationalist. The Kennedy Administration accepted this formula though it required the dispatch of marines to Thailand to deter Hanoi from completing the conquest of all of Laos in 1962. Hanoi treated this agreement with characteristic cynicism; it would win, hands down, the modern world's record for disregard of written undertakings.

At the 1962 Geneva Conference, Laos obtained the neutralist Prime Minister and neutralist government that Hanoi had demanded; all foreign troops were to be withdrawn through international checkpoints. But neither this, nor the fact that even the Soviet Union and the People's Republic of China recognized Souvanna Phouma, discouraged Hanoi from appropriating the two northeastern provinces under the exclusive control of its Communist stooges, the Pathet Lao. The area of the Ho Chi Minh Trail remained occupied by North Vietnamese forces. As for the withdrawal of foreign troops, all 666 American advisers left through international checkpoints; of the 6,000 North Vietnamese, exactly forty (yes, forty) presented themselves for repatriation — it must have been the weekly rotation quota or maybe officers in need of compassionate leave in Hanoi. The North Vietnamese did not even pretend to live up to the Geneva Accords, while trumpeting to the world the sins of American intervention. Each year the numbers of North Vietnamese on Laotian soil increased. By 1973, there were 60,000 North Vietnamese troops in Laos pressing toward Vientiane and occupying the entire border region contiguous to Vietnam.

Not surprisingly, Prime Minister Souvanna Phouma and his colleagues who greeted us on February 9 viewed the Paris accords with hope overshadowed by foreboding. It was not yet two weeks since the signature of the Paris Agreement and it was already becoming frayed.

In Laos no more than in Cambodia was there any sign of the North Vietnamese withdrawal required by Article 20. On the contrary, a new North Vietnamese division had been introduced into southern Laos in the previous week.

Such was Hanoi's contempt for bourgeois notions of legality that it did not feel the necessity even for hypocrisy — of going through the motions of recognizing that a signed agreement imposed any obligations. Le Duc Tho had given me in Paris a written undertaking that a cease-fire would come into being in Laos within fifteen days of the signature of the Agreement. That time period was nearly up and there was no sign whatever of implementation. Hanoi had suddenly made a cease-fire dependent — without a shred of legal basis and in plain conflict with the written understanding — on the conclusion of a political agreement. Then Hanoi topped this with another of its patented cynicisms. It stopped treating Souvanna Phouma as head of the neutralist faction; it suddenly discovered a new "neutralist" group that not even its most devoted adherents had heard of previously. Hanoi's stooges also insisted that they would sign no document that did not condemn American intervention, thereby incorporating Hanoi's warped interpretation into the legal instrument ending the conflict and inhibiting recourse to American power to uphold the Agreement.

Souvanna Phouma was determined not to accept such terms. He had fought tenaciously for his country's independence. Though willing, in his extremity, to accept American and Thai help, he wanted nothing so much as to have Laos disappear as a point of contention of international politics. Gentle and extraordinarily suave, he exemplified in his bearing the virtues of a people who have made their contribution to history through the grace of their life-style rather than martial qualities. It would in any case have been an uneven contest against an adversary possessing seven times the population. Laos, exposed daily to Hanoi's military and political blackmail, was no exception to the rule that no country actually dealing with Hanoi entertained a shred of the illusion of so many in our peace movement that North Vietnam was a benign nationalist power victimized by senseless and arbitrary American pressure.

Souvanna was prepared to continue his hazardous and complicated balancing act; he would play out the string of peace negotiations; he would run the risks of negotiating new arrangements. He neither complained nor whined. All he asked of us was not to remove the American weight on the scale.

On the evening of February 9 he gave a dinner for the American party in his simple villa at the outskirts of Vientiane. It looked like the residence of a French junior minister, without the trappings usually associated with presidential palaces. At the end of the meal Souvanna rose and delivered an eloquent and moving toast, which can serve as a summation of the hopes and fears of all in Indochina who wanted only to be left alone and looked to us for succor:

Dr. Kissinger and friends, we welcome you to Laos at this critical moment in our history. The very survival of Laos rests on your shoulders. But your shoulders are broad shoulders. We are counting on you to make our neighbors understand that all we want is peace. We are a very small country; we do not represent a danger to anybody. We count on you to make them know that the Lao people are pacific by tradition and by religion. We want only to be sovereign and independent. We ask that they let us live in peace on this little piece of ground that is left to us of our ancient kingdom. Our old kingdom used to be 17 million people; now it is just 3 million.

If pressure is kept on the North Vietnamese to understand the risk they run from violating the Agreement, then perhaps they will respect the Agreement. Laos must live in peace. The United States does not want its efforts to end in the hegemony of North Vietnam over Indochina. This was the desire of Ho Chi Minh, to replace the French as the dominators of Indochina. . . .

Therefore we must count on our great friends the Americans to help us survive. We hope, we dream, that this wish will be granted.

What a touching hope it was that a distant country, as far away as it is possible to be on the globe, would be able to convey to Laos's next-door neighbor a pacific intent that, given the latter's mind-set, may have spurred aggressiveness. And that we would be forever willing to defend the freedom of a distant people.

Perhaps because Souvanna's speech brought home to me as no formal negotiating session could have the fragility of these hopes and the nature of our responsibility, my reply did not rise to the nobility of my host. It was somewhat self-centered, as if a pedantic reassurance could ease an almost spiritual travail — though it made the essential point in which our Laotian hosts were interested:

Your Highness, I greatly appreciate the very moving things you have spoken. It is a very heavy responsibility you have assigned me. I have had the honor to serve in my present position for four years, and we have gone through great difficulties, and we have not come all this way in order to betray our friends at the beginning of a new Administration — after an election that was fought precisely on the issue of whether the United States would stand by its convictions.

The next morning, at Vientiane's airport just before leaving for Hanoi, I publicly called for strict implementation of the Paris Agreement and an early cease-fire in Laos.

At this writing, Laos is under Communist rule. Over 40,000 Vietnamese troops remain as an occupation force. Souvanna is under house arrest. Between 10,000 and 30,000 political prisoners are in labor camps in the name of "re-education." The Hmong (Meo) tribesmen who fought the North Vietnamese with our help are being systematically exterminated, some by poison gas. Hundreds of thousands of Laotians have fled in terror to Thailand.

All that has happened since 1973 has reinforced my conviction that the United States did nothing ignoble in attempting to safeguard the independence of small countries in Southeast Asia. America has nothing to be ashamed of in its resistance to the oppressors of the weak, even if in the end we set ourselves goals beyond our capacity to sustain. But I cannot, even today, recall Souvanna Phouma's wistful plea without a pang of shame that America was unable to fulfill his hopes for our steadfast support against a voracious enemy.

An Eerie Visit to Hanoi

For me, the sensation of landing in Hanoi on February 10 was the equivalent of stepping onto the moon. As over the course of a decade the war turned from a crusading mission into a national nightmare, the cool manipulators in Hanoi had exploited America's hesitations and self-doubt. Pilgrimages of antiwar Americans to this Mecca of revolutionary rectitude became a regular event. North Vietnam successfully advertised itself as an innocent, peace-loving country sorely beset by brutal foreigners. Its negotiators in Paris perfected the ambiguous pronouncement that left the impression of great opportunities being lost by American administrations insufficiently dedicated to peace. Hanoi had understood that one of the major battlefields was in the minds of Americans, and it conducted the campaign brilliantly. One cannot deny respect for the fanatics who in their youth had dedicated themselves to Communism, had suffered heroically for their beliefs, had fought with single-minded devotion and courage first against the Japanese, then against the French, and finally against the Americans, exhausting all adversaries through the test of arms and psychological warfare.

We had forced a tenuous compromise from these zealots; but it took a greater act of faith than I was capable of to believe that they would abide willingly by an inconclusive outcome. The purpose of my journey to Hanoi in February 1973 was to encourage any tendencies that existed to favor peaceful reconstruction over continued warfare, to stabilize the peace insofar as prospects of American goodwill could do so, and to warn of the serious consequences should these hopes be disappointed.

The Boeing 707 of the Presidential fleet landed at Noi Bai military airfield, about fifty miles north of Hanoi. It was a gray, misty morning. The landscape around the airport was flat and desolate, pockmarked from our B-52 bombing that had destroyed most of the buildings and cratered the runways, though they had been patched up well enough to permit the plane to come to a bouncing stop.

Le Duc Tho greeted me almost affectionately. That dour, dedicated revolutionary and I had developed a curious relationship over the nearly four years of secret meetings in Paris. On one level he undoubtedly hated me as the representative of an "imperialist" power seeking to deprive North Vietnam of what it considered its birthright — hegemony

over all of Indochina. As a professional Leninist he despised the bourgeois values of compromise I put forward. And there were times that I
deeply resented how he sought to manipulate our public opinion and
shatter our self-respect; the effrontery of his deceptions inside and outside the conference room could be enraging. At the same time I admired
Le Duc Tho's subtlety, his acumen, his iron self-discipline. In all the
years of negotiation with me he never lost his poise; he never made a
mistake. Nor did he abandon his courtesy — except once, in May 1972,
when, carried away by the prospect of seemingly imminent victory, he
was tempted into insolence.[6] He had stonewalled ingeniously for three
years. And when the occasion to settle had been imposed by Hanoi's
defeats in 1972, he did so with flexibility and speed.

What Le Duc Tho's real views of me were must await Hanoi's adoption of a Freedom of Information Act. Toward the end, at any rate, he
thought it expedient to maintain the facade of cordiality. He greeted me
at the military airfield with friendly smiles, almost as if it were a reunion of veterans of some ancient conflict. He took me by the hand to
a shabby little barracks beside the tarmac, its windows blown out. After
light banter over tea, we boarded a Soviet An-24 light transport aircraft
for the twenty-minute flight to Gia Lam International Airport nearer Hanoi, another landmark familiar to me from years of military briefings.
(The 707 could not land at Gia Lam because its runways were not long
enough.)

Gia Lam was heavily damaged; B-52s had scored a direct hit on its
main runway. Only the front facade of the control tower was standing;
one could look up through its windows and see the sky behind. We
were greeted by other officials and set off in a motorcade of Soviet
Volga sedans to the city. As it turned out these were virtually the only
automobiles I saw during my visit.

Both airports were on the north side of the Red River. Hanoi lay on
the south side looking like a sleepy French provincial town. The river
could be crossed only by pontoon bridges; the famous steel-girdered
Paul Doumer (or Red River) Bridge, so frequently cited as proof of the
ineffectiveness of our air campaign, had finally collapsed under the onslaught of the Christmas bombing.

The north side of the river was heavily cratered by our bombing,
resembling photographs of a lunar landscape. Once we reached Hanoi
proper, however, the scene could not have been more peaceful. It was
immediately obvious (and confirmed by surprised journalists a few weeks
later)[7] that the city itself was practically undamaged by our bombing,
contrary to the mythology of the alleged barbarity of our Christmas attacks. Along the streets we traveled, the only destruction we saw was
the shattered house of the French Delegate-General, hit accidentally several months earlier in the midst of our negotiations in Paris — endearing

us neither to our interlocutors nor to our French hosts. Totally absent too was the frantic bustle of Saigon. A visitor from another planet would never have known that the same people inhabited both cities. Nor would he have guessed correctly which of the capitals had sent forth the invading armies that had terrified every neighbor and absorbed the world's attention — proving that faith and discipline, not material strength alone, create their own advantage.

Hanoi's buildings were dilapidated, and in the style of southern France; it was evident that hardly any new urban construction had taken place since independence nearly two decades earlier. The wide tree-lined avenues were filled with cyclists. There was an occasional Soviet-built truck but no private cars. The streets were not crowded; the authorities had not yet brought back all who had been evacuated during the previous year. The people looked solemn, serious, aloof, indifferent. How incongruously the heroic presents itself! Whatever had motivated the unprepossessing men and women to fight and endure so tenaciously was not to be read in their faces. They glanced at our motorcade with no visible interest, though its length must have made it evident that something important was taking place.

I drove into Hanoi with strange detachment. My visit was the end of a long journey but it had no self-evident purpose. Ever since the climactic phase of the negotiation, Le Duc Tho and the Politburo had been eager for me to visit their capital. Their motive was elusive. It could not be the hunger for equal status with China, which had made Brezhnev press to receive me in Moscow after my secret visit to Peking: Hanoi's leaders were too self-contained for that; psychological insecurity was hardly their most notable feature. Did they seek to tranquilize us before launching a new wave of conquest? It was possible, but it was a double-edged tactic. From our perspective our demonstration that we had explored every opportunity for conciliation was a necessary condition in America for defending the Paris accords by other means if it came to that. Might Hanoi be content to rest on the frenzied exertions of a lifetime of struggle and begin meeting the needs of its people? That was what Le Duc Tho had been saying and what we were prepared to explore.

In any event, our choices were circumscribed. I had come to Hanoi in part to symbolize a commitment to national reconciliation at home — a subject of no interest to the North Vietnamese. We hoped to convince Hanoi's leaders of the futility of resuming military operations by insisting on a strict performance of the Paris accords. But deep down I knew, with a sinking feeling, that words would not impress them. Somewhere along the line we would be tested. We would have to show our mettle. At the same time I had to attempt to provide inducements for peaceful endeavors in the shadow of two imponderables: Could Hanoi so adjust its scale of values as to give building its economy a higher priority than it had in all previous periods in its history? And would Congress support us?

I understood, or rather felt inchoately, that I, the representative of a superpower, was at a strange disadvantage in this city so devoid of all the appurtenances of modern life. America had been obsessed by Vietnam, but in the long run it was for us only a small corner of a world for whose security we had become at least partly responsible. On the other hand, the epic poem the leaders in Hanoi were acting out was their sole cause. They had the capacity to damage us out of any proportion to what we could gain, by resuming the war or their assault on our domestic tranquillity. But they could do nothing positive for us. They were too egotistical to think of foreign policy in terms of an international system; too arrogant to believe in goodwill; too ambitious to restrain their purposes by ideas of concord. And so I drove into Hanoi uneasily aware that the best outcome would be the avoidance of a loss and the best hope only that soon Vietnam might recede into oblivion in our national consciousness.

I was housed in an elegant two-story guest house in the center of Hanoi that had once been the residence of the French Governor-General of Tonkin. Most of my staff stayed in the Reunification Hotel, a shabby old structure diagonally across the street, whose walls were covered with graffiti, mostly in Russian, the cultural contribution of various Soviet aid missions. Service there was based on the proposition that all foreigners were potential spies whose stay could be cut short by showing no mercy to any aspiration to elementary comfort.

Le Duc Tho accompanied me to my own room and then politely excused himself, to prepare for my first meeting with Prime Minister Pham Van Dong. Having some time, my colleagues and I decided to take a walk, much to the discomfiture of both the North Vietnamese protocol officials and my Secret Service protectors. For once, North Vietnamese pedantry deserted them. This possibility had not been foreseen; hence no instructions had been left and the flustered guards at the gate did not impede our departure. We strolled along streets that the dearth of motor traffic made appear both old-fashioned and serene, crowded with people calmly performing their chores. Two little lakes form the center of Hanoi. We walked along them, the first American officials to move freely in Hanoi in two decades, while a few hundred yards away other Americans, our prisoners of war, still languished in a cruel captivity.* Passersby stared at us with no evident emotion. They displayed neither

---

*The Paris Agreement of January 27 provided for the release of all our POWs in stages, in parallel with the withdrawal of all US troops from South Vietnam, within sixty days. The process had begun but would not be completed until March 27.

hostility nor friendliness, treating us as if we were some strange muta-
tion of no possible relevance to them. In front of one of the buildings
was a huge billboard with a map showing what Hanoi's rulers were
pleased to consider the "liberated areas" of the South. Though somewhat generous to Hanoi, it was not inaccurate. I wondered how the
people of North Vietnam reacted to it; it was precious little to show for
their twenty years of sacrifice.

We strolled back to my residence. And here North Vietnamese ad-
diction to formal regulations took its revenge for our flirtation with the
unexpected. At the gate everyone was asked to show a pass in order to
regain admittance. This was easy enough for my colleagues, who had
been handed identity cards at the airport. Unfortunately, I had been
given no such document. Bureaucratic rules in any totalitarian Communist state are not treated casually; in Hanoi they are an obsession. I
was refused admittance. The North Vietnamese guard had never heard
of me. This may reflect badly on the quality of the gossip columns in
Hanoi's newspapers but it was no consolation to me; I expressed displeasure, with my legendary humility and restraint. An officer showed
up, but he too hesitated to bend the regulations. A twenty-minute argument ensued. It finally took Le Duc Tho's intervention to keep me from
having to sleep in the streets. One of my staff later raised the matter
with a North Vietnamese protocol official. He, nervously apologetic,
explained that the head of a delegation was never given a pass; it was a
mark of special status! Obviously, neither had any head of a delegation
ever taken a walk. Eventually they provided me with a pass, to which I
held on for dear life.

My living arrangements were lavish but also a bit erratic. The dimensions of the bedroom were majestic; it was lit by a forest of lights hanging from the ceiling. Unfortunately, each light was controlled by a different switch, located in a different part of the room. Before retiring I
had to hunt down the appropriate switches, with varying degrees of
success; at any rate none was reachable from my bed, so that I had to
return to it in pitch-darkness. Getting into bed was itself not a simple
task. Every evening I found it immaculately made up, my pajamas laid
out, a book I was reading (by Henry Fairlie on the Kennedy Presidency)
carefully placed on my pillow. The only barrier was a mosquito net,
enveloping the entire bed, that was tucked in so thoroughly it was impossible to get in without lifting up the mattress and undoing the whole
arrangement, which in turn guaranteed that I would be pursued into bed
by a swarm of mosquitoes.

In my bathroom I had only scalding hot water in the bathtub but no
plug, and nothing but ice-cold water in the washbasin. Actually, my
hosts were making every effort to be hospitable. North Vietnam was a
small country of limited resources, burdened by a vast military estab-

lishment, not to mention a concerted American effort to disrupt its economy. Nevertheless I was paranoid enough to suspect my hosts of a further diabolical attempt at psychological warfare — especially since I was
awakened every morning at 5:30 by the sound of the citizenry conducting their compulsory calisthenics in the plaza in front of my bedroom
window.

I had requested some time for sight-seeing, especially of cultural sites,
as I usually did in visiting a country for the first time. Le Duc Tho
graciously accompanied me on these excursions. He found them quite
educational since he had never seen them before himself. We first visited Hanoi's History Museum, a collection of historical relics assembled
mostly by the French. As reorganized by the North Vietnamese, the
museum told of ancient battles against the Chinese or against smaller
neighbors, great migrations and rebellions. Each artifact was labeled
with its place of excavation. Le Duc Tho found the exhibits fascinating,
mainly because the excavation sites reminded him of nearby prisons
where the French had confined him as a guerrilla leader. The old revolutionary was clearly more interested in his fight to create a new culture
than in celebrating an ancient one. He gave me a detailed account of
the relative merits of solitary confinement in various prisons, and unhelpful hints on how to disguise myself as a Vietnamese peasant.

The next day I visited an art museum. I have to say it was rather
disappointing. It was as if this talented people had consumed its substance in a history of incessant struggle, leaving no time or energy for
the development of gentler qualities or pursuits.

Pham Van Dong

As we turned to serious talks, we soon found ourselves in the position
of survivors of an ancient vendetta who have reluctantly concluded
that their inability to destroy each other compels an effort at coexistence — though without conviction or real hope. We were both aware
of the dictates of prudence, but neither side could shake off its memories, nor could Hanoi abandon its passions. The attempts to behave in a
friendly manner were so studied and took so much exertion that they
created their own tension; the slightest disagreement tended to bring to
the fore the underlying suspicion and resentment.

Hanoi's leaders soon showed that they had lost none of the insolence
that for years had set our teeth on edge. My opposite number in these
talks was Pham Van Dong, Prime Minister of the Democratic Republic
of Vietnam for nearly twenty years. But the change of personality
brought no alteration in the familiar style of condescending superiority
or of deception masquerading as moral homily.

Pham Van Dong had come to my attention in January 1967, when he had given a brilliant interview to Harrison Salisbury of the *New York Times,* explaining why Hanoi was confident of winning against the mightiest power in the world. Dong had argued that the disparity in strength was illusory; the North Vietnamese were prepared to fight for generations; America's material superiority could operate only in a more limited time span. They would simply outlast us.[8] Pham Van Dong turned out to be right — aided not a little by an American military strategy massive enough to hazard our international position yet sufficiently inhibited to guarantee an inconclusive outcome.

Pham Van Dong, implacable and incisive, had stalked our consciousness, and occasionally our consciences, during the intervening years. His periodic Delphic pronouncements had both raised public expectations and dashed official hopes. In early 1972 he had denounced all talk of compromise as "the logic of a gangster"; when a compromise was reached later in 1972, his interview with an American journalist put the most tendentious interpretation on it and contributed to the breakdown of the negotiations.[9] In the last stages of the negotiation it was Pham Van Dong in whose name the most important communications from Hanoi were addressed to President Nixon.

Pham Van Dong was wiry, short, wary, his piercing eyes watchful for the expected trickery and at the same time implying that the burden of proof of any statement by an arch-capitalist would be on the speaker. He greeted me on the steps of the elaborate structure now called the President's House. From here French colonial administrators had ruled all of Indochina and established in the minds of their all-too-receptive Vietnamese subjects the conviction that the boundaries of Indochina should forever after coincide with those of the French colonial empire. Vietnamese expansionism, which had already proved the nightmare of its neighbors even before the arrival of the French, was thus given new impetus and legitimacy by colonial rule. We entered a large reception hall and seated ourselves in a semicircle for the introductory informal conversation — as in China. Also as in China, this was an occasion for subtle hints to establish the mood.

The meeting started pleasantly enough with Pham Van Dong and me protesting our eagerness to begin a new relationship, and pledging perseverance to that end. But then the Premier introduced a jarring note; less than two weeks after signature of the Paris Agreement, he dropped an ominous hint of renewed warfare. If a new relationship did not develop a solid basis of mutual interest, he averred, the just-signed Paris accords would be "only a temporary stabilization of the situation, only a respite." He immediately qualified this slightly by adding that such was not Hanoi's preference. As a devout Leninist he happily fell in with my somewhat irrelevant response that we based our new relationship on the existing facts. Pham Van Dong could not resist returning to the theme of his earlier interview with Harrison Salisbury: "We Vietnamese living in this area will remain forever. But you are from the other side of the ocean. Should we take account of this fact, too?" In other words, when would we abandon South Vietnam? I replied with a pointed allusion to North Vietnam's status as a separate country: "This is why we are no long-term threat — despite recent events — to your independence." But Pham Van Dong was no more inclined than Le Duc Tho to give away anything, even a philosophical point, for nothing. Nor would he forgo another subtle warning of Hanoi's implacable determination: "But we should think this over."

Pham Van Dong thus did not take long to dash my dim hope that he might prove to be another Zhou Enlai and become a partner in transforming old enmity into new cooperation. He was not — indeed, could not be — a partner, any more than Vietnam was China. Pham Van Dong represented a people who had prevailed by unremitting tenacity; Zhou Enlai was the leader of a country that had made its mark through cultural preeminence and majesty of conduct. Pham Van Dong's strength was monomaniacal absorption with the ambitions of one country; Zhou was quintessentially Chinese in his conviction that China's performance was morally relevant to the rest of the world. Pham Van Dong was of the stuff of which revolutionary heroes are made. Zhou, while a revolutionary himself, was of the stuff of which great leaders are made.

Pham Van Dong, it is now clear, sought to tranquilize us so that Hanoi could complete its conquest of Indochina without American opposition. Zhou Enlai acted on the conviction that China's security — at least in the face of imminent Soviet threat — depended on America's strong commitment to the global balance of power. To Pham Van Dong the encounter with me was a tactic in a revolutionary struggle. He was prepared to improve relations with America if, as he had implied in our banter, this gained him a free hand in Indochina; otherwise the struggle would resume. In no case did Hanoi see any benefit in heightened American strength and self-confidence. Zhou Enlai's aims were strategically compatible with ours at least in the foreseeable future; his strategy presupposed shared interests that we would consider worth defending. Far from desiring to undermine America's international position and national self-assurance, as time went on Zhou attempted discreetly to strengthen both.

After the initial thrust-and-parry, Pham Van Dong and I walked with our colleagues into a formal conference room of heavy furniture and drawn curtains, where we faced each other across a table and immediately ran into another squall. The North Vietnamese Premier made a little speech greeting me formally and graciously, expressing the hope for good results. I replied:

We clearly endorse different ideologies, and it would be idle to pretend otherwise, but we have proved in our relationship with other countries that this need not be an obstacle to good relations and cooperative action. In the long term, from an historical perspective, a strong and independent self-reliant Vietnam is in no way inconsistent with American national interests. We slid into war against each other partly through misconceptions on each side. We thought the war was directed from one central office that was not in Indochina. And perhaps you drew certain lessons from your history that were not exactly accurate. But whatever the conditions under which we are acting, our interest in Indochina is the maintenance of the independence and sovereignty of the countries of Indochina, and that, we understand, is not opposed to your interests.

Pham Van Dong was less than enthusiastic about the reputation I had given him to uphold. The independence and sovereignty of any of the other countries of Indochina had hardly been a North Vietnamese goal in the past. Nor did it turn out to be even remotely an objective for the future. In addition, he surely did not accept our view that South Vietnam was a sovereign country. But he exercised uncharacteristic restraint on these topics. What he could not permit to slip by was my implication of North Vietnamese fallibility:

I think that what has just happened between us — and Dr. Kissinger referred to it as a misunderstanding — in this connection we have repeatedly expressed our views. And on our part I think what we have done, we ought to have done. . . .

In other words, the misconceptions were all on *our* part. But, as before, the cloud passed again rapidly. Dong continued:

[I]t is something past, something bygone, and we should draw some conclusions about that for the present and the future. And we should, in the spirit we have just mentioned outside and we continue in this room, shift from war to peace, . . . shift from confrontation to reconciliation as stipulated in the Agreement, and . . . bring a new relationship, a solid relationship, on a basis agreed upon by the two parties and aiming at the long-term goals as Dr. Kissinger has just mentioned. As far as we are concerned, we will firmly follow this direction — that is to say to implement the signed Agreement, to implement all the provisions of the Agreement.

Unfortunately, Pham Van Dong's eloquence was not matched by his country's actions. Our agenda consisted of three items: observance of the Paris Agreement, normalization of relations, and economic reconstruction. No sooner had we turned to the first agenda item than we realized that Hanoi had no intention of making the Paris accords the first agreement it had ever observed.

The cease-fire established by the Paris Agreement had gone into effect at midnight Greenwich Mean Time on January 27. There were immediate reports of violations as both sides sought to seize as much territory as possible in the hours before the cease-fire went into effect; some battles continued for days afterward. In that early period both sides were guilty of stretching the letter as well as the spirit of the Agreement. Saigon, still the stronger side, gave as good as it received; it expanded its control over more hamlets than it lost. But from then on North Vietnam showed itself capable of uniquely gross challenges to the solemn undertaking it had just signed.

The international supervisory machinery immediately ran into Communist obstruction. Hanoi would not designate the official points of entry through which alone, according to the Agreement, military equipment was permitted to enter South Vietnam under international supervision. Hanoi seemed to feel that refusing to comply with the provision for international control also removed the inhibitions of another clause that limited new equipment to one-for-one replacement. In flagrant violation, Hanoi's resupply efforts down the Ho Chi Minh Trail, freed of American bombing, proceeded massively and at an ominously more rapid rate than during the war.

As for the political provisions, Saigon was clearly in no hurry to set up the National Council for National Reconciliation and Concord envisaged by the Agreement; Hanoi for its part thwarted any discussion of elections — to be supervised by that Council — which it knew it would lose. But while neither Vietnamese party was distinguished by concern for the political obligations, there can be no doubt that Hanoi's illegal infiltration of military equipment and personnel started almost immediately, proved decisive, and antedated all the alleged breaches of the Paris accords by Saigon cited later by Hanoi's apologists.

To make our point, I had brought along a compilation of North Vietnamese violations in the two weeks since the signature of the Paris Agreement. The list left no doubt that Hanoi accepted no constraints of *any* of the provisions it had signed so recently. We had incontrovertible evidence of 200 major military violations. The most flagrant were the transit of the Demilitarized Zone by 175 trucks on February 6 and the movement of 223 tanks heading into South Vietnam through Laos and Cambodia. Transit of the DMZ by military vehicles violated Article 15(a), on the wording of which we had spent nearly two months and which banned all military traffic, as well as requiring the concurrence of Saigon for civilian traffic. It also violated the explicit stipulation that new military equipment could be introduced into South Vietnam only on the basis of one-for-one replacement through previously designated international checkpoints (Article 7). The movement of tanks through Laos and Cambodia violated Article 20, according to which all foreign troops were to be withdrawn from Laos and Cambodia and the territory of those countries was not to be used as a base for encroaching on other countries. When the tanks reached South Vietnam they would also be violating Article 7's prohibition of the introduction of new matériel.

Pham Van Dong and Le Duc Tho were not fazed. With the casual brazenness I remembered so well from my encounters in Paris, they explained the violations in terms that were irrelevant to the issue but served marvelously to confuse it.

There is the story of a law professor who taught his students how to take advantage of every possible defense. If one's client is accused of stealing a black pot, the tactic should be to reply: "My client did not steal anything. In any case it was not a pot that he stole, and the pot was not black." Le Duc Tho, to whom Pham Van Dong deferred on this issue, followed the same approach. There had been no violations, he said. And in any case the trucks crossing the DMZ were carrying civilian goods. This, of course, still violated the provision according to which civilian traffic required the assent of Saigon. And the resupply restrictions of Article 7 would become absurd if Hanoi could avoid international control by the simple device of declaring all supplies civilian. As for the tanks, Le Duc Tho and Pham Van Dong halfheartedly denied the truth of my allegations but promised to look into them. They then suggested that perhaps the tanks had been en route when the Agreement was signed. This was, of course, quite irrelevant to the prohibition of their entry into South Vietnam. Vice Foreign Minister Nguyen Co Thach, who had negotiated the technical protocols in Paris with Ambassador William H. Sullivan, had the cleverest idea. Probably, he averred, such was the urgency of the need that the tanks, too, were carrying civilian goods to the civilian population.

Hanoi's solicitude for the comfort of the fewer than two million South Vietnamese civilians under its control was remarkable; it had shown little evidence of it while the war was still going on. I was developing the queasy feeling that we were being tested, that if we did not force a showdown soon on the issue of resupply and infiltration the war would resume whenever Hanoi was ready, and all we would have done was purchase a brief respite for the withdrawal of our forces.

Equally frustrating were our discussions of the American soldiers and airmen who were prisoners of war or missing in action. We knew of at least eighty instances in which an American serviceman had been captured alive and had subsequently disappeared. The evidence consisted of either voice communications from the ground in advance of capture or photographs and names published by the Communists. Yet none of these men was on the list of POWs handed over after the Agreement. Why? Were they dead? How did they die? Were they missing? How was that possible after capture? I called special attention to the nineteen cases where pictures of the captured had been published in the Communist press. Pham Van Dong replied noncommittally that the lists handed over to us were complete. He made no attempt to explain discrepancies. Experience had shown, he said, that owing to the nature of the terrain in Indochina it would take a long time, perhaps a year, to come up with additional information, though he did not amplify what the terrain had to do with the disappearing prisoners. We have never received an explanation of what could possibly have happened to prisoners whose pictures had appeared in Communist newspapers, much less the airmen who we knew from voice communications had safely reached the ground.

To calm the atmosphere, Le Duc Tho offered to release twenty prisoners of war ahead of schedule, ostensibly in honor of my visit, and gave me the opportunity to pick them from the POW list. While grateful for the early release, I refused to select the names. I had no basis for making individual selections among those who had already suffered so long. (Prisoners held the longest were being released earliest in any case.) This was one promise Hanoi kept; twenty additional prisoners were released with the first group.

The North Vietnamese were at their most adamant (and obnoxious) about Laos and Cambodia. Article 20 of the Paris Agreement explicitly stipulated that "foreign countries" should end all military activities in Cambodia and Laos and totally withdraw all their forces there.[10] In a separate written understanding, Le Duc Tho and I had agreed that Vietnamese as well as American troops were "foreign" within the meaning of this article. If words meant anything, this required immediate North Vietnamese withdrawal from Laos and Cambodia and an end to the use of Laotian and Cambodian territory for base areas, sanctuaries, or infiltration.

My conversations with Pham Van Dong had not proceeded far before it became apparent that the North Vietnamese proposed to drain Article 20 of all meaning. They took the position that the required withdrawal, unconditional on its face, would have to await not only a cease-fire in Laos and Cambodia but also a political settlement in *both* those countries. Hanoi would withdraw only after negotiations with the new governments there. Since Communist political demands were for what amounted to Pathet Lao predominance in Laos and a total Khmer Rouge victory in Cambodia, North Vietnamese withdrawal would take place, if at all, only after it had become irrelevant and the issue had been decided in favor of the Communist side. Hanoi was proposing in effect to negotiate with itself, or at best with its Cambodian and Laotian stooges, about implementing provisions of an undertaking with us. The achievement of political settlements in Laos or Cambodia — which Le Duc Tho had in fact refused to discuss at Paris — could not possibly be made a precondition for the fulfillment of obligations that made no ref-

erence to it whatsoever and, by their plain import, were without qualification.

Hanoi's outrageous interpretation was particularly ominous for Cambodia. In Laos cease-fire negotiations were at least taking place and we
had, for whatever it was worth, Hanoi's promise to bring them to a
conclusion within fifteen days. But in Cambodia the Khmer Rouge refused to talk to any representative of the non-Communist side; their
response to Lon Nol's unilateral proclamation of a cease-fire was a renewed military offensive. We had risked making peace in Vietnam in
the absence of formal arrangements for Cambodia because the American
Congress would never have tolerated any delay on account of Cambodia
alone and because our experts agreed that the Khmer Rouge could not
prevail by themselves. If they were deprived of North Vietnamese combat and logistical support, as the Agreement required, some form of
compromise settlement was probable. But if North Vietnamese troops
remained, in violation of the Paris Agreement, they would almost certainly tip the balance in favor of the Khmer Rouge. Moreover, almost
all our studies — the last at the end of January by the British antiguer-
rilla expert Sir Robert Thompson — indicated that a Communist takeover in Cambodia, by opening another enemy front and a sea route of
supplies through Sihanoukville, would wreck South Vietnam's chances
of survival.

In fact, we have since learned from Sihanouk's memoirs that the
Khmer Rouge, considering the Paris Agreement a betrayal, had asked
the North Vietnamese troops to quit Cambodia.[11] They stayed in violation of Article 20 *and* against the wishes of both their enemies and their
own allies, whom they used as an alibi in their talks with us.

Needless to say, my response to Pham Van Dong was sharp. It was
all very well, I said sarcastically, to note Hanoi's fastidious regard for
the sovereignty of its allies. But it was bizarre to maintain that Hanoi
could not make a unilateral decision to remove troops it had introduced
unilaterally, in compliance with an agreement to which it had pledged
itself barely two weeks earlier. Its soldiers were not prisoners in these
countries. Hanoi, having introduced its forces without the approval of
the legitimate governments, could certainly withdraw them on its own.

It cannot be said that my arguments left a deep impression. On the
other hand, experience had taught that Hanoi did not always hold to the
original version of its position; it had, after all, abandoned a similar
position over South Vietnam. The only immediate "concession" we
elicited was a promise by Le Duc Tho to use his "influence" to bring
about a rapid cease-fire in Laos — the third time they had sold us that
particular item. The Laotian cease-fire finally came about on February
22, but not without the spur of one more US B-52 strike on North
Vietnamese troop concentrations in Laos, to the accompaniment of out-

raged media and Congressional protests that once again we were "expanding" the war. Despite the cease-fire Hanoi withdrew no troops from Laos.

North Vietnamese stonewalling doomed Cambodia, however, to prolonged agony. Pham Van Dong and Le Duc Tho claimed that Vietnam was not involved in Cambodia — another flagrant misrepresentation; hence they needed to take no position with respect to the de facto cease-fire that Lon Nol had proclaimed. They spurned Lon Nol's offer to talk to Hanoi or to the Khmer Rouge; they maintained their position of 1970 — demanding the overthrow of the Cambodian government. As in the long negotiating stalemate over Vietnam, they insisted that the political structure in Phnom Penh be disbanded *before* any talks, after which, of course, the talks would have had no purpose. In fact, Hanoi did not even pretend to want a coalition in Cambodia; it insisted on an undiluted Communist takeover. Le Duc Tho in an offhand manner suggested that I talk to Sihanouk, but he was curiously vague about the Prince's status or even his whereabouts, implying strongly that the Khmer Rouge would be the decisive element in the future of Cambodia. Le Duc Tho — clearly the Politburo's expert on the other countries of Indochina — was quite condescending about Sihanouk. He made fun of a visit Sihanouk had recently paid to Hanoi and the Prince's love of personal luxury. He showed a propaganda film about Sihanouk's visit to Communist-controlled territory in Cambodia, the clear implication of which was that Sihanouk was there on the sufferance of the Khmer Rouge. The primary use that Le Duc Tho seemed to see in Sihanouk was as a means to demoralize and undermine the Lon Nol government.

Where Le Duc Tho miscalculated was in his estimate of the pliability of the Khmer Rouge, who refused to be Hanoi's tools on the model of the Pathet Lao. But perhaps he was willing to pay the price of temporary Khmer Rouge autonomy because the immediate consequence of a Khmer Rouge victory would be the undermining of the government in Saigon, which could not long survive the communization of Cambodia. Hanoi also, as it later transpired, had its tried and true remedy for Khmer Rouge independence if it got out of hand. Less than four years after the Khmer Rouge victory in 1975, North Vietnam sent its troops to invade and occupy Communist Cambodia with no more scruple than it had shown toward Sihanouk's neutral Cambodia in the mid-1960s and Lon Nol's Cambodia in 1970.

We were prepared to settle for a genuine coalition government for Cambodia with Sihanouk as the balance wheel. What Hanoi pressed for was a Communist government with Sihanouk as a transitional figurehead. As previously with South Vietnam, Hanoi's notion of our contribution to the negotiating process was the overthrow of our ally. It was the continued Communist refusal of any cease-fire, de facto or negotiated, or of any real negotiation over Cambodia, accompanied by a renewed Khmer Rouge military offensive, that induced us to resume our bombing in Cambodia in February. Our purpose was to create a balance of forces that would deprive the Communists of hope for a military solution and thus force a compromise. This attempt collapsed when Congress in June 1973 prohibited further US military operations in Indochina. (Our diplomacy to end the war in Cambodia in 1973 is discussed at length in Chapter VIII.)

As for a political settlement in Laos, the North Vietnamese leaders remained evasive. At one point Pham Van Dong suggested that it might occur no more than ninety days after a cease-fire; then, amazingly, he was disavowed by Le Duc Tho, who sought a private meeting with me to suggest that henceforth Cambodia and Laos be discussed by him and me alone since his Prime Minister was not familiar with all the nuances. In the event, a political settlement was not reached in Laos until September 14, 1973. The newly constituted coalition government held together tenuously for two years until it was finally engulfed in the general debacle of 1975. And no more than in 1962 did North Vietnam pay even token obeisance to its pledge to withdraw its troops. Between 40,000 and 50,000 North Vietnamese troops remained in Laos even after Hanoi's own absurd interpretation of the Paris Agreement had been fulfilled.

Economic Aid

THE one subject about which Pham Van Dong was prepared to observe the Agreement was something on which we alone needed to perform: economic aid from the United States. He almost made it seem that Hanoi was doing us a favor in accepting our money. Not that its eagerness would reach the point of modifying its peremptory negotiating methods: American assistance was requested as a right. Any reminder that it was linked to Hanoi's observance of the other provisions of the Paris Agreement was indignantly rejected as interference in North Vietnam's domestic affairs or as an unacceptable political condition.

How we reached the point where a voluntary American offer became transmuted into a North Vietnamese "right" shows at the least the degree to which the two societies were doomed to mutual incomprehension and at most the ability of the North Vietnamese to turn insolence into an art form. On our side the offer of economic aid grew out of our contradictory mixture of idealistic values and a materialistic interpretation of history according to which economic motives are thought to dominate political decisions. Perhaps no major nation has been so uncomfortable with the exercise of vast power as the United States. We have tended to consider war as "unnatural," as an interruption of our vocation of peace, prosperity, and liberty. No other society has considered it a national duty to contribute to the rebuilding of a defeated enemy; after the Second World War we made it a central element of our foreign policy. In Vietnam we thought it a device to induce an undefeated enemy to accept compromise terms. The reverse side of our faith in what we consider positive goals is a difficulty in coming to grips with irreconcilable conflict, with implacable revolutionary zeal, with men who prefer victory to economic progress and who remain determined to prevail regardless of material cost.

For years, all these strands had been woven through our Indochina policy. We had just begun to build up our forces in South Vietnam when President Lyndon Johnson in April 1965 offered Hanoi a program of postwar economic reconstruction. We do not know whether North Vietnam saw in this offer the first symptom of our declining resolution (so that it had an effect contrary to that intended), or evidence of bourgeois incapacity to grasp revolutionary dedication. The offer, in any event, was not taken up.

The Nixon Administration had a different perception of Hanoi's motivation, but it thought that such a humanitarian proposal was one way of calming domestic dissent. Hence it did not wait long to follow in the footsteps of its predecessor. On September 18, 1969, in a conciliatory speech before the United Nations General Assembly, Nixon renewed the offer of economic aid to North Vietnam as well as the rest of Indochina, to no better effect than Johnson. Undiscouraged, in the summer of 1971 during my secret negotiations with Le Duc Tho, we proposed yet another reconstruction scheme. Le Duc Tho noted it without any show of interest. Nixon reiterated the offer publicly as part of a comprehensive proposal on January 25, 1972. Briefing the press the next day, I explained that we were prepared to contribute several billion dollars to the reconstruction of Indochina, including North Vietnam. The President's Foreign Policy Report issued on February 9, 1972, was even more specific: "We are prepared to undertake a massive 7½ billion dollar five-year reconstruction program in conjunction with an overall agreement, in which North Vietnam could share up to two and a half billion dollars." In my "peace is at hand" press conference of October 26, 1972, I repeated this theme. And I did so again in a press conference on January 24, 1973, as did Nixon on January 31, 1973.

By then Hanoi's interest in the proposition had quickened. It would not admit that it would end the war for economic reasons. But once it had decided on a cease-fire out of military necessity, it was ready, if not eager, to extract the maximum aid from us. Characteristically, Hanoi couched this not in terms of an acceptance of our offer but as a demand for reparations. Nor were Hanoi's ideas of the appropriate aid level characterized by excessive modesty; Le Duc Tho simply demanded for Hanoi the entire package of $7.5 billion that we had earmarked for *all* of Indochina. We were prepared to accept neither of these propositions. We were willing to extend aid because it had been promised by two administrations and especially because we thought it useful as one of the inducements to encourage observance of the Agreement. But we insisted that our offer was an application of traditional American principles; it was a voluntary act, not an "obligation" to indemnify Hanoi. It may have been hairsplitting but to us it involved a point of honor. Through weeks of weary haggling we managed to reduce Hanoi's demand to $3.25 billion, which was put forward as a target figure subject to further discussion and Congressional approval.

The relevant documents were the Paris Agreement and a Presidential message. Article 21 of the Paris Agreement stated:

> The United States anticipates that this Agreement will usher in an era of reconciliation with the Democratic Republic of Vietnam as with all the peoples of Indochina. In pursuance of its traditional policy, the United States will contribute to healing the wounds of war and to postwar reconstruction of the Democratic Republic of Vietnam and throughout Indochina.

It was a promise given in the expectation that the war was ending and an era of reconciliation would then be possible. And I repeatedly emphasized to Le Duc Tho that any aid presupposed both Congressional approval *and* Hanoi's living up to the Paris Agreement.

Our intention to extend aid and even its order of magnitude were well known and had been stated many times on the public record. What was kept secret at the time was a cabled message from Nixon to Premier Pham Van Dong spelling out the procedures for implementing Article 21. In order to underline the fact that it was voluntary and distinct from the formal obligations of the Agreement, Le Duc Tho and I had agreed that the message would be delivered on January 30, 1973, three days after the Agreement was signed, in exchange for a list of American prisoners held in Laos. When on the appointed day the North Vietnamese failed to provide a list of the American prisoners of war held in Laos, we instructed our representative in Paris to delay handing over the note. This produced immediate action: The Laotian POW list was handed over on the afternoon of February 1; as agreed, we gave the North Vietnamese the Nixon message to Pham Van Dong at the same time.

Nixon's message — drafted by my staff and me — suggested the procedures for discussing economic aid. On my visit to Hanoi there would be a general discussion of principles, leading to the setting up of a Joint Economic Commission. Its purpose would be to work out a precise aid program. (The Joint Economic Commission actually began its discussions in Paris on March 15.) The Nixon message spoke of an amount "in the range of $3.25 billion" over five years as an appropriate "preliminary" figure, subject to revision and to detailed discussion between the two countries. (Food aid was included in the total.) Whatever emerged from the deliberations of the Joint Economic Commission, the Nixon message stressed, would have to be submitted to the Congress, as is any foreign aid program after discussions with a foreign government. A separate paragraph emphasized this point: "It is understood that the recommendations of the Joint Economic Commission mentioned in the President's note to the Prime Minister will be implemented by each member in accordance with its own constitutional provisions."

Le Duc Tho, never lacking in chutzpah, presumed to instruct me in January as to what was appropriate to include in a communication from our President. He insisted that such a qualification had no place in the President's message; our obligation had to be unconditional. I pointed out that whatever the more convenient decision-making procedures of Hanoi, our legislative process was a fact of life. We "compromised" by stating the need for Congressional approval on a separate page, sent simultaneously and of equal weight. Le Duc Tho seemed to draw comfort from this. It would enable Hanoi to publish the letter and to suppress the qualification — which is precisely what it later did, earning itself for the gullible one more demonstration of our duplicity.

The Politburo's confidence that they could use our domestic pressures to push us from one position of disadvantage to another — not unreasonable in the light of a decade of experience — caused them to shrug off another important qualification, one that was equally real and equally explicit in my discussions with them. When I briefed the press about the Agreement on January 24, 1973, I stressed that we would discuss aid to North Vietnam only after its "implementation is well advanced."

As it happened, the end of the war also reduced the fervid pressures against the Administration to make concessions to Hanoi; indeed, many who had urged an offer of economic aid as a means to end the war became notably less enthusiastic when it came to voting for it in the Congress. Nor was public opinion, which on the whole would have preferred victory to compromise, hospitable to the proposition that we should extend aid to a government whose brutality was becoming vividly clear through the tales of returning prisoners of war. Nixon was thus on safe ground when he instructed me to reiterate to my interlocutors in Hanoi that aid depended on strict observance of the Paris Agreement, with special reference to withdrawal from Cambodia. The North Vietnamese could not expect otherwise. If the war did not end, the "postwar" period could not begin, and the time for postwar reconstruction aid could hardly be said to have arrived.

Equally predictably, Pham Van Dong rejected this argument. He advanced the startling view that asking Hanoi to observe a signed agreement was to attach "political conditions." Our aid was to be "unconditional." In other words, Hanoi was to be free to use American economic aid to complete its long-standing ambition of conquering Indochina in violation of the very Agreement that it claimed obliged us to provide those resources.

Still, what roused the North Vietnamese to genuine outrage was our constitutional requirement of Congressional approval. I had brought with me to Hanoi a voluminous set of documents to educate the North Vietnamese in our constitutional processes. It was a compilation of some fifty-seven single-spaced pages outlining the American budgetary procedure in both the executive and legislative branches; the various types of bilateral and multilateral aid programs in which the United States had participated; the texts of all relevant legislation (including Congressionally mandated restrictions on aid to Hanoi); an outline of various projects that might be included in an aid program for Vietnam; and a list of pungent comments by leading Congressmen and Senators expressing growing skepticism about foreign aid in general. I handed over these documents to Pham Van Dong. He brushed them aside, pretending not to fathom these legislative matters (this despite the fact that he had shown great skill in manipulating Congressional opinion *against* the Administration while the war was still going on). He also suspected a trick:

First of all, I would like to express my suspicion. . . . I will speak very frankly and straightforwardly to you. It is known to everyone that the U. S. had spent a great amount of money in regard to the war in Vietnam. It is said about $200 billion, and in conditions that one would say that the Congress was not fully agreeable to this war. When the war was going on then the appropriation was so easy [laughs], and when we have to solve now a problem that is very legitimate . . . then you find it difficult.

He kept reiterating that he did not believe the legislative obstacles were anything but pretexts we were using to evade our "commitment":

We should not deem it necessary to go in[to] the complete complexity, the forest of legal aspects. I feel it very difficult to understand. Of course, when one is unwilling then the legal aspect is a means to this end.

Never, I must say, have I been more eloquent in defense of Congressional prerogative than on this occasion. Later Congressional critics who scolded me for not taking their legislative responsibilities seriously would have been proud of me. It was finally agreed, as anticipated, that we would set up the Joint Economic Commission to consider how to develop our economic relations and to work out an aid program that we would submit to the Congress.

There were some inconclusive exchanges about normalizing diplomatic relations between Hanoi and Washington, and about the pending

International Conference that was to be held in Paris to lend international endorsement to the Paris Agreement. Hanoi was not yet ready to establish any formal ties, not even offices that fell short of full diplomatic status. We proposed a number of schemes; they rejected them all. (Amusingly, one of our ideas was accepted by the Chinese a few days later.) With typical self-absorption Hanoi meant to use the prospect of permitting some American diplomats to join the ostracism and general discomfort of their colleagues from Western Europe — and probably the Soviet Union — in Hanoi as a boon that we first had to earn. As for the International Conference, Hanoi's preoccupation was to reduce the participation of the Secretary-General of the United Nations to a minimum, if not eliminate him altogether. We found an honorific role that preserved his dignity as well as took account of North Vietnam's touchy view of national sovereignty.

At a final banquet, Pham Van Dong expressed "delight" at my visit, as well as at its results — although as I reread the transcripts at this remove the source of his pleasure is not self-evident. My mood was somber but I had not yet given up hope.

After ten years of bitter warfare, perhaps not much more could be expected. Hanoi and Washington had inflicted grievous wounds on each other; theirs were physical, ours psychological and thus perhaps harder to heal. Our hosts had been courteous but it was too soon to expect a change in attitude. They were clearly applying to the implementation of the Agreement the methods by which they had conducted the war: pressing against its edges, testing our tolerance, violating key provisions tentatively to see where the new balance of forces would be established. And yet with all our doubts we were dedicated to making a major effort for a peaceful evolution; there had been too much anguish to enter lightly into a new confrontation. One could draw some hope from the prospect that Hanoi's nationalism might cause it to seek better relations with Washington to gain some margin of maneuver between its Communist patrons, Peking and Moscow. Perhaps Pham Van Dong's dour insistence on economic aid might be a sign that Hanoi's rulers were considering the option of building their own society rather than conquering their neighbors. In that case we were prepared to cooperate. But I was prey as well to skeptical experience; I left Hanoi with determination rather than optimism. I drove over the same pontoon bridge to Gia Lam airport and then flew in the Soviet transport to Noi Bai airport, where the Presidential aircraft awaited us. We entered it with relief. The soggy weather, the Spartan austerity, the palpable suspiciousness combined in Hanoi to produce the most oppressive atmosphere of any foreign capital I have ever visited. The wary elusiveness of North Vietnam's leaders inhibited real dialogue much more than I had experienced in talks with any other Communist leaders. I reported cautiously to Nixon, giving my sober estimate of the prospects of the Paris Agreement:

They have two basic choices which I frankly pointed out to them (as well as to the Chinese). They can use the Vietnam Agreement as an offensive weapon, nibbling at its edges, pressuring Saigon, confronting us with some hard choices. In this case they would carry out the release of our prisoners and wait till our withdrawals were completed before showing their real colors unambiguously; they would keep their forces in Laos and Cambodia through procrastination of negotiations or straightforward violations; and launch a big new attack soon. They would calculate that we would not have the domestic base or will to respond.

Their other option is to basically honor the Agreement and seek their objectives through gradual evolution. They would welcome a more constructive relationship with us, seek our economic assistance and concentrate on reconstruction and building socialism in the north. Their Indochina allies would be told to pursue their objectives by political and psychological means. They would, in short, adhere to a more peaceful course and let the forces of history work their will, at least for a few years.

The North Vietnamese naturally proclaim the second option as their settled course, but this means nothing. I could not judge from my talks whether their enormous losses, isolation from their allies, and the prospect of aid mean they are ready for a breather. For them the ideal course would be to follow both options at once: violating the Agreement to pursue their objectives and improving relations with us so as to get economic aid. Our essential task is to convince them that they must make a choice between the two. This was the primary objective of my trip. I emphasized that the first course would mean renewed confrontation with us and that they cannot have their aid and eat Indochina too.* On the other hand, if they showed restraint and honored their obligations, we were prepared to normalize relations as we are doing with Peking, and we would not interfere with the political self-determination of Indochina, no matter what its manifestations.

To navigate this passage successfully would have proved very difficult in the best of circumstances. It required a united country and a strong, purposeful, disciplined American government capable of acting decisively and of maintaining the delicate balance of risks and incentives that constituted the Paris Agreement. Watergate soon ensured we did not have it.

---

*This sentence reveals that Winston Lord was one of the drafters of the report. No one else could have produced such a pun, whose merit resided in its awfulness, than the author of the line about one of Hanoi's negotiators: "Xuan Thuy does not make a forest."

III

China: Another Step Forward

Peking Revisited

I FLEW out of Hanoi for a rest stop of forty-eight hours in Hong Kong. Whenever I have left a Communist country (with the exception of China) I have experienced an overwhelming sense of relief. When one breaks free of the monochrome drabness, the stifling conformity, the indifference to the uniqueness of the human personality, the result is a sudden easing of tensions, a feeling akin to exhilaration. Hanoi, as I have said, was probably the grimmest. In striking contrast, the very self-indulgence of Hong Kong's rampant materialism was a garish reminder of the manifold human spirit.

The Chinese used my stay in Hong Kong for one of those subtle signs of goodwill that conveys simultaneously the futility of trying to outthink a people who have specialized in awing visitors for three thousand years. We had delicately not informed the Chinese of our stop in Hong Kong, a British enclave on the Chinese mainland. Instead, we had matter-of-factly noted that as on all previous visits we expected to pick up the obligatory Chinese navigators in Shanghai. This meant a considerable detour for us.

The Chinese have grace as well as a competent intelligence service. Without mentioning our stop in Hong Kong, they suggested we take on navigators in Canton, which was much more convenient. Lest we miss the point, the senior Chinese representative in Hong Kong (technically the New China News Agency bureau chief) demonstrated that nothing occurred in the British Crown Colony beyond the ken of Peking. He inquired at our consulate about the time of my departure so that he could come to the airport to see us off. As indeed he did.

On the afternoon of February 15, 1973, we arrived in Peking for my fifth journey to the Middle Kingdom. By now Peking had become familiar. There was a warmth to our welcome that the settlement of the Vietnam war had clearly released. The Chinese felt free of the constraints imposed by the need to show solidarity with an embattled North Vietnamese ally. Our hosts stood at the bottom of the steps and applauded as my colleagues and I disembarked from the aircraft. We were immediately whisked off along the wide boulevards of Peking to the state guest house that served as our residence, where for the first time the military guards stood at attention and saluted as we passed through the gates. From then on military honors were shown wherever guards were stationed, including at the Great Hall of the People.

Soon after my arrival Chinese Premier Zhou Enlai came to the guest house to ask each of us what he could do to make us more comfortable. Though the Chinese are less formal than the Japanese, their sense of propriety is as subtle and highly developed. The correct answer to the query is "nothing," since it certifies that Chinese hospitality has not been found wanting. If a comment is unavoidable it is best to ask for something the Chinese could not possibly have thought of by themselves. One of my secretaries, whose necessity to respond to the Chinese Premier was not obvious, replied that she wanted a Peking duck dinner — something that had been served as a matter of course on each previous visit. She had a profound impact. Peking duck was not offered again on any of my subsequent visits while I was in office — a little lesson that the Chinese need no instruction in the self-evident!

This little contretemps of protocol aside, the Chinese did us the greatest kindness imaginable. On the evening set aside for a cultural performance they spared us the presentation of one of the revolutionary operas whose stupefying simplemindedness one could escape only by a discreet doze. (This required that to avoid embarrassment one came to just before the lights went on after the final curtain. I am told that West German Chancellor Helmut Schmidt, having opened his belt to be more comfortable, once missed this deadline, awakened only when the applause was well started, and had trouble hitching up his trousers and applauding at the same time.)

On this occasion the cultural program consisted of classical music, both Western and Chinese, performed by the Peking City Orchestra, newly revived after the Cultural Revolution. They attempted — if I may use the word — the Sixth Symphony of Beethoven. Not even my affection for things Chinese can induce me to report that the Chinese musicians were in their element when attempting the Pastoral Symphony after the destructive interruption of the Cultural Revolution; indeed, there were moments when I was not clear exactly what was being played or from which direction on the page. But the symbolism was what mattered: Zhou Enlai intended to modernize, that is, to throw off the shackles of China's recent past and to adapt his country not only to Western technology but also to an awareness of the Western culture that had spawned it. (He was premature. A year later the revolutionary opera had been reinstated; Zhou Enlai was mortally ill; and little more was heard of modernization and opening to the West until after Chairman Mao's death.)

Zhou, as always, was electric, quick, taut, deft, humorous. He greeted me warmly, his expressive face reflecting the fact that he needed no interpreter. (He nevertheless continued to insist on a Chinese translation, gaining an unneeded advantage in hearing my remarks twice and so having twice as much time to think up his reply.) His grasp of international realities was masterly. In the nineteen months since we had come to know each other, Zhou and I had developed an easy camaraderie not untinged with affection:

I think that the Prime Minister [I said early in our first talk] notices that I am especially inhibited in his presence right now.

ZHOU ENLAI: Why?

DR. KISSINGER: Because I read his remark to the press that I am the only man who can talk to him for a half hour without saying anything.

ZHOU ENLAI: I think I said one hour and a half.

The friendly banter indicated that with the peace in Vietnam signed, China could accelerate its move toward us without embarrassment. The growing warmth of Sino-American relations was surely not uninfluenced by Soviet military dispositions. The number of Soviet divisions on the Chinese border had grown from twenty-one in 1969, to thirty-three in 1971, to forty-five in 1973. A common danger clears the mind of trivialities; a further advance in our relations was clearly desirable to demonstrate that we had an interest in China's territorial integrity. In our exchanges before my trip I had suggested as agenda items "the normalization of relations, the current world situation, and future policies in South and Southeast Asia in the postwar period." Even this was not broad enough for Zhou. He replied that "other subjects of mutual interest can also be discussed." It was soon apparent what this other subject was: the establishment of diplomatic offices in each other's capital.

We had come a long way since the Sino-Soviet border clashes of 1969 had first alerted us to the desirability of restoring contact with Peking. More than a year and a half had been spent in finding an intermediary whom both sides trusted. We thought Peking might prefer a Communist country as a channel; we chose Romania. It turned out that the Chinese were too wary of Soviet penetration of Eastern European Communist parties. In time the significant messages reached us through Pakistan, the only country in the world allied with both the United States and China.

During my secret trip to Peking in July 1971, we reestablished direct communication and decided on a Presidential trip to China. But both sides were still too cautious to share their international assessments. On my second visit, in October 1971, under the pretext of preparing for President Nixon's trip, Zhou Enlai and I began an intimate dialogue on major world issues. Not the least paradox in this effort to achieve a joint foreign policy analysis was that Peking had no legal status as far as the United States was concerned. Legally Washington still recognized the Republic of China on Taiwan as the government of China; we had a mutual defense treaty with Taiwan, and American military forces were still stationed there, on what the People's Republic considered its own territory. But Peking had brought us into play despite this affront to its legitimacy to counterbalance the Soviet threat on its northern borders. In light of that threat from the Soviet Union, Peking chose to ignore the insult. In the Shanghai Communiqué at the end of Nixon's visit in February 1972, we and the Chinese agreed on a carefully crafted formulation that accepted the principle of one China but left the resolution to the future. For the time being these differences over Taiwan were being subordinated to what was stated in the Shanghai Communiqué as the common goal of opposing the hegemonic aims of others in Asia. Only one country qualified for this mischievous role: the Soviet Union. In plain language, China and the United States agreed on the need for parallel policies toward the world balance of power.

The visit in February 1973, a year after Nixon's historic journey, began under auspicious circumstances. Not only was Vietnam behind us, but with Nixon just reelected by a landslide, the Chinese felt they could count on dealing with a strong leader for four years. Taiwan did not detain us long. I pointed out that — as we had indicated in the Shanghai Communiqué — with the end of the war in Vietnam the forces supporting our effort there would be withdrawn. Zhou commented that China had no intention of liberating Taiwan by force "at this time." With this both sides decided to leave well enough alone and turn to global — which to Zhou meant Soviet — affairs, reviewing events with a frankness rarely practiced even by close allies.

To Zhou, China's conflict with the Soviet Union was both ineradicable and beyond its capacity to manage by itself. One of the ironies of relations among Communist countries is that Communist ideology, which always claimed that it would end international conflict, has in fact made it intractable. In systems based on infallible truth there can be only one authorized interpretation; a rival claim to represent true orthodoxy is a mortal challenge. On this level, the dispute between Moscow and Peking was over who controlled the liturgy that would inspire the political orientation of Communist and radical parties around the world. This dimension of the conflict could be resolved only by the willing subordination of one to the other, which was impossible; or the victory of one over the other, which in Peking's view was precisely Moscow's aim.

At the same time the conflict between the Soviet Union and China transcended ideology; it was primeval. The two tremendous continental countries shared a frontier of 4,000 miles in a vast arc from the frozen

tundras of Siberia to the stark deserts of Central Asia. The border ran
erratically through the cradle of conquerors of both of them — at times
called Huns, Mongols, Kazakhs — dividing sovereignty in huge areas
without regard to race or language; the peoples straddling the line generally spoke the same native tongue, different from either Russian or
Chinese, thus magnifying the insecurity and potential hostility of both
regimes. In this ill-defined vastness sovereignty in the contemporary sense
is a new phenomenon; borders have swayed back and forth throughout
history with the ambition and power of the contending parties. Much of
Central Asia was appropriated by the tsars only in the nineteenth century
and was now governed by the new rulers in the Kremlin who have
rejected the entire legacy of their predecessors except their conquests.
All this alone would have doomed China and Russia to reciprocal paranoia. The superimposition of ideological conflict and personal jealousies turned inherent rivalry into obsession.

No Soviet leader could overlook the demographic realities. Close to
a billion Chinese were pressing against a frontier that their government
officially did not recognize — in Chinese high school textbooks large
areas of Siberia are shown as Chinese — confronting a mere thirty million Russians in a barren Siberia so forbidding to the Soviet nationalities
that throughout history it has had to be forcibly colonized by convict
labor. In 1974, when I visited Vladivostok, after having been to Tokyo,
Osaka, and Seoul, I noted with a start of surprise that this was not a
teeming Asian city but a provincial European one; in fact it was geographically closer to Honolulu than to Leningrad and much nearer to
Peking than to Moscow. I began to understand how the sense of isolation and foreboding engenders near-hysteria in Soviet leaders brooding
on China.

Similarly, no Chinese leader could ignore the strategic realities. The
vast increase of Soviet military forces along the Chinese frontier since
1969, backed by a sophisticated arsenal of weapons of mass destruction,
hardly bespoke an intention to conciliate. The encounter between the
Soviet Union and China was the stuff of an enduring geopolitical contest.

No negotiation would be able to remove the Soviet military preponderance, which might last for decades, nor the Chinese demographic
edge, which would last forever. Even were Soviet forces "thinned out"
as part of some hypothetical deal, they could always return in a matter
of weeks. And no "compromise" of Chinese boundary claims could
alter the fact that sometime in the next generation the disparity between
Soviet and Chinese power in Asia would first narrow and then tilt the
other way; from then on, Siberia's future would increasingly depend on
Peking's goodwill, which no Chinese government could ensure for
eternity. To be sure, clumsy American diplomacy or demonstrations of

our impotence might drive China and the Soviet Union together. But whatever pattern of coexistence developed, it would not likely be perceived as natural or become permanent — though it could last long enough to damage us grievously.

The Chinese leaders, who were among the shrewdest analysts of international affairs that I have encountered, understood these realities very well indeed. They saw no possibility of compromise with the Soviet Union that was not debilitating. In their view the minimum aim of Chinese statecraft had to be that no other major country would combine with the Soviets; better yet would be to convince such countries to add their strength to the Chinese side. From their experience with foreigners, they could not exclude that others might settle their differences over the prostrate body of China; indeed, during my secret visit in 1971, Zhou had specifically mentioned the possibility that Europe, the Soviet Union, Japan, and we might decide to carve China up again, though he professed indifference to ambitions that he was confident of defeating. The attitude was characteristic: China sought its safety in a reputation of ferocious intractability, in creating an impression, probably accurate, that it would defend its honor and integrity at any cost. It acted as if the smallest concession would start it down a slippery slope and hence had to be resisted as fiercely as an overt challenge to the national survival. China identified security with isolating the Soviet Union, and with adding the greatest possible weight to its side of the scale — which meant a rapid rapprochement with the United States.

The single-mindedness of the Chinese leaders eased our opening to Peking; it also complicated our relationship thereafter. For the parallel commitments to the strategic objective of containment of the Soviet Union did not preclude differences in style, in tactics, and even in perception. For China, ideological intransigence was a method of domestic control as well as a weapon to discourage outside pressures; foreign policy and domestic needs coincided. But we, having just emerged from a divisive war in Vietnam — in which the dedication to peace of America's leadership had been the key domestic issue — could not afford to be perceived as courting confrontation. The Nixon Administration was determined to run what military risks were necessary to prevent Soviet expansionism. However, we could sustain this course at home and with our allies in Europe and Japan only by the demonstration that we had made every honorable effort to avoid confrontation. Nor were we free of the hope, however fragile, that the stabilization of US–Soviet relations achieved in 1972 might in time lead to a more positive era characterized by balance in armaments and restraint in behavior. We could never forget that those nations possessing weapons capable of destroying mankind have a moral obligation to coexist on this planet. American tactics were therefore necessarily more complex, more supple, less fron-

tal than China's — "shadowboxing," Mao called it sarcastically in a
later conversation.

Then there was a difference in the Chinese and American approaches
to international relations. China's was in the great classical tradition of
European statesmanship. The Chinese Communist leaders coldly and
unemotionally assessed the requirements of the balance of power little
influenced by ideology or sentiment. They were scientists of equilibrium, artists of relativity. They understood that the balance of power
involved forces in constant flux that had to be continually adjusted to
changing circumstances. Only one principle was inviolate: No nation
could be permitted to be preeminent, however fleetingly, over the combination of forces that could be arrayed against it, for in that fleeting
moment of neglect independence and identity could be irrevocably lost.
China would not risk its survival on the goodwill of a dominant power;
it would act against potential danger, considering it an abdication
of leadership to permit a possible opponent to amass overwhelming
strength.

But the United States possessed neither the conceptual nor the historical framework for so cold-blooded a policy. The many different strands
that make up American thinking on foreign policy have so far proved
inhospitable to an approach based on the calculation of the national interest and relationships of power. Americans are comfortable with an
idealistic tradition that espouses great causes, such as making the world
safe for democracy, or human rights. American pragmatism calls for the
management of "trouble spots" as they arise, "on their merits," which
is another way of waiting for events — the exact opposite of the Chinese
approach. There is a tradition of equating international conflicts with
legal disputes and invoking juridical mechanisms for their resolution, a
view considered naive by the Chinese, who treat international law as
the reflection and not the origin of the global equilibrium. The legacy
of America's historical invulnerability makes us profoundly uncomfortable with the notion of the balance of power, and with its corollary that
encroachments must be dealt with early (when they do not appear so
clearly dangerous) lest they accumulate a momentum stoppable only by
horrendous exertions, if at all. We in the Nixon Administration felt that
our challenge was to educate the American people in the requirements
of the balance of power. This implied a diplomacy in which our weight
had to be available to the weaker side even in a conflict among Communist states whose domestic practices we deplored. This meant that we
had an interest in preventing a Soviet assault on China and resisting it
if it occurred.

But even if we succeeded in bringing our public along in this intellectual leap, Chinese and American interests and perspectives were different enough to require careful consultation to avoid needless irrita-

tions. Moscow's ideological hostility toward America had a long history; every Leninist textbook had defined us as anathema. At the same time Soviet ideology dictated no particular schedule for our downfall; it could be adjusted to the expediencies of the moment. While our peril was therefore as inexorable as China's, it was more long-term. The United States in 1973 was still militarily more powerful than the USSR and would remain so in mobilizable strength for the indefinite future.

The United States therefore had a margin for maneuver unavailable to China. The Soviet Union was likely to recoil before confrontations with us, if we could only convey our determination sufficiently clearly; nor were we likely to be given ultimatums. A Soviet Union confined to its national territory posed no unmanageable threat to the United States. The danger to us was that the rate of Soviet armament would fuel Soviet global adventurism against others. Unlike the Chinese, we had it in our unaided power to match Soviet arms and to thwart Soviet adventures. With our superior productive capacity, and that of our allies, we would be able to outproduce the Soviets, and if we understood our interests — in light of recent events, not a small qualification — we possessed the means to contain aggressive moves. The United States therefore had the option of playing for time to see what modifications the Soviet system might undergo if it were firmly blocked and as it dealt with its inherent stresses.

Peking did not enjoy this luxury; it was far more immediately threatened. Its greatest peril would arise, ironically, when it had settled its own internal schisms and began to grow economically at a steady rate. This would face the Soviet Union with the prospect that at some clearly predictable point China would become an unmanageable obstacle, especially in conjunction with the other countries Moscow was driving into an adversary status. Whenever Chinese growth appeared self-sustaining the Kremlin would be sorely tempted toward a preemptive attack, unless China was prepared to make drastic concessions to the Soviet Union. The Soviet Union needed no growth in its military capabilities to attack China even if (in 1973) it was not yet strong enough to take on the West. The Chinese leaders could pretend otherwise; they had to put up a bold front; their argument that Moscow was simply feinting in the East to assault the West was a good bargaining pose. But they were much too shrewd to underestimate their danger; their actions contradicted their pronouncements (which in any event were not put forward with much persistence). Thus whatever our motive for negotiating with the Soviets, however sophisticated our explanations, Peking could see no advantage in deferring a showdown, which it saw as inevitable and which it could not really avert by its own action unless it was prepared to condemn itself to permanent weakness.

For Peking there was no benefit and some risk in America's dealings

with Moscow. Even if the Chinese had some personal confidence in
Nixon and me as his representative, they could not be certain how our
successors would use the freedom of maneuver we had gained between
the Communist capitals. And in any event no serious statesman of equilibrium rests his country's security on personal trust in individuals. From
the Chinese point of view, the worse US–Soviet relations were, the less
China needed to worry about its strategic nightmare of a US–Soviet
condominium; the better would be China's bargaining position with respect to both superpowers.

These theoretical considerations became especially relevant for Peking after the end of the war in Vietnam. So long as Hanoi was being
armed by the Kremlin in a bitter war with the United States there was
an inherent limit to the rapprochement possible between Moscow and
Washington. And periodically America would take some drastic action
in Indochina that forced the Soviets to respond if only by slowing down
its diplomacy with us. Zhou Enlai, who was a great diplomat, was not
a bit unhappy that the war in Vietnam restricted our options. By the
same token its end had the opposite effect: America's options would be
increased; they were in fact greater than Peking's. We would be closer
to both Moscow and Peking than they were to each other — an irritating
state of affairs to a country that for centuries had masterfully manipulated the rivalries of what it considered barbarians.

Zhou was far too intelligent to make the Chinese dilemma explicit.
He understood that if the United States and China could articulate parallel analyses of the world situation, compatible actions would follow
automatically, while if we failed to do so, verbal assurances meant little. And so Zhou and I spent long hours comparing our assessments in
a detail impossible between countries having a great deal of day-to-day
business to conduct and with a candor that was our best guarantee to
bridge the difference in perspective.

Zhou raised his concerns elliptically in the form of questions: Would
we emphasize containment even in Asia? Or would we seek our security
in the mutual exhaustion of the two Communist giants? With the war in
Vietnam over, were we prepared to face Soviet expansionism head-on?
Or was the West going to try to conciliate the Soviets in the desire to
"push the ill waters of the Soviet Union . . . eastward" — that is, to
encourage or at least acquiesce in its threats against China?

Zhou's dilemma, in truth, was somewhat different from the way he
posed it. Idealistic Americans, and even those who were fervent anti-
Communists, were unlikely to be capable of cynically and deliberately
embroiling China with the Soviet Union. At the same time, American
leaders such as Nixon, who basically accepted the principles of equilibrium, might not be able to implement their conviction that the United
States had a vital stake in *preventing* the dismemberment or humiliation

of China — even though it was not an ally, had recently been an enemy, and showed no prospect of becoming a democracy.

As far as Nixon and I were concerned, diplomacy toward Moscow
would always be bounded by a firm perception of the American national
interest, which in our view included the territorial integrity of China.
Should the Soviet Union succeed in reducing China to impotence, the
impact on the world balance of power would be scarcely less catastrophic than a Soviet conquest of Europe. Once it was clear that
America was unable to prevent major aggression in Asia, Japan would
begin to dissociate from us. Faced with a Soviet colossus free to concentrate entirely on the West, Europe would lose confidence and all its
neutralist tendencies would accelerate. Southeast Asia, too, would bend
to the dominant trend; the radical forces in the Middle East, South Asia,
Africa, and even the Americas would gain the upper hand. Thus we
could not possibly wish to encourage a Soviet assault on China. We
would have, in my view, no choice except to help China resist.

But I also knew that in the early 1970s such a proposition was as yet
unfamiliar and uncongenial to most public and leadership opinion in
America. Thus it was crucial, first, to strengthen the tangible links between our two countries.

I put these considerations before Zhou Enlai in one of the most candid
and comprehensive accounts of our foreign policy that I ever made to
any foreign leader. I stressed to the Chinese Premier that Nixon and I
had no illusions about Soviet motives, and that China should not be
misled by the tactical maneuvers that our strategy sometimes required:

[T]here are two theoretical possibilities. One is [that the Soviet leaders] genuinely want to bring about a relaxation of tensions in the world. If that is true,
it is in our common interest. . . .

The second possibility is, and the evidence seems to point more in that direction, that the Soviet Union has decided that it should pursue a more flexible
strategy for the following objectives: to demoralize Western Europe by creating
the illusion of peace; to use American technology to overcome the imbalance
between its military and economic capability; to make it more difficult for the
US to maintain its military capability by creating an atmosphere of détente and
isolate those adversaries who are not fooled by this relaxation policy.

["Such as China," interrupted Zhou.

["I was trying to be delicate," I replied and continued:]

Now what is our strategy? . . . We believe that the second interpretation of
Soviet intentions is by far the most probable one. Now first, very candidly, as
you must know from your own reports, we have had a very difficult period
domestically as a result of the war in Vietnam. So on many occasions we have
had to maneuver rather than to have a frontal confrontation. But now [that] the
war in Vietnam has ended, especially if the settlement does not turn into a

constant source of conflict for the US, we can return to the fundamental problems of our foreign policy. Even during this period, which the Prime Minister must have noticed, we have always reacted with extreme violence to direct challenges by the Soviet Union. . . .

[W]hat is our strategy? First we had to rally our own people by some conspicuous successes in foreign policy, to establish a reputation for thoughtful action. Secondly, we had to end the Vietnam war under conditions that were not considered an American disgrace. Thirdly, we want to modernize our military establishment, particularly in the strategic forces. . . . [Fourthly,] ultimately we want to maneuver the Soviet Union into a position where it clearly is the provocateur. Fifthly, we have to get our people used to some propositions that are entirely new to them.

The "new propositions" were that the United States had a vital national interest in the global balance of power in general and in China's territorial integrity in particular, and that we might have to resist challenges even when there was no legal obligation to do so.

At the same time, my discussion of American policy sought to make clear that China and the United States would have to pursue their parallel strategies with the tactics suited to their respective circumstances. As I have said, America had no interest in a policy of unremitting, undifferentiated confrontation with the USSR as China undoubtedly preferred. We saw no need to become a card that Peking could play. China had to be able to count on American support against direct Soviet pressures threatening its independence or territorial integrity; it must not be permitted to maneuver us into unnecessary showdowns. Complex as it might be to execute such a tactic, it was always better for us to be closer to either Moscow or Peking than either was to the other — except in the limiting case of a Soviet attack on China.

By the same token we had to resist the temptation of playing the China card in our turn. To strengthen ties with China as a device to needle the Soviet Union would run the dual risk of tempting a Soviet preemptive attack on China — inviting the very disaster we sought to avoid — and of giving Peking the unnerving impression that, just as we tightened our bonds to respond to Soviet intransigence, we might relax them in response to Soviet conciliation. China would be transformed from a weight in the scale into an object of bargaining — an approach quite incompatible with the necessities that brought about the rapprochement in the first place.

I stressed that despite Chinese reservations we would pursue negotiations with Moscow that we considered in the common interest. But we would give Peking advance information; we would take seriously Chinese views; we would make no agreements aimed against China. We were prepared to make three types of agreements with the USSR, I said: those

that eased tensions in danger spots such as Berlin, where we thought
the overall benefit was on our side; those that were in the mutual and
general interest, such as the recent limitations on strategic arms; and
those that were technically useful but of no major political significance one way or another, such as cultural and scientific exchanges, and
trade (within strict strategic controls and subject to political conditions).

The Chinese Premier, who did not miss a trick, interrupted me: "But
it can also be said that this is consistent with the Soviet policy which is
meant to lull, to demoralize Western Europe."

"I admit," I replied, "both sides are gambling on certain trends. The
Soviet Union believes that it can demoralize Western Europe and paralyze us. We believe . . . that through this policy we are gaining the
freedom of maneuver we need to resist in those places which are the
most likely points of attack or pressure."

Zhou Enlai for his part had no doubt. He called on us to take the lead
in organizing an anti-Soviet coalition. It should stretch from Japan
through China, Pakistan, Iran, and Turkey to Western Europe. The concept was correct, but it could not be implemented through exhortation
alone. Nixon and I agreed on the importance of Turkey, Pakistan, and
Iran — but the next five years would reveal how little domestic support
there was in America for viewing key allies in terms of the world balance of power. (In 1974 the Congress legislated an arms embargo against
our Turkish allies. Aid to Pakistan foundered on Congressional opposition and public indifference, while Iran collapsed with a new administration standing impotently on the sidelines.) And Europe and Japan
would require more delicate ministration, as they were to prove resistant
to Chinese as well as American advice on many crucial issues of the
global balance. Nevertheless, American conservatives would have found
much in common with the analysis of world affairs put forward by the
Chinese Communist Premier. He derided the very thought of negotiating
with the Soviet Union. In his view the expansionist tendencies of the
Soviet system were immutable; negotiations could lead only to confusion. Whatever America did, China's role would be to expose Soviet
motivation and thus provide an intellectual framework for concerted opposition.

It was a difficult passage to navigate, all the more so as Zhou Enlai
had unerringly identified the ambiguity of our policy. On the one hand,
we needed flexibility to ensure that the United States was not paralyzed
by public or allied pressures denouncing it as the cause of tensions. But
it was also true that détente could, as Zhou pointed out, lull the West,
free the Soviet rear for pressure on China, and undermine the general
will to resist. What was the greater risk? The question was never finally
resolved either in our dialogue with the Chinese leaders or in our do-

mestic debate because Watergate was soon to impose its own imperatives.

Tour d'Horizon

FROM these perspectives — similar premises, differing circumstances, parallel strategies — Zhou Enlai and I surveyed the international situation. Since his paramount goal was the containment of Soviet power, the old revolutionary supported anything that enhanced the cohesion and strength of the non-Communist world regardless of the ideology the key countries represented.

In the nineteen months since my first visit, for example, Zhou had done a complete turnabout with respect to Japan. Then, as I have noted, he had described Japan as a potentially aggressive nation that might join with others to carve up China. He had accused us of deliberately reviving Japanese militarism; both privately and publicly he castigated the US–Japanese Security Treaty.[1] By February 1973, although Zhou still uttered a formalistic warning about Japanese militarism, in practice he treated Japan as an incipient ally. (China and Japan had restored diplomatic relations, encouraged by us, when Japanese Prime Minister Kakuei Tanaka visited China in September 1972.) Zhou Enlai now acknowledged that Japan's ties to the United States braked militarist tendencies in Japan and gave Japan an indispensable sense of security. He asked me to note that Peking had ceased its attacks on the Security Treaty; indeed, China now urged the closest cooperation between the United States and Japan. Chairman Mao would later offer the friendly advice that to preserve Japan's dignity I should never visit Peking without also stopping in Tokyo. We had already decided that this was imperative. By the time I left office I had visited Tokyo more frequently than any other major capital.

Western Europe was seen in precisely the same context; the discussions were a primer on containment of the Soviet Union. Since Europe had been my field of study for twenty years and I knew many of its leaders, Zhou peppered me with questions about European politics, policies, and personalities. A number of Western European leaders had recently been invited to Peking to be lectured (to their amazement) about the importance of European unity, Atlantic cohesion, and a strong NATO defense. Later on I came to refer to China only half-jokingly as one of our better NATO allies.

Zhou, the student of balance of power, had difficulty coming to grips with European attitudes substantially at variance with his recollections of the Twenties. He could not understand why Europe was so reluctant to transform its economic strength into military power, or why a continent capable of defending itself would insist on relying on a distant ally.

It was clear that China, if it had comparable resources, would not accept a similar dependency. Because Zhou judged Europe economically strong, militarily weak, and psychologically uncertain, he urged us to get our priorities straight. Transatlantic trade disputes, he insisted, must not be permitted to get in the way of defense cooperation against the Soviet Union. American policy in Europe had to be wise enough, Zhou argued, to distinguish between form and substance, between healthy assertions of independence and unreliable submissiveness. We needed to be especially solicitous of French President Georges Pompidou, he said; French claims to independence might irritate us but we should never forget that France was conducting the strongest foreign policy in Europe, which inevitably enhanced Western security. However annoying French tactics might prove from time to time, Zhou emphasized, we must never forget that a strong France also restrained German temptations toward Moscow. For Zhou shared the view of several of West Germany's allies that Chancellor Willy Brandt's *Ostpolitik* (his Eastern treaties with the Soviet Union, East Germany, and Poland) contained the risk that what started as gestures of reconciliation would turn into a free-wheeling German nationalism that might demoralize Europe.

Zhou Enlai had high regard for the British Prime Minister, Edward Heath. The subject of Heath gave Zhou an opportunity for a homily on the general Chinese preference for conservative leaders over socialist ones; they were less likely to be taken in by Soviet blandishments and faced fewer internal pressures in supporting a strong defense. In fact, Zhou suspected that Europe, especially, might be tempted to channel Moscow's "ill waters" toward the East. The Chinese clearly looked to the United States to prevent this danger, though how we might do so if they truly suspected us of the same tendency they never explained.

Once the common interest in containing Soviet power was firmly established, Indochina appeared in a different light. Zhou understood that if the Paris Agreement came apart, one of two unfavorable scenarios would unfold: Either the war would resume, and with it the Chinese dilemma of having to run risks in its relations with us on behalf of North Vietnam, a country that it profoundly distrusted. Or, even worse from Peking's point of view, Hanoi would achieve hegemony in Indochina without a fight, discredit the United States internationally as a paper tiger, and create on China's southern border a powerful Vietnamese state, with a long tradition of anti-Chinese feeling, dependent for its military supplies entirely on the Soviet Union.

The fact was that in Indochina, American and Chinese interests were nearly parallel. A unified Communist Vietnam dominant in Indochina was a strategic nightmare for China even if ideology prevented reality from being explicitly stated. Zhou Enlai was therefore sincere when he protested his commitment to the strict implementation of the Paris

Agreement, for its result if successful would be to deny Hanoi hegemony and to buffer it with three independent states, Laos, Cambodia,
and South Vietnam. Interestingly enough, he had always urged a cease-
fire much like what we had achieved, the implication of which inevitably would permit the South Vietnamese government to survive. Unlike
many of our domestic opponents, he never pressed us to overthrow Thieu
and to install Hanoi's puppet regime.

On Laos and Cambodia, Zhou began with his favorite device for dissociating from Hanoi, well tested in the crises of 1972. He disclaimed
any special knowledge of events in these two countries — an unlikely
proposition considering the meticulousness of Chinese preparation for
meetings with American leaders and their historical relationship to Indochina. But the fiction permitted him to escape into ambiguity where
he did not want to make his differences with Hanoi explicit. As it turned
out, Zhou's emphasis was practical. In Laos, Zhou hoped that the peace
negotiations between the Royal Laotian Government and the Pathet Lao
would prosper and result in a truly neutral coalition; China would welcome an early cease-fire. He spoke highly of the Laotian King Savang
Vatthana ("a patriot and honest") — not one of Hanoi's favorites —
and supported the legitimacy of neutralist Premier Souvanna Phouma.
In other words, China favored what we did in Laos: a neutral, peaceful,
non-Communist regime independent of Hanoi.

Zhou also lifted a corner of the veil that had mystified us about one
of China's strangest projects during the Vietnam war. For nearly a decade Chinese troops had been building a road in northern Laos through
the forbidding mountains and jungles bordering the two countries. Up
to 20,000 Chinese soldiers, protected by Chinese antiaircraft batteries,
had been engaged in this project on the territory of another sovereign
state. Souvanna often asserted to us that it was done against Laotian
wishes; the Chinese claimed it was authorized by prior agreement. I was
never able to disentangle the legal claims. Souvanna refused to state
publicly that the road was unauthorized; whether out of fear or because
he knew something he was reluctant to affirm, it was impossible to tell.
Peking refused to substantiate its claim of Lao approval; again, we could
not know whether because it wished to grant us no status to inquire into
its activities close to its borders or because no unambiguous proof existed.

By February 1973, at any rate, the legal basis for Chinese road-build-
ing in Laos interested us much less than its strategic purpose. And on
this subject Zhou was elliptically clear. For most of the war we had
thought the road was intended to supply the Hanoi-controlled Pathet
Lao. We had occasionally made plans — never carried out — to bomb
it. Only gradually did it dawn on us that no supplies ever came down
the road and that it sat on the flank of the advancing North Vietnamese.

I put forward my theory through the device of telling Zhou of Thai fears that the road might be aimed at them. He replied that China was interested in good relations with Bangkok; road construction would continue, but the road would end well before the Thai border. If that was the case, the only purpose of the road could be to contain and if necessary to threaten Hanoi. For all the years of the Vietnam war, Peking had been building a foothold in Laos on the flank of the advancing North Vietnamese to counteract the possible domination of its presumed ally over all Indochina!

China's emerging split with Hanoi became even clearer when we turned to Cambodia. China's official position was similar to Hanoi's: support for the Communist insurgency formally headed by Prince Norodom Sihanouk. But there the similarity ended. Hanoi treated Sihanouk as a barely tolerated appendage to the Communist Khmer Rouge; Zhou gave the Prince pride of place. Hence Zhou did not — indeed, could not — adopt the peremptory insistence of Pham Van Dong and Le Duc Tho that we overthrow the Lon Nol government in Phnom Penh. Zhou was too familiar with Cambodian conditions not to grasp that Sihanouk's balancing act depended on the continued existence of two contending forces to be balanced. It was only natural for Zhou to say:

> I do not mean that the forces that he [Lon Nol] represents do not count. . . . We understand our respective orientations. Because it is impossible for Cambodia to become completely red now. If that were attempted, it would result in even greater problems.

It was astonishing for a leader of the country that considered itself the fount of revolution to state that the complete communization of a country might magnify its problems. But it was the truth. Complete communization would render Sihanouk irrelevant, demoralize Saigon, and virtually hand Indochina to Hanoi.

Zhou's attitude suggested that we might yet reach a practical agreement. If the forces represented by Lon Nol could survive a settlement, there was something to talk about. If our basic precondition — that those who had relied on us not be turned over to Communist rule —was met, Sihanouk might well emerge in an important, perhaps decisive, role as a link between contending forces and as their balancer. I therefore proposed an immediate meeting between a representative of Lon Nol's government and Sihanouk's Prime Minister Penn Nouth to negotiate a coalition structure. We would not insist, I said, that Lon Nol himself participate in such a government so long as the forces he led were represented.

Zhou replied that Cambodia was a complicated problem. It was not simply a civil war, he said; outside forces (meaning the North Vietnamese) were deeply engaged. There were also many factions in the Sihanouk-led insurgent movement with different points of view (meaning that some — the Khmer Rouge — rejected any compromise). Not every element of the insurgency agreed to the central role for Sihanouk I had outlined (meaning that the Khmer Rouge wished to use him as a figurehead at best). Still, Zhou said he would pass our ideas to the interested parties, primarily Sihanouk, "in our [China's] wording" — meaning that in conveying our position (flatly rejected by Hanoi's leaders only a few days before) he would identify himself with it to a degree. After consulting with the parties, Zhou said, he would be in touch with us again. For the first time, China was approaching an active role in Indochinese peace negotiations.

There was every reason to do so. For China's interest in Cambodia, so oddly parallel to our own, was much more urgent. What was involved for us in holding Hanoi to the Paris Agreement was above all our global credibility. What was involved for China was an issue of national security, the emergence at its southern border of a well-armed major power of close to fifty million people and a fanatic leadership allied with the Soviet Union. Cambodia in that sense was the linchpin of Indochina; its collapse spelled the disintegration of South Vietnam and hence hegemony for Hanoi. Zhou's major concern, therefore, was less for a Khmer Rouge victory than for a structure that would best guarantee Cambodian independence and neutrality. He understood that we had a common problem: how to transcend the passions of the Cambodian parties lest in their fratricidal hatred they destroyed each other and all hope for the survival of their country.

We agreed on the objective, Zhou said. The question was how to accomplish it. I used the occasion to remind Zhou why a decent outcome was important to the United States, in the common interest, for reasons transcending Indochina:

> [P]recipitate American withdrawal from Southeast Asia would be a disaster.
> . . . The most difficult task which President Nixon has in his second term is
> to maintain an American responsibility for the world balance of power, or for
> an anti-hegemonial policy by the United States. Therefore it is not desirable for
> the United States to be conducting policies which will support the isolationist
> element in America.

Zhou did not contradict this statement; in the months to come he acted as if he agreed with it.

The Liaison Offices

As our policies and China's were beginning to move in parallel, our clumsy means of communication became inadequate. Lacking diplomatic relations (because of America's recognition of Taiwan), we had communicated in two channels. Most of the day-to-day business had gone via Paris, where Peking's Ambassador was Huang Zhen, a former general and veteran of the Long March and a member of the Central Committee of the Chinese Communist Party. I knew him well as a colleague of many secret encounters. His counterpart was our Ambassador to France, Arthur Watson. But in the Nixon Administration, at least in Nixon's first term, especially sensitive messages to key foreign governments were passed in special "backchannels" directly under the control of the White House. We created a backchannel to China through China's mission to the United Nations in New York, headed since 1971 by the distinguished Huang Hua (who was later elevated to Foreign Minister).

Initially Peking stressed that it preferred the Paris channel. The UN mission was to be used only for emergencies — perhaps it did not want us to have the benefits of a Chinese embassy without diplomatic recognition. Soon the necessity of rapid communication and the importance of candid discussion had caused both sides to stretch the definition of "emergency" more and more widely. From November 1971 until May 1973, I traveled secretly to New York on a score of occasions for face-to-face meetings with Huang Hua, usually in a CIA–provided "safe house" in mid-Manhattan, a seedy apartment whose mirrored walls suggested less prosaic purposes.

But this romantic environment left much to be desired in diplomatic logistics. Furthermore, if our joint strategic assessment was correct, Peking and Washington needed to show in dramatic ways that the two nations were in fact drawing closer. From Peking's point of view — and, properly understood, from ours as well — such public gestures signaled that the United States would not be indifferent to military pressure against China.

I had come to Peking in February 1973 with no clear-cut plan for increasing visible contacts. I had intended to propose some modest step, such as an American trade office in China; we remained convinced that Peking still did not want to open any office in Washington so long as Taiwan's representatives were there. Unexpectedly, Zhou Enlai decided to make a major advance that amounted to establishing de facto diplomatic relations between our two countries. In the best Middle Kingdom tradition he maneuvered so that it appeared that the proposal had come from me. It was flattering and gave me a stake in what had been accomplished. It was only marginally true.

As we talked about bilateral relations, I mentioned the utility of a permanent point of contact. Zhou allowed himself to seem mildly interested. He asked me whether I had any idea how to implement it. Consular representation did not interest him; it was too technical. Neither did the idea of a trade office in any of its variations strike a spark. He obviously wanted to emphasize political and not commercial relation-

ships. So I dusted off the idea of a liaison office, which had been prepared for Hanoi and peremptorily rejected there. We had not yet, in
Pham Van Dong's view, earned the privilege of permanent association
and regularized harassment. Zhou perked up. I was neither very specific
nor did I presume to offer reciprocity in Washington, so certain were
we that Peking's envoys would never appear where Taiwan's representatives were established.

Zhou said he would "consider" my "proposal" of a liaison office.
It was not clear to me that I had formally made it. The next day he
"accepted" it. He added a subtle wrinkle, however. China *would* insist
on reciprocity: a Chinese liaison office should be established in Washington as well. He was prepared to discuss technical arrangements immediately — thus proving that he had given our "proposal" more
thought than we had. The liaison offices as envisaged by him were, as
an observer has remarked, "embassies in all but name."[2] Their personnel would have diplomatic immunity; they would have their own secure
communications; their chiefs would be treated as ambassadors and they
would conduct all exchanges between the two governments. They would
not become part of the official diplomatic corps, but this had its advantages since it permitted special treatment without offending the established protocol order.

At first the plan was for professional diplomats of middle rank to head
the liaison offices. Upon reflection Nixon and I decided to appoint David
K. E. Bruce, one of our ablest ambassadors and most distinguished
public figures. He would symbolize the importance we attached to the
assignment; we would trust him completely with our most sensitive information. He would not chafe at the absence of routine chores by which
a lesser man might have judged the importance of the job. And he had
the wisdom and experience to ensure the success of the essential business of the liaison office: to maintain the maximum degree of harmony
in the respective perceptions of two capitals professing contradictory
ideologies, evolving from diametrically opposite histories, and now
united by comparable necessities.

Zhou Enlai reciprocated by designating Huang Zhen from Paris. I had
come to like enormously this warm and sensitive man whose hobby was
painting. Like all Chinese diplomats he was rigidly disciplined. Yet he
always managed to convey the intangibles behind his instructions. He
was masterly, especially during the most complicated part of the Vietnam negotiations, in conveying unimpaired Chinese goodwill without
compromising his government with its fractious allies in Hanoi. He
managed to instill trust even when we later had to go through some
difficult periods caused by domestic pressures in both countries. Both
sides demonstrated the importance they attached to the evolving relationship by sending their very best men to each other's capital.

This was how we found a practical solution to the dilemma that our dispute over Taiwan prevented full normalization while our common concerns with the balance of power required regular and intimate political contact. The principle that formal diplomatic ties had to await an agreement over Taiwan remained intact. But the reality was that, when diplomatic relations were eventually established (on January 1, 1979), the event essentially consisted of changing the signs on the gates of the Liaison Offices to read "Embassy." In less than two years we had advanced from tentative handwritten notes sent through intermediaries to close political relations even more intimate than most countries with formal diplomatic ties enjoyed with Peking.

A Meeting with Mao

DURING his lifetime, Mao Zedong, Chairman of the Communist Party of China, was shrouded in mystery and reverence much as were the emperors whom he replaced. He lived in a modest house within the walls of the old imperial palace, the "Forbidden City." His pronouncements were cited with awe by our Chinese hosts, who seemed able to read precise meanings into his most obscure observations. Even Premier Zhou Enlai insisted that all critical decisions came from Mao, and he sometimes recessed a meeting with me on the excuse of needing guidance from the Chairman. When he returned with pithy, fire-breathing revolutionary rhetoric, it was highly plausible that it came, as Zhou said, on the specific orders of Mao and reflected his thought. Whether Zhou intended this as a measure of dissociation from the Chairman or to add emphasis to his remarks, I was never quite sure.

Mao's portrait was in those days everywhere in Peking; his calligraphy covered billboards and public buildings; his personal dominance of the polity he had created was all-encompassing. The emphasis on personality in a Marxist system that in theory asserted the predominant role of material factors and historical forces was astonishing. It was as if the titanic figure who had risen from humble origins to rule nearly a quarter of mankind did not trust the permanence of the ideology in whose name he had prevailed. Challenging the gods, he sought immortality in the adoration of those vast millions who had endured the passage of so many conquerors, who had absorbed so much forced transformation only to transcend events by their endurance, their practicality, and their pervasive humanity.

And Mao sensed the ephemerality of this acclaim; sycophancy was the device of the least trustworthy. Dreading the fate of the Emperor Qin Shi Huangdi, who had revolutionized China for twenty years only to sink into the oblivion reserved for those who presume to alter China's elemental rhythms, Mao may have accelerated what he was so eager to avoid. By attempting to inflict upon his country the tour de force of a permanent revolution he also reawakened the historical Chinese yearning for continuity. The Chinese people have survived not by exaltation but by perseverance, not by spurts but by a steady pace. They have become great by a unique blend of culture, common sense, and self-discipline. Their greatest leaders find themselves assimilated sooner or later by this enduring mass of individualists who will suffer but not change their essential character and who understand, even when they cannot articulate, that in China ultimate stature goes to those who can reduce historic goals to the human scale. The Chinese people are talented but also skeptical, aspiring but also conscious that no one man's intuition, however tremendous, can provide the answer to the dilemmas of history.

Thus by a remarkable irony the leader who seems to have survived in the hearts of his countrymen is not the epic giant who made the Chinese revolution but his much more anonymous disciple, Zhou Enlai, who worked unobtrusively to assure the continuity of life rather than the permanence of upheaval.

In February 1973, however, there was no question about who was preeminent. Mao towered above everyone. He rarely saw foreigners; almost without exception those were heads of state or the highest ranking Communist Party officials. I had met Mao once with Nixon's entourage during the first Presidential visit in Peking. The summons had come suddenly, for there was never a formal appointment. This was partly because the Chairman's frail health made it hazardous to predict when he would be in a condition to receive visitors. Design was likely involved as well, for remoteness enhances mystery and aloofness is an attribute of majesty. Not that Mao needed artifice to magnify his impact. I had been struck during his meeting with Nixon by the almost physical force of his authority. He had dominated the room as I have never seen any person do except Charles de Gaulle.

My summons this time came on February 17, when Zhou Enlai and I were meeting in the state guest house. It was around 11:00 at night, because Zhou liked to work late and we nearly always had a session after dinner. We met in the state guest house because Zhou made it a practice — despite the wide gap in our protocol rank — to call on me as often as I did on him. Suddenly the unfailing serenity of our interlocutors was ruffled by the appearance of Miss Wang Hairong, Assistant Minister of Foreign Affairs. Reported to be a relative of Mao's, with the look of an easily startled deer, she carried unobtrusiveness almost to the point of invisibility.

Now she placed a note before Zhou. He continued talking on Soviet motivations for another minute and then said: "I would like to let you know a new piece of news. Chairman Mao has invited you to a meeting.

You can go with your colleague, Mr. Lord.'' This neatly ruled out the rest of my party. It also gave Winston Lord an opportunity to appear for the first time in a picture with Mao; he had been present as note-taker at Nixon's meeting with Mao in 1972, but we had asked the Chinese to delete him from the communiqué and to crop him from the picture in order to ease the offense to the State Department, none of whose officials attended.

One always went to see Mao in Chinese cars. And the Chinese never permitted American security men on these visits. We set off in Zhou's battered old 1939-vintage automobile along the broad avenues leading from the state guest house to the center of town, which was almost completely deserted at this hour of the night. Before reaching Tien An Men Square and the Great Hall of the People, we turned off to the left through a traditional Chinese gate with red columns that interrupted a long vermilion wall paralleling the wide thoroughfare. The road took us past modest houses behind high, nondescript walls for another mile or so; it wound along a lake on one side and an occasional residence in the Soviet bureaucratic style on the other. Mao's domicile was modest, like that of a middle functionary. We drove up to a covered portico; no special security precautions were visible. Inside, across a small sitting room and a wide hallway, was Mao standing in front of a semicircle of easy chairs covered with brown slipcovers. Books were everywhere: on the floor in front of Mao, on the little tables between the armrests, on bookcases that lined the wall.

Mao uttered a few pleasantries while Chinese cameramen took pic-tures. We learned later that the press treatment in the *People's Daily* the next day was always a good barometer of the state of our relations. On this occasion in February 1973, the *People's Daily* gave banner head-lines to our meeting, with two front-page photographs; the lights were green for friendship.

The purpose of the meeting was to underline that friendship between the United States and China was to be consummated while Mao was still alive. Mao wasted no time in making this point. As we headed for the easy chairs and while the photographers were still in the room, he said: ''I don't look bad'' (anticipating my thought, which indeed com-pared his appearance favorably with that when he had met Nixon just a year before), ''but God has sent me an invitation.'' Somehow it did not seem incongruous that the leader of the most populous atheistic state, the dialectician of materialism, should invoke the Deity. No being of lesser rank could presume to interrupt the Chairman's labors. Even more striking was the matter-of-fact casualness with which Mao treated the imminent end of his rule and hinted at the urgency to complete whatever business required his personal attention.

As he had a year earlier with Nixon, Mao proceeded to engage me in a joshing Socratic dialogue that made its key points in seemingly spontaneous and accidental fashion. His observations seemed random but formed a pattern spelling out a series of directives for his subordinates. Mao drew a line under the past by one of his indirections. Both Presidents Harry Truman and Lyndon Johnson had died within the previous two months, he noted. With them the old China policy and the old Vietnam policy had been buried. In his mocking way, Mao challenged me: "At that time, you . . . opposed us. We also opposed you. So we are two enemies." He laughed.

"Two former enemies," I replied.

That was not enough for Mao: "Now we call the relationship between ourselves a friendship," he insisted.

And Mao immediately gave this commonplace significance by stressing one of the basic principles of Chinese statecraft: that maneuvering for petty advantage is shortsighted and that we should do nothing to undermine mutual confidence. "Let us not speak false words or engage in trickery," he insisted. "We don't steal your documents. You can deliberately leave them somewhere and try us out," he joked, though he gave us no clue as to where we might carry out this test and how we might know that the Chinese had not taken advantage of it. There was no sense in running small risks, Mao was saying. And while he was at it he questioned the utility of big intelligence operations as well. Indeed, he considered intelligence services generally overrated. Once they knew what the political leaders wanted, their reports came in "as so many snowflakes." But on really crucial matters they usually failed. The Chinese services had not known about Lin Biao's plotting* nor about my desire to come, he said. He suspected that our intelligence agencies gave us the same problem.

In short, large goals required farsighted policies, not tactical maneuvering. The challenge before our two countries was to fashion joint action despite ideological differences. In this both sides must remain true to their principles while pursuing common objectives. Mao recalled with approval Nixon's comment to him in 1972 that China and the United States in coming closer to each other were fulfilling their own necessities. Mao took the proposition a somewhat cynical step further by indicating that we would strengthen domestic support for our cooperation if we took occasional potshots at each other — just so long as we did not take our own pronouncements too seriously:

> So long as the objectives are the same, we would not harm you nor would you harm us. . . . Actually it would be that sometime we want to criticize you for a while and you want to criticize us for a while. That, your President said,

---

*Lin Biao, Mao's former defense minister and heir apparent, died in an air crash in September 1971, allegedly fleeing to the Soviet Union after his plot against Mao had been unmasked.

is the ideological influence. You say, ''away with you Communists!'' We say, ''away with you imperialists!'' Sometimes we say things like that. It would not do not to do that.

Mao Zedong, the father of China's Communist revolution, who had convulsed his people in his effort to achieve doctrinal purity, went to great pains to show that slogans scrawled on every wall in China were meaningless, that in foreign policy national interests overrode ideological differences. Ideological slogans were a facade for considerations of balance of power. Each side would be expected to insist on its principles; but each had an obligation not to let them interfere with the imperatives of national interest — a classic definition of modern Machiavellianism. ''I think both of us must be true to our principles,'' I replied, getting into the spirit of things. ''And in fact it would confuse the situation if we spoke the same language.''

In this almost jocular manner we reviewed the world situation until almost 1:30 in the morning. In Mao's view the Soviet threat was real and growing. He warned against a fake détente that would sap resistance to Soviet expansionism and confuse the peoples of the West. The United States and Europe should resist the temptation to ''push the ill waters eastward.'' It was a futile strategy, for in time the West, too, would be engulfed. The United States and China must cooperate. This required institutionalizing our relationship. Setting up the liaison offices in each other's capitals was a good decision. He urged an expansion of contacts and even trade, calling the present level ''pitiful.''

In Mao's view the United States would serve the common interest best by taking a leading role in world affairs, by which he meant constructing an anti-Soviet alliance. Long gone was the day when Peking denounced the American system of alliances as an imperialist device; in its current view they had become pillars of international security. American troops abroad, castigated for decades, were useful provided they were deployed intelligently. The Chairman criticized our military deployments in Asia only because in his view they reflected no strategic plan: They were ''too scattered.'' As had Zhou, Mao stressed the importance of close American cooperation also with Western Europe, Japan, Pakistan, Iran, and Turkey. We should build up our defenses and keep our eye on the fundamental (Soviet) challenge rather than squabble over short-term problems with our allies. He urged a strengthening of unity among the industrial democracies:

As for you, in Europe and Japan, we hope that you will cooperate with each other. As for some things it is all right to quarrel and bicker about, but fundamental cooperation is needed.

And yet for all his preoccupation with foreign policy, the Chairman could not avoid the obsession of his last years with Peking's internal problems, which as so often in China's history seemed to follow their own momentum. Repeatedly Mao warned me about the pressures on him from radicals, but he did it so allusively that my dense Occidental mind did not immediately follow his meaning. "You know China is a very poor country," said Mao. "We don't have much. What we have in excess is women."

Thinking that Mao was joking, I replied in kind: "There are no quotas for those, or tariffs."

"So if you want them we can give a few of those to you, some tens of thousands," shot back Mao.

"Of course, on a voluntary basis," interrupted Zhou.

"Let them go to your place," Mao continued. "They will create disasters. That way you can lessen our burdens." He laughed uproariously.

But Mao was not yet sure that I had got the point; he returned to the theme a few minutes later. "Do you want our Chinese women? . . . [W]e can let them flood your country with disaster and therefore impair your interests." Since Americans were notoriously slow-witted, Mao returned to the theme yet again —by which time I understood he was making a point, though not yet what. Afterward, Winston Lord's wife, Bette, explained it to me: that conditions in China were far from being as stable as they looked; that women — meaning Mao's wife, Jiang Qing, as leader of the radical faction — were stirring up China and challenging the prevailing policy.

Personalities were not, however, the heart of China's domestic problem. What confronted Mao in his last days was the centuries-old dilemma of Chinese modernization. Historically, China has established its preeminence more frequently by the force of its example and its cultural superiority than through the displays of raw power that have characterized the political history of Europe. Indeed, China has been so dominant in Asia for centuries that it has had no direct experience of the notions of balance of power or sovereign equality in its own sphere. (All the more remarkable how adept it became at it when the outside world gave no other choice.) Other societies have been considered not in equilibrium but in some sort of tributary relationship to China. So firmly established was the concept of Chinese majesty that its rulers often considered it prudent to make larger gifts to their vassals than they received in tribute.

It was a massive shock when in the nineteenth century China learned that the barbarians of the West had acquired a technology that could enable them to impose their will on the Middle Kingdom as well as on other Asian states. But while Japan reacted to the same challenge by deciding to modernize at whatever cost (and miraculously preserved its individuality in the process), China was not prepared to hazard its culture on which it based its claim to greatness. Modern technology is universal; it brings with it a degree of standardization that carries uniformity in its train. To be like everyone else was to the Chinese a repellent thought. Technology and modernization thus threatened China as no other nation, for they challenged its essence, its claim to uniqueness.

Deliberately, China rejected the Japanese route; it encapsuled itself in its traditions, relying on its marvelous diplomatic skill and self-assurance to ward off the hated (and feared) foreign devils. And China in fact fared better than any other nation where European colonizers established themselves. By manipulating the rivalries and greed of the imperialist powers, China maintained a larger margin of independence than any other country in a comparable position.

Mao's revolution reflected the same historic Chinese ambivalence. In a curious way it was both a rebellion against China's old values and a confirmation of them. Maoism sought to overcome China's past but like traditional Confucianism it saw society as an ethical and educational instrument, though infused with a diametrically opposite doctrine fashioned by the peasant's son from rural Hunan province. The object of the Great Cultural Revolution unleashed by Mao in 1966 — and where else but in China would a bloody political upheaval call itself "cultural"? — was precisely the eradication of those elements of modernity that were not uniquely Chinese, an assault on the Western influences and bureaucratization that threatened to level China and absorb it into a universal culture.

By February 1973, when we met, the aged Chairman had realized that while his latest grandiose conception had dramatized his country's independence, it had simultaneously doomed it to impotence. He knew now — if perhaps only as a transient conviction — that China's continuing to live apart from the rest of the world would ensure its irrelevance and expose it to untold danger. China, he indicated not without melancholy, would have to go to school abroad. He had halted the Cultural Revolution, and he remarked with sadness that the Chinese people were "very obstinate and conservative." The time had come for them to study foreign languages, he said, which was another way of stressing the importance of learning from abroad. That, too, had been the symbolism of playing Beethoven at the cultural event. He would send more Chinese to school overseas, he repeated. He himself was learning English. And something had to be done to simplify the Chinese written language to enable Chinese to grasp foreign ideas better.

But the aged Chairman was too old to carry through to its conclusion another revolution against the instincts of his Party, the traditions of his people, and deep down his own. Within a year of this conversation with me he overturned the maxims he had advanced late at night in his study, or at least he permitted others to do so. Zhou Enlai was retired and within another year his successor, Deng Xiaoping, was toppled by the very forces Mao seemed to be resisting in 1973, once again delaying the modernization that one side of Mao recognized as essential. Did Mao encourage the radicals who later came to be called the Gang of Four, or did they take advantage of his growing feebleness? Probably there was a little of both. Mao died still wrestling with the dilemmas and contradictions of his revolution and indeed of Chinese history.

After my session with Mao, the rest was anticlimax. My next day's talks with Zhou Enlai covered some details of setting up the liaison offices; I informed him of our plans for new diplomatic initiatives toward Europe and the Middle East. Zhou Enlai had also agreed to release two American pilots whose planes had strayed over Chinese territory during the Vietnam war. The Chinese held another prisoner, John Downey, captured during an intelligence operation in 1950 and sentenced to life imprisonment. Downey's sentence had already been commuted, making him eligible for release late in 1973. But Zhou dropped a hint that his release would be expedited if we put forward a compassionate reason. Within a month Downey's mother fell ill; we communicated that fact to Zhou Enlai. On March 12, 1973, Downey was released, clearing the slate at last of the human legacies of the period of hostility between the United States and the People's Republic of China.

Conclusion

M Y journey to Asia was my first foreign trip free of the incubus of the Vietnam war. Hanoi had been ominous; Peking was an augury of positive possibilities that lay ahead once we turned our attention to creative foreign policy. We were improving relations with both Moscow and Peking despite the fact that both capitals would have preferred a less ambiguous stance from us — and we were succeeding perhaps for that reason. My report to Nixon drafted on the plane home from the Far East noted:

With conscientious attention to both capitals we should be able to continue to have our mao tai and drink our vodka too. Peking, after all, assuming continued hostility with the USSR, has no real alternative to us as a counterweight (despite its recent reaching out to Japan and Western Europe as insurance). And Moscow needs us in such areas as Europe and economics.

But this is nevertheless a difficult balancing act that will increasingly face us with hard choices. . . . We are useless to Peking as a counterweight to Moscow if we withdraw from the world, lower our defenses, or play a passive international game. Mao and Chou [Zhou] urged a more aggressive American presence — countering Soviet designs in various areas, keeping close ties with our allies, maintaining our defense posture. If the Chinese became convinced that we were heeding the inward impulses of voluble sectors of Congress, the public and the press, we would undoubtedly witness a sharp turn in Peking's attitude. You and I have, of course, assured the PRC leaders privately, as well as proclaiming publicly, our intentions to maintain a responsible international role.

To ensure the cohesion and self-assurance in America for such a world role had been the preeminent purpose of the policies — and sometimes the anguish — of Nixon's first term. In the second term we hoped to give perspective and meaning to the struggles of the first. The visit to Peking had marked a great step forward, we thought, toward the better future we sought to build. Instead, it became the last normal diplomatic enterprise before Watergate engulfed us.

IV

The Gathering Impact of Watergate

A Rude Awakening

THE moment when all hopes for a period of healing dissolved can be precisely charted. It was on a weekend in the middle of April 1973.

On the evening of Friday, the thirteenth of April, the Federal City Club of Washington — its membership predominately Democratic — in a gesture of goodwill, bestowed its public service award on me, a senior representative of the Nixon Administration, and on Senator John Sherman Cooper, a senior Republican Senator. The Federal City Club of Washington was founded in the early 1960s as a protest against the admissions policies of the dominant, prestigious, and staid Metropolitan Club. Leading figures of the Kennedy Administration and sympathetic journalists had resigned from the latter and founded a new club a few blocks away in the Sheraton-Carlton Hotel. Unfortunately, its finances did not equal the idealism of its founders; it consisted essentially of one large dining room, a bar, and a small terrace wedged between high and undistinguished office buildings.

The Nixon Administration did not have much use for either club. Its key members mistrusted the Federal City as too liberal and the Metropolitan as too Establishment. Nothing could better signify their isolation from the permanent community of the nation's capital and political life — an isolation that contributed to their undoing.

That evening a distinguished group had assembled; nearly everybody of importance in Washington was there to honor two leading Republicans — except for other senior members of the Nixon Administration only recently reelected with the second largest margin in American history. Senator Cooper and I brought to the occasion an appeal for national unity. My theme was the hope that, with Vietnam behind us, the nation's foreign policy could combine the exuberant idealism of the Kennedy Administration (which I had served briefly and inconspicuously) with the unsentimental emphasis on national interest of the Nixon Administration:

As a nation, we have been shaken by the realization of our fallibility, and it has been painful to grasp that we are no longer pristine, if we ever were. Later than any nation, we have come to the recognition of our limits. In coming to a recognition of our limits, we have achieved one of the definitions of maturity, but the danger is that we will learn that lesson too well; that instead of a recognition that we cannot do everything, we will fall into the illusion that we cannot do anything.

Nothing is more urgent right now than a serious and compassionate debate of where we are going, because if we lose the capacity for great conception, we can be administered but not governed. I first saw government at a high level over a decade ago, at a time which is now occasionally debunked as overly brash, excessively optimistic, even somewhat arrogant. Some of these criticisms are justified, but a spirit prevailed then which was quintessentially American: that problems are a challenge, not an alibi; that men are measured not only by their success, but also by their striving; that it is better to aim grandly than to wallow in mediocre comfort. Above all, the Administration then in office, and its opponents, thought of themselves engaged in a common enterprise, not in a permanent, irreconcilable contest.

At a time which history will surely mark as one of the great revolutions, the world continues to need our idealism and our purpose, and in this respect the spirit of the early 60s was more nearly right than some of the present attitudes.

In the 1920s, we were isolationists because we thought we were too good for this world. We are now in danger of withdrawing from the world because we believe we are not good enough for it. The result is the same, and the consequences would be similar. So it is time to end our own civil war.

To be sure, we should leaven our optimism with a sense of tragedy, and temper our idealism with humility and realism. But we have had enough of the liturgies of debate, and what we need most is the unity of which Senator Cooper spoke, which is the prerequisite for mastering the future and overcoming the past.

My remarks were received warmly. There was in the room a glow of goodwill, conciliation, and budding optimism.

My awakening the next day, Saturday, April 14, was rude. I was still buoyed by the evening's mood of reconciliation and the geniality of the audience when Leonard Garment called at my office at the White House. What he told me shattered everything.

Len Garment was one of that small group of liberal Republicans whom Nixon had added to his entourage partly for protective coloration, partly because they genuinely appealed to his gentler and more sensitive side. Like their conservative counterparts — the speechwriter Patrick Buchanan, for example — some of the "liberals" imagined that they alone represented the "true" Nixon, although Garment was too perceptive for such a sentimental misjudgment. The fact was that there was no true

Nixon; several warring personalities struggled for preeminence in the same individual. One was idealistic, thoughtful, generous; another was vindictive, petty, emotional. There was a reflective, philosophical, stoical Nixon; and there was an impetuous, impulsive, and erratic one. Sometimes one set of traits prevailed; sometimes another; occasionally they were in uneasy balance. One could never be certain which Nixon was dominant from meeting to meeting. Nor was it wise to act upon an impulsive instruction without making sure that the reflective Nixon had had a crack at it. Indeed, it was the failure of some more literal-minded White House advisers to understand the requirements of his complex personality that gave such momentum to Watergate. Strangely enough, the thoughtful analytical side of Nixon was most in evidence during crises, while periods of calm seemed to unleash the darker passions of his nature.

Garment had met Nixon when they were partners in a New York law firm. Len was a man of many talents. He was at ease in the world of the arts as in that of the law — he was himself an enthusiastic clarinet player — and credit for the Nixon Administration's enormously expanded federal support for the humanities is due to him as to no other single person. If his decency reduced his effectiveness in the more brutal sparring of high-level government, it also gave depth to his role as a conscience for the President and as confidant to his friends. His title, Special Consultant to the President, was grand enough, but without a specific area of responsibility; he had no regular access to the President or a day-to-day schedule.

As a general rule, influence in the White House must not be judged by job descriptions. Many unwary neophytes are enticed into service by promises of constant contact with the President. But influence on Presidential decisions depends more on the substantive mandate than on theoretical access to the Oval Office. Whatever the President's intentions, he is usually overscheduled. Inevitably, he faces problems requiring more decisions than he can comfortably handle. Conversation not related to his agenda, no matter how stimulating or instructive, soon becomes a burden. If the adviser agrees with the bureaucracy, he is a waste of time. If he disagrees and even if he should convince the President, he raises the problem of how to marshal bureaucratic support so as to implement the suggested course. I can think of no exception to the rule that advisers without a clear-cut area of responsibility eventually are pushed to the periphery by day-to-day operators. The other White House aides resent interference in their spheres. The schedulers become increasingly hesitant in finding time on the President's calendar.

Garment had reduced these inherent disabilities to the maximum degree possible through unselfish conduct and the high regard others had for him. Still, his emergence into prominence was usually a good signal that Nixon was in some distress and required a steadying hand. It was also noticeable that in recent days he had spent an increasing amount of time with Nixon, though it was not clear what matters were discussed. To explain why was the purpose of Garment's visit to my office on April 14.

In his deceptively casual manner he slumped into the blue-covered couch against the wall that faced the ceiling-to-floor windows overlooking the White House front lawn and Pennsylvania Avenue. I sat in an easy chair at right angles to the sofa, next to my desk. Never one to beat around the bush, Garment opened the conversation by raising a question unlikely to receive an objective answer: "Have you lost your mind?"

Without waiting for a reply, Garment somewhat wearily unfolded an astonishing and shattering tale: Within a matter of days my evocation of national reconciliation would look like a plea for mercy and be submerged in a crisis that would make the turmoil over Vietnam seem trivial. Nixon's lifelong enemies were about to be handed the weapon that they had been seeking. In the tornado of suspicion about to overwhelm us, my appeal to idealism tempered by a stern perception of national purpose would sound vacuous if not cynical. The outcome of the recent election might well be reversed; there was likely to be a battle to the death.

"Watergate" was about to blow up; its ramifications went far beyond the break-in at Democratic National Committee headquarters in the Watergate Apartment complex. There had been other break-ins sanctioned from the White House for several different purposes, some as yet unclear. Also, a plan had existed to kidnap presumptive leaders of potential demonstrations against the Republican National Convention and to fly them to Central America. Prostitutes were to be used to compromise and to blackmail delegates to the Democratic National Convention. Garment said the "sordid mess" had many dimensions, only part of which he knew himself. It could not have developed without the cooperation of the highest levels of the Administration. Garment thought that Special Counsel to the President Charles W. Colson had probably been the "evil genius" behind it. Yet the scale of the wrongdoing really made it impossible to imagine that Assistants to the President H. R. (Bob) Haldeman and John Ehrlichman, whom the press had nicknamed "the Germans," had been unaware. There was a puzzle here, for Haldeman's and Ehrlichman's dislike of Colson was proverbial. And if Haldeman and Ehrlichman were involved, it was nearly inconceivable that the President had been completely ignorant.

Whoever was the culprit, in Garment's view, only radical surgery and the fullest admission of error could avert catastrophe. But if the President was involved even indirectly, full disclosure would not be the course selected; hence the Administration might bleed to death amidst a cascade of revelations gleefully exploited by the host of opponents Nixon had managed to acquire over the years. Garment was convinced that the Administration would have to be ripped apart and reconstituted in procedures as well as personnel. Nixon would have to put himself at the head of this movement of reform, brutally eradicate the rot, and rally the American people for a fresh start.

I was stunned. From the White House, somebody had implemented Presidential musings that could only be regarded as juvenile; had adopted the tawdriest practices of the hated antiwar radicals; and had set at risk both our social cohesion and our ability to fulfill our international responsibilities. For four years I had sustained myself through the anguishing turmoil of Vietnam with the vision of a united America turning at last to tasks of construction. And now through acts that made no sense, discord would descend once again on a society already weakened by ten years of upheaval. I felt like a swimmer who had survived dangerous currents only to be plucked from apparent safety by unexpected and even more violent riptides toward uncharted seas.

As I considered what this portended for foreign policy, my heart sank. A nation's capacity to act is based on an intangible amalgam of strength, reputation, and commitment to principle. To be harnessed, and applied with care and discrimination, these qualities require authority, backed by public confidence. But if Garment was right, political and moral authority inexorably would start draining from the Presidency. The dream of a new era of creativity would in all probability evaporate. Even preserving what we had achieved — the Indochina settlement, for example — would become precarious. There was real peril. Without the impression of American authority, aggressors would be tempted. Delicate balances in regions where American commitments were crucial to peace would be less stable. Our ability to mediate conflicts, or to inspire friends, would erode. We were threatened with stagnation in our foreign policy, and a rearguard struggle to avert a wholesale unraveling.

Exactly what had triggered this avalanche? When the Watergate break-in occurred in June 1972 I had been en route to China. I had paid little heed to the sparse news reports I read. I could not imagine that a President as politically experienced as Nixon would permit the White House to be involved in so pointless an exercise. I thought that at worst some egregious minion had conducted a childish private enterprise.

In the months that followed, Watergate — then specifically associated in the public mind, as in mine, with the June 17 break-in — was never discussed at the White House meetings I attended. The White House assistants are both partners in a joint endeavor and competitors for the President's attention and favor. The latter consideration often predominates — at least it tended to in the Nixon White House. Each

Assistant tenaciously defends his turf, which is best accomplished by maintaining some exclusive jurisdiction.

Thus in the Nixon White House there was an almost total separation between the domestic and the foreign policy sides. The relation of the various Nixon aides to one another was like that of prisoners in adjoining cells. They might hear something about the scale of the activity; proximity did not invite participation or intimate knowledge. To all practical purposes I was excluded from domestic issues and Ehrlichman, who handled domestic policy, from foreign policy discussions. Haldeman, who attended both, invariably confined himself to political and public relations concerns. There were large daily staff meetings, which both foreign and domestic advisers attended, but they were preoccupied with public relations; sensitive matters were never discussed there.

I was aware, of course, of the pervasive sense of beleaguerment that resulted from a combination of the President's personality and the violent, occasionally extralegal assaults of the antiwar critics. And I had come to know a dark side of Nixon. Nevertheless, in the summer of 1972 I did not believe it possible that the White House was involved in the Watergate affair; I accepted Press Secretary Ronald L. Ziegler's public position that it was a ''third-rate burglary attempt'' involving no White House personnel. The morning staff meetings seemed to bear this out. The few references to Watergate were always by junior staff members who complained of the media's unfairness. The avuncular approval this elicited from Haldeman, who presided, reinforced the sense that nothing serious had occurred.

Once, in the summer of 1972, I asked Haldeman what Watergate was all about. ''I wish I knew,'' he replied; and changed the subject. On another occasion I mentioned Watergate to John Ehrlichman. In late January 1973 I had run into Joseph Califano, a former Johnson aide and old friend from the other side of politics, and gossiped on the street for a few minutes with him. To my smug remark that I did not see how the Democrats could recover from their electoral debacle, Califano said Watergate would bring a Democratic revival. It was wrong to think of judges as unaffected by the public mood. Enough media attention had been focused on Watergate to make it extremely likely that the forthcoming trial of the Watergate burglars could cause the judge to crack down and force further revelations. I passed this view on to Ehrlichman. Ehrlichman, smarting under the media's tendency to contrast me favorably with ''the Germans,'' tended to give me short shrift whenever I ventured within the three-mile limit of domestic jurisdiction. He snorted, ''Wishful thinking! If that is what they are counting on, they will be out of office for thirty years.''

There was, hindsight makes plain, something that should have alerted me early in 1973. It was the behavior of Nixon himself. I found it difficult to get Nixon to focus on foreign policy, to a degree that should have disquieted me. In the past, even in calm periods, he had immersed himself in foreign policy to enliven the job of managing the government, which ultimately bored him. Now it was difficult to get him to address memoranda. They came back without the plethora of marginal comments that indicated they had been carefully read. On at least one occasion Nixon checked every box of an options paper, defeating its purpose.

I ascribed this lassitude to his characteristic depression after success. Through my acquaintance with him, absence of tension provoked not elation but lethargy. Nixon's most capricious actions had occurred in times of quiet, not in reaction to crises. Calm periods seemed to drive him to disequilibrium as if he could find his own balance only in tension.

Throughout this period I remember only one conversation with Nixon that related directly to Watergate. In early April 1973, as Senator Sam Ervin's Senate Select Committee on Presidential Campaign Activities (the Watergate Committee) began its investigations, we were in San Clemente. One afternoon the President called me to his office and asked whether Haldeman should testify. I replied, naively as it proved, that this would be an admission of guilt and that only those with direct knowledge of the break-in should appear. Nixon gave no sign that based on his knowledge I had just put forward a proposition that contradicted itself. Impassively, he told me to repeat my views to Haldeman, a suggestion whose extreme ambiguity did not strike me for several weeks. When I did, Haldeman listened equally impassively and urged me to repeat my views to Ehrlichman. Ehrlichman, in turn, shrugged off the observation with the air of a man whose patience was barely equal — but might not always be — to my invincible ignorance of political matters.

Now that Watergate was about to explode, I pondered Nixon's options. I had my doubts about Garment's proposed solution. The vision of Nixon's putting himself at the head of a reform movement to clean up his own Administration stretched credulity. Nor was it all that certain to work. A massive purge in the fifth year of a Presidency raises profound doubts about the incumbent's judgment for not having spotted the malfeasance earlier. Moreover, I thought that Garment's diagnosis precluded his remedy. Anyone familiar with Nixon's way of conducting affairs would know that he needed a strong chief of staff to carry out *any* plan, that in the absence of delicate pressure from those he trusted he would procrastinate; his usual coolness under fire always needed reinforcement by trusted aides. In other words, only Haldeman could get Nixon to fire Haldeman, an unlikely proposition. If Haldeman was involved even indirectly, there was no one else to shepherd such a program past our chief's psychological defenses. On Garment's diagnosis the Administration seemed headed for prolonged turmoil without a foreseeable outcome.

If this was true, my duty as I perceived it was to rally those unaffected by the catastrophe for the ordeal ahead. I asked Garment's permission to inform a few in the White House whose probity and integrity would help us preserve public confidence — George Shultz and Arthur Burns in particular. Garment agreed; I immediately set up a meeting for Sunday evening, the first time they were both available.

In the meantime, on Saturday evening, April 14, I attended the annual dinner tendered by the White House correspondents. The guest of honor is putatively the President, together with the Cabinet. I say "putatively" because a point is usually reached in an administration — it came rather early in Nixon's — where the President feels that his daily harassment by the media exhausts his tolerance for their company. Listening to the uneven sarcasm that is the staple of these evenings is not a duty foreseen by the Constitution. Presidential attendance begins to slip. Nixon used his absence to pretend an imperviousness to the journalists assigned to cover him — only reinforcing the reciprocal hostility and sensitivity of the President and the press.

On this occasion, however, Nixon decided to show up. The evening went well enough; at least I remember no untoward incident, though the atmosphere was redolent with resentment. Afterward, several newspapers gave parties in various suites. While attending one of them, I was called to a phone. It was the President and he was highly agitated. It was not unusual for Nixon to call at all hours, nor for him to pose an odd-sounding question and hang up. But this evening the question sounded weird even for a late night call. "Do you agree," he asked "that we should draw the wagons around the White House?"

We know today from the mountains of Watergate revelations that the day had been one of frenzied meetings between Nixon, Haldeman, Ehrlichman, and former Attorney General and campaign manager John Mitchell. But I was not aware of them. I would like to be able to report that I said something helpful or constructive to the obviously distraught President. But few advisers possess the fortitude to tell their President that they do not know what he is talking about, or that his query indicates a propensity toward melodrama. Nor did I feel up to it that evening. I mumbled something noncommittal that Nixon, not unreasonably, construed as assent. "All right," he said, "we will draw the wagons around the White House." He gave that enigmatic metaphor no further content before hanging up suddenly. Had it not been for my conversation with Garment a few hours earlier, I would not have known what agitated the President so much.

Stung, I mentioned Garment's worries to John Ehrlichman when he called me about something or other on Sunday, April 15. "Garment," replied Ehrlichman, equably enough, "is a nuclear overreactor. Pay no attention to him. Our major problem is to get John Mitchell to own up to his responsibility." Mitchell indeed! Did he have the major responsibility for the Watergate break-in — or was he chosen as the fall guy? I asked myself the question without any idea of the answer. What was clear was that if Mitchell was involved, the scandal would be uncontainable. John Mitchell, that epitome of loyalty, would never have acted without at least believing that he was carrying out Presidential wishes. Indeed, whatever hypothesis one considered — Garment's, which saw Colson as the chief villain with Haldeman and Ehrlichman in supporting roles; or Ehrlichman's, which now apparently placed the blame on Mitchell — Watergate was bound to rock the nation. It simply was not credible, least of all to those of us who knew how the White House operated, that Nixon's paladins had acted totally on their own on a matter with such grave implications for the President.

Thus, unless it could be shown unambiguously that the President was not involved, we would soon face a monumental crisis of institutions. Clearly, the President was severely wounded. Whatever the unimaginable outcome, Nixon would have to alter his system of management. He would no longer be able to dominate the government through White House assistants, harassing or bypassing the regular bureaucracy. The trusted political aides who, as part of the post-election shake-up, had been placed into every key department as a means of keeping an eye on the Cabinet member who was titular head, would lose their clout if not their positions. Challenges to White House predominance were increasingly probable. It was imperative to adopt rapidly a mode of government less dependent on solitary decisions at the top. However necessary existing procedures may have appeared to brave the Vietnam period, the moral, psychological, and political basis for them had now disappeared.

My meeting with George Shultz and Arthur Burns was the evening of that same Sunday, April 15, in Shultz's White House office. Shultz at that time combined the positions of Secretary of the Treasury and Assistant to the President in charge of economic policy. Burns was Chairman of the Federal Reserve Board but wielded a wider influence than that title would indicate. The later debacle of the Nixon Administration has obscured the extent to which it included men and women of extraordinary character and intelligence.

Shultz had entered the Cabinet as Secretary of Labor, had been moved to the Office of Management and Budget when it was given policymaking functions, and had succeeded John Connally as Secretary of the Treasury in the summer of 1972. I met no one in public life for whom I developed greater respect and affection. Highly analytical, calm and unselfish, Shultz made up in integrity and judgment for his lack of the flamboyance by which some of his more insecure colleagues attempted to make their mark. He never sought personal advancement. By not threatening anyone's prerogatives, and, above all, by his outstanding performance, he became the dominant member of every committee he joined. He usually wound up being asked to sum up a meeting — a role that gave him influence without his aiming for it. If I could choose one American to whom I would entrust the nation's fate in a crisis, it would be George Shultz.

It was easy to underestimate Arthur Burns. As he puffed on his pipe while considering a proposition, he seemed to be a fuzzy-minded, slightly abstracted academic, and indeed he had been a professor at Columbia University for three decades. His deliberate manner of speaking might be occasionally taken by the unwary as a reflection of the pace of his mind. But Burns had an unusual ability to get swiftly to the heart of any problem. He was both brilliant and incredibly persistent; and he proved to be one of the canniest bureaucratic infighters in Washington. He had not been filling his pipe reflectively throughout the Eisenhower and Nixon administrations without studying and learning what made government tick. He worked patiently at lining up support for his position; he lost few battles while I observed him in action. Yet this did not diminish the admiration for his integrity, dedication, and subtle intelligence held by those of us whom he usually outmaneuvered.

When I confided Garment's news to my two colleagues they were at first unbelieving. But we all shared a sense of impotence. We did not know the dimensions of the looming scandal. We agreed to keep each other informed of whatever we learned; we would tell each other of conversations with the President relevant to our concerns so that we would, if possible, offer unified advice. We would try jointly to develop policies and initiatives to maintain the confidence of the American people in their government even in the midst of a political crisis. The Administration had, after all, nearly four years to run; presumptuous as it may seem, we thought a duty had fallen on us to preserve as much moral substance for the national government as could be salvaged.

The Legacy of Vietnam

BEFORE continuing the tale of the unfolding of Watergate, I must stop to explain its context. Most of the voluminous literature of Watergate — a cottage industry — treats it as a personal aberration of Richard Nixon as if there had been no surrounding circumstances. And in truth Watergate is unthinkable apart from Nixon's driven personality. But there was also a deeper background. Historians will misunderstand Watergate who neglect the destructive impact on American politics, spirit, and unity of the war in Vietnam.

The United States had entered Vietnam during the Kennedy Administration, with sixteen thousand advisers, idealism, and a sense of mission producing an extraordinary activism. Communist aggression in Indochina was thought to reflect the cutting edge of a homogeneous ideology directed by a monolithic Sino-Soviet bloc. The Johnson Administration had escalated the commitment, sending more than 500,000 American troops to the inhospitable jungles of Southeast Asia to combat what it considered a test case of a theory of revolutionary warfare centrally directed from Moscow and Peking. That assessment proved to be mistaken. Hanoi was essentially acting on its own account though it could not have done so without the help of the two giant Communist powers, especially the Soviet Union.

The frustrations of the Johnson Administration in Indochina made it an easy target for later abuse, aggravated when many of the policymakers who had involved us in Indochina became so demoralized that they in effect joined the critics who had destroyed them and their President. But their original perception was not so mistaken as their own loss of confidence in themselves made it appear. The rulers of Hanoi were anything but the benign nationalists so often portrayed by gullible sympathizers; they were cold, brutal revolutionaries determined to dominate all of Indochina. The impact of a North Vietnamese victory on the prospects of freedom and national independence in Southeast Asia was certain to be grave, especially on governments much less firmly established than was the case a decade later; the much-maligned domino theory — shared by *all* the non-Communist governments in the area — turned out to be correct.

Whether the strategic stakes justified such a massive American involvement in Vietnam must be doubted in retrospect. But once American forces are committed, there is no logical or valid goal except to prevail. The Kennedy and Johnson administrations trapped themselves between their convictions and their inhibitions, making a commitment large enough to hazard our global position but then executing it with so much hesitation as to defeat their purpose. They engaged us in Indochina for the objective of defeating a global conspiracy and then failed to press a military solution for fear of sparking a global conflict — a fear that was probably as exaggerated as the original assessment. There are no awards for losing with moderation; neither domestic nor foreign critics are placated by failure.

But it must also be said that the task was so novel, the undertaking so unfamiliar, that these failures deserve compassion rather than scorn. The men who involved us in Vietnam were neither frivolous nor callous. They ventured American prestige beyond the strategic merits of the local issue and risked infinitely more than they intended. Yet their purposes were far from ignoble; later events confirmed the validity of the view that American impotence in the face of aggression could have wider, and catastrophic, consequences. The global turmoil that followed the final collapse of the non-Communist governments in Indochina owed not a little to loss of confidence in the stabilizing role of America; Soviet adventurism accelerated with American weakness; for a time, military force seemed to become the arbiter of all political conflicts. And the horrible fate of the peoples of Indochina since 1975 —the mass murders, the concentration camps, the political repression, the boat people — is now rendering a final verdict on whether it was our resistance to totalitarianism, or our abandonment of our friends, that was the true immorality of the Indochina conflict.

When the Nixon Administration came into office in January 1969, the wisdom of the commitment of over 500,000 Americans and nearly 100,000 allied soldiers had become moot. The troops were there. Thirty-five thousand Americans had already been killed. We did not question the desirability of American disengagement. Even before assuming office, we decided to withdraw American forces as rapidly as possible.* The Nixon Administration perceived also that far from coordinating their policies, Peking and Moscow were engaged in an intense geopolitical and ideological struggle. The difficulty was how to implement these judgments while maintaining our international responsibilities and our national honor.

Our definition of honor was not extravagant: We would withdraw, but we would not overthrow an allied government. We were prepared to accept the outcome of a truly free political process in South Vietnam even if it meant the replacement of the personalities and institutions that we favored. What we were not willing to do was to accept the unconditional surrender Hanoi was in effect demanding, to mock our people's sacrifices by collaborating in the imposition of Communist rule, betraying those who had believed the assurances of our predecessors and thereby putting at risk global confidence in the United States.

But a free political process was precisely what Hanoi was determined to prevent. Its dour and fanatical leaders had not fought and suffered for all their adult lives to entrust the outcome to an electoral procedure that they had never practiced in their own country. They were dedicated revolutionaries whose profession was guerrilla war and whose method was the exhaustion of their adversaries. Their faith was in the balance of forces — military, psychological, and political, in that order of priority. Within Indochina they worked tenaciously, indeed heroically, to

---

*I had published an article in the January 1969 *Foreign Affairs* with my ideas on the subject, written before I was appointed to be Nixon's national security adviser. After criticizing the Johnson Administration's strategy, I suggested a two-track approach: The United States and North Vietnamese should negotiate on the military issues (mutual withdrawal, cease-fire, and return of prisoners of war), while the South Vietnamese parties settled the political problems among themselves.[1]

frustrate our military strategy, to demoralize our troops, and to defeat our South Vietnamese allies. In negotiations they did not budge from their central demands: that America had to withdraw from Indochina unconditionally, that on the way out we must overthrow the governments allied to us. And they did not alter these terms until they were militarily exhausted.

By then America's national unity had been strained almost to the breaking point. Given the self-limiting strategies adopted by two Presidents — Johnson out of fear of expanding the conflict, Nixon to gain maneuvering room for an honorable extrication — the war was bound to be protracted and the outcome ambiguous. The process of an honorable withdrawal was inevitably confusing to a public that was still being asked to sacrifice in the name of an abstract, unprovable goal of maintaining America's global credibility. Many of the young, on whom the burden of conscription fell, found a messy war in a faraway country incompatible with their ideals. For the first time in history, the average person could see the ugliness of war every evening on his television screen. Thousands of decent and patriotic Americans from every walk of life were moved to protest against an enterprise that exacted such a human toll. At the same time, poll after poll showed the overwhelming majority of the American public unprepared to accept an outright, humiliating American defeat. The result was an intractable and increasingly bitter domestic stalemate.

In this impasse the attitude of two groups proved pivotal: the American foreign policy Establishment, and the tiny indigenous radical movement.

The leadership group in America that had won the battle against isolationism in the 1940s and sustained a responsible American involvement in the world throughout the postwar period was profoundly demoralized by the Vietnam war. They, indeed, had launched their country in the 1960s into this war of inconclusive ends and ambiguous means. When it ran aground, they lost heart. The clarity of purpose that had given impetus to the great foreign policy initiatives of the late 1940s was unattainable in Indochina. The Marshall Plan, the Greek-Turkish aid program, the Atlantic Alliance, the reconstruction of Japan, had been of a piece with our domestic experience. Those economic programs had seemed to vindicate the premise of the New Deal: that political stability could be restored by closing the gap between expectation and economic reality. And the alliances had harked back to the lessons of the Nazi period: The threat of war was perceived to come from large armies attacking across an internationally recognized line of demarcation. Such policies had worked brilliantly in postwar Europe and Japan. There, political institutions had a long tradition. Overcoming the economic dislocations of World War II had the immediate effect of restoring the vitality of political life. And since military danger could come only from overt aggression, security could be defined in terms of clear-cut force levels.

None of these conditions was fulfilled in Indochina. There was no massive attack by regular units across a well-defined boundary but the seeping in of hostile forces across trackless jungles. By some sort of weird bow to legality, the one frontier in Indochina relatively unviolated by Hanoi was the Demilitarized Zone between North and South Vietnam along the seventeenth parallel established by the Geneva Accords of 1954. To compensate for this uncharacteristic deference to a legal obligation, the North Vietnamese proceeded to bypass the Demilitarized Zone by establishing their supply lines in neutral countries that wanted only to be left alone. The Ho Chi Minh Trail ran through Laos; sanctuaries were established in Cambodia. By an even weirder turn of events, this logic was accepted by many domestic critics of the war. Whenever we reacted to these gross violations of international law and threats to the security of our forces, by seeking to intercept the totally illegal supply lines that sustained an aggressive and expansionist activity, it was we who were accused of violating the neutrality of Cambodia and Laos. This was the issue in several of the bitterest domestic controversies of the war.

The political situation in Vietnam was equally at variance with our preconceptions. The war concerned not the support of a particular government but the legitimacy of *any* non-Communist structure. Many Americans tended to judge the government we were defending by our own constitutional practices, which were only marginally relevant to a civil war in a developing country with a totally different historical experience. In the West the nation existed before the state, and indeed gave birth to it. In many developing countries the opposite is true; a state is trying to crystallize a sense of nationhood. In such circumstances government is often the only expression of national identity; political contests become a struggle for total power; there is no historical experience with the concept of loyal opposition, without which democracy cannot flourish. Conversely the attempt to force-feed constitutional government can hazard what little cohesion exists.

So it was in Indochina. South Vietnam, emerging out of a reluctant partition of the country in 1954, struggled for nationhood while a guerrilla assault, organized and run from Hanoi — there is no longer any doubt about this — rent the tenuous fabric of society. The South Vietnamese leadership, essentially brought into office by an American-backed coup in 1963, hung on precariously in the face of an escalating invasion of outside forces; its best officials were systematically assassinated by Communist guerrillas; its economy was ravaged. And while dealing with these challenges, almost unmanageable in their collective impact, the

Saigon administration faced relentless pressure for reform from its distant ally, America. Almost miraculously, South Vietnam endured these multiple pressures and even gained in strength — a tribute to the tenacity of its people and a measure of the price they were prepared to pay to avoid being ruled by the brutal totalitarians of Hanoi.

But, inevitably, the process bore no resemblance to the expectations of the liberal American leadership groups that had conceived the initial intervention. Wedded to an inconclusive strategy — or perhaps engaged in an inherently unwinnable conflict — they lost their self-assurance and sense of direction. They first abandoned victory, then faith even in the possibility of serious negotiation toward a reasonable compromise; finally they concluded that the postwar American role of global leadership was itself deeply flawed.

This moral collapse was not a minor matter for our country or for nations around the world that depended upon us. That those who had involved America in Indochina should come to argue for the necessity of settling the war was a tribute to their sense of reality. But their refusal — more of a sense of guilt — to admit that a negotiated settlement required national unity behind a minimum negotiating program turned the extrication from Vietnam into a nightmare. No negotiator, least of all the hard-boiled revolutionaries from Hanoi, will settle so long as he knows that his opposite number will be prevented from sticking to a position by constantly escalating domestic pressures. The myth that the obstacle to a settlement was the short-sightedness, if not worse, of our government and not the implacability of the aggressor was in the end endorsed by the very people who had heretofore sustained our foreign policy. The old foreign policy Establishment thus abandoned its preeminent task, which is to contribute balanced judgment, long-term perspective, and thoughtful analysis to the public discussion of our international responsibility.

As a result of this abdication, the so-called peace movement came to be driven by a relatively tiny group of radicals, whose public support in the country was close to nil. To that most vocal hard core of dissenters, the issue in Vietnam was not the wisdom of a particular American commitment but the validity of American foreign policy in general and indeed of American society. They saw the war as a symptom of an evil, corrupt, militaristic capitalist system. They treated the Viet Cong as a progressive movement, North Vietnam as a put-upon, heroic revolutionary country, and Communism as the wave of the future in Indochina, if not in the entire developing world. They were outraged by our incursion into Cambodia less because of the alleged extension of the war into sanctuaries (from which North Vietnamese had, after all, killed thousands of South Vietnamese and Americans for five years) than because they feared it might lead to success. Concern for the future of Vietnamese, Cambodian, and Laotian populations under Communism was contemptuously dismissed as a transparent subterfuge for continuing a war conducted for much more sinister purposes. By the same token, our fear of the decline of American global credibility and its impact on international security was interpreted in radical circles as using the peoples of Indochina as pawns in some overall American strategic design. Indeed, in these terms the decline in America's world position was welcomed as a contribution to world peace.

To this small but increasingly strident group a victory for Hanoi was not regrettable but morally desirable. It was not to be mitigated by negotiation but made brutally evident by, in effect, surrender. America's humiliation in that distant enterprise was seen as an object lesson in the immorality of America's postwar world leadership and as a convenient tool to demoralize the entire American Establishment — business, labor, academia, the media, Congress — which was perceived as an obstacle to the forward march of history. Thus the arrogant tone of moral superiority, and the flaunting of profanity that implied that its objects were beneath contempt.

Throughout the last year of the Johnson Presidency, the style, methods, and rhetoric of opponents of the Vietnam war descended to a level of nastiness from which our public life has yet to recover fully. During the 1968 Presidential campaign, the relentless harassment of so warm and generous a personality as Hubert Humphrey reached a bitterness that he could recall only with tears later on.

All these tendencies were tragically accelerated by the election of Richard Nixon. Nixon was probably the only leader who could disengage from Vietnam without a conservative revolt. Yet his history of partisanship had made him anathema to most of the responsible Democrats. Radical opposition to the war thus fed on and merged with hatred of Richard Nixon on the part of many who had no sympathy for radicalism in general. The virulence of dissent escalated and was not moderated by those who, presumably, stood for values of civilized discourse and civic responsibility. The latter's yearning to expiate a guilt that was in retrospect vastly exaggerated or nonexistent prolonged the war. It also shattered forever the existing foreign policy Establishment, whose members were ground up between a national policy they dared not support and a radical opposition that would not embrace them — indeed, which was determined to punish them for their past, however hard they might try to disavow it.

This process destroyed any compassion for the complexity of the task the Nixon Administration had inherited. To withdraw fast enough to ease public concerns but slowly enough to give Hanoi an incentive to negotiate, to show flexibility at the conference table while conveying a determination that there was a point beyond which our national honor would not permit us to go, required a firm strategy sustained by an understanding public. The persistent domestic pressures — however different the motives — turned this task into an ordeal. By the end of Nixon's first term, rational discourse on Vietnam had all but stopped; the issue was fought out by recrimination and vilification in the Congress and the media and by demonstrations and riots on the campuses and periodically in the streets.

The ugliness of the domestic battles was a national tragedy. The issue was posed as to who was "for" or "against" the war — a phony question. Nixon was determined to end our involvement and in fact did so. What he refused to do was to doom millions who had relied upon us to a bloody Communist tyranny. He believed that abject failure would vindicate the neo-isolationist trends at home, demoralize the American people, and make them fearful of foreign responsibilities. He was convinced that an America so weakened would dishearten allies who depended on us and embolden adversaries to undertake new adventures. And he was proved right. The collapse in 1975 not only led to genocidal horrors in Indochina; from Angola to Ethiopia to Iran to Afghanistan, it ushered in a period of American humiliation, an unprecedented Soviet geopolitical offensive all over the globe, and pervasive insecurity, instability, and crisis.

I will not rehearse here once again all the various arguments made in the debate over the war amid the emotion of the time. I am clearly a party to them; their intellectual and moral merit will have to be sorted out by others in the fullness of time. Whatever the conflicting positions, it was a national disaster that the discussion deteriorated by 1972 into an attack on motives, poisoning the public discourse that is the lifeblood of a democratic society. Critics claimed a monopoly on the desire for peace, ridiculing and condemning all other concerns as subterfuges for psychotic commitment to killing for its own sake. The systematic undermining of trust deflected us from what should have been our principal national debate.

In the early 1970s America needed above all a complex understanding of new realities; instead it was offered simple categories of black and white. It had to improve its sense of history; instead it was told by its critics that all frustrations in the world reflected the evil intent of America's own leaders. The Vietnam debate short-circuited a process of maturing. It represented a flight into nostalgia; it fostered the illusion that what ailed America was a loss of its moral purity and that our difficulties could be set right by a return to simple principles. Whatever our mistakes, our destiny was not that facile. A self-indulgent America opened the floodgates of chaos and exacerbated its internal divisions.

All this bitterness was compounded by Nixon's response. Nixon became convinced that he was faced with a hostile conspiracy. He was following a bolder policy of American withdrawal than any serious critic had dared offer before he came into office.[2] Nixon was incensed by what he saw as the cynicism of prominent Democrats who had taken America into the war and now assuaged their guilt (or sought to preserve their careers) by insistent attacks on a President who was trying to get us out. He was amazed that a callous unconcern for the fate of Vietnamese, Cambodian, and Laotian populations under Communist rule paraded under the banner of superior morality. And he was most outraged — and justifiably — at the radicals' resort to methods of pressure and sabotage at or beyond the borderline of legality: the terrorism of the Weather Underground, firebombings of research facilities at universities, massive theft of classified government documents, unauthorized leaks of sensitive military operations and negotiating positions, incitement of draft resistance and desertion, to name the worst.

There is no excuse for the extralegal methods that went under the name of Watergate. A President cannot justify his own misdeeds by the excesses of his opponents. It is his obligation to raise sights, to set moral standards, to build bridges to his opponents. Nixon did not rise to this act of grace. But no understanding of the period is possible if one overlooks the viciousness, self-righteousness, and occasional brutality of some of Nixon's enemies.

In truth, the animosities of the President and his opposition fed on each other. And if one lesson of Watergate is the abuse of Presidential power, another is that if a democracy is to function, opposition must be restrained by its own sense of civility and limits, by the abiding values of the nation, and by the knowledge that a blanket assault on institutions and motives can paralyze the nation's capacity to govern itself.

Watergate Accelerates

Two days after the dramatic weekend that first brought home to me the nature of Watergate, on Tuesday, April 17, Nixon hosted a State dinner at the White House for Prime Minister Giulio Andreotti of Italy, at which Frank Sinatra performed. One of the guests at my table told me that the President had stepped into the press room a few hours before the dinner (it had, in fact, been at 4:42 P.M.) and disclosed that a month earlier he had ordered a new investigation of the Watergate break-in; it had produced "real progress . . . in finding the truth." Contrary to his previous orders, White House personnel would now be permitted to appear before the Senate Watergate Committee; however, no wrongdoer on the White House staff would be granted immunity from prosecution. Nixon and his political aides clearly had thought that the announcement would have such a minimal impact on foreign policy that they had not informed me of it either before or after. The bearer of the tidings, a devout Nixon supporter, was certain that Nixon's statement ended Watergate. The culprits had obviously been discovered; the matter could now be left to judicial processes.

In the light of what Len Garment had told me, I doubted that it would prove quite so simple. In reality, the primary significance of the White House statement was to begin Nixon's mortal struggle with White House Counsel John Dean, the associate who Nixon feared was about to turn against him. Nixon was now throwing down the gauntlet by denying Dean immunity and thus attempting to deprive him of any hope of making a deal with the prosecutor to save his own skin.

The dinner was festive and relaxed. The White House, indeed, was like the *Titanic;* one part of the ship was flooding but no one else was aware, or affected to be aware, of the danger. The band played on. It was, as it happened, the last ''normal'' dinner of Nixon's term. Later I joined Sinatra at a small party that was also attended by Vice President Spiro T. Agnew.

There I received another phone call from the President. He asked me what I thought of his remarks. Thinking it was one of Nixon's frequent requests for reassurance, I complimented him on his toast at the State dinner. That was not what was on Nixon's mind. He wanted my reaction to the Watergate announcement. I said that I could not judge its import since I did not know who was involved or what the purpose of the announcement had been. Nixon replied that the refusal to grant immunity would throw ''the fear of God into any little boys'' who might attempt to escape their responsibility by dumping on associates. Sensing my hesitation, Nixon asked out of the blue whether he should fire Haldeman and Ehrlichman; he was heartbroken, he said, even to have to ask the question. I was dumbfounded; it was one thing for Garment to speculate along these lines; if Nixon himself held that view, he must be in mortal peril. I replied that I did not know enough to answer. However, adopting a formulation from which I never deviated, I ventured one piece of advice: Whatever would have to be done ultimately should be done immediately, to put an end to the slow hemorrhaging.

Agnew came into the room as I was putting down the telephone and asked me what I thought of Nixon's Watergate statement. I told him, too, that I could not assess its impact. In a somewhat contemptuous, unfeeling manner, Agnew said that Nixon was kidding himself if he thought he could avoid firing Haldeman and Ehrlichman. He would be lucky if he could save himself.

Agnew's acid comment dramatized, on one level, the ambivalent relationship that almost inevitably grows up between the only two nationally elected officials of our government. At the outset, Vice Presidents are always hailed as partners of the President; the new Chief Executive proclaims that he will avoid the tendency of all his predecessors to reduce the Vice President to — in Nelson Rockefeller's phrase — "standby equipment." He is promised a major role in policy formulation and execution. With rare exceptions these expectations have been disappointed, to the growing frustration of the Vice President, whose increasingly visible chagrin sets up a vicious circle by fueling the natural uneasiness and aloofness of the President. Natural because it takes a superhuman degree of self-abnegation to be at ease with a man whose most exhilarating moment is likely to be one's death — and men with that capacity for self-abnegation do not reach the Presidency.

There is also a serious bureaucratic obstacle to assigning the Vice President major responsibilities. The Vice President is the only member of the Executive Branch not subject to removal by the President. To give him a regular task is to gamble on his permanent willing subordination; in case of policy disagreement, the President's capacity to enforce discipline upon a Vice President controlling his own segment of the bureaucracy would be circumscribed. Hence, Vice Presidents usually wind up with odd jobs in widely different fields or with clear terminal dates. This prevents the articulation of a clear-cut, coherent policy position or the creation of a bureaucratic base. (As Vice President, Nelson Rockefeller used to joke that he was an avid reader of the obituary pages to see when he might be sent abroad as head of an American funeral delegation.)

To be sure, the Vice President sits in on National Security Council meetings, where the gravest decisions of national policy are considered. But no one in an advisory position can prosper without staff help or the ability to follow up. The Vice President either supports the existing consensus, in which case he enhances the prevailing prejudice as to his irrelevance, or he challenges it, in which case he usually lacks detailed tactical knowledge and he risks becoming a nuisance. On one or two occasions when Agnew took a position challenging Nixon's, he was excluded from a subsequent meeting even though the President adopted Agnew's point of view. Nixon just wanted to make sure that everyone understood who was in charge.

Moreover, Presidents are encouraged in this tendency by their White House entourage. These men and women derive their power exclusively from propinquity to the President. They guard this relationship jealously against *all* outsiders. Their stock in trade is loyalty, an attitude that easy access to the President fosters and that shared experience with White House stresses tends to institutionalize. The President and his aides are beset by the same critics and journalists; they fight the same importuning bureaucracies; they are subject to harassment by the same pressure groups. A community of interests is inevitable, as is a joint front against all those with autonomous sources of loyalty and, worse still, independent ambitions.

While Cabinet members are not infrequently the target of these attitudes, they at least have the solace of having responsibility for many
problems the President does not *wish* to touch because he lacks the staff
to do so or because they are too controversial. And Cabinet officers
have large bureaucracies of their own, more or less loyal to them. The
Vice President has no such safety nets; he is the natural victim of the
White House staff's zeal; any consistent attempt to assert himself runs
the risk of reducing his prospects for his paramount ambition: receiving
the President's endorsement for electoral succession.

The relationship between Nixon and Agnew illustrated these maxims;
indeed, the personalities of the two men accentuated all the latent tensions. Nixon was solitary and chronically suspicious. He started out
thinking of Agnew as a political bungler; always sensitive to being
overshadowed, he may well have picked him for that reason. Later he
came to see Agnew's utility as a hired gun, attacking targets not suitable
for Presidential assault or venting emotions that Nixon secretly shared
but did not dare to articulate. He never considered Agnew up to succeeding him. He once said, only partly facetiously, that Agnew was his
insurance policy against assassination.

Agnew in turn was ferociously proud. He suffered his peripheral roles
in dignified silence. He deeply resented not having been briefed in advance on my secret trip to China. I found him highly intelligent and
much subtler than his public image. But his frustrations turned him inward. And my impression on that evening was that Agnew was not
exactly heartbroken over the prospect that his tormentors on the White
House staff would now be taken down a peg. Throughout the initial
period of Watergate Agnew remained conspicuously aloof. And when
his own purgatory started, the White House, including Nixon, reciprocated by dissociating from him.

On April 17 that denouement would still have appeared fantasy. But
Agnew's icy detachment from his chief's travail brought a premonition
of imminent disaster. A Vice President eager to succeed would hardly
be so cutting unless convinced that Nixon would not be decisive in the
nominating process of 1976.

Another man I consulted was Bryce Harlow. Harlow had served on
President Eisenhower's staff and had been in charge of Congressional
relations in the early years of the Nixon White House, before retiring
again into private life at the end of 1970. An Oklahoman with a drawl-
ing voice, gentle manner, and wary eyes, Harlow had spent his adult
life studying the ways of Washington, alternating between participant
and observer. There has never been any doubt in my mind that Watergate could not have happened had Nixon been more confiding in Harlow
or others of comparable stature. Harlow was a man not of soaring imagination but of encompassing prudence. He knew what the traffic would

bear in Washington, but, more important, he understood what restraints must not be tested if democracy is to thrive. He had a deep sense for the Presidency, its power, its majesty, and the awful responsibility it imposes. His fundamental loyalty to a President was bounded by his personal integrity, his reverence for our institutions, and a sense of duty to the nation. With such a philosophy, Bryce found himself pushed to the sidelines by eager young votaries who were crudely assertive when it was not really necessary and craven when their careers were unexpectedly jeopardized.

I gave Harlow a brief account of what I knew and asked him what he thought had happened. "Some damn fool," drawled Harlow, "walked into the Oval Office and took literally what he heard there." Harlow mused that something like this had become inevitable. "If it had not been this, it would have been something worse." The procedures had been too erratic, the atmosphere too paranoid. A housecleaning now might be good for the nation and make Nixon a great President. Thus, even Harlow did not conceive of a threat to Nixon's Presidency itself, no doubt in part because the destruction of a President with its collapse of executive authority was too staggering to contemplate. Like Garment, he saw in Watergate a means to purify the Administration by getting rid of unsavory elements.

"The Germans": *Haldeman and Ehrlichman*

THE media tended to portray H. R. Haldeman and John Ehrlichman as Prussian drill masters implementing with their own sadistic frills malevolent orders from the Oval Office. I was generally contrasted favorably with them; it was believed that they "had it in for me," as the saying goes. I was awarded the white hat, they the black: I returned telephone calls from journalists; I met many leading critics from the Congress, academia, and the media at dinner parties, and some were my friends; I listened to opposing points of view. Whether my interlocutors considered a dialogue a sign of agreement or whether I misled them by ambiguous statements is impossible to reconstruct at this remove — there was probably a combination of both.

The conventional perception of my relationships in the White House vastly oversimplified everybody's role. For one thing, Haldeman and Ehrlichman was not a single firm; in some respects they were rivals. On the whole, Ehrlichman's views were on the liberal side of the spectrum; he was truly interested in substance; he sponsored or supported domestic policies that were humane and progressive. In our internal deliberations he spoke in favor of reducing defense expenditures beyond a point I considered prudent so as to free resources for social programs; several times I appealed his interventions to Nixon. Ehrlichman was shaken by the student protest following the Cambodian incursions. He had three teenage children caught up in the campus upheaval and their travail touched him deeply. But no one could survive the White House without Presidential goodwill, and Nixon's favor depended on the readiness to fall in with the paranoid cult of the tough guy. The conspiracy of the press, the hostility of the Establishment, the flatulence of the Georgetown set, were permanent features of Nixon's conversation, which one challenged only at the cost of exclusion from the inner circle.

Rough talk and confrontational tactics did not come naturally to Ehrlichman. Every Presidential Assistant is tempted to purchase greater influence by humoring a President's moods. Ehrlichman overcompensated; he felt compelled to translate some of Nixon's musings into action, and as the official in charge of Nixon's domestic programs he was in the front line of bitter tests of strength. To the mounting protest demonstrations, the massive leaks of documents, and the drift of the dissenters into extralegal activity, Ehrlichman responded with a zeal that was sometimes excessive and a boastfulness that later damaged him severely.

Toward me Ehrlichman showed a mixture of comradely goodwill and testy jealousy. He respected my views though not the assurance with which they were presented. But he would have been superhuman had he not resented the contrast drawn between us by the media. He had been associated with Nixon for too long for the President to tolerate on his part social contacts and attitudes that in my case were treated as a congenital, inherited defect. Torn between his prohibited predilections to conciliate and his political survival, Ehrlichman made a virtue of necessity. He adopted a supercilious manner. Outsiders considered it a mark of arrogance; its real fount was ambivalence.

He had some solace scoring points against me by pretending to be more watchful against Nixon's enemies than recent recruits from the Ivy League on my staff were and by conducting the investigation of some security leaks so as to reflect on my associates. But these were more in the nature of harassments than serious challenges. Despite occasional tensions, Ehrlichman and I were essentially friendly. I respected his goodwill and tough competence; he admired, as he envied, my prominence.

Haldeman was made of sterner stuff. He had been with Nixon for a decade and knew intimately the complexities and foibles of his master. Though by instinct conservative, he was at bottom uninterested in policy. Genuinely admiring of Nixon, he considered it his paramount duty to smooth out the roller coaster of Nixon's emotions and to project to the outside world the appearance of steady, calm, unflappable leadership.

Convinced that image defined reality, Haldeman went along with, and frequently encouraged, Nixon's nearly obsessive belief that all his difficulties were caused by inadequate public relations and that public relations was essentially a technical problem. Nixon never could rid himself of the delusion that only the inadequacy of his media staff kept him from receiving the acclaim he associated with John F. Kennedy (forgetting that after the first year his own approval rating in the polls was consistently higher than that of his martyred predecessor in office). Haldeman tended to confuse policy with procedure and substance with presentation. Much of the time between President and chief of staff was devoted to discussing how to manipulate the press — a quest doomed to futility so long as both rejected the most obvious, and indeed only possible, strategy: conducting a serious, honest, and continuing dialogue with the hated, feared, and secretly envied representatives of the media.

This was all the more remarkable because Nixon and Haldeman seemed to grasp very well that personal contact and credibility made a crucial difference. A shower of memoranda rained down on the hapless White House staff from the Oval Office via Haldeman, detailing the "line" to take with the press and meting out punishment to offending journalists, usually the denial of access to officials (which most of us ignored most of the time). This "line" was occasionally some dig at a political rival; more frequently it consisted of a recital of our leader's sterling qualities. Since I was considered to have special entrée, ascribed to my membership in the Georgetown set (whose members I had never met before coming to Washington), I was the recipient of a disproportionate number of these missives.

I never understood why the other members of Nixon's entourage did not strive for the same relationship with the Washington media as I had. Diffidence must have played a large part, a failing of which I am rarely accused. Even though I had never held a formal news conference before being appointed security adviser, I did well and as a result was treated in the White House as if I possessed some special advantage in public relations. Perhaps, so my associates reasoned, it was because of my Ivy League background and my tangential relation in the early Sixties with the Kennedy Administration. (The Kennedy White House, it must be recorded, saw no such gifts in me; I was kept miles away from any representative of the media.) At any rate, I was encouraged to cultivate the media and was then resented when my press relations were better than those of my associates.

Later, Haldeman was accused of exercising a baleful influence on Nixon by isolating him. This was unjust. Nixon's isolation was self-imposed. He dreaded meeting strangers. He was unable to give direct orders to those who disagreed with him. When he did see a new personality, he avoided any risk of tension by seeming to agree with everything his interlocutor said. The vaunted Haldeman procedures were an

effort to compensate for these weaknesses. Access to the President was
restricted because even a tightly limited schedule of appointments brought
forth constant Presidential complaints. A White House staffer sat in on
every meeting with an outsider so as to ensure some follow-up on Presidential promises (and to be aware on occasion of the need to disavow
them). As much staff business as possible was conducted by memoranda
because Nixon was much more likely to express his real views in writing than face to face.

At the same time, those White House aides with whom he felt secure
served frequently as lightning rods upon which Nixon released nervous
tension. One would sit for hours listening to Nixon's musings, throwing
an occasional log on the fire, praying for some crisis to bring relief,
alert to the opportunity to pass the torch to some unwary aide who
wandered in more or less by accident. But no one logged even approximately Haldeman's hours or listened with similar goodwill. And if
Haldeman was eventually destroyed because he carried out the President's wishes too literally, it is also my impression that many instructions given in the heat of emotion never went further than the yellow
pads where Haldeman dutifully noted them as if their execution awaited
only his exit from the Oval Office.

Haldeman's lack of interest in policy had its advantages. One could
be certain that he would report scrupulously to the President and not
skewer one's views on his own biases. Indeed, not infrequently I used
him as a conduit for views that ran counter to Presidential preferences,
because Nixon was less likely to brush off the bearer of unwelcome
intelligence than the originator and because Haldeman would do his utmost to see to it that Nixon would consider even subjects distasteful to
him (provided one succeeded in convincing Haldeman first that to ignore it would cause some damage to the President). Haldeman was free
of personal ambition or at least his ambition was fulfilled in the position
he occupied. Precisely because there was nothing more to achieve, he
had no need to engage in bureaucratic backbiting.

And yet, there resided in this almost inhuman detachment the seeds
of the eventual destruction of the Nixon Administration. Haldeman had
no deep experience in national politics; his feel for the propriety, scope,
and limits of Presidential prerogative was simply not equal to the role
he imposed upon himself. His second mistake was in the manner in
which he sought to cope with the erratic vacillations of his client, the
President. Haldeman's chilly discipline here was functional; he sought
unquestioning obedience from his staff in part to short-circuit apparently
wayward Presidential commands. But there are two ways of achieving
discipline: by motivating subordinates so that they *want* to agree with
the principal's objectives; or by establishing a rigid hierarchy, making
it inconceivable that an order is ever challenged because no subordinate

is granted the privilege of independent judgment. Haldeman chose the latter course. He selected miniature editions of himself — men and women (mostly men) with no political past, whose loyalty was determined by a chain of command and whose devotion was vouchsafed merely by the opportunity to play a part in great events.

But men who lack a past are unreliable guides to the future. They grow euphoric in authority and panicky at the thought of losing it. During Nixon's ascendancy, too many staffers were overbearing; they sought surcease from Haldeman's insatiable demands in the browbeating of their own subordinates, including the established Cabinet departments that were not technically subordinates at all. Thus Haldeman's lack of direction was aggravated by an even more rudderless group of associates.

The upshot was that the White House staff's attitude to the President resembled that of an advertising agency — whence indeed most came — to an exclusive, temperamental client. They might differ with some directives; they would seek to mitigate excessive demands insofar as they had standards for gauging them; but at the end of the day they would be judged by their efficiency in carrying out difficult assignments. They were expediters, not balance wheels. And once the machine started skidding, they accelerated its descent over the precipice rather than braking it in time.

Haldeman's relations with me had ingredients for friction. He was a conservative middle-class Californian, with all the sentiments, suspicions, and secret envy of that breed. He had rarely met and had never needed to deal consistently with a man of my background (though he overestimated how close I really was to the despised Establishment). He had stuck with Nixon after the gubernatorial defeat of 1962 when only a congenital outsider would remain with so unpromising a figure. He genuinely believed in Nixon's mission. It was bound to be irritating to him to see a newcomer, a member of the Rockefeller team, one who had consistently opposed Nixon, garner so much publicity. But he rarely showed jealousy. The key to our relatively quiescent relationship was that he did not feel competitive with me. He affected tolerant amusement about what he took to be my excessive passion for policy and, in fact, he treated any indication of more than routine interest in substance as excessive. We sometimes clashed when he insisted on his prerogative to screen access to the President in a manner that I considered mindless or when the obsession with public relations was pushed to a point where I thought it harmed policy. But such disagreements were in fact much less frequent than might be expected between chief of staff and national security adviser.

Haldeman's attitude to me was fundamentally a reflection of Nixon's. When Haldeman harassed me, I could be sure that it was to carry out some design of the President. For despite his pretense of being above the battle, Nixon did not really mind the tug-of-war that developed between Secretary of State Rogers and me. Usually Haldeman was instructed to side with me but also to make sure that no issue was ever settled conclusively. (And, of course, I had no way of knowing what Rogers was told behind my back.) Nixon, moreover, was convinced that my special talents would flourish best under conditions of personal insecurity; as I have noted, he periodically saw to it that I developed some doubts about his purposes or priorities or about my standing with him.[3]

But any tensions caused by these practices had largely evaporated in early 1973, once I had decided to resign. In the second half of April 1973, therefore, my feelings toward both Haldeman and Ehrlichman were tinged with sadness. Whatever the occasional frictions, we had been colleagues during turbulent years. I remembered their hopes and, yes, their dedication to service. I knew and liked their wives and their children. I had a better sense than almost anyone of the environment out of which — nearly imperceptibly — had grown the cancer of Watergate. The White House is both a goldfish bowl and an isolation ward; the fish swim in a vessel whose walls are opaque one way. They can be observed if not necessarily understood; they themselves see nothing. Cut off from the outside world, the inhabitants of the White House live by the rules of their internal coexistence or by imagining what the outside world is like. This in the Nixon White House became increasingly at variance with reality until suddenly the incommensurability between the two worlds grew intolerable; the bowl burst and its inhabitants found themselves gasping in a hostile atmosphere.

So Haldeman and Ehrlichman thrashed around at the end of April 1973, not able to gauge the implications of what was happening or even the degree of their own responsibility. As the days went by without exoneration I became more and more convinced that they were finished in their accustomed roles even if they survived in their official positions. The authority of a Presidential Assistant is like that of a trainer in a wild-animal act. His mastery depends on never being challenged; even if he survives an initial assault, he has lost the presumption of his dominance. Every command becomes a struggle; attrition is inevitable. Once Watergate broke and they were thought to be involved, Haldeman and Ehrlichman were doomed to an endless struggle as many who considered themselves abused would now test the limits of their power. And the President would soon tire of the constant contention; he would not want continually to reaffirm his orders to fractious Cabinet secretaries. It was, after all, precisely to spare himself that necessity that he had given so much authority to Haldeman and Ehrlichman in the first place.

As April drew to a close, I was given reason to believe Haldeman and Ehrlichman would not survive at all. In almost every conversation,

Nixon asked me in his elliptical manner whether his two closest aides should resign. It was a strange query, since Nixon never told me the reasons for which he was considering separating himself from the associates of a decade. Throughout the Watergate crisis, not once did Nixon tell me his version of events. He maintained in private the same posture he had adopted in public, that every revelation was new to him and that he was forced to deal with the scandal as it unfolded since he had no personal knowledge of its constituent elements.

On April 21, from Key Biscayne, Nixon telephoned to tell me that Haldeman and Ehrlichman were at Camp David over the weekend to reflect on their predicament. They were in great distress. Would I be willing to call them to fortify their morale? I was by now familiar enough with Nixon to suspect that in addition to offering psychological succor, I was expected to urge them into the desired course, all the more so as he told me ominously that he was planning something decisive. He simply had to wait, he said, for the right moment.

Over the next few days, I spoke with Haldeman and Ehrlichman several times. I listened to them in their travail with a sympathy incapable of generating true helpfulness. For no more than the President would his closest aides tell me exactly what had happened. They ruminated on their chances of survival but not on the circumstances that had produced their dilemma. And I am not sure that they really fully understood. What later came to be labeled Watergate was the composite of a series of ad hoc decisions, elliptical conversations, and uncoordinated acts by different individuals, many of whom were competing with each other for Presidential favor and therefore jealously guarding the bits of intelligence they had picked up in or near the Oval Office.

Which of these random events would emerge during the investigation — more important, which actions were legally wrongful — seemed obscure to Haldeman and Ehrlichman. They had not thought of their conduct as a "cover-up" but as a means to protect an elected Administration that still had much left to accomplish from opponents working against the national interest as they conceived it. Or else they were more skillful actors than I think possible. They had no difficulty agreeing with my by-now stereotyped recommendation, that anything bound to happen eventually should be carried out immediately. But clearly they did not believe that resigning was ultimately necessary; hence there was no reason to consider it immediately. They seemed to think that they would have to leave office only if they were criminally liable. I was convinced their survival depended on more rigorous standards. But I knew too little to argue the merits of the case. Nor was it my place to do so; that decision could only be made by the President, much as he sought to avoid it.

The Disintegration of the White House

D AY by day, Watergate grew into bewilderment and frustration for those seeking to keep the government operating and into panic for those directly involved. We had all become passengers in a vehicle careening out of control in a fog; but we had different perceptions. Those who might have taken control were inhibited by ignorance and by a frustrated mixture of pity, loyalty, and horror; they had but brief, blurred glimpses of the landscape. Those who knew the size of the looming precipice were incapacitated by the fear that a halt for safety would result in their being flung aside.

It was in this atmosphere that only ten days after my high hopes at the Federal City Club — now appearing so naive — I mounted the rostrum at the Associated Press Annual Luncheon in the grand ballroom of the Waldorf-Astoria Hotel in New York to make my first major public speech after four years of office. Its purpose was to unveil the Nixon Administration's new initiative toward the industrial democracies: the so-called Year of Europe. My theme was that, a generation after World War II, the Western Alliance had to articulate a new sense of purpose; military defense remained crucial but no longer seemed a sufficient motivating force. The nations that shared democratic values needed to join in a reaffirmation of common ideals and common goals if we were to maintain our cohesion in a new era of East-West diplomacy, economic and energy problems, and a changing military balance (see Chapter V).

The reception to my speech was friendly, but the question period afterward indicated what we were up against. The audience was preoccupied with matters other than our new initiative: problems with the cease-fire in Vietnam, my personal plans, and Watergate.

I will also discuss Vietnam elsewhere (see Chapter VIII). As for my personal plans, I used the occasion to hint at my preference to leave. But I stressed that I felt a duty to remain until the immediate domestic crisis was surmounted:

I have always believed that I should leave at a moment when some major task had been accomplished and when the transfer of responsibility could occur under conditions that assured continuity, and that made it clear that the position was not held for personal motives entirely, which is always difficult to separate.

Now, at this moment, it is not the time for senior officials of the Administration to talk about their resignations, until the framework of the future becomes clearer, and it depends, of course, also on the President's conception of what one's duties are.

I was committed to stay, but for how long I could not guess; privately, I estimated it as some additional months.

The Watergate questions were less easily disposed of. I now thought it probable that Haldeman and Ehrlichman would be forced to resign or inevitable that their roles would be much diminished. But I wanted to preserve to the greatest extent attainable the possibilities of a constructive foreign policy; for that I had to maintain that executive authority was unimpaired. Moreover, I felt pity for men who had been close associates over a long period. All these themes were in my extemporaneous reply:

On the [Watergate] case itself, of course, I know many of the people that you all read about, and, of course, I know them in a different way than you read about them, and it is difficult to avoid a sense of the awfulness of events, the tragedy that has befallen so many people who have, for whatever reason, or are alleged to have done certain things. So without prejudging anything, one should at least ask for compassion.

With respect to foreign policy, a great deal will depend on how foreign countries will assess the degree of authority in this country, the degree of dedication of the public to the objectives of its foreign policy.

I have no question that the President will insist, as he has said publicly, on a full disclosure of the facts. But when that is accomplished and the human tragedies are completed, the country will go on. Then we have to ask ourselves whether we can afford an orgy of recrimination, or whether we should not keep in mind that the United States will be there far longer than any particular crisis, and whether all of us do not then have an obligation to remember that the faith in the country must be maintained, and that the promise of the country should be eternal.

The moment proved as ill chosen for a new foreign policy initiative as for an appeal for compassion. The media reported my reply on Watergate almost to the exclusion of any reference to my carefully prepared speech on the Year of Europe. Part of the fault was organizational. To reduce the bureaucratic backbiting between the White House and the State Department, Nixon had suggested that I not announce the theme of my speech ahead of time. Therefore no briefing was given in advance; as a result, only the *New York Times* gave it major coverage, hailing my appeal for revitalization of the Alliance. The *Washington Post* led its news reportage with my answer on Watergate and consigned the Year of Europe to the concluding paragraphs. Some editorial opinion indeed treated my speech as a maneuver to divert attention from Watergate.

An editorial in the *Washington Post* of April 26 distinguished between compassion and an assignment of blame, which it insisted must take place. It refuted the idea that the authority and prestige of the Presidency abroad as well as at home could be salvaged only by insulating the normal functioning of government from the Watergate scandal.

Everything, including the Year of Europe and all foreign policy, was secondary to Nixon's "revealing the whole truth":

Richard Nixon can restore what is essential to the nation and to himself by trusting the American people with all the facts. Mr. Nixon is in a terrible predicament at the moment, and nothing that affects him fails to affect the rest of us. We believe the situation can be redeemed. But we also believe that it can be redeemed only by his bending his every effort to win that popular trust which is essential to the functioning of the presidency, and that the only way in which he can win such trust is by pursuing and revealing the whole truth. . . . It represents the only hope he has of regaining public trust and, with it, presidential authority.

The *New York Times* of the same date questioned even the appropriateness of compassion:

When Mr. Kissinger speaks of "the tragedy that has befallen so many people" involved in Watergate, can he really be insensitive to the tragedy of those who remain without hope for amnesty from this Administration for having broken the law, not in pursuit of political power but in protest against a war they regarded as immoral?

Faith in this country, both at home and abroad, will best be preserved through an unflinching demonstration by the President that a single standard of justice prevails here, with the most powerful as subject to punishment as the weakest — and with the always desirable qualities of compassion and forbearance impartially applied.

Watergate was thus linked with Vietnam, which had indeed spawned it.

If the media thought I was too compassionate toward my colleagues, many in the White House thought I had gone too far in speaking of human tragedies as if they were already accomplished. George Shultz told me that Ehrlichman was of the view that he could maintain his position while Haldeman's prospects were shaky. Len Garment reported that he had no idea what would happen next nor who was really responsible for what had already been disclosed. Also he had only a most fragmentary notion whence future revelations might descend upon us.

On the weekend of April 28–29, I was in New York on personal matters, mostly to see my future wife, Nancy. On Sunday afternoon, April 29, I received a phone call from Nixon at Camp David. Nearly incoherent with grief, he told me that he had just asked Haldeman and Ehrlichman to resign. Richard Kleindienst, the Attorney General, had also submitted his resignation. John Dean was being fired. The President said he needed me more than ever. He hoped I was abandoning any thought of resignation. The nation must be held together through this crisis.

My attitude toward Nixon had always been ambivalent, compounded of aloofness and respect, of distrust and admiration. I was convinced that he was at the heart of the Watergate scandal even if he did not know all its manifestations. He had set the tone and evoked the attitudes that made it inevitable. And yet there was another side to Nixon that made him a considerable figure and accounts for his surviving all his vicissitudes. I admired the self-discipline by which he wrested a sense of direction from the chaotic forces at war within him; I was touched by the vulnerability of a man who lived out a Walter Mitty dream of toughness that did not come naturally and who resisted his very real streak of gentleness. For all his ambiguities, he had by conspicuous courage seen our nation through one of its great crises. He had inspired and run the risks for a sweeping and creative revision of our foreign policy. He had effected a dramatic breakthrough to China; he had begun to construct a more positive relationship with the Soviet Union. He had attempted to free America from its historical oscillation between over-extension and isolation. His strange mixture of calculation, deviousness, idealism, tenderness, tawdriness, courage, and daring evoked a feeling of protectiveness among those closest to him — all of whom he more or less manipulated, setting one against the other.

It seemed quite natural both that I should speak to him warmly, urging him never to lose sight of the service he had yet to render, and that, having recovered his composure, he would make another of his elliptical sallies, at once a plea and a form of blackmail: "I hope you will help me protect the national security matters now that Ehrlichman is leaving."

I had no idea what he was talking about. I was baffled but made no response, on the assumption that like so many of his odd comments this did not necessarily have a concrete basis. Later that evening I saw my old friend and mentor Nelson Rockefeller, and mentioned it. What could Nixon have had in mind? "Nothing," replied Rockefeller, who was willing enough to support the President of the United States but could never bring himself to shake the personal dislike of Nixon developed over a decade and a half of rivalry. "He is trying to spook you." *

The next morning, Monday, April 30, Haldeman called the senior White House staff to a meeting in his office. In attendance were Haldeman, Ehrlichman, Shultz, Roy Ash (head of the Office of Management and Budget), and me. With great dignity Haldeman said that he and Ehrlichman had decided to resign to enable the President to go on with the tasks that had brought all of us to the White House in the first place.

---

*The next morning it became apparent that Nixon had been talking about the wiretap records. John Ehrlichman hinted to me that he had some "national security" records to turn over to me. I refused, and called Attorney General–Designate Elliot Richardson and suggested that he take custody of them.

(Neither made any reference to having been requested to do so by Nixon.) Those of us who stayed had to redouble our efforts, he said; we had important goals to reach; the President needed us more than ever. I replied for the others that we knew how much of their lives they had given to service; we would do our best; we wished them well.

That evening, Nixon went on television and, in a distraught presentation, announced the wholesale purge of his Administration. It was not easy to tell from his remarks whether he was concluding an era; it was impossible to believe that this rattled man could be ushering in a new one. His words were self-exculpatory; his demeanor did not convince one of his innocence. It was not the cold recital of available facts some of us had hoped for; but it was not a staunch defense of the record either. It fell between the two stools, defining rather than mitigating disaster. No one watching Nixon's genuine desperation and anguish could avoid the impression that he was no longer in control of events.

As after every major speech, I called the Residence to offer reassurance. Rose Mary Woods, his fanatically and touchingly loyal secretary, answered. Haldeman had banished her to the periphery so as to gain control of all access to the President; now she was back as one of Nixon's principal props. The President, she said, was too upset to come to the telephone. She would convey my good wishes to him.

But for me the evening would not end without a last, incongruous touch. The People's Republic of China was in the process of establishing its Liaison Office in Washington. Weeks earlier, the Chinese advance team had invited me to dinner on April 30 together with other American friends in the Yenching Palace restaurant. The Chinese would not hear of cancellation. They simply moved the starting time to ten o'clock, after the President's television address was completed.

We met in a festive setting, with the ubiquitous toasts to friendship and cooperation. Our Chinese Communist hosts clearly could not comprehend that a nation might destroy its central authority over the issues so far revealed — or anything comparable. Their principal concern was to get the strange period over with so that we could return to the fundamentals of the US–Chinese relationship. My host, Ambassador Han Xu, proposed an eloquent toast to the crisis that President Nixon had just so courageously transcended. Watergate, he averred, had found its proper conclusion.

For once the subtle Chinese analysis had failed them. Our travail had just begun.

The Transformation of the Nixon Administration

NIXON's dramatic speech on the evening of April 30 accelerated the disintegration of the Administration. Watergate had begun to turn into a national obsession. No doubt Nixon's distraught appearance, conveying an impression of both grief and evasion, did not offer the picture of a Chief Executive dominating a crisis. His assertion that Haldeman and Ehrlichman were two of the finest public servants he had known was difficult to reconcile with the decision to let them go; his implication that his closest associates and John Mitchell had kept him uninformed of major events over a period of years did not ring true to some and made him look weak to others. Nixon would probably have been better advised to forgo the speech and simply announce the restructuring of his Administration.

But no change in presentation could have altered the impact of the disclosures that now burst upon the American public: the details of the original Watergate break-in and wiretapping; the burglary of the office of Daniel Ellsberg's psychiatrist; the cover-up; the use of governmental investigative agencies to harass political opponents; and the juvenile escapades, such as the so-called enemies list — which in effect really amounted to a list of those not to invite to White House dinners, something that exists tacitly in every administration. The immature second level of the Nixon White House managed to turn this last triviality into another national scandal.

The disintegration of a government that only a few weeks earlier had appeared invulnerable was shocking to observe. The President lived in the stunned lethargy of a man whose nightmares had come true. The constant undercurrent of his life had been the premonition of catastrophe, which seemed to obsess him in direct proportion to his inability to define it and which dominated him especially when things seemed to be going well. Now at what should have been the height of his success it had all really happened; everything was crashing around him. Like a figure in Greek tragedy he was fulfilling his own nature and thus destroying himself. I am convinced that he genuinely believed his version of events, which was essentially that he had been let down by faithless retainers. And there was indeed an incommensurability between his punishment and his intentions. Anyone who knew him realized that the coarse side of his nature was a kind of fantasy in which he acted out his daydreams of how ruthless politicians behaved under stress. He thought he was imitating his predecessors; he had never meant it as a central feature of his Presidency.

In the weeks following Nixon's April 30 speech, I received many queries from friends, some in hope, others in trepidation, as to when Nixon would launch one of his characteristically vicious counterattacks. But while he occasionally made dark references to doing so, he never considered it seriously. The inchoately expected disaster having finally struck, he seemed unable to do other than endure it, and at the pace set by his critics. He was reluctant to transcend it by putting out the entire truth all at once — because he genuinely did not know it, or had suppressed it in his mind, or knew that he was already technically guilty of obstruction of justice. But he equally resisted entrusting his defense to a lawyer experienced in high-level Washington politics — partly, no doubt, because he was embarrassed to find himself in the position of needing such a lawyer. So he simply endured passively, never sharing his knowledge with anyone, defending himself lackadaisically with evasions and half-truths, going through the motions of governing without the concentration, the attention, or the frenetic bursts of energy that had produced the achievements of his first term.

In the weeks after the resignation of Haldeman and Ehrlichman he appointed John Connally, Melvin Laird, and Bryce Harlow to senior advisory posts on the White House staff. These men, seasoned in the ways of Washington, were supposed to give a sense of professionalism and solidity; they were meant to convey a new, respectable approach to governing. They certainly could have made a major contribution, but Nixon was too shattered to reach out genuinely. He did not institutionalize his government; he withdrew even deeper into his private resentments and terrors. Having invited distinguished leaders to the White House, Nixon could think of nothing for them to do. Without specific assignments they proved of little help. Within months they had all resigned.

In his growing loneliness, what Nixon needed above all was a keeper of the gate, someone to buffer him from the conflict that he now had even less desire to handle directly. This was reflected in the decision to bring in Alexander Haig to replace Haldeman as his chief of staff.

Al Haig and I had been colleagues for over four years. When Nixon had asked me in November 1968 to become Assistant to the President for National Security Affairs, I thought it important to have on my National Security Council staff a military assistant whose responsibilities ran to the White House rather than to the Pentagon. Previously there had been a liaison officer from the Joint Chiefs of Staff, and I proposed to continue that arrangement; but he would necessarily echo the position papers submitted by the Pentagon. What I was looking for, with a war in Vietnam to end, was an officer who belonged to my staff but had the confidence of the military, who could explain the military point of view without being bound by it, and who at the same time would be able to represent White House thinking to the Defense establishment.

It was a delicate assignment. General Earle Wheeler, then Chairman of the Joint Chiefs of Staff, was convinced that as a former professor I would be most comfortable with an officer with advanced degrees from world-famous academic institutions. Having taught there, I rated somewhat lower the wisdom evidenced by such degrees; at any rate, I was already reasonably familiar with it. I sought a more rough-cut type, someone with combat experience and therefore familiar with the practical complexities of operational planning. An old mentor, Fritz Kraemer, came up with the name of Alexander M. Haig, Jr., who was then a colonel on the staff of West Point. He was also strongly recommended by friends like Joe Califano and Robert McNamara, under whom he had served at the Pentagon during the Kennedy and Johnson administrations. With his endorsement by both conservatives and liberals, I offered Haig the position on the basis of one interview.

Haig soon became indispensable. He disciplined my anarchic tendencies and established coherence and procedure in an NSC staff of talented prima donnas. By the end of the year I had made him formally my deputy. Over the course of Nixon's first term he acted as my partner, strong in crises, decisive in judgment, skillful in bureaucratic infighting, indefatigable in his labors.

To be sure, nobody survives in the rough-and-tumble of White House politics — especially of the Nixon White House — without a good measure of ruthlessness. I could not help noticing that Haig was implacable in squeezing to the sidelines potential competitors for my attention. He was not averse to restricting the staff's direct access to me or at least making himself the principal intermediary to the outside world — even if I partly encouraged the practice in order to husband my time to concentrate on the major issues. At the same time, I am sure, he was not above presenting himself to my subordinates as the good guy tempering my demanding, somewhat unbalanced, nature. He worked assiduously at establishing his own personal relationship first with Haldeman and Ehrlichman, then with Nixon. I did not doubt that they considered him more of a loyalist than me. As time went on, I began to wonder whether Haig always resisted Nixon's version that I was a temperamental genius in need of reining in by stabler personalities; or whether Haig objected to the proposition that he could be helpful to my chief in fulfilling that need, making them partners in tranquilizing me, so to speak.

Yet this is no more than saying that I recognized Haig as formidable. One of the most useful tools of the trade of chiefs of staff is to present unpleasant orders as emanating from an implacable superior who has already been softened to the limit; it was a tactic I used myself in my relationship to Nixon. Nor had I strenuously objected when others had put me in the position of the good guy in the White House. In that sense Haig hoisted me with my own petard.

As for Haig's relations with Nixon and his entourage, in the context of White House psychology it was not easy to determine the dividing line between going along with the minimum prejudices required for the effective operation of my office and encouraging these prejudices to advance personal ambition; probably the dividing line occasionally became blurred even in Haig's mind. During the stormy closing phase of the Vietnam negotiations in 1972 and my gradual emergence as a public figure, making my relations with Nixon difficult, Haig drew closer to Nixon — partly out of genuine conviction (he probably would have preferred a purely military outcome), partly as a response to the conflicting pulls of loyalty to his immediate superior (me) and duty to his Commander-in-Chief, the President. This caused moments of extreme exasperation in my relationship with Haig and some tense long-distance exchanges. And yet in the end they were always superseded by my admiration for Haig's integrity, courage, intelligence, and patriotism.

At the beginning of Nixon's second term, Haig wanted to — and Nixon and I reluctantly agreed that he should — resume his Army career. Too long a period in a staff job, no matter how exalted, could only damage Haig's future advancement. He was made Vice Chief of Staff of the Army, a four-star rank culminating a spectacularly rapid rise from colonel within four years.

On the evening of May 2, 1973, I received a phone call from Rose Mary Woods. Nixon wanted to bring Haig in as chief of staff, she told me, for a week or two. He was afraid of my reaction; I might resent seeing my former subordinate in a technically superior position. She hoped that when Nixon told me the next morning I would not give him a hard time; I should remember that he was still distraught over the departure of Haldeman and Ehrlichman; he needed bolstering and support. She was, of course (she said), calling on her own without her boss's knowledge. (The odds were that he was standing beside her, prompting her while she talked.)

It was vintage Nixon: the fear of confrontation; the indirect approach; the acute insight into my probable reaction; and the attempt to soften it through a preposterous charade that would get him over the first hurdle. Anyone familiar with Nixon knew that his need for a chief of staff could not possibly end in a week or two. In the midst of Watergate the need would be greater than ever. I had often witnessed, and occasionally participated in, little games just like this: the sugarcoating of unpalatable decisions, first establishing the principle and then obtaining acquiescence in the measures it inevitably implied.

Nixon was right, as usual, in his psychological estimate of me. It is always difficult to reverse the relationship with a subordinate. And given Haig's interest in national security matters, there was the potential for rivalry on substance. Yet I realized, too, that the situation had gone far beyond normal bureaucratic rules or White House jockeying for position. If a national catastrophe was to be avoided, coherence had to be restored to the government and especially to its center in the White House. Nixon had depended on Haldeman during his entire first term; he clearly could not function without a strong chief of staff to shield him from the day-to-day management of the bureaucracy and to implement his decisions. Watergate made it impossible to bring in a completely new personality. In any event, no one was so well qualified as Haig, who was familiar with Nixon's personality, his style of operation, and his psychological needs. I therefore decided to put the best face on the situation and to make the inevitable easy on everybody.

Haig tactfully called on me the next morning. He would not accept the position without my blessing, he said; it was only for a week or so anyway. This was, of course, as much nonsense as Rose Woods's original proposition. Given his high commitment to service, Haig would not refuse a request by the President no matter how I might feel about it. Nor once established at the White House would he be able to leave after a few days; there could be no rapid change in the necessity that had brought him there. In any case Haig was the only possible choice. I told Haig with conviction that he had to accept, even though it would probably mean the end of his military career. Haig replied that when he had gone on patrol in Vietnam he risked not only his career but his life; he had no right to abandon his Commander-in-Chief in distress. He was shamingly right.

After these preliminaries were over, Nixon called me on the telephone (he was not yet ready to face a direct confrontation). Infinitely ingenious, he had come up with an irresistible argument for Haig's appointment: It was designed to *enhance* my influence; it was aimed at, of all people, Agnew. Haig was essential, said the President, to keep Agnew from "trying to step into things. Well, Agnew can't — we just can't allow that to happen." It was mind-boggling to think that a Chief Executive needed a high-powered chief of staff to control a Vice President who had been given little to do, had a skeleton staff, and was in no position to "step into things." At any rate, Nixon insisted, I should have no concern about my continued paramount role in foreign policymaking: "You and I are going to handle it. I've just got to get somebody that can — it's a curious thing — that can handle that so that you and I can do the other, see." I replied that the various functions would all sort themselves out in practice. Nixon seemed vastly relieved when I told him that I had urged Haig to accept.

So Haig became White House chief of staff. It was fortunate for the nation. His strength and discipline preserved cohesion in the executive branch and helped the government to traverse Watergate without totally disintegrating. He furnished psychological ballast to a desperate President. He did so without catering to Nixon's every prejudice; he ensured that Nixon's preferences and orders would be screened by a governmental structure capable of advising the President in a mature way about the national interest.

Haig's first act was to abolish arbitrary procedures. He understood that it was no longer possible — as it had never been desirable — to present decisions as emanating from Presidential fiat. He made a major effort to broaden participation in decision-making. By May 18 he reported to a rump session of the Cabinet that the Cabinet members' status had been raised, the profile of the White House staff lowered. A shakeup of White House personnel was under way. A sincere attempt would be made to improve relations with the Congress.

To be sure, Watergate imposed some of these measures. The fact remains that Haig gave substance to a vague necessity and a sense of direction to a demoralized Administration. No internal reorganization could ever quite catch up with the rate of disintegration impelled by the seemingly endless revelations, crises, and investigations; still, Haig served his country well and honorably in its extremity.

For the next fifteen months Haig and I worked in closest harmony. It did not exclude occasional petty squabbles over status — such as a debate over who got the bedroom closer to the President's in the Kremlin during Nixon's visit to Moscow in 1974 — but those were minor. Haig dealt with domestic issues; I was responsible for foreign policy and national security. I made no major recommendations to Nixon without discussing them with Haig; he kept me generally informed of key developments on the domestic side, and especially Watergate, that might affect foreign policy. Together with others we sought to hold the ship of state steady even while its captain was gradually being pushed from the bridge. And noble service was performed by people like George Shultz, Arthur Burns, William Simon, Leonard Garment, James Schlesinger, Anne Armstrong, and others, who considered our national tragedy as a call to duty, affirming through their conduct the continuing and overriding values of our nation.

The Taping System

IT was like living on a volcano: Those of us who sought to keep the government going had no idea when another eruption would start. Almost every meeting with Haig or Garment or the various lawyers ended with the query: Is it all out yet? To which the invariable answer was that no one knew. It was impossible to guess what other obscure staff member had sought to prove his dedication by extralegal or improper activities. For nearly two months the torrent of revelations seemed unending.

Among the most startling was the disclosure that Nixon had been tape-recording all his conversations since early 1971. I learned about it a few weeks after Haig took over as chief of staff. He told me to be careful about anything I said in the Oval Office; it contained a voice-activated tape-recording system.

Only Haldeman and Alexander Butterfield, his deputy who operated the system, seem to have known of its existence. Even Ehrlichman appears to have been kept in the dark. The idea was first suggested when Nixon found in the White House a taping system installed by President Johnson. He had it removed then, but he obviously looked more favorably on it as he found himself engulfed in leaks painting him as the villain of the Administration. (He forgot that Johnson's system was controlled from the President's desk and thus permitted selectivity before, during, and, if necessary, after a conversation.) Some taping seems to have taken place also during the Kennedy period.[4]

Nixon's tapes were made to be deposited in the Nixon Presidential Library for the use of future researchers. Haldeman has written that Nixon's motive was to protect himself against associates who might seek to disavow discussions in which they had participated. It was a high price to pay for insurance. Insofar as the Cambodia incursions gave impetus to his decision, I was apparently an unwitting cause as well as target. The purpose was to prevent me from emerging as the "good guy" on decisions in which I had taken part.[5] Obviously, Nixon had no idea that his own style of conversation, the degree to which the romantic and the real merged in his mind, would place him in jeopardy — not so much legal as historical. Even men less complex than Nixon might have trouble surviving so pitiless and literal a record as years of transcribed offhand comments or extended conversations separated from context — especially after the witnesses who might explain their real significance have passed from the scene. Since the tapes were activated by sound, the system was beyond the control of even its originator. This was ironically symbolic of a White House mood that had run essentially out of control: an excess of faith in mechanical procedure compounded by a literal-mindedness that, assigned the task of producing a record, did so with a vengeance — in a manner certain eventually to destroy the image Nixon was so passionately cultivating.

Anyone familiar with Nixon's way of talking could have no doubt he was sitting on a time bomb. His random, elliptical, occasionally emotional manner of conversation was bound to shock, and mislead, the historian. Nixon's indirect style of operation simply could not be gauged by an outsider. There was no way of telling what Nixon had put forward to test his interlocutor and what he meant to be taken seriously; and no outsider could distinguish a command that was to be followed from an emotional outburst that one was at liberty to ignore — perhaps was even expected to ignore.

How Nixon would have used these tapes, had his Presidency run its normal course, I cannot say. I doubt whether anyone had begun to think about the problem of even transcribing, let alone organizing, seven years of conversation: A psychiatrist friend once told me that he taped his patients until he realized "it takes an hour to listen to an hour." As for their value for historical research by some indefatigable listeners, it must be doubted. What could anyone uninitiated make objectively of the collection of reflections and interjections, the strange indiscretions mixed with high-minded pronouncements, the observations hardly germane to the issue of the moment but reflecting the prejudices of Nixon's youth, all choreographed by the only person in the room who knew that the tape system existed and could therefore produce whatever tableau suited his fancy? The significance of every exchange turns on its context and an appreciation of Nixon's shifting moods and wayward tactics. Remove these and you have but random musings — fascinating, entertaining, perhaps, but irrelevant for the most part as the basis for the President's actions.

One of Nixon's favorite maneuvers, for example, was to call a meeting for which everybody's view except one recalcitrant's was either known to him or prearranged by him. He would then initially seem to accept the position with which he disagreed and permit himself to be persuaded to his real views by associates, some of whom had been rehearsed in their positions, leaving the potential holdout totally isolated. It took a strong man to maintain his position when the contrary arguments had obviously convinced the President.[6]

If the President's own words are a quicksand for researchers, the responses of his interlocutors are hardly solid ground. A Presidential Assistant has to balance the wisdom of scoring a passing point against the risk of losing the President's backing in his area of responsibility. Presidents, by nature, desire to prevail. But it was especially tempting to fall in with Nixon's musings because experience had taught that his more extravagant affirmations rarely had operational consequences. No doubt many of us in the inner circle listened in silence to reflections we would have challenged in abstract intellectual debate; we sometimes made a contribution more to meet the needs of the moment — one of which was to be able to depart quickly in good grace — than to stand the test of deferred scrutiny.

After the taping became known, I understood various things in retrospect, both innocent and contrived. For example, I was present at practically every Presidential conversation with a foreign leader, formally as note-taker. In a bizarre memorandum in early 1971 Haldeman instructed the staff not to pay too much attention to substantive details in our records of Presidential conversations; we should concentrate on atmosphere and personal impressions. It was one of the orders I ignored, at least to the extent of making sure a good record existed. I thought it an undue burden for the President to have to dictate his own notes; they would, moreover, be highly unreliable and I said so to Haldeman. He did not enlighten me about the President's other methods for making a record of substance.

Other, more devious, patterns became clear when I knew about the taping. Many conversations that had made no sense at the time fell into place. I could see occasions where I was set up to prevent my dissociating myself from some course or to get me on record in supporting some complicated design. For example, on the day Nixon had ordered the bombing and mining of North Vietnam, I was called to his study in the Executive Office Building five minutes before the relevant order was to be signed. I was confronted by Haldeman, who listed all the arguments against proceeding, contrary to everything said the previous week. Nixon was silent. I defended the decision, insisted that it was now too late to change it, and rounded on Haldeman for mixing into substance. Nixon thereupon signed the order without comment. The tape will show counterargument by Haldeman, strong advocacy by me, silence by Nixon.[7]

As Watergate made only too evident, however, no one could possibly prearrange every conversation during every waking hour over a period of years. The spider got entangled in its own web. Even had Watergate not occurred, the tapes would have damaged Nixon's reputation severely and the more so the longer their release was delayed and the memory of Nixon's idiosyncrasies faded. Had matters gone as planned — and the tapes trickled out posthumously — Nixon would have managed the extraordinary feat of committing suicide after his own death.

Weirdly enough, I doubt that my new knowledge of the tape system in 1973 changed very much what I said to the President afterward. He was so much in need of succor, so totally alone, our national security depended so much on his functioning, that these goals overrode the knowledge that what was being said would be heard and read by posterity long after its context had been obliterated.

The tapes came to my consciousness again in late June during the week that John Dean, the former White House Counsel, was testifying against Nixon on national television before Senator Sam Ervin's Watergate Committee. Haig told me that consideration was being given to releasing a tape that contradicted the testimony. He had not listened to any tapes himself. The lawyers, who had apparently been given a few (by whom I never learned), thought they had caught Dean in a serious misstatement. I warned Haig that the release of one exculpatory tape would reveal the system and lead inevitably to the demand that all the tapes be released. It should be done only if Nixon was prepared to take this step. Whether on the basis of my recommendation or because the lawyers found the tape less helpful than they believed at first, I heard nothing further of the proposition.

The next time I thought about the tapes was when their existence was publicly revealed on television by Alex Butterfield before the Ervin Committee on July 16. Bryce Harlow and I chatted about it; he said his wife was jubilant; the foxy Nixon had once again confounded his opponents; the tapes were certain to exonerate him. Harlow and I were less confident. We had no knowledge of what the tapes might reveal with respect to Watergate. But from what we did know, about what happened when our leader was seized by either exaltation or despondency, we suspected that the release of the tapes would prove uniquely damaging.

The day that Alex Butterfield publicly disclosed the existence of the tapes I had dinner with Nelson Rockefeller at the residence he maintained in Washington. He held that the tapes should be destroyed forthwith. They represented a breach of faith with anybody who had entered the Oval Office. Since no one could go through all of them concurrently, they lent themselves to a form of selective blackmail either by Nixon and his associates or by whoever wound up controlling them. But Nixon was at that time in a hospital with pneumonia. He was not soliciting opinions. When he emerged it was too late; legal processes to claim the tapes had started.

In retrospect it is clear that from then on the Nixon Presidency was irredeemable. So long as the testimony of senior aides was in conflict, there was some possibility that once the Senate hearings had concluded, boredom and the impossibility of deciding among the different versions conclusively would cause the crisis to run out of steam. The revelation of the White House taping system ended any such possibility. The initial outrage at the practice of secret taping made it appear that Nixon had committed some unique wrong; the fact that his predecessors had also used taping systems was ignored. But if taping in the Oval Office was not unprecedented, it had never been given such painstaking publicity. Nor, more important, had there ever been an occasion when tapes could determine the potential criminal culpability of a President and his immediate staff. Thenceforth Watergate was transformed into a bitter contest between the President on the one side and the Congressional investigating committees and the Special Prosecutor (appointed in May) on the other, as Nixon sought to keep exclusive control over the tapes by invoking the constitutional principle of the separation of powers.

Whatever the fine points of the legal debate, it necessarily placed Nixon in the position of withholding information that on the face of it could settle the various allegations once and for all. From then on, the issue was no longer the relative credibility of the various witnesses but the President's attempt to withhold evidence. Regardless of the outcome of that litigation, its very nature — with the implication that there was guilty knowledge to hide — destroyed what was left of Nixon's moral position. It made him a lame duck six months into a Presidency won by the second largest plurality in American history.

The "Plumbers" and the Wiretaps

"WHAT did he know? When did he know it?" These questions by Senator Howard Baker became one of the hallmarks of the televised Watergate hearings conducted by Senator Ervin's Select Committee. As the investigations and allegations spread, more and more members of the White House staff were being asked to account for a wider and wider range of decisions. The break-in and cover-up at Watergate and the burglary of the office of Ellsberg's psychiatrist came to be linked with controversial foreign policy decisions that were totally unrelated. The bombing of Cambodia or covert operations in Chile were thrown into the cauldron and pursued in an effort to vindicate a philosophical and political point of view by quasi-judicial proceedings. Inevitably, I as security adviser during the period in question became involved in the controversy. Early in the Watergate ordeal, Nixon's enemies had a vested interest in focusing all attention on him and in leaving those conducting foreign policy out of the general assault. As Nixon weakened, even more after he left office, the few survivors of the debacle became the targets for those drawing emotional sustenance from Watergate. That small minority feeding on its resentments sometimes seemed to imply that there had been no President making decisions, only a security adviser.

I shall deal with Cambodia and Chile elsewhere. I knew nothing of the Watergate break-in, or the burglary of Ellsberg's psychiatrist. The area of activity that critics have emphasized is the effort to protect national security information. For the sake of a complete record I shall deal with it here.

The Office of the Assistant to the President for National Security Affairs must self-evidently be concerned with safeguarding military and diplomatic secrets. A nation that cannot be trusted to maintain the confidentiality of sensitive exchanges loses the ability to conduct diplomacy. It will be crippled in negotiations; it will be deprived of crucial information. If every exploratory contact immediately becomes public before even the reaction of the other side can be ascertained, the frank communications so necessary to clarify positions cannot take place. Diplomacy becomes trench warfare. If internal deliberations are leaked, foreign governments gain an advantage and candid advice to the President by his colleagues is inhibited.

No doubt administrations tend to confuse what is embarrassing politically with what is essential for national security — the Nixon Administration perhaps more than most. Fairness dictates acknowledgment, however, that few administrations since the Civil War faced a more bitter assault on their purposes, a more systematic attempt to thwart their policies by civil disobedience, or a more widely encouraged effort to sabotage legitimate and considered policies by tendentious leaks of classified information in the middle of a war.

As security adviser I thought it my duty to help stanch these leaks. We had to demonstrate to the world, to friends as well as adversaries, that we could conduct a serious foreign policy even in the midst of bitter controversy; that we were worthy of confidence and capable of guarding the secrets of others. If our government remained passive when stolen documents became media currency, confidence and the ability to negotiate would be undermined.

The issue became particularly acute in June 1971 when 7,000 pages of confidential files on Indochina from the Kennedy and Johnson presidencies — the so-called Pentagon Papers — were leaked to the press. None of these documents was embarrassing to the Nixon Administration. They could have been used to support the proposition that we had inherited a mess, and some in the Nixon White House urged that we exploit them in this way. Indeed, at the beginning I thought that our own people had leaked the documents for precisely that purpose. When I learned of their publication, I spoke to Haig from California demanding that the culprit be severely punished.

But from the beginning Nixon thought it improper to place the blame for the Vietnam war on his predecessors. In his view he owed it both to those who had given years to that struggle, and to the families of the dead, not to discredit their sacrifice as the error of one President. He was rewarded for this generosity by seeing many of those who had made the decisions to send troops encourage the civil disobedience that so complicated the efforts to extricate them. Thus, when the Pentagon Papers became public, Nixon was consistent. He rejected a partisan response. He took the view that the failure to resist such massive, and illegal, disclosures of classified information would open the floodgates, undermining the processes of government and the confidence of other nations. Nor was his a purely theoretical concern. We were at that very moment on the eve of my secret trip to Peking; we were engaged in private talks with Hanoi that we thought — incorrectly, as it turned out — were close to a breakthrough; and we were exploring a possible summit with Moscow, together with a whole host of sensitive negotiations from a Berlin settlement to SALT. All these efforts would be jeopardized if the impression grew that our government was on the run and its discipline was disintegrating. And it was obvious that the motive of both the theft and the publication of the Pentagon Papers was political warfare to force us to accept terms on Vietnam that we considered dishonorable.

I shared Nixon's views; I almost certainly reinforced them. I believed then, and do now, that our system of government will lose all coherence if each President uses his control over the process of declassification to smear his predecessors, or if he treats the defense of secret documents as a question of partisan expediency. I certainly felt strongly that the executive branch had to be perceived as resisting such a massive breach of trust. I was aware of the legal steps to attempt to enjoin publication in the courts; I was not formally consulted about them but I considered it the correct decision.

But until I read about it in the newspapers, I knew nothing of the White House "Plumbers unit" burglary of the office of the psychiatrist of Daniel Ellsberg, the admitted perpetrator of the Pentagon Papers theft. The break-in was sordid, puerile, and self-defeating: It aborted the criminal trial of the individual who flaunted his defiance of the laws against such unauthorized disclosures. I have difficulty to this day understanding the rationale for the break-in; had the psychiatrist's documents proved Ellsberg unstable it would have helped his defense rather than the government's cause. But if it was stupid practically, it was inexcusable on moral grounds; a White House-sponsored burglary conducted with no color of law enforcement authority cannot be anything but a disgrace.

The "Plumbers unit" — so called because its job was to stop leaks — was part of John Ehrlichman's office. As with several other aspects of Watergate — the enemies list, for example — the infantile nomenclature did more than the substance of the activities to raise the presumption of sinister purpose. In itself there was nothing startling about assigning two staff members to look into leaks of classified documents. The need for it appears to have been compounded in Nixon's mind by his growing distrust of J. Edgar Hoover, then the Director of the FBI. By 1971 Nixon had become convinced that Hoover would conduct investigations assigned to him capriciously, stopping at nothing to destroy individuals who had incurred his displeasure or jarred some personal prejudice, going easy on suspects where there was a personal link. Nixon believed that Hoover's friendship with Ellsberg's father-in-law would prevent a serious investigation of the Pentagon Papers theft. Moreover, Hoover was quite capable, Nixon thought, of using the knowledge he acquired as part of his investigations to blackmail the President. Nixon was determined to get rid of Hoover at the earliest opportunity after the 1972 election and he wanted to supply no hostages that might impede this process.*

What was striking about the "Plumbers" was not their existence but that the assignment should have been given to two such clean-cut, middle-class young men who had no investigative training whatever. Egil Krogh and David R. Young looked like advertisements of the decent, idealistic young American. And fundamentally that is what they were. I barely knew Krogh, but had brought David Young to Washington after

---

*Hoover died in early May 1972.

having made his acquaintance in Nelson Rockefeller's office. He became my personal assistant because I wanted near me somebody who I considered had ability, high moral standards, and dedication. The appointment did not work out because Young ran afoul of the redoubtable Haig, who carefully protected his access to me, and because Young was overqualified for the kind of work the position required. In January 1971 Young was shifted from my immediate office to a make-work job of research in the White House Situation Room. He was rightly dissatisfied with this assignment and happy when Ehrlichman hired him in July 1971, while I was on the secret trip to China. Upon my return the job was presented to me as — and indeed it was, at first — an interagency review of the declassification system. Ehrlichman's hiring of Young was not uninfluenced by the petty jealousies of the White House staff; he lost no opportunity to rub it in that he knew how to use talented men better than I. I, in turn, was displeased that Ehrlichman had recruited one of my staff members without consulting me and while I was out of the country. From this assignment, or as part of it — I never knew which — David Young found his way to the "Plumbers."

The essentially pointless question of whether "I knew about the Plumbers" became another controversy in the Kafkaesque atmosphere of Watergate. Unbelievable as it may appear to the outsider, it is difficult to reconstruct what others in a large bureaucracy thought one knew. I was, of course, fully aware that Ehrlichman's office had responsibility for investigating security leaks, though the details were carefully kept from me except when they affected my office directly. I did not realize, or bother to inform myself, that a special unit existed to investigate security leaks and that its members essentially had no other duties. I assumed instead that staff members were assigned to conduct these investigations on an ad hoc basis, including Krogh and Young, though it is quite possible that Krogh and Young thought I knew that theirs was a full-time mission all along. But even had I known this, I would not have found it improper that the White House sought to protect its classified information by an investigative unit, so long as it operated within the law. Nor do I think to this day that the "Plumbers unit" — apart from the burglary — was illegal or improper given the context of the time.*

Another episode, and one in which I did play a part, was the installation of seventeen wiretaps on individuals between May 1969 and February 1971. I reported on the wiretapping in my first volume,[8] but I return to it here because it became known in 1973. The mysterious "national security matters" that Nixon had spoken of the night before Haldeman and Ehrlichman resigned turned out to be the wiretap records,

---

*The "Plumbers" issue came up periodically afterward. See Chapters XVIII and XXIV.

which had been stored (unknown to me) in Ehrlichman's safe, were confiscated by the FBI when the latter resigned, and soon began to leak out. The wiretapping became a major controversy in 1973, and again in 1974. It was linked by some to Watergate to prove that the Nixon Administration had a pervasive inclination to unlawful behavior.

On this issue hypocrisy is rampant. The myth has been fostered that electronic surveillance was an invention of the Nixon Administration. Of course, that is absurd. Wiretaps may be unpalatable, but they are as ubiquitous as the telephone and almost as old. All major West European democracies — including Britain, France, and the Federal Republic of Germany — use wiretaps for investigative and intelligence purposes on a scale dwarfing the activities of the Nixon Administration. But that is only the beginning of the double standard. Wiretapping by past Presidents of both political parties seems to have been more widespread, with fewer safeguards and looser standards than in Nixon's relatively small number of cases so cherished by his enemies. That is what law enforcement officials indicated when Nixon assumed the Presidency and there is voluminous published evidence to the same effect: Franklin Roosevelt seems to have used wiretaps to monitor the activities of White House staff aides, isolationist leaders, political opponents, and journalists; the hoary practice apparently continued with vigor through all successor administrations until Nixon came into office.[9] Moreover, the wiretapping for national security purposes in 1969–1971 clearly complied with the administrative and legal procedures in effect at the time; judicial warrants for them were required only after a Supreme Court decision of 1972.[10]

That wiretapping is distasteful is unquestionable. But so is the willful and unauthorized disclosure of military and diplomatic secrets in the middle of a war. Those responsible for national security in early 1969 were warned by their predecessors — Presidents Eisenhower and Johnson, in particular — that a dangerous practice was growing in the bureaucracy: Some who disagreed with national policy felt free to try to sabotage it by leaking classified information in clear violation of the law. We found the warning borne out as negotiating positions, military operations, and internal deliberations cascaded into the media. The media took the position that they had no responsibility to the country but to print or broadcast. It was up to the Administration to keep its own secrets — which is precisely what it attempted to do.

By the spring of 1969 Nixon became convinced that the leaks of military operations and sensitive negotiations were jeopardizing American lives. He consulted Attorney General John Mitchell and FBI Director J. Edgar Hoover at a meeting on April 25, a portion of which I attended. Hoover recommended the institution of wiretaps, which he pointed out had been used in all previous administrations at least since

FDR's for these and other much less justifiable purposes. The Attorney General affirmed their legality. Nixon ordered them implemented on the basis of three categories: officials who had access to the classified information that had been leaked; officials in sensitive positions who had adverse information in their security files; and individuals whose possible involvement emerged from the FBI investigations. Later, Nixon courageously assumed full responsibility for the decision in a letter to the Senate Foreign Relations Committee on July 12, 1974:

I wish to affirm categorically that Secretary Kissinger and others involved in various aspects of this investigation were operating under my specific authority and were carrying out my express orders.

Remarkably, this did not still the semantic contortions that accused me of "initiating" or "authorizing" or "ordering" the wiretaps. Given the somewhat haphazard bookkeeping — only Hoover kept records and he was a master at protecting himself[11] — there is no clear-cut documentary record. But a little common sense is in order. It would have been unthinkable for a brand-new recruit to the Nixon entourage, widely distrusted for his liberal associates and with foreign policy responsibilities only, pulling off in his third month in office the initiative for and institution of a law enforcement program in the exclusive jurisdiction of such heavyweights as John Mitchell and J. Edgar Hoover.

The truth is simpler. I agreed strongly with Nixon that something had to be done to stem the leaks; Mitchell and Hoover recommended the program; Nixon ordered it; my office implemented the part of identifying to the FBI persons we knew to come under the first of the three criteria established by Nixon: that is, persons with access to the leaked information. In each case, the FBI requested authority from the Attorney General to wiretap these persons. The FBI sporadically sent to my office brief summaries, averaging about a page in length, of conversations that it considered to represent discussions of secret military or foreign policy matters.

Eventually under this program, wiretaps were established by the FBI on seventeen officials and newsmen. My office did not supply all the names nor was it aware of every wiretap.* (If someone was tapped but no conversation touched on military or foreign affairs, he would not be the subject of reports and I and my office would have no way of knowing about the tap. There was no opportunity, and even less desire, to

---

*Of the seventeen, only six were the subject of reports that were ever sent to my office. Three names (I learned later) were suggested by Haldeman's office, not mine. Of the names listed in the FBI memoranda as "requested" by Colonel Haig or myself, four or five were in fact specifically urged on Nixon by Hoover in the April 25 meeting (including three members of my staff), and additional names came up in the course of the surveillance of others and were called to our attention by the FBI. Another four seem to have originated with Nixon.

spend time pruriently reading over transcripts of personal conversations.) The short summary reports of conversations touching on what the FBI considered national security matters were sent to my office, the President's, and Haldeman's for a year. In May 1970, a year after the first tap, Nixon ordered that my office be dropped from the distribution; I no longer saw *any* reports. Thereafter Haldeman was apparently the sole recipient until the whole program was discontinued in February 1971.

In reflecting about the subject, I cannot add a great deal to what I have written in my first volume:

. . . I went along with what I had no reason to doubt was legal and established practice in these circumstances, pursued, so we were told, with greater energy and fewer safeguards in previous administrations. The motive, which I strongly shared, was to prevent the jeopardizing of American and South Vietnamese lives by individuals (never discovered) who disclosed military information entrusted to them in order to undermine policies decided upon after prayerful consideration and in our view justified both in law and in the national interest. I believe now that the more stringent safeguards applied to national security wiretapping since that time reflect an even more fundamental national interest — but this in no way alters my view of the immorality of those who, in their contempt for their trust, attempted to sabotage national policies and risked American lives.[12]

In retrospect it is also clear to me that while electronic surveillance is a widely used method of investigation in democracies, the wiretapping of one's associates presents an especially painful human problem. I was never at ease about it; it is the part of my public service about which I am most ambivalent. At the time, I simply preferred it to the alternative, which was to separate from their posts those who were suspected of unauthorized disclosures of information. No doubt Nixon and his inner circle savored the notion that some colleagues of the Harvard outsider and Rockefeller associate were suspected leakers. And some officials of the FBI used the opportunity to vindicate their judgment in cases where their reservations about security clearances for my staff had been ignored. For these reasons I may well have subconsciously leaned over backward in resolving my ambivalence about the program. It does not change the fundamental fact that, as far as I knew, the only motive was to protect classified information against unauthorized disclosure in the middle of a complicated war. I had no reason to challenge the claim of the Attorney General that the program was legal and proper. Still, I want to express my regret at the anguish that may have been caused to any individual by a procedure that has since been modified by court decision.

Having said that, I feel entitled to record my dismay at the harassment in lawsuits and print ever since by some who knew very well that I was torn between doing my duty as I saw it and sparing them personally. I even warned some of them about the suspicions of my superiors and cautioned them that they were under scrutiny. By the same token I am grateful to those who were tapped but have remained or become close friends, reconciling their sense of grievance with understanding of the practices, motives, and circumstances of the time.

The Impact on Foreign Policy

M Y predominant concern during Watergate was not the investigations that formed the headlines of the day. It was to sustain the credibility of the United States as a major power. We were tragically back to the domestic disunity of the first term. While this time the national trauma had not grown out of foreign crisis — Vietnam — it would nevertheless affect our international position profoundly. We could — and did — take diplomatic initiatives; we could — and did — utter fierce warnings against threats to our security. But the authority to implement them was beginning to seep away for reasons quite beyond the reach of those conducting foreign policy, in a purgatory in which there were no victors, only victims.

For a while, the real cost of Watergate to the conduct of foreign policy was not apparent. Patriotism and a sense of the awfulness of events induced many traditional critics to suspend their assaults. As an individual I led a charmed life; I became the focal point of a degree of support unprecedented for a nonelected official. It was as if the public and Congress felt the national peril instinctively and created a surrogate center around which the national purpose could rally. But that was a pale substitute for the real thing and it evaporated progressively.

Tawdry revelation was matched by a vile animus. A journalist not known for his friendship to Nixon called me to say he was shocked by the "bloodlust" surfacing among many of his friends: All they seemed to be able to think of was "get him, get him, get him. As if they were gladiators that wanted to kill." William Safire tells of a prominent editor who insisted to him, around this time in 1973, that a "bloodletting" was absolutely necessary.[13]

The symptoms of weakening authority were everywhere. By May 10, 1973, we were receiving reports that Chinese officials were discreetly asking visitors about the extent of the damage to Nixon's authority. They seemed to think that "organized groups" in the United States, determined to jettison the President's foreign policy, were orchestrating the opposition.

The same queries were put to me in the Soviet Union, where I spent May 4 to May 9 to prepare for Brezhnev's June visit to the United

States. At first the Soviet leaders seemed to treat Watergate as a passing phenomenon. But as the revelations began to accumulate and the investigations went on and on, one began to notice efforts to dissociate Brezhnev from Nixon. In early May, Brezhnev told me that he intended to bring his wife and children to America. On June 12, less than a week before his arrival, we were suddenly informed that his wife could not come: "[T]he doctors are flatly against that. As for the daughter and the son, they have had their own compelling reasons preventing them from making such a trip now." A stop by Brezhnev in Houston was also canceled without explanation or consultation. The impression that Watergate was a key factor in Soviet thinking became unavoidable when the same message explained that Brezhnev was going with Nixon to San Clemente against the judgment of his doctors because

if somebody speculates that my suggestion not to fly to California is somehow connected with the internal events in the United States, this is absolutely not true, Mr. President. There is no basis for such an interpretation. The President knows full well that from the outset we have unhesitatingly followed a consistent line in relations with him and our respect and my personal respect has not diminished a bit.

This apparent token of solicitude could equally plausibly be explained as a heavy-handed Soviet attempt to remind the President of his weakened position. In either case it was profoundly demeaning to think that the President required an assurance of continued personal esteem from the General Secretary of the Central Committee of the Communist Party of the Soviet Union.

The erosion of executive authority affected not only adversaries; it blighted as well relations with our friends. West German Ambassador Berndt von Staden told me that the cynical West German press coverage of Chancellor Willy Brandt's visit in early May was undoubtedly caused by its coincidence with the speech announcing the resignation of Haldeman and Ehrlichman. In my June 8 meeting with French Foreign Minister Michel Jobert, he insinuated that the purpose of the Year of Europe was to ease our domestic situation; it forced me to remind him that it had all been planned before Watergate (as Jobert knew very well from a conversation I had had with President Georges Pompidou in December 1972). The subject came up again when I met with the allied representatives to the North Atlantic Council in San Clemente on June 30 (they were touring the United States); with the Italian Ambassador on July 24; and on the visits of German Foreign Minister Walter Scheel and British Cabinet Secretary Burke Trend in July — always politely, even compassionately. But the policy of a great power is sustained by respect, not compassion.

On August 4 Lee Kuan Yew, Prime Minister of Singapore, a man of singular intelligence and judgment and a true friend of the United States, interrupted a meeting of Commonwealth heads of government in Ottawa to fly to New York for a private meeting with me at Kennedy Airport. His sole purpose was to have the opportunity to judge the impact of Watergate on the foreign policy of the United States. "You are the anchor of the whole non-Communist world," he said nearly in despair, "and because of righteous indignation this anchor is slithering in the mud." His fear was that if Nixon was overthrown, for whatever reason, the strong foreign policy that Nixon represented would also be undermined. In 1976, a new President would be elected who saw his election as vindication of the antiwar, neo-isolationist position. This must not happen: "My survival depends on it," he said.

As so often before, Lee Kuan Yew was prescient. Friendly countries needed then, and still need, a strong Presidency for their security; even adversaries are more comfortable with a predictable, coherent America. Against my premonitions, I was duty-bound to reassure my old friend from Singapore. We would maintain the nation's strength and purpose, I said; we would surely get through this crisis as we had overcome so many others. I asserted that the policy of our successors, whoever they might be, would maintain a strong America. I do not know whether the perceptive Lee Kuan Yew believed me; I tend to doubt it. I have been too embarrassed to ask him.

In mid-1974, the distinguished columnist of the *Washington Post,* Chalmers Roberts, wrote perceptively in *Foreign Affairs:*

> Foreign policy is made both by commission and omission. It is affected by mood and nuance, by judgments of strengths and weaknesses, by one government's measure of another's will as well as its ability to act, by one national leader's perception of a rival or friendly leader's political standing in his own country and its effect on both national power and policies.[14]

That was the issue precisely. With every passing day Watergate was circumscribing our freedom of action. We were losing the ability to make credible commitments, for we could no longer guarantee Congressional approval. At the same time, we had to be careful to avoid confrontations for fear of being unable to sustain them in the miasma of domestic suspicion. (When we went on alert at the end of the Mideast war in October 1973, I was asked at a press conference whether it was a Watergate maneuver.) Deprived of both the carrot and the stick, we could only watch with impatient frustration as first Hanoi and then Moscow began to exploit our discomfiture.

For better or worse it fell increasingly to my office to hold foreign policy together. There was now an entirely different atmosphere in the White House from that in the first term. Gone were most of the arrogant young men of the Haldeman era, cockily confident that all could be

planned and every problem would yield to procedure. Only Ronald Ziegler remained, as head of the press office, carrying out an impossible
task with loyalty and dedication. The White House staff, in any event,
no longer had the authority of a strong President or the self-assurance
of participating in a great cause. Senior members of the White House
had to establish their right from case to case by performance, conviction, and the ability to appeal to a sense of the national interest in excruciatingly difficult circumstances, of which the most serious was the
inability to articulate the extent of our peril.

At every press conference I was asked about the impact of Watergate
on foreign policy. I consistently denied any relationship. Though everyone knew it to be untrue, only a show of imperviousness would enable
us to salvage anything. A great power is given no quarter because it has
trouble at home. We could surmount our perils, if at all, only by demonstrating self-confidence and continuing to insist that we would defend
the national interest against all obstacles, foreign and domestic.

But I was filled with foreboding. The country seemed in a "suicidal
mood," I said to one friend in May 1973, and it was bound to erode
our world position: "Four or five years of amassing capital in nickels
and dimes is being squandered in thousand dollar bills." To another
friend in July I confided: "At no crisis in the last fifteen years did I
think the country was in danger. But I genuinely now believe that we
could suffer irreparable damage." And later:

[T]he difference in any effort you have ever known as between greatness and
mediocrity is a nuance. You can't describe it. And it took us two years when
no one understood what we were doing to get it. One success created the necessity of the other. When it unravels it will go the same way. For two years
you won't see anything, and then you start pulling the threads out. I can go to
the Hill and say, gentlemen, here are the dangers. You will have a Mideast
war if this keeps up.

This is more or less what happened, though self-pity was no help. I
could not go to the Congress with a warning because I would have been
at a loss to recommend a different course of action. The Senate hearings
were theatrical and procedurally unfair; there was no opportunity to cross-
examine, no advance information of charges. But the rot it exposed was
real enough. The essence of the problem lay within the Administration,
not with those who were exposing it, however self-righteously. Once
Watergate erupted, it was impossible to arrest its course. Many old-line
opponents of Nixon understood very well what was happening to their
country's prestige and were horror-struck. The best they could do was
to ease the task of those few in authority trying to steer the wreck.

In this manner I, a foreign-born American, wound up in the extraordinary position of holding together our foreign policy and reassuring our

public. It had nothing to do with merit; it was evoked by a national instinct for self-preservation. While I had not discouraged the public attention in the first term by which I was made the good guy, this new and higher responsibility was too elemental, too awe-inspiring, to be consciously sought. The responsibility that seemed to devolve upon me had to be used to foster the impression of continued American strength, resolve, and indeed active involvement in world affairs, to convey the conviction that amidst all our trials we remained masters of our fate.

I would not have chosen the role, and I surprised myself by not feeling up to it, though I tried hard not to show it. But all survivors of the debacle had an inescapable duty to contribute what they could to a sense of national purpose, and I did my best. It imposed a style of diplomacy leaning toward the spectacular; a show of driving self-assurance that would cause potential adversaries to recoil from a challenge. Some of it no doubt reflected vanity; much was conscious decision growing out of awed reflection. We needed a visible, if necessary theatrical, affirmation that America would survive its anguish and still build a better world. It was a measure of the straits in which Nixon found himself that he accepted this state of affairs; it was a tribute to his tenacity and patriotism that he did so with good grace.

Yet the political prerequisite for getting through this period was that decisions be seen to reflect a functioning Presidency. Nixon no longer had the margin of maneuver or the personnel for the intricate minuets with which he had managed affairs in the first term. Both he and I had been reduced to fundamentals. He governed by more conventional procedures. And I worked at holding together a national consensus on foreign policy. The rambling talks between us became more reflective just as the taping system stopped and, in a curious way, less anxious and frenetic; when the worst had already happened, only principles remained.

Increasingly, I sought bipartisan Congressional support. While it proved impossible on some neuralgic issues such as Indochina or Jewish emigration from the Soviet Union, there was more unity on foreign policy than in any other area. It was as if the Congressional leaders too had become horrified by the tidal wave that was carrying the country forward, threatening to engulf the just and the unjust alike.

By holding foreign policy together I no doubt eased the consciences of some of Nixon's more implacable adversaries. But there was no choice. And in the final analysis Nixon's fate was ordained once the White House staff began to fall apart and to turn on him. From that point the duty to the nation was to preserve its security and credibility by creating a facade of unity and purposefulness. The edge of a precipice leaves scope for only one imperative: to obtain some maneuvering room.

So it fell in part to me, in part to Haig, and to both our staffs, to bolster our wounded President whose fortitude compelled respect and whose suffering evoked a curious warmth. For the worst punishment that befell Nixon was the knowledge that in the final analysis he had done it all to himself. And in his extremity he acted with high purpose in the field of foreign policy; he seemed driven by the consciousness that even if his Presidency could not be saved, the nation must be.

V

The Year of Europe

Origins

LIKE the White House, the Elysée Palace serves as a combined residence and office of the French head of state. One approaches it through a majestic gate on the narrow and busy Rue du Faubourg-Saint-Honoré, then across a gravel courtyard that enhances the palace's simple and elegant facade. Inside, at the top of a wide staircase, is a landing that serves as a waiting area. Though the President's own room is not large by the standards of chief executives of major countries, it is exquisitely appointed with tapestries and French provincial furniture. It overlooks a peaceful, formal garden beyond which one can see the tops of the trees lining the Champs-Elysées; it is a bucolic refuge in the midst of a great bustling city.

The serenity of the view was matched by the demeanor of the large, portly man with bushy eyebrows who sat behind the ornate table that served as his desk. Georges Pompidou, whom I visited in early December 1972, was formidable. Before he succeeded President Charles de Gaulle in 1969, he had served the great general as Prime Minister for six years and then had been suddenly removed in 1968 in the aftermath of the student rebellion that briefly took over large parts of Paris. It was Pompidou's remarkable achievement to return from near-oblivion, at a time when de Gaulle was still alive, and to maintain his hold on the Gaullist majority even while changing the style, if not the substance, of France's foreign policy.

When de Gaulle resigned from office in April 1969, I wrote Nixon that the French Presidency was more fragile than it appeared. Its power was dependent on Presidential control of a parliamentary majority, control difficult to sustain indefinitely since elections for the National Assembly followed a different calendar from those for the Presidency. Whenever a parliamentary election produced a majority not of the President's party, or not controlled by the President, it would be able to nominate its own Prime Minister to whom the balance of power would then shift. The traditional pattern of French postwar politics — parliamentary instability — might then recur. De Gaulle had tried to close the door on France's past. But it was not locked.

My analysis was theoretically correct, but it has proved at least premature. Every French parliament since de Gaulle has been controlled by the President. Pompidou in his day was dominating French political life almost as de Gaulle had, and though his manner was less majestic, his style of government was no less regal. With a skeptical, penetrating intelligence that never descended to the cynical, he made up in analytical acumen and shrewdness what he lacked in international experience. He had been both professor and banker. He knew the world of letters as well as the world of affairs. While free of the anti-American bias of his predecessor (and of some of the top echelons of the Quai d'Orsay, the French Foreign Office), he shared the French intellectual's assumption that in the long run America was too naive, clumsy, and unstable to be entrusted with the fate of Europe. On the other hand, he was realistic enough to understand that America was too powerful to be ignored and France too weak to go it alone.

Pompidou had been deeply offended when demonstrators protesting French arms sales to Libya had jostled him and his wife in Chicago during their visit to the United States in early 1970. While it did not alter the courteous and conciliatory style of his diplomacy, it spawned an element of reserve, even of resentment, that was never completely dissipated; it burst forth with vehemence during his last tormented year when his reserves of self-control were strained to the utmost by a bone cancer whose ravages he managed to hide from all but a few intimates. I considered him a most farsighted and intelligent leader, a man who, whatever his doubts about America's grasp of global events, would work within his principles to strengthen the values, the power, and the resolution of the democracies.

During Nixon's first term, relations between the United States and France flourished. Nixon and Pompidou were akin in their unsentimental recognition of the importance of the balance of power; they shared a skeptical assessment of Soviet motivations. Pompidou was leery of potential German nationalism; Nixon was uneasy about Willy Brandt — operationally the attitudes merged. Pompidou appreciated Nixon's gallant gesture of announcing immediately his attendance at de Gaulle's funeral, thus setting a protocol level all other countries had to emulate; and of unexpectedly appearing at a dinner in Pompidou's honor in New York in March 1970 to show his disapproval of the anti-Pompidou demonstrations. Nixon was grateful for Pompidou's discreet and practical help in arranging my secret talks with the North Vietnamese in Paris. Nixon respected Pompidou's grasp of world affairs. Having admired de Gaulle, he had little difficulty with the Gaullist strain in Pompidou's approach; he considered a strong France, even when it was occasionally difficult, overwhelmingly a boon to the West.

On December 8, 1972, I called on Pompidou while I was in Paris for the final phase of the negotiations with the North Vietnamese. I briefed him in a detail not vouchsafed to our own Cabinet departments — a procedure that in retrospect strikes even me as astonishing. He never betrayed our confidence or sought any special favors for his assistance in making my journeys to Paris possible. He spoke French to me, which I believed I understood. I replied in English, which was translated for Pompidou by the brilliant interpreter Constantin Andronikov, whose accent in English was undoubtedly better than my own.

This occasion was one of the low points of the Vietnam negotiations and indeed of my public life to that date. Le Duc Tho was stonewalling after we had come excruciatingly close to a settlement in October. He seemed to be gambling that if he held out long enough, American domestic pressures might force us to dismantle the Saigon government and deliver total victory to Hanoi.

Pompidou listened to my recital with his characteristic courtesy before he calmly commented: "These are details. In my view you are condemned to succeed." Pompidou had gone to the heart of the matter. The two sides were too committed to an agreement to turn back; one way or another the war was bound to end soon; our maddening frustration was in fact the final spasm of a decade of struggle. And to underline his confidence in his judgment, Pompidou asked me another question, perhaps out of curiosity, perhaps to encourage me: "And afterwards, what will be the center of gravity of your policy?" It was oddly reassuring, even soothing, to be asked about a future no longer dominated by the nightmare of Indochina, to be invited in the midst of bitter divisions to speculate about a world of constructive ends.

I said that after the war was over we intended to give more emphasis to Atlantic relationships. Europe and North America had made no serious effort in two decades to chart their larger common purposes. A suitably prepared summit meeting of leaders of the Atlantic community might do so. Pompidou was avuncularly encouraging.

A few days later he showed that this was not simply politeness or an attempt to restore my flagging spirits; he took the unusual step of putting his authority publicly behind a new Atlantic dialogue. In an interview with *New York Times* columnist James Reston, Pompidou declared that in the new year of 1973 he favored consultations "at the highest level" to clarify economic and above all political relations among the democracies. He looked forward to discussions with his colleagues on both sides of the Atlantic to define and reaffirm the shared objectives of the United States, the European Community, and Japan in a new era. Matters of money and trade were secondary to these larger political and philosophical questions that had been neglected in recent years.[1] It was a farsighted comment. In light of the controversies between France and the United States to which it later gave rise, there is no little irony in the fact that the ill-fated Year of Europe was born in the office of the President of the French Republic.

Atlantic Relations in Disrepair

THAT Atlantic relations needed a fresh look was by early 1973 almost conventional wisdom. For conditions had changed dramatically and on many fronts. On January 1, 1973, three new members were admitted into the European Economic Community — Britain, Ireland, and Denmark — joining the six that had founded it in 1958 (France, West Germany, Italy, Belgium, the Netherlands, and Luxembourg). And the new Europe of the Nine was now committed to move toward political as well as economic unification. This expansion and strengthening of European unity marked the end of the matter-of-fact American preeminence in the West that had characterized the period since 1945. The two superpowers excepted, Europe's economic and potential military strength was now larger than that of any region in the world. With unity it was bound to articulate its own identity. We for our part, spiritually liberated from the trauma of Vietnam, looked to Europe to share in the regeneration of our purposes; it was, after all, that part of the free world with which we had most in common in history, culture, and moral values.

But I was not as sanguine as others were that this would come easily. For a generation, eminent Americans of both political parties had taken it for granted that a united Europe would ease our global economic burdens while continuing to follow our political lead. They remembered only the impotent Europe of the late 1940s, totally dependent on America for economic support and military security. They forgot the Europe that had invented the concept of sovereignty, whose centuries of statecraft had refined the philosophy of nationalism, and whose unwillingness to subordinate parochial interests to wider purposes had been a principal cause of the two catastrophic world wars of this century.

While much had changed since 1945, I had always doubted that Europe would unite in order to share *our* burdens or that it would be content with a subordinate role once it had the means to implement its own views. Europe's main incentive to undertake a larger cooperative role in the West's affairs would be to fulfill its own distinctive purposes. These no doubt could be harmonized with America's goals; on most issues European interests and ours indeed ran parallel. But it would be a different relationship from the "golden age" of the Marshall Plan, which had fitted in so well with the American penchant for taking charge and inundating problems with resources. After Europe had grown economically strong and politically united, Atlantic cooperation could not be an American enterprise in which consultations elaborated primarily American designs. A common focus had to be achieved among sovereign equals; partnership had to be evoked rather than assumed. This was easy enough to state as a theoretical proposition; it required painful adjustment and patience and sensitivity on both sides of the Atlantic.

Charles de Gaulle had been the first to identify the potential contradiction in the American position between our advocacy of European integration and our simultaneous nostalgia for continued American leadership. No doubt de Gaulle expressed this insight in the most wounding possible way for us. He implied not only that Europe should be *free* to pursue its own interests but also that these interests would in all probability diverge from ours — indeed, that Europe's identity derived in important measure from that proposition. It was therefore scarcely surprising that the debates of the Kennedy and Johnson administrations with de Gaulle over the nature of European unity and of defense cooperation resulted in bitter confrontation. In 1963, de Gaulle vetoed Britain's entry into the Common Market on the ground that Britain was a "Trojan horse" for America. In 1966 he withdrew France from NATO's integrated defense command and forced NATO headquarters to leave Paris. The sense of outraged hurt was reflected in Lyndon Johnson's query whether we should move our military cemeteries as well.

Pompidou stated Europe's case more tactfully. He was more receptive to European integration than de Gaulle, less insistent than de Gaulle that Europe could only be a loose grouping of national states. But he was no less adamant that Europe needed to play its own distinctive role in international affairs. On October 31, 1972, after the historic summit meeting of the European Community that decided to proceed toward full political unity, Pompidou stated his attitude toward the United States in terms of both cooperation and challenge:

> Our links with this great country, the world's foremost economic power, with which eight of our countries are united within the Atlantic Alliance, are so close that it would be absurd to conceive of a Europe constructed in opposition to it. But the very closeness of these links requires that Europe affirm its individual personality with regard to the United States. Western Europe, liberated from armies thanks to the essential contribution of American soldiers, reconstructed with American aid, having looked for its security in alliance with America, having hitherto accepted American currency as the main element of its monetary reserves, must not and cannot sever its links with the United States. But neither must it refrain from affirming its existence as a new reality.

The Nixon Administration had no difficulty with the concept that Europe should be free to conduct its own policy. We agreed with Pompidou's assessment that on fundamentals our interests were likely to run parallel. At the same time, for many years no attempt had been made to define what was fundamental. Nor had any American leader been required to live with the reality of an assertive Europe; de Gaulle had been considered an aberration rather than an augury. Neither side of the Atlantic had addressed seriously the issues that would determine the West's future: How much unity do we need? How much diversity can we stand?

The problems that Europe and America would face together were not simply a matter of adjusting the decision-making procedures in the Alliance, but challenges of substance reflecting major changes in world conditions since the 1940s, when the Alliance was formed. One crucial problem was European defense.

In the late 1940s and 1950s, the United States possessed overwhelming nuclear superiority over the Soviet Union. Europe's defense therefore rested essentially on the threat of American nuclear retaliation. The Eisenhower Administration's so-called doctrine of massive retaliation was not spelled out in precise operational terms; in practice it meant that if Europe was attacked we would strike at the Soviet Union with strategic nuclear weapons. So long as Soviet strategic forces were small and vulnerable — so long, in short, as "victory" in a general nuclear war could still be given some military significance — NATO's military establishment could afford the luxury of not facing up to the long-range menace of the Soviet Union's conventional predominance and geographic proximity. What concerned our allies was not the agreed strategy but the possibility that we might not be ready to employ it. Their own history gave them reason for concern; leaving allies in the lurch had not exactly been unknown in Europe's recent past. The European solution was to encourage a large American troop deployment *in Europe* even while the agreed strategy was that a Soviet attack would trigger nuclear retaliation *from America*. The purpose was as straightforward as it was impolitic to articulate: A Soviet attack that enveloped American as well as allied ground forces would force us into a nuclear response nearly automatically.

Since it was politically inconceivable that America would station forces abroad without at least some European contribution, each of our allies built up ground forces on the Central Front. But the result was a hodge-podge of national armies deployed in locations dating back to the occupation period, with neither standardized weapons nor agreed rates of consumption of supplies. This was not fundamentally a symptom of inefficiency; it reflected the psychological realities. European armies were not designed or expected to win a war in Europe. They were conceived as a "trip-wire" or a "nuclear threshold" — euphemisms for depriving America of choice in launching nuclear retaliation.

The American nuclear superiority on which this strategy depended began to change in the late 1950s, when the Soviet Union developed intercontinental ballistic missiles (ICBMs). For a few years the Soviets' buildup was slow and their missiles remained vulnerable. But the Cuban missile crisis of 1962 brought home to the Soviets the penalty for strategic inferiority and they began a relentless program to remedy it. By 1971 the Soviets had caught up with us in total numbers. Instead of stopping when they reached parity with us, as the Johnson Administration expected, the Soviets continued their buildup and forged ahead in numbers of missiles (though we retained a large edge in bombers). When numbers were frozen by the first SALT agreement in May 1972, they switched energetically to qualitative improvements.

Thus by 1973 the NATO strategy, dependent on American nuclear superiority, was in urgent need of revision. For a while, perhaps through the decade, the United States would retain a clear edge in numbers of warheads, because we were at least five years ahead in the art of multiple independently targetable reentry vehicles (MIRVs). But that only delayed the day of reckoning; it did not avoid it. The Atlantic Alliance faced the urgent necessity of recasting its military doctrine; pledges of American nuclear retaliation first given in the halcyon days of the 1950s and 1960s would begin to lose their credibility. As strategic parity approached, the historical Soviet advantage in ground forces in Europe would grow more ominous, especially in the light of the inexorable Soviet buildup in all other categories of weapons (including, for the first time, a navy capable of global intervention).

But serious analysis and effective response were for too long prevented in America by the passions of the Vietnam war. Essential new weapons were decried as wasteful and dangerous, the mindless mania of the military-industrial complex. "Reordering national priorities" was the slogan of the day; it was the euphemism for cutting the defense budget. We were fortunate to rescue our troop deployments in Europe from the Congressional ax; in 1971 we barely fought off the Mansfield amendment, which would have required the withdrawal of half of our troops from Europe.[2] Many who years later denounced the Nixon Administration as too "soft" were nowhere to be found in the early 1970s when the Administration was fighting these battles — or were on the opposite side. The damage went deeper than the statistics indicate: We paid a heavy price in ideas or programs never put forward because of the certainty of Congressional and media hostility. Forces suitable for local defense were especially hard hit because they ran counter to the obsession with reducing our foreign involvement.

Europe was even less willing to confront the changed real world. Many of our allies continued to treat their own military capabilities as a token payment for the American commitment to Europe; they stopped well short of developing a realistic option for local defense. They dreaded the devastation of their territories; they were loath to leave the familiar shelter of our nuclear guarantee even as its premises were being eroded by technology. They were as reluctant to deal with the implications of the looming strategic parity as we were to raise them. They resorted to the ancient device of responding minimally to our importuning for a greater effort without, in fact, changing the basic philosophy. The Alliance continued to be held together, as was once said about the British Commonwealth, by the highest common platitude.

Similar strains existed in economic relations, where, in contrast to the perhaps overly elaborate NATO coordinating machinery, no formal consultative mechanisms existed at all. As the economic strength of the European Community grew, its competition with the United States intensified and its distinguishing feature, a common external tariff, began to affect American products. This should not have come as a surprise. On the one hand, a revivified Europe absorbed more of our exports; on the other hand, what makes a Common Market advantageous to its members is that its arrangements favor internal industry over outsiders'. It nevertheless came as something of a shock to Americans to find themselves in serious economic rivalry with the nations they had sustained in the postwar period.

The impact of the European Community's newfound assertiveness was daily brought to the attention of the Oval Office by our economic departments. There was the complaint that the European nations maintained preferential trade arrangements with their former colonies, restricting our access to these markets. There was a growing network of special ties between the European Community and other nations in Europe and the Mediterranean littoral. There was perennial controversy over the Community's Common Agricultural Policy. For their part, the Europeans resented the shock tactics by which we had proceeded to reform the international monetary system in 1971. There were many complaints that by abandoning the modified gold standard we were exporting our inflation and penalizing our allies for our refusal to discipline ourselves domestically.

By the early 1970s, the liberal financial and trading system on which the West had built two decades of prosperity was at risk to competitive devaluations, currency crises, and protectionist rivalries. And beyond these immediate strains, little had been done to shape a common policy toward the developing countries and international commodity markets, not least of which was oil, the Achilles' heel of the West. As Pompidou told James Reston in that prescient December talk, a solution could not be found on the technical level; it required some political decisions subjecting the disputes to the overriding imperative of our political and moral unity.

The absence of agreement on political goals came to expression in the European reaction to our improving relations with the Soviet Union. It did not lack irony, for of all our policies détente had initially seemed most to reflect European wishes, even pressures. From the moment Nixon

came into office, he had been treated by our allies as a confirmed Cold
Warrior whose bellicose instincts needed taming by European wisdom.
West European leaders presented themselves to their publics as mediators between American intransigence and Soviet aggressiveness. Visits
to Moscow by Macmillan, Wilson, de Gaulle, and Brandt and the signing of declarations in favor of détente became a staple of European
diplomacy. No meeting with a West European statesman during the first
two years of Nixon's Presidency was complete without subtle hints to
us (or, if necessary, formal disquisitions) on the urgency of a relaxation
of tensions.

Until, that is, we took their advice and our own détente policy began
to bear fruit in 1972. We had many reasons for pursuing it, among
which were the need to separate the Soviet Union from its North Vietnamese ally and to gain maneuvering room at home for a strong foreign
policy amid the powerful neo-isolationist and antidefense pressures from
Congress and media. But we had an additional motive having to do with
trends in the Atlantic Alliance. We did not want NATO to be perceived
as an obstacle to peaceful coexistence. We sought to discourage the
Europeans from unilateral initiatives to Moscow by demonstrating that
in any competition for better relations with Moscow, America had the
stronger hand. The tactic served its purpose; European pressures for
concessions decreased in direct proportion as we developed our own
option toward Moscow. The Alliance stopped being controversial in almost all countries of Western Europe. The irony was that as Soviet-
American relations improved, some of the statesmen who had urged
conciliation began to see in it the harbinger of the long-dreaded Soviet-
American condominium, de Gaulle's nightmare of a "super-Yalta"
carving up the world.

Unjustified and occasionally irritating as we considered these European suspicions, the uneasiness was yet another sign that the Atlantic
nations had lost a shared sense of direction. Indeed, the reason for our
passionate commitment to the new initiative lay largely in the psychological and moral realm. The democracies, we were convinced, could
not continue simply to administer their patrimony. They had come this
far through successive acts of faith that had enabled them to transcend
the vicissitudes of history. A whole generation had grown up who knew
nothing of the perils of the 1940s that had produced the Alliance or of
the vision of man that had shaped their political institutions. In America
their formative experience was the nasty debate of the 1960s over Vietnam. In Europe it was the boredom of the welfare state. It had been a
long time since the idealism and self-confidence of the Western tradition
had found expression in a rededication to major positive tasks. Every
great achievement was a dream before it became a reality. We thought
we were tapping the idealistic tradition of the democracies when we put

forward the Year of Europe. We did not know what we were letting ourselves in for.

The Exploratory Phase

THE year began on a somewhat sour note. All our European allies, with the honorable exception of British Prime Minister Edward Heath, dissociated themselves in varying degrees from the last painful tremor of the Vietnam war — the Christmas bombing. Most European media swallowed the fashionable canard that we had been engaged in the massive extermination of civilians. Many European leaders made comments no less offensive for their allusive phrasing.

Nixon was beside himself. As a passionate believer in the Atlantic Alliance — in 1947 he had been a member of the Herter Committee that had studied European reconstruction for the House of Representatives and laid the basis for the Marshall Plan — he simply could not understand how our allies could turn on us at a moment of such importance and sensitivity. Over a month after the bombing and a week after the Paris Agreement was reached, on February 1, 1973, Nixon told Heath: "What you did, did not go unnoticed and what others did, did not go unnoticed either. It is hard to understand when allies turn on you." On February 15 Nixon made the same point to General Andrew Goodpaster, then Supreme Allied Commander in Europe. Nixon's bitterness did not keep him from pursuing his commitment to a new initiative in Atlantic relations. Indeed, while the photographers were still in the room with Goodpaster, Nixon repeated his intention to make 1973 the "Year of Europe."

There was one man impervious to obstacles, impatient with petty calculation, undisturbed by latent tensions: the father of the European Community, Jean Monnet. Amidst Europe's postwar chaos he had grasped that the traditional nation-state in Europe was finished and that the Continent, to recover from the ravages of war, needed the guiding light of a great idea: European unity. Monnet was a remarkable statesman, though ironically he had no state to represent. Great historical achievements often evolve from simple concepts, for an enterprise requiring the collaboration of multitudes rarely thrives on complexity. Monnet's contribution to European unity was two propositions of great seeming simplicity: First, the various European states, encapsuled in their jealous sovereignty, would not, without prodding, take the leap into the future implicit in the notion of European unity. Second, the United States might well provide that prod if it did not fear that a united Europe would turn on America.

What was most extraordinary was Monnet's inspiration to prod governments by means of a nongovernmental group. In 1955 Monnet created the Action Committee for the United States of Europe. With unerring intuition he brought together a remarkable collection of distinguished persons likely to be influential regardless of which parties governed their countries. By itself this would have barely elevated Monnet's efforts above those of the innumerable international study groups dedicated to worthy causes. What gave the committee impetus and conferred real power on Monnet was his unparalleled access to America's leading personalities and his ability to influence them, indeed almost to mesmerize them. Monnet had chosen America as the deus ex machina that would propel Europe toward unity. The choice reflected a shrewd assessment of American psychology, for his program appealed to every American preconception: the obsolescence of the traditional nation-state, the pragmatic approach to problems, the importance of economic well-being in promoting political stability, and the role of a united Europe in sharing America's burdens.

The man who achieved this influence was an unlikely candidate for such eminence. The quintessential Frenchman, slightly built, somewhat pedantic in his manner, only the bright eyes revealing the inner fire, he would be unnoticed in any large group. He was the embodiment of one of his maxims: "Everybody is ambitious. The question is whether he is ambitious to be or ambitious to do." Monnet clearly was ambitious to do. He was restless with pretentious rhetoric. He sought no glory for himself. His impact reflected anonymous dedication. Monnet was that rarest of all prophets who put people at ease; that most unusual of revolutionaries who overturned the prevailing order without alienating the upholders of existing institutions.

In the process it was barely noticed that his premises did not differ much from those of that other eminent Frenchman, Charles de Gaulle. Like him, Monnet believed that Europe needed to be strong to be influential; that cooperation was meaningful only when there existed the capacity for independent action. Unlike him, Monnet stressed that a united Europe would collaborate with, rather than challenge, us. But this was an elusive distinction, for neither Monnet nor de Gaulle could really be sure how Europe would use the strength that would flow from unity. Monnet did not reject European assertiveness in pursuit of conflicting interests; de Gaulle did not oppose cooperation where interests coincided — witness his staunch support during the crises over Berlin in the late 1950s and the Cuban missile crisis of 1962.

I often wondered what a conversation between Monnet and de Gaulle might be like. "You fool," says my imaginary Monnet, "don't you see that you frighten Americans to no purpose? You are seeking to extort what I can get them to hand to us for free. Only history will decide what we will actually do with our strength and unity."

"You dreamer," replies my hypothetical de Gaulle. "Don't you understand that some possessions are meaningless if received as a gift? We will be able to use them only if we seize them.''

It is quite possible that both would be right. There would have been no European unity without Monnet and no European identity without de Gaulle — producing the final paradox: that the most nationalistic country in Europe made the largest single contribution to the emergence of a European community.

In January 1973 I saw Monnet, then eighty-four years old and frail, on another of my visits to Paris to wrap up the Vietnam agreement. Monnet always liked to check on whether his friends and disciples were living up to his impossibly high standards. If they were not, the eternal twinkle of his blue eyes would give way to a steely cast. If he detected any slackening of effort Monnet would mobilize his army of powerful friends, especially in the United States — a contingency no official faced with equanimity.

On this occasion there was no need for pressure. He was convinced that his approach was good for at least one more act of creativity; I was eager to believe it. Monnet thought it imperative to tie the United States and Europe into a more coherent system on both economic and security issues; that was precisely what we intended with the Year of Europe. He urged that Nixon visit Europe, attend a meeting with the European Community's Council of Ministers, and join in a collective declaration of common goals and objectives. America should begin treating Europe as a political unit whether or not it had fully articulated its institutions. In other words, the United States should complete the process of European unification it had started with the Marshall Plan whether the Europeans were fully ready for it or not.

Nixon was receptive when I reported Monnet's views, but balked at the proposition that we start dealing with Western Europe as a unit immediately. Where I recounted Monnet's suggestion that we force our efforts on the Community, Nixon queried in the margin: "K— (1) is this possible? (2) is this in our interests?" In the end, no more than his predecessors could Nixon escape Monnet's relentless logic. But while Monnet's vision retained its intellectual force, his influence depended on Americans prepared to insist on their view of European institutions and on European leaders for whom Atlantic relations were the top priority. Both of these were in short supply in 1973. Nixon and I wished the European Community well, but we thought that it should evolve from European decisions, not American pressure; we were essentially agnostic about how and when political cohesion came about, provided it did not seek its identity in opposing us. And yet that is precisely the concept of European unity that was gaining ground. Those European leaders most dedicated to European unity were beginning to perceive a conflict between Atlantic unity and European identity. European unification was absorbing more of their energies and dedication than was the elaboration of Atlantic institutions, which they had come to take for granted. Some leaders, in fact, considered a new emphasis on Atlantic cohesion a diversion from their priority of constructing a united Europe; contrary to Monnet, they did not believe that we would be able to merge the two.

These trends were nearly all personified by Edward Heath, Britain's Prime Minister and the first European leader with whom Nixon discussed the Year of Europe. That we should choose Britain for the first of these consultations was natural; it was the essence of what was still called the "special relationship." For generations successive administrations had synchronized their moves with London, especially over the Atlantic Alliance. The British had fought for this tenaciously. Their way of retaining great-power status was to be so integral a part of American decision-making that the idea of not consulting them seemed a violation of the natural order of things. So able and self-assured were our British counterparts that they managed to convey the notion that it was they who were conferring a boon on us by sharing the experience of centuries. Nor were they quite wrong in this estimate.

But this pattern was precisely what Heath was determined to change. He preferred a leading position in Europe to an honored advisory role in Washington, and he did not consider the two functions compatible.

Heath was the first Conservative Prime Minister to have achieved party leadership by election of the Tory members of Parliament instead of by the traditional method — effectively an informal consensus of key Conservative leaders talking privately in their clubs and elsewhere. And his background was as unprecedented as the process that had produced him. A product of the lower middle class, he had risen to leadership of a party still essentially upper-class in its orientation if no longer in its composition. He had the insecurity that the British class system inflicts on those not born into the upper echelons. Some compensate by disguise, affecting the accent, postures, and bonhomie of the well-bred.

Ted Heath had clearly chosen a different course. He gave the impression of a man who was in essence warmhearted and must have been in his youth jolly and gregarious but who had steeled himself by iron self-discipline to rest his eminence not on personality but on performance. He eschewed any claim to personal charm even though at one time he must have had it in considerable measure; he insisted on prevailing through mental superiority and a somewhat aloof air. He made a citadel of personal excellence. In the process his smile grew mirthless; the few excursions into human warmth he permitted himself were tentative and sharply separated from his political actions. His personality and chilling integrity would have inhibited the "special relationship" even if his convictions had not.

In many ways Heath's psychology and complexes were similar to

Nixon's. Heath, however, was more versatile. He did not suppress entirely, as Nixon often did, the warm and generous side of his nature but sublimated it in his passions for music and sailing. As a result Heath rarely exhibited Nixon's crippling diffidence even as he shared his essentially solitary nature. He could travel with an approximation of ease if not enjoyment in the class that disconcerted him; Nixon was always in enemy territory. Heath was more of a piece than Nixon; the various segments of his personality fitted together more snugly. Strangely, this made him somewhat more ideological, even doctrinaire. He was less flexible, less subtle. He was a better, more assertive talker, a less adaptable statesman.

The similarity in psychological makeup was just great enough to make the ultimate differences unbridgeable. Nixon's relationship with Heath was like that of a jilted lover who has been told that friendship was still possible, but who remembers the rejection rather than being inspired by the prospect. Nixon began with enormous admiration for Heath; he had exulted in Heath's unexpected victory in 1970. He counted on establishing a close personal relationship. It was doomed.

Of all British political leaders, Heath was the most indifferent to the American connection and perhaps even to Americans individually. Personally, I liked and admired Heath immensely; in many ways I have had a longer friendship with him than with any other leading British political figure. Yet this did not keep him from being the most difficult British head of government we encountered. Whether it was the memory of the American pressure that had aborted the Suez adventure in 1956 when Heath was Chief Whip of the Conservative Party (and he did refer to it from time to time), or whether the reason was dedication to a vision of Europe quite similar to de Gaulle's, Heath dealt with us with an unsentimentality totally at variance with the "special relationship." The intimate consultation through which British and American policies had been coordinated during the postwar period was reduced to formal diplomatic exchanges. Heath disdained the occasional telephone calls I urged upon the British Ambassadors to establish the personal relationship that Nixon craved, lest he be accused by France, as his predecessor Harold Macmillan had been, of being an American "Trojan horse." Ten years before, Heath had led the British side in the negotiations for Britain's entry into the Common Market, which de Gaulle had abruptly vetoed at least in part because of Macmillan's Nassau agreement on nuclear cooperation with President Kennedy.

There was a stubborn, almost heroic, streak to Heath's policy: He sought to alter not simply a diplomatic pattern but the attitude of his people. The heart of most Britons was with America and the Commonwealth. Europe for them began not in the British Isles but across the Channel, reflecting a history in which peril had almost always arisen in

Europe and — recently, anyway — help had arrived from across the sea. To the majority of the British, entry into Europe reflected at best a distasteful adjustment to necessity. Heath, by contrast, not only accepted that Britain's future lay with Europe, he preferred it that way. And so, paradoxically, from 1970 to 1972, when the other European leaders strove to improve their relations with us — Willy Brandt in Federal Germany to balance his overtures to the East, Pompidou to end the isolation that had threatened his predecessor — Heath went in the opposite direction. His relations with us were always correct, but they rarely rose above a basic reserve that prevented — in the name of Europe — the close coordination with us that was his for the taking.

The very setting of the meetings between President and Prime Minister in early February 1973 highlighted the uncomfortable relationship. As a sign of special respect Nixon took Heath and his party to Camp David the second day so they could continue their conversations in a relaxed, informal, and personal atmosphere. But small talk was not the forte of either leader; they were both better off in set-piece encounters across a conference table. On the way to Camp David — about halfway there — the Presidential helicopter was forced to land because a heavy fog had suddenly enveloped the Presidential retreat. The journey had to be completed by automobile. British Cabinet Secretary Sir Burke Trend (now Lord Trend) and I in the follow-up car speculated on what our two chiefs might be talking about, assailed in part by the usual fear of advisers either that they would be proved dispensable, or — more altruistically — that they would be held responsible for the execution of decisions that their chiefs would neglect to pass on. But above all we had trouble imagining how these two withdrawn men would conduct a social conversation in the back seat of a car when there was neither agenda nor any of the normal supports of governmental ambience. I have never learned what, if anything, was discussed. All I got was Nixon's cryptic comment that it had been "tough going."

When we reached Camp David at last and managed to turn to the agenda, the meeting proved interesting but inconclusive. Nixon assumed that he was dealing with a kindred spirit and a partner in a common design. He was not wrong about the former. But for Heath, revitalizing the Atlantic relationship was simply not a priority. He agreed with Nixon's analysis of world affairs and added thoughtful elaborations. But when it came to drawing joint conclusions, there was a nearly impenetrable opacity about Heath's formulations, which, given his intelligence, had to be deliberate. Heath was acute in his assessment of Southeast Asia and the Middle East; he was scathing in his comments about the new, leftist Australian Prime Minister Gough Whitlam, whose uninformed comments about our Christmas bombing had made him a particular object of Nixon's wrath. But the harmony of views grew more complicated when we turned to Atlantic relations.

In one of his more eloquent expositions Nixon explained the fundamental issue. An America in a dangerously isolationist mood and an inward-looking, protectionist European Community risked finding themselves in serious conflict. Public opinion and the realities of nuclear weaponry demanded visible efforts to relax tensions. Yet they could disrupt the Alliance unless we had first elaborated a shared set of purposes. Nixon urged that Britain and America form study groups to coordinate goals and strategies. He proposed a summit meeting of all the leaders of the industrial democracies to symbolize a new impetus to the cooperation of the free peoples.

Heath could not have been more helpful on diagnosis or more evasive on prescription. He endorsed Nixon's presentation of the problem. He agreed that a new initiative in Atlantic relations was necessary. But he wanted to postpone any elaboration of a partnership until Europe's institutions had evolved further. He did not take up Nixon's proposal for joint study groups. Naively, we ascribed this to the fact that the still flourishing "special relationship" seemed to make new groups unnecessary. So many exchanges were taking place, including bimonthly meetings between Burke Trend and me, that all issues could be discussed in existing forums.

Heath's reluctance was based not on tactical but on philosophical considerations. He did not dismantle the existing machinery of consultation; it was useful as a source of intelligence on our thinking. But he was reluctant to give it new assignments. He wanted Europe *as a unit* to formulate answers to our queries; he was determined to avoid any whiff of Anglo-American collusion. Heath's attitude was partly obscured because his Foreign Secretary, Sir Alec Douglas-Home, and his colleagues in the Foreign Office were still following more established habits of collaboration and did their efficient best to hide their Prime Minister's foot-dragging. We in turn took silence as consent, especially since nothing very concrete needed to be decided right away, and counted on the British as supporters in what we took to be the common task of strengthening Atlantic unity. And so the meeting with Heath ended in ambiguity — though we did not at the time understand just how little progress we had made.

Whereas with Heath we thought we had harmony on policy (and did have on global issues) and difficulties on the personal level, the opposite was true of our relationship with Chancellor Willy Brandt of the Federal Republic of Germany. I personally liked him — Nixon less so — but his policy worried us both. I avoided a portrait in *White House Years* because I was afraid my ambivalence might lead to misunderstanding, but I must make the attempt now.

When I first met Brandt in the 1950s, he was the mayor of embattled Berlin, courageously vindicating the freedom of his people. He was bluff, strong, friendly, outgoing, and at the same time oddly remote from the drama in which he was a principal actor. He was committed to the liberties of his people but strangely detached from the issues that had imperiled them. I had the impression that had destiny not placed him on these particular barricades he would almost surely not have mounted them on his own. In part this was because while Brandt's nature was passionate, he seemed to respond more to his intuition of the moment than to the logic of a guiding philosophy. There was even then a gap between the role in which fate had cast him — and which he played to perfection — and his own compulsions. What he said was usually commonplace; what he did symbolized the issues of the time without defining them.

Brandt had lived through a decade of Soviet harassment. Inevitably, he was driven to thinking how the nightmare might be dispelled. American inaction during the trauma of the building of the Berlin Wall appears to have convinced him that German unity, or at least the easing of Germany's divisions, could not be achieved through unquestioning reliance on America and NATO. German nationalism reinforced his pragmatic conclusion. Imperceptibly at first but with gathering momentum, Brandt set out to pursue the German national interest by a new course: not the rigid anti-Sovietism of Konrad Adenauer but a determined effort to reduce tensions and suspicions between East and West, in the hope that this would encourage the Soviet Union to permit a lowering of the barriers between the two halves of divided Germany.

What started as a practical calculation was in time transmuted by Brandt's emotional nature into a psychological necessity. Psychologists have remarked that prisoners sometimes ease their captivity by endowing their jailers with extraordinary qualities; hatred and a strange kind of respect coexist. There was an element of this in Brandt's journey from endurance to conciliation, from resistance to Communism to the championing of a relaxation of tensions and to policies and, even more, rationales sometimes verging on a nationalist neutralism. Brandt's warm, responsive personality was ideal for his symbolic role in reversing and transcending Germany's postwar policy. Who can forget the historic, moving scene of the German Chancellor visiting Poland and kneeling spontaneously to the victims of the Warsaw Ghetto? And yet once Brandt had accomplished his destiny of breaking stereotypes, he possessed neither the stamina nor the intellectual apparatus to manage the forces he had unleashed. He in fact became their prisoner, wallowing in their applause instead of disciplining it with a sense of proportion or a long-range policy.

By 1973 Brandt was clearly under pressure politically and at war within himself. At first I ascribed his long moody silences to depression; later it occurred to me that having accomplished his major task he had in fact nothing left to say but could not admit to himself that he had no further contribution to make. He possessed the rare gift of embodying the hopes for a more humane world, but the very spontaneity of his gestures precluded him from managing his own achievements. He was a paradox: He had changed the course of history but by doing so had made himself irrelevant (and in some respects dangerous). Forever after, he sought the exultation of his moment of breakthrough, and that was attainable only by ever more daring and risky apologies for a version of East-West policy combining nationalism with resignation from any confrontation.

Brandt's historical accomplishment was to find a way to live with the partition of Germany, which for the entire postwar period his predecessors in Bonn had refused to accept. Under the so-called Hallstein Doctrine, Bonn had been pledged to break diplomatic relations with any government that recognized the Communist regime in East Germany. Under his new *Ostpolitik* (or Eastern policy), Brandt sought ties with East Germany, and relinquished German claims to the eastern territories that were now incorporated into Poland and the USSR. On one level Brandt's wrenching decision to recognize the division of his country was a courageous recognition of reality. For German unification was not achievable without a collapse of Soviet power, something that Bonn was in no position to promote. That part of *Ostpolitik* the United States endorsed and facilitated, though we bolstered it by insisting on an acceptable agreement to safeguard Berlin.

But there was always another aspect to Brandt's policy about which we could never overcome our reserve, especially as it was articulated by Brandt's political confidant, Egon Bahr. For Brandt did not really present his policy as an acceptance of the *division* of Germany. Rather, he put it forward as a means to achieve German *unity* by building good relations with the East and turning the Federal Republic into a magnet for Eastern Europe. As a first installment, there would be a better life for the 17 million East Germans. Travel and exchanges would multiply. Trade with Eastern Europe and the Soviet Union would increase. Gradually, so the argument went, the ties would become close; the dividing line between East and West in Europe would begin to fade.

The question in our minds was which side of the dividing line would in fact be the magnet. We feared that over time, at first imperceptibly, the Communist world would wind up in the stronger position. Détente was difficult enough to manage for the other Western allies because it might encourage euphoria, be confused with psychotherapy, and fail to insist on Soviet reciprocity. But for Bonn all these dangers were compounded because the Soviet Union in effect held 17 million Germans hostage. We worried whether West Germany could consistently face two ways at once. The danger was not withdrawal from NATO; no German government would be prepared to forgo this protection against direct attack. What concerned us was a tendency to avoid controversies outside of Europe even when they affected fundamental security interests; a creeping dissociation from Western policies except those for the physical defense of Western Europe; and a more cautious approach to Soviet challenges that tended to drain the Western response of meaning. On one occasion I said to an associate that I dreaded the moment when "no German Chancellor can afford the hostility of the Soviet Union. When that happens it will be a very dangerous situation." It has not yet happened with a German Chancellor but it came close to describing Brandt's personal odyssey.

This uneasiness about the drift of Brandt's policies was shared by his principal partners in the Western Alliance. It was a staple of the conversations of Pompidou, Heath, and Nixon that Brandt's Eastern policy would, however unintentionally, sooner or later unleash a latent German nationalism. A free-wheeling, powerful Germany trying to maneuver between East and West, whatever its ideology, posed the classic challenge to the equilibrium of Europe, for whichever side Germany favored would emerge as predominant. To forestall this, or perhaps outflank it, each of Brandt's colleagues — including Nixon — sought to preempt Germany by conducting an active détente policy of his own. In this sense *Ostpolitik* had effects far beyond those intended. It contributed to a race to Moscow and over time heightened mutual suspicions among the allies. As for Brandt, after he left office he became a passionate spokesman for a course that relied upon NATO for reinsurance but whose practical implication was European neutralism — at least with respect to issues outside of Europe.

What was sentimentality in Brandt was cool calculation for Egon Bahr, Brandt's chief aide for sensitive negotiations, whom I had first met in the mid-Fifties. Unprepossessing physically, extremely agile intellectually, indefatigable, Bahr showed what consistent commitment can achieve even from relatively subordinate positions. He was the intellectual driving force behind Brandt's *Ostpolitik*. His ingenuity and negotiating skill were indispensable in bringing about Bonn's treaties with the USSR, Poland, and East Germany, and the Four-Power Agreement on Berlin.

When, after some initial hesitations, Nixon and I had acquiesced in *Ostpolitik*, which overt American opposition would have wrecked, Bahr had been my counterpart in all sensitive backchannel discussions between the White House and the Chancellery. Bahr and I both knew that we started from different, even clashing, premises, but we found a common vocabulary reflecting parallel interests. Outsiders may debate who manipulated whom; serious students of international affairs know that common policies can endure only if both parties serve their own purposes.

Bahr at any rate did not view the prospect of separate approaches to Moscow — inherent in *Ostpolitik* — with reluctance; he actively sought them. He saw in them the key to German unification. This was not because, as some of our people thought, he was pro-Soviet. Rather, he was an old-fashioned German nationalist. After all, though half-Jewish, he had sought to become an officer in World War II and had been deeply hurt when he was refused. Like Bismarck, he sought to exploit Germany's central position for its national goals. Bahr had sufficient confidence in his dexterity to believe he would avoid the pitfalls that had produced disaster on earlier occasions when Germany had struck out on such a complicated course.

It was from this essentially nationalist perspective that Bahr reacted to the Year of Europe. I first broached the subject with him in a conversation in Washington in January; in early April I solicited his views in advance of my speech on the Year of Europe. Like most political leaders, Bahr used every development as a means to advance independently formed preconceptions. In a thoughtful reply he affirmed the conventional thesis of the importance of the Atlantic relationship. For the foreseeable future, he argued, Europe was dependent on the military protection of the United States; no disagreement on economic matters should be allowed to threaten these ties. But Bahr also held that the problem of security had altered fundamentally in recent years. Throughout the postwar period American strategic nuclear power had been the key to Europe's security. As it lost credibility, no European country — much less Europe as a whole — would be prepared to make the economic sacrifice to build conventional defenses capable of deterring a Soviet invasion. From these truisms Bahr produced a revolutionary conclusion. Soviet–American parity would lead to an attempt by the two superpowers to preclude nuclear war; they had a common interest in this that might well override their obligations to allies. If Europe could no longer rely on American strategic preeminence and if Europe would not — or in terms of its domestic politics could not — make the effort to defend itself, Europe and above all the Federal Republic had to seek safety in relaxation of tensions with the East. Military forces in Central Europe should be reduced, not augmented; contacts between East and West should be multiplied. The relaxation of tensions was in that view an alternative to security policy, not an outgrowth of it.

Bahr, therefore, opposed the key aim of our new approach; he would hear nothing of strengthening the political coordination within the Alliance because an Atlantic bloc would undermine the flexibility necessary for his version of détente. At a minimum, each European nation should be free to pursue its own approach to East-West relations. Bahr never explained why the Soviet Union, placed in a predominant position by the lassitude of the West, would relieve us of the consequences by playing Bahr's game of, in effect, matching our unilateral disarmament. Also, this proposition implied that in some circumstances it might be in Europe's interest to separate itself from the United States so as to improve its freedom of maneuver toward the Soviet Union. Here was the intellectual basis for Europe's playing along with the Soviet strategy of "differential détente," setting the democracies against each other and dividing Europe from America.

If Bahr's analysis was correct, nuclear parity would erode the relevance of American protection and Europe's conventional inferiority would dictate a "political" solution — an elegant phrase for accommodation to Soviet power. This might be camouflaged as closer East-West economic relations, but insofar as these worked they would also increase Western Europe's dependence on Moscow. The Kremlin would have another pressure point in an East-West trade that for some Western countries was becoming the crucial hedge against recession.

The Year of Europe was beginning to reveal hitherto unarticulated differences in perspective between the United States and at least some of its European allies. The common fear that had united the Alliance for the first two decades of its existence was either disappearing or, where it existed, providing arguments for appeasement of Moscow as readily as for a new approach to Western partnership. In Heath's case, we missed his essential point, ascribing his reserve to his personality rather than to his convictions. With Brandt we understood his basic point only too well. But we saw in it only a potential, not yet an actual, danger. We concluded we must ensure against it by tightening the bonds of the Alliance — which was our starting point for the Year of Europe.

It was time now to consult with France again about developments since my meeting with Pompidou in December. On March 29 I met with the new French Ambassador in Washington, Jacques Kosciusko-Morizet, to discuss how we might proceed.

Kosciusko would have won no prizes for charm. He was a classic product of the *grandes écoles,* those indelibly French institutions of whose graduates Pétain said in a perceptive moment: "They know everything. Unfortunately they do not know anything else." Kosciusko was brilliant, analytical, and unsentimental. Conducting foreign policy on the basis of the national interest was, for him, the implementation of a concept developed in France at least three centuries earlier. He understood immediately that we had no desire to reopen the controversies of the Sixties. We would raise no objection to European autonomy; we would break no lances over the issue of national identity that had so preoccupied de Gaulle. We did not, I told him, challenge Europe's right to conduct its own policy. What we sought was a harmonization of separate judgments, not a legal document that proscribed different opinions. On that basis, we welcomed Pompidou's idea of a summit gathering of allied leaders as outlined to Reston in December. As an initial step I proposed a meeting between Pompidou and Nixon. I stressed our fundamental concern: "The question is whether the Western world will have a good consistent policy, or will we be like the Greeks and be overwhelmed by the outside world?"

Kosciusko said that he would return to Paris for instructions. Before he could get back, the quadrennial parliamentary elections were handsomely won by Pompidou's party. In the resulting cabinet shuffle, Pompidou replaced the voluble Foreign Minister Maurice Schumann with the precise and austere Michel Jobert. This seemed promising at the time. In the White House we knew Jobert favorably for his unfailing helpfulness on many issues as assistant to Pompidou, indeed as my counterpart in the Elysée. Kosciusko returned to Washington early in April with French agreement to a Franco-American summit. Our general approach to the Year of Europe met no objection.

As usual, the venue for a Nixon-Pompidou summit caused trouble, reflecting the always prickly French pride. Nixon still owed Pompidou a return visit for the French President's journey to the United States in February–March 1970. But Paris remained reluctant to receive Nixon as part of a European tour. We in turn could not go to Europe for the sole purpose of visiting France without offending all other allies. We were driven, as on other occasions, to look for an island in the Atlantic. That reasoning had led us to the Azores in 1971; it caused us to choose Iceland in 1973 (and later Martinique in 1975). At that rate it was mathematically predictable when Franco-American relations would begin to stagnate for lack of suitable islands for their leaders to meet on.

On April 13, I gave Kosciusko an outline of a speech on the Year of Europe that I proposed to deliver on April 23. No objection was raised from Paris. We construed silence as assent.

That left only Italy to be consulted, a prospect customarily involving ambivalence on both sides. The Italian leaders wanted to be treated on an equal level with those of European countries of comparable size. But they were not eager to risk a domestic crisis over implementing American designs and, even less, risk relations with the other members of the European Community. They sought involvement without controversy; we settled on consultation without commitment.

The official visit to Washington of Italian Prime Minister Giulio Andreotti on April 17 gave us an opportunity to present our arguments. I wrote to Nixon before the meeting: "He [Andreotti] can probably be counted on to carry the ball for us with his fellow Europeans to the degree that his domestic position and Italy's modest political weight permit." The qualifications were more important than the assertions; they meant in effect that no help could be expected from Rome. For Andreotti's domestic situation was far from brilliant and his influence in the Community correspondingly marginal. His professorial manner hid a razor-sharp political mind, and he was more interested in foreign policy than any of his predecessors whom I had met. But the last thing he wanted was to add foreign policy to his bursting cupboard of problems. The Italian Prime Minister is chairman of a committee, moreover, not Chief Executive; his power to give orders to his Foreign Minister cannot be taken for granted. It depends much more on their relative position within the Christian Democratic party structure than on the hierarchy of government.

Andreotti's energies were absorbed in maneuvering a turbulent political system within an extremely narrow margin. For a decade, Italian politics had been dominated by the "opening to the left," partly engineered by the United States in the early Sixties and designed to bring the left-wing Socialists into the government as a presumed barrier against the Communists. The Socialists, while allies with the Christian Democrats nationally, were in coalition with the Communists on the provincial level. A coherent long-range program was therefore impossible. The only way out of this dilemma was an immobilism that magnified the crisis it was supposed to solve.

Andreotti sought to escape the structural deadlock by grouping into a working coalition the parties from the Social Democrats (the part of the Socialists that refused to work with the Communists) to the free-enterprise Liberal Party. But while such a grouping was ideologically more homogeneous than the "opening to the left," the parliamentary arithmetic was against it. Its majority was wafer-thin, especially since the Christian Democrats were not one party but a conglomerate of factions, with a left wing separated from the Communists primarily by religious convictions and a right wing divided from the Fascists largely by the memory of national catastrophe. Italy was in the position of having to choose between ideological cohesion at the price of parliamentary instability, and parliamentary stability at the risk of philosophical, and hence practical, chaos.

Not surprisingly, most of the conversation between Andreotti and Nixon concerned not the Year of Europe but the subtleties of the Italian domestic scene, whose intricate and ruthless maneuvers national unification had transposed from the city-state to the political arena in Rome. Andreotti could not restrain himself from expressing the perennial Italian illusion that Italy could contribute by reasons of propinquity to the solution of the Middle East problem. But while every Italian leader I met advanced this proposition, none acted as if he believed in it.

With respect to a new initiative on Atlantic policy, Andreotti promised his goodwill and his support without rising to precision. We could count on benevolent understanding, but the Italian government would not be in the forefront of a new initiative.

As I write these pages I find it astonishing that no record can be found of any effort to consult Japan in advance about its attitude, even though we planned to include it in our initiative. That we should do so in the first place was clearly a triumph of abstract theory over experience. It is a tribute to the self-fulfilling quality of bureaucratic momentum that the joke of naming an initiative including Japan the "Year of Europe" apparently struck no one. Japan was indeed part of the larger community of the industrial democracies, and to that extent we were justified; we would have been deservedly criticized for leaving Japan out.* But while Japan's role in the economic disputes was crucial, it had less interest in the defense and political issues racking the free world, which were centered clearly in Europe.

The enterprise could have led to severe embarrassment but for the skill of Japanese statesmen in deflecting unwarranted enthusiasms by means of a bland courtesy that never permits the interlocutor to get to the point. Only when forced into a corner by mortifyingly poor manners do Japanese leaders attempt a frontal refusal. Wherever possible they protract the negotiation until the protagonist throws up his hands in despair. Since the Japanese never had any intention of joining the Year of Europe, our failure to consult them about it did not enter the catalogue of "Nixon shocks," such as my secret trip to China and the abandonment of the modified gold standard in the summer of 1971. Japan was relieved not to be asked to take a position on what it wished to avoid. And for the rest of the time it was to stand on the sidelines watching the inscrutable Westerners tear each other apart about how to improve their friendship.

Our process of consultation was completed on April 19, 1973. Sir Burke Trend was in Washington for his regular meetings and I gave him an advance text of my speech announcing an Atlantic initiative. He seemed receptive; no critical comment — or anything else — was heard from London.

Perhaps we should have sensed from the lack of precise response to our approaches that our allies, who had urged us for years to give higher priority to Atlantic relations, were going to disappoint us. To the degree that we were conscious of European hesitations, however, we regarded them as yet another reason for a major effort to work on the elaboration of common purposes. We thought the best way to concentrate minds was to advance a formal proposal.

The "Year of Europe" Speech

IN four years in the Administration as national security adviser, I had never given a formal public speech on a substantive topic. The ad-

---

*Indeed, as it was, my speech on April 23 was criticized in some quarters for giving Japan too little a role in the exercise.[3]

dress on the "Year of Europe" was my first. The audience was the annual meeting of the editors of the Associated Press at New York's Waldorf-Astoria hotel on April 23, 1973. Neither Nixon nor I expected controversy. We thought we were ushering in a period of creativity in the Atlantic partnership.

I began by stressing that we had proclaimed 1973 as the Year of Europe not because Europe had been less important previously but because new conditions were a challenge to the free nations:

Nineteen seventy-three is the year of Europe because the era that was shaped by decisions of a generation ago is ending. The success of those policies has produced new realities that require new approaches:

— The revival of Western Europe is an established fact, as is the historic success of its movement toward economic unification.

— The East-West strategic military balance has shifted from American preponderance to near-equality, bringing with it the necessity for a new understanding of the requirements of our common security.

— Other areas of the world have grown in importance. Japan has emerged as a major power center. In many fields, "Atlantic" solutions to be viable must include Japan.

— We are in a period of relaxation of tensions. But as the rigid divisions of the past two decades diminish, new assertions of national identity and national rivalry emerge.

— Problems have arisen, unforeseen a generation ago, which require new types of cooperative action. Insuring the supply of energy for industrialized nations is an example.

These factors have produced a dramatic transformation of the psychological climate in the West — a change which is the most profound current challenge to Western statesmanship. In Europe, a new generation to whom war and its dislocations are not personal experiences takes stability for granted. But it is less committed to the unity that made peace possible and to the effort required to maintain it. In the United States, decades of global burdens have fostered, and the frustrations of the war in Southeast Asia have accentuated, a reluctance to sustain global involvements on the basis of preponderant American responsibility.

So firmly had a Presidential trip to Europe later in the year entered official — and probably even public — consciousness that I treated it as a given to which a program could be geared. By the time the President traveled to Europe toward the end of the year, I said, we and our allies should work out a "new Atlantic Charter," or declaration of common purpose. The agenda that we faced in common — defense, trade, and East-West relations — required coordination of our national approaches. I then used a formulation to describe those differing perspectives that I soon came to regret:

Diplomacy is the subject of frequent consultations but is essentially being conducted by traditional nation-states. The United States has global interests and responsibilities. Our European allies have regional interests. These are not necessarily in conflict, but in the new era neither are they automatically identical.

The purpose of my speech was to set forth how the United States was prepared to contribute to reinvigorating the Alliance, and what we hoped for from Europe. And (months before the Arab oil embargo and the OPEC price explosion) I highlighted energy as a key topic for cooperation:

We will continue to support European unity. Based on the principles of partnership, we will make concessions to its further growth. We will expect to be met in a spirit of reciprocity.

We will not disengage from our solemn commitments to our allies. We will maintain our forces and not withdraw from Europe unilaterally. In turn, we expect from each ally a fair share of the common effort for the common defense.

We shall continue to pursue the relaxation of tensions with our adversaries on the basis of concrete negotiations in the common interest. We welcome the participation of our friends in a constructive East-West dialogue.

We will never consciously injure the interests of our friends in Europe or in Asia. We expect in return that their policies will take seriously our interests and our responsibilities.

We are prepared to work cooperatively on new common problems we face. Energy, for example, raises the challenging issues of assurance of supply, impact of oil revenues on international currency stability, the nature of common political and strategic interests, and long-range relations of oil-consuming to oil-producing countries. This could be an area of competition; it should be an area of collaboration.

We had conceived the speech as a summons to a new period of creativity among the industrial democracies. At home we hoped to overcome the self-destructive legacy of Vietnam; abroad, we sought to surmount irritating economic and other disputes by rallying our allies to a new vision of the future. But the timing of the speech — established over a month earlier — proved disastrous.

At home, Watergate muffled the thrust of our initiative. The resignations of Ehrlichman and Haldeman were just a week away. So strong was the preoccupation with the scandal that, as described in Chapter IV, the *Washington Post* devoted most of its news coverage not to my speech but to my few remarks on Watergate, elicited in the question period, that called for compassion for some of the accused. There were, to be sure, several strongly supportive editorials in the *New York Times,* the *Christian Science Monitor,* and the *Washington Star,* but the *Washington Post* doubted whether the initiative could remain unaffected by

Watergate: "The damage will continue until the President, by his own remedial actions, can assure the world that his capacity to govern has not been undermined."[4] The *Post* turned out to be right. Even those sympathetic to the concept felt an understandable disinclination to rally around a reaffirmation of the moral unity of the West put forward by the tarnished Nixon Administration.

The response of our allies was as ambiguous as it had been during the prior consultations. There was no rush to get on the bandwagon, in sharp contrast to the memorable days of the Marshall Plan, when British Foreign Secretary Ernest Bevin had taken the lead in organizing a positive European reply. Following an April 26 meeting of the French cabinet, a French spokesman noted my speech "with interest" and said that our proposals deserved attentive study, which would be undertaken by France "in the spirit which had always been ours, that of faithfulness to the Alliance in the context of respect for our independence." This could mean anything.

The same day I reminded the French Ambassador that our proposals reflected Pompidou's observations of the previous December. I had outlined them in detail to Kosciusko-Morizet in March and April. Kosciusko did not deny this. He mumbled something about the unacceptability of confining Europe to a "regional role" as my speech implied. I answered: "We have no objection if Europe wants to play a global role. But until now we have not found any desire on their part to do so." Then Kosciusko got to the heart of the problem. It would be hard for Europe to respond with one voice to so vast an agenda, he said. We were forcing a major task on Europe in the very year of the Community's first fumbling attempts at political unity. This might prove to be too much. The attempt to foster Atlantic unity might wreck the tentative movement toward European community.

On April 24, the British Foreign Office made a warm comment that I had made "clearly an important speech, with a constructive intent," but that Britain planned to "study [it] closely with our European allies." Britain was essentially deferring to France. Foreign Secretary Sir Alec Douglas-Home, whom we revered for his integrity and his devotion to the American relationship, added a friendly — but noncommittal — observation on April 27:

The central theme of Dr. Kissinger's speech, and of recent statements by the American Secretary of State, is the need for continued trust and cooperation between the new and expanded Europe and the United States of America. The horizons of this cooperation must, he argues, be extended to include Japan and Canada. I agree with him. For although this adds to the complexity of negotiation nothing less is adequate to secure prosperity in a climate of security.

The West German government welcomed my support for European unity, but avoided further response on the ground that Chancellor Willy

Brandt was scheduled to meet with Nixon on a long-planned visit to Washington in less than a week. Italy expressed itself as favorable, if skeptical about Japan's participation — thus covering all bases. The smaller European countries postponed a position until the ministers of the European Community would meet in several weeks' time. Japan was understandably puzzled as to why it should be included in an Atlantic Charter at all. It was spared the necessity of immediate comment by the fact that its Foreign Minister was traveling to Europe. When he arrived in Paris, he remarked opaquely that he supported the plan for a new Atlantic Charter and considered the idea fully understandable. This left Japan's response wide open; it did not even imply that Japan would participate. Tokyo was not about to enmesh itself through an excess of explicitness.

It was hard to avoid the conclusion that all of our major partners had found excuses to postpone a response to a major American initiative involving them. This became even clearer when Willy Brandt arrived in Washington on May 1 for an official visit. It was a pity that Nixon's first European interlocutor on the Year of Europe should have been the European statesman whose policy made him most uneasy and whose personality was perhaps most incompatible with his own. Nixon's attitude was best summed up in his reaction to a letter he had received, before Brandt's visit, from the American-Hungarian novelist Hans Habe. Habe accused Brandt of deliberately undermining the Western Alliance and of being motivated by an anti-American bias. The White House procedure at this time was that letters to the President dealing with foreign policy passed through my office, where a summary or covering memorandum was often attached. I sent such a memorandum forward with Habe's letter on March 15. Nixon returned it with a note: "K— a very perceptive and very disturbing analysis. I think he is too close to the truth."

Brandt reciprocated Nixon's wariness. He was punctiliously correct but the very meticulousness of his conduct suggested that it would take an enormous effort of self-discipline to overcome his doubts, bordering on aversion, about the American President. Mutual suspicions were dwarfed, however, by our domestic upheavals. Nixon's speech announcing the resignation of Haldeman and Ehrlichman had occurred the evening before the first meeting of the two leaders. Nixon was more shaken by this decision than by any other until his own resignation a little more than fifteen months later. That Nixon managed to get through the Brandt visit without any show of emotion was a spectacular feat of will.

Instead, in his disciplined manner, Nixon conducted a thoughtful dialogue with the Chancellor. One had to know him well to note that while Brandt was speaking, Nixon's mind was elsewhere. If one watched carefully one could detect the glassy, melancholy look and the waxen expression that, as Watergate proceeded, became increasingly obvious signs of Nixon's inner torment; Nixon's thoughts were far away in some stark, remote universe that would more and more claim his energies and attention. He gave no other sign of his distress. His sole reference to Watergate was wistful; like a little boy giving himself courage by talking loudly in the dark, he expressed his certainty that our domestic controversies would not affect our foreign policy. He was too experienced for illusions, but he knew also that he could make no other statement.

I could not tell whether Brandt was aware of Nixon's distress; he could not avoid sensing some of it. How else to explain the change in Brandt's demeanor? It was only a nuance, but of the stuff that alters human relationships irrevocably. Whether he intended it or not, Brandt became a shade less deferential; he was uncharacteristically crisp and businesslike. There was neither the bonhomie of former times nor the long pauses with which Brandt had punctuated his earlier conversations and which had contributed no little to Nixon's restlessness. A little more than two years before, the President had salvaged Brandt's *Ostpolitik* by authorizing me to backstop the Berlin negotiations with Soviet Ambassador Anatoly Dobrynin. This time, though, Brandt was in no mood to reciprocate. The briskness with which he went through the agenda reflected his strategy — to settle nothing.

The Chancellor pretended to welcome our initiative, but abstract expressions of goodwill were not what was needed and Brandt made no concrete proposal on how to carry out what he said he favored. He saw merit in a comprehensive Atlantic dialogue on economic, political, and security issues. But he did not suggest a mechanism for accomplishing it, nor did he really consider it urgent to negotiate all topics simultaneously. Failure to agree on one subject should not block progress on the others, Brandt averred, thus taking away with one hand what he had given with the other. Indeed, his argument that there was no need to move forward on a broad agenda came close to turning our proposal into a platitude, for no one had ever questioned that controversial issues should be discussed individually.

Brandt expressed the hope that the negotiators on economic subjects be given political direction, but he was silent about the nature of the political purposes that were supposed to be achieved or the means by which they were to be articulated. He welcomed a Presidential visit to Europe. He put forward the idea that the President meet the allied heads of government at a large summit in the context of NATO. But there, too, Brandt built in a hedge. For a NATO summit — apart from the likelihood of a French objection — would make it procedurally impossible to discuss America's relationship with the European Community, since some of its members did not belong to NATO, while not all members of NATO belonged to the Community.

To deal with the newly enlarged European Community, Brandt suggested a meeting of the President with the *foreign ministers* while he was in Brussels. But one could scarcely ask the President to meet with the foreign ministers of the members of the European Community when the heads of government were in town for the NATO meeting. Such a gathering could not possibly reach any decisions if only because of the differences in rank. Brandt made no reference to our proposal for an Atlantic Charter. And he used his toast at the State dinner that evening to qualify even the astonishingly thin response he had made. He was not in a position, he now said, to make ultimate commitments on even the scant matters he had agreed to discuss:

None of us [meaning the European heads of government who had visited Washington] meets you any longer solely as the representative of his own country but at the same time already, to a certain degree, as a representative of the European Community as well.

So, I, too, am here not as the spokesman *of* Europe, but definitely as a spokesman *for* Europe.

We would happily have endorsed this as a theory for the relations between the European Community and the United States. The problem was to give them practical meaning in the gestation period of European unity. Since no European political institution yet existed, there was no focal point for contact with Europe. Brandt in fact faced us with a Catch-22 dilemma: If every European leader was a spokesman for Europe but could not represent it, and those who represented Europe were civil servants with no authority to negotiate, who then could act authoritatively?

Any doubt that Brandt had come to Washington to stall was removed by the way the German party handled their press briefings. To our astonishment we learned — it was all over the German media — that our final joint statement's reference to a "balanced partnership" was an indirect rejection of any attempt by us to dominate — an ambition of which we were unaware. The omission of the words "Atlantic Charter" from the communiqué was hailed as a success, as if avoiding an American offer to tie our destiny formally to Europe was a test of statesmanship. Nor could the briefers resist seeing in Watergate an opportunity to squeeze the United States: "Brandt's success," opined one of the leading dailies, the *Frankfurter Allgemeine Zeitung,*

is also due to the fact that in view of the tremors created by the Watergate scandal, Nixon needs reaffirmation of the world-wide significance of U.S. Presidential action in foreign policy. Brandt's presence, reflected in his reception by the Senate Foreign Relations Committee and the National Press Club, came in handy for Nixon and made him amenable to concessions.

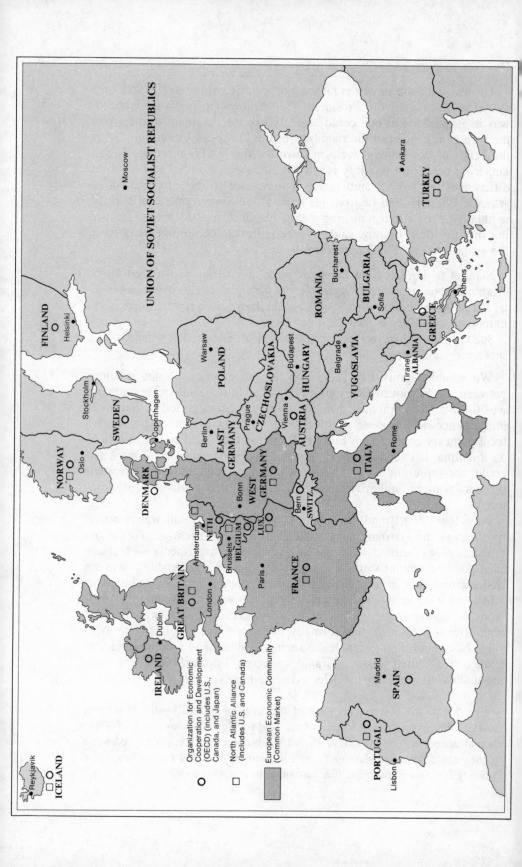

The new German Ambassador, the reliable Berndt von Staden, who later became a good friend, therefore started his mission in highly inauspicious circumstances. He had arrived some weeks earlier, but diplomatic custom prevents ambassadors from performing their function until they have presented their credentials. The protocol office of the State Department usually waits some weeks until several new ambassadors can be introduced to the President together. Von Staden was given the opportunity to present his credentials alone on the day of Brandt's arrival; this was done as a special courtesy to permit him to participate in the talks. Now, after his Chancellor's departure, he bore the brunt of our displeasure, which was hardly softened by the nervous strain of Watergate. Von Staden, unruffled and soothing as always, assured us that neither Brandt nor Foreign Minister Walter Scheel had made any such insinuation to the press. Von Staden was too honorable to lie. We assumed, therefore, someone else close to the top had done the briefing — probably the official spokesman. When all leading German newspapers reported essentially the same story, they must have had the benefit of some official guidance.

The next symptom of what still seemed to us nearly inexplicable European reserve was the reaction to the President's annual Foreign Policy Report published on May 3. It was the fourth such document issued in Nixon's term of office — a unique attempt by a President to give a comprehensive yearly account of his stewardship in foreign affairs. It was deliberately conceptual in approach, with major events used as illustrations rather than listed in a bureaucratic catalogue. The purpose was to give the Congress, the public, the media, and foreign leaders an insight into our thinking, something our secretive procedures, which often excluded the bureaucracy, made essential. It was the most concise guidance available to officials eager to carry out established policy but not always privy to its formulation. On occasion we used the Foreign Policy Report to indicate or hint at important changes of policy. Every year key members of my staff — Winston Lord, Peter W. Rodman, William G. Hyland, Richard T. Kennedy, Marshall Wright, and others — spent weeks producing essays that we hoped would be at once thorough, illuminating, and readable. I was general editor. To this end I would free two weeks to do nothing else.

Try as we might, we never succeeded in our principal objective of using the Foreign Policy Reports to spark a thoughtful public discussion. Part of the reason was the media's insatiable hunger for the new; concepts and goals are too abstract to be newsworthy. Part of the reason was the burgeoning length of the product (the first was 160 printed pages, the fourth, 234), which made it difficult even for journalists with the best of intentions to do justice to it. Perhaps we never briefed the press on it properly — though as the principal briefer I would hate to think

so. Whatever the reason, the only chapter that generally received attention by the American media — to the chagrin of the drafters and their
families, who had been deprived of their company for weeks —was the
one dealing with Indochina. In retrospect, this was inevitable, given the
national obsession with Vietnam, though careful study would have picked
up important clues to our unfolding policy toward China and the Soviet
Union. But the rest of the report was read attentively in foreign chan-
celleries and by thoughtful journalists and columnists who understood
that it provided an unusual insight into high-level thinking.

In 1973 we thought we had found a way to blunt the obsession with
Vietnam: We postponed the report until the subject had largely disappeared from the front pages. Nixon himself introduced the fourth report* in a radio speech on May 3, a stratagem devised by the ingenious
William Safire in 1968 as a means to get Candidate Nixon on record:
Radio, in Safire's view, was a safe medium for establishing a reputation
for thoughtfulness without risking a dispute over substance.

There was in the report a ringing affirmation of America's commitment to the Atlantic Alliance and an urgent appeal for a new dedication
to common purposes:

> As the relaxation of East-West tensions became more pronounced, some of
> our allies questioned whether the United States would remain committed to
> Europe or would instead pursue a new balance of power in which the older
> alignments would be diluted and distinctions between allies and adversaries
> would disappear.
>
> But the United States will never compromise the security of Europe or the
> interests of our allies. The best reassurance of our unity, however, lies not in
> verbal pledges but in the knowledge of agreed purposes and common policies.
> For almost a decade the Alliance has debated questions of defense and dé-
> tente — some urging one course, others a different priority. Now the debates
> should end. We must close ranks and chart our course together for the decade
> ahead.

For once we succeeded in banishing Vietnam from the headlines,
though hardly in the way we had planned it. This time we were totally
drowned out by the uproar following the resignation of Haldeman and
Ehrlichman that had occurred three days earlier.

European heads of government once again avoided a response to
Nixon's offer to revitalize the partnership. They hid behind their experts
and the experts procrastinated in glacial procedures. This left the field

---

*And also the last, because after I became Secretary of State in September 1973, I did not have
the time to produce a thoughtful document. It is an interesting commentary on the nature of bureaucracy and a pity because I continue to believe that an intelligent statement of basic purpose
and philosophy is important for public, bureaucratic, and foreign understanding of a President's
policies.

open to the media, which, briefed by the second level of the government, rallied the European public to resist American "blackmail" and pressure tactics. German newspapers were still celebrating Brandt's success in removing the term "Atlantic Charter" from the final communiqué of his visit. The French press reaction was hardly more charitable. It warned against the attempt to link the various issues to each other; it saw a threat to European autonomy; it welcomed a dialogue but seemed to prefer to drain it of all content. The influential *Le Monde* editorialized on May 1:

In proposing a global negotiation on relations among the U. S., Europe and Japan, President Nixon makes light of the existing European institutions, none of which encompasses all aspects of the problem. . . .

It remains to be seen whether Europe can best find its own individuality through opposition to the U. S., as Paris still appears to believe, or by continuing to go along with the U. S., as Bonn believes.

My reference to Europe's regional role in the Year of Europe speech was endlessly replayed and castigated, no one bothering to point out that I was describing a condition that we deplored. I was noting an observable fact that European conduct, both earlier and later, amply underlined. Europe had been shedding its overseas responsibilities throughout the postwar period. It had shown no shred of willingness to take on new ones. Despite our misgivings Britain had just withdrawn from the Persian Gulf. We had difficulty persuading our allies to strengthen their NATO defenses. It may not have been wise to make reality explicit, but European carping over the phraseology represented a mixture of hypocrisy and subterfuge. Before the year was over, many European nations played back the same phrases during the Middle East war and later in the decade in the crises over Iran and Afghanistan —as a means to evade American appeals for joint action.

The only papers that seemed to grasp what the Administration was really after were British. The *Times* of London described the report as "a broad and thoughtful review which must now be taken as the basic text on American thinking." For Europe, the paper said,

the most important point is that although he links trade and defense, he does not suggest that the American commitment to Europe will be bargained against the trade policies of the European Community or against political concessions from the Soviet Union. This is clearly right.

But even this sympathetic journal could not avoid the remark that the West Germans were "wonder[ing], like everyone else, how President Nixon's domestic disasters will affect his foreign policy."

The conservative *Daily Telegraph* found "some of the sharpest and most analytical passages'' of the President's report in the section on Europe and the Atlantic Alliance:

> At the present stage of the debate . . . it rather looks like a case of everyone telling everyone else that something ought to be done and then waiting for the other chaps to do it or suggest it. That is probably inevitable in a period when so many important developments are proceeding together, some in parallel, others apparently on collision courses. But it is the duty of statesmen to think ahead. European leaders, take note.

This, in our view, was the essence of the problem. A purely pragmatic approach could not solve even the technical issues. Above all, it would fail to inspire the generation that had grown up since the last great acts of Western creativity.

Jobert Leads Us a Dance

B Y May the demonstrations of European indifference should probably have caused us to postpone our initiative. After all, in any realistic assessment, our allies should have had at least as much to gain from a new impetus to Atlantic relations as we. But Watergate made us more persistent than prudent. Nixon knew that the very critics who charged him with putting forward the Year of Europe as a diversion would allege that its failure was due to his domestic difficulties. Since he pretended that his authority had been unaffected — and indeed could preserve its remnants in no other way — he became rigid in persevering on enterprises once launched. Moreover, he deeply believed in a strengthened Atlantic relationship; it was one of the legacies he was most determined to leave to his successor. Watergate thus became both a major cause of deadlock and the obstacle to its resolution. We soldiered on, winding up in the absurd position of appearing more eager to reaffirm and strengthen our commitment to Atlantic relations than Europe to accept it.

I pursued our elusive goals next in London. On May 10 I stopped there to brief the British leaders on the talks I had just had in the Soviet Union with Brezhnev (see Chapter VII). Whitehall could not have been more understanding or more noncommittal. The various ministers and officials, in their skillfully insinuating manner, steered the talks toward procedure, elegantly avoiding any discussions of the substance of our proposal. They were more than willing to explore forums for allied consultation as long as it did not involve a summit or a firm British obligation to any particular arrangements.

All sorts of ingenious ideas emerged. Heath proposed a steering group of four (France, Britain, West Germany, and the United States), either officially designated by NATO or meeting informally. We accepted. Sir

Denis Greenhill, then permanent head of the Foreign Office, said that this might be supplemented by ad hoc groups to address specific topics. We agreed. Someone else advanced the idea of a meeting of deputy foreign ministers of NATO further down the road. This too passed muster. The only trouble was that every British scheme left it to us to gain the approval of the other allies and kept open just exactly what would be discussed or, for that matter, what Britain would do should the other allies balk. Britain could not be counted on to take the lead in forming a European response to our initiative or, as it turned out, even to support its own ideas if we put them forward and France objected.

No clearer demonstration could be given of the new priority Heath attached to European over Atlantic relations than the British obsession with French attitudes. The British officials solicitously, and puzzlingly, inquired into France's point of view. They seemed vastly relieved when I informed them that I was planning to see Jobert and Pompidou a week later, as if the telephone circuits between London and Paris were out of order. Though it was not yet obvious to us, all the evidence was that Britain would supply goodwill and advice but in the final analysis it would follow the French lead.

Thus Paris wound up as the key to unlock the Year of Europe, and on May 17 I had my first encounter with the master locksmith in his new capacity as Foreign Minister — Michel Jobert, until a month earlier my opposite number as assistant to the French President. I had known Jobert as a discreet, anonymous figure of ability and cooperativeness. He had handled the French end of the technical arrangements for my secret Paris meetings with Le Duc Tho with unfailing tact. He was the man we had approached for solutions to delicate problems that occasionally arose in Franco-American relations during Nixon's first term. He had never failed us.

For that reason and for the warm relations cultivated in Nixon's first term, we expected nothing so little as confrontation with France. We were quite prepared to come to a prior understanding with the French leaders about the Year of Europe; in fact, we preferred it that way. We were convinced that France's unsentimental conception of the national interest would lead it to the same conclusion that we had reached: that Western solidarity was crucial to European security and freedom.

The assessment turned out to be badly mistaken. Before the year was out, we found ourselves embroiled with France in the same sort of nasty confrontation for which we had criticized our predecessors. The reasons for it are not fully clear to me even today. We were prepared to defer to France on procedures; we believed we were implementing ideas originally put forth by Pompidou. We did not mind if France used our initiative to enhance its role in Europe. We were quite willing to see Monnet's legacy implemented by French statesmen. The principal cause of our disappointment, in my view, was the ascendancy of Michel Jobert, coinciding with the physical decline of Pompidou and the political collapse of Nixon at home.

For about four weeks Jobert and I worked in harmony, or at least so he made me believe. He even offered to help draft the new "Atlantic Charter." And indeed major portions of the joint declaration ultimately signed in Brussels in June 1974 were written under Jobert's aegis by the thoughtful French Ambassador to the North Atlantic Council, François de Rose. But by then it had been drained of significance by Jobert's tactics. As the months passed, he worked to thwart our policies with demonic skill. This does not affect my view that no foreign minister I met surpassed Jobert in intelligence and very few equaled him. And strange as it may seem, I liked him enormously through all our conflicts, and a kind of friendship — tinged with exasperation — grew up between us. He was a cultured, charming man with whom it was a pleasure to exchange ideas. Slight, sardonic, with a sensitive face dominated by luminous eyes, Jobert was a formidable intellect and a fierce debater. As befits a nation where rhetoric is still an art form, his aphorisms were often as apt as they could be biting.

What Michel Jobert lacked was neither intelligence nor analytic ability but a sense of proportion. I do not believe that he started out seeking a confrontation with the United States. His initial aim was the traditional goal of French diplomacy in the Gaullist Fifth Republic: to create at least the appearance that France had shaped whatever it was that was happening. In a later conversation Jobert told me that it would not do for him simply to accept an American proposal. France needed "a certain space for maneuver," and he did not mind if journalists invented stories of confrontation; it would in fact facilitate agreement:

> There will be incidents, happenings, progress, uncertainties — this may help your project because it will make it more important. Otherwise, it would be too simple; people would lose interest. Therefore we should maintain an appearance of a difficult dialogue.

Jobert left me with the impression that in the end he would not only go along but take the lead in shaping an outcome consonant with our objectives. All he asked was that he be permitted to play the leading role, and that we not use the Year of Europe to isolate France within the European Community. He inquired whether we already had prepared a draft Atlantic Declaration. He seemed skeptical when I said we had not. In fact, we had hesitated to put pen to paper before we had an agreement with our key allies lest they unite in nitpicking it to death. Jobert urged us to give him a draft as soon as possible. If he agreed with it, he would present our case to Europe, he argued. But we should not attempt to wield our undoubted influence to outvote France in the

Community or invoke the Atlantic partnership to slow down the emergence of a European identity.

Given the eagerness of Britain and Germany to stay in step with France, I had no difficulty conceding Paris a leadership role. I readily accepted and stressed that we would not work within the European institutions to isolate France. Thus for the first weeks of the Year of Europe, we cold-shouldered the European Community — at France's request! The wily Jobert had confronted us with a Catch-22 even more impenetrable than Brandt's. To show our dedication to European unity we were asked to bypass European institutions, leaving it to France to shape the consensus through its relations with the other national capitals. The initiative had slipped from our hands.

It is always a mistake to give one's proxy to another sovereign state. It soon transpired that whether he had planned it or not, Jobert knew how to use opportunity when it came his way. Ruthlessly exploiting our aloofness toward the European Community, which he had encouraged, he organized its ministers and officials — a touchy group in the best of circumstances — against us, and made himself their spokesman. An American initiative enabled Jobert to pursue the old Gaullist dream of building Europe on an anti-American basis.

I cannot judge whether Jobert was playing a deep game from the beginning, or whether he gradually slid into a position beyond his intentions simply because the opportunity presented itself. I tend to lean toward the second alternative, partly because France had nothing to gain from the confrontation that Jobert's tactics made inevitable. Once the issue was joined and European nations were forced to choose between the United States and France, their dependence on our protection could leave no doubt about the outcome. Before it came to that, Pompidou's death removed Jobert from the Foreign Ministry, and for the rest of the decade Franco-American quarrels vanished like a puff of smoke.

What seems to have diverted Jobert on the way to cooperation with us was the heady wine of publicity distilled from the grape of Franco-American conflict. Like a character in a Pirandello play, Jobert became what he had started out pretending to be. When I first met him he thought my admiration for de Gaulle excessive. Gaullism, he said, was immobilism leavened by rhetoric. By the time he was through he had carried Gaullism to lengths unimagined by the great general, who was too much of an historian to give any quarrel a personal cast and who never would have stepped over the line that risked the global equilibrium. Having started in an adversary role to lay the psychological basis for cooperation later — or so he professed — Jobert became so intoxicated with it that he never again could find the language of cooperation. He forgot that disputes are not ends in themselves; they have value only as a stage toward a settlement, even between adversaries. I suspect — and I know some of Pompidou's entourage share this view — that what finally drove Jobert into obsessive exaltation was the heretofore inconceivable idea that he might be the successor to his mortally ill President if he could capture the public imagination as a strident defender of French nationalism.

The impasse was made worse by Jobert's passionate nature, which masqueraded as cynical nonchalance. The wheels of diplomacy are oiled by conciliatory forms that distinguish disagreements over policy from personal animosity. The elegant protocol rituals symbolize that the diplomat, however much he may differ with his interlocutor, pursues a cause, a principle, an interest, but never a personal vendetta. Jobert refused to act in this manner. Once launched on a confrontation, he quickly turned it into a personal assault. Though our private meetings remained pleasant and were cordial, he never missed an opportunity for the most cutting formulation in the presence of others. Nor did he confine his acid comments to Americans. At the Washington Energy Conference in February 1974, he attacked Helmut Schmidt, then German Finance Minister, with a personal animus impossible to reconcile with any rational French national objective.

Jobert was a great talent, who might have thrived had his President not been stricken just when he reached prominence. Pompidou was essentially measured, careful, and balanced. I cannot believe that he would have let matters slide so completely out of control had he been healthy. But Jobert, left without the guidance of his President, suddenly seized with visions of eminence unimaginable in his previous anonymity, turned into a meteor that briefly and brilliantly illuminated the firmament of diplomacy only to recede as quickly into obscurity.* It was a great pity.

At our first meeting on May 17, 1973, there was not a hint of the conflicts to come. Most of our talk concerned how Presidents Pompidou and Nixon could jointly advance the Year of Europe at their forthcoming summit meeting in Iceland. Jobert said he agreed with the objective. He counseled patience and hard work, in which he would cooperate. He thought my talk with Pompidou the next day would be productive.

And so it turned out. When I met the President on May 18, at the Elysée Palace, Pompidou emerged as the first European leader to deal seriously with the substance of the Year of Europe. He did not resort to procedural evasions and went straight to the heart of the problem. He had some comments to make about my April speech, he said. He did not share the general reaction to my reference to Europe's regional role. If I had asserted that Europe had no right to its own opinion, it would have been a different matter. But I had not done so — a point neglected

---

*He returned to official life in 1981 as Minister of Foreign Trade under President François Mitterand.

by most journalistic critics. I had merely stated an objective reality. It was "more or less true," Pompidou continued, that Europe represented a secondary power (an assertion that went much further than mine had). He also agreed that the Atlantic nations had before them a vast agenda of unresolved problems that needed to be solved simultaneously. It was not possible to overcome economic disputes, for example, without a framework of shared political and military strategy. He looked forward to discussing the whole range of outstanding questions with Nixon in Reykjavik.

Pompidou understood that East-West détente, in particular, high-lighted the need for some agreement on overall goals. Essentially he was worried that Nixon had gone too far in his overtures to the Soviets. What especially bothered him was the Agreement on the Prevention of Nuclear War, which was due to be signed by Nixon and Brezhnev in June and on which we were keeping Pompidou regularly informed (see Chapter VII).

He interpreted it — erroneously, in my view — as renouncing nu-clear war between the superpowers and thus opening Europe and China to pressures below the threshold of all-out war. Had Nixon a different policy from mine? Were we still pursuing a policy of balance between the various power centers, or were we siding with the Soviet Union against China? And what would be our attitude to a "camouflaged" Soviet advance, one that came, that is, "without recourse to force but . . . as a 'progressive tide'?" In other words, what would we do if Communist-dominated forces gained control of vital Third World coun-tries or perhaps even of European parliaments?

It was a penetrating, prescient set of questions, which identified the key problems of the next decade. The American strategy of détente was based on garnering support among moderate elements at home, avoiding appearing to our allies as a source of international tensions, giving the Soviets an opportunity for a reasonable accommodation, but it was never an end in itself. If Soviet expansionism continued, we were determined on a firm response and our policy was disposed to create the widest possible base for it. Still, it was true that Pompidou had spotted its weak point: Détente might confuse tactics with strategy, rhetoric with reality. If a leader as subtle as Pompidou was uncertain, there was a serious risk that in the effort to demonstrate a commitment to peace we might demoralize the traditional opponents to Soviet expansionism. In remov-ing the argument that NATO was an obstacle to peace, we might also confuse its perception of the danger. All this might give momentum to what Pompidou called the "progressive tide" — in 1973 still only a ripple on the horizon.

Whether the United States would have been able to square this circle in a normal Presidency will never be known. We obviously thought not only that we could but that in the long run we could strengthen the West's cohesion in no other way. In the fetid atmosphere of Watergate, when Nixon's hopes of broadening his base by a moderate policy were being shattered, we ran the dual risk that camouflaged Soviet advances would confuse the public while attempts to rally resistance would find no constituency.

Pompidou had indeed asked the basic question that Americans above all are reluctant to address: Do we, as the strongest free nation in the world, resist the fact of change or the method of change? Do we seek to prevent only that Soviet expansion brought about by illegitimate means (however "illegitimate" is defined), or do we have a stake in defending the geopolitical equilibrium whatever the method by which it is challenged — even if, as Pompidou put it, the assault on it is disguised as a "progressive tide"?

A tradition of faith in international law and an historical reluctance to think in terms of balance of power incline Americans to the view that we resist only the method and not the fact of change. And of course we cannot, and should not, be wedded to a blind defense of every status quo. Justice as well as stability must be a goal of American foreign policy, and indeed they are linked. Yet there are changes in the international balance that can threaten our nation's security and have to be resisted however they come about. For a century England went to war rather than permit the port of Antwerp to be acquired by a major power, by any methods. Control of the seas, the prerequisite to Britain's survival, was considered incompatible with the existence of a secure naval base so close to Britain's lifeline. As the product of a similar tradition, Pompidou was asking whether there were comparable limits to American forbearance. His question placed me in a quandary. Intellectually, I agreed with him. The security of free peoples depended on whether the United States could develop a concept of national interest that we would defend regardless of the guise that challenges to it might take. But I also knew that this ran counter to American stereotypes of foreign policy and that I was in no position to give him an unequivocal answer.

The philosophical thrust of the foreign policy of the Nixon Presidency was to develop such a perception of the national interest and to educate our people to its complexities. Unfortunately, the Vietnam war confused the terms of reference and Watergate was on the verge of submerging the debate. For reasons extraneous to our foreign policy we were losing the ability to make our fundamental point: that our nation had a duty to defend the security of free peoples if it wanted to preserve its own; that to resist challenges to the equilibrium in the early stages is an inherently ambiguous task. For if one waits till the challenge is clear, the cost of resisting grows exponentially; in the nuclear age it may become prohibitive.

Over a pontoon bridge into Hanoi, February 1973.

Meeting Pham Van Dong in Hanoi, February 1973 (in the middle, Le Duc Tho).

With Le Duc Tho at the Guest House, Hanoi, February 1973.

ABOVE: *Zhou Enlai, November 1973.*
LEFT: *With Premier Zhou Enlai and Chairman Mao Zedong in Peking, February 1973.*

A flock of Peking ducks at a commune near Peking, November 1973. With HAK are, second from left, Walter Bothe (Secret Service); to his left, Ji Pengfei, Foreign Minister; fifth from left, Robert McCloskey, State Department press spokesman; behind, to HAK's right, Richard H. Solomon, NSC staff; behind, to HAK's left, Arthur Hummel, Acting Assistant Secretary of East Asian and Pacific Affairs; and far right, Winston Lord, Director, Policy Planning Staff.

ABOVE: *Dinner for Edward Heath at Camp David, February 1973. Left to right: HAK, Ambassador Cromer, Secretary of State Rogers, Sir Burke Trend, Robert Armstrong, Ambassador Walter Annenberg, Prime Minister Heath, President Nixon, Foreign Secretary Sir Alec Douglas-Home, Sir Denis Greenhill.* BELOW: *Meeting with President Georges Pompidou in Reykjavik, May 31, 1973. Left to right: Pompidou, Mrs. Kristjan Eldjarn, President Nixon, President Eldjarn of Iceland.*

With Chancellor Willy Brandt after meeting in Bonn, March 4, 1974.

The Big Four Foreign Ministers before dinner in Br
December 9, 1973. Left to right: Sir Alec Douglas-
(United Kingdom); Walter Scheel (Federal Re
of Germany); HAK; Michel Jobert (Fr

*With Helmut Schmidt in Munich after Schmidt's accession
to the Chancellorship, July 7, 1974.*

*French Foreign Minister Michel Jobert at the
Washington Energy Conference, February 1974.*

Being greeted in Tokyo by Japanese Foreign Minister Masayoshi Ohira, November 14, 1973.

A nation and its leaders must choose between moral certainty coupled with exorbitant risk, and the willingness to act on unprovable assumptions to deal with challenges when they are manageable. I favor the latter course. Indeed, shrinking resources leave us no other realistic choice. But it carries with it the burden that it can never be proved whether the sacrifices it demands are in fact necessary. Had France resisted the reoccupation of the Rhineland by Hitler in 1936 — clearly the seminal event in the outbreak of World War II — it would have succeeded at minimal cost. But then Ph.D. theses would still be written debating whether Hitler was a misunderstood nationalist or a maniac bent on world domination. Four years later everyone knew what Hitler was; the knowledge was acquired at the cost of millions of lives.

The statesman's duty is to bridge the gap between his nation's experience and his vision. If he gets too far ahead of his people he will lose his mandate; if he confines himself to the conventional he will lose control over events. The qualities that distinguish a great statesman are prescience and courage, not analytical intelligence. He must have a conception of the future and the courage to move toward it while it is still shrouded to most of his compatriots. Unfortunately, while it is true that great are the statesmen who can transcend ambiguity, not everyone who confronts ambiguity is a great statesman. He may even be a fool.

And so in the year of Watergate and after a decade of Indochina, I spoke to Pompidou more as a professor than as a diplomat. We would maintain the world balance of power at all costs, I said. There were some changes we would not accept, however disguised the catalyst — even if it appeared as a "progressive tide." He was wrong, therefore, in believing that Nixon had opted for the Soviet Union over China. On the whole we would prefer not to have to choose, but if we did:

There is no sense in choosing the strongest against the weakest. If the Soviet Union managed to render China impotent, Europe would become a Finland and the United States would be completely isolated. It is therefore consistent with our own interests not to want and to try not to permit that the Soviet Union should destroy China. . . . How can one support China? Today, such an idea would not be conceivable for American opinion. We need several years to establish with China the links which make plausible the notion that an attack directed against China could be an attack on the fundamental interests of the United States. This is our deliberate policy.

As for the "camouflaged Soviet advance," I said that we would do our maximum to prevent the deterioration of Western vigilance in which such circumstances could arise. This was the reason we wanted to give a new moral dimension to Atlantic relations, to create a new commitment to common goals and values. It was in this spirit that Nixon would come to Reykjavik.

But even as I uttered these reassuring phrases, I was sick at heart. The America of Watergate would probably not be able to muster the domestic support to give effect to them, and the Europe of competitive approaches to Moscow might not listen even after America had recovered its unity. Yet to admit this would accelerate all the dangerous trends. Sometimes one can do no better than maintain the faith against seeming odds and trust to Providence to prevent the worst.

Pompidou replied with understanding. He knew the obstacles we faced, and ironically the time left to him was now too short for him to do more than concern himself with palliatives. In this mood he responded by emphasizing the tactical. He was going to Iceland to achieve a "positive thing." He was ready for "real discussion" of a new document by which the allies could reaffirm their solidarity and their long-range purpose: "We must talk to one another so that Europeans will not have the impression that things are dictated by the United States." And with this, after a month of fruitless exchanges, I began to think that we were at last on the verge of an important European-American dialogue of the kind we had envisaged.

Icebergs in Reykjavik

THE summit between Nixon and Pompidou at Reykjavik on May 31 and June 1, 1973, failed to fulfill these hopes. That we went there with every intention of making a breakthrough is shown by our internal debates. Our economic agencies, for example, were convinced that their goal of a floating monetary system had been nearly frustrated at the Azores in 1971, when Pompidou and Nixon had settled the monetary crisis initiated by our abrogation of limited gold convertibility.[5] Despite Nixon's promise to Pompidou then to defend the dollar — which implied fixed exchange rates — our neglect, or inability (depending on the point of view), to do so had by March 1973 brought about in fact the very practice of floating exchange rates that our Treasury had always preferred and the French had equally strenuously opposed.

As we headed for another Franco-American summit, my friend George Shultz was concerned that we might sell these hard-won gains — as they then appeared — for a mess of pottage, which is how the proposed Atlantic Charter appeared to economists. In his thoughtful, understated manner he submitted a memorandum to the President just before our departure. Its basic point was that Nixon should not retreat from our position on monetary reform for vague French promises of political cooperation. It was a reasonable position for Treasury to take; it was necessary for the political leadership to reject it. I mention it here only to stress the irony that our own associates' fears contradicted those of our European critics.

Nixon and I, caught between the hesitations of our bureaucracy and the suspicions of some of our allies, proceeded in what we took to be the spirit of my conversation with Pompidou. Jobert had asked me to send him a "private," that is, unofficial, paper — if such a thing is possible between senior diplomats. Pompidou and he, he said, would study our views in preparing for the summit and respond constructively. Whether this was another of Jobert's subtle traps or the product of his sardonic, playful cynicism that delighted in making us appear the supplicant, I saw no harm in responding; the French would have to come to grips with our views sooner or later. On May 26, I transmitted a memorandum through our Ambassador, John Irwin. It summed up our thinking. The paper was entitled "Proposed Outcome of the Meeting Between Presidents Nixon and Pompidou in Iceland." The operative paragraph described what we had in mind for an "Atlantic Declaration":

We would like to reach an understanding to begin the process of drawing up a set of principles of Atlantic relations by the time the President visits Europe later this year. The principles could be embodied in a document which could be published as a Declaration to which the countries that are members of the North Atlantic Alliance and the European Communities would subscribe. We are, however, flexible as to the precise form that such a set of principles would take or what name to give them. . . .

But we would like to reach some understanding on the categories of topics to be included, e.g.,

— a fresh statement of the values and broad interests shared by the Atlantic nations,

— a definition of common security interests and objectives under the strategic conditions of the seventies.

— basic approaches to East-West relations and to relations with third areas,

— principles of cooperation on such common problems as the environment, energy supply, exchange of technology, etc.,

— and the basic approach to economic relationships, including trade negotiations and the effort to reform the international monetary system.

There was no time for a French reply before we met in Iceland.

In the interval, Heath and Pompidou had had a private meeting, which once again underlined European reserve. Neither side gave us much of an account even though the principal topic of their conversation was an American initiative. The French told us nothing at all — as if their consultations with Britain did not concern us. Heath wrote a noncommittal letter friendly in tone, sparse in content, repeating what Pompidou had already told us himself: that the French President was going to Iceland with a "positive attitude." From that point on, Heath was to strike the pose of a pained bystander at an incipient family quarrel.

While we learned little of the private discussions, the public omens were bleak. The idea of an early Atlantic summit, which both Pompidou and Brandt had earlier endorsed, was pushed into the remote future. Heath and Pompidou now refused to set a date unless and until bilateral and multilateral consultations warranted a higher-level meeting. This was, of course, a tautology: Since the result of consultations would depend on the will of the governments involved, those reluctant to have a summit had the veto inherent in the capacity to drag their feet. Indeed, by refusing to establish a target date, Heath and Pompidou created incentives for procrastination. They thwarted any attempt at using the prospect of a summit, or even of a Presidential trip to Europe, as a deadline to accelerate talks. Lest any misunderstanding remain, the two leaders allowed the press to learn from their aides that they saw no chance of the consultations being completed by the end of 1973.

But Nixon was preoccupied with Watergate, I with another round of Vietnam negotiations, and neither of us had yet begun to understand that the Year of Europe might turn into an adversary procedure. Reluctant to face the debilitating impact of Watergate, constrained by procedures marvelously designed to confuse the issue, impelled more by righteous conviction than by cool calculation, we read the tea leaves to give us the answers we wanted. We would not face the fact that it was either too late or too early for the new era of creativity, the vision of which had sustained us through the anguish of Vietnam.

Before turning to the purpose of our visit to Iceland, we had to meet the leaders of that hard land of rockstrewn tundra and stark mountains, where amidst the nearly perpetual daylight of summer and the endless gloom of winter an admirable people wrests a living from the reluctant soil and the merciless seas. As is diplomatic custom, Nixon, Secretary of State Rogers, and I called on the Icelandic government to thank its key members for their hospitality. We found them polite but only slightly interested in the Franco-American summit. Their overwhelming concern was the war they were about to start with Britain over codfish.

The issue was territorial rights over offshore waters. Iceland claimed to have exclusive fishing rights in waters lying between it and Britain; it raised implications for defense and for access to deep-sea minerals. Whatever the merit of Iceland's legal position, the little country meant to enforce it by the threat of closing the NATO airbase on its soil and if necessary by war with Britain. British trawlers and a British warship had already been attacked by Icelandic speedboats, which made up in skillful handling for what they lacked in firepower. The Icelandic ministers were uttering dire threats of escalating military action while Nixon and Rogers implored them to withhold the final sanction.

I sat there in wonderment. Here was an island with a population of 200,000 threatening to go to war with a world power of 50 million over codfish, and here was a superpower that considered it necessary (a) to express a view and (b) to restrain not the stronger but the weaker. Nixon and Rogers made soothing noises while the Icelandic ministers implacably insisted on what in any previous period would have seemed suicide. I thought of a comment by Bismarck over a century earlier that the weak gain strength through effrontery and the strong grow weak because of inhibitions. That little tableau in the town hall of Reykjavik — the beseeching superpower, the turbulent tiny country threatening to make war against a nation 250 times its size and to leave NATO (without which it would be defenseless) — said volumes about the contemporary world and of the tyranny that the weak can impose on it.

That same evening — May 30 — I called on Michel Jobert for what I thought would be a routine preparatory meeting for the encounter of the two principals. As in the Azores in 1971, the French had managed to obtain the best accommodations on the island, a large villa where Jobert and I met around 10:00 P.M., which in Iceland at that time of the year was broad daylight. For some reason Jobert preferred that the room reflect the conditions that would have obtained farther south. Heavy drapes produced the darkness to which he was accustomed at this hour, necessitating the use of electric light. Jobert wasted little time in getting to the point, which was quite the opposite of Pompidou's encouraging goodwill of two weeks earlier. Indeed, it turned out to be a catalogue of grievances against the United States. If Pompidou was coming to Iceland to achieve something "positive," as he had told me, he would clearly reserve that for his personal encounter with Nixon.

But that was unlikely. Jobert's presentation was bound to reflect Pompidou's views, even if the acerbic formulations were no doubt his own, and it was impossible to tell to what extent he had influenced Pompidou's thinking. According to Jobert, the timing of our initiative was significant primarily from the point of view of US-Soviet, not Atlantic, relations. He presumed that it was an attempt by the United States to get the largest number of cards into its hands for the forthcoming Brezhnev visit to the United States. We wanted to face Brezhnev as the spokesman not of our own interests but of all Atlantic nations. At any rate, Jobert strongly implied that it was in France's interest to drag its feet until the Brezhnev-Nixon summit was past, and we could not use Atlantic cooperation to exact concessions to our own benefit.

Not content with this ingeniously perverse rationale, he added further objections: Granting my denial that our motive for proposing the Atlantic Declaration was leverage on Moscow, then it must have been designed to pressure Europe in the forthcoming trade negotiations. And even if we had no ulterior motives our initiative would still damage French interests because it had led to a procedural tangle in the European Community. If we were planning to work through NATO, the

Year of Europe might turn into a device to pressure France to resume full participation; if the European Community was to be our counterpart, the practical consequence would be an American attempt to lobby the other members, hence diluting (if not worse) the leadership role of France. Or were we perchance thinking of an entirely new organization that would merge all existing institutions in some supra-Atlantic concert?

France, according to Jobert, did not favor the European-American summit that he claimed we had encouraged Brandt to propose on his visit to Washington. (In fact, Pompidou had proposed it in his interview with Reston, and Brandt had surprised us by seconding it.) The sole purpose could be to isolate or to diminish France. And when were we going to float the draft of a Declaration that he was sure I had in my hip pocket? When would he be able to see it? He could not believe that no such draft existed. Lest we suffer from the illusion that we might do *something* right, Jobert added that our monetary policies disorganized the world. Either the United States did not know what it was doing or else we were deliberately seeking financial dominance by flooding the world with cheap and inconvertible dollars. And our insistence on a reappraisal of strategy was a subterfuge to obscure the fact that under conditions of nuclear parity we would run no real risks for the defense of Europe.

Jobert was turning the Year of Europe into a wrestling match. Whatever contingency he discussed became an attack on our purposes or a reason for stalling. He ascribed to us motives of nearly paranoid deviousness, the very articulation of which destroyed the significance of any reply: If we were capable of what Jobert was accusing us of, he was beyond reassurance.

I somewhat wearily recited our by-now conventional position. We sought a rededication to the moral and political purposes of the West, not a bargaining chip for an encounter with a Soviet leader or upcoming trade negotiations. We had put forward the Year of Europe precisely to transcend the obsession with East-West relations. We were convinced that without such an effort the democracies would lose their sense of direction and cohesion. As for the procedural points, we were here to settle them; we would not proceed except in cooperation with France. The economic issues could best be dealt with if Pompidou provided a detailed critique of our approach, perhaps together with suggestions for a solution. We would resolve the matter in the same spirit as at the Azores eighteen months earlier. The dilemmas of defense resulted from evolving technology, not our preference or design. We needed a sensible doctrine for the defense of Europe lest the contingencies now clearly foreseeable would someday produce the impossible choice between suicide and surrender that he too seemed to fear.

Jobert changed his approach; he suddenly was as sympathetic as his tense nature permitted. He indicated that he was putting forward Pompidou's ideas, while his own were more benign. (This is an old trick of Presidential confidants, designed to deprive themselves of negotiating flexibility without turning matters into a personality clash. I, too, used it on occasion.) He suggested that Nixon's presentation to Pompidou the next morning would be of crucial importance — though how any presentation would change suspicions so deeply ingrained Jobert did not tell us. The best construction one could put on the conversations was that Jobert had placed Nixon in the position of a graduate student who would be examined by a stern and testy professor.

I returned to the hotel in a far from buoyant mood. It was clear that the meeting of the leaders of government would get nowhere. We would be hard put to avoid a stalemate. But this was not the theory of the accompanying White House press corps prowling the halls for some stray intelligence. They bearded me with cynical questions that assumed we were on the verge of some coup to blunt the edge of Watergate. Was the meeting necessary? Had we not already agreed to the outline of an Atlantic Declaration, turning Reykjavik into a charade to give Nixon the credit and to pull the teeth of Congressional hearings? Would we, in short, have the temerity to deflect the public attention from the spectacle of a besieged Presidency by presuming to govern in the national interest?

The next morning Nixon proceeded to the museum that served as the meeting place with Pompidou. Two additional separate sets of meetings had been arranged: on foreign policy between the foreign ministers and their assistants, on economic issues between the economic ministers and their staffs. This gave Nixon a pretext for excluding Bill Rogers and Pompidou for doing without Valéry Giscard d'Estaing. At Nixon's request, I joined the two Presidents as note-taker. No doubt this added to Jobert's resentment. Having been "elevated" to Foreign Minister, he now found himself relegated to a secondary forum. Pompidou revealed the peevishness produced by his illness when he allowed a French spokesman to leak the point that their President, for one, could conduct a dialogue without the assistance of aides — a petty and unfair comment, especially since I had attended in the same role in the Azores.

Nixon was less sure of himself than usual, since Watergate had been taking a toll of his time and nervous energy. The change in Pompidou even in the two weeks since I had seen him last was likewise striking — or perhaps the monarchical environment of the Elysée Palace had obscured it. He was bloated from cortisone. Though his courtesy never flagged, it seemed to require a massive effort to maintain it. He had that withdrawn appearance of cancer patients, as if the private battle in which he was engaged made irrelevant the matters at hand. No doubt Pompidou's suffering contributed to the increasing irritability of French policy. It was a tall order to ask him to be a partner in launching a new initiative of undefined duration when he was contemplating his own demise. In normal times Pompidou might have assumed for himself the role of balance wheel to what he considered our impetuosity and inadequate understanding of European sophistication. And he might well have participated in our shaping a larger vision of our future. But now his lack of confidence in potential successors — congenital in heads of government, most of whom require the psychological reassurance of their indispensability — compounded Pompidou's native skepticism and caused him to avoid new courses that in other hands might lead to unpredictable and perhaps deleterious results. At the end of his life he returned to the Gaullist orthodoxy that had spawned him. He had no stomach for battle with the paladins of his predecessor whom he had ignored when the future still stretched as if infinite before him.

So the encounter at Reykjavik was dominated by a difference of perspectives. Nixon, though sorely beset, still thought of himself as a functioning Chief Executive planning early in his term a long-range program. Pompidou was suspended between the momentary, which he knew only too well, and the eternal, which he was afraid to get to know. And on this incommensurability the dialogue ultimately foundered.

Nixon, aware of Jobert's challenge, made one of his best presentations. After expressing his admiration for de Gaulle, he eloquently stated the rationale for our initiative. He took care to rebut Jobert's arguments of the previous night, sidestepping a confrontation by the clever device of ascribing Jobert's views to unnamed French journalists:

First of all, the timing of our initiative for Europe has nothing to do with the Russian summit or with U.S. political institutions. If we proclaim this year of 1973 the Year of Europe, it is because I feel that during this year of so-called détente with Russia, in this year when Europe is flexing its muscles, we would face a very great danger if Europe were to begin to disintegrate politically. It is wrong to go on saying the U.S. can just sit down with the Russians and Chinese because this downgrades the importance and concern we have for our real friends. When I meet with the Russians I have no more illusions than you do about what they want. But I do not complain.

What I see if we do not seize this moment is a race to Moscow — each country in the West and in Europe going to Moscow to negotiate and make deals. Of course there must be individual meetings, but there must be some underlying philosophy that animates all of us. Otherwise, those shrewd and determined men in the Kremlin will eat us one by one. They cannot digest us all together but they can pick at us one by one. That is why it is so important that we maintain the Atlantic Community — I think at the highest level, first of all, the Big Four, Heath, Brandt, Pompidou and the U.S., for some very frank talks about where we are going from here. . . .

I do not have a blueprint for the future; the future must come from all of us. In spite of what I read in the French press, I am very far from wanting to force France back into NATO or other institutions which France does not consider in its interest to return to. . . .

Despite its occasionally complicated grammar, this was a generous statement and a correct one. There was the danger of neo-isolationism in America and parochialism in Europe. Technology imposed the need for a new approach to defense; it was not an American policy preference but a recognition of reality. The Soviets surely were trying to create in Europe the impression that we and they were about to arrange a condominium. Something needed to be done to resolve Europe's ambivalence between indivisible defense and political autonomy. As I said later to Jobert on June 8, when he accused us once again of pursuing selfish motives in the Year of Europe: "We do it for a larger selfishness. In eight years, if Europe becomes obsessed with a sense of impotence because of isolation from us, both sides will have lost." That prediction, in fact, came true with a vengeance.

Pompidou replied in a lapidary manner that submerged the essence of the problem in elegant paradoxes. He began with an analysis of the international situation. It was acute but lacked his customary relevance. He simply would not bring it to a point; whatever aspect he considered was shrouded in complexity. The United States had accepted military, hence diplomatic parity, he said. Yet "how could you do otherwise unless you spent fabulous sums?" The United States sought to enmesh the Soviet Union, to freeze the status quo "by use of texts, agreements, treaties. . . ." Still, détente or not, the Soviets were pushing their pawns everywhere. And there were weak links, such as Yugoslavia because Tito was an old man. Where would all this lead? The new American relationship with China was an important factor. But could it survive the deaths of Zhou and Mao? Then there was the emergence of Japan, which was caught in a difficult position between China, the Soviet Union, and the United States, and "which has *temporarily* said it will be tied to the United States [emphasis added]."

In this elusive environment Pompidou was not optimistic about Europe. He did not believe that 1973 would be marked by the "advent of Europe"; there was therefore no clear-cut partner for our transatlantic dialogue. The best he foresaw was that Europe would become a major commercial power capable of resolving economic problems. In Britain, Heath was the only European; Pompidou had not met any other. Pompidou shared Nixon's worry about West Germany, which was, the Frenchman said, "beginning to talk of its two options and proclaims its attachment to the West as it is being pulled into the specific German problem which turns it to the East." And a little later again; "Germany

tries to look both ways simultaneously.'' The Italians were worried —
ready to agree to any American proposal but not to a prior arrangement
between the United States and other European countries in which they
did not participate. The same was true of Holland. As for the European
Community, it was fighting over the prices of carrots and wheat. ''Things
come out but they come out poorly. It is a poor system but right now
there is no will to pull out of it.''

All of this was true enough. Yet Pompidou offered no solution to the
perplexities he had delineated, no vision of a common future. For his
view finally came down to the proposition that nothing would work in
any forum. Only Americans, he said sardonically, could invoke *a* Year
of Europe; for France every year was *the* Year of Europe. But Europe
at the moment was moribund. On the other hand the concept of an
Atlantic Declaration was very vague:

> Who says what? If the Alliance, then it must come out of the Atlantic Coun-
> cil. Is it the U.S. plus one European country? Is it the U.S. and the European
> Community? This is difficult since the Community has no political reality, only
> an economic reality.

Pompidou had a point. The memberships of NATO and of the Community only partly overlapped. The functions of the two institutions
were different. Yet this quibble was not the essence of Pompidou's
problem. If the Atlantic Declaration was issued by NATO, which after
all contained the relevant nations save Ireland, it would give political
stature to an organization that France was seeking to confine to military
functions. But if it emerged in the European Community, it would make
the United States a partner in that organization's deliberations and thereby
frustrate France's ambition to preeminence. France wanted to curtail
neither its independence in the Alliance nor its claim to the leadership
of Europe. On this rock an aspiration to greater Atlantic coherence was
bound to run aground.

Pompidou made procedural sense, but it is the responsibility of a
statesman to resolve dilemmas, not to contemplate them. Pompidou's
presentation amounted either to a permanent perplexity or to the deliberate thwarting of a major initiative to give a sense of direction to the
democracies — exposing them to the risk of consuming their substance
over tactics while drifting gradually into a pervasive sense of impotence
that would weaken domestic structures and create mounting foreign
danger.

Nixon lamely brought the morning to a close by proposing an informal working group of individuals possessing the personal confidence of
the heads of government of Britain, France, Germany, and the United
States. Heath had advanced that idea to us earlier in May; it had been
the concept of a *directoire* put forward by de Gaulle in 1958; we had

included it in our memorandum to Jobert of May 26. Pompidou seemed at first to accept the idea, not unnaturally since it reflected a long-standing French proposal. At least we interpreted in that sense some ambiguous remarks made just before the luncheon break.

When Pompidou returned for the afternoon session he had thought better of it, or perhaps had been talked out of it by Jobert. Conceivably, though unlikely, we had misunderstood him in the first place. What Pompidou had in mind, it transpired, were consultations among the Big Four on a *bilateral* basis. France would participate in no new forum on the Atlantic Declaration. It would consult only in established forums or bilaterally. If I wanted to meet British and German representatives jointly, Pompidou would not object, though France would not participate. (Pompidou knew very well that this killed the prospect because neither Heath nor Brandt would agree to such consultations.) The only "concession" Pompidou offered was that the deputy foreign ministers could meet as part of the North Atlantic Council *provided* that sufficient progress was made in other forums, where, of course, France had a veto. To sugarcoat the pill, he suggested that Jobert and I could meet in Paris on the occasion of another round of my talks with Le Duc Tho in a week. And Pompidou was also willing to send Jobert to the United States at the end of the month — a good way to waste another four weeks and to keep us from raising unwelcome projects in other forums.

Pompidou was in fact saddling us with a procedural monstrosity. If the Four consulted bilaterally, then six negotiations on the same subject would be going on simultaneously (and if Italy joined, eight). There would be no way to agree, for everything discussed with one partner would have to be communicated to all others, with infinite potential for confusion, misunderstanding, and mischief. With no central focus and without any specific proposal, chaos was certain. But if we approached existing forums with a draft proposal — the only rational approach — we would be accused of organizing Europe against France and of seeking to dominate NATO with an American document.

When we had put forward the Year of Europe, we had expected to elicit an organized European response that would lead to a conclusion within a few months. It never occurred to us that after six weeks there would be no interlocutor (or so many as to amount to the same thing), no forum, and no draft document.

The remaining discussions were equally inconclusive. Pompidou made a devastating criticism of our monetary policies but, in contrast to the Azores meeting, he put forward no specific proposal to resolve the issue. In this he was probably wise. The differences between the two sides were too wide to be bridged by a directive from the chiefs of state. There was no obvious middle position between convertibility into gold (the French view) and nonconvertibility (ours).

The final session, in which all ministers participated, foreshadowed the stalemate. Nixon made an impassioned speech reiterating his admiration for de Gaulle. He deplored his predecessors' failure to understand that great leader; he was determined, he said, to overcome what suspicions remained. He would insist that members of his Administration treat France on the basis of trust and cooperation.

Nixon never fully understood that panegyrics on de Gaulle tended to irritate Pompidou more than reassure him. Heads of government generally prefer to distinguish themselves from their predecessors rather than be considered in their shadow. After all, de Gaulle had dismissed Pompidou as Prime Minister, and only his unexpected resignation had saved Pompidou from oblivion.

Pompidou, at any rate, felt no obligation to reciprocate. He replied sardonically: "President Nixon and I were matching Gaullisms but there was neither victory nor vanquished" — a formula always uttered by the side that believes it has won. Lest anyone suffer from the illusion that anything had been achieved, he added: "We did not try to decide anything." Pompidou was witty but opaque about just what had been accomplished:

We share our inner thoughts, we did not agree on all the methods, but we do agree on our general interests and that France and the U.S. are guided not only by a sentimental tradition but by a community of deep interests. I am convinced that this conference has not given birth to anything, but it bears a seed for the future, and conception is more fun than delivering.

What seed had been planted Pompidou would not reveal to us. There was little doubt, however, that its planting had not been that much fun and that the species had a long gestation period.

Almost immediately a new controversy broke out. The delegations had not left Iceland when a French spokesman, telling the press on background that further consultations would be bilateral, played down the idea of a deputy foreign ministers' meeting and oozed skepticism about an Atlantic Declaration. Our own briefing had necessarily given the contrary emphasis. The fact that I had personally cleared the text of our quite different public statement with Pompidou did nothing to cool tempers.

The next few days left no doubt that it was the French briefer who had correctly understood Pompidou, as we should have known from the beginning. The permanent head of the Quai d'Orsay, the elegant Geoffroy de Courcel, whom we knew as an old-line Gaullist, repeated to Ambassador John Irwin on the return trip to Paris from Iceland that France's obligation to the European Community stood in the way of a consultation by the Big Four. This delicacy toward its partners came as news to us; France had for years participated in restricted meetings of the Big Four finance ministers and had bitterly resisted the inclusion of any others. Nor did this solicitude extend to giving France's partners an opportunity to participate in the diplomacy of the Year of Europe. At a meeting of the European Community foreign ministers on June 5, Jobert opposed a summit meeting of the Community with the President because it would be unseemly for all the Europeans to flock around Nixon. While he was at it, Jobert also contradicted what he interpreted as our excessively optimistic briefing of the Reykjavik meeting, blocked the appointment of an ad hoc group to prepare a European position for the Atlantic dialogue, and flatly opposed any kind of Atlantic Declaration.

In these conditions, my meeting in Paris with Jobert on June 8 turned into a duel. If a restricted group was impossible and a meeting of all the Community members unseemly, what forum was left? Jobert, after reiterating his view that we were pursuing the Year of Europe for domestic reasons, insisted on bilateral consultations — the one result of Reykjavik he seemed eager to affirm. And he returned to his obsessive demand that we produce our nonexistent draft charter. Bilateral talks should start by our showing him whatever documents we had.

The unfortunate fact was that because of an excess of scrupulous concern for European and specifically French sensibilities, we still did not have any draft. We were waiting for some consultation so that we did not seem to be imposing our views. I suggested that the Four try their hand at a document, with each country taking primary responsibility for one section in first draft — all the exchanges to take place on a bilateral basis. This was a more than clumsy procedure but it reached out to meet French concerns.

Jobert at first seemed sympathetic. France would write the section on the political evolution of Europe. Later in the meeting he seemed to suggest that everybody — France, Britain, West Germany, and the United States — should be asked to produce a comprehensive draft. But, once again, before any work could start, Jobert wished to see our own document. Convinced that we would get nowhere unless we showed him something, I agreed to produce a draft by the time he came to America at the end of June. He in turn indicated that he would do some drafting of his own, perhaps in response to our version. Painful as it is for me to admit it, I had fallen into another trap. For once I gave Jobert a draft I was at his mercy. If I showed it to other allies he would accuse us of ganging up on him. If I waited for his response, he could begin undermining our position with his partners by nitpicking it or stop its going forward at all.

The anomaly of our position was illustrated the next day when, still in Paris, I had a meeting with Joseph Luns, who had recently become Secretary General of NATO. In many ways Joseph Luns was symbolic of the changes in the Atlantic relationship. When I first met him he was

Foreign Minister of the Netherlands in a cabinet of sturdy, moderately
conservative, strongly pro–NATO orientation. We knew Luns as a
staunch friend of the United States, a combative defender of NATO
unity. He had become such a fixture that when he visited Washington
in 1969 to convince us, with his affectionately browbeating tactics, that
we should grant additional landing rights to KLM, the Dutch airline,
Elliot Richardson, then Under Secretary of State, introduced him at a
State Department luncheon as follows: "Dutch-American relations go
back 300 years and Joseph Luns has been foreign minister for the greater
part of that period."

But within the space of a few years he had become an anachronism
in his own country. The Dutch political spectrum tilted sharply to the
left; the security dimension of NATO was de-emphasized; a spirit of
moralistic semineutralism flourished. Luns, with his insistence that the
West represented absolute values worth defending, had no place in such
a structure. He disappeared as Foreign Minister and his compatriots were
relieved when his appointment to NATO removed him from the Dutch
political arena. In Brussels his passionate nature earned him snickers
among the cool representatives of the modern trend as well as the admiration and affection of those of us who knew how essential it was
that the crucial post of Secretary General be filled by a strong personality deeply convinced of the moral importance of the unity of the democracies.

Luns had the distinction of being the first European leader to welcome
our initiative unequivocally. Unfortunately, he represented no government. And the institution for which he spoke was not one of France's
favorites. Luns told me that he had written to all Alliance foreign ministers commending our initiative and offering NATO's good offices in
any consultations. He was prepared to use the weekly luncheons of
NATO's permanent representatives to take soundings and even begin
drafting a document. He was asking for guidance. But France stood in
the way. As a result of Jobert's maneuvers, we were being precluded
from talking to those who wanted to be helpful (for fear of being accused of seeking to isolate France) and confined to those who were not
disposed to be cooperative.

I was not yet prepared to give up on Jobert or to cross Pompidou
without one more effort, so I evaded a recommendation. I told Luns
that I wanted to wait for the exchange of drafts with Jobert before involving NATO institutionally. We had no choice, I said, for if France
turned against the Year of Europe it would wither anyway. Luns went
along with me, though silent acquiescence was not his strong point. He
did not like maneuver; his normal style when confronted with an obstacle was to bulldoze it into submission. He warned that some of the
smaller countries were restive. He was right. But we thought we had to

choose between the irritation of the smaller countries and the outright opposition of France, whose stalling would have at least the moral support of Britain and the acquiescence of the Federal Republic.

Waiting for Jobert

B Y the end of June 1973 we were treading water. Two months after our initiative, no one had yet put forward any concrete idea of what the Year of Europe should contain. There did not exist a work program or a forum for discussion or even a formal European reply. I was waiting for Jobert. Two versions of my promised draft were being readied for his visit: a somewhat longish text prepared by the State Department putting forth our objectives in a manner so conciliatory that few sharp edges remained; and a more succinct and probably more contentious document prepared by my own staff.

On June 27 Etienne Davignon, the Director General for Political Affairs of the Belgian Foreign Ministry, visited Washington. A strong defender of European institutions, he had demonstrated that intelligence and dedication could, within the framework of a united Europe, achieve an influence disproportionate to the power of one's country. Before visiting me in San Clemente, he called on Under Secretary of State William Porter and Assistant Secretary for European Affairs Walter Stoessel. From the point of view of the European Community, Davignon carried approximately the same message as Luns. He feared that our bilateral dealings with France were undermining the ability of the other eight members of the European Community to move France toward conciliation. A redefinition of Community relations with the United States was imperative because most disputes would arise in the area of Community competence, not within NATO. Jobert, according to Davignon, was blocking progress at Community meetings with two arguments: that no decision should be taken pending his further consultation with the United States; and that there was no hurry anyway because the status quo was hardly disadvantageous and, as France had shown, it was not necessary to agree with Washington to have good relations with it. Everything thus depended on Jobert, who was coming to see me in San Clemente on June 29 and 30.

Important moments in diplomacy frequently occur in incongruous settings. The Western White House consisted of two rows of one-story, prefabricated buildings parallel to each other and separated by a cement walkway. The eastern row contained a conference room, a reception area, staff and administrative offices, and a small dining room. The other faced the ocean; it contained four offices each with an anteroom for secretaries. Propinquity to the President's office is one of the better ways of judging the relative importance of White House aides. On this

basis, the hierarchy of White House aides had been Haldeman, Ehrlichman, and me in that order. The whole edifice had been built, under the
pressure of Haldeman's merciless lashing, in three months between April
and July 1969 so that it was ready for Nixon's summer retreat. (Since
Nixon insisted that he never took vacations, his sojourns in
San Clemente were presented as moving the working White House to
the West Coast.) Each of the main offices had a little patio, helpfully
equipped with telephone console, overlooking the President's golf course.
Beyond it was the Pacific Ocean.

It was on my patio in the bright California sun that Michel Jobert and
I resumed our sparring — as yet maintaining the facade of being partners in a joint enterprise. Jobert had read enough of French military
history to be attracted to the value of an immediate attack. He opened
by requesting that we cease briefing his partners in the European Community — perhaps a reference to the Davignon visit. Jobert had brought
nothing — no draft, no proposed procedure, no forum for further discussion. Indeed, he strongly implied that his prime purpose in coming
had been to be briefed about Nixon's just-concluded summit with
Brezhnev. Most of our conversation was taken up by that. When we at
last returned to the Year of Europe, Jobert suggested his reason for
traveling all the way to San Clemente was simply to collect our draft of
the Atlantic Declaration — surely a time-consuming method in the age
of telecommunication. As a sign of good faith I gave him both our
drafts — usually a poor procedure because it enables the opposite number to choose what is most advantageous to him and to learn of one's
internal disagreements. Jobert refused to read them there. He would "read
and study" — or else he would "study and read." He would do almost
anything except make progress. If he agreed with our draft, things would
be easy; we would then move to multilateral forums. He did not say
what would happen if he disagreed.

Jobert's visit was best epitomized by a disastrous dinner I gave for
him in Los Angeles. I had invited distinguished representatives of politics, business, and the entertainment industry. Matters proceeded
smoothly enough until Jobert rose to reply to my toast, using the French
language. My friend the performer and unpredictable genius Danny Kaye,
not fully familiar with diplomatic protocol, interrupted to inquire into
the choice of language; he had noted that Jobert spoke excellent English. Would the French Foreign Minister not speak in a tongue most of
the guests understood? Jobert replied coldly that he was speaking in
French for the benefit of the party traveling with him. Danny Kaye
offered to solve this problem by interpreting.

To my amazement Jobert, perhaps because he had never encountered
someone like Danny Kaye at a diplomatic function, acquiesced. He delivered an elegant enough toast in English, which Danny proceeded to

render in a stentorian voice in his wholly nonsensical, double-talk version of French — a nonexistent language that had the maddening quality of catching the precise intonation of French and whole snatches of French phrases, so that the uninitiated required several minutes of straining to realize they were being put on. Jobert seemed not amused. On the other hand, it was a case of art not so much imitating as encapsuling life: Our dialogue was beginning to approach Danny Kaye's elegant gibberish.

While waiting for Jobert's reply or counterdraft, we sought to advance the transatlantic dialogue — this time with the Federal Republic of Germany. But nothing concerning the Year of Europe was to prove easy.

Since Willy Brandt had assumed the Chancellorship, Nixon's confidential exchanges with him had gone via Egon Bahr. I had discussed our project with Bahr at the beginning of the year; he had indicated support in a memorandum in early April; it was only natural that we would turn to him again. I had invited Bahr to come to Washington following my San Clemente meeting with Jobert. After accepting tentatively, he canceled his trip without explanation. On June 30 I repeated my invitation. Jobert, in the meantime, had done his bit to muddy the waters by informing the German Foreign Minister, Walter Scheel, that I considered Bahr my interlocutor on the Year of Europe, thus guaranteeing an internal German row over prerogatives.

On July 2 Nixon sent a cable to Brandt informing him of the conversations with Jobert (this was necessary in part to keep the French version from being the sole briefing available in Bonn). He invited Brandt to send a representative to Washington for bilateral US–German talks so that an Atlantic Declaration could be completed before Nixon's visit to Europe in the fall. He left it to Brandt to designate the representative.

Brandt replied coldly on July 7. He did not respond to the hint of a European trip by Nixon in the fall; he simply ignored it. He did agree to bilateral talks on the Atlantic Declaration, which he described modestly as "some general principles concerning the gradual development of relations between the United States of America and a uniting of Western Europe." Clearly, the Year of Europe was in no danger from excessive German enthusiasm.

Brandt's letter now designated Foreign Minister Walter Scheel for bilateral explorations. Either Bahr had lost a bureaucratic battle or else Brandt did not want to be too closely identified personally with the Year of Europe. Perhaps both.

Debonair and exuding soothing formulas, Walter Scheel arrived in Washington on July 12. His air of easy camaraderie tended to create the impression that he was veneer all the way through. But that was a grave error. A conciliatory manner was allied with a first-class intelligence. He skillfully pursued *Ostpolitik* but there was never the slightest question about his commitment to the unity of the West. That he was made of stern material was shown by the skill with which, as leader of the Free Democratic Party, he moved it from slightly right of center to slightly left, a subtle shift that preserved it as the balance wheel of German politics and gave it an influence out of proportion to its numbers. There was no doubt where Scheel, a devout believer in democracy, stood on the philosophical conflicts of our age. Yet I had the impression that he thought the wisest course for his country was to achieve the degree of freedom of maneuver that had been so crucial for his party in domestic politics. Scheel well understood the pivotal importance of the American connection for Germany's security and hence its diplomacy. He had brought with him the outline of a draft declaration. It was the meatiest draft anyone had produced and the one most in accord with our basic approach. I urged Scheel to turn it into a formal document. He promised to do so within two to three weeks. We never saw it again; it fell victim to French pressure and the disintegration of the dialogue a few weeks later.

Scheel's helpfulness on substance did not extend to procedures. His desire for a Presidential visit was as inhibited as Brandt's. The only hint as to a date he could bring himself to advance was that it should take place sometime before the end of the European Security Conference. Since the conference had just assembled the previous week and was guaranteed a run of a few years, this created no great pressure to begin the planning. Scheel repeated the by-now familiar procedural dilemma that it was relatively easy to assemble the heads of government at NATO but difficult to discuss economic subjects or European-American relations there, while it was possible to discuss these subjects within the framework of the European Community, though not in the presence of heads of government.

Scheel's solution was that there be two declarations, one on subjects within the province of NATO and the other for those applicable to the European Community. But in attempting this, the old perplexities returned. France would not stand for a meeting between the heads of government of the Community and the American President. Scheel offered the suggestion that the President might meet in Brussels with the President of the European Commission (a civil servant), the President of the European Community (who, in the rotation by which the post was filled, would be the Danish Prime Minister for the next six months), and the nine foreign ministers in their capacity as members of the Political Consultative Committee. It was a preposterous proposition that heads of government, having first guaranteed Western security at a NATO meeting, would refuse to discuss economic and political issues in the same town with the President and instead delegate these topics to their foreign ministers. I pointed out the additional absurdity that almost all our allies were pressing us to agree to a summit with Leonid Brezhnev at the conclusion of the European Security Conference. Why were they reluctant to commit themselves to a summit meeting with the President of the United States? What was it that made a meeting with Brezhnev so much easier? Scheel would not budge. We deferred a decision until the outcome of drafting.

The elephantine procedure Jobert had imposed on us was now creating its own havoc. Draft documents were like pollen in the spring air. In addition to the German outline which we had seen, a thin Dutch draft had been submitted to NATO, Jobert had promised a French draft to us alone, and there were two American drafts shown only to Jobert.

It was impossible to tell who had actually seen or approved what. I found it hard to believe that the German outline had been prepared without consultation with anyone. But it was sensless to have Jobert studying an American draft and permit Scheel to fill in his outline in ignorance of our position.

I therefore decided to give Scheel the two American drafts. And having gone that far, we also transmitted them to London on July 8. I knew that this would give Jobert a point to score against me because I had told him that I would await his reaction. But Jobert had had our draft now for ten days and the very bilateral process to which we had agreed on France's urging created its own necessities. It was impossible not to tell each of our principal partners what we were saying to the others.

As it turned out, I was too late to preempt another of Jobert's maneuvers. Jobert had visited London early in July and promptly asked the British leaders what they thought of the American drafts (before they had received them). When they honestly denied any knowledge, he accused them of colluding with us against France; it was unthinkable, he claimed, that we would not show such documents to our oldest ally. The wily Jobert thereby achieved two objectives. If we had given the documents to London, he had established equal status; if we had not, he would have soured Anglo–American relations just when decisions could no longer be avoided. He achieved the latter objective. Though I did not learn the details of Jobert's visit until after Heath and I were both out of office, it was clear in July 1973 that during the climactic part of the negotiations, Whitehall, feeling itself discriminated against, treated us more aloofly than even in the previous period of the Heath government.

The other shoe dropped on July 16. The French chargé d'affaires in Washington delivered a letter to me from Jobert rejecting *both* our drafts. The State Department document, which he thought "less generous" than mine, seemed to him to be also "more prudent." Still, vapid as it was, it too did not pass muster. Jobert would offer no ideas of his own: He did not now want to begin what could be a polemic, he said, for he would find one irritating. But out of "friendship" he advised me to engage in the bilateral talks I desired with more realistic documents. He would not offer a text, however, to convey the "sense of realism" that was acceptable. To do this, he feared, might embarrass me; on reflection, he wrote, he felt it better to remain silent. In other words, we could submit documents but would be given no clue to what was desired. Nor would we be told why our proposals had been rejected. In the meantime, Jobert used our drafts to weaken our relations with the other European countries. It was a very skillful performance of pointless diplomacy, for Jobert's victories brought him and his country no benefits and mortgaged its relations with the United States.

It served, however, to stalemate our initiative. On July 23 the foreign ministers of the European Community met in Copenhagen. Three months to the day after the Year of Europe speech, after weeks of bilateral consultation, they had at last gathered to address its substance. Once again our allies took refuge in procedure; but more than delay was involved. The formal decision was that the Community's political directors (senior civil servants in the foreign offices) would draft some principles for the ministers by mid-September. When the Community had concluded its deliberations, the Chairman of the Council of Ministers would transmit its results to us. There was no reference to Nixon's visiting Europe.

After a few more days, we began to understand that what had happened in Copenhagen was not only to put the Year of Europe on ice for two more months and to cold-shoulder a Presidential visit — two unprecedented events in Atlantic relations — but also to turn the European–American dialogue into an adversary proceeding. After insisting that we not consult the European Community, Jobert used our aloofness to convince the Community to adopt a procedure totally at variance with the practice of intimate consultations of more than two decades. It had become customary that the nations of the Atlantic — and especially the large countries — exchange ideas on outstanding issues in many informal contacts whose vitality was enhanced by their spontaneity. It now transpired that the European nations had decided that they would work on a paper (on Atlantic relations, no less) without any consultation with us. We would be shown no drafts; we would have no opportunity to express our views. After the Community foreign ministers had completed the document several months hence, it would be submitted to us by the Danish Foreign Minister, who would be in the chair for the remainder of the year. He would be empowered only to present the draft, register our comments, and report back to the other foreign ministers, who would consider our views at the next monthly meeting. After they had come to a consensus about the appropriate response, the same process would repeat itself. In the intervals between the appearances of the

Danish Foreign Minister, none of the other ministers could talk to us, even informally, about what had started out as an American initiative.

Heath made the new approach explicit in a cable to Nixon of July 25. He emphasized that henceforth the Nine would share among themselves all information "which they obtain in the framework of bilateral exchanges with the U.S." In other words, confidential bilateral exchanges — first demanded by our allies as the *sole* acceptable procedure — were at an end. What had already taken place would be shared. All at once, we understood why Burke Trend, the Cabinet Secretary and my designated contact in the British government on the Year of Europe, had been so elusive. He had avoided consultations since April, stalling until after the meeting in Copenhagen. Afterward, he no longer had the authority to consult bilaterally. This was made clear by Heath:

I think that we shall stand the best chance of achieving the success which you and I both want if we ourselves are now seen to adhere to this decision as regards the present exercise. To do so will improve the chances of an orderly response by the Nine in the autumn.

For the entire postwar period, Britain had prided itself on a "special relationship" based on a preferential position in Washington. But if every communication to London would automatically be distributed to the Nine, the relationship was hardly "special" any longer. Europe had responded to the Year of Europe initiative with a procedure in which those who talked with us were not empowered to negotiate while those who could have negotiated with us no longer had the authority to talk.

What made it all so painful was that we knew we had been outmaneuvered by Jobert, and that he had gotten away with it because we had not envisaged an adversary procedure. Jobert had ruthlessly used our effort to conciliate France as a device to isolate us. It was at Jobert's request that we had resisted the importuning of the smaller countries for a formal proposal or a wider forum. In the name of avoiding the isolation of France we had, with grave misgivings, proceeded to bilateral talks with France, Britain, and Germany and not appealed directly to the machinery of the Common Market. In order not to exacerbate old sensitivities we had put off Joseph Luns's proposal to use NATO as a forum for consultation.

It was clear what had happened after three months of waiting for Europe. Jobert had exploited the smaller countries' uneasiness about dictation from the Big Four, West Germany's reluctance to inhibit *Ostpolitik* within a larger grouping, and Heath's determination to demonstrate his European vocation, to weld together a coalition of negation. Jobert, backed by Heath, had had a free run at us because the possibility that the whole exercise might turn into a confrontation had simply never crossed our minds. No wonder that emotions were hardly at an even keel in an Administration already roiled by Watergate pressures.

The result was a Presidential reply to Heath of unusual coolness:

Although I accept your view that a certain amount of progress was made in the general direction of what we hope to achieve, I must tell you frankly that I am quite concerned about the situation in which we seem to find ourselves.

I thought we had agreed when we discussed what later became known as the Year of Europe initiative in our January meeting that this was a major enterprise in the common interest at a critical time. In that meeting and in numerous subsequent exchanges in this channel and in conversations with your representatives, it was common ground that the revitalization of Atlantic relationships is at least as much in Europe's interest as in our own and that extraordinary efforts with strong public impact were required. . . .

[W]e have no objection whatsoever to the idea that the Europeans should concert among themselves how they wish to conduct the dialogue with us. Not wishing to get delayed by procedural issues, we employed bilateral channels because that was the European preference and indeed because no other channels seem to be available. Every attempt at multilateral talks including some proposed by your government when Dr. Kissinger visited London in May has been rebuffed. We finally accepted bilateral talks because we agreed with your judgment that the French should not be isolated. But our preference for multilateral channels was always clear. We consistently stated that the various bilateral talks as well as discussions in existing multilateral forums should be pulled together multilaterally as soon as this was feasible. If we have sought to preserve the privacy of our bilateral exchanges it was largely at European request and because we agreed that under the circumstances it was the best way to make progress. I find puzzling what you say about the exploitation of our private bilateral contacts by the country that had initially insisted on them.

The same points were put even more sharply in a letter of July 30 from Nixon to Brandt, who had weighed in with the by-now standard European argument that the Copenhagen meeting represented a significant response to our initiative. Nixon used the opportunity to say he would not visit Europe in these circumstances and that he would sign no documents that were not signed by other heads of government — a slap at the idea that he meet with the foreign ministers, and not the heads of government, of the Community:

I must in all candor express to you my surprise at the approach that has emerged from the European deliberations. Three months after our initiative, and after numerous discussions which at European request we conducted on a bilateral basis, we now find that the Europeans are unwilling to discuss substantive issues with us until mid-September. After a number of European governments, including yours, had assured us that they would present us with their substantive views in response to ours, the Europeans have now decided to with-hold these views until they have first prepared a collective position among themselves through discussions from which we are excluded. The intention, as I understand it, is then to present this collective view to us and thereafter to conduct the exchanges by means whereby we are asked to deal with instructed European representatives. I must honestly tell you that I find it astonishing that an endeavor whose purpose was to create a new spirit of Atlantic solidarity and whose essence should have been that it was collaborative at all stages should now be turned almost into a European-American confrontation.

In these circumstances, you should know that we will take no further initia-tive in either bilateral or multilateral forums but will await the product of the Nine in September and then decide whether and how to proceed. . . .

Let me say now, however, that I have reached the following conclusions regarding my proposed trip to Europe: I will not come to Europe unless there is a result commensurate with the need for strengthening Atlantic relationships. I cannot consider meetings in multilateral forums in which my European col-leagues do not find it possible to participate. I do not believe that it will serve the purpose envisaged in our initiative and, I thought, agreed between us when you were here in May, for me to sign communiqués in Europe not signed also by other heads of government.

One cannot know what the impact of these letters would have been had they been sent by an unimpaired President. But our allies knew that Watergate had reached a new climax with the discovery of the White House taping system. There is little doubt that without Watergate, the need for the letters would never have arisen. As it was, our allies knew not only that I was the principal drafter — which had always been the case — but also that the President, for domestic reasons, could not give the matter his continuing attention. But in any event, it was too late for recrimination, as soon became clear in the next consultation with Great Britain.

Sir Burke Trend arrived in Washington for Anglo-American bilateral talks the day the letter to Brandt was dispatched (July 30). In light of the Copenhagen decision he had nothing to talk about. There was a painful session with my wise and gentle friend. We both realized that if these tendencies continued, we were at a turning point in Atlantic rela-tions. For the sake of an abstract doctrine of European unity and to score purely theoretical points, something that had been nurtured for a generation was being given up. Atlantic — and especially Anglo-Amer-ican — relations had thrived on intangibles of trust and consultation. They were now being put into a straitjacket of legalistic formalisms. Trend had lived too long in the old framework, based on mutual confi-dence, to be anything but uncomfortable with his brief. He came as close to showing his distress as the code of discipline of the British Civil

Service and his high sense of honor permitted. But matters had gone beyond his level in the hierarchy.

That the British government was determined to change the existing pattern became even clearer when, again without any prior consultation or warning, it introduced a draft text of an Atlantic Declaration at NATO in early August. What made the gesture more astonishing was that London had never responded to the texts we had transmitted on July 8. (We received a negative reply to those only on August 17.) The British draft was notable for its blandness. Moreover, it was to be kept separate from the Community effort — preventing a comprehensive document. And it was to be dealt with by the "natural timetable" of the Alliance. This meant that the earliest time for a summit would be at the next NATO Council meeting in December, a time when Nixon had specifically declared he could not visit Europe because of the need to prepare for the Congressional session. When, still caught up in old patterns, we complained about lack of consultation, Her Majesty's Government replied:

We are, however, in trouble already with some of the smaller members of the Nine for the delay with which they have learned of some of our discussion with the White House . . . We think wherever possible we should go for multilateral discussion from the outset . . . [T]he nature of the Atlantic relationship is not something that can be agreed through purely bilateral discussion. Action, as opposed to explanations, will have to be multilateral.

Simultaneously, we learned that the Community had submitted the text of a draft declaration to Japan, with the comment that a document negotiated between Europe and Japan would be concrete, while if we participated it would of necessity be vague. We had never been told of the existence of such a project, still less consulted about its contents. The snub was plainly intended because the tactic was unnecessary. Japan's primary concern was to stay out of the line of fire. Japanese diplomats from time to time inquired politely but with studied indifference about that anomalous Year of Europe in which they had been invited to participate. But they made it plain that while exclusion from a serious effort would be resented, they had little interest in participating in a Western family squabble. It was in this manner that what started as an effort to foster Atlantic unity turned into a device to organize all the democracies against the United States.

Though bureaucratic inertia and Watergate despair impelled us to continue to go through the motions, the Year of Europe had lost its meaning.

The Year That Never Was

THE formal part of our proposal, a new Declaration of Atlantic Relations, was finally accomplished a year later when Nixon was the sole surviving head of government of the Big Four — and he resigned six weeks afterward. But by then it had been drained of its moral and psychological significance by a year of bickering.

History, it became obvious, cannot be repeated on command. The idea of a dramatic speech by an American to inspire Europe was copied too self-consciously from Secretary George C. Marshall's unveiling of the Marshall Plan; the phrase "Atlantic Charter" was an echo of the famous Roosevelt-Churchill understanding of the Forties. Encouraged by European exhortations to shift our attention back to the West and away from Southeast Asia, and seduced by our own nostalgia for historic initiatives, we ran afoul of conditions that had changed drastically since 1947. Then Secretary Marshall had offered to nations that had no alternative what was in effect a free gift: massive American aid in the reconstruction of Europe. Europe's problem was to organize itself to make sure of the bounty — a pleasant assignment not unhelpful to politicians. The Atlantic Declaration of 1973–1974 conferred no immediate benefits; it forced every government to grapple with tough problems on a broad agenda — an assignment elected political leaders generally prefer to pass on to their successors.

There was a complex psychological reason at the heart of our frustrations. We were so eager to liberate ourselves from the trauma of Vietnam that we failed to give sufficient weight to the fact that Europe could not possibly share this largely American imperative — at least to the same extent.

There were other important obstacles, which I shall discuss in Chapter XVI. But the single most corrosive factor was Watergate. The Year of Europe might well have succeeded but for the way the scandal seeped into every nook and cranny of the project. A strong President at the height of his prestige, with an American consensus behind him, could have made a compelling case for the moral unity of the free nations. They would have been eager to share the limelight with him. As 1973 progressed, the opposite was the case. Association with Nixon had become dangerous; nor could the wounded President rally domestic American opinion in a manner our allies could not have ignored. Had not Nixon become a political liability to the European leaders, it is highly improbable that they would have been so insistently aloof. They had to wonder more and more about the risks to themselves of signing a solemn document with an increasingly discredited Chief Executive. Had there been immediate gains to show, they might have taken the chance. But the Atlantic Declaration highlighted the dilemma of the modern democratic leader: The time frame for a policy to bear fruit is longer than his term of office, while the down-side of the policy begins to operate immediately. Every European head of government had to calculate that for a vision of a more secure tomorrow he might share in the immediate opprobrium if he identified himself with Nixon just before Watergate engulfed him. And the issues we raised were all complex; better to bury them by ignoring them.

Still, in the perspective of nearly a decade, I regret the callousness with which some of our allies reacted to Nixon's loss of authority. Here was a man whose entire public life had been devoted to strengthening the Atlantic Alliance. In his first term he had gone to great lengths to win the confidence of European leaders. He had ended an ugly quarrel with France. He had overcome his predispositions and helped salvage Brandt's *Ostpolitik*. He had given Heath many proofs of his admiration. Despite some serious lapses in 1971, he had made extraordinary efforts to consult regularly with his European colleagues. Yet all these leaders, without ever failing to be polite, took steps that none would have dared to risk with a functioning President enjoying even modest public support.

When all is said and done I have to conclude that though the immediate attempt was doomed, it was right to try. For I still believe we asked the correct questions. The leaders of the industrial democracies had for too long avoided fundamental issues by using the American connection for domestic politics. During periods of international tensions the criticism was that American policy was jeopardizing Europe's security. When we had taken our partners' advice and eased relations with Moscow, they complained about a Soviet-American condominium. At bottom, Europe wanted America committed to its defense but hoped to deflect actual military operations from its territory. Its governments sought detailed assurances from us on every aspect of our negotiations with the Soviet Union but were not prepared to accept similar restraints on their own unilateral initiatives. These inconsistencies, if pursued long enough, would consume Western unity in a morass of conflicting policies driven by the most short-term domestic pressures. More important, the obsession with tactics deprived the politics of the democracies of moral sustenance. Without a vision of their future, publics were increasingly demoralized by technical issues beyond the ken of nonexperts. Fear, not purpose, became the dominant ingredient of the policies of too many democracies; adaptation, not taking charge of one's destiny, defined political prudence. The causes for this state of affairs run deep and are not soluble by foreign policy initiatives alone. Yet the ideas represented by the Year of Europe could have contributed to overcoming them.

As it was, most of the practical proposals of the Year of Europe were realized. Before Nixon's resignation the Atlantic Declaration was signed. In the Presidency of Gerald Ford, regular consultations on a broad agenda were begun and continue at this writing. But the task of evoking a vision of an inspiring future remains, in incomparably more difficult circumstances.

VI

The Middle East in Ferment

Time for a New Initiative?

STRANGELY enough, the domestic weakness produced by the traumas of Vietnam and Watergate had the least impact on our Middle East policy. No Middle East issues had yet erupted into major controversy at home; the countries in the area took less advantage than others of the growing embarrassments of our executive authority because they would all be stranded without their belief in a powerful America. Each in its own way relied on a strong American policy to achieve their widely differing purposes. Israel depended on American support for survival. The moderate Arabs counted on American influence with Israel for progress towards peace. Even the radical Arabs needed us if only as an alibi; they tended to exaggerate our malign influence as vastly as they considered it impervious to the stresses involved in Watergate.

Nixon began his second Administration with the firm intention of launching a diplomatic initiative for peace in the Middle East, though he had not yet formulated a plan. In an interview two days before his reelection Nixon had said that the Middle East would have "a very high priority" in his second term. On November 5 Secretary of State William Rogers had added his own prediction that the United States expected soon to be "very active."[1] And with the end of the Vietnam war, public attention turned increasingly to the Middle East. In the first week of February 1973, the columnists Rowland Evans and Robert Novak noted "growing pressure from Arab countries friendly to the United States" to get Nixon and me involved in Middle East diplomacy. The *New York Times* editorialized the same week that pending visits to Washington of various Middle East leaders would give Nixon a "natural opportunity to take some new initiatives." The *Baltimore Sun* stressed that such initiatives were "overdue." And the *Washington Post* urged Nixon to give the Middle East his "sustained personal attention" now that Vietnam was concluded, warning that Israel's attitude was "unacceptably shortsighted."[2]

Nevertheless, there were many reasons for caution. The first term had underlined the futility of overeager peace plans that had run aground amid the passions of the parties and the divisions in our government. An Israeli election was set for the end of October 1973; experience had taught us that no Israeli government could make the difficult decisions inherent in the peace process while its future hung in the balance. We intended to use the interval in exploratory talks between me and President Anwar el-Sadat's national security adviser, Hafiz Ismail; to formulate a workable proposal we needed a clearer understanding of Egyptian purposes.

Within our government, management of Middle East diplomacy was in transition. During the first term Nixon had initially left the Middle East to the State Department, partly to placate Rogers, partly because Nixon thought Middle East diplomacy was a loser from the domestic point of view and sought to deflect its risks from himself. Thus my influence on Middle East policy in Nixon's first term was far less direct than in other spheres. I could write memoranda; I could warn; occasionally I could delay. But except in the Jordan crisis I exercised no operational control. Until mid-1972 the system of White House backchannels — secret negotiations with other governments, bypassing the State Department — never applied to the Middle East. Though I occasionally chafed under the system that should in fact be the norm, it served, in truth, the strategy I favored: a prolonged stalemate that would move the Arabs toward moderation and the Soviets to the fringes of Middle East diplomacy. Late in 1971, Nixon began shifting responsibility to me. He was afraid that the State Department's bent for abstract theories might lead it to propose plans that would arouse opposition from all sides. My principal assignment was to make sure that no explosion occurred to complicate the 1972 election — which meant in effect that I was to stall. Necessity in the form of preoccupation with the concluding phase of the Vietnam negotiation reinforced Nixon's instructions. All I did was to set up a secret channel to Sadat's security adviser; little took place in the channel even after Sadat expelled Soviet military personnel from Egypt in July 1972.[3]

The reason for delay was, in fact, more substantive than political. The Middle East crisis had many components, all of which were traps for the unwary and argued for caution: the Arab-Israeli conflict; the ideological struggle between Arab moderates and radicals; and the influence and rivalry of the superpowers, especially the growing Soviet military role. These ingredients had separate origins but had grown intertwined; a solution to one could not be accomplished without grappling with the others. Creation of the State of Israel with American (and at the time Soviet) support had inflamed Arab nationalism and led to war. Israel established a nation by force of arms and lived thereafter unrecognized, ostracized, and bitterly resented by its neighbors. In June 1967 Israel erupted across the armistice lines after Egypt under Gamal Abdel

Nasser, spurred on by Soviet disinformation, declared a blockade of the Israeli port of Eilat and ominously moved its army into the demilitarized Sinai toward Israel. The war ended in six days with Israel in possession of large areas of Egypt and Syria as well as of the West Bank of the Jordan River, compounding Arab frustration with humiliation.

Israel, never having lived within accepted frontiers, saw no essential difference between locating its boundaries in one unaccepted place and another; condemned to Arab belligerency, it sought the widest imaginable security belt. The Arab countries were torn between their philosophical objection to the existence of the Israeli state and the practical reality that they could not alter the status quo except through some form of diplomacy. Moderate Arab governments like Jordan and (under Nasser ambivalently) Egypt felt their way toward a formula that accepted Israel on its prewar (1967) borders but, pending a settlement of the status of the Arab Palestinians, would grant no more than an end to the state of belligerency — another form of armistice — rather than the full peace that Israel demanded.

And the Palestinian issue was deadlocked by the attitude of the Arab radicals and Israel's perception of its security needs on the West Bank. Syria refused to negotiate for *any* conditions; it objected to Israel's very existence, not its borders. As late as December 1973, when I flew from Tel Aviv to visit Damascus for the first time, the controlled Syrian press reported that the American Secretary of State had arrived from "occupied territory" (that is, Israel). Iraq strenuously added its weight to that of the radicals, as did Libya and Algeria. The Palestine Liberation Organization (PLO), whose claim to represent all Palestinians was not yet recognized by the Arab states, called for the creation of a secular state in Palestine, that is to say, the disappearance of Israel. And Israel came more and more to identify its security with its presence on the West Bank. This impasse blocked Middle East diplomacy for all the years between the wars of 1967 and 1973.

The symbol of the deadlock was United Nations Security Council Resolution 242 of November 22, 1967. It spoke of a "just and lasting peace" within "secure and recognized boundaries" but did not define any of the adjectives. Rejected by some Arab states, interpreted by those that accepted it as well as by Israel to suit their preconceptions, it became more an expression of a stalemate than a means of its resolution. Those Arab leaders willing to negotiate at all construed it to require total Israeli withdrawal to the pre–June 1967 frontiers. Israel professed that none of its prewar borders was secure; it insisted on retaining some of the occupied territory of each of its neighbors. To make doubly sure that its interests were safeguarded, Israel put forward a demand as seemingly reasonable as it was unfulfillable: that the Arab states negotiate directly with it. In other words, Israel asked for recognition as a precon-

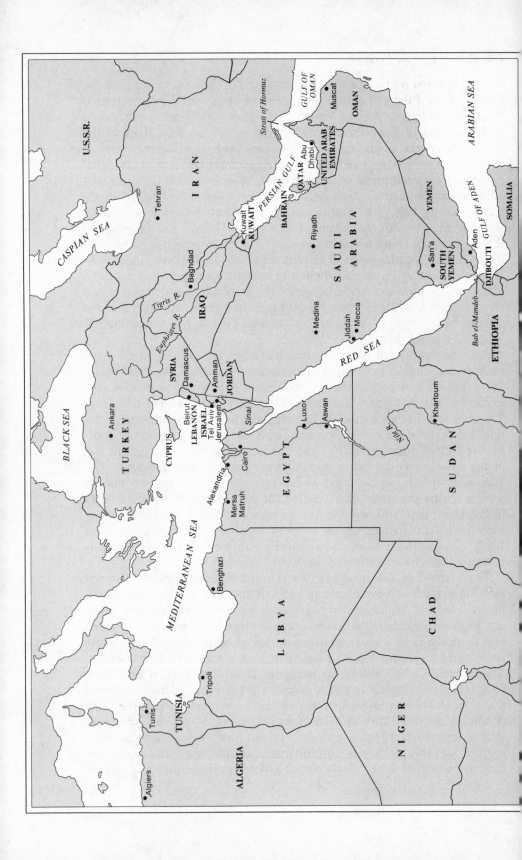

dition of negotiation. The Arabs, not to be outdone, demanded acceptance of their territorial demands before they would consider diplomacy. No Arab leader, however moderate, could accede to Israel's demands and survive in the climate of humiliation, radicalism, and Soviet influence of the period. No Israeli Prime Minister could stay in office for a day if he relinquished the claim to the occupied territories as an entrance price to negotiations. Israel chased the illusion that it could both acquire territory and achieve peace. Its Arab adversaries pursued the opposite illusion, that they could regain territory without offering peace.

Still, at the beginning of Nixon's first term Jordan and Egypt were tentatively feeling their way toward negotiation. King Hussein of Jordan was the most ready of the Arab leaders to accept Israel as a fact of life and to negotiate with it. But it was commonly believed — and he did nothing to discourage the view — that he should follow in the train of some less vulnerable Arab nation. Already the target of the hostility of Arab radicals because he had refused to break diplomatic ties with the United States in 1967 and had expelled the PLO in 1970, the moderate, pro-Western King was thought not strong enough to bear the certain radical assault on the peacemaking process. The conventional wisdom was that Jordan should be the *second* Arab state to make peace.

Thus Egypt became the key to Middle East diplomacy. Tactical necessity reinforced what Egypt had earned by its size, tradition, cultural influence, and sacrifice in a series of Arab-Israeli wars. Egypt was the most populous Arab country, the cultural hub of the area. Its teachers were the backbone of the educational system of the Arab world; its universities attracted students from all over the region. It had the longest continuing history of political organization of any nation, with the possible exception of China. And it had borne the brunt of the Arab-Israeli conflict. As both monarchy and republic, it had engaged itself in a struggle that went beyond narrow Egyptian national interests. It had sacrificed its young men to the cause of Arab unity and of Palestinian self-determination. In the process it had lost the Sinai peninsula and repeatedly risked its national cohesion. Egypt had earned the right to make peace.

For us a first step with Egypt had particular attraction. The territorial issue seemed easier because the Sinai was neither so strategically important to Israel nor so overlaid with historical memories as the other territories, especially the West Bank.

But so long as Nasser was President, he paralyzed Egypt by ambivalence. On the one hand, he indicated a general willingness to participate in the peace process — but his program was unfulfillable. He demanded Israel's withdrawal to the 1967 borders in return for Egyptian nonbelligerency; peace would depend on an Israeli settlement with Palestinians even then demanding the destruction of the Jewish state. Nor would

Nasser negotiate directly with Israel. Rather, *we* should achieve the Israeli withdrawal, in return for which Nasser would confer on us the boon of restored diplomatic relations. In the meantime Cairo Radio remained as the center of anti-American, indeed anti-Western, propaganda throughout the Middle East. In short, Nasser wanted to lead the Arab world from an anti-American position; to present whatever concessions he obtained as having been extorted by Arab militancy, backed by Soviet arms and Soviet diplomatic support. The United States had no interest in vindicating such a course. We were being given the privilege of meeting Nasser's peremptory demands in return for diplomatic relations, which if they meant anything had to be as much in Egypt's interest as in our own, and for a cease-fire with Israel, which already existed de facto.

In the resulting stalemate, the role of the Soviet Union oscillated between the malign and the confused. Its weapons encouraged Arab intransigence. But this achieved no more than to increase the dangers of the deadlock; it could not remove it. Moscow never managed to choose among its dilemmas. So long as it one-sidedly supported all the positions of its clients, it could not advance either the negotiating process or its own role. For we had no motive to support the program of the Arab radicals who were castigating us; in the unlikely event that we would change our view, we did not need the Soviet Union as an intermediary. In other words, Moscow could contribute effectively to a solution only by dissociating itself to some extent from Arab demands and thus jeopardizing some of its friendships in the Arab world. But if it did not do so, it risked backing objectives it could not bring about and thus earning disdain as being impotent. Moscow could stoke the embers of crisis, but once they exploded into conflagration it could use them for its own ends only by risking a great-power confrontation, something from which the Soviet Union had until then carefully shied away. Like the other parties, the Soviet Union temporized. It acted as the Arabs' lawyer but could not advance their case; it bought time through the supply of weapons, but this only escalated the level of possible violence without changing the underlying realities.

The Nixon Administration had confronted this impasse with divided counsel. The State Department was pressing for a diplomatic solution to reduce Arab resentment of the United States. It put forward the Rogers Plan for Israel's return to its previous borders. But it never solved the problem of how to persuade Israel to give up all its conquests when Syria rejected *any* terms and Egypt refused to make peace without Syria or the Palestinians, who were determined to destroy Israel. In these circumstances, diplomatic initiatives tended to exacerbate rather than reduce tensions. Our proposals were likely to fall flat, strengthening the Soviet and radical position. And Nixon considered us too fully engaged in Indochina to throw full White House support behind proposals he considered unrealistic to begin with. A negotiation can succeed only if the minimum terms of each side can be made to coincide. During Nixon's first term, neither side would state anything other than its maximum program — Israel unwilling to forgo wholesale alterations of frontiers, the Arabs demanding total withdrawal and reluctant to undertake significant commitments for peace or, for that matter, security.

On September 28, 1970, Nasser died. His successor, Anwar el-Sadat, was little known and vastly underestimated. Our experts generally believed that he was a transitional figure soon to be replaced by the better known Ali Sabri, Secretary General of the Arab Socialist Union, whom we knew to be close to Moscow. Nor did Sadat early on separate himself in any clear-cut manner from Nasser's course. He began a complicated maneuver strengthening his position in the Arab world while inching Egypt toward a more realistic, nationalist posture. On the one hand, he spoke of the need for a settlement in more urgent and concrete terms than his predecessor; on the other, he used Nasser's anti-Western rhetoric. In May 1971 he purged Ali Sabri and his associates; that same month he signed a twenty-year friendship treaty with the Soviet Union. We in Washington were baffled about his purposes; the gyrations that lulled Moscow about his real intentions also confused us.

To overcome the stalemate, the State Department attempted a new initiative. In March 1971 it put forward a proposal for a limited disengagement of forces along the Suez Canal. This failed because Sadat insisted that disengagement be only the first stage of an agreed total withdrawal. The Israelis, not to be outdone, demanded an equivalent pullback of the Egyptian army from the Suez Canal, suggesting that in return for an Israeli pullback from incontestably Egyptian territory, Egypt's armed forces had to withdraw even deeper into their own country. By 1972 there had been little diplomatic progress. The Soviets were pressing for an immediate overall settlement, the Israelis insisted on direct negotiations, the Egyptians demanded a phased comprehensive solution, the Syrians and PLO refused any negotiation — and the American State Department was pursuing an interim Suez Canal disengagement while the White House acted as if the State Department were a foreign sovereign power.

This welter of confusion ironically suited the strategy that I considered the only realistic American option. There was no American interest in imposing a settlement on Israel under radical pressure, for that would only reinforce the conviction that America was best dealt with by extortion. Within the Arab world we needed to strengthen the moderates as against the radicals, the governments associated with the West as against the clients of the Soviet Union. I therefore opposed, as a matter of principle, any concessions to Egypt so long as Nasser (or Sadat for that matter) relied on anti-Western rhetoric buttressed by the presence of Soviet combat troops. And I saw no point in proceeding jointly with the Soviet Union so long as Moscow's position was identical with the Arab program. Sooner or later, I was convinced, either Egypt or some other state would recognize that reliance on Soviet support and radical rhetoric guaranteed the frustration of its aspirations. At that point, it might be willing to eliminate the Soviet military presence —"expel" was the word I used in a much criticized briefing on June 26, 1970 — and to consider attainable rather than utopian goals. *Then* would come the moment for a major American initiative, if necessary urging new approaches on our Israeli friends.

During his first term Nixon never formally chose between the two strategies: my recommendation of stonewalling radical pressures or State's view of defusing them by offering compromise solutions. He leaned toward my analysis, but he implemented it not by making a decision but by simply letting State Department initiatives run their futile course. My relationship with Nixon, never easy, was in any event more complex with respect to the Middle East than with most other issues. Nixon was convinced that he owed nothing to Jewish votes and that he could not increase his Jewish support regardless of what he did. And what he deep down wanted to do was to impose a comprehensive settlement sometime during his term in office. Many of his comments, written and oral, testify to this visceral attitude. In October 1972, I forwarded to Nixon a memorandum from Secretary of Defense Melvin Laird urging secret contacts with Egypt to take advantage of Sadat's expulsion of the Soviets and to move closer to the Arab position. (Secret contacts with Egypt were already in train, unknown to Laird.) Nixon sent me back the memorandum with a note: "K— I lean to Laird's view. The conduct of the American Jewish community on the Soviet visa problem — clearly indicates they put Jewish interests above US concerns. This we *cannot* do."

Such comments by Nixon were as frequent as he was unlikely to act on them. I mention them here because to omit them would falsify the historical record but also because they illustrate the strange symbiotic relationship between the President and his adviser. Starting from opposite ends of the emotional spectrum with respect to Israel, we came together on policies and strategies because of a similar perception of the national interest. Nixon shared many of the prejudices of the uprooted, California lower-middle class from which he had come. He believed that Jews formed a powerful cohesive group in American society; that they were predominantly liberal; that they put the interests of Israel above everything else; that on the whole they were more sympathetic to the Soviet Union than other ethnic groups; that their control of the media made them dangerous adversaries; above all, that Israel had to be forced into a peace settlement and could not be permitted to jeopardize our Arab relations.

None of this kept him from having cordial personal relations with many individual Jews and from elevating them in his Administration to several key positions. Indeed, personally he sometimes seemed especially at ease with representatives of a group that shared with him the experience of being outsiders.[4] His prejudices would break forth in some of his commands reflecting the emotion of the moment, which his associates knew better than to implement; he never returned to them. I did not keep track of how often I was told to cut off all aid to Israel in retaliation for the actions of some wayward Jewish members of Congress; Senator Jacob Javits seemed to have a special ability to get under Nixon's skin. As late as three days before his resignation he issued such an order. Haig and I decided to draft a directive but to hold it for the new President to sign — or reject. (Ford did the latter.) Equally frequent were instructions to convey some Communist moral transgression to the Jewish leaders, as if Jews needed special instruction in the evils of Communism.

And yet when all was said and done, in every crisis Nixon stood by Israel more firmly than almost any other President save Harry Truman. He admired Israeli guts. He respected Israeli leaders' tenacious defense of their national interest. He considered their military prowess an asset for the democracies. Though convinced that Israel's occupation of Arab territories strengthened anti-Western radical forces, he was sophisticated enough to understand that the reverse was not true: Pressuring Israel in concert with radical forces was more likely to further Soviet than Western interests. And in crises — whatever his calculation of who was ultimately at fault — Nixon never lost sight of his priorities. He understood that we could not mediate effectively until it was clear that our actions had not been extorted by Soviet pressure. Thus at the end of the day — by a different route — Nixon came to the same conclusion as I: that the American national interest required a demonstration of Soviet and radical inability to achieve Arab objectives and that no progress could be made until at least moderate Arabs were willing to make a peace of genuine compromise.

My own starting point was at the other end of the emotional spectrum. Though not practicing my religion, I could never forget that thirteen members of my family had died in Nazi concentration camps. I had no stomach for encouraging another holocaust by well-intentioned policies that might get out of control. Most Israeli leaders were personal friends. And yet, like Nixon, I had to subordinate my emotional preferences to my perception of the national interest. Indeed, given the historical suspicions toward my religion, I had a special obligation to do so. It was not always easy; occasionally it proved painful. But Israel's security could be preserved in the long run only by anchoring it to a strategic interest of the United States, not to the sentiments of individuals. And on this basis that unlikely pair — the Communist-baiter from Southern California and the refugee from Nazi Germany — joined hands to break at last the deadlock of Middle East diplomacy.

Three circumstances in late 1971 and 1972 began to create the partnership between President and security adviser in Middle East diplomacy that already existed in other areas of our national policy. The first, as I have already indicated, was Nixon's desire to avoid a domestic blowup over the Middle East in an election year. Therefore in late 1971 he asked me to undertake secret exchanges with Israel and the Soviet Union on the Middle East to drag matters out through the Presidential election. That delay was inevitable in any event; we had our hands full with summits in Peking and Moscow and Hanoi's spring offensive.

The second event was the Moscow summit of May 1972. The Soviet Union has been justly criticized for its tendency to encourage conflicts, even at the height of détente. But in 1972 its influence in the Middle East was on the whole in the direction of restraint; at least, it was moderating its arms deliveries to Egypt and doing little more than going through the motions in diplomatic exchanges about Middle East peace. Sadat complained constantly of Soviet procrastination in the supply of arms.[5] The culmination was Foreign Minister Andrei Gromyko's agreement at the Moscow summit to a paragraph in the final communiqué so anodyne that it permitted no other interpretation than that Moscow was putting the Middle East on ice. Showing the exhaustion of long hours of talks, Gromyko also agreed to a set of "general working principles" to guide Middle East negotiations, which represented perplexing concessions to our point of view (for example, a clause that seemed to agree to border changes in favor of Israel).[6]

To be sure, Moscow in mid-1972 had good reasons of its own for not rocking the Middle East boat. It desperately needed to purchase American grain. It may have calculated that to add a Middle East crisis to the war in Vietnam might shred the gossamer fabric of East-West relations. It never could square the circle that its clients stood to lose any war resulting from pushing tensions beyond a certain point. But that is only another way of saying that the Soviets were willing to pay *some* price for détente.

That, in any event, was the perception of Anwar Sadat, and it led to the third seminal event of the period: the expulsion of Soviet troops from Egypt. For Sadat, the Moscow summit communiqué was the last straw. This apparent Soviet collusion with the United States came as a "violent shock" to Egypt, he records in his memoirs. He would not accept, he said in a speech at the time, seeing the Middle East as only the fourth or fifth priority of Soviet policy.[7] And so with one of the bold maneuvers that later became his trademark, he demanded on July 18, 1972, the withdrawal of Soviet military personnel from Egypt within a week. The move had a dual purpose: It removed an impediment to an Egyptian attack on Israel, for Sadat was convinced, probably rightly, that his Soviet advisers would not cooperate in initiating military operations. At the same time it made possible diplomatic overtures to the United States. Before the month was out he had reactivated the direct channel to the White House. The backchannel system had come to the Middle East.

During the fall of 1972, Cairo and the White House attempted to arrange a secret meeting between me and Hafiz Ismail, Sadat's national security adviser. A date was set for late October but postponed because the Vietnam negotiations took all our time and nervous energy.

Despite these delays, by the end of Nixon's first term we were approaching the fruition of our preferred strategy. The Soviet military presence was being eliminated from Egypt. Sadat was moving toward us, and though we could not yet discern his full design, it clearly would differ from the radical blackmail of his predecessor. The Soviet leaders were rattled, at a loss as to how to recapture their waning influence. For the time being, they confined themselves to ritualistic platitudes underlining their growing irrelevance. Time was working in our favor; nothing could happen without our cooperation; those who relied on Soviet support were bound to become progressively disillusioned. The way to an increased and more balanced American role was beginning to open.

Preparing for Ismail: A Diplomatic Minuet

APPEARANCE and reality rarely mesh in the Middle East. The situation on the ground in early 1973 showed no sign of the strategic shift that was in train. After Palestinian terrorists murdered Israeli athletes at the Munich Olympics in September 1972, Israel retaliated with a series of raids in Syria and Lebanon, and the cycle of violence escalated to a new high. The Arab nations moved to consolidate their common front against Israel. In late January 1973, eighteen Arab foreign and defense ministers convened in Cairo as the Arab Joint Defense Council and appointed Egyptian War Minister Marshal Ahmed Ismail Ali as commander-in-chief of the Jordanian, Syrian, and Egyptian fronts. The Arab ministers also agreed, with Jordanian consent, to "reactivate" the Jordanian front. (What that meant was far from clear because the Jordanians simultaneously announced that they stuck by their policy not to permit fedayeen to return to Jordan for operations against Israel. The practical result of these two decisions was that they canceled each other out — a not infrequent occurrence at Arab foreign ministers' meetings.)[8]

On February 11, 1973, Egyptian Premier Dr. Aziz Sidqi announced that Egypt was scrapping some domestic programs to free funds for the "battle with Israel." A "war budget" would be formulated. In the light of previous Egyptian threats that had not been carried out, we did not take this too seriously, especially as our intelligence estimates agreed in being unable to define a realistic Egyptian military option. Indeed, in the Arab world Sadat came under continuing attack for alleged do-nothing policies — demonstrating that none of the parties involved understood his intricate design.

For Sadat was moving toward war, using an extraordinary tactic that no one fathomed: If a leader announces his real intentions sufficiently frequently and grandiloquently, no one will believe him. Sadat had first declared 1971 as the "year of decision." We had believed him. In fact, one reason we had reacted so neuralgically to the Indian attack on Pakistan was to discourage a comparable incitement of Egyptian ambitions. Whether for that reason or his own, Sadat made no military move that year or in 1972. Ominous threats continued to issue from Cairo, but as of December 20, 1972, our assessment was that Sadat had few, if any, military options. Israel's military superiority appeared unchallengeable. Sadat could not escape his dilemmas by launching an all-out military offensive since it was bound to fail. Though the assessment granted that Sadat was capable of a limited attack, there seemed no rational military purpose for it. It too would be defeated; hence its sole function would be to heat up international concern and pressure for negotiation. Its failure would only deepen the diplomatic stalemate. Even should negotiations develop, it was expected that other complexities would follow: A cease-fire based on mere disengagement of forces along the Suez Canal would find no support in Egypt; yet full peace seemed precluded because Israel would not accept a comprehensive settlement based on the 1967 frontiers, and the other Arab states would block any separate Egyptian settlement. Thus it would follow that Egypt had no choice but to await the American diplomatic initiative.

But Sadat was not bound by our estimates. While we were preparing a new diplomatic approach, he was seeking for military ways to break the deadlock.

As the second term began, Nixon was pushing me deeper and deeper into Middle East negotiations but without revoking the authority he had given to the State Department. Whenever he met a Middle East leader, he avoided a clear-cut position by suggesting exploratory talks with me — a great way to get through an hour, though it risked chaos. Since Nixon did not withdraw the negotiating authority he had earlier assigned to Rogers, three parallel diplomatic tracks were developing: the formal State Department track aiming at an interim disengagement along the Suez Canal; my secret channel with Hafiz Ismail, in which I had agreed to take up as yet undefined Egyptian proposals when we finally arranged our secret meeting; and my special Channel with Soviet Ambassador Anatoly Dobrynin on the possibility of joint Soviet-American approaches to the Middle East. To provide a semblance of coherence, I sought to delay any new State Department initiatives in the second term and stall Soviet overtures until I could determine in the meeting with Hafiz Ismail what the Egyptians had in mind. This was no easy matter since I was the only person aware of all three tracks, and the State Department was being stonewalled for no discernible reason. Such a method of government could not have been sustained through another full term, regardless of Watergate.

The first off the mark, as usual in Middle East diplomacy, was the State Department. Between 1969 and 1971 its various schemes for a comprehensive solution had united both sides in opposition to American proposals. The Department now decided to throw itself anew into the quest for an interim disengagement along the Suez Canal with the method that had so spectacularly failed during the first term: launching an approach without having fully explored its feasibility with either of the parties.

To prove that two could play at the multitrack system, the Department on January 22, 1973 — only two days after Inauguration — sent instructions to Joseph N. Greene, Jr., the head of our Interests Section* in Cairo, without clearing them with the White House. (I cannot know, of course, whether Rogers had discussed them privately with Nixon.) Undeterred by Sadat's public rejection of a similar interim Canal agreement in September 1972, State now told Greene to put forward essentially the same proposal as "the only proposition in sight that offers [the] prospect of real progress at [the] present time."

As was inevitable — because Sadat wanted to await the outcome of Ismail's talks with me — Egypt rejected the approach. On January 27 Ismail told Greene that Egypt was not interested in an interim settlement, though it might be prepared to talk about an "opening phase" of a "comprehensive" process. This had been a nonstarter in 1971, for if Israel had been ready to agree to the 1967 borders, it did not need an interim settlement. While he was at it, Ismail enumerated Egypt's complaints about one-sided American support for Israel. On the one hand, Egypt would settle on the basis of what it considered just to the Arab

---

*When formal diplomatic relations are broken, sometimes a small diplomatic mission may be permitted to remain, technically as part of the embassy of some third country that is authorized to look after the interests of the country no longer formally represented. Thus in Cairo from 1967 to 1973 there was a small "US Interests Section" — in fact staffed by American diplomats — under the aegis of the Spanish Embassy. An Interests Section is usually, but not invariably, staffed by less senior personnel. But it can facilitate communications with the host government and even conduct negotiations in some instances.

people and would let no other nation veto it; on the other hand, it would make no separate peace. Ismail did not explain to Greene how he proposed to reconcile these propositions. It would be interesting to know what went on in his mind because our weird governmental procedures had put him into the position of dealing with two American representatives, neither of whom knew of the approach of the other.

Ismail played both channels for what they were worth. In the secret channel, he sought to bring subtle pressure by reminding us that he was about to embark on a long-scheduled round of talks with the Soviet Union in early February — implying that Egypt might take irrevocable steps if we did not set a date for a meeting. I replied that a secret meeting between us was impossible before the Vietnam negotiations were completed, but I invited "any preliminary views from the Egyptian side through this channel." Ismail did not take the bait. Instead, he informed me that he would be visiting London at the end of February; a meeting there would be highly convenient. Unfortunately, I was planning to leave for Hanoi and Peking; I had no pretext for going to London at the proposed time. Taking up an Egyptian suggestion for prior staff-level talks to arrange our meeting, I sent an emissary to Cairo to explain to Ismail the facts of our bureaucratic life. There was a limit to the secret trips I could take, especially after my role in various negotiations had become known and the press started following my movements.* And if I went publicly, the British government would have to be involved and a cover story would have to be invented to keep our bureaucracy out of the act.

Egyptians have undoubtedly witnessed many cultural peculiarities of foreigners in their history stretching over thousands of years, and little surprises them. In fact, when something is highly complicated and slightly devious, it immediately gains validity in Egyptian eyes. Ismail went to work with a will and after several exchanges we finally settled on a procedure acceptable to all and miraculously involving all interested bureaucratic parties: Ismail would be invited by the State Department for an official visit to Washington on February 23, 1973; he would be received by Nixon and would meet with officials at State. Then, his official program completed, he would betake himself on February 25 to New York. From there he would proceed to a secret meeting site in the suburbs — a private home hired for the purpose — where he and I would confer for two days for a full, private review of Egyptian-American relations.

So it happened that an astonished Jerry Greene in Cairo was suddenly instructed in normal channels to extend a formal invitation to Hafiz Is-

---

*After my secret trip to Moscow in April 1972, I did not, in fact, undertake any more secret missions abroad.

mail to visit Washington. The State Department could only ascribe to the inexplicable vacillations of the White House the fact that contacts conducted at arm's length for five years should suddenly turn into such an ostentatious embrace. As for Ismail, he would be exposed to our dual-track system right at the source, for neither I nor any member of my staff was included in the State Department sessions, while the State Department did not even know of my secret meeting with Ismail. It was not the best way to project unity of purpose. But it demonstrated to the Egyptians at least that we too could be Levantine without even half trying.

Cairo maneuvered not only within our bureaucracy but among the superpower rivals for Mideast preeminence. To strengthen Egypt's hand for the forthcoming talks in Washington, Hafiz Ismail and then War Minister Marshal Ali visited Moscow in February 1973. The Kremlin found itself in an uncomfortable position. The Soviet leaders realized that they had paid a heavy price for the insouciance with which they had treated Egypt's concerns at the Moscow summit in 1972. But they also knew that if they pressed for solutions unacceptable to Israel they would demonstrate their impotence (thus playing into our strategy), while if they forced the issue militarily they would bring about an Arab defeat. (Their estimate of Arab fighting capabilities was, judging by their cynical comments to us, extremely low.)

Subtlety is not a Soviet forte. They dealt with their dilemmas by mixing — perhaps unintentionally — an explosive brew. The Soviets seem to have repeated to Ismail their opposition to an interim settlement; their reasoning was undoubtedly that any agreement under our aegis would weaken Soviet influence. But while objectively heightening tension, they also appear to have warned against a conflict that might involve the risk of a Soviet war with the United States. This seemed to imply that short of that threshold, Egypt was free to consult its own interests — which left open the possibility of a limited war against Israel. The Soviet leaders soon afterward agreed to the largest arms package ever negotiated for the Middle East. The Soviet Union may have seen in this strange half-policy — of acquiescing in a limited but not an all-out attack — the safest means of procrastination; in fact, it tempted an explosion that it did not have the ability to contain. It encouraged a crisis that it thought it could exploit by appearing as the spokesman for Arab interests. But it lacked the capacity to shape what it had wrought. In the end, the Soviet effort caused it to lose everything in Egypt, proving that futile half-measures are not a monopoly of the bourgeois West.

A backchannel message came from Brezhnev to Nixon on February 18 informing us of what had transpired during Ismail's visit to Moscow. According to the Soviet message there could be a phased settlement, but it must be "within a framework of a single plan (in package), so that all elements of the settlement are coordinated and balanced among themselves. . . .'' Further, "there can be no separate Israeli-Egyptian settlement independent from the settlement between Israel and other Arab countries involved in the conflict." Finally, Brezhnev wrote, "we have got an impression from our talks with Mr. Ismail that, if at this time also no progress is reached towards political solution of this vital . . . problem, the Arabs can turn to the use of other possible means of its solution. . . .'' Having thrown the switches toward confrontation, the Soviets demonstrated characteristic insolence in warning us of what they themselves had encouraged.

In short, the Soviets were putting forward, under the threat of war, an intransigent Arab program certain to lead to deadlock or confrontation. By opposing both an interim agreement and a separate Israeli-Egyptian settlement, Moscow was objectively encouraging a blowup. The Kremlin may have calculated that a crisis would force the United States to engage itself. But excessive cleverness rarely pays in diplomacy. Moscow's dilemma was that it could contribute to a settlement only by urging its Arab clients to compromise. Unwilling to do this, it both encouraged a blowup and recoiled from its consequences, condemning itself eventually to a seat on the sidelines.

Ismail in Washington

WHEN Hafiz Ismail arrived in Washington for his visit on February 23, 1973, we knew astonishingly little of Egypt's real thinking. We considered the secret contacts a hopeful sign. But this had to be balanced against the frequent Egyptian consultations with Moscow and the continuing bellicosity of Egyptian propaganda. The expulsion of the Soviet forces was important. But we could not exclude that part of the reason might be Sadat's desire to gain a free hand for military initiatives. For all we knew, Sadat was pursuing a slightly more benign version of the Nasser strategy: to get *us* to deliver the maximum Arab program for concessions that could later be vetoed by the Palestinians, who were in turn heavily influenced by the Soviets. It was hard to be clear about exactly what Sadat wanted; perhaps he had not yet fully made up his mind.

For Sadat, too, was in the same box as other parties — perhaps, being more visionary, even more frustratingly so. He knew that the boilerplate program of Arab irredentism was doomed, but that deviation from it might bring him isolation in the Arab world without any assurance of Israeli acceptance. Indeed, judging by Israeli public statements, a settlement would require ceding some Egyptian territory, which Sadat would never accept. He was wise enough to know that peace would require Arab concessions; but these would be nearly impossible in the climate of frustration and humiliation growing out of the 1967 defeat. This is why he cooled on the idea of an interim settlement at that point, for he feared it would be ascribed to weakness and not statesmanship. It was to discuss a way out of these dilemmas that Ismail had come to Washington.

Nixon was prepared to engage the United States diplomatically, in an exploratory way now and fully after the Israeli election scheduled in October. But we would not be able to make any progress if we left illusions that we would be able to deliver any neat package, or that the whole process could simply be dumped into our lap. We could not agree to impose a peace. In suggested "talking points" (which Nixon marked "OK") I urged Nixon to define these limits to Ismail:

My [Nixon's] course in Vietnam also showed, however, that we do not betray our friends. A great power does not enhance its power by behaving in such a way. There are severe limits to what we can compel Israel to do. . . .

Egypt must have no illusions. It cannot achieve its maximum demands in any settlement that is conceivable. In the absence of a settlement, on the other hand, Egypt has little prospect of ever recovering anything. This is not our doing; this is the reality as we perceive it. Both Egypt and Israel will have difficult decisions to make.

In other words, we were prepared to urge Israel to make concessions but this required flexibility on the Egyptian side as well. My memorandum, in any event, triggered all of Nixon's ambivalences. In it I had described three options: first, to "stand back and let the two sides reflect further on their position"; second, to seek an interim agreement; or third, to work privately toward an agreement on the general principles of an overall settlement.

Nixon would hear nothing of the first option — to stand back — prophetically noting in the margin next to it that inactivity would lead to war:

K — Absolutely not. [Ambassador Yitzhak] Rabin must be told this categorically before I see her [Golda Meir]. I have delayed through two elections and this year I am determined to move off dead center — I totally disagree. This thing is getting ready to blow.

Nixon made no comment on the second option (an interim agreement). He favored the third option: secret talks aiming at an overall settlement. He wrote: "The preferred track for action. At the same time keep the public track going for external appearances — but keep it from interfering with the private track." In other words, the classic pattern of the first term: a public negotiation as a cover for a private one. It did not, however, fit the volatile Middle East. Nixon did not favor me with a hint as to how I might accomplish the feat of a "public track" consisting of State's scheme for an interim partial settlement which was an alternative to and in a sense incompatible with negotiation of an overall settlement.

The vehemence of Nixon's marginal comments revealed how strongly he felt about the need to move forward. At the end of my memorandum he appended another note:

> K — you know my position of standing firmly with Israel has been based on broader issues than just Israel's survival — Those issues now strongly argue for movement toward a settlement. We are now Israel's *only* major friend in the world. I have yet to see *one iota* of give on their part — conceding that Jordan and Egypt have not given enough on their side. This is the time to get moving — and they must be told that *firmly.* . . . .
>
> [T]he time has come to quit pandering to Israel's intransigent position. Our actions over the past have led them to think we will stand with them *regardless* of how unreasonable they are.

In this atmosphere, Mohammed Hafiz Ismail had his first exposure to the many layers of the American government. Within the space of forty-eight hours he would encounter the American President uttering generalities, the State Department pushing an interim agreement without White House backing, and Nixon's national security adviser discussing principles of an overall settlement at a secret meeting without State Department participation. Ismail moved through this thicket with extraordinary aplomb. Tall, erect, and with thinning gray hair, he had the bearing of the military officer he once was and the natural dignity of the educated Egyptian. For four millennia the peoples of Egypt have witnessed the foibles of eager foreigners and achieved a margin of maneuver by being conciliatory, impermeable, supple, and infinitely resilient. Through all the changes of racial composition brought by successive waves of conquerors, an archetypical Egyptian has survived, his face etched on the statues and temples that are the closest any nation has come to achieving eternity — an expression at once gentle and transcendent; a posture at once humble and enduring; a look both human and yet gazing into an infinity beyond the limitations of the human scale.

Hafiz Ismail was of this mold. I met with him twice in 1973; after the October war he stepped aside in one of Sadat's periodic personnel reshuffles. He did not show much flexibility, but then Egypt's position before the war did not allow it. He presented Egypt's maximum program in a manner so conciliatory that he appeared more pliable than he really was. He was so courteous that he obscured Sadat's basic strategy, which was to elaborate the conditions for a showdown. He did not achieve a breakthrough, which we had thought was his purpose, but he skillfully served Sadat's aim of maintaining a deadlock without creating the warning of a crisis.

Ismail's first appointment was with Nixon at 11:20 A.M. on Friday, February 23. As was his custom, Nixon expressed himself face to face with Ismail much more elliptically than in his marginal comments to me. Ismail handed the President a message from Sadat, the polite phrasing of which contained a threat backing up a request for an overall settlement: "Circumstances lend themselves now to exerting further efforts to achieve a full and just settlement"; otherwise, "the situation in our region has deteriorated almost to the point of explosion." Nixon regretted that progress had not been made in the past but said that the "important thing" was to "see where we stand to explore the possibilities that there might be some movement which could take place."

Ismail's presentation followed the same theme as his President's letter. The thirty-month-old cease-fire was not an end in itself, he avowed, for its practical consequence was to confirm Israel's conquests. Indeed, the cease-fire had to be ended by going either forward toward peace or back toward war. Two issues required resolution: Israel's occupation of Egyptian territory and the Palestinian problem, which was the "core" issue. If Israel agreed to withdraw from Egyptian territory, Cairo was prepared to discuss security guarantees and an end of belligerency; final peace between Egypt and Israel would require a solution acceptable to the Palestinians. Nothing was said of Syria.

Nixon, always uncomfortable with detailed negotiation, used my scheduled secret talks with Ismail as a device to avoid a clear-cut reply. Indeed, he pushed a program somewhat at variance from his marginal note to me. To my astonishment, he seemed to favor an interim Suez Canal settlement after all. He understood Egypt's fear that an interim solution might become frozen, he said. Still, it had the advantage of feasibility; hence Ismail should explore it with me as a bridge to further steps. We favored a permanent settlement, Nixon averred, and he pledged his best efforts in that direction. But he did not think it possible to solve the entire Middle East problem in all its aspects all at once. That, too, should be explored by Ismail and me, though in strictest privacy.

Having thus been given the task of achieving simultaneously an interim and a comprehensive settlement, an exploratory conversation and a final one, Ismail and I repaired to the outskirts of New York City for two days of talks on February 25 and 26. We had acquired for the occasion an elegant house in the sylvan setting of a middle-class suburban area. We held formal meetings across the dining room table and chatted informally in the living room, sharing a lunch on the second day.*

---

*Ismail was accompanied by Dr. Muhammad Hafiz Ghanim of the Central Committee of the Arab Socialist Union; Dr. Abd al-Hadi Makhluf, Ismail's Office Director, and two aides, Ahmad

Coherence in our government had by now disintegrated to the point where only Ismail knew what all of its elements were thinking. State was not even aware that I was meeting with the Egyptians. I was not immediately informed about Ismail's conversations with Rogers; only much later did a report reach the White House.

The opening of a complicated negotiation is like the beginning of an arranged marriage. The partners know that the formalities will soon be stripped away as they discover each other's real attributes. Neither party can yet foretell at what point necessity will transform itself into acceptance; when the abstract desire for progress will leave at least residues of understanding; which disagreement will, by the act of being overcome, illuminate the as-yet undiscovered sense of community and which will lead to an impasse destined to rend the relationship forever. The future being mercifully veiled, the parties attempt what they might not dare did they know what was ahead.

Almost invariably I spent the first session of a new negotiation in educating myself. I almost never put forward a proposal. Rather, I sought to understand the intangibles in the position of my interlocutor and to gauge the scope as well as the limits of probable concessions. And I made a considerable effort to leave no doubt about our fundamental approach. Only romantics think they can prevail in negotiations by trickery; only pedants believe in the advantage of obfuscation. In a society of sovereign states, an agreement will be maintained only if *all* partners consider it in their interest. They must have a sense of participation in the result. The art of diplomacy is not to outsmart the other side but to convince it either of common interests or of penalties if an impasse continues.

So it was this time. I began by explaining to Ismail the strange ways of our government. We had a two-channel system, which indeed Egypt had used by contacting the White House directly. This could work only if both sides acted in a manner wholly aboveboard. If Cairo sought to manipulate us by playing off one channel against the other, it could no doubt cause us embarrassment but only at the price of guaranteeing itself a deadlock. This was the tactical problem. The deeper challenge was to establish a basis of confidence. I invited Ismail to "tell me candidly what you think and feel." We had to find a concept before we drew up proposals:

There is no sense doing anything — drawing maps, and so on, unless we know exactly what we want to accomplish, unless we have some idea of what is doable. Otherwise we will just be buying ourselves three months of good will, and great distrust afterwards. You must have the sense that when you deal with

---

Mahir al-Sayyid and Dr. Ihab Said Wahba. I brought my NSC staff colleagues Harold Saunders and Peter Rodman, with Bonnie Andrews as note-taker.

the White House, our word counts. I would rather tell you honestly we can't do something than to tell you something we can do and later we would not deliver. . . .

When Hafiz Ismail and I met in suburban New York, we were far from that level of confidence. Indeed, he had come less to discuss mediation — and therefore compromise — than to put forward a polite ultimatum for terms beyond our capacity to fulfill. Spelling out what he had told Nixon, Ismail now argued that a settlement had to take place during 1973; at a minimum he hoped he could achieve by September an agreement on fundamental principles ("heads of agreement"). He never clearly explained what he understood by that or what would happen if such an agreement was not reached by the deadline. Ismail rejected an interim accord — a Suez Canal disengagement — except as part of an agreed comprehensive plan that was to be implemented in stages over a brief period of time, in which case it was of course nearly irrelevant. Above all, Israel had to agree, before anything else happened, that it would return to its 1967 borders with *all* neighbors, with some margin for adjustment, perhaps, on the West Bank. Only on that basis would Egypt join the negotiating process, and then only to discuss security arrangements. These could include, for example, demilitarized zones, which for reasons of prestige and equity should be established on *both* sides of the international border; international supervisory teams could function at strategic points like Sharm el-Sheikh at the tip of the Sinai. In return, Egypt would end the state of war with Israel — but not yet establish "full peace." It would open international waterways to Israeli ships and end hostile propaganda and the boycott of foreign companies trading with Israel; but it would not agree to full diplomatic relations or open borders. *That* degree of "full peace," or "normalization," would have to await a comprehensive settlement with *all* the other parties, including Syria and the Palestinians.

The same principle of total withdrawal, coupled with security measures, would have to apply to the Golan Heights. Ismail was more flexible with respect to the West Bank: There could be negotiations either with King Hussein or with some undefined group of Palestinian leaders. Egypt would accept any outcome agreeable to the parties, even along the lines of the so-called Allon Plan, which called for Israeli military outposts along the Jordan River. There were, however, two caveats: Arab control of East Jerusalem was essential and nonnegotiable. And Egypt reserved the right to express its view as to who should ultimately govern on the West Bank if Jordan negotiated a settlement — a hint of the growing influence of the PLO. This was ominous both for Hussein and for Israel. It meant that Hussein might be used to extract territory from Israel but not be able to retain it. And for Israel, negotiations with

Hussein were thus becoming only the admission price to confrontation with its mortal enemy, the PLO, still committed to its destruction. The only hint of flexibility was Ismail's statement that Egypt would not insist that the various negotiations be completed simultaneously. Cairo was prepared to work out an Israeli-Egyptian agreement as a first installment, but it would not sign it unless the Syrian and Jordanian negotiations were in train and it would not establish full peace until those negotiations were in fact completed.

This was far-reaching but one-sided and not essentially different from what had produced the deadlock. The price paid for the return to the prewar borders would be not peace but the end of belligerency, not easy to distinguish from the existing cease-fire. Formal peace would come only after the Syrians and Palestinians had settled in an extremely cloudy procedure — giving the most intractable parties a veto, in effect, over the whole process.

Hoping that further exploration might reveal prospects not apparent at first hearing, I asked clarifying questions, one of which hid a substantive suggestion: Would Egypt be prepared to separate the questions of sovereignty and security? If Israel accepted Egypt's sovereignty to the 1967 borders, would Egypt permit some Israeli defensive positions to remain on its soil? Ismail was noncommittal, clearly not overwhelmed by an idea of which I had been prematurely proud.[9] And so the talks with Hafiz Ismail ended.

They left us with little reason for optimism. The hint of a separate Egyptian-Israeli accord was so heavily qualified with unacceptable conditions that it was more compatible with a come-on to get us involved than with a serious effort to negotiate. We needed more time to determine what Sadat had in mind. Ismail and I promised to meet again after a few months.

In the meantime, we reviewed the bidding with King Hussein and Prime Minister Meir.

Hussein

Two conversations with our longtime ally King Hussein bracketed the meeting with Ismail. The first meeting was on February 6.

The King governed one of those states whose arbitrary frontiers reflected less the results of history or the necessities of geography than the spheres of influence established by France and Britain upon the conclusion of World War I. Created as a buffer between the French mandate in Syria, the British protectorate in Iraq — both historic founts of Arab nationalism — and the British Mandate of Palestine, it was tossed into an unpromising desert as a weight in a balance conceived and manipulated by distant powers. It was a testimony to the wisdom of the only two monarchs Jordan has known — Hussein and his grandfather, Abdullah — that they managed to wrest both independence and dignity from the initial disdain of Arab nationalists and the self-confident domination of the imperial power. They did so, moreover, at a time when the nationalist movements were aimed as much at the ruling monarchies as at the European colonial countries. The Hashemite kings were forced into a precarious balancing act. They needed outside support against radical pressures, especially as these increasingly were bolstered by other Arab states and by the growing Soviet power. But they did not behave as the surrogates of foreigners. Rather they strove for, and succeeded in articulating, a form of Arab nationalism that asserted an Arab identity while affirming friendship for the West, seeking to demonstrate that Arab aspirations could be fulfilled through moderation.

The creation of the state of Israel added a new dimension of special volatility for Jordan. Its rulers were drawn into asserting Jordanian sovereignty over the West Bank of the Jordan River; thus they inherited the passions of the Palestinians and a guaranteed admission to the main arena of Arab-Israeli confrontation. Though no happier about the new Jewish state than their Arab brethren, the Hashemite monarchs recognized the impossibility of destroying it and were the first to explore the possibilities of coexistence, an effort that cost King Abdullah his life to an assassin in 1951. For the next fifteen years Hussein joined his Arab colleagues in refusing to recognize Israel, always uneasily conscious that the radical forces in Egypt, Syria, and Iraq sought his downfall as surely as the destruction of Israel and perhaps as a first step toward that goal. He jealously guarded his independence while relying on Western support; in 1956 he expelled the British officers training and in some respects commanding his army. And yet when a radical wave threatened to engulf the Middle East following the revolution in Iraq in 1958, American forces landed in Lebanon and British forces entered Jordan for a few weeks.

Nearly ten years later, in 1967, Jordan was engulfed by the Six Day War. Though Nasser had treated the kingdom with aloof disdain, Hussein carried out his high conception of the requirements of Arab solidarity and entered a war that Nasser had already lost. The result was that Jordan was driven out of the West Bank and the Old City of Jerusalem. Jordan's involvement in the peace process thereafter only complicated its already precarious existence. For Hussein was caught between the passions of his Arab brethren and his own realism, for which he paid the price of several radical attempts on his life; and he was trapped in the paradox that he was the Arab leader most ready to make peace, yet of all the territories it had conquered Israel was most reluctant to relinquish the Jordanian portion, which it most intimately connected with its own traditions. Israel's fundamental demand for direct negotiations was in fact granted by Hussein, yet it did not speed a settlement. And so Jordan remained suspended between contending forces. It made an enormous sacrifice for Arab nationalism, but it was assailed by the radicals then dominating the nationalist movement. In 1970 it was driven to suppress the Palestinian guerrillas creating a state within a state on Jordanian territory, and yet did so while retaining its Arab vocation. It had grievances against Israel but did not want to engulf the area in a new conflict that might destroy those vestiges of moderation that were the essence of Hashemite rule.

Hussein's mastery of this challenge stamped him as a formidable personality. His legendary courtesy, which the uninitiated took for pliability, was a marvelous way to keep all the contending forces at arm's length. He was imperiled by the intransigence of Israel, the embrace of the West, the hegemonic aspirations of Egypt, and the revolutionary fervor of Syria and Iraq. He emerged as his own man. Hussein did not take refuge in blaming America for the humiliation of 1967. He did not break relations with us, as did several other Arab states, but he maintained his insistence on a solution just to the Arab cause — even the cause of those who sought to bring him down.

On the occasion of his first visit to Washington since Egypt's expulsion of Soviet personnel, Hussein did not share the general complacency about that event. He suspected — as it turned out correctly — that one of Sadat's motives had been to free himself of the Soviet reluctance to support military action. At the same time, according to Hussein, the Soviet setback was likely to produce three dangerous consequences in Soviet policy. The Soviets would increase their arms aid to Egypt to protect what was left of their position in Cairo. Second, they would stake out a rigid position insisting on a comprehensive settlement so as to complicate any Egyptian temptations toward separate arrangements — this explained why Gromyko had been so hostile to an interim agreement during the fall of 1972. Third, they would continue pouring arms into Syria to prevent it from following Cairo's example and to make it the new spearhead of Soviet policy in the area.

Hussein's gloomy prognosis was not confined to the Arab-Israeli conflict. He also warned about Soviet ambitions in the Persian Gulf, represented by Iraq, which, heavily armed with Soviet weapons, would work against all moderate governments in the area even if the regime in Baghdad continued to have its own differences with the Soviet Union. He offered Jordanian forces to help stabilize the Arab emirates in the lower Gulf. Our bureaucracy complacently haggled over the trivial aid sums involved to support such a policy; it took a White House order to break that bureaucratic logjam.

Hussein repeated his willingness to make peace with Israel. But despite secret contacts he faced an impasse. Hussein symbolized the fate of Arab moderates. He was caught between his inability to sustain a war with Israel and his unwillingness to make common cause with the radicals. He was prepared for a diplomatic solution, even a generous one, but Israel saw no incentive for negotiations so long as Hussein stood alone. Any return of conquered territories seemed to it less secure than the status quo. And the West Bank with its historic legacy would unleash violent domestic controversy in Israel — the National Religious Party, without which the governing coalition could not rule, was adamantly opposed to the return of *any* part of the West Bank.

We asked Hussein to come up with a plan suitable for negotiation. He promised to review one with us when he returned to Washington in two weeks after a vacation in Florida.

The February 6 meeting with Hussein was my first direct exposure to what turned out to be a tragedy for the peace process in the Middle East: the personal distrust between Sadat and Hussein. Sadat quite simply did not like Hussein, or royalty for that matter. At this early stage of his complicated diplomacy, Sadat needed the Palestinians, or thought he did, to burnish his Arab credentials. To back a negotiation with Hussein might alienate the Arab radicals, especially Syria, whose support was essential if the military option was to be maintained. Sadat therefore dealt with Hussein at arm's length, thus preventing the emergence of the one spokesman with whom Israel might have successfully negotiated over the West Bank. Hussein, on the other hand, was profoundly mistrustful of Egypt, fearing that Sadat's volatility might do harm to Jordan as had Nasser's. The pity was that these two moderate leaders failed to give each other the support that might have speeded up Middle East diplomacy; they wound up in an impasse from which the sole exit was war.

I cannot say that all these crosscurrents were as clear to me at the time as they became later. But no great subtlety was needed to discover His Majesty's profound distrust for the Egyptian approach when he returned to Washington on February 27 and I briefed him on the meetings with Ismail. Hussein and his principal adviser, Zaid Rifai, later Prime Minister, did not see anything new in the Egyptian proposals, which had been staples of Egyptian diplomacy for years; they recommended that we draw Cairo out to bring about greater precision. But our Jordanian friends considered it crucial to keep the Soviets out of the process. We thus had had two hints of separate approaches from two Arab leaders whose mutual suspicions kept them from combining. Sadat was using the Palestinians to gain a veto over Jordanian actions, while Hussein invoked our fear of Soviet intransigence to slow down a separate peace by Egypt.

Hussein, alone among the Arab leaders at that time, was prepared to be specific about peace terms. He gave me a paper that spelled out the elements he had described to Nixon and me a few weeks earlier. Jordan would negotiate directly with Israel about the West Bank. There would be some border changes provided the Gaza Strip was given in return. If Jordanian sovereignty was restored, there could be Israeli military outposts along the Jordan River or even Israeli settlements, provided they were isolated enclaves on Jordanian territory; he could not agree to the annexation of the Jordan Valley by Israel. Wryly the King said that all these proposals had already been made directly to Israel and been rejected. What was needed was an American proposal, not another Jordanian one. Perhaps, he said, two or three years were available for the peace process before the area exploded. It was his one misassessment. Unfortunately, it was crucial, because it lulled us by confirming our existing predilection for waiting for the outcome of the Israeli election on October 30.

Golda Meir

OUR next visitor, Israeli Prime Minister Golda Meir, did not share Hussein's sense of urgency. At an appointment with Nixon on March 1 she proclaimed that "we never had it so good" and insisted that a stalemate was safe because the Arabs had no military option. Golda Meir was an original. Shrewd, earthy, elemental, she felt herself to be the mother of her people. To her every square inch of the territory of Israel had been nourished by the blood of her children. She had seen too much of the human character to rely on such intangible and reversible assurances as recognition of Israel's existence. She knew only too well that recognition of their existence is where the security problem of all other nations begins, not ends.

Golda had come to Israel as a young pioneer. The idea of returning territory was almost physically painful to her. She demanded ironclad guarantees of security in return, and it was hard to imagine what guarantees she could possibly consider more secure than physical possession. She was skillful in raising issues that put us on the defensive or postponed the need for Israel to make difficult choices. In 1973 she fought under the banner of "direct negotiations," a demand that brought home the absurdity of the position of even the moderate Arabs who insisted that Israel relinquish its conquests but who refused to sit down at the conference table to discuss withdrawal. From us she demanded that we coordinate positions between our two countries, a reasonable-sounding proposal whose practical consequence was to give her a veto over our tactics.

In the meeting with Nixon, Mrs. Meir began a direct assault with the weapon of flattery, to which Nixon was rather vulnerable. She thanked him for "revolutionizing the world and creating for the first time hope in the hearts of people that we are approaching the end of wars.'' Nixon was not about to contradict this judgment but added cautiously: ''We are realistic about the dangers which still exist. Many here say that since the world is at peace we can reduce arms to spend on ghettos. But we need more [arms] until our adversaries really change.'' Mrs. Meir fell in with this line of reasoning by telling Nixon that she had warned her fellow socialist Willy Brandt not to become dewy-eyed or to drop his guard. Nixon, convinced that anyone suspicious of Brandt was bound to be a kindred spirit, volunteered somewhat irrelevantly: ''My rule in international affairs is: do unto others as they would do unto you.'' ''Plus ten percent,'' I added, based on an experience with my chief extending over more than four years.

The meeting turned to practical matters. Golda had two objectives: to gain time, for the longer there was no change in the status quo, the more Israel would be comfirmed in the possession of the occupied territories; and to achieve Nixon's approval of a new package of military aid for Israel.

With respect to negotiations, Golda's attitude was simple. She considered Israel militarily impregnable; there was, strictly speaking, no need for any change. But given the congenital inability of Americans to leave well enough alone, she was willing to enter talks though not to commit herself to an outcome. She felt Jordanian matters were well in hand because there was already direct contact (which no fair-minded observer could claim had speeded up the process of settlement). As to Egypt, she was prepared to make an interim disengagement agreement along the Suez Canal as a first step toward a final settlement. But she would not agree to final bourdaries before negotiations had even started: Egypt, she argued, was looking for someone to help it get everything for nothing. First Cairo had tried the Soviets, now the United States: ''The trouble with Egypt is that they want the end before they begin.'' She agreed to our bizarre two-track procedure: Together with the public negotiations over an interim agreement, she would be prepared to have me continue to explore in private with Hafiz Ismail some general principles of an overall settlement as long as Israel was kept informed. This was fair enough, though it gave no real reason for optimism, for it kept all options open.

The situation was further complicated by the perennial problem of military deliveries for Israel. One of the weaknesses of our military supply relationship with Israel was that it came up for renewal every year or two. Inevitably, each new delivery provided a focal point for Arab resentment and led to an internal debate within our government about priorities. Regularly, as domestic pressure reinforced strategic necessities, the outcome was a favorable decision on a new arms package, fueling a new outburst of outrage in the Arab world.

So it was this time. On March 1, pressed by Mrs. Meir, Nixon agreed in principle to a new schedule of airplane deliveries, including some plans for co-production in Israel. We sought to ease the impact in the Arab world by not making a formal announcement. But the domestic position of too many leaders here and in Israel was involved; the decision leaked within two weeks.[10] Coming so soon after Ismail's visit, it caused an explosion in Cairo.

We had a delicate task. We had to nudge Egypt toward direct negotiations on a realistic program and Israel toward greater concessions than it had ever envisaged. But if we raised Arab hopes too much and then could not deliver, we would evoke an anti-American backlash. If we pressed Israel too far, it might launch a preemptive war while it still had the upper hand. And we had to fend off Soviet importuning for a direct Soviet-American agreement to impose terms even more impossible to achieve than Ismail's (see Chapter VII). I never saw any sense in a deal with Moscow unless the Soviets were willing to press the Arabs as they urged us to press Israel. I expressed my doubts to Sir Thomas Brimelow of the British Foreign Office on March 5 when I briefed him on the Ismail visit:

A bilateral Soviet/American deal on the Middle East starting with pressures on Israel would do two things: it might create another Middle East war, and tempt the Soviets to intervene in this Middle East War because of a joint US/Soviet position. And thirdly, after a settlement it is obvious that the next round after the frontiers are settled is the dispute between the Palestinians and Israel over the future of Palestine. . . . It is obvious [from my talks with Ismail] that a peace settlement ultimately depends on the Palestinians — who have the least incentive to settle anything.

So the result will be the exact opposite from Vietnam. In Vietnam the settlement got us out; in the Middle East the settlement will draw us in, in order to protect what we have imposed.

I was convinced that we would have to reduce the Soviet role if progress was to be made:

They have no incentive to be softer than the Arabs, and they have much incentive to be harder, so that the onus for an unsatisfactory settlement falls on us or on Sadat. Because the next round will be between the radicals and moderates in the whole area.

If we propose a detailed paper we are in hock to all sides, and responsible for both a process and a solution.

For these reasons I was extremely wary of putting forward a detailed plan for which everyone was volunteering us. The worst diplomatic posture is to be committed without having the ability to bring about one's designs. We had to explore the terrain carefully lest booby traps go off all around us.

Second Secret Meeting with Ismail

WALKING through that minefield was even trickier than I expected. For right after my February meetings with Hafiz Ismail, the Middle East went through another of its periodic eruptions of violence. American diplomats Ambassador Cleo A. Noel, Jr., and Deputy Chief of Mission George Curtis Moore were taken hostage and brutally murdered in Khartoum on March 2 by Black September Palestinian terrorists; Libyan jet fighters fired upon a US reconnaissance aircraft over the Mediterranean on March 21; and there was a renewed spiral of raid and reprisal across the Lebanese border.

Simultaneously, our relations with Egypt grew strained. At first, after returning home, Ismail sent word back that he had been very pleased with his reception here; his secret talks with me had exceeded his expectations in terms of both comprehensiveness and frankness. He hoped to be more specific at the next meeting. Ismail even agreed to examine my suggestion to "separate sovereignty and security," and to seek to strike a balance between them. If Egyptian sovereignty over the Sinai could be restored, practical security arrangements meeting Israel's requirements might be worked out. On March 9 I sent Ismail a reply that I would talk to the Israelis to "develop an understanding of their position as it might relate to the possible heads of agreement in the plan you outlined."

But the mood soon changed. Egypt found itself in a quandary about what position to take on the Khartoum murders. It was torn between personal revulsion at the killings, the need to maintain radical support for the war planning even then going on (of which we were ignorant), and the desire to involve us in the peace process. The contemplation of its dilemmas increased Egyptian irritability. A senior Egyptian official in Cairo cautioned us that some in his government opposed the peace effort and that the press leaks of our sale of jets to Israel were "not making things easier for us." On March 20 Ismail replied to my message of March 9, warning that the sophisticated military equipment we were providing to Israel risked aborting the secret talks. I replied on March 23, without commenting on Ismail's charges, that I looked forward to hearing the detailed reactions promised by Ismail at the last meeting.

The Egyptians, meanwhile, made their own contribution to complicating the lives of those handling the American end of the dialogue. Given the nature of Arab diplomacy, they probably could not have done otherwise. In the exuberant atmosphere of the Arab world, "keeping a secret" has a special connotation. Since Arab leaders feel both a bond of solidarity with their brethren and the tug of a wild individualism, none of them would believe — indeed, would be profoundly disquieted by — any assurances from Sadat that nothing was going on. Judging their colleagues by their own proclivities, Arab leaders are convinced incessant maneuvers are always taking place whereby each "brother" seeks to advance his own position even while ostensibly defending the Arab cause. In this cacophony of voices secrecy, ironically, can best be maintained by drowning all one's partners in a Babel of conversation that eventually overwhelms the distinction between epic poetry and reality.

Thus we learned on March 6 that the Saudis had been briefed by Egyptian officials about my secret meetings with Ismail. Since the world of diplomacy lives by trading information, word soon spread. British officials in Cairo then queried their American counterparts about what was going on. Though I had briefed the top level of the British government via Sir Thomas Brimelow, Whitehall had respected our injunction of secrecy and had not passed the information to its representatives in Cairo. Sadat then gave an interview to Arnaud de Borchgrave of *Newsweek* in which he referred to some exchanges that had taken place prior to Ismail's visit to Washington. That revelation appeared only in the Arabic version of the interview released in Cairo — enough to alert Jerry Greene that something was going on behind his back.

There is no fury like that of a Foreign Service Officer bypassed, especially when he is head of a diplomatic mission, even a small, so-called Interests Section as in Cairo. The offended diplomat has two choices. If he is wise, he limits himself to inquiring discreetly of his superiors about what is going on and leaves the bureaucratic sorting out to Washington. But he also has the option of standing on prerogative; he can report his knowledge in regular channels, thus spreading it through the bureaucracy by means of the computerized distribution system. This will quickly churn out enough copies to explode any aspiration to secrecy. The upshot of such maneuvers almost invariably is not to increase the responsibilities assigned to the diplomat — who tends to become the victim — but to reduce the options of Washington.

Greene, at any rate, took the more aggressive route, or perhaps someone in Washington put him up to it. After the Sadat interview became public, Greene first discreetly queried his Secretary of State about any secret channels of which he (Greene) was unaware; he also queried the local CIA representative. That worthy man, contrary to the myth of CIA deceitfulness, was obliged for the sake of the peace of the diplomatic mission to acknowledge, in effect, that there had been secret exchanges, though he did not discuss their content. Greene, no mean bureaucratic infighter, responded by reporting in deadpan fashion in a regular State telegram — and therefore widely distributed — the Saudi version of my talks with Ismail, which a Saudi official had helpfully provided to him in the meantime. Greene, in fairness, was not in an enviable position.

It was not he who was at fault, but our system. There was no way now to negotiate over the Middle East without involving the interested departments. On April 9, therefore, I briefed Joseph J. Sisco, Assistant Secretary of State for Near Eastern and South Asian Affairs, on my exchanges with Ismail; Nixon saw Sisco on April 13 and soothingly invited State's participation; Sisco's deputy, Alfred L. (Roy) Atherton, Jr., attended my next meeting with Ismail a month later. It was clear that the dual-track system could not be sustained in the Middle East.

And all the time Sadat was stoking the embers of conflagration, safe from consequences because no one took his threat of war seriously. On March 23 we heard that Sadat was thinking of "warming up" the Canal. On March 26 Sadat reshuffled his cabinet in a move proclaimed as clearing the decks for "total confrontation" with Israel. In the published *Newsweek* interview with de Borchgrave, Sadat declared that "the time has come for a shock"; resumption of the battle was now "inevitable." [11] No one believed that he had the means to carry out his threat. It seemed to refer to commando raids and renewed shelling.

On April 7, Hafiz Ismail sent me a message saying that Cairo was operating on two assumptions:

(1) That the White House has in fact decided to engage itself directly with the Middle East problem. . . .

(2) That the U.S. side as a result of explorations with Israel feels that there are sufficient encouraging indications so as to render useful the Egyptian–U.S. dialogue. In other words, Israel has shown to the U.S. side its readiness to achieve substantial progress towards an overall settlement during the next few months.

Egypt was asking for a guarantee of a comprehensive settlement on its total program as the entrance price to another round of talks. To accept this would guarantee massive disappointment. I replied noncommittally on April 11, welcoming a second meeting. As for Ismail's "assumptions," I suggested that a discussion of what Ismail called "heads of agreement," or general principles, might serve as a link between a Suez Canal accord and an overall agreement. But I avoided specificity on final borders. I appealed again for secrecy, disputed some of the interpretations being spread in the Arab world, and added a reassurance: "The U.S. side recognizes the Egyptian concerns about past experiences. It would not, however, pursue these channels if it wished to repeat the patterns of the past."

But Sadat was implacably heading for confrontation There were disturbing reports that Arab arms were being moved around the area: Libyan and Saudi planes to Egypt, Moroccan and other troops to Syria. We still considered this psychological warfare, however, rather than serious preparation for war. On April 20 the Central Intelligence Agency submitted its assessment that Sadat may have begun to take his own talk more seriously, but the Agency did not think he was at the point of decision. After listing the various military steps that had been taken among Arab states, the CIA concluded that there were no indications of planning for any specific military operation at a specific time.

In fact, Sadat had decided on war during the summer of 1972. What drove him to the throw of the dice was not the immediate deadlock in the negotiations but the objective stalemate in the real positions of the parties. Sadat was shrewd enough to understand that he would not get his territory back all at once. Somewhere along the line he would have to make some significant concessions. But timing was crucial. If he suggested a phased negotiation — what later came to be called a "step-by-step" approach — he would lose the support of Syria and of the Soviet Union, on which he depended for the threats without which the negotiation would never get off the ground. If he hinted at a separate peace, he would stand naked without the means to negotiate it.

Sadat decided to cut the Gordian knot by war. He went through the motions of diplomacy but at a pace that made it impossible to crystallize the issues, much less resolve them, setting deadlines so short that they permitted no real exploration. The utility to Sadat of both the diplomacy and the military preparations was to raise a cloud of dust behind which he was forging what everybody considered the most improbable contingency: a unified Egyptian-Syrian attack on Israel. But Sadat was the only figure aware of the diplomatic revolution he was planning. We had maneuvered to bring his reorientation about but did not yet recognize that Sadat considered a war was necessary before he could take the decisive steps to fuel the peace process with some genuine give-and-take. For in the mood of Arab humiliation following the defeat in the Six Day War, concessions would in all likelihood be ascribed to military weakness rather than statesmanship.

Against this background, my second meeting with Ismail was bound to be stillborn, though I did not understand this then. Sadat knew the tenuousness of the Arab unity he was forging too well to believe that he could delay his military plans for more than a few months. He was too familiar with the mutual suspicions of Arab leaders to have any illusion that he could keep alive his military option through a protracted negotiation. If I had been able in mid-1973 to guarantee him the 1967 borders without his having to make peace, he would have accepted it — though with reluctance, as he later told me, since it would have done little for Egyptian pride. But this could hardly be realized, if at all, in any time frame relevant to the coalition he had so tentatively forged, and he knew it.

So Hafiz Ismail and I met one more time. It was in France on May 20, 1973, in a centuries-old French provincial farmhouse located between Paris and Chartres, refurbished by its American owner in the expensive simplicity of the very rich. It retained its beam-ceilinged, rustic quaintness, and an extensive garden and waterfall emphasized the pastoral setting. We had a formal meeting on the upper floor and, after lunch, I walked with Ismail in the garden in the spring sunshine. In these beautiful surroundings we had what the diplomats would call "useful"— that is to say, ultimately unproductive — talks. The difficulty was that Ismail would not deviate from his original program, which he must have known could never be sold to Israel in one stage. He pretended to take umbrage at my suggestion that Egypt come up with something new to get the negotiating process started. But it took no great acumen to grasp that Egypt's position — in effect what Egypt had been proposing since February 1971 and which had been consistently rejected — would not give us the means to start a new negotiating process with an Israel that saw no need for it to begin with. (Indeed, prior to my meeting with Ismail, Golda Meir had gone back on a previous understanding, now questioning in a personal communication the wisdom of pursuing the comprehensive and the interim routes simultaneously.) I objected to some of the more strident parts of the Egyptian briefing of the Saudis, which seemed to me to imply a confrontational tone that I had not noted at our meetings. Ismail did not deny this but implied that it reflected Arab psychological necessities.

I also suggested a formula for linking the interim to an overall agreement, but it was clear that Egypt would risk neither the isolation inherent in an interim agreement nor the protracted negotiation required for an overall settlement. Ismail remained cool to my scheme of separating sovereignty and security. He called this "diluted sovereignty," but said he would check with Sadat and let me know. I never heard from him.

The American official who had found the meeting place reported to me that after I left, Ismail, visibly dispirited and glum, had sat alone in the garden for a long time contemplating the waterfall behind the house, head cupped in hands. His staff had left him alone, but finally his young daughter joined him and appeared to cheer him up. He told the American later that he hoped to maintain contact with me whatever the vicissitudes of the peace effort. Our relationship would be important even in case of an armed clash, he said.

For Ismail knew that Sadat was determined on war. Only an American guarantee that we would fulfill the entire Arab program in a brief time could have dissuaded him. That was patently impossible. And Ismail, though a military man, was enough imbued with the extraordinary humanity of the Egyptian to dread what reason told him was now inevitable. The Middle East was heading toward war. We did not know it. But he did.

VII

Détente: Zavidovo to San Clemente

FOUR days after the resignation of Haldeman and Ehrlichman I was airborne for Moscow. No doubt the Soviets were bemused by this turn in our political scene; but it was too soon for even the most acute seismic ear to catch the scale of the pending earthquake. In the spring of 1973, Soviet-American relations were unusually free of tension. A second summit between Brezhnev and Nixon, this time on American soil, was due to take place in June and my few days in the Soviet Union, from May 4 to May 9, were to prepare for it. Away from the negotiating table on this trip I had a glimpse of Leonid Brezhnev that intrigues me today when I reflect on whether there can ever be a stable coexistence between us and the Soviet Union.

Upon arrival my colleagues and I were driven from Moscow's Vnukovo II airport, not to the ponderous guest houses in the Lenin Hills in the western part of the capital, but to Zavidovo, the Politburo hunting preserve — the Soviet equivalent of Camp David — some ninety miles northeast of Moscow. We took off in a motorcade traveling at a speed of close to 100 miles per hour with cars tailgating each other and security vehicles scissoring in and out of the column. This reflected either deliberate psychological warfare or the propensity for suicide described in nineteenth-century Russian novels. The American party and its Soviet escorts could not possibly have survived if the lead car had stopped suddenly.

For all its perils, the journey was intended as a great honor. No Western leader had ever been invited to Zavidovo; the only other foreigners to visit it, I was told, had been Tito and President Urho Kekkonen of Finland. In light of what has happened since, the atmosphere of jovial if heavy-handed camaraderie may seem transparent. But at the time our Soviet hosts, headed by Brezhnev, certainly did their best to convey that good relations with the United States meant a great deal to them. They went out of their way to be hospitable, on occasion stiflingly so. Our meetings were conducted with easy banter and a minimum of the squeezing for extra advantage that is the usual hallmark of Soviet diplomacy.

Was it a ruse to lull us while the Kremlin prepared a geopolitical offensive? Or were the Soviets sobered by Nixon's firmness into settling for a period of restraint reinforced by the possible gains from economic relations? Did they seek détente only as a tactical maneuver? Or was there a serious possibility for a long period of stability in US–Soviet relations? Could the Moscow summit of 1972 have been a turning point, or was it always destined simply to be an ephemeral moment of euphoria?

We can never know, and probably neither can the Soviet leaders. Within twelve months both Nixon's capacity to oppose Soviet expansion and his authority to negotiate realistically had been undermined by Watergate. We lost both the stick and the carrot. Whether our East-West policy was doomed in any event by the dynamics of the Soviet system or by the inherent ambiguity of our conception will be debated for a long time. The issue became moot when the executive power in the United States collapsed. Fortunately for our state of mind, that future was still obscure when we arrived in Zavidovo.

The American party was housed in an East German–built villa resembling an oversized Swiss chalet blown out of scale by the heavy stolidity that in the Communist world denotes status. The exterior looked vaguely Alpine; the inside was all velvet-covered Victorian opulence. Some junior members of my party were housed in an old dormitorylike structure diagonally across a wide lawn from my residence. They spread out happily in a number of suites that had formerly been reserved for the Politburo before a newer and more modern wing had been added.

The largest private residence in the compound belonged to Brezhnev. It was a two-story chalet built in the same style as my residence, though on an even grander scale. The ground floor contained a number of large reception rooms filled with heavily upholstered furniture, a dining room, and a movie theater. The upper floor had a large living room, a study, and a bedroom. Each upstairs room opened on a balcony shaded by an overhanging roof. At right angles to Brezhnev's villa and connected with it by passageways on each floor was a fully equipped gymnasium containing an Olympic-sized swimming pool.

Brezhnev came to my residence soon after my arrival and greeted me boisterously. A little later he invited my colleagues and me to dinner at his villa, which he first showed off with all the pride of a self-made entrepreneur. He asked me how much such an establishment would cost in the United States. I guessed tactlessly and mistakenly at four hundred thousand dollars. Brezhnev's face fell. My associate Helmut Sonnenfeldt was psychologically more adept: Two million, he corrected — probably much closer to the truth. Brezhnev, vastly reassured, beamed and resumed his guided tour. He showed us with boyish pride a scrapbook of clippings and congratulatory telegrams from various Communist leaders on the occasion of his being awarded the Lenin Peace Prize. The near-absolute ruler of the Soviet Communist Party seemed to see nothing incongruous in boasting of an award from his own appointees and congratulations from those whose careers and political survival depended on him.

Brezhnev conducted almost all the negotiations for the Soviets; only highly technical subjects, such as the European Security Conference, were left to Foreign Minister Andrei Gromyko. Brezhnev's repertory of jokes seemed as inexhaustible as the previous year's, now spiced with a new familiarity that probably went further than he intended. His drinking was less restrained; one of his jokes, allegedly a Russian folk tale, was vaguely anti-Semitic — indicating perhaps that I had been promoted to an honorary equal!

The timetable was, as usual, enigmatic. No schedule or advance indication of subject matter was ever given, even though Brezhnev had no other visible program. Meetings occurred randomly, with little, if any, advance warning. Except for concluding the Agreement on the Prevention of Nuclear War (which I shall discuss later), there was no definable agenda. Twice, when our conversations did not come up to Brezhnev's hopes — on the Middle East, and on some dispute over the nuclear agreement — he sulked in his villa and refused to schedule another session. The Soviet Ambassador to Washington, Anatoly Dobrynin, did his best to minimize tensions; making Brezhnev appear like a man whose tender feelings required careful cultivation, he explained that his chief needed to regain his composure. When I maintained my position — simply by putting forward no additional thoughts — Brezhnev suddenly materialized again as if nothing had happened. His ploy having failed, he would then do the best with what he had and set about to restore an atmosphere of ebullient goodwill.

My team — Hal Sonnenfeldt, Philip Odeen, William Hyland, Peter Rodman, and Richard Campbell — had the usual problem of how to communicate with one another without becoming immortalized in the KGB tape library. In a strange way we felt somewhat more secure in the Politburo hunting lodge than in our usual haunt of the state guest house in Moscow. We thought the KGB was likely to be somewhat less exuberant in wiring the vacation retreat of its own top leadership than in doing so to the residences specifically designed for foreign guests. We came equipped, of course, with the so-called babbler, the cassette tape machine emitting incoherent gibberish that allegedly drowned out the sound of our voices for eager listeners. I do not know whether it worked and I hate to think that I may have subjected my emotional balance to that infernal noise-making machine to no avail. It was a close race between KGB technology and our sanity. In any event, my colleagues and I occasionally escaped the babbler by identifying what we considered one absolutely secure place: the balcony outside Brezhnev's study to which we repaired during breaks in our meetings. We thought it improbable that Brezhnev would be so imprudent as to allow the Soviet secret police to install eavesdropping equipment in his own office.

The dominant impression from the potpourri of buoyancy, watchfulness, and random negotiation was Brezhnev's insecurity about his forthcoming trip to the United States. It is one of the glories of our country that it seems endowed with a special, almost magical quality even to its adversaries. Brezhnev might be the General Secretary of a party dedicated to world revolution, the leader of the assault on the capitalist system that we epitomize. Still, his major concern seemed to be whether he would be treated as an equal in what his media never ceased to describe as the citadel of imperialism.

The Communist form of government had not mellowed and had perhaps accentuated an age-old Russian ambivalence about America. This was reflected in a relentless insistence on status and a doubt that it would be conceded; a boastful assertion of strength coupled with uncertainty that it would be recognized. Whatever Brezhnev's systems analysts might tell him of the emerging parity in the military power of the two countries, to him America seemed to be what he had learned of it in his youth — a land of superior technology and wondrous industrial and agricultural capacity, a country of marvelous efficiency compared with the cumbersome Soviet colossus.

Brezhnev could not hear often enough my avowal that we were proceeding on the premise of equality — an attitude inconceivable in Peking, whose leaders thought of themselves as culturally superior whatever the statistics showed about relative material strength. Brezhnev endlessly sought reassurance that he would be courteously received in America, that he would not be exposed to hostile demonstrations, and that he would have the chance to meet "ordinary" people. This was a tall order and its various elements were not necessarily consistent with each other. He spoke of bringing his family with him and of a number of side trips he planned to take — always with a mixture of awe, wonder, and uncertainty. No doubt his gesture of spending five days in the Politburo hunting lodge with me was to establish a standard for us to emulate.

I confess that I was touched by this insecurity even while I recognized that the country he represented had a record of seeking reassurance in bullying and safety in domination. On this occasion Brezhnev's vulnerability allowed a human contact that was not to recur. He would suddenly appear and whisk me off to some excursion in the rolling countryside of lakes, meadows, and vast forests. One day he called for me in the black Cadillac sedan that Dobrynin had suggested might be a suitable State gift for Nixon to bring the year before. (Brezhnev, an automobile enthusiast, collected national cars as souvenirs on every State visit to every country; his ambassadors were not bashful about suggesting them.) With Brezhnev at the wheel, we took off along narrow winding country roads at speeds that made one pray hopelessly for some policeman's intervention, unlikely as it was that a traffic cop — if indeed they existed in the countryside — would dare halt the General Secretary. Thus propelled to a boat landing, Brezhnev bundled me off onto a hydrofoil — mercifully not driven by him — which nevertheless seemed determined to break the speed record established by the General Secretary in getting me there. My brain being addled by these multiple jolts, I lack a precise recollection of this excursion. Another morning, Brezhnev kidnapped my attractive secretary, Bonnie Andrews, and took her on a boat ride. She was returned, by her account, equally shaken and unharmed.

One afternoon I returned to my villa and found hunting attire, which our hosts had ordered for me since my arrival. It was an elegant, military-looking olive drab, with high boots, for which I am unlikely to have any future use. Brezhnev, similarly attired, collected me in a jeep driven, I was grateful to notice, by a game warden. Since I hate the killing of animals for sport, I told Brezhnev that I would come along in my capacity as adviser. He said some wild boars had already been earmarked for me. Given my marksmanship, I replied, the cause of death would have to be heart failure.

After more heavy joshing, Brezhnev nevertheless whisked me off to the hunting preserve. Simultaneously, Gromyko took Sonnenfeldt away in another direction. Deep in the stillness of the forest a stand had been built about halfway up a tree, with a crude bench and an aperture for shooting. Brezhnev, the interpreter Viktor Sukhodrev, the game warden, and I waited there for the wild boar to be lured by the bait that various foresters in green uniforms were spreading on the ground. All was absolutely still. Only Brezhnev's voice could be heard, whispering tales of hunting adventures: of his courage when a boar once attacked his jeep; of the bison that stuffed itself with the grain and potatoes laid out as bait and then fell contentedly asleep on the steps of the hunting tower, trapping Soviet Defense Minister Marshal Rodion Malinovski in the tower until a search party rescued him.

After about an hour of this, as dusk was settling, a herd of wild boar came toward the bait. I was struck by the grace and wariness of their movements, though clearly their desire for food overcame all prudence. While Brezhnev calmly selected his victim, I reflected on the vulnerability of the greedy — only to have my rudimentary philosophy quickly disproved by a very large wild boar that emerged from the forest. One could see easily why it had attained such a size. It was not greedy; it set about to investigate the bait. It examined the ground before every step. It looked carefully behind every tree. It advanced in a measured pace. It had clearly survived and thrived by taking no unnecessary chances. All its precautions attracted Brezhnev's attention, however, and he felled it with a single shot. Only Brezhnev's jubilation prevented me from launching on another train of thought about the perils of excessive intellectualism.

There is no telling what other contribution to pop philosophy I might have generated on this expedition had not Brezhnev's hunting instinct propelled him to move us to another stand even deeper in the forest. By then, fortunately for the boars — for whom I was rooting — night was beginning to fall and Brezhnev missed two shots at long range.

Brezhnev and I remained in the second stand for some hours, and someone brought cold cuts, dark bread, and beer from the jeep. Brezhnev's split personality — alternatively boastful and insecure, belligerent and mellow — was in plain view as we ate together in that alfresco setting. The truculence appeared in his discussion of China. He began describing the experiences of his brother who had worked there as an engineer before Khrushchev removed all Soviet advisers. He had found the Chinese treacherous, arrogant, beyond the human pale. They were cannibalistic in the way they destroyed their top leaders (an amazing comment from a man who had launched his career during Stalin's purges); they might well, in fact, be cannibals. Now China was acquiring a nuclear arsenal. The Soviet Union could not accept this passively; something would have to be done. He did not say what.

Brezhnev was clearly fishing for some hint of American acquiescence in a Soviet preemptive attack. I gave no encouragement; my bland response was that the growth of China was one of those problems that underlined the importance of settling disputes peacefully. Brezhnev contemptuously ignored this high-minded theory and returned to his preoccupation. China's growing military might was a menace to everybody. Any military assistance to it by the United States would lead to war. I reminded him (irrelevantly) that we did not even have diplomatic relations with Peking; I warned that history proved America would not be indifferent to an attack on China. But the Soviet leaders were not content to let the matter rest on that note; the next day Dobrynin took me aside to stress that the China portion of the discussion in the hunting blind was not to be treated as social. Brezhnev had meant every word of it.

Reflecting the duality of the national character and of his own personality, Brezhnev shifted suddenly from menace to sentimentality. He spoke of his youth in the Ukraine and his father's experience in the First World War. His father had learned from that carnage that peace was the noblest goal; he had never stopped insisting on this theme. Brezhnev agreed: We had reached the point in history where we should stop building

monuments for military heroes. Public memorials should be reserved
for peacemakers and not generals. His father had wanted one constructed on the highest point in the Ukraine (which, unless my knowledge of geography betrays me, is not a very towering eminence). Brezhnev wanted to dedicate his tenure to bringing about a condition in which
war between the United States and the Soviet Union was unthinkable.

Brezhnev reminisced about his rise through the Communist hierarchy,
his sudden elevation in 1936, and the human impact of World War II.
Before he went off to serve in that war, his wife and he had pledged
never to question each other about the interval no matter how long it
might be; it turned out to be four years. He described movingly their
reunion over the gulf of a long separation and how both of them kept
their promise and their trust. He told me of his difficulty in finding a
uniform for the victory parade in Red Square in 1945 under the conditions of wartime scarcity and how he succeeded, only to have his resplendent garment ruined by a daylong torrential downpour. In this account he spoke gently, with none of the braggadocio so evident even a
few moments earlier. His theme now was peace. And with his slightly
slurred and halting speech he was suddenly an old man somewhat drained
by a lifetime of struggle.

Which was the real Brezhnev? The leader who spoke so threateningly
of China or the old man who recited his devotion to peace? Probably
both were genuine. Was the peace of which he spoke only the stillness
of Soviet hegemony, or an acceptance of the imperatives of coexistence? Again, the answer is almost surely both. Which strand predominated would depend on circumstance and opportunity. And probably the
West's ability to address the two antiphonal trends of Soviet policy simultaneously and effectively would decide the issue of peace or war.
The Bolshevik believed in the prevalence of material and military factors; the aged leader was exhausted by the exaction of a pitiless system.
Doubtless no more than any Soviet leader would Brezhnev resist taking
advantage of an opportunity to alter the power balance; nothing can take
off our shoulders the imperative of preparedness. But within that con-
straint some leaders, driven by the impossibility of suppressing human
aspiration forever, may well emerge eventually to explore the requirements of genuine coexistence. The West's policy must encompass both
possibilities: uncompromising resistance to expansionism and receptivity
to a serious change of course in Moscow.

I give this account in full awareness of the brutalities of Brezhnev's
tenure, from Czechoslovakia to Afghanistan. It is quite possible that the
KGB suggested these basic themes as a way to display a human bond
and pretend a sincere desire for peace. But fairness compels me to say
that I know of no other Soviet leader who could have made it credible.
Perhaps this is a tribute to Brezhnev's acting skill. I doubt it. As a good

Communist Brezhnev was, of course, dedicated to the victory of his ideology; as a believer in objective factors he could not justify failing to take advantage of a superior position of strength that our domestic divisions increasingly presented to him. It was then — and remains — our principal responsibility to prevent such temptations from arising. But there was also in Brezhnev a clearly evident strain of the elemental Russia, of a people that has prevailed through endurance, that longs for a surcease from its travails and has never been permitted by destiny or the ambitions of its rulers to fulfill its dream.

The mellow mood of the evening in the hunting stand proved evanescent. Once returned to Zavidovo, we were engulfed again in the routine of the negotiations and preparations for Brezhnev's visit to the United States. And they, as well as other circumstances, soon overwhelmed this single, brief glimpse of humanity that was not repeated while I was in office.

Détente: What Was It?

NEGOTIATIONS with the Soviet Union have had a checkered history in the past decade. Urged on us insistently when we entered office, hailed exorbitantly as a turning point when three years later we carried it out, later blamed for all our contemporary dilemmas, détente has been more a barometer of our domestic controversies than a subject of serious analysis. For the statesman in any event, a foreign policy issue does not present itself as a theory but as a series of realities. And the realities of Nixon's first term were stark. We had to end a war in Indochina in the midst of a virulent domestic assault on all the sinews of a strong foreign policy. It was followed by the impotence of the Presidency as a result of Watergate. Détente was not the cause of these conditions but one of the necessities for mastering them. Any discussion of it must begin with understanding this fact.

Now in the retrospective of a decade, détente is being made to bear the burden for the consequences of America's self-destructive domestic convulsions over Vietnam and Watergate. The former made Americans recoil before foreign involvement and thus opened an opportunity for Soviet expansionism; the latter weakened executive power to resist Soviet pressure. For the better part of a decade policymakers had to contend with a public opinion that had turned inward and a Congress that systematically reduced defense programs and the scope of executive action. To court confrontation in these circumstances was to invite a debacle. Those of us charged with the nation's foreign policy could never forget that we were operating at the edge of a precipice.

A collective amnesia has seized the participants in that tragedy. Liberals have been understandably reluctant to assume any responsibility for the consequences of their two great causes of the 1970s. Conservatives have fudged the issue because an Administration they considered their own fell over Watergate and because many of them were more interested in an ideological anti-Communist crusade at home than in the geopolitical contest in the distant lands where the foreign policy issues are in fact decided. Many conservatives resurrected traditional isolationism, protecting American moral purity against contamination by the tactical and expedient. And some of the "neoconservatives," who had moved from the liberal to the conservative side after the end of the war in Vietnam, had the passion of the convert and few incentives to recall their own contributions to the collapse of international restraints. They forgot that they had assaulted as far too bellicose the same foreign policy that five years later they denounced as strategic retreat.* That the Nixon Administration manned the barricades almost alone against such critics, defending American military strength and geopolitical credibility, did not figure prominently in the later, revisionist analysis that blamed Nixon, not his opponents, for the weakening of both.[2] For years we had been ferociously attacked from the left for resisting the Communist takeover in Indochina — a policy we carried out precisely because we feared the global consequences of a collapse of American credibility. Now suddenly we had to ward off assaults from some of the same people, who had joined the right, for our attempts to navigate the ship of state through the turmoil we had both predicted and opposed.

It is therefore important to recall what détente was and what it was not.

Richard Nixon came into office with the well-deserved reputation of a lifetime of anti-Communism. He despised liberal intellectuals who blamed the Cold War on the United States and who seemed to believe the Soviet system might be transformed through the strenuous exercise of goodwill. Nixon profoundly distrusted Soviet motives; he was a firm believer in negotiations from positions of strength; he was, in short, the classic Cold Warrior. Yet after four tumultuous years in office, it was this man, so unlike the conventional intellectual's notion of a peacemaker, who paradoxically was negotiating with the Soviets on the broadest agenda of East-West relations in twenty-five years. And not long afterward he found himself accused of what had been a staple of his own early campaign rhetoric: of being "soft on Communism."

The paradox was more apparent than real. We did not consider a relaxation of tensions a concession to the Soviets. We had our own reasons for it. We were not abandoning the ideological struggle, but

---

*The distinguished, now neoconservative, journal *Commentary,* for example, in 1970 criticized Nixon for his ABM program, MIRV testing, and laxity in pursuing SALT. It bitterly opposed Nixon's Vietnam policy and once came close to welcoming an American defeat.[1]

simply trying — tall order as it was — to discipline it by precepts of national interest. Nor was détente without its successes. There is no doubt that our better relations with the Soviet Union (and China) isolated Hanoi. In 1972 Moscow acquiesced in the mining of North Vietnamese harbors and the bombing of Hanoi and Haiphong; by the end of the year Hanoi settled for terms it had contemptuously rejected for years. In Europe the knowledge that the Americans, too, could talk to the Russians reined in the temptation to blame all tensions on the United States and to seek safety in quasi-neutralism. And later on it helped us to bring about a diplomatic revolution in the Middle East.

I also believe that the evidence proves exactly the opposite of what our critics charged: Détente helped rather than hurt the American defense effort. Before the word détente was even known in America the Congress cut $40 billion from the defense budgets of Nixon's first term; even so dedicated a supporter of American strength as Senator Henry M. Jackson publicly advocated small defense cuts and a "prudent defense posture."[3] After the signature of SALT I, our defense budget increased and the Nixon and Ford administrations put through the strategic weapons (the MX missile, B-1 bomber, cruise missiles, Trident submarines, and more advanced warheads) that even a decade later are the backbone of our defense program and that had been stymied in the Congress *prior* to the easing of our relations with Moscow.

Détente did not prevent resistance to Soviet expansion; on the contrary, it fostered the only possible psychological framework for such resistance. Nixon knew where to draw the line against Soviet adventure whether it occurred directly or through proxy, as in Cienfuegos, Jordan, along the Suez Canal, and during the India-Pakistan war. He drew it with cool fortitude, and all the more credibly because there was national understanding that we were not being truculent for its own sake. If the Vietnam war had taught us anything, it was that a military confrontation could be sustained only if the American people were convinced there was no other choice.

Any American President soon learns that he has a narrow margin for maneuver. The United States and the Soviet Union are ideological rivals. Détente cannot change that. The nuclear age compels us to coexist. Rhetorical crusades cannot change that, either.

Our age must learn the lessons of World War II, brought about when the democracies failed to understand the designs of a totalitarian aggressor, sought foolishly to appease him, and permitted him to achieve a military superiority. This must never happen again, whatever the burdens of an adequate defense. But we must remember as well the lesson of World War I, when Europe, *despite* the existence of a military balance, drifted into a war no one wanted and a catastrophe that no one could have imagined. Military planning drove decisions; bluster and posturing drove diplomacy. Leaders committed the cardinal sin of state-craft: They lost control over events.

An American President thus has a dual responsibility: He must resist Soviet expansionism. And he must be conscious of the profound risks of global confrontation. His policy must embrace both deterrence and coexistence, both containment and an effort to relax tensions. If the desire for peace turns into an avoidance of conflict at all costs, if the just disparage power and seek refuge in their moral purity, the world's fear of war becomes a weapon of blackmail by the strong; peaceful nations, large or small, will be at the mercy of the most ruthless. Yet if we pursue the ideological conflict divorced from strategy, if confrontation turns into an end in itself, we will lose the cohesion of our alliances and ultimately the confidence of our people. That was what the Nixon Administration understood by détente.

The Nixon Administration sought a foreign policy that eschewed both moralistic crusading and escapist isolationism, submerging them in a careful analysis of the national interest. America's aim was to maintain the balance of power and seek to build upon it a more constructive future.[4] We were entering a period when America's responsibility was to provide a consistent, mature leadership in much more complex conditions than we had ever before faced and over a much longer period of time than we ever had had to calculate.

The late 1960s had marked the end of the period of American predominance based on overwhelming nuclear and economic supremacy. The Soviet nuclear stockpile was inevitably approaching parity. The economic strength of Europe and Japan was bound to lead them to seek larger political influence. The new, developing nations pressed their claims to greater power and participation. The United States would have to learn to base its foreign policy on premises analogous to those by which other nations historically had conducted theirs. The percentage of the world's Gross National Product represented by our economy was sinking by 10 percent with every decade: from 52 percent in 1950 to 40 percent in 1960, to some 30 percent in 1970 (it is at this writing 22 percent). This meant that if all the rest of the world united against us or if some hostile power or group of powers achieved the hegemony Peking warned of, America's resources would be dwarfed by its adversaries'. Still the strongest nation but no longer preeminent, we would have to take seriously the world balance of power, for if it tilted against us, it might prove irreversible. No longer able to wait for threats to become overwhelming before dealing with them, we would have to substitute concept for resources. We needed the inward strength to act on the basis of assessments unprovable when they were made.

How to avoid nuclear war without succumbing to nuclear blackmail, how to prevent the desire for peace from turning into appeasement; how to defend liberty and maintain the peace — this is the overwhelming problem of our age. The trouble — no, the tragedy — is that the dual concept of containment and coexistence, of maintaining the balance of power while exploring a more positive future, has no automatic consensus behind it. Historically, America imagined that it did not have to concern itself with the global equilibrium because geography and a surplus of power enabled it to await events in isolation. Two schools of thought developed. The liberal approach treated foreign policy as a subdivision of psychiatry; the conservative approach considered it an aspect of theology. Liberals equated relations among states with human relations. They emphasized the virtues of trust and unilateral gestures of goodwill. Conservatives saw in foreign policy a version of the eternal struggle of good with evil, a conflict that recognized no middle ground and could end only with victory. Deterrence ran up against liberal ideology and its emotional evocation of peace in the abstract; coexistence grated on the liturgical anti-Communism of the right. American idealism drove both groups to challenge us from different directions. The mainstream of liberalism found anything connected with the balance of power repugnant: Through the early part of the twentieth century the United States thought of itself as standing above considerations of national interest. We would organize mankind by a consensus of moral principles or norms of international law. Regard for the purity of our ideals inspired conservatives, contrarily, to put Communism into quarantine: There could be no compromise with the devil. Liberals worried about the danger of confrontation; conservatives about funking it.

I sought to convey a sense of the complexity of our policy toward the USSR in a speech before the Pacem in Terris Conference in Washington on October 8, 1973:

This Administration has never had any illusions about the Soviet system. We have always insisted that progress in technical fields, such as trade, had to follow — and reflect — progress toward more stable international relations. We have maintained a strong military balance and a flexible defense posture as a buttress to stability. We have insisted that disarmament had to be mutual. We have judged movement in our relations with the Soviet Union, not by atmospherics, but by how well concrete problems are resolved and by whether there is responsible international conduct.

Coexistence to us continues to have a very precise meaning:

— We will oppose the attempt by any country to achieve a position of predominance either globally or regionally.

— We will resist any attempt to exploit a policy of détente to weaken our alliances.

— We will react if relaxation of tensions is used as a cover to exacerbate conflicts in international trouble spots.

The Soviet Union cannot disregard these principles in any area of the world without imperiling its entire relationship with the United States.

But our effort simultaneously to resist expansionism and to keep open the option of historical evolution — in effect, to combine the analysis and strategy of the conservatives with the tactics of the liberals — proved too ambitious in a bitter period when a domestic upheaval over Vietnam was followed immediately afterward by another upheaval over Watergate. Conservatives at least remained true to their beliefs. They wanted no truck with Communism whatever the tactical motivation. They equated negotiations with Moscow with the moral disarmament of America. They rejected our argument that if we did not take account of the global yearning for peace we would isolate ourselves internationally and divide our nation again over the same issues that had polarized America over Vietnam.

The liberals' position was more complex. Viscerally they opposed the balance of power theory implicit in containment. But what could they say about détente, so long championed by them and now put forward by that hated Cold Warrior Nixon? Their frustration mounted when Nixon, in stealing some of their clothes, could not resist taunting them with some of their own rhetoric. The tendency to hyperbole, unnecessary for such a sensible case, provoked liberal critics at first into attacking détente as just another version of balance of power, as not going far enough, as a tactic — almost as a Cold War tactic — rather than as policy for the genuine relaxation of tensions.

But liberals soon left this uncomfortable position, which, however, had the merit of attacking our policy for what were, for better or worse, its premises. In early 1973, liberal critics suddenly shifted the vector of their assault. In that twilight period when Nixon was haunted by his looming perils even while his opponents were still obsessed by his seeming invulnerability, many liberals began to move in a direction that the master manipulator had considered inconceivable. They adopted the very positions that he had vacated in his march toward the center. Suddenly it was the liberal community that began to find ideological flaws in the détente that for so long it had passionately championed. The argument gained currency that Nixon had "oversold" détente; that he neglected human rights in his desire to get along with the Kremlin; that the Administration was insensitive to the moral problem of dealing with Communism. These arguments were natural from conservatives who were seriously worried lest the erosion of dividing lines sap the Western will to resist. They came with less grace from those who had systematically opposed higher defense expenditures and who had decried the resistance to Soviet expansion in distant theaters that was the essence of our commitment to containment.

The result was a dangerous contradiction. On the one hand, the lesson of Vietnam was alleged to be that we had no moral right to engage in distant enterprises. On the other hand, the Administration was now accused of amoral callousness in not insisting on the internal amelioration of all other societies, be they friendly or adversary. A new doctrine of political intervention into the domestic affairs of other states emerged, even while we were being pressed to withdraw American power from remote continents. With respect to the USSR, our liberal critics did not explain how we would handle the resulting confrontations with the Kremlin in the middle of a Watergate-inspired attack on both defense budgets and executive power.

In the process, our policy toward the Soviets was turned by its disparate critics into a caricature of itself. We had conceived it as managing the relations among adversaries; our critics faulted it for falling short of establishing friendship. In every crisis there were cries that détente had failed to prevent it. We measured the success of our policy in the ability to achieve strategic goals even in crises, while mitigating risks — the Middle East war of 1973 is a good example. Until there is a major domestic change in Moscow, no East-West policy can abolish crises altogether. This is especially true if both the carrot and stick are removed, as occurred in the attack on executive discretion from 1973 onward. The alternative offered by our critics, moreover, was simply to needle the bear, inviting constant crises without tactical flexibility. Every evidence of Soviet ulterior motive was eagerly seized upon as if it were a new discovery. We took it for granted that the Communist superpower did not wish us well. We thought we could defeat its designs more effectively by a policy of firmness, maneuver, and positive aspiration that had a better chance of sustained public and allied support over the long-term future than simply by the mindless reiteration of truculent slogans.

No doubt the Soviet leaders hoped to convince the democracies — abetted by Communist-sponsored front groups and the West's own hopeful interpretation of world affairs — that what had produced the seeming relaxation of tensions was not our vigilance but a basic change in Soviet purpose. More and more Western leaders, the hard men in the Kremlin reasoned, would gear their domestic positions to a relaxation of tensions, pay a growing price for it, and seek refuge from the perils of confrontation by blaming the United States for all crises. That danger was real. But the opposite course was even more perilous. Confrontations not perceived as necessary by the public will divide each country, split our alliances, and produce a quest for peace at any price. No self-respecting democratic leader can sustain himself by treating vigilance and peace as if they were opposites. Our alliances will be sundered if they appear as obstacles to peace. To be sure, détente is dangerous if it does not include a strategy of containment. But containment is unsustainable unless coupled with a notion of peace. The remedy is not to evade the effort to define coexistence; it is to give it a content that reflects *our* principles and *our* objectives.

The subtlest critique of our policy held that our emphasis on the national interest ran counter to American idealism and national character. Americans, on this thesis, must affirm general values or they will lack the resolution and stamina to overcome the Soviet challenge. In other words, America must commit itself to a moral opposition to Communism, not just geopolitical opposition to Soviet encroachment, or its policy will be based on quicksand.[5] But while I sympathize with this point of view, a statesman must relate general theorems to concrete circumstances. Crusades rarely supply the staying power for a prolonged struggle. Obsession with ideology may translate into an unwillingness to confront seemingly marginal challenges, depicting them as unworthy because they appear not to encapsulate the ultimate showdown. This happened over Angola and Vietnam (after the Paris Agreement), and later in the Persian Gulf. In an era of growing Soviet boldness and radical quests for ascendancy, an American failure to deal with the geopolitical challenge would risk the global equilibrium as surely as a failure to preserve the military balance. And the overemphasis on ideology would create a characteristically American vulnerability: The doctrine of redemption would make us peculiarly receptive to Soviet peace offensives that seemed to imply that Soviet purposes had changed. Our moral convictions must arm us to face the ambiguity inseparable from the long haul or else they will wind up disarming us.

Whatever policies they conduct, statesmen always gamble on their assessment of the future. Clearly, the United States and the Soviet Union each expected history to be on its side. Just prior to the summit of 1973, I analyzed Brezhnev's motivations in a memorandum to Nixon, and there is a glimpse of his own attitude at the time in the way he underlined some portions (in italics here):

Like all Soviet postwar leaders, Brezhnev *sees the US at once as rival, mortal threat, model, source of assistance and partner in physical survival.* These conflicting impulses make the motivations of Brezhnev's policy toward us ambivalent. On the one hand, he no doubt wants *to go down in history as the leader who brought peace and a better life to Russia.* This *requires conciliatory and cooperative policies* toward us. *Yet, he remains a convinced Communist* who sees *politics as a struggle with an ultimate winner;* he intends the Soviet Union to *be that winner.* His recurrent efforts to draw us into condominium-type arrangements — most notably his proposal for a nuclear nonaggression pact — are intended both to safeguard peace and to undermine our alliances and other associations.

Almost certainly, Brezhnev continues to defend his detente policies in Politburo debates in terms of a historic conflict with us as the main capitalist country and of the ultimate advantages that will accrue to the USSR in this conflict. Brezhnev's *gamble* is that as these policies gather momentum and longevity, their effects will not undermine the very system from which Brezhnev draws his power and legitimacy. Our goal on the other hand is to achieve precisely such effects over the long run. . . .

The major, *long term question is whether the Soviets can hold their own bloc together while waiting for the West to succumb to a long period of relaxation* and to the temptations of economic competition. Certainly, our chances are as good as Brezhnev's, given the history of dissent in East Europe.

In short, I rejected the proposition of our critics that the Soviet Union stands to benefit more from peaceful competition than do the democracies. It is a counsel of despair, the opposite of what I believe to be reality. It shows an unwarranted historical pessimism, a serious lack of faith in the American people. Nixon would have no part of it. In his famous 1959 "Kitchen Debate" in Moscow he scoffed at Khrushchev's boast that he would bury us — and Nixon was right. Nothing has changed in the intervening two decades to suggest that the Communist world, inferior in resources and organization, can outstrip the West in prolonged competition. If the Soviet Union overtakes the West in military power, this will be caused not by détente but by the failure of the democracies to do what is clearly necessary. The argument that the American people cannot understand a complex challenge and a complex strategy to meet it, that unable to handle both deterrence and coexistence it must base its policy on truculence, reflects a lack of faith in democracy.

If the West saw to containment, I was convinced that it would win its historical bet. The Soviet Union's economic system was glaringly weak; its ideological appeal had faded; its political base and empire were precarious. In the sixty-year history of the state, it had never managed a legitimate, regular, succession of leadership. There had in fact been only three changes of leader: Of the four General Secretaries of the Communist Party, two (Lenin and Stalin) died in office; the third (Khrushchev) was replaced in a couplike procedure; the fourth (Brezhnev) was still consolidating his powers in early 1973, though even then signs of declining health could be noticed. The system had failed to deal seriously with the desire for political participation of the intellectual and managerial elite that industrialization inevitably spawns. Or else it sought to preempt their political aspirations by turning the ruling group into a careerist "new class" bound to produce stagnation. Moreover, the Soviet Union has yet to cope with the looming reality of its growing non-Russian population, soon to be a majority, with the severe problem of adjustment that it will entail.

The increasingly intractable problems of the Soviet economy were already becoming apparent. In 1972 its growth rate was estimated to be

1.5 percent, about equal to the population growth; this was stagnation incarnate. Total planning seems to obstruct growth in direct proportion to the scale of the economy. All incentives work in the wrong direction. Factory managers understate their potential output lest they be locked into targets that bottlenecks outside their control will prevent them from meeting. Planners do not have the test of the market to gauge the preferences of consumers (even industrial consumers). In such a vacuum they produce merchandise that is both unwanted and inferior. Quality is impossible to guarantee by directives; hence each manager tends to fulfill his quota in the manner least dependent on other sectors of the Soviet system. (An East European planner once told me that if the quota for locomotives was expressed in weight, his country produced the heaviest locomotives in the world; when it was expressed in numbers, they were the lightest and shoddiest — in each case the line of least resistance was followed.)

With no discretion to change plans, managers are forced to operate at the margin of bureaucratic legality: to hoard scarce materials or to seek reliable suppliers on the sly. This culminates in the paradox that a totally planned economy requires a black market, that is, a secret free market, to function at all. But this only magnifies the classic weakness of Communist economies: chronic shortages and chronic surpluses side by side.[6] The dilemma of Communism is that it seems impossible to run a modern economy by a system of total planning, yet it may not be possible to run a Communist state *without* a system of total planning.

The Communist Party's *raison d'être* is its monopoly of power — but this produces another anomaly. The small group of votaries who arrogate to themselves superior insight into the processes of history derive from this conviction the monomaniacal intensity required to make revolution. But once they are firmly established in power, what is their function? They are not needed to run the government or the economy or the military. They are guardians of a political legitimacy that has long since lost its moral standing as well as its revolutionary élan. They specialize in solving internal crises that their centralized system has created and external crises into which their rigidity tempts them. The Party apparatus duplicates every existing hierarchy without performing any function. Its members are watchdogs lacking criteria, an incubus to enforce order, a smug bastion of privilege inviting corruption and cynicism.

In every Communist state — it is almost an historic joke — the ultimate crisis, latent if not evident, is over the role of the Communist Party. In Poland, the Party was almost swept away because it was irrelevant and impotent. And we are still only at the beginning of that process of transformation. If Moscow is prevented by a firm Western policy from deflecting its internal tensions into international crises, it is likely to find only disillusionment in the boast that history is on its side. I remain convinced that a long period of peace will favor the pluralism of a democratic system — the economic vitality, genius for technological innovation, and creativity of free peoples.

The Nixon Administration's hard-headed geopolitical approach to East-West relations, though not easily grasped at home, was in fact effective with the Soviet leaders. For while the men in the Kremlin do not mind playing on Western preconceptions that identify diplomacy with good personal relations, they really do not know how to deal with a senti-mental foreign policy. No Western leader who specialized in "under-standing" them, as if foreign policy were like personal relations, ever succeeded. Soviet leaders have come up through a hard school. They have prevailed in a system that ruthlessly weeds out the timid and the scrupulous. Only a great lust for power — or near-fanatical ideological conviction — can have impelled them into careers in which there are few winners and disastrous penalties for losers. Personal goodwill, that mirage of Western diplomacy, cannot move them. Their ideology stresses the overriding importance of material factors and the objective balance of forces. They cannot defend conciliatory policies toward the outside world amid the struggle for power that characterizes the Soviet system except by emphasizing that objective conditions require them.

This is why unsentimental realists seem to find greater favor in that capital whose ideology rejects the proposition that man can alter the foreordained course of history. And Nixon was nothing if not a realist. Few leaders were less likely to confuse coexistence with psychotherapy or peace with good personal relations. His personal insecurity made him doubt that he could charm anyone — especially the dour Soviet leaders. He knew that there was no substitute for posing calibrated risks that would make aggression appear unattractive; he strove mightily to pre-serve the balance of power. But he was not afraid to explore incentives to give the Soviets a stake in cooperation even while he sought to make expansionism too dangerous. Over time, as other factors came into play, a stable peace might be founded on conviction and not only on neces-sity. On this basis in May 1972 the erstwhile Communist-baiter and the General Secretary of the Soviet Communist Party had met in Moscow to explore the boundaries of coexistence.

I believe that a normal Nixon Presidency would have managed to attain symmetry between the twin pillars of containment and coexistence. Nixon would have been able to demonstrate to the conservatives that détente was a means to conduct the ideological contest, not a resignation from it. And he could have handled the liberal pressures by rallying a majority of moderates behind his policy of settling concrete issues. He could then have used his demonstrated commitment to peace to marshal the free peoples of the Alliance behind a new approach to defense.

But early in his second term Nixon was no longer a normal President. And the damage was nearly irreparable. Between the Moscow summit of 1972 and Vladivostok in 1974, the chances for stable long-term coexistence between the United States and the Soviet Union were the best they have ever been in the postwar period. The USSR suffered a major setback in the Middle East and accepted it; the conflicts between us, while real, were managed. We had laid extensive foundations through a network of agreements. We had assembled incentives and penalties that seemed to moderate Soviet behavior. Never were conditions better to test the full possibilities of a subtle combination of firmness and flexibility.

We will never know what might have been possible had America not consumed its authority in that melancholy period. Congressional assaults on a weakened President robbed him of both the means of containment and the incentives for Soviet moderation, rendering resistance impotent and at the same time driving us toward a confrontation without a strategy or the means to back it up. The domestic base for our approach to East-West relations eroded. We lost the carrot in the debate over Jewish emigration that undercut the 1972 trade agreement with the Soviet Union. And the stick became ineffective as a result of progressive restrictions on executive authority from 1973 to 1976 that doomed Indochina to destruction, hamstrung the President's powers as Commander-in-Chief, blocked military assistance to key allies, and nearly devastated our intelligence agencies. In time the Soviets could not resist the opportunity presented by a weakened President and a divided America abdicating from foreign responsibilities. By 1975 Soviet adventurism had returned, reinforced by an unprecedented panoply of modern arms.

Partly as a result of our domestic weakness and Soviet power, for many of our allies détente became what conservatives had feared: an escape from the realities of the balance of power, a substitution of atmospherics for substance. In a period of recession induced by the oil price explosion, several European countries turned to East-West trade as an economic lifeboat, not an instrument of a well-thought-out foreign policy. Their leaders played to a domestic gallery, appearing as "mediators" between the Soviet Union and the United States.

Thus America sacrificed a great deal to its domestic divisions. The process began with the debate over the relationship of trade with the Soviet Union to human rights.

Grain and Emigrants

No issue of foreign policy saw such a drastic reversal of positions as East-West trade. From the moment the Nixon Administration came into office in 1969, liberal critics pressed us to relax Cold War restrictions on trade.[7] Less than six months after the Soviet occupation of Czechoslovakia, leading journals, academics, and the Democratic Congressional majority (as well as liberal Republicans) attacked our doctrine of linkage that tied trade relaxation to Soviet foreign policy behavior. Since 1969 and 1970 were turbulent years in US–Soviet relations, we granted no export licenses whatever. This, we were told, was dangerous and ineffective: We were playing into the hands of Stalinist hard-liners in the Kremlin; trade with the Soviets was not a favor to them but to us; it would promote peace; it would speed the liberalization of the Communist regime; and in any case, if we did not trade, our allies would. Some conservative businessmen joined the liberal side of the debate, regarding the linkage of trade to foreign policy benefits as an illegitimate attempt to bargain with their assets for objectives in which they had no direct interest.

The Nixon Administration held to its course. We eased restrictions slightly after the first breakthrough in SALT in May 1971 and the completion of the Berlin negotiations in August of that year. Only after the 1972 Moscow summit did we agree to a progressive improvement — always taking care to relate our moves to Soviet restraint in foreign affairs. We granted credits only to specific projects, never on a blanket basis. The Soviets were given to understand that our relative flexibility would not survive a foreign policy challenge.

Later on, when the public mood changed, it was sometimes said that the Nixon Administration had naively relied on economic incentives to moderate Soviet behavior. In light of Nixon's firm commitment to military containment, and the grudging East-West trade policy of his first term, this is a serious misconception. We did believe that carefully controlled trade would reinforce a coexistence based on a balance of forces. Economic ties in our view could make a difference but only if the Soviets were deprived of the option of adventurism. Having blocked Soviet encroachment in 1970 and 1971, we were prepared to test the possibilities of coexistence soberly and carefully, but not by adopting arguments we had been refuting for nearly four years.

The first brouhaha was over the US–Soviet grain deal. In 1972 the Soviets exploited our free market, buying up nearly a billion dollars' worth of grain on concessional terms — almost the whole of our agricultural surplus — before anyone knew what was happening.[8] The real trouble, as it turned out, was not the eagerness of the government to sell, though Nixon was surely not blind to the political benefits of a grain deal in an election year. The Soviets' coup was due primarily to their shrewd calculation that each grain company would try to keep its sales secret from its competitors. Thus, if they spread their orders widely, the Soviets reasoned (accurately), the greed of the companies would obscure the extent of Soviet purchases until the contracts were signed.

The Soviets' task was eased because no governmental monitoring system existed; the event dramatized the difficulty of relating a market economy to foreign policy objectives. If any buyer can enter the market, the sole restraint on him is his ability to pay. Therefore to achieve foreign policy goals the government must be able to interfere with the market to hold up sales, regardless of economic conditions, until its political terms are met. A system of licenses or similar restraints is inevitable — which is anathema to many entrepreneurs, including some who consider themselves fiercely anti-Communist.

Early in 1973, we became aware of another potential shortfall in the Soviet harvest. As a quid pro quo for our help we sought to force the Soviets to spread their purchases over several years. The White House insisted on a five-year agreement with a ceiling on permitted purchases that would enable our farmers to plan, prevent disruption of our markets, and give us extended foreign policy leverage. But this was possible only if we held up the grain sales until our terms were met. Our farmers were happy enough about the objective of a long-term agreement. They were much less keen on postponing immediate sales in order to achieve it; and they had acquired in Secretary of Agriculture Earl Butz a wily, passionate, and indefatigable advocate. He had been schooled in the deadliest of bureacratic arenas, as the dean of a university. When I asked Butz to study whether he had the legal authority to delay sales (by ordering that grain sales be reported to the Department of Agriculture), he evaded a clear-cut answer. Several weeks later, on May 3, I jogged his memory:

My concern in this matter is that we should not permit the Soviets to corner, quietly, a large part of this year's grain crop, leaving the U.S. consumer and our other international customers to bid up the price on the remainder.

But Butz had no intention of facing the wrath of the farmers. Much better to blame the striped-pants boys of diplomacy. He therefore suggested that *I* induce the Soviets to limit their purchases. This was great advice: Instead of using our agricultural strength as leverage on the Soviets, he was suggesting that we ask the Soviets to do us the favor of buying less than market conditions allowed. In the real world this would work only if I implied that otherwise we would find another way of limiting sales. Butz's approach was an elegant way of preventing foreign policy criteria from interfering with Soviet grain purchases.

The pro-trade coalition of liberals and entrepreneurs was gradually overtaken by another grouping of conservatives and liberals who sought to hold East-West trade as hostage to changes in Soviet emigration policy. They accepted our doctrine of linkage but gave it its most extreme formulation — far beyond the original intention. Concessions on trade were now related not to Soviet foreign policy, with which we agreed, but to Soviet domestic practices. East-West trade thereby turned into a political issue in America that over time seriously jolted our relationship with the Soviet Union without supplying a strategy for handling the resulting tension. Ironically, the vehicle for this challenge was a measure that liberals had been pressing on us since early in the Nixon Administration: the extension of Most Favored Nation (MFN) status to the Soviet Union.

Most Favored Nation status is, of course, a misnomer. It grants no special favors; it extends to the recipient country only the tariff treatment already afforded to all other nations (over a hundred) with which we have normal commercial relations. In other words, MFN treatment ends discrimination against the country that receives it. It allows normal trade to develop as commercial conditions warrant. It benefits our traders as well as foreign ones. Even with MFN, Soviet exports to the United States were not expected to grow rapidly or significantly. The MFN status was important to the Soviets for symbolic rather than for commercial reasons; it conveyed the appearance of equality in the economic field.

In September 1972, we concluded the negotiations on the Soviet Lend–Lease debt (dormant for twenty-five years) that had been conducted with skill and ingenuity by Secretary of Commerce Peter G. Peterson. This cleared the way for the trade agreement with the USSR, of which MFN was a key part. On April 10, 1973 — as Watergate was about to explode — Nixon submitted the agreement to the Congress. And thereby, just as he was faltering, he sparked a debate that blighted US–Soviet relations ever after.

It was galling that the issue chosen by our critics was a subject in which we had every reason to take pride: Jewish emigration from the Soviet Union. Early in Nixon's first term we had decided to raise this in the special Channel we maintained through Anatoly Dobrynin to the Soviet leadership. We proceeded without publicity, calculating that the Soviets could alter practices within their domestic jurisdiction more easily if they were not overtly challenged. Starting in 1969, I approached Dobrynin with the proposition that we would take note of any voluntary Soviet regard for the moral concerns of our people with respect to Soviet emigration practices. The effort was low-key but persistent; we sought action, not acclaim. Whether as a result of our representations or for reasons of its own that it did not divulge to us, Moscow changed its emigration policy. Whereas only 400 Soviet Jews had been allowed to emigrate in 1968, the number rose to nearly 35,000 in 1973.

In addition, I periodically handed over lists of hardship cases: individuals who were barred from emigration by some technicality of security regulations or for other difficulties with Soviet authorities. I told Dobrynin if the Soviets heeded our humanitarian appeals we would not as a government exploit the propaganda value of those released. Do-brynin accepted the lists without comment. But we noted that a majority of the hardship names we submitted were permitted to leave. In one instance, Dobrynin formally gave us statistics summarizing the Soviet treatment of hardship cases.

Why the Soviet Union interrupted the process right after the Moscow summit will have to be left to the publication of the Soviet archives or the memoirs of Soviet leaders. Whatever the reason, on August 3, 1972, an administrative decree of the Presidium of the Supreme Soviet im-posed a substantial "exit tax" on emigrants. The tax was theoretically designed to refund the Soviet state for the expenses of the emigrants' education; the practical consequence was to slow emigration to a trickle. The decision was nearly inexplicable in light of the generally improved state of US–Soviet relations and the goodwill the Soviets had acquired from liberalizing emigration.

The least plausible explanation was the one advanced by Dobrynin: that some middle-level functionary had made a routine decision mechan-ically ratified by the relevant minister who himself was a technician. The Soviet system does not work that way, expecially on an issue of demonstrated foreign policy sensitivity. My guess is that the exit tax was a panicky reaction to Sadat's expulsion of Soviet troops from Egypt. Afraid for their position in the Arab world, the Soviet leaders sought for some way to refurbish their credentials (since most of the Jewish emigrants settled in Israel). But I took Dobrynin's lame explanation to indicate that the Kremlin was having second thoughts; it was looking for both a scapegoat and an exit.

By then the genie was out of the bottle. On October 4, 1972, the redoubtable Senator Henry Jackson sponsored an amendment to the trade bill that precluded granting Most Favored Nation status to any Com-munist country restricting emigration. Senator Jackson had a long record of opposition to Soviet tyranny. He had courageously warned of the Soviet military buildup when it was highly unfashionable to do so. He had cooperated closely with the Administration during Nixon's first term on the struggle for an adequate defense budget, an honorable exit from Vietnam, and a strong foreign policy. To my astonishment, I found myself in confrontation with a former ally in what became an increas-ingly tense relationship. What made the conflict both strange and painful was that I felt more comfortable with Jackson on most issues than with many newfound allies who questioned his amendment from a different philosophical perspective.

Up to a point Jackson's efforts and ours complemented each other. But gradually his amendment became for him an end in itself. Once it was passed, it was no longer useful as leverage; the Soviets could not possibly change their policies in response to the act of a capitalist legislature; they were more likely to move in the opposite direction. Far from spurring emigration, the Jackson amendment in fact wound up substantially reducing it.

But the times were not propitious for a rational dialogue. Jackson suddenly found supporters among liberals who had consistently fought his views on national defense and foreign policy. The *New York Times,* which in 1969 and 1970 had castigated us for what it considered the outrageous proposition that trade should be linked to Soviet foreign policy conduct, suddenly discovered the importance of using it to accomplish the domestic transformation of Soviet society. In an editorial on November 25, 1972, the *Times* began its conversion to its own definition of linkage:

> Russia's brutal repression of the civil rights of many of its own people, the imposition of a head tax on Jews to prevent them from leaving the Soviet Union and the threat of more serious restrictions still to come, the encouragement of other countries to expropriate American interests — all such actions are calculated to inflame American public opinion and to jeopardize the future growth of Soviet-American economic relations.

On February 21, 1973, the *Washington Post,* another long-time advocate of East-West trade, turned a hard-won and tacit change in Soviet practice into a nonexistent formal Soviet pledge:

> The strong Hill sentiment to tie trade and emigration gives the President the solid practical ground he needs to inform the Russians that in order for him to make good his pledge on tariff equality, they must make good their pledge on Jewish emigration.

Later in 1973 this debate, like many others, became mired in Watergate. On September 3 the *New York Times* professed to see no difference between Watergate and Soviet police-state repression of dissidents; indeed, it made its own contribution to the prevailing paranoia by discovering a Nixon-Brezhnev alliance to suppress opposition in both countries:

> The administration announced that Treasury Secretary Shultz will soon lead a high level delegation to Moscow to renew discussions on expanding Soviet-American trade. Soviet repression apparently disturbs the White House as little as Watergate bothers the Kremlin. The world now sees a de facto Nixon-Brezhnev alliance against dissent in each other's country.

On October 10, 1972, Representative Charles Vanik of Ohio introduced an amendment similar to Jackson's in the House. He was supported by such previous stalwart defenders of East-West trade as Representatives Donald M. Fraser of Minnesota and Benjamin S. Rosenthal of New York, who joined Representative John H. Buchanan, Jr., of

Alabama on a visit to the Soviet Union in December 1972. They published in April 1973 a report on "Tension and Detente" that concluded in hitherto most uncharacteristic fashion:

We are convinced that improved relations with the Soviet Union — and, specifically, improved trade ties — are useful to both countries and to the cause of world peace. But both the President and Soviets must understand that normal relations between our countries cannot proceed while Jews and others in the Soviet Union are harassed and prevented, by whatever means, from exercising their right of emigration.[9]

On the one hand, we were being pushed to do what we had already largely accomplished: to spur Soviet emigration. On the other, it was becoming clear that the pressure hid a deeper purpose: to extend the conventional criticism of Nixon's alleged moral insensitivity into new areas of policy, including foreign affairs, in which Nixon's competence had heretofore gone unchallenged. It was not free of recklessness, for while Jackson was prepared to face the consequences of a confrontation with the Soviet Union, many of his supporters, as they were soon to prove, were not. If baiting Moscow led to increased Soviet adventurism, which of the crusaders for human rights would support our determination to resist it? Within two years many of the rhetorical hard-liners had a chance to answer that question over the issue of Soviet-Cuban intervention in Angola. Most of the members of the liberal-conservative coalition that had spoiled for a confrontation over human rights avoided it over a blatant threat to international security.

At the beginning of the campaign on Soviet emigration practices, it was luckily not yet apparent that we were facing a fundamental challenge to one of the pillars of our foreign policy. We dealt with it on its merits, as an attempt to lift the newly imposed exit tax. And the threat of the Jackson amendment undoubtedly helped to convince the Soviet leaders that a change of course was indicated. On March 30, Dobrynin came to see me with a statement labeled "confidential for the President." It proclaimed, naturally enough, that emigration policy fell exclusively within the jurisdiction of the Soviet state; it complained of the "noisy campaign" on emigration that it denounced as "artificial and ill-meaning." But the upshot of all the tough talk was the good news that the tax was being lifted. The Soviet note claimed that the new law had always been intended to be discretionary; it would be applied only in "unusual" circumstances of state security. Accordingly, only such "usual and insignificant duties which were also being collected before the decree of August 3, 1972 are being collected. . . ."

Private messages from Brezhnev were generally not communicated to the Congress; hence, unless the Soviets made an exception, the note would not help us in dealing with Jackson. Moreover, the emphasis on the discretionary nature of the law did not preclude a future sudden tightening of the regulations. I therefore asked for permission to transmit the communication to the Congress; going far beyond diplomatic custom, I inquired whether I might inform the government of Israel. I also asked for more specific assurances than the mere statement that discretionary authority would not be applied — specifically a de facto ending of the tax.

The Soviets replied on April 10 in a manner that underlined how much importance they attached to US–Soviet relations; they authorized us to communicate Brezhnev's message to the Congress as an official statement. As for informing Israel, Moscow stressed that Israel had no standing to discuss Soviet emigration policies, especially via the United States. Still, this was only bravado: "It is a matter for the President to decide how to use our communication and whom he will inform about its contents." To avoid any misunderstanding, I worked out a formal statement of the Soviet position, including a proviso that the tax would not be reintroduced. I cleared it with Dobrynin for submission to the Congress. Dobrynin agreed to it on April 16. (The full text is reprinted in the backnotes.)[10]

Once the Soviet Union agreed formally to drop the exit tax, I informed Dobrynin that no outstanding issues stood in the way of implementing the US–Soviet trade agreement of 1972. I proved wildly off the mark.

For the growing enfeeblement of the President had changed all previous assumptions. Nixon expected to celebrate a great achievement when he called the Congressional leaders, including Senator Jackson, to the White House on April 18, to inform them of the Soviet note. The Soviet Union under American pressure had repealed domestic legislation and given written assurances to that effect, which we could transmit to the Congress. Nixon had removed the major obstacle to the granting of MFN and had proved the advantage of quiet diplomacy on human rights. Or so he thought.

By then Nixon was badly wounded. The day before, he had acknowledged the possibility that Watergate involved high levels of his Administration. In these circumstances the Congress was not seeking a collaboration; it was looking for opportunities to prove its independence. The legislators assembled in the Roosevelt Room of the White House listened politely. None had thought such a Soviet collapse possible. Yet it was difficult to avoid the impression that a few of them up for reelection in 1974 preferred to have the issue rather than its resolution. They sat in grumbling silence at another of Nixon's coups when they were rallied by the redoubtable Jackson. What the Soviets had done was not enough, he said coolly. The Soviets would have to give assurances not only as to the exit tax; they had to guarantee a minimum number of exit visas;

and they had to ease emigration not only for Jews but for all nationalities.

It was an amazing demand. Anyone even vaguely familiar with the Soviet system knew that there was no chance whatever that such terms would be met. The Soviet Union could not commit itself publicly to a fixed number, which implied that there was an unlimited mass of Soviet citizens eager to emigrate. And if it made that concession to all nationalities, there was literally no telling what would happen to the Soviet system. Yet in the prevailing public mood in America, no legislator could afford to dissociate himself from the demand and risk charges of being "soft" on Soviet emigration. And if Congressional pressures led to deadlock, one could always blame the Administration for not having pursued a Congressionally mandated objective with adequate energy and conviction. So Jackson's colleagues remained silent and we were left to sort out the confusion. It was our first exposure to what came to be a staple of Watergate and its aftermath: a Congressional mandate for an unfulfillable course that sapped our credibility abroad without giving us the tools to deal with the consequences of the resulting tension.

No doubt Communist nations are prepared to pay *some* price for increased trade; indeed, this theory lay behind our own linkage approach. But in our view concessions were more likely to be obtainable in the field of international conduct, with respect to which foreign countries have a defined interest and legal standing, than over matters traditionally considered within the domestic jurisdiction of a state, particularly a state historically and ideologically so obsessed with internal security. For the Soviet Union to alter its domestic practices in response to a frontal public assault by a foreign nation would be perceived by its already nearly paranoid rulers as a direct impairment of their authority. And it was likely to be resisted all the more strenuously because the Soviet Union had modified its emigration policy as a result of our private diplomacy.

The pity was that Senator Jackson and the Nixon Administration were both committed to the same objective: increasing emigration from the Soviet Union. The dispute was over tactics. The Administration doubted that overt pressure could succeed; Jackson insisted that no other method would work. Sometimes it was hard to avoid the impression that he was as interested in the symbolism of confrontation as in the result. He also sought to appeal to a Jewish constituency for his Presidential ambitions — a not unworthy motive for a public figure fortunate enough to be a native-born citizen of the United States.

A weakened Nixon was at a grave disadvantage. The Jackson amendment, originated to maintain existing levels of Jewish emigration, was being pursued even after the Soviets had lifted restrictions in order to bring about *increased* emigration of *all* nationalities. Nixon and I did not help matters by misunderstanding Jackson's thrust. We thought that eventually he would work out some accord with us for what was attainable. In fact, he kept escalating his demands.

The collapse of national civility and cohesion made it difficult for the disputants to hear each other. The Administration felt aggrieved, not the best attitude in dealing with the Congress; our critics sensed our vulnerability, not the ideal precondition for serious dialogue. My nightmare was that under the conditions of Watergate it was wildly risky to provoke a confrontation with Moscow over an issue on which it had already substantially yielded, our leverage was weak, and the resulting crisis might find us without public support. Jackson believed Watergate gave him the opportunity to insist on his total program, and once he was embarked on his course, his constituency gave him added impetus. To his banner flocked many willing enough to strike a pose, not nearly so prepared to face confrontation. In my speech to the Pacem in Terris Conference on October 8, 1973, I tried, almost despairingly, to point out the dangers:

> We shall never condone the suppression of fundamental liberties. We shall urge humane principles and use our influence to promote justice. But the issue comes down to the limits of such efforts. How hard can we press without provoking the Soviet leadership into returning to practices in its foreign policy that increase international tensions? Are we ready to face the crises and increased defense budgets that a return to Cold War conditions would spawn? And will this encourage full emigration or enhance the well-being or nourish the hope for liberty of the peoples of Eastern Europe and the Soviet Union? Is it detente that has prompted repression — or is it detente that has generated the ferment and the demand for openness which we are now witnessing? . . .
>
> These questions have no easy answers. The government may underestimate the margin of concessions available to us. But a fair debate must admit that they *are* genuine questions, the answers to which could affect the fate of all of us.

It was to no avail. The struggle over the Jackson amendment continued through 1974. (I shall describe the later negotiations with Jackson in Chapter XXII.) The Congress progressively weakened the constraints on Soviet conduct without providing us the tools to see it through in the form of increased defense (though Jackson himself was always in the forefront of the fight for a strong defense). It was a part of a larger pattern — the product of Vietnam trauma and the corrosion of Watergate — that stripped away both the incentives and penalties needed to conduct an effective policy toward Moscow.

Missiles and Fantasy

SENATOR Henry Jackson was the indispensable link between the two groups critical of our relations with the Soviets — the liberals, preoccupied with human rights; and the conservatives, who became anxious about any negotiations with the Soviets. Nixon, great tactician that he was, never conceived that he, the renowned Cold Warrior, would in the end be attacked from his old base on the right wing of the Republican party. But when in 1972 he culminated a year of negotiations with a summit in Moscow and a series of agreements, his erstwhile friends were at first baffled and then disillusioned. Some found solace in blaming me; others started a guerrilla war, attacking especially the agreement limiting strategic arms. Much of the issue was fantasy, much of it politics, and in the Watergate era it had perverse consequences. Conservatives tore each other apart, only to produce a more liberal Congress just as foreign perils were mounting.

There was a revolutionary element in the first strategic arms limitation treaty (SALT I). This lay in the agreement of the Soviet Union and the United States permanently to limit their deployment of antiballistic missile systems (ABMs) to no more than two sites 1,300 kilometers apart and to no more than 200 missiles. For the first time in history two major powers deliberately rested their security on each other's vulnerability. But it was not this unprecedented feature that led to acrimony. What drew fire was an issue few had thought controversial when the accords were being negotiated. This was the five-year Interim Agreement that pledged both sides to freeze their strategic offensive missile forces, whether land- or sea-based, at the levels of mid-1972. It was expected that during the five-year period a follow-on, long-term agreement would be negotiated.[11]

The Interim Agreement did not affect our strategic arsenal or our force planning; it was a snapshot, as of the moment of signature, of the strategic relationship as it had evolved over the previous decade. The Soviet Union had expanded its missile force at a rapid rate after the Cuban missile crisis in 1962. By 1971 it had equaled us in numbers of intercontinental missiles; at the time of the 1972 summit it had more. We retained a large advantage in the total number of warheads, however — an advantage that would, in fact, grow over the five years of the agreement. We were already equipping our missiles with multiple independently targetable reentry vehicles (MIRVs), whereas the Soviets had not yet tested such a system.

SALT imposed a sacrifice on the Soviets if it did on anyone. They had been building 200 new launchers a year. They had to dismantle some 210 ICBMs of older types to come down to the agreed ceiling.

We had stopped building during the Johnson Administration; we had no new missile program in production and the Vietnam-era Congress would not have approved one. For us the sacrifice was theoretical. The only area where we could have been inhibited by SALT was in submarine-launched ballistic missiles (SLBMs). But the Joint Chiefs of Staff were adamant in their opposition to building more of the submarine-launched Poseidon missiles then available or the submarines to carry them. They preferred to wait for the more powerful Trident submarine and missile, which would not be ready until at least 1978, or *after* the expiration of the Interim Agreement.[12] Moreover, SALT I did not count or limit strategic bombers, in which we were vastly superior, or our forward-based aircraft and carriers in and around Europe and the Pacific, or the nuclear weapons of France and the United Kingdom (or China). In short, if there was an imbalance, SALT did not create it; it reflected self-limiting decisions made over a decade. SALT did provide a time span in which they could be remedied. SALT I caused us to give up not a single offensive weapons program. The freeze was essential, indeed, if we were ever going to catch up. And we followed SALT I with a substantial modernization of our strategic forces.

But a man from Mars arriving to observe our domestic debate would never have known this. He would have read that SALT I "conceded" an inequality in missiles to the Soviets. He would have deduced that the treaty sanctified a missile gap — instead of reducing that gap. He would not have been aware of the strange phenomenon that a force level we had adopted voluntarily, and that we were in no position to change over the life of an agreement, suddenly became "dangerous" when it was reaffirmed as part of that agreement.

Instead of flailing about in this fog of obscurantism, the real debate should have been about how we got into the position in the first place. The roots of the discrepancy in numbers lay in the strategic doctrine of "mutual assured destruction" developed in the Sixties. According to this doctrine, it did not matter whether we had more or fewer missiles than the Soviet Union so long as we had enough to obliterate the citizens and factories of large parts of the Soviet Union.* Similarly, the Soviet Union was considered to possess a capacity to deter the United States so long as it had enough missiles to destroy American popular and industrial centers. Strategy thus turned into economic analysis: As long as enough of our weapons survived a Soviet nuclear strike to wreak the theoretically calculated havoc, deterrence would be maintained. Ac-

---

*In 1965, Secretary of Defense Robert McNamara defined the "assured destruction" requirement as the capacity to destroy one-fourth to one-third of the Soviet population and two-thirds of Soviet industry. Three years later, the requirement was *lowered;* in 1968 it was defined as one-fifth to one-fourth of the Soviet population and one-half of Soviet industry.[13]

cording to this rationale, our requirement for strategic forces was thought to be largely independent of the threat we faced. The vulnerability of part of our forces — such as ICBMs — was irrelevant provided enough warheads from all sources would survive to inflict "unacceptable" damage.

The reliance on nuclear retaliation had been developed when America enjoyed overwhelming strategic superiority. In an era of parity, the willingness of any President to put the American population at risk for the protection of distant countries was bound to lose credibility. The doctrine ignored or vastly underestimated the psychological and political inhibitions on leaders who have to give the orders. The targeting scenarios left a President with only two options in a crisis: to give in, or to initiate the extermination of tens of millions of people (first Soviet citizens and then our own in the inevitable retaliation). This strategy was morally questionable even in an era when we had superiority. In an age of approaching strategic equality it threatened to turn into a formula for either suicide or surrender. All would depend on the Soviet leaders' having enough fear of our intentions to be deterred from running risks. This could be sustained only by a reckless diplomacy through which it would become plausible that if pressed we would unleash a cataclysm even if it destroyed our population and urban centers — an approach most incompatible with the convictions of our people and most likely to evoke panic or appeasement among our allies.

In other words, it was not necessary to postulate a Soviet advantage in strategic weapons to be concerned about the altered military balance. Even US–Soviet equality in strategic weapons implied a revolutionary change in the assumptions on which the West's security had been based in the entire postwar period. For the first twenty-five years of the nuclear age, maintaining the military equilibrium was relatively straightforward. The Soviet Union was always superior in ground forces on the Eurasian continent, yet its military reach was generally limited to regions accessible to motorized ground transport, that is, adjacent territories in Europe and, to some extent, China. On the other hand, Africa, most of the Middle East, even Southeast Asia, were beyond the range of major Soviet military intervention. And even the areas theoretically hostage to Soviet ground armies were protected by three factors:

• First, by American strategic forces so preponderant that they could disarm the Soviet Union or at least reduce its counterblow to tolerable levels;

• Second, by a vast American superiority in so-called theater nuclear forces everywhere around the Soviet periphery;

• And third, in Europe, by substantial American and allied ground forces that posed a high risk to the Soviets that a ground attack would trigger nuclear retaliation from the United States.

Not surprisingly, the major crises in the first twenty years of the post-war period — whether in Berlin, Korea, the Middle East, or Cuba — were ultimately contained, because the costs of pushing them beyond a certain point always appeared exorbitant to Moscow.

Starting in the 1960s, the military balance began to change, almost imperceptibly at first, so great was our superiority, but with growing momentum as the years went by. By the 1970s it was already foreseeable that when the Soviets developed multiple warheads of their own, the larger size of their missiles (in technical language, their bigger throwweight) was bound to be translated eventually into more warheads of superior explosive power. Not only would we lose our "counterforce" capability (our ability to destroy their land-based missiles); our land-based missiles would become substantially vulnerable. The strategic equation of the entire postwar period would be reversed: Our threat to initiate a nuclear exchange would become hollow. If crises no longer produced fear of escalation to all-out war, they would also become more likely. There would be an exponential increase in the danger to allies at levels of violence below general nuclear exchange.

The imminent transformation of the strategic balance should have forced a reappraisal of the strategy of relying on the threat of general nuclear war even to protect Europe and certainly other areas; and it should have led to major efforts to strengthen local and regional conventional forces. Unfortunately, in the early Seventies the civil strife over Vietnam prevented a rethinking of old verities just when it became most urgent. The defense budget was the focal point of antiwar pressures, not of thoughtful analysis.

New weapons were decried as excessive, as symptoms of a military psychosis, as wasteful and dangerous. The ABM program passed the Senate by only one vote and was then emasculated in the appropriations process. The C-5A transport aircraft that later saved an ally in the 1973 Middle East war was challenged repeatedly. Even MIRVs, the only new strategic system available to us to offset the Soviet numerical superiority in the 1970s, were not immune; in 1970 forty Senators signed an appeal to stop MIRV testing. In 1973 the Trident submarine and missile, then the only strategic offensive program ready for production, escaped cancellation by one vote. Ironically, it was those most opposed to the arms race who rejected flexible military options; they clung to the most bloodthirsty nuclear targeting strategies because mass extermination of civilians, in the weird logic of the nuclear age, requires the smallest number of strategic forces.

In this atmosphere, maintaining even the arsenal inherited from the Sixties absorbed the energies of the Nixon Administration up to the end of the Vietnam war. Obtaining funds for new programs, nuclear or conventional, was enormously difficult. This is why the initiative for negotiating a freeze on offensive weapons originated in the Pentagon itself, in an October 1970 memorandum from Deputy Secretary of Defense David Packard — a fact later conveniently forgotten. The best that could be accomplished in the conditions of the early 1970s was to strengthen our military posture as much as the Congress allowed and to adjust the doctrine of assured destruction so that less catastrophic options were possible.*

In short, the first SALT agreement was not extracted from us by clever Soviet negotiators; the conditions it reflected were conditions we had imposed on ourselves by our earlier decisions and our domestic turmoil. It was therefore in our power to alter these. And the Administration set about to do exactly that. It used the debate over SALT to renew its request for a supplementary appropriation to strengthen our strategic forces — the B-1 strategic bomber; the Trident submarine and missile; cruise missiles; and more accurate missile warheads — *all* of which were to be available to go into production after the Interim Agreement expired (in 1977). We would then be in a position either to match the Soviets in an arms race or to trade bargaining chips in a new round of SALT.

But as Nixon's second term began, the political and moral authority he needed to pursue simultaneously the military balance and a sophisticated policy of arms control was beginning to erode. Congressional liberals resisted increases in the defense budget; it was not the "peace dividend" they had expected. (The Congressional climate did not begin to support major defense increases until about 1975.) And conservatives were uncomfortable with the ideological ambiguity of arms control. Erstwhile allies became adversaries. Watergate poisoned the atmosphere.

The fact of the matter was that each side in the debate had a point; Jackson and the Administration would have served the country better as allies than as opponents. The Nixon Administration deserves great credit for having preserved the sinews of our defense in the face of a relentless Congressional and media assault. Every new strategic program in existence a decade later (together with some canceled by the Carter Administration) had its origin under the stewardship of Nixon and Ford.

But Jackson and his friends were not wrong in their fear that theories of arms control may in fact have reinforced the reluctance of some in Congress, key opinion-makers, and even Administration officials, to face the relentless Soviet military buildup squarely. After arms control be-

---

*Nixon's Foreign Policy Reports of 1970–1973, written by me and my staff, called repeatedly for a change in targeting, but little was done until the stewardship of James R. Schlesinger as Secretary of Defense. Paradoxically, however, the decline of our *capability* for a counterforce strategy turned even the more sophisticated targeting into a risky tit-for-tat option with no logical stopping place once it was embarked upon.

came fashionable in the Sixties, new weapons systems had to overcome not only the traditional objection of liberals that they were unnecessary (because we already possessed an "overkill" capacity) but the added one that they endangered the prospects of SALT. Indeed, many new programs could be put through the Congress less on their merits than as bargaining chips. They were needed, various Administration spokesmen — including me — argued, so that they could be traded in a negotiation. Whatever the tactical utility of this argument, it tended to reduce the energy with which new programs were pursued. The Pentagon found it difficult to muster enthusiasm — or scarce resources — for projects that were defined as negotiable. After a while the Soviet Union began to play the game deliberately. From ABM to cruise missiles, it systematically sought to use SALT to inhibit our military and technological development; it tried to fuel our domestic debate, adding its own propaganda to Congressional pressures against new weapons.

The theory that new American weapons weakened the prospects of arms control thrived despite all evidence to the contrary. In 1967, before we had an ABM program, President Lyndon Johnson had suggested to Soviet Premier Alexei Kosygin at Glassboro that both sides renounce ABMs. Kosygin contemptuously dismissed the idea as one of the most ridiculous he had ever heard. By 1970, after the Nixon Administration had won its Congressional battle for ABM by one vote, Soviet SALT negotiators refused to discuss any other subject. Only by the most strenuous negotiating effort did we ensure that limits on offensive, as well as defensive, weapons were included. (Conversely, the Carter Administration's abandonment of the B-1 strategic bomber, its stretch-out of the MX missile, and slowdown of the Trident program did not speed up SALT II negotiations or improve the terms.)

As with all civil wars, the conflict between the Nixon Administration and its conservative critics was bitter. Shared premises inevitably caused disagreements to be ascribed to bad faith. Suspicion of motives came to overwhelm discussion of substance. Nixon, like me, was substantially in accord with Senator Henry Jackson. As on Soviet emigration, we differed with him primarily as to tactics: The Administration thought that we could best sustain domestic support for a strong defense if we had demonstrated that we were also concerned with arms control. Jackson was convinced that SALT would ultimately drain Congressional support for our military programs by creating a misleading impression that peace had arrived.

The two sides should have joined forces behind a strong defense program and a realistic arms control approach. Instead, Jackson insisted on a showdown, egged on by Nixon's traditional liberal opponents who seized the opportunity of this intramural squabble but whose newfound militancy on human rights did not divert their pressures for cutting the military budget. On March 8, 1973, Nixon gloomily told the National Security Council:

I had breakfast this morning with Senator [John] McClellan and Senator [Milton] Young. Both of them have always been strong supporters of our policy, particularly where military matters are concerned. They said that as far as the Senate was concerned, we were going to have real troubles on defense matters. Even Senator McClellan is talking of making cuts in our NATO forces. He said he is doing this not because he wants to, but he needs to take this position in order to avoid even deeper cuts that would be imposed by the Senate. The Senate, with the exception of Senators Jackson and [John] Tower, simply won't back us on these issues.

In these circumstances Nixon naturally had the greatest difficulty crediting the seriousness of those who accused him in effect of being soft in negotiating with the Soviets. And it was hard to take after the abuse we had suffered in the lonely determination to preserve American honor and credibility in the first term. A meeting of minds would have been difficult in the best of conditions; Watergate froze the mutual distrust beyond any hope of understanding.

The SALT II Stalemate

IN theory our defense problem should have been amenable to the rational weighing of carefully elaborated choices that outsiders see as the process of government. Reality is not like that. Decisions emerge from a combination of personal convictions, bureaucratic self-interest, administrative trade-offs, and Congressional and public pressures, with the dividing line between these elements often blurred in the discussion and even in the minds of the participants. In this instance, astonishing as it may seem, hawks and doves alike were reluctant to face the implications of our evaporating strategic superiority. The programs being pushed by the Pentagon — Trident, B-1, and improved warheads — generally enhanced our second-strike capacity. They were an insurance against a Soviet surprise attack. They did not deal with the dilemma of how to respond to Soviet expansionism when we no longer possessed a credible counterforce capacity and were inferior in conventional forces. The Defense Department did not dare address the issue of conventional forces when the national policy was to abolish the draft — which in turn was needed to defuse the antiwar movement. The doves thought even existing forces were excessive. They perceived no threat to international security in the fateful combination of nuclear parity and local inferiority.

In this environment our preparations for SALT II fell between two stools. Our deliberations neither rose to a true analysis of our long-term strategy nor addressed the fundamental question of whether a SALT negotiation was the right way to deal with our emerging security problems. The Defense Department generally defended its existing programs, though the rationale for them was growing threadbare. It was torn between its desire to support Presidential policy (which favored a new round of SALT talks) and its fear of retribution from Senator Jackson, the second ranking member of the Armed Services Committee, whose support was essential to steer military appropriations through the Congress. The State Department and the Arms Control and Disarmament Agency (ACDA) — before Fred Iklé took over as its director — were concerned with negotiability, defined at least in a general sense by what the Soviets had said they would accept. They were thus objectively opposing the few new strategic programs that had passed the Congressional gauntlet.

How Nixon would have reacted to these pressures in normal times is difficult to determine. He had an overwhelming mandate. He had pulled off more difficult feats than reconciling a strong defense with arms control. But the question soon became moot when Watergate deprived him of the attention span he needed to give intellectual impetus to SALT. Even in his first term I had had difficulty getting Nixon to focus on the technical issues of SALT. Now in the wake of the resignations of Haldeman and Ehrlichman, he explicitly told me (on May 1) to follow my own judgment in choosing among options. I did not do so. I continued to submit the options to him. But this merely added one bureaucratic step. His approval of staff recommendations on SALT was nearly automatic.

The practical result, however, was a governmental stalemate. Presidential assistants can be powerful in influencing Presidential decisions; they cannot make the decisions, especially when major departments have strong convictions. In the first term my influence had been greatest where the departments were eager to avoid the onus of public controversy (as on Vietnam negotiations), or where no one wanted to take the responsibility for a major change of course (as on China).

In that period, my chairmanship of interdepartmental committees had enabled me to learn the views of the various agencies, encourage analysis, and narrow the options. I could then use this knowledge in secret negotiations with some confidence as to where I had bureaucratic support and what would cause difficulties. The agencies still assumed that they shared responsibility for the outcome of a negotiation, including its failure.

But by 1973 they had discovered that the major negotiations took place without their knowledge. Hence I could be blamed for failure, or be made to bear the brunt of whatever controversy even success was sure to bring. Each department thereafter would stake out its maximum objective, whatever sense it made. If that pristine position was not

achieved, the agencies were not responsible. The inevitable compromise
that would be necessary for a solution, and which in normal procedures
they would have urged, could now be blamed on inadequate vigilance
by the negotiator. My position, in short, had become bureaucratically
untenable.

Our preparations for SALT II suddenly took on a theological cast.
For ten years we had deliberately designed a force structure quite asym-
metrical with that of the Soviets. Our missiles were small and presumably versatile; theirs were heavy and powerful. The Soviets put most of
their emphasis on land-based missiles with heavy payloads; we had di-
versified to include bombers and submarine-based missiles. The Soviets
were ahead in numbers of land-based missiles and throwweight; we in
multiple warheads. This was the force structure we had *chosen*.
Throughout my period in office not a single request came forward from
either the civilian or the military element of the Pentagon to change the
mix of our forces. What they did ask for, when SALT II negotiations
began, was that we demand in negotiations the perfect symmetry that
their own unilateral decisions had never sought, and had indeed prevented, and that they never attempted to achieve even once the principle
had been conceded.

Perhaps we should have declared a moratorium on SALT for a year
to get our intellectual house in order. But bureaucratic momentum, and
the fear that delay would be blamed on Watergate and thus weaken the
President, made it impossible. And we hoped to repeat the experience
of SALT I, in which we had clarified our thinking as we went along.
Our dilemma was that we were constrained by domestic pressures from
choosing either of the two options that made strategic sense: building
up massively to bring about Soviet restraint through the threat of a counterforce capability, or freezing the status quo while we still had an edge
in warheads.

The Defense Department had a clear-cut different view. It would be
prepared to live with the number of launchers we had decided to build
though they spelled inequality; it was not willing to see these numbers
written down in an agreement. For an agreement, it insisted on "equal
aggregates," or equality in every weapons system — ICBMs, SLBMs,
and heavy bombers. This was a symbolic objective that reflected domestic pressures, not a political or strategic analysis.* It is impossible

---

*The strategic significance of equal aggregates would depend on the level at which the numbers
were equalized. For example, one favorite proposal was to equalize missile throwweight. As a
result of unilateral procurement decisions made by each side in the Sixties, Soviet throwweight
was about four times our own. On the other hand, the weight of warheads on our airplanes more
than made up the difference. Advocates of a throwweight limitation, looking for the most advantageous definition for us, therefore urged that it be confined to ICBMs. Their argument was not
unreasonable; bomber throwweight was not, in fact, suitable for surprise attacks because of the
long time it took for airplanes to reach their targets. What was never explained was why the Soviets

to achieve by negotiation what one is not willing to pursue by one's own effort. In effect, the proposal meant asking the Soviets to reduce unilaterally without sacrificing any American program or threatening any American buildup if the proposal were not accepted. How to accomplish it was generously left to my discretion. The proposition reminded me of the story of the admiral who during World War II claimed to have found a solution to the submarine problem: He proposed heating the ocean and boiling the enemy to the surface. Asked how to accomplish this feat, he replied: "I have given you the idea; its technical implementation is up to you."

The State Department went to the other extreme. It proposed a moratorium on all MIRV testing and deployment. This was no more negotiable since it would have excluded the Soviets from the MIRV field altogether. It was also greeted with little enthusiasm in the Pentagon because it would have forced us to abandon the Trident, the only new American missile then under development. Such MIRV limits were also alleged to raise a host of verification issues. (These on closer examination proved soluble.)

So it was that for the first time since I had come to government I was bureaucratically isolated — and confronted with palpable absurdities.

While these esoteric debates were going on, and despite its obsession with equality, the Defense Department continued to *reduce* our forces by administrative decisions throughout the nearly seven years that SALT II was being negotiated. For example, under its published 1973 five-year program — without any White House guidance or any reference to SALT — the Pentagon planned to retire some 100 B-52s and to build only 250 B-1s to replace the remaining B-52s, for a total numerical decline in our strategic forces of some 290 units. It thus gave the Soviets for nothing benefits for which we could at least have attempted to exact some reciprocity in the negotiations.

It may seem strange that decisions of such consequence could be made

would accept our definition or how we would convince them to do so given known building programs. But assuming there were equal ICBM throwweight limitations, if the ceiling was set at the Soviet level and there were no limitations on MIRVS, *both* sides would develop a first-strike capability. This violated every precept of arms control because in a crisis it would give each side an incentive to strike first. But if we did not build up to the Soviet level – and there were neither programs nor proposals to do so — the "equality" would remain theoretical; only the Soviets would gain a first-strike capability. This was even more dangerous; it would compound conventional inferiority by strategic instability. A joint ceiling at the Soviet level was no doubt easy to negotiate, if we lost our sanity, since it was meaningless; it constrained no Soviet program and gave us a freedom we were unlikely to use. Pursuing the idea of equality in the other direction — getting the Soviets to come down to our levels — was chasing illusions. They would want us to give them something in return, such as accepting continued inequality in launchers. This was precluded by the Defense Department's near-religious dedication to equal aggregates. Or else we would have to threaten a massive buildup of our forces. In the fevered Congressional climate of the closing stages of the Vietnam war and the beginning of Watergate, there was no possibility of this either. We would be lucky to keep what we had.

by a department of the government without White House clearance. And technically they were not. But the White House faces a serious decision in determining at what point to intervene in the budgetary process. Our defense budget is larger than the entire expenditures of any European country. In the early phases the Office of Management and Budget in the White House can have considerable influence — but only on the gross totals. For the NSC to intervene in detail at this stage and to specify weapons systems that we wanted to preserve for a SALT trade-off would have affronted the Defense Department and the uniformed military. They are acutely sensitive about what they consider their prerogative in making the initial recommendation about how to divide up approved funds among the services.

The Pentagon had been too badly burned by what it considered interference by armchair civilian strategists in the Sixties to be hospitable to high-level review of its planning. In 1971 I had sent an inquiry to the Defense Department asking why Soviet weapons should cost less than comparable American ones. It was still under study five years later when I left the government. The same fate befell a request for a comprehensive review of naval strategy and requirements. In each case the Joint Chiefs objected, by the time-honored method of foot-dragging, to the principle that their detailed plans might be subject to review by officials outside the Department of Defense. It was not until James Schlesinger became Secretary of Defense in 1973 that we succeeded in obtaining the review of targeting for our strategic forces that we had requested in 1969. By then the growth of the Soviet strategic forces had severely constricted our choices.

Early in the Nixon Administration I thought some progress was being made when a Defense Program Review Committee was set up, including State and the economic agencies. Secretary of Defense Laird supported it because he wanted to bring home to the claimants for larger expenditures for social services the grave consequences of taking them out of the defense budget. I agreed happily because I thought it would give me the opportunity to influence strategic doctrine and force levels at an earlier stage than had been customary. As things turned out, Laird served his purposes better than I mine. As a practical matter Laird invoked the committee only to stave off gross cuts in the budget. The White House saw the outlines of the detailed defense program only during the summer before it was put into final form in October. By then the services had made their various trade-offs. Weapons considered obsolescent were the first to go, partly because as they disappeared they strengthened the case for entirely new systems. The unresolved issues were kept to a minimum and were usually highly technical, satisfying Presidential insistence on having the last word without enabling his staff to undertake a serious strategic review. So it happened that we continued to hand to the Soviets as part of our budgetary process what we should have used as bargaining chips — to my vocal but futile dismay; the budgetary and the negotiating cycles were simply out of phase.

It was hardly an environment conducive to conceptual thought when SALT II got under way in October 1972. The Soviets proposed the withdrawal of American ballistic-missile submarines from forward bases as well as mutual "restraint" in the development of new strategic weapons. Since our government had not yet formulated any position, and was preoccupied by the Presidential elections and the final negotiations on Vietnam, we arrived at a tried and true response: We proposed an "exploratory" meeting. Its purpose, as laid down in instructions to the SALT delegation on November 8, 1972, was to elicit Soviet reactions and to develop a "work program" — in short, to make sure that nothing much controversial could occur.

Our delegation carried out these instructions with the meticulousness that our own internal divisions made obligatory. For six months theoretical papers were pushed back and forth while we consumed ourselves in near-academic debates about options that, even had we been able to agree on them, had no relationship to any negotiating reality.

Early in 1973, SALT talks resumed. The negotiations met in Geneva and presented maximum positions to each other without a serious effort to bridge the gaps. This had to await internal review by both governments. I do not know what deliberations, if any, the Soviet leadership undertook. As for us, at NSC Verification Panel meetings* in February and March 1973, it became clear that there were political limits to any proposal that impinged on our MIRV program. The State Department was leaning toward proposing a moratorium on MIRV testing. Deputy Secretary of Defense William Clements and Chairman of the Joint Chiefs of Staff Admiral Thomas Moorer were strongly opposed. They argued that though we would still be able to test our new Trident missiles with single warheads, the Trident program without MIRVs would lose its rationale and be killed in Congress. The new Secretary of Defense, Elliot Richardson, agreed. In this they were undoubtedly right; with our budgetary process, a moratorium tends to kill the weapons system to which it applies. One cannot obtain appropriations for what one is seeking to ban through negotiations.

A National Security Council meeting on March 8, 1973, confronted the President with having to decide whether any kind of MIRV limitation should be included in our position. If so, which approach — a ban on MIRVing large Soviet missiles, a freeze and a MIRV test ban for

---

*The Verification Panel was an interagency subcommittee of the National Security Council with responsibility for SALT planning. It included representatives of the Departments of State and Defense, CIA, Joint Chiefs of Staff, ACDA, and NSC staff, under my chairmanship.

two or three years, or some other variation? And what were we prepared
to pay for limitations on Soviet multiple warheads? The desultory discussion merely reaffirmed old perplexities. Unbeknownst to his foreign
policy advisers, Nixon was already preoccupied with the unraveling of
Watergate. And technical discussions of throwweight, aggregates, or
fractionization (the number of warheads on each launcher) bored him in
the best of circumstances. His distracted look and sporadic sarcastic
comments underlined that he wanted nothing so much as for the meeting
to end without having to confront a decision that could only add a foreign policy controversy to his domestic agonies.

Nixon also had an acute instinct for the right moment to act. The
Soviets had given no indication that they were ready for serious discussion. Our own deliberations were largely exploratory and theoretical.
No one understood better than Nixon the principle that a President should
not spend political capital unless he can calculate high odds for success.
So the outcome of the meeting was the Solomonic decision that a new
interagency paper would be prepared, summing up — and possibly sim-
plifying — the many options before us. Given the raging disputes within
our government, even agreeing on a definition of the disagreements
would not be a simple matter. Resolving them would have taken months
without Watergate; Watergate caused the issue in effect to be deferred
into the Ford Presidency. While not prepared to rule on SALT, Nixon
had no hesitation in pronouncing on our strategic goals. He concluded
the meeting with a peroration that we could never afford to be Number
2; we had to do what was necessary to maintain at least equivalence.
But he gave no guidelines by which to measure whether this criterion
was met either in strategic planning or in SALT. That, after all, was
the issue.

The divisions in Washington were matched by foot-dragging in Moscow. The American debate about "inequality" must have had its counterpart in Moscow. After all, SALT I constrained no American program;
it stopped several Soviet programs. The Soviets had not yet tested any
MIRVs, moreover, and were undoubtedly not ready to undertake a serious negotiation on limiting them.

These inhibitions were reinforced by Brezhnev's eagerness to conclude the Agreement on the Prevention of Nuclear War (discussed below). He was afraid that to pursue intensive negotiations on both subjects simultaneously would delay his cherished project. At times he even
attempted to use SALT to speed that Agreement. This was reflected in
two conversations I had with Dobrynin in early March 1973. Dobrynin
alleged that the Soviet military did not see any point in a strategic arms
limitation agreement when the existing one had still four years to run.
We had to understand, said Dobrynin, that left to the Soviet bureaucratic processes SALT was bound to move very slowly. To intervene

personally, Brezhnev needed the excuse of a successful conclusion of the Agreement on the Prevention of Nuclear War.

To argue that the General Secretary of the Soviet Communist Party required a pretext to participate in Soviet bureaucratic decisions was to elevate chutzpah into an art form. But once launched on it, Dobrynin was infinitely inventive in developing variations on the theme of a beleaguered Brezhnev assailed on all sides by fractious colleagues. The Soviet Ministry of Defense, according to Dobrynin, did not have much use for SALT. It consistently put its most unimaginative and unenterprising general on the SALT delegation, he said, with instructions to block any initiative put forward by the Foreign Ministry, which was technically in charge of the negotiations. If the general was asked by the head of the Soviet delegation, Vladimir Semenov, to request new instructions, he refused to do so, arguing that if new instructions were needed the Ministry of Defense would issue them on its own. And the Defense Ministry's attitude was allegedly summed up in a remark on SALT by Soviet Defense Minister Marshal Grechko, to Dobrynin: "If you want my personal opinion, I'll give it to you. If you want my official opinion, the standard answer is no."

The idea that the head of a Soviet negotiating team would not have a Politburo mandate was preposterous. The proposition that elements of the Soviet government would squabble while dealing with foreigners was cleverly geared to American preconceptions of the "doves" in the Kremlin fighting a valiant battle against "hard-liners." The general assigned to SALT in 1973, Nikolai Ogarkov, eventually became Soviet Chief of Staff — a position unlikely to be given to a man perceived to be second-rate — though I do not doubt that the Soviet military were as suspicious of the newfangled theories of arms control as generals the world over.

The stalled negotiations in Geneva were enlivened from time to time by hopeful reports from our negotiating team, who in the best tradition of American negotiators soon developed a vested interest in their own success. Thus on March 27 the team reported an alleged hint by a member of the Soviet delegation to the effect that if we agreed to continue SALT I's inequality in total numbers of launchers, the Soviets might go along with limiting each side to 300–500 MIRVed land-based missiles of one type. This was not an uninteresting proposition from our point of view. It would have put off the day of Minuteman's vulnerability and prevented the Soviets from MIRVing their heavy missiles. And we never intended to MIRV more than 550 of our own. On the other hand, it sounded uncharacteristically complicated and conceptual for a Soviet opening position. Dobrynin never raised it, and he was the channel through which the Soviets pursued those issues about which they were serious. Nor did Dobrynin respond when I questioned him. It may thus

have been a case of an eager American representative construing stupe-
faction at one of his complex expositions as assent and reporting his
preferences as a Soviet proposal. It would not have been the first time.

What we received from the Soviets officially was a proposal so one-
sided that one wonders how any serious person could ever have believed
that it might be discussed, much less negotiated. Quite simply, the Soviets proposed to ban *any* new strategic weapons during the period of
the new agreement. Conveniently, they allowed modernization to proceed. By a strange coincidence every Soviet missile being tested (we
were aware of four new types) was defined as a "modernized" version
of an existing one. Since we were just beginning to develop our first
new strategic missile in ten years (the Trident), the scheme did not invite much dispassionate analysis in our government.

At the end of April 1973, as I was preparing for my trip to Zavidovo,
I convened three more Verification Panel meetings, on April 25, 27,
and 30. No one had any new ideas to offer. Defense and the Joint
Chiefs had only one position: equal aggregates in every category and
every weapons system, no matter how different the design of our own
forces from that of the Soviets. After hearing for years about the dangers of the Soviet heavy missile if MIRVed, we were now told that
stopping their MIRVing was "not worth much." This caused me to ask:
"If this is true, can someone explain what the hell this negotiation is
all about?" Clements modified the position slightly: MIRVing of the
Soviet SS-9 missile was not such a formidable prospect; halting it "would
be desirable but only if we don't pay too much" — in other words, not
at the price of giving up the negotiating goal of equal aggregates (for
which Defense continued to offer no building program in the absence of
a SALT agreement). But if there was no limit on MIRVs, what became
of all the fine theories of arms control based on discouraging a first
strike by reducing the advantage of the attacker? I stated my concern at
the Verification Panel meeting of April 25:

Equal MIRVs with equal numbers would give the first striker a great advantage. It would be only a cosmetic equivalence, not real. It would put a premium
on striking first. It may be unavoidable, but if you have five times as many
warheads as missiles, and your aiming points are fewer than your missiles, it
puts a premium on the first strike. That creates a massive element of instability.

Whereas Defense wanted SALT II to ratify all existing programs,
State and ACDA either were prepared to abandon all new programs or
were asking for the right to go on a fishing expedition in the name of
conducting a "probe." The proposition that we should probe without
having a position of our own — indeed, after we had explicitly failed
to reach an internal agreement — was guaranteed to elicit my sarcasm:

What do you probe for without knowing what we want? I'd rather go from our own position than from theirs. It's a sad commentary on the ability of our government if our own position would not be better for us than theirs would be.

Since the agencies could not agree on a position and the President was immobilized by Watergate, the instruction sent on May 3 to our SALT delegation was a mélange of every agency's preference. No one was overruled; everyone's pet project was included. The proposal called for equal aggregates at a ceiling of 2,350 delivery vehicles, some 250 *below* existing Soviet numbers and some 150 *above* ours. It included a freeze on, and a ban on further testing of, land-based MIRVs. This neatly shut the Soviets out of MIRVing their ICBM force, which comprised 85 percent of their total throwweight, without significantly curtailing any program of our own. We offered, in other words, to trade 450 warheads (on the 150 Minuteman IIIs that we would forgo) for a minimum of 5,000 Soviet warheads (depending on how many they would have put on each land-based missile). Not surprisingly, this proposal quickly disappeared into the limbo of one-sided proposals by which each side pleased its bureaucracy while it decided whether painful decisions were in fact necessary.

Thus when I reached Zavidovo in May 1973, SALT was stalemated. I tried out on Brezhnev the MIRV portion of the Presidential instructions, which had been sent to Geneva but not yet been presented there. (I had met our chief negotiator, the able and unflappable U. Alexis Johnson, on May 4 at the airport in Copenhagen on the way to Moscow and asked him to hold that part back so I could present it to Brezhnev as a special Presidential suggestion.)

Brezhnev was crude but far from stupid. He would not fall for transparent ploys. He could hear nothing of a scheme that precluded the Soviets from putting MIRVs on their best missiles. I hinted to Dobrynin at another scheme — just "thinking out loud," I said — namely, a Soviet promise not to MIRV their heavy missiles in return for an American pledge not to develop stand-off bomber weapons (cruise missiles) of a range of more than 3,000 kilometers. The trouble with that scheme was the Pentagon's reluctance to develop or produce such a weapon (a neglect I corrected as soon as I returned) and the range, which was too great to make the offer truly attractive to the Soviets. Dobrynin checked with Brezhnev, who showed some interest but said he would have to consult his military and therefore could not make a decision while I was in Zavidovo. He never came back to it. Almost certainly he was not ready to discuss *any* MIRV limits prior to the completion of the Soviet MIRV testing program.

We retreated to the idea of signing some "general principles" on

SALT at the June summit. This is the usual refuge of diplomats unable to agree, unwilling to admit the impasse, and skillful in finding formulas to permit each side to maintain its original position. On April 6 at Geneva, the Soviets had put forward a draft, which repeated their one-sided positions in the guise of general principles. We had ignored it, neither negotiating on it nor offering alternative formulations. On April 25 Dobrynin handed me a condensed version of the Geneva draft, still heavily loaded in favor of the Soviet position. It implied strongly, for example, that our airplanes based in Europe should be included in the aggregates. This would have forced us either to reduce the number of our strategic weapons (to compensate for the planes based in Europe) or to withdraw some of the air forces assigned to the defense of NATO. It was therefore worrisome to our NATO allies both on strategic grounds and because they did not relish having their security arrangements the subject of negotiations in which they did not participate. While they were at it, the Soviets sneaked in a clause that would require us, in effect, to end our nuclear cooperation with Britain. And they made the numbers of the Interim Agreement permanent, thus institutionalizing the inequality in launchers without any compensating Soviet concession. We had no incentive to pursue this scheme.

Our counterdraft will not be recorded by historians as a model of precision. It sought neutral ground, keeping open the options of each side. It finessed the Soviet desire to include our forward-based systems by the same formula employed in the SALT I agreement: a pledge that there would be no circumvention via third countries. This implied that there could be no significant increase in the number of our European-based weapons capable of reaching the USSR; but it did not require that the existing weapons be counted in the totals. Our draft also eliminated the proposal permanently to freeze the unequal numbers of the Interim Agreement. (Ironically, after fighting for years to exclude forward-based systems from SALT, we seem to have reached a point at this writing of negotiating about forward-based systems *without* SALT.)

Thus emerged a statement of "general principles" that did not exactly mark a memorable turn in the history of diplomacy or of arms control. The document enshrined the hallowed principle of "equal security." This could mean anything: equal aggregates and equal MIRVs without regard to overseas bases; unequal MIRVs in return for unequal aggregates; or any other schemes either government might devise. A little more specific was the clause that a new SALT agreement should include restraints on "qualitative" development; this was a euphemism for conveying that certain — as yet unspecified — MIRV limitations would be part of SALT II. The most concrete provision was that the parties would seek to conclude a new agreement before the end of 1974. Gromyko worried about this because he feared that a failure to meet the deadline, even for technical reasons, might sour our relations. We thought that a deadline was the only way to stop endless procrastination within our government and at Geneva. (We got in just under the wire with the Vladivostok agreement of November 1974.)

But none of this esoteric maneuvering, either by supporters or opponents of SALT, reached the central reality. During the course of the Seventies we would lose our residual counterforce capability (our ability to destroy Soviet ICBMs). Sometime in the Eighties our land-based missiles would become vulnerable, depending on the rapidity with which the Soviets placed multiple warheads on their land-based missile launchers and improved their accuracy. If each side had an equal number of MIRVed vehicles and if there was "freedom to mix" (another hallowed Pentagon principle allowing each side to decide on the composition of its force), then it was certain that the Soviets would MIRV many more of their land-based missiles than we and, since theirs were larger, would place more warheads on each than the three on our Minuteman. The result would be an overwhelming Soviet capacity to destroy our ICBM force, not offset by any American buildup in other categories of strategic weapons. Our only new program, the Trident submarines, gave us no counterforce capability because SLBMs were generally not accurate enough to pinpoint silos and presented technical problems of simultaneous launching.

Sooner or later, even if the overall number of warheads were equal, the Soviets would combine their growing counterforce capability with their traditional conventional superiority to bring about changes in the geopolitical balance. Two weeks after the June 1973 summit, the Soviets conducted their first MIRV test on their SS-17 ICBM, the new missile that was to replace the obsolescent SS-11. A strategic revolution was now only a question of time.

On July 13, 1973, I wrote to Bill Clements insisting that we proceed with a long-range cruise missile. The Pentagon was thinking of canceling this weapon both for budgetary reasons and to prevent its being used as an excuse to kill off the Air Force's cherished new bomber, the B-1. (Later events proved that the careful maneuvering of the services is not always the result of parochialism, as folklore has it, but the result of long experience. The B-1 was canceled by the Carter Administration, which indeed argued that the cruise missile, carried by the existing B-52 bomber, made the B-1 unnecessary.) I argued to Clements "that a long range bomber-launched cruise missile program makes sense strategically and could help our SALT position." Clements went along enthusiastically and the cruise missile program was saved.*

---

*Having saved long-range cruise missiles in 1973 did not keep me from being attacked two years later for allegedly slighting them in SALT negotiations.

The SALT process thus went on while both sides were developing new weapons — we, the cruise missiles, the Trident submarine, and the B-1 bomber; the Soviets, four new land-based ICBMs, and MIRVs. In America, our domestic divisions prevented a clear articulation of either strategy or an arms control doctrine, and in the resulting vacuum each issue became a philosophical as much as a technical one, settled on essentially political grounds. It was not until 1975 that Congress would take the Soviet threat seriously. A strategic nightmare was developing, in which the Soviets in the Eighties might use the "window" provided by the combination of counterforce capability (or even simply growth of its strategic arsenal) and local superiority to exploit or generate crises and to insist on geopolitical changes favorable to it. The issue of how to relate defense to arms control, how to maintain our strength while negotiating reciprocal limitations, has remained one of the central problems of American foreign policy.

The Agreement on the Prevention of Nuclear War

CURIOUSLY, there was another negotiation going on simultaneously with the debates on trade and SALT, which received very little attention: the diplomacy leading to the Agreement on the Prevention of Nuclear War. On the tactical level, the handling of the talks was rather subtle. We skillfully pulled the teeth of a dangerous Soviet maneuver to lure us into renouncing the use of nuclear weapons, on which the free world's defense after all depended. On the other hand, while it was a good illustration of the stamina required to deal with Soviet diplomacy, when it was all over we had avoided danger, but achieved little that was positive.

Soviet diplomacy knows no resting places. A scheme is presented as a major contribution to relaxing tensions; if we will only accept it there will be an "improvement in the atmosphere." But as often as not, no sooner has one agreement been completed than the Kremlin advances another, which is pursued with characteristic single-mindedness and with the identical argument that failure to proceed will sour the atmosphere.

The origin of these projects is obscure. They may represent a deep strategic design. They may be carried forward by habit and inertia. They may represent the banner of one faction in some arcane maneuvering of the Politburo. Whatever their immediate motivation, Soviet initiatives once launched are pursued with almost monomaniacal intensity. Starting in 1972, we were exposed to such a Soviet steamroller. On my secret visit to Moscow in April 1972, Brezhnev took me aside to propose what he was pleased to call a "peaceful bomb" — a treaty between the Soviet Union and the United States renouncing the use of nuclear weapons against each other.[14] This was at the height of North Vietnam's spring offensive, when the Nixon Administration had all but decided to cancel the summit if Hanoi's military push succeeded. And we were also determined to resume bombing of North Vietnam if the offensive were not halted in the next few days. To introduce the renunciation of nuclear weapons at that stage was a colossal piece of effrontery since NATO's defense depended on the American nuclear guarantee. Given the Soviet superiority in conventional weapons, such a move would demoralize our allies and deeply disquiet China, which would see it as a sign of the much dreaded US–Soviet collusion.

On the other hand, the moment was well chosen for avoiding a flat rejection. Our strategy was to obtain a free hand in ending the war in Vietnam by separating Moscow from Hanoi. We therefore did not mind setting additional bait that would give the Soviets a stake in not turning on us if we increased pressure on Hanoi. This led us into a delicate maneuver: We sought to give Brezhnev and his associates some hope that their project might lead somewhere, without committing ourselves to it in the form in which it was presented. Our first move was to play for time; I turned it aside by in effect deferring it to the summit.

After Nixon, on May 8, 1972, had ordered the resumption of full-scale bombing of North Vietnam and the mining of its harbors, we were preparing for a cancellation of the summit until on May 10 Dobrynin nonchalantly asked me whether the visiting Soviet trade minister Nikolai Patolichev would be received by the President. Needless to say, we arranged for Patolichev to meet Nixon the next day. When eager journalists afterward pressed him for a public statement, Patolichev turned away questions about whether the summit was still on with wide-eyed amazement. "Have you any doubt?" he asked with a smile, as if the bombing of a Soviet ally and the mining of its harbors were an everyday occurrence.

But the Soviets never waste time presenting their bill. The very next day — May 12 — Dobrynin appeared for his quid pro quo. In order to prepare Brezhnev's conversation with Nixon, he asserted blandly, his masters had armed him with a brief draft treaty to be signed as soon as convenient. In the first paragraph the United States and the Soviet Union renounced the use of nuclear weapons against each other. The second paragraph stated peremptorily that the two parties "shall prevent" situations whereby actions of third countries might produce a nuclear war. It was strong stuff. We were being asked to dismantle the military strategy of NATO and at the same time to proclaim a virtual US–Soviet military alliance designed to isolate or impose our will on China or any other country with nuclear aspirations.

The draft handed over by Dobrynin, while outrageous, presented a tactical problem. Nixon, as did I, wished to keep the discussion going, so as to give the Soviets an additional incentive to remain quiet while we broke the back of Hanoi's offensive. At the same time we could not accept the Soviet draft without grave peril. So we engaged in a complicated fencing match in which we sought to parry the characteristic Soviet lunge with fancy footwork. But we knew that sooner or later we had to take a stand.

During the Moscow summit of 1972, as we had expected, Brezhnev bearded Nixon on the treaty. Nixon and I had agreed that Nixon should be noncommittal while evincing ambiguous interest — a pose at which Nixon was a master. If Brezhnev pressed, we had prepared a counter-draft that emphasized our constant theme that peace ultimately depended on the restrained conduct of the superpowers. We evaded the Soviet proposal of banning nuclear weapons in war and substituted for it a clause abjuring the threat of force in peacetime. Nor would we undertake an obligation to concert US–Soviet actions toward third countries; we would go no further than to offer our best efforts to see that the actions of third countries did not lead to nuclear war between the United States and the Soviet Union. Brezhnev received the document without comment; Gromyko, however, was too experienced not to realize that we were stalling. Nixon extricated himself from embarrassment by airily suggesting that any difference between the two drafts could be dealt with by Dobrynin and me. How we were to reconcile the irreconcilable he did not explain to the baffled Soviets. As for me, I understood that he did not want to hear of the enterprise again until after the election.

But the Soviets were working on a different timetable. On July 21, back in Washington, Dobrynin presented himself to carry out the assignment given to him and me by our principals. Unfortunately, he said, our draft would not do. Moscow had helpfully tried its hand at a new version, which he handed over. It maintained the bilateral renunciation of the use of nuclear weapons but — aware that we would not abandon our NATO commitments — added a clause to the effect that nothing in the agreement affected existing obligations to third parties, or the right of collective self-defense. This seemed to take care of our allies, but only highlighted the vulnerability of nonallied countries, such as China, whose territorial integrity was also essential to the international equilibrium.

We still needed time to finish the war in Vietnam. To stall, I put three hypothetical questions to Dobrynin. If the new Soviet draft were accepted, would the United States have the right to use nuclear weapons in defense of NATO? Would either side have the right to use nuclear weapons in defense of traditional friends toward whom we had no formal treaty obligations (for example, in the Middle East)? Would either side have the right to use nuclear weapons in defense of a major nonaligned country, the loss of whose independence might affect the global balance? (I mentioned India as an example, although the Soviet leaders could have had no doubt that we were really talking about China.)

I had not expected a formal answer. Indeed, I had asked such pointed questions because I thought that the Soviet reluctance to reply would bury the increasingly awkward project. To my amazement, a written Soviet reply was received on September 7, 1972, articulating their purposes unabashedly. The answer to my three questions was as follows: The proposed agreement did not preclude the use of nuclear weapons in a war involving NATO and the Warsaw Pact; however, their use would have to be confined to the territory of allies; employment against the territory of the United States and the Soviet Union was proscribed. In a Middle East war, nuclear weapons could not be used by either side. Even less could they be used if there were a conventional attack on an important third country such as India.

It would have been difficult to draw up a more bald or cynical definition of condominium. The proposed treaty would protect the superpowers against nuclear destruction even in a European war while guaranteeing the devastation of each country's allies. Nothing would have been better designed to promote European neutralism or to depreciate the value of alliances. The defense of the vital Middle East would have to depend on conventional weapons, in which we were inferior, and even more so in the capacity to reinforce that distant theater. All other countries were to be left to their fate. For example, China could be attacked by Soviet armies that would be free of the fear of American nuclear response. On this interpretation of the treaty, our alliances would be shredded and friendly countries' confidence in us destroyed.

These propositions could not stand unchallenged. Despite our wish to gain time I replied on the very same day, September 7, to remove any doubt about our priorities. I handed Dobrynin a paper restating our willingness to explore general principles of restrained international conduct. But I emphasized as well the limits beyond which we were not prepared to go:

— We believe it important to avoid any formulation that carried an implication of a condominium by our two countries;
— We believe it important that an agreement between our two countries should not carry any implication that we were ruling out only nuclear war between ourselves but were leaving open the option of nuclear war against third countries;
— We think it important that in concentrating on the prevention of nuclear war we should not at the same time appear to be legitimizing the initiation of war by conventional means;
— We think it important that past agreements, whether alliances or other types of obligations, designed to safeguard peace and security should be enhanced by

any additional agreement between ourselves relating specifically to the prevention of nuclear warfare.

Our response owed no little to discussions we had initiated with the British government. During the summer we had briefed our major European allies, and China, on the outlines of the Soviet proposal. At the end of July 1972, I had used the regular visit to Washington by Sir Burke Trend, the British Cabinet Secretary, to show him the Soviet draft of July 21. I asked for British advice, and indicated that we would proceed only in tandem with London. On August 10 the Foreign Office sent its Soviet expert, Sir Thomas Brimelow, and a small group of advisers to Washington to review the project in detail.

London could not have made a happier choice. Cherubic, unflappable, not quite successful in obscuring his penetrating intelligence behind the bland exterior of the perfect civil servant, Brimelow became an indispensable part of the negotiations. He was a profound student of Soviet behavior. He had an unsentimental assessment of Soviet purposes. He was convinced that the threat of general war was one of the chief fears of the Soviet Union; anything that lessened Soviet concerns on that score would weaken deterrence. In his view, the Soviets wanted to reduce the margin of their own uncertainty while seeking to magnify allied inhibitions against the use of nuclear weapons. Our course must thwart those designs.

Brimelow, as did we, judged existing Soviet drafts unacceptable. I outlined a possible strategy of seeking to transform the Soviet approach into a statement of principles of political restraint proscribing the threat of force, nuclear or conventional. Brimelow agreed with the objective and counseled stalling — easy to accept since it coincided with what we were already doing. We knew that we would be able to achieve Soviet acquiescence only if we could slow down exchanges until some new deadline — like a summit — would produce Soviet anxieties sufficient to modify Brezhnev's proposal fundamentally. So we marked time, using the need to end the Vietnam war as a pretext.

Patience was not Brezhnev's strong suit. He used every opportunity to try to speed up negotiations. On my visit to Moscow in September 1972, he tried to lure me into a drafting session by urging me to indicate my objections to the Soviet text line by line. But this would make the Soviet draft the basic document and we objected to it in principle, not in details. I temporized by repeating at inordinate length the position that I had given to Dobrynin on September 7: no condominium; no implication that the United States and Soviet Union were seeking to protect only their own territory; no suggestion that conventional war was acceptable while nuclear was not. Brezhnev professed to be puzzled about such base suspicions of Soviet motives. If the Soviet Union renounced the use of nuclear weapons, he argued soothingly, we could be "two hundred percent" sure that it would also refrain from employing conventional weapons against us or our allies. (This, of course, left China and the Middle East conveniently uncovered.) Brezhnev sought to give force to this assurance — qualified by region as it was — with an appeal to Soviet constitutional practice: "Such a prospect would be completely contrary to the declarations of the Party Congress of our Party." It was mind-boggling to imagine what would happen if we presented an agreement to the North Atlantic Council, much less to Peking, based on our confidence in a pledge made to itself by the Congress of the Soviet Communist Party.

I suggested that we proceed in two stages as we had with SALT: a general declaration of principles, to be followed by a more formal agreement. This found no favor with Brezhnev, who under Gromyko's tutelage understood that the principles could only restate what had already been signed at the 1972 summit, that drafting them would take months, and that we would then claim that they exhausted the subject. But hours were consumed in debating this point — which served my purpose. I finally agreed to try my hand at another draft, which I promised to give Gromyko when he visited Washington in early October. This got us out of Moscow without a blowup.

When Gromyko arrived in Washington, I handed him on October 2 a draft that eliminated the obligation not to use nuclear weapons and stated a series of political conditions involving restraint in international behavior that had to be met before the renunciation of nuclear weapons could be considered. Gromyko was an expert draftsman. He understood immediately what I had done. He complained that we were not proceeding in the "spirit" of the initial exchanges. He noted (correctly) that "nothing" remained of the original Soviet proposal of the renunciation of the use of nuclear weapons.

To mount pressure, Gromyko told Nixon that Brezhnev's return visit to America in 1973 was conditional on progress on the nuclear treaty. But that maneuver had lost its effectiveness. We were becoming confident that we would be free of the Vietnam war by 1973; a summit was no longer important to separate Moscow from Hanoi.

Still, during the final phase of the Vietnam negotiations, we were not eager for additional disputes. So I went back to stalling. Using the tried-and-true tactic of Presidential assistants, I hid behind Nixon, claiming somewhat disingenuously that the nuclear field was an area in which I had less latitude than in others. Due to the Presidential campaign, I would not be able to get Nixon's attention until November; at that point I would work on a redraft. I doubt that Gromyko believed me. After all, in Moscow Nixon had evaded talking about the nuclear treaty by assigning the subject to Dobrynin and/or Gromyko and me. Now I was reversing the argument. But Gromyko had few cards to play. So he acquiesced, as the Soviets usually do when faced with an unchangeable reality.

During the final agony of our negotiations over Vietnam, even the persistent planners in the Kremlin understood that we had no time to deal with the nuclear draft. This did not keep Dobrynin from some not-too-subtle pressures over the forthcoming summit. In December, he suggested two dates, June or November 1973, and implied that in the absence of the nuclear treaty Moscow was leaning toward November. The flaw in his stratagem was that, all things considered, we preferred November as well. We wanted to complete the Year of Europe and progress further in our relations with Peking. So we ignored the heavy hint.

By the end of February 1973, the Paris Agreement on Vietnam had been achieved and our triangular diplomacy was beginning to operate. I was barely back from China with the announcement that liaison offices were to be established in Peking and Washington, when the Soviet chargé d'affaires, Yuli Vorontsov, asked for an appointment to deliver a letter to Nixon from Brezhnev. Dated February 21, the letter purported to be a reply to Nixon's acknowledgment of the good wishes sent by the Politburo on the conclusion of the Vietnam war. Nixon's letter had carefully avoided listing the nuclear agreement in a catalogue of issues on which we were ready to proceed. It had referred elliptically to our willingness to consider whatever points Dobrynin had submitted to me with ''a constructive spirit.'' (This could refer to a whole list of subjects, including the Middle East.) It was thin gruel, but enough for Brezhnev to resume his campaign.

Brezhnev's letter settled the issue of the summit first of all. It used the ploy of rejecting May as too early (a date that had never been discussed) and ''postponed'' the visit to the earliest date ever considered, the month of June. Nixon had enumerated SALT, European security, and Mutual and Balanced Force Reductions in Europe as the top items. Brezhnev listed the nuclear treaty and the Middle East as *his* priorities. He showed some interest in SALT, none in European force reductions. As always when the Kremlin wanted to make progress, Dobrynin suddenly reappeared in Washington from one of his frequent home consultations, catching me just before I was going on a vacation (which would have gained us ten more days).

But the bargaining positions had changed. Once the Soviets had set the date for the summit, time worked against them. We had next to no interest in the project; Brezhnev had made it one of his priorities. The Soviets had to move in our direction if they wanted to have anything to show for Brezhnev's visit. In early April 1973, Dobrynin tried halfheartedly to play games about setting the precise date of the summit, but they ended abruptly when I pointed out that unless we agreed soon, technical arrangements would prove impossible and the summit would have to be postponed to November after all. Shortly afterward I was invited to Zavidovo to complete preparations, and the date of the summit was firmly established for June 18.

Now, if ever, was the moment of truth. We had skillfully avoided any final commitment to the project. We should probably have dropped it now that the Vietnam war was over and the summit was settled. But the price of stalling had been the implication that we would negotiate something; abandoning the negotiation — though in retrospect correct — seemed then too drastic.

On March 5, 1973, I summed up for Brimelow my analysis of Soviet motives and our objectives:

> Their motives are obvious: to create the impression of détente, to create the impression of great power bilateralism and to give them a relatively free hand for blackmail — at the same time they are steadily increasing their strategic forces in an eerie way. Now it could also be to leave open the option of genuine détente further down the line. . . . So our objective . . . is to give them enough of the form without any substance.

I asked Brimelow whether, now that the Vietnam war was over and we had achieved Soviet agreement to a summit, we should drop the whole project. Brimelow remained suspicious, but he acknowledged that we seemed stuck on SALT, the Mideast, and the European Security Conference; our long-range objective was to enmesh the Soviets in "a less competitive relationship, and we cannot get there by telling them to go to hell."

Of course Nixon and I bore the ultimate responsibility for proceeding. Brimelow's job, after all, was not to make American policy but to help steer it in the safest directions. Once the strategy was settled, Brimelow applied his subtle mind to change the Soviet proposal from a renunciation of nuclear weapons to an agreement to renounce the threat of force in diplomacy. What emerged was like a Russian *matryoshka* doll that has progressively smaller models nested each inside the other. By a series of carefully hedged conditions, the avoidance of nuclear war became an objective rather than an obligation; the objective in turn was made to depend on refraining from the use or the threat of force by one party against the other, against allies of the other, or against third parties. Thus nuclear weapons would be renounced only after a renunciation of the threat of war in diplomacy, and if that condition was not fulfilled, the basic premise of the agreement disappeared. Indeed, it then worked the other way: It legitimized nuclear defense. To reassure allies, the draft continued to stress that the agreement did not affect existing obligations or the right of collective (or individual) self-defense.

Brimelow's role was an example of the Anglo-American "special relationship'' at its best, even at a time when the incumbent Prime Minister was not among its advocates. There was no other government which we would have dealt with so openly, exchanged ideas with so freely, or in effect permitted to participate in our own deliberations. All documents were made available to the British, sometimes with a time lag, but significant moves were always joint ones. Brimelow occasionally showed us British analyses. He did most of the actual drafting. The final version owed, in fact, more to British than to American expertise.

When I set out for Zavidovo on May 4, I was thus left with selling Brezhnev a draft about 180 degrees removed from his original design. It was a weird negotiation extending over several evenings of occasionally heated exchanges. Brezhnev's idea of diplomacy was to beat the other party into submission or cajole it with heavy-handed humor. My tactic was to reduce matters to easy banter to avoid personal showdowns and to give emphasis to our sticking points when I turned serious. The negotiation became a contest between a bull and a matador, except that at the end of the contest the matador for all his intricate cape-play had only slightly winded the bull, who was assembling his energies for a new charge.

During breaks, while Brezhnev and his team disappeared into other rooms, my colleagues and I stepped out onto a balcony in Brezhnev's office. We asked ourselves whether the text as it was evolving would help or hurt our ability to protect China and other third countries. We tended to think that it was marginally useful. In the meeting room Hal Sonnenfeldt attempted to apply in the Soviet Union the methods by which he kept abreast of my activities in Washington: He sought to read upside down Brezhnev's briefing paper, which the General Secretary had left on the table in front of him. For once Sonnenfeldt failed.

On the first day of talks Brezhnev began with a long speech extolling the virtue of his version of the nuclear treaty — a ''clear-cut and lucid agreement'' that would contain provisions causing ''no alarm,'' he reassured me. ''I wouldn't bet on that,'' I replied drily. Undeterred, Brezhnev rambled on about its historical importance for the United States and the Soviet Union, climaxing with the first of several sallies indicating that China was his real target:

And at least here in this group we should not pass over in silence the fact that there do exist in the world other nuclear powers as well, and there have to be such points in the agreement to show them it would be wrong to play with nuclear war.

Joining in a US–Soviet alliance against China was not exactly our idea of détente. Nor was I about to be bested in the department of long speeches, especially when the passage of each hour improved our bargaining position.

In my response I treated the proposed agreement as just one of many negotiations between the United States and the Soviet Union, not as a unique historical event. I took a weak run at linkage by arguing that simultaneous progress on SALT II would enhance the significance of each negotiation. I shudder to think what would have happened had I proved more persuasive; the state of our internal deliberations hardly lent itself to serious negotiations on SALT. I noted, slightly sarcastically, that without the President's personal relationship with Brezhnev the proposed agreement would have never gotten so far — implying that it was not a top priority for us from the point of view of national interest. I mentioned the necessity of informing allies (which we had already done, of course). Brezhnev replied that he would not prescribe how we should treat our allies; as for him, he was going to East Germany and Poland soon but would not inform them of the project. This was an unlikely proposition, not to mention that his equating East Germany with, say, France, would not, I suspected, have gone over well in Paris. Indeed, he added — perhaps to flatter me that our own procedures could be adapted to the Soviet Union — that only a few of his colleagues in the Politburo knew of the project. (This also raised a question in my mind about Dobrynin's constant theme that failure to complete the agreement would weaken Brezhnev's position in the Politburo. He could hardly be blamed for not finishing what his colleagues did not know about.)

The first session adjourned without going beyond general principles. On Saturday evening, May 5, after an introductory period of Brezhnev jokes, we turned at last to the text. At once a haggle broke out over which text to use. We had won three-quarters of the battle when it was decided to use our (more accurately Brimelow's) text as a point of departure. Then we found ourselves in a typical pettifogging debate. Hard as it is to believe that grown men could quarrel over such trivia, the issue was whether someone should read out the entire text or only the disputed portions and if so who. We favored concentrating on disputed points to avoid introducing new isssues, especially the idea of renouncing the use of nuclear weapons. Finally, it was agreed to read the entire text aloud. Brezhnev took upon himself that dubious honor.

This having consumed well over an hour, it became evident that the passage of time had not affected the underlying motivations. Once our basic approach was accepted, Brezhnev sought to turn it to his purpose. He opened with a long appeal for a clause that would emphasize the bilateral nature of the agreement. The American draft proposed that the United States and the Soviet Union would "act in such a manner as to . . . exclude the outbreak of nuclear war between themselves and between either party and third parties." Brezhnev wanted to drop the last seven words — leaving a glaring loophole for a nuclear attack on third parties. We finally settled on making the renunciation of nuclear war an objective, not an obligation, applying it to all countries and not simply to the superpowers, and making it dependent on a series of political conditions, especially the avoidance of the threat of war — substantially as Brimelow had suggested.

Immediately another wrangle broke out over the wording of an article saying that the document did not affect "obligations undertaken by the United States and the Soviet Union towards third countries in appropriate treaties and agreements." I sought to strengthen the clause by adding the phrase "other appropriate instruments" — to take care of countries, such as Israel, with which we had no formal alliance (and to emphasize the unspoken but well-understood implication that it would include China as well). Brezhnev grudgingly acquiesced. Similar haggling went on over each article. In order not to test the reader's patience further, I have included the entire text of the final agreement in the backnotes.[15]

To leave no ambiguity, on June 7 we drafted a Nixon letter to Brezhnev making clear that we would interpret the agreement as involving general obligations applicable to all nations; that it did not contain a renunciation of nuclear weapons but of the threat of force in diplomacy; that US–Soviet consultations must not be used to seek to impose any conditions on third countries:

My view is that we have set forth an objective and certain modes of conduct applicable to the policies of each of our countries in the years ahead. In doing this, we have not agreed to ban the use of any particular weapons but have taken a major step toward the creation of conditions in which the danger of war, and especially of nuclear war, between our two countries or between one of our countries and others, will be removed. In short, the obligations we have accepted toward each other we have also accepted as applicable to the policies which each of us conducts toward other countries. In subscribing to the agreement and, in particular, in agreeing to consult with each other in certain circumstances, we have made commitments to each other but have in no sense agreed to impose any particular obligation or solution upon other countries. At the same time we have left the rights of each of our two countries, and obligations undertaken by each of them unimpaired.

In short, in over a year of negotiation we had transformed the original Soviet proposal of an unconditional renunciation of the use of nuclear weapons against each other into a somewhat banal statement that our objective was peace, applying as well to allies and third countries and premised on restrained international conduct, especially the avoidance of the use or the threat of force. Another clause provided for consultation before any party resorted to the threat of force in circumstances endangering international peace and security. In case of a major military move the offender would stand in violation of the agreement. The whole document now constituted a web of conditions entangling the Soviets and making it impossible for them to turn on either NATO or the Middle East without violating the agreement. And it even gave us a kind of legal framework for resisting a Soviet attack on China.

Brezhnev and Nixon signed the agreement in Washington on June 22, 1973. We were sufficiently uneasy about possible misinterpretations that we had prepared a careful press briefing, which I read to Brezhnev before giving it. Its basic point was our by-now familiar one: The purpose of the agreement was not to prohibit the use of any particular weapon in wartime but to preserve the peace by refraining from the threat or use of force:

Each side has now set down in precise form its willingness to practice self restraint not only in relations with each other but with *all* other countries. . . . In other words, in their general conduct of international affairs, they must accept the constraints and implications that if their actions or policies increase the threat of war, they would be inconsistent with the objective of this Agreement. Thus, there is no condominium here, but rather the reverse. The two strongest nuclear powers explicitly accept a general responsibility to preserve the peace, not through intervention or pressures, but by refraining from the threat or use of force.

The underlying significance of this document, therefore, is that it is a reassurance for all countries.

Brezhnev grumbled that I seemed constantly to stress what the agreement was not, rather than its positive aspects. He had a point. But he had no choice except to go along with the briefing.

Peace between the two superpowers will hardly be ensured by legal documents. And whether we resist attacks on threatened countries depends less on artful interpretations of a complicated agreement than on our perception of the national interest. The Soviets proposed the document for symbolic reasons, and we had rewritten the content to render its symbolism either harmless or to the West's advantage. What had started out as a Soviet step toward condominium had evolved into an elaboration of the "Basic Principles of US–Soviet Relations" signed at Moscow the previous year. The Agreement on the Prevention of Nuclear War reflected our belief that control of arms presupposed restraint in international conduct; that coexistence between the superpowers would ultimately depend on adherence to standards of behavior by which they would learn not to threaten each other's vital interests.

The final agreement was thus in a sense a vindication of our basic approach. Technically, it was one of our better diplomatic performances. It represented ingenious drafting (mostly by Brimelow) and stubborn negotiating. Yet in retrospect I doubt whether the result was worth the effort. We gained a marginally useful text. But the result was too subtle; the negotiation too secret; the effort too protracted; the necessary explanations to allies and China too complex to have the desired impact.

The Europeans were especially sensitive. They had known about the project for months. I had personally briefed Pompidou, Heath, and Brandt several times. But allied unity eluded us despite the intensive consultation. Though Heath, Brandt, and Bahr had given support and the British had been partners in the drafting, Pompidou had always been wary, and for reasons of their own the leaders of Britain and Germany had not kept their bureaucracies informed. When the project finally surfaced in the North Atlantic Council in June 1973, this culminated in the absurdity that Britain's permanent representative strongly criticized what was to a large extent a British draft and he was supported by his German colleague.

The same difficulty arose with China. According to our interpretation of the agreement, the Soviet Union could not bring pressure on Peking without violating just about every provision of the agreement, including the requirement to consult before engaging in actions threatening international peace and security. Senator Jackson, so critical of other aspects of our Soviet policy, immediately recognized this and supported us. But the cool calculators in Peking did not see it this way. They did not believe their security enhanced by unenforceable obligations; they recognized the potential for a misleading euphoria in a document purportedly devoted to preventing nuclear war.

No wonder the Agreement on the Prevention of Nuclear War disappeared into desuetude, perhaps mercifully. It has been invoked only once in the decade since its signature — when during the Middle East alert of 1973 we warned the Soviets that their unilateral intervention would violate its provisions. But as that occasion demonstrated, the dangers of nuclear war are repelled not by a document but by strength, resolve, and determined diplomacy.

Brezhnev's American Visit

SUMMIT meetings are risky business. Nobody in politics reaches the top without a highly developed ego; the fortunes of political leaders are tied to their ability to achieve their objectives. They find it difficult to compromise — especially when their negotiations are conducted in public; they generally do not have the time to give the detailed attention to nuance that is the essence of successful diplomacy. Deadlocks become difficult to break. Agreement may be achievable only by formulas so vague as to invite later disavowal or disagreement.

Summit meetings between ideological opponents are particularly complex. Following a period of tension, they invite the risk of popular euphoria; during a crisis they may exacerbate tensions. They can generate both excessive expectations and excessive disappointments and indeed swing from one extreme to the other.

But if the risks are properly understood and if preparation is meticulous, there are also opportunities. The Soviet system of government is even less hospitable than bureaucracies in general to ideas that challenge assumptions. Disagreement with orthodoxy tends to be interpreted as lack of ideological vigilance; conformity is the prerequisite of political survival. Soviet leaders need periodic opportunities to form their own judgment of the moral fiber and conceptual apparatus of their Western counterparts or they run the risk of living in a series of Potemkin villages built by subordinates only too eager to flatter their preconceptions.

Precisely because the clash of US–Soviet national interests and ideologies encourages competition and occasionally confrontation, peace may well depend on the ability of the Politburo to form a correct judgment of the likely reaction of our leaders when challenged. A strong, confident American President should be able to use occasional summit meetings to impress the Soviet leaders with his determination, to reduce the risk of miscalculation, to keep open the possibility, however slim, of an ultimately constructive dialogue. Conversely, of course, if the Soviets conclude that their American opposite number is unsophisticated or weak or irresolute it may give them the courage to run additional risks.

From this point of view, Nixon's 1972 summit in Moscow took place under nearly ideal circumstances. Two weeks before, Nixon had ordered the resumption of bombing of North Vietnam and the mining of its harbors. When Moscow maintained its invitation nevertheless, the Kremlin showed that it would subordinate some of the concerns of its friends to Soviet-American relations. We in turn had demonstrated that we were fully prepared to risk détente for what we considered vital interests.

By the same token, the omens for the 1973 summit were much less propitious. Soviet leaders are extremely sensitive to the balance of forces. At first the Soviets were baffled by Watergate; they interpreted it as a right-wing plot aimed at détente. When I was in Zavidovo they said they hoped it would soon be over; they were not eager to have the General Secretary of the Soviet Communist Party buffeted by the treacherous currents of American domestic controversy on a visit to Washington. The complex Soviet system craves predictable partners. The capacity of an American President to make good on his threats or to fulfill his promises is the principal currency in which they deal. And precisely this was in question in 1973. Tempting as was the prospect of a weakened American executive, the Soviets seemed for many months restrained by the uncertainties involved. It took them nearly two years before they moved aggressively to exploit our domestic upheavals by supporting proxy forces in Africa.

As the Watergate battle gained momentum, however, in the spring of 1973 there occurred a barely noticeable hedging of bets. At Zavidovo in early May Brezhnev was still bubbling with enthusiasm about the summit. He would bring his wife and family. He wanted to visit several American cities — at least Houston and Los Angeles in addition to Washington. But during the month of May we were told that Brezhnev's doctors suddenly "forbade" travel by his wife; the visit of the children was dropped without any explanation. At one point the Soviets even proposed to confine Brezhnev's visit entirely to Washington.* When we expressed surprise at the curtailment of the schedule, the Soviets reinstated the sojourn at San Clemente, not without Brezhnev's woundingly explaining in a note that he did so to demonstrate his indifference to the criticisms made of Nixon (see Chapter IV).

At the same time, Senator Sam Ervin's televised Watergate committee hearings were gathering steam. Not a day passed without damaging revelations. The star witness before the Senate Select Committee, John Dean, the former White House Counsel, was scheduled to testify during the very week of Brezhnev's visit. The humiliation of spreading the malfeasances of the President on the public record while Brezhnev was in the country — or perhaps the unwillingness to share the television spotlight with the Soviet leader — induced the committee to postpone its hearings, but by only one week. It was not prepared to grant even one additional day of delay. The hearings thus resumed on the very day of Brezhnev's departure, giving the Soviet leaders an unprecedented personal opportunity to watch the public indictment of the President with whom they had just been negotiating.

These prospects had caused Senator Jackson to propose publicly a week before Brezhnev's arrival that the summit be postponed. In the abstract, Jackson was right. In practice a cancellation after so much preparation and on such grounds would have gravely undermined the authority of the United States government. It would have signaled that we had lost the capacity to negotiate — and therefore also to protect our interests — during the unforeseeable course of a prolonged investigation. Once this principle was admitted to the Soviets, it would have

---

*American officials in charge of the planning may have contributed to Brezhnev's reluctance to take side trips. They proposed to a Soviet advance team a visit to Pittsburgh, where Brezhnev could meet American steelworkers — mostly of Polish, Czech, or Serbian ancestry — and could walk along a catwalk overlooking the blast furnaces. The Soviets quickly ruled this out, testifying either to the rapid communications with Moscow or the prudence of Brezhnev's trip planners. A Soviet politician who has survived to reach the Politburo probably has learned not to get too close to blast furnaces, particularly if run by East Europeans.

to be applied to all other relationships. We would have made ourselves an international basket case long before events imposed that condition upon us.

We had no choice except to pretend that our authority was unimpaired. For that, we had to do business as usual; we could afford no appearance of hesitation; we needed to project self-confidence no matter what we felt. Of course, Nixon also had a more personal motive. For him to concede that his ability to govern had been impaired would accelerate the assault on his Presidency. He could not bring himself to admit the growing disintegration of what he had striven all his life to achieve.

So the second Nixon-Brezhnev summit proceeded inauspiciously. Fortunately, there were no unfinished negotiations. The Agreement on the Prevention of Nuclear War had been completed at Zavidovo. All that remained to be done on the SALT principles was to agree on a target date for completing the agreement — a secondary issue. Several subsidiary agreements were also ready for signature — on agricultural cooperation, transportation, oceanography, cultural exchanges. The major utility of the summit in those respects was to provide the momentum of a deadline.

The slate being clean, the Washington summit of 1973 provided an unusual opportunity for the two leaders to explore each other's minds. It is the best use of summit diplomacy, but Nixon's mind was troubled and distracted. He conducted the discussions ably enough but without the sense of direction and self-assurance of the previous year. As for Brezhnev, his boisterousness never quite managed to obscure his insecurity. A visit to the United States was obviously a big event for him. He desperately wanted to make a good impression. In his public appearances he sought to hide his vulnerability behind heavy-handed clowning. He clearly wanted to be perceived as being more human and outgoing than Khrushchev. In a normal environment it might have been appealing as it was in some respects touching. In the miasma of Watergate it fell flat. Indeed, the press tended to interpret it as a Brezhnev rescue operation for Nixon, which helped neither party. It was also unfair since at that point Brezhnev could not yet have fully grasped the extent of Nixon's difficulties.

Brezhnev arrived in Washington on June 16. Something of a hypochondriac, he turned the necessity of getting used to the time change into an obsession. He wore two watches, one set at Moscow time, the other for Washington time. He kept forgetting whether Moscow was ahead of or behind Washington. When we reached San Clemente and three more hours were added, he gave up keeping track of the time difference but never ceased his grumbling about it.

Nixon made Camp David available to Brezhnev and his party to rest before the summit began. The cabins in capitalist America were considerably more rustic, smaller, and less elegant than the villas in Zavidovo. Since Nixon and I were in Key Biscayne that weekend, I called Brezhnev to inquire into his comfort. Even through the screen of interpretation, he was bubbling with enthusiasm and anticipation and at the same time worried lest everything not go smoothly. He made it clear that he would be reassured if he could go over the schedule before the official welcome set for the next day. I flew to Camp David on June 17 to greet a buoyant Brezhnev. He kissed me — the only time in our acquaintance — and immediately showed me his new toy: a cigarette case that released its contents one at a time, at preset intervals. Brezhnev had all sorts of ingenious schemes to beat the system; one was to carry two of these pocket safes around at the same time.

There was as well the unquenchable anxiety: Were we looking for a way out of signing the Agreement on the Prevention of Nuclear War? I assured him that there was no such possibility. Would he be confronted with demonstrations? Would Senators treat him respectfully? Would there be attempts to interfere in Soviet domestic affairs? I expressed my confidence in his ability to handle any foreseeable situation. Fretfully, Brezhnev let himself be reassured.

The arrival ceremony for State guests at the White House is simple and impressive. It was set for 10:30 in the morning on the expansive South Lawn. A few minutes before, to the tune of "Hail to the Chief" played by the Marine Band, the President and the First Lady appeared at the entrance of the South Portico from the Diplomatic Reception Room on the ground floor. Nixon greeted the dignitaries waiting on the lawn, who invariably included the Secretary of State, the Chairman of the Joint Chiefs of Staff, the dean of the diplomatic corps, the ambassadors to and from the visitor's country, and other officials. Another blare of trumpets signaled that the limousine carrying Brezhnev had entered the Southwest Gate and was moving slowly past an honor guard toward the President.

All this went well enough. The limousine halted before the South Portico for the President to greet Brezhnev and they jointly mounted a platform to listen to the national anthems. But then things began to go awry. A contingent of troops in ceremonial dress representing each of our military services and exhibiting a colorful array of flags waited for review, but Brezhnev's ebullience welled over. As he moved toward the soldiers, brought crisply to attention, he was distracted by a crowd waving American and Soviet flags. He rushed over to them and began to shake hands like an American politician on the campaign trail. Nixon managed to preserve the sanity of the escort officer and our Chief of Protocol by gently nudging Brezhnev back in the direction of the troops still standing at attention. Brezhnev returned to the stand while the Marine Band marched by; he and Nixon each made brief statements. The two leaders then walked up the curved stairway to the South Portico itself to wave to the crowd before disappearing into the reception rooms, where the President and his guest formed a receiving line for the assembled dignitaries. Here again Brezhnev sabotaged the schedule. The reception line moved with something less than its traditional briskness because Brezhnev could not forgo extended commentary to several old acquaintances. Brezhnev's disdain for capitalist planning meant that a reception scheduled to last half an hour, or until eleven o'clock, was delayed by almost as long again and with it the opening of formal talks in the Oval Office. But we were not yet through with the unforeseen.

The first Oval Office meeting between Brezhnev and Nixon was supposed to include Secretary of State William Rogers, me, and Hal Sonnenfeldt as note-taker on our side; Foreign Minister Andrei Gromyko, Ambassador Dobrynin, and the splendid interpreter Viktor Sukhodrev for the Soviets. (Sonnenfeldt on our side understood Russian.) First, Nixon and Brezhnev posed alone for photographs. After the preeminence of the principals was established, the rest of the party was supposed to join them. As it happened, we waited over an hour in the Cabinet Room for a call that did not come.

The full record of what was discussed will have to await the relevant Nixon tapes. The President did not tell me what had transpired. It is probable that Brezhnev repeated some of what he had told me in Zavidovo. The talks must have remained general because Dobrynin — who undoubtedly had Sukhodrev's record available — never referred to them or implied that any conclusions had been reached. (Sukhodrev had promised to give me his record but never got around to providing it.)

Finally, the rest of us came in at 12:35 P.M. Brezhnev, who took literally Nixon's invitation that he outline his views on US–Soviet relations, launched into an extended discourse on the history of Soviet-American relations that with translation lasted nearly forty-five minutes. In that recital the 1972 Moscow summit was marked as a turning point in East-West contacts. All problems were soluble, Brezhnev insisted, so long as both parties renounced unilateral advantage and were prepared to compromise:

All that was done in Moscow and that we have to do here therefore acquires unusual significance and importance. As you know, we Russians have an adage — life is always the best teacher. I believe that the life of our two great peoples and of our leaders had led us to the conclusion that we must build a new relationship between us now and in the future. Therefore, I am deeply gratified to emphasize that human reason led us both at the same time to recognize this and that is what led us to the successful meeting last year in Moscow. I very firmly believe, and will go on believing, that what was done in

Moscow took place in the profound awareness of the importance of our joint ventures for the future and for peace. We met in Moscow last year not to compare our strength or to compete but to adopt important decisions. And I know that they won the unanimous support of our people and of yours.

With John Dean's testimony one week away, the unanimity of Nixon's support among the American people was a wistful thought, at least to the Americans present, who were grimly aware of the turmoil ahead. On the other hand, our capacity for serious reflection was progressively impaired by growing hunger pangs as the meeting stretched into the afternoon with no sign of drawing to a conclusion. Indeed, it could not end since the President had not yet responded. Brezhnev, aware of a certain restlessness on the American side, kept checking his two watches. He did this, he said, in order to keep track of his body rhythm and to know when to call his colleagues in Moscow. Gromyko and Dobrynin, for the tenth time in my hearing, set him straight that Moscow was seven hours ahead of Washington, without much conviction that the lesson would stick. Brezhnev interrupted his own monologue repeatedly to ask the President, Rogers, and me whether he was tiring us out. We gamely denied it as a point of national prestige, though we had a sinking feeling that we said it with decreasing conviction as the afternoon wore on.

Nixon proceeded to respond, mercifully more tersely than Brezhnev. He had not been prepared for a prolonged meeting. The briefing memorandum supplied by my office had suggested that he and Brezhnev agree on the agenda of the summit and that he disabuse the General Secretary of any idea of a condominium. Nixon was not about to be bested by Brezhnev in philosophical discourse, however. He drew a contrast between the mood when Eisenhower met Khrushchev in 1959 in the Oval Office and the present one. I suppose he meant that this time there was no threat to Berlin, the challenge that had generated the invitation to Brezhnev's predecessor. Then Nixon lauded the nuclear parity that had developed since then. This was the only time in my association with him that his usual sure touch deserted him in talking to a Communist leader. Strategic parity, unless the democracies increased their conventional forces, was bound sooner or later to turn into a strategic nightmare for us, freeing the Soviet superiority in conventional forces for intervention in regional conflicts.

Nixon recovered quickly by stressing that we would have no part of any superpower condominium. "While we as practical men know what our strength is we also, as strong nations, can afford and should follow a policy of respect for the rights of other nations." Nixon thus made sure that Brezhnev did not misunderstand the significance of the Agreement on the Prevention of Nuclear War, which, he said, "recognizes

the rights of all countries and at the same time the responsibility of the
two of us to develop methods that will avoid nuclear and other confrontations between us.''

Nixon concluded by listing a long agenda of topics for the later sessions: European security, SALT, Vietnam, Cambodia, economic relations. Brezhnev agreed to it in great good spirits. "I hear Vietnam,"
he said when Nixon raised the subject. "I did not raise it. But if you
want we can have a discussion later. I remember we talked about it at
the dacha.''

His reference was to the tongue-lashing administered to Nixon in 1972
by Brezhnev, Kosygin, and Podgorny, who spoke seriatim at Brezhnev's dacha, forty minutes from the Kremlin.[16] The session had been at
once brutal and irrelevant because it had been made for a record, not
for practical effect — as the next exchange made clear. "Yes," replied
Nixon suavely, "it was a late dinner." Brezhnev was equal to the occasion: "We had a very good time." I do not doubt he meant it. What
can be jollier than to have threatened without risk an ideological opponent engaged in its private purgatory in a faraway corner of the globe?

The Oval Office meeting ended at 3:30 P.M. with the famished
American delegation sprinting for the White House mess. Brezhnev,
whether seven hours behind or ahead of us, apparently was in no need
of sustenance.

The rest of the summit followed the jagged rhythm characteristic of
Soviet negotiations. Meetings would be canceled without explanation;
or our Soviet counterparts would simply fail to show up. The meetings
would be rescheduled just as suddenly and unpredictably. This happened not only in Moscow, where after all the Soviets controlled everybody's movements, but also in the United States. At Camp David, to
which the whole group repaired on June 20 for two days, Brezhnev's
cabin was diagonally across from the President's retreat. On one occasion Brezhnev and his colleagues sat on their veranda in boisterous conversation in full view of the President's quarters for two hours past a
scheduled meeting, without so much as sending a messenger to explain
their delay. Suddenly, just as if it was Moscow, they indicated they
were ready. Whether by design or because of the difficulty of adjusting
to Eastern Daylight Time, they chose the luncheon period once again.
Nixon was more patient than I felt. He knew the Soviets could see that
he was free. He agreed to the meeting, which dealt with the European
Security Conference; it was largely a recital by Brezhnev of which
Western European leaders had already agreed to the Soviet proposal to
conclude the conference at the summit level. (Much of this was news
to us and not without its irony, since these same European leaders were
dragging their feet about meeting the President at a Western summit.)

The rest of the week passed in discussions between the principals, signing ceremonies, and State dinners. One meeting was devoted to prospects of increasing Soviet-American trade. The mood of that now faraway period is reflected in Brezhnev's expression of hope that the USSR would purchase twenty billion dollars' worth of consumer goods from the United States. This, if true, was an extraordinary reflection on how skewed toward military production the Soviet economy is — and how inefficient. At another meeting John Connally, now a part-time Presidential adviser and practicing lawyer, made an appearance to urge on both delegations the importance of proceeding with the natural gas development of Siberia, causing the Secretary of State to mutter to me that he hoped someone would keep him in mind so benevolently when he returned to his law firm.

After an effusive dinner at the Soviet Embassy on June 21, the delegations flew to San Clemente in the President's plane on June 22. Having been a guest on Brezhnev's far more lavishly appointed aircraft in 1972, I wondered whether the relative simplicity of Camp David and of *Air Force One* did not convince our Soviet guests that status conferred greater benefits in a classless society than in a capitalist one. We had left a cowboy hat and a Western belt replete with toy gun and holster for Brezhnev in his cabin on the plane. He eschewed the hat but found the belt irresistible. As we crossed the Grand Canyon, Brezhnev entered into the spirit of the occasion by imitating his allegedly favorite movie star, John Wayne, and drew the six-shooter from the holster.

In San Clemente, Brezhnev insisted on staying in the same compound as the President. As Nixon had the only suitable residence, Brezhnev was lodged in a small cottage usually reserved for Nixon's daughter Tricia; it had only a medium-sized living room connected to two small bedrooms with floral designs. Gromyko wound up with Julie Eisenhower's even smaller cottage. San Clemente, of course, immediately brought to the surface again Brezhnev's mania about time changes, this time driving him to retire as soon as he arrived, around 6:00 P.M.

As it turned out, the two most significant conversations of the summit occurred on that last full day in San Clemente, June 23. They were unscheduled and descended upon us without warning. At a noon meeting between Nixon and Brezhnev, attended only by me and the interpreter Sukhodrev, Brezhnev vented his hatred for the Chinese. It was a replay of Zavidovo. His ire was not free of racial overtones. The Chinese were perfidious and they were sly in concealing their real aims. He considered the Chinese Cultural Revolution an example of moral degeneracy, asking what kind of leaders would oppress their people while making propaganda all around the world — as if the Gulag Archipelago of concentration camps and extermination had never been heard of in his fatherland of socialism. He strongly implied that Soviet doctors believed that Mao suffered from a mental disorder. At any rate, sane or not, "Mao had a treacherous character."

But Brezhnev was not interested in simply making a theoretical point. His purpose was eminently practical. He proposed a secret exchange of views on China through the Presidential Channel. He warned that in ten years China's nuclear program might be equal to the Soviet program of 1973. That would not be acceptable to the Soviet Union, though he did not say what the Kremlin would do about it. In the immediate future the USSR would expose China's bellicosity to the world by offering to sign a nonaggression treaty, which he was certain would be rebuffed by Peking. (He turned out to be correct.) Brezhnev added that he had no objection to state-to-state relations between Washington and Peking. Military arrangements would be another matter: "The peoples of the world would lose trust in us," he said, with uncharacteristic concern for world opinion. The Soviet Union had no intention of attacking China, but a Chinese military arrangement with the United States would only confuse the issue, asserted Brezhnev with a subtlety that showed Gromyko's fine drafting hand.

Nixon replied coolly that he was prepared to be in touch through the Channel "on any subject," but he gave no analysis of his own of Chinese motives or purposes. I added that we had never had any military discussions with China. Neither Nixon nor I offered any reassurance about the future. Brezhnev seemed to imply a quid pro quo when he remarked out of the blue that the Soviet Union had stopped military deliveries to North Vietnam after the signing of the Paris accords. "There may be rifles but nothing of considerable significance. We will urge them to adhere to the Paris Agreement."

In the afternoon, just before a poolside reception, Gromyko took me aside. He was obviously worried that Brezhnev had been insufficiently explicit — though not even his worst enemy is likely to list vagueness of expression among Brezhnev's faults. At any rate, the Foreign Minister wanted to reaffirm unambiguously, for the third time in six weeks, that any military agreement between China and the United States would lead to war. I said I understood what he was saying. But I gave him no clue as to our intentions. I saw no sense in giving blanket reassurance in the face of a threat, all the less so as I was convinced, as I have already explained, that while we should be careful not to provoke a Soviet attack on China, we could also not remain indifferent if it occurred. The impact on the global balance of power would be nearly as disastrous as a successful attack on Western Europe.

The second surprise event started undramatically enough that final day with a conventional haggle between Gromyko and me over the Middle East portion of the joint communiqué. Gromyko was very wary. After all, the previous summit and its communiqué had been a major factor in the expulsion of the Soviet advisers from Egypt (see Chapter VI). This time Gromyko refused even to include a reference to Security Council Resolution 242, the different interpretations of which were the heart of the liturgy of Middle East negotiations, because we refused to go along with the Soviets' pro-Arab interpretation of the resolution. In 1972, Gromyko had sought to avoid any expressions of differences on the Middle East; in 1973, he insisted on it. It was only a brief sentence, but it would prevent the debacle of the preceding year, when a vague anodyne formulation had been interpreted by Sadat as a Soviet sellout of Arab interests. (The agreed-upon paragraphs are in the backnotes.) [17]

But the conversation with Gromyko was only shadowboxing. Brezhnev was concerned not so much with the status of current negotiations as with the whole trend of events in the Middle East. At Zavidovo in May I had summed up for Brezhnev our assessment in light of Soviet support for the Arab maximum program: "It is hard to convince Israel why they should give up the territory in exchange for something they already have [a cease-fire], in order to avoid a war they can win — only to have to negotiate then with the most intransigent element of the Arabs [that is, the Palestinians]." We were planning a major diplomatic initiative after Israel's elections in late October and were in the meantime stalling. But at Zavidovo, Brezhnev had invoked the threat of war; he hinted at increasing difficulty in holding back his Arab allies. He growled that we were counting on a state of affairs that might not last: "It is impossible not to take some steps or President Nixon and I might find ourselves in an impossible situation. . . . After all, nothing in the world is eternal — similarly the present military advantage enjoyed by Israel is not eternal either." Brezhnev had offered me no program. I thought the veiled threat of war was bluff because in our view a war would lead to a defeat for the Arabs from which the Soviets would not be able to extricate their clients. Gromyko had given me a set of principles at Zavidovo, but they were identical to the Arab program. Since Brezhnev in his talk with me had not been prepared to retreat one inch from it, we had deferred discussion until the June summit.

Now that the summit was here, the Soviets had, strangely, indicated no special desire to discuss the Middle East. There was the sparring with Gromyko over the communiqué, but neither in Washington nor on *Air Force One* nor in San Clemente had there been any sign that Brezhnev wanted to talk to Nixon about the Middle East.

I thought we could relax from serious business at last when, at 4:30 P.M. on June 23, Nixon gave a cocktail party around the swimming pool of his residence for those members of the Hollywood community willing to come to San Clemente in the middle of Watergate. There were not many. Brezhnev seemed to enjoy himself. A family dinner for just ten people in Nixon's small dining room was to follow at 7:00 P.M. But even before the party had started, Brezhnev suddenly pleaded fatigue — that time change again — and asked that dinner be moved up to six.

Nixon obliged, providing thin gruel indeed for those loyal and hardy few who had risked opprobrium to travel for two hours from Los Angeles to attend a reception lasting barely an hour.

The dinner went off jovially enough. Brezhnev felt at ease in the family atmosphere. Nixon gave a sensitive toast about the responsibility of both leaders for the well-being of the children of the world, a responsibility both men had to feel deeply in light of their attachment to their own children. When Nixon concluded, Brezhnev walked around the table and embraced him. At about 7:15 P.M. the Soviet party excused itself. Brezhnev needed all the rest he could get in view of the fact that another of those debilitating time changes was coming up. He was returning to Washington the next morning to rest at Camp David before departing for Paris on June 25. Nixon retired to his bedroom, I to my residence about ten minutes away.

At ten o'clock my phone rang. It was the Secret Service informing me that Brezhnev was up and demanding an immediate meeting with the President, who was asleep. It was a gross breach of protocol. For a foreign guest late at night to ask for an unscheduled meeting with the President on an unspecified subject on the last evening of a State visit was then, and has remained, unparalleled. It was also a transparent ploy to catch Nixon off guard and with luck to separate him from his advisers. It was the sort of maneuver that costs more in confidence than can possibly be gained in substance. Concessions achieved by subterfuge may embarrass; they are never the basis for continuing action between sovereign nations because they will simply not be maintained.

I told the Secret Service to inform the Soviets that nothing could be done until I saw the President. About fifteen minutes later I awakened Nixon. His initial grogginess was replaced by immediate alertness when I told him what was afoot. "What are they up to?" he asked. "Who knows?" I replied, "but I fear we are not going to get through a summit without a dacha session." Nixon told his valet, Manolo Sanchez, to light a fire in his study in the small tower overlooking the Pacific. Meanwhile, I looked for Gromyko, to find out what this was all about and to make clear that I would be present. It transpired that Brezhnev had been seized with an all-consuming desire to discuss the Middle East. Rather coolly, I said I would inform the President and let the Soviet party know when he was ready.

So it happened that around 10:45 P.M. on Brezhnev's last night with Nixon, the Soviet leader made his most important proposition of the entire trip: that the United States and the Soviet Union agree then and there on a Middle East settlement, based on total Israeli withdrawal to the 1967 borders in return for not peace but an end to the state of belligerency. Final peace would depend on a subsequent negotiation with the Palestinians; the arrangement would be guaranteed by the great powers. This was, of course, the standard Arab position. Brezhnev must have understood — and if he did not, Gromyko was much too experienced not to know — that there was no chance whatever of implementing such a proposal or of reaching any such agreement in the remaining few hours. It did not stop Brezhnev. He wanted no public declaration, he said. It could be a secret deal, known only to the people in the room. He did not vouchsafe to us how so revolutionary a scheme as a peace imposed by the United States and the Soviet Union on the Middle East could be kept secret if it were to be implemented.

Nixon, as always calm under pressure, replied that there was nothing to be done that night. Nor could we accept the "general working principles" given to me at Zavidovo. I would try my hand at revising them and get the text to Brezhnev before he left Camp David on June 25. This idea found no favor with the General Secretary. As at the dacha, he went back to bullying:

If there is no clarity about the principles we will have difficulty keeping the military situation from flaring up. . . . Without an agreement on general principles we don't see how we can act. . . . I am categorically opposed to a resumption of the war. But without agreed principles . . . we cannot do this.

In other words, twenty-four hours after renouncing the threat of force in the Agreement on the Prevention of Nuclear War, Brezhnev was in effect menacing us with a Middle East war unless we accepted his terms.

And he was vehement as he did so. Dobrynin told me afterward that he had told Sukhodrev to refrain from translating some of Brezhnev's more pointed remarks. But what got through was clear enough. Brezhnev wanted to settle the Middle East conflict that summer and the terms he proposed were the Arabs' demands. The facts were that there was no chance even of launching a serious peace process before the Israeli election four months away, and there was no possibility at any time of achieving the terms Brezhnev was proposing. For Nixon to force the issue at the height of Watergate hearings would have added the allegation of engaging in a diversionary maneuver to the charge of betraying an ally. In any event, the program put forward by Brezhnev was unacceptable to us on its merits.

To be sure, Brezhnev was probably threatening as much from frustration as from conviction. He must have heard the same Egyptian threats as we had and may have shared our own estimate that such an attempt was bound to end in Arab defeat. He knew that our ally was militarily stronger and that we held the diplomatic keys to a settlement. He wanted to bulldoze us into solving his dilemmas without paying any price. At a minimum he sought to build a record for shifting the onus of a deadlock onto us and to prevent a further erosion of the Soviet position in the Arab world.

These explanations do not detract from the egregiousness of Brezhnev's performance. It was a blatant attempt to exploit Nixon's presumed embarrassment over Watergate — to the visible discomfiture of Dobrynin, who knew that what was being asked was as impossible domestically for us as it was senseless diplomatically. This also must have accounted for the icy aloofness of Gromyko. We were prepared to discuss overall principles with Moscow in consultation with our ally Israel and, for that matter, with Egypt, with which preliminary talks had already started. We were not willing to pay for détente in the coin of our geopolitical position. After an hour and a half of Brezhnev's monologue, Nixon brought matters to a conclusion firmly and with great dignity by stating that he would look over the record of the discussions in the morning; the problem was not as simple as Brezhnev had presented it; the best he could do was to ask me to present a counterdraft to the principles submitted at Zavidovo by Gromyko:

I will take it into account tomorrow. We won't say anything in terms of a gentlemen's agreement. I hope you won't go back empty-handed. But we have to break up now. It would be very easy for me to say that Israel should withdraw from all the occupied territories and call it an agreed principle. But that's what the argument is about; I will agree to principles which will bring a settlement. That will be our project this year. The Middle East is a most urgent place.

That was the end of it. As at the dacha in 1972, Brezhnev subsided. He gave us a synopsis of what he proposed to discuss with Pompidou when he stopped in Paris on the way home. But the bad taste remained, and we could not forget the conversation in Nixon's study when the Middle East exploded a little more than three months afterward.

On the final day, June 24, as is always the case in meetings with Soviet leaders, the squalls had lifted. Brezhnev and Nixon said goodbye on the lawn in front of the residence in San Clemente. Brezhnev thanked Nixon profusely and stressed that he was leaving with "a good feeling." He looked forward to welcoming Nixon to the Soviet Union the following year and expected that further progress would be made then. Nixon asserted that the improvement of US–Soviet relations served the cause "not only of peace between our two great countries but of building an era in which there can be peace for all the peoples of the world."

Nixon accompanied Brezhnev on the short helicopter ride to El Toro Marine Corps Air Station. Brezhnev took the occasion to suggest that the talks on mutual force reductions in Europe might be given impetus if the Soviet Union and the United States began them with a symbolic reduction of perhaps ten thousand men.

Nothing came of the idea. When Nixon bade Brezhnev farewell, it

was the last time they met as equals. The next summit a year later in
Moscow took place little more than a month before Nixon's resignation.

A Summing Up

THE 1973 summit laid bare the ambiguities of East-West relations in
the nuclear age. Both sides were painfully aware of the risks of war.
I continue to believe that Brezhnev was sincerely prepared for a prolonged period of stability. But no Soviet leader can step out of his philosophical skin and abandon the Leninist postulate that a country's influence is ultimately determined by the correlation of forces. The physical
energy of the aging Soviet leadership may have had its limits; its willingness to run risks may have been reduced after a lifetime of struggle.
But Soviet leaders literally have no framework for exercising restraint
when faced with a propitious balance of power. An opportunity for strategic gain would not be left unexploited indefinitely because of bourgeois scruples or personal relations with Western leaders.

From this perspective, the impact of the 1973 summit was almost
certainly unfortunate — not for foreign policy reasons but because of
the dramatic demonstration of America's internal disarray. By the end
of the visit the Soviet party understood that the summit had been overshadowed by Watergate, as Dobrynin told me needlingly two weeks
later. More gravely, the summit began to convince the Soviet leaders
that Nixon's problems might turn out to be terminal. This did not yet
tempt them to adventures staking Soviet assets. But it undoubtedly made
them less willing to expend capital on preventing adventures by friendly
nations — and thus it surely contributed to the Middle East war.

Almost immediately the perception of Watergate slowed the pace of
diplomacy. Brezhnev took himself out of the direct line of fire in US–
Soviet negotiations. There was no sense involving the prestige of the
General Secretary with the possible collapse of the Nixon Presidency.
As in negotiations on the Year of Europe, diplomacy became more bu-
reaucratic, less bold. The 1974 Moscow summit between Brezhnev and
Nixon turned into a pale imitation of the first two without thrust or
underlying purpose.

The strategy of the Nixon Administration presupposed a decisive
President willing to stake American power to resist Soviet expansionism
and ready to negotiate seriously if the Soviets would accept coexistence
on this basis. But both of these courses of action were being destroyed
by our domestic passion play. Therefore many of our critics missed the
fundamental point. Liberals accused us of being too Machiavellian; conservatives, of being too accommodating. Neither fully understood that
we had no real choice. Watergate did not permit us the luxury of a
confrontational foreign policy, and it deprived conciliatory policies of

their significance. Moderation, after all, is a virtue only in those who are thought to have an alternative. In the nuclear age there is no substitute, I am convinced, for a long-range policy that avoids either confrontation for its own sake or acquiescence in Soviet expansion. We must resist marginal accretions of Soviet power even when the issues seem ambiguous. And we must be ready for real coexistence should the opportunity appear. That is a challenge of unprecedented complexity, requiring acute judgment, resolution, and faith. In the early Seventies it was engulfed by our domestic crises. But the challenge remains, and the way America responds will determine whether a free society can preserve its security and advance its values.

VIII

Indochina: The Beginning
of the End

Broken Promises

WHEN the Agreement on Ending the War and Restoring Peace in Vietnam was signed in Paris on January 27, 1973, it fulfilled a national longing shared by the Nixon Administration and its critics. To most Americans it signaled the end of the war. But the millions in Indochina who had suffered and struggled knew that their freedom was precarious.

All too soon, the leaders of North Vietnam showed that the cease-fire was merely a tactic, a way station toward their objective of taking over the whole of Indochina by force. Before the ink was dry on the Paris Agreement they began to dishonor their solemn obligations; in truth, they never gave up the war. On the occasion of my February 1973 trip to Hanoi, it was possible, stretching goodwill and credulity to the utmost, to explain the already blatant violations of the Agreement as a reflex twitch after ten years of struggle (see Chapter II). During March that excuse vanished; it became apparent that the cease-fire was a barely disguised cover for moving men and weapons into position for another offensive. The violations were not technical; they were flagrant preparations for a new stage of war by means explicitly prohibited in the Agreement.

The scale was staggering. In a three-month period, as we protested to the Soviets in early May, 30,000 troops were infiltrated into South Vietnam through Laos. War matériel could legally be introduced only as replacement for outworn equipment on a one-for-one basis and only through a system of international checkpoints. The United States kept its word throughout; the North Vietnamese sent in over 30,000 tons of military equipment in thousands of trucks — *none* through international checkpoints, whose establishment in any event had been made impossible by North Vietnamese obstruction. They added 400 tanks and 300 pieces of heavy artillery to their inventory for war, and set up a network of antiaircraft installations. The North Vietnamese systematically blocked the operation of the International Commission of Control and Supervision (ICCS), which was supposed to monitor the cease-fire. Since two of its four members were Communist (Poland and Hungary), it was hamstrung also because the Communist members refused to confirm Communist violations, thereby canceling out the observations of the Canadian and Indonesian participants in the Commission.

Article 20 of the Paris Agreement had required the withdrawal of all foreign forces from Laos and Cambodia; a separate written understanding had defined North Vietnamese forces as "foreign" within the terms of the Agreement. Article 20 also prohibited the establishment of base areas in other countries of Indochina and the use of their territory for infiltration. Both of these provisions were being ignored. The North Vietnamese refused also to withdraw from Cambodia, though, as we now know, even the Cambodian Communists demanded it.[1] Hanoi's troops in Laos were actually augmented. More than 18,000 trucks entered Laos. North Vietnamese forces took part in combat operations in Cambodia and used both countries for logistical purposes.[2]

South Vietnam was not virginally pure. In the first few months it more than held its own in minor engagements over control of territory. There was some harassment of Viet Cong liaison officers who were assigned to a Joint Military Commission. And South Vietnam dragged its feet on the formation of the National Council for National Reconciliation and Concord, because Hanoi, for its part, would not agree to countrywide elections. But these matters could not begin to compare with Hanoi's immediate, unprovoked — and eventually decisive — efforts to transform, wholesale, the balance of forces in Indochina.

By March 1973, less than two months after signing an agreement to end the war, we were thus facing a crass challenge that mocked every significant provision of it. This raised two issues: Should we act to enforce the Agreement? And did we have the right to do so?

We were not naive when we made the Agreement. As I have indicated in Chapter II, I never believed that Hanoi would reconcile itself to the military balance as it emerged from the Paris Agreement without testing it at least once more. In our estimate, Saigon could handle most North Vietnamese encroachments, especially if American military and economic aid (permitted by the Agreement) was adequate. But we recognized that there might be gross breaches of the Agreement that could topple the military balance it ratified and that would be discouraged only by the threat of American retaliation. American air power was thus always seen as an essential deterrent to the resumption of all-out war. Nixon gave assurances on this score to South Vietnamese President Nguyen Van Thieu to persuade Thieu to accept the Paris Agreement. It was self-evident that Saigon could not survive if Hanoi were free to infiltrate all countries of Indochina and to strike against South Vietnam wherever it chose along a frontier of seven hundred miles.

The obvious fact that the peace settlement was not self-enforcing has been evaded by some who have questioned whether we had a right to defend the Agreement by military action, or even to pledge to do so. The President's legal authority to continue air operations after the Paris Agreement was spelled out in a memorandum that Secretary of State William P. Rogers submitted to the Senate Foreign Relations Committee in April 1973; a Library of Congress study commissioned by the committee agreed in early April 1973 that there was "no bar to resumption of hostilities in Vietnam or Laos and the President retained whatever legal power he had had to carry on the war before the Paris Agreement."[3] Nevertheless, since then various arguments have been advanced to suggest that Nixon's assurances to Thieu that we were prepared to defend the Paris Agreement by military action if necessary were improper, illegitimate, or unwarranted.

One argument is that Nixon's pledges were improper because the letters containing them were never made public or endorsed by the Congress.[4] There are several flaws in this line of criticism. One is that similar instances of unpublished Presidential letters indicating a President's intention to vindicate his perception of the national interest have been written by most postwar Presidents. For example, President Kennedy made such commitments to both Pakistan and Saudi Arabia.[5] Such Presidential assurances obviously are not legally binding; they define an intention that the recipient is entitled to take seriously, however. Nor did Nixon ever invoke his letters to Thieu as a legal obligation, as the formal basis of his threats of retaliation, or as arguments against the later legislation that barred their implementation. There is ample constitutional precedent for the validity of what Nixon (and Kennedy) did in the national interest.

From the perspective of a decade it is possible to argue that Nixon would have been well advised to seek formal Congressional approval of the Paris Agreement, as a basis for enforcing it. I certainly think now — though I did not propose it then — that he should have demanded an authorization from the Congress in 1969 to conduct the war he inherited when he assumed the Presidency, giving the Congress the choice of pursuing the existing strategy or ending our involvement. In his first term Nixon took too much on his own shoulders in his effort to end a war he had not started, in the face of harassment by many who had brought about the original involvement, and against constant Congressional pressures that deprived our strategy of impetus and our diplomacy of flexibility.

Nixon refused such a course in 1969 and did not consider it in 1973 because he believed it incompatible with the responsibilities of a President. In 1969 he thought it an abdication to ask the Congress to reaffirm his authority to conduct a war that was already taking place. In 1973 he was convinced that to ask a hostile Congress to give him authority to enforce the Agreement would be a confession that he had no authority to resist while the Congress was deliberating, and would thus invite an all-out North Vietnamese assault. He therefore proceeded to do what in his view the national interest required, in effect challenging the Congress to forbid it.

The most direct rebuttal to the charge of "illegitimate secret agreements" is that Nixon's assurances to Thieu were not secret. His policy and intentions were totally public. Indeed, the *public* nature of Nixon's pledge was the essence of the assurance that helped persuade Thieu to sign the Agreement.* Nixon, his Secretary of Defense, and other officials repeatedly stated the Administration's intention to enforce the Agreement. Sometimes this took the form of refusing to rule out the use of force, as I did in my press conference on January 24, 1973, explaining the terms of the Agreement, and as Secretary of Defense Elliot Richardson did even more explicitly in a television interview on April 1, 1973, and in remarks to newsmen on April 3, 1973. Sometimes it was stressed that there was no formal inhibition on our use of air power, as Deputy Assistant Secretary of State William Sullivan pointed out on television on January 28, 1973, and as I reaffirmed in a television interview on February 1, 1973. There were ominous assertions that we had resorted to force before and could do so again, as Nixon warned in a news conference of March 15, 1973: "I would only suggest that based on my actions over the past four years, that the North Vietnamese should not lightly disregard such expressions of concern, when they are made with regard to a violation." (These and other warnings are quoted later in this chapter and more fully in the backnotes.)[6] However indirectly phrased any one statement may have been, their overall impact was correctly summed up in the President's annual Foreign Policy Report published on May 3, 1973: "Such a course [massive violations] would endanger the hard won gains for peace in Indochina. It would risk revived confrontation with us. . . . We have told Hanoi, privately and publicly, that we will not tolerate violations of the Agreement."

The media's reaction — especially to Nixon's scarcely veiled threat at his March 15 press conference — is the clearest possible evidence that there was nothing secret about the President's intentions. For example, the *Washington Post* editorialized on March 18, 1973:

We do not doubt at all that, if he chose, the President could resume the bombing — even now, B-52s continue to rain death daily on Cambodia and no one seems to mind. More than that, we don't doubt at all that President Nixon

---

*Thus, Nixon wrote to Thieu on January 14, 1973: "To this end I want to repeat to you the assurance that I have already conveyed. At the time of signing the Agreement I will make emphatically clear that the United States recognizes your Government as the only legal government of South Vietnam; that we do not recognize the right of any foreign troops to be present on South Vietnamese territory; and that we will react strongly in the event the Agreement is violated."

is "tough" enough to bomb; nor do we know of anyone else who doubts it. Given his overwhelming margin of victory over Mr. McGovern; given his evident determination to run the government in a way avoiding the need to depend on or cooperate with the Congress; and given the new associations he has forged with Moscow and Peking, we would not even argue that a resumption of bombing would significantly undercut his political or diplomatic plans for his second term. He is in an enviable position to conduct his Vietnam policy on the merits alone.

The same interpretation was put forward by the *New York Times* of March 17, 1973:

The President left little doubt that he regarded resumption of bombing and harbor mining as a viable option against North Vietnam. Hanoi's leaders recently tried to test Mr. Nixon's resolve on the cease-fire terms by delaying the process of releasing American war prisoners, and when they saw the Administration's firmness they returned to the agreed upon schedule. A similar response is looked for now.

The President's determination to use force was thoroughly understood; and his right to do so early in 1973 was unimpaired. The issue, at bottom, is not really a legal question but turns on one's perception of the national interest. Our determination to enforce the Agreement came up against all the passions unleashed by the Vietnam war. Those who had always wanted us to wash our hands of the non-Communist peoples of Indochina sought to vindicate their course upon the war's conclusion. Letting free Indochina go as the result of an agreement seemed to them no more pernicious than their previous insistence on unilateral withdrawal. They saw the Paris Agreement not as the honorable compromise it was, but simply as a fulfillment of their old prescription to disengage unconditionally. They wanted to impose *their* version of an agreement that in fact constituted much more. It was inevitable, and just as predictable, that we could not accept this. We had opposed unconditional surrender during the war. All the reasons that impelled us to pursue the war to an honorable settlement argued for maintaining its terms. We had no intention of letting slip by inaction what 50,000 Americans died to achieve, or of abandoning the millions who in relying on our promises had fought at our side for a decade. We were convinced that the impact on international stability and on America's readiness to defend free peoples would be catastrophic if we treated a solemn agreement as unconditional surrender and simply walked away from it. And events were to prove us right.

How was the Paris Agreement then to be maintained? "By diplomacy," the favorite answer of our critics, was no answer at all. It was diplomacy, after all, tedious years of it, that had produced the very

Agreement that was being violated. But it had not been diplomacy in a vacuum. We had brought military pressure to bear on Hanoi. Effective diplomacy depends on other countries' assessment of incentives and penalties, not on the eloquence of some individual. To argue otherwise is a bromide, an evasion of the problem.

No one who had gone through the agonies of Nixon's first term could contemplate with an easy mind the domestic eruption that a new recourse to force — even if only a few days' duration — would bring. Radical critics, of course, wallowed in charges of blood lust and esoteric psychological theories of our alleged propensity to violence. But they were acting out their own inner turmoil, not advancing a reasoned analysis. These traditional foes of the war were joined in this new phase by a different group — people of distinction who had supported the Administration in the war but felt that America had done enough. We had done our duty, they felt, by achieving an honorable extrication; no national interest was served by insisting on an honorable outcome. The ambivalence of this group — at once deploring the threat of force and hoping that it would deter the circumstance in which it might be used — was expressed in a column in *Newsweek* of March 26, 1973, by my late dear friend, the irrepressible and sage Stewart Alsop:

> A lot of people (including, for example me) went along reluctantly with the President's Vietnam policy because the McGovern alternative was shameful. If the President again sends the bombers over Hanoi, such people are going to begin asking themselves some hard questions.
>
> The White House estimate is that the North Vietnamese cannot mount a successful main-force attack on South Vietnam for many months — at least until next autumn. Can the South Vietnamese not learn to defend their own turf within these many months? If not, why not? And if not, when? Must we really send the bombers north again, in order to prove the integrity of the President's rhetoric? Will it work if we do? Won't the Senate rescue Hanoi, as the Senate was ready to do in December, before the Paris pact was signed?
>
> It is most earnestly to be hoped that these questions need never be asked. Paradoxically, the best reason for so hoping is that the President, trapped by his own rhetoric, has very little choice but to make good on his threat if the violations continue. Moscow and Peking no doubt know that this is so, and they will no doubt let Hanoi know that it is so.

Alsop's argument — the new conventional wisdom — was that if the South Vietnamese could not take care of themselves after a decade of assistance, they would never be able to do so. This amounted to turning over millions of non-Communist Vietnamese to a totalitarianism they clearly hated and feared. Nor was this argument applied to Europe, where 300,000 American troops remained twenty-four years after NATO was formed, and 50,000 American troops were still stationed in Korea twenty years after the armistice, in areas much better able to defend themselves than South Vietnam. The reason for our continued commitment is the same in both Europe and Korea: We doubt the ability of our allies to assume their own defense completely and we fear that the removal of our shield might tempt aggression.

Nixon, like me, hoped that Alsop's second proposition would turn out to be right: that Nixon's renown for ruthlessness would deter gross violations. No doubt there was an element of braggadocio in our pronouncements. But if the bluff did not work, what then was to be our policy? Should we let South Vietnam, Laos, and Cambodia be engulfed by Hanoi's imperialism within months of signing an agreement guaranteeing their survival? What would this tell others about American reliability as an ally? If we were prepared to abandon Indochina, why not South Korea or for that matter any other friendly country? These were the considerations that drove Nixon and me, with reluctance, to the conclusion that we had no choice except to resist Hanoi's cynical testing of the Agreement. As I said in reply to a question at a press conference on April 23, 1973:

Concerned people should ask themselves: What should the United States do? What is our position if we can neither threaten nor offer incentives, if we are criticized for attempting to maintain the agreement by force and pressed not to provide the economic incentives which might be another motive for keeping the agreement? And we should ask ourselves: Where will we be if what was a very solemn agreement, very painfully achieved, in which we made very major concessions, is simply disregarded?

*   *   *

The profound problem we face as a nation today is whether we should sign an agreement, and when it is totally violated, act as if the signature which was then endorsed by an international conference should simply be treated as irrelevant.

The American people would have been entitled, of course, to take a different view of our national interest. But the people never chose abdication. Nixon's massive mandate over McGovernism and steady public opinion polls justified our course. Three clear majorities had emerged in American public opinion after the 1968 Tet offensive: a majority that held it had been a mistake to get involved in Vietnam in the first place, a majority who wanted that involvement ended, but an even larger majority that rejected the peace movement's policy of immediate and unconditional withdrawal.[7] It was left to us who inherited the war and the national ambivalence to square the circle. There is no doubt many people were simply tired of the war, fearing it would go on forever, but they also did not want to lose it. Exhaustion is no guide to policy.

Here, indeed, is the central dilemma of the statesman. Nixon was not the first American President, nor will he be the last, to face the core question of leadership in a democracy: To what extent must a national leader follow his conscience and judgment, and at what point should he submit to a public mood, however disastrous for the nation or the peace of the world he considers it to be? The question permits of no abstract answers. The extreme cases are easy. The dilemmas arise in the gray area where the national consensus is itself vague or contradictory, or where its convictions are ill founded and likely to lead to a debacle though the statesman cannot prove it. The consequences of the totalitarian victory in Indochina, for the people concerned as well as for global stability, like all prospective dangers, were unprovable in 1973. There would be few who would doubt them at this writing (1981).

A President who identifies leadership with public opinion polls dooms himself to irrelevance; a President who substitutes his judgment totally for that of other elected representatives undermines the essence of democracy. Weak Presidents try to hide behind a public opinion that, in the end, will not forgive debacles even when caused by its own preferences. In 1938 after Munich, Neville Chamberlain was the most popular man in Britain; appeasement exactly reflected the dominant opinion. Twenty months later it had become a byword for weakness of will. Strong Presidents sometimes rely excessively on their judgment; some are later revered as great because they did so. Nixon's fate was to fall before he had a chance to vindicate or even act on his convictions with respect to the settlement in Vietnam.

Thieu Visits San Clemente

BEFORE we could turn our full attention to the North Vietnamese violations, one last vestige of the Paris negotiations had to be taken care of: our promise that our ally, President Nguyen Van Thieu of the Republic of South Vietnam, could visit the President of the United States. It had been an extra inducement to go along with the cease-fire. Thieu had held out for months against the peace agreement that effectively partitioned his country. The Paris terms were better than either our critics or supporters thought possible. As negotiating proposals, Thieu himself had approved them for three years — when the North Vietnamese seemed unlikely to accept them. Once they did, he maneuvered to put the onus for compromise on us. What he really wanted was to go on fighting until the last invaders were expelled. It was not his fault that American public opinion would not tolerate it.

Thieu fought us with Vietnamese methods of tenacity and single-mindedness not unleavened by duplicity. We both wanted the same conclusion, an independent South Vietnam secure in its territory. Those of us who negotiated the Paris Agreement were neither cynical nor naive. We expected North Vietnam to continue to press, but we had brought about a balance of forces, and Congress would have surely voted us out of the war unconditionally if we had tried to go beyond that. The United States hoped that military stalemate would at least ensure security and perhaps someday lead to political dialogue among the Vietnamese.

Thieu had his eye on the other end of the telescope. What he saw close up was not the ultimate peace but the immediate enemy. After the cease-fire, our troops withdrew halfway around the globe; his people would remain facing an army dedicated to the destruction of every flicker of independence in Indochina. We were sure of our own resolve to control Hanoi's ambitions; his eye focused on the long-term uncertainties. And he was essentially right, for it turned out that the Nixon Administration could not sustain its determination domestically, and even if it had, a successor administration was likely to funk our conception of our responsibilities. Thieu developed a bitter hatred of me as the architect of the peace agreement. While I had deep sympathy for Thieu's anxieties, we had no choice. The United States could not reject, when Hanoi accepted them, the very peace terms we had been offering with Thieu's acquiescence for three years. To this day I respect Thieu as a gallant figure who fought for the freedom of his people and who was ultimately defeated by circumstances outside of his, or his country's, or our, control.

Thieu visited the United States from April 2 to 5, 1973. There was little about the visit of which we could be proud. Throughout the war, though his countrymen fought side by side with ours, it had been impossible to receive him in America for fear that his presence might spark civil disorders. He had met American Presidents furtively in Guam, in Hawaii, and at Midway. He had never been permitted to set foot on the continental United States.

Thieu's 1973 visit to America was intended to make up for that, to symbolize a new peacetime relationship and our dedication to a free South Vietnam. It turned into almost the exact opposite. The end of the war had not ended the risk of public disturbances. It was therefore decided to receive the leader of an allied country, for whose freedom tens of thousands of Americans and their allies and several hundred thousand Vietnamese had given their lives, at the Western White House in San Clemente. The arrival and departure ceremonies could be held inside the well-guarded Presidential compound. Even the State dinner was dispensed with and transformed into a small family gathering. The pretext was that Nixon's dining room had room for no more than twelve guests; the real reasons were doubt that we could generate a representative guest list and fear of hostile demonstrations.

To fulfill the promise of a visit to Washington, Vice President Spiro

Agnew was chosen to play the host in the nation's capital. The atmosphere there was revealed by a telephone conversation I had with Agnew shortly before Thieu's plane touched down. Agnew complained that only one Cabinet member — Secretary of Labor Peter J. Brennan — had been willing to join him for Thieu's arrival ceremony. The guests ready to attend the dinner tendered by the Vice President were appallingly few. Most senior members of the Administration had found some excuse for being out of town. It was a shaming experience. In my days in Washington, several Communist leaders had been received with honor. Senior officials had vied to attend State dinners in honor of neutralist leaders who specialized in castigating the United States. But the staunch President of a friendly country was a pariah. His alleged failings as a democrat were, for a decade, used as an excuse — by those who wished us to abandon his people to the enemies of democracy. There were no boat people fleeing from Vietnam while Thieu was there. Vietnamese by the million voted with their feet during his rule, pouring into areas under his control and away from Communist-held territory. Conventional wisdom blamed this on our bombing; since it continued after our bombing ended, it was almost certainly a reaction to the brutality of Communist rule. Thieu took steps to liberalize his government — however inadequately — even in the midst of Communist terrorism of which his best officials were the primary targets. None of this profited him with his critics.

To be sure, South Vietnam was hardly a democracy in our sense. There were justified criticisms of harshness and corruption. But when Thieu's disgruntled opponents in Saigon's turbulent pluralistic politics expressed these to our press, no contrast was drawn with Hanoi, where no opposition was tolerated, the press was controlled, and access to foreign media was prohibited. It was not, in short, a fastidious assessment of degrees of democracy that was at work on American emotions about Thieu. He was the victim of a deeper, more pervasive confusion that manifested itself in double standards in all the democracies. When we sounded out our European friends about a visit by Thieu either in connection with his trip to the United States or separately, there was an embarrassed silence. Neither he nor his Foreign Minister was ever received in allied capitals, except in Paris, which was the site of the negotiations; the process of delegitimizing the Thieu government — the first stage toward abandonment — was well advanced. Meanwhile, Madame Nguyen Thi Binh, the so-called foreign minister of the phantom Communist Provisional Revolutionary Government, which could not boast even a capital, was lionized in Eastern Europe.

It is a curious phenomenon, this self-hypnosis that persuades honest and serious men to concentrate their moral indignation on what is considered conservative. Between the wars it was known in Europe by the slogan, "No enemies on the left." In the postwar years we have seen Western newspapers replete with the transgressions of the regimes in Spain, Portugal, South Korea, Greece, Iran, South Vietnam, and others, while being much more restrained — almost apologetic —about the cruelties of the "people's democracies" of Eastern Europe, the left tyrannies of the Third World, and of course Communist North Vietnam.

Never mind that the "progressive" regimes maintain domestic order — the test apparently applied for the loyalty of the population — because they are also totalitarian and that some conservative regimes face turmoil simply because they have neither the theory nor the apparatus for effective repression. Never mind that conservative regimes leave their neighbors alone and occasionally evolve into democracies (Spain, Greece, Portugal), while Soviet military power imposes its will on a global basis in the name of a universalist doctrine. Nor does the postwar period record the amelioration of many radical regimes in the Third World. The terrible migrations of our time have always been away from Communist countries and never toward them. Yet down the years disdain and outrage have disproportionately been reserved for friends of the West, such as Thieu in 1973 and the Shah of Iran later in the decade.

In an ideal world, our democratic principles and the needs of our security would coincide. But the reality is that constitutional democracy, which we consider "normal," is, in fact, a rarity both in the sweep of history and on the breadth of this planet. This is no accident. Constitutional democracy places authority in an abstraction: obedience to law. But constitutionalism can function only if law is believed either to reflect an absolute standard of truth or grow out of a generally accepted political process. In most parts of the world and in most periods of time, these conditions have not existed. Law was the verdict of authority, not of a legislative process; politics has been about who has the right to issue orders. Personal authority has been made bearable by a concept of reciprocal obligation, as in feudal societies, or when limited by custom, as was the authority of kings who ruled by the claim to divine right in the seventeenth and eighteenth centuries. In each case tradition was a limiting factor; certain exactions were impossible not because they were forbidden but because they had no precedent. No ruler of eighteenth-century Europe could levy income taxes or conscript his subjects; authoritarianism, in short, was quite precisely circumscribed.

It was, paradoxically, the emergence of popular government that expanded the scope of what authorities could demand. The people by definition could not oppress itself; hence its wishes, as expressed by assemblies or rulers in its name, were absolute. The growth of state power has gone hand in hand with the expansion of populist claims.

In this context modern totalitarianism is a caricature, a reductio ad absurdum, of democracy; modern authoritarianism is a vestige of traditional personal rule. This is why some authoritarian governments have been able to evolve into democracies and why no totalitarian state has ever done so. Personal rule has inherent limits; government that claims to reflect the general will countenances no such restraint.

But for this very reason, authoritarian governments are infinitely more vulnerable to internal subversion than totalitarian ones. When the personal bond of reciprocal obligation is broken, both rulers and subjects become demoralized; the former because they have no legitimacy for governing on a sustained basis by naked force, the latter because once the criteria of obedience have evaporated, every directive appears oppressive. Our dilemma is that in almost all developing countries on this planet, authority is still personal. The transition to constitutionalism is a complex process that, if force-fed, is more likely to lead to totalitarianism than to democracy.

One of the premises of the democratic process is that the loser accepts his defeat and in return is given an opportunity to win on another occasion. It depends on a moderate center. Such an evolution is almost inevitably thwarted in a developing country when a totalitarian element succeeds in organizing a guerrilla war. This impels the government into acts of repression, starting a vicious circle that traps both government and opponents and destroys whatever moderate center exists — fulfilling the central purpose of the insurgency. Moreover, the victims of terrorist attacks are almost invariably the ablest and most dedicated officials, leaving in place the corrupt, whose transgressions multiply as they attempt to make up for the peril of their station by accumulating the maximum material compensations.

The American response to this historical phenomenon is usually expressed in the conviction that a government under siege can best maintain itself by accelerating democratic reform and by expanding its base of support by sharing power. But the fundamental cause of a civil war (of which guerrilla war is a special category) is the breakdown of domestic consensus. Compromise, the essence of democratic politics, is its first victim. Civil wars almost without exception end in victory or defeat, never in coalition governments — the favorite American recipe. Concessions are ascribed to the weakness of those holding power, not to their magnanimity, and hence accelerate rather than arrest the disintegration of authority. The proper time for reform is *before* civil wars break out, in order to preempt their causes — though this does not always work when the insurrection is inspired, financed, trained, and equipped from outside the country. The next occasion for conciliation is *after* victory (as in America as Lincoln intended, or in Nigeria after 1970), but Western inhibitions about force and authoritarian incompetence usually combine to prevent the testing of this hypothesis. As for the so-called "political solution" to civil wars — the much-touted recipe of negotiation among the parties — it too is belied by historical experience. It is against all probability that groups that have been assassinating each other would govern jointly; this is why it is next to impossible to think of a civil war that ended in coalition government. It is at best a temporary expedient to preserve one group to fight again under better circumstances. Thus guerrillas generally refuse political negotiations when they seem to be winning and conduct them generally to gain time for a later showdown.

This is why the perennial American pressures for political talks tend to demoralize allied governments with which we are associated. When the crying need is for an assertion of authority, our advice usually dilutes it. And hard-pressed governments beset by an implacable domestic enemy are often reduced to paralysis by advice which they know is dangerous if not disastrous but which they dare not reject. This was the fate of Nguyen Van Thieu, as it was later of the Shah of Iran.[8]

Thieu's country was assaulted on every frontier, first by guerrilla forces trained and equipped by Hanoi and then by a large invading army from North Vietnam. Nevertheless, the United States government pressed for an electoral process and flexibility in negotiations, partly out of conviction and partly to placate insatiable critics at home. By a miracle of fortitude Thieu managed to navigate this passage, fighting a determined enemy and propitiating an uncomprehending ally. He emerged in 1973 with an agreement in which Hanoi gave up its political demands of many years in return for a cease-fire better than we had expected, though more precarious than he had hoped.

I had little personal affection for Thieu but I had high regard for him as he continued his struggle in the terrible loneliness that followed America's withdrawal. He received scant compassion or even understanding. It did not dent his dignity. Though the sole head of state to have his reception ceremony in the absence of the public, he acted as if this were the most natural thing in the world. At the San Clemente arrival, Nixon made a polite speech that referred to South Vietnam's capacity to defend itself — a dubious proposition if Hanoi launched an all-out attack with Soviet weapons. Thieu fell in gracefully with this fairy tale, not, however, without contrasting South Vietnam's position to that of Europe, which still required 300,000 American troops a quarter-century after the end of World War II.

This ritual completed, the two leaders repaired for their private talks. There was, in fact, not much to discuss. Thieu did not whine about the task we had left him or Hanoi's malevolence. He gave a matter-of-fact account of North Vietnamese violations. Nixon assured him privately — as he had already done publicly on March 15 and elsewhere — that he would resist blatant violations by force if necessary.

At the same time he urged Thieu to lean over backward to carry out South Vietnam's obligations under the Agreement. If there was to be a breakdown of the Paris accords, Nixon advised, the onus must fall unambiguously on Hanoi. Thieu pointed out that the main obstacle to assembling the National Council for National Reconciliation and Concord, as required by the Agreement, was Hanoi's refusal to hold the elections that the Council was to supervise. The "political contest" so passionately advocated by some in America during the war would never be undertaken by Hanoi in peacetime. It would not risk a generation of struggle on ballots that it disdained in its own country.

Nixon's and Thieu's second day of discussion mostly concerned aid for South Vietnam. It had a slightly unreal quality because the American participants knew that Congressional support even for economic development assistance was eroding fast. The liberals were losing interest because they had little commitment to the survival of South Vietnam, and the conservatives believed that they had discharged their obligations by supporting the war to an honorable conclusion. Both reflected the war-weariness of the nation. Nixon promised to use Saigon's aid request as a target figure; the final result would depend on Congressional consultation. Thieu did obtain a pledge in the final communiqué that the two allies would maintain "vigilance" against "the possibility of renewed Communist aggression after the departure of United States ground forces from South Vietnam." Furthermore, "actions which would threaten the basis of the Agreement would call for appropriately vigorous reactions" — yet another clear *public* statement of Nixon's intention to enforce the Agreement.

The ambiguities of the response to his economic requests did not dim Thieu's high spirits as he left San Clemente. As his plane took off from California, he had a champagne celebration to mark his pleasure and relief at his talks with Nixon.[9] Despite his usual suspiciousness and the gathering omens of future difficulties — our hesitation over both Hanoi's violations and economic assistance — Thieu had an unshakable conviction that the United States would come to South Vietnam's aid in a crisis. It was a confidence entertained before and since by other allies of the United States, a faith that has constituted one of our principal assets in the world and that we were determined not to dissipate.

The Aborted Retaliation

THERE was a fashionable slogan that we could not guarantee the future of South Vietnam for all eternity. This was probably true. But eight weeks hardly qualified as "eternity." What our reactions should have been after a few years might be debated; but failure to react after a few weeks was certain to turn the Paris accords into ashes and make

a mockery of American credibility. As early as March 6, 1973, I said
to a meeting of the Washington Special Actions Group (WSAG):*

[The President] is concerned that if we permit ourselves to be nibbled to death
in Laos and Cambodia it will also happen later in Vietnam. Our critics give us
no awards for our restraint. . . . [W]hat do you think they'll say if we lose
Vietnam? They will attack the agreement as a sellout and forget that they were
advocating a real sellout just a few months ago. The President held firm for
four years in rejecting a simple exchange of POWs for our withdrawal. He's
not going to let Vietnam go down the drain now.

All intelligence estimates, moreover, confirmed that Hanoi was being
restrained from large-scale hostilities by fear of American reaction. A
WSAG meeting of April 16, 1973, was told by James Schlesinger, then
Director of Central Intelligence, that Hanoi was not doing very well in
gaining popular support in the South but had improved its military position there since the cease-fire:

This gives the third factor — Hanoi's judgment of how the U.S. would react
to a resumption of larger-scale hostilities — a more important influence than
ever on Hanoi's future decisions.

One of our concerns was how to react to violations without wrecking
the entire Agreement. We were prepared to give Hanoi a jolt; we had
no desire for all-out war. We judged that a prompt retaliation could
enforce a prolonged pause in which both sides might be forced to engage in political rather than military competition. There was another
reason for acting swiftly: I learned that the Pentagon was planning to
withdraw air power from Southeast Asia at a faster rate than I had appreciated. As I have explained, the jealous independence by which Defense guarded its budgetary decisions meant we often presented
with a fait accompli. We had to act quickly.

At the end of February, there were two brief tests of strength that
validated our reasoning. The first was over Laos. Despite the fact that
during my visit to Hanoi it had been agreed that a cease-fire for Laos
would go into effect within days, the Pathet Lao — Hanoi's Laotian
clients — continued what Premier Souvanna Phouma called a "general
offensive." On the very first day of the truce, the Communists broke it
no fewer than twenty-nine times. Souvanna therefore requested American B-52 strikes against the Pathet Lao. The President and I discussed
it on the evening of February 22. Nixon was reluctant because he feared

---

*The Washington Special Actions Group, or WSAG, was an interdepartmental group responsi-
ble for coordinating policy during crises and reviewing contingency plans. It was formed in 1969.
It was chaired by me and included the Deputy Secretaries of State and Defense, the Director of
the Central Intelligence Agency, and the Chairman of the Joint Chiefs of Staff, together with
whatever other experts the subject required.

Hanoi would use it as a pretext to delay the release of American prisoners of war. I argued that Hanoi would refuse the release of our prisoners — our most insistent demand — only if it was prepared for a showdown for other reasons. Nixon authorized an immediate B-52 strike. Within forty-eight hours the cease-fire in Laos was established.

The second mini-confrontation in late February was indeed over the release of American prisoners of war (though almost certainly unrelated to the Laos incident). Hanoi failed to produce, on February 26, a list of the POWs who were due to be released the next day. It gave no explanation, though it hinted that the release of our POWs was dependent on Saigon's release of its political detainees — a linkage we had spent weeks of negotiation to avoid. This happened at almost the same time that Washington and Saigon were protesting the appearance of three SAM-2 surface-to-air missile sites at Khe Sanh in violation of the standstill cease-fire.

We responded very sharply by suspending American troop withdrawals and mine-clearing operations in North Vietnamese harbors. Secretary of State Rogers declined to attend any sessions at the International Conference in Paris. A terse message was sent to Hanoi simply informing it of our actions. In addition, White House press secretary Ronald L. Ziegler was instructed to read at his noon briefing a tough statement making clear that the release of American prisoners was an unconditional obligation of North Vietnam not linked to any other provision of the Agreement. A day later I told Ziegler that I was certain the pressures would work (in a conversation that also clearly indicates my plan to leave government soon): "A year from now when I'm out of here, they're really going to put it to us. Not for that reason but a year from now, they're going to be tigers but now they're not ready." The POWs were released on schedule.

But these were harassments at the fringes of the real challenge, which was the massive infiltration of personnel and war matériel through Laos and Cambodia and across the Demilitarized Zone, violating almost every provision of the Agreement. Schlesinger estimated that at this rate of resupply, Hanoi would by fall be at least as strong in the South as it was prior to the 1972 offensive. The WSAG held many meetings on the subject. As a preliminary step it was decided to send a crescendo of protests to Hanoi with increasingly ominous warnings about retaliation. Notes were sent on March 4, March 6, March 14, and March 15, 1973. The note of March 14 warned that if infiltration continued and culminated in military action by Hanoi, "the consequences . . . would be most grave."

On March 8 I warned Soviet Ambassador Anatoly Dobrynin. I stressed that a continuation of substantial Soviet deliveries of military supplies would be considered an unfriendly act; a new offensive by

Hanoi would have "the profoundest consequence for US–Soviet relations."

Dobrynin was equal to the occasion. Nothing was ever the fault of the Soviet Union. My information, he argued, was either incorrect or outdated. Indeed, he hinted darkly that the wily Chinese were probably to blame for the continued flow of Soviet military equipment into North Vietnam. The fact was, he told me with a straight face, that several hundred tanks and some supply trains had inexplicably disappeared during the war as they transited China. The Kremlin was convinced that the Soviet war matériel showing up in North Vietnam now was being introduced by the Chinese in their eternal effort to undermine a relaxation of tensions between the United States and the Soviet Union. Dobrynin said that it would be appropriate for me to raise the issue with Brezhnev during my scheduled visit to Moscow (eight weeks hence). It was obvious from this we could expect little help from the Soviet quarter. We also warned the Chinese; they replied ambiguously.

On March 13, there was another meeting of the WSAG on this subject. The group concluded that:

> We have no intention, under any circumstances, of letting the enemy mount a big offensive this year. We will be meticulous in honoring the agreement ourselves, and we want to make public their continuing violations. There will be no press statements issued that belittle the enemy violations.
>
> The best military option appears to be a resumption of bombing the trails in Laos as soon as possible after the third tranche of POWs is released, possibly followed later by bombing of the DMZ and the area between the DMZ and the South Vietnamese lines, if necessary. The final decision will be made by the President.

But the President was in an uncharacteristically indecisive frame of mind. It was not unusual for Nixon to approach a major decision crabwise. Long recitals of the dilemmas he faced were his way of reflecting on the options. During his first term the process had led inexorably to a decision. Each successive conversation, however apparently interminable, would lead gradually, almost imperceptibly, to a sharper definition of the issues. In stages Nixon worked himself to a fever pitch emotionally so that intellectual and psychological readiness tended to coincide with the point of decision. I would often frame the issue earlier than he; but he had the better instinct for the jugular. His final decision would cut through equivocation to the heart of the matter.

But it was a different Nixon in March 1973. He approached the problem of the violations in a curiously desultory fashion. He drifted. He did not home in on the decision in the single-minded, almost possessed, manner that was his hallmark. The rhetoric might be there, but accompanied this time with excuses for inaction. In retrospect we know that by March Watergate was boiling. At the end of February, he was closeted for long periods with John Dean, his White House Counsel, devising strategy for the investigations by the newly constituted Senate Select Committee chaired by Senator Sam Ervin and worried about the hearings opening in the Senate Judiciary Committee on the nomination of L. Patrick Gray as permanent director of the FBI. It was on February 27 that Dean warned Nixon the cover-up might not be contained indefinitely. Nixon was a distracted man. On March 6, for instance, he ordered a bombing strike of one day's duration on the Ho Chi Minh Trail — timed for the following weekend. The illegal bumper-to-bumper military truck traffic down the trail promised profitable targets. The next day, March 7, he canceled the order. Again he said he did not want to give the North Vietnamese a pretext for delaying the release of the next batch of American prisoners. I doubt whether this was a considered reason. Gray was in difficulties over the FBI's Watergate inquiries and was daily dragging in John Dean and the White House. The Senate Judiciary Committee was demanding that Dean appear despite the President's assertion of executive privilege. Nixon clearly did not want to add turmoil over Indochina to his mounting domestic perplexities.

I submitted a memorandum urging acceptance of the WSAG recommendations for an air strike to the President on March 14. I outlined the North Vietnamese leaders' possible motivations: They might believe that we would not react to their violations so long as they held American prisoners; they might simply be testing the limits of our tolerance; they might have decided to resume offensive operations as soon as their resupply effort was completed. Whatever their purposes, we should exhaust every diplomatic avenue, but we would not be able to avoid the preparation of military contingency plans:

[T]he North Vietnamese are exposed both in the trail area of the Laotian Panhandle and in the northern reaches of South Vietnam's MR-1. In both areas they are operating in daylight and the traffic is so heavy as to be congested. They clearly are taking advantage of the fact that all air action against them has ceased. A series of heavy strikes over a 2 or 3 day period in either of these areas would be very costly to them in both personnel and material.

The future of the Paris Agreement indeed depended on action now to enforce it:

[An air strike] would signify clearly that we will not tolerate continued violations and will react decisively to them. It is precisely this sort of U.S. reaction on May 8 [1972] and again in December [1972] which caused the North Vietnamese to reexamine the course on which they were then bent. If they now believe that we may not react and we fail to do so, we will encourage increasing and even more blatant violations. If we react we will demonstrate the costs which they must expect to bear if they abrogate the Agreement. . . . There will be recriminations. But in my judgment if we do not react, the Agreement may well break down precisely because we did not. The recriminations in that event will be no less severe.

To meet Nixon's concern about the American prisoners of war, I recommended that we launch an attack on March 24–26, after the third but before the fourth group of our prisoners due for release.

The increasingly insolent tone of Hanoi's response to our protests required a sharp reaction, in my view, lest the Paris Agreement simply fall apart. Hanoi repeated its by-now familiar interpretation of Article 20, that withdrawal of its troops from Laos and Cambodia had to await a political settlement, which in turn was identified with Communist control. Hanoi rejected our documented evidence of infiltration. Since no military matériel had been introduced through checkpoints as the Agreement required, no evidence of illicit equipment existed, averred Hanoi with characteristic brazenness. In any event the United States had no standing to raise the issue, which should be taken up by the International Commission of Control and Supervision (on which, of course, the Communists had a veto).

In crises the most daring course is often the safest. The riskiest course in my experience has been gradual escalation that the opponent matches step by step, inevitably reaching a higher level of violence and often an inextricable stalemate. Hanoi had to reckon with the fact that holding up release of American POWs would halt our implementation of all other provisions of the Agreement: the mine-clearing, the troop withdrawals, the prospects for economic aid; it might trigger an even fiercer American retaliation, this time against North Vietnam. As I said in my memorandum:

If we act immediately after the third prisoner release, which will be completed by the end of this week, we can minimize the risk of a hold on the remaining POWs. There will be a 2-week period prior to the final release. There will be time after the strikes to reestablish the arrangements for that final release and for our coincident final withdrawal. Meanwhile we would cease all withdrawals as additional leverage to bring about the final release.

But the President temporized. He approved contingency planning but told me again that he was worried about delaying the release of our POWs. On March 15, he issued a warning to Hanoi in his news conference. I spent from March 17 to March 26 in Acapulco on vacation. During that period the Watergate cover-up really began to come apart, with incessant demands for money by E. Howard Hunt, one of the Ellsberg break-in team, though I and my NSC colleagues had as yet no inklings of that. Nixon's indecisions were compounded on March 19 when Ambassador G. McMurtrie Godley backchanneled to the White

House from Vientiane, Laos, questioning the timing of the proposed strike. It might disrupt the scheduled formation of the new Laotian co-alition government (which in the event was not finally formed until the following year). Premier Souvanna Phouma might find it difficult to go along. Informed of this message, I instructed General Brent Scowcroft, who had replaced Al Haig as my deputy, to raise Godley's argument with the President. I cabled to Scowcroft via secure communications from Acapulco:

I want you to discuss the question of the strikes in Laos with the President. I believe Godley is making a good point concerning the possibility of fouling up the Laotian negotiations. However, none of the considerations advanced last week have really changed. I don't believe the North Vietnamese decision on withdrawal will depend on one series of strikes. Another danger is that they will delay release of POW's. The counter argument is that they will tend to be ruthless next fall.

I want you to discuss this issue with the President personally and the final decision should be made by him. The President should be made aware of the Godley argument. We should not in any case go before Thursday night [March 22]. My recommendation, on balance, would be that we go then.

Scowcroft on March 20 reported to me the now familiar symptoms of Presidential ambivalence. Nixon had avoided a decision but had rumi-nated on adverse political consequences. On March 21 Nixon indicated that he would prefer to hold up our troop withdrawals rather than strike. He would order an air attack but "only if it is felt that it will do some real good" — a condition almost surely unfulfillable for a single air strike.

This was the very day John Dean told Nixon that John Mitchell, Charles Colson, Jeb Stuart Magruder, Herbert Kalmbach, and others were not the only ones with a problem. He said the President, too, had a problem — there was "a cancer growing on the Presidency." Un-aware of all of these pressures, I reiterated my position on March 21:

There is one principal argument for conducting the strikes at this time and that is to make it clear to the North Vietnamese that we may do something totally unexpected if pressed in defense of the agreement. If the North Vietnamese believe we will not act after the POWs are out, an offensive by the end of the year is almost a certainty. If an offensive succeeds, all those who have fought every move the President has made will be vindicated and the whole basis of the President's policy undermined. I consider one of the key objectives of our foreign policy to be to get as much time as possible before the resumption of hostilities by the North.

That same day Nixon again philosophized to Scowcroft about the utility and timing of our plan; he asked Scowcroft to query me again. Obviously, I was not giving the desired advice. Nevertheless, I repeated my view on March 22:

The operation is likely to cause considerable though not decisive damage. If they do not react to our strikes it will be seen as a sign of weakness on their part but I do not see what action they can take. . . . Basically, my view remains somewhat similar to my feeling during the Korean situation in early 1969. There is no pressing necessity to strike but failure to react now will cost us later.

Nixon was stung by this reference to the EC-121 incident,[10] which awakened his usual instinct to appear at least as tough as his advisers. He ordered an immediate one-day strike on the Ho Chi Minh Trail. This combined every disadvantage: It was too short to be effective, too blatant to be ignored, and too hesitant to have the desired psychological impact on Hanoi. But Nixon's order had outmaneuvered me. It induced me to recommend postponement until we could discuss matters after my return from Acapulco — in other words, after the final release of our prisoners.

We kept up our warnings. We had by this time reassurance, if any were needed, that retaliation would not do any lasting damage to our relationship with the Soviet Union. For what it was worth, Dobrynin on March 23 formally assured us that Moscow had stopped arms for Hanoi after the Paris Agreement and argued again that Soviet supplies reaching Hanoi were probably those delayed in transit through China. As for retaliation, Moscow merely hoped that "things would not turn in that direction" — a form of dissociation so mild as to cause us no concern. When Nixon addressed the nation on March 29 to mark the return of our last prisoners of war, he included another tough reminder to the North Vietnamese leaders that they "should have no doubt as to the consequences if they fail to comply with the Agreement."

Other Administration spokesmen took up the theme. On April 3, the following dialogue took place between Secretary of Defense Elliot Richardson and newsmen questioning him prior to an appearance before a House Appropriations subcommittee:

QUESTION: Mr. Secretary, under what conditions might we have to begin bombing in support of the South Vietnamese?

RICHARDSON: It would be one of those questions that it's impossible to answer in general terms. We can only see what develops, and hopefully, what will develop is the full and complete implementation of the cease-fire agreements.

QUESTION: But is it possible that we will have to bomb either North Vietnam or in support of the South Vietnamese army again?

RICHARDSON: It's certainly something we cannot rule out at this time.

On April 2, I sent Nixon a memorandum outlining further possible responses, both diplomatic and military. My memorandum was labeled "information"; it asked for no decision. Nixon was in San Clemente with Haldeman and Ehrlichman. They were under siege by the Ervin Committee, with the chairman threatening to arrest any White House aide who refused to give testimony in public. Nixon simply placed a check mark on my memorandum to indicate that he had noted it. The paper was returned with none of the underlinings and marginal comments that normally showed he had studied a paper carefully.

Planning by the WSAG, meanwhile, revealed that the North Vietnamese, in complete violation of the Agreement, had built up an extensive complex of surface-to-air missiles south of the Demilitarized Zone, especially around Khe Sanh, where activity had been noted before, and in the Ashau valley threatening the old imperial city of Hué. The result was that the Joint Chiefs of Staff now insisted on three days of bombing for antiaircraft suppression before we could attack the North Vietnamese supply complex in Laos that was our real concern.

This put back our timetable once again. To bomb for the better part of a week, we needed to lay the ground with diplomacy. Hanoi, pursuing its own stratagems to head off bombing, gave us something of an opportunity for a dual-track approach by replying to our protests with a hint that it might be ready to talk about violations. It had made a vague reference on March 27 to private meetings to review the Agreement. More explicitly, in a message of March 31, Hanoi suggested that private meetings between Le Duc Tho and me could "resolve difficulties or snags which may arise in future in the implementation of the Agreement." Of course, being Hanoi, it blamed all breaches on the United States and Saigon. Indeed, it denied us any standing with respect to insisting on the observance of the Agreement. After the completion of our withdrawal, only the Vietnamese parties could deal with such issues. We told Thieu about these messages but waited until he had departed from the United States before responding to Hanoi. We left no doubt that our patience was approaching its end:

The DRV messages are an insult to the intelligence of the U.S. government and the American people in view of the record of the DRV performance, for which no explanation is offered, and their repetition must prevent the normalization of relations which the U.S. government is seeking.

The U.S. side rejects emphatically the DRV contention that responsibility for implementation of Article 7 of the Paris Agreement [regarding infiltration] rests only with the two South Vietnamese parties. All four parties to the Agreement are responsible for its strict implementation. The U.S. side holds the DRV side fully responsible for the continued violation of Article 7 and insists that the DRV side accept its responsibility and cease the infiltration of men and materiel into South Vietnam in violation of that article and Article 20. The U.S. side further insists that the DRV side withdraw its forces from Laos and Cambodia unconditionally as required by Article 20. . . . The U.S. side wishes to point out that continuation of these violations will have most serious consequences.

But the end of our message coupled another warning with a proposal for a meeting with Le Duc Tho:

In order to arrest any further deterioration, Dr. Kissinger proposes a meeting in Paris with special adviser Le Duc Tho at a mutually agreeable time during the first week of May.

Our strategy at this point was to launch a three- or four-day air attack on the North Vietnamese supply bases and trails in Laos and on both sides of the Demilitarized Zone sometime during April. Against this background, we expected my scheduled negotiations with Le Duc Tho in May to help dampen the controversy at home while inspiring Hanoi with increased caution.

But as always, Hanoi had strong nerves. By the end of April, the Ho Chi Minh Trail would be shut down as the rainy season turned it into a quagmire. So Hanoi played for time while continuing its illegal infiltration. It took ten days to reply, then on April 15 accepted the meeting for any day after May 15. Le Duc Tho wanted as long an interval as possible, calculating that we would not attack until after negotiations had taken place. His calculation was wrong; but he prevailed for reasons connected with Watergate, not diplomacy. But for Watergate we would surely have acted in April.

By mid-April, 35,000 fresh North Vietnamese troops had entered South Vietnam or nearby sanctuaries; the total increase in combat personnel and supplies was greater than before the 1972 Easter offensive. The normal Nixon would have been enraged beyond containment at being strung along like this; but Watergate Nixon continued to dither. He had, on April 8, sent Al Haig, now Vice Chief of Staff of the Army, on a five-day fact-finding trip to Indochina. In the past this had been the precursor to strong decisions. Not now. When Haig reported on April 15, the same day as the Hanoi message, Nixon engaged in further procrastination, which would soon make the projected attack pointless as the rainy season rendered the Ho Chi Minh Trail unusable. We were instructed to call yet one more WSAG meeting to consider our options.

Nixon was simply unable to concentrate his energies and mind on Vietnam. The records show that he was engaged in incessant meetings and telephone calls on Watergate. April 14, for instance, we know now was the day the President concluded with Haldeman and Ehrlichman that his old friend John Mitchell must be pressured into admitting that he was "morally and legally responsible." It was on April 15, the day of our Vietnamese discussion, that Henry Petersen, heading the Justice Department's Watergate inquiry, urged Nixon to fire Haldeman and Ehrlichman.

I was convinced at the time, as I told Elliot Richardson a few days later, that hesitation was the most dangerous course: "[T]he only chance we have got is not to let the other guys calibrate the price that they have to pay at each stage." We reviewed the options the next day in the WSAG. In addition to the resupply down the Ho Chi Minh Trail threatening South Vietnam's safety, we were now faced with a new North Vietnamese offensive in northern Laos. We recommended that this should be attacked by bombing, and that we should suspend mine-clearing. These narrower decisions were carried out almost immediately. But they fudged the fundamental issue, which was the transgressions in the main theater — South Vietnam itself. American B-52 bombers and fighter planes struck targets in Laos on April 16 in retaliation for the North Vietnamese seizure of Tha Vieng, south of the Plain of Jars. On April 17 the raids continued for a second day, and Defense Secretary Richardson at a news conference described them as a response to "a flagrant violation" of the Laotian cease-fire. But no action was taken against the North Vietnamese infiltration down the Ho Chi Minh Trail or against the illegal infiltration across the DMZ, and that was after all the heart of the matter.

Pursuing the track of negotiations simultaneously, on April 17 we sent a sharp message to the North Vietnamese responding "with indignation and dismay" to their message of April 15. We agreed to a meeting between me and Le Duc Tho, to be preceded by a preparatory meeting between Hanoi's Vice Foreign Minister Nguyen Co Thach and Deputy Assistant Secretary of State William Sullivan.

The WSAG met again on April 17. The Joint Chiefs still insisted that they could not attack the Ho Chi Minh Trail in southern Laos — the only segment still in active use with the approach of the rainy season — unless they first destroyed the Communist surface-to-air missile complexes just south of the DMZ.

Therefore, the military extended the length of military operations once again, insisting on a full seven days of bombing. This was a turning point. Three days before this meeting I had been shaken to hear from Leonard Garment how Watergate might touch the President himself. I was appalled by the knowledge, seeing, for the first time clearly, how the Watergate challenges could reach to the heart of the Presidency and destroy all authority. I have described in Chapter IV how I and others responded, but on April 17 I did not see how I could urge Nixon to put his diminishing prestige behind the new prolonged bombing campaign that the situation required and that his own hesitations had made necessary. I therefore suggested at the WSAG that we wait for a clear-cut provocation from Hanoi while continuing with our planning. The members of the WSAG, who were finely tuned to bureaucratic intangibles, understood correctly that this represented a sea change. Up to then our strategy had been to prevent a major challenge rather than wait for it to occur. (Our estimate was that it would not occur for the better part of a year.) The decision meant that we were postponing a preemptive strike indefinitely. Thus sooner or later South Vietnam would have to cope with the full fury of the unimpeded North Vietnamese buildup.

It was a great lost opportunity, as Hanoi's mild reaction to the air strikes in Laos demonstrated. For five years it had been an article of faith among critics that strong actions marred the climate for negotiations. The truth was quite different. We had invariably found that Hanoi was never more tractable than after a violent American blow. In this case, too, Hanoi responded to our bombing of northern Laos and our tough note of April 17 by *accepting* on April 20 the preliminary meeting between Thach and Sullivan. There was a Freudian typographical error in its message (or else in someone's transcription of it) to the effect that Hanoi "strictly respects and *unscrupulously* [sic] implements" the Paris Agreement — one of the few communications from Hanoi that we could endorse without qualification.

But our strategy was becoming unhinged, for it was clear that we were in no position to carry out the military half of our original plan. In its absence the meeting with Le Duc Tho took on quite a different significance. I informed Nixon on April 21 of Hanoi's message. We chatted about an NSC meeting planned for April 26 to make the final decision. The meeting never took place. In any event, Watergate would have predetermined the outcome. I made clear to Nixon — in less than good taste — that we were simply in no position to implement our planning: "If we didn't have this damn domestic situation, a week of bombing would put this Agreement in force," I said to him. And to demonstrate that my tactlessness had been finely honed, I added another sentence of exquisite infelicity: "[O]ne good thing about Watergate, it puts it all [the Laos bombing] on page 20 [of the newspapers]." To which Nixon, getting into the spirit of things, replied: "It even puts the ten percent increase in inflation on page 20."

By April 23 it was clear that the President was not prepared to order any kind of retaliation. I told Haig:

> My problem is I don't see how we can get anything done in this climate. I mean supposing we start bombing. This will crystalize all the Congressional opposition. . . . I have no doubt that if it weren't for this mess we'd back them off [that is, the North Vietnamese].

By the end of April 1973, therefore, our strategy for Vietnam was in tatters. In the light of flagrant North Vietnamese violations and the horrible stories told by returning prisoners of war, the carrot of economic aid to Hanoi was understandably all but eliminated by the Congress: The Byrd amendment, barring direct or indirect assistance unless specifically authorized by Congress, went through by 88 votes to 3. Then the stick of bombing was lost by our own domestic incapacity. The Congress in June was to prohibit a military response by law, but the "window" we had in those few months of early 1973 was closed by Watergate's enfeeblements.

In this climate my next meetings with Le Duc Tho registered a new reality. I went not as a representative of an America that had just demonstrated there was a penalty for treachery, but as someone with almost no cards to play.

A Charade with Le Duc Tho

I SET out for Paris for what turned out to be an extended series of negotiations with Le Duc Tho lasting (intermittently) from May 17 to June 13. The ill omens did not cease, the most extraordinary being an intelligence report I received while en route to Paris. It was a North Vietnamese account that described how the Viet Cong leaders were briefing their subordinates in the field. The report confirmed our knowledge of Hanoi's buildup, referring to a "general offensive" that was in preparation. But it was being postponed, the briefing stated, to give Watergate an opportunity to complete the paralysis of our Presidency and the demoralization of our South Vietnamese ally. It accurately predicted that the wounded President now lacked the authority to retaliate against North Vietnamese transgressions.

The Watergate investigations . . . have already proved that the last U. S. Presidential election was fraudulent, and many members of the White House staff have submitted their resignations. Therefore, . . . President Nixon must also resign because he no longer has enough prestige to lead the United States. His weakened authority over the US government is now generating a favorable influence in South Vietnam for the struggle of the NLF,* and will result in a new US policy in Indochina. Even if President Nixon remains in office . . . he will not dare to apply such strong measures as air strikes or bombing attacks in either North or South Vietnam, because the US Congress and the American people will violently object.

Just as it did in the years of peace negotiations, Hanoi was orchestrating its moves with our domestic politics. It had plenty of evidence for its shrewd judgment. Beginning in early May, antiwar measures in

---

*The National Liberation Front (NLF) was the original formal name of the Viet Cong, the South Vietnamese Communists. Later they called themselves the Provisional Revolutionary Government (PRG). They purported to be an indigenous insurgency within South Vietnam. When the North Vietnamese Army occupied South Vietnam in April 1975, the fiction was dispensed with. Some PRG leaders are today in jail, apparently for taking too seriously the propaganda that the PRG was independent of Hanoi.

the Congress that had usually been blocked in the House of Representatives began to *pass*. For example, on May 10, the House of Representatives voted 219–188 to cut off funds for the bombing of Cambodia. On May 31, the Senate voted the same by a margin of 63–19. Only three Democratic Senators — James Eastland, Henry Jackson, and Russell Long — voted with the President, along with sixteen Republicans. Twenty Republicans joined forty-three Democrats in voting for the bombing cutoff.

Why did the Administration begin to lose Congressional votes that it had won consistently over the preceding four years? To some extent it was because the Paris Agreement to most Americans spelled "peace"; it signified our disengagement from the war. More concretely, the President's previous — and usually successful — plea that military measures were necessary to protect American troops lost its rationale after all American forces were withdrawn. Nevertheless, Nixon could have taken his case to the American people, arguing that we could not abandon what 50,000 Americans had died to preserve. A Nixon reelected by one of the largest majorities in history might well have prevailed, as he had so many times before. In the swamp of Watergate the President's political strength drained away and this option did not exist.

If Hanoi had been able to penetrate our inner councils as well, it would have found a bureaucratic deadlock that a weakened President was unable to resolve. The White House, the Joint Chiefs of Staff, and CIA Director Schlesinger favored early preemptive action against the continuing infiltration. Some CIA experts and the civilian element of the Pentagon favored turning over enforcement of the Agreement to the South Vietnamese — a disguised way of acquiescing in its collapse since the South Vietnamese army was fully occupied in static defense and had no planes of a range to interdict the North Vietnamese supply routes. The State Department wanted to wash its hands of the whole affair, only too happy in this case to have me prominently responsible. There was a division of opinion in the CIA about what Hanoi was up to. One school reasoned that it would act soon to thwart the political gains Thieu was making; another argued that it was building up secure base areas for an assault much later. This was a normal pattern for the role of intelligence in finely balanced policymaking. It usually mirrors the prevalent division of opinion, following rather than creating policy preferences.

There is almost always in a crisis a division between doves who seek evidence for delay, wrapping their hesitation in the mantle of "diplomacy," which without leverage is bound to be dilatory and inconclusive, and hawks who want early preemptive action. Generally the advocates of passivity seem to have the stronger case in the beginning of a crisis because the risks of action are evident while those of passivity are deferred or conjectural. The bane of preemptive action is the impossibility of proving it was necessary. The penalty for gradualism is that one becomes the prisoner of events. The temptation is nearly irresistible to try to combine both courses, striking bureaucratic compromises rather than seeking real solutions, or to confuse the two. A hawkish policy is coupled with dovish methods that deprive it of effectiveness (the Bay of Pigs syndrome). Or a dovish policy is carried out with hawkish rhetoric (the Iran hostage syndrome). With respect to the violations of the Paris Agreement we had used the rhetoric of hawks, but were forced to be doves. For the first time we had threatened and not followed through.

Le Duc Tho responded by turning his customary insolence into a new art form. He knew I was bluffing and let me feel it. An exchange at the outset of our talks showed him once again exploiting our domestic divisions:

LE DUC THO: You have given air support to the troops of the Vientiane administration, launching encroaching operations against the regions under the control of the Pathet Lao in violation of the Agreement on Laos.

With regard to Cambodia, you have stepped up very fierce air attacks in Cambodia, and the U.S. Senate and the House of Representatives are opposed to the air attacks in Cambodia by the Nixon Administration.

KISSINGER: May I recall to the Special Adviser a rule we discussed three years ago that should be enforced? You have been consistently wrong in your assessment. You will be wrong again. But other than that let us not discuss it.

LE DUC THO: Let me finish the first sentence. Considering the bombing of Cambodia as an illegal act, therefore, the Senate and the House of Representatives refuse to appropriate funds to carry out these attacks in Cambodia. I just point out this fact that the stepped up bombing of Cambodia is a wrong deed; not only we are opposed to that but even the American people are opposed to the bombing in Cambodia. This is what I wanted to mention.

KISSINGER: The American people are our problem, not the Special Adviser's. And if he remembers, he has not always been right in his assessment.

LE DUC THO: Whether I was wrong or right, you are aware of that.

KISSINGER: But we do not need to delay on that. We will continue to other matters.

It was an almost verbatim replay of many exchanges of previous years. The trouble was that both Le Duc Tho and, deep down, I knew that this time he was *not* wrong. Nixon would not be able to pull another rabbit out of his hat. The military actions we were still carrying out (in Cambodia) were under unprecedented Congressional attack. Our forces capable of intervening — in Thailand and at sea — were being drastically reduced; I was fighting a desperate but losing struggle against the Pentagon's desire to redeploy air and naval forces out of Southeast Asia in order to devote scarce funds to the procurement of new weapons.

Perhaps I should have called off the negotiation when it became apparent that we would not conduct the air strikes that had been intended to precede it. Unfortunately, our domestic divisions had left us bankrupt. We had nothing much left we could do except negotiate and hope that peaceful pressures — and bluff — might work. We were reduced to relying on naked diplomacy just as our critics had urged. Cancellation of the talks followed by military inaction would merely advertise what Nixon could not admit even to himself: that he was losing the authority to conduct a coherent foreign policy. There was no point making the tragedy explicit. That could only have accelerated the weakness at the center and tempted other international challenges.

So I persisted in the charade with Le Duc Tho, emerging without success but without significant setback. In three negotiating sessions — from May 17 to May 23, June 6 to June 9, and June 12 and 13 — we went through all the provisions of the Paris Agreement, attempting to set new deadlines for implementing provisions where we agreed that there had not been compliance.

We achieved a joint communiqué on June 13 that refined some obligations. But that was shadowboxing. There was no reason why, in the absence of the ability to enforce it, a new accord was any more likely to be observed than the existing one; and it was not. The talks did have an incidental effect — not a happy one, which I will discuss shortly — but the substance of the negotiation was a tour de force of effrontery by Le Duc Tho while I polished a few one-liners.

"It is a contribution to the history of relations among states," I said, "to find 350 tanks, 300 pieces of long-range artillery and several battalions of anti-aircraft guns and missiles classified as civilian goods not subject to the restrictions of Article 7." As I mentioned in Chapter II, the North Vietnamese had come up with the ingenious idea that everything that entered South Vietnam outside the international checkpoints was civilian goods by definition, however it looked to us. Le Duc Tho opened his response by saying: "Your intelligence service has been mistaken. I would like to point out your intelligence service sometimes mistakes an elephant for a tank." I asked him if he was pumping water through his newly built oil pipeline so that the elephants in South Vietnam had enough to drink. Le Duc Tho was quite bland: "You have seen it wrong. But I think you understand also that, militarily speaking, in military operations the PRG must have some reserves. So now if the Saigon Administration continues its military operations, this reserve will be sufficient to cope."

Would he, I asked, do his utmost to keep all the elephants in North Laos? "When the elephants are hungry and thirsty," said Le Duc Tho, laughing, "they must look for food and drink!" He denied my charge that Hanoi had systematically violated the Paris accords and I replied: "If it wasn't systematic I would hate to think what you would do if you did it systematically. If this was accidental, then I hate to think of what you are capable of." Le Duc Tho insisted that cease-fire violations were secondary issues, because the two sides had much practice in implementing cease-fires on "some festival or national day" (meaning the annual Christmas truces, for example). I sarcastically recalled the Tet offensive: "Except in 1968. A slight problem arose in '68 when the word didn't get to all the units of North Vietnamese. . . ."

Le Duc Tho now made observance of the ban against infiltration dependent on the achievement of an effective cease-fire, which in turn Hanoi prevented from coming about. He finally agreed that three specific points of entry for replacement equipment should be designated within fifteen days. He never kept this promise.

Negotiations do not prosper by debating points or sarcastic remarks of the kind we had exchanged; they require a balance of interests and risks. In 1972 we had achieved our objective of preserving an allied government in Saigon because Hanoi could not force the withdrawal of our troops from South Vietnam, because our mining of its harbors was draining its resources, and because our bombing was exhausting its capacity to conduct large-scale offensives. No pressures of any kind were left to us in 1973. I was reduced to finessing at the conference table.

Many was the time, when I tried to pin down Le Duc Tho, that I wished those who urged us to rely on diplomacy and to eschew resort to force could witness what I was experiencing. Le Duc Tho denied, for example, that North Vietnam held any South Vietnamese civilian prisoners. This exchange shows the brazenness that he was capable of when he did not have to worry that we might respond belligerently:

LE DUC THO: As to the civilian prisoners that the Saigon Administration had alleged we are holding, [that] there is a big number of them, . . . in fact this is not true. Because in the PRG region there cannot be conditions to have so many prisoners and jails. Moreover, when we captured them we release them right afterward.

KISSINGER: If you release them right afterward, why do you capture them?

LE DUC THO: Because we have no accommodation to keep them in custody. Also the food is difficult.

KISSINGER: Then why do you bother to capture them?

LE DUC THO: They have committed a crime and therefore we have to capture them. But the question of their food is not easy and moreover, we do not have prisons enough to keep them. The question of food supply for our troops requires a lot of efforts on our part. It is only a pretext they invoke to delay the return of civilian prisoners.

KISSINGER: I must say the Special Adviser never ceases to astonish me. But I always learn. It is a new approach to criminal justice that you arrest people who have committed a crime for the specific purpose of setting them free.

LE DUC THO: There are two jurisdictions. Your jurisdiction is different from ours. You see, in our jurisdiction we capture them, educate them, and release them. As for your jurisdiction, you capture innocent people, you torture them morally and physically. So these are two different jurisdictions. So you are not aware of this.

KISSINGER: Well, we have had a few prisoners who were aware of your jurisdiction.

North Vietnam's imperial ambitions, so strenuously disbelieved in our domestic debates, were now flagrant. Article 20 of the Paris Agreement required the removal of all foreign forces from Laos and Cambodia. Le Duc Tho evaded this obligation by repeating the argument already made to me in February in Hanoi, that the implementation of that provision depended on a political settlement in both countries — a point we had rejected during the peace negotiations because no political settlement was remotely in sight in either country. With respect to Laos, we managed to extract yet another written understanding to the effect that a political settlement would be achieved by July 1, 1973. In fact, it took until July 29 to achieve a preliminary agreement, until September 14 to agree on a coalition, and until April 5, 1974, to set up the coalition — without having the slightest effect on the withdrawal of North Vietnamese troops. Over 50,000 North Vietnamese troops remained in Laos until the country was finally overrun and every vestige of independence eliminated in 1975. Most of them remain as an occupation force to this day.

It was over Cambodia that Le Duc Tho outdid himself. As with Laos he insisted on a political settlememt *before* a troop withdrawal. But the only political settlement he would consider was the elimination of Lon Nol and a complete Communist victory. "So you are saying," I told Le Duc Tho in exasperation at one point, "we have to kill Lon Nol or he can kill himself?" The implication did not faze Le Duc Tho in the slightest — after all, two years before he had cheerfully proposed the assassination of Thieu and offered his help.[11] "You asked me a question," he answered equably enough, "and I am frankly speaking. I told you my personal views. I am just raising the real situation."

In other words, only a complete Communist takeover would count as a political settlement. No negotiations were going on, because the Khmer Rouge — the Cambodian Communists — were adamantly opposed, as I shall describe later in the chapter. My suggestion of a negotiation with Sihanouk failed to interest Le Duc Tho, in part no doubt because he could not deliver the Khmer Rouge to it, in part because he considered Sihanouk too much under Chinese influence. But Le Duc Tho must have been looking to the future and reflecting on the fractiousness of his Khmer allies, because he built himself an escape hatch for a Hanoi role in Cambodia even *after* a Khmer Rouge victory. To do this he had to admit that there were indeed Vietnamese troops in Cambodia. However, according to him they did not come from North Vietnam. They were, Le Duc Tho averred, Cambodian citizens of Vietnamese ethnic background, native to Cambodia and locally recruited. It followed that they were not "foreign" in the meaning of Article 20 of the Paris accords; hence they were not required to leave, even should the Communists win.

All that I could achieve on Cambodia was a joint reaffirmation of Article 20 requiring the withdrawal of foreign troops, to which Hanoi continued to apply its eccentric interpretation. In addition, both North Vietnam and the United States agreed privately to put forward "their best efforts to bring about a peaceful settlement of the Cambodian problem." This was no more than Hanoi had been willing to pledge at the time of the Paris Agreement, when Le Duc Tho pointed out that Hanoi had little influence over its Cambodian ally. Le Duc Tho also refused our proposal that we jointly work for a cease-fire in Cambodia. Hanoi's "best efforts" for a settlement consisted of maintaining 40,000 troops on Cambodian soil and supplying arms, training, and logistical support to the murderous Khmer Rouge. Our efforts will be described in the next section.

But the May-June 1973 negotiations in Paris were not without impact. In retrospect, I believe that they contributed marginally to the further demoralization of Saigon. In most respects our disputes with Saigon over the peace talks were a replay of the controversies of 1972. As before, Saigon knew that we were proposing a meeting with Le Duc Tho and gave its approval; it certainly never offered an objection. (It may have well believed that the meeting would follow some American military retaliation against Hanoi's violations, as we planned, though we never promised explicitly.) I was determined not to repeat the misunderstandings of the previous year. Every draft text was checked with Saigon. A South Vietnamese negotiating team met with me every evening in Paris at our Ambassador's residence. In the early stages of the negotiation, Saigon offered many helpful suggestions. There was no hint of controversy. Then Saigon's method of doing battle began to dawn on us. The South Vietnamese negotiating team more and more frequently found itself without instructions. Or else it had received apparently innocuous but lethal instructions. For example, at one point Saigon proposed that the paragraphs in the document be renumbered; all North Vietnamese obligations were to be listed together at the beginning, to be followed by all South Vietnamese obligations. It seemed a weird alteration since the numbers of the paragraphs in the new document exactly paralleled those of the Paris accords — not surprisingly since they specified their implementation.

Nevertheless, I put Saigon's request forward and received yet another lesson in the convolutions of the Vietnamese mind. Le Duc Tho saw nothing strange in that request. On the contrary he thought it a capital idea. He accepted it, only he proposed reversing the order of Saigon's proposal, with South Vietnamese obligations stated first and Hanoi's second. As I pursued the reasoning of my Vietnamese interlocutors it emerged that contrary to every maxim of international law and practice, both groups of Vietnamese seemed to think that the order of the paragraphs would determine the sequence of the performance — at least psychologically. Each side wanted its opposite number to carry out *all* of its obligations before undertaking *any* of its own.

From harassment Saigon graduated to specific objections, some of surpassing pettiness, in which, moreover, it shifted its stand whenever we seemed about to accept its point of view. But these maneuvers, if maddening to us at the time, were not mere mischief. Saigon's concerns were better founded than its presentation of them. It was in a mortal struggle for survival. Its enemy had violated every key provision of the Agreement without being penalized. The very fact that a negotiation was taking place at all between the United States and Hanoi, as if their actions were of equal moral significance, tended to weaken Saigon's legal position, not to speak of its morale. Much more was involved than hurt pride.

A good example is the constant friction over the treatment of Viet Cong liaison officers assigned to the Two-Party Joint Military Commission and stationed in various district towns; they were virtually under South Vietnamese house arrest. We suggested moving the officers of the commission and the liaison officers away from towns to the demarcation line in the jungle between the two areas of control, where in fact they were supposed to function. Moving them from populated areas was sensible from our point of view. But it touched a raw nerve with South Vietnam. It ran up against the reality that it would clearly separate South Vietnam into two areas of control, however minimal the Viet Cong area, disproving Saigon's claim to undisputed sovereignty. This is why Le Duc Tho readily accepted the idea.

Saigon was successful in making the point that its views counted; it brought about a number of changes in already agreed clauses. It won its point about the location of the Two-Party Joint Military Commission as well as its demand to be signatory of the final text. But no adjustment of clauses could alter the underlying reality. It was well summed up by Deputy Assistant Secretary William Sullivan, whom I had sent to Saigon during a break in negotiations to consult with Thieu:

Essentially, what is dawning on them is that a territorial division of the country, even if it means a PRG retreat from the political contest, is a pretty definitive action. If, as they fear, it may be coupled with a Communist controlled Cambodia, they realize this could lead to a military balance in which they have a precious narrow patrimony threatened from well developed base areas in an impregnable cordillera.

Nor was Thieu wrong when he wrote to Nixon on June 6 that Hanoi, instead of being punished for violating a solemn agreement, was only being asked to sign another one:

We are the victims of aggression. The Communist aggressors have systematically violated the Agreements. However, while they suffer no "violent reactions" from our side, as they have been warned, they now want to enjoy unilaterally all the gains from the Communiqué.

The crux was that the new joint communiqué of June 13, like the original Agreement, depended on the willingness to enforce it. That was being eroded in Vietnam by the declining American aid and the demoralization induced by our evident passivity. And it was draining away in the United States under the combined impact of war-weariness and domestic crises finally culminating in an act of Congress legally banning all American military actions in Indochina. The impetus for that last nail in the coffin came from a debate over that unhappiest of countries: Cambodia.

Cambodia: A Certain Hypocrisy

N o country has endured such a succession of miseries as Cambodia in the last decade. Invaded and partially occupied by its North Vietnamese enemy in 1965, bombed by America after 1969, devastated by a civil war whose victors practiced genocide on their own compatriots, reinvaded by North Vietnam in 1978 and racked yet again by guerrilla warfare, it has enjoyed neither peace nor order for nearly two decades. Little more than half its people have survived the exactions of its Communist rulers and the starvation in the wake of Hanoi's uncertain conquest.

It is not surprising, perhaps, that Cambodia's fate has induced a certain amnesia about its antecedents; but Cambodia has also come to have a special place in the history of hypocrisy. It is one thing to have opposed, at the time, the measures the Nixon Administration considered necessary to help Cambodia, thereby to preserve South Vietnam. I can understand the fears there were then in the passions of the moment that America might get "bogged down" in Cambodia as it had in Vietnam. That represents an honorable difference of judgment and I do not seek to stir the embers of those debates. We have all learned from them. But it is another matter when the tragic sequence of events produces among critics not sober second thoughts, not revulsion against the mass killings by the Cambodian Communists, not anger at North Vietnam's unending aggressiveness, but a campaign to shift the indictment for all those *Communist* misdeeds to those who tried to save Cambodia and spare it the horrors that befell it.

The absurd myth by which guilt for abandoning Cambodia has been assuaged runs like this: Cambodia was a peaceful, happy land until *America* attacked it. There was no reason for this attack; it was the product of the psychosis of two American leaders determined to act out their own insecurities on the prostrate body of an innocent people. They covertly dislodged the only political leader, Sihanouk, who held the fabric of the country together. Then American bombing turned a group of progressive revolutionaries, the Khmer Rouge, into demented murderers. By this elaborate hypothesis American actions in 1969 and 1970 are held principally responsible for the genocide carried out by the Cambodian Communist rulers *after we left* in 1975 — two years after all American military actions ceased — as well as for the suffering imposed by the North Vietnamese invasion of 1978.[12]

The thesis has had some appeal to professional Nixon-haters and others because Cambodia can be presented as entirely a Nixon initiative, unlike Vietnam and Laos, where our involvement was inherited from two liberal Democratic administrations. It is a fevered absurdity, but it has to be dealt with. It is important for Americans and those who rely upon us to understand the sequence of events and the true responsibility for them.

The master architect of disaster was North Vietnam, the impulse its imperial ambitions for Indochina. I will not go over in detail the reasons why we raided the North Vietnamese sanctuaries in Cambodia, first from the air and then by land; these are set out in *White House Years,* and the wisdom of those tactical actions will ultimately be judged by others. But the crucial point is that it was North Vietnam that dragged Cambodia into war. It was North Vietnam that occupied portions of Cambodia in 1965 to implant military bases from which it killed Americans and South Vietnamese for four years before there was any American response — and that response was limited to the narrow border where the North Vietnamese sanctuaries were located.

On March 18, 1970, the neutralist chief of state Norodom Sihanouk was deposed by his own government and national assembly. The reason was Cambodian popular outrage at the continued presence of the North Vietnamese occupiers, and Sihanouk's inability to get them to leave. When Cambodia's new leadership demanded the departure of the North Vietnamese, the latter responded by a wave of attacks all over eastern Cambodia designed to topple the new government in Phnom Penh — a month *before* the US–South Vietnamese "incursion" into the sanctuaries, which lasted eight weeks. It was Hanoi that had spurned our proposal immediately to restore Cambodia's neutrality, which I made to Le

Duc Tho in a secret meeting on April 4, 1970. It was Hanoi that refused to talk of peace except with the prior condition that any non-Communist structure in Cambodia should be destroyed. It was Hanoi that rejected offers of cease-fire in October 1970, May 1971, October 1971, January 1972, and from October 1972 to January 1973. It was the Communist Khmer Rouge, organized, armed, and sponsored by Hanoi, that blocked Cambodia's inclusion in the Paris Agreement, something the United States had repeatedly sought. The Khmer Rouge wanted to fight on to victory. Hanoi provided the military wherewithal and thereafter disclaimed any responsibility for negotiating a Cambodian peace settlement, dooming any diplomatic solution.

It was Hanoi, therefore, if it was anyone, that brought the war to Cambodia and made possible the genocide by the Khmer Rouge. No doubt we overestimated Hanoi's influence on the Khmer Rouge at various times; the Cambodian Communists were intractably different from the submissive Pathet Lao. Whether all our actions were wise must be left to future historians with no vested interest in refighting the contemporary debates. But there can be no doubt that the decision on a fight to the finish was Hanoi's. Hanoi promoted the unconditional victory of the Communists, calculating — correctly, as it turned out — that the collapse of Cambodia would speed the demoralization of South Vietnam and that it would be able to deal with a fractious Cambodia at leisure afterward.

Cambodia was misperceived in America as a separate "war" that we must avoid. But it was not any such thing. The enemy was the same as in Vietnam. North Vietnamese troops shifted back and forth across the border as if the concept of sovereignty did not exist. They did with impunity for years what produced for us in 1970, over eight weeks, a national crisis.

America contributed to the disaster in Cambodia not because it did too much but because it did too little. In 1970, after American and South Vietnamese troops withdrew from their brief incursion into the sanctuaries — designed to destroy North Vietnamese base areas from which American and South Vietnamese had been killed for years — antiwar critics sought to achieve by legislation what had eluded them in the street demonstrations of May 1970. Between 1970 and the end of the war, the following restrictions on American assistance to Cambodia were passed into law, always over Nixon's veto or vigorous objection:

• The Fulbright amendment to the Armed Forces Appropriation Authorization for Fiscal Year 1971, enacted on October 7, 1970, specified that South Vietnamese and other free world forces (such as Thailand's) could not use funds provided by the act to furnish military support and assistance to Cambodia. It also prohibited South Vietnamese or other free world forces from transferring to Cambodia any military supplies furnished under the act. Thus the ceiling placed on our aid was imposed as well on our allies in Southeast Asia, as if our primary national problem was to close every loophole by which Cambodia might be aided. It was passed three months after our incursion was over and on the same day that Nixon offered a cease-fire throughout Indochina — which the Communists quickly rejected.

● The Cooper-Church amendment to the Supplementary Foreign Assistance Act of 1970, enacted on January 5, 1971, prohibited the use of funds for "the introduction of United States ground combat troops into Cambodia, or to provide United States advisors." Thus the United States was barred by law from giving the Cambodians the kind of advice and training that they needed to become an effective fighting force.

● The Symington-Case amendment to the Substitute Foreign Assistance Act and Related Assistance Act, enacted on February 7, 1972, limited the total number of "civilian officers and employees of executive agencies of the United States Government who are United States citizens" in Cambodia to 200 at any one time. It also limited the number of third country nationals employed by the United States in Cambodia to 85. This made any effective military *or civilian* advice to the Cambodians impossible.

● The Second Supplemental Appropriations Act for Fiscal Year 1973 (signed into law reluctantly by Nixon on July 1, 1973) prohibited the use of funds appropriated in the act to "support directly or indirectly combat activities in or over Cambodia, Laos, North Vietnam and South Vietnam or off the shores of Cambodia, Laos, North Vietnam and South Vietnam." Also, it prohibited any funds appropriated under *any* act to be used after August 15 for the above purposes. Thus any American military action anywhere in or around Indochina became illegal. With it vanished any Communist fear of a penalty for violating the Agreement.

● The Continuing Appropriations Act for Fiscal Year 1974 likewise prohibited the use of any funds to finance directly or indirectly combat activities by US forces "in or over or from off the shores of North Vietnam, South Vietnam, Laos or Cambodia." This continued the prohibition of the previous year.

● The Foreign Assistance Act of 1973, which became law on December 17, 1973, provided that no funds authorized or appropriated under any provision of law would be available to finance military or paramilitary combat operations by foreign forces in Laos, Cambodia, North Vietnam, South Vietnam, or Thailand unless such operations were conducted by the forces of the recipient government within its borders. This meant that allies like Thailand, threatened from Indochina, could not use our equipment — and therefore not their forces — to assist the countries whose survival they judged important to their security.

In addition, the Congress limited any aid for Cambodia to $250–$300 million a year, about 2 percent of what was being spent to help Vietnam.

These cumulative constraints not only prevented effective American assistance; they also precluded our allies in Southeast Asia from committing the horrible offense of helping their Cambodian neighbors. Military advisers were prohibited, which our Embassy in Phnom Penh interpreted to bar even field trips by our military attachés. Thus the Cambodian army grew in size but not in competence. Our restrictions forced it to rely on firepower rather than mobility (and the rigidity our critics imposed was then used by them as an indictment of the Cambodians' military effort). To stave off disaster we could look only to American air power — until that too was prohibited.

Sadly, Cambodia became a symbol and a surrogate for the whole controversy over Vietnam. To Nixon it was "the Nixon doctrine in its purest form,"* meaning that our policy was to help it defend itself without American troops. To his opponents it was an opportunity retrospectively and symbolically to defeat by legislation both our incursion into the sanctuaries and Nixon's very effort to achieve a defense against aggression by building up local forces. They sought, and succeeded, in imposing on Cambodia the restrictions they had failed to inflict on South Vietnam. Their failure over South Vietnam meant that we were strong enough there to prevent collapse; but their success over Cambodia doomed that country and therefore South Vietnam as well. The restrictions made inevitable the diplomatic impasse that served Hanoi's purposes. Once Hanoi was committed to conquest and the Khmer Rouge to total victory, the only way to extricate ourselves honorably was to demonstrate that these goals were unfulfillable. Our domestic divisions produced the opposite result. The restrictions on our aid saved the Khmer Rouge from defeat in 1970–1972 when it was still an embryonic force; and thereafter they prevented the leverage over the Khmer Rouge and Hanoi that was essential to induce a political negotiation. Antiwar critics who made the collapse of Indochina inevitable then turned on those who had sought to resist the Communist takeover and blamed them for the resulting carnage.

The Lost Opportunity

EVER since Cambodia achieved independence in 1954, Prince Norodom Sihanouk had performed a masterful if precarious balancing act. By maneuvering between the contending forces pressing on his country, Sihanouk preserved Cambodia's peace, neutrality, and safety. An hereditary ruler, he anchored himself in the affection of his people.

---

*Nixon used the phrase in his news conference of November 12, 1971.

Western in his style of life, he nevertheless managed to deal with his Communist neighbors, preempting their demands and thereby mitigating some of the worst of their ambitions. The Laos settlement of 1962 convinced him that the United States would be unable in the long term to stem Hanoi's domination of Indochina. He attempted to cope with the inevitable by loosening his ties with the United States and turning a blind eye to North Vietnamese violations of Cambodia's sovereignty, territorial integrity, and neutrality. After 1965 he acquiesced when Hanoi established sanctuaries on Cambodian soil, in effect expelling Cambodian authority from a strip of territory paralleling the South Vietnamese frontier.

But Sihanouk welcomed — though he could not always avow it — American efforts to stem the Communist tide in South Vietnam. Starting in 1968, he privately invited American attacks on the Communist sanctuaries, hoping that we could drive the North Vietnamese out of his country. When in 1969 the Nixon Administration took the hint and started bombing the sanctuaries, Sihanouk in public took the not excessively subtle position that, as long as Cambodians were not hurt, it was an affair between the Americans and the North Vietnamese, and that indeed he did not know what took place on territory from which Cambodian authorities had been expelled. While our air attacks on the sanctuaries were going on in 1969, he reestablished diplomatic relations with Washington and warmly invited President Nixon to visit Phnom Penh.

In January 1970, Sihanouk went for his annual cure to southern France. He announced that he would return via Moscow and Peking to plead with the two Communist giants to use their influence with Hanoi to reduce its presence in Cambodia. Just as he was getting ready to start his return journey, there were riots in Phnom Penh against the North Vietnamese. While he was in Moscow, Sihanouk learned on the way to the airport that he had just been deposed by his own national assembly. Deeply stung by what he considered betrayal by his colleagues at home, he flew from Moscow to Peking, where he was embraced by Zhou Enlai and accepted as the legitimate ruler of Cambodia. Sihanouk virulently blamed the United States for his overthrow; in his bitterness he placed himself at the head of the Communist Khmer Rouge, then a tiny organization (whose leaders he had just a short while before sentenced to death for treason), and vowed a war to the finish against his erstwhile associates in Phnom Penh. In the process he all but forfeited his role as a mediator and balance wheel between the factions of his country.

Conscious that Congressional limitations prevented a clear-cut military outcome, the United States tried hard to find a peaceful political settlement for Cambodia. We offered a cease-fire on at least a half-dozen occasions between 1970 and 1973. After the settlement in Vietnam, we were ready to negotiate with Prince Sihanouk as part of a political structure in Cambodia in which he could play a meaningful role. But if Sihanouk was to reclaim his position as the balance wheel, arbiter, and neutralist leader, this required the survival and participation of the non-Communist forces associated with Lon Nol, though not necessarily of Lon Nol himself. Hanoi never showed the slightest interest in either Sihanouk or a compromise — but China did. As early as June 22, 1972, Zhou Enlai had told me that he did not favor Hanoi's conquest of either Laos or Cambodia or of a Communist takeover in either country. A negotiated settlement was the right course:

In solving the Indochina question it is not Vietnam alone — it is still a question of Cambodia and Laos, but they are comparatively easier. Because no matter what happens we can say for certain that elements of the national bourgeoisie will take part in such a government; and we can be sure in Cambodia Prince Sihanouk will be the head of state, and in Laos the King will be the head of state. So if it can be solved through negotiations such an outcome would be a matter of certainty.

We were in no position to pick up this lead in the middle of a North Vietnamese offensive threatening to engulf Saigon, but in November 1972, I told Chinese Vice Foreign Minister Qiao Guanhua that if there were a cease-fire in Cambodia we would be prepared to have discussions with Sihanouk and that he could play a major role in postwar Cambodia, provided he did not simply act as front man for the Khmer Rouge. "Whoever can best preserve it [Cambodia] as an independent neutral country, is consistent with our policy," I told Qiao, "and we believe consistent with yours."

As 1973 began, we dedicated ourselves to bringing about a cease-fire in Cambodia to follow the cease-fires in Vietnam and Laos. On the day the Paris Agreement was signed, January 27, 1973, the Cambodian government, on our advice, made a bid for peace by halting all offensive military operations and declaring a unilateral cease-fire. Simultaneously, we stopped American air operations. But the Khmer Rouge rejected the cease-fire appeal and launched a new offensive. Reading the tea leaves, my NSC staff at the end of January nevertheless experienced a flurry of hope. A briefing paper prepared for my February visit to China analyzed several statements by Sihanouk, the Khmer Rouge leaders, Hanoi, and China. From this my staff concluded that "a recent series of developments strongly suggests that the other side may soon be seeking negotiations on Cambodia and will positively, if indirectly, respond to Lon Nol's call for a cessation of offensive military actions."

In retrospect this judgment was totally wishful thinking. A careful reading of the statements suggests that whatever desire Sihanouk may have had for conciliation, he was himself a prisoner of the Khmer Rouge and of his own 1970 declaration of total war against the Cambodian government. The official position of the Khmer Rouge was the extreme statement that Sihanouk had issued on March 23, 1970, less than a week after he was deposed. He had called then for dissolution of the Lon Nol government and legislature and for formation of a "Government of National Union," a "National Liberation Army," and a "National United Front," whose essential task was to fight "American imperialism" at the side of the Vietnamese and Laotian Communists. It was a ringing call for a complete Communist takeover of all of Indochina.

In the period leading up to the Paris accords, Sihanouk reiterated this maximalist position. And the signs of flexibility afterward, that so raised our hopes, evaporated in the sunlight of closer inspection. In an interview with Agence France Presse (AFP) on January 29, 1973, Sihanouk noted that "our friends" (probably Hanoi and China) had urged his government in exile not to maintain its intransigent stance. He was willing to talk to the United States, he said, but he would never negotiate with Lon Nol and would never accept a solution like that reached for South Vietnam. In any case, he said significantly, the ultimate position would be determined not by him, but by the "Cambodian resistance, which is operating in the interior" — that is to say, the Khmer Rouge. An official four-point statement of January 26, 1973, issued in the name of Sihanouk, his Prime Minister Penn Nouth, and Khmer Rouge leader Khieu Samphan, intransigently reiterated that the solution to the Cambodian problem could be found *only* on the basis of Sihanouk's declaration of March 23, 1970 — that is to say, a complete Communist takeover.

In remarks to journalists in Hanoi on January 31, Sihanouk spoke of willingness to make an "overture" to the United States. Nevertheless, he stressed once again his subordinate role; he had "not yet received the definitive green light for the reevaluation of the GRUNK's* policy from the leaders of the domestic resistance, the Red Khmers led by GRUNK Deputy Prime Minister and Defense Minister Khieu Samphan, who has the last word." He could not have made his dependence on the Communists more plain.

On February 2, the Khmer Rouge radio broadcast an official statement by the Khmer insurgent leadership — Khieu Samphan, Hou Youn, and Hu Nim. It was a bloodcurdling diatribe against the United States and the Lon Nol government, insisting on the March 23, 1970, position, and explaining that "the Cambodian nation and people are obliged to continue their struggle against the U.S. aggressors and the traitors Lon Nol, Sirik Matak and Son Ngoc Thanh in order to liberate the

---

*The GRUNK was, by its initials in French, the Royal Government of National Union of Kampuchea, or Sihanouk's government in exile. It is not to be confused with the FUNK, or the National United Front of Kampuchea, Sihanouk's political movement in exile.

people . . ." The statement contemptuously ruled out all negotiation with the "U.S. imperialists," declaring that "it is necessary to obstruct and oppose their diplomatic maneuvers. . . ."

These statements were not just propaganda. On February 2, the Khmer Rouge command issued orders that the fighting would continue, that any political negotiations or compromise with the Cambodian government was ruled out, and that Sihanouk was not to engage in negotiations with the Americans or anyone else. In short, by the time I left for my Asian trip in February 1973, the Cambodian Communists had decided on war to the finish.

So much for the self-flagellation that *we* were responsible for the failure to negotiate.

By the time I visited Peking later in February, a measure of congruence between the American and Chinese positions was emerging. As I discussed in Chapter III, Peking was beginning to understand that the domination of Indochina by Hanoi might be an ideological victory but a geopolitical defeat for China, since it would place at China's southern border a major power drawn to Moscow and with a record of historical enmity. Perhaps China had always understood it but — like many other nations — could not believe that the United States would accept military defeat, much less engineer it. Both of us, in any event, wanted an independent and neutral Cambodia and both of us were moving toward the return of Sihanouk — we hesitantly because we saw no other unifying force, the Chinese with conviction because they considered him their most reliable friend in Cambodia. Both Peking and Washington were convinced that the best solution for Cambodia was some sort of coalition headed by Sihanouk, whose influence would depend on the continued existence of some of the non-Communist forces represented by the Lon Nol government.

Zhou Enlai picked up the theme when he told me that if Cambodia became completely red "it would result in even greater problems," meaning that it would doom Sihanouk and assure Hanoi's hegemony over Indochina. I responded by proposing an immediate meeting between Sihanouk's Prime Minister Penn Nouth and a representative of Lon Nol. We would not insist on the participation of Lon Nol in a government that might emerge from such a negotiation, I pointed out, so long as the forces he represented were included. Zhou offered to take this proposition to the Cambodians "in our wording," meaning that he would identify himself to some extent with our position.

The scene was confused. The Chinese saw the best guarantee of Cambodian independence in Sihanouk. But the Soviet Union continued to recognize Lon Nol — thus transferring the Sino-Soviet rivalry to Cambodia. The irony was that everybody's estimate of the Cambodians turned out to be wrong; each of the major Communist rivals backed the wrong horse because both overestimated our determination to back the existing structure in Phnom Penh, for without this both the Lon Nol group as well as Sihanouk were doomed. Thus American abdication made the Khmer Rouge the major force, supported by Hanoi logistically, using Sihanouk for a while to give themselves respectability, but ready to turn him out as soon as they felt strong enough to govern alone.

Our analysis was that the Khmer Rouge would agree to a negotiated settlement only if deprived of hope of a military victory. That the Khmer Rouge had made exactly the same analysis became evident in July. We learned that in the spring of 1973, the executive committee of the Khmer Communist leadership had made a crucial policy decision. It decided to keep open two basic options: total victory or a compromise. The choice between them was to be determined by the military situation in Cambodia later in the year. In the event that military victory was out of reach and a stalemate emerged, the Khmer Rouge would negotiate for the best conditions obtainable. If, on the other hand, the military situation was favorable, negotiations would be avoided and total victory sought. It was thus a contest between our quest for equilibrium and the Khmer Rouge determination to prevail.

Upon my return from Asia at the end of February I called a series of WSAG meetings. My attitude was summed up by what I told the group on March 28:

We've been meeting here for four years and we've been through it all. I'm not looking for alibis from you for losing this whole thing. There are a hundred ways we could make it look good while turning it over to the Communists, but that's not what we're here to do.

If there were officials favoring an elegant collapse of the free Cambodians, they did not speak up at the meetings. One of the participating agencies at the WSAG had indeed sent me a thoughtful analysis of the situation in a memorandum of February 27: Our dilemma was that we seemed to have two mutually dependent objectives in Cambodia. One was to strenghten the present government in Phnom Penh; the other was to achieve a cease-fire — which probably only a strengthened government could accomplish. Yet, reluctant to repeat the Vietnam and Laotian experience in Cambodia, we had deliberately kept our profile there low, and although supplying the Cambodian government with both military and economic aid, we had largely adopted the attitude that it was up to the Cambodians to apply this aid successfully. Also, by Congressional constraints we were limited in the funds and personnel we could apply to the Cambodian problem and prohibited from the use of US military advisers. Thus, we were caught in a vicious circle. We could not achieve a cease-fire without a stronger government in Phnom Penh, and the government could not be strengthened without a more active American policy, which in turn was prevented by legislative restrictions.

Not unnaturally, the strain began to show in Cambodia. The guerrilla war conducted with unparalleled cruelty by the Khmer Rouge, assisted by the North Vietnamese, drove refugees from the countryside into the cities, especially into Phnom Penh, distorting the social equilibrium of the country. It imposed a war on a Cambodian army that had first been deliberately kept small and ineffective by Sihanouk to discourage any temptation for a coup and then had been deprived of effective training by our legislative restrictions. Assaulted by battle-tested North Vietnamese and ferocious indigenous Communists, the free Cambodians fought with extraordinary bravery that was both made possible and shackled by an American aid program perversely legislated to prevent any decisive success. Lon Nol accepted his unhappy fate with grace and dignity. He took our advice readily (unlike Thieu). But his government showed symptoms of progressive demoralization in factionalism, corruption, and inefficiency.

The Lon Nol government was in reality Sihanouk's without the Prince; its institutions and personalities were the leadership groups that had governed Cambodia since independence. As in many authoritarian societies there had always been corruption — under Sihanouk and his family as under his successors. This is partly because in traditional societies the distinction between the private and public sectors tends to be less sharply defined and partly because the insufficient power to tax invites corruption as a means of financing the costs of government. It was perhaps inevitable that Lon Nol should lean increasingly on the few people he trusted, who tended to be his family, especially his younger brother, Lon Non; the latter unfortunately carried corruption and favoritism to new heights beyond what could be explained by sociological analysis. Lon Nol came to be described in the world's press as paralyzed and arbitrary and Lon Non as the "evil genius." It resembled a similar drama a decade earlier in Saigon when the Ngo Dinh Diem government began to disintegrate under the impact of Communist guerrilla war, American pressure to reform, and its own inherent rigidities, and Diem's brother Ngo Dinh Nhu was blamed. Diem and Nhu were killed (in an American-encouraged coup) — and the situation almost totally unraveled.

In Washington, participants at the WSAG proposed that to lay the ground for a negotiated return of Sihanouk we should persuade Lon Nol to "broaden the base of his government" and indeed to resign. I had, of course, already privately indicated to Zhou Enlai that we were ready for talks on these lines (though, unlike some of my colleagues, I saw the iniquities of the Cambodian government as primarily a symptom of the crisis, not its cause). A scheme was hatched to send Lon Non to military school in the United States and Lon Nol abroad for medical treatment. Prince Sisowath Sirik Matak, perhaps the ablest Cambodian leader (who had been Sihanouk's Deputy Prime Minister until the 1970 coup), was to become Vice President and acting President during Lon Nol's absence. In early April, Al Haig visited Phnom Penh to present the scheme. Lon Nol agreed to send his brother into exile and to bring Sirik Matak into the government. We decided to delay Lon Nol's departure as a bargaining chip for an eventual negotiation.

Sihanouk gave us no help. It is hard to believe that the Chinese did not indicate to him that in the right circumstances he could go back as head of state. But to make himself more acceptable to the implacable Khmer Rouge, the Prince kept on parroting their insistence on a fight to the finish. Despite his obvious self-interest in Peking's preferred solution, Sihanouk understood that the Khmer Rouge and Hanoi were determined to block such an outcome. He was too weak to abandon the only base he had — whatever his convictions. Sihanouk repeatedly let it be known that the "interior resistance," that is to say, the Khmer Rouge, opposed all compromise. On April 19 he said from Hanoi:

I tell you solemnly that the leaders of the interior will never accept any compromise with the Phnom Penh clique. It is completely illusory for countries like the United States, France or the Soviet Union to count on a compromise solution.

And on April 28 he again stressed his own irrelevance. "He said," reported an AFP dispatch,

that the strategy and tactics of the people's forces were worked out in Cambodia itself by Khieu Samphan, Deputy Prime Minister of the Cambodian Royal Government of Popular Union and his general staff, and nowhere else.

As for eventual negotiations between himself and the United States, Prince Sihanouk toughened his position in declaring that even for preliminary contacts before any negotiations the decision rested with the "interior resistance" and not with himself.

That Sihanouk's assessment of Khmer Rouge dominance was accurate soon became evident. Sihanouk made a brief visit to the "liberated zone" of Cambodia in March 1973, widely publicized afterward. But the Communists were trying to undermine Sihanouk's standing in the country even while exploiting his prestige internationally. The Khmer Rouge made every effort to ensure that his prestige would not be reinforced by disseminating what he said within Cambodia. Other reports revealed that the Khmer Rouge were systematically purging pro-Sihanouk elements from their organization and launching a propaganda campaign to discredit him and eliminate all vestiges of his popularity in the countryside.[13]

So much for the argument that it was American opposition that prevented the return of Sihanouk to power in Cambodia.

Our only remaining card was to produce a military stalemate. And to achieve this our sole asset was American air power — advice and training to improve Cambodian military performance and increases in American aid having been precluded by our legislation. Part of the new Cambodia guilt-shifting myth is that our bombing was indiscriminate, that it produced monstrous civilian casualties, and that the "punishment" we inflicted on the Khmer Rouge turned them from ordinary guerrillas into genocidal maniacs driven by "Manichean fear."[14] The reality is otherwise.

Ambassador Emory C. Swank, often critical of our policy, and his deputy Thomas O. Enders, have set out the facts about the bombing in a document submitted to the Historical Division of the Department of State. (The document is in the Appendix. The analysis here follows their account.) On January 27, 1973, when the Cambodian government unilaterally halted offensive military actions in the hope of achieving a cease-fire, American tactical air and B-52 operations also stood down. The bombing was to be resumed only if the Khmer Rouge insisted on continued hostilities, and only at the request of the Cambodian government.

These conditions were unfortunately fulfilled early in February 1973. The Khmer Rouge answered the cease-fire appeal by launching an offensive; the North Vietnamese refused to withdraw their forces and continued to give logistical and occasional rocket and artillery support to their Cambodian allies. The United States had to respond or face the collapse of free Cambodia — and probably South Vietnam as well. American air operations were resumed, as Swank and Enders demonstrate, through regular channels (not, as some hyperactive imaginations would have it, through clandestine procedures devised by me in my Bangkok meeting with Swank in February behind the back of Secretary of State Rogers).[15]

The accusation that B-52 operations were conducted sloppily, with large-scale and out-of-date maps in the US Embassy, turns out to be a canard as well. In fact, the targeting was controlled by the Seventh Air Force, which relied on up-to-date photography, precision radar, and infrared sensors and conducted reconnaissance both before and after every strike. Our air operations were subject to careful rules of engagement that prohibited the use of B-52s against targets closer than one kilometer to friendly forces, villages, hamlets, houses, monuments, temples, pagodas, or holy places. These rules were observed. There were tragic accidents — only two serious ones, Swank and Enders note — but they hardly amounted to systematic bombing of civilians. On a number of occasions the Seventh Air Force turned down Cambodian requests for strikes because our reconnaissance showed risks to the civilian population that we were unwilling to take.

Today it is clear that the Communist Khmer Rouge, not the Americans or Sihanouk, were the obstacle to peace in Cambodia. My repeated, vain efforts in 1972 and 1973 to extract a commitment from Le Duc Tho for a cease-fire or political settlement ran into Hanoi's plea, probably truthful, that it had little influence over Khmer Rouge decisions. Indeed, the Khmer Rouge bitterly denounced Hanoi for signing the Paris Agreement; they saw the Vietnam settlement as a betrayal, and not only because they thought it allowed us to shift the brunt of our military operations to Cambodia. In a document published after they came into power, they admitted that they resisted all pressures for a cease-fire because "if the Kampuchean revolution had accepted a cease-fire it would have collapsed."[16] Later they blocked a settlement because they were bent on total victory.

The myth that Khmer Rouge brutality was the result of our bombing may fulfill some masochistic imperatives; it, too, does not stand up to serious analysis. Not only is there no evidence for it; what evidence there is suggests something completely different. As early as 1971 or 1972, the Khmer Rouge were carrying out deliberately, in all areas of Cambodia they controlled, the same totalitarian practices that horrified the world when applied to Phnom Penh after their victory in 1975. The forced uprooting and dispersal of village populations; destruction of traditional local social organization, religious practices, and family structures; forced collectivization of agriculture; deliberate liquidation of the middle class as an obstacle to a "new society"; and the systematic terror of the Communist police state — all these features of the post–1975 holocaust in Cambodia were in evidence in Khmer Rouge–controlled areas for several years before 1975. They represented *deliberate policy*, founded in ideological fanaticism.

A French priest who worked in Cambodia until the end, and who has written perhaps the best account of Cambodia's tragedy, called it "a perfect example of the application of an ideology pushed to the furthest limit of its internal logic." And he states flatly that it was "traditional revolutionary practice" dating back at least to 1972.[17] Another expert analyst, who interviewed hundreds of Cambodian refugees in South Vietnam from 1972 to 1974, methodically sketches the outline of a brutal program of social transformation — "everything that had preceded it was anathema and must be destroyed" — and points out that the process "actually began in some parts of the country as early as late 1971."[18] It was not American bombing that produced the flood of refugees and the horror of Cambodia. It was a demonic ideology, ruthlessly applied.

We had no more fervent desire in the summer of 1973 than to end the Cambodian war. Both the broadening of the Phnom Penh government and the intensification of the bombing were only means to prompt resumption of negotiation. Sihanouk's public remarks, unfortunately, continued virulently negative about its prospects. On April 13, after returning from his visit to the "liberated zone" in Cambodia, undoubtedly reflecting what he had been told by the Khmer Rouge inside Cambodia, Sihanouk told a press conference in Peking that he would "never accept a cease-fire nor compromise."

This news of current Khmer Rouge policy could not have been entirely welcome to his Chinese hosts. They knew that a total Khmer Rouge victory would ruin the viability of their carefully nurtured Sihanouk card and guarantee Hanoi's domination of Indochina. China doubtless also calculated that we would not permit a total defeat of the forces with which we had been associated. A continuation of the war would therefore increase Peking's foreign policy problems without altering the outcome. At a minimum it would delay the rapprochement with the United States that my February 1973 visit had shown was a principal objective of Chinese policy.

Zhou Enlai tried to cut through these perplexities — at first a bit too obliquely for us to grasp. He used the occasion of Sihanouk's return to Peking to articulate Chinese preferences. At a state banquet for Sihanouk on April 11, Zhou condemned the United States for continuing its "wanton bombing" in Cambodia and its support for the "traitorous Lon Nol clique." An authoritative editorial in the *People's Daily* gave added emphasis to Zhou's observations; the Prince's visit to the "liberated zone," it argued, showed that he was "the legitimate ruler of Cambodia." In our anger at one of Zhou's rare public statements critical of us, we overlooked the thrust of his remarks: China's emphatic backing for Sihanouk as Cambodian head of government. According to Zhou, Sihanouk's visit to Cambodia had proved what the Khmer Rouge, as noted earlier, had sought to deny: that Sihanouk was "beloved and supported by the Cambodian people."

We noticed mainly the explicit criticism of the United States — which was in fact one of Mao's "empty cannons" — rather than the subtle dissociation from Hanoi and the Khmer Rouge. On April 13, therefore, we sent an unusually sharp note to Peking expressing our "extreme disappointment" at Zhou's remarks. We called attention to Hanoi's flagrant violations of the Paris Agreement, especially of Article 20, which required withdrawal from Laos and Cambodia. But even this note, which must have made the Chinese wonder whether we were ever capable of understanding anything complex, ended with an affirmation that we were willing to proceed with negotiations on the basis of compromise:

The US side wishes to reiterate its continued willingness to adhere to the Vietnam agreement, end all military operations in Cambodia, and work for a political solution in that country that brings about true neutrality and independence. The US side believes, however, that it is the responsibility of all interested countries to work for moderation on these matters.

That Peking was stung was apparent in the rapidity of its reply. Huang Hua, then Chinese Ambassador to the United Nations, spoke to me on April 16 in a "personal" capacity — an inconceivable procedure for a Chinese diplomat unless he wished to say something that could be officially disavowed. He could not understand, he averred, our expression of extreme disappointment; China had done no more than restate its previous positions. He urged that the United States end its support of Lon Nol; the formulation, aimed at an individual and not a structure, left open the prospect discussed in Peking in February of including other elements of the Phnom Penh government in a coalition without their present chief.

I picked up the theme in my response:

With respect to Cambodia, we are prepared to work with you to bring about some coalition structure along the lines that the Prime Minister and I discussed in Peking. We are not committed to any particular personality. And we would encourage negotiations between representatives of Prince Sihanouk and the other forces.

Our objective in Southeast Asia seems to us not totally dissimilar from yours. We want to prevent a security system extending in South and Southeast Asia controlled by one unit and one outside power. We believe this is best achieved if each country in the region can develop its own national identity.

On April 24 I reiterated this theme in a written message to Zhou Enlai:

With respect to the Cambodian situation, the U.S. side wishes to repeat its willingness to see a settlement which includes all political forces, including those of Prince Sihanouk. The U.S. side is prepared to undertake discussions with the Chinese side looking towards this objective either in Washington or Peking after Ambassador Bruce's arrival.

The Chinese did not respond immediately. However, on May 18, 1973, in his first meeting with David Bruce, recently appointed the head of our new Liaison Office in Peking, Zhou turned the conversation to Cambodia: He told Bruce that "the only way to find a solution was for the parties concerned to implement fully all the subsidiary clauses of

Article 20." China thus agreed with our interpretation that North Vietnamese forces had to vacate Cambodian territory. And Zhou reiterated this point in another allusion. Though our viewpoints differed, he said, China and the United States shared the goal of a peaceful, neutral, and independent Cambodia, in fact "more peaceful, neutral, and independent than ever before" — which could only mean that North Vietnamese base areas had to be eliminated. Zhou added that Huang Zhen, the newly designated head of China's Liaison Office in Washington, would leave on May 25 for the United States and would be authorized to pursue the subject. Clearly, Zhou hoped for an answer by the time Huang Zhen reached Washington.

Meanwhile, I was engaged in the Paris negotiations with Le Duc Tho, whose definition of Cambodian neutrality and independence spelled North Vietnamese hegemony. He would hear nothing of implementing Article 20 before there was a political settlement, and he would not discuss a political solution out of respect for the "sovereignty" of his Cambodian allies. So tender was Hanoi's regard for the independence of a country it had first invaded in 1965 and was to invade again in 1978 that Le Duc Tho would not even agree to my plea that we jointly recommend a cease-fire to both parties in Cambodia. My May-June negotiations with Le Duc Tho ended irrelevantly. As noted, Le Duc Tho would commit himself to no more than a pledge that both sides would put forward "their best efforts to bring about a peaceful settlement." By now, "best efforts" was a clear euphemism for doing nothing. If it depended on the North Vietnamese, Cambodia would be settled on the battlefield. Our diplomacy would have to seek other channels.

During a hiatus in my talks with Le Duc Tho, I therefore approached the Chinese with a formal proposal to follow up the exchanges with Zhou Enlai. On Sunday, May 27, my fiftieth birthday, I told Huang Hua in New York that in my view American and Chinese interests were compatible. We both sought to prevent "a bloc which could support the hegemonial objectives of outside powers." In other words, we did not want an Indochina under Hanoi's tutelage aligned with the Soviet Union. To achieve this purpose I made the following proposal:

We are prepared to stop our bombing in Cambodia, and we are prepared to withdraw the very small advisory group we have there. And we are prepared to arrange for Lon Nol to leave for medical treatment in the United States. In return we would like a cease-fire — if necessary, say for ninety days — a negotiation between the Sihanouk group and the remainder of the Lon Nol group; and while this negotiation is going on in Cambodia, we would authorize some discussions between the staff of Ambassador Bruce and Prince Sihanouk in Peking. And when this process is completed, in some months, we would not oppose the return of Prince Sihanouk to Cambodia. But it is a process that has to extend over some time, and it must not be conducted in a way that does not take into account our own necessities.

Huang Hua was a thoroughgoing professional. He asked a few clarifying questions. I told him I had presented the basic idea to Le Duc Tho. Huang Hua knew that Hanoi would not favor such a scheme but might not be able to block it. He reminded me that Premier Zhou Enlai had told David Bruce that both Sihanouk and the Khmer Rouge were in principle willing to talk to the United States. This might not mean much if the precondition was the destruction of the non-Communist forces; but the Chinese had to have something more in mind. For after all, Zhou himself had said in February that a completely "red" government would compound everybody's problems.

Interestingly enough, Huang Hua did not reject my proposition as he surely would have done had it been Peking's policy to keep aloof from events in Indochina. He said he would report to Peking what I had said.

On May 29, I reiterated our proposal to Huang Zhen on his first call on me at the White House. He, too, said he would report back; he too pointedly reminded me of Zhou's conversation with Bruce and its emphasis on the strict implementation of Article 20. The next day Nixon used the occasion of an Oval Office courtesy call by Huang Zhen to stress the importance he attached to a peaceful solution for Cambodia.

The Chinese were swift to follow up. On June 4, eight days after my original proposal, Huang Hua in New York requested a meeting with me to hand over a message. It noted our "tentative thinking on the settlement of the question of Cambodia." It stressed that all parties concerned — and therefore by implication Hanoi as well — needed to respect the sovereignty of Cambodia. China could not conduct talks with the United States on behalf of Cambodia; direct talks with Sihanouk would be necessary at some point. Nevertheless China was now prepared to:

communicate the U.S. tentative thinking to the Cambodian side, but as Samdech [Prince] Sihanouk is still visiting Africa and Europe, it is inconvenient for us to contact him through diplomatic channels. For the sake of accuracy, the Chinese side would like to repeat the U.S. tentative thinking. . . .

In an unusual step, the Chinese note then repeated absolutely verbatim the proposal that I had read to Huang Hua, and concluded: "If there are any inaccuracies in the above, it is expected that the U.S. side will provide corrections."

Thus did the Chinese offer themselves as intermediary and step into the middle of a Cambodian negotiation. Anyone familiar with Zhou Enlai could be certain that he would not check so meticulously except to signal that he was committing himself, and he would not act as intermediary unless he expected to succeed. The careful Chinese would never risk demonstrating their impotence to affect events in Southeast Asia; they would never offer to pass on a message that they thought would be turned down. And it was significant, too, that Peking designated Sihanouk as our interlocutor; no reference whatever was made to the ''internal resistance,'' that is to say, the Khmer Rouge. Still, it was inconceivable that the Chinese would expose themselves in this manner without having checked with the Khmer Rouge. And if the Cambodian Communists were ready to deal, the military stalemate that they had decided in March would cause them to negotiate by July must be imminent.

Zhou had clearly committed China to a compromise that preserved key elements of the Lon Nol structure — that was the thrust of everything we both had been discussing for nearly a year. The proposal, reflecting the military balance, would stop short of the total victory the Khmer Rouge had heretofore demanded. The cease-fire would preserve the structure of free Cambodia; Sihanouk would return with the support of the United States and China not simply as a temporary figurehead as the Cambodian Communists preferred, but with the power inherent in the necessity of reconciling different factions.

Zhou Enlai could have sold any such proposition to the Politburo in Peking — and especially to Chairman Mao — only with the argument that a total Khmer Rouge victory was impossible because Washington would never tolerate it and that it would in any event aid the hegemonic aims of Hanoi. Nor could he possibly have made it palatable to the Khmer Rouge without the argument that only this scheme would bring about the end of American bombing. And the Khmer Rouge would not have acquiesced unless convinced that they could not prevail militarily in the face of continued bombing. Hence, even though he would not admit it, Zhou needed our military actions in Cambodia for the effectiveness of his policy almost as much as we did. Our bombing was a bargaining chip for two parties even though one of them condemned it.

But our domestic situation, it soon appeared, would not sustain our policy as it was nearing its culmination. By early June, the President was at bay. He was spending time, we now know, playing back tape recordings of his conversations in the Oval Office to see whether they were damaging to him. In Los Angeles on June 5, a grand jury began hearings on the break-in at Daniel Ellsberg's psychiatrist's office. On June 6 Nixon agreed, under pressure from the Senate Watergate Committee, to reverse a refusal two days before to release the logs of his taped conversations with John Dean. And on June 8, one of the Watergate burglars, James McCord, asked Judge John Sirica for a new trial on grounds that the government withheld evidence and perjury was committed at his trial.

Neither Zhou Enlai nor I appreciated quite how far Presidential au-

thority had been eroded by Watergate, so we proceeded buoyantly
enough. On June 13 in a meeting in Paris with Chinese Acting Foreign
Minister Ji Pengfei, I confirmed the accuracy of what Zhou intended to
convey to Sihanouk. I emphasized the importance of a transition period
of several months before Sihanouk could return to Cambodia. There was
no disagreement between us about the Prince's ultimate role as head of
state. Each of us agreed to respect the requirements of the other. I promised that as soon as a cease-fire was brought about in Cambodia we
would, as requested, consult Sihanouk himself; Ji agreed on our transition period "for a certain period of time." Ji Pengfei observed that the
sole obstacle to further progress straight away was Sihanouk's globe-
trotting and the difficulty of communicating rather delicate and complex
matters while he was traveling (not to speak of the unpredictability of
his temperament if he dealt with matters at long range). If he enjoyed
his African and European trip too much, he might extend it and delay
the negotiations he had been seeking.

That was the sense, too, of a conversation I had with Huang Zhen
the next day, June 14, in Washington. I briefed him on my negotiations
with Le Duc Tho. We both expressed our impatience for Sihanouk's
early return to Peking and our frustration at the unpredictability of his
movements. Huang Zhen and I began to discuss a trip by me to Peking.
Ostensibly it was to brief Zhou on the results of Brezhnev's imminent
visit to the United States. It would also be the occasion for beginning
contact with Sihanouk.

On June 19 I told Huang Zhen that if a cease-fire existed in Cambodia
by the time of my visit to China — expected around August 6 — I would
be prepared to meet Sihanouk for political discussions. We had gone to
the limit of what was possible. Meantime, Sihanouk continued his travels, apparently oblivious to my talks with the Chinese. He seemed above
all concerned that Le Duc Tho and I might settle Cambodia over his
head. Sometime in June, while visiting Yugoslavia, he gave an interview to my old nemesis Oriana Fallaci; it is a tribute to his skill that he
emerged from the encounter with that formidable Italian journalist in
much better shape than I had the previous year. Sihanouk emphasized
that Hanoi had no right to speak for the Khmer insurgents. Then he
repeated the Communist hard-line position, again in the subtle form of
reporting the views of his allies — not his own: "The Khmer Rouge
will never accept a cease-fire. They will never bow to an agreement.
Never."

Sihanouk paid tribute to the American bombing: it was "the only
thing that prevents us from entering Phnom Penh right now." But he
also showed his awareness of Watergate and the Congress's efforts to
terminate American military activities: "Nixon is in a very difficult situation. The Watergate scandal has done him a great disservice and in

the end the Senate and Congress will oppose his expenditures." As for his relationship with the Khmer Rouge, Sihanouk had few illusions and many premonitions: "The Khmer Rouge do not love me at all. I know it! . . . I am useful to them. . . . I understand very well that when I shall no longer be useful to them, they'll spit me out like a cherry pit." Cambodia would one day be Communist, he said. He disdained any ambition, saying he had no desire to be a figurehead like Queen Elizabeth or Hirohito.[19]

We did not learn of the interview until August 12, when the die had already been cast. It would not have meant much to us in any event. We would have believed that Sihanouk in his travels was almost surely out of touch; that Zhou knew what he was doing; that he would not have committed himself to a course unless confident that he would succeed in it.

In mid-June we believed for better or worse that we were on the homestretch. We could envisage a cease-fire, Sihanouk's return, and then Sihanouk's dealing with existing political forces so as to give himself room to maneuver between them and the Communists. We nearly made it, with all that it would have meant for Cambodia's future. But our inability to maintain domestic support was to doom our proposal and Cambodia — and to shake Zhou Enlai's position at home to its foundation.

Congress Halts the Bombing

MANY factors contributed to the final series of events that led to the abandonment of Cambodia. There was simple war-weariness in the United States. Some legislators sincerely thought they were conferring a great boon on the peoples of Indochina by prohibiting any American military action there. For others, humanitarian pretensions were probably secondary to the opportunity to score on a hated adversary, now a crippled President; liberals sought to vindicate the antiwar positions of four years. Congressman Thomas P. O'Neill, Jr., then Democratic Majority Leader, remarked in the House that Cambodia was not worth the life of one American flier.[20] Conservatives, already disheartened by the ambiguities of ten years of war, were demoralized by the travails of their old standard-bearer, Nixon. In the event, Congress marked the final breakdown of domestic consensus by taking the United States out of military operations in Indochina. Thus were the people of Cambodia abandoned to their fate.

Congressional agitation against the bombing started to boil up in April and May. Our air operations were denounced as "illegal," though their constitutional basis was substantial (as elaborated in the backnotes).[21] The series of Congressional votes against the bombing in May was de-

scribed earlier in this chapter. Le Duc Tho had gloated to me in May
of the Congressional pressures on us. For the first time there was no
conviction in my brusque rejoinder that we would handle our own domestic situation. I feared that only a miracle would enable me to
convince Congress of a truism that I stated in a press conference on
May 12:

> No one can expect that an agreement for a cease-fire will be observed simply
> because it is written down, and the Congress and others have to ask themselves
> whether it is possible to maintain an agreement without either sanctions or
> incentives.

I was straining to bring off a cease-fire in Cambodia before the Congress
acted. But at almost the same moment in mid-May, John F. Lehman,
NSC staff aide in charge of Congressional relations, sent me a shrewd
report forecasting a rough season of Congressional votes attempting to
halt the bombing. The White House was doing its best to block or delay
these attempts. According to Lehman, Watergate was *"the* factor in the
adverse votes"; he optimistically considered it a temporary phenomenon.

By early June, the legislative scene was bleaker still. On June 4, the
Senate approved the Case-Church amendment to cut off all funds for
military operations in Indochina. In a memorandum of June 5, Lehman
told me that a bombing cutoff might be delayed until the end of the
month: "After that it will be touch and go, but not hopeless." Some
success had been achieved in persuading Senators at least to wait until
the conclusion of my negotiations in Paris with Le Duc Tho; a success
there might further strengthen our hand.

I was desperate. A bombing cutoff would destroy our only bargaining
chip — and the sole stimulus for Chinese involvement. Zhou Enlai
needed to be able to argue to the Khmer Rouge that he had brought
them the end of our bombing, in exchange for a compromise involving
Sihanouk and parts of the existing structure. The negotiations now in
tenuous train were our last throw of the dice. If they failed, Cambodia,
and soon thereafter South Vietnam and Laos, would be doomed. On
June 18 I appealed to Mel Laird, after Watergate temporarily brought
him back to government as Counsellor to the President for Domestic
Affairs. I told Laird that the Chinese had promised to intercede: "I can't
imagine that they would commit themselves to saying that they would
do something unless they felt they had a chance of bringing it off." I
offered to make a gentleman's agreement with the Speaker of the House,
Carl Albert, and the venerable Chairman of the House Appropriations
Committee, George Mahon, that, succeed or fail in the negotiations, we
would stop bombing on September 1. But they had to give us their word
not to reveal the deadline; once it was known, our capacity to use the

end of bombing diplomatically was gone; the Khmer Rouge would simply wait until the deadline passed. Laird agreed to put forward my proposal but he was not optimistic. That master manipulator of Congressional committees was convinced we had reached the end of the line: "Mahon says it's never been as tough as it is right now."

Every day counted. We learned that Sihanouk would return to Peking from his travels on July 5 and that our plan could then unfold. But Congress would brook no further delay. On June 25 — the day Brezhnev left the United States and John Dean started testifying before the Senate — came a crucial vote in the House on the so-called Eagleton amendment, a Senate-passed rider to cut off funds for Cambodian bombing. Attached to a supplemental appropriations bill to fund the activities of the US government after the end of the current fiscal year (June 30), it was hard for the President to veto. For if the bill did not pass, *all* government agencies would be out of funds. From San Clemente I appealed by telephone to a number of Congressmen: We would end the bombing by September 1 come what may, but this pledge had to be kept secret if prospects for a cease-fire in Cambodia were not to be derailed. I could not be explicit about the Chinese initiative, but I gave enough hint about negotiations.

But the secrecy of the September 1 deadline could not be preserved. Only by a public "compromise" in which September 1 was named as a cutoff date could Administration supporters hope to stave off the pressure for an immediate end to bombing. Yet once the deadline was public our strategy was dead; the Khmer Rouge would simply wait it out. Then on June 25, we failed on a tie vote, 204 to 204, to obtain even this scant relief. The House by voice vote approved the Eagleton amendment, which cut off funds immediately.

The next day, June 26, antiwar amendments were attached to a Continuing Resolution, the means by which existing budgets are extended pending Congressional consideration of new appropriations. The same amendments were tied to the bill raising the national debt ceiling. Our opponents, in short, were prepared to stop the operation of the entire government so as to emasculate military operations in Indochina and our sole means to preserve the freedom of our allies.

The Congress was determined to impose the withdrawal that had been thwarted by the executive for half a decade; it was no longer prepared to listen to arguments about the complexities of diplomacy. Legislators would not risk the bitter media opposition to prevent a Communist takeover of what seemed to them an obscure corner of Indochina. Our political system can work only through a set of delicate understandings sustained by the confidence in each other of coequal branches of government. But that confidence had been destroyed by the bitter struggles over Vietnam policy, capped by Watergate. The debate was dominated by the desire to settle scores rather than by consideration of a common objective. There was little understanding of the Administration's basic anguish. We knew that the public was tired and the Congress hostile. But we also thought that if the American executive abandoned its friends of years' standing to Communist domination, confidence in us worldwide would be undermined in a manner that would exact an even heavier toll later on.

So we went on seeking an honorable cease-fire even as Mel Laird in Washington called me in San Clemente on June 26, pointing out the grim prospects (and implicitly discouraging me from insisting on fighting the looming amendments). John Dean had begun his televised appearance the day before; Laird attributed the two days of unfavorable votes to Dean's damaging testimony. I was firm: "Everything is just going to come apart in Cambodia if we stop bombing. I think we can get it done in two months. Can you help us?" But there was no help on substance and no surcease from publicity. Another "compromise" attempt to postpone the cutoff to September 1 failed, this time by 24 votes. It was a Catch-22: We might have won the September 1 postponement if the Administration had supported it openly. But we could do so only at the price of destroying our negotiations. The only hope now for a delay — even for sustaining a veto — said Laird, was for the Administration to *agree* to a forty-five-day deadline, putting us right back on the horns of our dilemma: An announced deadline was marginally better than an immediate cutoff but equally certain to destroy prospects for a cease-fire. Laird was not too upset about this prospect: "Politically, you'd be better off — I don't think Cambodia will ever work out very well anyway and I'd like to be able to blame these guys for doing it, myself." I was less interested in an alibi than an outcome. I was sickened to see the chances of bringing even a fragile peace to Cambodia being destroyed by a senseless orgy of partisanship and the venting of the accumulated resentments of a decade.

On June 27, the President vetoed the second Supplemental Appropriations Act with the "Cambodia rider." A bombing cutoff, he announced correctly, would jeopardize not only Cambodia but the "fragile balance of negotiated agreements, political alignments and military capabilities upon which the overall peace in Southeast Asia depends and on which my assessment of the acceptability of the Vietnam agreements was based." The House sustained the President's veto on June 27. It mustered its largest antiwar margin yet — 241 to 173 — but fell 35 votes short of the two-thirds majority needed to override the President. However, its failure was technical and parliamentary; the steamroller could not be arrested for long. The House and Senate then passed a similar antibombing amendment as part of the Continuing Resolution that was needed to enable all federal agencies to continue functioning after June 30 — and also as an amendment on raising the debt ceiling. It was only a question of time.

Not only our allies in Congress were losing heart, but also our own Administration. Only Haig really supported our policy. Understandably, perhaps, no one had the stomach to refight the Vietnam debate in the midst of Watergate. White House Congressional experts were convinced that we would face one cutoff bill after another until a veto was overridden. Mel Laird kept urging a "compromise": Presidential acceptance of an August 15 cutoff date. I told Laird that it was senseless and self-defeating: "They are going to throw everything down the drain for nothing." Laird insisted that we had no choice if we wanted the government to continue to function. I was bitter:

This is one of the most vindictive, cheap actions that I've seen the Congress take. And it's not just in Cambodia, it's going to hurt us murderously with the Chinese because if they think that the Congress can do these things to us in Cambodia, what are they going to do to us elsewhere?

On June 29, the August 15 "compromise" won support from the Senate Foreign Relations Committee and was passed by the Congress. But to grant this meaningless extension of Cambodian bombing, opponents exacted the price of banning *all* military activity in *all* of Indochina after that date. Mel Laird apparently gave the go-ahead to Republican Minority Leader Gerald R. Ford to accept the compromise. In any event Ford called Nixon and confirmed the decision personally. When I protested to Nixon, he said it was too late; he had yielded to *force majeure* — a surrender that would have been inconceivable had not the John Dean testimony drained all his inner resources.

On June 30, leading newspapers were jubilant that Nixon had agreed to stop bombing in Cambodia by August 15. The *New York Times* claimed that this compromise would permit "delicate negotiations" to continue. It was an illusion; the negotiations had been killed. Nixon had second thoughts — too late. On August 3, shortly before the bombing halt went into effect, Nixon wrote House Speaker Carl Albert and Senate Majority Leader Mike Mansfield:

This abandonment of a friend will have a profound impact in other countries, such as Thailand, which have relied on the constancy and determination of the United States, and I want the Congress to be fully aware of the consequences of its action. . . . In particular, I want the brave and beleaguered Cambodian people to know that the end to the bombing in Cambodia does not signal an abdication of America's determination to work for a lasting peace in Indochina. . . .

I can only hope that the North Vietnamese will not draw the erroneous conclusion from this congressional action that they are free to launch a military offensive in other areas in Indochina.

But the threat had become empty bluster. To widespread applause, the end of military operations in Indochina had been legislated. In Vietnam, we had no counter left to a North Vietnamese offensive. As for Cambodia, the media's themes were familiar: Lon Nol was corrupt; there was little to choose as between him and the Communists. The bombing was "murderous"; therefore ending *our* military activity was a humanitarian gesture to the people of Cambodia. The consequences for the rest of Indochina, or for Presidential authority in future generations, or for America's reputation as a reliable ally, were not admitted as valid. The bombing, it was held, did not spur negotiations; it gave Lon Nol an excuse to avoid them and antagonized the Khmer Rouge. All these themes appeared in a *Washington Post* editorial, which was essentially representative of a broad range of public comment:

The President professes to fear installation of a "Hanoi-controlled government in Phnom Penh" — while ignoring whatever Hanoi may feel about a Washington-controlled government. But it is indisputable that no matter what government sits in Phnom Penh, Hanoi will be able to keep using Cambodia for purposes of supply and sanctuary in South Vietnam. Mr. Nixon and everybody else knew this perfectly well in January. He signed the cease-fire agreement anyway — for the good reason that he counted on South Vietnam's coping for itself despite the problem of the Cambodian flank. For him now to claim that a bombing halt would shake the Southeast Asian "balance" which he negotiated in January is the kind of reckless overstatement which, if even partially true, calls into question the durability of the whole January deal.

As for Mr. Nixon's contention that a bombing halt would deal "a serious blow to America's international credibility," it is nonsense — a relic of a way of thinking about international affairs which has been rendered obsolete by, among other things, Mr. Nixon's own considerable achievement in improving relations with Russia and China. It cannot possibly be the President's purpose, or to his advantage, to suggest that his new "structure of peace" will tremble to its foundations if he is not allowed to continue dropping bombs on hapless Cambodians. This is tantamount to conceding that his entire foreign policy is a fraud — a judgment, we might add, which we do not share.[22]

In fact, it was held that a Communist victory might be a good thing, somehow leading to a neutralist government and the return of Sihanouk — oblivious to the reality that Sihanouk now had no bargaining power and the non-Communist elements needed for such a coalition had been doomed to military destruction. The *New York Times* on August 14 repeated the theme that American military actions having blocked the peace, Congress by prohibiting them had in fact opened the road to negotiations:

. . . there are indications that both sides to the Cambodian conflict are interested in a peaceful solution, now that the prop of direct American military support is about to be removed from the Lon Nol regime by Congressional order. From Phnom Penh come reports — disputed in Washington — that high-ranking government officials there have asked the United States to arrange the removal of President Lon Nol and the return of Prince Sihanouk. From North Korea, where he travelled to avoid a possible meeting with Henry Kissinger in Peking, the Prince has cabled his old friend, Senate Majority Leader Mike Mansfield, offering the United States "peace with honor" if it will withdraw all support from Lon Nol.

Although there would be little honor for Washington in any effort at this late date to reinstall a leader whom it has sought to ostracize from his country for the last three years, the Prince's offer is the best proposition in sight, especially if there is support for it within the existing Cambodian regime. Sihanouk has frankly cast his lot "100 percent" with the Cambodian Communists in his struggle to return to power, but his credentials as a dedicated nationalist who would resist subservience to any foreign power are beyond dispute.

A similar theme was struck by the *Washington Post* on August 28.

We agreed with the desirability of a neutral Cambodia ruled by Sihanouk. Our diplomacy had for six months painstakingly put the pieces into place for just such an outcome. But our military pressure was one such piece, and the legislated end of military activity destroyed all possibility of a neutral free Cambodia. With a total Communist victory now guaranteed, Sihanouk became nearly as irrelevant as Lon Nol — barely tolerated by the Khmer Rouge for international consumption, rapidly discarded when total power was achieved. The Congress thus doomed Sihanouk as surely as it did the Phnom Penh government.

The Negotiations Unravel

FOR a few weeks the existing plan kept going by momentum, perhaps in part because our Communist interlocutors suspected a trick. They needed time to adjust to the spectacle of a superpower voluntarily abandoning all commitments. On July 6, coinciding with Sihanouk's return to Peking, the Phnom Penh government officially offered to negotiate with the "other side." This step had been planned to provide a diplomatic framework for the Chinese initiative, which we now expected to unfold. Murrey Marder of the *Washington Post,* one of the most judicious and objective foreign correspondents, on July 11 complained that the offer was belated:

If such a move had been made back in February, when Sihanouk was publicly signaling his readiness to bargain with Kissinger in Hanoi or Peking, the opposing sides by now might have been at, or near agreement.

Marder's comment illustrated the perils and price of secret diplomacy. First of all, the Khmer Rouge would have vetoed a Sihanouk negotiation with me in Peking in February. Secondly, such a compromise proposal had not been made once but several times since the beginning of the year; it had been consistently rejected. It seemed to be feasible in early July only because we had brought about a military stalemate on the ground. This had now been wrecked.

The clearest proof was Sihanouk's own conduct. For months he had been denouncing me for failure to negotiate, while at the same time blaming his side's totally intransigent position not on his preference but on the Khmer Rouge's quest for total victory. Returned to Peking, he must have been aware that we had offered a bombing halt, negotiations, and a meeting between him and me early in August. Clearly, too, Zhou Enlai favored such a course. Yet after the Congressional action, Sihanouk reversed himself. Obviously the Khmer Rouge had studied the military situation, as they had planned to do in the early summer (according to the report mentioned earlier), and had concluded that with the bombing ended there was no need for compromise after all. On July 5, Sihanouk's public line eschewed all hints of a willingness to negotiate: It was now "useless" to talk, he said. It was now "too late." The Khmer insurgency, he announced candidly, had decided "to struggle to the end."

Around the same time (the first week of July), the Soviet Union also shifted its position. Throughout, it had recognized Lon Nol and maintained an embassy in Phnom Penh — probably because it calculated that this was one country in Indochina where a Communist victory was not foreordained. Now *Pravda* and *Izvestia* both began to refer to Sihanouk as chief of state, for the first time since his ouster on March 18, 1970. Communist diplomats briefed newsmen in Moscow that Moscow was shifting its bets — an augury that these cold-blooded practitioners of power politics, who pride themselves on their assessment of objective factors, had grasped the significance of the Congressional action.[23] Two weeks later, Soviet Ambassador Dobrynin informed me that the Soviets, Chinese, and North Vietnamese had all come to the conclusion after July 1 that negotiations were dead and the Khmer Rouge were going to win.

Hoping against hope, we nonetheless tried to pursue the negotiation through the Chinese. On July 6, 1973, Ambassador Huang Zhen was my guest in San Clemente. He brought with him a message hinting that Zhou Enlai was getting nervous and looking for an exit. The Chinese complained about "rumors" and "speculation" in the American press about a negotiation between the Lon Nol "clique" and Sihanouk. The message tactfully attributed the leaks in part to the Lon Nol government, although "US officials" had recently "made some disclosures" on this question. Interestingly, the Chinese did not claim the speculation was wrong; on the contrary, they expressed concern that such speculation "is extremely disadvantageous to seeking a settlement of the Cambodian question and will even cause trouble.'' (The ''disclosures'' of a negotiation, of course, had been provoked by the Administration's desperate attempt to head off the Congressional bombing halt.)

I replied by reiterating our plan. Huang Zhen confirmed that Peking would, as promised, inform Sihanouk of our ''tentative thinking'' now that Sihanouk had returned from abroad. If Zhou was still willing to transmit an offer whose central element — the cease-fire — had been made irrelevant by legislation, the Chinese must have been nearly as desperate for a political settlement as we were. Huang Zhen confirmed that a visit by me in Peking in early August would be welcome. Zhou Enlai clearly would not give up our joint plan easily. At the very least, it reflected the extreme reluctance with which the Chinese break their word once given.

The tension in Peking caused by the new and unexpected turn of events in Washington was revealed in an encounter that same day between the Chinese Premier and a visiting Congressional delegation headed by Senator Warren Magnuson. Zhou Enlai made the standard boilerplate criticism of our Cambodian policy, including the bombing. The agreed plan, indeed, depended on his ability to claim later that he had induced Washington to end the bombing as his contribution to the peace process. Suddenly Zhou Enlai found handed to him in front of many witnesses what his design required to appear to be extracted from us. Senator Magnuson informed Zhou grandiloquently that he need not worry about the bombing; Zhou should be patient; it would soon be over — specifically, on August 15; Zhou had Congress to thank for it. Zhou grew visibly irritated. Desperately seeking to preserve his bargaining chip, he said that it was hard to be patient while bombs were falling. Not to worry, intoned Magnuson, the Congress would take care of everything. ''Zhou was visibly angered,'' to the growing bafflement of the Congressional delegation, David Bruce reported to me. And Zhou's annoyance seemed to mount uncontainably when Magnuson continued to mutter: ''We stopped the bombing.''

I understood. Zhou saw emerging before him his geopolitical nightmare: an Indochina dominated from Hanoi and allied with the Soviet Union, brought into being by an obtuse superpower that did not deign to give its own diplomacy a chance to succeed.

And the prospect raised premonitions of a yet deeper sort for him. Watergate had heretofore appeared as an incomprehensible domestic squabble in America, its impact on our foreign policy obscure. But now it seemed possible, even likely, that China would have to deal with a President whose authority was so weakened that his commitments had become unreliable; that — to use a favorite Chinese phrase — his word no longer counted. If America proved so incapable as a superpower it had profound implications for China's security; indeed, it undercut the premise on which the Chinese rapprochement with the United States had been based. If a decision could be imposed by Congress so contrary to American interests, could Peking continue to rely on America?

Unsurprisingly, after the Zhou-Magnuson exchange, signs of hesitation from Peking multiplied. On July 11, David Bruce backchanneled an assessment of the Cambodia diplomacy in light of my projected visit to China. The Chinese seemed to be backing away from involvement in a Cambodia negotiation. Bruce did not think they had much leverage left:

> The Chinese will imply it will fall like a ripe apple into the eager hands of Sihanouk, but they may have private doubts about his ability to control the Khmer Rouge and other insurgents. . . . Meanwhile, they may calculate they have little to lose from delay.

On the same day there was another straw in the ill wind. The Chinese had already agreed to receive me in Peking in the first week of August; they had invited us to pick the date. When at the end of June we proposed August 6, they had even allowed that date to leak to the press in Peking. We had then suggested an announcement for July 16. On July 11 we received the bland reply that Huang Zhen had been recalled to Peking — in itself an unexpected development — and that the announcement would have to await his consultations. This was a clear hint that there were second thoughts.

We decided to play out the string. I asked General Scowcroft to call in the deputy chief of the Chinese Liaison Office, Ambassador Han Xu, and remind him that we had been told to pick any day in the first week of August. Scowcroft reiterated our preference for August 6 and proposed an announcement for July 19 or 23. I instructed him to add as a "semiofficial" comment that should I return from Peking empty-handed on Cambodia, my ability to maintain an unsentimental policy based on national interest would be jeopardized. Therefore, Scowcroft hoped the Chinese could let us know "what he may be able to bring back regarding the Cambodian situation."

Insolence is the defense of the weak. I was staking too much on a losing hand. To link Sino-American relations this explicitly to the outcome in Cambodia would compound the Chinese quandary without adding to China's leverage. The simple fact was that Zhou had lost the ability to shape events — as a result of *American* actions. We had overturned the framework of the negotiations we had ourselves proposed and there was no way for even the best-intentioned Chinese leader to ask the Khmer Rouge to forgo the total victory we had handed to them.

On July 16, Sihanouk made clear that he understood the new balance of forces. In a prepared statement more definitive and authoritative than his usual erratic off-the-cuff interviews, he revealed clearly what Khmer

Rouge policy was. China's Xinhua News Agency in Peking broadcast Sihanouk's "Forty-third Message to the Khmer Nation." It denounced all "meddling" attempts to promote a negotiation; the only terms for a solution were total Communist victory. And the next day Sihanouk's defiance was tinged with despair that Communist domination of his country spelled the doom of all his hopes. He told a Reuters correspondent in Peking that he was "washing his hands of the state of affairs after Phnom Penh is liberated. Let the Khmer Rouge take over the running of the country!"[24]

The guillotine finally fell on the evening of July 18. Han Xu delivered a note to General Scowcroft declaring that for a variety of rather contrived reasons, China was no longer willing even to communicate the American negotiating proposal to Sihanouk. The Chinese note simply repeated the most extreme demands of the Khmer Rouge, all of which had been known in the months in which the Chinese had engaged themselves in the search for a compromise. But now it insisted that we accept them — abandoning the previous position that a completely red Cambodia would complicate everybody's problems:

The origin of the Cambodian question is clear to the U.S. side. It is up to the doer to undo the knot. The key to the settlement of the question is held by the United States, and not by others. If the United States truly desires to settle the Cambodian question, the above reasonable demands raised by the Cambodian side should be acceptable to it. It is hoped that the U.S. side will give serious consideration to this and translate it into action.

And since the Chinese could never be sure that the Western mind fathomed the intricacies of any situation, Zhou Enlai sent us another unmistakable signal: The very next day — July 19 — we were informed that my visit on August 6 was no longer "convenient." The most appropriate date would be August 16. Even we could grasp that August 16 was the day *after* the bombing halt we had imposed on ourselves. If Cambodia were to be discussed in these circumstances, we would be supplicants. The implication was clear. We had become largely irrelevant to Chinese policy in Indochina — and so had Sihanouk. They might continue to pay lip service to Sihanouk but henceforth they had to place all their bets on the Khmer Rouge. Chinese mediation was over.

And thus gradually the scheme so laboriously put together unraveled. It was clear that in order to obtain a "solution" as outlined in the Chinese note we did not need to "negotiate"— least of all with the Chinese. Nor could we leave the impression that we were being panicked. As de Gaulle once replied to Churchill when chastised for being too intransigent: "I am too weak to be conciliatory." We let Peking wait for nearly a week for our reply. It was stiff:

As to the substance of the Chinese note of July 18, the Chinese side will not be surprised that the US side rejects a "solution" so arbitrarily weighted against it. This is inconsistent with the requirements of reciprocity and equality. It is beyond the bounds of logic to be asked to negotiate on an issue when the other side, clearly and from the outset, leaves no room for negotiations. In such circumstances the US side will leave negotiations to the Cambodian parties.

Simultaneously, Scowcroft read the following sharp "oral note" to Han Xu:

My government notes, with regret, that this is the first time in the development of our new relationship that the Chinese word has not counted.

The Chinese side has often expressed its devotion to principle. The US side is no less serious. One of its firm principles is not to betray those that have relied on it. The US side believes that the Chinese side will welcome US adherence to this principle in other contexts.

Following the Chinese sequence, we waited a day before commenting on the Chinese proposal of August 16 for my visit to Peking. We proposed instead a period four weeks later: September 13 through September 16. This the Chinese found a reason to avoid. In the end, my trip did not take place until November.

It was, of course, pointless to rail against the Chinese for failing to deliver a negotiation that our own domestic processes had aborted. The fact was that it was not the Chinese who had changed their minds; it was we who had changed the situation, undercutting the premises of the previous understanding. At a meeting on July 19 of all my close associates — General Scowcroft, Larry Eagleburger, Winston Lord, Jonathan T. Howe, Richard H. Solomon, and Peter Rodman, the veterans of the reconciliation with Peking who had helped nurture the policy and were committed to it emotionally — I summed up my analysis:

The bombing cut-off had fundamentally changed the situation in Cambodia. Formerly, Sihanouk's utility to the Khmer Rouge had been that he gave them legitimacy they had not had. Now they didn't need legitimacy; they saw they could win. Sihanouk's utility to the Chinese had been that he gave them influence over the Khmer Rouge and could resist other outside influences. The utility of the Chinese to us was that they had some control over Sihanouk. Sihanouk's utility to us was that, once he returned to Cambodia, he might be able to keep things balanced. Ironically the Chinese needed the Lon Nol group — this was a restraint on Sihanouk and on the Khmer Rouge. The Congressmen had totally misjudged the situation. Now this was all lost. Sihanouk couldn't deliver the Khmer Rouge and the Chinese couldn't deliver Sihanouk.

On August 4 I made the point to my friend Lee Kuan Yew, the Prime Minister of Singapore:

We have suffered a tragedy because of Watergate. When I saw you [in early April] we were going to bomb North Vietnam for a week, then go to Russia, then meet with Le Duc Tho. Congress has made it impossible. . . .

The Chinese offered to act as an intermediary. Now the Chinese lose if the Khmer Rouge win, because Sihanouk loses. The ideal situation for the Chinese is if the Khmer Rouge need Sihanouk and they can maneuver between. But if the Khmer Rouge will win anyway . . .

Sihanouk's rhetoric escalated with his irrelevance and illuminated the grim prospects. He gave another interview to AFP on August 12, confirming that the Khmer Rouge remained "inflexible in the position they have already fixed once and for all." Negotiations were impossible; the insurgents had "absolutely decided to continue armed resistance" until the Lon Nol government was "radically and irreversibly eliminated." And on August 15, in Pyongyang, North Korea, Sihanouk repeated that any formula that asked the Khmer Rouge to share power with any other group would never be accepted.

In these circumstances, there was nothing left for us to negotiate. In a news conference on August 23 I was fatalistic:

The Cambodian negotiations now inevitably with the end of American bombing will depend more on the decision of the Cambodian parties than on American decisions, and if the Congressional intent means anything, it is that the United States should not play the principal role in these activities.

And I spoke in this sense, too, when Chinese Vice Foreign Minister Qiao Guanhua came to the United Nations General Assembly for his annual visit and we met over dinner on October 3. Like a veteran of a battle in which we had been essentially on the same side and had been defeated by a totally unpredictable and senseless event, Qiao said wistfully that it was now clear that neither of us should have gotten involved — a rare admission of Chinese fallibility. He claimed that Cambodia was not that important; it was only a "side issue."* (Devotees of the thesis that Cambodia was a "sideshow" should note its origin here.)

The best way to handle defeat is to minimize it. Qiao did his best to dissociate China from what was going on in Cambodia; clearly, he wanted to pay no further price in Sino-American relations on a matter we both had lost the capacity to affect. He said little about Sihanouk. He did not contradict me when I said that Peking's interests and Hanoi's were not identical on this issue. But he had no other solution than "to let the flames burning in Cambodia extinguish themselves, by themselves."

---

*See p. 682.

It did not, of course, happen like that. The Congressionally mandated bombing halt was succeeded by a series of disasters. The prospect of rounding out the Paris accords in Indochina vanished. Sihanouk returned to Cambodia but only to face humiliation, house arrest, and the murder of several of his children. He had no independent forces left to balance, no chance at a pivotal role as head of state. Sihanouk confirmed to other interlocutors what we had already deduced: that he indeed favored negotiation himself, but the Khmer Rouge leadership rejected it.

Perhaps the most grievously wounded victim of the Congressional action was Zhou Enlai. The Chinese Premier had staked his prestige on a complicated scheme, the essential premise of which was that strong American military action had produced a Cambodian stalemate and required a compromise. He must have presented our plan as the best attainable, given our determination not to yield to force. The Khmer Rouge — judged by their publicly proclaimed program — could not have been happy with this approach, but the Chinese seemed to think that the moment was propitious in the month of June, and that the Khmer Rouge had been brought around, or could be brought around, to accept it as the only course possible.

But Zhou's effort also ran up against the pressures of the radical faction inside China, who saw China's security best assured by militancy in defense of revolutionary rectitude. Those who later came to be known as the Gang of Four were at this time beginning to influence Mao strongly, if not control him, and he was prone to second thoughts about the moderate and pro-Western trends that had emerged since his opening to Washington. Possibly he would have turned on Zhou whatever the circumstances. Zhou, having risen to the undisputed second post, ran the inherent risk of sharing the fate of his predecessors in that position. But I have convincing reason to believe that a significant event in the ascendancy of the Gang of Four during the summer of 1973 was the collapse of the Cambodian negotiation. Our Congressionally imposed abdication humiliated Zhou. He had staked ideological capital and we had not been able to pay in geopolitical coin. He would never have recovered his domestic position after this even if illness had not put an end to the public career of my extraordinary friend.

There is no guarantee that this negotiating effort would have succeeded. Indeed, in retrospect, as I read over the records of all our negotiating attempts from 1970 to 1975, the possibility is strong that the Khmer Rouge would have violated any agreement they did not block. The fact remains that even if the plan we were negotiating ultimately failed, it would have bought a transitional period to ease the fate of the Cambodian people and perhaps spare them the genocidal suffering that the abdication of their friends and the ferocity of their conquerors eventually inflicted on them. This was the most promising negotiating opportunity if not the only one — with the Chinese and us working actively in parallel — and it was torpedoed by the United States Congress and our domestic turmoil.

In fairness the participants on both sides of our domestic debate shared one vast gap of understanding: They could not possibly imagine the incarnate evil represented by the Khmer Rouge. Those who sought to end the war by throttling Lon Nol — even the radical fringe — cannot be blamed for the holocaust they helped bring about. Incapable of imagining that a government would murder three million of its own people, they thought nothing could be worse than a continuation of the war and they were prepared to ensure its end even at the price of a Communist takeover.

The fashionable critics who apply their ingenuity to blame those who sought to resist Cambodia's doom thus have a right to ask to be spared opprobrium; they meant well. But they should have the decency not to reverse the truth by blaming those who sought to resist the Communist takeover all along. If they cannot bring themselves to admit fallibility, they should at least in the stillness of their souls ask themselves whether self-righteousness cannot exact its own fearful penalties.

The Administration was perhaps too abstractly analytical when it sought to sustain by executive action alone one more exertion to complete what had already cost so much. Our critics had passion without analysis; we had concept without consensus. Watergate destroyed the last vestiges of hope for a reasonable outcome. For the first time in the postwar period, America abandoned to eventual Communist rule a friendly people who had relied on us. The pattern once established did not end soon. We will have to pay for a long time for the precedent into which we stumbled that summer, now seemingly so distant. While the disputants will never agree on the merits of their controversy, if they cherish their country they should resolve never again to permit such a gulf to open in our nation, and never again to engage in such an orgy of assault on motives rather than analyzing substance. By our self-indulgence we damaged the fabric of freedom everywhere. And by our abdication we have already caused more suffering than we ever did by our commitment.

Nobel Peace Prize

AFTER the summer of 1973, I knew that Cambodia was doomed and that only a miracle could save South Vietnam. North Vietnamese communications to us grew progressively more insolent. There was no longer even the pretense of observing the Paris Agreement. And our legislated impotence added humiliation to irrelevance. We struggled to furnish what economic and military aid for South Vietnam and Cambodia was obtainable from Congress. But the reasoning that had led to the legislated bombing halt also produced a systematic drop in aid levels. By the spring of 1975, Congress was considering a derisory "terminal grant" — as if Saigon and Phnom Penh were the beneficiaries of some charity — when the accumulated strains led to their collapse and spared us that ultimate disgrace. In 1973 in my bones I knew that collapse was just a question of time.

Such was the dark mood when shortly before eleven o'clock on the morning of October 16, 1973, a Situation Room officer interrupted a WSAG meeting on the Middle East to hand Brent Scowcroft an Associated Press news bulletin announcing that Le Duc Tho and I had been awarded the Nobel Peace Prize. Scowcroft passed it to me without comment:

30
B U L L E T I N
PEACE PRIZE
OSLO, NORWAY (AP) — U.S. SECRETARY OF STATE HENRY KISSINGER AND NORTH VIETNAMESE POLITBURO MEMBER LE DUC THO WERE AWARDED THE 1973 NOBEL PEACE PRIZE TODAY FOR THEIR EFFORTS TO OFFICIALLY END THE VIETNAM WAR.
CB1050PED OCT 16

I had not even known that I was a candidate. I threw the dispatch on the table. My colleagues read it with astonishment rather than jubilation; they congratulated me but without real passion. For we all were ill at ease.

There is no other comparable honor. A statesman's final test, after all, is whether he has made a contribution to the well-being of mankind. And yet I knew that without the ability to enforce the Agreement, the structure of peace for Indochina was unlikely to last. I would have been far happier with recognition for a less precarious achievement. Without false modesty, I am prouder of what I accomplished in the next two years in the Middle East.

Mrs. Aase Lionaes, chairman of the Nobel Committee of the Norwegian Parliament, issued a statement explaining the award in terms of the world's relief at the end of the Vietnam war:

News of the Paris Agreement brought a wave of joy and hope to the entire world. The two chief negotiators brought their talents and goodwill to bear in order to obtain a peace agreement. The Norwegian Nobel Committee hopes that the undersigning parties will feel a moral responsibility for seeing that the Paris agreements are followed.

Shortly thereafter, I received a telegram from Mrs. Lionaes, confirming that Le Duc Tho and I would share the prize, amounting to 255,000

Swedish crowns (or about $65,000) each. I was invited to Oslo to receive the Nobel gold medal from King Olav V on December 10 and to deliver a Nobel lecture then or within six months thereafter.

The moment must have been painful for Nixon. There was no recognition for which he yearned more than that of peacemaker. And in fact the major decisions that had ended the Vietnam war had been his, whatever my contribution in designing or executing the underlying strategy. He might well have won the award for the Vietnam peace and other achievements — the diplomatic revolution he brought about with China and the USSR — had not Watergate destroyed this dream together with all the other aspirations that had sustained the incredible self-discipline of his march to the top.

I called on him immediately in the Oval Office. It happened to be the day that Melvin Laird became the first senior official publicly to discuss possible impeachment proceedings: Laird disclosed that he had warned the President he ran this risk if he defied a Supreme Court ruling on releasing the Oval Office tapes. Only those who knew Nixon well could perceive beneath the gallant congratulations the strain and hurt that I was being given all the credit for actions that had cost him so much. I sought to restore some perspective in a formal statement that mentioned him twice:

> Nothing that has happened to me in public life has moved me more than this Award, which represents a recognition of the central purpose of the President's foreign policy which is the achievement of a lasting peace.
>
> I am grateful to the President for having given me this opportunity and also for creating the conditions which made it possible to bring the negotiations on Vietnam to a successful conclusion.
>
> When I shall receive the Award, together with my old colleague in the search for peace in Vietnam, Le Duc Tho, I hope that that occasion will at last mark the end, or symbolize the end, of the anguish and the suffering that Vietnam has meant for so many millions of people around the world — and that both at home and abroad it will mark the beginning of a period of reconciliation. . . .
>
> But beyond all these immediate crises, perhaps the most important goal any Administration can set itself is to work for a world in which the Award will become irrelevant, because peace will have become so normal and so much taken for granted that no awards for it will have to be given.

Normally the award of a Nobel Peace Prize is the occasion for great national pride. But our divisions had been too deep; to many, treating the Nobel Peace Prize as a national accomplishment would have meant acceptance of a course they had bitterly fought. Media reaction was restrained, to put it mildly. A *New York Times* editorial of October 17 snidely called it "the Nobel War Prize." The *Hartford Times* of October 22 spoke of "Honor without Peace?" The *Richmond Times-*

Dispatch of October 23 called it an "Ignoble Nobel." My old sparring partner George W. Ball was quoted in the October 17 *Washington Post* as remarking that "the Norwegians must have a sense of humor." Many objected to the award to Le Duc Tho, and I could share a certain wonder that a representative of a country that had invaded all neighboring countries could win a peace prize for making a cease-fire that even then it was violating in every provision. Nevertheless, in the spirit of the occasion I sent a friendly message to Le Duc Tho on October 16, hoping to inject a human note into the tedious exchanges on the deterioration of the Paris Agreement:

Let me congratulate you, Mr. Special Adviser. You and I have shared a great honor — not so much the award we have been given but rather the historic privilege we had of playing a role in ending a war.

On January 23, when you and I initialed the Paris Agreement on Ending the War and Restoring Peace in Vietnam, you made an eloquent statement. You said that the event was a subject of great satisfaction for both of us personally and that we should not forget that historic day. I echoed this sentiment.

I also expressed my conviction that our work would not be complete until we brought a lasting peace to the people of Indochina and a spirit of reconciliation between the people of the Democratic Republic of Vietnam and the people of the United States.

This continues to be my profound conviction, and my sincere intention.

Not until eleven days later did Le Duc Tho reply. And he was beyond being moved by bourgeois sentimentalities like "peace" and "reconciliation." In the interval he had written to the Nobel Committee declining the award because the Paris Agreement, he said, was not being implemented. It was another insolence by North Vietnam, whose transgressions had, in fact, turned the Agreement into a farce. Le Duc Tho cabled me in a similar vein on October 27, proving that no occasion was too solemn for him to forgo scoring debating points:

. . . At the ceremony for the initialling of the Paris Agreement on Vietnam, I still remember, when offering you the pen used for the initialling as a souvenir, I told you that the Agreement being now concluded, you should keep in mind the strict implementation of the Agreement, and you promised me to do so. I have not forgotten that promise of yours.

It is very regrettable that so far the Paris Agreement on Vietnam has been very seriously violated. The war has not yet ended, peace has not been really restored in South Vietnam. Therefore, I am of the view that all the parties signatory to the Paris Agreement must strictly carry it out. Only on this basis can we proceed to the normalization of relations between our two peoples. This is what I wish to see and what I will actively work for. I hope you will do the same.

On November 29, 1973, I asked Mrs. Lionaes and the Nobel Committee to donate the entire proceeds to a scholarship fund for children of American servicemen killed or missing in action in Indochina. The Paula and Louis Kissinger Scholarship Fund, named in honor of my parents, was established for this purpose. (On April 30, 1975, as Saigon fell, I wrote to Mrs. Lionaes returning the Peace Prize and the equivalent of the cash award.* The Nobel Committee refused to accept them, replying that intervening events "in no way reduce[d] the Committee's appreciation of Mr. Kissinger's sincere efforts to get a cease-fire agreement put into force in 1973.")

I had learned that my presence at the award ceremonies would lead to massive demonstrations by anti-Vietnam groups in Oslo. The Norwegian government, though unfailingly courteous and helpful, seemed relieved when I used the pretext of a NATO ministerial meeting to have the award accepted on my behalf by our Ambassador to Norway, Thomas Byrne. Slipping into the auditorium at the University of Oslo through a rear entrance in order to evade snowballs and anti-American demonstrators, Ambassador Byrne read my statement:

To the realist, peace represents a stable arrangement of power; to the idealists, a goal so preeminent that it conceals the difficulty of finding the means to its achievement. But in this age of thermonuclear technology, neither view can assure man's preservation. Instead, peace, the ideal, must be practiced. A sense of responsibility and accommodation must guide the behavior of all nations. Some common notion of justice can and must be found, for failure to do so will only bring more "just" wars. . . .

Certain war has yielded to an uncertain peace in Vietnam. Where there was once only despair and dislocation, today there is hope, however frail. In the Middle East the resumption of full-scale war haunts a fragile cease-fire. In Indochina, the Middle East and elsewhere, lasting peace will not have been won until contending nations realize the futility of replacing political competition with armed conflict. . . .

If peace, the ideal, is to be our common destiny, then peace, the experience, must be our common practice. For this to be so, the leaders of all nations must remember that their political decisions of war or peace are realized in the human sufferings or well-being of their peoples.

As Alfred Nobel recognized, peace cannot be achieved by one man or one nation. It results from the efforts of men of broad vision and goodwill throughout the world. The accomplishments of individuals need not be remembered, for if lasting peace is to come it will be the accomplishment of all mankind.

With these thoughts, I extend to you my most sincere appreciation for this award.

---

*The full text of my letter to Mrs. Lionaes is in the backnotes.[25]

IX

Chile: The Fall of Salvador Allende

The United States and Allende

IT may seem strange that in a book describing my stewardship of affairs I should feel obliged to include a chapter on the downfall of Chile's President Salvador Allende Gossens in September 1973. It is a testament to the power of political mythology — for, contrary to anti-American propaganda around the world and revisionist history in the United States, our government had nothing to do with planning his overthrow and no involvement with the plotters. Allende was brought down by his own incompetence and inflexibility. What happened, happened for Chilean reasons, not as a result of acts of the United States. In the mass of documents that make up modern government, unfriendly investigators have failed to unearth any evidence that, even taken out of context, would prove otherwise. A suspicious Senate investigating committee was forced to admit that it could find "no evidence" of American complicity.[1]

To prove the negative is logically nearly impossible. So this chapter offers a brief history of Allende's Chile between his inauguration as President in 1970 and his collapse in 1973 as well as a description of American policy during that period.

The record leaves no doubt that Chile was not a major preoccupation of the American government after Allende was installed as President. Indeed, Allende's overthrow occurred while I was myself in transition from my position as national security adviser to my new appointment as Secretary of State (see Chapter X). Much of my time was taken up with confirmation hearings and the preparation for them.

This fact, which no doubt affected the sense of urgency with which we dealt with the immediate crisis in Chile, was essentially irrelevant, however, to the events leading up to the military coup. The truth is that the coup was indigenous; Allende was brought down by the forces in Chile that he himself had unleashed and by his inability to control them.

In the Presidential election of September 4, 1970, the overwhelming majority of Chilean voters — 62.7 percent — voted *against* Salvador Allende. But in the three-man race this opposition vote was split between the two democratic candidates, and Allende won with 36.2 percent, by a razor-thin plurality of 39,000 votes out of the nearly three million cast. The Chilean Constitution provided that if no candidate won 50 percent of the popular vote, the Chilean Congress would choose the President six weeks after the election. By tradition, however, the Congress usually confirmed the candidate who had received a plurality of the popular vote no matter how narrow the margin. And this they did. From this inauspicious beginning, Allende undertook a radical, wholesale transformation of Chile's social structure and political institutions for which he had no mandate. This proved to be his undoing.

It was the first, and so far the only, time in modern history that a democratic process has come so close to producing a Communist takeover. For Allende was not the classic Chilean President who would serve his six-year term and then be replaced through another democratic election. Once he was in office, his proclaimed intention was to revise the Chilean Constitution, to neutralize and suppress all opposition parties and media, and thereby to make his own rule — or at least that of his party — irreversible. More immediately worrisome from our point of view was his implacable ideological hatred of the United States and his determination to spread his revolutionary gospel throughout Latin America. I have described our judgment of Allende's purposes in *White House Years* in terms I have seen no reason to alter:

> Allende's later martyrdom has obscured his politics. Socialist though he may have proclaimed himself, his goals and his philosophy bore no resemblance to European social democracy. Allende had founded the Socialist Party of Chile, which set itself apart from the Communist Party by being more radical in its program and no more democratic in its philosophy. He was willing enough to come to power by an election *before* undertaking the revolution; but the social and political transformation he promised afterward did not differ significantly from the Communist platform. It was a central tenet of the party's program that "bourgeois" democratic practices would be made irrelevant; by definition his would be the last democratic election.[2]

This was no mere campaign rhetoric. It had been Allende's conviction throughout his political career. In 1967 he had been a founder of the Organization of Latin American Solidarity, a Havana-based coalition of leftist groups dedicated to armed struggle against the United States and to violent revolution throughout the hemisphere. Allende was not a reformist democrat; he was an avowed enemy of democracy as we know it. To imply that he was not loyal to his stated convictions is to insult the intellectual integrity of a man who was proud of his steadfast commitment to principle. Before confirming him as President, the Chilean Congress evidenced its mistrust of him by requiring his assent to a Statute of Democratic Guarantees — in effect, a negotiated Bill of Rights.

He agreed to this only as a "tactical necessity," as he proudly admitted
to his French revolutionary colleague, Régis Debray, after taking office.
While constitutional President of Chile, Allende told Debray that his
assurances of democratic liberties should be viewed as comparable to
Mao's permitting private enterprise for a brief period after coming to
power in China. His true objective in Chile, he told Debray, was "total,
scientific, Marxist socialism," which meant the "overthrow" of the
"bourgeois State."[3]

Nixon and his principal advisers were convinced that Allende represented a challenge to the United States and to the stability of the Western Hemisphere. Allende's commitment to nationalizing American-
owned companies was not our principal worry. True, we believed that
policies which discouraged private investment were likely to defeat
Chile's hopes for economic development. And we inherited legislation — the so-called Hickenlooper amendment — that required a cutoff
of American aid if American property was expropriated without fair
compensation. But the Nixon Administration did not view our foreign
policy interests through the prism of the financial concerns of American
companies. In 1969, we had cooperated with Chile's Christian Democratic President, Eduardo Frei Montalva, and negotiated fair terms for
the nationalization of majority ownership of the Anaconda copper company. That same year, in Peru, we stretched the Hickenlooper amendment almost to the breaking point to avoid cutting off aid after Peru's
seizure of the International Petroleum Company. We repeatedly sought
a basis to avoid invoking the legislation and finally worked out a modus
vivendi with Peru despite the fact that its government leaned toward the
more radical factions of the Third World.

Allende was different, not merely an economic nuisance or a political
critic but a geopolitical challenge. Chile bordered Peru, Argentina, and
Bolivia, all plagued by radical movements. As a continental country, a
militant Chile had a capacity to undermine other nations and support
radical insurgency that was far greater than Cuba's, and Cuba has managed to do damage enough. If Chile had followed the Cuban pattern,
Communist ideology would in time have been supported by Soviet forces
and Soviet arms in the southern cone of the South American continent.
Our apprehensions had been heightened by the discovery, in the same
month as Allende's election, of a Soviet attempt to build a nuclear submarine base in the Cuban port of Cienfuegos.[4]

Two Democratic administrations preceding Nixon's had made the same
judgment that a victory for Allende would imperil our interests in the
Western Hemisphere. They had given substantial sums of money to the
Christian Democratic Party to block Allende in the Presidential elections
of 1964 and his coalition in the Congressional elections of 1968. No
one ever felt happy about these activities; successive Presidents of both

parties recognized them as essential. There is a gray area between military intervention and formal diplomacy where our democracy is forced to compete against groups inimical to it.

Many developing countries provide a fertile ground for the network of political parties, front groups, pseudo-press agencies and so-called research institutes by which Communist and radical forces seek to dominate. Small, disciplined groups can have a disproportionate impact; control of the media will not be balanced by the checks and balances of a pluralistic society. If we cede a monopoly of support to organizations financed, disciplined, and trained by our adversaries, many of them with direct links with the Soviet Union, only one of two outcomes will be possible: Either radical, anti-Western groups will intimidate and suppress moderate alternatives; or else extreme conservative elements will preempt this evolution and govern by repressive methods, alienating themselves from our support despite our security interests.[5]

In Chile, a relatively advanced society with a long democratic tradition, we agreed with our Democratic predecessors that groups standing for democratic values needed our help against those who openly threatened them. Our support for democratic forces in Chile was conceived as being justified only by special circumstances because important interests were truly engaged and all else had failed. The Soviet Union had no doubts that international issues were involved. The importance it attached to its adherents in Chile was demonstrated by an extraordinary event toward the end of 1976. For the first time the Soviet Union traded a Soviet citizen it had jailed (the dissident Vladimir Bukovsky) and it did so in exchange for a non-Soviet Communist — the Chilean Communist leader Luis Corvalán, together with other Party colleagues arrested after the overthrow of Allende.*

I have described in *White House Years* the belated and confused efforts made by the Nixon Administration to prevent Allende's accession to the Presidency. First was a vain attempt to persuade the Chilean Congress to select another candidate. Then came a haphazard and amateurish exploration of a military coup, designed to bring about not military rule but a new electoral contest between Allende and the leading democratic candidate so that the Chilean people could make a clear-cut choice between democratic and totalitarian alternatives. These efforts were called off before they could produce any result. (More precisely, the American part was called off; the Chilean component was bungled.)[5]

Allende was inaugurated as President on November 3, 1970. There was no American involvement in coup plotting afterward.

---

*The trade took place in Switzerland, worked out under the auspices of the Ford Administration.

Allende in Office

THE mythology that the United States relentlessly assaulted Allende after he was installed is the opposite of the truth. We had not changed our original judgment but we were prepared to make an effort at coexistence. So many other problems were clamoring for our attention that Chile kept sliding on our list of priorities except when some provocation by Allende forced us to react. But these started as soon as Allende was inaugurated.

Allende showed at once, practically and symbolically, that he was not interested in either a democratic process in Chile or an accommodation with the United States. His inaugural speeches made clear that he had not the slightest intention of changing the anti-American convictions of a lifetime; the new government's ideological orientation was reaffirmed early in a series of gestures. He invited the leaders of the Puerto Rican independence party to his inauguration and unveiled a statue of Ché Guevara a few days later. Within nine days of being sworn in, he established diplomatic relations with Cuba, in contravention of the 1964 resolution of the Organization of American States (OAS) ostracizing Cuba within the inter-American system. He moved rapidly toward relations with North Korea and took up contact with North Vietnam, with whom we were at war. More ominously, within a month Allende amnestied hundreds of jailed members of the Movement of the Revolutionary Left (MIR), a Chilean terrorist organization dedicated to the seizure by violence of total power. Over the next months, between 10,000 and 15,000 visa-less foreigners entered Chile; their mission was never published; it was widely reported and never denied that they were supporters of militant movements in neighboring countries and formed the nucleus of a paramilitary force inside Chile.

The Administration decided its basic strategy toward Chile in the period immediately before and after Allende's inauguration. A series of meetings in late October and November 1970 considered three policy alternatives: accommodation with Allende; open confrontation; and a cool but correct posture that left it to Allende to set the tone and pace of the subsequent relationship.

There was less to these choices than met the eye. They were, in fact, the classic troika of bureaucratic options: the one possible course surrounded by two fictitious ones. Both Nixon and Allende were sure to reject accommodation. Nixon had not railed against the coddling of Fidel Castro for a decade to head now for the conciliation of a Latin leader he considered a crypto-Communist. Allende showed no receptivity to such a course; his supporters would not have tolerated it.

Confrontation was a slogan, not a policy. We would not want to make Allende a martyr in Latin America or give him a pretext for accelerating his pace toward his stated objective of absolute control.

At a National Security Council meeting on November 6, 1970, Nixon therefore chose, more or less by default, the "cool and correct" option favored by all elements of the bureaucracy. I issued a directive on November 9 elaborating his decision and defining the limits between which our policy was to navigate: (a) "to avoid giving the Allende government a basis on which to rally domestic and international support for consolidation of the regime"; and (b) "to prevent the consolidation of a communist state in Chile hostile to the interests of the United States and other hemisphere nations." The two goals were not easy to reconcile. To prevent the consolidation of a Communist regime required that we should not go out of our way to help Allende; hence no new bilateral economic aid commitments were to be undertaken. At the same time, to keep open the possibility of improving relations (should Allende decide, against our expectations, to moderate his course), humanitarian programs were continued, and the pipeline of existing aid commitments was maintained.

The President's decision not to approve new aid projects was not as drastic as it sounded. Grant aid to Chile had been terminated by President Johnson in 1968. Loans of $40 million in 1969 and $70 million in 1970 had been approved; disbursements of funds under these commitments were continued. The ban on new aid appropriations would not take effect before the fall of 1971 — nearly a year away — leaving enough time to reverse ourselves should Allende's policies prove more restrained than the evidence indicated.

In late November 1970, the State Department issued a formal policy statement, approved by the Senior Review Group* of the National Security Council, which left the future of US–Chilean relations up to the new Chilean government:

> The new President has taken office in accordance with Chilean constitutional procedures. We have no wish to prejudge the state of our relations with Chile but naturally they will depend on the actions which the Chilean government takes toward the U.S. and the inter-American system. We will be watching the situation carefully and be in close consultations with other members of the OAS.

The door might as well never have been left open. Allende himself slammed it shut. He began to move against American property on November 20, 1970, in a manner that gave us no choice except to resist. He ordered the takeover of two firms controlled by American companies, charging that they had deprived Chileans of their jobs. Six days later he announced, to a meeting of the Communist Party leadership, a

---

*The Senior Review Group brought together the Under Secretary of State for Political Affairs, the Deputy Secretary of Defense, the Director of Central Intelligence, and the Chairman of the Joint Chiefs of Staff, under my chairmanship as Assistant to the President for National Security Affairs.

program of large-scale nationalization of basic industry, beginning with foreign interests but not confined to them. Allende's Finance Minister, in explaining these decisions to a committee of the Chilean Congress, placed the blame for Chile's economic problems on the "capitalist system" and on foreign, especially American, investors.

On December 21, Allende proposed a constitutional amendment expropriating all foreign copper mines. This decision affected American interests almost exclusively and abrogated the earlier takeover agreement negotiated between the government and the copper companies with our encouragement. Even after these unfriendly acts, President Nixon declared on January 4, 1971, in a televised interview:

> [W]hat happened in Chile is not something that we welcomed, although . . . that was the decision of the people of Chile. . . . What we were interested in was their policy toward us in the foreign policy field.
>
> So, I haven't given up on Chile or on the Chilean people, and we are going to keep our contact with them.

In January the United States made another gesture; we supported two loans from the Inter-American Development Bank amounting to $11.5 million to aid two Chilean universities.

On March 23 our Ambassador in Santiago, Edward Korry, was instructed to offer his good offices to help the companies and the government achieve a negotiated solution of the expropriation problem. Korry's involvement continued after the companies' own efforts toward direct negotiations were rebuffed. Our objective was to assure fair compensation as required by international law and our domestic legislation. Whatever prospects existed for an equitable settlement were negated by a constitutional amendment put forward by Allende, providing for the retroactive application of "excess profits taxes," which had the potential for offsetting any compensation that might be agreed upon. The amendment was signed into law by Allende on July 15, 1971, and applied in a manner that indeed in all but one case — a new mine where no excess profits determination was possible — left the copper companies owing money to the government *in addition* to losing their property. Then, on November 9, 1971, Allende took on other foreign creditors. He proclaimed a moratorium on Chile's foreign debt payments and three days later Chile began to default on most debts to major international creditors, including the United States government and American financial institutions. This led the United States Export-Import Bank to halt further disbursement on its loans a month later, in keeping with standard banking practices, though it continued its loan guarantees until February 1972.

I have traced this sequence of events because it gives the lie to the charges that the United States, without provocation, initiated economic warfare against Chile. A country defaulting on its foreign debts is scarcely creditworthy whatever its form of government. It was not American pressure but Allende's doctrinaire radicalism that dried up the flow of funds from Western lending institutions.

Allende's challenge was not limited to the economic field. In November and December 1971, Fidel Castro spent nearly a month in Chile, concluding his visit with a joint communiqué that hailed the "common struggle" and "common outlook of both governments and peoples in analyzing the world situation." Allende and Castro joined in condemning America's "imperialist intervention" in Vietnam, hailing "the crisis of the capitalist monetary system" and "the gradual, substantial increase of the economic, political, social and technological power of the socialist camp."

Simultaneously, Allende launched his assault on Chile's constitutional system. On November 11, 1971, he sent Congress a constitutional "reform" bill that would broaden Presidential powers, reduce the independence of the Supreme Court, and replace Chile's Senate and Chamber of Deputies with a unicameral Popular Assembly elected coterminously with the President — an attempt to destroy the checks and balances of Chilean democracy. The bill had to be withdrawn in response to vociferous and widespread objection.

Allende next turned to stifling his domestic opponents. Our new Ambassador in Santiago, Nathaniel Davis* — not one of my more uncritical admirers — called Allende's strategy a deliberate effort to "starve out the opposition."[6] A prime goal was to suppress all media opposed to the government. Allende seized control of the supply of newsprint, and he used the regulatory powers of the government to hold down the prices that opposition media could charge — a move certain to be economically devastating in a period of rampant inflation. While progressive nationalization was shrinking the resources available from the private sector, the government systematically withdrew official and institutional advertising. Ambassador Davis has described other pressures used against opposition media and political parties:

> [S]piraling inflation produced officially-decreed wage and salary hikes every month. Bills for back taxes were presented under new interpretations of the law. Fire code and other violations were found against opposition newspapers and radios. When leftists seized and illegally operated the University of Chile's TV station, the authorities turned a blind eye. Import licenses and foreign exchange permits to import radio and television tubes and printing equipment were denied. Smaller radios and newspapers did go under — and were bought up by the parties of the government.

---

*Davis succeeded Edward Korry as Ambassador in October 1971 and served in that post until October 1973.

As for the parties, their expenses were in large part the costs of their media — newspapers, radios and publications — plus posters, campaign expenses, and of course salaries. They were vulnerable in the same ways the media were.

While opposition was being systematically throttled, the entire state apparatus was put at the disposal of Allende's party and its coalition partners. They received a subsidy in the form of a percentage of all foreign trade operations. Government transport, communications equipment, supplies of paper and printing facilities were made available to the ruling coalition — including the Communists — on a large scale and on generous terms. There was substantial assistance to the official parties from Cuba and other Communist countries.

Such were the ominous developments in Chile in the first year of Allende's term that led us to reexamine our covert action program. No effort to promote a coup was considered. What we sought was to help the democratic parties and groups to resist Allende's systematic efforts to suppress them. Our aim was to keep the opposition groups alive so that they might compete in the various elections provided by the Chilean Constitution and ultimately in the next Presidential election in 1976.

To that end, the 40 Committee* unanimously approved financial support for political parties or media threatened with extinction: $3.88 million was authorized in 1971; $2.54 million in 1972. (Actual expenditures were somewhat less.) A cynic might list this as a form of economic aid for Allende, since most of the funds wound up in the Chilean treasury in the form of confiscatory taxes and other exactions on the media we were helping. A small portion of the aid was earmarked for the "private sector," such as shopkeepers and labor unions, subject to the approval of Ambassador Davis. He decided against disbursement.

In the mania of investigation that followed Watergate, these actions have entered the folklore as a campaign to "destabilize" Chile — a word ascribed to CIA Director William Colby. The phrase was in fact the invention of Congressman Michael J. Harrington; neither Colby nor any other US official ever used such a term.[7] Indeed, it is wildly inaccurate. We believed then — I am convinced, correctly — that democratic institutions in Chile would have been destroyed without our assistance. We sought to maintain the possibility of another election. As Ambassador Davis has written:

In looking back on the experience of the opposition parties and media, some US commentators have engaged in circular argument. They have noted that, by and large, the newspapers, TV and radio of the opposition survived; and have

---

*The 40 Committee was the interagency committee supervising covert intelligence activities. It consisted of the Deputy Secretaries of State and Defense, the Director of Central Intelligence, the Chairman of the Joint Chiefs of Staff, the Assistant to the President for National Security Affairs, and intermittently the Attorney General.

concluded that we therefore need not have helped them. The real question is whether they could have survived without our help. I believe not. And institutional democracy could not have long survived their extinction.[8]

Chilean democracy was "destabilized" not by our actions but by Chile's constitutional President.

1972: The Accelerating Polarization of Chilean Politics

BEYOND the policy of helping Chile's democratic parties to survive the assaults on them, the United States government did nothing. We were confident that Chile's democratic tradition and processes would prevail if we could keep Allende from stifling them. And there was little continuing high-level attention to Chilean problems. No further NSC meetings were held on the subject. I was not deeply engaged in Chilean matters. The Senior Review Group, which I chaired, handled such issues as arose, mainly in response to the economic chaos and intensifying polarization of Chilean politics that Allende's policies were fomenting.

Salvador Allende had come into office as the leader of a coalition :alled Unidad Popular (UP, or Popular Unity). It consisted of the Communist Party; Allende's own Socialist Party, which lacked the tactical prudence of the Communists while sharing their ideology; and splinter groups for the most part even more radical and explicitly dedicated to revolutionary violence. (The coalition contained one small democratic left-wing party, the Radical Party, which split apart in 1971 as Allende's orientation became more obvious, with many of its leaders joining the opposition by early 1972.) The coalition never had a majority in the Chilean Congress. To govern, Allende needed the left wing of the Christian Democratic Party, which shared many of his socialist objectives without, however, giving up its dedication to Christian values and democratic processes. Allende thus faced a dilemma. If he adopted Christian Democratic methods he would alienate his radical wing, dedicated as it was to violent change of the existing order. If he failed to resist the violent tactics of his principal partners he would risk the support of the left-wing Christian Democrats and his ability to pass legislation through the Congress. Through incompetence, conviction, or overconfidence in his manipulative skills, Allende never faced up to that dilemma. He did not crack down on his revolutionary left wing. He acquiesced in their violent takeover of Christian Democratic radio stations and other enterprises. He failed effectively to oppose — indeed, he was suspected of encouraging — a mutiny of noncommissioned navy officers and illegal seizures of land by peasants in the countryside. Large quantities of arms were imported into Chile via the Cuban Embassy, outside the control of either the Chilean military or police.

Allende's policies thus drew the democratic parties together. It was he who unintentionally brought about the alliance between the right-wing National Party and the Christian Democrats, the absence of which in 1970 had made his own electoral victory possible. The absence of a Congressional majority for his increasingly radical policies in turn tempted Allende to resort to extraconstitutional legerdemain: physical occupation of enterprises, exploitation of ingenious loopholes to evade constitutional provisions, and the use of century-old laws for purposes never intended.

Polarization turned to confrontation toward the end of the first year of Allende's rule. The Chamber of Deputies impeached Allende's close confidant and Minister of the Interior, José Tohá Gonzalez, on the ground that he had failed to oppose the growing violence of extremist groups. The Chamber voted on January 6, 1972, to suspend Tohá from his post — an extraordinary procedure in a system based on separate, co-equal branches of government. On January 7, 1972, Allende showed his disdain for the Congressional action by merely switching Tohá to the equally important post of Minister of Defense. The government suffered a major electoral setback on January 16, when its candidates lost two by-elections, one for the Senate and one for federal deputy. In a memorandum to Nixon dated January 20, 1972, I summed up the implications:

It will almost certainly increase the polarization of Chilean society and political life which has been developing quite rapidly in recent months. The outcome will increase the confidence of the opposition parties and should demonstrate to them the benefits of cooperation. The results may also lead to a schism in Allende's UP coalition. The Socialists are likely to insist that the Government turn away from the democratic path it has followed up until now and take the reins of power into its own hands in order to impose a socialist revolution, by force if need be. However, the other two major parties in the UP, the Communists and the Radicals, as well as Allende himself, will probably be reluctant to do this out of fear of the Armed Forces, which have remained neutral and apolitical thus far but made clear that they will react sharply to any violation of the Constitution.

The prediction was only partially borne out by events. Allende continued his efforts to alter constitutional practices. By September 1973 the Congress and the Supreme Court had declared his administration outside the law and Constitution. They charged, in short, that the democratic process was being undermined by the constitutional President of Chile.

As Chile moved toward totalitarianism at home, it set a course for confrontation with the United States in its foreign policy. On January 1, 1972, Pablo Neruda, the poet who served as Chile's Ambassador to

France, charged that the United States was trying to overthrow Allende through economic pressures and encouragement of subversion. On January 3 Luis Herrera, the Chilean Ambassador to the OAS, on assuming the chairmanship of the OAS Permanent Council, spoke of the US–Latin American relationship as one of "serfdom in the economic, political, social and even cultural realms."

Chile was pursuing the policy that has since become standard among radical governments. On the one hand, it was assaulting American economic and political interests; on the other it denounced as "imperialism" our inevitable reaction to its provocation. Allende was acting — as have several other Third World leaders after him — as if he had a right to be subsidized by the United States in pursuing anti-American policies. He attempted, and even partially succeeded in, an extraordinary feat: to default on his debts, expropriate American companies without compensation, win a rescheduling of Chile's foreign debt, and at the same time maintain all previous aid and credit relationships with American and international lending institutions.*

Allende's actions produced the need for decisions, many of which were more significant for the light they shed on the balance of forces within the Administration than on our strategy toward Chile. There was, in fact, a gap between the internal rhetoric of the Administration and its actions. The language of our decisions was usually tough; the outcome of our actions, on the contrary, quite forthcoming.

Our reaction to Allende's repudiation of Chile's debt on November 9, 1971, illustrates this. Since Allende had repudiated almost all foreign debts, our actions had to be concerted with other creditor nations. A meeting of the creditors — in effect, the industrialized Western countries — was scheduled for early 1972 in Paris (informally called the Paris Club). As is too frequently the case, the United States's position was less the product of an overall strategic assessment than the uneasy result of interdepartmental feuding. For once, the conflict was not between my office and the State Department but between State and the Treasury Department, headed by the redoubtable John Connally, who was once again seeking to confirm his predominance in economic matters.

Connally had been appointed Secretary of the Treasury in December 1970 when Nixon, shaken by the unexpected Democratic success in the midterm Congressional elections, coopted the man whom he considered

---

*Chile reached tentative agreement with a group of private United States banks on February 9, 1972, on the refinancing of $300 million of its total foreign debt; this was the basis for new loans of $250 million and $50 million to cover public sector debts for 1972–1974 and the obligations of the Chilean Copper Corporation through 1976. Chile remained some $20 million in arrears to the US Export–Import Bank and $1 million in arrears to the US Agency for International Development (AID) and the Department of Agriculture.

the most formidable Democratic opponent for the Presidency. There was
no American public figure Nixon held in such awe. Connally's swaggering self-assurance fulfilled Nixon's image of how a leader should act;
he found it possible to emulate this conduct only in marginal comments
on memoranda, never face to face. As a result, Connally was spared the
maneuvers by which Nixon pitted his associates against one another.
Nor did Nixon ever denigrate him behind his back — a boon not granted
to many. He could identify with Connally, who had arisen from similar
humble origins without seemingly being driven by his insecurities.

I suspect that the difference was not in the existence of insecurities
but in the way Connally and Nixon handled them. Neither cherished
being challenged; neither was really quite sure of himself. But Connally
sought to cow opposition while Nixon's strategy was to outmaneuver it.
For Connally a victory was meaningless unless his opponent knew he
had been defeated; for Nixon the most exquisite triumphs were those in
which the victim did not know who had done him in, or maybe even
immediately that he had been done in.

It did not take Connally long to grasp that the combination of Nixon's
fear of confrontation and genuine admiration gave him a headstart in the
maneuvering that determines the pecking order of Presidential advisers.
He wasted little time before exposing the fragility of the vaunted White
House staff system by the simple device of refusing to submit his memoranda to the President through any White House Assistant. Fortunately
for my bureaucratic position, I had ceded my responsibilities for foreign
economic policy to Peter G. Peterson, my opposite number in the area
of international economics. Connally proceeded to give Peterson —
himself an able and strong man — a short course in the fact of life that
no Presidential Assistant can stand up to a strong Cabinet member determined to insist on his prerogatives. When he had something to take
up with the President, Connally would simply walk across the street that
separated the Treasury Department from the White House and insist on
an appointment. He personally delivered any memorandum in which he
was interested; he was prepared to demand an immediate reply. And
Nixon was incapable of turning down even a less formidable personality
to his face — this indeed was the reason for the staff system in the first
place.

By January 1972 Connally had defeated Peterson utterly for leadership in international economic policy and was ready to take on the State
Department. He used the identical methods. He personally brought to
Nixon's attention a memorandum implying that his opponents in State
were prepared to reschedule Chile's debt payments, that is, agree to
stretching them out, and that this in turn would stampede other creditor
countries into the same cowardly course. Connally argued that the real
purpose of the Paris meeting should be to isolate Chile.

All this was grist for Nixon's mill. It sounded tough. It confirmed his worst suspicions about the effete State Department. It had an anti-Allende thrust. He did not concern himself with the central contradiction of Connally's position: If the objective was to isolate Chile, we would have to overcome European reluctance about confrontation and the preference of our allies for rescheduling. If we insisted on being tough and opposing rescheduling, the chances were that it was the United States that would end up isolated.

Connally was aware of this, of course. His real point was to ensure that the Treasury Department would be in charge of our delegation so that "we fully protect our economic interests and keep the pressure on Chile." Nixon covered the memorandum with marginalia that any agreement to reschedule Chilean debt was "*totally* [Nixon's underlining] against my instruction" and that the isolation of Chile was our policy. How we could combine these objectives was not explained. In short order and without consultation with anyone (including me), a memorandum emerged from the Oval Office addressed to the Secretary of the Treasury with copies to the Secretary of State and me:

With reference to your [Connally's] memorandum of January 15, I hereby appoint Treasury to head the United States Delegation to Paris on the Chilean loan matter. Any suggestion, expressed or implied, that I favor U.S. support of an agreement to renegotiate the Chilean loan is in total contradiction to the views I have expressed on a number of occasions in various meetings on this matter with representatives of the departments involved.

As was usually the case with Connally, his actual conduct was far more subtle than his brutal insistence on prerogative. For one thing, State had made no such proposal as Connally alleged. He undoubtedly was not far off the mark in analyzing its predilections. But at this point we did not even know officially the attitude of the other creditors and had not yet taken a formal position. Moreover, Connally's insistence that we work with other nations to isolate Chile only clothed in the language of confrontation the course that I also preferred (and I suspect State too) as a matter of deliberate strategy. My view, as expressed in several staff memoranda, was that while we should take a strong line at the Paris talks, we should in the end act in concert with the other creditor nations. If we separated from them, Allende would be able to transform a repudiation of *all* foreign debts into a confrontation with "Yankee imperialism." This would rally patriotic support among the democratic opposition and the armed forces against the Yankee colossus. Allende would then be free to settle with his other creditors and cancel only his American debts, which constituted 60 percent of Chile's total foreign obligations. Much better, in my view, to develop a common front with the other creditors and to insist that Chile adhere to an agreed formula for renegotiating *all* its obligations. If the terms were unsatisfactory, we could always dissociate at that point.

Conversations with Connally confirmed that he agreed the United States should maneuver to bring about a consensus of the creditor nations so that the onus for a showdown would not fall on us. If the European nations insisted on rescheduling, we would go along. In short, for all the tough rhetoric, the decision was to postpone Chile's debt repayments — an indirect form of economic assistance.

While the debt talks proceeded in Paris, the Administration also continued to show public restraint. In a statement on January 19, 1972, Nixon reaffirmed that the law of the land as a result of the Hickenlooper amendment required that nations expropriating American property without adequate compensation could not receive new American aid. Nixon offered to work out, together with other interested nations, agreed criteria for what constituted just compensation. And on February 9, 1972, the President's annual Foreign Policy Report held out the olive branch once again:

Chile's leaders will not be charmed out of their deeply held convictions by gestures on our part. We recognize that they are serious men whose ideological principles are, to some extent, frankly in conflict with ours. Nevertheless, our relations will hinge not on their ideology but on their conduct toward the outside world. As I have said many times, we are prepared to have the kind of relationship with the Chilean Government that it is prepared to have with us.

This too was rebuffed. Allende seemed in the grip of his ideological zeal and that of his fanatical adherents. He continued the expropriation, in effect without compensation, not only of foreign but also of Chilean companies. In early January 1972, his government listed 53 firms subject to nationalization, with 38 others slated for a combination of state and private ownership. A month later (February 7), in a speech in Concepción, Allende vowed to nationalize another 120 companies over the coming year, to expropriate 2,000 farms, and to complete the state takeover of banking and foreign trade.

Meanwhile, the democratic majority in the Chilean Congress had become increasingly determined to resist Allende's policies. On February 19, 1972, the Chilean Congress passed a series of constitutional amendments attempting to restrict the state's right to take over the private sector. The measures, retroactive to October 1971, prohibited the government from expropriating any enterprise without specific authorization by Congress. On February 21, Allende announced that he would veto the bill. If Congress overruled the veto, he threatened, he would appeal to the Chilean Constitutional Tribunal (a special court on which a majority were his appointees). The opposition parties challenged Allende to hold a plebiscite on his plans for socializing the national economy.

The battle lines were now drawn. Allende was heading for a show-down both within Chile and in Chile's relations with the United States.

ITT and the Mounting Crisis

THE first explosion was triggered, strangely enough, by an American newspaperman. The syndicated columnist Jack Anderson published alleged internal documents of the International Telephone and Telegraph Company (ITT) outlining an effort in 1970 — nearly two years earlier — to prevent Allende's election as President. Anderson's column of March 21, 1972, claimed that on October 9, 1970, the head of ITT's Washington office, William R. Merriam, had reported to ITT director (and former CIA chief) John McCone that his CIA contact was "very, very" pessimistic about the prospects of "defeating Allende." Nevertheless, "approaches continue to be made to select members of the armed forces in an attempt to have them lead some sort of uprising. . . . Practically no progress has been made in trying to bring on economic chaos."

Anderson's March 22 column described a phone conversation of September 11 between J. D. Neal (ITT's director of international relations) and Viron P. Vaky, my NSC staff associate responsible for Latin America, in which Neal spoke of ITT President Harold S. Geneen's "concern about the Chile situation." Neal allegedly asked Vaky to tell me that ITT was "prepared to assist financially in sums up to seven figures." The Anderson column noted the "generally polite but cool reception" given this ITT initiative at the White House, by the NSC staff, and at the State Department, but went on to note its "more friendly" reception at the CIA.

I do not know how accurate the internal ITT documents were, but the thrust of Anderson's revelations about the NSC was true enough. I had, in fact, seen two officers of ITT in September 1970 at the request of Peter Flanigan, then a Presidential aide. They had offered financial assistance to an effort to prevent Allende's accession to office. I turned them away, politely, because I considered this sort of activity inappropriate for private enterprise.

But in the heated atmosphere of 1972, the Anderson columns added momentum to Allende's rush toward radicalization. The plan to which they referred had, in fact, never been accepted by the United States government — as indeed Anderson's columns made clear. Our governmental efforts in the same direction — of which Allende was presumably unaware — had been abandoned as well nearly two years earlier. Still, the Allende government wasted no time in seeking to implicate the democratic opposition in an alleged CIA–directed plot. On March 23, 1972, four marches were organized by the Central Labor Confederation (CUT) to support the government against "imperialist intervention." Exploiting the mood of nationalist indignation, ultra-leftist Interior Minister Hernán del Canto charged on March 28 (without producing any evidence) that right-wing conspirators — by implication abetted by the United States — had planned to assassinate Allende and seize power a few days before.

When the Chilean Congress reconvened, it voted on March 28 to appoint a thirteen-member commission to investigate the allegations of ITT interference in Chile in 1970. Opposition leaders, on the defensive now and angrily denying any dealings with the CIA, demanded that a commission also investigate another allegation by Anderson: that the Cuban Embassy in Santiago was a center for fomenting armed revolution. Jack Anderson, for a brief period, had become a central figure in Chilean politics.

On April 11, 1972, the NSC Senior Review Group met under my chairmanship to analyze Chilean developments. A paper prepared by my new NSC staff assistant on Latin American affairs, William J. Jorden, accurately summed up our policy:

We have sought to isolate Chile as much as possible politically and economically, while avoiding actions that would support the charge we are acting out of simple anti-Allende spite.

We have been working hard to get prompt and fair compensation for and debt repayment to American companies, and to protect the principle of the inviolability of repayment of just debts and compensation for nationalized properties.

So far, we have been able to pursue these goals simultaneously. However, the Anderson affair has raised our posture and brought into question our political motivation. More important, the Paris talks on renegotiation of Chile's debts force us to decide what blend we wish to make of "maximum pressure" and a "correct outward posture."

To deduce the trend of American policy from government documents, one must go beyond the analysis to the operational decision facing the senior officials. In this case it was not how to influence Chile's internal affairs; it was to decide the tactics for the next session of the Paris creditors. There was a dispute over whether we should seek binding arbitration of the expropriation disputes, particularly the compensation issue. This was favored by State, characteristically, because it would make a major contribution to international law. Treasury — for reasons no longer clear to me now — opposed putting forward arbitration as an American idea but was willing to accept it if it emerged as a Chilean proposal.

In the event, the outcome of the Paris talks was unaffected by the deliberations of the Senior Review Group. After all his tough talk, Connally accepted the strategy of not separating from the other creditor nations and not giving Allende an opportunity to saddle the United States with the onus for his debt problem. Connally went along with the consensus to reschedule Chile's debts (amounting to roughly $250 million). In return, Chile accepted the principle that its international obligations were valid, a minimum requirement if it wished to retain any creditworthiness.

Chile also agreed to negotiate nationalization problems with each affected country — but on the basis of two criteria that canceled each other out. Chile expressed a willingness to pay ''just'' compensation for nationalized property in accordance with both Chilean law (effectively meaningless since Chilean law provided for the retroactive excess profits tax that could take away whatever sum might be defined as ''just'' compensation) and international law (which Chile immediately declared contained no principles to cover expropriation). The practical result was that without any change in its policies Chile obtained relief from nearly all its debts due for one year — a form of economic aid exceeding any received in one year by the previous democratic government. Pending negotiation of specific bilateral agreements with each creditor nation, Chile continued to benefit from a de facto moratorium on debt repayments.

Nevertheless, Allende's domestic problems multiplied. The massive inefficiency of his administration and the galloping inflation promoted by his policies were eroding governmental stability and social cohesion with every month. Even a Communist Party leader, Orlando Millas, admitted in March 1972 that the central problem was how to make the nationalized enterprises operate ''with the same immense profits that they had used to give the capitalists.'' The fact was that expropriation seemed to magnify costs and reduce productivity. This in turn fueled inflation that reached an officially admitted annual rate of 163 percent in 1972 (and eventually climbed to 350 percent), with devastating impact on the economy and social fabric. Domestic political tensions reached such a point that at the end of March 1972 Allende suspended the Chilean Congress for a week.

All this happened while foreign assistance to Chile was in fact larger than during any earlier comparable period. The agreement to reschedule the $250 million of Western debts was accompanied by a steadily growing flow of credits from the Communist world. By the time Allende was overthrown, Communist credits had exceeded $600 million. And, contrary to the mythology, closer ties with the Communist world proved no obstacle to gradually improving economic relations with the West, with which Chile was again negotiating private credits. On June 12, Chile and a group of twenty-eight private American banks agreed to refinance

$160 million in Chilean debts.* American banks began to relax the restrictions they had imposed on short-term credits to Chile.[9] One day later the Chilean government announced a $100 million credit from Brazil, Mexico, Colombia, and Peru to be used for the purchase of capital and consumer goods.

Neither the debt relief nor the new international assistance stemmed Allende's rush toward confrontation with the United States. On April 13, he opened the third United Nations Conference on Trade and Development (UNCTAD) in Santiago with a passionate denunciation of the industrial nations — singling out the United States especially — for creating a world where "the toil and resources of the poorer nations pay for the prosperity of the affluent peoples." On April 14, Chilean Under Secretary of Foreign Affairs Anibal Palma, in a speech to the OAS General Assembly, accused us of trying to block development loans for Chile in multinational lending agencies and — contrary to the record outlined here — of frustrating Chile's efforts to win rescheduling of its debt payments. At a May Day rally, Allende charged that the United States was imposing an economic blockade against Chile. It was obvious that, regardless of what we did or did not do, Allende needed the demonology of a hostile United States to shore up support for the increasingly unpopular march toward his version of socialism.

Yet, if Allende's domestic problems were not caused by the United States, neither could they be exorcised by focusing frustrations on us. His essentially unconstitutional procedures produced a running battle with the Chilean Congress of a bitterness unprecedented in Chile's history. On July 5 the Chamber of Deputies voted to suspend Interior Minister del Canto for failing to enforce laws protecting private property and human rights, refusing to bring legal action against leftist agitators involved in land and factory seizures, and allowing the entry of thirteen mysterious crates from Cuba without proper customs inspection.[10] The government maintained they were personal gifts for Allende. The opposition charged they contained illegal arms.** The Senate held a special session on July 26 to discuss the issue and on July 27 voted (27– 14) to censure and oust del Canto. Thus for the second time the democratic parties in the Congress removed an Interior Minister for violating the Chilean Constitution and flouting Chilean laws.

The summer of 1972 completed the polarization of Chilean society.

---

*According to information released by the Chilean Embassy in Washington, repayment of three-quarters of the total debt (originally due in 1974) was delayed eight years and the payments due in 1972 and 1973 were reduced.

**After Allende's overthrow, documents revealed that the crates had contained over a ton of armaments. Government officials, including Allende, had repeatedly claimed the crates contained "works of art." Thus the Allende government was by March of 1972 already seeking to arm its supporters clandestinely.

In the guise of controlling inflation, Allende sought to push through tax increases whose practical consequence would be the expropriation of the middle classes and the nationalization of most of the remaining private sector. The Congress responded with measures to block these initiatives. Thereafter the government never seemed able to regain control over events. Every month from July 1972 until the September 1973 coup, prices increased while production declined. Dissension within the governing coalition and strong opposition from the legislature made it impossible for the government to pursue a coherent policy. The century-old Chilean tradition of civility between the government and the opposition parties came to an end. Relations between Allende and the judiciary collapsed after del Canto, on July 12, denounced the legislature and the judiciary for "collusion with the great imperialist interests." The Supreme Court responded with an open letter to Allende protesting the executive's actions.

The political process turned more and more into a test of strength between Allende and his opponents. On August 21, 1972, shopkeepers went on strike charging that inflation, the scarcity of goods, price controls, and other restrictions were forcing them out of business. Marches were held in Santiago and Valparaíso. After police clashed with the demonstrators Allende declared a state of emergency in Santiago province. The government denounced a "wave of sedition" by opposition groups and instituted a series of repressive measures. The Los Angeles radio station was closed by the government; there was a police crackdown against right-wing groups; controls were imposed on the activities of resident foreigners. The Christian Democratic Party laid the blame for the disruptions on Allende and his "erroneous and socially negative" economic policies. Concepción was placed under army control on August 31, when thousands of pro-Marxist youths battled with opponents of the government in the streets.

This slide toward chaos owed nothing to American intervention. We had no involvement through the CIA or otherwise with the strike leaders or protesting groups. We authorized no overt or covert assistance to them; we offered them no advice.

On September 14 Allende repeated his earlier charges that "fascists" were plotting against his administration, but he could name only one retired major who was in exile in Bolivia. Rumors that the military might step in continued to circulate throughout September and were explicitly denied on September 29 by the army commander-in-chief, General Carlos Prats Gonzalez, who pledged support to the government.

As the confrontation grew, the Chilean Congress passed three laws seeking to limit the government's nationalization program, to curb its assault on the media, and to halt its encouragement of terrorist activities. The first measure was a constitutional amendment to prohibit the expropriation of all landholdings under forty hectares (98.84 acres). A second bill provided public financing for the hard-pressed radio and press and guarantees against their expropriation. (This was prompted by the imminent bankruptcy of the Alessandri paper company, which had been allowed to raise its prices only 19 percent while having to absorb cost increases of 200–300 percent in mandatory salary increases. Another factor alarming the Congress was the government's closing of two opposition radio stations for alleged distortion of the news.) Allende vetoed the media bill.

The third crucial action by the Christian Democratic Party was the introduction of a law aimed at halting the illegal importation of arms by Allende's leftist supporters. The Arms Control Law gave broad powers to the armed forces to carry out searches and to prosecute violators in military courts. Although Allende had been expected to veto the bill and his own Socialist Party urged him to do so, he had no choice but to accept it. For starting in October 1972 he was faced with burgeoning strikes that he could end only with the assistance of the military, whose price for joining Allende's government this time was the new Arms Control Law.

By then Chile had fallen into a classic revolutionary pattern. At some point in the disintegration of authority, there is not enough force left for repression nor sufficient legitimacy to derive any benefit from concessions. In fact, after that stage is reached, repression as well as conciliation tends to accelerate the collapse: the use of force because it will prove inconclusive and concessions because they are ascribed not to a generous policy but to the strength of the opposition. So it was in Chile. Allende could assemble the force needed to deal with the strikes only by enhancing the role of the military on whom in turn the democratic opposition relied to curb the government's unconstitutional actions. When Allende yielded on the Arms Control Law, he encouraged other groups to press their claims. The method they chose was a strike aimed not at employers — indeed, some strikes were by employers — but against the government.

The most serious of these erupted on October 10, 1972, when the Confederation of Truck Owners called a nationwide walk-out to protest the government's announced intention to create a competing regional public trucking firm. It quickly snowballed into a popular protest against the government amounting to a general strike. The Christian Democratic Party backed the truckers; its National Council declared the government in violation of the Statute of Democratic Guarantees — the negotiated preelection Bill of Rights that had enabled Allende to take office. Among its conditions for resolving the conflict, the Christian Democrats listed effective guarantees of liberty of expression. On October 16, the Engineers' Association joined the strike, followed by bank employees, gas workers, lawyers, architects, taxi and bus drivers, doctors, and dentists.* The government established a curfew in twenty of Chile's twenty-five provinces and took over all the radio stations.

The strikes finally ended on November 5, but only at the price of a further enhancement of the role of the military. Four representatives of the armed services were brought into Allende's cabinet. The Interior Ministry responsible for public order was turned over to Army Commander General Prats, who had negotiated an end to the strikes. The breather proved to be shortlived.

In Washington, meanwhile, the 40 Committee had decided on October 26 to extend financial support to the democratic parties for the March 1973 Congressional elections. The sum of $1,427,666 was approved. Once again $100,000 was set aside for private-sector organizations (for voter registration efforts) subject to the approval of the Ambassador — approval that Ambassador Davis withheld. Eager investigators for a Senate Committee hostile to the CIA later struggled hard to find some violation of Washington's strict guidelines. They discovered exactly *one* diversion of $2,800 to striking truckers, "contrary to the Agency's ground rules."[12]

On October 17 the responsible NSC staffer, William Jorden, passed on to me the CIA's judgment that despite mounting chaos the odds were 60–40 against a military overthrow of Allende. Jorden, who had served in Washington for a long time (including a period as an assistant on President Johnson's NSC staff), added: "My experience is that 60–40 means you are certain something won't happen, but you don't want to be too wrong if it does." An interagency report came to the same conclusion. There would be no coup unless the government violated the constitutional order more unambiguously than heretofore.

Thwarted at home, Allende sought to restore his fortunes by departing on November 30 on a fifteen-day foreign trip that took him to Mexico, the United Nations, Algeria, the Soviet Union, and Cuba. He used the excursion to burnish his anti-American credentials and vent his usual anti-American themes. Addressing the Mexican Congress on December 1, he hit hard on ITT's alleged aggression against Chile. On December 4, he delivered a blistering attack on the United States to the United Nations General Assembly in New York.

Allende continued his anti-American campaign during his nineteen-hour stopover in Algiers. "Future relations between Algeria and Chile will be those of revolutionary friendship because we have the same

---

*According to one source, all the taxi drivers and most bus drivers were on strike. Strike leaders estimated that at its height, 100 percent of transport, 97 percent of commerce, 80 percent of professions, and 85 percent of the peasant cooperatives had joined in the strike, with the total on strike estimated at between six and seven hundred thousand Chileans.[11]

enemies," he declared. In Moscow he was warmly received by Soviet leaders from December 6 to 8. Premier Alexei Kosygin declared that Chile and Cuba were blazing a new path for Latin American socialism. President Nikolai Podgorny assured Allende that the USSR and all socialist countries supported Allende's "revolutionary renovation" in Chile. The final communiqué contained a Soviet pledge to continue political and economic aid to Chile.

In his spiritual home, Havana, Allende received an ecstatic welcome befitting the first head of a Latin American country to visit Cuba since Castro's rise to power. The joint communiqué celebrating the end of the visit on December 14 repeated the call for Latin American unity against "foreign economic exploitation and oppression," which it said sought to crush Latin America's "struggle for emancipation" — all codewords for a revolutionary anti-American crusade.

Unfortunately for Allende, travels in radical capitals did not translate into approval at home. On his return to Chile on December 14, Allende immediately faced charges by the opposition Christian Democrats that he was "leading Chile to a dependence on and a subordination to the Soviet Union." They demanded an investigation of all agreements concluded on the trip, calling them a dangerous threat to the economic future of Chile. The next stage in the struggle between the constitutional President bent on subverting the Constitution and the democratic opposition would be the Congressional elections scheduled for March 1973.

1973: Allende's Final Crisis

ALLENDE'S collapse overlapped Nixon's and it had the same doomed quality. In Chile in 1973, the intervals between governmental crises grew ever shorter. Allende reacted not by conciliation — perhaps he calculated that he had burned his bridges behind him; perhaps his even more radical allies on the left gave him no choice — but by speeding up the seizure of Chilean companies and muzzling the media — the actions that had triggered the convulsions in the first place. He behaved as if his only salvation was to drive matters out of control and then bend the resulting chaos to his will. The conflict turned more and more into a question of political life and death for all sides. It seemed to more and more people that either Allende had to go or democracy would collapse. On December 5, 1972, the highly respected former President, Christian Democrat Eduardo Frei, had opened his electoral campaign for the Senate by accusing the Allende government of bringing about a "catastrophic" situation, of seeking to divide Chileans irreconcilably, and of spreading hate and violence.

Frei's forebodings were soon borne out. On January 10, 1973, Allende announced a new system for the distribution of basic foodstuffs —

oils, rice, meat, sugar, coffee, and wheat — that amounted to government control over who could purchase these necessities, in what quantities, and at what prices. The plan assigned responsibility for retail distribution to "cooperating" neighborhood merchants. The system was to be run by Price and Supply Boards dominated by members of Allende's governing coalition. While participation in the plan was to be "voluntary," merchants and families outside it would not be able to purchase vital foods at the subsidized prices.

This was not only an assault on private enterprise; it amounted to a strict system of rationing. Inevitably, it led to a resumption of strikes. Equally predictably, Allende reacted by stepping up his abusive attacks on the United States. In part this was a device to rally support for his Congressional campaign. On February 5, Allende's coalition published a campaign platform proposing once again constitutional "reforms" he had offered unsuccessfully in November 1971, subordinating the legislature to Presidential dominance. Even more ominously, Allende began uttering threats of violence. He declared in a speech that if the democratic opposition persisted in its obstruction, the "Chilean revolution would be forced to abandon the democratic road and embrace physical violence as an instrument."

The Congressional elections on March 4, 1973, ended in a stalemate. Allende's coalition, with its predominant influence on the media, gained six seats in the Chamber of Deputies and two in the Senate. But its vote was still only 43.4 percent of the total. The democratic opposition's margin in both houses remained substantial (87 to 63 in the Chamber of Deputies and 30 to 20 in the Senate), though in the Senate it fell short of the two-thirds majority necessary to override presidential vetoes or to annul executive orders. In other words, Allende would be unable to implement his constitutional changes, but his opposition could not block his method of government. The practical result was to harden the battle lines.

From this stalemate Allende drew the astonishing conclusion that he was entitled to bypass the Congress and implement by executive order the more radical planks of his original electoral program. Two days after the elections he published an executive decree providing for a thorough reorganization and reorientation of primary and secondary education, of the private as well as the public school systems. The aim was, in the words of the Ministry of Education, "the construction of a new socialist society" and the "harmonious development of the personality of the young people in the values of socialist humanism." This crude attempt to politicize the educational system, with its clear totalitarian implications, had the practical consequence of uniting all of Allende's political opponents: the democratic political parties, the military, and for the first time the Catholic Church. And as so often before, Allende, in mid–

April 1973, yielded. The Minister of Education accepted the Church's request that the program be postponed pending full and open debate. To end an attempted usurpation by surrender inevitably weakened Allende's authority further.

In late April, demonstrations and strikes had spread to the provincial cities and to the copper mines. Violence broke out in the streets of Santiago. An incident outside the Christian Democratic headquarters gave Allende a pretext for the extraordinary step of closing down that opposition party's central office. On May 6 Allende declared a state of emergency in the province of Santiago, which remained in effect for twelve days. Workers, the supposed beneficiaries of Marxist policies, were in open confrontation with a socialist government, now the mine owner in consequence of nationalization.

On May 15, the National Assembly of the Christian Democratic Party accused the government of "seeking the totality of power, which means Communist tyranny disguised as the dictatorship of the proletariat." The statement promised to use "all [the Party's] power" to stop the government's "totalitarian escalation." Former President Frei, whose democratic credentials were beyond challenge, was elected President of the Senate. A Christian Democrat was chosen to preside over the Chamber of Deputies. The polarization of Chilean political life was symbolized by the refusal of Frei to attend when Allende presented his annual message at the opening session of the Congress.

No sooner had it resumed its session than the Congress began once again to impeach Allende's ministers for alleged violations of the Constitution. This extraordinary device of introducing the methods of a parliamentary democracy into a presidential system caused unending cabinet crises. On May 25 the Christian Democrats impeached Allende's Ministers of Labor and of Mines, charging them with precipitating the copper strikes. Congress also had suspended a number of regional administrators for leniency toward left-wing terrorism. While Allende sought to revolutionize Chilean society, the Congress attempted to dismantle his government.

All this occurred against the background of growing economic chaos. In the twelve months ending in May 1973, the cost of living in Chile rose by an almost unbelievable 238 percent; inflation was encouraged by the government as a means of expropriating the middle class; it triggered a new epidemic of strikes. On May 22 private bus owners stopped operations, demanding higher fares and relief from the severe shortage of spare parts. The government responded by requisitioning all buses.

On May 24, my staff aide Bill Jorden forwarded intelligence warnings that the Chilean military were plotting. Jorden thought that these reports should be treated with some skepticism, however: "This bears watching carefully, and we will be doing that. But in the meantime, I do not think we should get too excited. Above all, there should be no effort to involve the U.S. in these developments in any way.'' Jorden's recommendation easily carried the day. No one proposed any action and no action was taken; we had no dealings at any point with military plotters; there were no NSC meetings to consider the subject.

The only overture to the Chilean military during this period was as part of a military assistance package to key countries in Latin America. The purpose was to forestall the sale of Soviet arms. In a memorandum to Nixon dated May 15, I endorsed Secretary of State Rogers's recommendation to sell F-5E aircraft to major Latin American countries, including Chile:

Up to now they [the Chilean military] have resisted Allende's pressures on them to accept Soviet offers of credits for arms purchases. If we foreclose the possibility of Chile obtaining U.S. aircraft we could not only alienate the Chilean military but also give them no alternative but to yield to Allende's pressure to purchase Soviet equipment with a concomitant increase in Soviet influence.

Events in Chile developed a momentum of their own. On June 5, the forty-eighth day of the strike in the copper mines, the government was obliged to suspend foreign copper shipments — thus depriving itself of its principal source of foreign exchange. Street fighting broke out in Santiago again, and on June 15, Allende met with six strike leaders to dampen the violence. (That meeting was denounced by the leadership of the Communist and Socialist parties as appeasement.) There was more street violence in Santiago on June 15; sixty-three were injured as striking miners marched on the city. On June 20, thousands of students, teachers, and physicians struck in solidarity with the miners and in protest against the government's economic policies. The following day the Communist-led Central Labor Confederation organized a counterstrike in support of the government. Between the strike and the counterstrike, transportation and business ground to a halt, not only in Santiago but in Valparaíso, Concepción, and Arica as well. The armed forces had to be called out to quell violence.

On June 21 the government closed the prestigious newspaper *El Mercurio* for six days allegedly for ''inciting subversion'' by printing a National Party statement criticizing the President. Once again the measure proved more provocative than effective and underlined both Allende's growing weakness as well as his antidemocratic proclivities. The paper stopped publication for one day only because an appeals court overturned the lower court order. The government also tried to strip Senator Onafre Jarpa, president of the National Party, of his Congressional immunity. On June 25 the *New York Times* editorially warned against civil war, laying the major blame at the feet of Allende:

Chile Near the Brink

"Civil war must be avoided" declares President Salvador Allende, but his Marxist-dominated coalition perseveres with policies and tactics certain to accelerate the polarization that has pushed Chile close to the brink. The government's attempt, only temporarily successful, to close down the conservative but widely respected Santiago newspaper, El Mercurio, for carrying a National Party advertisement accusing Dr. Allende of violating the Constitution, is a case in point.

It will be a confession of bankruptcy in leadership if Dr. Allende, in order to head off a major explosion, brings high-ranking military officers into his Cabinet as he did briefly after paralyzing strikes last November.

Leaders and backers of Dr. Allende's Popular Unity Government rail incessantly against "fascists and traitors" but they cannot obscure the cardinal fact about the present crisis: it was precipitated by a bitter strike against the state-owned Copper corporation by workers at El Teniente mine, many of whom voted for Dr. Allende in 1970 and hailed his nationalization of copper. . . .

Sinister elements on the extreme right, including the fascist type youth organization Patria y Libertad, have exploited the El Teniente strike in an effort to paralyze government and provoke military intervention. But Dr. Allende could still isolate and disarm these forces if he would stand up to the radicals in his own ranks and invite genuine dialogue with his opponents in Congress, especially the Christian Democrats, on how to pull the country out of crisis and confrontation.

This approach would inevitably mean that Dr. Allende would have to forgo much of the pervasive socialist program for which he has no mandate in any case, but it might save Chile from either a military takeover or the civil war that the President rightly fears.

But Allende was not interested in a democratic dialogue. He was marching inexorably toward a fate that he both dreaded and invited.

The Military Begin to Move

O N June 29, 1973, forty-two years after the last previous military effort to oust a Chilean government, about 100 troops from the Second Armored Regiment attacked the Presidential Palace and the Defense Ministry in Santiago. Allende declared a state of emergency and loyal forces suppressed the rebellion in a matter of hours. Twenty-two people, mostly civilian bystanders, were killed and another thirty-four wounded in the fighting, which left the area a shambles.

So strong was the constitutional tradition in Chile that this violent shock brought disparate forces to the defense of the Allende government. The navy and air force commanders-in-chief gave Allende their immediate backing. The Christian Democratic Party also called for defense of the constitutional order. I summed up the aborted coup for Nixon at the end of the day: "All indications are that the coup attempt was an isolated and poorly coordinated effort. Most of the military leaders, including the commanders-in-chief of all three branches of the Armed Forces, remained loyal to the government."

Once again Allende reacted not by conciliation but by deliberately stepping up the pace of his radical policies. His government acquiesced in, if it did not encourage, the occupation of hundreds of enterprises by militants. The number of companies taken over by the government almost doubled in a single day from 282 to 526.[13]

On July 10, Bill Jorden transmitted the latest intelligence assessment: that another military coup was unlikely. Jorden's own judgment remained that we should continue our hands-off policy:

The US lacks powerful or reliable levers for influencing the final outcome. Continued encouragement of constraining forces within Chile and continuing economic pressures could have some limited impact. But a policy of open, all-out economic pressure would help Allende more politically than it could hurt him economically.

We followed Jorden's recommendations.

Still, Allende continued his collision course with disaster. He rejected the austerity program advocated by the International Monetary Fund that might have restored Chile's financial position. He would not declare a moratorium on expropriations, which might have patched up relations with the democratic opposition parties. And he disdained improved relations with the United States, which, while it had not caused his difficulties, was in a position to help ameliorate them.

A new wave of strikes broke out. The vicious circle of strike followed by government requisition started up again. On July 26, truck owners throughout the country struck. Allende ordered their trucks confiscated. On the same day, the Christian Democrats agreed to negotiate with Allende in order to ease tensions. Talks began on July 30. By August 1 the Party listed its demands in a letter to Allende: Paramilitary groups of both the extreme left and right should be disarmed; properties seized after the abortive coup should be returned to their owners; a constitutional reform bill should clearly delimit the private, mixed, and state sectors of the economy; and military officers should join the cabinet to provide "constitutional guarantees."

The same day a dozen private businesses and professional organizations joined ranks to form a "civic front" with the proclaimed objective of bringing down the Allende administration. By August 3 public transportation in Santiago was virtually at a standstill; the owners of buses and taxis had joined the strike of the private truckers. Employees of the Santiago waterworks also struck, and physicians and copper miners were threatening to do so. Allende denounced the wave of strikes as "seditious" and placed all public services under a state of emergency. He ruled out military participation in the cabinet. The Christian Democrats responded by declaring the talks with Allende ended.

Nothing symbolized better the collapse of Chile's constitutional order than the opposition demand that the military be included in the government as a guarantee of democratic practices. Even the leader of the Christian Democratic left wing — which in 1970 had supported most of Allende's social and economic goals — called for military participation so that conditions would be "normalized." On August 9, six days after having formally refused to do so, Allende finally yielded and brought the military into the cabinet. In this third cabinet reorganization of the year, General Prats, a former Interior Minister as well as army commander-in-chief, was appointed Defense Minister. Three other military leaders took over the portfolios of Finance, Transport, and Lands. Apart from the military members, the new cabinet had approximately the same political balance as the one it replaced — with three Socialists, three Communists, two Radicals, one independent, and other left-wing splinter party leaders.

It was an odd combination of revolutionaries and conservatives — and inherently unworkable. Allende's sole remaining card was to appeal to anti-American passions. The left-wing press began accusing the American Embassy in Santiago of backing the strikes and encouraging violence. An editorial in *Ultima Hora* on August 13 signed by former Interior Minister Hernán del Canto, recently removed by the Chilean Congress for failing to curb terrorism, charged that Ambassador Davis was helping finance the antigovernment agitation through the CIA. On August 15, bombs were discovered outside the homes of three American Embassy officials. Ambassador Davis received assurances that attacks on American diplomats would not be tolerated, but on August 21 the Communist newspaper *El Siglo* continued the charges of a foreign conspiracy against Chile's independence and sovereignty.

Allende was trapped. He could not defy his critics without the support of the military; yet he would not abandon his radical program that the military had joined the government to brake. Prats, his government's most loyal military supporter, was obliged to resign as both Defense Minister and army commander-in-chief by restive military colleagues one day after the Chamber of Deputies passed by 81 to 47 a resolution accusing the government of "constant violations of the fundamental rights and guarantees established in the Constitution." Once again the Chamber asked that the Defense Ministry "direct the government's action" in order to guarantee democratic institutions. The President of the Christian Democratic Party, Patricio Aylwin, echoed the demand.

The impending coup of September 11 was thus in a sense invited by the recently elected Chamber of Deputies and Chile's leading democratic party.

The Coup

THROUGH all this turmoil Chile was a peripheral concern of Washington policymakers. It was eclipsed by the Year of Europe, the Soviet summit, the Middle East. Decisions were made only as they were forced by events, and were almost invariably related to economic issues, such as the periodic debt rescheduling meetings of creditor nations or the bilateral debt talks that stalled in March 1973. On those matters Treasury was the dominant agency, and its primary interest was to defend economic principles: compensation for the expropriations and the avoidance of a precedent-setting default. The 40 Committee continued to confine our covert assistance to financial support of democratic political parties and media threatened with extinction.

That no senior official considered a coup likely is shown by the fact that as late as August 20, 1973, the 40 Committee approved — by telephone vote — another $1 million to support Chile's democratic parties through mid-1974. Of the approved amount, $225,000 was allocated for private-sector organizations subject to Ambassador Davis's approval. Once again, as was the case with the funds set aside by the October 26 decision, the Ambassador withheld approval. On August 25, CIA Director Colby sought to bypass the Ambassador by requesting authority from the White House to channel some of the funds to the strikers. On August 29 Bill Jorden recommended disapproval:

> The Ambassador believes (correctly) that present U.S. policy is to keep the pressure on, but not to take action in overthrowing Allende. He believes the new proposal would move us toward the latter.

I agreed with Jorden. No action was taken on Colby's recommendation; it was never even forwarded to the President. Events soon made it irrelevant.

Seventy-two hours before the explosion — on Saturday, September 8 — I met Nathaniel Davis for the first time. This encounter has entered the mythology of American culpability as a conspiratorial meeting to fine-tune the plot against Allende. The truth is that my appointment with Davis had nothing to do with Chile at all. After I was nominated as Secretary of State on August 22, I asked for a list of the ablest senior State Department officers for possible elevation to key positions. Davis's name appeared on that list. Since I had never met him, I asked the State Department to invite him for an interview. I suggested the weekend of September 8–9 because it was the first free moment after my return to

Washington from San Clemente. Davis was told to pick another date if that proved inconvenient or if his presence was required in Santiago.

The subject of our meeting was internal State Department organization and personnel. It resulted in my appointing Davis Director General of the Foreign Service. Before turning to my principal concern, however, I asked him to bring me up to date about Chile. Davis emphasized that Chile was sliding toward crisis; there was a growing chance of a military coup. Less certain was whether a coup would result in a pro-Western nationalist regime like Brazil's or a Third World radical regime like Peru's. The military might yet back off at the last moment. In that case — and perhaps in any event — Allende might succeed in establishing a Cuban-type dictatorship. I speculated that if Allende were forced to resign, the Senate President, Eduardo Frei — for whom we had high regard as a patriot and a democrat — would take over according to the Chilean Constitution. Davis warned that if the military did overcome their inhibitions against a coup, they would not give up power in a hurry. He was prescient.

I told Davis to keep the American Embassy out of the developing crisis. He emphasized that his "firm instructions to everybody on the staff are that we are not to involve ourselves in any way." Davis stuck to that resolve meticulously. Because of the retroactive importance that has been (erroneously) given to this meeting, I have placed the transcript of the Chilean portion of the conversation in the backnotes.[14]

That conversation leaves no doubt of the state of our knowledge and of our intentions immediately before the coup. We were aware of what was well known to every Chilean, including Allende: that the military who already controlled key positions in the government were seriously considering the takeover that had been virtually invited by the Chamber of Deputies and the President of the Christian Democratic Party. But we were unaware of any specific plan or date. And we were party to none.

The move came at approximately 6:30 A.M. on September 11, 1973. Opposition radio stations broadcast a proclamation by the commanders-in-chief of the army, air force, and national police and the chief of naval operations calling on President Allende to resign immediately. The commanders declared that the armed forces and the police were united in their fight against Marxism and against an incompetent government that was leading the country to chaos. They assured the workers that their social and economic gains would be maintained. All pro-government media were ordered to stop broadcasting.

Allende arrived at the Presidential Palace at 7:30 A.M. with a heavily armed escort. On nationwide radio he refused to resign; he called upon workers to occupy their factories and mount resistance. After the air force bombed the Presidential Palace, army troops entered it around noon. They found Allende dead. Our Embassy conveyed to Washington the report that he had committed suicide, apparently with a submachine gun that had been a gift from Fidel Castro. I am unable to assess the contrary allegations which have been made.[15]

I have described Allende's fall in some detail as a case history of political mythology. In some quarters our alleged "destabilization" of Chile has become the code word for all that they consider baleful in American policy. The only difficulty is that nothing of the sort took place. It was not the United States but Allende's own government, aided by Cuba, that plotted paramilitary insurgency and subversion, supplying arms clandestinely to the radical Communist element. What we did was fund free newspapers and political parties that sought our help against a heavy-handed, calculated campaign to suppress them before the next election.

The United States was hardly the crucial determinant of events. It was Allende who brought the economic and political system so close to breakdown by 1973 that our Ambassador withheld our subventions to the private sector for fear of being blamed for the inevitable collapse. Perhaps the most astute postmortem on Allende was expressed by that old revolutionary veteran, Chinese Premier Zhou Enlai, who was strongly sympathetic to Allende's Marxist experiment. On my visit to China a few months after Allende's death, Zhou told me he had urged Allende to go slower, to be less doctrinaire. But Allende had systematically ignored Chinese advice:

We told them about [the risks], but they didn't believe us. That kind of phenomenon was caused by themselves. . . . . I only wrote one letter to President Allende, asking him not to do too many things in [a] hurry. It only concerned economic problems, that they should make preparation beforehand. They shouldn't do everything at one go; they should take steps. They should not promise too many things to people; otherwise, they would not be able to honor these things. Because we believe the life of the people can only be improved on the basis of production. Whenever one speaks of Socialism, also think of welfare. And my letter to President Allende was carried in the newspaper, but it was useless because the word of a foreigner meant nothing.

Either by design or through the dynamics of his radical coalition — most likely a combination of both — Salvador Allende had by 1973 produced such a polarization in Chile that it could end only in one of two ways: a Cuban-style dictatorship or a military government. All the democratic parties had come to the same conclusion, though they no doubt underestimated the eagerness of the military, once it had abandoned its historic stance as guardian of the Constitution, to maintain itself in power. The Chilean junta was triggered into action by incipient chaos and the pleas of the democratic parties. It moved, and from all the evidence with extreme reluctance, only when it felt it had the support of the majority of Chileans. When it took on political responsibility its political inexperience, if not naiveté, became apparent — though one should not lightly dismiss its basic judgment that the existing party structure, having brought Chile to the brink of civil war, was unlikely to be able to overcome the conditions that had made military intervention necessary.

It is important to remember what so dedicated a democrat as former President Frei said immediately after the military coup:

The military have saved Chile and all of us whose lives are certainly not as important as Chile's, but they are human lives, and many, and all of them are not yet safe because the armed forces continue discovering hideouts and arsenals. A civil war was being well prepared by the Marxists. And that is what the world does not know, refuses to know.[16]

Washington Reaction

As it happened, the coup occurred in the middle of my confirmation hearings for Secretary of State. This slowed down American responses; it did not affect our ultimate attitude.

A meeting of the Washington Special Actions Group (WSAG) was called for the next morning, September 12. William Colby's briefing, which began the meeting, was extremely cautious but on the mark. Colby characterized General Augusto Pinochet, the coup leader, as a heretofore not especially forceful officer with a reputation for being pro-American. Colby correctly predicted that the military would insist on fundamental changes in the political system. Their distrust of civilian politicians made early elections highly unlikely. He predicted that the junta would not reverse all of Allende's social programs but would permit a gradual return to private ownership. In foreign policy, Colby expected an end to invective against the United States and a mellowing of Allende's Third World stance. The new government was breaking relations with Cuba and had expelled 150 Cubans.

Against this background, the WSAG turned to operational questions: Should we recognize the junta? What should be our attitude to Chilean requests for aid, either economic or military? And what public position should we take toward the new regime? As is often the case in the midst of upheaval, two random, accidental decisions preoccupied the policymakers. There was the problem of what to do about the imminent visit to Chile of a US Air Force stunt-flying team and a US naval exercise on the high seas off the coast of Chile and Peru — both events scheduled months before. The consensus of the WSAG undoubtedly was relief at Allende's overthrow (though not his death). We were conscious of the danger that we might be blamed for both. In the post-Vietnam, Watergate atmosphere, the United States had to bend over backward to avoid charges of American complicity in an event that everyone in the room considered in our national interest.

With this in mind, the WSAG advised the President that the issue of diplomatic recognition be muted. As a general proposition we recognize countries, not governments. Practically, however, we would do our utmost to avoid being among the first to acknowledge and deal with the new government. We would, as I wrote the President, favor "a low-key posture to allow time for Latin American governments and possibly some Europeans to announce the continuation of their relations." Such a course, I argued — with wild optimism — would "defuse any charge of our implication which would not only be damaging to us but more importantly to the new Chilean government." We recommended, however, that Ambassador Davis inform the new Chilean authorities discreetly and through an intermediary that our basic disposition was favorable. The delay in formal recognition, they should understand, was in our mutual interest.

With respect to economic aid, an interagency task force was assigned to anticipate requests from Chile and propose suitable responses. We decided routinely to fulfill the military supply obligations undertaken while Allende was in office. As to the stunt fliers, we would let the Chilean government decide whether it wanted the visit to go forward. (It did not.) The naval exercise was canceled and the US Navy ordered to stay away from the Chilean coast even beyond Chile's territorial waters. The Joint Chiefs of Staff representative objected, reasonably enough, that we could not forgo our rights to use of the high seas near every country that had undergone a revolution. To defend ourselves against the expected charge of complicity, the WSAG requested the CIA to prepare a list of all its activities in Chile over the past three years — an assignment that would hardly have been given had we planned the coup. The list would enable us to rebut inaccurate charges and to assure ourselves there had not been any unauthorized action that might be used to implicate the United States. The CIA turned up no such event. This did not, however, prevent the charges.

The first contact between the military junta and United States officials occurred the day after the coup, on September 12, when General Pinochet initiated a secret meeting with the head of the US Military Assistance Advisory Group.* Pinochet stressed, as I reported to Nixon, that

---

*The date is not certain. My memorandum to the President reporting the conversation is dated September 19. The first draft of the memorandum, prepared by NSC staff aide Bill Jorden, is dated September 12. I cannot explain the long interval except by my preoccupation with my Senate confirmation hearings.

"he and his colleagues had not even hinted to us beforehand of their planned action and said he thought it had been better that way." The junta's fundamental desire was to restore the traditional ties of friendship with the United States. Chile needed help with food and one year's debt relief. My report concluded:

> Pinochet understands and is relaxed about the matter of recognition. He volunteered that obviously the U.S. should not be the first to announce its intention to continue relations with the new Chilean Government. He also recognized the advisability of avoiding too much public identification with us for the moment.

On September 13, I reported to Nixon that the Christian Democratic Party and the Social Democratic Party had issued statements supporting the junta, as had the President of the Supreme Court. The WSAG met again on September 14. The key question was what assistance the United States could provide the new regime without becoming tarred by repressive actions it might take.

No specific decisions were reached at the meeting. I resisted pressures from William Simon, then Deputy Secretary of the Treasury, to "use the coup as a bargaining point" to settle the expropriation and debt issues. To do so, I argued, might make the new government appear to be the tool of the economic interests of multinational companies.

The pattern of ambivalence continued throughout September. At a WSAG meeting of September 20, we sidestepped a Chilean request for 1,000 helmets and 2,000 flares for night-fighting. But it was decided to announce on September 24 that the United States considered its relationship with the government of Chile to be a "continuing" one — which amounted to a recognition of the junta. By then Brazil, Argentina, Peru, Mexico, France, and Switzerland had already extended some form of recognition. Delay had thus served our strategy of not being out front. Self-interest, too, may have been the handmaiden of good policy. Nobody was eager to complicate my confirmation as Secretary of State.

Similar ambivalence marked our response to Chile's requests for economic aid. Ambassador Davis was authorized to inform the Chilean government that we would assist with emergency food and medical supplies. We were prepared to discuss middle- and long-term economic needs. The WSAG decided to send a team to assess those needs if the junta requested it.

The junta was meanwhile tightening its grip. On September 21, it outlawed the Marxist political parties and declared the non-Marxist parties to be "in recess." On September 25 it abolished the pro-Allende Central Labor Confederation, removed all mayors and city councilmen, and shortly thereafter took control of the universities by replacing the rectors with military delegates.

On September 27, the junta appealed to the International Monetary Fund and the World Bank for assistance to rescue Chile from "the brink of bankruptcy." It promised to "create the conditions that will form an environment in which external assistance can prove effective." On September 28 the new Foreign Minister, Rear Admiral Ismael Huerta, declared Chile's willingness to resume negotiations on compensation for American copper companies whose Chilean properties had been nationalized. Agencies administering food and price controls were abolished, and the government pledged to restore lands illegally expropriated under Allende. The Chilean escudo was devalued by 143 percent.

We continued to walk our tightrope, trying to balance our conviction that developments within Chile were geopolitically in our national interest with our view that too ardent an embrace might embarrass us domestically with the Congressional majority, always suspicious of conservative governments. Publicly we maintained some distance from the military government; privately we responded to several of its requests. On October 1, I told my State Department staff:

that so far as the new government of Chile is concerned, we should not support moves against them by seeming to dissociate ourselves from the Chileans and on the other hand should not be in a position of defending what they are doing in Santiago.

In accordance with this, it was decided the following day that Foreign Minister Huerta, who was in New York for the UN General Assembly, should not be excluded from the Secretary of State's luncheon for the heads of the Latin American delegations on the ground that his government was not yet fully recognized; he should be seated in accordance with regular protocol. And I agreed to meet Huerta during his stay in the United States. That all these matters should have required formal decisions was a reflection of the atmosphere of the times in which the overthrow of a radical government by its own people would be almost ritualistically ascribed to America's pernicious influence.

Our meeting took place on October 11. A naval officer of great courtesy but no experience in diplomacy, Huerta was genuinely baffled on how to deal with this strange country whose press and Congress were increasingly antagonistic to a friendly government in Santiago while they had largely ignored, or been mildly sympathetic to, a Marxist predecessor explicitly whipping up anti-American radicalism throughout the Western Hemisphere. He was convinced that the Chilean military had saved Chile from a totalitarian regime and the United States from an enemy — and he was right in both judgments. When I warned that Chile would pay a heavy price in its international image if it resorted to brutal repression, he replied that his government's first priority was to control the "internal situation." I stressed that we considered the new government basically in our interest but that I would feel free to call to his attention actions by the junta that might weaken its international standing — a delicate way of raising the human rights issue.

It soon emerged that there were major obstacles to assisting the new Chilean authorities. To be sure, loans from private banks increased sharply as the expropriation issues were settled and the austerity program began to take effect. But the intensity of feeling against military governments in the post-Vietnam, Watergate Congress made it very hard to obtain governmental aid. The Commodity Credit Corporation loaned $24 million to replace food shipments from Eastern Europe and the Soviet Union that had been turned around on the high seas on the day of the coup. (This gave dramatic proof of the political motivations of Soviet aid programs.) In mid-November, our Department of Agriculture granted Chile an additional loan of $28 million. For the rest, we relied primarily on the PL–480 food program as a vehicle for meeting Chilean needs. Food assistance was less controversial since it would go to the hungry and because the Administration had considerable discretion in allocating it.

Ironically, the Nixon Administration was reluctant to carry out agreements on military supply even when they had been made with Allende's government, lest they cause an explosion in Congress jeopardizing our entire foreign aid program. For this reason the delivery to Chile of three destroyers — promised to Allende! — was delayed by several weeks until the foreign aid bill had passed.

A Chilean economic delegation arrived in Washington on December 12, and on December 21 State and Treasury announced that an agreement had finally been signed rescheduling Chile's debt payments to the United States (totaling $124 million) for the period from November 1971 through December 1972. Chile began making payments in accordance with the new schedule. It reiterated its commitment to fulfill all the provisions of the creditor nations' agreement of April 1972 and, in particular, its intention to negotiate with the companies on just compensation for nationalized properties. Rescheduling of Chile's debt for 1973 and 1974 was to be taken up at a meeting of the Paris Club in February 1974.

All of these maneuvers obscured the fundamental problem: How was the United States to reconcile its geopolitical interests and its concern for human rights? It would be idle to deny that we felt a sense of relief at Allende's collapse. The new Chilean government, whatever its faults, would not assault our interests in every international forum as its predecessor had done. It would not be a haven for terrorists from all over the world threatening to solidify totalitarianism in Chile and to subvert neighboring Western Hemisphere governments. We could not convince ourselves that undermining the new government would serve either the cause of human rights or our own security. Yet there was no blinking the fact, either, that the very opposition parties and newspapers that we had attempted to keep alive under Allende were suppressed by the junta. The imposition of an authoritarian regime in a country with the long-standing democratic tradition of Chile was a special pity — but the circumstances that brought it about were extraordinary, too.

Unfortunately, the issue arose in America at the worst possible time. In the aftermath of Vietnam and during Watergate, the idea that we had to earn the right to conduct foreign policy by moral purity — that we could prevail through righteousness rather than power — had an inevitable attraction. There was a mood of resignation from the world of hard tactical choices, reinforced by the historical American animus toward the concept of equilibrium. It was not the first time in our history that the aversion to power politics took the form of a moral crusade. And the fetid climate of Watergate endowed the charge of the Administration's moral obtuseness with a certain credibility.

Chile thus became caught up in a domestic debate transcending it; it had to carry the burdens of Watergate as well as of Vietnam. The Nixon Administration was not so insensitive to the Chilean junta's clumsy and occasionally brutal practices as our critics alleged. But we considered that the change of government in Chile was on balance favorable — even from the point of view of human rights. We were therefore prepared to give the military leaders a chance; we made repeated private approaches to ease their methods. There is no doubt that our insistence on quiet diplomacy weakened our case at home even as it succeeded with Chile in many individual cases. It is equally true that many of our critics were retroactively blind to the totalitarian implications of Allende's policies, ignored the danger of his alliance with Cuba and the Soviet Union, invented a role for us in bringing him down, and acted as if overthrowing the junta was now the sole valid national objective.

Within weeks of Allende's overthrow, his incompetence, corruption, and violation of democratic procedures — all widely acknowledged while he was alive — disappeared from public comment. There was recurring reference to Allende as a "democratically elected leader," with nary a mention that he never had a majority mandate to impose the transformation that he was attempting; that his antidemocratic policies, had they succeeded, would have meant the end of Chile's constitutional system; and that he was viciously hostile to the United States.

The new plight of the democratic parties in Chile under the junta shifted the focus, blotting our historical memory. The continuing roundup and detention of civilians in Chile was a source of much anguish, particularly for us. Although several American citizens were known to be detained at the National Stadium in Santiago, our Embassy officials were denied access to them. Other Americans were reported missing; some died. Unofficial estimates of the total number of prisoners ranged from 3,500 to 20,000. Rumors of torture were widespread. The impression was being created that all arrests were arbitrary; there was no reference to the thousands of revolutionaries imported and armed by Allende and his associates.

On September 22, the junta confirmed that high officials of the former Allende government were being held at a naval base prison on Dawson Island. Communist Party Secretary General Luis Corvalán was also arrested, which generated immediate international pressures on his behalf. Even UN Secretary-General Kurt Waldheim, at the request of the Soviet UN delegation, later made an appeal for Corvalán's life. This was a symptom not of Waldheim's sympathies but of the double standard of the dominant group in the United Nations; there was no similar appeal on behalf of the victims of Iran's later revolution, who were far more numerous and far more badly treated. Ironically, it was the United States that obtained Corvalán's release three years later in the exchange for the Soviet dissident Bukovsky.

On September 26, two days after the United States announced that it considered its diplomatic relations with Chile to be "continuing," Chile released six American citizens arrested during the coup. Two appeared two days later at hearings held by Senator Edward Kennedy's subcommittee on refugees to relate claims that they had heard, but not witnessed, the execution of several hundred prisoners in the National Stadium in Santiago. Senator Kennedy deplored the Nixon Administration's "policy of silence." On October 2, he proposed an amendment to the Foreign Assistance Act stating that it was the sense of Congress that the President should cut off aid, other than humanitarian assistance, to Chile "until he finds that the government of Chile is protecting the human rights of all individuals, Chilean and foreign — as provided in the Universal Declaration of Human Rights."

The Foreign Assistance Act as finally approved by the Congress in December 1973 did not contain this provision but did include a request that Nixon call on the Chilean government to respect human rights. Senator Kennedy mounted another effort to cut off aid to Chile in 1974. Both houses of Congress voted in December 1974, in the foreign assistance legislation for 1975, to end all American military aid to Chile "unless the President reports to Congress that Chile is making fundamental improvements in the observance of human rights." By 1976 all aid to Chile was effectively cut off — a step never taken against Allende.

The Chilean junta was being judged with exceptional severity while it faced near–civil war conditions. It probably continued authoritarian practices for too long, but two questions remain: Was it America's duty to single out Chile for the harassment to which it was subjected, far exceeding in scope anything ever undertaken against Allende? Was there not involved a double standard that continued to be demonstrated at an ever-accelerating pace throughout the 1970s? No radical revolution, no matter how bloody — one thinks of Cuba, Iraq, Algeria, many African states, Vietnam's occupation of Indochina, Khomeini's Iran — has confronted the worldwide press campaign and the global indignation evoked by the clumsy authoritarians of Santiago. Was its crime in its methods, or its position on the right of the political spectrum? Was its sin the lack of civil freedoms, or the abandonment of the leftist embrace? Why is the argument so widespread that left-wing governments like Nicaragua's are supposed to be moderated by economic assistance while conservative governments like Chile's must be reformed by ostracism? The socialist government of Sweden cut off aid to Chile on September 13, within forty-eight hours of the coup, before its implications could possibly be known. Had it ever acted with such alacrity, or at all, against left-wing tyrants? Indeed, it had lavished aid on Hanoi throughout the Vietnam war and afterward.

I do not mean to condone all the actions of the junta, several of which I consider unnecessary, ill-advised, and brutal. Nor do I question the humane motivation of many of its critics. But it did inherit a revolutionary situation in which government-sponsored violence played an important role. A serious analysis must come to grips with these issues.

In the domestic anguish through which we went, it was impossible even to pose such questions. We were being driven much further on a course of isolating Chile than we thought wise. As with the Jackson amendment, we were convinced that our methods would have produced an easing of the situation more rapidly without running the risk of driving the junta toward anti-American nationalism or collapsing it in favor of the totalitarian left.

More pressing events — above all, the Middle East war — turned Chile into a secondary issue. The junta solidified itself. The United States Congress imposed increasing restrictions. In June 1976, I attended an OAS General Assembly in Santiago and delivered a major speech on human rights. The state of human rights in Chile did ease without becoming satisfactory; it was far more acceptable than in many radical left-wing regimes that have escaped censure. The world fashionably condemned the junta — and the United States — conveniently forgetting that Allende's ambitions and incompetence, not American imperialism or the generals' lust for power, brought about the breakdown of the constitutional system. In the theology of the left, Allende's collapse *had* to be the malign work of others.

But over time, Chile gradually faded as a major issue both in American public opinion and for American policymakers. History, evolution, and the spirit of the Chilean people would determine the future of Chile's institutions, and with it that country's relationship with the United States.

X

Becoming Secretary of State

Crisis of the Executive

ONE of the more cruel torments of Nixon's Watergate purgatory was my emergence as the preeminent figure in foreign policy. Richard Nixon wanted nothing so much as to go down in history as peacemaker. He had organized his government so that he would be perceived as the fount of foreign policy, in conception and execution. To this end he had insisted on launching all major international initiatives from the White House; he had excluded the State Department and Secretary of State William P. Rogers relentlessly, and at times humiliatingly, from key decisions.[1] I was his principal instrument because I seemed ideally suited for a role behind the scenes. As a Harvard professor, I was without a political base; as a naturalized citizen, speaking with an accent, I was thought incapable of attracting publicity; in any event, since I was a member of the President's entourage, my access to the media could be controlled by the White House.

In the beginning things had worked out as Nixon planned. My office dominated the policymaking process; several sensitive negotiations were entrusted to me. It was not true, as was later alleged, that the complex interdepartmental machinery of the National Security Council was designed to generate busywork for the bureaucracy while the real business of our foreign relations was conducted through my office. We were neither so farsighted nor so devious. The interdepartmental machinery was applied to real problems; it was designed to elicit the best thinking within the government and to define the range of choices available to the President. The final decision was often made alone by Nixon or in consultation with me; but though the bureaucracy did not participate in the decision it played — paradoxically — a major role in the process of reaching it. For the options produced by it were the raw material of our deliberation.

At the outset, too, my office was conducted with the anonymity that Nixon had desired. When I dealt with the media it was invariably at Nixon's request. I briefed the press occasionally, usually in connection with major Presidential speeches or actions and always on "background'' — the ground rule according to which the briefer could be identified only as a ''senior White House official.'' I had great influence but not prominence.

Three events brought me into public view. The revelation in July 1971 of my secret trip to China and in January 1972 of my secret negotiations on Vietnam appealed to the American sense of adventure and perhaps to the nation's yearning to shape a hopeful future even in the midst of national division. The *Washington Post* accelerated the emergence of a public persona by refusing to honor background rules (a fit of puritanism from which it later recovered): It insisted on identifying me as the official spokesman, even when I briefed on background. And when I appeared on live television for the first time in October 1972 to present the breakthrough in the Vietnam peace negotiations, a wide audience witnessed the dramatic disclosure that a decade of anguish was ending.

So against all expectations — and indeed against Nixon's desires — I had become by the start of the second term something of a public figure. Since Nixon had not wanted a strong Secretary of State, it could never have crossed his mind that he would wind up with a security adviser having a constituency of his own. In normal times my newfound prominence would almost surely have speeded my departure from government. No ordinary President would have accepted such a state of affairs, least of all one so jealous of his public image as Nixon. Throughout 1972, the President and Haldeman missed few opportunities to reduce my visibility, to dissociate from me when I was involved in controversy, and to demonstrate my dependence on Presidential favor. It was one of the reasons, as I have pointed out in Chapter I, why I began Nixon's second term firmly determined to resign by the end of 1973.

All this was changed by Watergate. Once the erosion of executive authority set in, my resignation would have compounded difficulties and added to the impression of disarray. It would have been irresponsible to leave when all hands were needed to stabilize the ship of state. Nor were there White House pressures to do so. In fact, the relationship between Nixon and me improved subtly. Nixon no longer insisted on keeping me in the state of insecurity that he had fancied was essential to my sense of proportion.[2] He had never been willing to engage personally in the petty harassment by which this strategy was implemented, and with Alexander Haig installed as chief of staff he now lacked subordinates prepared to do it for him. Nor did Nixon retain the nervous energy to play the little games that generally so delighted him, designed to exploit, and if necessary to generate, tensions between Rogers and me, so that both of us had to appeal to him or Haldeman for support. Nixon's attention span for foreign policy was also declining. He would sign memoranda or accept my recommendations almost absentmindedly now, without any of the intensive underlining and marginal comments that in the first term had indicated he had read my papers with care. He stopped engaging me in the long, reflective, occasionally maddening conversations that were his means of clarifying a problem in his own mind. Increasingly, he went through the motions of governing, without the bite or the occasional fits of frenzy with which in more normal times he had driven issues to decision and steeled himself for a characteristic act of courage.

My position was thus at the same time unprecedently strong and precarious. On the one hand, there were no competitors in the White House for the attention of a distracted and discredited President. The senior staff, instead of vying for the President's favor, sought to put the maximum distance between themselves and him. Yet there was also an air of unreality about anybody's residual power in the White House; it was now increasingly vulnerable to challenge from the long-suffering bureaucracy as well as from the Congress.

In those circumstances Nixon reversed his attitude toward my growing celebrity. He no longer showed resentment at public attention to me (though he must have felt it); political calculation caused him to welcome it as a means of cementing the claim that Watergate was a trivial aberration from a Grand Design. But Nixon's position had declined to a point where no matter what he did, it tended to weaken him. The more Nixon emphasized his foreign policy achievements, the more he tempted his critics to assign most of the credit to me. In the end Nixon had no choice but to fall in with the notion of *my* central role, however wounding to him — and however unfair.

I found myself in a truly extraordinary position. I, a Presidential appointee on the President's own staff, unconfirmed by the Senate, totally dependent on the President's goodwill and confidence, had become a Presidential surrogate. Amid the wholesale assault on the Administration, most critics seemed willing to spare me, even to protect me, from the mounting rancor as if to preserve one public figure as a symbol of national continuity. No doubt my vanity was piqued. But the dominant emotion was a premonition of catastrophe. A weakening of authority of such dimensions must sooner or later lead to major foreign policy reverses. I tried to erect a facade of imperviousness and self-confidence, but I had no illusions. It merely delayed the inevitable erosion; it could not prevent it.

Nixon was too experienced not to recognize the peril to our foreign policy. He did his best to shield me from the consequences of his travails. By tacit agreement, I was excluded from the inner circle of White House deliberations on Watergate. Nixon and Haig insulated foreign policy to the greatest extent possible from the scandal. Haig would give me brief advance warnings of such explosions as might affect the conduct of our diplomacy, but as a general rule I was not involved in the discussions of either strategy or tactics. Whenever there was a plan to refer to foreign policy in a Presidential statement on Watergate, I was given a chance to comment.

As I have already said, my general view was that Nixon's only hope was to disclose everything all at once. I made this point consistently to Len Garment and, whenever the occasion arose, to Al Haig. Nothing short of it would stop the tidal wave of successive shocks. Only in this manner would the Administration be able to return to the task of government. Garment and Haig agreed in principle, but they were in no position to put it into practice. Neither of them had any personal knowledge of the events that gave rise to the disaster. With the departure of all key White House assistants except Ron Ziegler, there was no institutional memory left in the White House. By now Nixon himself had no longer — if he ever had — a clear view of the activities lumped under the rubric of Watergate. Given his style of conversation, he genuinely had trouble distinguishing his own serious orders from his familiar rhetorical outbursts not intended to be acted upon. His Walter Mitty tendencies allowed him to perceive evasions as reality and endowed wishful thinking with the attributes of truth.

So the summer of 1973 passed with periodic White House statements on Watergate, which almost invariably lagged behind events and only served to stimulate the national hunger for further disclosure. Nixon had promised a comprehensive statement for the middle of August. He toyed with the idea of coupling it with a plea to bring the various inquiries to an end so as not to increase our foreign policy perils. The argument was valid in the abstract; in the climate then, it would only have drawn foreign policy into the maelstrom without easing the pressures on Nixon. There was no way to stop the inquiries at this stage; the Congress, the media, and the public would not have permitted it. I appealed to Haig, Garment, and Nixon's special Watergate counsel Charles Alan Wright not to link foreign policy and Watergate. They agreed. In the end Nixon accepted our unanimous advice without demur. In Nixon's hierarchy of values, even at the height of his private suffering, the international position of the United States took precedence over his personal fortunes.

The statement finally issued on August 15, 1973, suffered the same fate as all the Presidential "explanations" that had preceded it. It was too little too late. It repeated the version already advanced in the Presidential speech of April 30: that Nixon had become aware of interlocking malfeasances only late in the day as a result of investigations ordered after March 21. As earlier, Nixon was torn between shifting the blame to his subordinates and avoiding so antagonizing them that they would turn on him. The statement added little of either fact or explanation to

what investigations had already brought to light. It sidestepped the issue
of whether the tapes should be made available to the Special Prosecutor,
Archibald Cox. Predictably, media and Congressional reaction ran the
gamut from hostility through exasperation to indifference. Failing in its
prime objective, the August 15 statement generated neither sympathy
nor understanding.

By August, in short, Nixon's style of government by means of Pres-
idential assistants had become unworkable. The power of a Presidential
Assistant derives from a strong — if necessary, a ruthless — President.
If the President wishes to rely on his assistants he must be able to give
them unambiguous and decisive indications of support. As President
Eisenhower wrote to his Budget Director Joseph Dodge in 1953:

> [Y]ou must act as my authoritative agent in working on these problems.
> While, of course, each Department head always has direct access to me, I think
> it vastly important that if any appeal from your decisions is made, that you
> must be present at the time — and even more important, that you and I ap-
> proach these problems so definitely from the same viewpoint that the occasion
> for such appeals will be minimized.[3]

Ultimately, this means that the Assistant is no longer challenged; it is
taken for granted that he speaks for the President. (At that point the real
danger of arbitrary action by the Assistant arises; from then on it will
rarely be tested whether he in fact reflects the President's wishes or is
implementing his own preferences in the President's name.)

That was essentially the state of affairs by the end of 1971. I had
unique access to the President; my office cleared the key policy cables
instructing our diplomats abroad. All this placed Secretary Rogers in an
impossible position. If he approved a telegram or option before it was
passed to the White House, he might see his judgment overruled in full
view of his own subordinates. If he waited until I had stated my view,
he was in the position of either rubber-stamping or challenging what for
all he knew had already been approved by the President. (And if a
Presidential Assistant is wise, or simply bureaucratically adept, he will
have discussed any controversial item with the President.)

Theoretically, this problem could have been avoided if the Assistant
for National Security Affairs and the Secretary of State had been so
close that they exchanged ideas constantly and thus avoided a confrontation — much as Brent Scowcroft and I did at a later time. But for
Rogers and me, conflict between the Secretary of State and security
adviser seemed almost to have been built into the design of our offices.

Nixon had always distrusted the State Department, which he considered both fuzzy-minded and a nest of holdover liberal Democrats. In
addition, I remain convinced that he wished to establish, for once, a
relationship of primacy over his old friend and mentor Bill Rogers, to

whom he had so often turned during the periods of his own weakness (such as in the crisis that led to the "Checkers" speech and during Eisenhower's first heart attack). Nixon seemed eager to prove that there were some areas in which he was the more masterful; he had studied foreign policy all his life while Rogers came to it as a novice from a distinguished career in the law. For all these purposes I was a useful, often indispensable, instrument. But this did not mean that I was spared all exposure to Nixon's complicated, at times convoluted, maneuvers. Nixon was not the first President deliberately to encourage rivalry between subordinates, while claiming to disdain it, so long as he did not himself have to adjudicate the resulting disputes. And Haldeman, Mitchell, occasionally Ehrlichman, stood ready to contain the fires without extinguishing them.

Whether Nixon planned it that way or simply permitted it to happen — probably a combination of both — the relationship between Rogers and me soured beyond recovery. We had begun with the customary protestations that we would not repeat the frictions of the previous administrations. We soon found ourselves at loggerheads. I was too arrogantly convinced of my superior knowledge, Rogers was too insistent on his bureaucratic prerogative, for the acts of grace that would have permitted both of us to escape the treadmill on which we found ourselves, and, more important, to serve the nation better.

By the beginning of Nixon's second term, the pattern was frozen. Rogers and I had no social contact. Officially, we dealt with each other correctly without being forthcoming. I was the preeminent Presidential adviser; Rogers controlled the machinery by which much of our foreign policy had to be carried out. The stalemate deepened; I considered the situation unworkable. Rogers had been told in November 1972 that he would be replaced in the summer of 1973, but either he thought that his chief would recoil at the last moment as he had so often before, or else his imminent departure freed him of previous restraints.

In any event, Rogers launched an attack on the system of clearances by which White House control had previously been exercised. For example, early in December 1972 the State Department decided to open discussions with Cuba on the hijacking of airplanes. Obviously, any negotiation with Cuba, whatever the issue, had profound foreign policy implications — especially with a President so neuralgically sensitive on the subject. Nevertheless, the White House was informed on a Saturday afternoon that the Secretary had authorized the discussions to begin on the following Monday morning — giving the NSC staff thirty-six hours to consider a major policy move and daring it to veto a negotiation that had already been scheduled. There was a fifty-fifty chance that the instructions requiring White House clearance might need another thirty-six hours over the weekend to work their way through the bureaucracy — so that even the formalities of clearance might be short-circuited. Similarly, at a time when the White House had ordered a cool attitude toward India, the State Department published without any White House clearance whatsoever an enthusiastic public response to an Indian feeler for improved relations. And I have already recounted State's initiative toward Egypt at the end of January 1973, of which the White House was unaware.

All this occurred even before Watergate stripped me of the backing of a strong President. Watergate left no doubt that the existing system could no longer be sustained. Sometime in the spring of 1973, Melvin Laird, then serving his brief turn as Presidential Counsellor, told me that my position as Assistant would soon become untenable. I would be ground down between the Congress and the increasingly assertive bureaucracy. I would have to become Secretary of State or resign. (I do not know whether Laird spoke to Nixon in the same vein; if so, neither of them informed me.) A little later Al Haig told me that he had come to the same conclusion: If I wanted to remain effective I would have to leave the White House and take over the State Department. He would raise the subject with Nixon, he said, but he knew it would not be easy to sell; it would lead to painful and possibly prolonged exchanges.

I had not sought Cabinet office. Bob Haldeman has correctly described my attitude at the end of 1972 in a book containing many unflattering comments about me: In an undamaged Nixon Presidency, the national security adviser's post was decisive; Nixon had no intention of moving me into the State Department.[4] Nor do I believe that Nixon would have made John Connally Secretary of State but for the fear of losing me, as has been claimed. He knew I intended to leave by the end of 1973 anyway, no matter who was Secretary. And in a normal Presidency so politically powerful a personality as John Connally would run counter to all Nixon's ideas of how to conduct foreign policy.[5] Without Watergate, Kenneth Rush, then Deputy Secretary of State, who had played a decisive role in achieving the 1971 Berlin Agreement, would have been made Secretary in the summer of 1973 and I would have left the White House a few months later.

But by the summer of 1973 all these plans had become irrelevant. Once Watergate descended, I could not operate effectively as a Presidential staffer; Nixon was fed up with the Rogers-Kissinger rivalry and had already decided in principle that Rogers had to go; Rush was too little known to be promoted. I would have been prepared to continue as national security adviser had Nixon insisted on going through with his original plan of appointing Kenneth Rush. I never changed the position I had announced when Watergate broke upon the nation: I would serve so long as the crisis continued, without conditions.

The process of arriving at the decision caused all the anguish Haig had foreseen. It must have been torture for Nixon to consider assigning the principal Cabinet post to someone who was being lionized by his opponents precisely in order to make the President seem dispensable. All the arguments in favor of appointing me also underlined the mortal peril to his Presidency. So Nixon reacted to Haig's recommendation by enveloping himself in silence. He did not accept Haig's recommendation and he did not reject it. According to Haig, he simply noted it without comment; he never mentioned it to me even elliptically. It was an enormous strain for everybody: for the President fighting against the acceptance of his vulnerability; for Haig, who had run the risk of Presidential disfavor by raising the matter; and for me now in an almost untenable position should Nixon simply maintain his silence.

Washington abhors a vacuum. In the middle of July, my opponents accelerated a decision that my friends so far had been unable to advance. While Rogers was on a trip to the Far East, on July 13 Dan Rather broadcast on *The CBS Evening News* that consideration was being given to having me replace Rogers. Other commentators soon took up the theme. The White House reaction would now give a crucial clue.

Washington is like a Roman arena. Gladiators do battle, and the spectators determine who survives by giving the appropriate signal, just as in the Coliseum. Barely noted by the rest of the country, leaks to media serve Washington as clues to power and influence. Once a controversy begins, the outcome importantly depends on what influential person will back which version. This is not necessarily a function of truth; it more often reflects ulterior motives. Reputations can be damaged, or made, by leaks that find no rebuttal from the powerful, even if untrue. A particularly subtle version is the untrue leak that is permitted to run its course uncontested by those in a position to rebut it, and is denied only when the news cycle has passed it by. This has the advantage of damaging the victim almost as much, while preserving the reputation of the source.

The journalists act simultaneously as neutral conduit and tribunal, shielding their witnesses by the principle of "protection of sources" and often determining the outcome by the emphasis they choose to give competing versions. The press is thus both spectator and participant. The people may have "a right to know" — but only what the press chooses to tell it. In bureaucratic infighting, masking the identity of the leakers is frequently a suppression of the most significant part of the story. The journalist may strive for objectivity, his competitors may have an incentive to knock down his story, but leakers can always initiate a drama that creates its own momentum through the reactions of the victim and the power brokers. Rarely, it seems, does anyone worry about the motives of the source, though there are serious ethical problems when the journalist's interest in a scoop and the source's self-interest coincide, as in some "investigative" journalism. It becomes difficult to determine who is using whom.

In this case the story died quickly, but not before it made its mark. Nixon, though no doubt nonplussed, continued to keep his thoughts to himself, torn between his emotions, which rebelled against my promotion, and his judgment, which underlined its inevitability. Haig kept White House comments noncommittal. I denied to the press ever having discussed the subject with the President, which was true but only part of the story. The Secretary's party in Tokyo naturally blamed the leak on me. Dan Rather — with whom I was later to have my disagreements — would not tell me his source but generously confirmed to me that he had received the story from opponents eager to thwart the prospect. They in turn had apparently exhausted their store of knowledge. The Secretary of State's entourage in Tokyo soon realized that impugning motives would do no good; further pursuit of the story could only dramatize the weakness of Rogers's position. No supporters for him had come forth; no Senators had rallied; the White House had not denied the story. The leak had backfired.

In early August, Haig told me that Nixon, who still had not said a word to me, had agreed to appoint me in Rogers's place, provided he did not have to dismiss Rogers personally. Accordingly, Haig called on the Secretary of State on August 8 to suggest his resignation. Rogers, who throughout behaved with extraordinary strength, honor, and aplomb, in effect threw Haig out of his office. If Nixon wanted his resignation, he said, he would have to ask for it himself. He would not give up the senior Cabinet post to an intermediary. To anyone familiar with Nixon's dread of personal confrontations, it was clear that this requirement would bring about another, probably prolonged, delay.

By now the uncertainty was growing hard to bear; perhaps it was a deliberate price exacted by Nixon for taking a step essentially so repugnant to him. Haig was told nothing; Nixon hid behind the need to prepare his statement on Watergate and withdrew to Camp David. As usual when drafting speeches, he refused to answer the telephone for days on end, even for routine foreign policy business. Finally on August 16, with only a few hours' warning to Haig and no notice to me at all, Nixon called in Rogers, intending to ask for his resignation. To everyone's surprise and Nixon's immediate intense relief, Rogers made it easy for his old friend. Without letting Nixon speak he submitted a letter of resignation free of recrimination or argument. It was a classy performance.

And still Nixon had said nothing to me. Even after he had Rogers's resignation in his hand, he did not speak to me for several days. Although I knew about Rogers's visit and Haig had told me that Nixon would announce my appointment at his next news conference, Nixon continued in silence. I heard from him only on the late afternoon of August 21, in San Clemente, about eighteen hours before my appointment was to be announced. Nixon took me to a corner of the swimming pool with the pretext of wanting to go over some questions and answers for his news conference the next day. Then he told me matter-of-factly, while floating on his back, without warmth or an expression of anticipation of close cooperation, that he would open the news conference by announcing my appointment as Secretary of State. I made a reply that would have been sarcastic had I been less moved; it was in fact simply: "I hope to be worthy of your trust." We both realized that for Nixon my appointment was less an act of choice than a step taken against his will in the hope it would mitigate catastrophe.

On August 22, at 11:30 in the morning Pacific Daylight Time, Nixon announced my appointment in a televised outdoor news conference with the sparse comment that "Dr. Kissinger's qualifications for this post, I think, are well known." He did not elaborate.

Waiting for the Senate

I N the first few hours after my nomination, I was as if suspended in a vacuum. I was numb from weeks of uncertainty, and seized by wonder at what had transpired. Thirty-five years earlier I had come to America as a refugee from persecution. I had worked in a shaving-brush factory, joined the US Army as a private, and become a naturalized citizen. America had been a distant dream when as a young boy I experienced intolerance and hatred under totalitarian rule. Now I was being given the responsibility to help steer my adopted country through one of the gravest constitutional crises of its history. I felt a stirring emotion, and not a little awe.

And I was also oddly relieved. On being made Prime Minister, Churchill remarked that he felt liberated: At last he alone would bear the responsibility. I had not reached that eminence. Nor were my feelings quite so unambiguous. But I did feel the quietude that comes with the knowledge that one's convictions would stand or fall on their merits without being strained through the uncertainties of clashing personal ambitions.

Congratulatory phone calls cascaded in. Those from the veterans of many battles meant a great deal to me. From Dean Rusk, for example, suffering in noble silence the ostracism inflicted on him for the sin of having stood by his President in a bitter war. He spoke of the small community of ex–Secretaries of State who had a national duty to support each other across partisan divisions. And from Robert McNamara, nearly destroyed by many of those who had urged the war in Indochina and who had then left him alone to conduct it with all his inward doubt caged by a sense of duty to his President and his nation. No one had sustained me more on the human level during Nixon's first term than McNamara, even though he was uneasy about many of the policies we thought necessary for our nation's honor. And there were, of course, many calls from members of the Administration, including Elliot Richardson, who had been a strong partner when he had served as Under Secretary of State and who was now carrying out with some distaste the job of Attorney General during the Watergate period.

Members of the diplomatic corps offered their good wishes. While no special significance attached to this — getting along with the Secretary of State is, after all, the principal task of foreign chiefs of mission — I sensed that they welcomed the approaching end of our bureaucratic controversies. No doubt a few had seen the opportunity inherent in the White House–State Department split and used it skillfully. But it is easy to overestimate the ease with which foreigners can understand, much less manipulate, our internal conflicts. For most diplomats the rivalry between White House and State Department was a nightmarish complication of our already excessively complex political process.

And then, of course, there were the calls from the State Department itself. Kenneth Rush must have been aware that but for Watergate he would have been the recipient of these congratulations. And he had to realize that his role as Deputy Secretary would be diminished by the appointment of a Secretary with strong views and likely to bring his own circle of advisers into the Department. None of this, however, was reflected in his cordial call to me offering full cooperation during the transition. I invited him to an early meeting in San Clemente.

William Rogers telephoned from Washington even before Nixon's press conference. He said he would do his utmost to bring about a successful transition in the national interest. "You'll find it's a great department," he said. I told him that his personal staff would receive responsible assignments. I would be guided to the greatest extent possible by his recommendations about the future of his associates. We promised to consult frequently. It was a pointless assurance. Not having relied on each other's judgments while we were both in office, it was unlikely that we should become confidants while Rogers was in retirement. In fact, we have had little contact with each other since that conversation.

Yet I owe it to Bill Rogers to point out that he left office with grace as he had conducted it with dignity. He showed none of the resentments he must justifiably have felt. And he behaved in an exemplary manner ever after. He engaged in no fashionable second-guessing; he did not join attacks on me, even though he had far more legitimate grievances than most. He reacted evenly to accounts — including mine — that showed his influence to have been less than dominant. He showed that to him national service was its own reward.

The guest house at Zavidovo, May 1973 (see Chapter VII).

ABOVE: *Ambassador Anatoly Dobrynin, Foreign Ministe,*
Andrei Gromyko, General Secretary Leonid Brezhnev
interpreter Viktor Sukhodrev, and, standing, Foreig
Ministry official Georgi Korniyenko, at Zavidovo, Ma
1973

RIGHT, ABOVE: *With Brezhnev at the huntin*
tower, Zavidovo, May 1973 (the picture is autographe
by Brezhnev)

RIGHT, BELOW: *Brezhnev, HAK, Sukhodrev in hunting ga*
at Zavidovo, May 197.

On the Presidential yacht Sequoia *on the Potomac, June 19, 1973. Clockwise, from far left: Andrei Gromyko (partially obscured); Nixon; Brezhnev; Viktor Sukhodrev; William Rogers; Anatoly Dobrynin; NSC staff member William G. Hyland; Brezhnev aides A. M. Aleksandrov and G. E. Tsukanov; Treasury Secretary George Shultz; HAK.*

Brezhnev's arrival in Washington, June 18, 1973.

Actress Jill St. John, Leonid Brezhnev, and Andrei Vavilov (interpreter) at Nixon's San Clemente reception, June 1973.

Nixon, Brezhnev, and HAK at San Clemente, June 1973.

Len Garment and Ron Ziegler answer press questions on Watergate, May 22, 1973.

New White House Team, June 1973: Melvin Laird, President Nixon, Alexander Haig.

After being sworn in as Secretary of State, September 22, 1973. Left to right: David Kissinger; HAK; Elizabeth Kissinger; President Nixon; Paula and Louis Kissinger.

Luncheon in the White House Mess after the swearing in, September 22, 1973. Clockwise from left: Paula Kissinger; Governor Nelson Rockefeller; Nancy; HAK; Louis Kissinger; Deputy Secretary of State Kenneth Rush; Pat Mosbacher; Joseph Alsop.

*Waiting for a ride
at the White House
with Brent Scowcroft.*

First day at the State Department after being sworn in, September 1973.

Testifying before Congress
as Secretary of State, September 1

The traveling State Department press corps.

ABOVE: *With the House Congressional Leadership, 1973. Left to right: Minority Whip Leslie Arends, Majority Leader Thomas P. O'Neill, Jr., Foreign Affairs Committee Chairman Thomas Morgan, HAK, Speaker Carl Albert, Minority Leader Gerald Ford.* BELOW: *Opening of the Washington Energy Conference, February 11, 1974.*

Nor should my tales of Rogers's bureaucratic setbacks — put forward to explain the pathology of the Nixon Administration — obscure the fact that Rogers's judgment on foreign policy was superior to the role that circumstances and his own personality permitted him to play. Rogers's conciliatory instincts caused him to shy away from the public confrontations that marked Nixon's conduct of the Vietnam debate; within the councils of government he tended to oppose strong policies on Indochina even when he offered no strategic alternative. All this deprived him of influence on the one issue that obsessed Nixon's first term. His advice was generally sensible; his values were humane. His predictions of the domestic consequences of actions that he opposed were usually correct. His special talent was the analysis of individual cases rather than the development of an overall conception. His views on particular plans, such as the ill-starred Laos invasion of 1971, were acute. He would have done yeoman work as a private counselor; his temperament and training caused him to recoil from extracting a coherent strategy from an ambivalent bureaucracy or from defending it against hostile media and Congress. There is no doubt that Nixon counted on these inhibitions to assert his own dominance. I certainly exploited them mercilessly. Yet nothing can deprive Bill Rogers of the final verdict: He was a man of decency and good judgment, qualities overwhelmed by the complex psychology of his President, his colleagues, and the passions of a divided country.

Confirmation Hearings

THE mood of exaltation passed rapidly. Within days I had to face the confirmation process before the Senate; in the Watergate atmosphere this was not without complexity. I was the first Secretary of State in many years — the last one had been Christian Herter — to be appointed in a Presidential mid-term and the first to reach the office *after* being perceived as a chief architect of the prevailing policy. And Nixon's foreign policy, for all its successes, had been highly controversial even before Watergate. My confirmation thus lent itself to the public airing of many pent-up grievances. It provided, as well, an opportunity to publicize whatever peripheral aspects of Watergate involved the National Security Council, the principal of which was the wiretap issue I have described in Chapter IV.

The Senators on the Foreign Relations Committee found themselves in a dilemma. The influence of the committee parallels the importance of the Secretary of State. He is its channel to the executive branch; it is he who can be held accountable; it is he to whom the committee can convey its policy views systematically. When he is influential, the committee plays a major role. When the Secretary of State's role dwindles, so does the committee's. Yet the Secretary and the committee are also inherently competitive. The Secretary must seek to preserve a margin of discretion for executive authority; the committee will inevitably seek to impose its preconceptions. When both parties are restrained and compassionate about each other's needs, they can be mutually reinforcing. If either the Secretary or the committee presses its claims to an extreme, the result can paralyze foreign policy.

The committee had been troubled by my preeminence as security adviser because as a White House staffer I was not subject to its control. From that perspective, most of the committee members welcomed the nomination of a Secretary certain to be the President's principal architect of foreign policy. On the other hand, few of the Senators wanted to be perceived as having gone easy on an executive branch that had defied them on Vietnam and was deeply enmeshed in Watergate. And they had the pretext of looking into the seventeen wiretaps.

The result was one of the most extensive hearings on the appointment of a Secretary of State in the postwar period, extending over the two weeks from September 7 to 21, 1973. It was a strange ritual because the members of the Committee were to a man personally well disposed toward me and eager to confirm me. They were well aware that I had softened Nixon's refusal, on the basis of executive privilege, to let his White House assistants testify before Congressional committees. With his approval I had met twice a year with the committee in circumstances we pretended were social but that soon came to resemble a Congressional hearing. At first we gathered in the home of the Chairman, Senator J. William Fulbright, later in a hideaway office in the Senate. The sessions grew increasingly formal; by 1972 the staff director of the committee, Carl Marcy, kept an official record. Throughout I had stayed in touch with many of the members of the committee on a personal basis. Senators Hubert Humphrey and Jacob Javits, in particular, were friends of long standing. I greatly respected Senator Fulbright across the chasm of our policy differences for his erudition, fairness, and patriotism. Now that Vietnam, the principal source of our disagreements, was behind us, the committee had reason to look forward to a new era in executive-legislative relations. My confirmation was a certainty.

Yet the committee had to be seen in diligent pursuit of any hint of executive malfeasance. It therefore spent over half its time on the wiretap issue. Despite its extraordinary exertion on the subject, it was accused, to its great chagrin, of letting me off too easily.[6] In these strained circumstances I was not able, as I had hoped, to turn the confirmation hearings into the auspicious beginning of a bipartisan approach to foreign policy.

I tried to set a conciliatory tone. In my opening statement on September 7, which was nationally televised, I stressed how important a strong, self-confident America was for the peace of the world and why this required putting an end to our national divisions:

Americans have recently endured the turmoil of assassinations and riots, racial and generational confrontations, and a bitter, costly war. Just as we were emerging from that conflict, we were plunged into still another ordeal.

These traumatic events have cast lengthening shadows on our traditional optimism and self-esteem. . . . Where once a soaring optimism tempted us to dare too much, a shrinking spirit could lead us to attempt too little. Such an attitude — and the foreign policy it would produce — would deal a savage blow to global stability.

But I am hopeful about our prospects. America is resilient. The dynamism of this country is irrepressible. Whatever our divisions, we can rally to the prospects of building a world at peace and responsive to humane aspirations. In so doing, we can replenish our reservoir of faith.

The committee was in no position to respond to this overture during the confirmation hearings. It was not lack of goodwill on its part but the political requirements of public hearings. In addition to the Watergate atmosphere, there were the dynamics of television. Elected officials depend on publicity for survival. They know that the evening news programs rarely give more than two minutes to any news event and they are far more likely to use a segment reflecting confrontation or controversy than harmony. I used to joke with Jacob Javits that when he saw the red light of the television cameras he would ask even his most constructive questions in a loud voice, set off by a pointed finger and a throbbing vein in his forehead, leaving the unwary viewer with the impression that what I had been eager to put forward had been extorted from me by this vigilant defender of the public weal.

So it happened that Senator Fulbright responded to my opening statement by raising the subject of wiretaps. As in the periodic reexaminations of this issue that were to recur with almost annual regularity, no new facts emerged; this investigation and every other since has confirmed the sequence of events I have described in Chapter IV. Elliot Richardson, Attorney General, and William D. Ruckelshaus, Deputy Attorney General and Acting Director of the FBI, submitted a statement that no previous or subsequent inquiry has seriously challenged:

As best can be determined from the FBI records, Dr. Kissinger's role included expressing concern over leaks of sensitive material and when this concern was coupled with that of the President and transmitted to the Director of the FBI, it led to efforts to stem the leaks, which efforts included some wiretaps of Government employees and newsmen. His role further involved the supplying to the FBI of names of individuals in the Government who had access to sensitive information and occasional review of information generated by the program to determine its usefulness.[7]

The problem with recurring investigations of old issues is not the facts. When there is controversy about the propriety of governmental actions, it can be stilled only by the fullest and most candid disclosure. The difficulty arises in determining what is relevant and what is self-serving, and in sorting out the different perspectives of the participants. Even if the investigator is fair and all witnesses are honorable, it is next to impossible to recreate the context of individual decisions made years before. For one thing, the investigator, be he journalist or Senator, finds it difficult to grasp the pressures of decision-making. To him the subject being investigated is paramount; he is not concerned with other governmental duties or contexts. He operates as if what he is looking into had been the *sole* activity of the participants and had commanded their undivided attention.

A distinguishing feature of high office, however, is the disproportion between the gravity of actions and the time available to deal with them. To tear any decision from its whole context distorts its essence. The decision-maker will almost certainly not have known as much of its ramifications as the ex post facto investigator now does. He may have spent a few minutes on it; the later investigator has days and weeks, the opportunity of acquiring different perspectives — and hindsight.

If there are several participants in the decision, some of the evidence is likely to be contradictory. Each department or agency keeps its own records, which are generally unavailable to other agencies. Its version of events is heavily influenced by its mission and the natural tendency to shift responsibility for controversial decisions. Even when the intention is to be scrupulously fair, each agency views events through the prism of its own preconceptions. When documents surface years later, one may be forced to comment on versions that are difficult to rebut so long after the event, and indeed on happenings of which one was only dimly aware.

My confirmation hearings spent more time on the wiretap issue than on any international problem. There was lengthy discussion in open session. Senators John Sparkman and Clifford Case were then designated as a subcommittee to review the FBI files, take additional testimony in closed session, and submit a report. There was another day of hearings in executive session in which I reviewed each individual wiretap case with the committee — though my recollection of several was hazy at best.* It was during these hearings that I saw for the first time the files kept by J. Edgar Hoover (who had died in May 1972). These included the listing of officials whom Hoover had recorded as having "requested" or "authorized" each tap. The authorizing individual was invariably Attorney General Mitchell. Equally invariably the request was listed as having come from some official outside of the Justice Depart-

---

*The transcript of my testimony in executive session was later published, with relatively minor deletions for security and to spare embarrassment to those individuals tapped.[8]

ment (in about a dozen cases either then–Colonel Haig or me) even when — as I knew in four or five instances from personal knowledge — it was J. Edgar Hoover who had first proposed to Nixon that the individuals be tapped. What the "request" usually amounted to, in fact, was my office's submission of names of those who fulfilled the first of the categories established by the President: officials who had had access to the classified information that had been leaked. Nearly a year later the question of whether I had "initiated" or "requested" the wiretaps became a huge public issue again (see Chapter XXIV).

No attempt was made in the hearings to compare the practices of the Nixon Administration with those of its predecessors to determine whether any unusual amount of wiretapping occurred or whether, as I believe was the case, the seventeen taps so obsessively pored over were no greater a number than previous administrations had on average conducted. In any event, I strongly endorsed the Supreme Court ruling of 1972 — three years *after* the wiretaps in question had occurred — that specified for the first time that wiretaps for national security required a court order. And I summed up my attitude in my testimony:

Since the time that [Nixon's wiretapping] decision was made in May, 1969, the Supreme Court has made a new definition of the procedures to be followed in the use of wiretaps, and therefore, many of the issues that have been raised with respect to the previous wiretapping by this or by previous administrations have to a very large extent become moot. In any future national security cases we would expect to observe scrupulously the division between the concerns of national security and the requirements of liberty.

But beyond this, the issue of wiretapping raises the issue of the balance between human liberty and the requirements of national security. I would say that the weight should be on the side of human liberty, and that if human liberty is to be ever infringed, the demonstration on the national security side must be overwhelming.

The Foreign Relations Committee, following the recommendation of Senators Sparkman and Case, concluded without dissent that the wiretapping episode should not bar my nomination.

In addition to wiretapping, the so-called secret bombing of Cambodia received a great deal of attention, as did the coup that toppled Salvador Allende in Chile while the hearings were going on. Various Senators asked questions about particular concerns: Javits with respect to the War Powers Bill, about which I expressed serious reservations; Humphrey about a more comprehensive and humane use of our food assistance abroad. I promised Humphrey that I would put forward a new American policy to combat world hunger — a promise fulfilled the following year at a United Nations World Food Conference in Rome held at American initiative and at which I unveiled a comprehensive new program. A

number of Senators raised the matter of Jewish emigration from the
Soviet Union as if it were their invention.* They took a run at implying
that we neglected human rights or the moral dimension of foreign policy, seemingly oblivious to the fact that under the Nixon Administration
the rate of emigration had increased from 400 to nearly 35,000 *before*
there was serious Congressional agitation on the subject. Senator Edmund Muskie, who in January 1971 had told Soviet Premier Kosygin
in Moscow that he thought Nixon's policy toward the Soviet Union was
too tough and would be eased by Congressional pressures,[9] now insisted
in his separate statement supporting my nomination that "progress toward détente must be accompanied by continued pressure on the Soviet
Government for greater respect for human rights."

At last, after two weeks, the hearings drew to a close. They had
performed their function: The imperative of a show of Congressional
vigilance had been fulfilled without impairing a subsequent relationship
of confidence between the nominee and the committee. The Senators
had been persistent but, by and large, constructive. If the hearings repeated disputes of the past more than they sketched visions of the future, they drained some of the venom from the controversies and permitted a fresh start to be made. And they contributed importantly to the
good relations that continued between me as Secretary of State and the
committee while Watergate moved inevitably to its conclusion. This relationship was never ruptured even when the accession of President Ford
made it safe to reassert traditional partisanship. The Senate Foreign Relations Committee under Senator Fulbright and then Senator Sparkman
remained for the next three and a half years true to the wise words with
which it concluded its report on my nomination:

It would be naive to assume that the Executive and Legislative Branches will
always agree. But, if the issues are debated openly and clearly, it should be
possible to avoid the public confusion, mistrust and alienation which have developed during the last decade.

Each of the branches has its respective powers and responsibilities. Some
conflict between the two is inevitable and may, on occasion, serve the national
interest. From time to time in recent years each of the branches may have
become overly assertive of its own powers but it is clear that the American
constitutional system works best when each branch has a clear sense of the
limits of its authority and of the rights of the other. We hope that this balance
can be restored for neither branch is all-wise or all-powerful.

On September 18, the committee voted 16–1 in favor of my nomination. Senator George McGovern, the lone dissenter, had telephoned
the evening before to tell me of his high personal regard. He thought

---

*See Chapters V and XXII.

the Senate should confirm me; his negative vote, he said, was a debt
owed to those who had supported his Presidential campaign and did not
reflect his high regard for me or his eagerness to cooperate with me
after my confirmation. I was not put off by McGovern's attempt to carry
water on both shoulders. Circumstances impose on any public official
some demand for a show of hypocrisy, and he can only hope that when
the final balance is struck the causes for which he fell short were worthy
ones.

On September 21 the full Senate voted 78–7 to confirm me. On September 22 Chief Justice Warren Burger administered the oath of office
in the East Room of the White House in the presence of my parents and
children, and under the genial but ambivalent auspices of President
Nixon. The East Room is not large. It can seat no more than perhaps a
hundred and fifty people at formal events, especially since a large part
has to be given over to the news media. A lectern and platform were
set up on the east side, facing an array of seats arranged in a semicircle.
White-gloved military aides unobtrusively ushered the invited guests to
their places. Congressional leaders from both parties attended, as well
as Robert Strauss, Chairman of the Democratic National Committee,
whose friendship then and thereafter was a testimony that the foreign
policy of the United States reflects purposes that transcend the fluctua-
tions of partisanship. Chief Justice Burger had interrupted a European
trip to swear me in — a moving gesture. My parents were as in a dream;
they had been driven out of their native country; thirteen members of
our family had become victims of man's prejudices. They could hardly
believe that thirty-five years later their son should have reached our
nation's highest appointive executive office. I had set out to prepare
some written remarks but found myself so tense that I gave up, and
relied on the inspiration of the moment.

Only Nixon seemed driven by his own demons. He did not join in
the family gathering in the Red Room with the Chief Justice just before
I was sworn in. His remarks at the swearing-in ranged from the perfunctory to the bizarre. He began by pointing out that I had overcome
intense Congressional opposition to win confirmation — perhaps implying that he was not alone in having trouble with the legislative branch.
He then sought to explain that my appointment represented yet another
historic first, for three reasons: I was the first naturalized citizen to become Secretary of State; the first Secretary who had visited Peking and
Moscow before his appointment; and the first Secretary of State since
World War II who did not part his hair. He did not amplify the first two
points but he pursued the last topic relentlessly, speculating as to what
category Dean Rusk, who had no hair, belonged: "But then my barber,
who is a very wise man and seldom wrong — I said, 'But what about
Secretary Rusk?' And he said, 'Well, Mr. President, he didn't have

much hair, but what he had, he parted.' '' I replied, evading this fascinating subject but saying what was in my heart:

Mr. President, you referred to my background, and it is true, there is no country in the world where it is conceivable that a man of my origin could be standing here next to the President of the United States. And if my origin can contribute anything to the formulation of our policy, it is that at an early age I have seen what can happen to a society that is based on hatred and strength and distrust, and that I experienced then what America means to other people, its hope and its idealism. And therefore, in achieving a structure of peace under your leadership, Mr. President, we will strive not just for a pragmatic solution to this or that difficulty, but to recognize that America has never been true to itself unless it meant something beyond itself.

And as we work for a world at peace with justice, compassion and humanity, we know that America, in fulfilling man's deepest aspirations, fulfills what is best within it.

The ambivalence, to put it mildly, of the Nixon family to my appointment was shown by the fact that Mrs. Nixon — whom I admire — refused to join the receiving line after my swearing-in. Nixon disappeared immediately afterward, not mingling even for a few moments with the guests at the traditional reception in the State Dining Room.

The following cable went out from the State Department to all diplomatic and consular posts a few moments later:

DR. HENRY A. KISSINGER TOOK HIS OATH OF OFFICE AND
ASSUMED THE DUTIES AS 56TH SECRETARY OF STATE AT 1106
EDT SEPTEMBER 22, 1973.

The Department of State

IN the West Wing of the White House, all the working offices are rather austere and small, even the President's. The national security adviser, despite his supposedly fearsome power, has always had to make do with humble and compact quarters, sometimes on the ground floor, sometimes in the basement. The Department of State, in contrast, like most Cabinet departments, lavishes on its Secretary a spacious and elegant suite of offices on a regally high floor with a magnificent view of the city of Washington and its monuments. It provides a beautiful panorama of the Lincoln Memorial, the Potomac River, and Arlington National Cemetery. It took some getting used to. In my White House warren, if I wanted to express displeasure at some untoward happening in my usual emphatic way, it was a short walk to my door and my deputy was an available target a few steps beyond. In the State Department, my deputy seemed to be almost a mile down the corridor, and in any case by the time I reached the outer door of my own office I had usually forgotten what had triggered my charge. If I made it through the door I encountered the disapproving gaze of Jane Rothe (now Jane Rothe Mossellem). Coolly beautiful, unflappably efficient, Jane had served four previous Secretaries, imposed her own standards of how Secretaries of State should behave, and in the end proved as indispensable to me as to my predecessors.

This was not the only or the most significant contrast. The qualities for the job of national security adviser do not translate so readily into the responsibilities of the Secretary of State as some incumbents may be tempted to believe. The Assistant for National Security Affairs is the President's creation; he operates solely by Presidential mandate. He presides over a microscopic staff. His task as originally conceived is to advise the President whether the foreign affairs departments and agencies of the government are placing the appropriate information and options before him. Usually, of course, the security adviser does much more. Propinquity to the Oval Office tempts the President to use his security adviser as confidential troubleshooter. (Psychologists may explain someday why physical proximity to the Oval Office gives one such an advantage over officials only a ten-minute car ride distant.)

The security adviser, in turn, is human; he seeks status; he is only too well aware that his power depends on his ability to demonstrate a unique kind of usefulness. Since his only responsibility is that assigned to him by the President, he can afford to take the "big view." He can present geopolitical analyses unconstrained by the flood of detail or pressing problems that are the lot of the Secretary of State. If he is skillful, he can position himself in bureaucratic debates close to the President's predilections, which he usually has the possibility to learn more intimately than his competitor in Foggy Bottom.

The Secretary of State's responsibility is vastly different. He presides daily over a vast catalogue of international relationships that are not always reflected on the Presidential agenda or in the labors of the National Security Council and many of which are far from glamorous. He must contend hour to hour with a hundred and fifty countries and an array of multilateral issues and international organizations — economic problems, arms control, foreign assistance, visa and immigration policy, and so forth. He is responsible for a colossal enterprise.

In the short run, this vast effort places the Secretary of State at a bureaucratic disadvantage. Inevitably, he must grapple with many mundane or highly technical subjects. He is forced to champion unpopular causes, such as the annual appropriations for foreign aid. There is always the risk that the Secretary of State begins either to bore the President with arcane problems that require urgent Presidential decision, or to appear to him like some special pleader.

And yet a President who succumbs to impatience with the ponderous State Department damages the country in the long run. A foreign policy achievement to be truly significant must at some point be institutionalized; it must therefore be embedded in permanent machinery. No government should impose on itself the need to sustain a tour de force based on personalities. A foreign policy to be lasting must be carried by the understanding of those charged with the regular conduct of diplomacy and over time must be implanted in the heart and mind of the nation.

That can only be accomplished by a confident partnership between the President and the Secretary of State, such as existed between Harry Truman and Dean Acheson, Dwight Eisenhower and John Foster Dulles, or the Presidents I served and me. The security adviser can fill a gap in confidence only for short periods of time and then at the risk of demoralizing the bureaucracy and confusing foreign governments. If the President does not trust his Secretary of State he should replace him, not attempt to work around him by means of the security adviser. Any other course complicates the problem it is supposed to solve. Nixon's fear of State Department leaking was such that he excluded it wherever possible from all sensitive negotiations. He had some cause for his suspicions. But it was also a self-defeating course — though I did not understand that when I was in the White House. The more the State Department was excluded from policymaking, the less incentive it had to safeguard any information it managed to acquire on its own. Indeed, it was tempted to snipe at whatever emerged, out of wounded pride or ignorance of the difficulty of negotiating. And it was untenable to have several allied foreign ministers better informed about major negotiations than our own. We were not to remedy this administrative schizophrenia until I became Secretary of State in the fall of 1973.

At the same time the State Department bureaucracy has a tendency to tempt fate. The permanent career service of the State Department has endured so much abuse that its sense of beleaguerment is accompanied by an acute consciousness of bureaucratic prerogative. Convinced of the importance of State Department preeminence, it insists passionately on its formal role, sometimes at the cost of the intangible bond between President and Secretary that is the essence of its real influence. Even before Nixon was sworn in on January 20, 1969, the Department fought a bitter battle to preserve its chairmanship of various interdepartmental subcommittees that had been established in the Johnson Administration. Never mind that these groups were moribund and that the real decisions had been made at the so-called Tuesday lunches President Johnson held with an inner circle of Cabinet members. The symbolism of status seemed to outweigh its reality.[10]

The contretemps confirmed all of Nixon's prejudices. He did not want the State Department preeminent in any event; State's tenacious struggle for prerogative multiplied his suspicions. Whatever slight chance the State Department had to gain Nixon's confidence evaporated in this essentially meaningless battle over turf. And while Nixon's judgment of the State Department was too harsh, his instinct was sound. The State Department is simply not equipped to handle interdepartmental machinery. As I shall explain, its key personnel by style and training are usually uncomfortable with conceptual approaches; its organization is better suited to dealing with the immediate than the long-range. A Secretary of State seeking to run the interagency process imposes a heavy burden on himself. For even should he succeed in overcoming the proclivities of his Department — as he eventually must, however interdepartmental machinery is organized — he would be in a hopeless position bureaucratically.

Our government tends to operate by adversary procedures. But the chairman of an interdepartmental group must develop a reputation for objectivity. When a department chairs an interagency committee, either it will be tempted to skew the process in favor of its predilections or else it will not adequately represent its own point of view — an ironic outcome of a grab for preeminence. Even should a Solomonic group of chairmen emerge from the Department of State, they would be forced to use up a great deal of energy in defending themselves against the criticism that they exploited their position. No department in our system will for long accept the formal preeminence of another one. It will challenge decisions that go against it, on procedural as well as substantive grounds. In the end, the result is not the predominance of one department but Presidential adjudication of a disproportionate number of disputes.

I experienced these problems when I attempted a variation of the scheme. When I became Secretary of State I also remained national security adviser, giving me control over interdepartmental machinery by what in dynastic times would have been called personal union. It did not work. The State Department representatives at interagency meetings were my subordinates when I wore my Secretary of State hat; when I chaired a meeting they had to reflect my point of view or else all interdepartmental matters would be outside my control even within the State Department. But that meant in practice that I would either push my department's view as chairman or dissociate from my subordinates, an inherently absurd proposition. For two years I was exposed to the charge that I had an unfair predominance over the policymaking process. Insofar as this was true, it grew out of my close relationship with the Presidents I served, not from the organizational framework of their administrations. My dual position was, in fact, a handicap and a vulnerability. In November 1975 President Ford took away my job as national security adviser. I resented the decision bitterly because I thought

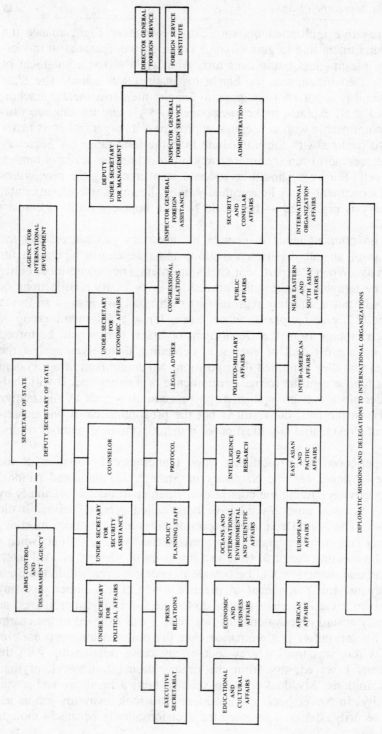

DEPARTMENT OF STATE IN 1973

* A separate agency, with the director reporting directly to the Secretary and serving as principal adviser to the Secretary and the President on Arms Control and Disarmament.

that it would undermine the perception of my position. For a few weeks I was even thinking of resigning.

It would have been a childish gesture. My influence was unaffected by the organizational change and my peace of mind greatly improved. I prevailed where I did because I managed to convince Ford and when I failed it would have been no different had I remained technically as chairman.

I have become convinced that the running of interdepartmental machinery ought to be preeminently the responsibility of the security adviser (except perhaps in a crisis). A determined Secretary of State cannot fail to have his view heard whoever chairs the committees. The security adviser's contact with media and foreign diplomats should be reduced to a minimum; the articulation and conduct of foreign policy should be left in the main to the President and the Secretary of State (and of course their designees). The preparation of options, which is in the main what interdepartmental machinery does, should be the province of a security adviser chosen for fairness, conceptual grasp, bureaucratic savvy, and a willingness to labor anonymously. (General Andrew Goodpaster under Eisenhower and General Brent Scowcroft under Ford are two outstanding examples.) The influence of the Department of State would flow from the personal confidence between the President and the Secretary and the quality of the analytical work produced by the Department.

To elicit that quality of work is a most daunting task for even the most strong-willed Secretary of State. For he runs up against the organization of the Department and its allergy to conceptual thought.

The internal structure of the Department is wondrous to behold. (The chart on page 436 shows its organization in 1973.) At its apex is the Secretary of State, in whose name all actions are taken; all instructions and cables are issued over his name. He cannot possibly read them all. Thus to produce with great flourish a cable signed by the Secretary of State proves only that he was in town, not that he wrote the cable or even knew of it. In my time the Secretary was assisted by a Deputy Secretary and three Under Secretaries (for Political Affairs, Economic Affairs, and Security Assistance). There is also the Counselor, who is a sort of free-wheeling adviser to be used for whatever role the Secretary finds most useful. (My Counselor was Helmut Sonnenfeldt, a distinguished specialist in European affairs and US–Soviet relations.) These officials have offices on the Seventh Floor of the State Department together with the Secretary and serve as his general staff, at least in theory. At the next echelon are the Assistant Secretaries: In my tenure there were five for various regions of the world, one for international organizations, and seven for functional areas like economic affairs, educational and cultural affairs, oceans and scientific affairs, public affairs,

Congressional relations, administration, and security and consular affairs. Then there is the Legal Adviser, as well as the Policy Planning
Staff and the Bureau of Intelligence and Research, both headed by officials with the title of Director. In addition, the Secretary of State has
a myriad of special assistants — for press relations, international labor
affairs, narcotics, refugees, and human rights, in my time. Each of these
officers theoretically reports directly to the Secretary regarding his or
her specialty. But no executive can possibly direct so many individuals
in a personal relationship. There has to be some intermediary staff.

According to the organization chart, the Under Secretaries on the
Seventh Floor are supposed to help the Secretary coordinate the Sixth
Floor, where the Assistant Secretaries are located. But the real world is
not so tidy. The organization chart that reflects real lines of authority
has not yet been devised. For one thing, the Deputy Secretary's role
depends importantly on the personalities involved and the Secretary's
own style. In Dean Rusk's tenure, he and George Ball tended to divide
the world between them. Others acted as chiefs of staff across the board,
as Walter Bedell Smith did for Dulles. I assigned to my Deputy Secretaries general supervision over foreign economic policy as well as over
the functional bureaus. I personally worked with the regional bureaus.

As for the Under Secretaries, their impact varies. The Under Secretary for Economic Affairs has a staff too small for his assignment; the
Under Secretary for Security Assistance has a title larger than his responsibilities. The economic Under Secretary must deal with the entire
gamut of foreign economic policy aided by only a handful of staff assistants and backed up by a bureau (headed by an Assistant Secretary)
that is far too small — and also too low in rank — to deal with all the
powerful Cabinet departments and agencies whose duties impinge on
our foreign economic policy. The job of Under Secretary for Security
Assistance was created when military assistance played a larger role
than proved to be the case later. He thus has responsibilities smaller
than those of some Assistant Secretaries; I used the position to handle
newly developing crises, like the early phases of the energy emergency
in 1973.

The key Under Secretary is that for Political Affairs, which is traditionally the highest policymaking position occupied by a career Foreign
Service Officer. It is responsible for interdepartmental coordination in
the political field and above all for imposing some coherence on the
regional bureaus. In practice, two factors vitiate the assignment. First,
an officer with the grasp and toughness to make these individualistic
bureaus follow a common concept is not easy to find. The temptation is
great for the Under Secretary for Political Affairs to take over some
area of operational responsibility that has been his specialty, thus adding
an additional official to the multitude already reporting directly to the

Secretary. Second, the Assistant Secretaries will generally resist having intermediaries between themselves and the Secretary; they tend to insist on their day in court. And they have the technical ability to do so because the officers of the Seventh Floor have tiny staffs. With only one or two special assistants, these run the risk of becoming prisoners of the bureaus below them unless there is a clear allocation of responsibilities that makes it impossible to bypass them.

These tendencies account for the mushiness and slow pace by which the State Department has driven so many outsiders to distraction. Since the Department at any moment threatens to disintegrate into practically autonomous fiefdoms — and surely does so under a weak Secretary — a great deal of time is spent on "clearances," meaning that each bureau has to be consulted on any problem remotely involving its formal responsibilities. No bureau likes to be overruled — nor does it really want to win, because this implies that it might lose next time. All the incentives are thus skewed toward compromises reflecting the lowest common denominator and paralyzing the imagination.

Left to its own devices, the State Department machinery tends toward inertia rather than creativity; it is always on the verge of turning itself into an enormous cable machine. Too often policy filters up from the bottom in response to events, complaints, or pleas that originate abroad. Each significant country is assigned to an officer with the revealing title of "country director"; indeed, some of these officials seem more interested in directing "their" country than in shaping the foreign policy of the United States. Or rather they tend to identify the two, becoming spokesmen for the country assigned to them. The country director drafts a cable to respond to a specific situation. He clears it with interested bureaus and sends it up through the hierarchy, sometimes with an explanatory memorandum, frequently not. The memorandum in any event is typically focused on the immediate problem, is heavily influenced by the local context, and, if it deigns to present options, does so in a manner that all but imposes the bureau's preference. If it survives all obstacles, and if it is one of the minority that are of special policy importance, the cable winds up on the desk of the Secretary of State. He does not know which ideas were eliminated by the clearance process, what modifications occurred on the cable's journey to him, or — unless he has studied the subject himself — what long-range purpose is to be served, if any. He can rewrite the cable, though he will rarely have time or the detailed knowledge to do so. He can reject it, though if he is not extremely vigilant the cable is likely to come back to him in only slightly modified form. (In the summer of 1976 I received so many essentially identical cables on one particular subject I did not wish to act upon that only the threat of transferring the entire bureau stopped the pressure.)

The most difficult task for any Secretary of State is to impose a sense of direction on the flood of papers that at any moment threatens to engulf him. Even someone who, like me, had spent his lifetime on the study of foreign policy — and whose hobby it was, to boot — was sometimes overwhelmed. The system lends itself to manipulation. A bureau chief who disagrees with the Secretary can exploit it for procrastination. For example, in 1975 the Assistant Secretary in charge of Africa managed to delay my dealing with Angola by nearly ten weeks because he opposed the decision he feared I would make. He simply used the splendid machinery so methodically to "clear" a memorandum I had requested that it took weeks to reach me; when it arrived it was diluted of all sharpness and my own staff bounced it back again and again for greater precision — thereby serving the bureau chief's purposes better than my own. Alternatively, the machinery may permit a strategically placed official's hobbyhorse to gallop through, eliciting an innocent nod from a Secretary unfamiliar with all the codewords and implications.

I came to the office too late in Nixon's term to attempt a fundamental reorganization — a task that should be undertaken in the early phase of the first term of an administration. Such a reorganization would see to it that each bureau reports to some Under Secretary; that the Deputy Secretary is freed to act as an alter ego; and that some formal apparatus is created on the Seventh Floor to insist on the development of a long-range policy.

In an Administration racked by Watergate and buffeted by a war in the Middle East that broke out within two weeks of my confirmation, reorganization requiring legislation was out of the question. I tried to impose coherence by three steps. First, I sought to carry out what I consider one of the key responsibilities of the head of any department: to elicit from his subordinates a standard of performance of which they do not know they are capable. I insisted on thoughtful memoranda; I drove my staff mercilessly. Many could not stand the pace or my temperament and resigned. They are the sources of much unfriendly publicity regarding my administrative methods. Those who stayed — and they were the majority — responded nobly to the challenge; many became close personal friends. The analytical work of the Department improved remarkably.

Secondly, I moved into positions charged with long-range planning key associates whom I had recruited for the National Security Council staff. They were familiar with my methods. They understood my insistence on a strategy. I put Helmut Sonnenfeldt, in the essentially free-floating office of Counselor, in charge of East-West relations. He was later to be traduced for alleged "softness," an absurd accusation reflecting a woeful ignorance of the convictions and contributions of an outstanding public servant. Many times in these volumes I have quoted from his superb analyses, which the passage of time has confirmed to be penetrating, shrewd, and wise.

I placed William G. Hyland in charge of the Bureau of Intelligence and Research. A brilliant analyst trained in the Central Intelligence Agency, he subjected all information and preconceptions to skeptical and informed scrutiny; he saw to it that intelligence guided rather than followed policy prescriptions.

Two other key transfers from the White House were Lawrence Eagleburger and Winston Lord, who combined high ability with a deep personal friendship. Eagleburger's skill was the management of men and organizations. An experienced Foreign Service Officer, he understood the foibles of his colleagues without succumbing to their parochialism. He had the virtue of being deeply attached to the Foreign Service; he used this dedication as a challenge to seek to turn his service into a great institution. First as my executive assistant, later as Deputy Under Secretary for Management, he saw to the translation of concept into policy. He stood up to me when necessary. He was incorruptible in his judgment; he was one of the outstanding public servants of my experience.

Winston Lord was largely responsible for giving an impetus to conceptual thinking as the new director of the Policy Planning Staff. He had been a close collaborator during my White House years on key enterprises, including the opening to China and the Vietnam negotiations. In 1970 he was close to resigning over the incursion into Cambodia. I appealed to him with the argument that if the young men of his generation channeled their idealism into protest, there would be none left to build a better world. He would serve his principles better by working for an end to the war within the government than by striking a pose outside. Fortunately for me, he stayed on — no little influenced by his marvelously strong wife, Bette. He became one of my best collaborators, a resident conscience, and a close friend. More than almost anyone, he was familiar with my views; he had a global, not simply a regional, perspective. I gave him priority in choosing the best men and women for his staff. He and his associates screened most key cables coming to me for consistency with policy and provided me with additional papers on fundamental or long-range issues that the operational bureaus often missed. Together with Peter W. Rodman, they helped me write the speeches by which I sought to articulate the premises and goals of our foreign policy.

Peter Rodman had written one of the most outstanding undergraduate theses of my tenure as professor at Harvard. After Oxford and law school he joined my NSC staff in the summer of 1969. He remained in the White House after I became Secretary of State as an informal liaison to my office. Self-effacing, brilliant, indefatigable, he came as close to being indispensable as it is possible to be in a large government. His role was hard to define. In addition to speechwriter, he functioned as my institutional memory. He did research projects; he made sure that what was being said in negotiations or publicly was consistent with previous statements on the subject and with our internal planning. He attended nearly every sensitive conversation, technically as a note-taker, in reality as confidant and adviser. He was a constant if unsung hero of my tenure as Secretary of State.

Thirdly, I formed out of this group, plus the Deputy Secretary, the Under Secretary for Political Affairs, and the regional Assistant Secretaries, a kind of political staff group to help me plan strategy. I met with them as a body practically every day on key issues. Still, the Department's central structural problem remained throughout my period in office.

The Foreign Service

THAT foreign policy nevertheless succeeded as well as it did I owe in large measure to a group of men and women who have sustained Secretaries of State through the modern period: the Foreign Service of the United States.

On one level, gaining control of the machinery of the Department of State is relatively easy. The Secretary's unambiguous orders are scrupulously carried out, at least at the outset, because the Foreign Service begins with the presumption that the Secretary deserves its support — until it has tested the limits of his tolerance. The difficulty is that it is not always easy to formulate orders unambiguously. The competent, proud, clannish, and dedicated Foreign Service Officers soon spot the lacunae in the knowledge or endurance of their chief, and fill them with recommendations derived from a philosophy honed through the common trials of a close-knit fraternity. They justly take pride in their professionalism; they abhor ''lateral entry'' — the jargon for political appointees who have not risen through the ranks. The difficulty is that they sometimes treat the Secretary as a lateral entrant — an appointee who could never have made it on his merit through the competitive rigors of the Foreign Service.

In the hands of a determined Secretary, the Foreign Service can be a splendid instrument, staffed by knowledgeable, discreet, and energetic individuals. They do require constant vigilance lest the convictions that led them into a penurious career tempt them to preempt decision-making. In American folklore, our professional diplomats tend to be maligned as a collection of striped-pants fuddy-duddies, excessively internationalist in outlook, soft in defense of the national interest, as often a contributory cause of our difficulties abroad as agents of their resolution. The need to "clean out" the State Department has become a staple of our political oratory. Several Secretaries have begun their tours of duty with that expressed determination. I know of none that has left office without having come to admire the dedicated men and women who supply the continuity and expertise of our foreign policy. I entered the State Department a skeptic, I left a convert — with the perhaps unbalanced conviction of one who has overcome earlier prejudice on the road to Truth.

Until the so-called Wriston reforms of 1954, the Foreign Service was a small, elite organization that supplied our diplomatic personnel overseas and staffed some of the key positions in the Department of State. Its formal title, Foreign Service of the United States, implied that it was a Presidential instrument; in reality its chain of command has always run to the Secretary of State. Before the reforms the Department of State was staffed by two types of officers: those who stayed permanently in Washington and were part of the civil service, and those who divided their service between the United States and overseas but generally preferred to serve in embassies — the traditional Foreign Service. During this period the Foreign Service Officers were drawn largely from the upper-class, predominantly Protestant, private-school background of the Eastern Establishment — from the social groups, in short, most likely to be interested in America's international role. Many had the financial means to support a style of life not possible on government salaries.

The Wriston reforms created a unified Foreign Service. It was no longer possible to serve only in Washington or exclusively abroad. Each officer had either to join the Foreign Service or leave the departmental career ladder. Most chose to stay. The rationale for Wristonization was sound. In the old system, the civil servants in Washington issuing orders to embassies did not always understand what it was like to be on the firing line. And Foreign Service Officers always abroad gradually lost the perspective of Washington; they rarely had the experience of dealing with Congress or pursuing interagency battles. They lost touch with America and therefore represented it less effectively abroad. (Imagine, for example, someone leaving the United States in 1970, being abroad almost continuously for ten years, and trying to reflect the American scene to foreigners.)

Wristonization was designed to make Foreign Service Officers whole, to give them both experience with America and broad overseas knowledge. The official writing cables of instructions in State could imagine what it would be like to carry them out. The diplomat overseas would have some understanding for the context of American society and the clash of priorities and agencies that are at the heart of government.

After Wristonization, the key positions in the Department were manned by career personnel. Except at the highest political level, advancement was through stages of increasing responsibility in the Foreign Service. At the same time strenuous efforts were made by successive Secretaries of State to broaden the base of the Foreign Service to make it more representative of the American people as a whole, opening it to women, members of ethnic and racial minorities, and people with a wider variety of geographical and academic backgrounds.

Amazingly, the value structure of the earlier period persisted through all these changes. The Foreign Service remained self-consciously elitist. Serving abroad, especially as an Ambassador, rated higher on the scale of values than almost any assignment in Washington, partly because successive pay adjustments had made overseas service financially more rewarding, but above all because the men and women who chose the career were genuinely dedicated to fostering America's relationship with the world around us. The conventional criticism, that they were a group of "cookie pushers," contributed to a sense of beleaguered solidarity. And the cohesiveness was reinforced by many shared experiences in far-flung posts forever inaccessible to the regular civil servants with whom the Foreign Service came into contact or, for that matter, to their superiors. All these tendencies, it cannot be emphasized often enough, developed among a group of men and women of truly exceptional ability and dedication who came to their elitist convictions naturally by passing one of the most difficult and comprehensive written and oral examinations required for any career.

The Foreign Service's approach to foreign policy nevertheless reflected much of American attitudes and historical experience. The Foreign Service had developed in the earlier years of our history when no direct physical threat to America's security was apparent. America's foreign involvement was considered to flow less from a concept of national interest — which was thought morally myopic — than from enlightened notions of freedom of trade and the implementation of moral, or at least legal, principles. We believed that the decision to be involved with matters beyond our shores was entirely ours to make. We would engage ourselves against overwhelming dangers, but we would take no responsibility for the day-to-day management of the balance of power; indeed, we tended to deny its importance and even demonstrated our moral superiority by denouncing it as a contributory cause of international tensions. American diplomats proclaimed their faith in international law. They were more likely to concern themselves with the illegality of another state's conduct than with whether the latter's actions represented an assault on the international equilibrium and hence to our long-term security. They were not called upon to develop a geopolitical design. They tended to resist the concept as reflecting values that America had transcended.

Until the end of the Second World War, the Foreign Service saw its role as a negotiating instrument, not as the designer of a foreign policy; more as solving concrete issues as they arose than as conceiving a strategy and shaping events. Long service abroad created greater sensitivity to the intangibles of foreign societies than to those of our own. Conscious of the isolationist tradition in America, Foreign Service Officers had a tendency to seek to balance it by becoming spokesmen for the countries in which they were stationed or for which they were given responsibility in the Department of State. This is referred to in the Department as the disease of "localitis," or "clientism." A Foreign Service Officer's job is always easier, or more pleasant, if he is able to produce good news for his client country — more aid or backing in a dispute, or an invitation to meet the President, for example. A diplomat abroad faces the same dilemma that a Congressman does. How much should he represent his constituents' view, even be an advocate — at the risk of parochialism, not to mention loss of credibility in Washington? How much should he try to take the overall view that reality imposes on the President and Secretary of State — at the risk of not giving them the full flavor of local views they need to make a decision, and knowing that fellow ambassadors or country directors will be pushing hard for their clients while he is trying to be "fair"?

The Foreign Service emphasizes negotiability — which is another way of saying consciousness of what the other side will accept. There is less sensitivity to the pressures and incentives that, if boldly applied, can alter the perceptions that in turn define negotiability. Institutionally, the Foreign Service generates caution rather than risk-taking; it is more comfortable with the mechanics of diplomacy than with its design, the tactics of a particular negotiation rather than an overall direction, the near-term problem rather than the longer-run consequences.

Most foreign policies that history has marked highly, in whatever country, have been originated by leaders who were opposed by experts. It is, after all, the responsibility of the expert to operate the familiar and that of the leader to transcend it. What the Department of State needs is strong and consistent leadership grounded in a philosophy of the world and guided by a sense of purpose. Frequent gyrations in our national direction demoralize the Foreign Service, as they do foreign nations. Leadership clearly incapable of grasping the complexity of the office or in constant need of briefing on the most elementary issues elicits the most self-willed assertions of Foreign Service parochialism. The wholesale purge so often advocated would accomplish no good. Any alternative group is likely to have the same biases, which are after all rooted in our society and our history. A climate of fear would arrest a healthy maturation. But under strong Secretaries of State — like Dean Acheson — the Foreign Service is a marvelous tool, and under all of them a loyal one.

The Foreign Service, in fact mirroring the same biases as the society it represents, has had to undergo the same painful adjustment to a new postwar world unprecedented in our experience. Once the last resort in defense of freedom, the United States has since 1945 become the principal protector of the global equilibrium. Our diplomacy must be prepared to act on assessments of whose truth it cannot at the time be sure. We must resist seemingly marginal changes because to wait until the challenge is unambiguous may also make it unmanageable. All this requires much greater self-assurance and intuition and daring and above all conceptual skill than have been traditionally fostered.

Early on, I abandoned my own preconceptions and decided that it was impossible to conduct a creative foreign policy of the United States without the Foreign Service, even less against it. We had a joint task of mutual education while helping to move our society to an understanding of its new circumstances. In the process it became soon clear to me that no foreign minister in the world is served by a more creative, skilled, professional, and loyal group of men and women.

I used the four-week interval between my nomination and confirmation to conduct a systematic talent search in the Foreign Service. Despite all the clichés about my alleged hostility to the bureaucracy, the truth is that during my tenure as Secretary of State, the highest percentage of all my appointments at the policymaking level were Foreign Service Officers. I elevated those who enjoyed the respect of their peers and represented the ablest younger men and women. And I took care to give serious assignments to those I replaced, including some who out of loyalty to Rogers had publicly criticized my appointment.

There is no doubt the Foreign Service served me with distinction. It stuck by me when I came under attack. It made possible my successes. It is not to blame for those areas of policy in which I fell short.

Taking Over

M Y biggest immediate challenge in taking over the State Department was to fulfill the purpose for which, in effect, I had been appointed: to conduct a strong foreign policy despite the growing weakness of our executive authority; to use the premier Cabinet office to inspire hope in a future worthy of our nation's ideals amidst a political crisis unprecedented in our modern history. My acceptance remarks in the East Room were intended to establish the main themes of my tenure at the State Department. In the face of the disintegrating authority, we had to project serenity and strength and purpose to discourage pressures by adversaries and to give hope to those who depended on us.

If history was any guide, crises were now unavoidable. And we would be able to weather them only if the American people saw our foreign policy as a design for peace and international order, not simply as tactical responses to upheavals tempted by executive weakness. We had to put forward a vision that would put into perspective the squalid spectacle of the destruction of a Presidency unfolding daily in the headlines and newscasts. It was imperative, at that moment most of all, to remind Americans and our friends around the world that our government was functioning and purposeful and the master of events.

This is why I scheduled three speeches during my first two weeks as Secretary. Within forty-eight hours of my taking the oath of office, I addressed the General Assembly of the United Nations. Since I had not felt free to call on State Department personnel until I had been sworn in, the speech was prepared in a round-the-clock frenzy of some thirty-six hours. It went through many versions during the final night while the State Department support and secretarial staffs received their first exposure to my compulsive methods. When all was done, technology threatened vengeance for our presumption. I was standing in the doorway of my office at the Waldorf Towers, impatient to depart for the UN across town, waiting for the final text of my speech to be photocopied for a file copy. My new secretary, Jane Rothe, courageously informed me that the overheated machine had just eaten a page of our only complete typed draft. The original page had gone into the machine; nothing had come out. Fortunately, the handwritten pages remained. Jane sat down calmly and typed the missing page over again. There was no way the actual delivery of my maiden speech could match the drama of its preparation.

In my address to the General Assembly I asked the nations of the world "to move with us from détente to cooperation, from coexistence to community." I then stated the main goals of our diplomacy, which in that forum obligates one to list every key region and trouble spot in some more or less meaningful sentence. The omission of a part of the world is likely to cause a diplomatic incident; frequently banality is the better part of valor. (In my inexperience I forgot that lesson and omitted Europe. I paid the price; the gap was added to a catalogue of my neglects.) Less conventionally, I called for international cooperation on an agenda reflecting the interdependence of the modern world:

We are, in fact, members of a community drawn by modern science, technology, and new forms of communication into a proximity for which we are still politically unprepared. Technology daily outstrips the ability of our institutions to cope with its fruits. Our political imagination must catch up with our scientific vision.

Keeping my promise to Senator Humphrey, I called for a World Food Conference for 1974. I promised that the United States stood ready to define its responsibilities in the dialogue between rich and poor nations in a humane and cooperative spirit.

On October 8, I delivered a long-prepared speech in Washington at the Pacem in Terris Conference. In Chapter VII, I quoted from the portion on US–Soviet relations, but its central theme was an appeal for a new national consensus on America's role in the world. There had been controversy over the Administration's emphasis on the balance of power, the alleged amorality of my approach to world affairs. I tried to set forth a philosophical view of the relationship between morality and pragmatism:

This country has always had a sense of mission. Americans have always held the view that America stood for something above and beyond its material achievements. A purely pragmatic policy provides no criteria for other nations to assess our performance and no standards to which the American people can rally.

But when policy becomes excessively moralistic it may turn quixotic or dangerous. A presumed monopoly on truth obstructs negotiation and accommodation. Good results may be given up in the quest for ever-elusive ideal solutions. Policy may fall prey to ineffectual posturing or adventuristic crusades.

The prerequisite for a fruitful national debate is that the policymakers and critics appreciate each other's perspectives and respect each other's purposes. The policymaker must understand that the critic is obliged to stress imperfections in order to challenge assumptions and to goad actions. But equally the critic should acknowledge the complexity and inherent ambiguity of the policymaker's choices. The policymaker must be concerned with the best that can be achieved, not just the best that can be imagined. He has to act in a fog of incomplete knowledge without the information that will be available later to the analyst. He knows — or should know — that he is responsible for the consequences of disaster as well as for the benefits of success. He may have to qualify some goals, not because they would be undesirable if reached but because the risks of failure outweigh potential gains. He must often settle for the gradual, much as he might prefer the immediate. He must compromise with others, and this means to some extent compromising with himself.

It was still a hopeful period. I was convinced that a thoughtful debate could even help the nation regain its bearings. Our historic idealism was the best compass course through the new perils that were now inevitably ahead of us. On October 4, I spoke in New York at the Metropolitan Museum of Art at a dinner for the delegations attending the UN General Assembly:

Of the species on this planet, man alone has inflicted upon himself most of his own suffering.

In an age of potential nuclear cataclysm, in an age of instant communication amidst ideological conflict, our most urgent task is to overcome these apparently iron laws of history. The vision of a world community based on justice, not power, is the necessity of our age. . . .

I pledge you that the United States is ready to begin the journey toward a world community. Our sights will be raised even when our tread must be measured. We will make no excessive promises, but we will keep every promise we shall make. We look upon stability as a bridge to the realization of human dreams, not as an end in itself. We know that peace will come when all — the small as well as the large — have a share in its shaping, and that it will endure when all — the weak as well as the strong — have a stake in its lasting.

Two days later the Middle East war broke out.

XI

The Middle East War

An Awakening for Us All

AT 6:15 A.M. on Saturday, October 6, 1973, I was sound asleep in
my suite at the Waldorf Towers in New York City, my headquarters for the annual session of the UN General Assembly.
Suddenly Joseph J. Sisco, the energetic Assistant Secretary of State for
Near Eastern and South Asian Affairs, barged into my bedroom. As I
forced myself awake, I heard Sisco's gravelly voice all but shouting that
Israel and two Arab countries, Egypt and Syria, were about to go to
war. He was confident, however, that it was all a mistake; each side
was really misreading the intentions of the other. If I set them right
immediately and decisively, I could get matters under control before the
shooting began. It was a flattering estimate of my capacities. Unfortunately, it turned out to be exaggerated.

What had triggered Sisco was an urgent message from our Ambassador in Israel, former Senator Kenneth Keating. Two hours earlier, Prime
Minister Golda Meir had summoned Keating to her office in Jerusalem.
It was extraordinary for an Israeli leader to be at work that day — for
it was Yom Kippur, the Day of Atonement, the holiest day of the year
for Jews. It is a day spent in fasting, prayer, and reflection; it reminds
man of his insignificance in relation to God and climaxes a High Holy
Day season in which, according to tradition, God decides the destiny of
all mortals for the coming year.

Golda's startling message was in effect that Israel's encounter with
destiny had already begun: "We may be in trouble," she told Keating.
Egyptian and Syrian troop movements, which both Israel and the United
States had assumed to be simply military exercises, had suddenly taken
a threatening turn. Keating reminded her that not twelve hours previously he had been assured by Israeli defense officials that the situation
was not dangerous. This was no longer accurate, Mrs. Meir replied; the
Israelis were now persuaded that a coordinated Egyptian and Syrian attack would be launched late that afternoon. Since the Arabs were certain
to be defeated, she suggested, the crisis must result from their misunderstanding of Israeli intentions. Would the United States convey ur-

gently to the Soviet Union as well as to Israel's Arab neighbors that Israel had no intention of attacking either Egypt or Syria? Israel was calling up "some" reserves, but as a proof of its peaceful intentions was stopping short of general mobilization. Keating asked whether Israel was planning a preemptive strike. Golda emphatically reiterated that Israel wished to avoid bloodshed; it would under no circumstances initiate hostilities.

When Sisco awakened me there were only ninety minutes of peace left for the Middle East. So skillfully had Egypt and Syria masked their war preparations that even at this stage the Israelis expected the attack to come four hours later than the time actually set. I knew that no diplomacy would work if an Arab attack was premeditated. But my view was still colored by the consistent Israeli reports, confirmed by our own dispatches, that such an attack was nearly impossible. I therefore plunged into a frenetic period of intense diplomacy to head off a clash, more than half convinced that Egyptian and Syrian actions grew out of a misunderstanding of Israeli intentions.

A crisis does not always appear to a policymaker as a series of dramatic events. Usually it imposes itself as an exhausting agenda of petty chores demanding both concentration and endurance. One is forced to react to scraps of information in very limited spans of time; longing for full knowledge, one must chart a route through the murk of unknowing. Operationally, a crisis resolves itself into minutiae that must be attended to with painstaking care, which includes the need to ensure that all parties work from the same body of information. So it was that morning of the Day of Atonement when war stalked the Middle East.

At 6:40 A.M. I called the Soviet Ambassador, Anatoly Dobrynin, at his Embassy in Washington. Roused from bed, he was sleepy and confused (or pretended to be). I asked him to assure Moscow urgently, as well as Cairo and Damascus, that Israel had informed us it was not planning any offensive action.

Dobrynin at first claimed that the whole episode must be an Israeli maneuver to justify a preemptive attack. I told him that my point in calling him was precisely to guarantee the opposite. Next, pedantically diplomatic, he wanted to know who was sending messages to whom — was it an assurance from Israel to the Arab countries or from the United States to the Soviet Union? I cut him off impatiently: "If this keeps up there is going to be a war before you understand my message." Dobrynin found another excuse for procrastination: He doubted that his communications were fast enough for Moscow to act in time. I offered our end of the Hot Line; he implied the Soviet end was too far from the Foreign Office. (I found myself wondering what use it would be in a major-power crisis.) So I put the White House switchboard at Dobrynin's disposal. He accepted with a show of gratitude.

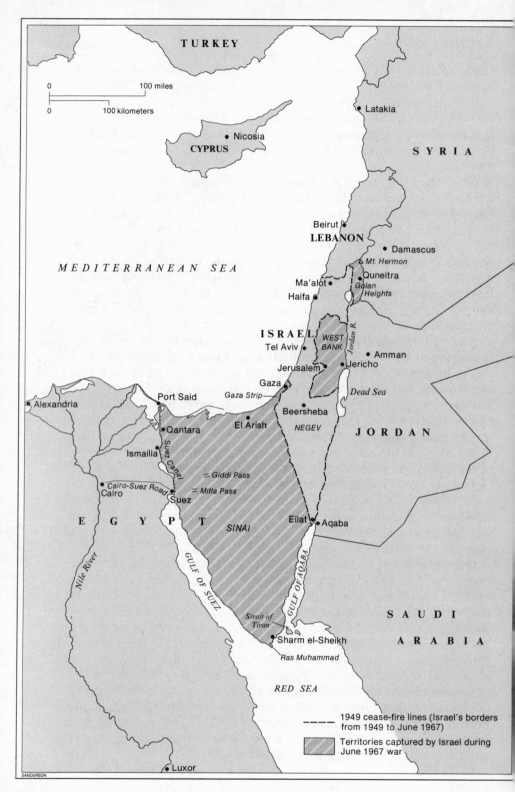

Israel and Its Neighbors before the October 1973 War

All this was nonsense. Dobrynin had superb communications. He could get an answer from Moscow within minutes (as he demonstrated later in the crisis). I now think that, expecting to be overheard, he wanted to use open American communications to establish an alibi against the charge of collusion between the Soviet Union and its Arab friends.

At 6:55 A.M. I called Mordechai Shalev, the chargé d'affaires at the Israeli Embassy, a senior diplomat of great sagacity, warmth, and quiet dignity. (Ambassador Simcha Dinitz was in Israel because of the death of his father.) I told Shalev that Golda's assurance that there would be no Israeli preemptive strike had been conveyed to the Soviets. He should pass this to Jerusalem, along with my personal plea to avoid a rash move.

At 7:00 A.M. I telephoned Egyptian Foreign Minister Mohamed el-Zayyat, who was attending the UN General Assembly in New York. To save time and explanation I read him the Israeli message verbatim. A day earlier, ironically, Zayyat and I had discussed how to begin negotiations for Middle East peace, which the United States intended to pursue immediately following Israel's parliamentary elections scheduled for October 30. Zayyat, I am convinced, had not been dissembling. Sadat had not shared his plans with many.

Diplomacy at the edge of war is an incongruous instrument. All one's instincts make for haste, while precision requires time-consuming repetition. Zayyat, like Dobrynin, made me reread the message. In his case, I am reasonably sure, it was confusion, not dissimulation. He said he would transmit it immediately, though he professed to be very apprehensive that it was a pretext on Israel's part. I told him we would stand behind the Israeli assurance.

Next, I tried to reach the Syrian Vice Foreign Minister, Mohammed Zakariya Ismail, who was also in New York, but to no avail. Syria's UN mission did not answer its phone.

By 7:15 A.M. Shalev had reiterated to me Golda Meir's assurance that Israel would not launch a preemptive attack. At 7:25 A.M. I called the Soviet Embassy, only to find that Dobrynin was on the phone to Moscow via the White House. I told Oleg Yedanov, an aide, to make sure Dobrynin did not hang up without conveying the renewed Israeli assurance to Moscow.

At 7:35 A.M. I called Egypt's Zayyat again to tell him of Israel's reiterated pledge and our guarantee of it. At 7:47 A.M. I checked in with Dobrynin. Our message had been passed to Moscow, he said. I told him about my conversation with Zayyat and asked for his help in reaching the Syrians. We would "play no games," I said; Moscow would be informed of our communications with the parties.

Meanwhile, I instructed my NSC deputy in Washington, General Brent Scowcroft, to call a 9:00 A.M. meeting, in my absence, of the Washington Special Actions Group (WSAG) to canvass the views of the rest of the government.

At 8:15 A.M. Zayyat called me with Cairo's reply: He claimed there had been an Israeli "provocation"; Israeli naval units supported by aircraft had attacked Egyptian positions in the Gulf of Suez; they were being repulsed; a communiqué had been issued. This was preposterous. It was improbable that Israel would break a pledge to the United States only a few hours old; inconceivable that it would start a war on the Day of Atonement; uncharacteristic for it to strike without mobilization; nonsensical for Israel to initiate hostilities with a naval action at the farthest distance from its borders. I told Zayyat coldly that I hoped Egypt would confine its military "response" to the locale where the "attack" had occurred. I would immediately contact Israel to seek clarification. I put White House communications at the disposal of Zayyat to reach Cairo. Luckily for our heroic White House telephone operators, they had become accustomed to me; otherwise the sudden plethora of foreign accents might have proved too daunting.

At 8:25 A.M. I called Israeli Foreign Minister Abba Eban, who was also in New York, and told him of Zayyat's charge of an Israeli attack in the Gulf of Suez. Eban and I considered such a move inconceivable on Israel's holiest day; he would check with Jerusalem immediately.[1]

At 8:29 A.M. Shalev was on the line from Washington with the report from Israel that Egyptian and Syrian planes had been attacking along all fronts for the past half-hour.* He had no word yet on ground operations, if any; of the alleged Israeli "naval attack" he knew nothing.

At 8:30 A.M. I dispatched flash messages to the kings of Jordan and Saudi Arabia urging that they use their influence to avert hostilities. (Flash messages have top priority and reach their destination in minutes.) I had little hope: If the attack was premeditated, these two moderate Arab states could not halt it; if it resulted from misunderstanding they were in no position to remove it. Their replies late that night showed that they were bystanders. Hussein conveyed his concern at the outbreak of hostilities, Faisal emphasized Arab solidarity. Both remained at the fringes of the military conflict thereafter.

At 8:35 A.M. I called Al Haig, the President's chief of staff, who was with Nixon in Key Biscayne, Florida, to inform the President that war appeared to have started. Haig and I speculated inconclusively about the Soviets' role. What might have happened, I thought, was that they had recommended to Egypt that a little stirring was needed to encourage diplomatic activity and "those maniacs have stirred a little too much." I suggested that the White House spokesman in Florida, deputy press

---

*The combined Egyptian-Syrian attack began at approximately 2:00 P.M. Middle East time, or 8:00 A.M. Washington time. As will be seen, it was some time before our bureaucracy agreed that war had actually begun, or that the Arabs had started it.

secretary Gerald L. Warren, say no more than that the President was getting regular reports on events and was on top of things.

At 8:40 A.M. I phoned UN Secretary-General Kurt Waldheim with a brief summary of what I knew. He would not be able to influence substantive discussions, but he was well disposed and could be helpful on procedural problems. He was in a position to delay or speed up Security Council or General Assembly meetings. And he was a great gossip. One could be sure that he would convey what one was reluctant to say directly — veiled threats or plans for compromise too delicate to put forward under one's own name. At this point I wanted above all his cooperation in allaying any fears of Israeli preemption. I urged him to use his influence for restraint with the Syrians, with whom we still had no contact, and the Egyptians. Waldheim observed somewhat mournfully that he had sat next to the Syrian Foreign Minister at lunch the previous day but had been told nothing. I sympathized; the same had happened to me with Zayyat, though it was asking a bit much to expect Syria and Egypt to inform us that a surprise attack was imminent.

At 8:50 A.M. Eban called to convey the same reassurance as Shalev, that there would be no Israeli preemption; redundant channels of communication were obviously not an American peculiarity. He knew nothing of an alleged naval engagement in the Gulf of Suez or anywhere else.

My next task was to give Scowcroft instructions for the WSAG meeting. If this was the outbreak of a full-scale war (we were still not sure), we had two problems: what to do, and what to say. Like everyone else, I expected a rapid Israeli victory; but history taught that at some stage every Mideast war had turned into an international crisis. Arab frustrations would elicit Soviet threats. There was a danger that Europe would dissociate from us: It had never been comfortable with American support for Israel and, as I have pointed out in Chapter V, some of its leaders were looking for pretexts to build European autonomy in separation from, if not in opposition to, the United States. And it was obvious to all that Nixon was wounded by Watergate. We would need to show that we were determined to prevent Soviet intervention, but we had to do so in a low-key way, conveying confidence without weakness.

From New York I asked Scowcroft to obtain by noon, first, a plan to move the US Sixth Fleet — at the moment scattered among ports in Spain and Greece — into the eastern Mediterranean; and second, plans to reinforce our Mediterranean naval units if necessary. No troop movements should take place, but the readiness of our forces should be enhanced. Departments should do no briefing on their own. When anything was to be said, Haig or I would clear it. The President or Haig should decide whether the White House or some other agency would do the briefing.

Then at 9:00 A.M. Shalev informed me urgently that Egypt's forces

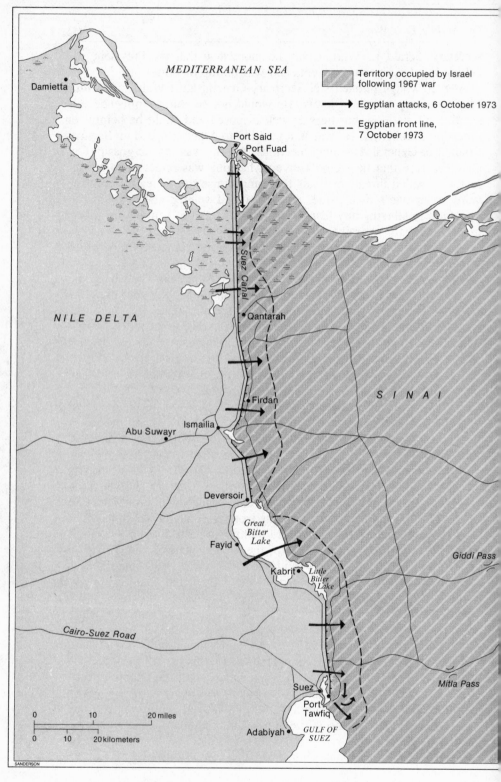

The Sinai Front: Egyptian Attack, October 6, 1973

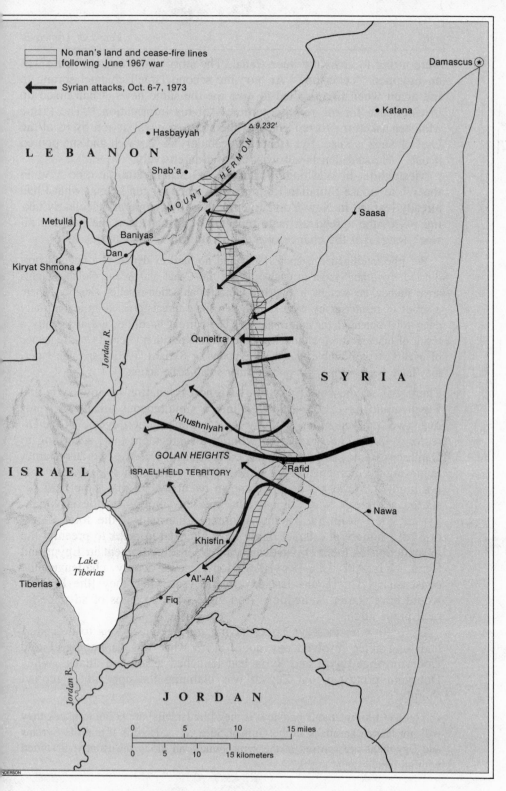

The Golan Front: Syrian Attack, October 6–7, 1973

were trying to cross the Suez Canal. The story about a naval battle was
an Egyptian "cover-up." At 9:07 the second Israeli channel sprang to
life again when Eban called to give me the same news. Eban made up
in eloquence for the relative tardiness of his information: "The Prime
Minister asked me to tell you that the story of naval action by us at the
Gulf of Suez is false. Her Hebrew vocabulary is very rich and she poured
it out." He said that Israel was reacting defensively.

Meanwhile, in Washington, the WSAG was meeting at 9:00 A.M. in
the White House Situation Room. Intelligence lagged behind what I had
already learned in New York: Even with military operations clearly taking place, the agreed estimate repeated what had been the position all
week long, that the chance of a deliberate full-scale war was low:

> We [the intelligence agencies] can find no hard evidence of a major, coor-
> dinated Egyptian/Syrian offensive across the Canal and in the Golan Heights
> area. Rather, the weight of evidence indicates an action-reaction situation where
> a series of responses by each side to perceived threats created an increasingly
> dangerous potential for confrontation. The current hostilities are apparently a
> result of that situation, although we are not in a position to clarify the sequence
> of events. It is possible that the Egyptians or Syrians, particularly the latter,
> may have been preparing a raid or other small-scale action.

There was no dissent. There was also no explanation of how Syria and
Egypt could have been triggered into a simultaneous attack on fronts
over two hundred miles apart by the "action-reaction cycle." CIA Director William Colby reported without disagreement that, according to
Damascus Radio, Israel had launched the attack. Defense Secretary James
Schlesinger commented that while Syria's reputation for veracity was
not high, it would be the first time in twenty years that Israel had *not*
started a Mideast war: "I just don't see any motive on the Egyptian-
Syrian side." Admiral Thomas Moorer, Chairman of the Joint Chiefs
of Staff, thought that Israel might have attacked in order to preempt the
introduction of more sophisticated air defense equipment in Egypt and
Syria. Only Alfred L. (Roy) Atherton, Sisco's deputy, challenged the
consensus: "This is the last day in the year when they [the Israelis]
would have started something. And there were no signs of advance Israeli preparations."

By 9:20 A.M. in New York, having no preconceptions to defend, I
had long since resolved any doubt as to what was happening. I told
Dobrynin that Egypt and Syria had launched a surprise attack. When
Dobrynin protested that Zayyat was claiming the opposite, I replied
sharply:

> You and I know that is baloney. If they [the Israelis] are going to attack they
> will not launch an attack in the Gulf of Suez. . . . How is it that the Syrians
> and Egyptians are starting at the same minute all along the front if it started
> with an Israeli naval attack?

I warned Dobrynin that everything that had been achieved in East-West relations might be at risk if the Middle East went out of control. It was the beginning of a protracted duel in which Washington and Moscow, each protesting its devotion to cooperation, sought to weaken the other without risking an open confrontation.

Why We Were Surprised

SURPRISE attack has been the subject of military writing and analysis since the beginning of warfare, and in America particularly since December 7, 1941. A pioneering study of the intelligence failure at Pearl Harbor, by Roberta Wohlstetter, relates surprise to the potential victim's inability to distinguish significant information from trivia. Evidence of an impending attack is usually overwhelmed by background "noise," that is, the barrage of other information that is either ambiguous, irrelevant, or contradictory.[2] A perceptive academic study of Hitler's attack on Russia in June 1941 takes Wohlstetter's analysis a step further: The attacker may reveal his activity but deliberately deceive as to its purpose.[3] Thus Hitler in 1941 made no attempt to conceal the German military buildup on the Soviet frontier; indeed, its scale was such that it could not be hidden. But Hitler created the impression — and Stalin chose to believe — that there would be some specific German ultimatum that would trigger a negotiation rather than a war. The concept is hardly new. "All warfare is based on deception," wrote the Chinese analyst Sun Tzu around 500 B.C.[4]

The Egyptian-Syrian attack was a classic of strategic and tactical surprise. But the surprise of the October war is not explained fully by either background "noise" or deception. It resulted from the misinterpretation of facts available for all to see, unbeclouded by any conflicting information. Sadat boldly all but told what he was going to do and we did not believe him. He overwhelmed us with information and let us draw the wrong conclusion. October 6 was the culmination of a failure of *political* analysis on the part of its victims.

Every Israeli (and American) analysis before October 1973 agreed that Egypt and Syria lacked the military capability to regain their territory by force of arms; hence there would be no war. The Arab armies must lose; hence they would not attack. The premises were correct. The conclusions were not. After the October war, the Israelis learned from prisoners that Egypt had no serious expectations of even reaching the Sinai passes twenty to thirty miles from the Suez Canal. Egyptian forces had drilled for years to perfect the technique of crossing the Suez Canal; beyond it they had no operational plan except to hang on. The Egyptian army never did reach the Sinai passes. The Syrian and Egyptian armies both suffered heavy setbacks. Yet Sadat achieved his fundamental objective of shaking belief in Israel's invincibility and Arab impotence, and thus transformed the psychological basis of the negotiating stale-mate.

What literally no one understood beforehand was the mind of the man: Sadat aimed not for territorial gain but for a crisis that would alter the attitudes into which the parties were then frozen — and thereby open the way for negotiations. The shock would enable *both* sides, including Egypt, to show a flexibility that was impossible while Israel considered itself militarily supreme and Egypt was paralyzed by humiliation. His purpose, in short, was psychological and diplomatic, much more than military. Sadat knew from two secret meetings in early 1973 between his national security adviser, Hafiz Ismail, and me that we were willing to engage in the diplomacy of the Arab-Israeli conflict. But he must have drawn two conclusions: one, that the full Arab program of total Israeli withdrawal was unattainable; two, that what was achievable im-mediately was insupportable for Egypt so long as it seemed to flow from weakness. So Sadat fought a war not to acquire territory but to restore Egypt's self-respect and thereby increase its diplomatic flexibility. (Syria fought for more conventional and literal objectives: It simply wanted to regain occupied territory and at a minimum to inflict casualties on Is-rael.) Rare is the statesman who at the beginning of a war has so clear a perception of its political objective; rarer still is a war fought to lay the basis for moderation in its aftermath.

The boldness of Sadat's strategy lay in planning for what no one could imagine; that was the principal reason the Arabs achieved sur-prise. The highest policymakers in both Washington and Jerusalem did not lack facts. The error lay in the conclusion drawn from them.

Sadat, in fact, paralyzed his opponents with their own preconcep-tions:

• He had been threatening to go to war every year since 1971. One year after another had been loudly proclaimed as the "year of deci-sion." No threat had ever come close to being implemented. New threats of war were therefore dismissed as bluff.

• Israeli planners simply assumed that Egypt would not attack as long as it lacked air superiority, and that no attack would come without at least twenty-four to forty-eight hours' warning.[5] The United States would have time to intervene diplomatically and Israel time to mobilize.

• The Arab nations were not expected to go to war without giving diplomacy one more chance. They would therefore wait for the results of our peace initiative, promised for after the Israeli election on Octo-ber 30.

All these assumptions turned out to be false. Sadat's unfulfilled threats camouflaged his intentions. Israel had barely ten hours' warning. And Sadat saw no point in awaiting our diplomacy. Its probable outcome — some sort of interim agreement moving forces back from the Suez

Canal — would serve none of his political purposes unless he could present it as having been exacted by Arab strength. The imminence of negotiations thus probably spurred rather than delayed his decision; he could afford to let us neither succeed, which would have mortgaged his domestic position, nor fail, which might have undermined our interest in mediation. The approaching diplomacy distorted the Israelis' perspective as well. They acquired a vested interest in belittling Arab threats lest the United States use the danger of war as a pretext to press Israel for concessions.

Storm clouds had been evident since the spring and particularly in May, five months before the war. Brezhnev and Gromyko warned of the danger in my meetings with them in Zavidovo in early May and at the summit with Nixon in June. But we dismissed this as psychological warfare because we did not see any rational military option that would not worsen the Soviet and Arab positions. In May also, King Hussein had sent us warnings that Syrian and Egyptian military preparations were too realistic to be considered maneuvers. I assured him that we were "watching the situation very carefully" — smug bureaucratese for our conviction that there was no real danger of war. Almost concurrently, Arnaud de Borchgrave, *Newsweek*'s senior diplomatic correspondent, told me over lunch that war fever was rising all over the Middle East, especially in Egypt. In May, too, Israel considered Egyptian preparations sufficiently threatening to order partial mobilization. It turned out to be a false alarm.*

As a result of these danger signals I had assembled a WSAG meeting on May 15 to review the possible threat of war. Nothing seemed to have affected the reassuring tone of the Israeli government. My staff summed up the Israeli view, which was that an Egyptian attack was unlikely:

> There is low probability that Sadat will renew fighting to break the deadlock, not because Sadat would not want to go to war but because he is conscious of the severe results of such a step in view of the balance of power in the area, the relative weakness of Egypt and the current international circumstances.

The report went on to characterize Egypt's military preparations as not being practical steps toward war. And it regarded a joint Egyptian-Syrian move as out of the question.

Our own assessments were substantially the same, perhaps because of our respect for Israel's judgment. On May 5, 1973, James Schlesinger, then CIA Director, had sent me a report that the Egyptian General Staff had been ordered to prepare a detailed plan for crossing the Canal. But the CIA added soothingly that it did not believe that the plan de-

---

*The cost of mobilizing for the false alarm in May 1973 added to Israel's hesitation when the real crisis came in October.

scribed matched up with Sadat's objectives. It made the standard assumption about Sadat's definition of rationality, noting Egyptian and other Arab military preparations but concluding that they were for psychological purposes. Overall the CIA did not believe that an outbreak of hostilities was likely before the next UN debate (scheduled for midsummer). Similarly, an interagency report of mid-May noted that even if the UN debate passed without useful results, "this does not mean that hostilities will then become inevitable or even probable."* Schlesinger told the WSAG meeting of May 15 that Egypt's military capabilities were limited to a sneak air attack on Israel, a move that would be "extremely ill-advised." Egypt would not be able to hold even a small amount of territory across the Suez Canal for as much as one week.

No wonder that the May 15 WSAG meeting lasted less than forty-five minutes and that it drifted off into a discussion of Lebanon's chronic crisis. I did, however, ask for two contingency plans. The first was for the eventuality that Lebanon might get out of control. The second I outlined as follows:

. . . the kinds of things the Egyptians might do, the various ways in which the Israelis might react and the diplomatic issues that might ensue. Short of actual Soviet intervention, it's hard to envisage any direct US action. But we should consider what to do to keep the Soviets out; the ways in which we might use the crisis to get diplomatic movement, if that is what we want, or to return to the status quo ante if it is decided that is desirable.

I would like to claim prescience for raising questions that defined fairly accurately the very issues that were to confront us abruptly a few months later. Unfortunately, the acuteness of my analysis was not matched by a sense of urgency. The contingency study had not been completed when war broke out on October 6.

Between June and September, the reporting from our various diplomatic posts converged on the proposition that war was improbable. Egypt and Syria were said to be suspicious of Soviet motivations and were thought to be relying increasingly on economic pressures, especially the oil weapon. Those evaluations were maintained during September while Egypt canceled leaves, called up large numbers of reserves, and began major military exercises; and while Syria built up its forces in the Golan Heights. Lulled by the false alarm of May, both Americans and Israelis interpreted these activities as merely more realistic exercises.

---

*The State Department's Bureau of Intelligence and Research (INR), directed by Ray S. Cline, prepared the only farsighted estimate, in late May 1973. Amazingly, it did not dissent from the interagency report, noted above, that war was improbable. But it presented an Information Memorandum to Secretary Rogers on May 31 that viewed the threat of a war for political purposes with "a little more urgency" than the interagency paper. It predicted that if the diplomatic stalemate continued, "our view is that the resumption of hostilities by autumn will become a better than even bet." Strangely enough, INR abandoned its prediction as war actually approached.

On September 28 Gromyko visited Nixon at the White House and warned once again that it was dangerous to treat the Middle East as quiescent: "We could all wake up one day and find there is a real conflagration in that area." But the warning in fact lulled us, for Gromyko then agreed to a schedule for dealing with the incipient crisis, including preliminary talks with the Middle East parties starting in November, followed by an exchange of views with the Soviet Union in January 1974, when I was planning to visit Moscow.

But on Sunday, September 30, by pure chance, I experienced alarm. I was spending my first full weekend in Washington as Secretary of State and I leafed through some intelligence reports by State's intelligence bureau (INR) in order to acquaint myself with its capabilities. I came across one that noted concentrations of unusual numbers of Syrian tanks on the Golan Heights. Would Syria so expose itself to Israeli preemption unless it intended to attack? I asked myself. I caused our intelligence to be reviewed at once.

There are two ways by which intelligence reaches top officials. One is through an agreed National Intelligence Estimate of all the different agencies represented on the US Intelligence Board. This usually requires several days to accomplish. Another is the individual assessment of the intelligence agency serving a particular Cabinet member — the Defense Intelligence Agency (DIA) for the Secretary of Defense; INR for the Secretary of State. The CIA is technically available to all agencies of the government; however, it usually undertakes special studies for the President. Its director is the titular head and actual coordinator of all the various departmental intelligence units.

On this occasion I covered all bases. I asked for an interagency estimate as soon as possible. Pending it, I requested separate assessments that day from INR (as Secretary of State) and from CIA (as Presidential national security adviser).

As it happened, I had also that Sunday scheduled a meeting with Israeli Ambassador Simcha Dinitz to review our plans for starting Middle East negotiations later in the year. Dinitz arrived worried — but not about Syrian tanks. He passionately pressed another problem. Soviet Jews who left the Soviet Union under the liberalized emigration policy of the détente period generally did so via a transit camp in Austria, at Schönau near Vienna. On September 28 a train traveling from Moscow to Vienna with Soviet Jews aboard was attacked by Arab terrorists as it crossed from Czechoslovakia into Austria; some emigrants were taken hostage. Austrian Chancellor Bruno Kreisky agreed to the terrorists' condition for release: that the transit facilities at Schönau be closed. The result was a furor in Israel and the riveting of attention, during the crucial week before the war, on Austria, not on Egypt or Syria. As Abba Eban later observed of that week, "Historians who read the Israeli newspapers published in the first days of October will be startled to find that there was no hint of any crisis, let alone of imminent war."[6]

Thus it was I who first raised questions with Dinitz about the Arab military buildup. Had he any information? His instructions, it proved, were to convey to our intelligence officials what Israel knew of Arab deployments but not to raise it at a "political" level unless there was a specific query. Israel, especially as it was taking a relaxed view, did not want to stir up our diplomacy. Clearly it would have insisted on intense consultation at the highest levels if it saw a serious danger of war. Its judgment was that Arab deployments were maneuvers or psychological warfare. I remained uneasy, however, and asked Dinitz to review the assessment every forty-eight hours. I asked our own intelligence agencies to do the same when they, too, reported that day (in response to my request) essentially the same conclusions. INR said:

> In our view, the political climate in the Arab states argues against a major Syrian military move against Israel at this time. The possibility of a more limited Syrian strike, perhaps one designed to retaliate for the pounding the Syrian Air Force took from the Israelis on September 13,* cannot of course be excluded.

But the qualification referred only to the familiar small-scale raids and reprisals. Such diffidence calmed rather than alerted us.** The CIA reassured us on September 30 that the whole thrust of President Sadat's activities since the spring had been in the direction of bringing moral, political, and economic force to bear on Israel in tacit acknowledgment of Arab unreadiness to make war.

My sense of alarm thus dispelled, I turned my attention to other problems, among them getting to know the Arab foreign ministers attending the UN General Assembly. Subsequent intelligence reports completed the process of reassurance: On October 3 an Israeli foreign ministry official expressed the view that Egyptian military movements were routine and that "the voice of reason" would prevail in Damascus as well. Eban spoke to me in the same vein on October 4 in New York. Our own reporting was a mirror image of Israel's. DIA's morning summary of October 3 concluded: "The movement of Syrian troops and Egyptian military readiness are considered to be coincidental and not designed to lead to major hostilities." Two days later — the day before the war —

---

*On September 13 the Israeli air force had ambushed and shot down thirteen Syrian Soviet-built jets.

**Ray Cline, head of INR, later argued in print that while this analysis did not predict an attack, it was "far from saying it was not at all likely." Mr. Cline is one of our nation's most distinguished intelligence experts. This does not make him infallible. The reader will have to judge whether a harassed policymaker could possibly draw the inference suggested by Mr. Cline from the conclusion of the INR report.[7]

the CIA reiterated its judgment of September 30 that Egypt did not appear to be preparing for war with Israel.

Clearly, there was an intelligence failure, but misjudgment was not confined to the agencies. Every policymaker knew all the facts. The Israelis were monitoring the movement of every Egyptian and Syrian unit. The general plan of attack, especially of the Syrians, was fairly well understood. What no one believed — the consumers no more than the producers of intelligence — was that the Arabs would act on it. Our definition of rationality did not take seriously the notion of starting an unwinnable war to restore self-respect. There was no defense against our own preconceptions or those of our allies.

Our mind-set was dramatized by the events of October 5, when we woke up to the astonishing news that for twenty-four hours the Soviet Union had been airlifting all its dependents out of Egypt and Syria. Technical and military advisers seemed to be staying, however. It is now inexplicable how that development was misinterpreted. Still, despite this event and the Egyptian military exercises, our morning briefings assured us that Egypt and Syria were not planning for war.

As it turned out, my White House office was unusually alert to events in the Middle East that day because it had received cryptic word from Shalev that a special message was coming from Jerusalem about "alarming developments overnight." A meeting was arranged for early afternoon between Eban, Shalev, and me in New York. In preparation, Peter Rodman tried to determine from my NSC office what the "alarming developments" might be. He could find only the overnight report from our Defense Attaché in Tel Aviv on the evacuation of Soviet civilian dependents. A check with the Situation Room turned up no other cables reporting any other significant occurrences.

At Rodman's suggestion, General Scowcroft called CIA to ask for a fresh political and military assessment to arm me for the meeting. Received at the White House around noon of October 5, it added nothing to the previous judgment denying the likelihood of war:

It appears that both sides are becoming increasingly concerned about the activities of the other. Rumors and agent reports may be feeding the uneasiness that appears to be developing. The military preparations that have occurred do not indicate that any party intends to initiate hostilities.

Whatever had alarmed the Israelis obviously failed to produce a sense of urgency in the delivery of their message. My appointment with Eban was repeatedly postponed because the promised cable had not yet arrived from Jerusalem. In the meantime, I started a heavy schedule of talks with foreign ministers attending the United Nations. Then Jerusalem decided that Shalev should deliver the message to me; a meeting with Eban was no longer thought necessary. This, of course, downgraded the importance of the message. By late afternoon Rodman suggested to Shalev that it would speed matters if he delivered the message, when it came, at the NSC office in the White House rather than flying up to New York himself. My schedule there was jam-packed and secure cable communications between my Washington office and my New York suite were excellent.

Shalev checked with Jerusalem and finally appeared at the White House around 5:30 P.M. to give Scowcroft *two* messages for me that tended to cancel each other out. The "urgent" message was that I inform the Soviet Union and the Arabs that Israel intended no preemptive strike; if Arab military preparations were for defensive purposes they were therefore unnecessary; at the same time Israel would react with firmness and great strength if the Arabs initiated a war. Simultaneously, Shalev delivered the latest Israeli estimate, which coincided exactly with that of the CIA six hours earlier, reinforcing the existing complacency. After cataloguing the by-now familiar Arab preparations, Israel concluded:

> Our assessment is that the alert measures being taken by Egypt and Syria are in part connected with maneuvers (as regards Egypt) and in part due to fears of offensive actions by Israel. We consider the opening of military operations against Israel by the two armies as of low probability.

Scowcroft heard Shalev out and wired the messages immediately to my New York office.

In the event, I did not see the messages until the next morning. On that Friday night I closeted myself in my Waldorf Towers suite for a private dinner and work on a major speech I would give in Washington three days later. It was the first evening I had had to myself since my nomination as Secretary of State on August 22. I did not ask for additional paperwork and my staff saw no urgent reason to interrupt me. Nor am I sure I would have done anything immediately with the messages had I received them. It was now the middle of the night in all capitals concerned; nothing menacing seemed afoot. We were not informed that Israel had taken any special precautions — and it had not called up reserves. It is also clear in retrospect that any effort by us then would have been academic. The Arab assault was deliberate, not even remotely prompted by fear of an Israeli attack. Any last-minute message to Egypt and Syria reassuring them that Israel would not preempt would only have been greeted with elation in the war rooms of Cairo and Damascus.

The breakdown was not administrative but intellectual. At the latest on October 5, as we learned of the Soviets' evacuation of their dependents from the Middle East, we should have known that big events were impending. We uncritically accepted the Israeli assessment that the reason was either a "crisis in relations with Egypt and Syria or the result of a Soviet assessment that hostilities may break out in the Middle East." But the only danger of hostilities foreseen lay in the "action-reaction cycle": each side's fear that its adversary was about to attack.

There were questions crying to be asked that would have rapidly reached the heart of the matter. That they occurred to no one, including me, seems inexplicable in retrospect. What crisis could possibly occur in Soviet-Arab relations that involved *both* Egypt and Syria simultaneously? Why would the Soviets evacuate dependents but not the advisers if there was a political crisis? Why would they undertake an emergency airlift if they were not working against a deadline? And what could that deadline be other than the opening of hostilities? The Israeli view that the Soviets might fear the outbreak of war should have given us pause. For if we had reflected, it would have been clear that the Soviets could not be fearing an *Israeli* attack. Had they done so they would have made urgent representations in Washington to get us to dissuade Israel, and perhaps added public threats. If the Soviets evacuated dependents because they feared a war, they must have had a very good idea that it would be started by the Arabs.

Policymakers cannot hide behind their analysts if they miss the essence of an issue. They can never know all the facts, but they have a duty to ask the right questions. That was the real failure on the eve of the Mideast war. We had become too complacent about our own assumptions. We knew everything but understood too little. And for that the highest officials — including me — must assume responsibility.

Shaping a Strategy

WHEN the war did break out, we had to face up to a number of seemingly contradictory concerns. We had to assure the survival and security of Israel; we needed to maintain our relations with moderate Arab countries, such as Jordan and Saudi Arabia. We knew that in a prolonged crisis Europe and Japan would be restless and, if we faltered, pursue a course different from ours. And while the Soviet Union would no doubt maneuver warily, it could not be expected to rescue us from our dilemmas; indeed, it would probably do all it could to intensify them.

From the first, I was convinced that we were in a good position to dominate events. Our de facto ally Israel stood to win. Our moderate Arab friends — though they could not admit it — were nearly as afraid of a victory achieved by Soviet arms as of a defeat of their Arab brethren. European dissociation might be mitigated by a conspicuous assertion of American leadership. And we might induce Soviet caution by threatening the end of détente while assembling the means for a confrontation should diplomacy fail.

This would not be an easy assignment, however, especially while the American Presidency was in trauma. It was not clear that Nixon retained enough authority to manage the manifold pressures about to descend on him. But we could not sit on the sidelines if the Middle East should rage out of control; the world would view it as a collapse of American authority, whatever alibi we put forward. We had to protect our country's ability to play its indispensable role as the guarantor of peace and the repository of the hopes of free peoples. We were like a tightrope walker: To stop was to fall; our only hope was to move forward, to ignore the chasm yawning below us.

Here at last was the critical test of the strategy we had been pursuing in the Middle East ever since Nixon entered office. We had seen no chance of serious negotiation while radical tendencies fed on the conviction that Soviet pressures and Arab blackmail would obviate the need for compromise. To demonstrate the futility of Soviet-backed blackmail had been for some time the key to our diplomacy; it was now culminating in an unexpected showdown. At its end — if we played our hand well — the Arab countries might abandon reliance on Soviet pressure and seek goals through cooperation with the United States.

Once war had started, it was plain that the diplomatic stalemate would be broken. But it would not be easy. If Israel won overwhelmingly — as we first expected — we had to avoid becoming the focal point of all Arab resentments. We had to keep the Soviet Union from emerging as the Arabs' savior, which it could do either by pretending that its bluster stopped the Israeli advance or by involving itself directly in the war. If the unexpected happened and Israel was in difficulty, we would have to do what was necessary to save it. We could not permit Soviet clients to defeat a traditional friend. But once having demonstrated the futility of the military option, we would then have to use this to give impetus to the search for peace. In sum, we had the opportunity to dominate events; but we ran the risk of becoming the butt of every controversy.

From the outset, I was determined to use the war to start a peace process. "There is no longer an excuse for a delay," I told Haig on the morning of October 6, in our first lengthy discussion of strategy. "After we get the fighting stopped we should use this as a vehicle to get the diplomacy started." Nixon in the following days enthusiastically agreed. On October 8 he told me:

We must not under any circumstances allow them [Israel] because of the victory that they're going to win — and they'll win it, thank God, they should — but we must not get away with just having this thing hang over for another four years and have us at odds with the Arab world. We're not going to do it anymore.

A big piece of the puzzle was Soviet intentions. What had the Soviets known about the imminence of war? Would they encourage its continuation with equipment and diplomatic support? Or would they cooperate in ending it?

How much the Soviets knew of Arab plans, or encouraged them, is still unclear. There is no doubt that they realized no later than the evening of October 3 that war was imminent, because their Ambassador in Cairo was then officially informed.[8] And they reacted immediately with their evacuation. Units of the Soviet fleet in Alexandria and Port Said put to sea on October 5. Did the Soviets expect us to pick up the signals, and did we fail to ask the right questions? Was it a form of warning to us without betraying their allies, or simple precaution?

There are no obvious answers, especially to the last one. Détente was conceived as a relationship between adversaries; it did not pretend friendship. No Arab leader whom I met immediately after the war gave credence to the charge of Soviet-Arab collusion. Sadat, Algerian President Boumedienne, Syrian President Asad, whatever their differences, agreed that Moscow had been grudging in its support for the Arab cause, slow in its delivery of arms, and eager to press for a ceasefire from the first day of the war. Indeed, in his autobiography Sadat insisted that while the Soviets were ignorant of his precise plans, Moscow had sought to impede any possible Egyptian move by slowing down military deliveries and working against him in Syria.[9] On the other hand, after Hafiz Ismail visited Moscow in February 1973, Egypt apparently concluded that it was free to consult its own interests short of actions that might lead to a US–Soviet war. In diplomatic language this was an invitation to limited war. Then there was the strange incident of the terrorist attack on the trainload of Jews emigrating from the Soviet Union through Austria. Was this attack, a week before the war, a coincidence or a planned diversionary move? If the latter, did the Soviets acquiesce or know of the purpose? It was reported at the time that the guerrillas had boarded the train in Czechoslovakia, then seized the hostages as the train crossed the border into Austria.[10] It seems inconceivable that armed men could board a train in a country as heavily policed as Czechoslovakia without the cooperation of the authorities, who in turn would never act on a matter of such serious consequence without Soviet approval.

My view is that the Soviet Union stopped short of encouraging the war but made no effort to halt it. Soviet intelligence undoubtedly deduced that some sort of military operation was being planned. Brezhnev must have decided that his warning to us in May and June fulfilled his obligation to us. The Soviets did nothing further to alert us more concretely (unless one regards the evacuation of dependents as an indirect warning). The likelihood also is that the Kremlin believed that its interests were served whatever happened. If the Arabs did well, the credit would go to Soviet arms and Soviet support. If they did poorly, Mos-

cow thought it could emerge, as in 1967, the champion of the Arab
cause; the consequent radicalization of the Arab world would strengthen
Soviet friends and perhaps even get rid of Egypt's troublesome Sadat,
who had expelled Soviet personnel in July 1972.

On October 6 I had not yet reached a conclusion about Soviet fore-
knowledge. But there was no doubt in my mind about the geopolitical
stakes. About ninety minutes after we learned of the fighting, when we
fully expected a rapid Israeli victory, I told Haig for Nixon:

> I think the worst thing we could do is to now take a sort of neutral position
> while the fighting is going on, unless the Soviets take a neutral position with
> us. . . . If the Soviets are all-out on the other side we have a mischievous
> case of collusion and then we have September 1970 all over again and we had
> better then be tough as nails.

We both knew, of course, that our situation was far different from
that in the 1970 Jordan crisis. Then, Nixon was at the height of his
power; now, his authority was deteriorating daily. In September 1973
the issue of whether Nixon should surrender tape recordings from his
office had moved inexorably through the courts, and was reaching a
climax at the very moment war broke out. The first indictments spawned
by Watergate had been handed down, including one against John Ehrlichman. Campaign aide Donald Segretti had just pleaded guilty to three
misdemeanors relating to "dirty tricks" during the 1972 Presidential
race. On top of all this, Nixon was about to lose his Vice President,
Spiro Agnew, in a scandal concerning alleged payoffs when Agnew was
Governor of Maryland. Agnew resigned on October 10, the fourth day
of the war. And the "Saturday night massacre" — the firing of Special
Prosecutor Archibald Cox and the resignation of Attorney General Elliot
Richardson — occurred ten days later, precisely when I was in Moscow
discussing a cease-fire to end the war.

Nixon was thus preoccupied with Watergate and its ramifications
throughout the Middle East crisis. This did not keep him from being
informed, or from making the key decisions. But it did inhibit the frenetic, restless, penetrating leadership that had characterized his performance in previous crises. His courage had not been impaired; it was if
anything reinforced by the fatalism with which he faced the last phase
of his Presidency and by his desperate desire to be seen to vindicate the
national interest in the area of foreign policy that was his forte. But he
was too distracted to shape the decisions before they reached him; that
responsibility now descended on me. I was painfully aware that whatever we did, we were likely to be accused of ulterior motives; we would
have great difficulty rallying public support as we pursued the seemingly
irreconcilable aims of thwarting the military designs of the side armed
by the Soviets and trying to win Arab confidence, so we could both

emerge as mediator and demonstrate that the road to peace led through Washington.

The first issue after the war opened concerned tactics at the United Nations. We did not want a General Assembly debate, which would have meant a diatribe of the nonaligned in support of the extreme Arab position, with the Soviets acting as the Arabs' lawyer, our European allies maintaining at least an embarrassed silence, and the United States isolated. We were better placed in the Security Council, though there too we faced problems. One was that the Soviets, or a proxy of theirs, might introduce a resolution supporting the unattainable comprehensive Arab program, forcing us to veto and undermining our position with the Arab moderates. There would also be a strong temptation to adopt a resolution in favor of an immediate cease-fire in place. We wanted to avoid this while the attacking side was gaining territory, because it would reinforce the tendency to use the UN to ratify the gains of surprise attack. And within a short time — less than seventy-two hours, according to our experts — the tide of battle would turn, with Israel pushing the Arabs back. We would then face the complexities of an Israeli victory, Arab rage, Soviet meddling, and the danger that all frustrations would turn on us.

I therefore recommended to Nixon that we should seek to draw the Soviets into a *joint* approach in the Security Council. It would keep Moscow from harassing us with its own proposals; it might separate Moscow from its Arab clients. According to my scheme, the two superpowers would not assess blame but instead call for a prompt return to the lines at which the conflict had started. If the Soviets agreed and the Arabs acquiesced, the conflict would have been contained. Our losses in the Arab world would be balanced by those of the Soviets, who, as in 1972, would have been perceived in the Arab world as giving priority to their ties with Washington. If the Soviets refused, as was probable, we would have gained the time for Israel to restore the status quo ante by military means. At that point we could accept a simple cease-fire solution, and insist that Israel return to prewar lines if it had crossed them. Once we had made our balanced position clear, this would cool the ardor of our European allies who might be tempted to rush in with more one-sided approaches.

I quickly put our proposition to Dobrynin at 9:35 A.M. on October 6. I warned that if the Soviets acted irresponsibly we would have no choice except to let nature take its course, that is to say, simply await the inevitable Israeli victory. "That," I said ominously, "will affect a lot of our relationships." I told Dobrynin that we would not proceed in the Security Council until we had a reply from Moscow to our proposal and expressed the hope that Moscow in its turn would refrain from unilateral action.

Dobrynin now was cool and professional. He avowed understanding, verging on sympathy, for our approach. There was the usual discussion of the quickest means of communication, and this time he thought the Hot Line would be fastest. Since he had to assume that we would read his message, this was undoubtedly designed to show, once again, that Dobrynin had nothing to hide. I gave him permission to use the Hot Line. He did not avail himself of it. We had played our little game. We could now return to serious business.

Our first need was to gain time. Whatever the future might hold, America's options would increase with Israeli mobilization (which would take two days to complete). Around 10:20 A.M. I briefed Kurt Waldheim on our latest thinking, emphasizing that we would oppose a General Assembly debate and wanted to wait for the Soviet response before going to the Security Council. He agreed. I also told him that we would favor a restoration of the status quo ante. Waldheim was likely to get that word around in no time, slowing down passionate advocates of radical solutions with the hint of US–Soviet cooperation. During the day I briefed several NATO allies. They were sympathetic but above all eager to get out of the direct line of fire. As I had expected, they favored a cease-fire in place but not a return to the status quo ante. In other words, they were prepared to ratify Arab military gains and to dissociate from us in the first hours of a conflict in which we bore the principal burden for the common interest — a hint of things to come. I also began phoning Congressional leaders; they were at the moment mostly confused and therefore generally supportive.

At 11:25 A.M., I told Dobrynin that we had heard rumors of an Egyptian appeal to the General Assembly; we would resist such a "grievous suggestion." Moscow should not "destroy everything that it has taken us three years to build up." I argued that our offer of a joint cease-fire resolution advocating a return to the status quo ante was to our mutual advantage:

[W]e don't believe this will last 72 hours and after that the problem will be to get the Israelis back to the cease-fire line. If we agree on this course no matter what the military operations, no matter how successful the Israelis may be, we will stick to this proposal and we will be prepared to oppose them.

I asked Dobrynin for an urgent reply.

We were well positioned now. As I explained to Haig shortly afterward, if the Soviets rose to the bait of joint action, the war would end quickly. If they refused, we would let the Israelis "beat them up for a day or two and that will quiet them down. . . . [W]e should be tough in substance but not have any dramatic moves." The only thing wrong with that smug assertion was the forecast: It took the Israelis much more than a day or two to restore their military situation and before that they were on the edge of catastrophe.

I was fortunate to have Joe Sisco as my "chief of staff" for the crisis. He was indefatigable in maintaining contact with the many diplomats in New York and Washington who were aching to play a role. He was ingenious in devising formulas for negotiations. Moreover, it did not hurt that he had a loud voice and a slightly frenetic manner. The former was useful in getting himself a hearing from me; the latter kept the staff to high standards of performance.

Meanwhile, I was devouring every shred of information available on the course of the battle. Israeli air power and ground troops were struggling to meet the coordinated Arab assault in the Golan Heights and along the Suez Canal, where Egyptian armored forces were crossing at several points.

At 2:30 P.M. I left New York for Washington. While I was airborne, Dobrynin delivered to the White House the first communication from Moscow since fighting had started. It was a stall, cast in the Soviet Embassy's version of English:

The Soviet leadership got the information about the beginning of military actions in the Middle East at the same time as you got it. We take all possible measures to clarify real state of affairs in that region, since the information from there is of a contradictory nature. We fully share your concern about the conflagration of the situation in the Middle East. We repeatedly pointed in the past to the dangerous situation in that area.

We are considering now as well as you do, possible steps to be taken. We hope soon to contact you again for possible coordination of positions.

Soviet procrastination was not inconsistent with our own strategy of waiting for Israel to restore the military situation. And so long as Moscow was hinting at coordination, we were relieved of the danger that it would mount a political assault against us at the United Nations. Still, I thought it best to keep up the pressure. From Washington, I gave Dobrynin my assessment of the note: "Anatol, I have your message. I can't say it is a model of solidity. It either means you are confused or you are cooperating with them." Dobrynin volubly protested that Moscow needed only a few more hours to chart its course; meetings were taking place that very moment. I warned that we would consider a General Assembly debate a "frivolous act." And I ratcheted our warnings another notch:

If it turns into a General Assembly debate, then we will let it take its course. We are certain it will turn out to be a military victory for the Israelis. Then everyone will come to us. If it turns nasty we will shut off communications for a while.

By evening we faced conflicting pressures. In New York, Eban favored delay at the UN, to give Israel an opportunity to complete its mobilization and reverse the Egyptian and Syrian advance. In Key Biscayne Nixon was eager to announce something showing he was giving orders: Taking the issue to the Security Council would serve that purpose. Theoretically, he was right. Had the UN been equal to its stated purpose of maintaining world peace, it would have been in session that very moment. But the UN had fallen short of its early hopes. Now, under the tutelage of its "nonaligned" majority egged on by Communist pressures, it in effect ratified military gains (when that majority was sure one of its side was winning; at this early stage nobody was sure enough what was happening to commit himself). A Security Council meeting was likely to generate rhetoric that put us on the defensive, or a resolution we might have to veto. I therefore urged delay.

When I finally received the Soviet answer at around 6:00 P.M., I found it amounted to another procrastination: Moscow still had not heard from the Arabs, so it was in no position to accept our proposition; none of the parties had yet asked for a Security Council session; the Soviet Union would only embarrass itself by proceeding to a Security Council vote in such circumstances. Like everyone else, the Soviets were waiting on the outcome of the battle.

I tried to find a way through this thicket by telling Haig in Key Biscayne that we were soon going to involve the Security Council without convening a meeting. To that end I instructed our nimble UN Ambassador, John Scali, to consume the evening in "consultations" — the process of informal meetings among the delegates, usually bilateral, by which the Security Council establishes its jurisdiction without holding a formal session or forcing matters to a vote. At 7:20 P.M. I told Dobrynin what we had decided and spelled out the options once again; we were not asking for any favors; time was on our side:

> Our reading of the situation is that the Arab attack has been totally contained, that now they are going to be pushed back and this process will accelerate as the [Israeli] mobilization is completed which will be no later than Monday morning and after that we will see what we have seen before.

The Arabs, I said, had made their point; they had crossed the Suez Canal. It was important promptly to end the war and return to the diplomatic schedule we had established before hostilities. Dobrynin rejoined with Moscow's main concern: "As I understand our position the difficult[y] we are now facing is that the Arabs are trying to regain the lands occupied by Israel. They have been using that argument to us and for us to tell them you cannot free your land, it is ridiculous."

He had a case. Our proposal was not easy for the Soviets, especially in the Arab mood of exultation. On the other hand, in those early hours

Soviet prospects seemed far from brilliant. If they did nothing, Israel would prevail and they would appear impotent. If Moscow accepted our proposal it would hazard its Arab friendships. But it could not help its Arab associates without involving itself in the war, and that in turn risked the entire structure of détente. Thus emboldened, I concluded our phone conversation by giving Dobrynin until 9:00 A.M. the next day, Sunday, to let me know whether we could count on either a common approach to the Security Council or an independent Soviet effort to end the war at the latest by Tuesday (October 9). If your side is winning — or you think it is — you can afford such abrupt procedures. But they should not be the staple of diplomacy.

At the end of a hectic day — still October 6 — I chaired a WSAG meeting. According to our reports, the Israelis were containing the fighting on the Golan Heights and preparing for a major ground assault the next day; but the Egyptians were establishing positions east of the Canal and preparing to transfer more forces over several bridges they had built. The consensus was that after two or three more days, Israel would nevertheless have the upper hand. Indeed, I had a message from Eban that evening that the Israelis believed "there are good prospects" of forcing the Egyptian and Syrian troops out of their positions within three days. Therefore, all concerns focused on the potentially dangerous impact of the war on our long-term relations with the Arab countries. Beyond general philosophizing, only one actual decision was made: to move the Sixth Fleet closer to the fighting. This was no laughing matter on a weekend. One of the two aircraft carriers was anchored in Greece; the other in Spain. Their crews were on shore leave. It would take a couple of days to move both carriers to a point off Crete, a position that the Soviets would read as indicating that the United States was preparing for any contingency — close enough for us to act in an emergency, far enough to bespeak no aggressive intent. The rest of our fleet lay farther west; we would be able to indicate heightened concern by moving it off Cyprus. Interestingly, Soviet naval units that had left Egyptian ports on October 5 moved *west*. They, too, were demonstrating noninvolvement while retaining the capacity for rapid action. (The two fleets, signaling parallel intentions, later met off Crete and started milling around there. A few days later Dobrynin delivered a low-key protest about our fleet's movement but without much conviction. Not even the Soviets would have the gall to complain of our fleet's moving to a point where the Soviet squadron had been maneuvering for days.)

Close to 9:00 P.M., I talked once more with Zayyat, Egypt's Foreign Minister. He did not readily embrace my suggestion of a return to the status quo ante; he was even less receptive to my hint that since Israel would start advancing soon, Egypt would stand to benefit from our formula in a few days. He considered my ideas at first "very strange,"

and then, as he warmed to the subject, "madness." And yet Zayyat did
not speak like a conqueror. There was no braggadocio, no claim that
the Middle East problem could be settled by military means. Egypt's
purpose was limited, he declared. It was to demonstrate to Israel that a
defense line along the Suez Canal did not represent real security; that
security with a country like Egypt could be based only on mutual respect. I allowed that the point had been made. It was now time to turn
to peace. Zayyat agreed. "I don't care very much for war," he said. I
urged that Egypt and the United States keep in mind, during the passions of a war that found us at least in part on opposite sides, that
afterward we would need to cooperate in the making of peace. Zayyat
took aboard this odd message. America had a "cool head," he said.
We should make a proposal: "Now is your chance to speak to them
both [Egypt and Israel] without the great confidence that Israel had and
the great lack of confidence which we had."

Zayyat had gotten to the heart of the matter. Every war ends in some
peace, but too often leaders let military operations dictate their intentions. They ignore Bismarck's warning of woe to the statesman whose
arguments at the end of a war are not as plausible as the day he started
it. The problem between Israel and the Arab states, especially Egypt,
was to a significant degree psychological. Insecurity ironically pervaded
the military overconfidence on one side; a sense of humiliation underlay
the superior numbers on the other. The war might narrow the gulf. With
care and patience, with restored self-respect on the Arab side and a new
Israeli recognition of the need for diplomacy, we might help forge in
the crucible of conflict a structure of peace that in the end might do
justice to the sacrifice.

October 7: A Sunday of Stalling

THE second day of the war, October 7, was a Sunday. Washington
was muggy and mild. Overnight, heavy fighting had continued on
both fronts. Egypt seemed to have established an unbroken line about
five miles across the Suez Canal; Syria had made inroads on the Golan
Heights. Our Defense Attaché in Tel Aviv, Colonel Billy Forsman,
whose cables throughout the war were models of precision and insight,
wired Washington that Israeli forces remained on the defensive, buying
time until mobilization was complete. Moreover, by day's end Israel
admitted to losing thirty-five high-performance aircraft. Some in Washington doubted the figure, suspecting that it was the prelude to a request
for replacements. But it was true, and it showed the effectiveness of the
Arabs' Soviet-built surface-to-air missiles, especially on the Egyptian
front. Still, there seemed as yet no reason to change our basic estimate
of a rapid Israeli victory. Israel's counterattack was not scheduled to

start until the next day. Israel contributed to the general complacency by telling us that it had destroyed nine of eleven bridges across the Canal. (This proved to be hyperbole; they were at most damaged for brief periods.)

At 9:30 Sunday morning, Chargé Shalev delivered a personal message from Golda Meir that reinforced our view. "Our military people estimate," she wrote, "and I rely on their estimates since they have never deceived themselves or the government before, that we are engaged in heavy battles, but with our reserves of men and equipment the fighting will turn in our favor." Golda could not resist a dig that would have raised our blood pressure even more than it did had we felt less affection for her and less sympathy for her anguish:

You know the reasons why we took no preemptive action. Our failure to take such action is the reason for our situation now. If I had given the chief of staff authority to preempt, as he had recommended, some hours before the attacks began, there is no doubt that our situation would now be different.

It is true that in years past I had expressed my personal view to Ambassador Simcha Dinitz and his predecessor, Yitzhak Rabin, that America's ability to help Israel in any war would be impaired if Israel struck first. But as this crisis approached, the subject of preemption had not been discussed. How could it have been, since Israel had repeatedly told us that there was no danger of war? The morning the war started, Golda had volunteered to Keating that Israel would not preempt. The decision had been her own, without benefit of recent American advice; [11] it confirmed what she had — entirely on her own — asked us to transmit to the Arabs the day before. I remain sure she was right. Had Israel struck first, it would have greatly complicated the prospects of American support. As it was, the majority at the first, early-morning WSAG thought Israel *had* struck first. Moreover, at that late hour it is doubtful whether a preemptive strike would have made much military difference. Moshe Dayan wrote afterward that the only proposal for preemption before the cabinet was Chief of Staff David Elazar's scheme to attack the surface-to-air missiles deep inside Syria — a measure that could not have blunted the ground attack that was about to surprise Israel. [12]

In her current message Golda now asked us to postpone a vote in the Security Council until Wednesday or Thursday (October 10 or 11), by which time Israel expected to be on the offensive on all fronts. "I would not have come to you," Golda reiterated, "if I did not think the situation would improve in the next few days." To make success doubly sure, Golda confirmed Israel's interest in some special military equipment — especially Sidewinder heat-seeking antiaircraft missiles. A Boeing 747 jumbo jet was on the way to New York to pick up what we might make available. Shalev affirmed another request, a speedup of delivery of items routinely approved during the previous weeks as part of the existing supply program. I had no difficulty promising Shalev delay on a Security Council vote, though I thought the wiser tactic was actually to request the Council to meet and then stall by calling for a return to the prewar lines:

If we call for the meeting and put in our resolution, we would be the first to speak and ours would be the first resolution on which there would be a vote.

If we are forced, in the first instance, to veto a simple cease-fire resolution, it will not be understood.

We would intend to move slowly; we are in no hurry to get to a vote. Surely if there is a debate others will be called on to speak, including Foreign Minister Eban. I am confident that he could speak for at least two hours without getting through his introduction. I think this is the best way to go. We would tell our man in New York to go slowly as well.

With respect to military supply, attitudes within our own government were sharply divided. They have also been the subject of much controversy. The cardinal fact was that all agencies, the State Department included, expected a repetition of the Six Day War of 1967. No senior official of *any* department believed, at that stage, that any significant resupply could reach Israel before the war had ended — limited quantities of specialized equipment excepted. The general view was that anything else we sent would arrive too late to affect the battle.

By the time of the very first WSAG meeting early on October 6, held in my absence, the Israelis had made a preliminary request for hardware. Deputy Assistant Secretary of Defense James H. Noyes argued that "they don't really need the equipment." No one present disputed that judgment. By the second WSAG meeting later that day, a request for specialized equipment had been received. Defense Secretary Schlesinger suggested delay on the Israeli arms list since "shipping any stuff into Israel blows any image we may have of an honest broker." And Deputy Secretary of State Kenneth Rush volunteered that "they have no real shortages."

I was the sole dissenter, for foreign policy, not military, reasons. I did not then doubt that Israel would win before any major aid could reach it. But I favored some arms aid to Israel unless the Soviets cooperated at the UN to bring about a rapid end of the war. If we refused aid, Israel would have no incentive to heed our views in the postwar diplomacy. If on the other hand Israel realized that in an extremity it would not stand alone, this would affect and perhaps moderate its territorial claims in the negotiations I was certain would follow the war. I was not, of course, insensitive to the threat of Arab displeasure. But in my view the *outcome* of the war would determine postwar relationships, not whether we supplied arms. If the Arabs won with Soviet support,

Moscow would emerge as the dominant power; the radical course — the military option — would appear vindicated, and moderate Arabs would be in an even weaker position. Then the United States would lose influence no matter how restrained we had been during the war. If our arms aid blocked an Arab victory, then our central role would be confirmed. The time to show understanding for the Arab position was *after* the war, when the peace process started.

This is why on the morning of October 6 I had told Haig that if the Soviet answer for cooperative action at the UN was negative, we ought to give Israel some limited arms. And I had told Shalev that day that "we will almost certainly approve tomorrow the military equipment within reason that you may need; especially if the Soviets line up with the Arabs, then we will certainly do it."

Now on the morning of October 7, right after my meeting with Shalev, I reported to Haig for Nixon: ". . . if the Arabs win they will be impossible and there will be no negotiations." Haig agreed: "We'll have to provide the stuff to which we have been committed unless they can stabilize this thing — quickly — two or three days." That settled our basic supply policy. At the middle levels of the Defense Department, there was undoubtedly some lack of urgency. Officials were convinced that we were risking the goodwill of moderate Arabs and the supply of oil for essentially unnecessary gestures. But even that foot-dragging resulted, ironically, from an expectation of immediate Israeli victory, not from an intention to complicate its conduct of the battle.

At 10:15 A.M. Dobrynin provided the pretext for the diplomatic procrastination that both Israel and we considered in the common interest. He telephoned that a message from the Soviet leadership was expected but not for two hours. I immediately informed Nixon and urged that we postpone any formal announcement calling for a Security Council session. As it turned out, waiting for the Soviet message consumed the better part of the day — which suited our strategy of waiting for the completion of Israeli mobilization.

In the meantime we had heard contradictory reports of Sadat's attitude. Sadat allegedly had told one West European ambassador that he wanted no Security Council meeting and would accept no cease-fire until Egyptian forces had recovered all territories captured by Israel in 1967. This, if true, would doom any cease-fire initiative; it also seemed inconsistent with the behavior of the Egyptian army, which remained stationary on the line it had now reached a few miles from the Canal. By contrast, according to another European ambassador in Cairo, Sadat's position was that he would not ask for a Security Council meeting but might comply with a cease-fire resolution passed at the request of others. But a simple cease-fire resolution at that point would ratify the gains of the attack — exactly what we wished to avoid.

Thus on the second day of a major war the United Nations Security Council, the institution specifically designed to deal with breaches of the peace, was paralyzed by obstruction from all sides. The Soviets were stalling; Egypt, depending on which ambassador to believe, was either stalling or preparing for a cease-fire in place; Israel wanted time to complete its mobilization; Syria had not been heard from. Only the United States was prepared to go to the Security Council, but our preferred resolution amounted only to a sophisticated delaying tactic because no other Council member was likely to support us. Since everyone wanted time and we wanted to keep the issue out of the General Assembly, we had decided to call for a formal Security Council meeting toward evening, to postpone the debate until the next day, and to aim for a vote by Tuesday or Wednesday. By then, if our intelligence estimates were to be believed, Israel would have restored at least the original lines. Everyone might then be prepared to accept a cease-fire in place.

By 1:00 P.M. the message from Brezhnev, promised for an hour earlier, still had not arrived. I pressed Dobrynin, telling him that we had held up doing anything with the UN until we heard from Moscow. There is never any harm in establishing a claim by ascribing to consideration for the other party what fits in with one's preferred strategy. In the absence of Soviet cooperation to end the war, we decided to get ready to undertake a limited arms supply to Israel. At 1:30 P.M. I told Schlesinger that he should make arrangements for ammunition and other high-technology equipment — especially Sidewinder missiles — to be picked up at an out-of-the-way naval base in Virginia by Israeli El Al commercial planes with markings painted out. He would receive the final go-ahead after I had one more discussion with the President. Schlesinger speculated that the apparent absence of a strong Israeli counteroffensive, especially in the south, might be intended to show that they had made themselves vulnerable by not preempting, thereby to establish a claim for American assistance. I expressed my doubt: "I think they were really surprised this time."

At 3:10 P.M., still not having heard from Dobrynin, I told Haig that we should move ahead on some Israeli requests for both psychological and military reasons. The Soviets would have to learn that the position of their clients could not be improved through procrastination; the Arabs must not win with Soviet weapons or they would become intractable. Haig agreed and told me that the President held the same view. At 3:45 P.M. I told Schlesinger to proceed.

This was all the easier to decide because in the meantime, close to 3:30 P.M., we received Brezhnev's reply: It turned out to be essentially another stall. Either Moscow was genuinely baffled as to what to do or it was operating on a different estimate from ours. If Arab prospects were as grim as we believed, the Soviet leaders should have welcomed the idea of a return to the status quo ante; it would have given them a formula to arrest further Israeli advances deep into Arab territory. But instead Brezhnev's letter to Nixon avoided any reference to joint action at the Security Council. It dealt not with how to terminate the war but with Brezhnev's favorite Mideast theme: joint US–Soviet diplomacy to impose a Mideast peace on Arab terms, based on the familiar total Israeli withdrawal in return for security guarantees that were not spelled out. Pending that, Brezhnev wrote, it would be "very important" for Israel to indicate "without any reservations" its willingness to withdraw from all Arab territories. Brezhnev implied that this would speed the end of the war but indicated no firm reciprocal Arab step. We were generously given the task of obtaining Israel's acquiescence by using our "influence." Clearly, the Soviets wanted to let the war run its course a little longer or else they did not have as much influence with their Arab friends as we had thought.

Sadat Gets in Touch

SHORTLY afterward we had our first direct word from Cairo. (In contrast, we never had a single direct communication from Syria during the war.) Its tone was friendly; its substance reflected a mood, not a policy. In a message addressed to me through intelligence channels, Sadat's security adviser Hafiz Ismail informed us of Egypt's terms for ending the war. They were identical with what had been put forward in May and had not become more realistic with the passage of time: Israel had to withdraw from all occupied territories; only *after* this withdrawal could a peace conference discuss other matters, such as freedom of navigation in the Strait of Tiran guaranteed by a temporary international presence at Sharm el-Sheikh. The message explicitly rejected partial or interim agreements.

These terms were clearly only an opening position. From his earlier contacts with us, Sadat was well aware that we considered such conditions unattainable. I did not think that he was at this stage seeking agreement; he was looking for a dialogue. Communicating with us was risky enough. He could not compound the risk of alienating Syria and perhaps the Soviet Union — whose support was essential for the conduct of the war — by immediately offering concessions that might drive Syria to abandon the common struggle or the Soviet Union to reduce its supplies.

What was significant was the fact of the message, not its content. Sadat was inviting us to participate in, if not take charge of, the peace process, despite the fact that at the UN we were advocating that he give up territory that he considered his own and that his armies had just captured. The message included an avowal that showed Sadat knew very well the limits of what was attainable: "We do not intend to deepen the engagements or widen the confrontation." If that phrase had any meaning, it was that Egypt did not propose to pursue offensive operations with Israel beyond the territory already gained or to use America as a whipping boy — as Nasser had done in 1967. But if we understood Sadat and the war correctly, a gap would inevitably develop between Egypt's military dispositions and its political objectives; this must sooner or later lead to a political negotiation.

Ismail's message inaugurated a strange dialogue with a country that had attacked our ally and whose aims were being thwarted by American arms. Throughout the war, hardly a day went by without a communication from or to Cairo. And even as our later airlift to Israel turned the battle gradually against Eygpt, Sadat kept his promise not to whip up anti-American hatred in Egypt. This was not a favor to us, but a means to avoid pushing us irrevocably to Israel's side in the diplomacy to follow. His plan was to establish a relationship with us in which we would be not only formally but also psychologically the mediator, that is to say, in which we would treat Egypt's claims on a par with Israel's — a stunning conception for Nasser's successor after two decades of hostility.

Until this message, I had not taken Sadat seriously. Because of the many threats to go to war that had not been implemented I had dismissed him as more actor than statesman. Now I was beginning to understand that the grandiloquent gestures were part of a conscious strategy. They had guaranteed surprise: Dramatic pronouncements not followed by action create the premise that no action will ever be taken. The expulsion of the Soviet advisers from Egypt in 1972 suddenly took on a new significance. Then I had had trouble understanding why Sadat had not sought to negotiate their departure with us instead of giving it to us for nothing. But Sadat was right. If the Soviet advisers were to depart, it had to be done all at once. Negotiating about it might have left him in the paradoxical position of having to maintain a Soviet presence if we could not offer satisfactory terms. Sadat wanted to be rid of the Soviets to remove an encumbrance both to the war he was planning and to his projected move toward the United States. Acts of historic magnitude must not be mortgaged by petty maneuvers that risk their ultimate purpose for marginal and temporary benefits.

Sadat's ability from the very first hours of the war never to lose sight of the heart of his problem convinced me that we were dealing with a statesman of the first order. Hafiz Ismail's message, while avowing sweeping terms, stated a modest and largely psychological objective: "to show," so the message said, "that we were not afraid or helpless." That objective Sadat achieved brilliantly. It was the precondition of his subsequent peace diplomacy.

With the Soviet and Egyptian messages now in hand, our course settled itself. For reasons that were hard to grasp in the light of our preconceptions, the Soviets as well as Sadat were maneuvering to allow the fighting to determine the outcome of the war. Since we were convinced that Israel would soon gain the upper hand, this suited our own purpose as well. We therefore implemented our warning to Dobrynin of the previous day. We would make a virtue of necessity; we would let nature take its course and we would conduct the forthcoming UN debate so as to soften the disappointment we were sure was awaiting the Arabs. Late that Sunday afternoon, October 7, we issued the call for a formal Security Council meeting. I summed up our strategy at the WSAG meeting at 6:00 P.M.:

Egypt doesn't want a confrontation with us at the UN and the Soviets don't want a confrontation with us period. Our general position will be a restoration of the cease-fire lines. The Arabs will scream that they are being deprived of their birthright, but by Thursday [October 11] they will be on their knees begging us for a cease-fire. . . . We're trying to get this over with a limited amount of damage to our relations with the Arabs and the Soviets. If we can also put some money in the bank with the Israelis to draw on in later negotiations, well and good.*

That evening Ambassador Dinitz arrived from Israel. His presence guaranteed a certain drama. Dinitz had replaced the taciturn Yitzhak Rabin in March in what is one of the three or four most important positions the government of Israel can entrust to one of its citizens. For Israel is dependent on the United States as no other country is on a friendly power. Increasingly, Washington is the sole capital to stand by Israel in international forums. We are its exclusive military supplier, its only military ally (though no formal obligation exists). The Arab nations blame us for Israel's dogged persistence. Israel sees in intransigence the sole hope for preserving its dignity in a one-sided relationship. It feels instinctively that one admission of weakness, one concession granted without a struggle, will lead to an endless catalogue of demands as every country seeks to escape its problems at Israel's expense. It takes

---

*The following exchange reflects, however, the beginning of my doubt about our intelligence appraisals of an early Israeli victory:

KISSINGER: How do you explain the cockiness of the Arabs? Why aren't they calling for a cease-fire?

SCHLESINGER: Euphoria has set in.

COLBY: The Syrians think they're doing well. They're not looking at the long term. Egypt may have intended to make only a limited move across the Canal.

KISSINGER: Why aren't they clinching their gain? Every foreign ambassador who saw Sadat today was told that Egypt didn't want a cease-fire until they were at the Israeli border.

SCHLESINGER: You're being logical. You can't ascribe that kind of logic to them.

RUSH: It's difficult to think Sadat would cross the Suez and just sit there.

KISSINGER: My judgment is that he *will* cross the Suez and just *sit* there. I don't think he will penetrate further.

a special brand of heroism to turn total dependence into defiance; to insist on support as a matter of right rather than as a favor; to turn every American deviation from an Israeli cabinet consensus into a betrayal to be punished rather than a disagreement to be negotiated.

And yet Israel's obstinacy, maddening as it can be, serves the purposes of both our countries best. A subservient client would soon face an accumulation of ever-growing pressures. It would tempt Israel's neighbors to escalate their demands. It would saddle us with the opprobrium for every deadlock. That at any rate has been our relationship with Israel — it is exhilarating and frustrating, ennobled by the devotion and faith that contain a lesson for an age of cynicism; exasperating because the interests of a superpower and of a regional ministate are not always easy to reconcile and are on occasion unbridgeable. Israel affects our decisions through inspiration, persistence, and a judicious, not always subtle or discreet, influence on our domestic policy.

Through this thicket the Israeli Ambassador must move, wielding an influence he cannot admit in America but that his cabinet for its own electoral reasons may overstate in Israel. He must extract assistance unparalleled in America's relationship with any other country. And yet he has to anchor Israel not just in the acquiescence but also in the moral conviction of Americans.

Dinitz was equal to the challenge. Witty and belligerent, insistent and defiant, intelligent and challenging, he had many great qualities; like his predecessor, Rabin, he was never ingratiating. Heroes do not wheedle; they take their stand. We read about them with admiration. But I suspect that heroes have always been hard to live with. Without self-assurance they would never dare what they undertake; it is the price that convention must pay to faith.

Dinitz had earned his spurs as Golda Meir's personal assistant in the office of the Prime Minister, which meant that he had to navigate in a cabinet whose members, while appointed by the Prime Minister, could not in practice be dismissed by her. Each government in Israel's history has been a coalition. To remove a colleague, the Prime Minister runs the risk of losing the support of an indispensable party or faction and thus hazards the survival of the government. No wonder that Israeli politics tends to belie what professors have written about the cohesiveness of cabinet government. There is no discipline. Each faction has an incentive to seek to place the onus of difficult decisions on its colleagues. Leaking secrets becomes a method of administration because it enables cabinet members to demonstrate their importance or vigilance.

Dinitz was well prepared for his Washington role. Tough, warmhearted, with a superb sense of humor, he would come on like a slightly distressed hornet inquiring what harm a little creature like him could possibly do to a powerful figure like me. He would buzz about the many grave injustices that had been done to Israel by shortsighted American bureaucrats and politicians. Those few at the very top of our system capable of understanding him were given the privilege of undoing the wrongs. But there was always the implied threat that if they failed to do their moral duty, the whole swarm of hornets would descend on them.

Dinitz and I became fast friends — and that friendship, I am proud to say, has survived now that we are both out of office. Later on, the myth developed that we had been too friendly, that Dinitz was excessively influenced by me; not to put too fine a point on it, that I had taken him in. Israel is probably the only country allied with us whose ambassador can be criticized at home for having too much contact with the American Secretary of State. (Most countries complain that their ambassadors cannot get to see the Secretary of State.) I have repeatedly pointed out that trickery is not the path of wisdom but of disaster for a diplomat. Since one has to deal with the same person over and over again, one can get away with it only once at best, and then only at the cost of permanent stifling of the relationship. At any event, nobody could trick even once somebody as resourceful and tough as Dinitz. Simcha and I worked together in war and peace. Yet neither of us ever forgot that our first duty was to serve our respective countries, which at a very minimum brought different perspectives to our common problems.

Like all experienced diplomats, we took great pains to keep our disagreements from becoming personal. One device is to blame — usually transparently — someone else for painful decisions. Dinitz was brilliant at mobilizing media and Congressional pressures but much too wise to make his prowess explicit. Listening to him, one could only be astonished how it had happened that so many normally individualistic Americans had come spontaneously to the conclusion that we were not doing enough for Israel. In turn, when I had bad news for Dinitz, I was not above ascribing it to bureaucratic stalemates or unfortunate decisions by superiors. Neither of us fooled the other. I knew Dinitz was orchestrating most pressures, and he understood that I had not reached eminence by losing too many bureaucratic battles.

At 7:40 P.M. that Sunday, October 7, our first meeting during the war, Dinitz brought optimistic news from Jerusalem. "We are on the move in terms of optimum power on both fronts," he said. He repeated what we had been told the day before, that nine out of eleven Egyptian bridges across the Suez Canal had been destroyed. Israel would need forty-eight hours from the next day, Monday noon (when mobilization would be completed), to finish the military operations under way. I was confident of being able to delay any UN–sponsored cease-fire at least through Tuesday. We spent some time on military resupply. In light of the military prognosis, Israel's needs did not appear desperate. I told

Dinitz that an El Al plane — with markings painted out — could pick up eighty Sidewinders and bombracks at the Virginia naval base during the night. The middle levels of Defense were now taking advantage of our injunction for secrecy to drag their feet, interpreting it so literally as to preclude any Israeli plane (even without identifying markings) from landing. But Scowcroft, on my behalf, put an end to the little game. The delay was less than twenty-four hours. It did not seem to matter because all were still convinced that the war would soon be over. The Sidewinders were conceived as a morale booster. In Israel's own projection, they could not arrive in time to affect the battle.

October 8: True to Scenario

B Y midday Monday, October 8, the strategy seemed to be in train. The Security Council had been called into session but was proceeding at the stately pace we had encouraged. It had not yet gone beyond consultations; a formal session would take place late in the afternoon at the earliest. No resolutions would be tabled, much less voted on, for quite some time. The morning intelligence report seemed to confirm our interpretations. A joint estimate by CIA and DIA held that the Israelis should turn the tide on the Golan Heights by Tuesday night; "pressing the offensive against the Syrians might take another day or two" — presumably to complete the destruction of the Syrian army. On the Egyptian front it was predicted that the outcome would be clear by Wednesday at the latest. This relatively neutral statement was amplified in a manner indicating little doubt about the prospect: "Several more days of heavy fighting might follow as the Israelis work to destroy as much as possible of Egypt's army."

In these circumstances, diplomatic delay seemed to fit our needs perfectly. With every passing hour, the difference that divided us from the rest of the Security Council — whether there should be a cease-fire in place or a return to the status quo ante, as we sought — would be overtaken by events. Once the Israeli army reached the lines at which the war had started, we could accept a simple cease-fire. If Israel advanced beyond these lines, a Security Council majority could be counted on to adopt our original position of restoring the status quo ante and we would go along with it, thus saving the Arab armies from a debacle. It was in our interest, or so it seemed, to keep everything as calm as possible lest the impending Israeli victory inflame friendly Arab nations against us or tempt the Soviets into a grandstand play.

A message was received from Brezhnev early Monday, October 8:

We have contacted the leaders of the Arab states on the question of cease-fire. We hope to get a reply shortly. We feel that we should act in cooperation with you, being guided by the broad interests of maintaining peace and developing the Soviet-American relations. We hope that President Nixon will act likewise.

When Dobrynin read me Brezhnev's message on the phone, I thought it served our immediate purpose very well. Since we did not intend to introduce a resolution and the Soviet Union was offering to coordinate with us, we were certain to get through the day without confrontation or embarrassing proposals. By the next day, we were convinced, the Israeli offensive would prevail; the Security Council would then call for a cease-fire in place. Our ally would have repulsed an attack by Soviet weapons. We could begin our peace process with the Arabs on the proposition that we had stopped the Israeli advance and with the Israelis on the basis that we had been steadfastly at their side in the crisis. I therefore did not hesitate to tell Dobrynin that we would act in the spirit of Brezhnev's message. We would put forward no resolution that day, nor without giving the Soviet Union several hours' advance warning. We would instruct Ambassador Scali to speak philosophically in the Security Council; we would avoid inflammatory statements. We expected the Soviet Union to follow a similar course. Dobrynin agreed.

The parties with which we were in touch — the Soviets, Egypt, Israel — were tacitly with us on a scenario in which no country would push a resolution and each would keep the rhetoric to a low decibel level. I told Eban to sacrifice eloquence to length if possible — a painful sacrifice for the Israeli Foreign Minister. I urged Zayyat to keep matters calm. It was becoming apparent even at this early stage that we were the only government in contact with both sides. If we could preserve this position, we were likely to emerge in a central role in the peace process.

To further these prospects I returned, at 11:40 A.M., a reply to Hafiz Ismail's message of the previous day. Clearly, the terms that Sadat had outlined through Ismail did not offer a basis for negotiations. But they were not likely to be Egypt's last word. I therefore thought it best to maintain communication without discussing terms that would depend to a large degree on a battle even then taking place. Instead, I put two questions and offered an assurance. My first query was whether Egypt's terms meant that Israel would actually have to withdraw from all occupied territories before there could be a peace conference, or whether it was enough for it to accept the principle of withdrawal. It was the sort of esoteric question that was the stuff of Middle East negotiations; it could use up time without a conclusion. The second request was for Ismail to clear up some ambiguity in a message we had received through the Shah of Iran telling us that Egypt was willing to permit a UN presence in territories evacuated by Israel.

The purpose of both questions was to hint that we envisaged *some*

Israeli withdrawal and thus to whet Egyptian appetites without committing ourselves to Ismail's precise terms, the assumption still being that Egypt's army would not be able to advance much farther. I concluded the message with the assurance of our intention to help in negotiations. Egypt had made its point; no more could be gained militarily; no more was required to get us involved diplomatically:

I would like to reiterate that the United States will do everything possible to assist the contending parties to bring the fighting to a halt. The United States, and I personally, will also actively participate in assisting the parties to reach a just resolution of the problems which have for so long plagued the Middle East.

I next turned to our domestic base. Senators Mike Mansfield and Hugh Scott, the majority and minority leaders, offered to put the Senate on record in support of our approach. I urged that any resolution not assess blame for the outbreak of hostilities; that the Senate express its approval for the manner in which the crisis was being handled; and that it state as a "desirable objective" the restoration of the cease-fire on the basis of the status quo ante. Such a resolution passed unanimously in the Senate the same day, to the enormous benefit of our diplomacy. (There was some grumbling that I had argued against condemnation of the Arab nations. That was overstated but reflected my dominant concern: Convinced that an Arab defeat was imminent, I saw no sense in making us the target of the expected wave of frustration.)

Fresh intelligence reports during the day reinforced the mood of complacency. At noon, the CIA reported heavy Israeli attacks on both the Syrian and Egyptian fronts. It mentioned unconfirmed Israeli claims that its forces had crossed the Suez Canal at both its northern and southern ends. The CIA prematurely added its own judgment that heavy Israeli air activity near Port Said suggested that the Israelis had crossed the Canal in the north. It was another case of the preconception fathering the prediction. There was not the slightest evidence that Israeli ground forces were anywhere near crossing the Canal. But such a move had been so widely anticipated that all operations — even some that in retrospect appear to have been defensive acts of desperation, like the bombing of Port Said — were interpreted to be consistent with it.

Dinitz called at 1:14 P.M. to confirm the optimistic assessment:

The situation on the front . . . looks considerably better. We have gone over from the containment to attack both on the Sinai and Golan Heights. Our military people think that [there is] a good possibility we will push the Syrians all the way across the cease-fire line and we are also moving out the Egyptian forces in the Sinai.

The Prime Minister's office had not "yet" been able to confirm, Dinitz added, that Israeli forces had crossed the Canal — implying that it was only a question of time. That he guessed such a move was imminent emerged inevitably from his next point, which was a hint of what I had suspected since the war broke out: Israel might well decide to go beyond the lines at which the war had started and take up new positions deeper in Arab territory, to ensure itself against a repetition of the surprise attack. We had decided early on that we could not support such a move. As we would ask the Arabs, Israel too would have to stop on the prewar line.

Things were going so smoothly that we succeeded in aborting even the General Assembly debate which had worried us so much. I worked out with the President of the General Assembly, the Ecuadorean Leopoldo Benites, that only the parties directly involved would speak in that forum, which would then defer to the Security Council. In the Security Council John Scali was instructed to make a bland, philosophical statement referring to the desirability of reestablishing the prewar line but stopping short of tabling a resolution. In the event, the Security Council debate was devoid of drama. Zayyat focused blame on Israel in standard terms, avoiding serious contention with the United States. Eban with customary eloquence gave exactly the opposite historical interpretation. Between the two they proved the saying that wars are about whose version of history will predominate.

At 5:40 P.M., Dobrynin telephoned to assure me formally that the Soviet Union was "not going to do anything at the Council. No kind of resolution in the Security Council. Our representative in the Security Council has instructions not to have any polemics with the American representative. Meanwhile we continue to consult urgently with the Arab side." He expressed the hope that we would introduce no resolution until the Soviets had completed consultations with their allies. I promised with alacrity to pursue the course that was in fact our preference.

Immediately afterward, I joined the daily WSAG meeting, which had started in the Situation Room. The CIA reported that the Israelis were pressing their counterattacks on both fronts and had virtually retaken the Golan Heights. We seemed to have reached our goal; Israel would probably win a decisive victory within the next forty-eight hours. Thus the focus was on how we could pick up the pieces and prevent an explosion in the Arab world and a possible oil embargo. The conciliatory attitude of the Soviet Union seemed to reflect its assessment that its Arab friends were losing. Yet again I raised the question that had begun to nag at me: If all this was true, why were the Arabs not grasping at a cease-fire? What did they know that we didn't? But I permitted myself to be reassured by the consensus of my colleagues: The Arabs were so astonished at their success in getting across the prewar line at all that it had turned their heads. They had talked themselves into an exaltation that would permit retreat only after they had been soundly beaten.

Dinitz and I met at 6:40 P.M. We joked about everybody's relaxed attitude at the Security Council. Dinitz, convinced that the prewar lines would look very attractive to Egypt and Syria "in two or three days," reported optimistically:

This morning, our attacks on both fronts were successful. In Syria, they are pushed out of the Heights except Mt. Hermon area. Our people have returned to their settlements to care for the livestock. There was a new charge in Quneitra and now a counterattack. We now have almost complete control of the air situation in spite of the SA-6s which were deployed. At the Egyptian front, we succeeded in destroying part of the Egyptian forces. Tomorrow we will continue. Our air force and armor prevented the Egyptians from bringing further forces across. By tomorrow I'll be able to tell you of our future plans.

I said that the major task now was to get through the week without an oil cutoff. Dinitz even began to speculate on Israel's cease-fire conditions. All Israeli prisoners of war in Egypt and Syria would have to be released, even those captured in the years of the "war of attrition" that preceded full-scale war. I replied that we had no objection to the prisoner point but warned that we would not hold still for territorial acquisition. "The only thing I urge strongly is a return to the prewar battle lines." We would be speeding up delivery of some F-4 Phantom jets that had been approved on the prewar schedule, and we were moving ahead on the earlier requests for special equipment: "Anything you can get on a[n El Al] plane, you can have tonight," I told Dinitz. In this complacent mood there was only one jarring note. We had learned that Sadat, Asad, and King Faisal were urging Hussein to enter the war. Perhaps their plight was even more desperate than we thought — or else they did not know when they were beaten. We did not give the information much serious thought.

When Nixon and I spoke soon afterward, we were concerned primarily with the postwar diplomacy. "If we bring it off," I said cockily, "if this thing ends without a blowup with either the Arabs or the Soviets, it will be a miracle and a triumph." And Nixon entered the spirit of the occasion, his mind also on the postwar period:

Right. The one thing we have to be concerned about, which you and I know looking down the road, is that the Israelis when they finish clobbering the Egyptians and the Syrians, which they will do, will be even more impossible to deal with than before and you and I have got to determine in our own minds, we must have a diplomatic settlement there.

I even found time to deliver my long-prepared speech at the Pacem in Terris conference in Washington that Monday evening, October 8. I had inserted a few sentences warning the Soviet Union: "Our policy with respect to détente is clear: We shall resist aggressive foreign policies. Détente cannot survive irresponsibility in any area, including the Middle East." But the warnings were intended less as a threat than as an artist's flourish on a nearly completed canvas. By the end of the third day of the war we went to bed expecting a repeat of the Six Day War of 1967.

But the gods are offended by hubris. They resent the presumption that great events can be taken for granted. Historic changes such as we sought cannot be brought off by virtuoso performances; they must reflect an underlying reality. And that reality caught up with us in the middle of that night.

October 9–10: The Tide Turns Ominously

DINITZ phoned me at 1:45 A.M., shortly after I had gone to sleep, waking me with a puzzling question: What could we do about resupply? I was baffled. By his prognosis of only a few hours earlier, the battle should be turning at about this time toward a decisive victory. What then was the problem? What was needed and why the hurry? The Israeli requests to date had been in the main for special types of ammunition and electronic gear. Almost all the requests had been granted; there had been some bureaucratic foot-dragging by Defense but the Sidewinder missiles had already been picked up. The primary unfulfilled request was for F-4 Phantom jets beyond those in the pipeline whose delivery we had already agreed to accelerate. This presented a special problem in that we had few surplus Phantoms except those coming off the production lines at the rate of about two per month to Israel, and those in our own combat units; to take the latter was bound to raise an outcry both in our armed services and in the Arab world. The unworthy thought crossed my mind that perhaps the Israelis wanted to commit us to a schedule of deliveries now before their probable victory removed the urgency. I told Dinitz that we would talk first thing in the morning, and I went back to bed.

At 3:00 A.M., Dinitz called again with essentially the same urgent message. Unless he wanted to prove to the cabinet that he could get me out of bed at will, something was wrong. I suggested that we sort things out in the morning.

Thus on Tuesday, October 9, we met at 8:20 A.M. in the elegant but little-used Map Room on the ground floor of the White House. Many of my private encounters with Dinitz and his predecessor Rabin (and with Dobrynin) had taken place there when I was national security adviser and wanted the meetings kept secret. It is a little dark, as the view from its windows is nearly obscured by rhododendron bushes. Its walls had been covered with battlefield maps when President Roosevelt used it as his military command post and communications center during World War II; hence its name. Dinitz had brought along his Armed Forces Attaché, General Mordechai ("Motta") Gur, to brief me. I was accompanied by Scowcroft and Rodman.

Dinitz and Gur wasted no time. Grimly, they explained that Israel's losses to date had been staggering and totally unexpected. Forty-nine airplanes, including fourteen Phantoms, had been destroyed. This figure was high but not completely surprising since both Syria and Egypt possessed large quantities of Soviet surface-to-air-missiles. The real shocker was the loss of 500 tanks, 400 on the Egyptian front alone. Dinitz implored me to keep the numbers secret from everyone except the President. If they were known, the Arab countries now standing aloof might join for a knockout blow. Many puzzles cleared up instantly. "So that's why the Egyptians are so cocky," I exclaimed. "How did it happen?" Gur explained that a significant number of Israeli tanks were lost on the way to the battle by being run too fast in the desert after having been inadequately maintained in reserve depots. I was so shocked that I indelicately reminded Dinitz of his prediction two nights before of victory by Wednesday. He admitted that "obviously something went wrong." He did not know what.

Nor did it make any difference. For what Dinitz was reporting would require a fundamental reassessment of strategy. Our entire diplomacy and our resupply policy had been geared to a rapid Israeli victory. These assumptions were now overtaken. But something deeper was involved. I pointed out that the Syrian army, though suffering serious casualties, had not broken. Israel would therefore find it difficult to shift its forces from the Golan to the Sinai. And Israel's equipment losses on the Egyptian front were about equal to Egypt's. Israel stood on the threshold of a bitter war of attrition that it could not possibly win given the disparity of manpower. It had to do something decisive. Gur suggested that Israel's best chance was against Syria. Unless the Egyptian armor ventured significantly beyond the belt of surface-to-air missiles, an Israeli offensive in the Sinai would be too costly. I said that in my judgment Egyptian forces would not make a reckless move. Gur thought differently, that they would try to reach the Mitla and Giddi passes — especially if Syria were under pressure. Luckily for Israel, Gur proved to be right.

Such was Israeli consternation that Dinitz and Gur did not know exactly what Israel's priorities were, except planes. Tanks, which Israel desperately needed, were in short supply and difficult to transport quickly. Gur suggested shipping some from Europe, but even that would take several weeks. It was agreed that El Al planes could begin to pick up more consumables and electronic equipment immediately. But clearly this small fleet of seven civilian aircraft would not be able to handle heavy equipment. As for the larger items, I promised to assemble a special meeting of the WSAG and give Dinitz our answer before the end of the day.

Gur asked for intelligence information. I instructed Scowcroft "to give them every bit of intelligence we have." I never doubted that a defeat of Israel by Soviet arms would be a geopolitical disaster for the United States. I urged a quick victory on one front before the UN diplomacy ratified Arab territorial gains everywhere. "We are concentrating now on a fast Syrian victory," replied Dinitz. "With the Egyptians, it will take longer."

At the end Dinitz asked to see me alone for five minutes. Prime Minister Meir, he told me, was prepared to come to the United States personally for an hour to plead with President Nixon for urgent arms aid. It could be a secret visit. I rejected the visit out of hand and without checking with Nixon. Such a proposal could reflect only either hysteria or blackmail. A visit would take Golda away from Israel for a minimum of thirty-six hours. Leaving while a major battle was going on would be a sign of such panic that it might bring in all the Arab states still on the sidelines. It would leave Israel leaderless when Golda's dauntless courage was most needed and major decisions might have to be made. (I learned after the war that at this very moment Dayan was recommending a withdrawal deep into the Sinai.) And because her visit could not be kept secret, we would be forced to announce a massive supply policy, destroying any possibility of mediation. The Arab world would be inflamed against us. The Soviet Union would have a clear field.

At 9:40 A.M. that Tuesday, I urgently convened a special meeting of the WSAG confined to the most senior departmental representatives. Staff was barred to enhance security. I reported the conversation with Dinitz and Gur, omitting the figures for tank losses. My colleagues were skeptical. Colby reported that Israel was doing well on the Syrian front and holding its own in the Sinai; Israel was simply trying to obtain the maximum military aid from us before victory, as a sign of unrestricted support not so much for the war as for the period afterward. Since I chaired the meeting as Presidential Assistant, Deputy Secretary Kenneth Rush spoke for the State Department. There had been no time to give any instructions; Rush supported Colby. Schlesinger saw no problem with sending auxiliary equipment not requiring American technicians. But his concern was that meeting Israel's requests and thus turning around a battle that the Arabs were winning might blight our relations with the Arabs. Schlesinger pointed out the distinction between defending Israel's survival within its pre–1967 borders and helping Israel maintain its conquests from the 1967 war. Other participants concurred.

My own view was that events had gone beyond such fine-tuning.

Theoretically, the best outcome was an Israeli victory that pushed back the Arabs without producing an Arab debacle. But matters had progressed too far: "Israel has suffered a strategic defeat no matter what happens," I argued. "They can't take two-to-one losses."

Meanwhile, I was becoming dubious about the Soviets' conduct. They had acquiesced in our stalling tactics because they apparently had better intelligence about the battle than we. Even if that were not so, they must have caught up with events by this time; they were clearly seeking to fish in troubled waters. During a break in the WSAG deliberations I learned from our Ambassador in Amman, Dean Brown, that the Soviet chargé in Jordan had now urged Hussein to enter the battle, promising full Soviet diplomatic support. Later in the day Brezhnev's appeal on similar lines to President Houari Boumedienne of Algeria was made public. "There are two issues," I told the WSAG, "supply and the indication the Soviet Union is stirring up the Arabs. We can't let the Soviet Union get away with this." How different were our prospects now from those of the night before! I adjourned the meeting and requested that various options for resupplying Israel be prepared by noon. I urged Schlesinger to ship straight from the production line to Israel any Phantoms not yet delivered to American units.

Meanwhile, I sought to thwart the Soviet design to turn the conflict into an Arab holy war. King Hussein had so far declined to enter the battle, even refusing King Faisal's request the day before to move a Saudi brigade stationed in Jordan into Syria. I sent a message to Hussein appealing to his statesmanship, promising an active American peace effort as soon as the war was over. He replied by expressing his solidarity with the objectives of his Arab brethren and castigating Israel's refusal since 1967 to make peace. He would exercise self-control for as long as possible, but unless we were able to arrange an early cease-fire he could not hold out. A prolonged war would strengthen the Soviet position in the Arab world.

It was clear to me that there would be no cease-fire unless Israel seemed to be gaining; Israel would have to pull itself together and overcome what was beginning to look like incoherence. To restore confidence, tangible evidence of American assistance was required. At the same time we had to keep the Soviets from seeking to exploit the sudden (at least to us) change in the military situation. During the day I warned Dobrynin against encouraging other nations to enter the conflict. He claimed that the report from Jordan had to be a misunderstanding and that Brezhnev's appeal to Boumedienne was boilerplate Soviet rhetoric. But when a superpower is "misunderstood" the same way in widely separated capitals, it is a pretty good working definition of design.

When the WSAG reconvened at noon on Tuesday, October 9, it had before it six options to meet the Israeli arms requests, ranging in ascending order from continuing our low-key resupply to commencing all-out support delivered by American planes. There was some skepticism about whether there was an emergency. Colby reported, for example, that Israel had ammunition for at least two more weeks.

But the issue had gone beyond logistic calculations. If Golda was willing to leave Israel in the middle of a war for survival, Israel must be close to panic. (I could not side with cynics on the WSAG who argued that if Golda felt free to come, the war must be close to being won.) Something substantial had to be done for psychological as well as military reasons. But it was in our interest — which on this issue was not identical with Israel's — to seek the least conspicuous method of delivering supplies. I told the WSAG that I would submit the options to Nixon, who would not be available, however, until the conclusion of a state visit by President Félix Houphouët-Boigny of the Ivory Coast later in the day.

Dinitz was not idle while we were waiting. Telephone calls descended on me from Capitol Hill urging me to stop dragging my feet on arms supply. Dinitz, of course, professed innocence; many Senators had spontaneously come to the same independent conclusion. My low boiling point was exceeded when Senator Frank Church, our scourge on Vietnam and constant critic of "deceitful" methods, urged us to "slip in" a few Phantoms into Israel, presumably without anyone knowing it. I replied that I would not mind if he went public with his appeal — a reversal of our usual positions. I thought there was some advantage in being seen to be pressed by Congress to do more for Israel; it might deflect some of the Arab resentment.

At 4:45 P.M., Haig, Scowcroft, Ziegler, and I met with Nixon. I outlined the problem. Diplomatically, we were not badly off. We were the only country in touch with most of the parties, including the Soviet Union. Once diplomacy took over, we would put our central position to good use. But the theoretical advantage would mean nothing if Israel appeared to be losing: "If the Arabs sense that the Israelis have lost more than they have admitted, they might rush in."

Nixon was preoccupied with his domestic scandals. He had spent much of the day tidying up Agnew's resignation, to be announced within twenty-four hours. But while this might have deflected him from details, it had not dimmed his eye for essentials. "The Israelis must not be allowed to lose," he said, and acted accordingly. His decision was to speed the delivery of consumables and aircraft. Heavy equipment would not reach Israel before the end of the fighting. We would guarantee to replace Israel's losses; thus Israel would be freed of the need to maintain exorbitant reserve stocks during the battle. At 6:10 P.M. that Tuesday, I conveyed Nixon's crucial decision to Dinitz:

On your special requests, the President has approved the entire list of consumables, that is, ordnance, electronic equipment — everything on the list except laser bombs. The President has agreed — and let me repeat this formally — that *all* your aircraft and tank losses will be replaced. Of the tanks you will be getting, a substantial number will be M-60s, our newest. As for the planes, for immediate delivery, you will be getting 5 F-4s, 2 plus 3. For the rest, you will work out a schedule. . . . On the anti-tank ammunition and anti-tank weapons, Schlesinger is all set. You know whom to get in touch with at Defense. If there is any trouble, contact Scowcroft. This is everything else on the list, except the laser bombs and aircraft. On tanks, you will have to work out a schedule. . . . The problem of tanks isn't what you need in this battle, but the situation after this battle. You have assurances that you will have replacements. You have the additional assurance that if it should go very badly and there is an emergency, we will get the tanks in even if we have to do it with American planes.

I had told Schlesinger that he would have discretion to determine the degree of Israel's need while the war was still going on. If he judged that Israel needed tanks during the battle, he should ship them immediately. Dinitz volunteered that Israel would pick up everything possible in unmarked El Al planes. There was no talk of an American airlift — except if tanks were urgently needed in an emergency.

So much for the canard that the Nixon Administration deliberately withheld supplies from Israel to make it more tractable in negotiations. After the prospects of a quick Israeli victory vanished, we faced two dangers: a prolonged military stalemate or a sudden proposal for a cease-fire in place while Israel still had not regained the prewar lines on either front. We sought to give Israel the confidence and the means to face the next few crucial days when the outcome hung as much on Israel's self-assurance as on its arms. But we also strove for a low profile in the method of resupply; we were conscious of the need to preserve Arab self-respect.

To maintain the dialogue with Egypt, I replied late that day to Hafiz Ismail's newest message, which we had received that morning and which had expressed appreciation for our government's "good intentions." I told Ismail ambiguously that our actions were the minimum that public opinion would tolerate — giving Egypt a face-saving formula for acquiescing in them. I stressed that the United States "now understands clearly the Egyptian position with respect to a peace settlement." But I avoided any comment on it. In diplomatic usage, that was tantamount to indicating it was a nonstarter.

Instead, I moved the exchange one notch closer to concreteness by asking Ismail another question that was more operational and permitted a specific response. It had the additional advantage of presenting our strategy of procrastination in the Security Council as a sign of concern for Egypt's point of view:

The U.S. side is less clear, however, as to the views of the Egyptian side on how the present fighting can be brought to an end. These views would be very useful to the U.S. side in formulating its position in the current debate in the Security Council. In the hope of hearing the views of the Egyptian side, the U.S. side will hold off as long as possible in presenting a definitive U.S. position in the Security Council.

The U.S. side wishes to reiterate its willingness to consult urgently with the parties concerned in order to achieve a just peace settlement in the Middle East. In these difficulties, it is important to keep this long-term perspective in mind and to avoid confrontations and bitter debate as we seek to resolve the present crisis. . . .

On Wednesday morning, October 10, we awoke to the ominous news of a Soviet airlift to Syria. Some twenty transport aircraft were on the way via Hungary and Yugoslavia. An airlift of such magnitude could not have been improvised; it must have been organized for several days. At this stage it seemed confined to consumables, paralleling our decision made the previous Sunday for Israel, though the Soviet effort was on a much larger scale and more overt. Was the purpose to stoke the fire of conflict, or to support a client and keep a Soviet hand in the postwar negotiations? Was it to encourage Arab intransigence, or to establish Soviet bona fides for a peace effort? Were they helping their most hard-pressed associate to keep it from collapsing, or were they encouraging a new onslaught?

Even now the answer is not clear. Probably the Soviet leadership tried to keep several options open and managed to combine all disadvantages. It did enough to ensure the continuation of the war but failed to affect the outcome. It may have sought a cease-fire, as all Arab leaders told us disdainfully after the war. But it did so tentatively — and, according to Sadat's published version, so duplicitously — that it magnified Egypt's doubts about its ally's good faith.

Sadat wrote that almost from the opening of hostilities — by 8:30 P.M. Cairo time on October 6, or six and a half hours after the war started — Moscow was urging him to accept a cease-fire. The Soviet Ambassador said to him then that President Asad of Syria had told the Kremlin *before* the war broke out to seek a cease-fire within forty-eight hours. It sounds sufficiently heavy-handed to be plausible. Although Asad denied having made such a request (not, in the context of Arab politics, definitive proof), the Soviets repeated their request daily for several days until Sadat finally ended it by insisting on continuing the war until he had shattered Israel's "theory of security." [13]

Sadat's account — unlikely to be colored by sympathy for the Soviet leadership — coincides with what the Soviets were telling us over the same period. Shortly after 8:00 A.M. on Wednesday, October 10, Dobrynin called me with a message he declared important: The Soviet consultations with Egypt and Syria had been "protracted" and "not easy." Nevertheless, Moscow could now tell Nixon that the USSR "is ready not to block adoption of a cease-fire resolution in the Security Council." In other words, the Soviet Union would abstain from a resolution favoring a simple cease-fire in place; it would not support — that is, it would veto — a call for a return to the prewar lines. In addition, the Soviet note expressed willingness to work for a negotiated settlement "on the basis of liberation of all Arab lands occupied by Israel."

The Soviet initiative for a cease-fire in place was now on the table in the worst possible circumstances for our strategy: If the Soviets pushed their proposal at that juncture, it would have had nearly unanimous backing, including by our European allies. On the other hand, Israel, with the prewar situation not yet restored, would have refused. Had we gone along with the Soviet plan and pressured Israel to agree, the war would have ended in a clear-cut victory for the Soviet-supplied Arab forces. The United States's position in the postwar diplomacy would have been severely impaired. The proposition that we alone among the superpowers could produce progress would have been exploded. Soviet arms would have achieved success; Soviet diplomacy would have protected it. The probability of another war would have been high, since Israel would want to regain its previous supremacy; the Arabs would become convinced that they could break every negotiating deadlock with a new assault.

Had the Soviets conducted a decisive policy or had the Arab nations not been carried away by euphoria, they might have clinched their gains by pressing for that cease-fire in place on October 10. We would have been hard put to resist. But Egypt and Syria either underestimated Israel's recuperative power or did not know how to end their mutual suspicions — probably a combination of both. What the Soviets hoped to achieve is hard to fathom. Their ambivalence gave us a chance to play for time and recoup. If they hoped to slow down our resupply of Israel, it was a false hope. The Soviet airlift to Damascus settled that once and for all. So I decided to accept the Soviet proposal "in principle" to inhibit a Soviet diplomatic offensive at the UN, but to delay its implementation long enough to test the latest Israeli prediction of victory within forty-eight hours on the Syrian front.

I therefore told Dobrynin that he could tell Moscow the cease-fire proposal was "constructive" but we needed time to consider it. A little while later I called him back to say that the President would not be able to make a formal reply until after another visitor from Africa, President Mobutu Sese Seko of Zaire, had left around 11:30 A.M. But my real purpose was to let Dobrynin know that we were aware of the "very substantial" Soviet airlift, which I told him was "not helpful." Dobrynin professed surprise. I said sarcastically: "I am sure [Soviet Defense Minister] Grechko knows it. . . . They are coming through Budapest just in case they are looking for the last airport." Dobrynin, who given the pedantry of Soviet bureaucratic procedures could not have been totally uninformed, said he would ask Moscow. Whatever happened now, I replied, the Soviet airlift would "force us to do at least the same."

Watergate provided a pretext for another delay. Agnew's resignation as Vice President was due to be announced at 2:00 P.M. that day. At 11:45 A.M. I called Dobrynin again on the pretext of alerting him, claiming that this would prevent the President from turning his attention to the Soviet proposal for hours. I asked Dobrynin to make sure that we would not be forced into premature decisions. He gave a flat assurance that the Soviets would introduce no resolution in the Security Council.

In between the conversations that morning with Dobrynin, I reviewed the situation with Dinitz. He read me a message of gratitude from Golda Meir to Nixon for the "vital" resupply decision communicated the day before, which would, she said, "have a great beneficial influence. . . . We are fighting against very heavy odds, but we are fully confident that we shall come out victorious. When we do we will have you in mind." I told Dinitz that with resupply assured, Israel did not need to hoard reserves. There was no time for complicated moves. Everything depended on the Israelis' pushing back to the prewar lines as quickly as possible, or beyond them on at least one front. We could not stall a cease-fire proposal forever.

Our dialogue with Egypt told us that there still was some time before there would be movement at the Security Council. At 1:00 P.M. that Wednesday we received Ismail's reply to my query of the day before about cease-fire terms. He made it clear that Cairo was not yet ready to clinch its gains; it continued to insist on a comprehensive peace plan, though in a much modulated manner:

> Mr. Ismail would also like to express that while the Egyptian side has taken note of the motivations of the position taken by the U.S. government, it would appreciate Dr. Kissinger's understanding of the political and other factors related to the Egyptian position, which makes it essential to consider a general program for the establishment of peace in the Middle East.

This delicate formulation — which implied that Egypt's terms went beyond the dictates of national interest, strictly speaking — indicated that in the right circumstances Egypt's insistence on a comprehensive program might be negotiable. In the rest of the message Ismail modified his position on the cease-fire, in five points, the most important of which were: Egypt no longer insisted on the *prior* withdrawal of Israeli troops to the pre–1967 boundary but would accept an Israeli pledge to that effect provided it had a specified time limit; the state of belligerency would end as soon as the withdrawal was completed; a peace conference would follow.

Ismail must have known very well that there was still no possibility of obtaining Israeli agreement to these terms short of total military defeat. But in delicate negotiations it is not the substance of the modification that matters; it is the fact that it is offered at all, especially as Ismail did not put it forward on a take-it-or-leave-it basis but "for the consideration of Dr. Kissinger" — in effect inviting a counterproposal.

With all my newfound admiration for Egyptian subtlety, I was convinced that serious talks would not take place until there was a change in the military situation. But first it was essential to keep the war from spreading. During the day we learned that Sadat was now pressing King Hussein to join the battle. Dean Brown reported that the King was thinking of sending an armored brigade into Syria in order to escape a more dangerous decision, such as opening up a new front by attacking along the Jordan River. But any Jordanian move might well encourage other Arab states to enter the war and encourage persistence in pursuing the military option. I urgently appealed to the King to delay any decision for at least forty-eight hours: I told him I was making a major effort through quiet diplomatic channels to bring about an end to the fighting. I needed time and his help. Hussein did not reply, which was prudent, but accepted the recommendation, which was statesmanlike.

Our own government remained divided on the urgency of resupplying Israel (though there was no dispute over making good its losses eventually). Everyone was convinced that the decision would be reached on the battlefield before heavy equipment could arrive and affect the outcome. There was a legitimate concern lest we ruin our relations with Arab moderates without really helping Israel — especially when we learned early on the tenth that King Faisal, having been rebuffed by King Hussein about moving the Saudi brigade stationed in Jordan to Syria, had now decided to send a brigade direct from Saudi Arabia. Schlesinger had called me with that news about 8:30 A.M., urging a rapid move to a "straight cease-fire." He was worried enough to canvass the idea of involving American troops in an "occupation." This I rejected. I told Schlesinger:

On the Saudi thing, I think everybody's just got to stay calm now. One Saudi brigade on the move means it will be two days before it can be anywhere near action and probably the Jordanians may move a brigade in there too, which is fine; that's the least they can do. We are going to hold our course another day or so, because we think we are going to get this thing taken care of on the course on which we are. I don't think there is any need to consider occupation of anything at this time.

During a lunch I gave at State for Belgian Foreign Minister Renaat van Elslande, I was called by prearrangement to the White House to receive Agnew's resignation. For some obscure legal reason, the resignation of the President or the Vice President must be made to the Secretary of State. The rule had never before been implemented. I trust that no other Secretary of State will find himself accepting the resignation of both our highest elected officials in the space of ten months.

While I was thus engaged with the Agnew resignation, Scowcroft met with Dinitz to brief him on the Soviet proposal for a joint abstention (on a simple cease-fire) and to discuss speeding up the resupply. Dinitz was no more eager for a cease-fire along existing lines than we. As instructed, Scowcroft urged that Israel make the maximum military effort in the next forty-eight hours. We would not be able to stall forever and we could not find ourselves trying to insist that Arab states return Arab territory that Israel had failed to recapture. But Dinitz could not provide Scowcroft with any sense of Israel's timetable or its operational plan, either because it did not exist or because his government chose not to share its intentions with us (or him).

This same conversation made clear that Israel could not pick up all the promised equipment in the seven jets of the El Al airfleet. After consultation among the WSAG principals, it was therefore decided that Israel should be given US government permission and support to employ private air charter companies to carry the additional equipment.

The resort to air charters turned out to be a fiasco; after forty-eight hours, as a result, an American military airlift was organized. Subsequently, it was alleged that the airlift was deliberately delayed as a maneuver to pressure Israel to accept a cease-fire.[14] The present description of our strategy can leave little doubt that this was not the case. On the morning of October 13, when we finally realized the extent to which bureaucratic foot-dragging and logistical problems had delayed the charter plan, I restated our strategy to the WSAG, asking on the President's behalf for the resignation of any official unwilling to support it: "[W]e needed to get the stuff in when we needed an offensive. Now it is going in afterwards, when we want the diplomacy to work. . . . If Israel feels we have let them down and the Arabs think they have done it themselves, we are sunk."

The reasons for the delay were manifold. No charter company was eager to court an Arab boycott or to risk its planes in a war zone. The Defense Department could have brought pressure on the charter companies, which rely on Pentagon business, but it felt no urgency because it estimated that Israel still had stocks for two weeks — or longer than any projection of military operations. The Department of Transportation (which was the other option) wanted to stay out of a military confrontation. The two departments adeptly pushed the ball back and forth into each other's court. Brent Scowcroft and Joe Sisco, who tirelessly worked to organize the charters, were in effect given the runaround. But fundamentally the problem was that we explored all alternatives before being brought face to face with the reality that since no private company would assume charters to Israel, the United States government would have to run the risk either by undertaking the airlift itself or by chartering the planes in its own name. I am not sure the delay made a substantial difference. Even had the military airlift started immediately, it could not have influenced Israeli military operations prior to the launching of the first cease-fire initiative of October 12–13, which aborted.

But on October 10, whatever our perception of the resupply problem, we had to delay the diplomacy until there was a change on the war front. We thought the optimum military circumstance for the postwar diplomacy we were planning was if Israel could restore the prewar situation or perhaps go slightly beyond it. This would demonstrate that the military option backed by Soviet arms was an illusion; that diplomatic progress depended on American support. Failing that, it might be possible to negotiate on the basis of an Israeli military advance on one front, even with a setback on the other — though this would be a much more complicated state of affairs.

On October 10, however, neither of these conditions yet existed. Israel had barely recaptured the Golan except for some Syrian outposts in the Mount Hermon area. Two Egyptian armies were firmly established across the Suez Canal. There was no prospect of an offensive in the Sinai; the only Israeli option was an offensive against Syria scheduled for the next morning. We would stall the Soviet overture until the results of this operation became clearer. (It must be remembered we had been told that very day that Egypt was not yet ready to give up its demand for total withdrawal. And we had heard nothing from Syria.)

To gain time, I told Dobrynin at 5:40 P.M. on October 10 that we had not had the time to consider his proposal for joint abstention from a simple cease-fire proposal. I would be in touch later. I added soothingly that we took the idea of a cease-fire seriously even if the mechanics were complicated. This was thin gruel but it prevented acrimony. That evening, Kurt Waldheim called to say that there was no majority in the Security Council for *any* resolution and that only Peru, Kenya, and Guinea were inscribed as speakers for the next day. Neither the Arabs nor Israel seemed to want any kind of cease-fire. This suited us fine. But Waldheim was worried: "More and more people are asking me, what is the [Secretary-General] doing to stop the fighting" — a fair enough question considering that nearly a week of a major war had passed without any formal UN action whatever.

At 9:45 P.M., I called Dobrynin again: "Anatoly, we won't be able to give you an answer till tomorrow." Dobrynin, who understood very well what I was doing, responded with affable menace: "You are playing quite well. Don't overplay the theme of Russian irresponsibility." I warned him again about the "massive" Soviet airlift.

Late in the day of October 10 we received another message, through Beirut, from an unexpected source: Yasir Arafat, head of the Palestine Liberation Organization (PLO). It is difficult to remember now the relatively marginal role played by the PLO until after the October war. In 1967 the hallowed UN Security Council Resolution 242 had made no reference to the PLO; it mentioned the Palestinians only as refugees. In "Black September" of 1970, King Hussein had uprooted the PLO from Jordan, inviting a crisis with Syria, whose backing of the PLO stemmed more from long-held designs on Jordan than political affinity with Palestinians. Until well into 1974, the common assumption was that Jordan, not the PLO, would negotiate with Israel over the West Bank. We had no political contact with Arafat. Occasionally, inconsequential messages were exchanged through low-level channels. Arafat's message now declared that it was

99 percent sure that the Israelis will rout the Egyptian and Syrians in the next few days. The United States therefore should not intervene or provide any more aid to Israel until after hostilities. The United States should seek a cease-fire soonest without preconditions.

This suggested that the Arabs, having crossed the prewar lines by their own efforts, had regained enough "face" to undertake real negotiations, even if they eventually would lose the battle, as Arafat seemed to predict. According to Arafat, the PLO was willing to participate in these talks though it reserved the right to settle its old score of 1970 with Jordan. This could mean, if taken at face value, that the PLO might conceivably make peace with Israel though never with Jordan. Arafat promised no hostile actions against American personnel or installations — unless America undertook a resupply effort while the war was going on. Did Arafat really believe this assessment and seek an entry into the negotiations? Or was he playing the same game as everybody else, trying to stall — in that case, prevent our resupply effort — in order to accelerate a victory of his allies? It made no real difference, for we did not return a reply until the war was over (see Chapter XIII).

That evening I reviewed the day's events and our progress. We would maintain contact with the parties. Our aim was to slow down diplomacy without appearing obstructionist, to urge a speedup of military operations without seeming to intervene, and then to force a cease-fire before the impatience and frustration of the parties or unforeseeable events could rip the whole finely spun fabric to smithereens.

October 11: Israel Drives into Syria

THE next day, Thursday, October 11, it became apparent that Dobrynin had not threatened idly. Ten new Soviet flights to Syria were detected in the early hours; indeed, the Soviet airlift now included flights to Egypt and even Iraq. Later in the day we learned that three Soviet airborne divisions had been put on alert.

That morning Israel's strategy also became clear. Israel was sweeping across the prewar lines on the Syrian front and carrying the air war deep into Syria. Defense Minister Moshe Dayan was quoted by news tickers as saying that the Israeli army was heading for Damascus. By the end of the day, Israel occupied a salient on the Golan Heights eleven kilometers deep and twelve kilometers wide, beyond the prewar lines. Forward Israeli positions were only about thirty-five kilometers (or twenty miles) from Damascus. This Israeli gain accorded with our preferred strategy if only the Israelis had kept quiet about it. After all, we had been stalling the Soviets for over twenty-four hours on a cease-fire in place — a position we could hardly maintain if Israel announced that it was advancing on the capital of a Soviet ally. I put the problem to Shalev around 11:00 A.M.:

It is not very good for you on the one hand to ask me to slow down the UN and you get Dayan to say on the radio and TV that you are heading for Damascus. How can we get the UN to slow down when you make this kind of announcement by your Defense Minister? . . . This looks like the most extreme form of collusion and bad faith.

But I continued to stall with Dobrynin, this time using the excuse that we needed to consult with Israel and other parties before a meaningful cease-fire proposal could be put forward. In fact, I was in urgent consultation with Israel, though not about a cease-fire. But this time there were increasing public complaints, led by Senator Henry Jackson and some columnists, that we were procrastinating in resupplying Israel and that détente was being exploited by the Soviets to lull us. The latter charge was especially ironic since, as we saw it, we were seeking to calm Moscow via détente to restore the situation. And it was highly unfair. Haig, Scowcroft, Sisco, and I were making strenuous efforts to assure resupply. We were trying to find our way through the unfamiliar world of air charters; and we were working on the assumption, encouraged by the Israelis, that by the time the supplies got through, the war on the Syrian front would be won. We were also doing our best to protect Israel from other attack: Tempers became so frayed that Nixon asked me to warn Dinitz he would hold Dinitz personally responsible if the hostile news stories continued — one of the emptiest threats imaginable.

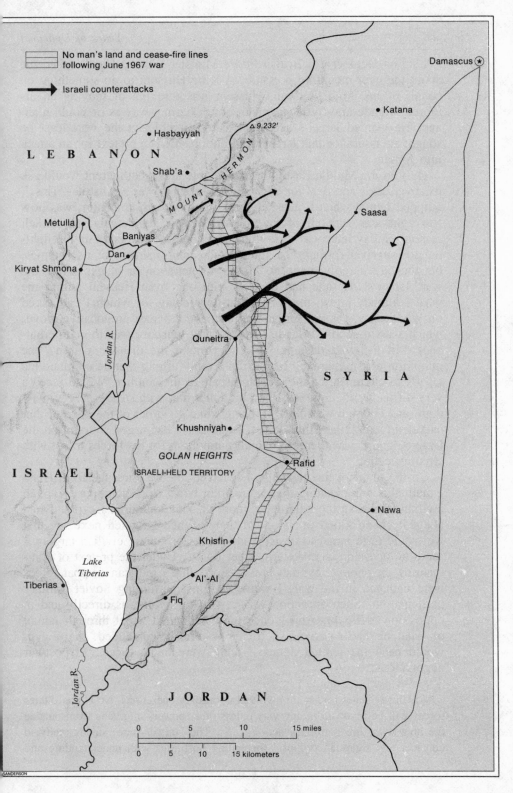

The Golan Front: Israeli Counterattack

Late on October 11, British Prime Minister Edward Heath called me about the ever-mounting pressure on King Hussein to do something on behalf of his Arab brethren. Hussein was thinking of moving an armored brigade into Syria, as much out of harm's way as he could manage. He wanted Israel's acquiescence if possible; at the very least he sought an assurance that Israel would not use it as a pretext for an attack into Jordan.

Only in the Middle East is it conceivable that a belligerent would ask its adversary's approval for engaging in an act of war against it. "This," quipped Dinitz when I later submitted the proposition to him, was how "to fight war with all of the conveniences." Predictably, the Israeli response a day later was to say no. One could not expect a nation fighting for survival formally to agree to the reinforcement of its enemies; but the Israeli reply made no threat of retaliation or of expanding the war. Israel's message had crossed with one from Hussein telling me what I already knew: the forty-eight-hour delay for which I had asked on Wednesday was up; Jordan had to make the least provocative move, which was to send a brigade to Syria. The purpose was to counterbalance "Iraqi-Soviet designs" and to contain the disaster within "the minimum possible area." I sent him a reply urging that he continue his efforts to circumscribe the area and scale of the conflict. We all faced a very difficult situation, but I had no doubt that with steady nerves, wisdom, and courage we could yet bring some good out of the disaster that had again struck the Middle East. I told him I had urged restraint on the Israelis, and it was therefore equally important for his forces to act with circumspection.

On the night of the eleventh, I received another message from Hafiz Ismail, this one pleading that we restrain Israel from bombing Egyptian civilian targets in the Nile delta; more than five hundred Egyptians had allegedly been killed or wounded there. When I replied next day that we would urge Israel to desist from attacks on purely civilian targets, I used the occasion to make two other points. Under the pretext of commenting on phony Egyptian press reports that American combat forces were engaged in the war, I warned against permitting Soviet military participation. Such an action was certain to involve us directly and in opposition to Egypt. And I once more reminded Sadat through Ismail of what he had — unknown to me — already concluded, that Egypt would need the United States if there were to be successful postwar negotiations:

No United States forces are involved in military operations. No United States forces will be involved in any way unless other powers intervene from outside the area with direct military action. . . . The United States stands ready to consider any Egyptian proposal for ending hostilities with understanding and good will. It will attempt to be helpful when hostilities are ended. Whatever the inevitable pressures of the moment, the U.S. hopes that both sides will not lose sight of this objective.

October 12–13: Our Airlift Begins

AT the end of the first week, with even the Golan Heights battle undecided and a cease-fire proposal seemingly almost on the table, it was clear the Soviet-American relationship was becoming a case history of both the possibilities and the limitations of détente. The Soviets were certainly giving vocal support to their Arab friends. Their airlift was disturbing. And now we learned that seven, not just three, Soviet airborne divisions were on alert. But this support was as yet far short of what the Soviets were capable of doing. After the war, all Arab leaders complained to me that the Soviet airlift was grudging and the sealift was slow, as if to rub in the Arabs' dependency. And the Soviet Union never launched a diplomatic offensive to embarrass or isolate us at the United Nations. I do not believe that history will judge that we were the party being used. The war was contained, and the United States maneuvered successfully to reduce the Soviet role in the Middle East.

This perception of East-West relations is fundamental to an understanding of my first news conference during the war, on Friday, October 12. My remarks were the subject of criticism because I refused to bury détente even while warning the Soviets that they were approaching its outer limits. But a verbal assault on Moscow would have accelerated events when it was our purpose to slow them down; it could have forced a confrontation while the military situation did not yet favor our strategy. That is why I spoke in carefully measured terms:

We did not consider the Soviet statement to the President of Algeria helpful. We did not consider the airlift of military equipment helpful. We also do not consider that Soviet actions as of now constitute the irresponsibility that on Monday evening I pointed out would threaten détente. When that point is reached, we will in this crisis, as we have in other crises, not hesitate to take a firm stand. But at this moment we are still attempting to moderate the conflict. As of this moment we have to weigh against the actions of which we disapprove — and quite strongly — the relative restraint that has been shown in public media in the Soviet Union and in the conduct of their representatives at the Security Council.

With respect to the Soviet airlift I employed the same combination of menace mitigated by restraint:

The Soviet airlift, at this moment, is moderate. It's more than light. It's a fairly substantial airlift. And it has to be addressed in relation to the possibility of influencing immediate military operations.

As far as we are concerned, you all know that we do have an ongoing military relationship with Israel, which we are continuing. And we are having discussions with Israel about the special situation created by recent events. . . .

A journalist asked whether Arab threats to cut off our oil supplies would affect our decision to resupply Israel. I replied:

We have made a very serious effort, in this crisis, to take seriously into account Arab concerns and Arab views. On the other hand, we have to pursue what we consider to be the right course; we will take the consequences. . . .

Asked whether the United States was prepared to be as firm now as in the Jordan crisis of 1970, I replied with a thinly veiled warning: "Situations are never comparable, but the basic principles that governed our policies throughout this administration remain constant. . . ." And I summed up publicly the strategy I had been articulating to my colleagues privately:

We have not gratuitously sought opportunities for confrontations in public forums which might harden dividing lines and which might make it more difficult to move toward a settlement. . . . Our objective is to bring about an end of hostilities in such a manner that we will be in contact with all of the parties, as well as with the permanent members of the Security Council, after hostilities are ended, because we believe that in this manner we can make a maximum contribution to a just and lasting peace in the Middle East.

I spoke to Nixon on that Friday morning at the end of the first week. He was preoccupied with selecting a new Vice President, the first time a President in office was able to appoint his own successor. I told him where we stood with respect to the air charters and our stalling on the Soviet cease-fire proposal, now forty-eight hours old.

Dobrynin, meanwhile, was getting restless. At a testy lunch he brought an unsigned note to express the "surprise" of his leadership at my complaint about Soviet public statements supporting the Arabs. Were we not making many statements in support of Israel? (His question was not without merit, though sidestepping the issue of who had opened hostilities.) The note also objected to the eastward deployment of our Sixth Fleet, which was now milling around near Crete with the Soviet fleet. This was basically low-order griping, designed to show that the Soviets were getting impatient. Dobrynin stiffened when I mentioned the alerting of Soviet airborne divisions. Nothing irritates Soviet officials more than evidence of our intelligence capabilities — particularly diplomats if they are not being kept informed of military deployments. Dobrynin rather heatedly emphasized that the Soviet Union could not be indifferent to threats to Damascus. If Israel continued its advance, matters might get out of hand. I warned that any Soviet military intervention would be resisted and wreck the entire fabric of US–Soviet relations.

Israel had informed us before my press conference that it was now agreeable to proceeding with a standstill cease-fire. I could have acted on that assurance, but to make sure nothing would get unstuck I had inquired whether there was any recommendation on timing. At 3:15 P.M. Shalev replied that Israel would prefer — but did not insist — that the resolution not be put to a vote until the afternoon of the following day, Saturday. However, we could start the process of consultation at our discretion. At 5:50 P.M. I told Eban in New York that we would aim for a vote not before late the next afternoon. To concert tactics we scheduled a meeting for 9:00 A.M. the next morning, Saturday, October 13 — the eighth day of the war — in Washington. At 6:50 P.M. I contacted the British Ambassador, Lord Cromer, to propose that Britain introduce a cease-fire in place at the Security Council the next day. Cromer thought it a good idea, but was obviously without instructions. We would have to wait to see what Prime Minister Heath and Foreign Secretary Sir Alec Douglas-Home thought.

Then at 7:00 P.M. the Soviet Minister, Yuli Vorontsov, requested an immediate appointment for Dobrynin, who was said to have an "urgent" message to deliver to me. Since Nixon was going to announce his choice for Vice President at 9:00 P.M., I would have to be at the White House at 8:30. (Haig had told me in the afternoon that Gerald Ford was the choice.) I could see Dobrynin for fifteen minutes at the State Department at 8:00 P.M.

At 7:45 P.M. I warned Dinitz of the coming Soviet message. He told me that Israel was very concerned about the implied Soviet threats conveyed to me over lunch by Dobrynin. Golda had authorized him to tell me to submit the cease-fire resolution that evening if I thought it wise. I demurred. No one would be ready to proceed on such short notice; any sudden show of American anxiety would invite new pressures. More important, I said, "once you have been threatened it is better to stick to your course."

It was a rule I sought to follow whenever possible. A leader known to yield to intimidation invites it. A statesman with a reputation for intransigence in the face of menace does not avoid all pressures but he reduces them to those that adversaries consider unavoidable. No leader can skirt all confrontations, but if he maneuvers carefully and with determination he can avoid provoking them by either excessive bellicosity or excessive pliability.

Things were clearly getting tense. Either the Soviets sensed an imminent victory or they feared the approaching demoralization of their clients. The first threatening public statement from Moscow preceded Dobrynin into my office. TASS, the Soviet news agency, attacked the "criminal actions of the Israeli military" in bombing civilian targets in Syria and Egypt, which they said had resulted in some Soviet casualties.

The Soviet Union, said TASS, could not regard these actions "indifferently." When Dobrynin arrived in bubbling good cheer, he had with him not one but two messages on the same theme. The first assailed the "barbaric bombings by the Israeli aviation of peaceful population centers in Egypt and Syria, Damascus includ[ed]. . . ." It added ominously that Israeli population centers would not remain immune indefinitely. That message also sharply protested an attack by Israeli torpedo boats on a Soviet merchant ship in a Syrian harbor, culminating in another threat: "The Soviet Union will of course take measures which it will deem necessary to defend its ships and other means of transportation."

The second Soviet message was pure insolence. The Soviet Union had been running an airlift into Syria and Egypt amounting to some eighty-four planes over three days; I had protested this from October 10 onward. This did not keep them from responding by accusing us of resupplying Israel. They were referring, if to anything at all, to the seven El Al planes that had been shuttling back and forth picking up equipment. Our massive American resupply effort had not yet started.

I curtly dismissed this protest. As to the bombing, I told Dobrynin what I had already communicated to Hafiz Ismail, that we would do our best to discourage attacks on purely civilian targets. I warned that any Soviet military intervention — regardless of pretext — would be met by American force. (It would have been a more convincing threat had I made it on any other day. For that very day the Congress passed the so-called War Powers Act, whose purpose was to reduce Presidential discretion in committing American military forces.) Dobrynin pointed out that Moscow's message reaffirmed its willingness to "direct the events toward a cease-fire in the Middle East," first communicated to us two days before. I told him that I had asked Britain to explore the idea of submitting a cease-fire resolution the next day.

Dobrynin had barely left when Cromer called to tell me that London was willing in principle to put forward such a resolution, but only if convinced that it would succeed. Whitehall frankly doubted that what I proposed was realistic; it felt that Egypt would not accept a cease-fire unless Israel agreed to return to the 1967 borders. (This was, of course, what Ismail had also told us.) London even had some doubts that Israel would go along. On that last point I knew better; Israel was, if anything, too eager to proceed. Still overestimating the closeness of Cairo and Moscow, I assured Cromer that Dobrynin would not be proceeding without Cairo's approval. But I would shortly double-check with Dobrynin at the White House ceremony where the new Vice President would be announced.

There was just enough time to give Dinitz a brief summary of the Soviet messages. I told him that we would move an additional aircraft

carrier into the Mediterranean and, as my personal view — not yet
checked with the President — that we would intervene if "any Soviet
personnel, planes or ground personnel appear in the area." Dinitz and I
agreed to meet around 11:00 P.M.

The ceremony in the East Room of the White House turned into an
eerie interlude in the Watergate bitterness. Assembled were the leaders
of the Congress, the Cabinet, senior White House staff, and the senior
members in terms of service of the diplomatic corps (which included
Dobrynin as second in longevity in Washington). There was an air of
expectancy as if noisy goodwill could drown out the uneasiness that the
constitutional crisis would not end this evening, that the worst in fact
was yet to come. The selection of the popular Gerald Ford evoked a
wave of enthusiasm that for a moment stilled the worry about the future
of a country with a visibly disintegrating executive authority. For fifteen
minutes everyone submerged his private fears and doubts in warm feelings toward this quintessential American who all subconsciously felt
would soon take over leadership of our country. Unhappily, the euphoria ended with the ceremony.

On the way out I had a word with Dobrynin. The British, I told him,
were under the impression that Sadat did not favor a cease-fire in place.
Dobrynin was equal to the occasion. With the air of a man much put
upon by the incurable obtuseness of Americans, he said that of course
he had no right to promise that Egypt would accept a cease-fire resolution. He could assure me, however, that we would be taking a "good
gamble" if it were put forward on the assumption that Egypt would
accept. I took this to mean that the Soviets knew Egypt would not give
advance approval, but that it would acquiesce in a cease-fire achieved
without its cooperation.

This was the line I took with Cromer in reporting my conversation
with Dobrynin. Cromer said that Home would be in touch with me early
the next morning — with the time difference, this would give him eight
hours of consultation in various capitals. I urged that he trigger the
cease-fire appeal "before any of these maniacal parties change their
minds."

That the parties might change their minds — if indeed they had ever
made them up — was evident not only from the ambiguity of their responses but also from their military dispositions. It was beginning to
appear that Egypt, instead of aiming for a cease-fire, was heading for a
new offensive in the Sinai to break out of its bridgehead along the east
bank of the Suez Canal. Artillery was being moved across; there were
reports that two armored divisions would follow. I still did not believe
that Egypt would permit its tanks to advance beyond the protective umbrella of its surface-to-air antiaircraft missiles. But if I were wrong, the
cease-fire initiative was certain to prove stillborn. Then, too, the Soviet

airlift was growing in magnitude. On Saturday, October 13, we were to detect sixty-seven new flights, the bulk to Egypt — was it a sweetener for a cease-fire or a way to stiffen resolution? We also learned that the Soviet Union had sought permission to fly military planes over Iran into Iraq or Syria; the Shah had refused, permitting only one plane allegedly carrying spare parts for Aeroflot civilian jets stationed in Syria. Even if one disbelieved the story about the cargo — as I did — the Shah stood by us in our hour of need, a service we did not reciprocate.

As I waited for the result of Home's consultations, Dinitz showed up at my White House office at 11:20 P.M. that Friday evening and launched us into one of the decisive encounters of the week. For it led the United States to undertake an all-out military airlift.

The security adviser's office had been moved three years previously from the basement to a high-ceilinged room on the ground floor whose huge windows stretched from floor to ceiling. As a result, the office appeared larger than its dimensions would suggest; it seemed almost at one with the White House Lawn stretching toward Pennsylvania Avenue, where one could see the distant lights of the passing traffic but barely hear its sounds. In this peaceful atmosphere Dinitz somberly began with a military briefing. He reviewed the military dispositions and reiterated Israel's willingness to begin moving toward a cease-fire in place. It took a few minutes to find the various locations on a map. Suddenly I realized that Israel's armed forces had not advanced significantly during the day. I had been stalling the diplomacy for nothing. This led to the following exchange:

KISSINGER: Do you want us to start it [the diplomacy] tonight? Did you make the offensive today? I have the impression no.

DINITZ: No.

KISSINGER: If we could synchronize your moves better — I think the urgency will disappear if there are no military moves tomorrow. If I knew there was no offensive today, I would have started earlier.

DINITZ: I must tell you: Our decision whether to start a new offensive or not depends on our power. We thought we would have by now in Israel the implements to do it — the bombs, the missiles, etc.

KISSINGER: So did I. What exactly is the obstacle?

Dinitz said that he had had a difficult meeting with Schlesinger at 6:00 P.M. and could not get a clear-cut decision on arms aid from the Defense Secretary. This was puzzling. At 5:40 P.M. Schlesinger had briefed me in advance that he would be offering Dinitz a large replacement package worth $500 million that included sixteen F-4 Phantoms, thirty A-4 Skyhawks, 125 tanks (including 65 M-60s), three Hawk missile battalions, and "a whole range of other things." I had even half-facetiously pleaded that he make sure to give the White House some of the credit. Now Dinitz complained to me that those replacements of heavy equipment would come too late and that the charters carrying consumables — needed for the current counteroffensive — had been delayed three days. Dinitz in particular stressed that Israel was running out of ammunition; if it was not replenished immediately, Israel would exhaust its supplies in two or three days. The Syrian offensive would have to be slowed and the Sinai front would be in severe jeopardy.

There were a number of aspects that did not make sense. Dinitz had been urging a cease-fire since early that day without alluding to specific shortages or informing us of the need for ammunition. (In fact, a DIA estimate we received early the next day said Israel could continue military operations at the existing rate of expenditure for another ten days.) On the other hand, previous estimates had proved most unreliable and average figures might still leave Israel short of critical items. We could not take another chance.

I immediately called Schlesinger, who expressed astonishment; he simply did not believe that an army could run out of ammunition without warning. (And he told Haig a few hours later that it seemed to him more a maneuver to lock us in than a military necessity.) By then it made no difference. Only a show of determination could now arrest the creeping Soviet escalation and persuade the Arabs to settle before the conflict drew in other states.

At 12:50 A.M., after checking with Haig, Schlesinger and I decided on three interim steps: We would load with ammunition and dispatch ten C-130 transport aircraft that had already been promised to Israel; we would haul supplies to the Azores to be picked up by the Israelis, shortening the distance their planes had to fly and greatly increasing the volume of cargo that could be carried (since less fuel was needed); and we would continue to press for charters. I stressed to Schlesinger that those who were afraid of Arab reaction should remember that the gravest threat to our Arab interests came from a prolongation of the war and the concomitant radicalization of the area. Schlesinger agreed. Shortly after 1:00 A.M., I informed Dinitz of the steps we had decided upon.

As for the charters, the next issue to be decided was whether the aircraft were to be chartered by Israel or by the United States government; perhaps we should use American military planes, such as the long-range jumbo C-5A. After a few hours' sleep, on Saturday morning, October 13, I had a brief meeting with Abba Eban. Jerusalem had not informed him in detail about the discussions of the previous evening (though Dinitz was with him now). So we went again through the airlift discussion. Eban saw no difference in the impact on the Arab world between chartered or government-owned American aircraft. That would be the heart of the discussion of the special WSAG that was assembling in the White House Situation Room at 10:30 A.M.

I spoke to Nixon before the WSAG met. He was in good form, still exuberant over achieving surprise in naming Ford, who (he reasoned) would be a short-term asset with the Congress. His selection would dampen desires to impeach him because the Congress would not want to run the risk of placing a supposedly inexperienced man in charge of foreign affairs — a symptom of how profoundly Nixon was still misjudging the determination of the forces arrayed against him and the extent to which he had shredded the tissue of confidence on which a Presidency ultimately depends. And Ford, he thought, would not stand in the way of Nixon's ultimate aim: designating John Connally as his successor in 1976.

As always after a successful public performance, Nixon was exhilarated. He still reveled in the applause that had greeted his brief, graceful speech the night before. He failed to recognize that it was a tribute above all to Ford. Nor did he yet understand that his fate could no longer be changed by tactical maneuvers. Indeed, Nixon's travail had reached the point where even if Ford was as inconsequential as Nixon thought — which he emphatically was not — his designation as Vice President would accelerate Nixon's collapse rather than delay it. It was more tempting for Democrats to remove Nixon if his successor seemed to be someone they thought they could beat in the Presidential election of 1976.

When we turned to the airlift, Nixon showed his old courage once again. By now the Pentagon had located three giant C-5A jet transports that were available to fly sixty to eighty tons of supplies each directly to Israel. Nixon immediately agreed to the proposal. "Do it now!" he urged.

With this guideline, the Saturday morning WSAG meeting moved to a crisp conclusion. It was attended by Schlesinger, his deputy Bill Clements, Admiral Moorer, Ken Rush, Bill Colby, and me. I opened it by warning in Nixon's name that any further foot-dragging would result in the dismissal of the offender. The rest of the meeting was devoted to the mechanics of the airlift. There was still unanimity that planes chartered by Israel would be the safest course for us. But it was becoming clear that we would, in fact, have to charter the planes in the name of the United States government. The difference between that mode and a direct American military airlift was so esoteric as to seem academic. It was also decided that F-4 Phantom deliveries would be vastly accelerated; Israel would get ten planes by Sunday and another four by Monday at a minimum. Schlesinger reported to the WSAG that the first of these planes were already moving.

By 12:30 P.M. I was able to report to Dinitz that we would fly the C-5As direct to Israel until we had the charter issue sorted out, that supplies already in the Azores and beyond El Al's capacity would be moved to Israel in American C-141s, and that Israel would shortly be receiving fourteen F-4 Phantoms.

By Sunday morning — twenty-four hours after the airlift had started — we were to recommend to Nixon that it be a straightforward American military operation. Nixon was buoyed by crisis, as always. "We are going to get blamed just as much for three planes as for 300," he told me with respect to the C-5As. He was right.

The history of the resupply effort has become entangled in American domestic politics and the strategy underlying it has been obscured in a fog of conflicting charges and rebuttals. A summary of the sequence of events after Golda's dramatic appeal on the morning of Tuesday, October 9 is therefore in order. By the evening of October 9, Israel had been assured that its war losses would be made up. Relying on this assurance, it stepped up its consumption of war matériel, as we had intended. Israeli predictions led us to believe that the main battle would be over first by Wednesday, then, after an Israeli reassessment, by Saturday. At that point a cease-fire would have been triggered as proposed by Dobrynin on Wednesday morning and accepted by Israel on Friday. Hence no one believed that military urgency prevented us from exploring the method of resupplying Israel that would least jeopardize our interests in the Arab world and the dependence of the industrial world on imported oil. The duty of those of us responsible for our nation's security was to relate all vital considerations to an overall design.

I consistently pressed for more urgent deliveries than my colleagues not because I thought supplies would affect the immediate battles but because I wanted a demonstrative counter to the Soviet airlift. Fundamentally, however, Israel's problem lay not in the pace of our resupply but in the complacency induced by the memory of great victories. Israel's strategy had been based on repeating the lightning thrusts of 1967. In the meantime the Arab countries had learned that if they kept from losing, their position would steadily improve by a war of attrition. Their lines bent but did not break. They inflicted casualties that a small country of fewer than three million people, however heroic, found difficult to bear. It was not until Israel adjusted its tactics in the second week of the war, aided by a grievous Egyptian strategic blunder *and* the psychological impact on both Israel and the Arabs of a massive American resupply, that the tide of battle turned decisively.

As it turned out, the concatenation of circumstances did ensure that the massive American airlift took place in a diplomatic context least likely to inflame Arab passions. After Saturday, October 13, we could present our massive resupply of Israel as a reaction to the Soviet airlift as well as to Moscow's failure to deliver on its own cease-fire initiative. For when we began to implement the proposal Dobrynin had earlier advanced on Wednesday, October 10, it quickly emerged as empty.

October 13–14: The Failed Cease-Fire

AFTER our Friday night discussion with the British, I had expected to have early on Saturday morning, October 13, their considered response to the cease-fire initiative proposed by the Soviets; the plan was for Britain to introduce in the Security Council late that afternoon a resolution calling for a cease-fire in place. I was perturbed when we heard nothing by 9:30 A.M. that day, since by then it was late afternoon in the Middle East and Sir Alec's consultations should have been completed.

Therefore, I called Dobrynin to say that if we did not have a British decision by noon, we would ask Australia to introduce the cease-fire resolution. Dobrynin said he would have to check with Moscow but "I don't really see that there is any difference." I said that we had ominous indications that an Egyptian offensive into the Sinai was imminent and warned that trickery would seriously harm our relations. Dobrynin thought that we should stick to the agreed course regardless of the unpredictable actions of the parties. He saw no insurmountable obstacles to a joint abstention from a Security Council appeal for a cease-fire.

No sooner was I finished with Dobrynin than Sir Alec telephoned. To understand his impact, a word must be said about our estimate of him. While he was not truly analytical, he was one of the wisest men I have known. He was that rarest of statesmen, one whose integrity disarms even his critics. He exuded a rectitude so matter-of-fact that he never needed to appeal to it. Because he was totally trustworthy, his word counted, even if it was painful. Because his judgment was prudent, his insights were central to any consultation. For a statesman, values lived are more reliable than postulates articulated. Home inspired confidence in full measure. He was deceptively underemphatic; he would lead his interlocutor to the desired conclusion by a Socratic dialogue that was as penetrating and relentless as the manner in which it was put forward was diffident. He was an unconditional friend of the United States. He stood for the common values of freedom. There was quite literally no one whom we trusted more.

Home's assessment now was that a cease-fire in place was a mirage. Sadat would not accept anything less than an Israeli commitment to return to the 1967 frontiers. Our proposal would not fly unless Moscow was willing to pressure Sadat by cutting off his military supplies; he doubted the Soviets were prepared to go this far. Home proposed instead a compromise including a cease-fire in place, an international police force for the rest of the occupied territories, followed by an international conference. There was no chance that Israel would accept this scheme, which in some ways was even more disadvantageous to it than Sadat's. After all, the introduction of an international force presupposed an almost immediate Israeli withdrawal to the 1967 boundaries, while Sadat was asking now for only an agreement to it in principle. I told Home it was too complicated; we would not support it. (Within the hour I told Cromer for Home that we would in fact veto it.)

I explained to Home that Dobrynin's overture seemed to be based on the assumption that Sadat would not agree to a cease-fire ahead of time but would yield to a Security Council consensus backed by the superpowers. I could not conceive that the Soviets would risk our confidence by deliberately misinforming us about what was possible — especially as they were bound to be found out almost immediately. What were they going to get from it? I must say that even at this remove I cannot answer the question. Therefore, what did Britain stand to lose if it tested this hypothesis by introducing a cease-fire resolution? Home feared that acting without Sadat's prior acquiescence would hurt Britain in the Arab world without benefit to us. However, he would check again in Cairo to see whether my hypothesis was correct.

I immediately told Dobrynin of Home's negative view. Dobrynin was nonplussed. He reaffirmed that the Soviet Union would abstain from a cease-fire resolution, whatever Sadat's preferences. The only hitch to this scheme was that Britain would put forward no resolution of which Sadat disapproved. "Maybe we should go with Australia," suggested Dobrynin. I told him that we might do so after we heard again from Home.

At 1:40 P.M. Dobrynin called back with the astonishing news that the "Australian variation" was "not really a good one." This made no sense whatever. If Moscow wanted a cease-fire and if it was confident of being able to get Sadat aboard, it could make no possible difference who introduced the resolution. Refusing Australia could only mean that the Kremlin, deciding that Home was probably right in his assessment of Sadat, was not willing to pay the price of his displeasure. (Unless of course it had been an elaborate trick all along.) I told Dobrynin to keep in mind that "there are no easy victories" in international affairs.

While waiting for the final British reply I told Scowcroft to get ready "to pour stuff in there." If the cease-fire initiative failed for lack of Soviet cooperation, it must be because they anticipated an Arab victory or because they were not prepared to pay the price of a compromise. In either case our course was clear. We had to create a situation on the ground that would force the principal parties to reassess their positions: "We can't let Israel lose. If the Soviet side wins we will be in very bad shape." I then told Haig that if the cease-fire initiative collapsed, we would have to step up the airlift to maximum capacity using all available planes, no matter what the risk of confrontation. We could talk again only when the battle had turned once more.

At 3:35 P.M. on October 13 Home called with the final British reply:

Sadat rejected any variation of a cease-fire. If it were introduced over his objection and if it threatened to pass because of Soviet and American abstention, Sadat would ask China to veto it. The French Ambassador had exactly the same impression of Sadat's views. Home asked whether détente remained our motivating consideration. "Détente is not an end in itself," I told him. "I think developments now are going to drive us towards a confrontation."

All our information seemed to point in that direction. Egypt's 21st armored division — carefully husbanded until now — had crossed the Suez Canal. At least one other armored division was preparing to follow.

The die was now cast; matters had reached a point where maneuvering would be suicidal and hesitation disastrous. The parties could not yet be brought to end the war — or the Soviets to support this course — by a calculation of their interests. All that was left was to force a change in the perception of their interests. We would pour in supplies. We would risk a confrontation. We would not talk again until there was no longer any doubt that no settlement could be imposed.

Conciliation is meaningful only if one is thought to have an alternative. We could not know, when we decided to engage in massive resupply, whether the Arab states would take out their frustration in bitter hostility or whether the Soviet Union would pick up the challenge and organize a bloc of countries working against our interests throughout the region. But we had no alternative anyway. If the Soviet-armed states won, the Soviets would control the postwar diplomacy. If Israel did not force a decision, it would be enmeshed in a war of attrition in which courage and ingenuity even in Israeli measure could not overcome a population ratio of thirty to one arrayed against it.

But events of the past week had also demonstrated how precarious was the base from which our diplomacy was operating. As we forced a showdown, we would be alone with Israel; inevitably, we would be isolated at the United Nations. Whatever our judgment about Soviet duplicity or obfuscation — and at the moment it was not kindly — they had not yet sought to embarrass us there. They had not introduced the Egyptian idea of linking a cease-fire with a return to the 1967 borders, which would have forced us to veto a cherished Arab goal. Still, Moscow had been far from helpful. It was clear that we faced a combination of Arab pressures, European fears, and Soviet opportunism that placed a floor under Arab risks. Egypt and Syria would be able to find a majority for a cease-fire in place whenever things got too hot. And we would not be able to block it for any lengthy period without enormous political costs.

Informing Dinitz of our decision to operate the airlift at maximum capacity and exclusively with American military planes, I urged that Israel accelerate its military offensives so that they could be completed

within forty-eight hours of the issue's going to the Security Council —
whenever that was. We could not stall much longer than that, and we
would not be able to justify vetoing what many nations knew we had
advocated a short time previously.

Soviet behavior remained puzzling. Had they been stringing us along,
never intending to have a cease-fire? Did they maneuver to prolong the
war? I accused Dobrynin of this when I informed him of the British
refusal to introduce a cease-fire resolution. He was defensive, but asked
what Soviet purpose would be served by such tactics. This puzzled me
as well, so I halfheartedly invoked the Egyptian offensive expected for
the next day. That I knew made little sense. We had done the procrastinating for seventy-two hours to help the Israeli offensive in Syria; the
Soviets were willing to proceed on Wednesday. Dobrynin, who did not
miss a trick, had understood our strategy. Did I suggest, he asked, that
the Soviet Union had procrastinated for Israel to defeat the Syrians? "It
is a very interesting presumption." Sadat's autobiography, as I have
noted, asserts that the Soviets were pressing him for a cease-fire in place
from the first day of the war. They did not start resupplying Egypt until
Thursday, October 11, and did not put in substantial quantities until that
very morning (Saturday, October 13), a week after the war began.

What seems to have occurred is that the Soviets sought to combine
the advantage of every course of action: détente with us, enough support
for their Arab friends to establish their indispensability if things went
well, but not so much as to tempt a confrontation with the United States.
The Kremlin may also have calculated that the Soviet position in the
Middle East would be stronger if it could lure us into a cease-fire while
the Arab armies had made net gains of territory with the aid of Soviet
weapons and before the Israeli counteroffensive had achieved conclusive
results. Even by October 13, after Israel's successes against Syria, a
cease-fire would have left at least Egypt in a very strong military position. But Sadat was either carried away by his successes or driven by
his loyalty to Syria to relieve the pressures on his ally. We did not hear
directly from the Syrians, but it would have been uncharacteristic of
them to avow less intransigence than their ally and rival in Cairo. The
Europeans were seeking to curry Arab favor and thereby objectively
encouraged Arab euphoria. The Soviets were not willing to bring the
sort of pressure that might have made Sadat go along with a cease-fire
proposal at that point.

It is as wrong to overestimate the strategic insight of one's adversary
as it is dangerous to underrate it. In the beginning the United States and
the Soviet Union were, in fact, pursuing comparable strategies, each
seeking to enable its friends to gain the upper hand on the battlefield.
When a stalemate developed, each side began to support its friends with
consumables. We started earlier (on Sunday, authorizing use of El Al

planes); the Soviets jumped in on Wednesday, much more massively than we, with an airlift. We would have matched this by Thursday evening or Friday morning but for the confusion over charters. We finally more than matched the Soviets' moves by Sunday.

We had two assets, however. Our ally was ultimately stronger and better able to take advantage of resupply. And we were prepared to risk more than Moscow. Once a stalemate had become apparent, either by Soviet design or confusion, we moved decisively, even brutally, to break it. I had learned in Nixon's first term, largely under his tutelage, that once a great nation commits itself, it must prevail. It will acquire no kudos for translating its inner doubts into hesitation. However ambivalently it has arrived at the point of decision, it must pursue the course on which it is embarked with a determination to succeed. Otherwise, it adds a reputation for incompetence to whatever controversy it is bound to incur on the merits of its decision.

That, at any rate, is how we acted as soon as London declined to put forward the cease-fire proposal and Moscow rejected the Australian alternative. I immediately warned Dobrynin: "We are now going to wash our hands of it and let nature take its course." What that meant I then conveyed to Scowcroft: "Since we are going to be in a confrontation we should go all-out." I instructed him to load ships with equipment for Israel so that a cease-fire that ended each side's airlift would not suddenly cut Israel's lifeline. I informed Cromer that we were starting an airlift to Israel, implying — with less than total accuracy — that it was due to the failure of the cease-fire initiative. Cromer asked: "What will be your posture when the Arabs start screaming oil at you?"

"Defiance," I replied, playing Churchill.

"Just defiance?" queried Cromer, reasonably enough; "it is going to be rough, won't it?"

"We have no choice," I said.

Meanwhile, we had obtained Portuguese permission to use Lajes airfield in the Azores for refueling. When the first approach had been made on Friday, October 12, the Portuguese government had stalled. It had no national interest in antagonizing the Arab nations. It sought to extract some military equipment for its colonial wars in Mozambique and Angola. To this we were not prepared to agree. I had therefore drafted a Presidential letter of unusual abruptness to Portuguese Prime Minister Marcelo Caetano that refused military equipment and threatened to leave Portugal to its fate in a hostile world. By the middle of Saturday afternoon, the Portuguese gave us unconditional transit rights at Lajes airbase.

At 5:30 P.M. on October 13 — with the airlift under way — Nixon and I had a lengthy review. We realized that if the Egyptian offensive succeeded, in the next twenty-four hours the war could turn decisively against our interests. I speculated that once Egyptian tanks ventured outside their antiaircraft missile screen the Israeli air force might bloody them and break the back of the offensive. But the Arabs were certainly cocky. If they prevailed in these circumstances, we would really have to "tighten our belts." Nixon did not think that Israel's armed forces had deteriorated so rapidly that they would lose a pitched battle. But he agreed we were now in a test of wills, saying that this was "one of those times" and "that's what we are here for."

Nixon, whatever his travail, would see it through. No faint heart would be able to appeal to him to reverse our course. And if his ordeal deprived him of his previous intensity, it gave him the composure of a man who had seen the worst and to whom there were no further terrors. Indeed, he probably welcomed staking his future on defending the interests of free peoples as he understood them rather than on the outcome of a sordid litigation over events that had clearly gotten away from him.

As so often before when confronted with decisive American action, the Soviets began to pull back. Late in the day we received an "oral message" from Brezhnev. Moscow had been prepared for two days to implement the cease-fire, it said, but when the United States procrastinated, the Arabs had changed their minds. I remarked sarcastically to Dobrynin that perhaps the growing Soviet airlift (now 140 planes) contributed to this Arab determination. Dobrynin reiterated the hope of his leadership that what happened should not undo all the good that had been accomplished. But the time for soothing generalities was over. A tolerable conclusion depended on our ability to convince the Soviets that there would be no flinching on our part, either to protect détente or for fear of the Arab reaction. "We will not under any circumstances let détente be used for unilateral advantage," I said. "[D]on't think we will accept a military setback in the Middle East." Making a virtue out of our bureaucratic confusion over charters, I claimed that we had delayed to give diplomacy a chance. But the Egyptian proposal that a return to the 1967 borders be a precondition of a cease-fire was, and would remain, "unacceptable." At most, we could consider a reference to Security Council Resolution 242 as part of a cease-fire but not go beyond it or define the words "secure boundaries" more precisely. Basically, I said, we would let matters develop for three or four days and then see what the situation was. We were ready to discuss a Middle East settlement but only *after* a cease-fire. Moscow should not believe that it could pressure us by military means. Dobrynin was not eager for controversy. He would report everything I had said, "quote . . . unquote," he assured me.

In almost every crisis there occurs a moment, however fleeting, which conveys an unmistakable signal that the other side is not prepared to push matters to a confrontation. Brezhnev's message and Dobrynin's subdued behavior hinted that unless Moscow changed its mind, we would be able to see our new course through to a conclusion. The curtain had been raised on a new act, the first scene of which would be the tank battle in the Sinai.

October 14: Deadlock on the Battlefield

Now everything depended on our playing our hand coolly and deliberately. Egypt launched its new thrust into the Sinai as expected on Sunday, October 14 — largely to relieve the pressure on Syria. But that battle was out of our hands. While it was raging, we reviewed our plans and sought to minimize the impact of our decisions on the Arab world. That Sunday morning Nixon and I talked again. We both agreed that the battle in the Sinai would not last long. Supplies for both sides would have to come long distances and would soon be exhausted; the desert did not lend itself to protracted warfare.

The WSAG meeting that assembled at 9:16 that morning settled the technicalities of the airlift once and for all. We would skip charters and keep moving with a straight-out US military airlift. The next, perhaps most important, task for the remainder of the day was to make sure the key actors knew our purposes and to keep in view an ultimate end to the deepening conflict. At midday, I told Dobrynin that Soviet actions had provoked us into an airlift of considerable magnitude. I warned him against raising the ante; we had the capacity to expand the scale of the airlift to match any Soviet escalation. By the same token we were prepared to stop the airlift soon after a cease-fire was achieved. Dobrynin, subdued, said he would report this to his leaders as a "direct quotation"; it was "important for them to know the mood."

That evening I sent a message for Sadat to Hafiz Ismail in Cairo. As I have pointed out, only amateurs believe that clever diplomacy consists of telling each party a different story. In fact the only safe assumption is that the various parties will exchange information, especially in the Middle East, where tale-telling is an art form. I laid heavy stress on our aborted effort to arrange a cease-fire based on the Soviet claim that Egypt was prepared to accept it. I emphasized that the United States could not ignore the Soviet airlift into the Middle East. It was not self-evident, of course, that Sadat would find persuasive the reasoning that we had the right to arm Israel because the Soviet Union was arming Egypt or that our thwarting of the Egyptian military effort was an argument for an American role in the peace process:

The U.S. side wishes to inform the Egyptian side that it is prepared to cease its own airlift resupply efforts immediately after a cease-fire is reached.

The United States wishes to emphasize again that it recognizes the unacceptability to the Egyptian side of the conditions which existed prior to the outbreak of recent hostilities. The U.S. side will make a major effort as soon as hostilities are terminated to assist in bringing a just and lasting peace to the Middle East. It continues to hope that the channel to Egypt established with so much difficulty will be maintained even under the pressure of events.

The U.S. will do all it can in this sense.

There was another country on which we counted for moderation, which we needed to inform of our decision: Saudi Arabia. Nixon had great regard and affection for the staunchly pro-Western King Faisal, without necessarily embracing the principles of the complex domestic structure he represented. At that time I had no experience with Saudi Arabia at all or of the indirect, adaptable, and subtle method by which Saudi policy is conducted. Underdeveloped in the midst of unimaginable wealth, in transition from feudalism to a future it cannot yet define, the Kingdom of Saudi Arabia aims above all to avoid open confrontation or unambiguous pronouncements, striving to advance its security without exposing itself to direct challenge. Its rulers seek to have its policy emerge as the result of a balancing of the interests of others rather than as an assertion of Saudi self-will. They can acquiesce in what they are reluctant to advocate; they can be privately relieved at the thwarting of radical designs to which they have to pay lip service publicly. Later on, I learned that one does the Saudis no favor by asking for their approval on matters that they cannot influence and on which taking a position can only imperil their careful balancing act.

But as yet I did not possess this insight. Therefore on October 14 we sent two communications to King Faisal: the first a letter from Nixon, the second a message from me. Given the established procedures and Nixon's preoccupation with Watergate, both messages were apparently drafted under my guidance at State. But in retrospect it would be hard to prove that from the content — unless we deliberately decided to follow a high road–low road approach, which at this writing I do not recall. Nixon's letter was psychologically just right. It did not refer to the airlift. It simply asked for Saudi understanding of our efforts to end the war and to engage ourselves in the search for a permanent and just peace. It called attention to Nixon's press conference of September 5, in which he had asserted that the United States was neither pro-Israel nor pro-Arab but pro-peace. It waxed eloquent about Nixon's desire to work cooperatively toward common objectives. Faisal was not asked to agree to anything nor formally apprised of developments that, once noted, he could only oppose.

The moral terrain seized by the letter drafted for Nixon's signature was nearly lost in the heavy-handed missive drafted for me, formally notifying Saudi Arabia of our airlift to Israel, thus forcing it to take a position. I explained our reasoning in terms almost identical to those used in messages to Egypt. But where Egypt, fighting its own battle, had the option of conceding part of its objectives for larger purposes, Saudi Arabia as a bystander did not have that luxury; it had to support the other Arab states unconditionally.

Finally, I approached the Shah of Iran. His country was the eastern anchor of our Mideast policy. His armed forces, equipped by us, restrained Iraqi ambitions in the Persian Gulf and limited the forces that radical country could commit to the Middle East war. In April 1972, Iraq had concluded a treaty of friendship with the Soviet Union, which everywhere else had always implied not only weapons supply but synchronization of foreign policy. In addition, Iran had a long border with the Soviet Union. Iran's role in Western strategy was to pose a barrier to Soviet encroachment that could not be surmounted short of all-out invasion, and to help shield the vital Persian Gulf regime from disruption. It was a mutuality of interests. Iran in protecting its independence was also serving to thwart designs inimical to the well-being of our country and our allies, the industrial democracies.

The continuing nightmare that has befallen the Persian Gulf since the Shah's overthrow is the most eloquent demonstration of what he contributed to free world security. To us he proved it dramatically during the October war. Iraq did not dare to send more than one division into Syria, nor did it threaten Jordan or Saudi Arabia, its other neighbors. Iran remained the only country that refused a Soviet request for overflights — some of our NATO allies did not feel strong enough for a similar act of resistance. Our fleet in the Indian Ocean was fueled from Iran. And the Shah remained close to Sadat. When after the war Sadat launched on his bold and yet precarious course toward peace, the Shah lent him moral, political, and material support.

But the Shah, in conducting parallel policies, nonetheless insisted on a demonstration that the proposed course in fact strengthened the moderate regimes of the area. When major decisions were involved, we made sure he understood our reasoning. It was in that sense that I now addressed the Shah on October 14 in a message that shows the difference between ally and puppet:

The United States is attempting to conduct itself in respect to the Middle East conflict in such a way as to be able to play a useful role in the resolution of the problems of the area, both in ending current hostilities as well as in achieving a permanent peace based on justice. . . .

[T]here is one factor which must be kept constantly in mind. We hope that the Shah will understand that an Arab victory in the present conflict obtained as it would be by the use of Soviet arms, coupled with the victory obtained by Soviet arms in the Indo-Pakistan conflict of 1971, would most certainly lead to a radicalization of regimes in the area and, at least to some extent, globally.

The Shah should know that we are trying our best to bring the war to a conclusion, with all the above considerations fully in mind. We sincerely hope that the Shah will not let himself be swept along by tactical considerations of the moment to the prejudice of the greater strategic goals which both our countries are pursuing jointly. The President is, of course, greatly appreciative of the courage and leadership shown by the Shah in refusing the Soviet request for military overflight of Iran.

A stalemate ends either when a battle turns or when one of the principals reassesses the situation. Monday morning, October 15, dawned to both of these developments. The Egyptian offensive into the Sinai had been defeated. Some 2,000 tanks were joined in one of the biggest tank battles in history. Once outside their antiaircraft missile screen, the Egyptian tanks were vulnerable to Israeli air power; at least 250 were destroyed by a combination of Israeli armor, antitank weapons, and air assaults. It was the reversal of the Israeli setback of the week before. The tank was losing its supremacy on the battlefield, unless it was supported by artillery and antiaircraft defense. Now the Israelis would begin to move forcefully on the southern front.

Also, the Soviets began to nibble at our bait. Dobrynin informed me that Moscow was studying our proposal to link a cease-fire not to Israel's withdrawal to the 1967 borders but to a general reaffirmation of Resolution 242, which — at least in Israel's interpretation, not challenged by us — was ambiguous on that point. If such a formulation were finally accepted, this would lead to rapid progress in the Security Council.

October 15–16: The Tide Turns Again

At the WSAG on the morning of October 15, Admiral Moorer estimated that after the Egyptian offensive was finally repulsed, it would take Israel three or four more days to break the Egyptian front. This estimate turned out to be conservative; in fact, the Egyptian front was never finally broken but bypassed.

Our airlift was proceeding in stunning fashion. Once over its second thoughts, our Defense Department put on the sort of performance no other country can match. Flights of the C-5A began at a rate of four per day, then rose higher. The total of all aircraft — C-5As, C-130s, and C-141s — was twenty flights a day, carrying an average of 1,000 tons of equipment daily, or about 50 tons each hour. In the first full day of the airlift we had more than matched what the Soviet Union had put into all the Arab countries (Egypt, Syria, and Iraq) combined in all of the four previous days. We were bound inexorably to pull ahead of the Soviet resupply effort. Eighteen hundred tons had already landed; three thousand more tons were on the way. I said somewhat cattily to Schlesinger: "I must say when you want to work you are terrific. You are equally awe-inspiring when you don't." It was not incorrect but unnecessary, fueling some later tensions in the Ford Administration when Schlesinger gave as good as he received. Colby wisely proposed that we announce no figures for the airlift and let the Soviets find out its magnitude for themselves.

I had learned in Nixon's first term that one must never relax pressures when the opponent is weakening. The right strategy is to combine two seemingly contradictory courses: to *increase* the pressure and to show a way out of the adversary's growing dilemma. I put both of these approaches to the WSAG. As for pressure I argued:

> The only way we can wind this up is if the Soviets see we won't quit and won't panic; if the Europeans see that they are pushed between losing their NATO relationship and lining up with us. . . . It will help with the PRC [People's Republic of China] and will limit adventurism in the Soviet Union. When the Europeans are restored to balance, they will realize that we help our friends.

At the same time I instructed agencies to avoid confrontational rhetoric and not to crow about the airlift. This was to keep the Soviets from trying to raise the ante and to calm the atmosphere for the Security Council deliberations that, if Moorer's estimate was correct, were likely to occur by the weekend.

Nixon almost simultaneously was interjecting on his own initiative a public comment certain to increase the sense of menace to the Arab side. At a ceremony that day to award the Congressional Medal of Honor to nine members of the armed forces, he extemporized that our policy was like the one we had followed in Lebanon in 1958 or Jordan in 1970: to defend the right of every Middle East nation to live in independence and security. The analogy left something to be desired. In 1958 moderate Arabs regarded our move into Lebanon as a major assurance of their security. In 1973 the security of Israel, the country we were now upholding, was not considered a major interest — to put it mildly — by even the most moderate Arab state. The reference to Lebanon could only imply that we were not excluding military intervention on the side of Israel. When press queries cascaded in, I did not back off the implied threat though I would not have recommended it. I instructed State Department spokesman Robert McCloskey to say simply that the President had spoken about "principles," not tactics — a comment so opaque that its precise meaning eludes me even at this writing.

In light of our tough stance, the response to our messages of the previous day astonished me. The various Arab countries may not yet have grasped the size of our airlift, but they were bound to know that it was substantial. Nevertheless the immediate reaction was milder than expected. On October 15, the Shah responded. His only comment was that he had been warning for some time of the effect in the area if Soviet arms were decisive in another military victory. In other words, he went along with us.

Late on October 15, Ismail replied in a manner that under the circumstances can only be called extraordinary. He reaffirmed Egypt's "determination" to keep open "this special channel of contact." No other party spoke in Egypt's name; in other words, we should pay no attention to interpretations from Moscow that differed from what Cairo told us directly. Ismail denied any intention to humiliate Israel "because Egypt tasted what humiliation means." He expressed his "appreciation" for our efforts to achieve a cease-fire as a *preliminary* to a political settlement — contrary as they were to Egypt's views. However, experience caused Egypt to doubt that such a separation would work in practice. In short, Ismail spoke to the principal armorer of Egypt's enemy as would one urbane man of affairs to another. His objection to our approach was its impracticality; presumably if we could demonstrate how our diplomacy might succeed, Egypt might change its attitude.

Only then did Ismail refer to the airlift, dismissing it as "unacceptable," as he had previous arms sales to Israel. But he did not linger over it nor did he threaten any consequences. Instead, he urged me to redouble my efforts to link a political to a military solution. And then — amazingly — he invited me to visit his country:

> Egypt will welcome Dr. Kissinger in appreciation for his efforts. The Egyptian side will be prepared to discuss any subject, proposal or project, within the framework of two principles — which, it is believed, Dr. Kissinger does not reject, neither does any one — that Egypt cannot make any concessions of land or sovereignty.
>
> With warmest regards. Hafiz Ismail.

It was the message of a statesman, for there could be no doubt that Ismail was speaking in Sadat's name. It is easy to go with the tide; more difficult to judge where the tide is going. But only the wisest of leaders have the foresight to look at a distant objective and in its name stand up against all pressures. Sadat knew that we were working to thwart his military designs. He could easily have used the airlift as an alibi for the setbacks that the defeat of his Sinai offensive had made inevitable; he could have unleashed the mobs in the Arab world against us, as Nasser had done with far less provocation in 1967. But Sadat was tired of spilling blood for futile causes. He was willing to forgo posturing for attainable progress. Unlike Nasser, he saw no future in being the leader of radical Arabs who confused rhetoric with achievement. He had taken the measure of Soviet support: always enough to keep tensions high, never enough to bring about a settlement.

But Sadat should not be conceived as a sentimentalist. He knew how to defend the interests of his country. While restrained in public utterance, and courteous, he saw to it that we were aware he had other options. There is no doubt that he was the godfather of the oil embargo soon to descend on us. In this complicated manner he performed the amazing feat of beginning to turn away from the Soviet Union, on whose supplies he was yet totally dependent, and to move imperceptibly toward us, who were thwarting his short-term designs. In the midst of war he began to walk the path to peace.

The Saudi reaction to my message was much more complex. Prince Fahd, Deputy Prime Minister, informed us that the situation was deteriorating. He felt that America's friends were now in a hopeless dilemma. If the Arabs "won," the Middle East was forfeit to the Soviet Union. If the Arabs "lost," the Soviet Union could be relied upon to rebuild the Arab armies; Soviet advisers would be invited back into Egypt. It would grow impossible for any Arab to say with pride that he was America's friend.

We did not disagree with Fahd's analysis of the two choices before us and him. But we drew up a different balance sheet. The risk of the Soviet Union's rebuilding the Arab armies after a defeat seemed to us a lesser evil than a victory achieved by Soviet arms. We thought it far from preordained that the peace we were seeking would find the Soviets in an improved position. Indeed, our whole strategy aimed for the opposite. Egyptian messages indicated an intention to break free of Soviet tutelage; we were determined to explore the prospect.

The next day, Tuesday, October 16, King Faisal replied to my message of October 14. In a response more pained than insistent, he apparently charged my letter off to inexperience with things Saudi. He expressed his "great sorrow" about the bitter struggle between the great powers that threatened ruin to all countries in the area. Faisal stopped well short of recrimination; much less did he blame the United States for the current crisis. He restated Sadat's proposal that Israel return to its 1967 borders. He urged that we stop all arms shipments to Israel. But he defined a penalty for noncompliance that was vague and indirect: If we did not end our support for Israel, Saudi-American relations would become only "lukewarm." We believed that we had to run this risk in order to arrange a balance of forces that would enable the moderate Arab states to breathe more easily — even if they felt compelled to oppose the tactics by which we arrived at this state of affairs.

More ominously, Saudi Deputy Foreign Minister Ibrahim Masuud called in the ambassadors of the European Community to warn that unless they pressed us to change our policy, Saudi Arabia would reduce its oil production. We were aware that oil minister Sheikh Ahmed Zaki Yamani was already en route to a meeting of his Arab colleagues in

Kuwait that had been called before the airlift. I had not learned then —
though I would soon enough — that Saudi Arabia was no more willing
to confront the radical Arabs than to confront us directly. The Kingdom
judged that its safety depended on presenting itself as the reluctant im-
plementer of decisions of others. Even had we understood Saudi methods and the prospect that the Kingdom was likely to ascribe its decisions to the requirements of Arab solidarity, we had no other choice
than to continue the course on which we were embarked. Vacillation
would prolong the war and the attendant risk of its spread. Saudi Arabia's long-term attitude would be determined by our contribution to the
peace process after the war. And for that, Egypt was the pivot. It was
in Egypt, too, that Saudi fears of a reintroduction of the Soviet Union
into the Middle East would be tested.

These considerations caused us to return a speedy reply to Ismail's
message of the night before. At 9:08 A.M. on October 16, I reciprocated
Ismail's expression of the importance of our special channel. But I also
sensed that with matters nearing a showdown, the psychological moment to speak more concretely had arrived. It was essential to bring
Egypt to a sense of what was possible. We had to give Sadat a pretext
for climbing down from the impossible conditions that he publicly repeated within the hour in a speech to his Parliament, cast as an "open
message" to President Nixon: a cease-fire conditioned on immediate
Israeli withdrawal to the 1967 borders. "We are not ready," said Sadat
in clear reference to his experience with Security Council Resolution
242, "to accept ambiguous promises or elastic phrases subject to all
[kinds of] interpretations thereby wasting time and returning our case to
a stalemate."

The necessity was to convince Sadat of both the limits of the attainable and our seriousness in pressing to the full extent of these limits.
There is a temptation to assign intractable problems to a personality who
is then endowed with mythical qualities commensurate with the difficulty of the problem. Nowhere is this more true than the Middle East,
that home of romantic figures. The various diplomatic spectaculars in
which I had engaged — from the secret trip to China to the conclusion
of the Vietnam negotiations — had put the idea into the head of the
Middle East leaders that I could perform the same role for them. While
this was an asset, it also contained the danger that each party would ask
me to take from its shoulders the burden of difficult decisions. That
would be the road to disaster. Any negotiator who seduces himself into
believing that his personality leads to automatic breakthroughs will soon
find himself in the special purgatory that history reserves for those who
measure themselves by acclaim rather than by achievement. They begin
by deluding themselves; inevitably, they will disappoint others.

In now conveying to Cairo what it could expect from the United States,

I separated the cease-fire from subsequent negotiations. I stressed that Egypt had redeemed its honor and changed the strategic environment. It could risk a cease-fire first and rely on negotiations later. Subsequent diplomacy closely corresponded to what my message to Ismail of October 16 put forward:

> Dr. Kissinger wishes to present his frank assessment of the present situation.
>
> The objective of the U.S. side continues to be to terminate the present fighting in circumstances that will facilitate progress toward a final settlement. Egyptian forces have already accomplished much. The humiliation which Egyptians and, indeed, the Arab world felt after 1967 has been erased. A new strategic situation has been established in which reliance by any country on permanent military supremacy has become illusory. Hence, the necessity of a political settlement is becoming much clearer to all parties.
>
> What can the U.S. do in these circumstances? Dr. Kissinger has often said that he would promise only what he could deliver but deliver everything he promised. With its five-point proposal contained in Mr. Ismail's message of October 10, the Egyptian side is asking, in effect, for Israeli agreement, as part of a cease-fire, to Egyptian terms for a total settlement. In Dr. Kissinger's judgment, this is not achievable except by protracted war. No U.S. influence can bring this goal about in present circumstances.
>
> What the U.S. side can promise and will fulfill is to make every effort to assist in achieving a final, just settlement once a cease-fire is reached. Dr. Kissinger believes that recent events may well serve to make it less difficult for the U.S. side in the future to exercise its influence constructively and effectively on behalf of such a settlement. . . .
>
> The Egyptian side therefore has an important decision to make. To insist on its maximum program means continuation of the war and the possible jeopardy of all that has been achieved. The outcome will then be decided by military measures. The U.S. side will not speculate on this outcome but doubts whether it will be clear-cut. In any event, circumstances for a U.S. diplomatic effort would not be propitious.
>
> If diplomacy is to be given a full opportunity, a cease-fire must precede it. Only in these circumstances can the promised U.S. diplomatic effort be developed. Egypt will find the guarantee for the seriousness of this effort in the formal promise of the U.S. side to engage itself fully as well as in the objective situation.
>
> The goal must be to achieve a cease-fire and turn it rapidly into a real and just peace which reconciles the principles of sovereignty and security.
>
> The U.S. side believes that progress could be made on the basis of a cease-fire in place, accompanied by an undertaking by the parties to start talks under the aegis of the Secretary General with a view to achieving a settlement in accordance with Security Council Resolution 242 in all of its parts, including withdrawal of forces envisaged by that resolution.

Dr. Kissinger greatly appreciates the thoughtful invitation of the Egyptian side to visit Egypt. Once a cease-fire has been achieved, he would be glad to give that invitation the most serious and sympathetic consideration as part of a serious effort to bring a lasting peace to the Middle East.

With warmest regards. . . .

The WSAG convened shortly after 10:00 A.M. Since the decision to resort to the airlift, its mood had been almost magically transformed. Gone were the hesitations of the previous week, the attempts to shift the potential blame for dangerous consequences. The most important role of a leader is to take on his shoulder the burden of ambiguity inherent in difficult choices. That accomplished, his subordinates have criteria and can turn to implementation. Nixon performed this role in the Middle East war when he made the airlift decision. I stated the principle that should govern our resupply effort: "Our only interest in this semi-confrontation situation is to run the Soviets into the ground fast. Give them the maximum incentive for a quick settlement. Bring in more each day than they do." And as a rough guideline I suggested that we keep our resupply at least 25 percent ahead of the Soviets'. We decided to supplement the airlift with a strengthened sealift, for in the Black Sea the Soviets had been loading ships with enormous quantities of matériel, including their most modern equipment.

We had to conduct this confrontation for high stakes in the midst of a Watergate crisis that pitted Nixon against Special Prosecutor Archibald Cox and in the face of an assault by some in the Congress and the media on our alleged softness over détente. Senator Henry M. Jackson on October 14 publicly accused me of having been beguiled by the Soviets. Columnist George F. Will on October 16 asserted that ideological blinders — undefined — left me unable to recognize a "dead détente" when I saw one. Joseph Kraft on October 18 claimed that I had been "taken in" by the Soviets.[15] The *New York Times* on October 17 even reported a growing split between me and Counsellor to the President Melvin R. Laird, of all people, about Soviet intentions. As usual with Laird, I was the last to know that he had any views on the subject — much less different ones. True, I consistently urged a low-key public approach to the Soviets. Among superpowers the winner in a crisis must carefully judge when to rub in this fact to his opponent. I stressed this theme to my WSAG colleagues:

We must keep this whole thing low key today no matter what happens. There should be no backgrounders. If we can finish this off without a confrontation with the Soviets and without ripping our relations with the Arabs we will have earned our money. Everything else is grandstanding. We will take a very hard line on substance and keep the stuff going into Israel.

All morning the news continued to be favorable. Even before the WSAG met on October 16, we learned that a Soviet VIP plane was en route to Cairo; we guessed it carried Premier Alexei Kosygin, who had unexpectedly canceled an appointment with the visiting Danish Prime Minister. This had to mean that the Soviets would urge Sadat to accept our approach to the cease-fire; he needed no persuasion to persist in his proclaimed course. And Soviet pressure was likely to sour Soviet-Egyptian relations.

Almost concurrently we were informed that a small force of twenty-five Israeli tanks had crossed to the west side of the Suez Canal at Great Bitter Lake and was beginning to tear up the surface-to-air missile fields. If it continued, this guaranteed an Israeli victory because it exposed the Egyptian forces across the Canal to the full fury of Israeli air power. But it was too early to tell whether the Israelis could sustain themselves on the west side of the Canal. The WSAG considered the move as only a raid, as indeed the Israelis first presented it. It was during this meeting discussing war strategy that the news bulletin was brought in reporting that I had won the Nobel Peace Prize, as described in Chapter VIII.

At the end of Tuesday, October 16, I reported to Nixon that the odds were two out of three in favor of a rapid conclusion of the war. The previous cease-fire effort of October 13 had looked too easy; we had done it "too much with mirrors." The solution would be more reliable now because we were no longer dependent on the actions of others. Our own commitment of resources would, with every passing day, improve the prospects for our strategy. Kosygin would either deadlock with Sadat — and thus undermine Soviet relations with Cairo — or get him to accept our formula. Either outcome would strengthen our hand in Cairo. The Israeli crossing of the Canal might only be a raid, as we continued to believe. But it would weaken the SAM missile screen and thus enhance Israel's ability to squeeze the Egyptians back across the Canal. Time was now clearly working for us.

October 17: Heading for a Cease-Fire

WEDNESDAY, October 17, was once again a day of waiting for the unfolding of events, though events now were increasingly turning in our favor. Early in the morning Dobrynin informed me officially that Kosygin was in Cairo. He had as well a message from Brezhnev that underlined what we already knew: that while the Soviet Union might be willing to fight the Middle East war by proxy, it would stop well short of a confrontation with us. Brezhnev could not resist calling attention to his previous warnings about the danger of a Middle East explosion. He repeated the familiar Soviet position that if Israel returned to the 1967 borders its security could be guaranteed by the superpowers or the

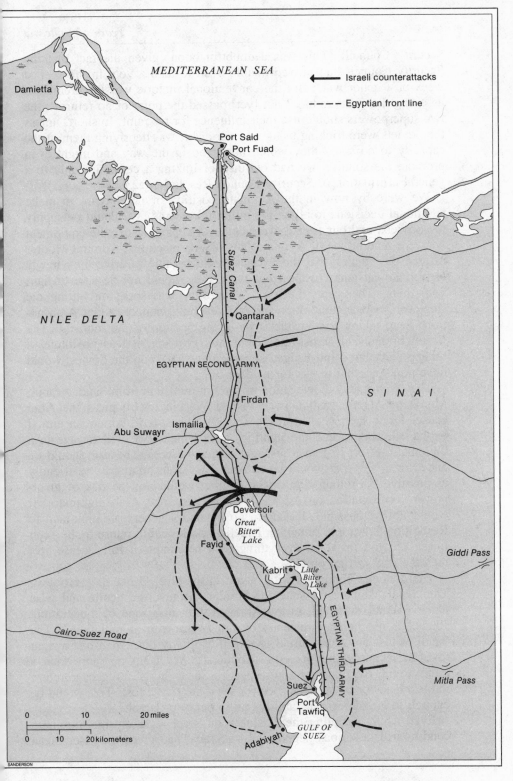

The Sinai Front: Israeli Canal Crossing and Breakthrough

Security Council. (This was a doubtful boon, given the fact that the Security Council had proved unable even to take a vote in the second week of a major war.) But the conventional rhetoric was the prelude to asserting that matters had "not [yet] passed the point of no return"; the two superpowers should use their influence for restraint. In short, unless the Soviets were tricking us — and our airlift was depriving them of the capacity to do so — they would not stand in the way and might even promote the solution we had outlined of linking a cease-fire only to a general affirmation of Security Council Resolution 242.

We were by now in the fortunate position of not having to make additional decisions to affect the military outcome. We could outsupply the Soviets, and our friends were better organized to use the equipment we were sending them. At one of the WSAG meetings, Admiral Moorer offered the opinion that the Syrians might be able to drive their newly arrived Soviet tanks to the front lines; they would not be able to fight with them. Therefore, much of Wednesday was spent on setting the stage for postwar diplomacy and on preventing noncombatant Arab nations from taking irrevocable steps in the passion of the moment. The Israeli bridgehead across the Canal was growing; it was no longer a raiding party but a full-fledged counteroffensive. Soon the Soviets would have no choice but to ask for a cease-fire.

That Wednesday a delegation of foreign ministers from Saudi Arabia, Morocco, Algeria, and Kuwait visited Washington to press the Arab cause. I saw them first at 10:15 A.M. The short-term American aim, I explained, was to end the fighting, after which "we will engage in a diplomatic effort to find a just and lasting peace." The war should be ended in a way that would leave Arab-American relations "as friendly as possible." Prolongation of the conflict would run the risk of great-power confrontation on Arab soil — the perennial Arab nightmare. It would not be possible, I said, to go beyond a general commitment to Resolution 242 nor to obtain an Israeli commitment to return to the 1967 lines: "If you insist on everything as a precondition for a cease-fire, then the war will go on."

The dialogue continued with Nixon in the Oval Office at 11:10 A.M. The Saudi Minister of State for Foreign Affairs, the gentle and wise Omar Saqqaf, summed up the Arab position in a tone of moderation: "Israel is not being threatened by the Arabs with annihilation." The Saudi Minister was not afraid to affirm explicitly that Israel had a right to exist, albeit within its 1967 frontiers: "We want no more than a return to the 1967 borders and respect for the rights of refugees to return to their lands or be compensated for what they have lost. This would be enough to guarantee the stability and integrity of Israel."

Even while accepting the existence of Israel — surely the minimum condition for a serious negotiation — Saqqaf had given us a Herculean task. Israel would not return to the 1967 borders as the result of a war imposed on it by its neighbors, in which, moreover, the tide of battle was now beginning to turn in its favor. On the other hand, without United States support there could be no progress even toward more limited objectives. And several of the Arab countries represented in the President's office needed the United States to fend off threats from rapacious neighbors (often Arabs) and to stabilize domestic turbulence. They and we had to cope with this seeming paradox without ever making it explicit.

Nixon with his mastery of intangibles knew exactly how to strike the right note: to promise a major diplomatic effort without committing himself to a particular outcome. Though Nixon no longer had the time or nervous energy to give consistent leadership — he was even then arranging the face-off with Archibald Cox that was to lead to the beginning of impeachment proceedings against him — he handled his meeting with the Arab ministers masterfully and without a sense of strain. He tried to bring the Arab leaders to a sense of limits, if more obliquely than I:

I will work for a cease-fire, not in order to trick you into stopping at the cease-fire lines, but to use it as a basis to go on from there for a settlement on the basis of Resolution 242. I make this commitment to you. It is very important to use restraint now. I know how people feel, I understand. We will use restraint, and we hope you will. . . . You have my pledge. I can't say that we can categorically move Israel back to the 1967 borders, but we will work within the framework for Resolution 242.

As he warmed to the subject, Nixon grew exuberant. He promised me as a negotiator. He implied — to my horror — that this ensured success. He returned to a familiar theme from his first term, assuring his guests that despite my Jewish origin I was not subject to domestic, that is to say Jewish, pressures. Saqqaf, who had already earlier in the conversation avowed that I was "doing a great job," turned this point deftly aside: "We are all Semites together."

Saqqaf, upon leaving the Oval Office, made a conciliatory public statement expressing great confidence in President Nixon — to the discomfiture of Nixon-haters eager to announce that Watergate was wrecking our ability to handle crises: "The man who could solve the Vietnam war, the man who could have settled the peace all over the world, can easily play a good role in settling and having peace in our area of the Middle East."

Thus the American airlift resupplying Israel had not impaired — and had perhaps enhanced — Arab conviction that the United States was the key to a peace settlement. The ministers seemed determined to refrain from confrontation. On my part, when I met them afterward once again, I urged our visitors not to ask the impossible:

We know Israel is not prepared to accept any of the present Arab ideas. The Israeli Prime Minister said so yesterday. In any case, and whatever the pressures may be, U. S. influence will have to be used. There is no substitute for U. S. influence. While the Arab armies have done better than expected, these armies cannot attain Arab diplomatic objectives without a long war and the high risk of Great Power involvement.

I cannot say that these observations evoked wild enthusiasm; but neither were they rejected. The four foreign ministers urged me to involve myself despite all my reservations; once you are committed to a medicine man, his sense of reality is interpreted as an act of modesty. I was the deus ex machina — for what, unfortunately, no one could describe.

While I was meeting with the Arab foreign ministers, I asked Scowcroft to have Dinitz obtain his government's reaction to the idea of linking a cease-fire only to some call for implementing Resolution 242. We expected little difficulty; after all, Resolution 242 had been the basis of Mideast negotiations for six years.

The daily WSAG deliberation took place at 3:00 P.M. on October 17 in a relaxed atmosphere. Clements reported that our airlift was meeting the criterion of exceeding the Soviet airlift by 25 percent. I complacently observed that the mood of the Arab ministers seemed to confirm that there would be no immediate oil embargo. Somewhat more accurately, I predicted that diplomacy would be dormant until Kosygin returned to Moscow. "But we have to keep the stuff going into Israel. We have to pour it in until someone quits."

At the end of the meeting I took my WSAG colleagues to the Oval Office for a pep talk by Nixon, who even in the midst of his preoccupation with the Watergate tapes decision showed his grasp of the situation:

No one is more keenly aware of the stakes: oil and our strategic position. We can't go down the road to a cease-fire without a negotiating effort which will succeed. The purpose of the meeting this morning [with the four Arab ministers] was to contribute to this. Some of these — not the Algerians — are desperately afraid of being left at the mercy of the Soviet Union. The Saudis, Moroccans, and even the Algerians, fear this. The other aspect is our relations with the Soviet Union. This is bigger than the Middle East. We can't allow a Soviet-supported operation to succeed against an American-supported operation. If it does, our credibility everywhere is severely shaken.

But as the WSAG adjourned, a news ticker spelled out more complications. The Arab oil producers meeting in Kuwait had just announced an immediate production cutback of 5 percent, to be followed by successive monthly cutbacks of 5 percent until Israel withdrew to the 1967 frontiers. Further, in a separate development, the six Persian Gulf members of OPEC unilaterally increased the price of oil by 70 percent, from $3.01 to $5.12 a barrel. We were so focused on the danger of an embargo that we thought the production cutback, which the CIA estimated as initially one million barrels a day, largely a symbolic gesture. This it was — but it had revolutionary implications. As it became progressively evident that the producer cartel could set prices nearly arbitrarily by manipulating production, a new phase of postwar history began. It took some months for all parties to grasp its ramifications. I shall discuss this in Chapter XIX.

One result was immediately apparent. Vague European uneasiness was congealing into panic. Dissociation from the United States was accelerating. Europe seemed to have no specific aim except to seek the goodwill of the oil producers; it had no underlying strategy except to ease immediate pressures. Michel Jobert was in the lead. Not a week before, on October 11, he had sat in my office for a briefing on the war's diplomacy and expatiated on the desirability of leaving things alone and not pushing matters at the UN. But now Reuters reported a highly critical speech by Jobert in the National Assembly attacking the United States for fraternizing with Brezhnev while both sides were pouring arms into the area.

Hussein, too, was getting nervous. He saw the West Bank (to him the most tempting prize) denuded of Israeli troops. Speculation on a peace settlement had consistently played down Jordanian claims. Would the most restrained of Israel's neighbors, the King inquired in a letter to me, have to pay the price of being excluded? He could not avoid some melancholy reflections that previously we had refused to complete deliveries of some new tanks to Jordan because of alleged shortages and yet scores were now being sent to Israel.

In the meantime we pressed on with the airlift, kept in contact with the parties, and urged a cease-fire linked to Resolution 242. We had to appear implacable. But we also needed to show an honorable way out. We had to walk this narrow path, moreover, while Watergate once again approached one of its climaxes.

Much of Nixon's attention during the week of the airlift was absorbed with the Court of Appeals decision on the Watergate tapes. On October 16 Melvin Laird became the first White House official publicly to discuss possible impeachment proceedings. The next day Attorney General Elliot Richardson transmitted a White House proposal to Special Prosecutor Cox that Nixon would allow John Stennis, a prestigious Senator, to verify the accuracy of proposed White House summaries of the disputed tapes. Haig had given me a brief sketch of the compromise, adding ominously that the President was prepared for a showdown with

Cox. By coincidence I had had on my schedule for several weeks a lunch Wednesday, October 17, with Richardson. He was not happy as Attorney General. The most important legal case of the century, Watergate, had been taken away from him and assigned to a special prosecutor. He told me he had the uneasy feeling that the White House was trying to jockey Cox into a position where it could fire him. That Richardson would not accept. I do not recall making any comment.

That afternoon I told Dinitz that Israel should base its military operations on the assumption that we would not be able to stall a cease-fire more than forty-eight hours after we were approached. We knew that a tank battle was raging on the central part of the Sinai front along the Suez Canal, but we received only a few reports from Israel, none of them very illuminating. But clearly the war could not go on much longer.

October 18–19: An Invitation to Moscow

O N Thursday morning, October 18, Israel announced that it was reinforcing its bridgehead across the Suez Canal, which now extended about eight miles wide to the north and about four miles wide to the south. In getting Ron Ziegler ready for the morning press briefing, I told him that I expected a cease-fire by Sunday or Monday (October 21 or 22).

King Faisal finally replied to Nixon that day, along the lines of his communication to me of two days earlier. Prolongation of the war would help the Soviets, he averred. The war could be ended only if Israel returned to the borders of 1967. The letter closed with the same ambiguous warning as the earlier message: "If the United States continues to stand by the side of Israel, then this [US–Saudi] friendship will risk being diminished." But the gesture of restraint was more than offset by — it may indeed have been designed to obfuscate — Saudi Arabia's announcement that very day, October 18, that it had doubled, to 10 percent, the production cutback agreed by the Arab oil ministers the day before. The Saudis promised to make further monthly cutbacks and even threatened a possible total suspension of oil to the United States if these steps did not achieve "quick, tangible results."

Shortly afterward, around 6:25 P.M. on October 18, Dinitz brought Golda's reaction to our query about a cease-fire linked only to Resolution 242. It was a classic illustration of Israeli negotiating tactics — produced by a combination of an extraordinary sense of vulnerability and a complex domestic political system. All Israeli leaders I have known have agreed almost instinctively on one proposition: never to accept the first proposal put forward by the United States, whatever its merit. If Israel submits without a struggle — never mind the substance — the

United States may come to think of it as a docile client and God knows what we then might take it into our heads to impose.

What the international environment encourages, Israeli domestic politics makes inevitable. Israel's domestic political procedures explain its maddening negotiating method, which is to haggle over even the slightest concession, never to make an unexpected compromise, and to settle only when everyone has reached a state of exhaustion that deprives the conclusion of exaltation or even goodwill. For only by demonstrating either duress or ultimate tenacity can those responsible for Israel's national security prove to skeptical or ambitious colleagues that there was no alternative. They can afford no grand gesture because they might not hold their government together if they attempted it. Negotiation for Israel is a process of self-education. A Prime Minister runs the risk of being accused of softness if he (or she) simply accepts an American proposal without at least testing what else may be obtainable.

So it was that Golda now demurred at a cease-fire that she had asked for a week earlier, rejecting especially the linkage with Resolution 242 that had been Israel's holy writ in six years of negotiation. That resolution, Golda now argued, grew out of the war of 1967 and was irrelevant to the current war; it was not "a panacea"; there was "no reason for undue haste."

The message was not intransigently phrased. Nor did I have any intention of going along with it. We had seen Israel through two weeks of mortal peril. We had stalled at the UN when it served our common strategy; we had proposed a cease-fire when Israel was ready; we had poured in supplies during Israel's extremity. We could not now jeopardize relations with Europe and Japan, tempt an oil embargo, confront the Soviets, and challenge our remaining Arab friends either by forever delaying a cease-fire proposal or by jettisoning Resolution 242, in the name of which we had fought off Soviet and radical Arab pressures for six years. Nor would it have been in Israel's interest that we do so. Without Resolution 242, there would be no legal basis for any future negotiations. Given the voting lineup in the United Nations, any substitute was certain to be worse. But as yet we were still talking only about theories. So I told Dinitz once again that I felt a cease-fire proposal would soon emerge and I urged a speedup in military operations so that they could be terminated in forty-eight hours.

My premonitions were realized at 8:45 P.M. that Thursday night, October 18, when Dobrynin called me with an urgent message from Brezhnev. All of a sudden the Soviets were ready to deal seriously. Dobrynin read me a three-part Soviet draft proposal for submission to the Security Council: (1) a call for a cease-fire in place; (2) an appeal for immediate phased Israeli withdrawal "from the occupied Arab territories to the line in accordance with Resolution 242 of the Security Council, with com-

pletion of this withdrawal in the shortest period of time''; and (3) an
appeal for ''appropriate consultations'' aimed at establishing a just peace.

Point 1 was clearly acceptable; it was what we had proposed with
Israel's agreement five days earlier; it would leave Israeli forces twenty
miles from Damascus and on the other side of the Suez Canal. Point 2
was obviously preposterous; one could not as the condition of a cease-
fire ask Israel to begin a withdrawal to an undefined line ''immediately''
and to complete it in the ''shortest period of time.'' Point 3 was just as
obviously a come-on. ''Appropriate consultations'' could mean anything; if it was the usual negotiation under UN auspices with an intermediary moving between the parties, it meant little. If, however, it could
be made to lead to direct negotiations between the Arabs and Israel it
would mark a significant new turn in Middle East affairs. For the first
time since Israel came into being, Arab states would be engaging in
public face-to-face negotiations with it.

I immediately called Nixon. ''They are moving in our direction,'' I
said, ''but are not quite there yet.'' I estimated that it would take us
''another forty-eight to seventy-two hours'' to wrap it up.

Next I notified Dinitz, certain of his reaction. I omitted the offer of
Point 3 because I knew Israel would never agree to Point 2 and I hoped
to shape Point 3, before presenting it, into the direct negotiations between the parties that Israel had claimed it was seeking.

As for Dobrynin, I procrastinated. I told him the Soviet proposal had
constructive elements. However, Point 2 was not acceptable and Point
3 required precision. To gain time by maintaining a civil atmosphere
and to give the Soviet system something to analyze, we sent, around
10:30 P.M., a reply from Nixon to Brezhnev's general message of the
day before, which had not dealt with the cease-fire at all. It was long
on rhetoric, waxed eloquent about the need to cement relations between
our two countries, and pledged major joint efforts to promote peace in
the Middle East after the end of hostilities. But we studiously avoided
any comment on the Soviet draft cease-fire proposal. Dobrynin was much
too subtle not to grasp that we were stalling — the usual tactic of the
putative winner whose position is likely to improve with every passing
hour.

With a cease-fire approaching, it was vital to maintain close contact
with key Arab leaders. I wired King Hussein:

I want you to know specifically what I am doing. We are talking to the
Soviets with a view to agreeing to a Security Council resolution which calls
for a cease-fire in place to be followed promptly by negotiations between the
parties on a fundamental settlement. In such a settlement, Your Majesty, it is
inconceivable that the interests of Jordan, which you so eloquently explained
to me, would not be fully protected. . . . Your views will, I can assure you,
be given the full weight they deserve.

The party most in need of contact with us was our semi-adversary in Cairo, undergoing — we thought — deep travail. The Egyptian army was now in serious difficulties. But it was not in our interest that the war end with Egypt's humiliation. We had wanted to prevent a victory of Soviet arms. We did not want to see Sadat overthrown or Egypt radicalized by total defeat. At 10:45 P.M. on October 18, when I discussed the Soviet proposal with Scowcroft, I said:

The fact of the matter is when all is said and done it is a Soviet defeat. The same reasons why we could not accept an Israeli defeat will operate against them and even if they [the Arabs] say the supplies did it, that should make them realize they better get on our side.

Thus, at midnight, I sent a conciliatory message to Ismail for Sadat. Its basic point was to reaffirm the offer made two days earlier of a cease-fire linked to a reaffirmation of Resolution 242. To make clear that we respected Egypt's dignity, I paid special attention to the fact "that Egypt and its Arab allies have brought about important changes in the situation as a result of the strength and the valor demonstrated on the battlefield. None of this should be jeopardized by further prolongation of the fighting." I concluded by reiterating our appeal for a cease-fire even in the changed military conditions (though I did not refer to the latter). So near to our goal, I hoped that passing frustration would not destroy the complex design on which Sadat and we had been working in parallel:

Mr. Ismail knows the importance we attach to a prompt end to the hostilities in conditions that make possible a serious effort toward a fundamental settlement. This remains our view. To this end, it is important that both sides maintain a restrained attitude, keeping in mind the imperative need for a long-term relationship. With warm regards.

We were close to ending the war on terms we had sought. But we could not be reckless. At any moment the Soviet Union might rush its cease-fire resolution into the Security Council or get someone else to do so. It would almost certainly pass with the aid of European and non-aligned votes; even China might support it. In the name of what could we veto? And if we vetoed, we would be alone in the crisis that followed, tempting Soviet threats, European dissociation, and Arab radicalism. At the end we would have achieved nothing. For if we acquiesced in the Israeli desire to delete Resolution 242, there would be no agreed legal framework left in which to negotiate. Our only realistic option was to take charge of the process of negotiation, to gain a little more time for Israel's offensive, and then to settle so that we could start the postwar diplomacy in the best setting.

I was pondering the appropriate tactics when Brezhnev's impatience showed us a way out.

I had just completed the daily WSAG meeting that Friday morning, October 19. Our information on Israeli intentions was sketchy. We knew their offensive was proceeding, with 300 tanks now on the west bank of the Canal; they were trying to cut Egyptian communications in all directions. Later in the day we learned they were moving north toward Ismailia and south to surround Great Bitter Lake and to cut the Cairo-Suez road. But the Israelis did not define for us either their immediate objectives or their strategic plan. Nor were we ever given any optimum time frame for whatever strategy they were pursuing. The morning WSAG decided to keep the airlift going until a cease-fire was well established. We also speeded up the sealift so that we would not be caught short by a sudden cease-fire and the Soviets would not encourage their Arab friends to try a war of attrition.

Minutes after 11:00 A.M., Dobrynin called with an urgent message from Brezhnev to Nixon. It spoke of the increasing danger in the Middle East which might even do "harm" to relations between the Soviet Union and the United States. Prompt and effective decisions were needed:

> Since time is essential and now not only every day but every hour counts, my colleagues and I suggest that the US Secretary of State and your closest associate Dr. Kissinger comes in an urgent manner to Moscow to conduct appropriate negotiations with him as with your authorized personal representative. It would be good if he could come tomorrow, October 20. I will appreciate your speedy reply.

When I read the invitation, I felt it solved most of our problems. It would keep the issue out of the United Nations until we had shaped an acceptable outcome. It would discourage Soviet bluster while I was in transit and negotiating. It would gain at least another seventy-two hours for military pressures to build. Nixon and I talked in this vein together with Haig and Scowcroft. We concluded that a trip to Moscow would advance our strategy.

There was one technical embarrassment. Ambassador Huang Zhen, Chief of the Chinese Liaison Office, had invited me to a large dinner in my honor that evening at the Mayflower Hotel. I could not possibly cancel it for a trip to Moscow, of all places. But we could put it to good use. It gave a pretext for postponing my departure at least until the early hours of Saturday, delaying my arrival in Moscow so that negotiations could not start until Sunday, or forty-eight hours away.

I promptly called Dobrynin back from my White House office to tell him that we were giving Brezhnev's proposal serious consideration. But why could not Gromyko come to Washington? Dobrynin argued that Soviet decisions would require the participation of Brezhnev and Kosygin (who had just returned from Cairo). I promised an answer during the course of the afternoon.

In the meantime, I briefed Dinitz and reviewed the situation once again with Nixon and Haig. At 1:35 P.M. from my State Department office, I called Dobrynin to give him the final word. I would leave early Saturday morning, arriving in Moscow in the evening. I would not be prepared to start negotiations before Sunday morning; there could be no discussion of any final settlement or any subject except the cease-fire. I was "assuming that no unilateral actions will be taken while I am in transit," which I defined either as threats or initiatives at the UN or elsewhere. The announcement had to state that I was going at the "invitation" of the Soviet government so that I did not appear as a supplicant.

Dobrynin accepted these terms on behalf of Brezhnev at 4:30 P.M. I reiterated that I would not be prepared to discuss any aspect of a political settlement. Dobrynin thought that this had been made sufficiently clear. I then had a meeting with Dinitz to compare notes on where we stood.

In the meantime, Watergate had intervened in its most explicit form. Nixon was even more driven than had become usual; October 19 was the day the Stennis compromise was to go into effect (and the next day he was to fire a defiant Cox). At 3:30 P.M. that Friday, Haig informed me that Nixon was planning a statement about the Stennis compromise and intended to couple it with an announcement of my trip. I objected violently, calling the linking of foreign policy with Watergate a "cheap stunt" that Nixon would regret: "It will forever after be said he did this to cover Watergate. I really would plead with you. If he wants to, make it as an announcement separate from the other."

Haig was being a good soldier. He had delivered Nixon's message; he was equally meticulous in transmitting my reaction. Within a few minutes he reported back to me that Nixon accepted the primacy of foreign policy considerations. The two announcements would be separated. He just wanted to make sure that the Moscow trip would be announced by the White House, not the State Department, at whatever time had been agreed with the Soviets.

At 6:30 P.M. I briefed the Chinese, at 6:50 P.M. the British Ambassador. At 7:10 P.M. I reviewed everything once again by phone with Dinitz. I told him that I would begin negotiations with their preference, linking the cease-fire only to peace negotiations among the parties. Above all, I would not accept the Soviet thesis that Resolution 242 meant immediate and total Israeli withdrawal. But I stressed to Dinitz that I would probably not be able to exclude all references to 242; indeed, I thought it undesirable to destroy the only existing legal framework for negotiations. I asked Dinitz to supply me with detailed military reports during my Moscow sojourn. I expected no results before Sunday afternoon, Moscow time, and they would then be transmitted immediately to Israel. Israel should keep this schedule in mind. As it turned out, that schedule was not far off the mark.

At 7:15 P.M. I had a brief session with my colleagues of two weeks of WSAG meetings: Jim Schlesinger, Tom Moorer, Bill Colby, Brent Scowcroft. We had conferred daily, sometimes tensely. We had not always agreed; but we had managed a difficult crisis to a tolerable outcome. We could all see the end of the road now; the worst dangers had been overcome. A great opportunity for a new approach to Middle East problems lay before us. We felt an immense sense of relief. I sketched the strategy of the trip to Moscow:

Sending me would delay it a few days, give them a face-saver, and avoid Gromyko coming here with tough instructions. Brent will keep you informed. I will work for a simple cease-fire, with maybe a call for negotiations. The trouble is Israel doesn't want anything, but I may have to include a reference to 242. I may have to go back to our original status quo ante.

Everyone knows in the Middle East that if they want a peace they have to go through us. Three times they tried through the Soviet Union, and three times they failed.

Later in the day I sent messages to King Hussein and the Shah to inform them of my impending trip, stating that we had made this decision "in response to Soviet urging. . . . My objectives during these talks will remain as they had been since the beginning — an immediate end to the fighting on a basis that will make possible early progress toward a final, just and lasting peace."

I have since asked myself whether we accepted the Soviet invitation too quickly. Possibly I could have delayed my departure another twenty-four hours — and strengthened Israel's military position even further. On the other hand, the Soviets would have understood exactly what we were doing, and might have sought to counter our blatant stalling by surfacing a formal resolution at the United Nations or raising the military ante. And Arab frustration would have turned a unified Arab world against the United States. A week earlier I had counseled Israel to delay seeking a cease-fire because I thought the military situation unpromising for postwar diplomacy. But just as it is important not to flinch on the road to strategic success, so it is essential not to press beyond what is sustainable. We had been riding many wild horses simultaneously. We could not now confuse virtuosity with a long-range strategy. We had to avoid risking everything for marginal gains, for we had achieved our fundamental objectives: We had created the conditions for a diplomatic breakthrough. We had vindicated the security of our friends. We had prevented a victory of Soviet arms. We had maintained a relationship with key Arab countries and laid the basis for a dominant role in postwar diplomacy. And we had done all this in the midst of the gravest constitutional crisis of this century.

We held the cards now. Our next challenge was to play our hand.

XII

Moscow, the Cease-Fire, and the Alert

Journey to Moscow

MY associates and I left for the Soviet Union at two o'clock in the morning on Saturday, October 20, almost exactly two weeks after the outbreak of the war. I gave a lift also to Soviet Ambassador Anatoly Dobrynin, for whom this was the quickest means to get to Moscow. My departure was secret, but shortly after takeoff the White House announced that President Nixon had sent me to Moscow for "direct discussions with the Soviet leadership on means to end the hostilities in the Middle East."

While we were en route and until negotiations actually started, we enjoyed temporary relief from the anxiety that the Soviets might attempt to exploit Arab passions for an anti-American crusade. But later that day we had a glimpse of other dangerous prospects, with Saudi Arabia's dramatic announcement that it and other Arab oil producers were embargoing *all* sale of oil to the United States.

I had told Dobrynin that I never negotiated immediately after a long flight across many time zones and would not be prepared to begin talks until Sunday morning Moscow time, more than thirty-six hours away. In the interval, as he and I both knew, the military situation could only change in our favor. I had consistently told Israeli Ambassador Simcha Dinitz that Israel would be well advised to conduct operations in the knowledge that we would not be able to stall on a cease-fire proposal for more than forty-eight hours. (My trip to Moscow, in the end, doubled that interval.)

While in transit I received two reports from Dinitz. Both matter-of-factly described the location of Israeli forces in terms of place names in Arabic, but gave no indication of Israel's strategic objectives or of any time-scale required to achieve them. One report made clear that the Israelis indeed understood that a cease-fire was approaching; it also hinted that the exhaustion of Israeli forces might set a limit to their further advances, whatever happened in Moscow:

All our actions have to be guided by considerations related to the possibility of a rapidly approaching cease-fire/standstill. When the cease-fire comes into force it should find us holding a line that makes sense from a politico-military point of view. The further drive that we still have to develop will be made possible by the magnificent fighting spirit of our forces. However, we must bear in mind that they have been engaged in heavy combat almost incessantly since October 6th.

The second report asserted that Israeli forces had cut the road from Cairo to the city of Suez, though the Egyptians were expected to try to reopen it. Egypt's forces across the Suez Canal consisted of two so-called armies each about 35,000 strong. The Second Army held the northern sector; the Third Army was installed in the south opposite Suez City (see the map on page 566). If the Israelis had cut the Cairo-Suez road, the Third Army was virtually encircled.

In acknowledging these reports I cabled Brent Scowcroft back at the White House:

I cannot overemphasize the urgent need to keep me fully informed of the military situation. I need exact assessments, and I need them quickly and frequently.

Dinitz must, repeat must, report to you at least three times a day, and I must then have those reports immediately. Tell him to get his communications set up now if he has not yet done so. These reports must be clearly identified.

I cannot avoid mistakes if I am not kept fully up to date and know exactly what the situation on the ground is.

We were not to receive another Israeli military report while I was in Moscow, only information from American sources. I was never given an explanation for this hiatus. Israel's leaders may themselves have been in the dark about the location of their rapidly moving forces, or about which prong of a multipronged attack would turn out to be the line of most rapid advance.

It was a busy and, as it turned out, fretful journey. I was particularly anxious not to be robbed of bargaining chips in Moscow by some untoward development at home. So I instructed Scowcroft from the plane to resist Defense Department tendencies to ease budgetary pressures by cutting down on our airlift to Israel while I was in Moscow. I reminded Scowcroft: "If the Israelis win, what we do on resupply in the next few days will make no difference; if the Israelis cannot pull it off and bog down I will need all the bargaining leverage I can muster."

As we approached Moscow, then, I felt we were in a very strong negotiating position. Israel seemed poised to achieve a decisive victory. But my confidence was suddenly shaken by an unexpected message from Nixon. We, on our way to Moscow, were not to know what a fateful day October 20 was for the Presidency. We were ignorant of the dramas of what came to be known as the "Saturday night massacre": Special Prosecutor Archibald Cox refused to accept summaries of the Nixon tapes reviewed by Senator John Stennis; he wanted the tapes themselves, and he rejected Nixon's alternative proposal that in exchange for them he renounce the right to subpoena further documents. Nixon forced a showdown by sacking Cox, which led Attorney General Elliot Richardson and Deputy Attorney General William Ruckelshaus to resign as well.

None of this was communicated to the plane carrying me toward Moscow. What was apparent, rather, was an unusual flurry of diplomatic activity on Nixon's part. It was not unprecedented that on the way to a negotiation I would be bombarded with White House missives. Nixon did this partly to calm his nerves, partly to show he was in charge. It had in the past led to some testy exchanges but not to any serious consequences. This time, however, Nixon took a step that had a significant and irreversible impact on the negotiation. It started with an urgent cable from Scowcroft transmitting the draft of a letter that Nixon intended to send to Brezhnev immediately through the Soviet Embassy in Washington. Its essence was that Nixon was granting me "full authority" and that "the commitments that he [Kissinger] may make in the course of your discussions have my complete support." Nixon's letter further appealed to Brezhnev for:

a firm commitment from both of us to devote our personal efforts toward achieving that goal [a final peace] and to provide the strong leadership which our respective friends in the area will find persuasive. I am sending a message to Dr. Kissinger which he will convey orally to you, of my strong personal commitment in this regard.

I was horrified. The letter meant that I would be deprived of any capacity to stall. "Full authority" made it impossible for me from Moscow to refer any tentative agreement to the President for his approval — if only to buy time to consult Israel. Moreover, the letter implied that the Soviets and we would impose an overall Mideast settlement on the parties and that I was empowered to discuss that subject as well — a concession totally contrary to our strategy until now, which sought to separate the cease-fire from a political settlement.

Undoubtedly, Nixon's eager involvement reflected a desire to be identified with something more elevating than the interminable and sordid legal disputes over the Watergate tapes. The trouble was that Nixon's communication to Brezhnev lacked his usual fine touch. His desire to tell the Soviet leader that I had his complete confidence was helpful. But his phraseology went far beyond his intention; it did not strengthen my hand. On the contrary, in a situation in which time was our most important ally, it deprived me of the opportunity to procrastinate, hence of maneuvering room.

I therefore flashed a message to Scowcroft uncharacteristically objecting to the grant of full authority: "I must be in a position to insist to the Russians that I must pass the proposals back to the President for his consideration. Any reference to full authority would undercut this ability." As for the "strong leadership which our respective friends in the area will find persuasive," I warned Scowcroft delicately that "if the language was ever published, it could prove difficult for the President."

My message arrived too late. His despair masking as exaltation, Nixon had pressed Scowcroft to have the letter typed for his immediate signature without waiting for my comments. When Nixon threatened to have it prepared and sent by his trusted secretary Rose Mary Woods, Scowcroft yielded. For students of White House lore it is significant that what made the final typed letter irreversible was that Nixon added to it a handwritten postscript: "Mrs. Nixon joins me in sending our best personal regards to Mrs. Brezhnev and to you." Scowcroft added dryly: "This eliminated any flexibility I may otherwise have had for modification" — meaning that in its absence he might have had the letter retyped with my suggested changes. The letter was delivered to the Soviet Embassy at 11:25 A.M. Washington time.

The Soviets recognize a windfall when they see it, especially when they are in a hurry to settle. Within hours a reply from Brezhnev arrived in Washington — a turnaround time never before or again equaled for an exchange of letters while I was in the White House. Brezhnev fully grasped what had happened:

> I understood it exactly the way you stated that Dr. Kissinger being your closest associate who enjoys your full confidence, will this time as well speak on your behalf, and that the commitments he may make in the course of our discussions with him will have your complete support.

And just to keep matters in the family, Brezhnev added a handwritten postscript of his own: "Mrs. Brezhnev is grateful for the regards and in turn joins me in sending our best personal regards to Mrs. Nixon and to you." I did not find out about Brezhnev's reply until I saw him in the Kremlin.

History will not record that I resisted many grants of authority. This one I resented bitterly; it was a classic example of how "full powers" can inhibit rather than enhance negotiating flexibility.

We arrived in Moscow around 7:30 on Saturday evening, October 20, for my first visit as Secretary of State. Foreign Minister Andrei Gromyko, now my counterpart, was at the airport to greet me. He escorted us at the customary racing-car speed to our guest villa on the Lenin Hills overlooking the Moscow River. It was the same stodgily opulent residence that had housed me previously; only this time, in honor of my new status as Secretary of State, it flew the American flag — a protocol courtesy that gave me an odd thrill. No sooner had we been installed than we were served the obligatory heavy meal that immediately cut down our mobility. Then our hosts attempted to get around my insistence to Dobrynin that I would not be prepared to negotiate before the next morning. They came up with a clever dodge. Brezhnev invited my party and me to a "private" dinner late Saturday night in the Politburo office in the Kremlin — never mind that I had just eaten.

A social invitation by the General Secretary could not be refused, whatever our assessment of his motivation. Our minds addled by a fifteen-hour plane trip and our bellies distended by a Russian dinner, we set off at breakneck speed to the Kremlin. Just after nine o'clock Brezhnev received us in what looked like a Churchill jumpsuit in sky blue and ushered us into his inner sanctum. It contained a conference table that could easily seat forty people, opposite the end of which stood a huge desk with a telephone console the shape and dimensions of a medium-sized organ.

Soviet psychological warfare was so effective that we were almost relieved that Brezhnev suggested an "informal" discussion before feeding us yet again. He kept pretty much to the understanding that there would be no negotiation during the first evening — though idle conversation with the ruler of a Communist state is a contradiction in terms. Brezhnev waxed eloquent about the special relationship between the Soviet leadership and Nixon — no doubt as a device to keep me from being too hard-nosed when we got down to serious business. He did not neglect to remind me that I had "full powers" and therefore would have no need to refer matters to Washington. To procrastinate, I fell in with the spirit of the occasion, discoursing on the principles of forswearing unilateral advantage and avoiding exacerbation of tensions.

The conversation seemed a small price to pay to gain time, though its bizarre quality was not lost on us. The relationship of the two superpowers was being extolled, after all, at the very moment when both sides were introducing thousands of tons of war matériel daily to opposite sides in a desperate war, each seeking to reduce if not eliminate the influence of the other. Brezhnev's contribution to the pleasant mood was the claim that the Soviets were doing nothing unusual in their air- and sealifts to the Middle East; they were simply fulfilling long-standing, four-year-old agreements "according to which we must send so many guns." The idea that Moscow, in fueling the Middle East war, was motivated simply by its well-known adherence to legal obligations was a bit much to take, even in the interest of maintaining a noncontentious atmosphere for an evening of stalling. "To us," I replied sarcastically, "it looks like you are fulfilling the four-year agreement in two weeks. It is an impressive performance."

No evening with the Soviet leadership could be complete without some bluster. Once again more in sorrow than in anger, Brezhnev invoked the threat of war that was inherent in the Middle East crisis. He used this to press his favorite theme from Zavidovo and San Clemente that the superpowers should impose a comprehensive peace of their own in the Middle East. I turned him down. I had come to discuss a cease-fire, not a settlement, I said. There was some minor sparring, but it was agreed that we would get down to business the next morning, Sunday, at eleven o'clock. The late hour was undoubtedly designed to enable Dobrynin to attend church services, I joked. "That is his innermost desire," quipped Brezhnev. Both of us knew, in fact, that we would need the time to assess military reports to determine our bargaining positions.

I was convinced that we were in a strong position to conclude the negotiations on substantially the terms we sought: a cease-fire in place, a vague reference to Security Council Resolution 242, and the breakthrough to direct negotiations between Israel and its Arab neighbors for the first time since the creation of the Jewish state. When I returned to the guest house, however, there was another unnerving surprise. Waiting for me were the instructions to which Nixon had referred in his letter to Brezhnev together with a White House announcement of the fact that instructions had been sent. Nixon's message to me came in two parts: his analysis of the current situation in the Middle East, and specific points I was to convey orally to Brezhnev. The message, dictated personally by Nixon, was, however much I disagreed with it, an acute discussion of the Middle East problem, a remarkable feat of concentration considering the Watergate storm raging around him. The analytical part — intended for me alone — expressed Nixon's conviction that the Soviet Union and the United States should jointly use the end of the war to impose a comprehensive peace in the Middle East: "The current Israeli successes at Suez must not deflect us from going all out to achieve a just settlement now." We would serve even Israel's best interests if we now used "whatever pressures may be required in order to gain acceptance of a settlement which is reasonable and which we can ask the Soviets to press on the Arabs." Nixon then listed the obstacles that had so far prevented a solution: Israel's intransigence, the Arabs' refusal to bargain realistically, and our own "preoccupation with other initiatives." These could no longer stand in the way of a permanent settlement. "U.S. political considerations," Nixon wrote to me in a euphemism for the Jewish vote, "will have absolutely no, repeat no, influence on our decisions in this regard. I want you to know that I am prepared to pressure the Israelis to the extent required, regardless of the domestic political consequences.''

The oral message to Brezhnev did not differ significantly. I was to point out that in contrast to the implementation of the US–Soviet trade agreement, Nixon could act in Middle East diplomacy without Congressional veto. Too late, Nixon wrote, he had realized the essential correctness of the views Brezhnev had put forth in San Clemente in June:

> The Israelis and Arabs will never be able to approach this subject by themselves in a rational manner. That is why Nixon and Brezhnev, looking at the problem more dispassionately, must step in, determine the proper course of action to a just settlement, and then bring the necessary pressure on our respective friends for a settlement which will at last bring peace to this troubled area.

It was a blessing that I had been ignorant of this message during my just concluded "informal" session with Brezhnev. American strategy so far had been to *separate* the cease-fire from a postwar political settlement and to reduce the Soviet role in the negotiations that would follow the cease-fire. What Nixon seemed to envisage now would involve us in an extensive negotiation whose results we would then have to impose on Israel as the last act of a war fought on the Arab side with Soviet weapons. Moscow would receive credit with the Arabs for having forced us into a course we had heretofore avoided. Our leverage on the Arab states would disappear. Their tendency would be to rely on the Soviet Union — unless the Soviets were willing to separate themselves from the hard-line Arab program, for which we had never seen one shred of evidence. But even should Nixon now wish to reverse our settled strategy, Moscow was not the place to do it. It would complicate the cease-fire negotiations. We would emerge at best with an agreement in principle that would haunt us for years. This is why with Nixon's approval I had made it a precondition of my trip to Moscow that the sole agenda item be a cease-fire. Expanding the agenda now to include a comprehensive settlement would land us in a morass.

The strain of two weeks of too great tension and too little sleep translated itself into my rather strident cable to Scowcroft:

> The letter to Brezhnev has already been used against me; the General Secretary refused to accept it when I told him I would have to refer any scheme back to Washington for consideration, citing the fact that I already had full powers granted me by the President.
>
> As a result, my position here is almost insoluble. If I carry out the letter of the President's instructions it will totally wreck what little bargaining leverage I still have. Our first objective must be a cease-fire. That will be tough enough to get the Israelis to accept; it will be impossible as part of a global deal. If

the war continues the consequences will be incalculable. We can pursue the
course the President has in mind after a cease-fire made with Israeli acquiescence, but not before. In the meantime, a continuation of public comment can
only ruin us all around.

When aggrieved, I would rarely rely on only one channel of communication. I therefore telephoned Al Haig and expressed on an open
line to Washington my extreme displeasure at the orders I had received.
"Will you get off my back? I have troubles of my own," said Haig,
uncharacteristically testy.

I insisted on my injury: "What troubles can you possibly have in
Washington on a Saturday night?"

Haig replied wearily: "The President has just fired Cox. Richardson
and Ruckelshaus have resigned and all hell has broken loose."

That is how I learned what troubles one can have in Washington on
a Saturday night.

Agreement on a Cease-Fire

IT was now even more imperative to end the war before the Soviets
were tempted to take advantage of our domestic debacle. Therefore,
I adhered rigidly to the earlier, more restricted plan approved by Nixon
before my departure. Brezhnev in turn was in such a hurry for a cease-
fire that he never inquired as to what instructions Nixon had referred to
in his letter.

My meeting with Brezhnev the next day, Sunday, October 21, was
delayed until noon, which suited us. Despite my entreaties via Dinitz,
no special military briefings were being sent to me by the Israeli government. The CIA reported the declaration of a senior Israeli defense
official on late Saturday that Israeli forces had cut all highways and
railroads from Cairo to Ismailia and Suez, thus isolating Egyptian forces
on the east bank. Like many other Israeli claims during the war, this
turned out to be premature. But to us in Moscow it seemed further
evidence that Israel's major strategic goals on the Egyptian front were
being achieved.

We continued to note that Moscow had alerted forces capable of intervening in the Middle East, including seven Soviet airborne divisions.
Brezhnev obviously did not get so carried away by his protestations of
peaceful intentions that he neglected to give himself an alternative should
negotiations fail.

Our own information on Sunday morning, October 21, was more ambiguous. The CIA reported heavy fighting around the Suez Canal and
suggested that both sides might have been encountering difficulties. The
major focus of Israeli activity was described as being between Great

Bitter Lake and Ismailia — implying a northern thrust, not the flanking movement south toward Suez that was actually developing. (In reality, Israeli forces were probing in both directions, north and south, but the southward thrust proved more productive.) Scowcroft wired me that he had told the President of steady but "fairly slow" Israeli progress. I heard nothing directly from Israel about its prognosis or intentions.

The clearest statement came instead from a radio broadcast by Defense Minister Moshe Dayan. He declared that Israel's position was bound to improve with every day the war continued; nevertheless, Israel was not in a position to oppose a cease-fire. He suggested a cease-fire based on one of two conditions: a return by both sides to the lines prior to the war, or the retention by both sides of positions occupied at the time of the cease-fire. We were well on the way to achieving the second condition by the time the report of Dayan's speech reached us.

Early on October 21 a message from Cairo reached me, via Washington, before my meeting with Brezhnev. Hafiz Ismail for the first time indicated that Sadat might be willing to separate a cease-fire from an overall settlement. Cairo would content itself, he wrote, with the convening of a peace conference and a "guarantee" by the United States and the Soviet Union of the cease-fire and the speedy subsequent withdrawal of Israeli forces. We were in no position to give such a guarantee, much less in conjunction with the Soviets. On the other hand, I did not consider Ismail's message Egypt's last word on the subject either.

Due to the time difference — it was very early morning in Washington — I heard nothing more about the "Saturday night massacre." Nor did I receive any further instructions until the negotiations were already concluded and I was on my way back.

While our intelligence was skimpy and conveyed no particular sense of urgency, the Soviets seemed to be better informed. For when we met Sunday noon in Brezhnev's Politburo office, we found the Soviet team so eager to settle that there was really no negotiation in the strict sense. Brezhnev began with some extended remarks suggesting that he was equally prepared to discuss principles of a general settlement or a cease-fire. When I told him that I was ready to deal only with a cease-fire, he accepted with alacrity.

Brezhnev opened with the normal Soviet ploy alleging I had accepted in principle the Soviet three-point plan presented by Dobrynin in Washington (see Chapter XI). This was news to me since I was under the impression that I had rejected two of the three Soviet terms. So I spelled out our position once again. The first Soviet point, I said, calling for a cease-fire, was acceptable. The second point, requiring "immediate" Israeli withdrawals to "the line in accordance with" Security Council Resolution 242, was meaningless because the parties had never yet agreed on such a line, because it was senseless to ask Israel to return to a nonexistent line, and because negotiation of a postwar settlement should be separated from the cease-fire. The third Soviet point, the appeal for "appropriate consultations" for negotiation, had to be elaborated into a clear obligation of direct talks between Israel and the Arab states.

Usually, the Soviets stick to their formal positions for extended periods and then sell their abandonment of an outrageous proposition as a concession. On this occasion Brezhnev conceded my points before I had even raised them: "I am not claiming the proposals are ideal or can be accepted as they stand right now."

To avoid talking from a Soviet draft, I then submitted a counterproposal that Joe Sisco and I had worked out during the night. Our first point called for a cease-fire in place. Our second point eliminated the Soviet demand for an immediate Israeli withdrawal to new lines; indeed, it made no reference to withdrawal at all, calling on the parties simply to begin implementation of Security Council Resolution 242 "in all of its parts" — a mandate sufficiently vague to have occupied diplomats for years without arriving at agreement. Our third point required immediate negotiations "between the parties concerned" under "appropriate auspices"; in other words, the cease-fire would lead to the direct negotiations with Israel that the Arab states had consistently refused and that a succession of Israeli cabinets had claimed would unlock the door to their concessions. We said nothing about guarantees.

To our amazement, Brezhnev and Gromyko accepted our text, with only the most minor editorial changes.* They then took a run at turning the "appropriate auspices" for the direct negotiations into a US–Soviet guarantee of the outcome — a euphemism for an imposed peace. I rejected the proposition. I defined "auspices" as meaning the presence of Soviet and American diplomats at the opening of the negotiations and thereafter only when key issues were dealt with. That too was accepted by Brezhnev and Gromyko with a minimum of haggling.

After only four hours of negotiation the text of the cease-fire resolution was agreed, together with a US–Soviet understanding on the meaning of "auspices." This was phenomenal considering the need for translating everything, checking the texts, and frequent interruptions as each side huddled together for consultation.

The agreement indeed improved what we had been proposing for two weeks. The original American proposal had been a cease-fire linked to a general reference to Security Council Resolution 242. Four months earlier in the summit communiqué, Brezhnev had refused *any* such reference. Then and during the war the Soviets had insisted that we jointly spell out the meaning of Resolution 242 and impose terms that in the

---

*The text agreed between us became UN Security Council Resolution 338. It is printed in the backnotes.[1]

Soviet formulations were indistinguishable from the hard-line Arab program. We prevailed with our approach, which left the elaboration of Resolution 242 to direct negotiations between the parties. The vaguely defined US–Soviet "auspices" had the advantage, as I cabled Scowcroft, of preventing the intrusion into the negotiating process of other parties liable to bring pressure on us — I fear I meant some of our European allies.

The only subject left for discussion in Moscow was the timing of introducing our joint cease-fire resolution in New York. Brezhnev and Gromyko wanted it put to the Security Council immediately, with the cease-fire to take effect the moment the resolution was passed. This underlined the extremity in which Arab armies found themselves (but of which I had not yet received any formal word either from our sources or Israel's). It was, however, totally impractical. It was now 4:00 P.M. in Moscow and 9:00 A.M. in Washington. It would take us an hour to draft a report and instructions and at least another hour for cable transmission to Washington. There would have to be discussions with key members of the UN Security Council and above all with Israel. Assuming our estimate held, these could start at 12:00 noon Washington time. I therefore proposed that the American and Soviet representatives issue a call at 6:00 P.M. New York time for a Security Council meeting to convene at 9:00 P.M. (leaving nine hours for consultation). The cease-fire should not go into effect until twelve hours *after* the resolution had been adopted, which in turn would require several hours of debate. Brezhnev reluctantly accepted this timetable, which put the cease-fire at best some twenty-eight hours away. Brezhnev also pledged to exert maximum Soviet influence to bring about an early exchange of prisoners of war, which I had pressed on Israel's behalf.

The American team returned to the state guest house to begin its labors. My staff and I urgently drafted a report to the President and a letter for him to send to Prime Minister Meir, which Scowcroft in Washington would hand to Dinitz as soon as it arrived. We estimated that this would be no later than 12:00 noon Washington time, or nine hours before the Security Council was to convene and some twelve hours before it would vote. Nixon's letter to Mrs. Meir spelled out what we had accomplished:

Madame Prime Minister, we believe that this is a major achievement for you and for us and supportive of the brave fighting of your forces. [First:] It would leave your forces right where they are. [Second:] There is absolutely no mention whatsoever of the word "withdrawal" in the resolution; third, for the first time, we have achieved the agreement of the Soviet Union to a resolution that calls for direct negotiation without conditions or qualifications between the parties under appropriate auspices. At the same time we and the Soviets have agreed privately to make our joint auspices available to you and to the Arabs to facilitate this process, if this is agreeable to the parties.

The letter pointed out the vast difference between the cease-fire resolution now being proposed and Sadat's program publicly put forward five days earlier. A prompt reply was requested.

Messages were also drafted for Hafiz Ismail, the Shah, King Hussein, and our UN Ambassador John Scali. This process was completed by about 5:30 P.M. Moscow, or 10:30 A.M. Washington, time.

At 6:30 P.M. I met with the British, French, and Australian ambassadors to Moscow, the first two in their capacity as permanent members of the Security Council, the Australian because his country's representative in New York was president of the Security Council for October as the consequence of rotation. Diplomats are congenitally careful in expressing their opinions on issues with respect to which their governments have not yet taken a stand. In this case they were sufficiently confident of their governments' views to offer warm congratulations before rushing off to inform their capitals. Because of a horrendous communication mix-up, it is likely that their reports arrived before ours.

I then lay down to rest for an hour. When I awoke around 8:00 P.M. (1:00 P.M. Washington time) I found out to my horror that none of my messages had been received in Washington. My staff had first sought to send the messages through our Embassy in downtown Moscow, forty-five minutes away. The Embassy had great difficulty, however, because its procedures for sensitive messages were cumbersome and time-consuming. We then resorted to transmitting via our Presidential aircraft, parked at Moscow's Vnukovo II Airport, for a satellite hookup to the White House Situation Room. But the messages sent from the plane were arriving in practically unreadable form in Washington. My associate Larry Eagleburger was in touch with our Embassy and then with Brent Scowcroft in Washington on an open phone line. Scowcroft could make out that we had agreed to a cease-fire, but the letter to Golda Meir had come in too garbled to pass to Dinitz. We thereupon had no choice but to switch back to sending the messages through the Embassy.

My reaction to this was later described by Larry Eagleburger in a reminiscence he sent to me:

As if it were yesterday, I recall sitting at a desk in a fairly large room in the villa, yelling over the phone at the communications people in the Embassy. (I was yelling because of the bad telephone connection, *not* because I thought it would help move the cables faster. Unlike certain Secretaries of State, I never believed that a loud voice had much impact on inanimate objects, no matter how badly they functioned.) There were some twenty to thirty people in the room, all talking, with Joe Sisco (never a quiet fellow) taking the lead. In short, the room was crowded and noisy, but I was more-or-less hidden from view (and hearing) by the crowd.

. . . Unbeknownst to me, you walked in at that moment and obviously heard what I was saying (I still haven't figured out how). There was a bellow along the lines of: "What, the cables aren't out yet!?!" I looked up, to find you standing in the middle of the room with smoke issuing from nose, eyes, and ears, and *no one* else (with an exception I'll mention in a minute) in sight. All twenty or thirty people — no doubt led by Sisco — had exited with a speed and facility that would have put Houdini to shame. The single exception was Winston Lord, who was sort of huddled in a corner, but — God bless him — prepared to hang around for the pyrotechnics and to clean up the blood (mine) when it was all over. Winston, ever since, has had a special place in my heart, as well as my great respect for his outstanding courage.

The situation was far from funny. Altogether, at least four hours were lost and much Israeli confidence in us. At first I thought it was an inexplicable technical malfunction; I was told that electrical storms in the atmosphere were disrupting all radio communications. The next day it struck me as weird that *all* transmission channels should break down simultaneously on a Presidential plane that was outfitted for instant communications and that over five years of diplomatic missions had never failed. Then I recalled the delays and garbling I had experienced when cabling Nixon from the parked aircraft during my secret visit in April before the 1972 Moscow summit.[2] If the interference was indeed deliberate (which I cannot prove),* it served Soviet purposes only marginally; but this of itself does not exclude the possibility. What is so maddening about much of Soviet maneuvering is the loss of confidence that Soviet bureaucrats seem willing to accept for relatively slight benefits.

There is no doubt that the interference reduced the time Israel had available for gearing its last-minute military operations to the imminent cease-fire. This should not have mattered. Israel knew that I was in Moscow to negotiate a cease-fire; it had always been told that it would have only a limited time to complete its operations after negotiations began; we had by now already nearly doubled the forty-eight hours that I had told Dinitz for a week would be available; and it was probable that Israel was moving at full speed anyway. Moreover, I got one of the "lost" hours back by cabling John Scali in New York that we did not have the same interest the Soviets had in adopting the cease-fire by

---

*The aircraft radio operator routinely reserved a wide range of frequencies across the radio spectrum as insurance if atmospheric interference rendered some frequencies unusable. This time, frequencies all across the radio band were disrupted by interference — an extraordinary occurrence. Transmissions from both the aircraft and the US Embassy were garbled. The problem was unusual enough to prompt investigations. The majority of the experts concluded that atmospheric interference and other technical difficulties were responsible; the aircraft radio operator remained convinced that such prolonged and extensive interference could only have been man-made.

midnight as we had implied to Brezhnev. (It finally passed at 12:50 A.M. New York time.)*

The main impact of the Soviet maneuver, if it was such, was on US–Israeli relations. The hours we lost to communications problems gave Israel only about eight hours to deliberate rather than the twelve on which we had counted. It therefore appeared in Jerusalem as an ultimatum, which we had never intended. It also delayed our informing the rest of our government, Congressional leaders, and other countries, especially the People's Republic of China. Scowcroft attended to these duties with his customary efficiency. Huang Zhen, chief of the Chinese Liaison Office, was, as is the habit of Chinese diplomats when uninstructed, affable but impenetrable. He surely did not like the implication of condominium in a joint US–Soviet proposal to the Security Council. But we had kept the Chinese meticulously informed of our strategy. (China finally did not participate in the Security Council vote — the mildest form of dissociation available.)

I believed then and I still believe that we achieved the maximum attainable. Any effort to squeeze out more would have involved risks of major crises for inconsequential gains that might well have jeopardized the peace process we were determined to start — and to dominate. We had made clear that Soviet weapons gave the Arabs no realistic military option. But to benefit from this demonstration, we had also to show that moderation had its rewards; we had no interest in driving our potential Arab partners in a peace process into radical or Soviet arms. With respect to the Soviets, we would be courting a confrontation to no purpose. As we were to show later that week, we did not flinch from confrontation when vital interests were challenged. But we did not think that turning an Arab setback into a debacle represented a vital interest.

Shortly after, Scali reported that the Security Council passed the joint US–Soviet cease-fire proposal, Resolution 338. At 12:50 A.M. in New York in the early morning of October 22, it was already 7:50 A.M. Moscow time. I breakfasted with Gromyko at the state guest house, which made me technically the host. There was the exuberance that accompanies the end of any negotiation involving great exertions and commensurate risks. The major purpose was to review the meaning of "appropriate auspices." The Soviets were obviously eager to show their Arab clients that they had maneuvered us into a guarantee of achieving their program; our purpose equally plainly was the opposite. We initialed a document that defined "auspices" as follows:

[T]he negotiations between the parties concerned will take place with the active participation of the United States and the Soviet Union at the beginning

---

*Actually, it was 12:52 A.M. when the resolution passed, but the United Nations rounded it off officially to 12:50 A.M.

and thereafter in the course of negotiations when key issues of a settlement are dealt with.

There was much maudlin talk about the importance of close US–Soviet relations and some heavy joshing, reflecting the relief that the need for irrevocable decisions seemed to have passed. Gromyko's contribution consisted of calling his ally, Sadat, a "paper camel." Despite the early hour, everyone drank toasts of brandy, though we all knew that at best we had shifted our rivalry to the diplomatic plane. The passions of the Middle East combatants, the difficulty of implementation, and the inherent competitiveness of the American and Soviet interests would dominate our relations soon enough again.

A Tense Visit to Israel

DURING the hectic evening of exchanges between Washington and Jerusalem over the proposed resolution, Prime Minister Golda Meir had come up with the idea that I should visit Israel on the way back from Moscow. That was a nice way of putting it; Tel Aviv is hardly on the direct route from Moscow to Washington. Delicately, Golda had not made Israeli acceptance of Security Council Resolution 338 dependent on my agreeing to the visit. But though she did not say so, it was clear that she needed reassurance for the postwar phase and for handling her cabinet.

When I agreed to go, I immediately notified Sadat, Hussein, the Soviets, and the NATO ambassadors. I also created an entirely new set of problems. I made the decision at about 6:00 A.M. on October 22; I would depart four hours later. This required obtaining new flight clearances for our change in plans. It is not the easiest thing to find a responsible Soviet official awake at that hour, much less to get him to approve immediately a flight plan that would take us over much of the Soviet Union not usually open to foreigners — particularly when they had expected us to go due west rather than south. Our chargé d'affaires in Moscow, Adolph (Spike) Dubs (a distinguished diplomat who was murdered in 1979 while serving as our Ambassador in Afghanistan), took care of this problem by means that Foreign Service Officers jealously guard to maintain their indispensability; he had all arrangements completed in record time.

Around 10:00 A.M. Moscow time, we were airborne. About halfway to Tel Aviv, it dawned on me that we were heading into a war zone. The cease-fire, after all, was not scheduled to go into effect until several hours later. I realized, without excessive immodesty, that it might be a good idea to arrange some protection by aircraft from the US Sixth Fleet. Larry Eagleburger contacted the Pentagon from our aircraft, and the Pentagon's National Military Command Center (NMCC) promised that everything would be arranged immediately. And it was. In an outstanding demonstration of American military efficiency, we were met over Cyprus by a large number of US Navy aircraft that stayed with us until we landed at Tel Aviv's Lod Airport.

There was more to the story than I knew at the time. The Commander of the Sixth Fleet then was Vice Admiral Daniel Murphy, a former aide to Secretary of Defense Melvin Laird and later chief of staff to Vice President George Bush. Months afterward, Eagleburger ran into Murphy at a Washington party and congratulated him on his superb performance in October 1973. Murphy described to Larry what had really happened.

The fleet was conducting aircraft-launching exercises when the request for air cover for the Secretary of State came from the Pentagon. Admiral Murphy reasonably inquired into our location. The NMCC helpfully told him we were somewhere between Moscow and Tel Aviv. (Perhaps our pilot was reluctant to give too exact a fix for fear it would help other, less friendly aircraft also to locate us.) Murphy immediately launched the rest of his aircraft on a sweep of the eastern Mediterranean and ordered those already airborne to search for us as well, so long as their fuel (already substantially depleted) permitted. Murphy spent anxious moments frantically asking his pilots if they had found us yet, getting negative replies, all the while answering Pentagon queries with a nonchalant "we haven't found him yet, but soon will." Which they did, much to the Admiral's relief. But the planes were low on fuel and barely made it back to their carrier. Murphy told Eagleburger it was one of the more hair-raising experiences of his Sixth Fleet tenure.

I have often been asked to describe the most moving moment of my government service. It is difficult to compare memorable events in such a variety of cultural and political settings. Yet surely my arrival in Israel on Monday, October 22, 1973, ranks high on the list.

We reached Lod (now Ben-Gurion) Airport in Tel Aviv at 1:00 P.M. local time. Much was written afterward about how eager Israel was to continue the war and how painful it found the cease-fire. No one would have guessed that from our reception. Soldiers and civilians greeted the approaching peace as the highest blessing. Israel was heroic but its endurance was reaching the breaking point. Those who had come to welcome us seemed to feel viscerally how close to the abyss they had come and how two weeks of war had drained them. Small groups of servicemen and civilians were applauding with tears in their eyes. Their expression showed a weariness that almost tangibly conveyed the limits of human endurance. Israel was exhausted no matter what the military maps showed. Its people were yearning for peace as can only those who have never known it.

The same attitude prevailed in Herzliyya, near Tel Aviv, in the mysterious modernistic building called the Guest House, on the top of a hill, where Golda and her cabinet received me. It was surrounded by barbed wire; security was tight. The rooms were furnished in a contemporary style not quite rising to the level of elegance. I had several other occasions to visit it; the one purpose it clearly was never used for was to house "guests." It was a safe house for secret meetings with foreign visitors.

We were greeted by Golda; Dayan; David Elazar, the Chief of Staff; and other officers and ministers, including former Ambassador Yitzhak Rabin, who, without an official position at the time, sat in on the conversations saying nothing and looking enigmatic. Weariness, physical and moral, was stamped on each face. The characteristic Israeli show of bravado was not absent, but it required so much effort that it seemed to exhaust the participants rather than armor them. They spoke of imminent victories but without conviction, more as if to prop up the image of invulnerability. There were grumbles about how Egypt's Third Army might have been fully encircled and destroyed in another *three* days of fighting. But these were the same leaders whose repeated predictions — "we need three more days" — had consistently been proved overoptimistic. Besides, there was no scenario by which Israel could have been given three more days without risking a superpower crisis and destroying the American position in the Arab world. And Israel's leaders knew this. Their tone was wistful, rather than recriminatory; more a nostalgia for the glories of 1967 than a reflection of the reality of the hour.

The Third Army, in any event, did not loom large in the discussions at the Guest House. When I asked Golda what Israel's next objective would have been had the cease-fire not intervened, she mentioned Port Fuad — at the far northern end of the Canal, in the area of the Second Army, as far away from the Third Army as it was possible to be. And if there was one thing clear in Israel on the announced day of the cease-fire, it was that she had had enough casualties — its 2,000 killed being the equivalent of 200,000 Americans.

Deep down, the Israelis knew that while they had won the last battle, they had lost the aura of invincibility. The Arab armies were not destroyed. The Arab nations had not won but no longer need they quail before Israeli might. Israel, after barely escaping disaster, had prevailed militarily; it ended up with more Arab territory captured than lost. But it was entering an uncertain and lonely future, dependent on a shrinking circle of friends. What made the prospect more tormenting was the consciousness that complacency had contributed to that outcome.

Each of the Israeli leaders we met handled the trauma differently according to the stage of his or her career. They vaguely realized that the war had blighted their personal futures; indeed, within the year they were all out of power. For Golda, who had already held every office worth having, this was close to a welcome relief. She was anguished not about her political future but the casualties that she believed foresight might have averted. She had sacrificed her private life by adopting all of Israel as her family. Every Israeli casualty was a personal loss to her. And she was heartbroken not simply by the suffering but by her vision of what was ahead, which she understood better than her associates.

Golda had no difficulty assuming responsibility for the intelligence failures prior to the war; she made no excuses and offered no explanations. Freed of political ambitions, she prepared herself for what her instinct told her would now be Israel's challenge: that the direct negotiations Israel had demanded with such fervor for so many years would undoubtedly have to be fueled by Israeli concessions. To her the war was already a thing of the past. Alone among her colleagues, she was getting ready for the next battle, which she saw as depriving the outside world — and especially the United States — of any temptation to ease its problems at Israel's expense (or what she considered Israel's expense, which usually was any alteration of the status quo). Warily she prowled the lair of the Guest House, ready to defend her country's interests, insistent on selling Israeli compromises for the highest possible price. I knew that I, as her interlocutor, would bear the brunt of her tenacity and strength.

General David ("Dado") Elazar, the Chief of Staff, was at the other end of the spectrum. He knew that each war has its victims; he would be the sacrifice offered up for Israel's complacency. His career in the military or the government would end as soon as the political process could turn to a postmortem. I will not venture into the debate about the precise degree of his responsibility for Israel's failure to mobilize in time, for it is irrelevant to my purpose. Elazar struck me as a man of rare quality, noble in bearing, fatalistic in conduct. He briefed us matter-of-factly but with the attitude of a man to whom the frenzies of the day were already part of history. He resigned the next year when an Israeli governmental commission laid the blame for Israel's unpreparedness largely on him. He entered private life, which did not interest him. A year later he died. The medical diagnosis was heart attack; it is the best term those trained in tangibles can find for a broken heart.

Dayan's case was the most complex. One of the ironies of Israel's history is that a people often persecuted for being cosmopolitan and excessively intellectual has created a new type of leader in the process of forming its own state: the peasant-hero rooted in the soil, matter-of-fact, not burdened by excessive imagination (except in the sense of a premonition of catastrophe), a pioneer defending every square inch of his acquisitions not only as if diplomacy were another form of warfare — which Clausewitz had already noted — but as if it obeyed exactly the same rules. Dayan was a singular blend of the old and the new. Among his colleagues, he was unique in the sweep of his imagination, the nimbleness of his intellect, the ability to place Israel in a world context. His hobby was archaeology; this gave him an historical perspective beyond even the long history of his own people. He understood that the experience of catastrophe was not peculiar to Jews, even if destiny seems to have meted it out to them more amply than to most other peoples. He therefore had more understanding, and more tolerance, of the viewpoints of other societies — especially the Arabs' — than was characteristic of most Israeli leaders. He had the intuition of a poet. Sometimes he was able to see so many sides to a question that he lost the single-mindedness essential to all leaders and very marked in his own Prime Minister. Still, I had always believed that his special qualities would prove most needed whenever a peace process started; that indeed Dayan was the Israeli statesman most likely to lead Israel toward peace.

It was Dayan's tragedy that like Moses he was permitted a glimpse of the Promised Land but the journey to that mountain top had deprived him of the ability to implement his own vision. Like most talented and artistic men, he knew his own worth; he was not free of vanity. He had served for twenty years in positions that underutilized his extraordinary capabilities. He had sustained himself by his public image as a hero of the war of 1956; later, as the savior summoned in 1967 to engineer the stunning victory (whatever Rabin might think about who deserved the real credit). Yet, by a cruel irony, at the precise moment made for his talents Dayan was losing his aura. If the Chief of Staff was to be blamed for Israel's being taken by surprise, so inevitably would be the Defense Minister. Fundamentally, every criticism of the Chief of Staff applied as well to his immediate superior.

What made his fate so unendurable was that Dayan, the preeminent visionary among Israeli leaders, failed to recognize his own predictions when they at last came true. For years he had warned that war would be inevitable if Israel insisted on remaining along the Suez Canal. He had favored disengagement of forces, or if necessary a unilateral Israeli withdrawal to create a buffer zone. He had never been able to persuade his cabinet colleagues or Golda. They simply had no category of thought for unilateral withdrawals. Dayan's foresight was vindicated but in circumstances that nearly destroyed him. There were a host of explanations for his failure to recognize that the very attack he had been warning against was imminent; many others had drawn the same wrong conclusions about Egypt's intentions. But heroes lose something of their faith in themselves when they admit fallibility. Dayan had so identified himself with his own public image that he could not bring himself to take the only course that might have enabled him to transcend his misfortune, and the one, in fact, taken by Golda: to admit an honest miscalculation.

Instead, Dayan after 1973 was never the same again. Throughout the war he had oscillated between despair and euphoria, at one time recommending deep withdrawals in the Sinai, then constantly proclaiming premature victories whose announcement threatened our agreed diplomacy. He reminded me of a gambler who, having lost at roulette, sought to recoup by constantly doubling his bet. He was too close to his dream of becoming the Prime Minister of peace to let that dream go and yet too far from his destiny to be able to grasp it by an act of will. He had neither reached the pinnacle as had Golda, for whom the length of her stay on it had become irrelevant, nor had he fallen into the abyss like Elazar. He was suspended between his ambition and his premonition, too big to attack, too insecure to withdraw, too sure that this was his hour to admit that it was the wrong moment and thereby perhaps preserve himself for his ultimate mission. And so at the Guest House he was alternately taunting and encouraging. Only when he thought himself unobserved could one discern the underlying melancholy and frustration that were to embitter thereafter the life of that extraordinary personality.

On this emotion-laden visit, I had three meetings with Golda: first privately from 1:35 to 2:15 P.M.; then over lunch with a larger group of officials of both sides from 2:30 to 4:00 P.M.; and then at a military briefing from 4:15 to 5:00 P.M.

Golda's first question when we sat down in a back room concerned not the war but her nightmare for the future: Was there a secret US–Soviet deal to impose the 1967 borders? When I denied this forcefully, she asked whether there was a deal to impose any other frontiers. I denied this as well. As she explored all possible permutations of American duplicity, she exemplified the enormous insecurity inherent in Israel's geographic and demographic position and its total dependence on the United States. For two weeks we had stood by Israel's side, supplied its armories, risked and finally suffered an oil embargo, synchronized diplomacy, and achieved far more in Resolution 338 than foreseen in the first week when direct negotiations between Arabs and Israelis were never even being considered. Yet now the almost palpable relief at the war's end gave rise to acute uneasiness about its implications. For twenty-five years, Israeli diplomacy had striven for direct negotiations. Now that this achievement was at hand, Golda was nearly overwhelmed by the realization, still mercifully obscure to her colleagues, that the agenda for these negotiations would face Israel with the awesome dilemmas it had avoided for too long.

Israel's historic dread was clothed in Talmudic exegesis. A great deal of time was spent on whether Paragraph 2 of the cease-fire resolution —

the pledge to implement Resolution 242 — was organically related to the direct negotiations provided for in Paragraph 3 of the resolution. In other words, would the direct negotiations be confined to implementing a return to the 1967 borders, or would Israel have the right to put forward its own interpretation of 242? I reassured Golda and her colleagues that there were no secret deals nor any restrictions on what could be put forward by any of the parties.

In short, Israel's insecurity was so pervasive that even words were daggers. Golda knew very well that not even the attainment of its stated goals could compensate for the altered psychological balance. I asked whether she thought Sadat could survive the military setbacks of the last phase of the war. Golda replied matter-of-factly: "I do. Because he is the hero. He dared." She was right. Israel was at a disadvantage, even though the war ended in success, because its task was beyond the human scale. It could not prevail by force simply by defeating its enemies; it had to crush them so that they could not revive. Given the disparity in numbers — the city of Cairo alone having twice the population of the entire State of Israel — no nation, however heroic, could sustain such a task indefinitely. This is why for Israel peace is as necessary as it is terrifying. The real issue on my visit to Israel was whether peace could be made while the heroic spirit still held and before the pounding waves submerged the lonely rock.

During the luncheon, a message was brought in informing us that Egypt had accepted the cease-fire, effective at 5:00 P.M. Cairo time (actually two hours ahead of the deadline). The Israeli reaction around the table was a mixture of relief, exultation, and resignation — veering uneasily between hope and suspicion. A desultory discussion about ground rules ensued, soon submerged by a confusion that so often occurs at historic moments. There was uncertainty about whether Cairo and Tel Aviv were in the same time zone; so wide was the gulf between the two societies that no one seemed to be able to find out. I sent Eagleburger to a phone to check it out with Washington. While waiting for the official word, I suggested that Israel solve the issue by setting the time for 6:52 P.M. Israeli time — exactly twelve hours after the cease-fire resolution — and let Cairo translate that into Egyptian time. (It turned out to be the same.)

Later in the afternoon, a military briefing told us for the first time what we had attempted to extract from the Israelis for a week: the exact location and objectives of their forces on the west bank of the Suez Canal. Maps showed all Egyptian routes of supply to the Third Army cut except one secondary road in the extreme south. The Israeli officers praised the fighting qualities of the Egyptian and Syrian armies; they were less impressed by Iraqi units they had encountered.

I left Israel elated and yet somber. We had achieved our strategic

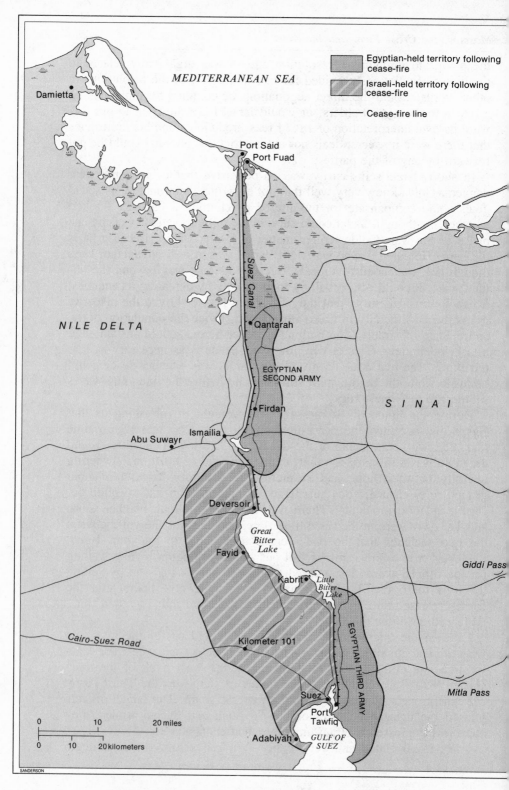

The Sinai Front: Cease–Fire Line after the October War

objective, but it had only opened the way to an unknown terrain that would require discipline, unity, and purpose to traverse. That Egypt was eager to negotiate was reflected in a new message from Hafiz Ismail inviting me to stop in Cairo on my return trip from Israel. I did not think Israel's anxieties could stand this or that we were in fact prepared for a serious dialogue with Egypt ourselves. I therefore turned it down politely:

Secretary Kissinger thanks Mr. Ismail for his kindness in inviting him to visit Cairo. Unfortunately, the invitation was received only after the Secretary had left the area and was well enroute to London. However, now that the cease-fire has been achieved, he accepts with pleasure Mr. Ismail's kind invitation to visit Cairo at an early date. He looks forward to fixing a mutually convenient time in the very near future, and to the continuation of exchanges with Mr. Ismail, using this channel.

In the meantime Washington had exploded after the "Saturday night massacre." Flying west, I had had only two brief reports. One from Scowcroft had noted in a message on other topics:

The all-consuming preoccupation of the moment is with the Richardson/Cox/Ruckelshaus affair. Comments about impeachment are rife in all media. The cease-fire news, of course, made big front page headlines but this latest Watergate crisis has the effect of overwhelming everything else.

Haig cabled me in greater detail:

Unfortunately, you will be returning to an environment of major national crisis which has resulted from the firing of Cox and the resulting resignation of Richardson and Ruckelshaus. Because the situation is at a state of white heat, the ramifications of the accomplishments in Moscow have been somewhat eclipsed and their true significance underplayed. For this reason, it is essential that you participate fully in maintaining the national perspective and that a major effort be made to refocus national attention on the President's role in the Middle East settlement. An impeachment stampede could well develop in the Congress tomorrow although we are confident that cooler heads will prevail if the President's assets are properly applied.

As of now, the President believes that it is essential that we have a bipartisan leadership meeting tomorrow at the White House during which you can report in detail on the Middle East situation, lacing this report with heavy emphasis on the President's accomplishments thus far and the need for national unity and a steady hand in the critical days ahead.

It was Monday evening, October 22, during my stop at Heathrow Airport near London to brief Sir Alec Douglas-Home, that I got from British newspapers the full flavor of what had happened. Impeachment proceedings were beginning. I was heading back toward the capital of a nation that, even while contributing to peace in the Middle East, was consuming its authority at home.

The Cease-Fire Unravels

SIR Alec was relieved that the war had ended, but uncertain about whether the cease-fire would take hold. He had information that Syria's President Hafez al-Asad was planning an offensive to start the next day; the war might erupt all over again. So as not to waste time with further communications via Washington, Home's Foreign Office aides got the Soviet Ambassador to London on the phone for me. Reacting with initiative to the unexpected is not a specialty of Soviet diplomats. It took me some time — and no little assistance from the British Foreign Office personnel — to convince him that I was not an impostor. The hapless Ambassador, probably wishing he had accepted a dinner invitation for the evening, made me dictate exactly what I wished to convey, turning a conversation into a message. I told him Israel had accepted the cease-fire resolution. If Syria started an offensive, we would not be responsible for the consequences. He did not run the risk of volunteering a comment.

But the Middle East never fails to teach one the limits of human foresight. The cease-fire indeed unraveled, though not in the manner we feared at Heathrow Airport. Just as the war seemed to be winding down under the aegis of the superpowers, and our media were beginning to rediscover a measure of merit in US–Soviet détente, the confrontation we had managed to avoid for seventeen days suddenly burst upon us.

The trouble was along the Suez Canal. I reached Andrews Air Force Base near Washington at 3:00 A.M., early Tuesday, October 23, and went home to bed after a long day that had begun in Moscow with intermediate stops in Tel Aviv and London. When I arrived in my office later that morning after four hours' sleep, I found two messages: one from Cairo, the other from Jerusalem. Hafiz Ismail tersely informed me that Israeli forces had broken the young cease-fire and were in the process of occupying new positions. Egypt was taking "all necessary measures to ensure its security." Ismail inquired what the United States and the Soviet Union were doing to secure Israeli compliance.

The message from Ambassador Kenneth Keating in Israel was much longer and infinitely more complex. Golda had just invited him for a long review. She began by pointing out that there was considerable domestic opposition to the cease-fire; she would win the approval of the Israeli Parliament though not without tough sledding. She then complained, quite rightly, about the incongruity of the Jordanian position: Hussein had publicly accepted the cease-fire on the West Bank (where no shooting had been going on) but was hiding behind Syrian failure to issue cease-fire orders in the area where there was actual fighting (and where Jordan had sent forces). Since she studiously avoided discussing the Suez front, Keating mentioned a briefing he had received earlier in the day from the Israeli military alleging wholesale cease-fire violations by Egypt. Some might view these claims with skepticism, Keating said delicately, since the Israeli forces seemed to be gaining ground. He was sure Golda was aware of this danger. Golda admitted that her military commanders had pleaded for "two or three days more" to complete the encirclement of the Third Army in the south (a fact never communicated to us while we were in Moscow), but the cabinet had overruled them. Unfortunately, during the night and well after the cease-fire had gone into effect, she maintained, the Egyptians had broken the truce and mounted a massive attack. In these circumstances she had ordered the Israeli army to continue fighting until the Egyptians stopped.

I shared Keating's skepticism. The previous day's military briefing in Tel Aviv did not suggest a substantial Egyptian offensive potential; nor did the first part of Golda's remarks to Keating imply that Israeli commanders would be meticulous about the cease-fire. I also had a sinking feeling that I might have emboldened them; in Israel, to gain their support, I had indicated that I would understand if there was a few hours' "slippage" in the cease-fire deadline while I was flying home, to compensate for the four hours lost through the communications breakdown in Moscow. But this new fighting was continuing far beyond the brief additional margin I had implied. We were by now nearly twenty hours beyond the deadline. Nor did the Israelis claim — then or ever — that they had any sanction for their efforts save self-defense. On the other hand, Ismail's and Golda's comments were still relatively mild. They did not suggest an imminent crisis.

The import of the two messages had obviously not yet been absorbed in Moscow. Or else the Kremlin, like us, considered any violations the normal final pangs of a bitter conflict. Rather, at 7:50 A.M., Soviet Chargé Yuli M. Vorontsov (Dobrynin not having returned yet from the Soviet capital) transmitted to us a positive reply from Moscow to my warning sent from Heathrow about an imminent Syrian offensive:

Having received Secretary Kissinger's communication we made appropriate steps. Now we would like to inform Dr. Kissinger that in connection with the latest resolution of the Security Council no actions of that type as we have learned are being contemplated on the part of Syria.

Around 9:30 A.M., UN Secretary-General Kurt Waldheim called to report that Egypt had formally complained of Israeli cease-fire violations and wanted a Security Council meeting. Waldheim suggested introducing an international force from Scandinavia and other countries to police the cease-fire. I told him I would consult my colleagues and the Soviets.

A few minutes later I discussed methods of policing the cease-fire with David Popper, the Assistant Secretary of State in charge of United Nations affairs. He thought that the handiest means available was the UN observers group that had previously been stationed along the Suez Canal.

I then spoke to Vorontsov. To get matters started on a positive note, I asked him to thank Brezhnev for Soviet hospitality. At the same time I stressed that the agreed joint "auspices" for negotiations — to which the Soviets had paid so much attention — presupposed the rapid fulfillment of Brezhnev's promise to bring about the release of Israeli prisoners of war. I then turned to the main purpose of my call, which was to inform Vorontsov of the reported cease-fire violations, with each party accusing the other. The best remedy, I said, would be to have the Security Council instruct Waldheim to call on the parties to observe the cease-fire immediately. We would go along if the Security Council wished to send UN observers or a UN force. Vorontsov was clearly without instructions. He confined himself to cryptic grunts of "yep" and "right" to indicate that he had understood. When I offered Vorontsov the White House switchboard to speed up communications with Moscow, he declined, assuring me he would be able to get through "in no time." In other words, as I had presumed, Dobrynin had pleaded poor communications on the first day of the war and asked for our facilities as a device to demonstrate the absence of Soviet-Arab collusion.

Within five minutes Vorontsov was back on the phone. Obviously, my message had crossed with one from Moscow, which by now was clearly alarmed. There was a note for me from Brezhnev — a highly unusual procedure, since in the past the General Secretary had invariably addressed his communications to Nixon. It took an hour for Brezhnev's message to be translated and sent over from the Soviet Embassy. In it he told me that Israeli forces were moving southward along the west bank of the Suez Canal. This news came from Moscow's "own reliable information" — in other words, not from Egyptian sources but presumably from the supersonic MiG-25 Foxbats that were flying reconnaissance missions from Egyptian airfields. Brezhnev called Israeli actions "unacceptable" and a "flagrant deceit," from which one had to conclude that the Egyptians were in deep trouble. He suggested a Security Council meeting at noon — less than two hours away — reconfirming the cease-fire, and ordering all forces to be withdrawn to the line they occupied when the October 22 cease-fire resolution had passed, or twelve hours *before* the cease-fire was required to go into effect. (A clever Soviet ploy, this would have put the Israelis well behind the lines from which they obviously jumped off when the current fighting started.) Brezhnev enclosed a Soviet draft of a Security Council resolution embodying his ideas.

We were now in a serious predicament. The urgency of Brezhnev's appeal suggested that the plight of the Egyptian Third Army was far more serious than our own intelligence had yet discovered or the Israelis had told us. If the United States held still while the Egyptian army was being destroyed after an American-sponsored cease-fire and a Secretary of State's visit to Israel, not even the most moderate Arab could cooperate with us any longer. We had to move quickly.

At 11:04 A.M. I urgently contacted Simcha Dinitz to see whether he had anything to add to Keating's report. He did not know the location of the new battle lines. He could tell me, however, on behalf of the Prime Minister "personally, confidentially and sincerely that none of the actions taken on the Egyptian front were initiated by us." With all my affection for Golda, I thought she was imposing on my credulity with her definition of "initiate." It was not plausible that the Egyptian Third Army should launch attacks after a cease-fire that had saved it from being overwhelmed; and that it should then immediately ask everyone within reach for yet another cease-fire, shooting all the time at passive Israelis who were only defending themselves while advancing.

But this was not the time for abstract debate. I went through the Soviet draft UN resolution with Dinitz. I told him we would not go along with the Soviet formulation that the parties return to the lines existing when the cease-fire resolution was adopted by the Security Council. But I did not see how we could refuse an appeal to return to the lines existing when the cease-fire went into effect (twelve hours later). I said we favored the introduction of UN observers. Dinitz promised to seek instructions.

A few minutes later Golda called primarily to assure me that Egypt had been the first to break the cease-fire. I mumbled something about my impression that her soldiers were obviously not heartbroken by that unexpected turn of events. Having proved my skill at repartee, I explained my thinking on the UN resolution. I suggested that Israel pull back a few hundred yards from wherever it was now and call it the old cease-fire line. "How can anyone ever know where a line is or was in the desert?" I said. Golda's melancholy at my obtuseness was palpable even at a distance of six thousand miles. She replied: "They will know where our present line is, all right."

Now I understood. Israel had cut the last supply route to the city of Suez. The Egyptian Third Army on the east bank of the Canal was totally cut off (see the map on page 566). A crisis was upon us.

My first effort was to gain time to defuse it. At 11:32 A.M. I contacted Vorontsov. We would not mind calling the Security Council for noon, I said, but we would not be ready to vote until considerably later. In any event, we were not prepared to accept the Soviet proposal demanding withdrawal to lines occupied at the time of the Security Council vote on the cease-fire.

At noon, Dinitz called with a rather complicated message. Its essence was that Israeli forces would not withdraw from the positions they now held. The Israeli government agreed, he said, with the argument that no one could tell where the original cease-fire line had been, so it would not accept a call to withdraw to it. Israel did not wish to undermine the authority of the UN by agreeing to an inherently unenforceable new resolution. Such delicacy showed a solicitude for the UN for which little in previous Israeli practice had prepared us. Nor did it solve our problem. We instructed Ambassador Scali in New York to stall until we had decided how to proceed.

At 12:36 P.M. an urgent message arrived from Brezhnev, this time to "Esteemed Mr. President." It spoke heatedly of Israeli "treachery"; it offered absolute assurance that the Arab leaders would observe the cease-fire. The message's passion was achieved at the cost of precision, for it omitted the issue likely to give us the greatest difficulty — whether Israel should withdraw and to what line. It concentrated simply on stopping the fighting. In the name of a nonexistent US–Soviet guarantee of the cease-fire — perhaps misleadingly put about by the Soviets to induce Cairo to accept the original cease-fire — it asked us to take "the most decisive measures" jointly "without delay" to impose the cease-fire. My assessment was that if a new cease-fire was all that was wanted, our task would be relatively easy; if an Israeli withdrawal was envisaged, we were in for a tempestuous time.

To preempt a more concrete Soviet proposal, we interpreted Brezhnev's message in the first sense in our reply, which went out under Nixon's name within the hour and which treated the available facts as more clear-cut than we really felt they were:

I want to assure you that we assume full responsibility to bring about a complete end of hostilities on the part of Israel. Our own information would indicate that the responsibility for the violation of the cease-fire belongs to the Egyptian side, but this is not the time to debate that particular issue. We have insisted with Israel that they take immediate steps to cease hostilities, and I urge that you take similar measures with respect to the Egyptian side.

At 1:35 P.M. I conveyed our decision to Vorontsov. We would support a new call for a cease-fire and for a return to the positions occupied by the two sides when the cease-fire became effective. I warned Vorontsov that the location of that line would have to be negotiated between Egypt and Israel. And I left no doubt that we expected that argument to be prolonged. "We want you and us to be slow about that debate," I said. Vorontsov seemed eager to enter into the spirit of my approach: "Let them argue but just not fight." For good measure I added that everything would be simpler if Egypt released Israeli prisoners.

It took Vorontsov only five minutes to check with Moscow and confirm its acceptance. At 2:26 P.M. Brezhnev took the unheard-of step of reiterating it in another message to Nixon. We still did not know exactly where the Israeli army was located. But the urgency of Soviet communications left little doubt that the Egyptian army was in perilous straits.

We thought we had given Israel the maximum flexibility to bargain; it could use this negotiation to press some of its other concerns, especially the release of prisoners. But Israel wanted what we could not grant: a veto over all our decisions regardless of the merits of the issue and a free hand to destroy the Egyptian Third Army.

That Tuesday afternoon, October 23, we received a blistering communication from Golda, which Dinitz read to us. She chose to construe the proposed new Security Council resolution as an Egyptian-Soviet imposition growing out of an Egyptian violation of the cease-fire: "It is impossible for Israel to accept that time and again it must face Russian and Egyptian ultimatums which will subsequently be assented to by the United States." It was, of course, hardly an ultimatum to ask Israel and Egypt to cease firing and to negotiate a return to a line we had carefully not specified. We had modified the original Soviet proposal substantially in Israel's favor. But all the frustrations of the three difficult weeks found expression in Israel's reaction. Golda informed us that Israel would not comply with the proposed resolution or even talk about it. Israel seemed determined to end the war with a humiliation for Egypt. We had no interest in seeing Sadat destroyed — even less so via the collapse of a cease-fire we had cosponsored. And if Israel had been less shaken by the events of the previous weeks, it too would have understood that what it sought would end any hope for peace and doom it to perpetual struggle. For if Sadat fell, the odds were that he would be replaced by a radical pro-Soviet leader; Soviet arms would in a measurable time reconstitute the equivalent of the Third Army; and sooner or later there would be another war reviving the same dilemmas we had just barely surmounted. The peace process dominated by us would end before it was even started; when restored in an uncertain future, it would be under much less favorable auspices.

The Israeli cabinet was too absorbed in its national travail to share that perspective. Its goal was revenge and the restoration of its reputation for invincibility. Never having known peace, it saw little point in giving up a tangible gain — however acquired — for a vague American intuition about a possible peace process. The victim of several past wars erupting out of armistice conditions, Israel did not consider the violation of the latest one a major international event.

Matters looked dramatically different in Cairo. At 3:15 P.M. an urgent message from Sadat direct to Nixon was delivered through intelligence channels — the first time Sadat's name was cited explicitly as the originator, demonstrating the gravity of the situation. Sadat made the extraordinary proposal that the United States, with which Egypt had not had diplomatic relations for six years, should "intervene effectively, even if that necessitates the use of forces, in order to guarantee the full implementation of the cease-fire resolution in accordance with the joint US–USSR agreement." The letter went on to allege (based probably on Soviet misrepresentation) that the United States had offered a "guarantee" of the cease-fire: "What is happening now, in the light of your guarantees, does not induce confidence in any other future guarantees." Though threatening the end of the budding US–Egyptian relationship, the letter nonetheless concluded: "with warmest regards."

The Egyptian proposal that we use American forces against our ally Israel was, of course, no more tenable than the Israeli desire that we run diplomatic interference while it strangled an Egyptian army trapped *after* the cease-fire. So we decided to stick to our course of working to stop the fighting and then to encourage a negotiation over the location of the cease-fire lines. At 5:15 P.M. I replied to the Brezhnev message of early in the day that had been addressed to me (before the messages to Nixon). Duplicating Nixon's reply but going beyond it in specificity, I affirmed that we had agreed to a new joint resolution, despite some reservations, because of the importance of making the cease-fire effective. Support of the cease-fire was coupled with considerable vagueness as to what the parties were supposed to do afterward. I stressed the difficulty of determining the actual positions at the time the October 22 cease-fire went into effect:

> As I said to Mr. Vorontsov, and as he confirmed, our willingness to accept the principle of your Security Council proposal was made possible when your government assured me that it will show moderation when differences ensue between the parties, as to the [cease-fire] positions in dispute.

And I stressed again that an immediate exchange of prisoners would be extremely helpful in assuring an "effective cease-fire."

Late Tuesday afternoon, we replied to Sadat on behalf of Nixon. We disposed first of the Soviet claim that the United States had "guaranteed" to enforce the cease-fire: "All we guaranteed — no matter what you may have been told from other sources — was to engage fully and constructively in promoting a political process designed to make possible a political settlement." Nevertheless, our message continued, we had on our own urged Israel to comply with Resolution 338. At the same time we recommended that Egyptian forces, too, maintain the cease-fire.

At 8:30 P.M. Dinitz informed me that I could pass Golda's solemn pledge to Sadat that if Egypt actually observed the cease-fire, Israeli forces, too, would stop shooting. The generosity of this proposal was somewhat diluted by Dinitz's admission that all roads to the Third Army had been cut. Starving the Third Army out would be a slower process than destroying it militarily. But it would lead to the same result and was almost certain to bring about a confrontation with the Soviets. They could not possibly hold still while a cease-fire they had cosponsored was turned into a trap for a client state.

Still, that problem was, I hoped, not yet upon us. Israel had agreed to a new cease-fire, and, not unanxious to claim credit for our part, I sent a conciliatory note to Hafiz Ismail. I urged that Sadat ask his army to stop firing. To leave no loophole I added: "Should he decide to issue such an order Mr. Ismail may, if he wishes, inform Dr. Kissinger of this fact for the guidance of the US side should other governments approach us."

Thus by the end of Tuesday, October 23, calm seemed to have been restored. The Security Council passed Resolution 339, which reaffirmed the October 22 cease-fire and "urged" (not "demanded" — a minor drafting achievement in which I took a pride not requited in Israel) the parties to return to the previous lines.* Israel and Egypt agreed to observe it effective at 7:00 A.M. local time the next morning, October 24 (1:00 A.M. in Washington). In addition, late on October 23, Syria finally announced its formal acceptance of the cease-fire.

At a minimum we seemed to have regained maneuvering room for diplomacy. Haig had told me Tuesday night that Nixon was "down, very down" over Watergate. Eight impeachment resolutions had that day been submitted to the House of Representatives Judiciary Committee. But I knew that whatever happened in his personal tragedy, Nixon would be firm and acute in the complicated diplomacy ahead of us.

The Alert: October 24–25

CRISES have their own momentum. A halt of military activities suited our diplomatic purposes but it ran counter to military realities. Egypt's Third Army was bound to try to break out of its encirclement; cease-fire or not, Israel would be reluctant to give up the opportunity to end the war with a knockout blow.

Waiting for me in my White House office at 8:00 A.M. Wednesday morning, October 24 — the new cease-fire theoretically seven hours old — was a message from Hafiz Ismail informing me that "the Israelis have resumed their attacks." Sadat would be communicating with Nixon again urgently to seek "effective measures to oblige Israel to observe the cease-fire."

Dinitz was reached at home but said he needed time to get to his office, which had a direct line to Israel. At 9:22 A.M. he was at last

---

*The text of Resolution 339 is in the backnotes.[3]

ready to talk. He told me the trapped Egyptian Third Army had tried to break out of its siege in three directions: west toward Suez City, east toward the Mitla Pass, and north toward the Egyptian Second Army. It was being repulsed everywhere; all Israel was doing was defending itself and just "blocking" the Egyptian offensives (in the process of which Israel somehow seized the Egyptian naval base at Suez). I cannot say that I gave Dinitz's report credence equal to my affection for him. I could understand efforts by a trapped army to attempt to lift the siege, to break out toward its supply base. But an attack toward the Mitla Pass would be *away* from its cut communications; it could have no strategic objective. I could more easily understand an Israeli effort to collapse the Egyptian bridgehead on the east bank of the Canal. "If you wind up tonight having captured 20,000 Egyptians," I warned Dinitz a few minutes later, "you won't be able to tell us that they started the fighting."

No sooner had I finished with Dinitz than Sadat's message to Nixon arrived. Israel had resumed the assault, Sadat charged, pleading with Nixon once again "to intervene, even on the ground, to force Israel to comply with the cease-fire. That much you have promised." It did not sound like the communication of a man who believed his army to be on the offensive.

I immediately informed Dinitz. It was clear that if we let this go on, a confrontation with the Soviets was inevitable. Gone too would be all hopes for a new relationship with Egypt, together with all prospects for negotiation. Late the previous evening, the Soviets had issued an official statement warning Israel of the "greatest consequences" if it did not stop its "aggression." All the factors that had elicited the alerting of the Soviet airborne divisions and the augmentation of the Soviet fleet in the Mediterranean had increased in ominous importance now with Brezhnev's personal involvement. I told Dinitz that the art of foreign policy was to know when to clinch one's victories. There were limits beyond which we could not go, with all our friendship for Israel, and one of them was to make the leader of another superpower look like an idiot. I said to Dinitz that if Sadat asked the Soviets, as he had us, to enforce the cease-fire with their own troops, Israel would have outsmarted itself.

Dinitz replied that Israel would stop fighting if the Egyptians did, and he offered to allow American military attachés from our Embassy in Tel Aviv to go to the front to verify that the cease-fire was being honored. I recognized these as essentially time-wasting devices. By then a battle had already been going on for the better part of a day. It would take many hours of exchanges to establish another cease-fire and to get American military observers to the farthest part of the Sinai.

But in foreign policy one must do with what one has. We promptly replied to Sadat. Whatever our suspicions, the message from Nixon steered a carefully neutral course, informing Egypt of our opposition to offensive operations and holding out the carrot of opening peace negotiations:

The Israeli government has replied to the effect that the attacks are being initiated by the Third Egyptian Army; that Israeli forces are on the defensive and have been ordered to only shoot back on attack. From here, the true facts are impossible to determine. I want to assure you that the U.S. is unalterably opposed to offensive Israeli military action and is prepared to take effective steps to end them. In the meantime, could you make sure that all military action is stopped also by your forces. Secretary Kissinger is getting in touch with Mr. Ismail later today about the possibility of direct conversations between our two sides about post-war diplomacy.

We had not yet heard from Moscow. But it was probable that Sadat had sent a similar urgent appeal to Brezhnev. Transmission, translation, and deliberation would waste some time. But I was certain that we would not have to wait long for a chilly blast from Moscow.

I decided to preempt it. At 9:45 A.M. I called the just-returned Dobrynin to tell him that "the madmen in the Middle East seem to be at it again." Without much conviction, I said that each side was claiming to be the victim of attack by the other. Since there was no point in being on the defensive, I asserted that "this time the Egyptians may have started it but we are not sure. We have no real basis for judgment. I just want you to know what we are doing." I explained that we had asked the Israelis to stop offensive operations. They had agreed if Egypt reciprocated; we would do our utmost to see that the cease-fire was enforced. Dobrynin had no instructions; he would have to report to Moscow. That suited me fine. Twenty minutes later, around 10:10 A.M., I gave the Soviet bureaucracy something else to ponder. I told Dobrynin, as if it were a major concession, of Israel's suggestion that American military attachés visit the front to observe the cease-fire until UN observers arrived. I was also sending him a copy of the latest Nixon message to Sadat. This would give the Kremlin a face-saving formula if it was seeking one; it was also a general sign of goodwill.

On the theory that so long as other countries are studying your communications they cannot be thinking up initiatives of their own, we briefed Sadat on the latest developments:

We have just been informed by the Israeli Prime Minister that strict instructions have been issued to Israeli armed forces to stay in defensive positions and not to fire unless they are fired upon.

In response to your proposal for U.S. ground observers, the Israeli Government has also agreed to permit U.S. military attachés to proceed immediately

578 *Years of Upheaval*

to the area of the conflict in order to observe that these orders are being carried out.

It would be very helpful at this time if you could instruct your own forces accordingly.

But events in the Middle East had developed a momentum not controllable by such maneuvers. At 10:19 A.M. Dobrynin called with the news that another message from Brezhnev was on its way. It was sharp but as yet unspecific. Its salutation was simply to "Mr. President," dropping the "Esteemed" of the previous day. It informed us in some detail of "defiant" Israeli attacks on both sides of the Suez Canal within hours of the agreement to the latest cease-fire resolution. Its conclusion was as vague as its tone was menacing:

We, naturally, have questions as to what is behind all this. I wish to say it frankly, Mr. President, that we are confident that you have possibilities to influence Israel with the aim of putting an end to such a provocative behavior of Tel Aviv.

We would like to hope that we both will be true to our word and to the understanding we have reached.

I will appreciate information on your steps towards Israel's strict and immediate compliance with the decision of the Security Council of this October 22 and 23.

I told Dobrynin he would hear from us when we had formulated a reply. In the meantime I had to impress on Israel the gravity of the crisis. Whenever I needed to enhance a message or avoid a personal confrontation between me and the Israeli cabinet, I would ask Haig to call Dinitz on behalf of Nixon. I did so on this occasion. At this stage of Nixon's agony, I doubt that Dinitz took the stratagem too seriously — but at a minimum it showed that painful decisions were needed. Haig demanded an end to offensive Israeli military operations.

At 10:30 A.M. on Wednesday, I chaired a WSAG meeting, briefing my colleagues on what had happened, and urging a steady course:

The Arabs may despise us, or hate us, or loathe us, but they have learned that if they want a settlement, they have to come to us. No one else can deliver. Three times they have relied on Russian equipment, and three times they have lost it. So, strategically we have a very good hand if we know how to play it.

After the WSAG, I continued my efforts to calm tempers and to gain time for diplomacy. I sent a message to Ismail accepting Sadat's invitation to visit Cairo and proposing an early date, November 7, "to review the situation and plan appropriate actions toward a permanent settlement."

Meanwhile, I learned that Haig's phone call had elicited an ambiguous Israeli response. Dayan sent a message through Dinitz, and Golda saw Ambassador Keating. Both made the same points: The Israelis were trying "to absorb fire without answer"; they had not tried to advance during the day and "they will not try to do so." (This left open the possibility of a war of attrition designed to use up Egyptian supplies and force the surrender of the Third Army.) Israel had asked UN observers to come from Cairo to the west bank of the Canal but the Egyptians appeared to be detaining them. (This left open the issue of what was happening on the east bank.) Israel had concrete evidence that Egypt planned to continue fighting, supported by tanks sent from Cairo to break through the Israeli line on the west bank. The Israelis had no intention of attacking Egyptian forces on the west bank. (We were concerned, of course, about Israeli activity on the east bank.) Dayan added that Keating would be kept fully informed and given access to Israeli information "in a further effort to calm the Secretary and to demonstrate Israeli good intentions."

Whatever our private thoughts, we treated Dayan's information at face value. Thus a Presidential message went to Brezhnev at 1:00 P.M. summarizing the Israeli assurances. A similar communication went from me to Ismail. But mine to Cairo crossed with a climactic new message from Sadat to Nixon. Sadat claimed that Israel had once again initiated offensive operations, and he then agreed to what we had *not* offered: the immediate dispatch of American observers or troops for the implementation of the Security Council cease-fire resolution on the *Egyptian* side. What was new was what I had feared three hours earlier: Sadat told us that he was "formally" issuing the same request to the Soviets. Shortly after Sadat's private message, I learned through a news bulletin that Cairo had announced publicly that it was calling for a Security Council meeting to ask that American and Soviet "forces" be sent to the Middle East. The makings of a crisis were appearing.

We were not prepared to send American troops to Egypt, nor would we accept the dispatch of Soviet forces. We had not worked for years to reduce the Soviet military presence in Egypt only to cooperate in reintroducing it as the result of a UN resolution. Nor would we participate in a joint force with the Soviets, which would legitimize their role in the area and strengthen radical elements. Anti-Soviet moderates like Saudi Arabia, the Emirates, Jordan, and Kuwait might well panic at this demonstration of US–Soviet cooperation. The Soviet force might prove impossible to remove; there would be endless pretexts for it to intervene at any point against Israel, or against moderate Arab governments, for that matter.

While we were waiting to see whether the Cairo report would turn out to be a false alarm, the Soviets stepped up the tension. At 3:35 P.M. Dobrynin called with a message, this time from Gromyko. The fact that it was at the foreign minister's level was a slight blessing because it de-escalated the level of the confronters, but the substance was ominous enough. Gromyko alleged that Israel was intensifying military operations and that Israeli assurances to the contrary were false. No specific action was requested other than that I inform the President — leaving it to us to solve an undefined problem, thereby creating a basis for holding us accountable. I told Dobrynin to come by my office at 4:00 P.M. In the meantime, I checked with Dinitz. He emphasized that he had been told not five minutes earlier that all was now quiet on the Sinai front.

There were several explanations for the conflicting Soviet and Israeli claims. They could both be telling the truth; Gromyko and Dinitz might be operating on different time scales. Allowing for transmission time, word of the end of military operations might not have reached Moscow when Gromyko's message was sent. If that was the case, Moscow would calm down once the facts reached it. Or, one side or both might *not* be telling the truth. If Israel was continuing military operations contrary to its report to us, a confrontation was certain. If Gromyko knew the Israelis had stopped but sent the message anyway, Moscow either wanted to garner credit in Cairo, pretending that it had extracted an already accomplished cease-fire, or else it was seeking a pretext for a showdown to free the Third Army and send its troops back into Egypt. In any event, a cease-fire would not solve our basic problem. Even should military operations have stopped, the Third Army was still encircled and imperiled.

We were determined to resist by force if necessary the introduction of Soviet troops into the Middle East regardless of the pretext under which they arrived. When Dobrynin called on me shortly after 4:00 P.M., I told him that we would veto any UN resolution calling for the sending of troops by permanent members of the Security Council — both a delicate way of phrasing the issue and a face-saving formula for the Soviets to back down.

Dobrynin was without new instructions but spoke in a most conciliatory fashion. Since it was now after 11:00 P.M. in Moscow, he must also have decided that it was too late for new instructions and therefore matters might be quieting down. He speculated that perhaps the best way to proceed was not to bother with any formal new Security Council resolution. Rather, the President of the Security Council could simply express a "consensus" favoring another cease-fire appeal. I agreed, with some relief, that this was a good way to defuse the crisis. The atmosphere seemed calm enough then — as I recounted at a press conference the next day — for us to exchange ideas on the site, participation, and procedures for a Mideast peace conference. If Dobrynin knew what he was talking about (and he generally did) the Soviet leadership had decided to make the best of a bad situation and steer matters rapidly toward a peace conference as the best way out of its dilemmas, including the fate of the Third Army. In this we were willing to cooperate.

In the same spirit I asked the Near East Bureau of the State Department to prepare papers on procedures and composition for a peace conference. In New York, Soviet UN representative Yakov Malik had as yet given no sign of supporting Sadat's request for American and Soviet forces. It was getting to be past midnight in Moscow. It seemed that we had managed to avoid a crisis at least for the better part of another day — and every hour gained improved the prospect of a diplomatic outcome.

Then suddenly at 7:05 P.M. that Wednesday evening, October 24 (2:05 A.M. Moscow time), the Soviet leaders decided on a showdown. Dobrynin announced to me that Malik had just been instructed to support a resolution calling for the dispatch of American and Soviet troops to the Middle East if someone else introduced it. This, I knew, would be easy to arrange; at a minimum Egypt would do so. I just had time to tell Dobrynin that we would never agree when I had to interrupt for a call from the President.

Nixon was as agitated and emotional as I had ever heard him. Talk of his possible impeachment increased daily. He expressed the hope that at a briefing scheduled for the next morning I would tell the Congressional leadership about his central, indispensable role in managing the Mideast crisis. He had already urged me to call some Senators to make this pitch — a symptom of the extremity in which this proud man felt himself. He spoke of his political end, even his physical demise: "They are doing it because of their desire to kill the President. And they may succeed. I may physically die." I tried to soothe him. He was at his best in adversity, I said. But for once he was not to be reassured:

What they care about is destruction. It brings me sometimes to feel like saying the hell with it. I would like to see them run this country and see what they do. . . . The real tragedy is if I move out everything we have done will crumble. The Russians will look for other customers, the Chinese will lose confidence, the Europeans will — They just don't realize they are throwing everything out the window. I don't know what in the name of God. . . .

Here was the Watergate tragedy encapsuled in a brief phone conversation. Nixon was correct in his perception of the probable international consequences of Watergate and not too far from the mark about the motives of some of his tormentors. Yet it was also true that he had given his lifelong enemies the opportunity to settle old scores. And now each side was trapped on a collision course it could not alter: his critics in the passions of a lifetime; Nixon in the paralysis of an approaching nightmare, unable either to avert it by timely disclosure or to transcend it by an act of grace.

We were heading into what could have become the gravest foreign policy crisis of the Nixon Presidency — because it involved a direct confrontation of the superpowers — with a President overwhelmed by his persecution and with a Congress that had just, in the War Powers Act, restricted the President's authority to use military force. It was in a somber mood that at 7:15 P.M. I turned from the conversation with the President to resume talking to Dobrynin. He admitted that what he told me three hours earlier was "wrong." The Soviet Union now wanted the United Nations to send troops — including Soviet troops — to the Middle East to enforce the cease-fire. I said curtly that we would veto it.

Urgent preparations had to be made. In the next ten minutes I took several steps. I instructed Scali to veto any peacekeeping force that included the superpowers, and also to veto any condemnation of Israel since that could provide the pretext for later intervention. The alternative we favored was augmentation of the UN observer force already called for in Resolution 339. I also told Scali to inform Chinese Ambassador Huang Hua of my instructions, as I was pretty certain that China did not want to see Soviet forces under UN auspices in the Middle East. China was likely to join our veto if it knew our views. Since I did not know which Chinese ambassador had the better communication, I simultaneously asked Scowcroft to inform Huang Zhen, head of the Liaison Office in Washington, of our decision and preference.

With the preliminary battle lines thus drawn, I called Dobrynin again, at 7:25 P.M. I urged him not to push us to an extreme. We would cooperate on sending more UN observers; we would not accept Soviet troops in any guise. Dobrynin replied that in Moscow "they have become so angry they want troops." He blamed us for allowing "the Israelis to do what they wanted." I urged him to prevent such a resolution from being introduced: "It would be a pity to be in a confrontation." In a crisis there was nothing congenial about Dobrynin; he was all business. He would mention any comments to Moscow, he said, but he was sure they had already discussed it and made up their minds.

I immediately called British Ambassador Lord Cromer to ask London to join our veto. At 7:35 P.M. I briefed Dinitz. Just after 8:00 P.M., I called Dobrynin again. According to our best information, I told him, *no* fighting was now going on in the Middle East. There was still time to avoid a confrontation. It was a way of warning without turning it into a test of manhood. Dobrynin played it the same way. "Let me know what the exact situation is," he said coldly and matter-of-factly, as if Moscow needed our intelligence on Middle East deployments, "and I will send a telegram."

Incongruously, in the midst of the building confrontation, a message from Hafiz Ismail arrived accepting my proposal to visit Cairo on November 7.

At 8:25 P.M. Dobrynin told me that Egyptian Foreign Minister Zayyat, in his speech minutes before in the Security Council, had formally asked the United States and the Soviet Union to send forces. I urged "great restraint." The Egyptian proposal was not yet in the form of a resolution. If it became one, "it would be that from the closest cooperation we turn to a very dangerous course." Dobrynin had no new instructions; he was "only saying what he [Zayyat] said in the Security Council."

I immediately sent an urgent message to Sadat in Nixon's name telling him that we would veto any resolution embodying the Egyptian appeal. It also warned that such a course might cause me to cancel my trip to Cairo. Sadat would be jeopardizing his careful edging toward us if he insisted on the dispatch of superpower forces.

Then there was somewhat better news from the Security Council. John Scali called to tell me that the Soviet speech, while condemning Israel and bordering on an attack on the United States, fell short of actually endorsing the Egyptian call for superpower intervention. I told Scali to present our position; in a strong speech he opposed the intervention of the great powers and urged the rapid deployment of more UN observers. He did not blame either Egypt or Israel.

At 9:32 P.M. I informed Haig, for the President, of the state of play at the UN and we discussed a possible opening statement for a Presidential news conference scheduled for the next day. The President had retired for the night. Haig and I agreed we might be heading for the most explosive crisis of an unquiet tenure.

Within minutes, the forebodings were dramatically fulfilled. There was a call from Dobrynin at 9:35 P.M. It was 4:35 A.M. in Moscow but he had a letter from Brezhnev so urgent that he had to read it to me on the phone. I could see why. It was in effect an ultimatum: It proposed joint Soviet and American military forces to ensure the implementation not only of the cease-fire but also "of our understanding with you on the guarantee of the implementation of the decisions of the Security Council" — in other words, the imposition of a comprehensive peace:

. . . Let us together, the USSR and the United States, urgently dispatch to Egypt the Soviet and American military contingents, to insure the implementation of the decision of the Security Council of October 22 and 23 concerning the cessation of fire and of all military activities and also of our understanding with you on the guarantee of the implementation of the decisions of the Security Council.

It is necessary to adhere without delay. I will say it straight that if you find it impossible to act jointly with us in this matter, we should be faced with the necessity urgently to consider the question of taking appropriate steps unilaterally. We cannot allow arbitrariness on the part of Israel. . . .

It was one of the most serious challenges to an American President by a Soviet leader, from its peremptory salutation, "Mr. President," to its equally peremptory conclusion demanding an "immediate and clear reply." In between it proposed that American and Soviet military forces impose not just a cease-fire but a final settlement on terms that were not specified but that had been repeatedly spelled out by Moscow during the year and had just as often been rejected by us. And it threatened to send troops unilaterally if we refused.*

The proposal was unthinkable. If we agreed to a joint role with the Soviet Union, its troops would reenter Egypt with our blessing. Either we would be the tail to the Soviet kite in a joint power play against Israel, or we would end up clashing with Soviet forces in a country that was bound to share Soviet objectives regarding the cease-fire or could not afford to be perceived as opposing them.

But the impact would go far beyond Egypt. If Soviet forces appeared dramatically in Cairo with the United States as an appendage, our traditional friends among Arab moderates would be profoundly unnerved by the evident fact of US–Soviet condominium. The strategy we had laboriously pursued in four years of diplomacy and two weeks of crisis would disintegrate: Egypt would be drawn back into the Soviet orbit, the Soviet Union and its radical allies would emerge as the dominant factor in the Middle East. China and Europe would be shocked by the appearance of US–Soviet military collaboration in so vital a region. If the joint effort collapsed and turned into a US–Soviet crisis — as was probable — we would be alone.

There was no question in my mind that we would have to reject the Soviet proposal. And we would have to do so in a manner that shocked the Soviets into abandoning the unilateral move they were threatening — and, from all our information, planning. For we had tangible reasons to take the threat seriously. The CIA reported that the Soviet airlift to the Middle East had stopped early on the twenty-fourth, even though ours was continuing; the ominous implication was that the aircraft were being assembled to carry some of the airborne divisions whose increased alert status had also been noted. East German forces were also at increased readiness. The number of Soviet ships in the Mediterranean had grown to 85 — an all-time high. (It later reached more than 100.) We discovered the next day that a Soviet flotilla of twelve ships, including two amphibious vessels, was heading for Alexandria. There were other ominous reports in especially sensitive areas. And I could not avoid the conviction that Nixon's evident weakness over Watergate had not a little to do with the Politburo's willingness to dare so crass a challenge.

---

*Dobrynin told me later that I had misunderstood the word "adhere" in the first sentence of the second paragraph quoted above; what he had dictated was "act here." Aside from the fact that this would not change the meaning of the letter, we never received an official correction, though in one of Nixon's messages to Brezhnev we quoted our version to make our point.

Some of these thoughts ran through my mind as I read Brezhnev's letter back to Dobrynin to make sure I had understood it correctly. I warned him against a unilateral move. He said he would report the warning to Moscow. Both of us were now caught in the rhythm of confrontation, which has its own logic. One side or the other would have to veer away from collision.

At 9:50 P.M. I informed Haig. He first thought the Soviets were bluffing: "They're not going to put forces in at the end of a war." I did not see it as a bluff but it made no difference. We could not run the risk that they were not. If we remained passive in the face of the threat, the Soviet leadership would see no obstacle to turning it into a reality. We had no choice except to call the bluff, if that was what it was, or face the reality if it was serious. I asked Haig whether I should wake up the President. He replied curtly: "No." I knew what that meant. Haig thought the President too distraught to participate in the preliminary discussion. It was a daunting responsibility to assume. From my own conversation with Nixon earlier in the evening, I was convinced Haig was right.

The decision before us urgently required a meeting of our government's most senior officials. I called a WSAG meeting to convene at the State Department at 10:30 P.M. Meanwhile, at 10:00 P.M., I told Dinitz of the Brezhnev letter, and asked him for Israel's views. We had no intention of accepting the proposal, I said.

At 10:15 P.M. I called Dobrynin to make sure that he knew where we stood, and to discourage precipitate action:

KISSINGER: We are assembling our people to consider your letter. I just wanted you to know if any unilateral action is taken before we have had a chance to reply that will be very serious.

DOBRYNIN: Yes, all right.

KISSINGER: This is a matter of great concern. Don't you pressure us. I want to repeat again, don't pressure us!

DOBRYNIN: All right.

In a subtle way, this conversation added to the impact of Brezhnev's threatening letter. It would have been easy for Dobrynin to say that the Soviets would in no case act until they had heard from us. He might have indicated in the hundred ways available to a seasoned professional that we were overreacting, that the threat of unilateral action was a figure of speech, the normal recourse of a sovereign country that feels pushed against the wall. Instead, Dobrynin permitted the impression to stand that a crisis was indeed impending, and that nothing had changed to defer the possibility of a unilateral Soviet military move in the Middle East. That awareness dominated the deliberations that our government was about to start.

Haig and I conferred again at 10:20 P.M. We were now both convinced that we faced a genuine threat of Soviet intervention. Haig urged that we move the WSAG meeting to the Situation Room, to demonstrate White House control and because he thought — correctly — that I should chair it in my capacity as Presidential Assistant and not as Secretary of State. We discussed again whether to awaken the President. Haig reasserted, somewhat ambiguously, that my best move would be to hold the meeting at the White House. The implication was that he would handle the internal White House notifications. Nixon has written in his memoirs:

When Haig informed me about this message, I said that he and Kissinger should have a meeting at the White House to formulate plans for a firm reaction to what amounted to a scarcely veiled threat of unilateral Soviet intervention. Words were not making our point — we needed action, even the shock of a military alert.[4]

The meeting started in the White House Situation Room, in the basement of the West Wing, with me in the chair, at 10:40 P.M., Wednesday, October 24. It went on with various interruptions until 2:00 A.M. early Thursday. Present were Secretary of Defense James Schlesinger; Director of Central Intelligence William Colby; Chairman of the Joint Chiefs of Staff Admiral Thomas Moorer; Presidential chief of staff Alexander Haig; Deputy Assistant to the President for National Security Affairs General Brent Scowcroft; Commander Jonathan T. Howe, my military assistant at the NSC; and me.

The White House later described it as a National Security Council meeting. There has been some discussion since of whether it was a "proper" National Security Council meeting if the President did not attend. (We were also without a Vice President, since Gerald Ford, nominated by President Nixon on October 12, had not yet been confirmed by the Senate.) It was in effect the statutory membership of the National Security Council minus these two men.*

---

*The National Security Act of 1947, which established the NSC, authorized the President, if he so desired, to designate another Council member to preside in his place. The NSC's statutory membership included not only the Secretaries of State and Defense (with the CIA Director and Chairman of the JCS as statutory advisers), but also the heads of organizations such as the National Security Resources Board (since defunct) and others such as the Service Departments, long since reduced in effectiveness. The act did not mention departments such as Treasury, whose participation was often essential to a realistic discussion of world affairs. The practice therefore developed since the Fifties, as envisaged by the act, that others could be invited at the pleasure of the President. Johnson often had Justice Abe Fortas sit in; Nixon frequently included Attorney General John Mitchell. By the same token, the President was not deprived of his right to call a meeting of key advisers without designating it in any particular fashion — NSC or otherwise. In short, the composition and agenda of an NSC meeting — or whether it was an NSC meeting at all — has over the practice of a generation been left to Presidential discretion and is an issue of no practical or legal consequence.

I now discover that our internal records called it a WSAG "meeting of principals" — a rare but not unprecedented occurrence. Since my elevation to Secretary of State, I thought it proper that the Defense Department representative be of Cabinet rank as well; therefore Secretary Schlesinger attended. Nixon had never attended WSAG deliberations in the past (though he occasionally appeared for brief pep talks). No one present thought it unusual that he did not do so now.

I began the meeting with a detailed briefing. There had been no particular cause for alarm for most of the day. In fact, matters had seemed to be calming down when suddenly, at about 7:00 P.M. our time (or 2:00 A.M. Moscow time), the Soviets decided at first to support and then to insist on the introduction of a joint US–Soviet military force into the Middle East. I said that in my view, joining the Soviets would be "a mug's game" for us, with devastating consequences to our relations in the Middle East, China, and Europe — all fearful, for various reasons, of a US–Soviet condominium. There were three possibilities: (1) The Soviets had intended this move all along and had invited me to Moscow to gain time for it; (2) they decided on it as the consequences of the Arab defeat began to sink in; or (3) they felt tricked by Israel and by us as the Israelis moved to strangle the Third Army after the cease-fire. I thought that the likely motivation was a combination of 2 and 3.

This was preliminary to one of the more thoughtful discussions that I attended in my government service. The participants weighed Soviet actions, motivations, and intentions. During the night, the consensus emerged that the Kremlin was on the verge of a major decision. We expected the airlift to start at dawn in eastern Europe, about two hours away. At 11:00 P.M. I interrupted the meeting to see Dinitz in the deserted lobby of the West Wing of the White House. I repeated to him that we would reject the Soviet proposal out of hand; only the tactics remained to be decided. We still were eager to hear Israeli views on this.

When I returned to the Situation Room, agreement was quickly reached to test whether we could slow down the Soviets' timetable by drawing them into talks. This suggested an American reply conciliatory in tone but strong in substance. There was consensus, too, that this would have no impact unless we backed it up with some noticeable action that conveyed our determination to resist unilateral moves. Ideally our response should be noted in Moscow *before* our written reply reached there. We therefore interrupted the drafting of a Presidential reply to Brezhnev for a discussion of various readiness measures.

Our forces are normally in various states of alert called DefCons (for Defense Condition), in descending order from DefCon I to DefCon V. DefCon I is war. DefCon II is a condition in which attack is imminent. DefCon III increases readiness without the determination that war is likely; it is in practice the highest stage of readiness for essentially peacetime conditions. Most of our forces were normally at DefCon IV or V except for those in the Pacific, where as a legacy of the Vietnam war they were in 1973 permanently in DefCon III. The Strategic Air Command was usually at DefCon IV.

We all agreed that any increase in readiness would have to go at least to DefCon III before the Soviets would notice it. Even then, they might not recognize the significance of the change rapidly enough to affect their diplomacy. We agreed to discuss additional alert measures not foreseen in DefCon III. In the meantime Admiral Moorer — at 11:41 P.M. — issued orders to all military commands to increase readiness to DefCon III.

Just before — at 11:25 P.M. — Dinitz gave the Israeli reply as to how to deal with the Soviet overture. It was in effect to offer a variant of the Israeli disengagement proposal of 1971: Israeli forces would withdraw to the east bank of the Suez Canal, Egyptian forces to the west bank in a territorial swap; a demilitarized strip of ten kilometers would then be created on each side of the Canal. It was an impossible scheme. Sadat would consider it an insult to be asked to vacate territory that not even the Israelis challenged as Egyptian. Nor could he end the war by withdrawing ten kilometers from where he had started it. And it was too complicated to negotiate in time to head off a Soviet intervention if indeed one was imminent. It might even accelerate the move if Sadat was sufficiently infuriated by it to *insist* on great-power participation. I told Dinitz that I would discuss the proposal with my colleagues but that I knew it would not work. In the event, we grew too preoccupied with forestalling the Soviet move to take up the Israeli scheme.

Our next decision was to seek to close off Moscow's diplomatic options by inducing Cairo to withdraw its invitation to the Soviets to send in troops. At 11:55 P.M. the meeting approved a message to Sadat in Nixon's name reiterating our previous rejection of a joint US–Soviet force. In its operative paragraph the message warned that should Soviet forces appear, we would have to resist them on Egyptian soil. At the very least, in these circumstances my planned trip to Cairo to start the peace process would have to be canceled:

> I ask you to consider the consequences for your country if the two great nuclear countries were thus to confront each other on your soil. I ask you further to consider the impossibility for us undertaking the diplomatic initiative which was to start with Dr. Kissinger's visit to Cairo on November 7 if the forces of one of the great nuclear powers were to be involved militarily on Egyptian soil.

Immediately after we instituted DefCon III, I asked Scowcroft to leave the meeting to call Dobrynin with the following instructions:

[T]ell him to desist from all actions until we have a reply. Tell him you are not empowered to give any reply. I am in a meeting and can't be pulled out. There should be no unilateral actions and if they are taken it would have the most serious consequences. If he says anything you can say you have instructions not to comment. They may as well know that we mean business.

But two could play chicken. Dobrynin made no comment except that he would transmit our message to Moscow. No reassurance; no claim of having been misunderstood; no suggestion that at midnight we all go to bed and resume our discussions in the morning because there was no real threat. Only the laconic comment that he would stand by for our reply.

If Dobrynin's pose was designed to heighten our sense of menace, it succeeded admirably. Our conviction that we were facing an imminent Soviet move was hardly diminished when we learned during the evening that eight Soviet An-22 transport planes — each capable of carrying two hundred or more troops — were slated to fly from Budapest to Egypt in the next few hours. And we discovered too that elements of the East German armed forces had been put on alert effective at 5:00 A.M. Washington time, or five hours away. We estimated that the Soviets could lift 5,000 troops a day into Egypt. We decided that going to DefCon III would not be noted quickly enough by Soviet decision-makers. Something more was necessary. At 12:20 A.M. we alerted the 82d Airborne Division for possible movement. At 12:25 A.M. we ordered the aircraft carrier *Franklin Delano Roosevelt* — now off Italy — to move rapidly to the eastern Mediterranean to join the carrier *Independence* south of Crete. The carrier *John F. Kennedy* and its accompanying task force were ordered to move at full speed from the Atlantic to the Mediterranean.

There was some desultory talk about whether the Soviets would have taken on a "functioning" President. I said: "We are at a point of maximum weakness but if we knuckle under now we are in real trouble." There was some discussion about whether the United States — in response to the Soviet dispatch of troops to Egypt — would be able to make a countervailing move by putting its own troops in the area. There was concern whether our domestic political situation would permit such a military move. But I was adamant that we would have to act in the national interest regardless of media skepticism or political opposition: "If we can't do what is right because we might get killed, then we should do what is right. We will have to contend with the charge in the domestic media that we provoked this. The real charge is that we provoked this by being soft."

The readiness measures were our signal to Moscow. At 12:30 A.M. we returned to drafting the President's formal reply to Brezhnev. We decided to deliver it around 5:30 in the morning Washington time. Insofar as the Soviet decision to intervene depended on our message, it gave us additional time to complete our preparations. And by then the Soviets would notice our troop movements. At 1:03 A.M. I informed Ambassador Cromer for the British government of our various alert measures and of the letter from Brezhnev. I told him that we would formally brief the North Atlantic Council an hour after delivering our reply to the Soviets, or about noon Brussels time. We hoped that Britain would support us in the North Atlantic Council as well as in other capitals.

It was a classic example of the "special relationship" with Britain as well as of the limits of allied consultation. We shared our information with Britain as a matter of course, despite the fact that the Heath government was doing its utmost to distance itself from us in Europe and had rather conspicuously underlined its different perspective in the Middle East. We could not consult the other allies in advance because we wanted the Soviets to pick up our readiness measures themselves and not through allied leaks, which would inevitably include any reassurances we might have given and thus lessen the sense of determination we thought it essential to convey. In retrospect I think this procedure was wrong. We could have informed our allies an hour or two before delivering our reply to Moscow; we should have risked the leaks.

At 1:35 A.M. Dinitz reappeared. He urged on behalf of the Prime Minister that we not ask Israel to pull back to the line it occupied at the time the original cease-fire went into effect (on October 22). I assured him that we had no intention of coercing Israel in response to a Soviet threat.

At 1:45 A.M. Scowcroft, at my request, called Dobrynin again with the same message as before, adding only that we had still several more hours of deliberation ahead of us. Dobrynin could infer from my refusal to talk to him that we were in no mood for negotiations. Once again he replied that he would report, offered no reassurance, and said that he would stand by. Concurrently, we notified the commander of our forces in Europe that he was to delay the scheduled return to the United States of troops participating in an annual NATO exercise designed to test our ability to reinforce Europe rapidly.

At 2:09 A.M., minutes after the conclusion of our formal meeting, I told Dinitz that we had completed our reply to Brezhnev. We would offer no new proposals except to augment the UN observer force. We would unequivocally reject joint military action and we would resist unilateral intervention by force, if necessary. I also asked Dinitz, for my information, how long it would take Israel to destroy the Third Army if a showdown became unavoidable.

At 3:30 A.M. as instructed, the Joint Chiefs of Staff ordered the return of Guam-based B-52s to the United States. They were there as a vestige of the Vietnam war, to deter resumption of the fighting in Indochina. Congressional action in the summer of 1973 had made this impossible. But hoping that Hanoi might feel some uncertainty about our constitutional procedures, we had not moved the planes, recognizing that we could not fool these experts in protracted warfare for long. Now we used the opportunity to end this empty game and in the process give the Soviets another indication that we were assembling our forces for a showdown.

At last, at 5:40 A.M. the reply to Brezhnev was delivered to Dobrynin in Nixon's name. It rejected all Soviet demands. We sent it by messenger, avoiding any softening via an explanation. The letter offered American approval of — and willingness to participate in — an expanded UN truce supervisory force composed of noncombat personnel on a temporary basis whose sole task would be to provide "adequate information concerning compliance by both sides with the terms of the cease-fire." Our reply added:

> You must know, however, that we could in no event accept unilateral action. This would be in violation of our understandings, of the agreed Principles we signed in Moscow in 1972 and of Article II of the Agreement on Prevention of Nuclear War. As I stated above, such action would produce incalculable consequences which would be in the interest of neither of our countries and which would end all we have striven so hard to achieve.

The Crisis Abates

AT 6:30 A.M. Thursday morning, October 25 — after three hours of sleep — I discovered that the American public had already learned of the worldwide alert of American forces. It was all over the morning news. I was shocked. This unexpected publicity would inevitably turn the event into an issue of prestige with Moscow, unleashing popular passions at home and seriously complicating the prospects of a Soviet retreat. It also showed the change in the discipline of our government in the three years since the Jordan crisis of September 1970. Then we had gone through similar alert measures; their extent had not become known until the crisis was already over, three days later.[5] The current alert had leaked within three hours in the middle of the night; we would now have a *public* confrontation, and not with a Soviet surrogate as in 1970, but with the Kremlin itself.

But at my White House office the day began well, minutes before 8:00 A.M., with two messages that had come from Egypt an hour apart. They were responses to my message to Ismail and Nixon's to Sadat.

Showing a degree of care appropriate to the seriousness of the situation, the Egyptians had numbered them sequentially to help us follow the evolution of their thinking. The Message number one was Ismail's answer to my account (midday on October 24) of the efforts we had made to secure Israeli compliance with the cease-fire. Despite the plight of the Third Army — to which he proudly did not refer — Ismail expressed his appreciation for our offer of help. He did not consider the sending of American military attachés adequate; he maintained that a combined US–Soviet force was the best guarantee. However, "since the U.S. refuses to take such a measure, Egypt is asking the Security Council to provide an *international* force" (emphasis added). This meant that Egypt was withdrawing the request that had produced the crisis. And it was substituting a proposal for an "international force," which by United Nations practice *excluded* forces from the five permanent members of the Security Council and therefore the US–Soviet force urged by Brezhnev.

This was made explicit in message number two from Sadat to Nixon. It agreed with not only the substance but also the reasoning of the message sent in Nixon's name the previous night:

> I understand the considerations you have put forward with respect to the use of a joint US–USSR force, and we have already asked the Security Council for the speedy dispatch of an international force to the area to review the implementation of the Security Council Resolutions. This we hope will pave the way toward further measures as envisaged in the October 22 Resolution of the Security Council aimed at establishing a just peace in the area.

We were on the verge of winning the diplomatic game. Without Egyptian support it was very unlikely that there could be a UN resolution calling for a US–Soviet force. If the Soviets sent troops it would be unilaterally, without the sanction of either the host country or the UN. This would be much easier for us to resist and we were determined to do so. It showed — though we could only guess this at the moment — that Sadat was staking his future on American diplomatic support rather than Soviet military pressure.

The second silver lining was an early morning report from John Scali at the UN. After his strong opposition to a joint US–Soviet force the previous evening, enthusiasm for the idea had cooled noticeably. The Security Council is rarely prepared to vote against the determined opposition of one of the superpowers if it is given any alternative. And it will be ingenious in finding alternatives. The nonaligned, faced with a United States veto, had early on October 25 tabled a draft resolution asking the Secretary-General to increase the number of UN observers and "to set up immediately a United Nations Emergency Force under [Security Council] authority." Though vaguely phrased, the draft resolution would open the way to excluding the superpowers from the Emergency Force. The Council was to meet at 10:30 A.M. to consider the draft.

Later in the morning we received the British reaction to Brezhnev's letter — which was the same as ours. Cromer informed us that "they [London] certainly take Brezhnev's message just the same as you do." The British Ambassador to Moscow had been asked to make urgent representations to Brezhnev to warn against unilateral military action.

It was thus in a hopeful, if still tense, mood that Haig and I briefed Nixon shortly after 8:00 A.M. that Thursday, October 25. I did not know what conversations Haig had had with Nixon in the early hours of the morning. To make sure, I reviewed the diplomatic and military moves of the night before. As always in crises, Nixon was clearheaded and crisp. We agreed that it would be unprecedented — and hence a major challenge — if the Soviet Union put organized combat units into an area far from its periphery and against the will of the local government. Despite the War Powers Act passed a few days earlier, Nixon was determined to match any Soviet troop buildup in the area and leave it to the Congress to terminate his move — as the new law made possible.

After the meeting with Nixon, a Presidential reply to Sadat was dispatched. It welcomed Sadat's "statesmanlike approach to the issue of peacekeeping" and indicated American support for an international force excluding the permanent members of the Security Council.

From 8:40 to 10:00 A.M. Nixon and I briefed Congressional leaders about the night's events. These distinguished men were at once supportive, rudderless, and ambivalent. They approved the alert; they were enthusiastic about our refusal to accept a joint US–Soviet force. But their support reflected more the Vietnam-era isolationism than a strategic assessment. They opposed a joint US–Soviet force because they wanted no American troops sent abroad; the *American* component of the proposed force bothered them a great deal more than the Soviet one. By the same token, they would object to the dispatch of American forces even if, in our view, they were needed to resist a unilateral Soviet move. That such an abdication might shake the global equilibrium and vital American interests was not considered conclusive. The spirit of cooperation thus cooled noticeably when Nixon outlined our determination to match a unilateral Soviet troop presence with an American one either in Israel or in friendly Arab countries. Several of the Congressional leaders expressed the gravest reservations. And while they did not go so far as to indicate outright opposition, they made it clear enough that support for the alert should not be interpreted as endorsing the movement of troops.

This sobering encounter was on my mind when, after another WSAG meeting at 10:15 A.M., I met the press at noon. Contradictory crosscurrents in the mood of the public and the Congress were buffeting us. There was a growing debate over détente, a mounting clamor that in some undefinable way we were being gulled by the Soviets. The opposite was true; our policy to reduce and where possible to eliminate Soviet influence in the Middle East was in fact making progress under the cover of détente. An end to détente would have triggered the Soviets into a political assault on us in the Middle East that would, at a minimum, have greatly complicated our strategy. And an open confrontation with the Soviets would be taking place at a point of maximum weakness of our executive authority. Could we sustain it, and for what purpose? What stronger course would the rhetoricians of toughness have proposed than the policy we were in fact pursuing? Détente was not a favor we did the Soviets. It was partly necessity; partly a tranquilizer for Moscow as we sought to draw the Middle East into closer relations with us at the Soviets' expense; partly the moral imperative of the nuclear age.

Hence I began the press conference — without notes — with a cold yet philosophical explanation of our conception of US–Soviet relations:

The United States and the Soviet Union are, of course, ideological and, to some extent, political adversaries. But the United States and the Soviet Union also have a very special responsibility. We possess — each of us — nuclear arsenals capable of annihilating humanity. We — both of us — have a special duty to see to it that confrontations are kept within bounds that do not threaten civilized life. Both of us, sooner or later, will have to come to realize that the issues that divide the world today, and foreseeable issues, do not justify the unparalleled catastrophe that a nuclear war would represent. . . .

In a speech — Pacem in Terris — I pointed out that there are limits beyond which we cannot go. I stated that we will oppose the attempt by any country to achieve a position of predominance, either globally or regionally; that we would resist any attempt to exploit a policy of détente to weaken our alliances; and that we would react if the relaxations of tensions were used as a cover to exacerbate conflicts in international trouble spots. We have followed these principles in the current situation.

It is easy to start confrontations, but in this age we have to know where we will be at the end and not only what pose to strike at the beginning.

I left no doubt of our determination in the immediate crisis:

The United States does not favor and will not approve the sending of a joint Soviet–United States force into the Middle East. The United States believes that what is needed in the Middle East above all is a determination of the facts, a determination where the lines are, and a determination of who is doing the shooting, so that the Security Council can take appropriate action. It is inconceivable that the forces of the great powers should be introduced in the numbers that would be necessary to overpower both of the participants. It is inconceivable that we should transplant the great-power rivalry into the Middle East or, alternatively, that we should impose a military condominium by the United States and the Soviet Union. The United States is even more opposed to the unilateral introduction by any great power, especially by any nuclear power, of military forces into the Middle East in whatever guise those forces should be introduced.

I went on to explain, deliberately vaguely, that "the ambiguity of some of the actions and communications and certain readiness measures that were observed" had led to the decision to order precautionary military measures on our part. If crisis management requires cold and even brutal measures to show determination, it also imposes the need to show the opponent a way out. Grandstanding is good for the ego but bad foreign policy. A public challenge could provoke the Soviets to dig in beyond what the Politburo might consider prudent. Many wars have started because no line of retreat was left open. Superpowers have a special obligation not to humiliate each other. Precisely because we were well on the way to success — and the Soviets knew it — I presented the outcome in terms compatible with Soviet self-respect:

> I would like to make clear that as of now the Soviet Union has not yet taken any irrevocable action. It is our hope that such an action will not be taken.
> I repeat again what I have said on many occasions in this press conference. We are not seeking an opportunity to confront the Soviet Union. We are not asking the Soviet Union to pull back from anything that it has done.
> The opportunity for pursuing the joint course in the Security Council and in the diplomacy afterward is open. The measures we took and which the President ordered were precautionary in nature. They were not directed at any actions that had already been taken. And therefore there is no reason for any country to back off anything that it has not yet done. . . .

I said nothing about the Brezhnev letter, preferring not to involve the General Secretary's personal prestige. It did little good. Somehow Senator Henry M. Jackson had learned of the letter, despite the small number of people aware of its existence, and had publicly described it as "brutal" and "threatening." One reporter asked me about Jackson's statement. I evaded a comment, subsequently indicating — unwisely — that in a week's time more of the facts would be made available.* My responsibility was not to score debating points; it was to defend American interests in a hazardous environment. And history teaches that the most perilous moment is often when an adversary is seemingly prepared

---

*Congressional committees in executive session were briefed on the alert and its surrounding circumstances; Secretary Schlesinger and I in our separate news conferences spelled out the essence of what had happened. But not every detail was made public, for the reasons explained above. The committees concurred in this decision.[6]

to retreat and is then jolted into new defiance by an assault on his self-esteem.

The alert was immediately engulfed in the cynicism spawned by Watergate. Two kinds of questions were hurled at me: whether Soviet actions had been caused by our domestic disputes; and its opposite, whether we had generated the crisis for domestic rather than foreign policy reasons — whether, in the unsubtle question of one journalist, our actions had indeed been "rational." The query about Soviet motives gave me an opportunity to hint at my recurrent nightmare: "One cannot have a crisis of authority in a society for a period of months without paying a price somewhere along the line."

The queries as to our motives were even more wounding to us who had agonized through a night of desperate uncertainty. Yet it showed how narrow was our margin for policy. If we courted confrontation, following the advice of the anti-détente zealots, we would almost surely be undermined by the Watergate bloodhounds who would treat every challenge to the Soviet Union as a maneuver by which their hated quarry, Nixon, was trying to escape them. To broaden our maneuvering room, I replied rather heatedly:

> We are attempting to conduct the foreign policy of the United States with regard for what we owe not just to the electorate but to future generations. And it is a symptom of what is happening to our country that it could even be suggested that the United States would alert its forces for domestic reasons. . . .

And in reply to another question:

> We are attempting to preserve the peace in very difficult circumstances. It is up to you ladies and gentlemen to determine whether this is the moment to try to create a crisis of confidence in the field of foreign policy as well. . . .
>
> There has to be a minimum of confidence that the senior officials of the American government are not playing with the lives of the American people.

I tremble at the thought of what fate would have been in store for us in such an environment if we had had to sustain a crisis for very many days. It was fortunate that the Soviets, too, feared to run the risks of a prolonged confrontation, even in the context of our fragile domestic balance.

Immediately after the press conference, at 1:10 P.M., I found a message from Sadat formally accepting an international force composed of nonpermanent members of the Security Council (the reference to the Security Council was a drafting error; he meant to exclude permanent members of the Security Council but leave participation open to any other UN members). A few minutes later I learned from Waldheim that Soviet Ambassador Malik would support the same scheme.

At 2:40 P.M. Dobrynin phoned to say he had another letter from Brezhnev. It was written as if the crisis of the night before had never occurred. Without any reference to the previous night's threat of unilateral intervention, Brezhnev informed Nixon instead that he had dispatched seventy Soviet "representatives" — apparently not military personnel — to observe the implementation of the cease-fire. Indeed, Brezhnev with characteristic swagger presented his standdown from confrontation as if *we* were yielding to *his* proposal: "Since you are ready now, as we understand, to send to Egypt a group of American observers with the same task, we agree to act jointly in this question." And he advanced the startling thesis that the events of the past twenty-four hours should be the prelude to even more conspicuous cooperation:

Following the dispatch of observers we in an urgent manner will continue also our other political measures which correspond to the decision of the Security Council and to the understanding between us, reached in Moscow with Dr. Kissinger, who conducted negotiations on your behalf.

The Soviets had backed off. The immediate danger was over. We were still navigating a narrow passage. But we now knew that with luck and skill we would enhance our influence on the peace process; indeed, that prospect had already helped persuade Sadat to refrain from inviting Soviet military forces back on Egyptian soil.

There was the usual aftermath of a crisis: the mixture of relief, letdown, and premonition that some other, if lesser, challenge would take its turn. I phoned Jim Schlesinger, my partner in the all-night session in the Situation Room, and thanked him and Tom Moorer and Bill Clements for their contributions. I did so with conviction, for their dedication and strength had carried us through the crisis of authority, enabling us to act with rare decisiveness and unity. I recommended that Schlesinger stand down the alert starting at midnight.

Phone calls came in from leading journalists with the common plea that more information be made public to convince a skeptical press corps that the crisis had indeed been genuine. One columnist was bothered because "the evidence given for so important an act seemed so flimsy as not to be credible." My answers were more charitable than were my sentiments. At this point, adding to the Soviet Union's public humiliation would have been a decidedly unwise course.

At 3:05 P.M. Thursday, I reviewed the situation with an elated Nixon. We discussed the Security Council resolution, plans for standing down the alert, Brezhnev's letter. I told him that I had not characterized the October 24 letter at my own press conference because it seemed to me dangerous to turn the issue into a personal confrontation between the President and the General Secretary. Nixon was outraged at the media's insinuation that he had personally generated the crisis to ease his domestic difficulties — an allegation he knew better than his critics to have been inherently impossible.

During the course of the afternoon, Security Council Resolution 340 was passed. It reiterated the call for a return to the lines of the original cease-fire of October 22; we had succeeded in substituting the more neutral word "return" for the original word "withdraw." It established an international force comprised of UN members excluding the great powers. (The text of Resolution 340 is in the backnotes.)[7] By phone I pressed Waldheim to exclude other Soviet-bloc nations by the formula that no member of existing military alliances should be invited to participate.

Golda adamantly objected to this resolution as she had to the one the previous day. She would take no chance — alert or no — that even tactical divergences with Israel might become habit-forming.

Meanwhile we had been exchanging messages all day with Cairo, which had asked for help with blood plasma and other medical supplies to the beleaguered Third Army. Israel, while agreeing in principle, was in no hurry to expedite any kind of supplies; it was still hoping for surrender of the Third Army.

My own thoughts turned increasingly to the diplomacy by which we might alter the moment's delicate balance. Having barely surmounted the crisis, I wanted to fix Arab minds on the prospects of peace. Late on October 25, on the pretext of inquiring about technical arrangements for my visit to Cairo, I sent a message to Hafiz Ismail elaborating on the purpose of my visit:

> I look forward to meeting with you and whomever else you feel appropriate, and to constructive preliminary discussions on the range of issues that are of concern to both our countries. In the period before we meet we must both seek to ensure that a constructive atmosphere is maintained in relations between Egypt and the United States.

At the end of the day Nixon called from Camp David to congratulate me on the television coverage of my press conference. He was understandably obsessed by Watergate — the "Saturday night massacre" had, after all, occurred only five days earlier and Congress was even then moving toward impeachment. Where public relations was concerned, Nixon believed in overkill. He now wanted me to bring the heads of major news organizations into the White House the next day and brief them about the alert. He wanted me to stress his indispensability. What if House Speaker Carl Albert — at that moment next in line to the Presidency — had been faced with the problem? A few minutes later he had the idea that I should make the same pitch to Jewish leaders: "Get the whole bunch in a room and say you are American first, and members of the American Jewish Community, and interested in Israel. Who is going to save Israel and who will save it in the future?''

It was pathetic but accurate. He had taken the responsibility and faced its implications with panache and determination. And yet we could preserve the strength and coherence of our foreign policy only if we ensured beyond peradventure that we would not let Watergate affect our actions. If a link were established in the public mind, the hopes for our diplomacy and therefore of peace would be destroyed. So I urged Haig to drop these schemes. They were bound to backfire. Haig agreed and nothing was heard of them again.

Only one loose end was left. The Soviet naval force of twelve ships was still approaching what some of our governmental reports were pleased to call the "landmass" of Egypt. They continued on their course even after Security Council Resolution 340 — perhaps because they had been forgotten in Moscow, more probably as insurance against another hitch in the implementation of the cease-fire. Finally, the CIA reported late on October 25 that the flotilla had stopped 100 nautical miles north of Mersa Matruh; it dispersed the following day and no such threatening Soviet naval activity took place again.

Thus ended the day of the alert.

Aftermath

AMERICAN newspapers on Friday morning, October 26, were awash with commentary on our military alert, most of it relieved that a serious confrontation with the Soviets had been avoided and unusually supportive of our decision to reject the Soviet-Egyptian proposal for superpower troop intervention.

The *Washington Post* on that day ran two editorials. One, on "the Watergate connection," bridled at any implication in my press conference that it was the press that was undermining public confidence: "Our crisis at home was created by the President." The other editorial suggested that the crisis demonstrated both the limits and the utility of détente. Nixon "responded, in our view, with admirable firmness and restraint:"

Whether in this crisis we were in fact that close [to danger] is something we may know more about when the administration produces, as Dr. Kissinger said it would, the appropriate texts and facts. A judgment on that can wait. What is important now is to note, with sober thankfulness, that the relationship created by Mr. Nixon and Mr. Brezhnev in recent years served both of them well in their contest this week.

The *New York Times* in two editorials on October 26 also suggested that the crisis demonstrated "how tenuous the Soviet-American détente still is.'' The *Times* favored early negotiations: ''Mr. Kissinger indicated yesterday it might take several weeks to organize them. This, in our view, is not good enough.''

The *Wall Street Journal* strongly backed the Administration: ''It is incredible that some reporters at the press conference suggested that the President had stagemanaged an international crisis to divert attention from the domestic one.'' The *Los Angeles Times* editorialized that ''the partial American mobilization . . . was the right thing to do,'' and endorsed the handling of the crisis from the outset of the war. It strongly opposed any superpower troop intervention and praised the Administration for rejecting the idea. The *Chicago Tribune* opined that ''the Mideast policy that Mr. Kissinger defined is admirable'' and ''this is a time for Americans to have confidence in the foreign policies of our government.''

We sought to defuse the crisis now by avoiding any attack on Soviet self-respect. It was not a time to crow, lest Moscow seize on the inevitable next pretext to reverse the outcome of the previous night.

Brezhnev did his part by giving a conciliatory speech on October 26 to the World Peace Congress meeting in Moscow. He extolled the importance of détente; he did not mention the American alert, but he castigated Israel for violating the cease-fire ''perfidiously.'' He repeated the standard Soviet line on a Mideast settlement, which amounted to blanket support of the hard-line Arabs. But he was no more specific now on how to achieve his program than he had been during the previous four years — a void that represented our strategic opportunity.

My associate Helmut Sonnenfeldt well summed up the ambivalence of our public debate:

> In this crazy town this conciliatory speech [by Brezhnev], in part induced by the firmness of our reaction to Soviet threats the other night, in part by Brezhnev's own stake in his détente policy, will further stimulate allegations that we manufactured a crisis for domestic reasons. And any efforts we make to show that we were justified in doing what we did will either have the effect of emphasizing the tenuousness of détente or of arousing the Russians to show that they were not faced down by us in a confrontation.

Clearly, détente had not prevented a crisis, as some of our critics with varying degrees of disingenuousness were claiming it should have — forgetting that détente defined not friendship but a strategy for a relationship between adversaries. After all, a principal purpose of our own Mideast policy was to reduce the role and influence of the Soviet Union, just as the Soviets sought to reduce ours. But I believe détente mitigated the succession of crises that differences in ideology and geopolitical interest had made nearly inevitable; and I believe we enhanced the national interest in the process.

We still sought, for instance, to limit the role and the number of the observers whom Brezhnev had sent to Egypt as he stood down from the crisis. They were in any event an anachronism now that the United Nations force had been approved. Nixon replied to Brezhnev's October 25 message nearly twenty-four hours later, at 1:00 P.M. on October 26, leaving no doubt that we intended to reduce the superpower observers to minimal proportions:

Now that the United Nations Truce Supervisory Organization has been augmented and a United Nations emergency force created, a separate US–USSR supervisory force would be inappropriate. I propose that at this time we leave the composition of the U.N. Observer Force to the discretion of the Secretary General. Our own preference is for the limitations on its composition to be the same as those agreed upon for the U.N. emergency force. We would, however, be prepared to consider a request by the Secretary General to supply a few U.S. observers should he desire to do so. The Soviet observers should be integrated in the same manner. We do not believe it necessary to have separate observer forces from individual countries operating in the area.

For the rest of the day, Dobrynin and I sparred about the size of the US–Soviet observer contingent; I opened the bidding by insisting on no more than twenty from each side. Finally, there was an agreement on thirty-six each. It was a needless effort, for Egypt promptly changed its mind about the desirability of the observers. Egypt's new Acting Foreign Minister, Ismail Fahmy, said in Cairo that Egypt neither wanted nor needed the observers. The Soviet ploy for a special US–Soviet contingent never got off the ground, and the issue was buried in the diplomacy that followed.

We had dealt with the threat of Soviet intervention. But the problem that had given rise to it remained. The Egyptian Third Army was still trapped; it was not under assault but was slowly being starved into submission. The medical convoy we had been attempting to arrange for twenty-four hours had been stalled by the Israelis under one pretext or another at the outskirts of the city of Suez. Israel claimed that it was transferring medical supplies directly. We had no means of checking. At any rate, this too was designed to humiliate the Egyptians by emphasizing their dependence on the Israeli armed forces. It was not something that Sadat could accept indefinitely.

And he did not. Shortly after 9:30 A.M. Friday, October 26, Sadat sent an urgent message direct to Nixon charging that the Israelis were exploiting the situation "to establish themselves astride the lines of communication of the Third Egyptian Army in an attempt to isolate and oblige it to surrender" and that the Israelis continued to prevent UN observers from reaching the area. Sadat threatened unilateral action to reopen the supply lines. He was also informing the Soviets, he told us.

He went on to suggest that prolongation of the impasse would jeopardize the atmosphere for "constructive" talks with me. "I would like to inform you," he wrote, "that in preparation for this visit, we are working out comprehensive proposals which we hope will provide a turning point toward a final peace settlement." A trip sold so often by each side to the other would require something of a miracle to fulfill all the expectations raised for largely extraneous tactical reasons. Obviously, both we and Cairo were trying to use my trip to maneuver for position — we to drive a wedge between the Soviet Union and Egypt and to keep Sadat from invoking Soviet help; Sadat to induce us to prevent Israel from destroying the Egyptian Third Army. As it happened, these objectives merged.

We had supported Israel throughout the war for many historical, moral, and strategic reasons. And we had just run the risk of war with the Soviet Union, amidst the domestic crisis of Watergate. But our shared interests did not embrace the elimination of the Third Army.

The issue of the Third Army was quite simply that Israel had completed its entrapment well *after* a cease-fire (that we had negotiated) had gone into effect. But while Israel could do this much, it could not cause the Third Army to surrender. Late the preceding night (October 25), Israel had replied to my query that it would take three or four more days of fighting along the *entire* front *and* the assurance of large quantities of modern equipment to destroy the Third Army. There was no way this could take place without another major crisis with the Soviet Union, the permanent enmity of all of the Arab states, and the humiliation of Sadat.

Nor would the final destruction of an Egyptian army after the cease-fire have been in Israel's long-term interest. Maddened by the fact that they had been surprised, beside themselves with grief over the high casualties, deeply distrustful of Sadat, who had engineered their discomfiture, Israel's leaders wanted to end the war with his destruction. Their emotion was understandable. But one of our interests was to give Arab leaders an incentive for moderation. Our exchanges with Cairo had convinced us that Anwar Sadat represented the best chance for peace in the Middle East.

Now that we had prevented Soviet intervention, it was essential to begin the peace process. This required some immediate relief for the Third Army — a difficult tactical problem. There was unanimity in our government as to goals, disagreement as to methods. The Defense Department had come up with a plan for resupplying the Third Army with American C-130 airplanes. There was also much pressure to cut off our airlift to Israel. I was uneasy about both ideas. We could not in the space of two weeks run an airlift to the two opposing sides in a Middle East war. At the same time, an abrupt halt of the airlift to Israel would risk being interpreted as dissociation from our ally and thus would tempt Arab intransigence and perhaps renewed Soviet intervention.

So we spent Friday, October 26, attempting instead to persuade Israel to volunteer some type of relief for the Third Army and thus avoid forcing us into open opposition. It was not an easy assignment. A prickly, proud, and somewhat overwrought friendly nation had to be convinced not to persist in a course promising great domestic benefits in the run-up to an election,* and we had to accomplish the goal while maintaining a public posture of close association. We had to preserve Egypt's confidence in us through the agonizing hours required to convince Israel. It was a close race between our persuasiveness and the endurance of the Third Army and with it the prospect of a moderate government in Egypt. And, having just coaxed and pressured the Russian bear back into his cage, we had to be watchful lest he come charging out again. It turned out to be another long day.

Within minutes of receiving Sadat's message, I contacted Dinitz. Meanwhile, the Third Army was trying to break out of Israeli encirclement north of Suez City. This indicated its desperation and would aggravate its plight by depleting its resources. It would also face us with another round of disputes over cease-fire violations. I urged that Israel take two steps: invite UN observers to proceed immediately to points between the two armies to monitor the cease-fire; and permit convoys of food, water, and medical supplies to the Third Army. The latter would remain surrounded, incapable of combat, useful as a bargaining counter but not subject to the humiliation of surrender. Dinitz promised an answer within a short time. I also told Dinitz of my plan to visit Egypt.

Nixon was at Camp David, where he had gone to prepare for a television news conference that evening. At 10:30 A.M. I sent a message in his name to Sadat, relating the proposals we had made to Israel:

> It will of necessity require several hours to get a definitive response on these points. It is our earnest hope that in the interim you can avoid taking any irrevocable actions.
>
> I am very encouraged by your substantive preparations for discussions during Secretary Kissinger's upcoming visit. You can be sure he will adopt a constructive attitude. We hope that his visit may represent a milestone on the road toward a permanent and just settlement.

Around noon I talked to Nixon at Camp David and briefed him on what we had been doing. When he heard of Sadat's urgent message earlier that morning, he wanted it passed to the Israelis "strongly," in his words. (I had already done so.) "Let's keep our side of the bargain."

Not having received a reply from the Israelis for nearly four hours, I finally called Dinitz. He was without instructions, but he had a "per-

---

*The Israeli general election, originally scheduled for October 30, was rescheduled during the war to December 31.

sonal'' idea: Any Egyptian wishing to leave the Third Army might be permitted to do so, but all equipment would have to be left behind. In other words, a public humiliation for Egypt — no wonder it was put foward as a ''personal'' idea. I repeated our proposal that emergency, nonmilitary supplies be allowed through — mostly food, water, and medicines. I added: ''You will not be permitted to capture that army. I am certain.'' After some desultory talk I warned again: ''I frankly think you will make a mistake if you push into a total confrontation.'' Once more I requested an urgent reply.

Around 2:30 P.M., still not having heard from Israel after five hours, we received another frantic message from Sadat for Nixon:

> At that moment when I am receiving your encouraging message with respect to the future of peace, the Israelis are launching air and ground attacks against the Third Army under the false pretext that it has initiated the attack.
>
> I wish to advise you that the moment is critical and that the future of peace is in danger. Your guarantee of the Security Council Resolution is being defied under false pretenses.
>
> I hope that we can act swiftly to stop that deterioration of the situation immediately.

Shortly afterward, Kurt Waldheim informed me that Zayyat in New York, in a highly emotional state, had contacted him about the possibility of a special Security Council meeting to protest alleged new Israeli cease-fire violations. The Egyptian army would not surrender; Egypt would be forced to take unilateral action. It was, said Zayyat, at a turning point.

When I reported the Egyptian message to Dinitz at 4:15 P.M., he was still without instructions — seven hours after my urgent request. Clearly, the Israeli government was stalling, hoping to force the Third Army into surrender. The only suggestion Dinitz had was that the cabinet would send a general to explain the situation to me and present a ''complete proposal.'' But this would take time, which we did not have. I warned Dinitz that there was a limit beyond which we could not be pushed. Dinitz replied, revealing the Israeli calculation: ''We cannot let them [the Third Army] out without getting something in return.'' Of course, if I threw the issue into our own bureaucratic machinery, it would almost certainly result in *American* resupply of the Third Army, which the Defense Department was recommending. I suggested that Israel had a good bargaining position and could get something for it, though not the surrender of the Third Army. We would do our utmost to arrange for direct discussions between Egypt and Israel — a long-stated Israeli goal. But a continuation of the current tactics would be disastrous:

> [Y]ou have to buy time for this discussion. We will be glad to propose that there will be immediate discussions between you and the Egyptians to solve this problem. We are willing to be cooperative but I tell you what will happen

is another maximum Soviet demand and you cannot put the President in confrontation day after day.

I requested a reply before the start of the Security Council debate set for 9:00 P.M. that evening.

Still wishing to avoid a clash with Israel and hopeful that eventually we would elicit a constructive reply, I sent a procrastinating message to Sadat in Nixon's name. It told Sadat of the locations at which Israel had agreed to accept UN observers, as well as Israel's agreement in principle to a medical convoy for Suez City. The message also pointed out that the Israeli and Egyptian versions of the cause of cease-fire violations were exactly opposite: "You must recognize that it is impossible for us to make proper judgments on who is keeping and who is violating the cease-fire." It promised that as soon as impartial observers were in place, the United States would be prepared to identify and condemn violators of the cease-fire.

This was thin gruel for Sadat. Disaster was incipient — in the pressures of Egyptian honor, the dwindling supplies of the Third Army, and our struggle to work out a complicated diplomacy.

Finally, at 7:10 P.M., during Nixon's press conference, a formal Israeli reply arrived. It was another stall. Prime Minister Meir now accepted my suggestion of direct talks with the Egyptians on "how to solve this problem." In the meantime she offered no relief for the Third Army. What Golda had in mind seemed simple enough:

> We believe we have something to offer to them — something which is neither surrender nor humiliation, but an honorable way out of the situation. All the Egyptians have to do is suggest the time, place, and rank of their representative.

But the reality was more complicated. The psychological difficulty for the Arabs in accepting direct talks was hardly likely to be eased by the deliberate humiliation of the Third Army. At a minimum it would take time to arrange a meeting, with each elapsed hour further weakening the Third Army. Golda recognized the problem and sought to soothe us: "They [the Third Army] are not in a desperate situation; Sadat is." But that did not answer our concerns at all, for we were even more interested in preserving Sadat than the Third Army; the fact was, however, that they were symbiotic. One had become the surrogate for the other. At 7:55 P.M. I passed the essence of Golda's message — proposing direct Egyptian-Israeli talks — to Hafiz Ismail in Cairo.

In the meantime, two events had further inflamed affairs. Around 4:30 P.M. we were alerted that yet another Soviet message was on the way. In the past, the time lag after notification had rarely exceeded fifteen minutes. Two hours later the message had not yet arrived. I queried Dobrynin. He professed ignorance. Was it psychological warfare to wear us down for a replay of the crisis of forty-eight hours earlier? Was Moscow having second thoughts about whatever it was proposing to send? We could only wait, though I thought it highly unlikely that we would so soon be faced with another threat as stark as the one we had just surmounted.

While waiting for the Soviet message, Nixon began his press conference at 7:00 P.M. in the East Room of the White House and it all but wrecked the delicate balance we had been seeking to maintain between firmness and absence of provocation. From my study of history I was convinced that the period just *after* any diplomatic victory is frequently the most precarious. The victor is tempted to turn the screw one time too many; the loser, rubbed raw by the humiliation of his defeat, may be so eager to recoup that he suddenly abandons rational calculation.

Nixon, however, had other imperatives. He was determined to show that despite a week's hue and cry over the "Saturday night massacre" and despite the threat of impeachment, he was in control — indeed, indispensable. He needed to convince the public that there had been a real crisis, which was not Watergate-imposed. Nixon, therefore, had an incentive to paint the crisis to the media in the darkest possible terms.

"We obtained information," he said, "which led us to believe that the Soviet Union was planning to send a very substantial force into the Mideast, a military force." He had ordered a military alert the purpose of which was "to indicate to the Soviet Union that we would not accept any unilateral move on their part."

This explicit challenge was moreover drawn to Brezhnev personally by a somewhat melodramatic rendition of the messages that had been exchanged: "Rather than saying that his note to me was rough and brutal, I would say that it was very firm, and it left very little to the imagination as to what he intended. And my response was also very firm and left little to the imagination of how we would react." Nixon went on to ruminate about how Brezhnev understood American power and Nixon in particular. This was so, Nixon mused, since he had been the President who had bombed North Vietnam in defiance of all public pressures: "That is what made Mr. Brezhnev act as he did." And Nixon capped his presentation of Brezhnev's backdown by claiming that it was "the most difficult crisis we have had since the Cuban confrontation of 1962" — a comparison that I in my news conference had deliberately downplayed.

Most of this was true enough. But it was not the most propitious moment to summon Brezhnev to a test of manhood. Somewhat overwrought by several nights with little sleep, I protested vehemently to Haig as if he could undo what was already on the public record. Haig had his own problems, for the hungry media had not been deterred by a tense international situation from pursuing their Watergate quarry through persistent, tough, and occasionally insolent questions on that subject. Coupled with Nixon's defensive answers, these had tended to defeat one of the purposes of the press conference: to convey the image of calm, purposeful, determined leadership. No wonder that Haig told me: "If you talk to him tonight take it easy. He is right on the verge." And Haig's next phone call a few minutes later showed how strong was the need for reassurance: "I am with the President. We noticed you are the only one who hasn't called." I knew only too well the nearly frantic insecurity felt by Nixon after every public performance, compounded now by the agony of Watergate. It was pointless and would have been cruel to engage in a debate on the nuances of crisis management. So I told Haig, not without ambiguity: "It was quite a tour de force."

The mood among journalists at the two press conferences raised the likelihood that if there were another early test, the psychological balance might not be so favorable. And it was true not only at home. Scali reported to me from the UN later that evening: "I think unless we get the Israelis to back up we are not going to have a friend in the house."

At 8:45 P.M. I called Dinitz "not as Secretary but as a friend." I told him a Soviet message was on the way. I had the impression, I said, that Israel preferred to be raped than to make a decision of its own accord. I wanted to avoid the appearance of Israel's yielding under pressure, if at all possible; it would set a bad precedent for the future. I urged Dinitz once again to come up with some forthcoming proposal that could blunt the UN debate. But Dinitz was as impervious to personal appeals as he had been impenetrable in the face of official approaches. He recited Israeli losses during the war; he argued that the Third Army would start an offensive if resupplied. (This was hardly the issue. No one proposed *military* resupply; the only issue was bare nonmilitary necessities to keep the troops alive.) Israel seemed determined to starve out the Third Army. I said impatiently: "You will be forced if it reaches that point." The best I could promise was to see to it that "you won't be pressured one second before it becomes inevitable."

The message from Brezhnev started arriving shortly after 9:00 P.M. The Soviet leader was threatening but much more ambiguously than he had been two days earlier. He confined himself to the charge that actions by Israel jeopardized the interests of universal peace. Brezhnev recapitulated what we knew: Sadat had asked the United States to take action to stop Israeli aggression and to provide relief for the Third Army. We had promised to be helpful in several hours but the time had passed and Sadat's request had not been met:

[I]f the next few hours do not bring news that necessary measures have been taken to resolve the question raised by President Sadat, then we will have the most serious doubts regarding the intentions of the American side. . . .

Brezhnev requested a positive US response in a matter of hours. He also, for the first time, discussed our alert, stating that though he had not reacted, our action was unprovoked and not conducive to the relaxation of international tensions.

It was a strange message. It spoke of threats to universal peace but not about what the Soviet Union would do about them. It asked for an American response within a few hours but threatened no consequences other than serious doubts about our intentions. It was plaintive about the alert, but the cautious phrasing indicated that some important lessons had been learned. Still, there would be a limit to the demonstrations of their impotence that the Soviet leaders would tolerate.

I had resisted the bureaucracy's pressures to undertake an American resupply of the Third Army. I understood that Israel's intransigence reflected a combination of insecurity and despair — molded of a fear of isolation, a premonition of a catastrophe burnt deep into the soul of a people that had lived with disaster through the millennia of its history, and the worry that if it once yielded to pressure it would invite an unending process of exactions. It also reflected the deadlock of a divided cabinet, none of whose members dared to appear "softer" than his colleagues. I had maneuvered all day to avoid a public American dissociation from Israel, to preserve Israel's psychological substance even while persuading it not to press its advantage to an extreme. But it was becoming clear that Israel was in no position to make a decision. It seemed to prefer being coerced to release its prey rather than relinquishing it voluntarily. My ultimate responsibility was as Secretary of State of the United States, not as psychiatrist to the government of Israel. With the utmost reluctance I decided that my duty was to force a showdown. The only act of friendship I could show to Israel was to keep it private, if Israel would let me.

Thus at 10:58 P.M. Friday evening, I called Dinitz on behalf of Nixon. I do not remember checking in advance with the President; whether I did or not, there was no doubt the President would back me. In all probability, he would have forced the issue earlier or accepted the option of American resupply of the Third Army had he not been preoccupied with his press conference and Watergate. I said to Dinitz:

Let me give you the President's reaction in separate parts. First he wanted me to make it absolutely clear that we cannot permit the destruction of the Egyptian army under conditions achieved after a cease-fire was reached in part by negotiations in which we participated. Therefore it is an option that does not exist. . . . Secondly, he would like from you no later than 8:00 A.M. tomorrow an answer to the questions of non-military supplies permitted to reach the army. If you cannot agree to that, we will have to support in the UN a resolution that will deal with the enforcement of [Resolutions] 338 and 339.

We have been driven to this reluctantly by your inability to reach a decision. Whatever the reasons, this is what the President wanted me to tell you is our position. An answer that permits some sort of negotiation and some sort of positive response on the non-military supplies, or then we will join the other members of the Security Council in making it an international matter. I have to say again your course is suicidal. You will not be permitted to destroy this army. You are destroying the possibility for negotiations. . . .

I told Dinitz that we would not inform Cairo of the démarche; that we would transmit any Israeli proposal to Egypt; that we would support Israel's refusal to permit *military* resupply of the Third Army. Dinitz, who was one of the sharpest minds among the ambassadors in Washington, could not have missed — and was probably relieved — that we had not demanded an Israeli withdrawal to the October 22 cease-fire line. I did not inform any other government of the pressure on Israel.

About 2:30 A.M. Saturday morning, October 27, we sent a Presidential reply to Brezhnev. It was polite but vague. It expressed our commitment to the cease-fire. Nixon promised to press the Israeli government to permit nonmilitary supplies to get through to the Third Army. The message did not indicate that we had already done so nor the deadline we had established. We did not want to tempt Soviet ultimatums riding piggyback on our deadlines. It promised Moscow a reply by late Saturday afternoon Washington time, well after the time limit we had given the Israeli cabinet, to leave room for any clarification that might be needed. Nixon's message concluded with a reference to the alert:

As to the actions which the United States took as a result of your letter of October 24, I would recall your sentences in that letter: "It is necessary to adhere without delay. I will say it straight that if you find it impossible to act promptly with us in this matter, we should be faced with the necessity urgently to consider the question of taking appropriate steps unilaterally." Mr. General Secretary, these are serious words and were taken seriously here in Washington.

Barely had we sent the message to Moscow when we heard from Israel in the form of a message from Golda to me. Even though I had transmitted our demand in the name of Nixon, Golda was too surefooted to tackle the President head-on. She made sure that her quarrels were always with subordinates. Placing the President on a pedestal gave him one more opportunity to change course by disavowing those who were undermining the harmony Golda postulated. And, if this failed, an ultimate concession to the President, with some skill and luck, could at least be turned into a claim for a future favor.

The letter itself was vintage Golda, passionate, self-centered, shrewd. It was written as much for its impact on the Israeli cabinet as for the

United States government. She chose to put the matter into the context of superpower imposition, implying that we were yielding to the Soviets — an argument which, if it surfaced, was certain to mobilize maximum domestic pressures against us: "I have no illusions but that everything will be imposed on us by the two big powers." This, about a request she had refused to answer for eighteen hours, that Israel make *some* proposal we could defend before the Security Council *against* Soviet pressures. All she asked, the letter said, was that we tell Israel precisely what it was to do "in order that Egypt may announce a victory of her aggression." This, about the proposal to let food and water through to an army trapped forty-eight hours after a US-negotiated cease-fire and that would remain trapped even after having received these minimal supplies. But if she had to make some concession, nothing could force the lioness to be graceful about it: "There is only one thing that nobody can prevent us from doing and that is to proclaim the truth of the situation; that Israel is being punished not for its deeds, but because of its size and because it is on its own."

It was a great letter for the Israeli cabinet: David defying Goliath and maneuvering so that he had conceded nothing.

Her profession of outrage did not hide from me that her reply once again evaded the essential point: She was still refusing to put forward a proposal. She was insisting that we impose it — exactly what I had been trying to avoid. It was a reflection partly of conviction, partly of the complicated Israeli cabinet politics, partly of the upcoming elections that made it easier for Golda to yield than to initiate.

Torn between admiration and exasperation ("they are mad heroes," I exclaimed to Scowcroft), I was drafting a reply when Sadat solved the problem for us — though at the cost of another sleepless night. At 3:07 A.M. that Saturday, I received word from Hafiz Ismail that Egypt accepted direct talks between Egyptian and Israeli officers of the rank of major general "to discuss the military aspects of the implementation of Security Council Resolutions 338 and 339 of October 22 and 23, 1973." Talks should take place under UN supervision at the route marker denoting Kilometer 101 on the Cairo-Suez road. The only conditions would be a "complete" cease-fire, to go into effect two hours before the meeting proposed for 3:00 P.M. Cairo time that day (Saturday), and the passage of one convoy carrying nonmilitary supplies to the Third Army under UN and Red Cross supervision.

Golda's rage had been premature. Through our mediation, Israel was about to enter the first direct talks between Israeli and Arab representatives since the independence of Israel. It retained control over the access route to the Third Army even while the UN almost unanimously was pressing for Israeli withdrawal back from that to the October 22 line. All this in return for permitting one convoy of nonmilitary supplies to pass.

At 4:31 A.M. I told Hafiz Ismail that his message, with our strong endorsement, had been passed to Israel "on a most urgent basis." By 6:20 A.M. Israel accepted the Egyptian proposal in total; I immediately informed Sadat. Three hours later — we wanted to reduce the time available for Soviet mischief — a letter was sent in Nixon's name to Brezhnev informing him of the imminent Egyptian-Israeli talks and of Israeli agreement to the convoy.

But the Middle East is not hospitable to clean-cut solutions. Every step forward requires testing the ground ahead for shifting sands. At 11:00 A.M. Washington time (or 5:00 P.M. in Cairo), we were informed by Israel that the Egyptians had not showed up at the appointed time or place. A flurry of exchanges followed. It transpired that the Egyptian military representatives en route to the meeting at Kilometer 101 had been stopped at the Kilometer 85 marker by Israeli sentries who had not yet received instructions to let them through. They seemed strangely lax in communicating with their headquarters on the unprecedented phenomenon of an Egyptian major general who insisted on speaking directly to his Israeli counterpart! The mix-up was soon straightened out. I talked personally to Golda. Apparently, Israel had neglected to notify UN General Ensio Siilasvuo to make the necessary arrangements as I had told Ismail it would.* I urged that a new time be set and all notifications be decided ahead of time. After considerable back-and-forth — produced by the need for messages between parties a few hundred miles apart to travel via Washington, or a total distance of 12,000 miles — it was decided that the two generals would meet at midnight.

Ultimately, at 1:30 A.M. local time on Sunday, October 28, an hour and a half behind the new schedule, Israeli and Egyptian military representatives met for direct talks for the first time in twenty-five years, under the auspices of UN observers. But throughout that day the Israelis managed to delay the passage of the convoy. They had told me late on the twenty-sixth that the Third Army had food and water for forty-eight hours; they were determined to keep it on short rations; if the army collapsed while a convoy was on the way, no tears would be shed in Jerusalem. Finally, on Monday morning, October 29, I was able to report to Hafiz Ismail that the convoy had arrived at its destination. Egypt agreed to further meetings. While these remained inconclusive, the turn toward negotiations had begun. It soon became irreversible.

Prospects for Peace

W E were nearly at the goal of our strategy. The war was ended and with it the most urgent perils to the American position in the Mid-

---

*I have since had an opportunity to check my impressions with General Siilasvuo. He confirms that it was a genuine mix-up, even though at the time I suspected an Israeli maneuver.

dle East. We had emerged as the pivotal factor in the diplomacy. Egypt
was beginning to move in our direction, thereby creating an incentive
even for radical regimes to reexamine the premises of their policy. Sadat
had clearly signaled his intention to change course — no other explanation was compatible with his disciplined, restrained, and farsighted
conduct. And all this had been achieved while we stood by our friends
in Israel in wartime and prevented their isolation in the chaotic diplomacy over the cease-fire.

Our growing preeminence was reflected in the tone of Soviet communications. On October 29, Brezhnev sent another letter to Nixon alternately plaintive, accusatory, and threatening about the delay in getting the Egyptian-Israeli talks under way and in permitting the relief
convoy to get through. Brezhnev spoke of a crisis of confidence produced by actions that objectively amounted to support for the Israeli
"military clique" (a view obviously not shared by some American critics who saw us in collusion with Moscow). Brezhnev urged cooperation
against "aggression" and "deceit" designed to worsen Soviet-American relations.

His letter illustrated the Soviet dilemma, together with the complexity
of the course we had charted. Once Brezhnev's big bluff had failed,
Soviet threats had lost much of their credibility. At the same time, their
protests and complaints inevitably tended to lag behind events. With the
interval needed for communication between Cairo and Moscow and then
Moscow and Washington, the problems now were usually overcome or
well on the way to solution by the time we heard from the Kremlin.
"Only we can really deliver the Israelis," I said to Nixon on October
31, "so they [the Soviets] are constantly trying to get themselves into a
position where they can claim by threatening us or by pressuring us by
doing this or that they have made us do what we were going to do
anyway."

A symptom of the Soviets' frustration was their attempt to create
some bilateral forum with us outside the UN that would give them an
official status to supervise the cease-fire. To calm Soviet concerns without getting them involved in day-to-day diplomacy, I proposed to Dobrynin on October 31 that both countries designate a representative to
develop the "auspices" for the peace negotiations foreseen by Security
Council Resolution 338. The very next day Gromyko pretended that the
representatives were supposed to supervise the cease-fire. So committed
was Sadat by then to an American role that I could evade the proposal
by shifting it to the Acting Egyptian Foreign Minister, Ismail Fahmy,
who was then visiting Washington. He was no more eager for a Soviet
supervisory role than we, and he stalled it. It soon died.

Clearly, if we played our hand boldly, we might gradually reduce
Soviet and radical influence in the Arab world or else force the Soviets

into a more moderate course. On November 3, we answered Brezhnev's letter of five days earlier by affirming once again our commitment to peaceful coexistence. Nixon's letter insisted on the principle of restraint and the forswearing of unilateral advantage. But it also reviewed in a matter-of-fact way the status of current US–Soviet negotiations from the Strategic Arms Limitation Talks to the prospects of economic relations. Our purpose was to show that there was a positive alternative to confrontation, and to put into perspective both the crisis just surmounted and the tensions that surely lay ahead.

In a society used to relatively simple answers and in a body politic racked by Watergate, however, the public ambiguities of our policy increasingly tempted domestic opposition. Conservatives resented the very fact of a Soviet-American dialogue. Liberals suspected its pragmatism. Both shared the classically American nostalgia for policy based on concepts more "elevated" than the national interest. I was preparing a journey to the Middle East that would test not only our diplomacy but also our ability to manage the conflicting pressures at home. Could America, emerging in the decisive role in the struggle for peace in the Middle East, unfreeze and reshape the lethal alignments of a quarter century?

XIII

First Middle East Breakthrough

Fahmy and Golda

AT the end of October 1973, the war was over, but there was a good deal of high explosive lying around. The Egyptian Third Army was cut off in the Sinai. The Arab oil producers had imposed an embargo and production cuts. The Soviet Union was brooding over its frustrations and loss of influence. We had managed to achieve a cease-fire and were beginning to move into a pivotal position as the arbiter of the peace process. Therefore, what had been conceived of as a visit to Egypt — my first to an Arab country — turned into a journey through several nations of the Middle East.

My trip would not be a celebration, however, but only an opportunity, and perhaps a trap. Its best outcome would be to extend the maneuvering room for our strategy; if it failed, disaster was probable. In the face of a demonstration of American impotence, Saudi Arabia and Jordan would no longer dare to support the moderate course; Syria would stiffen its intransigence; Egypt could wind up again in the Soviet camp. The Soviets would more than recover the ground they had lost. Moscow had shown in the crisis just surmounted that it was prepared to back its words with threats if not always its threats with actions.

The general nervousness was such that Cairo was not content to await my arrival there. We did not fully grasp it yet, but Sadat had almost as big a stake in a demonstration of America's crucial role as we did. On October 28 I was suddenly informed that Acting Foreign Minister Ismail Fahmy was being dispatched to Washington by President Sadat, without advance notice to us. Furthermore, as I would not be stopping in Israel on this trip (having been there earlier in October), Prime Minister Golda Meir was arriving in Washington for pre-trip discussions beginning October 31.

The immediate trap I faced, as Fahmy and Golda headed for Washington, was that we might consume our strategic opportunity in acrimony over the fragile cease-fire. And there were real problems. If the Third Army remained cut off, constant alarums were inevitable. Would

Israel permit more than one supply convoy to reach the trapped Egyptian army, or seek to starve it out? And how could supply to it be assured without dangerously turning the tables? If the Egyptians received unlimited supplies, the Israeli forces that had crossed to the west bank of the Suez Canal might themselves face encirclement (see the map on page 566). There was also Israel's demand for release of its prisoners of war. In order to speed the cease-fire, Brezhnev had promised me his full support in bringing about a rapid exchange of POWs. I quickly found that neither Egypt nor Syria was aware of this pledge — which Israel reasonably insisted should be honored. Israel was also demanding free passage through the Strait of Bab el-Mandeb, the southern entrance to the Red Sea, which was under an undeclared Egyptian naval blockade (see the map on page 198).

If the debris of conflict provided one peril, the temptation to aim immediately for a permanent, comprehensive settlement was another. Indeed, I have been criticized for not seizing this "opportunity" for such a solution.[1] But it was a mirage. We knew that Israel adamantly rejected a return to the 1967 borders, including relinquishment of the Old City of Jerusalem. No Arab state, even the most moderate, would ask for less in the context of a comprehensive peace. Israel, recovering from the stunning shock of the Arab attack, was as if paralyzed. It faced an election; it sought to regain its bearings; pressures for a comprehensive negotiation were more likely to lead to desperate measures, such as ending the cease-fire, or to psychological collapse, than to a settlement. As for the Arabs, in a comprehensive approach all concerned parties would have to agree, and radical elements in the Arab world would have a veto. Egypt would lose control over its own decisions. And the Soviet Union would inject itself as the lawyer of the Arab side, putting forth a maximum program that years of experience had taught us was unfulfillable. Our allies, both Europe and Japan, would support the Arab position, leaving us completely isolated.

It was the contemplation of these alternative risks — of bogging down in niggling detail and of consuming our energies in the pursuit of comprehensive goals more yearned for than attainable — that induced us to decide instead on a "step-by-step" approach. A more ambitious effort, if it failed, would make us the target for everybody's frustrations — the Israelis would blame us for our exactions, the Arabs for our reticence, the allies for their impotence; the Soviets would exploit the resulting turbulence for their hegemonic aims. The statesman must weigh the rewards of success against the penalties of failure. And he is permitted only one guess. Unlike the observer, he is not given the privilege, if his judgment turns out to be wrong, of revising it in another treatise. The statesman's errors are likely to be irrevocable. We needed to set objectives within the psychological capacities of the parties, goals that could not be vetoed by the intransigent or the fanatic. Each step had to show that we could achieve results. Thereby each advance would build confidence and make further steps easier. At a WSAG meeting of November 2, I said:

> We can reduce Soviet influence in the area and can get the oil embargo raised if we can deliver a moderate program, and we are going to do it. If not, the Arabs will be driven back to the Soviets, the oil will be lost, we will have the whole world against us, and there will not be one UN vote for us. We must prove to the Arabs that they are better off dealing with us on a moderate program than dealing with the Russians on a radical program.

But as yet, all was theory. I had never visited an Arab country nor dealt extensively with Arab leaders. Except from their infrequent visits to Washington, I had no way of knowing whether what seemed logical to me appeared in the same light to them. Nor was it yet clear whether I could establish a relationship of confidence with them. When I had been named Secretary of State, there had been some unease in the Arab world about my Jewish background — but also appreciation of my reputation for negotiating the Vietnam cease-fire and of the possibility that I could have a moderating influence over Israel.

I was fortunate that my first interlocutor from the Arab world was Ismail Fahmy, soon to be full (no longer Acting) Foreign Minister of Egypt. (He was confirmed in his post on October 31.) He came bounding into my State Department office on Monday, October 29, straight from the airplane without an appointment, taking the fortress by storm. "The President has sent me to make your acquaintance," he said matter-of-factly, "to report to him about you and to prepare your visit." In other words, Sadat was having me looked over; Fahmy was going to give me a grade.

Sadat could not have made a happier choice. Fahmy was at once transparent and subtle, convivial and abrasive, suave and prickly. He had lived for many years in the United States while serving at the United Nations; one of his children had been reared here. He had suffered for his alleged pro-American bias during Nasser's time. It was a misunderstanding on Nasser's part. Genuinely dedicated to better relations with the West, Fahmy was also a fervent Egyptian nationalist. Like Sadat, he did not move toward us from sentimentality but from a cool analysis of Egypt's interests. Nasser's policies had brought disaster; the flirtation with the Soviet Union had failed to recover Egyptian territory. What could not be exacted from us by pressure might perhaps be attained through trust and a spirit of cooperation. Fahmy was adaptable in tactics but he was clear about his objectives and implacable about his principles.

Fahmy had come both to charm and to bully me. His romantic nature saw fit to endow me with diplomatic skills exceeding even my own not excessively low estimate. It seems to be in the Arab nature to believe that some epic event or personality will miraculously transcend the humdrum mess that is the usual human condition; a miracle worker is a mechanism for avoiding hard choices. A related tactic of Fahmy's was to ascribe to me some outrageous design of astonishing complexity — which also put me on notice that a man capable of seeing through imaginary maneuvers of such stupendous subtlety would not be diverted by the cruder designs I might in fact produce. Yet Fahmy was also a skilled diplomat, particularly good at translating Sadat's instructions, which were more often visionary than detailed, into practical negotiating proposals. Roly-poly in appearance, Fahmy had no difficulty appearing jolly; he was a genuinely nice man. But the watchful eyes spoke of a penetrating intelligence. In the final analysis, while he used the conciliatory manners of the upper-class Egyptian to avoid unnecessary confrontation, he left no doubt that confrontation was inevitable if differences could not be reconciled.

Fahmy was my first extended contact with that extraordinary collection of Arab foreign ministers who spoke of themselves as "brothers" but seemed never to find anything else good to say about each other. Morbidly suspicious of one another's designs, they exchanged information with breathtaking rapidity, obscuring their real aims with a reticence masquerading as volubility. They were fun to be with even if slightly nerve-racking. Fahmy's "brothers" used to grumble that he belonged at a NATO ministerial meeting, not at the Arab League; he considered them ignorant amateurs more interested in heroic failure than in practical achievement. They both had a point. Fahmy did have more sympathy for the West and much more understanding of it than most of his colleagues. He also knew what seemed to elude some of the confreres: how to get from exalted declaration to practical achievement. Yet one forgot Fahmy's Arab vocation at one's peril. His nationalism included broader Arab goals. We became good, if wary, friends.

Fahmy's assignment in Washington was largely psychological. He offered an Arab program for peace but did not expect immediate success since he knew this would involve protracted negotiations with Israel, and Sadat could afford neither delay nor failure. Fahmy therefore stressed that his purpose was broader, to remove the tensions that had characterized Egyptian-American relations for nearly twenty years.

He engaged in no recriminations about the breakdown of the cease-fire, though it would have been natural to blame us for not being able to implement what we had negotiated. Indeed, he gave us credit for having brought about the cease-fire as well as for starting the process of negotiation between Israel and Egypt at Kilometer 101. Egyptians have not been manipulating foreigners for thousands of years without having learned that one of the best ways to induce someone to engage himself on your behalf is to give him a reputation to uphold. And the safest form of flattery is to praise him for what has already been accomplished.

Fahmy would not be deflected by our domestic upheaval; it pleased his fancy to pretend that Sadat's problems at home were much greater: "You have a small thing like Watergate here; in our country the whole situation is a crisis." I hoped, for all our sakes, that he did not know what he was talking about. If Egypt's crisis was worse than ours, a policy based on bringing about an Egyptian reversal of alliances could not succeed. Despite his difficulties, Fahmy continued, Sadat was eager for a basic change not simply toward the United States but toward Israel as well: "We have no interest in putting Israel into the sea or invading Israel, irrespective of the Palestinian situation." In other words, not only did Egypt accept Israel's existence — this was becoming the staple of Middle East rhetoric for ever more countries — but Fahmy left no doubt that it would not let the Palestinians stand in the way of a solution, a marked change from the stand Hafiz Ismail had taken with me earlier in the year.

Fahmy knew that the real issue in the Middle East, too, was psychological: "Confidence is the key. . . . Israel and Egypt must establish confidence, otherwise we can't go ahead." The minutiae of the negotiations over supply to the Third Army must not, in short, obscure the real and revolutionary goal, which was to alter the terms of reference of the Israeli-Arab dialogue.

Fahmy did have a number of ideas, however, on how to solve the problems of supply for the Third Army, release of prisoners, and the blockade of Bab el-Mandeb. None of them seemed particularly workable, based as they were on the proposition that Israel had either to pull back to the cease-fire line of October 22 (the line it held before it surrounded the Third Army) or at least to vacate a corridor ten kilometers wide on each side of the Cairo-Suez road — which would realize Israel's fear of seeing *its* army on the west bank of the Suez Canal caught between two hostile forces. To ease this concern, Fahmy offered the assurance that no military supplies would pass on this road — the germ of an idea, provided we could find an adequate inspection system.

Pending Golda's visit, I avoided detailed negotiation, but the study of Fahmy's ideas enabled us to move very rapidly when the opportunity arose. In the meantime, my primary concern was to avoid endless guerrilla war over these issues. As I said to Fahmy:

If I spend my capital on every point of the cease-fire, there will not be any capital left to spend on the peace negotiations. If peace negotiations do not succeed, we can take the present line or the October 22 line — it does not mean anything for there will be another war. The question is how we get cease-fire arrangements that are good enough to get us through peace negotiations over the next three to six months.

And I warned Fahmy that the oil embargo would hamper, not spur, our peace efforts: "If the oil embargoes and curtailments are not stopped, we will have to stop our diplomatic efforts. There can be no pressure." Fahmy was too sophisticated to imagine that regardless of pressures he could leave it all to us without making any concessions. While not yielding his position on the October 22 line, he indicated that if Israel agreed to regular nonmilitary supplies to the Third Army, Egypt would consider lifting the blockade of Bab el-Mandeb and releasing the Israeli prisoners of war. But would Israel permit any kind of supply to the trapped enemy army? Only Israel's Prime Minister would have the answer.

The Golda Meir who arrived in Washington on October 31 was a different person from the leader who had so confidently, even cockily, told Nixon a few months earlier: "We've never had it so good." The war had devastated her; she maintained her strong leadership but she suffered with every bereaved Israeli family. And in that psychological condition, she had to guide her people into a new and largely unfamiliar international environment.

The realization was beginning to sink in that the war had been tactically victorious but strategically inconclusive. Israel's aura of invincibility had disappeared as well as the self-confidence that went with it. A divided people approached with confusion what a year earlier it would have celebrated as a triumph: The direct negotiations that had been the stated goal of Israeli diplomacy since 1947 were already taking place on the military level with Egypt, yet their fruits turned to ashes as the implications became evident. All the tangible concessions — above all, territory — had to be made by Israel; once made, they were irrevocable. The Arab quid pro quo was something intangible, such as diplomatic recognition or a legal state of peace, which could always be modified or even withdrawn. Hope that Israel might at last be accepted by its neighbors was dimmed by knowledge that for other countries recognition is where diplomacy begins, not ends; by doubt that any change of Arab policy would be either genuine or permanent.

America's involvement in the diplomacy only partially eased the difficulty. As we became the mediator, Israeli-American relations were bound to change in many subtle ways. What Israel wanted from the United States was two nearly irreconcilable courses of action: unconditional support of Israel's negotiating position, which Israeli domestic politics usually drove toward the tactically intransigent; and influence on the Arab countries to accept the State of Israel and conclude a peace.

To fulfill the first role, we would have to act in effect as Israel's lawyer; to achieve the second objective, we would have to gain Arab confidence and a reputation for fairness. If we were serious about the peace process, we had to take Arab views seriously; on occasion we would have to dissociate from Israeli positions or actions we considered unreasonable. Several years earlier, I had told Ambassador Yitzhak Rabin that so long as the American policy was simply to frustrate Arab reliance on Soviet support, American and Israeli policies would be identical. But once Arab disillusionment was complete, and once Arab states began to turn to us in a spirit of cooperation, differences in perspective or tactics might well emerge. That moment was now approaching, at least as far as Egypt was concerned. All this produced an almost elemental fear in Israel that the United States might become so committed to a new relationship with the Arab world that its support would become less certain and Israel would lose its only friend.

That this fear had as yet no concrete basis made it all the more nagging. By any normal standard of relations among nations, we had stood by Israel to an unprecedented degree both during the war and in its tumultuous aftermath. We had saved Israel by the airlift and by running diplomatic interference. In the week before Golda's visit, we had prevented UN condemnation of Israeli cease-fire violations and we had faced down the Soviets in the alert. But for the first time, we had indicated that our support was not unconditional. We had drawn the line at the destruction of the Third Army trapped after that cease-fire. Our dissociation from Israel on that issue was, we thought, the gentlest imaginable in the circumstances. We did not ask for Israeli withdrawal to the October 22 line, only for the passage through Israeli lines of a convoy with humanitarian supplies. But in Israel the substance was less important than the symbolism. If our dissociation should become habit-forming, Israel was lost.

At any other time, Golda would have coolly taken stock of the situation and decided that Israel's security would be well preserved by elaborating a joint strategy with an American administration clearly sympathetic to Israel's strategic concerns. But this visit began nine days after the cease-fire, a week after the Soviet threats leading to the alert. She was drained; she hid her fears behind defiance. She spoke darkly of the one supply convoy as an Egyptian "victory."

All this was a surrogate for Golda's real worry, which went to the very heart of the process of peacemaking. If Israel's negotiating positions were not sacrosanct, where then was the stopping place? If America reserved the right not to follow Jerusalem's lead, what could Israel count on? There were answers to these questions, and we found them over the next few weeks. But at that particular moment it seemed to Golda that her country had escaped the specter of military defeat only to encounter the peril of slow diplomatic attrition. "I have left home now," Golda said on November 1, setting the tone at the first meeting at Blair House:

> because things have reached the stage where, beyond the issues of substance, things must be made clear. . . . We need to know the plans that are being discussed. We need to know, do we get things after they're done? After it is worked out by other parties? . . . Maybe Israel has to do everything Egypt wants. But we have to know what is being planned between the parties. Are there plans for the negotiations? We're responsible to our people.

The issue, of course, was not even remotely one of imposing Egyptian preferences on Israel. As we saw it, keeping the Third Army from being destroyed was the minimum prerequisite for *any* peace process — which no country needed more than Israel. But Golda had no confidence that we or anybody else knew how to get from here to there. And until she saw a road map, she preferred to stay where she was. She had, moreover, got hold of a real problem. The mounting demands on Israel had less to do with abstract analysis of their merits than with the pressures felt by major countries. "Suppose we start peace negotiations," she said two days later. "What happens to us then? The Soviets won't change, the Europeans, Japanese won't change. Oil is still in Arab hands. How do you know it won't just be more pressure to do more?" And if that was Israel's destiny, why not face it at the Suez Canal rather than at some point closer to Israel's borders?

Golda had put a good question, permitting no theoretical answer. We sought to ease Israel's fears of isolation. But dependence is not an easy relationship, especially dependence on a superpower. A small country's survival in a hostile world can turn on nuances not easily grasped by faraway nations with wider margins of safety. The readiness to run risks for peace was bound to be greater in America than in Israel. And these risks involved America only indirectly; for Israel they were issues of survival. America could afford experiments; for Israel a single miscalculation could spell catastrophe.

The problem thus boiled down to a challenge as old as international relations themselves. In an interdependent world, each nation must adjust goals and policies to some extent to those of others; no country has the possibility of acting as if only its preferences mattered. For many a decade, Arab intransigence and Soviet pressure had created the illusion that Israel did not have to conduct a foreign policy, only a defense policy. But the October war and Egypt's turn toward moderation had ended that simple state of affairs. Golda was railing not against America's strategy but against a new, more complicated, reality:

MEIR: We didn't start the war, yet . . .

KISSINGER: Madame Prime Minister, we are faced with a very tragic situation. You didn't start the war, but you face a need for wise decisions to protect the survival of Israel. This is what you face. This is my honest judgment as a friend.

MEIR (her voice shaking): You're saying we have no choice.

KISSINGER: We face the international situation that I described to you.

MEIR: You're saying we have to accept the judgment of the U.S. . . . . We have to accept your judgment? Even on our own affairs? On what is best for us?

KISSINGER: We all have to accept the judgment of other nations. We're deferring to your judgment.

Golda's apprehension was that if she once accepted our judgment of what was best — even if we were right — this would whet the appetite for even further Israeli concessions. So she went to the other extreme and insisted that Israel need not take into account the view of any other nation — an autonomy and luxury enjoyed not even by the superpowers.

As for us, we needed badly to work out a common approach with Israel, or else our strategy would be in tatters. If Israel was adamant, our central position in the diplomacy would disintegrate. We were able to reduce, often substantially, what the radicals and Soviets demanded, but, as I said to Golda, "we can do it only if we can show we can deliver and they can't." We could not, in other words, shrink the diplomatic agenda for the Middle East to nothing. If we produced no progress at all, the Arabs would have little incentive to deal with us; it would become impossible to split Egypt from the Soviets; there would be no moderate alternative to Arab radicalism. Not even the best friend of Israel could avoid the need for negotiations and concessions altogether; indeed, no true friend could encourage an intransigence that guaranteed the gradual erosion of Israel's position, as well as another explosion.

Golda recognized this in theory but at this early stage was not yet ready to face the implications. So she fought a tenacious rearguard action on the issue of supplies for the Third Army. She chose her battlefield cleverly — as a good strategist should — not by pleading Israel's national interest but by warning of Soviet-American collusion. This tactic was skillfully designed to stir up powerful elements of Israel's supporters in the United States, but it drove those of us who had gone through three weeks of crisis to a level of irritation that nearly matched our high regard for Golda.

Nor was she on this occasion a respecter of rank. When she met with Nixon in the Oval Office, he sought to win her to a policy of negotiation:

The problem you have to consider is whether the policy you have followed — being prepared with the Phantoms and the Skyhawks — can succeed, lacking a settlement. The question is whether a policy of only being prepared for war — although even with a peace settlement you will have to be prepared — is sufficient.

This last war proves the overwhelming conclusion that a policy of digging in, telling us to give you the arms and you will do the fighting, can't be the end. Your policy has to be to move as you are moving toward talks.

Golda would have none of it. She did not propose to rest her people's survival on assurances from neighbors fresh from launching a surprise attack. She had no category of thought that included supplying a trapped enemy army, no matter when it had been encircled.

And she reflected her cabinet's convictions. Indeed, in their despair and panic, Golda's colleagues dug themselves into total immobility. To break the deadlock, I proposed that Israel accept the "principle" of the October 22 line but then offer to negotiate with Egypt over its precise location. Such a negotiation was bound to be very time-consuming; it would, in effect, shelve the issue. While the negotiations were going on, nonmilitary supplies would be sent to the Third Army through UN checkpoints on the Cairo-Suez access route. In the process we would seek to transform these discussions into a broader negotiation on disengagements of forces that would ultimately make the issue of the cease-fire line moot. At first, Golda accepted this proposal, subject to cabinet approval. The next night she was obliged to reject it because her cabinet would not go along either with accepting the principle of the October 22 line or with permitting UN checkpoints on the Cairo-Suez road. They were prepared to do no more than discuss a general disengagement of forces.

But the Israeli concept of disengagement of forces was what had been put forward during the night of the alert: a territorial swap, with Israel pulling back to the east bank of the Canal and Egypt to the west bank, each side withdrawing ten kilometers from the Canal. There was no way Sadat would accept such a proposal. Egypt was being asked not only to relinquish all its territorial gains in the recent war but, on top of it, to vacate ten additional kilometers on the west bank where its forces had been deployed without restrictions before the war. This was certain to be rejected — as Golda herself admitted. Indeed, there was a chance that if we associated ourselves with such a scheme, Sadat might decide that American mediation was fruitless and he had no choice except to resume hostilities.

In the event, Golda permitted one more nonmilitary convoy to proceed, prior to my visit to Cairo.

Tempers at our daily WSAG meetings were growing short. Some of my colleagues were still urging that the trapped Third Army be resupplied by an *American* airlift; at one point the Defense Department even identified transport planes for such a mission. Despite my own irritation — after all, Israeli nerves were not the only ones frayed by three weeks of almost sleepless, nearly nonstop tension — I opposed this strongly. An American airlift to an Egyptian army would signal so profound a shift of American diplomatic priorities that it would undercut our own bargaining position. I urged my WSAG colleagues not to show any public displeasure with Israel, for our influence in the Middle East depended on Israel's being perceived as a close ally difficult to move. A visible split between us would invite mounting outside pressures; it would encourage the Europeans, the Soviet Union, and the nonaligned to press for solutions much less achievable, and therefore more likely to exacerbate the problem, than the ones we were discussing. We would get no benefit from breaking a deadlock by brute force — only escalating demands to do it over and over again.

Golda too, however difficult she was in private, understood that it was against Israel's interests to drive matters to the breaking point. Indeed, one of her purposes was pedagogical. She wanted to teach us that an attempt to solve our problems at Israel's expense was not free and might be painful. And she served a tactical necessity: She knew perfectly well that the issue of the Third Army would be solved one way or the other, but she did not want to saddle her cabinet with making the decision. It was too much to ask of a people so soon after a near-disaster inflicted by an attack by Arab armies. It was easier for Israel to yield to American pressure than to take on the burden of initiating generous proposals. She saw no sense in showing her hand too early. After she had heard what Sadat had to say to me, she would begin to bargain seriously. Her cabinet might overrule her when she was at Blair House; they would not hold out once she was in the chair and facing them.

Contact with the PLO

OF all of Israel's nightmares, none was more elemental than the Palestine Liberation Organization (the PLO), founded in 1964. The possibility that a group claiming all of Palestine for itself might gain any legitimacy whatever was considered a basic threat to Israel's survival. On the other hand, the imminence of negotiations increased the PLO's ambitions for a role, and our diplomacy, about to unfold, would be more difficult in the face of its active sabotage — confronting us with a delicate problem.

Of course, at this point the Palestinians had not yet achieved ultimate political recognition even by the Arab states. Security Council Resolution 242, passed in November 1967, had spoken only of a "refugee" problem; it accorded them no distinctive political role. The Middle East crisis had had its origin in Palestine, but all parties showed extraordinary ambivalence in their approach to the Palestinians. In 1973 they were still treated as refugees in the UN, as terrorists in the United States and Western Europe, as an opportunity by the Soviets, and as simultaneous inspiration and nuisance by the Arab world. After the October war, as the PLO became increasingly prominent, the ambivalence of some of its supporters mounted. It was never easy to tell how much of the Arab attitude reflected real commitment, fear of the Palestinian terrorist potential, or desire to appeal to domestic radical groups.

As for the United States, our experiences with the PLO had not been of a nature to inspire much confidence. In 1970, Palestinian terrorists had hijacked three airplanes to Jordan and taken hundreds of passengers hostage, including scores of Americans, holding them for several weeks. Having in the past organized several attempts to assassinate Hussein, this time the PLO attempted to take over his Kingdom; in the bloody struggle of "Black September," Hussein expelled it from Jordan. In 1972 it assumed responsibility for the massacre of Israeli athletes at the Munich Olympic Games, further forfeiting American sympathy, and in March 1973 PLO supporters assassinated two American diplomats in Khartoum. The PLO was thus overtly anti-American as well as dedicated to the destruction of two important friends of the United States: Israel and the Hashemite Kingdom of Jordan. In these circumstances, we did not have a high incentive to advance the "dialogue" with the PLO, as the fashionable phrase ran later — not because of Israeli pressures but because of our perception of the American national interest.

We were aware that the PLO contained many divergent elements, some avowedly terrorist, others more ambiguous in the formulation of their objectives, though none of them accepted the State of Israel. And various Arab nations controlled factions of the PLO as a means of protecting their own domestic tranquillity by influencing Palestinian policies. But this created its own complexities. For example, Syria's favorite group was the Saiqa, which was certainly more responsive to the government in Damascus than to the PLO leadership in Beirut.

Thus before 1973, the PLO rarely intruded into international negotiations. In the 1972 communiqué ending Nixon's Moscow summit, there was no reference to Palestinians, much less to the PLO. Neither did the abortive "general working principles" on which Gromyko and I worked in 1972 mention them except as refugees.[2] The 1973 US–Soviet summit communiqué spoke of the "legitimate interests of the Palestinian people" but did not define them. All planning and discussions with other governments regarding the West Bank of the Jordan River had assumed that King Hussein would be Israel's negotiating partner.

The issue of contacts with Palestinians was therefore not in 1973 a major policy problem for the United States. It arose most infrequently, almost invariably in low-level intelligence channels. The idea of a Palestinian state run by the PLO was not a subject for serious discourse.

Then in mid-1973, the PLO took an initiative toward us. In late July, our Ambassador to Iran, Richard Helms, in the United States in connection with a visit of the Shah, informed me that one of his aides had been approached by a close associate of PLO leader Yasir Arafat. Arafat was reported to be interested in a dialogue with the United States, which would be based on two premises: that "Israel is here to stay"; and that Jordan should be the home for a Palestinian state (in other words, that Hussein must be overthrown). The PLO also wanted clarification on certain questions: What did we understand by "Palestinian interests" in the Brezhnev-Nixon communiqué? How did we intend to pursue them? How committed were we to the continued existence of the Kingdom of Jordan? "The issue is whether you want to have policy talks with the fedayeen or not," Helms correctly pointed out.

I told Helms I would think about it. My reflections were unlikely to be positive, however. I considered King Hussein a valued friend of the United States and a principal hope for diplomatic progress in the region. Our aim should be to strengthen his position, not to encourage a group that avowed its determination to overthrow him in its very first communication with us. A Palestinian state run by the PLO was certain to be irredentist. Even should it change its professed aims, it would not likely remain moderate for long; its many extremist factions would see to that. Its Soviet ties, too, would lead it in the direction of becoming a radical state like Libya or South Yemen. Any Palestinian structure on the West Bank had every incentive to turn on Jordan — if only to gain a secure base for later operations against Israel and to avoid the provisions of a peace accord that would inevitably demilitarize the West Bank.

The PLO's hints of possible coexistence with Israel were contrary to the 1964 Palestinian National Covenant, the founding document of the organization; PLO policy at its most moderate called for a mixed Moslem-Jewish-Christian secular state in Palestine — a euphemism for the dismantlement of Israel. Of all the Arabs, the Palestinians had the bitterest grievance against the Jewish state. Even should Israel return to the 1967 borders on the West Bank and relinquish the Old City of Jerusalem — and there were few who thought this in the realm of possibility — the Palestinians would covet the territories to which their very name connected them. To them a West Bank mini-state could be only an interim step toward their final aims.

On August 3, I told Helms that we had "a nothing message" to send back, largely taking refuge in the generalization that our goal was peaceful coexistence among the states and peoples of the area. The United States would be interested to hear the ideas of the Palestinians on how this objective could be promoted through negotiations. We were unequivocal in response to the third question: The overthrow of existing governments in the Arab world was not acceptable; we were committed to the survival of the Kingdom of Jordan.

Interestingly enough, on August 13 we received essentially the same kind of PLO approach through Morocco. King Hassan passed the identical questions to Lieutenant General Vernon A. Walters, then Deputy Director of the CIA, who was visiting the King in Casablanca. The next day, I took care to inform Israeli Ambassador Simcha Dinitz of Arafat's two approaches and of our response:

[W]e will tell him we can't enter into discussions having to answer three questions. The one thing he wants, of course, is that we make Jordan dispensable. We will never agree to anything like that. You can tell the Prime Minister that.

Dinitz made no response then or later. On August 17, I told Israeli Foreign Minister Abba Eban that our policy was based on Jordan, not the Palestinians. (I made it as a general comment, leaving it to Golda to inform her Foreign Minister of the Arafat approach.) Eban suggested we leave no doubt "that when you talk about the Palestinians you mean it in the context of an Israeli-Jordan settlement." I had no difficulty agreeing to a proposition that reflected American policy.

On September 3, 1973, King Hassan told General Walters that it would be possible to establish a dialogue with the PLO; Morocco offered to help arrange it. On October 10 — four days into the Middle East war — we heard from Arafat, though not through Morocco. Instead, as I have described in Chapter XI, that message reached us through Beirut. Arafat predicted that though Egypt and Syria would be routed, they had achieved enough "face" to engage in serious negotiations. The PLO was prepared to participate in Arab negotiations with Israel; the "score" it had to settle was with Jordan, not Israel, but this need not be part of the current phase of diplomacy.

We returned no reply while the war was going on. But its tense aftermath caused us to take another look at the Palestinian feelers. In case of a confrontation with the Soviets it was important to minimize Arab support for Soviet intervention. And once that danger had passed, it was in our interest to create the best environment for moderate governments to join the peace process. The PLO had a high potential for causing trouble all over the Arab world. We wanted it to be on its best behavior during the delicate early stages of our approaches to Egypt and while we were seeking Saudi support. On October 23, moreover — the day that the confrontation over cease-fire violations was heading for its first climax — we received a further message reiterating Arafat's interest in talks.

On October 25, the day of the alert, we decided to take up the offer in order to gain some maneuvering room. In the only significant communication to the PLO while I was in office, a message was sent via Morocco that we were prepared to send a representative to meet with PLO officials in order to enable us to develop a United States reaction to Arafat's proposals. (In other words, our emissary would not be empowered to negotiate; a formal reaction, if any, would follow his report.) We designated General Walters as our representative. He had acted as our secret channel to the North Vietnamese and Chinese in Paris and was an expert at discreet missions. A meeting was suggested for the beginning of November, just preceding my trip to Cairo, thus ensuring PLO quiescence during this delicate phase.

The meeting took place on November 3 in Morocco's capital, Rabat. My instructions to Walters were to gain the maximum amount of time and to get as clear a view of Palestinian thinking as possible. He was to make no proposals; he should take the postion that as an intelligence officer he had only a "listening brief." As to the future political role of the Palestinians:

> The United States has no proposals to make. It is not so expert in the history of intra-Arab politics and culture that it can invent solutions. The Palestinians must understand, however, that the United States has a fixed principle that it does not betray its friends. We regard the King of Jordan as a friend. We would expect, nevertheless, that in the context of a comprehensive settlement, the relationship between the Palestinian movement and the Hashemite Kingdom could develop in the direction of reconciliation.

In other words, we proposed to treat the Palestinian problem not as an international but as an inter-Arab concern. It was up to the PLO to straighten out its relationships with the other Arab states — with one proviso: We would participate in no maneuver aimed at Jordan; the PLO's real option was reconciliation with the Hashemite Kingdom, not its overthrow.

What applied to Jordan was even more true of Israel. Walters was to make clear that the United States would oppose any threat to the survival of Israel and any challenge to its legitimacy. And we would go over to active opposition if any more American blood was spilled by the PLO.

Walters carried out his assignment with his characteristic swaggering efficiency and discretion. The PLO representative, a close associate of Arafat's, described the injustices done to the Palestinians. The thrust of his presentation was aimed at Jordan: Palestinians could never live in a Hashemite state; nor could they build a state of their own confined to the West Bank and Gaza. It followed that the Hashemite dynasty would have to be overthrown to provide a national homeland for the Palestinians. He evaded the question of under what conditions, if any, the PLO would recognize Israel. He spoke of a secular state (code words for the destruction of Israel), or of possibly reducing Israel to its status under the UN partition plan of 1947 — which meant truncating even pre-1967 Israel. The PLO representative did not make a concrete proposal any more than Walters did. First meetings always involve this tentative kind of exploration, neither side wanting to put itself at the disadvantage of having been rebuffed, each probing for flexibility in the other's position.

As it turned out, the beginning of our dialogue with the PLO was also its end. There was only one more meeting, in March 1974, but it did not advance matters beyond the point of the first one.

This was no accident. At this stage, involving the PLO was incompatible with the interests of any of the parties to the Middle East conflict. Even should some PLO leader accept Resolution 242 and the legal right of Israel to exist — something the organization has refused to do to this day — the dynamics of the movement made it unlikely that such moderation could be maintained indefinitely. The talk in Rabat made clear in any event that the 1967 borders were considered only the first phase; a PLO nation would be ideologically committed to the dismantling of the Jewish state. And Jordan faced even more immediate dangers; the PLO contact left no doubt of the organization's designs on the Hashemite dynasty.

Though the meeting in Rabat was supposed to be secret, it was potentially too explosive to risk its uncontrolled leakage to other countries. Moreover, if word spread only through the Arab gossip mill, it would take on a more dramatic significance than we intended, disquieting especially those countries on whose support we relied for a moderate evolution. I therefore informed Hussein, Sadat, and Boumedienne, and later discussed it with Asad. Brent Scowcroft briefed Ambassador Dinitz.

Walters's meeting achieved its immediate purpose: to gain time and to prevent radical assaults on the early peace process. After it, attacks on Americans — at least by Arafat's faction of the PLO — ceased. Otherwise the meeting yielded no lasting results.

My First Middle East Journey

I LEFT Washington on Monday, November 5, bound for Morocco and Tunisia prior to the critical visit to Egypt. I hoped that King Hassan and President Habib Bourguiba, old friends of the United States, would give moral support to our efforts with their brethren in the Arab world.

We reached Morocco around 10:00 that evening, for my first step on Arab soil. It was also my first experience with a guard of honor. The latter was a daunting event, all the more so because nobody had briefed me what to expect.

As I emerged from the airplane, I was greeted by the stunning sight of a rifle company of tall Berber troops in flowing red and white robes and white turbans. The next day at the King's palace I encountered an even more impressive corps of Royal Guardsmen wearing baggy scarlet and green uniforms and wielding swords. An officer with drawn saber invited me to review them. I had not the foggiest notion of the correct procedure. Impelled by an overwhelming desire to get it over with as quickly as possible, I moved along the front row of the soldiers at a clip obviously faster than expected. It may even have been a world's record, for when I turned around, my escort officer was goose-stepping behind me, still halfway down the line. I waited and, when he caught up with me, extended my hand — a gesture frustrated by the unsheathed sword thrust outward at a 45-degree angle in the perplexed officer's fist. He proved equal to the occasion. Throwing at me a look of mixed pity and condescension, he sheathed his sword, removed his immaculate glove, and offered me a handshake — by which time I had withdrawn my hand and was offering him a salute. Finally, I shook his hand and departed quickly. The same day at the Royal Palace, Joe Sisco was seated in one of the ornate gold and red velvet chairs in King Hassan's sitting room, tipping it back while reflecting on some profound matter. It collapsed, leaving Joe prostrate, just as His Majesty came into the room. Moroccan-American relations managed to survive these setbacks.[3]

Morocco is at the crossroads of Africa, Europe, and the Arab world, bordering the Atlantic and the Mediterranean. Its dramatic mountains and barren deserts have spewed forth conquerors who ruled North Africa and Spain, sometimes brutally, occasionally magnanimously, for several hundred years. But its pivotal location has also exposed it to periodic invasions. Alternately anvil and hammer, Morocco has seen the glories and the foibles of man, his triumphs and his degradations. Its upper classes are elegant and jaded, influenced by French rationalism but molded by Moslem certitudes. The mass of the population endures, as it has through the centuries, largely oblivious to what geography has imposed. Morocco has been for the past century at the intersection of the grand strategies of others, forcing its rulers to navigate by skill, shrewdness, and self-assurance.

A tradition of hereditary rule, dating in the existing dynasty from the seventeenth century, was reinforced by the fact that the father of Hassan was the principal leader in the struggle for independence against France. The monarchy mirrored the duality of Morocco's soul. A man of the world with sophisticated tastes, King Hassan II never made the Shah's mistake of professing an ostentatious secularism. At the same time a Moslem scrupulously sensitive to the religious conservatism of his country and a polished and rationalistic politician, King Hassan practiced the ceremonial authoritarianism rooted in Moroccan history. Ruler of the Arab state farthest from the conflict with Israel, he used his influence for moderation, making his country available not only for Walters's clandestine meetings with the PLO but also for the secret meetings between Israelis and Egyptians that led to Sadat's historic visit to Jerusalem in 1977.

Morocco's neighbors had styles of government less rooted in history. Socialist Algeria was always looking for an opportunity to weaken its neighbor and rival; revolutionary Libya fomented subversion. In the face of these radical challenges, the King maneuvered to avoid appearing backward or feudal. He has been among the most persuasive supporters of the Palestinians, never failing to press their case. He loyally sent a contingent of Moroccan troops to fight on the Syrian front in the 1973 war. Withal, the King had no illusions about radical policies. He knew that he could deflect the pressures on his country only if the balance between moderates and radicals within the Arab world tilted in favor of the moderates. For this, American support was essential, and he earned it through many acts of friendship as well as wise counsel.

In our first meetings, I explained the necessity of our airlift to Israel with the argument that we could not permit Soviet arms to defeat American weapons in the Middle East without turning the whole area over to radical and Soviet influences. The King shared our perspective. "We could not have survived," said the King. We conducted our review in the enormous palace in Rabat, first in a large plenary meeting and then alone in his private office. I wanted him to know our strategy: to avoid wasting our diplomatic capital on the cease-fire line and to move instead straight to a broader disengagement of forces. Hassan was supportive. He told me he would send a message to Cairo on my behalf, assuring Sadat that

[Kissinger] does not follow classic diplomatic intentions and he prefers to remain far from emotions and imagination, preferring to tackle problems and realities in a cool, calm and objective fashion. We insist upon our chief impression that if he gets into a commitment, he will honor it.

Where so much depended on intangibles, giving Sadat psychological reassurance was the greatest service the King could render to us.

I took my leave of King Hassan and flew on to Tunisia on November 6 to line up the support of another moderate leader and friend of the United States, President Habib Bourguiba. Bourguiba was of the original generation of independence fighters whose driving ambition was to be permitted to join the Western system of values, not to destroy it. Of middle-class background, he had been educated in France; not even frequent periods of imprisonment or exile extinguished his desire to bring the culture and modernity of the metropole to his country. Having achieved independence as long ago as 1956, Tunisia was already in danger of becoming a relic. Bourguiba remained staunchly pro-West, moderate in his pronouncements, measured in his policy. As with his colleague in Morocco, support of the Palestinians was a way of showing devotion to the Arab cause. But Tunisia, coveted by its neighbors Algeria and Libya and surviving in part because of their rivalry, needed a world of restraint. It could survive best by cooling passions; it feared the growth of Soviet influence and Arab radicalism.

Bourguiba lived in a palace he had built overlooking the ruins of Carthage — another reminder, if any was needed, that history is written by the victors. Bourguiba's palace was the fantasy that might sustain a man in prison. It seemed almost a plaything. Its corridors were covered with paintings, busts, and photographs of Bourguiba; I recall no other subject. Its rooms were of gargantuan dimensions. And through it all moved the slight, elderly figure, a French intellectual in bearing, with the fidgety restlessness of the man who has known confinement.

I had been warned that he was beginning to show signs of arteriosclerosis. It did not affect his lucidity, though his comments were not always directed to the subject one had raised. He expressed grave suspicion of Soviet intentions; he thought Soviet power was growing ominously and that the West lacked the discipline for effective resistance. He hoped for a major American role in the Middle East. I explained our strategy: "Others can give weapons, but only the United States can give territory." But we must not be blackmailed by oil; we acted on our convictions, not as the result of pressure. Bourguiba agreed sadly — and wisely — that the "attitude of hostility is a major error committed by the Arabs."

And so we left at last for Cairo, the stop that would make or break our journey.

The Six-Point Agreement

THE airport at Cairo was blacked out when I arrived late Tuesday, November 6, the cease-fire being only two weeks old. Foreign Minister Fahmy was barely discernible at the bottom of the stairs. The darkness did not inhibit his jocular grumbling, which he had developed into an art form. But he had hardly begun his catalogue of unfulfilled promises — American and Israeli — before a stampede of footsteps came rushing toward us across the darkened tarmac. It was the Cairo press corps, eager to observe the arrival of the first senior American since the war. Suddenly, television floodlights came on. My security personnel deployed. It was a losing effort. Like so many foreigners before them, they were engulfed by a sea of Egyptian humanity advancing inexorably like the nearby desert until the visitors stood there immobilized, finally surrendering to a fate made bearable by the obvious goodwill of those who had so flagrantly breached security. It was just as well that no terrorist decided to masquerade as a journalist, as Fahmy and I were jostled by this enthusiastic group that seemed more interested in some tactile contact with the visitors than with any particular set of questions. At last, a phalanx of soldiers rescued us and rushed us to a waiting

Mercedes limousine that had in better days served as Nasser's personal vehicle.

At my domicile, the Nile Hilton, Fahmy told me what the program would be: an early morning tour of the Egyptian Museum; a meeting with Sadat; a visit to the Pyramids; and a dinner at Fahmy's house. My meeting with Sadat was thus sandwiched between the contemplations of antiquity, perhaps to warn me that Egypt had prevailed over all outsiders — if not by defeating, then by outlasting them.

My first view of Cairo, the next morning, was from the balcony of my hotel. It showed a flat landscape divided by a muddy river. No building of any distinction was visible except the Tower of Cairo, built by Nasser in the early Sixties, allegedly with CIA money that he wanted to spend on "something unidentifiable, but very large, very conspicuous, very enduring and very expensive."[4] He got his wish, and the purposeless edifice is visible from every vantage. Like so many of Egypt's monuments, its main attribute is permanence, not function. And for all we know it may endure, for in that eternal country the dry air and brilliant sunshine preserve man's follies together with his triumphs.

The Egyptian Museum was still prepared for war. Artifacts were stored in boxes on the lower floors; strips of tape covered the glass cabinets, making viewing difficult. Sandbags were everywhere. What struck me most was the impact of Egypt on the art of its temporary conquerors. In one great hall one could observe the progressive "Egyptification" of the Hellenistic statuary after Alexander the Great. When the Greeks first arrived, their statues were realistic, on a human scale with a stern look and practical countenance. As the generations passed, they raised their sights quite literally; their gaze was no longer into the eye of another man but toward distant horizons. It transcended the limitations of Europe's fields and valleys and focused on the infinity of Egypt's sea of sand. The sternness left the faces, which became more abstract, almost beatific and detached as if the time allotted to mortals was irrelevant to their concerns.

A notable memory of my stroll across Tahrir Square to and from the museum was the friendliness of the passersby. I could hardly have been a household name in Egypt. Yet the bodyguard of security officers must have made it clear that I was the American visitor described in the newspapers. The mood was exuberant and, I judged, full of expectation. As in Israel a little over two weeks earlier, one sensed a people yearning for peace and for a signal of hope.

Mine was a fateful responsibility, not eased by a conversation I had had early in the morning with Arnaud de Borchgrave of *Newsweek,* who told me that Sadat had all but decided to resume hostilities; all his senior officers considered the encirclement of the Third Army an intolerable affront to Egyptian honor. Though de Borchgrave had been correct in his prediction of an imminent Arab-Israeli war six months earlier, I did not think he would be proved right this time. I could not believe that Sadat would have been so insistent on my coming or so flexible in his diplomacy if he intended to force a showdown. Still, this warning, at the least, increased my sense of the gravity of the occasion.

The multitudes in the streets of Cairo made vivid as no words could why Israel had such premonitions about its security. The city of Cairo, as noted, has almost twice the population of Israel. Every three years Egypt's population grows by the size of all of Israel's. It was a nearly insoluble dilemma: Israel had the power but not the faith for peace. The Arabs were still at a military disadvantage but they had the numbers and the time. They could wait for the Israeli mistake that would prove fatal. And the consciousness of this danger was what made Israeli diplomacy tense and rigid.

I was also aware that neither the domestic nor the international environment gave me much room for maneuver. Nixon was growing restless; he knew that his critics would blame Watergate for any failure of my mission, accelerating both his demise and the decline of credibility that must in time erode our world position. On November 5, Edward Brooke of Massachusetts had become the first Senator of the President's own party to call for his resignation; so had *Time* magazine, the *New York Times,* and the *Detroit News.* As always when in a tight corner, Nixon decided on attack, and attack seemed to mean a spectacular breakthrough in the Middle East. At a Cabinet meeting on energy on November 6, while I was in Cairo, Nixon unexpectedly raised the Middle East problem. Brent Scowcroft cabled me:

> At the end of the Cabinet meeting the President surprised everyone with a short speech on the Middle East. . . . The President said he wanted no notes taken and no discussion whatever but wanted the Cabinet to know in connection with energy that it might be necessary to apply pressure on Israel to avert a serious oil shortage. He said that Golda had first indicated some flexibility but then had become completely intransigent, apparently believing that the Israelis could just stay in possession of all they now held. He said it may be necessary for the US to go to the UN and perhaps to apply other kinds of pressure on Israel. He hoped it would not be necessary but if it was he expected the Cabinet to understand and to support whatever happened. . . .
>
> The whole thing was a bolt out of the blue and we can only hope it does not leak. . . . I feel confident that there will be no impact within the bureaucracy.

Turning on Israel over oil would have been a self-defeating act of desperation. Having committed ourselves to squeezing Israel to end the embargo, we would have set a precedent for use of the oil weapon over and over again as demands were being raised. We might wind up losing on all sides: neither achieving the Arabs' program nor — if we helped destroy Israel's reputation for intractability — gaining credit for compromise solutions. Miraculously, Haig and Scowcroft kept Nixon's comments from leaking. But there was little doubt that Nixon would order this strategy if my mission failed.

As we were approaching Cairo I had learned, too, that the European Community on November 6 had adopted a declaration on the Middle East strongly urging Israel's immediate withdrawal to the October 22 cease-fire line, and had thrown in a wholesale endorsement of the Arab interpretation of Security Council Resolution 242 for good measure. This abdication not only betokened Europe's abject weakness but did harm: It reduced Sadat's maneuvering room. Could he settle for less than the Europeans were proposing? The answer would determine what could be achieved, for the European program guaranteed a prolonged stalemate. To push Israel back to the October 22 line was too little a goal for the effort required. But if linked with an implied commitment to force Israel to accept the 1967 borders, it was too ambitious to be achievable. Caught between accomplishing too little and failing if we aimed for too much, we would expend capital better husbanded for the attainable disengagement of forces that was our objective.

Thus, Sadat and I both had our backs to the wall. Sadat had the Third Army at risk together with all hopes for a negotiated solution and the continuation of his switch from the Soviet Union to the United States. I was hazarding America's position in the Middle East in a talk with a leader I had never met and had only recently learned to respect. Sadat's asset was that he could produce a deadlock; mine was that deadlock served none of Sadat's long-term objectives and that I might help break it.

Tahra Palace is located in Heliopolis, a once-fashionable Cairo suburb now fighting to maintain appearances, squeezed between the urban slums spreading outward and the military housing associated with the Cairo airport creeping toward the city. Once occupied by one of King Farouk's wives, the palace reflects the Egyptian notion that royal pomp is the merger of the facade of Fontainebleau with the appointments of British country homes. It is situated in a spacious garden that seemed unusually empty for a Presidential headquarters.

When I arrived on the morning of November 7, two old acquaintances greeted me at the foot of the steps leading to the entrance. One was Hafiz Ismail, still security adviser to Sadat, ramrod-straight and urbane — the Cairo end of the "channel" to Washington. The other was Ashraf Ghorbal. I had enormous affection for this distinguished Harvard-educated diplomat who performed skillfully as head of Egypt's Interests Section in Washington in the absence of full diplomatic relations. He passionately believed that Egypt's destiny was on the side of the West. (In the tense days of Nasser's flirtations with Moscow, Ghorbal had once sent me a poem subtly pleading for patience.) He now embraced me. I knew his heart was with the success of my mission. In such situations, little gestures can give confidence. Ismail's and especially Ghorbal's presence made me feel more relaxed and hopeful.

I was hurried up a broad stairway toward a gallery overlooking the gardens. And at the top of the stairs the reason for the preternatural silence in the garden became evident. It seemed that every correspondent in the Middle East and half the President's staff were assembled in the gallery in another packed mob scene. Once again there were no visible security procedures. I was being jostled from several directions, nearly blinded by television lights, when suddenly I heard behind me a deep baritone: "Welcome, welcome."

Sadat had emerged, dressed in a khaki military tunic, an overcoat slung carelessly over his shoulders (for in November the inside of Egyptian palaces is cold). He was taller, swarthier, and more imposing than I had expected. He exuded vitality and confidence. That son of peasants radiated a natural dignity and aristocratic bearing as out of keeping with his revolutionary history as it was commanding and strangely calming. He affected nonchalance. I too did my best to pretend that there was nothing unusual about a meeting two weeks after a war in which we had armed Egypt's enemy and then — during the alert — had threatened to intervene militarily on Egyptian soil. Neither of us wanted to show that we had a great deal at stake, even while we knew that we would soon begin one of the few diplomatic exchanges that can be called seminal. We sat on a sofa, measuring each other through the banalities of the obligatory dialogue to make ourselves appear natural for the benefit of the photographers:

"How was your trip?"

"Excellent, Mr. President."

"You are welcome here."

"Thank you, Mr. President."

Sadat then ushered me into a large room that served as his office. On one side were French windows overlooking a lawn in which wicker chairs had been placed in a semicircle for the benefit of our aides. "I have been longing for this visit," said Sadat and started filling a pipe. "I have a plan for you. It can be called the Kissinger plan."

With these words he walked over to some situation maps covering the wall opposite and showed me a disengagement scheme according to which Israel would withdraw two-thirds of the way across the Sinai to a line from El Arish to Ras Mohammed (see the map on page 452). Sadat must have known this was an impossible assignment. If it was proving difficult to convince Israel to withdraw the few kilometers to the October 22 line on the *west* bank of the Canal, it was beyond all reason to imagine inducing such a dramatic retreat eastward, abandoning the Canal, the strategic Giddi and Mitla passes, and most of the Sinai. And what would Israel get in return? Sadat's vagueness on the subject showed that he was testing me. He puffed on his pipe and asked for my comments.

I did not think it wise to begin by rejecting one of the President's ideas, however unrealistic. And I had no wish to play the bull to Sadat's picador. So I changed the subject. Before we talked about the business at hand, I said, would the President tell me how he had managed to achieve such stunning surprise on October 6? That had been the turning point; what we were doing now was in a way its inevitable consequence.

Sadat narrowed his eyes, puffed again on his pipe, and smiled. He understood that I was paying him a compliment and establishing his status. He was not negotiating from weakness; he was not a supplicant; he had earned Egypt's right at the conference table; he had, in short, restored Egypt's honor and self-respect.

Slowly at first, but with growing animation, Sadat told his tale of lonely decision-making, his conclusion after the failure of the 1969 Rogers Plan that there would never be a serious negotiation so long as Israel was able to equate security with military predominance. It was impossible for Egypt to bargain from a posture of humiliation. He told me how he had grown disenchanted with the Soviet Union. Moscow prized its relations with the United States above support of Egypt; the bland treatment of the Middle East question in the communiqué of Nixon's 1972 summit in Moscow had removed any lingering doubts on that score.[5] Sadat had demanded the removal of Soviet troops in July 1972 because of the disrespect shown by Soviet leaders toward Egyptians and above all because they would surely seek to impede his planned military move or else exploit it for Soviet ends.

Sadat had wanted to launch an attack in November 1972 but his military had not been ready, indeed had been dubious about the entire enterprise. He had replaced his Chief of Staff with a commander who had confidence in his plans and in whom he had confidence. He had used the interval to line up Syria. His repeated mobilizations caused his threats of a showdown to dull Israel's vigilance. In May 1973 Israel mobilized in response to the Egyptian mobilization designed to culminate in the crossing of the Canal; Sadat had responded by postponing the attack once again to October, gambling that the false alarm would help his design. When his armies mobilized yet again, Israel was more likely to remain quiescent. And this is exactly what happened.

Why had he been so persistent, I asked? Why not wait for the diplomatic initiative we had promised? To teach Israel that it could not find security in domination, replied Sadat, and to restore Egypt's self-respect — a task no foreigner could do for it. Now that he had vindicated

Egyptian honor, Sadat told me, he had two objectives: to regain "my territory," that is to say, to restore the 1967 boundary in the Sinai, and to make peace. And he would be as determined and patient in the pursuit of these objectives as he had been in preparing for war.

Sadat had spent his years in prison under the British improving his English by reading novels and short stories in that language; he and a fellow prisoner had taught themselves German by the same method. Perhaps for this reason, his language was somewhat stilted, rather precise and formal. But an extraordinary passion lay just beneath the discipline of his manner of speaking — as if that self-control represented a dam necessary to contain elemental forces that once unleashed would know no restraint. As he spoke, Sadat kept his eyes slightly narrowed, viewing not his interlocutor but some distant horizon, much like the Egyptian statues seen a little while ago in the museum.

I listened to his tale of foresight and cunning, of honor and daring, of determination and suppleness, with the realization that I was in the presence of a remarkable man. Sadat seemed free of the obsession with detail by which mediocre leaders think they are mastering events, only to be engulfed by them. I could not tell yet whether it was possible to achieve both peace and the 1967 frontiers, nor whether Sadat had the endurance for the long journey inevitably required to find out. But I sensed that Sadat represented the best chance to transcend frozen attitudes that the Middle East had known since the creation of the State of Israel. The test would be if he was prepared to move by stages that reversed the momentum of conflict without offering a guarantee of final success — which required above all an act of faith. Therefore he had to understand our judgment of what was possible, and what he would have to do to make it possible.

And so I turned for the next half-hour to a conceptual discussion. Cooperation would depend on understanding of our long-term purposes; the tactics would follow almost automatically. I explained the American strategy in much the same terms as I had to my colleagues in the WSAG. History had shown, I said, that progress toward peace depended on two factors: an Arab leader willing to relate rhetoric to reality and an America willing to engage itself in the process. We would not exercise our influence under pressure; our actions had to be seen to reflect our choice and not submission to threats. We had no incentive to be forthcoming to clients of the Soviet Union. Nasser's policy of trying to extort concessions by mobilizing the Third World against us with Soviet support had not worked in the past and would not be permitted to work in the future. Peace in the Middle East could not come about by the defeat of American allies with Soviet arms — as we had just shown. But an Egypt pursuing its own national policy would find us ready to cooperate. We sought no preeminence in Egypt. I could discern no inevitable clash of interests between us.

"And Israel?" asked Sadat. Israel, I insisted, need not be a source of conflict. No Egyptian interest was served by the destruction of Israel; no Arab problem would be solved by it. Egypt had lost thousands of lives for a cause that had never been reduced to terms America could possibly support. We would never hold still for Israel's destruction, I continued, but we were willing to help allay reasonable Arab grievances. All we had ever heard from Arabs were sweeping programs put forward on a take-it-or-leave-it basis. Experience had shown that this course guaranteed deadlock. Israel was indeed stubborn, occasionally infuriating. But as someone who had spoken so movingly of national dignity, he had to understand the psychology of a country that had never enjoyed the minimum attribute of sovereignty, acceptance by its neighbors.

I urged Sadat to think of peace with Israel as a psychological, not a diplomatic problem. If, as he rightly insisted, Israel could not base its security on physical predominance, it also could not be secure without confidence. And that was the contribution required of the most influential Arab nation, Egypt. If Egypt supplied that component, we would do our best to obtain territorial changes, though they might not be so vast as in his "Kissinger plan."

Sadat listened intently to these heresies of Arab thought, impassively puffing on his pipe. He showed no reaction except: "And what about my Third Army? What about the October 22 line?"

I had gone too far to try stratagems. He had two choices, I replied. Relying on the declaration of the European Community and Soviet support, he could insist on the October 22 line. It would be difficult, even embarrassing, for us. Eventually, we might be induced to go along. But weeks would go by, and for what would he have mobilized all these pressures? To get Israel to go back a few kilometers on the *west* bank of the Suez Canal — a process that would then have to be repeated under even more difficult circumstances for a real separation of forces leading to an Israeli retreat across the Suez Canal. The better course was to live with the status quo, made bearable by a system of nonmilitary supplies for the Third Army. With immediate tensions defused, the United States would do its utmost to arrange a genuine disengagement of forces, moving the Israelis back across the Canal — although not as far as in his scheme, probably not even beyond the passes. Still, it would be the first Israeli withdrawal from Arab territory occupied for any length of time; it would create the confidence for further steps. The diplomacy to induce Israel to return to the October 22 line was about the same as the persuasion needed to produce a disengagement scheme and we would not be able to accomplish both in a brief period. Paradoxically, forgoing the October 22 line would speed up Israeli withdrawal from the Canal. Sadat should choose. I would do my best either way.

Sadat sat brooding, saying nothing for many minutes. I had given him a difficult problem. I was saying in effect that the key to peace was his acquiescence in keeping an Egyptian army cut off in the desert for weeks on end, relying on the assessment of an American he had just met and who had no experience in Middle East diplomacy. And then he astonished me. He did not haggle or argue. He did not dispute my analysis. He did not offer an alternative. Violating the normal method of diplomacy — which is to see what one can extract for a concession — he said simply that he agreed with both my analysis and my proposed procedure. It had been folly for Egypt, he averred, to seek its goals through harassing the United States. Egypt had had enough of war; there was no intention to destroy Israel. Having restored his nation's self-respect, he could now turn to the peace for which his people longed. He was prepared to accept the proposition that Israel needed confidence to engage itself in the peace process. But it was a great deal for him to be asked to win the confidence of a country occupying "his" territory.

That point was made analytically, not to generate a bargain. He would gamble on disengagement across the Canal. He would accept my strategy, he said. The Third Army would have to wait. And it could if supplies were assured, which was my responsibility to achieve with Israel. To give the diplomacy I had outlined a chance, he would defer the issue of the October 22 line. Anything less was too trivial to justify the suffering and risks of the war.

It was, in truth, an act of considerable courage. Against what we later learned was the near-unanimous sentiment of his advisers, Sadat decided to take his chances on the word of an American whom he did not know, that we would attempt to make significant progress over a period of three months. If anything went wrong — if I had overestimated what was possible, if I had deceived him, or if the Third Army's morale cracked while it remained cut off in the desert — Sadat would be ruined and Egypt humiliated.

The Third Army, Sadat added, was in any case not the heart of the matter between America and Egypt. He was determined to end Nasser's legacy. He would reestablish relations with the United States as quickly as possible and, once that was accomplished, he would move to friendship. Formal diplomatic relations required some pretext, however, before the Egyptian public and his Arab brethren would understand the steps. He would wait for some tangible diplomatic success.* But the delay was purely tactical and connected largely with inter-Arab politics; it was not intended as blackmail. He was prepared to announce his intentions immediately — upon the conclusion of our meeting, in fact. In

---

*Formal diplomatic relations were restored three months later, on February 28, 1974, shortly after the first Egyptian-Israeli disengagement agreement.

the meantime he would raise the head of his Interests Section to the status of Ambassador. He hoped that we would join such an announcement. We had sought for four years to restore relations; I had brought with me a proposal to do so. We agreed that the ambassadors would assume their functions immediately, operating from Interests Sections indistinguishable from Embassies.

Sadat showed no nervousness about the dangers of the course to which he had committed himself. Like a surgeon coldly considering the best course of action, he invited me to suggest a specific proposal; he averred that I knew better than he what Israel would accept. It was another exhibition of daring, psychological insight, and guile. I indeed knew what Golda would accept and what the cabinet had refused. More important, since the course on which we had agreed depended on our exertions, he would commit us more surely by a show of confidence in us than by haggling over technicalities.

I said that success later depended on restraint now; it would be best to reduce controversy to a minimum. Egypt's basic requirement was uninterrupted nonmilitary supply to the Third Army through checkpoints that were colorably not Israeli. Building on what Golda had accepted at Blair House before the cabinet overruled her, I therefore suggested the concept for what was refined later into the following six-point plan, signed by both sides a few days afterward:

A. Egypt and Israel agree to observe scrupulously the cease-fire called for by the UN Security Council.
B. Both sides agree that discussions between them will begin immediately to settle the question of the return to the October 22 positions in the framework of agreement on the disengagement and separation of forces under the auspices of the UN.
C. The town of Suez will receive daily supplies of food, water and medicine. All wounded civilians in the town of Suez will be evacuated.
D. There shall be no impediment to the movement of non-military supplies to the East Bank.
E. The Israeli checkpoints on the Cairo-Suez road will be replaced by UN checkpoints. At the Suez end of the road Israeli officers can participate with the UN to supervise the non-military nature of the cargo at the bank of the Canal.
F. As soon as the UN checkpoints are established on the Cairo-Suez road, there will be an exchange of all prisoners of war, including wounded.

The provision for observance of the cease-fire was boilerplate; it added no new element. The innovation was Point B, that discussions about Israel's return to the October 22 line would take place in the framework of a disengagement of forces. Golda Meir herself had put forward this formulation during her trip to Washington. When I had asked her what it meant, she had replied, "nothing." Its practical significance was to bury the controversy over the October 22 line. Either disengagement would work and move the line to *east* of the Canal, far *beyond* the October 22 line, or else we would be in a crisis that would submerge the issue. Either way, the October 22 line was now irrelevant.

The same attitude led to a solution for control over the disputed access route to the Third Army. In Washington, Golda had been obliged by her cabinet to refuse UN control over the Cairo-Suez road. On the other hand, to ask Sadat to send nonmilitary supplies through Israeli check-points was a humiliation to which I did not choose to submit him. The solution was to avoid the issue altogether by making the sort of compro-mise the acceptance of which marks a triumph of faith over substance. The checkpoints were placed under the United Nations; at the same time Israeli officers were permitted to participate "to supervise the non-mil-itary nature of the cargo." The Israelis could claim that the UN posts were there on sufferance on "their" road; Egypt could insist that the UN presence effectively removed the road from Israeli control. The Is-raelis could point to the fact that their officers participated in the inspec-tion; the Egyptians could argue that this was as part of a UN procedure. The fundamental fact was that there would now exist a mechanism for uninterrupted nonmilitary supply to the Third Army.

What unlocked the door to all these concessions was that Sadat also agreed, in the sixth point, to an exchange of prisoners of war as soon as the UN checkpoints were established — an issue I had raised as of critical importance to Israel.

Sadat made only the most trivial changes in what was essentially our draft. He saw it rightly as an investment in confidence as well as a spur to rapid implementation of the agreement.

There was also a private understanding that Egypt would "ease" the blockade of the Strait of Bab el-Mandeb if the Israelis promised to make only "moderate" use of it. Since the blockade had never been formally declared, Sadat argued, it could not be formally lifted. And too many public concessions would hurt his position with his Arab brethren. Sadat — and later Fahmy — defined "ease" as meaning that Egypt would not interfere with the normal flow of traffic through the strait. The whole issue was a contribution to metaphysics, since we could find no evidence that any ships had ever actually been stopped in the first place.

Like all good agreements, the six-point plan had something for every-body. Egypt obtained guaranteed supply for the Third Army and an international presence on the Cairo-Suez road. Israel secured the release of its prisoners and relief from pressure over the October 22 line. Sadat had followed the method I grew to know very well: to cut through trivia to the essential, to make major, even breathtaking, tactical concessions in return for an irreversible psychological momentum. His acceptance of our draft proposal committed us to try to bring about the disengagement he really wanted. By being forthcoming on the issues of the October 22 line and release of prisoners, he helped ease Israel's chronic suspicions of his motives. And yet what he conceded was essentially marginal: the improvements he might have achieved by haggling would have been cosmetic or a bow to vanity. Wise statesmen know they will be measured by the historical process they set in motion, not by the debating points they score.

Sadat, of course, must not be viewed as everybody's genial uncle. He was as tough as he was patient. He was, after all, the man who had relentlessly, patiently, and against all probability prepared the October war. He was not ready to sheath all his weapons. He turned a deaf ear to my pleas to help undo the oil embargo; he replied firmly that he could be persuasive with his brethren only after substantial progress had been made in the negotiations.

When we had finished going over the six points, Sadat clapped his hands and an aide appeared. Sadat asked him to call in Joe Sisco and Ismail Fahmy, who were sitting in full view in wicker chairs on the lawn. They would refine what we had discussed into the formal language of the six-point plan. While we were waiting, Sadat turned to me and reminded me of how much distance we had yet to travel: "Never forget, Dr. Kissinger. I am making this agreement with the United States, not with Israel." That was indeed the heart of the problem — but also part of the solution. Confidence in America could be the bridge across the gulf of four wars.

We agreed that once the six-point plan was put into formal language, Joe Sisco and Hal Saunders would go to Israel to present it. An Egyptian plane would take them to Cyprus; we would arrange for an Israeli plane to meet them there. I thought that Israeli acceptance was foreordained since the plan contained nearly all the points on which the Israeli cabinet had insisted and indeed went beyond what Golda had accepted. Sisco and Saunders would seek formal confirmation. I would stay in Cairo because Fahmy had invited a number of distinguished guests to his dinner for me and especially because I wanted to avoid the drama inherent in a sudden unplanned trip to Israel. It proved that I did not yet know the Middle East. What mattered to the parties was not only substance but psychological intangibles. Jerusalem, I learned later, should never be treated as if it could be taken for granted — its survival depends on its being perceived as a tough defender of its interests. Much as I enjoyed Fahmy's dinner, things would have gone more smoothly had I changed my schedule.

Usually, any one negotiation is a part of a long sequence; the conclusion more often yields exhaustion than relief. One participates in few events one recognizes as turning points. I had come to Cairo hoping for a step forward in a strategy that had been inching ahead for four years. Now in a single encounter with Egypt's President, one month after the beginning of the war, we had achieved a breakthrough. Sadat had clearly staked his policy on the American connection; if we pursued that strategy wisely, it would become increasingly difficult for him to reverse course. The reduction of Soviet influence was now only a matter of time and skill; the prospects of a peace of moderation loomed bright — provided we could find the balance between Israeli fears and Arab impatience.

My more mundane worry was to keep our accomplishments secret until the White House could announce the appointment of ambassadors and Golda could learn of the six-point plan from Sisco and Saunders. If the announcement was made in Cairo, there would be hell to pay at the White House and in Jerusalem. The normal tendency of any President to reserve to himself the privilege of announcing good news was magnified by Nixon's Watergate agonies. Sadat and I settled that the announcement would be made jointly at the White House and in Cairo at noon Washington time that day, some seven hours away. And we would say nothing about the six-point plan until Sisco and Saunders had presented it in Jerusalem. The touchy Israeli cabinet might balk if the issue emerged as an Egyptian proposal.

The desire to preserve the deadlines accounted for the difference in our respective moods as Sadat and I rejoined our aides in the garden at the end of our three hours of talks. Seated in the middle of the semicircle of wicker chairs, Sadat and I posed for what was in Haldemanese called a "photo opportunity" — an occasion for the press to take pictures but not to ask questions. The ground rules almost never restrain enterprising journalists, who hold the view that it is not questions that violate the rules, but answers, which are in the control of those who made the rules in the first place.

The irrepressible Sadat responded to every question the reporters put to him. "Mr. President," a reporter asked, "will the US now curtail its airlift of military supplies to Israel?"

"You should ask this question of Dr. Kissinger," Sadat answered, knowing full well that I had told him confidentially of the imminent end of the airlift. (We had, in fact, kept it going a few extra days precisely so that I might tell him.)

"Luckily I didn't hear the question," I shot back. I was not so lucky next time.

"Dr. Kissinger, will there be a reestablishment of diplomatic relations between Egypt and the United States?" asked a shrewd reporter. Mindful of Nixon's wrath but reluctant to lie, I squirmed and said nothing. Sadat had no such inhibitions. "We will have news for you later in the day, be patient," Sadat boomed, all but giving the game away.[6]

The rest of the Egyptian trip was anticlimax. In the evening I attended the dinner hosted by Fahmy in his apartment overlooking the Nile, to which he had invited the ambassadors of the other permanent members of the Security Council (Britain, France, the Soviet Union, and the People's Republic of China), together with leaders of the Egyptian government and the influential journalist Mohammed Heikal. The Chinese made excuses, probably because of the presence of the Soviets; the other ambassadors appeared. (Heikal has since published a poetically imaginative account of our dinner conversation.)[7] The evening was a theatrical performance by Fahmy and other senior Egyptians designed to demonstrate that Egypt was increasing its options beyond the Nasserite reliance on the Soviet Union.

The next morning, Thursday, November 8, Fahmy and I met to discuss plans for the Geneva peace conference and to define the "appropriate auspices" that had been part of the cease-fire agreed to in Moscow. On October 21, Moscow had no doubt urged the cease-fire on Sadat with the argument that Soviet partnership in the "auspices" would guarantee pressure on the United States and Israel. But now Egypt was shifting its emphasis to the United States and switching from a comprehensive to a step-by-step approach. A major Soviet role seemed much less desirable, perhaps even dangerous, because Moscow could appear as the spokesman of radical concerns and thus obstruct what Sadat considered attainable. Both Egypt and the United States, therefore, sought to prevent the "auspices" from turning into a Soviet veto. If in the guise of pressing for an overall solution the Soviets and their radical allies insisted on an all-or-nothing approach, the war would have ended in the same deadlock that produced the explosion in the first place. It was not yet clear that Syria would even participate in negotiations; it would probably countenance no other agenda than the one that had led to six years of stalemate; it would surely not take a position less Arab than that of Moscow. We were opening the door a crack by getting Egypt and Israel to agree that disengagement be the first agenda item of a peace conference. But we still had a long way to go.

Our approach was to segment the diplomacy into a series of steps during the negotiation of which the Soviet capacity for obstruction would be at a minimum. But we could obtain Soviet acquiescence in this course only by putting before the Kremlin the prospect, at some point, of participation in an overall peace conference. Moscow no doubt went along with the disengagement phase, in part because it had no solution of its own to the plight of the Third Army, in part because it believed that the American solo role could not be sustained beyond the opening stage, and above all because it calculated that its time would come when the Geneva Conference opened. We did nothing to disabuse the Soviets of that view; we consulted with them meticulously about the procedures for assembling the peace conference. On my October trip to Moscow, we had reduced the joint "auspices" to a minimum: American and Soviet representatives were to participate only at the beginning of the conference and when key issues were dealt with. For the future we intended to be extremely restrictive in our definition of what was "key." But we kept alive the prospect of a peace conference as a safety net and to discourage the Soviets from interfering with the disengagement phase.

My first visit to Cairo exceeded my hopes. For it, I received some public plaudits for negotiating skill. But if this implies that I talked Sadat into something he might otherwise not have done, the point was missed. What looked like a negotiating breakthrough to outsiders was in fact the merging of Egyptian and American perceptions that had been approaching each other for many years. Each side for its own reasons sought partnership with the other — a partnership that unlocked the door to peace and advanced the interests of all peoples of the Middle East.

Anwar Sadat

IN the years following that first meeting with Anwar Sadat in 1973, he became a world figure. At the time he was little known in the United States, at best considered one of the many volatile leaders in the Arab world whose posturing, internecine quarrels, and flowery eloquence were as fascinating to contemplate as they were difficult to fathom. But from that meeting onward, I knew I was dealing with a great man.

I had the honor of working in tandem with Anwar Sadat for the first few steps of his journey to peace. Then I left office and he went on within a year to new, bold strides that I had thought might take decades. When within sight of his dream, he was murdered. Prophets perform their service by inspiring ordinary men and women with their vision, but they pay the price of being consumed by it. So the reader will forgive a brief diversion as an appreciation of my fallen friend.

Isaiah Berlin once wrote that greatness is the ability to transform paradox into platitude.

When Anwar Sadat appeared on the scene, the Arab countries had too little confidence in their arms and too much faith in their rhetoric. The majority of them relied on the Soviet Union, which could supply weapons for futile wars but no programs for progress in diplomacy. Negotiations consisted of exalted slogans incapable of achievement; the Arab countries seemed to want the fruits of peace without daring to pronounce the word. The nations of the West stood on the sidelines, observers at a drama that affected their destiny but seemingly without the capacity to influence it.

Within a few years, Sadat overcame these riddles. When he died, the peace process was a commonplace; Egypt's friendship with America was a cornerstone of Mideast stability. By his journey to Jerusalem in 1977 he had demonstrated to all those obsessed with the tangible the transcendence of the visionary. He understood that a heroic gesture can create a new reality.

The difference between great and ordinary leaders is less formal intellect than insight and courage. The great man understands the essence of a problem; the ordinary leader grasps only the symptoms. The great man focuses on the relationship of events to each other; the ordinary leader sees only a series of seemingly disconnected events. The great man has a vision of the future that enables him to put obstacles in perspective; the ordinary leader turns pebbles in the road into boulders.

Sadat bore with fortitude the loneliness inseparable from moving the world from familiar categories toward where it has never been. He had the patience and the serenity of the Egyptian masses from which he came. I visited him once in the simple house to which he regularly returned in his native village of Mit Abul-Kum in the Nile Delta. For someone used to conventional topography, the unequivocal flatness of the countryside came almost as a shock. There was no geographic reference point, nothing to mediate between the individual and the infinite; one's relation with the universe was established through the medium of a pervasive, enduring mass of humanity. The population pressure in Egypt is a standard feature of the literature on the country. In Sadat's village, as I suppose in all the villages of Lower Egypt, one sensed it almost palpably though one saw it only in the smoke rising from innumerable chimneys over the trees and hedges that screened Sadat's small property from his neighbors'. A pensive stillness cloaked the activity one knew was all around one; the rhythm of a civilization was intuited but neither seen nor heard. One felt strangely sheltered, as if in a womb. Sadat said to me once, seemingly enigmatically, that he felt most relaxed at dusk when he knew all the villagers were preparing their meals at home. Sadat's inner security and his instinctive sense of his people's yearning for peace were periodically renewed here at their source.

But there was also another Sadat not content with resting with his origin: a man on restless peregrinations around his beloved country. Mrs. Sadat once told me it was a legacy of his time in prison; he felt confined if he stayed too long in one place. Sadat's dread of confinement was not only physical; he felt psychologically ill at ease with anything that limited the meaning of life to the status quo. He raised his people's gaze toward heretofore unimagined horizons. In the process he accomplished more for the Arab cause than those of his Arab brethren whose specialty was belligerent rhetoric. He recovered more territory, obtained more help from the West, and did more to make the Arab case reputable internationally than any of the leaders who regularly abused him at meetings of the so-called rejectionist front. He moved his people toward a partnership with the West, knowing that a sense of shared values was a more certain spur to support than a defiance based on striking poses. And when he had thus transformed the paradox and solved the riddle, he was killed by the apostles of the ordinary, the fearful, the merchants of the ritualistic whom he shamed by being at once out of scale and impervious to their meanness of spirit.

Sadat's passion for peace grew in intensity and profundity as his mission proceeded. When I first met him, peace had been a tactic in the pursuit of Egypt's interests. By the time he died it had become a vocation in the service of humanity.

Early in our acquaintance, in a military hospital he was inspecting, he spoke movingly to me of how much Egypt had suffered, how an end had to be put to pointless conflict, how he did not want to send any more young men to die. Egypt needed no more heroes, he said. The last time I saw him was on his plane from Washington to New York in 1981, during what turned out to be his final visit to our country. He had just met his fourth American President in the eight years since he had begun his cooperation with us. He seemed a little tired and perhaps the slightest bit discouraged that our political process forced him at such short intervals to start over again building confidence and explaining his vision. But then the old buoyancy returned. He was planning a week's celebration on the occasion of the return of the Sinai to Egypt, he said, at the end of April 1982. Perhaps I could join him for at least part of it, considering that we had started the journey together. And on the day afterward we might go to Mount Sinai; there he could show me the place overlooking the desert where he planned to consecrate the peace by building three chapels — Moslem, Jewish, and Christian — side by side. And then he and I could meditate there for a while.

But a statesman must never be judged simply as philosopher or dreamer. At some point he must translate his intuition into reality against sometimes resistant material. Sadat was neither starry-eyed nor soft. He was not a pacifist. He did not believe in peace at any price. He was conciliatory but not compliant. I never doubted that in the end he would create heroes if no other course he considered honorable was left to him.

Any simple assessment of Sadat is therefore likely to be mistaken. Dozens of visiting Americans were charmed by him. But he was also aloof and reflective and withdrawn. Like many men of power, he had an almost carnal relationship with authority. He could hold his own with small talk, but on deeper acquaintance it became clear it bored him. He much preferred to spend idle time in solitary reflection. Most of his bold initiatives were conceived in such periods of seclusion and meditation, often in his native village. I know no other leader who understood so well the virtue of solitude and used it so rigorously.

Walking in the garden with President Sadat's national security adviser, Hafiz Ismail, Paris, May 20, 1973 (see Chapter VI).

T, ABOVE: *With King Hassan of Morocco in Rabat, on HAK's
t trip to the Middle East, November 5, 1973.*

T, BELOW: *With President Habib Bourguiba in Tunis,
vember 6, 1973.*

OW: *Meeting President Houari Boumedienne in Algiers,
cember 12, 1973. In the middle are Joseph Sisco and Foreign
nister Abdelaziz Bouteflika.*

FT: *With King Hussein in Amman, November 8, 1973.*
LOW: *A call on King Faisal in Riyadh, February 1975.*

*With President Hafez al-Asad
in Damascus, January 20, 1974.*

ABOVE: *The US delegation at the Geneva Middle East Peace Conference, December 21, 1973. Front row: Ellsworth Bunker, HAK, Joseph Sisco. Second row: Ambassador Walter Stoessel, John Ready (Secret Service), Harold Saunders, Alfred L. Atherton, Jr. Third row: George Vest, Peter Rodman, Michael Sterner, Lawrence Eagleburger.* BELOW: *Geneva Middle East Peace Conference, December 1973: The Man in the Middle.*

ABOVE: *Cocktails at Abba Eban's house, Jerusalem,*
January 13, 1974. Left to right: Abba Eban, HAK, Moshe Dayan.
BELOW: *Negotiating the Egyptian-Israeli disengagement agreement, Aswan,*
January 1974. Left to right: Ellsworth Bunker, HAK, Joseph Sisco, Peter
Rodman, Foreign Minister Ismail Fahmy, President Sadat, Chief of Staff
General Gamasy.

Vice President Hosni Mubarak and President Sadat. With backs to camera, Joseph Sisco and HAK.

Anwar el-Sadat.

ABOVE: *Completion of the Egyptian-Israeli disengagement, at the Prime Minister's Residence in Israel, January 18, 1974. Left to right: Abba Eban, Joseph Sisco, HAK, Ephraim Evron, Prime Minister Golda Meir.* BELOW: *Signing the Egyptian-Israeli disengagement agreement at Kilometer 101, January 18, 1974. Signing the agreement, at center top, Lieutenant General David Elazar (for Israel); at bottom, back to camera, Major General Abdel Ghany el-Gamasy (for Egypt); at center right, UNEF Commander Lieutenant General Ensio Siilasvuo (witnessing for the UN). American officials present are State Department Legal Adviser Carlyle E. Maw (top right) and NSC staff member Harold Saunders (lower right).*

ABOVE: *Ismail Fahmy and Omar Saqqaf say goodbye after a visit to the White House, February 19, 1974.* BELOW: *"Photo opportunity" on the veranda at Giza.*

Shuttle scene; working in the compartment on SAM 86970.

Poster presented by the traveling journalists on the Syrian shuttle, May 1974.

ABOVE: *Getting ready to board King Hussein's helicopter, Amman, May 6, 1974.* BELOW: *Arriving home after the thirty-four-day shuttle, at Andrews Air Force Base, May 31, 1974.*

His urbanity made it easy to forget his early career as a revolutionary struggling for his country's independence and suffering for it in a succession of prisons. Such men are never "regular fellows," however charmingly they present themselves. Revolutionary leadership is a career that attracts only the deeply dedicated; its votaries forswear all the normal attributes of success because to them their cause transcends normal calculation. One can challenge the convictions of such men only if one is prepared for struggle; standing in their way is never free. Sadat took a long view but he would also insist on achieving it.

Sadat had an uncanny psychological discernment. He handled each of the four American Presidents he knew with consummate skill. He treated Nixon as a great statesman, Ford as the living manifestation of goodwill, Carter as a missionary almost too decent for this world, and Reagan as the benevolent leader of a popular revolution, subtly appealing to each man's conception of himself and gaining the confidence of each. He worked at identifying Egypt's interest with America's own. He repeatedly challenged us to enter the negotiations not as mediator but as participant, or else he offered to accept what we put forward — an offer one could embrace only if one understood that it was part of a strategy, not an abdication. And yet there was a true act of faith involved here beyond advancing his country's aims. Sadat deeply believed in America's sense of justice. He sustained himself by confidence in our leaders and, in the process, made them live up to the best within them.

Sadat analyzed correctly that Arab radicalism tended to reinforce America's special relationship with Israel. This offered America no alternative: It added the argument of strategic necessity to the existing moral ties. So Sadat set out on a course that would have been considered mad until he proved it possible: to woo the United States into a more "evenhanded" posture, to create another moral bond that would produce an incentive for American assistance in recovering lands the Arabs considered theirs. In this sense the 1977 journey to Jerusalem was at one and the same time an act of nobility and a method of disarming Israel psychologically: a unique gesture of reconciliation and a device to isolate the Jewish state.

This explains Israel's ambivalence toward Sadat. Israelis, for decades the object of their neighbors' hatred, greeted Sadat's overtures at first with incredulity, later with hope, even exaltation. But there was also a gnawing fear that his seduction of the United States would ultimately leave Israel alone and friendless in a hostile world. Therefore the Jewish state was torn between embracing Sadat's overture and haggling over its terms, between its own hopes and nightmares. And the last page has not yet been written in a history in which both Israel's hopes and its nightmares could come true.

Like all great men Sadat had the defects of his virtues. The same qualities that caused him to transcend obstacles made him impatient with the sensitivities of those incapable of sharing his lofty vision. He found it difficult to believe in the good faith of his critics, even allowing that he had more than his share of critics who could not be granted that attribute by the widest extension of charity. When challenged he moved further in the direction he had chosen to emphasize his opponents' impotence to stop him; thus did his dauntless courage turn into a provocation of those who resisted his march toward peace. He became so consumed in the peace process that he seemed at times to subordinate to it even the day-to-day longings of ordinary Egyptians — especially after they had come to take peace so much for granted that they no longer listed it among their unfulfilled aspirations. Great men are needed to break a mold; afterward, it is often their destiny to be so out of scale as to evoke a nostalgia for less demanding leadership.

But Sadat was more than the sum of his parts. By one of the miracles of creation the peasant's son, the originally underestimated politician, had the wisdom and courage of the statesman and occasionally the insight of the prophet. Yet nourishing all these qualities was a pervasive humanity. Who can forget his offer of haven to the fallen Shah of Iran, abandoned by friends who owed him more but succored by Sadat with a grace and nobility that redeemed the honor of all those who had failed their test?

On a visit I paid to Egypt after I had left government, Sadat invited my wife, my son, and me to dinner at his villa by the sea in Alexandria. The table had been set at the exact spot on the lawn where we had negotiated and signed the second disengagement agreement. During the course of the evening, I said that all Americans who had worked with Sadat owed him a great debt; he had made all of us look good. The remark disturbed him; he kept coming back to it. He did not want his labors to be considered personal; it was his duty, not his preference, to restore dignity to his people and give hope to his country and perhaps the world.

For once Sadat was wrong. He did make us look good. Only he made it seem too easy, too natural, so that we took him too much for granted. And when he was no longer with us and we had to journey toward peace alone, it was starkly clear how much we needed him.

No other people has been so obsessed with immortality as the Egyptian. None has sought to capture time so persistently — at times with defiant boldness, at times passively; now relying on endurance rather than the grand assault, now raising tremendous edifices to faith in the future. The Pyramids at Giza, at once simple and monumental, have withstood the elements and man's depredations for as close to eternity as man can come. At no other place in the world is man forced into humility so exclusively by one of his own accomplishments. In that sea of sand, split by the green valley of the Nile stretching man's vision in a narrow line for hundreds of miles, there is no natural monument to dwarf him; the most breathtaking landmarks are all man-made. They inspire awe by their immensity and grace and above all by the presumption of their conception. The tremendous Egyptian statuary evokes the same emotions: The figures are larger than life; yet their faces are infinitely human and their gaze leads us toward distant horizons.

Such a man was Anwar Sadat. Only the future will tell whether he started an irreversible movement of history or whether he was like that ancient Pharaoh Ikhnaton, who dreamed of monotheism amidst the panoply of Egyptian deities a millennium before it was accepted among mankind. Either way, none who knows history will ever forget that the journey to peace in the Middle East began with Anwar Sadat, and could not have progressed without him. Whether we reach our destination is up to us. For his part, Anwar Sadat has already earned the immortality of which his Egyptian ancestors dreamed — as an inspiration if we succeed, as a shaming example if we fail. One way or another, the cause of peace will be his pyramid.

Sisco and Saunders in Israel

I SENT Joe Sisco and Hal Saunders to Israel, as I have said, because I did not want to offend the many distinguished guests Fahmy had assembled for dinner. Moreover, moving my entire caravan — including press — could have been construed as a crisis in America and as pressure in Israel. Also, I could not believe that there could be much controversy in Jerusalem. After all, Israel would receive its prisoners, be relieved of pressures to withdraw to the October 22 lines and of the blockade of Bab el-Mandeb — all in exchange for permitting a few UN checkpoints, on a road the shoulders of which it continued to control, to assure the resupply of an army that the international situation (and its own interest, if it understood it properly) would not permit it to destroy. To make doubly sure, I had armed Sisco with the assurance that if Israel accepted the six-point plan, we would veto any future UN resolution requiring a return to the October 22 line.

Still, the symbolism was unfortunate. For a nation seeking some sense of control over its future, my sending subordinates, however able, tended to raise the nightmare of being taken for granted in an American arrangement made behind Israel's back — despite the fact that I had just concluded talks with Mrs. Meir four days before.

Sisco and Saunders met the Israeli negotiating team on Wednesday evening, November 7, in the Guest House, the scene of my encounter with Golda two weeks earlier. The session began auspiciously enough. Golda congratulated Sisco on what had been accomplished. But soon the basic realities asserted themselves. Sadat, representing an ancient country with the innate sense that time was on its side, could afford the grand gesture. Israel, fighting for its right to exist, could salvage its identity only by struggle — or so its history had taught it. Israeli domestic politics combined with the insecurity of a nation denied legitimacy to produce a maddening, nitpicking style of negotiation.

With the thoroughness of a bloodhound, Golda — one eye on preelection polls — probed all issues she anticipated the opposition might raise in Parliament or that coalition partners might exploit to her discomfort. The Israeli negotiators raised questions about what specifically was meant by "moderate" use of the Strait of Bab el-Mandeb; where the checkpoints would be on the Cairo-Suez road; who actually controlled the road between checkpoints — in fact, all the points on the fudging of which the whole agreement hinged. On the surface we seemed to be in a kind of never-never land; the Israeli negotiating team tended simply to "bank" what had been achieved and to talk as if Israel, suddenly confronted with Egyptian acceptance of its own proposal, had the option to take back the marginal concessions that had made the Egyptian breakthrough possible in the first place. However, Golda was wise as well as tough. After putting Sisco through the wringer for several hours and making a record of vigilance, Golda asked Sisco to tell me what no doubt she had concluded immediately:

We will meet with the Cabinet tomorrow morning. I hope we will have no difficulty. If so, we will try to overcome it. Give him my best and tell him that this is a fantastic achievement.

Dinitz conveyed a similar message to Scowcroft during the morning of November 8. Nevertheless, within hours things began to unravel. Golda had overestimated the pliability of her cabinet, which insisted on another hallowed ritual of Israeli negotiating tactics: a "Memorandum of Understanding" between the United States and Israel. The consciousness of having only one friend among the nations of the world produces an endless quest for reassurance in the form of additional concessions or side letters on the interpretation of existing agreements. In this case the Memorandum of Understanding was a detailed statement of how Israel intended to interpret the provisions of the six-point accord. These interpretations were not unreasonable; we were prepared to accept them privately and commit ourselves to support Israel should there be a dispute. What we could not do was what the cabinet seemed to want: turn the Israeli-American Memorandum of Understanding into the basic Egyptian-Israeli agreement. This would have required going back to Sadat and asking him to confirm formally what he could only accept de facto: such as lifting of the blockade at Bab el-Mandeb; Israeli control over the Cairo-Suez road; and the details of resupply of the Third Army, which would have brought home its plight to every Arab. Saunders wisely suggested that Golda declare Israel's interpretation to the Parliament and we would not contradict it. However, we could not ask Sadat to agree to it formally even while he acquiesced in practice. That seemed to settle things.

Sisco and Saunders caught up with me in Riyadh. We planned to announce acceptance of the six-point agreement by means of a public letter from me to UN Secretary-General Kurt Waldheim the next day, Friday, November 9. I sent messages to that effect from Riyadh to both Cairo and Jerusalem.

Everything seemed in train when early Friday morning a cable from Fahmy informed me that Israel was insisting on a new interpretation of the agreement. The Israeli negotiator at the Kilometer 101 talks, General Aharon Yariv, had gone ahead with what Sisco and Saunders had told Israel was impossible; he had in effect demanded Egypt's formal acceptance of the agreed Israeli-American interpretation. Fahmy also complained that Jerusalem had leaked the private understanding regarding the blockade and was insisting that Israel "controlled" the road. He suggested delay of the announcement until matters were clarified.

I had been afraid of something like this. Private understandings are useless to an Israeli cabinet, especially at election time; they leave the government open to the charge of having failed to achieve all it could. I can think of few memoranda of understanding that did not become public in short order. As for General Yariv, he had clearly decided to try to prove erroneous our judgment of what the traffic would bear.

I feared that if we delayed, the negotiations would be smothered in endless detail. I decided to split the difference. Still in Riyadh, I immediately sent a message to Fahmy that gave him a face-saving way out. We could not prevent speculation about the easing of the blockade at Bab el-Mandeb, but we could commit ourselves not to confirm such speculation. The other issues should be discussed between the military representatives at Kilometer 101; they seemed to me all technical and not matters of principle. I repeated our interpretation of them along lines Sisco had agreed with Israel but I did not ask Fahmy to take a position on that interpretation. I ended with a strong plea to announce the agreement at the appointed time, now less than ten hours away, lest new complications prevent any agreement altogether.

I cabled in the same vein to Golda from Islamabad. (I was in Pakistan on my way to Peking.) I recounted Egyptian complaints and urged the Israelis to avoid inflammatory press and public interpretations. I also told her Sadat had taken the position that "a visible [Israeli] presence on the road will make his position with respect to the agreement untenable." I reviewed the reply already sent to Fahmy, then urged Golda to go ahead with the agreement on schedule: "It is important that Israel proceed now to follow through on the terms of the agreement in a positive spirit and that your negotiators not act in a harassing manner."

Fahmy replied positively within three hours. He understood that it was in everybody's interest not to put forward too detailed an exegesis for an agreement that sought a face-saving formula for what was imposed by reality. So Fahmy professed to be satisfied by my "explanations" and urged me to proceed with the letter to Waldheim as planned.

Golda reached the same conclusions, though in a stormier manner. She professed to be outraged by the suggestion that an Israeli negotiator would harass anyone. She called in the American Ambassador, Kenneth Keating, and portrayed my cabled message as another "ultimatum" — a description not easy to follow since Egypt had accepted Israel's basic program and we had agreed to support Israel's interpretation of it. All we had asked for was a little less explicitness to permit practice and not theory to determine the arrangements. Golda spoke darkly of resigning in favor of a tougher negotiator — a truly frightening prospect, which we happily knew was unfulfillable.

But the conclusion she drew from her outrage was moderate indeed. As so often, Golda used the language of challenge to achieve the reality of cooperation. Since we were talking about an *American* letter to Waldheim, she said, she had no right to prohibit it. As far as she was concerned, Israel would announce its acceptance in principle subject to "clarifications" that she knew very well she had already received. It must be a pleasure to issue an ultimatum to which you already have the answer in hand. (It was also a good way to leak out the substance of the Memorandum of Understanding.)

We decided to go ahead. At the last moment Fahmy wanted us to delete a phrase from my letter to Waldheim on some esoteric point. We told him it was now too late. Announcement of the six-point plan was made in the United States midday on November 9. (Israel, however, delayed the signing ceremony until the eleventh because of the Sabbath.) From Islamabad I answered Golda with a conciliatory letter belying my less-than-calm mood. (I took my frustration out on the genial Ken Keating, who in my view had not responded firmly enough to Golda's diatribe — proving that he was wiser than I.)

Like Fahmy a day earlier, Golda now professed to be extremely pleased by the outcome; Keating found her "relaxed, warm and forthcoming." Having proved that she was no pushover — a point she felt more need to confirm than did we, who still bore the scars of her earlier assaults — she maneuvered the agreement through her cabinet with record speed. It was signed on November 11 at Kilometer 101 while I was in China.

In the two months the agreement was in effect before it was superseded by the disengagement accord, no major trouble appeared in implementing it. The Memorandum of Understanding was never invoked, proving that the parties had understood each other much better than had been suggested by the raucous posturing of which I had been the foil.

Amman

THESE Egyptian and Israeli exchanges had to be conducted from the various far-flung capitals to which I was making flying visits. My first stop after Egypt, on November 8, was Jordan. It was quite a transition from cosmopolitan Cairo to dusty Amman, clinging to the hills on the east bank of the Jordan River, from which on clear nights one can see the lights of Jerusalem. The arrival gave me another opportunity to practice the reviewing of troops. This time I managed to slow my pace to that of my escort officer, though the art of moving in rhythm with the band's music still eluded me.

We were driven to the King's palace, which by royal standards in the Middle East was modest indeed. The King greeted us with his accustomed courtesy and the comradeship that at that time still informed the relations between our countries. It was one of our sorrows that our best Arab friend was only at the periphery of this phase of the peace process. Having stayed out of the war (except for a brigade in Syria), he had no cease-fire line to stabilize: Having remained friendly to us (and because of the historic quarrel of the Hashemites with the Saudi dynasty), he had no oil pressures invoked on his behalf. The result was that the conversation was confined to abstractions or recollections.

Hussein deplored the sequence of events that had led to the war, the timing of which, he said, had taken him by surprise. He stated his dilemma accurately:

Jordan is the Arab country most involved in terms of both land and population. Participation in the war could have led to the destruction of Jordan and the creation of a vacuum which radical elements would have filled. Nonparticipation could have led to the total isolation of Jordan and to our becoming the scapegoat.

It was an acute analysis. Unfortunately, the middle road provided few incentives for outside support — and as the peace process reached the Palestinian issue, Jordan's unique role would become increasingly crucial. Hussein summed it up as follows:

Our situation is different from that of Syria and Egypt, which are not connected with the Palestinian problem and which already had international boundaries before the 1967 war. Jordan's 1967 border was the armistice demarcation line. The West Bank is both Jordanian territory and part of Palestine. The population is Jordanian and Palestinian. The rights of the Palestinians have to do not with the West Bank and Jordan but with Israel. The question is who represents the Palestinians. Our position is that the West Bank is Jordanian-Palestinian territory occupied by Israel. It is Jordan's duty to recover that territory with minor changes on a reciprocal basis. In addition, we cannot give up responsibility for the Moslem and Christian parts of Jerusalem which should, however, remain a unified city.

In short, Hussein rejected a role for the PLO on the West Bank as firmly as Israel. If Palestinian territory was to be recovered for the Arab nation, Jordan, according to the King, should do the negotiating. Afterward, a process of self-determination would operate. The King was clearly concerned lest his interests be neglected. He would not oppose disengagement agreements on other fronts but he urged a delay in their implementation until a comprehensive settlement could be concluded as a "package." The trouble was that in the immediate aftermath of the war, the disposition of the opposing armies did not give us this choice. The Third Army could not remain in the desert or for that matter the Israeli army twenty miles from Damascus while the Palestinian issue was being sorted out.

I told Hussein that disengagement would have to be the first step. The best way to protect Jordan's interests on the Palestinian question was to invite Jordan as a founding member of the Geneva Conference; this made it the spokesman for the Palestinians. I also briefed him on the six-point plan.

We were playing for time to overcome the vestiges of the war before turning to the issue of peace. Sometimes it is the best that can be done. But time is neutral; it is not a substitute for policy. In this case, as I shall discuss, time was to run out on the Jordanian option, because of Israel's (and America's) domestic situation, Arab passions fueled by radicals, and the necessities of the disengagement process. It was a great pity.

Riyadh

DURING my peregrinations across the Middle East, Watergate was winding its inexorable way through Congressional and judicial procedures. The House Judiciary Committee, in the wake of the "Saturday night massacre," was considering eight impeachment resolutions. On November 5, Leon Jaworski was sworn in as Special Prosecutor to replace Archibald Cox; he had exacted a promise from Nixon that he would not be dismissed or have his independence limited unless it was approved by designated members of Congress. On November 9, while I was in Riyadh, six of the Watergate defendants were sentenced by Judge John Sirica.

Understandably, Nixon was eager to demonstrate that none of these disasters had affected his mastery of foreign policy; indeed, that his foreign policy achievements buttressed his claim to continue in office. Haig reported that Nixon was "elated" at the just-announced six-point agreement. He had every right to take pride in what had been made possible by his fortitude — all the more remarkable in the face of the adversity he was enduring. By now, however, no foreign policy success could overcome the crisis; since the attack was on Nixon's domestic conduct, it could not be resisted by achievements abroad. This was less clear at the White House, which became seized with the idea that a spectacular outcome could be engineered at every stop on my itinerary. Agreement in Cairo should be topped by an end to the oil embargo in Riyadh, where I arrived on November 8. This, Haig stressed, must not be announced on my trip; it must be seen as resulting from an initiative by Nixon. Therefore Haig wired me:

He hopes that progress made in this area could be announced by him from the White House after your return. In conjunction with such an announcement and as Scowcroft advised you earlier, he would hope to have meeting as early as next week with Faisal in Washington. Following that meeting he would hope to announce progress on oil issue.

Long hours and heavy buffeting by conflicting Mideast pressures produced in me a reaction far less understanding than Nixon's genuine travail warranted. It was natural for any President to want to be viewed as the chief architect of a triumph; given Nixon's high standing in Saudi Arabia this was, moreover, a reasonable reflection of reality. But it was academic. There was no chance that Saudi Arabia would lift the embargo within two weeks of imposing it. If by chance it did, it would not be possible to keep this fact secret for the remainder of my trip, which was to last ten more days. A visit by Faisal to Washington so soon after the war was absolutely inconceivable; it would defeat the entire thrust of Saudi strategy, which had been to build credit with radical Arab regimes.

I cabled Haig:

An attempt to set up meeting with Faisal in Washington is total insanity. Every Arab leader I have talked to so far has made it clear that it is far easier for them to ease pressures de facto than as public Arab policy. Only repeat only course that can work is course we are now on. Invitation to Faisal would be interpreted throughout Arab world as US collapse. It would magnify, not reduce, Arab incentives to keep pressure on US via oil weapon. Nor is there any conceivable reason for Faisal to be willing to come to Washington for friendly meetings at this early phase of peace settlement process. If it should turn out that Faisal is willing for any public announcements of accord on oil matter, I of course would have no repeat no objection to having President announce it in Washington.

The occasion that Nixon longed for never presented itself. There turned out to be no possibility of any dramatic move in Riyadh, for the spectacular is against the very tradition of the country and the psychology of its leaders.

By the fall of 1973, the Kingdom of Saudi Arabia had been drawn reluctantly into the vortex of world affairs. It had to brave the turbulence all around it from an historical and psychological background differing from that of almost every other Arab state.

Mecca and Medina are the holy places of the Moslem world. The Prophet had preached his message first across Arabia's stern deserts and craggy mountains; from there issued forth the armies that spread his faith across a large part of the then known world. Shortly afterward by the reckoning of history, the curtain was drawn again and the succeeding centuries have been etched more deeply in the memory of the tribes and rulers inhabiting its vast territory than in an historical record. Little is known of the turmoil, the suffering, the victories and defeats that must have occurred in that vast plateau where man sustained a marginal subsistence by a noble faith.

What is today Saudi Arabia emerged from Turkish rule after World War I. The Kingdom bears the family name of Ibn Saud, the first dynastic ruler, who unified the various feudal principalities scattered across the Arabian peninsula and held them together by patriarchal allegiance and religious devotion to an exacting, puritanical ethic. The Saudi is wary of the infidel and suspicious of the foreigner. In this he does not differ from many peoples in this dramatic region. But where the Egyptian trusts his suppleness to manipulate the stranger, and the Syrian half believes that he can defeat him in battle, the Saudi seeks to protect himself by remoteness; this is why the Saudis appear withdrawn, impervious, detached. One cannot conquer a mystery, for its essence is immune to the accidents of political power. So Saudi Arabia obscures its vulnerability by opaqueness and hides its uncertainty about the motivations of outsiders by an aloof pride.

The royal family faces daunting tasks. It governs tribes living in the traditional nomadism and fiercely loyal to the crown, as well as urban concentrations approaching those of western metropoles. An emerging middle class here exists in the context of an age-old, semifeudal sense of reciprocal obligation. It is a tribute to the subtlety and wisdom of the ruling princes that they have combined a monarchy with a system of consensus by which the far-flung members of the extended royal family have some share in decisions. Unknown but surely substantial numbers of foreign workers — Palestinians, Syrians, Lebanese, Egyptians, Pakistanis, and Yemenis — combine in a mosaic held together by the bond of Islam and respect for traditional authority.

There is no doubting the sense of vulnerability of a country now unimaginably rich yet incapable of achieving security through wealth alone. Its rulers live with the nightmare that the covetousness of its neighbors might translate itself into attempted conquest. Conscious of the fate of nearby nations, they cannot but be ambivalent about economic and social modernization, which might undermine their traditional rule. Contemporary Saudi policy has been characterized by a caution that has elevated indirectness into a special art form. For if the Kingdom pursued a very forward policy, if it made itself the focal point of all disputes, it would be subjected to entreaties, threats, and blandishments, the cumulative impact of which could endanger either independence or coherence.

Thus there has grown up a style at once oblique and persistent, reticent and assertive. The Kingdom has maneuvered to keep itself out of the forefront of confrontation even when its resources have sustained it — as was now the case with the oil embargo. It has been skillful in avoiding the impression that its unilateral views are decisive. It has always striven to gain the protection of a consensus for which somebody else must assume the blame — at various times the Shah of Iran, the radical majority in OPEC, intransigent Israel. Something always has to be done by someone else before the Saudis can act. It is a marvelous way to avoid pressures and one absolutely consistent with the needs of the Kingdom.

Nor is it simply tactical expediency. The Kingdom has to navigate among certain fixed poles: a deeply felt friendship for the United States; a profound sense of Arab loyalty; a consciousness of internal and external danger. It is not Saudi Arabia's fault that the requirements of these goals occasionally clash. In this sense the ambiguity of Saudi policy is imposed by events, not by preference.

There is thus no point in trying to sweep the wary rulers of the Kingdom off their feet. Most leaders' vanity causes them to exaggerate their own significance; the Saudi princes under Faisal were immune to this temptation and they have not changed the basic pattern since. The opaque Saudi style is equally resistant to eloquence and to threats. To yield to either would imply a degree of latitude in decision-making that would invite endless repetition of foreign entreaties or demands. Much better to maneuver so that everything appears as the consequence of something outside Saudi control. Riyadh is not the place for scoring dramatic breakthroughs.

I understood little of this as my plane rolled to a stop near dusk in front of a modernistic arrival lounge flung on what a few short years ago had been a barren plateau. At the foot of the stairs was Omar Saqqaf, Minister of State for Foreign Affairs (Faisal reserved the title of Foreign Minister to himself). I had last encountered the urbane, worldly Saqqaf in Washington a few weeks earlier, meticulous in tailored Western clothes. Now he wore flowing white robes and Arab headdress and fingered worry beads. He led me between two rows of soldiers to the marble royal reception hall — an opulent room whose furniture was placed along the walls so that nothing obscured the view of the exquisite Oriental rugs covering every square inch of the floor. Small cups of bitter coffee were served to us by robed and turbaned waiters.

Riyadh, like Brasília, testified to a conscious choice to move the center of gravity of the country inland. But unlike Brasília, Riyadh had no great edifices or monuments of state serving as a symbolic focal point. The city was thus a Saudi bow to Western technology and a testimony to its ultimate irrelevance. An urban complex was needed; but in the Saudi scale of values it merited no central plan. Enormous palaces co-existed with hovels without either the charm of a traditional city or the nervous thrust of a modern creation. There was not even a royal palace; or rather, the royal palace was the private residence of the prince who was chosen to be the King. By 1973 very few ministries had as yet moved to Riyadh from Jiddah, and they made do in temporary concrete structures. Even when later the ministries became larger, sometimes verging on the gargantuan, they were thrown about as if at random, making it impossible to describe any part of Riyadh as the governmental center. It was the same with the residences of sheikhs and princes, which, hidden behind high walls, were cheek by jowl with the most ordinary dwellings; the royal family had, after all, been of Bedouin stock and lived in their austere traditional style before the colossal boom in oil wealth.

The edifice used as a state guest house in 1973 (it has since been replaced) was one of those accidents — at once out of scale and seemingly transitory. After a brief opportunity to get settled, I was taken to the King's palace for a reception and dinner given for me by King Faisal — a signal honor.

Faisal's palace was on a monumental scale. Preceded by two sword carriers, I was taken to a tremendous hall that seemed as large as a football field. Dozens of the distinguished men of the Kingdom (women, of course, being strictly segregated) in identical black robes and white headdresses were seated along the walls, immobile and silent. There was incense in the air, circulated by the air conditioning. What seemed like a hundred yards away on a slightly raised pedestal sat King Faisal ibn Abd al-Aziz Al Sa'ud, aquiline of feature, regal of bearing. He rose as I entered, forcing all the princes and sheikhs to follow suit in a flowing balletlike movement of black and white. He took one step toward me; I had to traverse the rest of the way. I learned later that his taking a step forward was a sign of great courtesy. At the time, I was above all conscious of the seeming eternity it took to reach the pedestal. His Majesty and I sat side by side for a few minutes overlooking the splendid assemblage while I reflected in some wonder what strange twists of fate had caused a refugee from Nazi persecution to wind up in Arabia as the representative of American democracy. Next, I was introduced around the room by the royal chief of protocol, walking past the lined-up dignitaries and shaking their hands as their names were given to me.

The King then took me to dinner. He and I sat at the head table at right angles to two long extensions along which Western clothes, looking strangely clumsy in this Arab environment, marked the few members of my party as intruders in the elegant uniformity of Saudi robes. It was like an eerily rehearsed symphony. When the King spoke, all was silent; my comments were drowned in a buzz of conversation. The silences for the King heightened my awareness in my first exposure to what throughout the Arab world, and in many more outlying regions, was immediately recognizable as Faisal's standard speech. Its basic proposition was that Jews and Communists were working now in parallel, now together, to undermine the civilized world as we knew it. Oblivious to my ancestry — or delicately putting me into a special category — Faisal insisted that an end had to be put once and for all to the dual conspiracy of Jews and Communists. The Middle East outpost of that plot was the State of Israel, put there by Bolshevism for the principal purpose of dividing America from the Arabs.

It was hard to know where to begin in answering such a line of reasoning. When Faisal went on to argue that the Jewish-Communist conspiracy was now trying to take over the American government, I decided the time had come to try to change the subject. I did so by asking His Majesty about a picture on the far wall, which I took to be a decorative work of art. It was a holy oasis, I was informed — representational art being forbidden in Islam. This faux pas threw Faisal into some minutes of deep melancholy, causing conversation around the table to stop altogether. In the unearthly silence my colleagues must have wondered what I had done so quickly to impair the West's oil supplies. I did not help matters by referring to Sadat as the leader of the Arabs. His Majesty's morose reaction showed that there was a limit beyond which claims to Arab solidarity could not be pushed.

The King always spoke in a gentle voice even when making strong points. He loved elliptical comments capable of many interpretations, thus protecting himself against being quoted in contexts that he could not control and that might ultimately prove embarrassing. He conducted audiences by sitting in the center of the room with his interlocutor at his right and the interpreter facing them, while each side's advisers were lined up along the walls beyond whispering range — indeed, given the size of the room, barely within shouting distance — and thus effectively excluded from the conversation. In talking to me he would look straight ahead, occasionally peeking from around his headdress to make sure I had understood the drift of some particular conundrum.

All this was so unprecedented in my experience that at first it was difficult to find criteria for judgment. It was easy for a Westerner to make light of King Faisal's standard rhetoric. But as I learned to know him I realized that he was a man of rare quality, highly intelligent, formidable, and yet wise enough never to display his strength. The imperatives of conviction and tactical expediency merged, so that he both believed in what he was doing and did what served his purposes. The speech on Communism and Zionism, however bizarre it sounded to Western visitors, was clearly deeply felt. At the same time it reflected precisely the tactical necessities of the Kingdom. The strident anti-Communism helped reassure America and established a claim on protection against outside threats (which were all, in fact, armed by the Soviet Union). The virulent opposition to Zionism reassured radicals and the PLO and thus reduced their incentive to follow any temptation to undermine the monarchy domestically. And its thrust was vague enough to imply no precise consequences; it dictated few policy options save a general anti-Communism.

Faisal combined religious intensity and diplomatic shrewdness — not for nothing had he been Foreign Minister of Saudi Arabia for years before ascending the throne. Religion gave him the inner strength to face Saudi Arabia's perils and seek to overcome them with serenity. It also provided cohesion to a country moving, however fitfully, toward modernization, as well as protection against the covetous. It was one thing to tackle an ordinary statesman and to subject him to the normal pressures of diplomacy, which in the Middle East can be quite rough. It was quite another to seek to blackmail a holy man who placed himself above the battle. By his reputation for piety Faisal combined exaltation and anonymity, great influence and aloofness from the fray. Faisal managed the extraordinary feat of positioning himself exactly into the calm eye of the hurricane, though he never forgot the storms raging all around him. It took great skill and inward detachment.

Faisal deserved his reputation for rectitude. He was as honorable as he was subtle. He weighed his words scrupulously. He never spoke idly; each sentence had its significance, even if it took slower minds a while to catch on. We were fortunate that toward the United States Faisal maintained a feeling of genuine friendship — which we reciprocated — balanced by doubt about our acumen and ultimate steadiness. He was close enough to the Bedouin tradition to anchor essentially political acts in personal relationships. He was a man of his word; indeed, generally he delivered more than he promised. On the other hand, in thirty years in high office he had seen enough of the volatility of American politics not to entrust the future of his country without qualification to the unpredictable shifts of mood he had witnessed. Therefore he always hedged his bets, wherever possible in favor of the United States but not if that jeopardized the interests of Saudi Arabia as he understood them. Above all, he knew the weakness of his own country. He never sought the role of mediator because he was convinced that for all its wealth — and perhaps because of it — Saudi Arabia could not stand being made the formal arbiter of all crises.

When I understood him better, I found that it was easier for Faisal to act seemingly spontaneously than in response to a request. It enhanced his standing in the Arab world if he was able to say truthfully that no assistance had been requested and hence no promises had been made. This would not keep him from doing on his own — as a totally voluntary act, as it were — what supported our objectives. It then did not have to be reported to his brethren as a commitment or promise to the Americans. I made sure that he was always well briefed about our negotiations; frequently I stopped in Riyadh to inform him personally. After the first few meetings I never made a specific request. But often I found through other channels a helpful Saudi footprint placed so unobtrusively that one gust of wind could erase its traces.

King Faisal brought off a tour de force. Under his leadership his country was taken seriously but reserved the right to define its role. Whether he intended it or not, he made possible a revolution in world economics and an upheaval in the world balance of power by lending Saudi Arabia's weight to the use of the oil weapon and turning the Kingdom into a major factor in world affairs. But he managed to present this revolution as a reluctant decision taken with a bleeding heart, an act imposed by the greed of others and the uncontrollable passions of the region.

And if one understood Saudi policy as the result of all the forces at work in the area rather than as the shaper of them, that perception was right. If the statesman acts as the helmsman in storm-tossed seas, Faisal performed masterfully in keeping his fragile bark always heading into the wind and having it emerge intact — no mean achievement when one considers the fate of countries all around him.

All these tendencies emerged when, following dinner, I sat down with Faisal for talks. Unlike Sadat, he was not a man for the dramatic initiative; his greatness was clothed in anonymity. I needed his goodwill for our Middle East diplomacy and I wanted to impress upon him that the oil embargo was a severe blow to our relations. The two levels of the conversation — what I wanted him to understand and what he was prepared to acknowledge — were not always the same. We warily circled each other like wrestlers before a match, studying each other's moves without, in the end, ever going beyond this preliminary phase.

I explained our Middle East strategy along the lines of my presentation to Sadat, omitting the tactical details. Faisal understood what I was saying well enough; his bearing indicated attention and sympathy. But his words, which would no doubt be communicated to other Arab leaders, including the PLO's, were elegant restatements of a comprehensive program incompatible with our strategy. Peace with Israel was possible — an unusual acknowledgment for Faisal — but he immediately qualified the statement by making it conditional on Israeli withdrawal to the 1967 frontiers and the return of *all* Palestinian refugees to their homes, which in practice would mean an influx of over a million Arabs into pre-1967 Israel. Faisal elaborated the shape of that state: "There must be established in Palestine, by agreement, a mixed Jewish-Moslem state" — in other words, exactly the PLO platform. I objected that this was not possible. Faisal replied cannily: "Israel would withdraw the moment Israel saw that you would no longer protect it, cuddle it." This was put forward regally, without intensity, but also without flexibility, as if Faisal's role was primarily to lay down principles, not guides to action. With respect to the Arab-Israeli problem, Faisal put forward an attitude, not a program.

Matters became more complicated when we dealt with oil. Goaded on by Nixon, I was concerned with persuading Faisal to lift or ease the embargo. Had I understood the mechanism of oil pricing better, I would have realized that Saudi production cutbacks were more dangerous than the embargo since they critically affected world supply and therefore provided the precondition for the impoverishing price rise. My misapprehension made no difference. Faisal, who understood the pricing mechanism very well indeed, made clear that he would increase production when he lifted the embargo; indeed, he professed to be "red hot with anxiety to expedite this as fast as possible." Unfortunately, Saudi Arabia was in an "embarrassed" position; it needed some proof of tangible progress before a proposal to sheath the oil weapon could be put forward to the other Arab states. Faisal, precisely because he was a friend of the United States, could not act alone.

The geopolitical approach having failed, I appealed to psychology. It was painful, I said, to be pressured by a friend. It was unseemly to yield to such pressure. Faisal turned the appeals against me by insisting: "I have suffered even more than you." He suggested that the strain might give him a nervous breakdown. We could not be perceived to be giving in to blackmail, I argued. Faisal was equal to the occasion. He appreciated my "valid" explanations. But unfortunately Saudi Arabia did not have a free hand since the decision was made jointly by all Arabs. "What I need is the wherewithal to go to my colleagues and urge this."

I tried the route of compromise. If Saudi Arabia was not prepared to lift the embargo, perhaps it could ease its application. Faisal was all for compromise. Perhaps the happy medium could be agreed upon if we, unable to induce Israel to give up all its conquests and permit the return of the Palestinians, would announce this as an objective in the form of a United States demand on Israel. I gently turned this aside.

In our stately minuet we went through our paces but failed to harmonize our movements. Faisal had given no hostages to his note-taker.

And yet as he walked me to the door, he bestowed in a minute the blessing for our diplomacy that I had sought in vain in hours of complex talk. He did so cryptically, when records were no longer being kept, and yet in the hearing of the other princes, almost as if the most important sentence he uttered were an afterthought or a formal courtesy: "We pray to Almighty God that He will continue to grant you success in all these noble efforts. I spoke very frankly to Your Excellency because I respect your proven ability and wisdom." Nothing Faisal said was idle; if he called the step-by-step approach "noble," he meant to support our policy, albeit in his own complicated way. Nor was it mere politeness or flattery that he had given me — in front of his senior advisers — a personal endorsement despite my religious background.

Since Faisal could not be sure that I had got the point, two visitors called on me, one after the other, at the guest house within minutes of the end of my audience with the King. The first was Prince Fahd, then Minister of the Interior and generally considered the strong man of the Kingdom after Faisal. As I got to know Fahd better, I learned that he was less indirect than his half brother the King but equally subtle and intelligent. And he was a good friend of our country. He had sat in on the meeting with the King and was thus by conviction as well as occasion in a position to affirm all that the King, with the spotlight on him, had been reluctant to make explicit. The record of this meeting, being unannounced, did not have to be distributed to the Arab world. "I appreciate," Fahd said:

listening to your explaining so brilliantly to His Majesty the King the difficulties for the U.S. and the particular difficulties that would not be understood by those who do not know the U.S.

And I would assure Your Excellency that I for one will be instrumental among those who will help you on the path you have marked out. . . .

While we feel at ease hearing you outline the steps you have embarked upon, I feel inevitably the results will be good. And we appreciate the fact that things cannot be done overnight and have to be done step-by-step, but expeditiously.

This was a royal imprimatur to our step-by-step approach, a precious vote of confidence. Fahd then pledged to do his utmost to remove obstacles to US–Saudi relations, including the oil embargo. He would visit the United States soon to demonstrate Saudi friendship.

When I bade him goodbye at the door of the guest house, Omar Saqqaf — also a participant at the royal audience — was already waiting, equally unannounced. He, too, clearly came at the King's bidding to speak more openly than had been possible at the formal audience. Saqqaf was concerned that I might be discouraged because the King's subtleties had eluded me. He came straight to the point: "You both were difficult, as far as I can see. But this was among friends. You will see results." He said that the Saudis appreciated my efforts; the alternative to Sadat was the Soviet protégé Ali Sabri. "If Arab radicals win with Soviet arms," I said, "you yourself will be threatened." Saqqaf, having studied Mideast trends all of his life, agreed. He stated in moderate terms the essence of the problem between the Arabs and Israel: "Both sides need to learn that the other doesn't want to kill them. Now it's a vicious circle." Saqqaf, like Fahd, conveyed Saudi eagerness that I continue my mission. This in turn gave the Kingdom a stake in its success. It would place no obstacles in my path; it would almost surely be helpful.

As the King had already done, Saqqaf told me that Syria was eager to establish contact with me at the highest level; this meant President Hafez Asad. I told him I would contact Asad upon my return to Washington. This I knew would give Saqqaf a chance to communicate with Damascus before I did, enabling him both to smooth my way and to garner some credit for the Kingdom.

My November trip marked the real end of the Middle East war. It stabilized the cease-fire; it settled the immediate postwar lines. By November 14, Egypt and Israel had worked out a detailed accord at Kilometer 101 for implementing the six-point plan. We had been instrumental in all these negotiations. We were gradually getting into a position where our support was essential for progress while the Soviet capacity for mischief was being systematically reduced. We could now focus on the next step — to assemble the Geneva Conference and to chart the road toward peace. But first we had to move some other pieces on the chessboard of diplomacy.

XIV

Persian Gulf Interlude

I LEFT Riyadh for countries that would contribute relatively little to the solution of the immediate crisis in the Middle East but that were important to our conception of a secure and more peaceful world: Iran was key to the balance in the Persian Gulf; Pakistan was a long-standing friend whose independence we had sought to protect; China was essential to the global equilibrium; Japan was a mainstay of our system of alliances. (The Peking and Tokyo visits will be discussed in later chapters.)

Our first stop was Tehran on November 9, 1973, to meet with America's ally of thirty-seven years, the Shah of Iran. Time and his people have not treated the Shah of Iran kindly. America and its allies shamed themselves by their later behavior toward him, abandoning a friend not only politically — which can result from the brutal dictates of national interest — but also humanly, when he was adrift without a refuge and required succor. History is written by the victors; in this case they have been cruel.

There have been many falsehoods about America's relationship with the Shah. The impression has been created that personal friendships or a predilection for authoritarian rulers shaped American support for the Iranian leader. Reality was more complex; a relationship that thrived under eight American Presidents of both political parties must have resulted from deeper causes than personal idiosyncrasy. America's friendship with Iran reflected not individual proclivities but geopolitical realities. Iran's intrinsic importance transcended the personalities of both countries' leaders. Iran, the state with the longest history of self-rule between Egypt and China, can be the landbridge between the Soviet Union and the Arab Middle East; under the Shah it was a barrier shielding vulnerable Pakistan and Afghanistan from the pressures of both Soviet expansionism and Middle Eastern turbulence. Iran is by far the strongest nation along the Strait of Hormuz, through which passes over 40 percent of the industrial democracies' imported oil. It is itself capable of producing well over six million barrels of oil a day (its production has been as high as eight million) — an important contribution to world oil supply, the reduction in which after the Shah's overthrow in 1979 caused a global economic crisis. It requires no complicated theories of a preference for authoritarians or personal seduction to explain why American Presidents from Franklin Roosevelt to Jimmy Carter affirmed the parallelism of interests between the United States and a friendly Iran.

Nor were the benefits one-sided — as indeed they could not be in a relationship extending over such a long period. Whatever the Shah's fanatical and misguided successors proclaimed, historically the gravest threat to the independence of Iran has come not from America, eight thousand miles away, but along the traditional invasion routes: from the north, where stood a covetous Soviet Union; from the west, where Iraq sought to undo the borders imposed half a century earlier. A prudent Iranian ruler would consider it safer to rely on a country separated by two continents than on a neighbor that had not accepted true independence anywhere along its frontiers. And the United States considered itself fortunate that the most populous and potentially the strongest nation in the Persian Gulf did not follow the fashionable trend of a non-alignment that grew less and less distinguishable from anti-Americanism.

The Shah, a shrewd analyst of foreign policy, based Iran's security not on maneuvering ambiguously among the superpowers but on alliance with America. At the same time, having seen Britain abandon its presence in the Gulf and America become mired in Southeast Asia, he foresaw that Iran would have to rely as well on its own strength. He therefore sought modernization and economic development partly to anchor his own rule in popular support, partly to enable Iran to carry its own share of the defense burden. He realized that outside assistance was more likely in a gross emergency if Iran could by itself resist threats from within the area and could force even the Soviets, if they chose to menace Iran, into a scale of adventure that would leave no doubt about their design.

Later, when our interests were beyond salvage, it grew fashionable in America to exorcise guilt feelings by blaming Iran's fate on Nixon's decision in 1972 to sell advanced weapons to our ally. This critique seems to have united two disparate groups otherwise severely at loggerheads. On the one hand, there were neoconservatives, some recently converted from having opposed all American military commitments abroad, who argued that the "Nixon doctrine" was fundamentally flawed. Since Iran and other threatened countries would never be able to defend themselves, we should have known all along that only the stationing of American forces in the Persian Gulf could establish the requisite security umbrella.[1] Others adopted an opposite, more fashionable, rationale, that appealed to liberal clichés about the evil of weapons

sales as well as the Shah's alleged repressiveness. Neither made historical or geographical sense.

For what Nixon faced in 1972 was not a theory but a reality. Britain's
withdrawal from the Gulf at the end of 1971 had been followed in April
1972 by a Friendship Treaty between Iraq and the Soviet Union, which
led to the heavy supply of modern military equipment to that then most
radical of Arab states. To keep Iraq from achieving hegemony in the
Persian Gulf, we had either to build up American power or to strengthen
local forces. America's eagerness to forget Vietnam, and the later conservative resurgence, have obliterated the mood of that period. That
America had to reduce its foreign involvements was the universal wisdom — unchallenged, indeed supported, even by conservatives. Every
military budget was slashed by the Congress. The one military base we
sought to build in the Indian Ocean, at Diego Garcia, was under constant Congressional attack. Funds for it could be obtained only by calling it a support facility and explicitly forgoing building an airport capable of handling heavy bombers. The stationing of troops there was
specifically proscribed — and Diego Garcia is 2,000 miles from the coast
of Iran. Creating a credible military capability for the defense of the
Persian Gulf by America alone is a task of enormous, perhaps insuperable, practical and logistical difficulty in the best of circumstances —
as we are discovering at this writing. Our choice in 1972 was to help
Iran arm itself or to permit a perilous vacuum. Nor did the Nixon doctrine ever look to any country to defend itself alone against a superpower; it explicitly offered assistance if a nuclear power — a euphemism for the USSR — attacked an ally willing to defend itself.[2] For
decades, Iran under the Shah contributed importantly to the stability of
the region and to international security. And he — or groups holding
his views — might have continued to do so with a wiser policy by our
successors.

A variation of the critique of our policy is that the error was not the
decision to arm the Shah but to give him a "blank check" to purchase
arms without limit. This is disingenuous; there was no blank check.
Nixon's decision was triggered by the Shah's request to buy new advanced aircraft, the F-14 or F-15. For a variety of reasons the Pentagon
dragged its feet, partly because it preferred to sell some of its obsolescent equipment, partly because of preference for stocking our own in-
ventories — though it did not frontally challenge Nixon's decision. When
Nixon visited Tehran in May 1972, the Shah raised the issue, pointing
out that he had the alternative of buying comparable if slightly inferior
French planes. Nixon approved in principle the sale of either F-14s or
F-15s. A directive to that effect was issued upon his return. The Defense Department replied with a counterproposal: that the Shah delay
any decision on the purchase of either aircraft until operational experi-

ence was acquired with *both* aircraft. Whereas the F-14 would be ready in 1973, the F-15 would not be ready until 1976 or 1977 — delaying the decision by four years. In order to put an end to the procrastination, Nixon ordered that the decision on these aircraft purchases and their timing should be left to the government of Iran. In the context, that is the meaning of the oft-quoted directive, which ended with a general *obiter dictum* that the Pentagon not try to second-guess Iranian decisions on what equipment to select.

In any event, only one ignorant of our governmental processes or eager to score debating points could argue that this single directive by Nixon survived Watergate and his resignation and drove all the decisions of two subsequent administrations — during which 90 percent of the major arms sales were in fact made. I doubt that Presidents Ford and Carter were even aware of the directive — as I had forgotten it — when they approved later arms purchases that were incomparably larger than those approved under Nixon. Presidents Ford and Carter encouraged the Shah's military strength for the same reason that Nixon approved the first increment: It was considered in the overwhelming strategic interest of the United States, of Iran, and of the stability of the region. (Secretary of Defense James Schlesinger maintained his own representative in Iran to handle Iranian arms requests.) That the strategic judgment had merit is shown by the fact that after the Shah's death, revolutionary Iran was attacked by Soviet-armed Iraq (an event inconceivable while the alliance with the United States was still intact) and was saved from catastrophe by the much-vilified American arms; and that the Iranian government holding American hostages would at various times ask for American spare parts as a condition of the hostages' release.

In the perspective of a decade, the Shah's overthrow had little to do with his purchases of military equipment. Indeed, had America played its hand differently when that upheaval started, Iran's military establishment might have provided a political counterweight to radicalism during the period of the monarchy's disintegration. The single most important factor in the Shah's collapse was the policy he learned from the West: the modernization of a feudal, Islamic society, the rapid economic development that absorbed far more of Iran's revenues than did arms purchases. The Shah took literally the Western academic doctrines according to which the source of political instability was the gap between economic expectation and achievement. And as the "revolution of rising expectations" was met, so the argument went, political stability would follow almost automatically. Western liberal maxims caused the Shah to build a secular, modern state in the reformist mold of Kemal Ataturk and to force-feed industrialization to a population that had barely left the feudal age. For nearly two decades he seemed to be succeeding.

Iran's gross national product rose at the rate of nearly 10 percent a year. Land reform was instituted, public education and women's rights fostered, workers' profit-sharing and public health spurred.

But the result was hardly the political stability foreseen by academic theory. Industrialization uprooted rural populations and drew them into the congested cities where they found themselves morally and psychologically adrift. The increase in the GNP spawned a new social class that, just as in comparable periods of European history, sought a larger role in government. Education produced intellectual ferment and the temptations of radicalism; it was surely hostile to absolute monarchy in the Shah's style. The modernizing cultural influences from the West, flooding over the broken dam of Iran's cultural isolation, overwhelmed Iran's religious and social traditions. The rootless, the newly powerful, the orthodox, and the spiritually dispossessed came together with disparate, often conflicting, motives and swept away the Shah's rule in an orgy of retribution and vengefulness.

But retribution for what? To be sure, there was corruption at the Shah's court, though not unusually so by the standards of the region or even by the standards of the regime that followed. The excesses of the secret police, the dreaded SAVAK, were inexcusable, even allowing for the mass of exaggerations.* Undoubtedly, the Shah lived in an isolation that prevented him from understanding that his economic successes were creating new political realities which could not be dealt with by repression. However, his accumulated failures were almost certainly less severe than the practices of other nations in the Persian Gulf or among the nonaligned that have not been exposed to opprobrium. And nothing that happened can compare with the witch trials, executions, terrorism, and lunacy that followed, reminiscent in bloodiness and judicial hypocrisy of the worst excesses of Robespierre.

What overthrew the Shah was a coalition of legitimate grievances and an inchoate accumulation of resentments aimed at the very concept of modernity and at the Shah's role as a moderate world leader. The Shah was despised less for what he did wrong than for what he did right. He was brought down by those who hated reform and the West; who were against absolute rule only if it was based on secular principles. The immediate victors were not enlightened dissidents of liberal democratic persuasion but the most regressive group in Iranian society: the religious ayatollahs who identified human dignity not with freedom and progress but with an ancient moral and religious code. It was, in fact, a declaration of independence directed against all the homogenizing cultural influences of global progress, against the alien doctrines of Communism

---

*SAVAK continues to exercise its powers, albeit under a new name and new auspices, in the revolutionary regime.

as well as of the West, a groping for identity and faith in a world perceived as representing rootless corrupting uniformity.

The valid criticism of our policy in the Seventies is our failure to perceive this almost metaphysical rebellion against modernization. We were blinded not only by the loyalty to the Shah for which we are criticized — and there are worse indictments to be made of a nation than steadfastness in support of an ally — but also by the Western notions of economic and social progress that are the patent medicine of the very critics who gloated at the Shah's downfall. I remember saying once to the traveling newsmen as we were leaving Tehran that, on historical precedent, a rate of economic advance like Iran's was bound to lead to revolution. But it was idle musing, for I added immediately that apparently the momentum of a very rapid rate of growth could overcome the political perils of industrialization. I was wrong. In fact, the rate of modernization accelerated the onset of political upheaval. The surface stability of 1976 was deceptive. Two years after I left office the cauldron exploded; the clumsy response in both Tehran and Washington compounded the tragedy and destroyed the domestic achievements of two decades — as well as the international ties that had served the cause of peace in the Persian Gulf.

But the problem is deeper than a simple mea culpa. Assuming we had understood the peril, what should the United States have advised? Do we possess a political theory for the transformation of developing countries? Do we know where to strike the balance between authority and freedom, between liberty and anarchy in feudal, religious societies? It is easy to argue that a more rapid liberalization would have saved the Shah; that moves toward parliamentary democracy to broaden political participation would have defused the pressures. Leaving aside the question of whether we had the power to bring this about, it is likely that these "enlightened" nostrums would have speeded up the catastrophe. The challenge to the Shah's rule came in the main from groups who had no interest in such Western ideas. His truly implacable enemies were the conservative, feudal group deprived of their social privileges; or radical leftists. Neither was remotely interested in parliamentary democracy. Indeed, after the Shah's overthrow, they crushed the few advocates of democratic institutions before turning to settling their own quarrels by mutual extermination.

It was no accident. The concept of representative democracy requires a social cohesiveness unattainable in many developing societies. Where government provides the principal social bond, the distinction is not always made (or even possible) between opposition to government and undermining of authority and indeed of the state. Clearly, in Iran the leader of the revolution was not a democrat of reformist tendencies but an embittered reactionary who, as soon as he attained office, garnered to himself dictatorial powers far exceeding those of the Shah.

The fact is that we lack a coherent idea of how to channel the elemental forces let loose by the process of development. Liberal democracy developed over centuries in essentially aristocratic and bourgeois societies; universal suffrage did not become general in the West until after the First World War. (Even in the United States, the Senate was elected by indirect vote as late as 1913.) In this cultural environment, the minority has a chance to become a majority and the political contest does not destroy the loser. It is different in countries with deep tribal or religious or racial divisions, or where a state has been created to govern populations whose principal common experience is colonial rule. Forcefed mass participation is more likely to lead to totalitarianism than to democracy. The contemporary irony is that Leninism has proved attractive to many developing countries not because of its economic theories, which have clearly failed, but because it offers legitimacy for staying in office — which is after all why most leaders of independence movements entered politics in the first place. Our dilemma is that we cannot abandon our own values, yet we have not yet learned how to build institutions capable of sustaining the political strains of development — at least in its initial phase.

In the Persian Gulf today, many traditional friends of the United States face this perplexity with us. We know that their domestic base is precarious, but we have no conclusive insight into how to strengthen it; indeed, to buttress the current rulers is as surely incompatible with democratic theory as it may be vital for our national interest. In the Persian Gulf the alternative to friendly authoritarianism is almost inevitably hostile totalitarianism. And the political concepts we try to transplant must appear to them as essentially destructive of their social cohesion; if that is the only way out, they may well prefer to make their own accommodation with radical currents sweeping the area. The dilemma remains one of the foremost intellectual challenges to American and Western political thought.

On November 9, 1973, reflections such as these would have seemed least relevant to Iran of all the countries in the Middle East. I was stopping in Tehran for both symbolic and substantive reasons: symbolic, to underline the importance we attached to our relationship with Iran, thereby to discourage adventurist policies by covetous neighbors; and substantive, to learn the Shah's analysis of world affairs and especially of the Middle East. Above all, I wanted to express our appreciation for the Shah's staunch support during the past month's crises.

We owed the Shah a great deal for his unflagging loyalty during the October war. NATO allies had permitted overflights of their territory by the Soviet airlift to the Middle East; the Shah had adamantly refused. While basically sympathetic to Sadat, he brought no diplomatic pressure on us. He kept us informed of what he understood to be Arab purposes. He was available as an intermediary — though Sadat's direct contact with us made that role only marginally necessary. Above all, he refused to join the pressures organized by the other oil producers in the Persian Gulf. Iran did not participate in the Arab oil embargo, nor did it curtail its oil production. Those were the measures that produced first panic and then a shortage of oil and finally made possible the massive increase in oil prices. (This did not stop revisionist historians from blaming the Shah for the oil price rise for which others shared equal if not greater responsibility.)* He continued to supply oil to Israel. When we moved a carrier task force into the Indian Ocean, it was fueled from Iran without argument about compensation. A hostile Iran could have blocked the diplomacy that had seen us through the crisis; an indifferent one would have greatly complicated our task. I always thought I had a duty to remember those services of the Shah to our country and to free peoples, especially in the vicissitudes that later befell him.

If the world is indeed destined to become one global village, airports will serve as their marketplace; their terminals have banished cultural as well as national characteristics. The gleaming royal pavilion at Tehran's Mehrabad Airport could have been the VIP reception area anywhere in the world — except for the exquisite Persian carpets that covered its floors. We lingered there for only a few minutes of greeting by the distinguished elderly Foreign Minister, Abas Ali Khalatbari. He accompanied me and Ambassador Richard Helms to the Imperial Palace at the outskirts of the town. As always, the Foreign Minister left us at the door of the imperial study. He did not participate in that or any other conversation with the Shah. In truth, his position was closer to that of chief of protocol than head of Iranian diplomacy; he greeted visitors of less than head of state rank; he represented Iran at conferences not worthy of imperial attention. But the overall conduct of foreign policy the Shah reserved for himself. I go into this much detail because after the revolution this inoffensive courtier of impeccable manners was executed senselessly after an absurd trial lasting less than an hour.

Mohammed Reza Pahlavi as always was gracious and aloof — an attitude composed in equal parts of shyness, consciousness of the difference in our protocol rank, and his conception of the attitude required of emperors. This posture had been drilled into him by his primitive Cossack father, who had usurped the throne in the 1920s; but one never had the sense that the Shah felt comfortable with it. Loneliness had been imposed upon him by his upbringing until his exile consummated it in a cruel abandonment by nearly all who had sought his favor for four decades.

The Shah was acute in his analysis of grand strategy. Radical Iraq,

---

* See Chapter XIX.

he thought, would be used as a battering ram against all moderate pro-Western regimes in the area. Though not strictly speaking a Soviet satellite, once fully armed with Soviet weapons Iraq would serve Soviet purposes by intimidating pro-Western governments, such as Saudi Arabia; simultaneously, it would exert pressure on Jordan and even Syria, which while leaning to the radical side was far from being a Soviet puppet. The Soviet Union would try to squeeze Iran between Afghanistan and its Iraqi client. The recent revolution in Kabul, which had replaced the Afghan King with a new President, Mohammed Daoud, was especially worrisome to the Shah. Led by officers with distinctly pro-Soviet tendencies, it sowed the seeds of future trouble. Daoud's revolution might well be the preview of even more radical upheavals — a prescient forecast, as matters turned out. Though Daoud was a nationalist, even his goals could easily serve Soviet purposes by destabilizing the area. Afghan irredentism, aimed at stirring up disaffected ethnic groups in border regions of both Pakistan and Iran (the Pushtoons and Baluchis), could produce a pincer movement whose practical consequence would be to project Soviet power closer to the Indian Ocean. The Shah would support Pakistan to the extent that our legislation regarding his use of American arms permitted. We must try to prevent the Fertile Crescent — Iraq, Syria, and Jordan — from being ruled from Baghdad. He would keep Iraq occupied by supporting the Kurdish rebellion within Iraq, and maintaining a large army near the frontier.

With all his sympathy for Sadat, the Shah considered Israel a strategic linchpin in the area. Indirectly, it contributed to the independence of Jordan by deterring Syrian or Iraqi military action against it. For the same reason it was a guarantee of Lebanon's independence. Unfortunately, in the Shah's view, Israel's foreign policy was not as wise as its contribution to overall security was strategically significant; its diplomatic intransigence complicated the position of the moderate Arab governments on which its own survival ultimately rested and threatened to weaken American influence. The Shah applauded our conduct during the Middle East war — especially the alert. He welcomed our rapprochement with Egypt. I briefed him on the six-point plan. He considered Sadat the best hope for a moderate and peaceful evolution. The United States should do its utmost to encourage him.

I stressed that the Arab oil embargo and production cutbacks put us into an impossible position. We were prepared to respond to legitimate Arab concerns; we were bound to resist any impression that the so-called oil weapon could be used to force us into decisions we would not make otherwise. All our friends in the Arab world had an interest in demonstrating that radical pressures were futile and that America held the key to the settlement. If we abandoned this posture, any diplomatic achievement would backfire and would simply encourage further blackmail. The Shah agreed. He promised to intercede with Egypt and Saudi Arabia to urge an end to the embargo. Within days he sent an emissary to Saudi Arabia and a message to Sadat, as he had promised.

My conversation with the Shah illustrated the basis of the Iranian-American relationship during his reign. Some of his analysis was, of course, self-serving in the sense of providing a rationale for existing policy. But self-interest is no inhibition against accuracy. It is precisely the collapse of a pro-Western Iran that led to an upheaval in the Gulf and the Indian Ocean that has not subsided at this writing.

The Shah's fate and that of his country are a permanent warning that there are no simple answers. Those who seek a more peaceful world must have a conception of its nature. Those who strive for justice must understand that it consists of more than the venting of resentments. And we have to become more thoughtful about the political evolution of friendly countries whose stability is important to our security. In that case we may still learn a lesson from that costly tragedy.

We stopped overnight in Islamabad in friendly Pakistan. Its volatile leader, Zulfikar Ali Bhutto, also later came to a tragic end. It does not alter my evaluation of him as a man of extraordinary abilities whose ruthlessness was matched by his brilliance. Whereas his neighbor the Shah fell because he maintained personal autocratic rule for too long, Bhutto destroyed himself by seeking a popular mandate too rapidly and then manipulating the electoral result. This self-indulgence was probably an attempt to score a debating point on his hated adversary, Mrs. Indira Gandhi, who had just established ''emergency'' rule by decree in India. But it must also be said that Bhutto's arrogance reflected a fair assessment of his talents. There was no blinking his skillful — some might say opportunistic — ideological gyrations throughout his public life. But I had also been present in 1971, when he extricated his country from a shattering defeat in the war with India that left Pakistan dismembered, with its eastern half seceding to become the new independent state of Bangladesh. Bhutto had acted with panache and wisdom in that tragic period and had been a steady friend of the United States afterward.

Bhutto had been variously accused of ''softness,'' now toward the Soviet Union, now toward China. And I never doubted that he was capable of drawing close to any country that served his perception of Pakistan's national interests. The fact was that after 1970, Pakistan's interests were best served by cultivating the two great powers it helped to bring together — the United States and the People's Republic of China. Pakistan was unique in being allied to both. But if this fact provided considerable diplomatic support, it also increased the precariousness of Pakistan's position. For the Soviet thrust toward the Indian

Ocean, combined with Indian resentment over the partition of 1947, tempted pressures from both directions. Nor was the gratitude of its powerful friends easily translated into concrete measures. The United States Congress would not approve military assistance to Pakistan or the transfer of American-supplied military equipment from Iran. China did not have the industrial base to provide substantial military supply. Throughout my term in office, the dilemma of how to preserve the independence of Pakistan was an excellent example of the conflict between our national interest and our domestic inhibitions. We were as conscious of Pakistan's importance as our inability to match our analysis with assistance was being brought home to us by each session of Congress. We managed one extremely modest military package, fulfilling a promise made by President Johnson over five years earlier; yet we arranged many ostentatious meetings to make good a pledge by President Kennedy a decade earlier: to demonstrate that America was not indifferent to threats to the independence of Pakistan. In the Watergate era, we had to stitch together a grand strategy from a tangle of expedients.

Bhutto's analysis of Soviet strategy was not much different from the Shah's. He, too, feared that the new Afghan leader Daoud might be encouraged by the Soviets to press into Pakistan and toward the Indian Ocean under the banner of Pushtoon and Baluchi autonomy. As it turned out, Daoud started on this course but gradually recoiled from it as he became aware that it made no sense to claim additional territories when Afghanistan's independence was itself threatened from the rear by the Soviet Union. From then on, Daoud ceased his mischief-making against Iran and Pakistan and began to move cautiously toward genuine non-alignment. Five years later, he paid for his presumption with his life in a Communist coup, and the Soviet design then unfolded precisely as the Shah and Bhutto had predicted.

The southern rim of Asia — Iran, Pakistan, Afghanistan — is a region of the world that may seem remote and strange to Americans, and yet it is a pivot of the world's security. Within a few years of my 1973 journey, it became an area of upheaval. From the Iranian revolution to the Soviet invasion of Afghanistan to the Iran-Iraq war, events dramatized the vulnerability of the Persian Gulf — the lifeline of the West's oil supply. The vital importance of that region had long been one of the themes of the shrewd strategic analysts I was to visit next: Mao Zedong and Zhou Enlai. We had much to talk about.

XV

The Eclipse of Zhou Enlai and
Another Talk with Mao

Zhou under Fire

I WRITE with sadness about the last exchanges I had with the Chinese Premier, Zhou Enlai. They took place about three months later than we had planned, and when they did, Zhou was on the way out of office, though we did not know it then.

As I have described in Chapter VIII, Zhou had agreed in late May and June to lend China's weight to an American compromise proposal to end the war in Cambodia; the formula envisioned a cease-fire, an end of American bombing, and immediate negotiations with Prince Norodom Sihanouk to set up a coalition government under the Prince's neutralist rule. Zhou would not have committed himself this far unless he had reason to believe that the Khmer Rouge could be brought to go along with the plan; and they could not have come to this uncharacteristic posture other than because our bombing had prevented the unconditional victory they sought. The scenario was to unfold once Sihanouk returned to Peking from a lengthy trip during the first week of July. I was to visit Peking in August 1973 for regular consultations and for a meeting with Sihanouk to begin a political dialogue.

A few days before Sihanouk's return, Congress voted to prohibit *all* American military action in Indochina; we had to agree to cut off the Cambodian bombing by August 15. Our principal bargaining leverage was lost. The Khmer Rouge saw no reason to negotiate a cease-fire we had already legislated. Zhou Enlai, politically wounded at home by our failure, dropped the initiative with Sihanouk and pointedly postponed my trip to August 16, the day after the bombing halt. It was a slap in the face and Zhou could have no doubt I would refuse. I did so on July 25.

After that misfortune, little passed between Peking and Washington. Both sides were frustrated; each sulked about the other's reaction. And Zhou's difficulties at home were mounting. There were long delays in our exchanges attempting to set up another visit. The Chinese, preoccupied with a National Party Congress, let us wait until August 17 before accepting September 6. But on August 22, my nomination as Secretary of State was announced. Since I could not travel while my confirmation was pending, I postponed my visit to the end of October. On the day after my nomination, I sent a personal message to Zhou saying that I considered Chinese-American relations "a cornerstone of US foreign policy." I informed him that I was calling Ambassador David Bruce home from Peking to help with the transition to my new assignment. Bruce had been instructed to request an appointment with the Premier and with Vice Foreign Minister Qiao Guanhua, then acting head of the Foreign Ministry, to obtain their assessment of the state of Chinese-American relations.

On August 29, Qiao received Bruce at the Foreign Ministry. He made no reference to Zhou except to convey the Premier's congratulations on my appointment. The Chinese "welcomed" my forthcoming visit. But pending it they had in effect nothing to communicate. Qiao considered the development of our relations to be "normal." The Liaison Offices set up in each other's capitals were creating an objective reality. In other words, there was no reason to be concerned; our relations now had their own dynamics. To be sure, on many aspects of these relations I had my own views and "the Chinese had theirs" — an oblique reference, no doubt, to my bitter response when Zhou broke off the talks on Cambodia. ("This is the first time in the development of our new relationship that the Chinese word has not counted.") But Qiao referred to the differences primarily to emphasize the underlying community of interests. The new style introduced into diplomacy by the Sino-American relationship and the Shanghai Communiqué, he said, was "not to attempt to hide our differences but to admit them frankly." In Bruce's laconic words: "Although Ch'iao [Qiao] was as usual polite and amiable it was clear that he had no desire to prolong a conversation that was degenerating into pleasantries."

There were many explanations for Chinese aloofness. They were undoubtedly smarting at my harsh reaction to their cancellation of the Cambodian initiative. The fact was, after all, that it was not the Chinese who had changed their minds but the United States Congress that had destroyed the premise on which the negotiations were based. The Chinese were surely confused by our domestic turmoil and no longer sure how steady or reliable a partner we would prove to be. And the collapse of the Cambodian negotiations accelerated the internal attacks on Zhou Enlai, who apparently found himself accused of having been taken in while we sought to play off the Soviet Union against China.

During September we noted confusing signals in statements that senior Chinese diplomats were making in various capitals around the world. For the first time in our experience, the hitherto coherent and uniform line was missing. This almost surely reflected an internal struggle in China that made Chinese representatives unsure of which side was going to prevail and caused them to adjust their pronouncements to their estimates of the probable outcome. Some claimed that US–Chinese relations were "stalemated," largely on the issue of Taiwan. Others hinted that progress would be easy if only the United States recognized the "principle" of one China — which sounded more like a face-saving formula than an operational policy. Since there had been no recent discussion of Taiwan with us and surely no controversy, the issue must have been raised as part of a domestic power struggle over the value of the rapprochement with the United States. We heard a report that the reason for the postponement of my August visit was that Zhou Enlai lacked the support of the Central Committee for his policy and needed to build up his domestic base first. This was reinforced by the sudden transfer of one of Zhou's principal aides to the ambassadorship in Ottawa because he allegedly criticized the United States for trying to manipulate the Sino-Soviet rivalry. All this, it must be stressed, became clear only in retrospect. At the time all we noted were confusing signals.

Another puzzling phenomenon was the "anti-Confucian campaign" building in the Chinese media. There were several schools of thought in the West as to the purpose of attacking a philosopher dead nearly 2,500 years, however influential he had been in shaping Chinese culture and turning the state into an all-pervasive educational institution. The Aesopian indirectness in Chinese media gave few clues; there was even a dispute among our analysts whether the campaign was pro- or anti-Zhou in its aim. Considering that Confucius was an aristocrat whose style and philosophy of restraint had dominated Chinese public life for so many centuries, the weight of the evidence suggested that Zhou was the target. The brilliant China scholar on the NSC staff, Richard H. Solomon, called my attention to a significant article in the Chinese party journal *Red Flag* in November, criticizing an "aristocrat" of ancient times who had favored a policy of making friends with "distant countries" to deal with menacing neighbors but found himself sitting on a volcano.*

---

*This transparent allegory is an example of the style of the Chinese debate. The Zhou figure criticized his opponents

for advocating the policy of "making friends with neighboring countries [i.e., the Soviets] and attacking the distant ones [the U.S.]" in order to preserve their own hereditary prerogatives, and went further in putting forward the policy of "making friends with distant countries and attacking the neighboring ones." San Sui's [Zhou's] line won the approval of King Chao [Mao], and he was accordingly appointed as a guest minister in charge of military affairs.

However, although San Sui [Zhou] had become Prime Minister, he was actually perched on the top of the crater of a volcano that could erupt at any time. In the Chu state the power of the old aristocrats [the regional military commanders?] was still rather powerful.

Even Zhou Enlai seemed to be seized by doubts. He told one visiting diplomat of his uncertainty about how US–Chinese relations would develop in the future. If the two superpowers reached an accord, Zhou felt, the China card would not have as much value for the United States as it did before. But Zhou Enlai was too astute to rail against reality. It was clearly not in the American interest to side with one of the Communist giants against the other; it was even more against our interest to permit the Soviet Union to overwhelm or to humiliate Peking. Therefore Zhou added what sounded like a non sequitur. Despite his doubts he would continue to improve relations with the United States. But there were objective limits to what China could do, Zhou indicated; on Cambodia it could not support American policies, however much importance it attached to its ties with Washington.

By early October, Chinese internal controversies seemed to us (erroneously) to be on the way to being ended. Vice Foreign Minister Qiao Guanhua arrived in New York as head of the Chinese delegation to the United Nations General Assembly to deliver the standard Chinese fire-breathing speech and (on October 3) to join me in the by-now equally standard amiable dinner in my suite at the Waldorf Towers.

Qiao was full of good cheer. He thought his speech at the UN had "rendered [us] quite a bit of help," which given his revolutionary rhetoric was not self-evident to me.

"Not everywhere," I objected politely.

"If I rendered you help everywhere, then I could not do it anywhere," replied Qiao, who was a Hegelian scholar. He used this occasion to clear the books on Cambodia. Speaking "as a philosopher," Qiao said he had come to the conclusion that we had *both* erred in getting involved with Cambodia — a rare admission of Chinese fallibility. Even more striking was his assertion that China was basically indifferent as to who won in Cambodia:

Whether Cambodia turns red, pink, black, white or what, what difference will this make in the end for world history? The best way out is for neither of us to get involved in Cambodia. You have some difficulties which we do not have, I know. Your difficulties with Congress and with the press.

In other words, China absolved the Administration of blame for the fiasco; it was the fault of the Congress and the media. I had suggested that Chinese and North Vietnamese interests were not the same with respect to Cambodia. Qiao evaded this by putting his Hegelian training to good use once again: "I would not say that it is a question of our interests being different, but rather that our circumstances are not the same." It was a distinction without a difference, which admitted that there were clashing perceptions between Hanoi and Peking. But the clever Qiao also preempted any American temptation to lure China again into the Cambodian bog. It did not really matter, he said. China had not known anything about Cambodia before 1954; it was beyond its historical horizon — the implication was that China would cultivate its traditional indifference. The best course for both China and the United States was to forget about it, averred the Chinese Foreign Minister:

The Cambodian problem is in some respects the same to both of us. You have not asked for our help, and we have not asked for yours. What I wish to emphasize is that, considering the overall situation, the Cambodian issue is very definitely only a side issue.

Peking, the fount of revolutionary orthodoxy, was clearly washing its hands of Cambodia. It expressed no preference as to the outcome; it subjected our policy to no harangues. The Chinese as shrewd analysts could have very few doubts indeed about the future course of events in Cambodia; nor could they fail to understand that a collapse of Cambodia would precipitate the same result in South Vietnam. They had miscalculated our perseverance and our geopolitical insight. They had thought that the United States would understand the impact of defeat on its global position. Therefore they believed we would stay the course in Indochina, sustaining the existence of four independent states in the former French colonial territory, the outcome that suited Peking's national interest best. That would have avoided one of China's strategic nightmares: the emergence on its southern border of a powerful unified state controlling all of Indochina and closely allied with the Soviet Union. Now that our domestic divisions had brought the hitherto-unthinkable into view, China's only course was to deprecate the importance of the almost certain outcome without really believing it. Zhou Enlai saw no sense in compounding his geopolitical setback by having it encumber the overall relationship with the United States. Qiao's remarks suggested that we understand each other's dilemmas on Indochina; they must not be permitted to magnify the disaster by impeding the overriding common objective of containing Soviet military power.

So the meeting ended on a conciliatory and friendly note. Qiao advised a more "two-handed" American policy in the Middle East, dealing evenly with both Israel and the Arab states; as friends "now for quite a number of years, we can talk frankly," he said. He might be obliged to criticize some of our policies from time to time; he would as a friend never criticize me as an individual. Apparently the struggle in Peking had ended with a victory for the line of conciliation. The switches had been thrown in the direction of continued elaboration of Chinese-American rapprochement.

Before my visit to Peking — delayed yet again to November by the Mideast war — there was one more opportunity for a show of goodwill. Its locus ironically was Cambodia, the country that would not let us go, however the Chinese and we might wish to minimize its significance. On October 15, Huang Zhen, Chief of Peking's Liaison Office in Washington, brought me a message from Zhou Enlai: Prince Sihanouk's mother was gravely ill in Phnom Penh; Sihanouk wanted to see her once more before she died. He promised not to make use of the Queen Mother in his political struggle. On October 16, I replied that we had made the necessary arrangements: The Queen Mother and her doctors could leave for China on a special Air France flight. To Sihanouk's credit, he meticulously kept his promise not to exploit his mother's presence in China.

I reached China toward the end of my round-the-world flight. Bhutto had seen me off at Islamabad airport with a flattering parade of horse guards normally reserved for heads of state. Bhutto explained on television that given the number of ''nincompoops'' occupying that office who had visited Pakistan, it was only fair to the horses that they get to see an intelligent example of the human species.

We retraced the route of my secret journey. Once again we crossed the Himalayas; Zhou had sent almost the same welcoming party to escort me into China. One can, of course, never repeat an experience; the thrill of the unknown could not be recaptured. And as Secretary of State I was surrounded by much more machinery than on that essentially solitary venture. But this was balanced by the knowledge that in the little more than two years since the first journey, we had built solidly. We were visiting a country that shared a comparable view of our major security problem and whose leaders possessed an acute insight into world affairs.

I arrived for my sixth visit to Peking to an extraordinarily warm welcome, late Saturday afternoon, November 10, 1973. Premier Zhou Enlai greeted us in the Great Hall of the People prior to a banquet for almost two hundred guests (modest by Chinese standards). Zhou and I had already met informally, with only a few advisers each, for about half an hour. Zhou congratulated me on my ''whirlwind diplomacy'' in the Middle East — the term ''shuttle diplomacy'' not yet having been invented. He urged me to convey his good wishes to President Nixon (a hint that Watergate had not altered China's high regard for him) and his admiration for the resolution shown during the October alert. He applauded our efforts to reduce Soviet influence in the Arab world. He confessed that he had originally thought that we had missed the opportunity represented by Sadat's expulsion of Soviet personnel. He now understood our strategy to wait for a propitious time when decisive action was possible.

With that Zhou escorted me into dinner, which for protocol reasons was hosted by Foreign Minister Ji Pengfei. And in Chinese fashion, everything was orchestrated to suggest approval and cooperation. For the first time on one of my visits a military band was playing (it had, of course, during Nixon's), alternating American and Chinese songs. The Foreign Minister's toast applauded the progress in our relationship, mentioning particularly the Liaison Offices and expressing confidence that normalization would be achieved. My response proved that I was loath to let go of a good line. For the fourth time on my six trips I referred to the fact that China had once appeared to us as a mysterious country but was so no longer. Zhou, who had first put that idea forward, hid his boredom behind an indulgent smile.

The friendly atmosphere set the tone for the rest of the visit. Our discussions were conducted at two levels. A group of experts reviewed bilateral problems, especially the expansion of exchanges and trade and a residue of the period of conflict: the unfreezing of blocked Chinese assets in return for a settlement of claims of American citizens. On previous visits we had kept the State Department personnel occupied with technical issues while I conducted political talks. Now that I was Secretary of State, we no longer needed to play such games. But the procedure had meanwhile proved efficient and was therefore continued — proving, I suppose, that some bureaucratic maneuvers can even have substantive merit.

Following the now well-established practice the heart of the visit was a detailed review of the international situation by Zhou and me, together with our senior associates. My opening comment — that we had developed between us a habit of candor, honesty, and long-range thinking — was not a diplomatic courtesy; it had, in fact, become the key to the Chinese-American relationship at a point when few concrete results were achievable and our bonds depended on intangibles. Our ties were cemented not by formal agreements but by a common assessment of the international situation. The media, which for the first time had accompanied me to China, tended to judge the visit in terms of progress on Taiwan. Zhou understood that what was then possible on Taiwan was not desirable, because it would make US–Chinese ties controversial in both countries, though for obvious reasons of Chinese domestic politics he could not say so. Most of our conversations, as usual, traced our shared analysis of the world situation, though for the equally obvious reason of Soviet sensitivities we could not announce that fact either. So what was perhaps the most cordial of all my visits to China took place against a backdrop of media comment on a stalemate in our relationship.

In contrast to my February visit and to what we knew of China's internal debates, Zhou did not raise the issue of the US–Soviet relationship. Nor did he inquire, as he had earlier in the year, whether our policy was to "push the ill waters eastward." Perhaps he had won this particular internal debate; perhaps, more likely, his domestic position had so weakened that he did not dare legitimize the arguments of his critics by raising questions about them with me.

So it happened that, for the first time, I volunteered an analysis of our strategy toward the Soviet Union. It added little to what I had told him nine months earlier (see Chapter III). Nor could it. After all, strategies do not change every few months, and if they do, it undermines confidence. Statesmen prize steadiness and reliability in a partner, not a restless quest for ever-new magic formulas.

I chose to meet head-on the conventional criticisms of détente. I did not doubt, I said, that the Soviet Union sought to use a period of relaxation of tensions to erode the unity of the West and to weaken its defense. This only meant that the Soviet leaders had purposes of their own, as was to be expected in the policy of a great power. We, in turn, thought that time was on our side. We could stand a relaxation of tensions better than the Soviet system, which seemed to depend on an artificial sense of crisis. The disintegrating tendencies in the Soviet bloc already evident in Hungary and Czechoslovakia would inevitably recur. I reminded Zhou that in my Pacem in Terris speech on October 8 I had warned that we would not permit détente to undermine our relationship with friendly nations, and that we would resist any attempts by the Soviet Union to use international crises to expand its influence:

When aggressive action occurs, we will act decisively, and if necessary brutally, but we require the prior demonstration that we have been provoked. And I think we have proved this in our handling of the Middle East crisis.

Zhou did not challenge these propositions. Either he had been persuaded or, more likely, thought our policy too settled to be altered by debate. He was baffled by the uncertain attitude of our European allies. He could not understand their ambivalence either about the alert or about my trip to the Middle East. After all, he said, China had not been consulted about the alert either, yet it had applauded our action. It was symptomatic of the strained state of US–European relations (see Chapter XVI) that I replied without an excess of generosity, if accurately:

If you want to play for high stakes with very little risk, then you are likely to be in a continued state of dissatisfaction. The secret dream of our Western allies in the Middle East is to restore their position of 1940 without any risk or effort on their part and therefore, to the extent that we are more active, there is a vague feeling of jealousy and uneasiness.

Moreover, European leaders had become used to posing as mediators between East and West. They pretended to their publics that they were more peace-loving than the United States, secure in the knowledge that we would continue to hold the ring against the Soviet Union:

[E]ach of them faces the problem that for domestic reasons he has to say one thing while deep down he understands that what we are doing is essentially correct. Therefore, they very often, particularly after the event is already over, take a public position which is at variance [with] their understanding of the real situation.

A more flexible American policy deprived European leaders of this luxury. It forced them to take their own defense more seriously and to assume responsibility for their own proposals. In another session on the same topic the next day, I said:

[I]f in these efforts we keep slightly to the left of the West Europeans, this is a means to prevent them from going further because then they will be afraid we will make a separate arrangement with the Soviet Union and that will worry them sufficiently so that they start thinking about their own defense.

Zhou nodded understanding. But he raised a point that over time proved unanswerable: "[A]s for this point, the people would not be able to comprehend it." This was indeed our dilemma. If we were to sustain prolonged crises, we had to demonstrate our peaceful intentions to our public. To maintain allied unity, we could not permit our European associates to claim a monopoly on détente. But if we went too far down that road, we might confuse our public about Soviet purposes or start a race to Moscow among our allies. The Watergate era proved inhospitable to a policy based on such complicated maneuvers. Nor has the West as a whole squared the circle at this writing; yet its cohesion and purposefulness, its security and its self-confidence, will ultimately depend on its ability to do so.

Over the course of the next few days, Zhou and I systematically reviewed a wide range of international issues. Zhou had correctly analyzed our basic Middle East strategy before we arrived. I told him on November 11 that the significance of the six-point plan — which happened to be signed by Egypt and Israel that very day — resided not in its specific terms, important as they were, "but that it was negotiated between Egypt and the United States without the Soviet Union." Zhou had already grasped the point: "I had thought of toasting you on that last night, but I was afraid the correspondents would hear us." I explained our strategy with respect to the Geneva Conference: We would use the plenary sessions for the formal reiteration of the familiar; the real negotiations would take place under our aegis outside the conference on a bilateral basis between the various Arab countries and Israel.

With respect to Indochina I repeated our policy toward Sihanouk:

[W]e are not, in principle, opposed to Sihanouk. In many of his private statements and public statements, he seems to be under the misapprehension that the United States government is, in principle, opposed to him. That is absolutely incorrect. If he could return to Cambodia in a position of real independence for himself, we would be very interested in him as a leader. We are not interested in him if he is a captive of one particular faction that is simply using him for a very brief period of time in order to gain international recognition.

But Zhou, once burned, would not get involved again. He replied that Cambodia could not be discussed except in the context of all of Indochina, and in that case, we should devote an entire session to it later on during my visit. In fact, he did not return to the subject except to tell me that his conversations with North Vietnamese leaders indicated they had "no intention of launching a major offensive now"— a judgment that, by a strict definition of "major" and "now," proved correct.

Zhou abandoned his passive role only on Iraq and Afghanistan. According to Zhou's analysis, the Soviets after their expulsion from Egypt had made Iraq the pivot of their Middle East policy. The United States needed to take great care to prevent radical Iraq from achieving hegemony in the Persian Gulf; the Shah of Iran, in contrast, was a farsighted leader who understood the world situation — illustrating once again that for Peking geopolitics took precedence over ideology. As for Afghanistan, Zhou was gravely concerned about the coup that had brought Mohammed Daoud to power. The officers close to Daoud were pro-Soviet; we probably had not yet seen the last of Afghan upheavals. Afghan irredentism against neighboring Pakistan and Iran, even if not Soviet-inspired, would serve Soviet designs. It would weaken Pakistan and Iran and give Moscow a corridor to the Indian Ocean. The United States should strengthen Pakistan, which found itself in dire peril.

Unfortunately, Zhou and I, however much we respected each other, had diametrically opposite problems. Zhou represented a country capable of a powerful intellectual analysis but without the physical means to implement it. I was the foreign minister of a country that had the physical means and shared the geopolitical analysis but in post-Vietnam, Watergate conditions lacked the domestic consensus to execute its conceptions. Much as I agreed with Zhou's recommendations, I knew there was no chance of Congressional approval of a serious effort to strengthen Pakistan. Military assistance was out of vogue; the predominant conviction in the Congress was that India was more important to us and would be irritated by a military relationship with Pakistan. The best we could do, I told Zhou, was to strengthen Iran to back up Pakistan. Thus the Shah's role as protector of his neighbors was impelled in part by our internal disarray.

By all standards of ordinary diplomatic exchange, the dialogue with Zhou Enlai was of a high order. But those of my colleagues who had been with me on previous visits, especially Winston Lord, noticed that the old bite and sparkle were missing. Zhou asked penetrating, clarifying questions; he made intelligent comments on our presentations. And yet something was missing. For the first time he avoided the long, brilliant analyses that had made previous encounters so stimulating intellectually. Had he lost authority? Or were our approaches so comparable that it was no longer necessary?

Zhou seemed uncharacteristically tentative — as if he knew he needed to plant as many seeds as possible on this visit without being sure that he would be there for the harvest. He seemed eager to remove Taiwan as a rallying point for the anti-American faction in Peking. He listened patiently while I explained the impossibility of the "Japanese formula" for Taiwan — whereby the United States would have to break diplomatic relations with Taipei as a condition for normalization with Peking. I suggested that perhaps normalization was possible short of the Japanese formula so long as the United States recognized "the principle of one China." Zhou did not reject this approach. To my astonishment, he asked me the next day whether I had a precise formula for it. It seemed almost like a replay of the exchanges that had established the Liaison Offices. Zhou even included a sentence in the communiqué to the effect that normalization required that the United States recognize the "principle" of one China — something that had never been at issue. We were never to find out what exactly Zhou had in mind, for he was removed from office or incapacitated before we had a chance to learn what the phrase meant in practice.

In this mood of almost anxious goodwill, the group dealing with bilateral issues made considerable progress. There was agreement to expand the staffs and the functions of the Liaison Offices. Additional cultural exchanges were arranged; trade was increased. The claims and assets issues approached a solution — though Zhou could not avoid pointing out that our threat of legal action to vindicate claims was empty: How could one sue a government one did not recognize? Yet strangely enough, all this progress on what is normally the standard fare of diplomacy made us slightly uneasy. We could not tell why Zhou seemed so eager to get things settled; he did not supply, as was his wont, the rationale or the ultimate objective. One was put in mind of a brilliant, slightly stifling summer day whose beauty is the harbinger of a distant thunderstorm.

Another Meeting with Mao

THAT this time the authoritative line on foreign policy would not be laid down by Zhou Enlai became clear on Monday, November 12, when late in the afternoon we were invited to see Chairman Mao Zedong. The summons came as peremptorily as it had on all previous encounters with the Chairman, in the midst of a regular review session. We traveled in Chinese cars, I with Zhou, along the now-familiar route to the simple residence in the Imperial City where Mao lived. The entrance hall with its Ping-Pong table and the booklined study with its semicircle of easy chairs had become almost familiar. But one could never become accustomed to that incarnation of willpower who greeted us with his characteristic mocking, slightly demonic smile. Mao looked better than I had ever seen him, joking with my companions David Bruce and Winston Lord about Bruce's age, Lord's youth, and his own seniority over both of them. He was eighty.

All this was standard. What was new was that Mao, while continuing the elliptical Socratic dialogue of my first two encounters with him, substituted precision for his usual characteristic allusions. On this occasion Mao would not leave it to Zhou to give texture to his indirections; he would take over Zhou's role of articulating policy. He was not content with indicating a general direction; he intended to fill in the road map. He began by asking what Zhou and I had been discussing.

"Expansionism," replied Zhou, making clear that containing the Soviet Union remained the top priority for China.

"Who's doing the expanding, him?" inquired Mao, pointing at me — as if all this were new to him and Zhou had not been reporting daily.

"He started it," answered Zhou, "but others have caught up." Mao went along cheerfully with Zhou's implication that the Soviets were now the principal threat, but he used it to discourage any undue sense of danger that might tempt accommodation. Soviet expansionism, he retorted, was "pitiful"; the Soviets' courage did not match their ambitions, as had been demonstrated during the Cuban missile crisis and America's recent alert. He illustrated his contempt for Soviet leaders once again by the story of his encounter in 1969 with Soviet Premier Alexei Kosygin, who had come uninvited to Peking airport to discuss the easing of Sino-Soviet tensions:

I said that I originally said this struggle was going to go on for ten thousand years. On the merit of his coming to see me in person, I will cut it down by one thousand years. [Laughter] And you must see how generous I am. Once I make a concession, it is for one thousand years.

And then there was another time [a Romanian official] came also to speak on behalf of the Soviet Union. This time I again made a concession of a thousand years. [Laughter] You see, my time limit is becoming shorter and shorter.

And the fifth time the Romanian President Ceauşescu came again — that was two years ago — and he again raised the issue, and I said "this time no matter what you say, I can make no more concessions." [Laughter]

Committed now to a struggle of eight thousand years, the Chairman saw no point in tactical maneuvers. American diplomacy depended too much on "shadowboxing," he said; his strategy was based on more direct blows. Of course, it was also true that he had no choice; a million Soviet troops right up against the Chinese border discouraged thoughts of flexibility. But I saw no sense in arguing tactics. I said that however different our tactics we had proved our determination to resist challenges. On that point he and I could meet. He replied: ''I believe in that. And that is why your recent trip to the Arab world was a good one.''

It turned out that Mao's principal concern was not our Soviet policy but our domestic situation, specifically Watergate. What good was a strategy of containment if at the same time we sapped our capacity to implement it by our domestic divisions? He simply could not understand the uproar over Watergate; he contemptuously dismissed the whole affair as a form of ''breaking wind.'' The incident itself was ''very meager, yet now such chaos is being kicked up because of it. Anyway we are not happy about it.'' He saw no objective reasons for an assault on a President who had done a good job:

[I]t seems that the number of unemployed has been cut down by an amount and the U.S. dollar is relatively stable. So there doesn't seem to be any major issue. Why should the Watergate affair become all exploded in such a manner?

It was not possible to explain to the absolute ruler of the Middle Kingdom the finer points of a constitutional system of checks and balances, which placed even the highest officials under the rule of law. At the same time, Mao had a point. He was not concerned with the intrinsic merits of our domestic drama. Watergate interested him primarily for its impact on our fitness to resist Soviet expansionism. And with respect to that, the geopolitical consequences threatened to dwarf the original offense.

Zhou had avoided articulating Chinese anxieties about our long-term policy toward the Soviet Union; he had not raised the dreaded US–Soviet condominium. Mao was not so delicate, though he was far too proud to seek reassurance directly. He chose the elliptical route of implying that there might be secret arrangements between us and Moscow. Once upon a time, he said, he had doubted our ability to keep secrets. Now he was confident that we could do so; my first visit to China had, after all, remained secret. And finally his real point: ''And another situation would be your recent dealing with the Soviet Union.'' There were no secret dealings with the Soviets, and I said so; we would not give a hostage to the Kremlin by conducting talks that, if leaked, might leave us isolated. Peking was being fully briefed about any discussions.

I knew well enough that my reassurance was no more credible than protestations of affection to a person racked by jealousy. The very insecurity that engenders the suspicion discounts the value of the assurance. Still, Mao chose to treat my remarks at face value, using them as a point of departure for a brilliant analysis of the overall strategic position of the Soviet Union.

Moscow, according to Mao, looked strong but it was actually over-extended. It had to be wary of Japan and China; it had to keep an eye on South Asia and the Middle East; and it faced another front in Europe, where it had to maintain forces larger than those facing China. In fact, only a fourth of the entire Soviet military forces were deployed against China — something of an underestimate. Hence, Mao concluded, the Soviet Union could not attack China "unless you let them in first and you first give them the Middle East and Europe so they are able to deploy troops eastward." And the converse was, of course, also true. We were thus the key to global security. The real danger was the potential victims' lack of understanding of the requirements of the geopolitical balance. If all those threatened by Soviet aggression cooperated, each of them was safe and the Soviets would confront increasing difficulties; if they did not, each was in peril. In other words, containment.

Mao then reviewed the attitudes of various European countries in these terms. It was astonishing how much the aged leader knew about the domestic politics of faraway countries and how he could move inexorably to his conclusions without a note in front of him. It was Mao's core conviction that while our European allies were wavering for various reasons, they would not in the end abandon their vital interests by succumbing to Soviet blandishment. It was important, therefore, not to confuse temporarily irritating tactics with long-term trends. We must stick to a firm line even if some of our friends seemed hesitant, and in time they would gain courage from our leadership.

Mao did not put forward these ideas in a single presentation. Instead, he spoke in lapidary sentences each of which required physical effort to articulate. Perhaps his stroke-induced infirmity imposed the need for the dialogue form to give him the chance to regroup. Perhaps he had always preferred to involve his opposite number in a dialogue. Whatever the reason, Mao spoke in short paragraphs, each of which tended to end in a query that implied its own answer — indeed, permitted no other conclusion — yet nevertheless forced me to become a partner in the journey to his intellectual destination.

Having established the basic analysis of the international situation in about an hour, Mao suddenly turned to the issue of Taiwan, and then not to state a challenge but to hint obliquely at a solution. He had heard that the three Baltic states still had embassies in the United States, he said. I affirmed it. "And the Soviet Union did not ask you first to abolish those embassies before they established diplomatic relations with you?" That was not exactly accurate, since at the time relations were established the Soviet Union recognized the Baltic states. But if Mao was implying that relations with Taiwan were no necessary obstacle to normalization with China, I saw no reason to draw fine historical distinctions; so I assented to his proposition. Zhou helpfully chipped in that though maintaining diplomatic relations with the United States, the

Baltic states did not have access to the United Nations. Did all this mean, I wondered, that China might acquiesce in a separate legal status for Taiwan, contenting itself with excluding Taiwan from the UN?

Mao veered in another direction that hinted at the same thing in a more convoluted way. A believer in the unity of opposites, he began by affirming a contradiction. As a matter of principle we had to sever relations with Taiwan if we wanted diplomatic relations with Peking. Nor did he believe in peaceful transition; after all, Taiwan's leaders were "a bunch of counter-revolutionaries."

But this was not an insoluble dilemma. He was in no hurry about implementing his unshakable principles: "I say that we can do without Taiwan for the time being, and let it come after one hundred years. Do not take matters on this world so rapidly. Why is there need to be in such great haste?" At the same time, relations between Peking and Washington need not march to the slow drumbeat of internal Chinese disputes; there was no need to wait so long: "As for your relations with us, I think they need not take a hundred years. . . . But that is to be decided by you. We will not rush you."

What did all this mean? Was it another hint that normalization could be separated from the issue of Taiwan? And that the rate of normalizing relations was up to us? At a minimum, it suggested that China would not attempt to swallow Taiwan quickly afterward; certainly, that the Taiwan issue would not be an obstacle to our relations, that contrary to public perception we were under no pressure with respect to it. I am inclined to believe that like Zhou on the day before, Mao was indirectly inviting a proposal that combined the principle of a unified China with some practical accommodation to the status quo. We cannot know, because the domestic situation in China changed too rapidly to permit an exploration of all the implications of Mao's remarks. And for the immediate future it made little difference. Mao had made clear that for "a hundred years" China would draw no political conclusions from his general principles. And lest we miss the point — one could never be too sure about Westerners' acuteness — he compared the situation in Taiwan with that in Hong Kong and Macao, where China was in no hurry either (and had, in fact, diplomatic relations with the countries "occupying" them). Taiwan was not an important issue, he said: "The issue of the overall international situation is an important one."

Taiwan being thus disposed of, not only with no hint of pressure but with its explicit renunciation, Mao turned to the Middle East, embedding Taiwan, as it were, between two treatises on how to contain Soviet power in different areas of the world. He demonstrated the attention he paid to relations with America by recounting his reaction to a conversation I had had with the head of the Chinese Liaison Office on the day of the alert. The unfortunate Huang Zhen had been taken by surprise when I briefed him; he therefore responded with boilerplate Chinese support of the Arab position. Mao took pains to put the conversation in perspective. Huang Zhen had been correct in mentioning Chinese support of the Arab goals, but ''he didn't understand the importance of US resistance to the Soviet Union.'' China ''welcomed'' our ''putting the Soviet Union on the spot, and making it so that the Soviet Union cannot control the Middle East.'' In other words, containment had priority over all other considerations — including Chinese courtship of the Arab countries.

Mao then launched on another review of the strengths and weaknesses of various states in the area, almost country by country. He stressed the importance of Turkey, Iran, and Pakistan as barriers to Soviet expansion. He was uneasy about Iraq and South Yemen. He urged us to increase our strength in the Indian Ocean. He was the quintessential Cold Warrior; our conservatives would have been proud of him. All this without notes or any prompting by his colleague, who maintained a deferential silence.

Mao concluded his *tour d'horizon* by turning to Japan. He applauded my decision to spend a few days in Tokyo on my way home. Japan must not feel neglected by the United States; Japan was inherently insecure and sensitive. He would see to it that China did not force Tokyo to choose between the United States and China. That might polarize Japanese politics; it would surely enhance Japanese insecurity and might give rise to traditional nationalism. ''Their first priority is to have good relations with the United States,'' he said approvingly. ''We only come second.'' The apostle of world revolutions would do his best to keep Japanese priorities that way; he did not want a free-floating Japan playing off other countries against each other, for that would whet chauvinistic appetites. We should do our part by staying in close touch with Japan. As one of the architects of the first ''Nixon shock'' — my secret visit to China — I personally had an important task: ''They are afraid of you and you should try to lessen their fear.'' The incongruity was almost palpable: China's enthusiastic support for the US–Japanese alliance was a complete reversal of the suspicions displayed during my first visit. Barely two years after establishing contact, the grizzled revolutionary was giving a tutorial to the American Secretary of State on how to keep America's alliances together. Starting from opposite ends of the ideological spectrum, we had become tacit partners in maintaining the global equilibrium.

After two and a half hours, Zhou indicated that it was time to leave. But the Chairman had to put his mind at rest about America's domestic situation. The last thing Mao wanted at that point was the very domestic upheaval in America that his political theory foresaw and advocated. Like the composer of a symphony, he ended by returning to his opening theme: Would Watergate sap the authority of a President with whom he more or less agreed? What kind of a new President might emerge from all this turmoil? He was "suspicious" that isolationism might return if a Democratic President came into office; what did I think? My conviction was that it could not be in America's interest to pretend that only a single personality whose term of office could not run beyond 1976 in any event — and might end sooner — was capable of guaranteeing American policy toward China. I said that reality would impose the main lines of our policy regardless of which party was in office; there might be some hiatus while this lesson was being learned, however. Mao missed no nuance. "Then you seem to be in the same category as myself. We seem to be both more or less suspicious," shot back the Chairman.

He was particularly uneasy about possible American troop withdrawals from Europe, a perennial proposal of Senate Democrats. I said there was also a difference between our two parties in the willingness to be "very brutal very quickly in case there is a challenge." Mao mused that it was not necessary to put up a diplomatic front; what I really meant was the willingness to risk war. Though he was known as a warmonger, he added, laughing, he hoped that a war would be confined to conventional weapons. I sought to curb the speculation: "We will not start a war in any event." Mao was not all that pleased with such a reassurance. It elicited a parting warning: "As for the Soviet Union, they bully the weak, and are afraid of the tough." In other words, do not deprive Moscow of the fear that we might prove bellicose.

We were stirring in our easy chairs on the verge of leaving when Mao suddenly reverted to the theme of our conversation in February, that we should be wary of China's women — meaning his wife's machinations. "And you shouldn't try to bully either Miss Wang or Miss Tang* because they are comparatively soft." I denied that I had detected any softness in either. But Mao persisted mystifyingly: "She [Miss Tang] is American, while she [Miss Wang] is a Soviet spy." He laughed again. And so the meeting ended after nearly three hours. The Chairman rose ponderously, though without assistance, and with slow shuffling steps escorted us to the outer reception room — a signal honor. As he bade us goodbye, more pictures were taken. He told me: "And please send my personal greetings to President Richard Nixon."

Zhou took me aside to agree on an announcement that spoke of a "wide-ranging and far-sighted conversation in a friendly atmosphere" and mentioned the Chairman's greeting to Nixon. This by Chinese standards came close to exuberance in putting Mao's imprimatur on US–Chinese relations.

---

*This referred to Miss Wang Hairong, Assistant Foreign Minister and reported to be Mao's niece, and Miss Tang Wensheng, or Nancy Tang, the American-born interpreter.

It was an astonishing performance. David Bruce, who had met all the great leaders of Europe over a period of thirty years, said that we had witnessed the most extraordinary and disciplined presentation he had ever heard from a statesman — all the more impressive for seeming so spontaneous and random.

But what did it all mean? Why did Mao consider it necessary to place his enormous authority behind so detailed an assessment of the international situation? There was no doubt that the Chinese attached great importance to the encounter. This was reflected in its unusual length (doubly significant for someone not a head of state), in the warmth of the announcement, in the attention it was given in the Chinese press, and in the choice of pictures that accompanied the news stories, showing a beaming Mao clasping my hand in both of his with a more solemn Zhou distinctly in the background.

Even the scheduling was bound to attract attention. For it coincided with a reception David Bruce had planned in my honor at the Diplomatic Club for the diplomatic corps. The meeting with Mao went on so long that the guests had given up by the time I appeared. From the Chinese point of view, that had the advantage that each ambassador was forced to report on the lengthy meeting to his capital — a meeting considered sufficiently weighty by the Chinese to stand up the entire diplomatic corps. Nor was it unconscious, for toward the end of the meeting Mao apologized to David Bruce for having "taken up time originally set aside for other activities." (Was a secondary purpose to teach Bruce that as only Chief of a Liaison Office he should not have invited accredited ambassadors to a semipublic event?)

Undoubtedly, there were many motives behind the actions of our multifaceted hosts. I think now that Mao's extended dialogue had two basic and perhaps related causes: the depth of the internal controversy and the imminent retirement of Zhou. It is possible that Mao's overwhelming authority was needed to end the debates over Chinese foreign policy that had been raging since the summer and had been fueled by the Cambodian fiasco. But Mao rarely put himself unambiguously behind one faction; he usually maintained freedom of maneuver. He might well have adopted Zhou's policy while personally favoring some, at least, of Zhou's opponents. This would explain why in the middle of the conversation Mao suddenly asked me whether I had met Guo Moro, "who understands German" — hardly a prerequisite heretofore for an encounter with me. When I said that I had never met the gentleman, Mao said: "He is a man who worships Confucius, but he is now a member of our Central Committee." Why would I meet a worshipper of Confucius in the midst of an anti-Confucian campaign? And who in China would have the temerity to arrange such an encounter? Or did it imply that being a Confucian was no obstacle to serving on the Central Committee of the Communist party, hence that the anti-Confucian campaign was over? And there was another brief flare-up when I referred to the dinner conversation I had had with Vice Foreign Minister Qiao Guanhua. "Lord Qiao," replied Mao, jocularly or menacingly, implying that Qiao came from the soon-to-be eliminated upper class — the very charge being made against Confucius.

Whatever the state of Chinese domestic play during my visit, Premier Zhou Enlai disappeared from the direction of affairs within two months. The official explanation was illness. Was the Premier's tentativeness due to the knowledge that his cancer was drawing his physical life to a close? Or was it the result of his imminent political demise? Did Mao engineer it as he had with every other deputy, or did he yield to the inevitable, either political pressures or the specter of mortality? Was the reference to the women a warning, or was the statement that they were soft intended as a reassurance? The one thing of which one could be certain was that Mao never spoke at random; he always had a purpose even if we were not able to divine it.

I was never to have another serious talk with Zhou Enlai. A year later I visited him with my wife and children in what was called a hospital but looked like a guest house. We chatted casually; Zhou looked unchanged to my amateur eye. But whenever I raised a serious topic, Zhou changed the subject. His doctors, he said, had prohibited him from discussing such problems. Why political problems impaired his health more than small talk was never explained. It was a painful session — probably for both of us.

Before my November 1973 trip ended, I caught a glimpse of the pressures closing in on Zhou. At the final dinner, a festive atmosphere and lavish toasts tempted me to raise the subject of Confucius. My mind must have been addled by the many changes of time zones. Or maybe the toasts of *mao-tai* had finally gotten to me. I cannot now explain what caused me to raise the explosive topic. China had always been Confucian, I ventured, in the sense that it seemed natural for the Chinese to see the state as a vast educational institution, regulating conduct, morality, and politics. This concept seemed to have survived, I argued, though of course the content of what was being taught now was diametrically the opposite of Confucian.

At this statement, which — with rare absence of tact — in effect called Mao a Confucian, Zhou lost his composure, the only time I knew him to do so. Although only the interpreter had heard my remarks, he insisted in an extremely agitated fashion on the absurdity of my parallel. Nor would he accept my disclaimer that he should ascribe any misunderstanding to ignorance. Zhou persisted, making certain that the ubiquitous Nancy Tang — later accused of radical sympathies — had a detailed record.

Whatever the cause of Zhou's decline, his name was never mentioned by any of my Chinese interlocutors after this trip. Whenever I referred to a previous discussion with him, the Chinese would reply by invoking Mao's conversation, which as it turned out had covered every area and practically every country of mutual interest. In that sense the meeting with Mao served both an immediate and a long-range purpose, though the latter remained obscure to me for quite a long time. For the remainder of my term in office, this dialogue with Mao became for the Chinese the bible of US–Chinese relations. And from our point of view it was a constructive one. While it did not prevent the rise of the radical faction, later called the Gang of Four, it provided a floor below which they could not drag Zhou's work even when our relations became temporarily stagnant under by the increasing influence of the radicals over the daily management of affairs.

None of this, of course, was apparent to me in those heady days when I seemed to travel from success in Cairo to acclaim in Peking. With Mao's apparent imprimatur, all negotiations ended rapidly and favorably. The claims issue was resolved, pending only some technical and legal details not expected to prove an obstacle. We agreed on a final communiqué that represented a major step forward; only the media's preoccupation with Taiwan caused its significance to be underrated: It extended the joint opposition to hegemony from "the Asia-Pacific region" (as in the Shanghai Communiqué of 1972) to the global plane. It affirmed the need to deepen consultations between the two countries at "authoritative levels" to this end. Exchanges and trade were to be increased. The scope of the Liaison Offices was to be expanded. Zhou Enlai added a sentence that "the normalization of relations between China and the United States can be realized only on the basis of confirming the principle of one China." After we had completed the text, Zhou almost playfully suggested that we review what was new in the communiqué. He called the sentence about Taiwan to my special attention — on the theory that subtle hints were likely to elude barbarians. "Confirming the principle" was not an impossible requirement; we had gone far toward it in the Shanghai Communiqué. We had indeed not challenged it at any phase of our China policy. Mao's and Zhou's elliptical references were clearly openings, but toward what was as yet obscure. Zhou said that he would call back Huang Zhen to instruct him on the nature of the intensified dialogue that should flow from the communiqué.

No wonder that the visit ended on a note of extraordinary goodwill. At our last session, Zhou thanked me for our help in facilitating the departure of Sihanouk's mother from Phnom Penh. He also told me that his protocol officers had handed him a list of Western newsmen missing in Cambodia — which I had left deliberately on a table in the guest house to spare us both the embarrassment of having to debate whether

China had any influence with the Khmer Rouge. Zhou said that he would do what he could, though I knew it was not much. And so our last official meeting ended with a sense of hope that a new course had been set and yet, on a mellow note, as if there were a premonition that somehow things would never again be the same:

ZHOU: Perhaps it is the national character of the Americans to be taken in by those who seem kind and mild. [He was referring to India.]

KISSINGER: Yes.

ZHOU: But the world is not so simple. . . . We wish you success and also success to the President.

KISSINGER: Thank you and thank you for the reception we have received as always.

ZHOU: It is what you deserve. And once the course has been set, as in 1971, we will persevere in the course.

KISSINGER: So will we.

ZHOU: That is why we use the term farsightedness to describe your meeting with the Chairman.

Zhou had compared the visit with my secret one; he saw it as the starting point of a major advance. It was not to be. Both Zhou and I were engulfed by our nations' domestic dramas. Huang Zhen was recalled to Peking as Zhou had promised. But he did not return to Washington for over four months and when he did he had nothing to say. The claims-assets talks were broken off by the Chinese under transparent pretexts. Exchanges languished. The overall orientation of the policy was maintained but its substance was substantially frozen. Subsequent trips in 1974 and 1975 either were downright chilly or were holding actions — through relations never went backward.

Two concurrent domestic crises contributed to this state of affairs. A Washington riven by strife was a less interesting partner for China. Our credibility was bound to decline with the evaporation of Presidential authority, whatever my brave words to the contrary. At a minimum, even a cohesive China would have had every incentive to hedge its bets until our Watergate drama had played itself out.

We know now that China was going simultaneously through its own leadership crisis. And while Mao's conversation with me laid down the main lines of the policy, no single document could encompass all the shades of interpretation, which increasingly fell into the control of the radical Gang of Four.

But if the hopes of the end of 1973 were not to be fulfilled, at least the philosophical premises of the dialogue with Zhou and Mao were maintained. In that sense the aged Chairman had in his conversations with me bought insurance against his own propensity to radicalism. There were periodic high-level exchanges of view with Zhou's de facto successor, Vice Premier Deng Xiaoping, and with Qiao Guanhua, soon elevated to Foreign Minister. They lacked the warmth of the previous conversations but did not alter their substance. We preserved the essence of a relationship crucial to world peace amidst the turmoil of the times and the stresses in both countries unrelated to our foreign policy design. Statesmen have often done much worse.

XVI

Troubles with Allies

BY the fall of 1973 we had run into unexpected obstacles in the effort to revitalize America's alliances with its fellow democracies. Europe gave priority to the elaboration of European unity; its governments faced domestic stress; America was racked by Watergate. The October war and the oil shortage completed the process: Each ally became absorbed in its national dilemmas; most governments lost the domestic base for farsighted action — indeed, none of the principal leaders survived 1974 in office. With Europe and with Japan, we then entered a period of strain. The oil crisis produced similar tensions in our Atlantic and in our Pacific alliances, but with emphases that differed with the culture and the history of the regions.

The End of the Year of Europe

NO grand design has produced more frenetic choreography than did our Year of Europe. The trouble was that most of the footwork it elicited was evasive. We wanted to give a new political impetus to the Western Alliance with a so-called Atlantic Declaration — a resounding statement of common positive goals to give perspective to the necessary containment of Communist aggression. We thought that the new generation that had grown up since the end of the Second World War needed to see its leaders dedicate themselves to purposes beyond the prudent management of technical decisions if governments were not to lose their legitimacy and the Alliance its cohesion. But our allies were preoccupied; they used our initiative for an Atlantic Declaration as the anvil for forging their own emergent institutions. They were less interested in a new basis for Atlantic unity, some considering it an interruption — perhaps even intentional — of their dominant preoccupation. I am not saying that we were right and our allies all wrong. As in most tragedies, each side was right from its perspective and both pursued worthy causes.

It was certainly a year in which the democracies exhibited symptoms of collective paralysis. Richard Nixon was a prisoner of Watergate; Georges Pompidou was dying; the erosion of Willy Brandt's authority was more evident by the day; Edward Heath, zealous for his European relationships, was increasingly absorbed by domestic crisis. No leader managed to combine authority with the act of grace that could have enabled them all to disenthrall themselves from the obsession with the tactical. European and American purposes were, at a minimum, out of phase with each other.

In all this Michel Jobert, the French Foreign Minister, was the impresario of elegant obfuscation. I have described in Chapter V how he induced us to bypass the European Community, leaving it to France to shape the European consensus, and then switched course to insist that discussions on the Year of Europe should be conducted exclusively by the Community, which he had meanwhile organized against our proposal. The cleverest device was a time-consuming and humiliating procedure that to all practical purposes forced Europe to define its identity if not in opposition to us, then in sharp distinction. It was in Copenhagen in July 1973, without warning or prior consultation with us, that the European leaders decided that until a Community view had emerged, no member would deal individually with us on what was after all an American initiative. Each would report our approaches to the others without responding; the European foreign ministers would then develop a draft declaration. Only when it was completed would it be shown to us by Danish Foreign Minister Knut Borge Andersen, in the chair at the foreign ministers' meetings of the Nine on the basis of the semiannual rotation. This estimable gentleman would not have the power to negotiate. He could listen to our comments and transmit them to his colleagues. They in turn would receive his report, discuss it, and deliver themselves of the new dispensation, which would then undergo the same process.

Instead of revitalizing consultation, we were invited to a bureaucratic exercise that stifled it. We were being asked to negotiate with a minister who had no authority while those who did have authority would not talk to us. We had hoped to fashion a new commitment to shared purposes, a new vision of a common future. Instead, the proposed procedure for an Atlantic dialogue turned out to be more rigid than even encounters with Soviet negotiators, who with all their stiffness and inhibitions generally had more of a brief than simply to listen.

The scenario envisaged by our allies for the President's proposed trip to Europe was equally incongruous. On security matters, the President could meet at NATO perhaps — though not yet certainly — his fellow heads of government. On political and economic issues, the President was supposed to meet with the Danish Prime Minister, whose country was chairing the Council of Ministers, and, provided the French agreed, with the foreign ministers of the other countries. But European heads of government would stay away from the forum embodying their unity.

All this made perfect sense if fostering the internal arrangements of the European Community were the sole priority of Western policy. But if there was any merit in our concept that transatlantic ties needed a new moral compass course, the legalism of the Europeans defeated its purpose. By the time a declaration of common goals emerged from so formalistic a procedure, it would be robbed of all inspiration and meaning.

The problem came to the surface in an exchange between Sir Alec Douglas-Home and me. "But how can we make a reality of the European entity if we don't speak together?" said the venerable British Foreign Secretary. "Who else can we use as our representative rather than the Chairman of the Council, who is appointed every six months?" That was not what bothered us. We objected not to dealing with the Chairman of the Council but to the refusal of all the other members to deal with us. I told him:

> We welcome a common European position and we support the idea of European unity. However, if the price for this is that we cannot talk with our traditional European friends, then over time this could create a massive change in our relations.

The question was why Europe should deal so formalistically with its closest ally, shutting off the bilateral channels of consultation elaborated over two decades and more. Our allies did not handle their diplomacy with any other part of the world in this manner. Indeed, the odd — let us be frank, infuriating — aspect of the dialogue was that the very leaders who found such ingenious formulas for avoiding the American President were at the same time pressing us to attend a collective summit with Leonid Brezhnev to conclude the European Security Conference. On that occasion, all of them intended to meet with their counterparts from Eastern Europe and especially the Soviet Union, without putting forward their Chairman as the sole spokesman.

At other times, we might have pulled out of the enterprise. But we had a residual hope and were in something of a dilemma. Indeed, weakness can tempt governments into a persistence they would never risk in happier times. With Watergate we were not eager to advertise any loss of Presidential authority, and beyond that debacle there was the ironic problem that we could terminate our initiative now only at the cost of being accused of undermining European unity. All our allies, having geared their cumbersome Community machinery to the Atlantic dialogue, were eager to continue the process, for it was a useful foil against which to elaborate their European identity. No one wanted a crisis; and no one knew how to conclude the project without one. Suspended between success and failure, we waited, if not patiently, at least in relative silence.

In September 1973, after a summer hiatus, the Year of Europe twitched into life again. We heard that the Community members' political directors (the equivalent of our Under Secretaries of State) would present a draft Atlantic declaration to the foreign ministers on September 10. We were not told officially, but rather on an unauthorized basis by old friends dedicated to Atlantic ties. And on September 8, our Ambassador in Paris, John Irwin, reported that Jobert thought that we would be satisfied with any draft document, however vacuous; endowing it with substance would be superfluous:

Since we [the United States] wanted a paper (i.e. a written declaration of principles), there would be a paper to which everyone, we and the Europeans, could agree. He recognized that we would prefer a paper with some substance in it but implied that he thought we would settle for the paper for its own sake.

Where Jobert turned out to be wrong was in the extremity of his cynicism: Contrary to his prediction, we were not ready to sign a meaningless document; we would rather abort the project.

On September 25 Foreign Minister Andersen at last presented Europe's response to my speech of five months earlier. It was a feeble document; it evoked a dialogue of the deaf. The atmosphere was not improved by the fact that the document we had been waiting for all these months had been leaked to the *New York Times* just before. After Andersen had read a prepared statement and presented the Community's text, with no power to negotiate it, there was not much I could say. Andersen, a man deeply devoted to the Atlantic Alliance, was mortified at having to conduct an essentially confrontational diplomacy with Denmark's powerful ally. But he had been given no latitude by his colleagues, and Denmark's influence within Europe was not such that he could essay a solitary initiative.

Andersen had been instructed to propose that any future negotiations on the draft declaration take place at the political director level. So as to run no risk that an alternative might emerge, he was to suggest a meeting almost immediately. This amounted to abandoning one of the chief purposes of the Year of Europe. No document symbolizing a new era could possibly emerge from such a process. In European foreign offices the political directors are civil servants; they cannot make political decisions. Any topic assigned to them is certain to receive careful, professional scrutiny; acts of vision and imagination they must leave to their political masters. The proposed dialogue was therefore at a minimum very time-consuming, since every new idea or disagreement would have to be passed to a higher level where it would undergo the same laborious process that produced the document in the first place. An exchange between Andersen and me defined the transatlantic gap:

KISSINGER: Our problem is that from July 23 to September 19 there had been no consultation at all. You present us with a document and within a week you want to meet with the political directors. We are proceeding in an area which is of utmost importance but there are no continuing consultations.

ANDERSEN: You must understand how difficult it is for the Nine to achieve what we have.

KISSINGER: Yes, it is a considerable achievement for Europe but not for Atlantic relations.

Nor was the draft produced by the European Community worth all the effort that was about to be bestowed on it. It was little more than a summary of two other documents: the declaration of the European Community summit of the previous October and the principles adopted by the Tokyo round of international trade negotiations. It stressed the separate identities of the European Community and the United States; the United States was specifically asked to recognize the European Community as a "distinct entity" in world affairs, a wounding proposition that implied we might otherwise oppose what owed so much to American initiatives. There was no mention of "interdependence." The draft failed even to refer to the idea of Atlantic "partnership," much less to the need to broaden or strengthen it. The proposed declaration was neither innovative nor elevated; it amounted to little more than an American endorsement of what the Europeans had decided at their own summit nearly a year earlier about their own internal arrangements.

I summed up my reaction to German Foreign Minister Walter Scheel the same day:

> We felt that, more than 20 years after NATO was created, we needed a new vision of where we were going. We wanted to unite people on both sides of the Atlantic to join together to do something useful. The procedure should be less of an adversary negotiation.

Normally, this sort of bickering could have been overcome at a summit meeting. But the reluctance of our allies to meet with the wounded President was palpable. No allied leader saw any benefit in meeting Nixon while Watergate revelations were cascading into the media. Several thought it would weaken their domestic positions. A Freudian revelation of this occurred in Scheel's reply to my observation that the process might drag on beyond the first of the year: "We would favor a meeting this year. This would be better for psychological reasons, since we will be in the chair next year" — meaning that Brandt would not wish to preside during a Nixon visit. (In fairness, Scheel may have thought it unwise for a German Chancellor to act as spokesman for Europe in the concluding phase of the Atlantic dialogue — a problem that would have been easily avoided, however, had the other heads of government consented to join him.)

For his part, Jobert was blocking tangible progress lest Europe's identity be subordinated to Atlantic partnership. On the other hand, he did not want a demonstrative failure either, for that might have weakened our commitment to the defense of Europe. And so when I lunched with him the next day, September 26, he did his utmost to keep matters suspended between these two poles. We went through our entire repertory. There was the incongruously jovial repartee. I admired Jobert's intelligence and sardonic wit; he envied the discretion granted to me by Nixon. "I will speak in English," opened Jobert, "although it is difficult for me." "You do not need to know much English to say 'no,' " I replied. There was the almost paranoid assault on our motives. In talking to the other Europeans we were really seeking to wreck a united Europe, Jobert insisted; Britain undoubtedly had given us a text of the Community declaration when it was still in draft form. (It was not clear why this would have been a crime; it also happened not to be true. In any event, if Heath's dedication to Europe did not satisfy Jobert, there was not much help for either of them.)

This was preliminary to a malicious interpretation of Nixon's motives in proposing a European trip: "About the President's visit, what do you think? Are there domestic problems which would indicate that he could not come, or do you really want him to come?" I replied sharply:

Whether or not the President goes depends on two things. First, is that of substance. He does not want to go just to tour capitals. There would be no point in that. Secondly, under no circumstances will he sign a document with persons who are not at his level. He will not meet multilaterally with people below his level.

Jobert had a capital idea to deal with the last problem. Why not defer the whole exercise by a year and conclude it in the second half of 1974, when Pompidou would be in the chair? This, of course, would promote French leadership in Europe. How it would solve the problem that I had mentioned — the impossibility of our President's meeting with a delegation of foreign ministers led by only one head of government — Jobert did not vouchsafe to me.

Yet, just when it appeared that the merry-go-round would never end, Jobert made the most constructive gesture of any European minister in the Atlantic dialogue. He tabled a draft declaration for the Atlantic Alliance that was as thoughtful as the declaration of the European Community had been grudging. Drafted largely by the splendid French Ambassador to NATO, François de Rose, it was an eloquent affirmation of the importance of strengthening the common defense. It had serviceable language about the need to adapt strategy to changing situations and about the relationship of nuclear to conventional forces. It was an excellent statement of the goals of the Alliance, not the least of its virtues being an explicit admonition that a period of relaxation of tensions made the Alliance more rather than less necessary.

What was missing was any political dimension. The reference to coordinated foreign policy toward the East was as ambiguous as the French practice in this field. The need for Europe to increase its defense effort was not mentioned. We thought it essential because Congress had just passed the so-called Jackson-Nunn amendment, which made burden-sharing a major American objective; ignoring the problem might resurrect Congressional pressures to reduce our forces in Europe. But these were manageable blemishes surely removable in a serious negotiation.

However, it soon became clear that this was another variation of Jobert's basic maneuver. On the Atlantic Alliance Declaration Jobert was so forthcoming and on the European Community one so ruthlessly obstinate because in his mind success in the Alliance and failure on Europe were two sides of the same coin. Jobert wanted America fully committed to defend Europe but he wished to reduce our political links to Europe to the greatest extent possible. It was vintage Gaullism. After all, de Gaulle and all of his disciples had held as an article of faith that Europe need pay no price for American military protection because the United States was defending Europe in its own interest; it could not afford to let Europe be occupied by the Soviets. In Jobert's view, there was no harm — indeed, there might be some benefit — in periodically reasserting the need for the common defense. But this implied no obligatory political consultation. What would serve these goals better than a strong NATO declaration and a weak Community declaration? Hence the paradox that Jobert was the assiduous supporter of the one and the indefatigable roadblock to the other.

But foreign policy is not an exercise in abstract logic; if it neglects psychological reality, it builds on sand. American public opinion would not hold still indefinitely for risking the lives of great numbers of American troops on a continent refusing to articulate the word "partnership" or "interdependence" or hedging on stating shared objectives. It was precisely to strengthen the American moral commitment that we had put forward the Year of Europe. Without a community of purpose with Europe, America's role would be reduced to supplying combat forces; the psychological bond of Atlantic relations would disintegrate. The French analysis was rational; yet there is in the relations among nations a moral and psychological component that statesmen ignore at their peril.

By the end of September, enough had happened to give each party to the Atlantic dialogue an excuse to persevere. The advocates of a united Europe saw in it a means to further their goal. The smaller European nations were seeking a formula to strengthen both Atlantic ties and European unity. We finally had a text with which to work and we were loath to proclaim our disappointment. Admitting failure might whet Congressional appetites for troop withdrawals (the Senate had by then overwhelmingly passed a resolution recommending a 40 percent cut in our worldwide troop strength overseas); it could also accelerate solitary diplomatic initiatives toward Moscow by our allies.

So we soldiered on, not rejecting the political directors' forum and still seeing the positive features of the French draft of the Atlantic Declaration. In a press conference of September 26, 1973, I put a hopeful face on things:

What we are confronting in the dialogue with the Europeans is the merging of several processes. There is the process of European integration. There is the process of the debate on security within NATO. And there is the redefinition of the Atlantic relationship which covers all these areas. . . .

We believe that we are now well on the way toward accomplishing what we set out to do earlier this year. The discussions have been useful, and they will proceed in a constructive spirit.

The disputes so far largely concerned procedures rather than substance, timing rather than purpose. Everybody — even Jobert — had shied away from open confrontation and had taken pains to insist that disagreements reflected misunderstanding or technical disputes rather than conflicting interests. In all likelihood, if the initiative had been allowed to play itself out, it would have been brought to a tolerable conclusion; there was, after all, a limit beyond which procedural obstructionism could not be pushed. The outcome would probably have been short of the ultimate hopes of my Year of Europe speech but it would have reflected enough of its aspirations to indicate a positive direction.

But the outbreak of the Middle East war ended what was either an illusion or a charade. On some issues of major concern to the allies, differing and occasionally even clashing interests emerged. And what was even more painful, some of our allies seemed to be looking for an opportunity to make them explicit.

The Impact of the Middle East War

LIKE the deep frustrations suppressed by a family for the sake of appearances that then explode with disproportionate fury at the first pretext, the accumulated tensions in our alliances suddenly erupted with the outbreak of the Middle East war. The hitherto theoretical arguments about whether American and European interests were always parallel, the until-now abstract debate about the nature and limits of détente, burst forth from the first day of the war.

It was not that our allies did not have a case from their perspective. Most were genuinely convinced that our failure to press a settlement on Israel had produced the war, that we had in effect put vital European interests at risk for reasons of American domestic politics. The always latent view that Mideast tensions would suddenly disappear if only Israel would return to the 1967 borders was put forward with increasing explicitness. Our arguments to the contrary — that Arab radicalism derived partly from ideology and not solely from the Arab-Israeli conflict; that concessions achieved under Soviet pressure would strengthen rather than weaken the radical position; that to set unachievable goals would undermine the prestige of the democracies — were even less persuasive when panic replaced analysis. Our European allies had no faith in the step-by-step approach; they thought that they could win over the radical Arab states. Before the Middle East war, the dispute had rested uneasily beneath the surface; neither side of the Atlantic had pushed its views to a showdown. But once the war was under way, many of our allies made up for their earlier restraint.

For present purposes, the issue is not whose analysis was correct. I have explained our reasoning at length in previous chapters. The European position was certainly not frivolous; Europe's dependence on oil was compounded by frustration at being a bystander to crisis in a region of its previous preeminence. The deeper problem raised by the October war was the proper conduct of allies in an emergency when they sincerely disagree with one another either about causes or about remedies: Should they use the occasion of their partners' embarrassment to vindicate their own views? Or do they have an obligation to subordinate their differences to the realization that the humiliation of the ally who, for better or worse, is *most* strategically placed to affect the outcome weakens the structure of common defense and the achievement of joint purposes? In 1956, when faced with this choice during the British and French attempt to seize the Suez Canal, the United States imposed its own assessment on its allies. While dubious about British and French military plans, I had bitterly opposed Eisenhower Administration policy then. I have always believed that many of our later difficulties have stemmed from our insensitive conduct toward our allies at that time, which both stimulated a long-festering resentment and fostered a sense of impotence that accelerated their withdrawal from overseas commitments and added to American burdens.

Now the tables were turned and Europe showed no greater wisdom than we had nearly two decades earlier. On the first day of the war, October 6, Britain and France were unwilling to go along with our suggestion for a UN cease-fire resolution that would urge the parties to return to the status quo ante. On October 10, our NATO ally Turkey advised us that Incirlik Air Base and other American facilities in Turkey were available for NATO purposes only; they could not be used for anything to do with the Middle East war. On October 11, Turkey went public with its position. With its arch-rival thus publicly committed, Greece could not be far behind. On October 13, Foreign Secretary Christos Xanthopoulos-Palamas announced that "US bases have nothing to do with the Arab-Israeli war.''[1] (October 13 happened to be the start of our all-out airlift.)

Franco's Spain, though not a member of NATO, was tied to the United States by a treaty of friendship and cooperation. Nevertheless, on October 11 the Spanish government declared that it would not permit the United States to utilize Spanish bases "in a local conflict such as the Arab-Israeli war." In case that statement was not sufficiently explicit, a second statement issued later left no loopholes: Our bases in Spain could not be used in connection with the Middle East war "at any time, in any way, directly or indirectly."[2]

Whatever one's view of the wisdom of our past Mideast policy, which our allies had criticized, by then the die had been cast; the longer the war continued, the greater the risks for all democracies. The best hope for avoiding disaster was to end the war as rapidly as possible and in this a show of Western unity could have played an important role. Instead, all our NATO allies except Portugal, the Netherlands, and the Federal Republic of Germany (for a time) either directly or indirectly dissociated from the airlift and banned our overflight of their territories. Henceforth American planes from Germany had to fly out over the Atlantic, skirt France and Spain, enter the Mediterranean at Gibraltar, and fly directly to Israel — a detour of nearly 2,000 miles. (After the war I complained to Sir Alec Douglas-Home that the Soviet Union had been freer to use NATO airspace than the United States, for much of the Soviet airlift to the Middle East overflew allied airspace without challenge.)

Throughout the war we were given to understand, in the many indirect ways available to a government as close to us as Britain's, that it would be appreciated in London if we did not use British bases either for the airlift or for intelligence collection in the Middle East. There was never a formal refusal on the airlift because it had been made plain that we should not ask. Our occasional overflights of the combat zone by SR-71 supersonic high-altitude reconnaissance — essential for our decision-making process — had therefore to originate in the United States, adding to our expenses and reducing their effectiveness. There was the additional difficulty that the bases on allied territory for the tankers that refueled the planes were also closed — a proscription we could avoid only by some complicated maneuvers.

Typical of the attitudes we faced, on October 11 Jobert had told me in Washington that France had no wish to participate in the diplomacy to end the war. Only the United States and the Soviet Union were in a position to succeed: "If the two great powers do not agree, then we can't do anything ourselves." Jobert stated that France would not take any precipitate action and — unusual for him — had some kind words for our tactics. None of this stopped him only six days later from violently attacking us in a speech before the National Assembly while the war was still going on. After depicting Israel as the country that had consistently prevented Middle East peace, Jobert castigated both the United States and the USSR for keeping the war going, in the process postulating the moral equivalence of the two sides — the intellectual presupposition of European neutralism: "We see Mr. Brezhnev, the apostle of détente, and Dr. Kissinger, now a Nobel Peace Prize winner, shaking hands while sending thousands of tons of arms by air."

Dissociation from us in the Middle East war was thus coupled with an attempt to opt out of any possible crisis with the Soviet Union. There was a tendency to gloat about the flimsiness of "our" détente with the Soviets — as if our allies had not preceded us on that road by several years and pressed us to follow them. At the same time, they expected the crises to be resolved by our ability to use that very détente.

It was true, as NATO Secretary General Joseph Luns publicly pointed out on October 14, that during some phases of the Middle East war the Soviet Union had violated the principles of international conduct signed between Brezhnev and Nixon in 1972,[3] specifically the pledge not to seek unilateral advantage. But why was the comment addressed exclusively to the United States? Since the principal European countries had signed similar documents several years before, they had every possibility to protest in their own names. Instead, they left the containment of the Soviets in the Middle East to us. Soviet expansionism was an exclusively American problem only if one assumed that American and European objectives in the Middle East were divergent, if Europe had less to fear from a radicalized Middle East. This was absurd, for the impact of Soviet domination of the Middle East would be even more serious for Europe than for us. Moreover, if it was important to hold the Kremlin to its commitments not to exacerbate conflict, Europe and America had to do this together. Economic pressures, slowing down or even abandoning the European Security Conference, reducing exchanges — all this, as was seen in subsequent years, required joint action on *both* sides of the Atlantic.

But as the fear of confrontation mounted, several of our allies moved in the opposite direction. They continued to press for concluding the European Security Conference at the summit level; they would not risk over the Middle East the web of their economic relations with the Communist world — which grew increasingly vital to them for economic reasons as the oil crisis triggered a worldwide recession. Once again Jobert gave the concept its most rigorous cast.

If during the war Jobert had seemed to postulate the moral equivalence of both the United States and the Soviet Union, immediately afterward he was more positive in detailing areas of cooperation with the Soviet Union than with the United States. Indeed, one of his principal objections to Soviet-*American* détente was that it might deflect the Soviet Union from multiplying its contacts and trade with Europe.* Détente served a triple purpose, each part aimed at the United States: It was blamed for not preventing the Mideast crisis; it was invoked to end the tension; and it was supposed to furnish for Europe an alternative to exclusive reliance on the United States.

Once the Middle East erupted, the issue ought not to have been whether American policy before or even during the war had always been wise. The problem was whether Europe could protect its interests best by separation from us or by closing ranks. Did flirtation with the radical Arab position guarantee oil supplies, or did it encourage intransigence that might prolong the war and paralyze diplomacy? Did proposals that had no chance of being accepted help the peace process, or did they undermine the position of Arab moderates like Sadat who were prepared to move in a series of attainable steps? Did detachment from the United States moderate Soviet policy, or did it tempt the Kremlin to play the Western allies off against one another, imperiling the security of all free peoples? We thought that unity promised the greatest benefits; most of our allies chose the route of dissociation.

Europe avoided facing this painful reality by means of an essentially legalistic argument to the effect that obligations of the North Atlantic Treaty did not extend to the Middle East. But our case for allied cohesion was based not on a legal claim but on the imperatives of common interests. When close allies act toward one another like clever lawyers, if they exclude an area as crucial as the Middle East from their common concern, their association becomes vulnerable to fluctuating passion.

The stampede of dissociation began with the cease-fire and the Arab cutback in oil production. The prospect of my trip to Moscow had been

---

*The following excerpt from Jobert's November 12 speech to the French Assembly illustrates this point:

> Like all peace-loving peoples, we want détente. . . . The Conference on Security and Cooperation in Europe is, for that matter, the natural outcome of a trend that has characterized the international scene over the past ten years during which time the countries of the East and West, hostile and imprisoned by the prejudices of the cold war, gradually engaged first in a few talks and then developed increasingly close scientific, technical and economic relations. France's move in this direction, taken at General de Gaulle's initiative, has set an example. And we consider it imperative that this should be further consolidated and expanded: contacts on the highest level between France and the USSR and between France and many other socialist countries, such as those visited by the Premier during his trip to Hungary and Bulgaria, stem from our desire to show that a country like ours can overcome the obstacle caused by differing régimes and reveal the profound need people have for peace and knowledge of each other.

> But although these consultations have often made it possible to point up the same analyses, notably between the Soviet Union and France, of some of the world's or Europe's problems, we are worried — and we've said as much to our Soviet friends — that in placing too much importance on dialogue between the two superpowers we would lose the opportunity of increasing the cooperation that is so useful to Europe.

warmly welcomed by Home in a personal message on my departure; in Moscow on October 21 I had briefed the British and French ambassadors within an hour of the completion of my cease-fire talks with Brezhnev; indeed, thanks to the communications breakdown described in Chapter XII, it is probable that London and Paris learned the results of my discussions in the Kremlin before Washington and certainly before Jerusalem. But when the October 22 cease-fire came under stress, the tenuous allied cohesion evaporated. On October 23 our Ambassador in Bonn, Martin Hillenbrand, was abruptly informed that the Federal Republic would no longer approve shipments of American equipment to Israel from German ports; a second strong German démarche was made the next day. The formulation of the German request was symptomatic: State Secretary Paul Franck of the Foreign Office suggested to Hillenbrand that the Federal Republic, having shown understanding for our interests during the war, was now entitled to ask for our understanding of their interests (as if German interests had not been involved and they had done us a favor).

The alert screwed tensions tighter. Our allies did not take comfort from the fact – as they might have — that even during the crisis of authority over Watergate, the United States was prepared to run a major risk to defend the global equilibrium. Instead, they concentrated on the indisputable fact that there had been no prior consultation over an alert that involved US troops stationed in Europe. The alert had been brought about by our conviction that the Soviets were contemplating sending troops into the Middle East and that we had only a few hours to warn them off. We sought to demonstrate that we took the prospect of Soviet intervention seriously.

Afterward, there were press reports of the "shock wave" that had crept over Europe after the "explosive news" of the American alert.[4] There were widespread complaints that some allies had learned of the alert only from news tickers. This was, of course, not true of all governments. As noted in Chapter XII, we had informed British Ambassador Cromer early on October 25 of both Brezhnev's threatening letter and our readiness measures, barely an hour after making the preliminary decisions and well before they had been implemented. And Cromer had later confirmed that London agreed with our assessment of the seriousness of Brezhnev's threat. However, Britain had the same problem with our advance notice of the alert as with our special consultations on the Agreement on the Prevention of Nuclear War (see Chapter VII). Unwilling to draw attention to the fact that they still enjoyed preferential status in Washington, British officials did nothing to stem the tide of criticism from the other allies — and fell in with the prevailing brouhaha over inadequate consultation. On October 31 the *New York Times* reported that Prime Minister Heath on the previous day had pointedly refused to endorse the nuclear alert — raising temperatures in Washington a few more notches.

Abstractly, our allies were justified in their complaints. Realistically, we had little time and we had to balance serious considerations. Our eye was on an imminent Soviet military move; our plan was to increase readiness and permit the Soviets to detect our preparations. This, we hoped, would give the Soviets pause; our written reply to Brezhnev, to be delivered around 5:30 A.M. Washington time, would give them a pretext for resolving the issue. Our Ambassador to NATO, Donald Rumsfeld, would be instructed to brief NATO an hour after our note to the Soviets was delivered. We chose this timing above all because we knew that to obtain allied support we would have had to give reassurances of the limits of our commitment; we preferred that these not reach Moscow via our allies until the Politburo had made at least a preliminary decision.

The allies were really objecting not so much to timing as to the absence of opportunity to affect our decision. But imminent danger did not brook an exchange of views and, to be frank, we could not have accepted a judgment different from our own. There was no middle position between alert and no alert. At issue were only readiness measures, not actions. In our perception, nevertheless, it was a clear emergency, and it fell to us to act as custodians of Western security. Whether our estimate of the danger was correct must be decided by more impartial students of the period. But on that night of potential crisis, our duty was to act on the facts as we perceived them. Of course, unilateral steps such as the alert can only be a last resort; allies should be consulted whenever possible. But emergencies are sure to arise again; and it will not be in anyone's interest if the chief protector of free world security is hamstrung by bureaucratic procedure in the face of imminent Soviet intervention.

Dissociation from the alert ironically extended even to the diplomacy by which we sought to end the looming US–Soviet confrontation. In order to give the Soviets a face-saving way out — and to erect a legal obstacle to a unilateral Soviet move — we had promoted the idea of a United Nations Emergency Force from which all permanent members of the Security Council were excluded. We thought we had won when Sadat had accepted our proposal. But Britain and France objected to their exclusion, though I do not understand to this day what benefit participation in a UN force would have conferred on them. Their UN ambassadors briefly threatened a veto even though this would have risked reopening the issue of Soviet troops in the Middle East.

The Federal Republic of Germany on October 25 — the day of the alert — chose to make public what it had already told us privately; a peremptory government statement was issued:

Weapons deliveries using West German territory or installations from American depots in West Germany to one of the warring parties cannot be allowed. The West German government is relying on America to finally halt deliveries from and over West Germany.

Since we were already carrying out the Federal Republic's private request, the purpose of the public statement could only be to distance Bonn from Washington for the benefit of a presumed Arab constituency in the midst of an acute crisis. Similarly, the Spanish government took it upon itself to declare after October 25 that the US alert did not apply to American bases in Spain because the consent of both countries was required for their use. On October 26 our allies, at the request of France, suspended work on the NATO draft declaration as a sign of displeasure over the fact that the American alert had been called without adequate consultation. On October 27 an Italian government spokesman stated that membership in the Alliance did not oblige Italy to assist the United States in its Middle East policy.

Infuriated by a sense of abandonment in a crisis, our nerves taut from several all-night vigils, we reacted in a manner bound to escalate tensions even further. On October 25 we sent a sharp note to Bonn:

The US G[overnment] believes that for the West to display weakness and disunity in the face of a Soviet-supported military action against Israel could have disastrous consequences.

Similar complaints were made to the British and others. The accumulated irritation and nervous tension burst forth in a galaxy of public statements on October 26 that confirmed the public impression of Western disarray. I instructed State Department spokesman Robert McCloskey to inform reporters that "we were struck by a number of our allies going to some lengths to in effect separate publicly from us." McCloskey said pointedly: "We would have appreciated a little more unified support." Joining the fray, Defense Secretary James Schlesinger told a Pentagon press conference that American actions in Europe had the purpose of enhancing our readiness. However,

the reactions of the foreign ministry of Germany raised some questions about whether they view readiness in the same way that we view readiness and consequently we will have to reflect on that matter.

As luck would have it, Nixon also held a press conference that same evening, less than forty-eight hours after the alert.* Nixon associated himself with these criticisms, specifically mentioning McCloskey's briefing with approval. He added his own twist: "Europe, which gets 80

---

*This was the occasion on which he described his dramatic confrontation with Brezhnev (see Chapter XII).

percent of its oil from the Mideast, would have frozen to death this winter if there hadn't been a settlement." Nixon thus implied that our actions, including the alert, had contributed more to assuring European oil supplies than did Europe's distancing itself from the United States. I had made the same argument to German Ambassador Berndt von Staden earlier in the day:

> We recognize that the Europeans are more dependent upon Arab oil than we, but we disagree that your vulnerability is decreased by disassociating yourselves from us on a matter of this importance. Such disassociation will not help the Europeans in the Arab world. The Arabs know that only the US can provide the help to get a political settlement. Not only will European capitulation to the Arabs not result in their insuring their oil supply, but it can have disastrous consequences vis-a-vis the Soviet Union who, if allowed to succeed in the Near East, can be expected to mount ever more aggressive policies elsewhere. To the degree Soviet influence can be reduced, we will gain a long-term advantage even if we pay a short-term price.

Our allies were by no means prepared to pay even a short-term price to reduce Soviet influence. A letter from Willy Brandt to Nixon of October 28 was immediately leaked to the press by the Germans — suggesting that its line of argument was thought to have a certain popular appeal in Germany. What minimum support Brandt expressed for American actions he gave not on their merit but primarily because no other country was strong enough to deal with the crisis. He thought it necessary to add the wounding point that he made this judgment without knowing details of the actions or reasons that had caused us to act as we did; at this point, more than seventy-two hours after the alert, after days of public and private briefings, he had been given a very full account; the implication was therefore that he had not been convinced by our briefings and that we had either acted unwisely or were holding back information. The major purpose of his letter was to explain the German ban on our resupply of Israel from German depots. Germany acted because common Alliance responsibilities did not extend to the Middle East — as if NATO allies were *prohibited* by their alliance from supporting each other outside of Europe.

But if our analysis was correct, all allies had an interest in preventing the Soviets or Arab radicals from dominating the Middle East. This point was sharply made in Nixon's reply to Brandt on October 30:

> You note that this crisis was not a case of common responsibility for the Alliance, and that military supplies for Israel were for purposes which are not part of the Alliance responsibility. I do not believe we can draw such a fine line when the USSR was and is so deeply involved, and when the crisis threatened to spread to the whole gamut of East–West relations. It seems to me that

the Alliance cannot operate on a double standard in which US relations with the USSR are separated from the policies that our Allies conduct toward the Soviet Union. By disassociating themselves from the US in the Middle East, our Allies may think they protect their immediate economic interests, but only at great long term cost. A differentiated détente in which the Allies hope to insulate their relations with the USSR can only divide the Alliance and ultimately produce disastrous consequences for Europe.

That was the essence of the American dispute with Europe. Six months before the Middle East war, we had proposed an effort to define common global purposes. Our allies had evaded the initiative on a variety of substantive and procedural pretexts. They had gone so far as to refuse to include such terms as "partnership" and "interdependence" in the various declarations designed to symbolize Western unity. The crisis in the Middle East suddenly brought home to us that the European objections were not simply formalistic or institutional as had been professed. Nor were they provoked by tactless American statements — though our phraseology was not always at its most felicitous. Europe, it emerged increasingly, wanted the option to conduct a policy separate from the United States and in the case of the Middle East objectively in conflict with us. Suddenly, the same countries that had complained of my phrase that they had primarily regional interests now claimed that their obligations were solely regional.

To be sure, from the European point of view serious criticisms could be made against American policy. But this is another way of saying that the Atlantic Alliance, to remain vital, must do its utmost to prevent conflicting perceptions of fundamental interests from festering by being left unattended. This was the purpose of our Year of Europe. And if a crisis arises, each side of the Atlantic should weigh carefully the risks of dissociation as against the risks of closing ranks. In fact, it is an interesting question whether allies can *afford* to prevail against whichever partner is placed by circumstances in the position best able to shape events. An alliance for whose vitality partners are not prepared to curtail their freedom of action is on the way to disintegration. In the Middle East in 1973, failure for America spelled disaster for the West — even if Europe's assessment was superior to ours, which I still seriously doubt. The beneficiary of the collapse of American policy would not have been Western Europe but forces unlikely to make fine distinctions among the various industrial democracies.

In reviewing the history of the period, I find it striking that while our European allies left little doubt of their distaste for our policies, they never articulated a coherent alternative. Nor did they address themselves to the consequences for them if our strategy failed — though they seemed to base their policies on this expectation. With the exception of a thoughtful letter from Heath to Nixon on October 31, one looks in vain for any attempt to present a strategy different from our own or for a serious effort at consultation. Our allies were content to saddle us with the responsibility for the diplomacy, but they were not prepared to share its risks.

Major substantive differences existed over two aspects of Middle East policy: the objectives of postwar diplomacy; and the response to the oil embargo and production cuts.

With the possible exception of the Netherlands, our European allies were clear about what should follow the cease-fire: American pressure to induce Israel to return immediately to the 1967 borders. They assumed that we had the power to force Israel to do our bidding; if we hesitated, it must be because we were willing to subordinate European interests to our domestic pressures, which they now urged Nixon to face down regardless of his Watergate plight. None of them had any clear-cut idea of how to accomplish this. Nor did it occur to them that the Middle East faced a more immediate problem, with the Egyptian and Israeli armies perilously athwart each other's lines of communications and an Israeli army perched twenty miles from Damascus. Disengagement of these forces was seen as a priority by most Arab leaders, even those of Algeria and Syria — as I was told repeatedly on my second trip through the Middle East in December (see Chapter XVII). And our allies showed little awareness that their rhetoric tended to strengthen the radical Arabs over the moderate ones and enhance the Soviet influence over both; they betrayed no perception of the obstacles and risks involved in attempting to settle all issues comprehensively at this stage — when we had not yet had any high-level contact with Syria, we were not yet sure of Egypt's orientation, and the military dispositions at war's end created their own necessities. All such arguments, if they found a hearing at all, were dismissed as rationalizations for a misconceived policy or subterfuges for maintaining American control of the negotiating process. As in the Atlantic dialogue, our allies clothed substance in procedure; they argued that they should, in some undefined way, participate in the postwar diplomacy. But their pro-Arab tilt and support for what amounted to an unworkable all-or-nothing approach ruled them out as mediators. They chafed at the fact that they were on the sidelines — though this wallflower role was brought about largely by their own actions, accentuated by their reluctance to adopt joint policies on oil.

The European Community's policy placed great stock in gaining the goodwill of the oil producers. Our allies adamantly refused any measure remotely appearing "confrontational," such as forging a common position among the oil consumers. Oil combined with conviction to drive Europe into ever-sharper opposition to our Middle East strategy.

In this situation, the insistent statements by European leaders that

Europe's unity was essential to make its weight felt were not simply theoretical avowals of new institutional arrangements, with which we in fact agreed. Their context gave them a more ominous cast. On October 31, Pompidou called for a common European policy on the Middle East. Europe, he argued, must be given a larger role in world affairs, for US–Soviet efforts to settle world crises could be dangerous, leading to generalized clashes. This, if it meant anything, implied that Europe should have the option to oppose both sides in the Middle East and to stay out of some East-West conflicts; it was the only way to keep them from becoming generalized. To achieve this capability, he proposed regular summit meetings of France's European partners, starting immediately. Pompidou's colleagues accepted in short order.

What an independent European policy on the Middle East might look like became apparent less than a week later. On November 6, 1973, the foreign ministers of the Community met in Brussels. Even though I was on the way to Cairo and they had been briefed on our strategy of giving priority to disengagement rather than haggling over the October 22 cease-fire line, they thought it appropriate to put forward a program that was a direct challenge to our policy. Without notice to us and without waiting for the outcome of my mission to Cairo, our European allies called for an immediate Israeli withdrawal to the October 22 line to solidify the cease-fire and to the 1967 borders to achieve peace. Whoever was right, the European statement would either undercut our diplomacy or demonstrate Europe's irrelevance, neither of which was desirable. The only rational explanation for the Europeans' haste was that they wanted to stake out a position in advance of ours even if we succeeded — before, as it were, the ground was cut from underneath them — and to have a platform from which to oppose us if we failed.

On November 9 a European "diplomatic source" in Brussels was quoted by the *New York Times* to the effect that the Middle East crisis had reinforced opposition to our efforts to include such words as "partnership" and "interdependence" in the proposed US–European Community declaration.[5] Independence as the precondition of opposition seemed to be the watchword.

On November 12, as noted, Jobert roiled the waters with one of his acid presentations to the French National Assembly. He denounced the United States for not consulting its allies during the Middle East war. He attacked the superpowers for their attempt to monopolize the Mideast settlement while Europe, he said, was left

a forgotten victim of the conflict, but a victim nevertheless, even though it perpetually denounced the perils. Its distress and its bitterness are obvious. But it also noted that it was more of a pawn than an instrument or an asset in the arbitration of the great powers. It can and should learn a basic lesson from this.

Many people expect Europe not merely to react but to actually be born at last. . . .

Jobert's speech amounted to a suggestion that Europe articulate its identity as a permanent challenge to the United States. European and American interests were assumed to be divergent. Europe could vindicate its views only by a readiness for confrontation with its ally across the Atlantic — even while Jobert proclaimed that that ally remained indispensable to the common defense.[6] How long it would be possible to maintain a credible American security guarantee for a Europe that dissociated over vital interests we considered common was the subject of little private and no public discussion.

In mid-November, Brandt picked up the theme in a speech to the European Parliament: "In a world whose destiny cannot and should not be determined by two superpowers alone, the influence of a united Europe has become indispensable." On November 20 the foreign ministers of the European Community met in Copenhagen to prepare for a European summit to deal with the Mideast crisis. We were given no hint of their preliminary conclusions even though we were then engaged in delicate negotiations designed to move the Mideast toward peace and to assemble the Geneva Conference.

Normally, such an assault by our allies would have produced a closing of ranks in America. The bipartisan leadership group that had sustained America's involvement in world affairs with NATO as its cornerstone would have rallied to defend its achievement — much as it had done in 1971 against the Mansfield amendment to withdraw troops from Europe.

But 1973 was not a normal year. In the Watergate atmosphere, the European accusation of high-handed American diplomacy found a receptive audience; many traditional supporters of Alliance ties could not bring themselves to believe that there was any issue on which Nixon might be right. A *New York Times* editorial on October 31 echoed other leading journals:

> Washington's failure to consult, despite countless promises to do so, and its decision not to give its allies advance warning of a military alert that inevitably affected their interests, fits a dismally familiar pattern for this Administration. Mr. Nixon and Secretary Kissinger can speak eloquently about the indispensable American-European connection; but their actions, particularly in crisis, do not match their words.

In early November, Senator Edward M. Kennedy published a five-page paper accusing the Nixon Administration of "heedlessly creating a crisis in the Atlantic alliance" and urging a reaffirmation of "the principle of allied consultation."[7] On November 21, Professor Zbigniew Brzezinski repeated in a newspaper article what was beginning to turn into a partisan refrain: "It is difficult to imagine a course more calculated to damage alliance relationships, and especially the notion of alliance consultations, than the one the U.S. unilaterally followed in recent days."[8]

The problem went much deeper, of course, than the inadequacy of consultation. This was shown in the British reaction to a press conference I held on November 21. I had made three points: First, the Atlantic Alliance remained the core of American foreign policy. At the same time,

one cannot avoid the perhaps melancholy conclusions that some of our European allies saw their interests so different from those of the United States that they were prepared to break ranks with the United States on a matter of very grave international consequence and that we happen to believe was of very profound consequence to them as well.

Finally, the lack of consultation was not the principal problem:

It is a root fact of the situation that the countries that were most consulted proved among the most difficult in their cooperation and those countries that were most cooperative were least consulted.

My last comment in an otherwise conciliatory presentation brought Heath into the fray, for he assumed — correctly — that Britain had been one of the countries I had in mind as having been most consulted. He unburdened himself at a dinner with American correspondents on November 28 that started out "off the record" but whose ground rules were relaxed as he warmed to the subject. In the process Heath unintentionally underlined my basic point. The difference between Europe and us was caused only superficially by inadequate consultation; the real trouble was a clash in political perspectives that no amount of consultation would be able to remove. Our Embassy reported Heath's views as follows:

There has never been a joint understanding between the U.S. and Europe on the Mideast. "I don't want to raise the issue of Suez but it's there for many people." The Mideast is outside NATO. During the past six years — since the 1967 war — the US had ample opportunity to bring pressure on Israel to negotiate and has done nothing. When we have had Four Power meetings, we have been warned off by the Americans. We all knew what would happen and it did. Another war was inevitable. (The tenor of Heath's comments made it clear that, in his view, Britain has disagreed with US policy since 1967 and British views have been given no consideration on the part of the US in formulating Mideast policy.)

In this situation, each side's unilateralism fed on the other's and turned into a self-fulfilling prophecy. It was grating, even humiliating, for

countries like Britain and France to be excluded from a peace conference on the Middle East. But their conduct guaranteed that Israel would
not accept them as impartial, and even to us the Europeans seemed
closer to the Soviet position and therefore objectively served to frustrate
the only strategy that, in our view, had a chance of working. We were
under the impression that the overriding concern of some of our principal allies was not to elaborate a long-range strategy but to end Arab oil
cutbacks aimed at them — if necessary at our expense. The line between building a safety net for the contingency of our failure and engineering it was eroding.

America and its democratic allies were drifting not only apart but into
a competition. We were not alone in our uneasiness about these trends.
Sir Alec Douglas-Home was sufficiently concerned about them to write
me a personal letter on November 29, the day after his Prime Minister's
outburst. He insisted that NATO was the linchpin of Britain's foreign
and defense policy. At the same time, "I don't think you would feel us
to be of much value as a friend and ally if we support American policy
blindly, even when we think it wrong." He went on to explain that
Britain for years had advocated a consistent course on the Middle East;
it had not changed under the impact of recent events. He then summed
up his views on how to transcend the crisis:

> We are firmly alongside the United States on East/West issues which could
> lead to serious confrontation. In any case of uncertainty the benefit of doubt
> would weigh decisively on the American side of the scales. But you must from
> your side do everything possible to reduce the area of uncertainty — that is to
> take us more systematically into your confidence and consult with us during
> the period of build-up towards crisis and confrontation. I think this applies to
> the Middle East also where, if I may say so, I think that over the years Amer-
> ican Administrations have not given enough weight to such policies of our-
> selves and others, which have a lot and, perhaps more than a lot, to be said
> for them. . . . I am sure that our aim should be to restore the old intimacy
> and I can see no reason why this should not be possible.

Home, as I have already emphasized, was one of the wisest and most
decent men I have had the privilege to meet. We never questioned that
for him, Atlantic partnership was a moral necessity; unlike his Prime
Minister, he did not see Britain's European vocation as requiring the
loosening of transatlantic ties built up over three decades. There was
little in Home's letter with which I disagreed. He had a point in his
criticism of previous American policies. We, in turn, were willing, nay
eager, to improve the process of consultation. My concern was that the
new procedures of the European Community were working against this
objective. None of us had a pat answer for how to reconcile European
identity and Atlantic partnership, especially when that "identity" was

flatly contradictory to ours in the Middle East. But under Home's prompting we decided to give it another try.

The North Atlantic Council and the Pilgrims Speech

ALL the foreign ministers of the Alliance convened in December in Brussels for the semiannual ministerial meeting of the North Atlantic Council. The atmosphere was far from ideal. We were conscious of our grievances, probably too insistently so. The allies who belonged to the Nine seemed as if mesmerized by the process of European unification. They acted as if it was a sufficient answer to our concerns on substance to point out how complex the task of achieving a European consensus was and how it was proceeding more rapidly than anyone could have expected.

Yet the meeting was bound to have a soothing effect. The North Atlantic Council is the institutional expression of the Alliance. Its basic reason for existence is to strengthen common security — an objective not disputed by any ally even in the most intense controversies. Its procedures tend to stress consensus. And just as France used the consensus procedure to dominate the European Community, so we, as the country providing the nuclear umbrella, had a decisive voice in the Council. Allies that did not belong to the European Community did not wish the transatlantic squabble to undermine their security. Most members of the Nine, when freed from Community procedures, were eager to avoid having to choose between France (backed by Britain) and the United States. Joseph Luns, the vigorous Secretary General of NATO, could be avuncularly intimidating toward anyone straying from his conception of the requirements of allied unity.

On the whole, the Brussels meeting did help heal the wounds. I made a conciliatory arrival statement reiterating that NATO was the cornerstone of our foreign policy — a cliché that appeared to calm tempers even while invoked to embrace obviously divergent policies. And I called for a new act of vision to enhance the Alliance's vitality. The next day I devoted to individual meetings with other foreign ministers. The principal vestige of recent unpleasantness was that my first two conversations were with the ministers of allies that had stood by us through the Mideast crisis: the Netherlands and Portugal. As with many gestures in whose subtlety one takes pride, its significance apparently was lost on my colleagues. Or else they decided that no point would be served by noticing it.

Each NATO meeting provides the occasion for a dinner of the foreign ministers of the United States, Britain, France, and the Federal Republic. NATO does not recognize a hierarchy based on size or influence, so the pretext for what amounts to a meeting of the Big Four is their special responsibility for the governance of Berlin. Since the Berlin agreement of 1971, there has not been much Berlin business; what there is can be disposed of in a few minutes. The remainder of the time is devoted to a review of the international situation. The December 9 dinner went off agreeably enough. Home did his valiant best to put a good face on recent disagreements, stressing the familiar legalism that NATO had never been thought to have Mideast responsibilities. There were polite European complaints about lack of consultation on the alert. I replied that our efforts had prevented a victory for Soviet arms and were in the process of reducing Soviet influence — an objective of benefit to all allies. Jobert restrained his mischievous side. He confined himself to asking penetrating factual questions and promised a calm speech for the plenary session the next day.

Given our central contribution to Western defense, the plenary sessions inevitably revolve around the American Secretary of State, whose speech is an important feature. On December 10, I urged a three-part program: to complete as rapidly as possible the two joint declarations; to work out procedures for consulting about common problems outside the NATO area; and to deal jointly with the energy crisis. To reduce complaints about inadequate consultation, I offered regular meetings at the deputy foreign minister level to concert policies outside the NATO area. That idea had been halfheartedly accepted by the French at Reykjavik in May — or so at least we understood — but it had never been implemented.

Whether Jobert, who had insisted on speaking last, had always intended to go on the attack or whether my remarks triggered him, I do not know. Whatever his motives, he sidestepped my proposal for improved consultation. Instead, he used the occasion for his by-now well-rehearsed assault on the condominium allegedly established by the two superpowers. He cited the consultation provision of the US–Soviet Agreement on the Prevention of Nuclear War as the most flagrant example (see Chapter VII). Europe, he implied, was better served elaborating its own policy. I used the rarely exercised right of reply for a sharp rebuttal. I explained the provisions of that agreement, whose meaning and history Jobert knew full well, and concluded: "I am repeating these facts for the public minutes. If a misinterpretation of them continues to be repeated, it cannot be inadvertent."

But the squall passed quickly. NATO was a poor forum for Jobert's sallies. The memory of twenty-five years of cooperation was not to be erased by scoring debating points. The next morning Jobert and I met over breakfast. Without exception our private encounters passed pleasantly, even entertainingly, for my French colleague was a man of unusual charm, penetrating intelligence, and sharp wit. To show his goodwill he withdrew his previous objection to a meeting between me and the foreign ministers of the European Community.

That a meeting with nine foreign ministers, eight of whom were also members of NATO (the sole exception was Ireland), should have become a problem in Atlantic relations showed the degree to which Atlantic cohesion was being suffocated by the elaborate procedures of the emerging Europe — or at least by the way Jobert was applying them. Having banned the words "partnership" and "interdependence" from the projected declaration between the United States and the European Community, Jobert had also vetoed any discussions between America and Europe at the ministerial level. The absurdity of this position must have been too much for Jobert's colleagues. That was certainly the view of Danish Foreign Minister Andersen, who was performing the duties of President of the Community Council of Ministers with dignity and ability. Or perhaps Jobert sensed that he had overplayed his hand during the NATO meeting. Whatever the explanation, my encounter with the nine Community foreign ministers took place on the afternoon of December 11 following the adjournment of the North Atlantic Council.

The situation was bizarre. I had just spent nearly three days with eight of them. I had seen them as a group and individually. There was quite literally nothing new to talk about. Moreover, to take care of French sensitivity that the European Community not be "dissolved" in NATO, my colleagues thought it unwise to meet in the NATO headquarters outside of Brussels where we all happened to be and which would have been most convenient. Jobert would not meet in any official building, such as an embassy, for reasons that now escape me if I ever knew them. The compromise was Andersen's suite at the Brussels Hilton.

The meeting will not be recorded in diplomatic history as having added to anybody's store of knowledge except that of the puckish Irish Foreign Minister, Garret FitzGerald, who had never before witnessed transatlantic tribal rites. For his benefit I repeated the arguments on behalf of the Year of Europe with which by now my other colleagues were surely surfeited. There was some obligatory and perfunctory comment by two or three ministers who were no more creative than I had been in finding something original to say. FitzGerald, to whom all this persiflage was new, had a marvelous time. But even his wit and sharp mind could not extend the meeting beyond an hour — much to the relief of Jobert, who wanted to make sure there were few incentives to make the meeting a regular one.

Afterward, a beaming Andersen, in his last month as chairman of the group, descended with me to the ground floor and told the waiting media of the "historic" meeting. The Dane had been an innocent victim of the tussle between the legal formalism of the Community and our abstract concepts of partnership. He seemed relieved that it was all over, which for him at least it was in his capacity as chairman. In my view the meeting underlined the malaise in US–European relations rather than easing it.

Therefore, I made another conciliatory overture to end the squabble. Many months earlier I had agreed to address the Society of Pilgrims in London, a prestigious group dedicated, as its name implies, to the affirmation of the Anglo-American relationship. My visit had had to be canceled once because of the Middle East war. When it was rescheduled to follow the NATO meeting, Sir Alec had volunteered to introduce me. Throughout the difficult period he had spared no effort to improve European-American ties. He had generously praised my visit to Brussels as having "strengthened the alliance." And he had taken part of the blame for Atlantic tensions on Europe's shoulders when he said to the press that Europeans "did not recognize as quickly as the United States" the strategic significance of the Middle East war.

Addressing the black-tie dinner on the evening of December 12, I summed up again the reasons that had led us to propose the Year of Europe: the growth of European strength, the emerging nuclear parity, the impact of a period of relaxing tensions, the growing interdependence of our economies. All this was occurring in a changed psychological environment that tended to weaken the moral basis of allied cohesion:

The next generation of leaders in Europe, Canada, and America will have neither the personal memory nor the emotional commitment to the Atlantic alliance of its founders. Even today, a majority on both sides of the Atlantic did not experience the threat that produced the alliance's creation or the sense of achievement associated with its growth. Even today, in the United States over 40 Senators consistently vote to make massive unilateral reductions of American forces in Europe. Even today, some Europeans have come to believe that their identity should be measured by its distance from the United States. On both sides of the Atlantic we are faced with the anomalous — and dangerous — situation in which the public mind identifies foreign policy success increasingly with relations with adversaries while relations with allies seem to be characterized by bickering and drift.

I then listed four principles of American policy that would be the basis of our dialogue with our European allies: the imperative of East-West coexistence, leavened by the caution that "we must take care that the pursuit of détente not undermine the friendships which made détente possible"; the necessity of common defense; the reality of European unity; and the fact of growing economic interdependence. We were prepared to consult intensively on this agenda or any other agenda Europe might propose. At the same time, I cautioned against giving these consultations too formalistic a cast:

But let us also remember that even the best consultative machinery cannot substitute for common vision and shared goals; it cannot replace the whole network of intangible connections that have been the real sinews of the transatlantic and especially the Anglo-American relationship. We must take care lest in defining European unity in too legalistic a manner we lose what has made our alliance unique: that in the deepest sense Europe and America do not think of each other as foreign entities conducting traditional diplomacy, but as members of a larger community engaged, sometimes painfully but ultimately always cooperatively, in a common enterprise.

As we look into the future we can perceive challenges compared to which our recent disputes are trivial. A new international system is replacing the structure of the immediate postwar years. The external policies of China and the Soviet Union are in periods of transition. Western Europe is unifying. New nations seek identity and an appropriate role. Even now, economic relationships are changing more rapidly than the structures which nurtured them. We — Europe, Canada, and America — have only two choices: creativity together or irrelevance apart.

As an example of this new creativity I invited the industrial democracies to form an Energy Action Group

of senior and prestigious individuals with a mandate to develop within three months an initial action program for collaboration in all areas of the energy problem. We would leave it to the members of the Nine whether they prefer to participate as the European Community.

And I concluded with another appeal for moral unity:

We have every reason of duty and self-interest to preserve the most successful partnership in history. The United States is committed to making the Atlantic community a vital positive force for the future as it was for the past. What has recently been taken for granted must now be renewed. This is not an American challenge to Europe; it is history's challenge to us all.

I have quoted at such length from that speech because there was no goal that meant more to me than to maintain the vital partnership between the United States and Europe. In the Pilgrims speech I sought to meet previous European complaints. I offered a carte blanche for closer consultation. I specifically affirmed Europe's global responsibilities, formally burying the canard that we sought to confine Europe to a regional role. I put forward a proposal to deal jointly with the energy problem that had caused near-panic among our allies (see Chapter XIX).

Whatever grievances could be dealt with by words should have been removed by the Pilgrims speech. And since many of the complaints had addressed formulations in my original Year of Europe speech that I either withdrew or placed into context, there should have been a return to a spirit of cooperation.

But subsequent events proved that the problem went far deeper. We wanted to give a new sense of purpose to Atlantic relations; our allies gave priority to constructing a united Europe. And they believed — in our view wrongly — that both causes could not be advanced simultaneously. In any event, both efforts were constantly interrupted by domestic upheavals, foreign crises, and the clashing time frame of two important enterprises. Soon the pattern that had developed over the past year reclaimed us.

I left London to pursue the peace process in the Middle East — essentially unilaterally. Within days, the heads of government of the European Community convened in Copenhagen to define their identity equally unilaterally. They did not respond to the Pilgrims speech, ignoring both the suggestions for new consultative devices as well as the proposal for an Energy Action Group. The subject on which they were prepared to be specific was the Middle East. They reiterated their call for a comprehensive solution — while I was seeking to assemble the Geneva Conference and start a disengagement process on a step-by-step basis with the support of even radical Arab states. This time it was in Riyadh that the news of the European statement reached me. I learned too that our allies would not be content with declarations: The French were urging a separate "European-Arab dialogue." Given Europe's stated objectives, this was bound to be at cross-purposes with our own efforts. And the European summit added another reminder of the growing divergence. A group of Arab foreign ministers had showed up in Copenhagen and they seemed to have no procedural difficulties in meeting with the heads of government of the Community — far fewer obstacles, in fact, than Nixon had encountered in pursuing the Year of Europe. There was no suggestion, as had been the case with the American President, that the foreign ministers meet only the President of the Community. To be sure, some allies claimed the Arab appearance was a surprise; the whole affair had been arranged on the spur of the moment. We knew better and they knew we did.

In this atmosphere I called on Jobert at his Quai d'Orsay office on December 19 to brief him on my just-completed Middle East trip and the Geneva Conference coming up. There was the customary mixture of personal goodwill and wary fencing. Jobert asked how I felt among my real friends. I said I would settle for being among friends, real or not. He loved paradox and was playful. It pleased him to pretend that his personal views differed from the policy that the national interest or his President imposed on him; he told me that he really agreed with our step-by-step approach to the Middle East. Unfortunately, as Foreign Minister of France he had to take a different position. He would do so as slowly and as subtly as he could. I asked why it was in the interest of France that he should act against his personal convictions. France had to keep up appearances in the Mideast, he said. After all, we had dropped Europe out of the area. This I denied. What would France do if it were in the area? I asked. In principle it would be a great satisfaction, but in fact he really did not know what France would do, Jobert replied.

Were all the postures and frictions a matter, then, of appearances? Jobert did not reveal his thinking. Rather, having in effect stated his personal agreement with our Middle East policy, he began to harass us over Europe. He accused us of using, of all countries, Luxembourg to block the unity of the Nine. This was too absurd even for Jobert to pursue, so he ended the discussion with another paradox: "Well, you will never have a strong Europe anyway." Then why all the fierce speeches and challenging statements? Jobert acted like a man doomed to act out failure for the honor of his country. He was similarly ambiguous about the various Atlantic declarations. He might or might not try his hand at a European Community draft; he would let me know early in January (in fact he never did). Anyway, he averred, the result would not make much difference. Jobert saw the complexities of the situation but not the direction that might lead to their resolution. Or perhaps he felt that any resolution would threaten France's preeminence in Europe. In that case, the best outcome for France was that nothing should happen; Jobert on that reading had a vested interest in stalemate.

And that was in effect Georges Pompidou's theme when I saw him for the last time the next day, December 20, 1973. Pompidou was made of sterner stuff than Jobert. He was less playful and he knew that he was dying. He showed no sign of the excruciating pain that I learned later racked him almost constantly. He was courtly and polite as always. But perhaps the foreshortened perspective that fate had imposed on him accounted for the uncharacteristic abruptness with which he dismissed every conceivable initiative. He declared France's lack of interest in the Geneva Conference, since it had been excluded by the Soviet Union and the United States. As for relations between the United States and Europe, he was leery of any attempt to codify them:

> I can tell you as a Frenchman that we see no need to have a formal declaration as a basis for relations between Europe and the U.S. But we don't feel strongly about it — we would rather prefer that there be no declaration at all or that it be a very brief declaration and more at the European initiative, which would eliminate the need for an American "nihil obstat."

And he was opposed as well to my proposal of an Energy Action Group. Any grouping of oil consumers involved a risk of confrontation with the producers. He would not accept the slightest chance of a cutoff in oil supplies to France; hence, there was no point in a grouping of consumers.

If France insisted on freedom of action on the Middle East, refused to participate in a consumer grouping on energy, and saw no point in any Atlantic declaration, little was left of the Atlantic dialogue. When two views of the future clash, only one of them can turn out to be right. What cannot be created by foresight must then be brought about through experience. And it was to this, the most painful method of education, that the Atlantic nations had by their disunity doomed themselves. The Year of Europe was over.

What Went Wrong?

MANY factors combined to produce disappointment. Most of the criticisms that were made in 1973 have since paled in significance and some were petty and partisan: that we were more at ease negotiating with adversaries than with allies; that we had insufficient consultation with European nations; that we were pressuring friends.

To be sure, it was less complex negotiating with authoritarian governments, but we were much more deeply committed to the Year of Europe than to any initiative toward the Communist world. That is why we turned the other cheek to so many rebuffs. As for consultations, the account I have given leaves little doubt that the Year of Europe was awash with them.

No doubt we made tactical errors. To attempt a major foreign policy initiative of this kind from the office of national security adviser was awkward. That was the way the President wanted it and with Secretary Rogers on the way out, I was certainly keen to try. We had achieved our successes in other areas without the State Department. But relations with Europe did not lend themselves to secret diplomacy followed by spectacular pronouncements. There were too many nations involved to permit the use of backchannels. North Atlantic diplomacy had well-established patterns for consultation that were guarded jealously, sometimes ferociously, by their bureaucracies. Had I been Secretary of State at the beginning, instead of national security adviser, I might well have been more sensitive to the need to engage allied foreign offices. But from the White House it was easier to deal with heads of government, and this antagonized the experts in the ministries whose goodwill was essential for the kind of detailed negotiations required by our initiative.

These were only the superficial difficulties. The real problems were deeper and they lay in four areas: the Mideast conflict; East-West relations; the movement toward greater political unity in Europe; and Watergate.

The Middle East crisis brought to the surface two basic issues in Atlantic relations: What is the correct behavior for allies in an area not covered by formal treaty obligations but affecting the vital interests of each partner? And how should allies conduct themselves when they fundamentally disagree with one another's policies? Not all allied disagreements present the same problem, of course. There are issues that so predominantly affect one party that not much is gained by seeking a consensus. In such instances, understanding and acquiescence — or maybe quiet consultations — can prevent dangerous disagreement. Our attitude toward Brandt's *Ostpolitik* was a case in point. The difficult issues are those that involve comparable interests of the two sides and different perceptions of them. That emphatically was the case in the Middle East.

With respect to juridical obligation, I reiterate my belief that if the Atlantic Alliance is reduced to its legal content, it will sooner or later fail even in the area covered by formal obligation. The lifeblood of an alliance is the shared conviction that the security, in its widest sense, of each ally is a vital interest to the others; in crises they must not have the attitude that they will check with their lawyers to determine their legal duty. Ultimately, the Western Alliance must be sustained by the hearts as well as the minds of its members. It follows that a threat to the vital interests of a partner cannot be treated with indifference even if it is not technically encompassed by any provision of the Alliance treaty. Clearly, if Western security is jeopardized, it cannot make a decisive difference whence this threat originates. If the Soviet Union came to dominate the Middle East, it would have a grip on NATO's lifeline; the collapse of Europe would follow as surely as if Soviet armies marched to the English Channel. If the radical Arab regimes gained the upper hand, the same results would occur if by some more circuitous processes — though some European countries do not share this judgment.

But what does the theoretical importance of allied unity outside the NATO area imply for circumstances in which views radically differ? Are allies required to submerge their judgments to the unilateral decisions of a senior partner? This is how the issue was frequently posed by our European allies and it permits no theoretical answer. Major efforts must be made, far beyond what has been the case, to prevent such a clash from occurring. If differences cannot be reconciled, one or the other partner must be wise enough to stand aside at least long enough to permit one policy to prevail. If each ally insists on implementing its clashing views, competition or conflict must mathematically ensue. Each side runs the risk of thwarting the other without being able to achieve its own purposes. Divisions will tempt new outside pressures; the Alliance runs the risk of disintegrating.

In the fall of 1973, the Atlantic Alliance seemed unable to break this vicious circle. Whatever the judgment of some of our allies about our Mideast policy prior to the war, the practical consequence of their actions described in this chapter was to paralyze our strategy if they succeeded or to underline European impotence if they failed. And for better or worse, we were the only ally in a position to produce rapid progress, which in turn was the prerequisite to defusing the crisis and reducing Soviet opportunities for political gain. That Europe differed with us on how to handle cease-fire violations was understandable; that it published its views on the day I arrived in Cairo complicated both our strategy and Sadat's, to the ultimate benefit of no free country.

The word "Europe" as used in this chapter is in fact a misnomer. The opposition to us was led by France in the person of Michel Jobert, supported by Heath and tolerated by Brandt for their own reasons. The Benelux countries, Denmark, and Italy were uneasy about the growing confrontation. They were not inclined to challenge our policies on the Middle East even when they had private reservations. But they also prized the newfound Community political institutions, which put a premium on the appearance of monolithic cohesion. The European Community seemed to find political consensus by one of two methods: either a lowest common denominator of vacuity or vagueness, or any policy advocated passionately by one partner that the others who felt less strongly (or might even disagree with mildly) considered themselves obligated to support for the sake of European unity.

As for East-West relations, they helped to prompt our initiative, and were a principal cause of its failure. We wanted to provide a psychological ballast to the democracies' approaches to the Communist world. As I said in the Pilgrims speech, it was important to overcome the anomaly that the public tended increasingly to identify foreign policy successes with relations with adversaries. We were serious about a reaffirmation of Atlantic solidarity. We were prepared to subordinate détente policy to the consensus of our allies. But not all our allies were ready for similar undertakings. Several of them had developed a large stake, both domestic and international, in their unilateral overtures to the East. As the speech of Jobert quoted on page 711 shows, some of our partners wanted us to slow down our détente efforts so that they could accelerate their own.

France and Germany, eager as they were to circumscribe *our* freedom of action, were not prepared to pay in the coin of a coordinated Western policy. Brandt did not wish to see his *Ostpolitik* constrained by the need to seek a larger Atlantic consensus. A free-wheeling German diplomacy aroused uneasiness in Paris. Earlier in the 1970s Pompidou had sought to counterbalance Germany by moving closer to us; in 1973, under the influence of Jobert, suspicion of Bonn brought Pompidou's Gaullist instincts to the fore — seeking to tie down Germany by stressing European interests in contradistinction to American and competing with Germany in separate approaches to the East. That a European race to Moscow might sooner or later represent the first steps toward the possible Finlandization of Europe — in the sense that loosened political ties to America could not forever exclude the security field — was either lost, ignored, or ridiculed in the obsession with immediate tactics that for statesmen too often covers a deep uneasiness about the future.

The third major cause of deadlock was that Europe's political body-clock was out of phase with ours. Now that the Vietnam war was over, we sought creative tasks that would transcend our domestic traumas. But our allies had no such compulsions. On the contrary, they felt that they had enough on their plates. After much delay, the Common Market had expanded from the Six to the Nine at the beginning of 1973. Our proposal to discuss Atlantic relations inevitably if unintentionally raised the question of who would speak for Europe, and the Europeans sought the answer by evolving procedures so formalistic as to be incompatible with any normal idea of consultation. Even leaders who saw no incompatibility between strengthened Atlantic ties and European unity were afraid that Europe could not handle the two processes simultaneously. Sir Alec Douglas-Home came close to asserting this when he said:

> In an ideal world, we would have chosen a different time scale. We would have preferred that the new community of nine had time to shake down and find its way towards common positions with greater deliberation. But the pressure of events on both sides of the Atlantic and in Japan obliges us all to quicken the pace.

Others, especially the smaller countries, agreed with Jean Monnet's thesis that a transatlantic dialogue might actually assist European unity by forcing Europe to speak with one voice. But this only landed us in the middle of the decade-old European dispute between France, which insisted on leadership in a united Europe, and countries like Belgium that insisted on formal equality, with the Federal Republic maneuvering uneasily in between the different conceptions.

For some Europeans — especially for France — the fact of European unity was inseparable from the manner in which it came about. They did not want unity to emerge from an *American* initiative. Heath, in Britain, had a similar view: At a minimum it raised for him the hateful prospect of having to choose between Paris and Washington, which he believed had aborted his negotiations for British entry into Europe in 1963. He preemptively opted for Paris before a choice was even demanded. Brandt was initially the most forthcoming, though in the context of 1973 that is a relative term. But even he was not willing to make an issue of it with his colleagues in France and Britain, especially as he preferred to avoid a tightening of Atlantic bonds in order to preserve his freedom of action for *Ostpolitik*.

Our dilemma was that if we followed Monnet's advice and pressed European unity, we would guarantee a repetition of the Franco-American disputes of the 1960s because Paris would construe it as contesting its claim to leadership in Europe. By taking account of French sensibilities and dealing through France rather than the European Community, however, we alienated many of the natural supporters of our initiative. In order to prevent being excluded, the smaller European states clung to the consultative procedures of the European Community, which were untried, time-consuming, and a major source of difficulty. And so, by a different route, we too wound up in a quarrel with France, after all — proving, I suppose, that success does not always lie in doing the exact opposite of what had failed in the previous decade.

The contending pressures might have been shaped into a creative response by a dominant European statesman. Unfortunately, the key European leaders who might have reached for such a role were all facing problems of their own. In 1973, Pompidou had already begun the physical martyrdom which, together with the drugs to combat the disease, deprived him of the concentration and the inward aloofness essential for sustained policymaking. He needed all his strength to marshal his energies for the display of stoicism by which he obscured his agony so well that even our intelligence analysts debated the seriousness of his illness. Knowing his time was limited, he was in a hurry to arrange affairs, easily peeved, and understandably more resentful of heavy-handed tactics than he would have been had he been vouchsafed a longer perspective. We had counted on Pompidou as an ally in the Year of Europe, and I believe he would have been, in ordinary conditions.

By a twist of fate, each of the other principals in the Atlantic dialogue was robbed nearly simultaneously of perspective and authority either by personal or by domestic circumstance. Willy Brandt, having accomplished his symbolic breakthrough to the East, was now confronting a host of mundane problems in economic policy and day-to-day diplomacy that were less suited to his special talents. Increasingly there was talk of replacing him. Within six months his own party found a pretext for removing him from office. When we put forward our initiative, Edward Heath seemed dominant in Britain. As 1973 proceeded, he too found himself consumed in struggles over industrial policy in Britain.

But while Europe's various hesitations had a reasonable basis and we were not always sensitive to them, there is little excuse for the brusque, indeed dismissive, manner with which the European nations, for all their problems, dealt with the country that had restored their economies and on which they continued to rely for their security. It was one thing to assert Europe's identity and to work for its cohesion; it was another to seek it through tactics of deliberate confrontation with the United States.

That Europe might not wish America to be involved in defining its own internal arrangements was understandable enough; European integration, even in the Monnet version, was always partly motivated by a desire to achieve independence from Washington. But our allies could have achieved this objective as easily, and more constructively, by bringing the Year of Europe to a rapid conclusion and then turning to the elaboration of their institutions on the bedrock of a newly defined Atlantic relationship. What a year later became the Declaration of Atlantic Relations could have been drafted within three months of the offer and culminated at a summit meeting within the framework of the Alliance. Instead, our allies chose a procedure that was wounding, unworkable, and disruptive. It was never followed again.

The various procedural and technical objections by European leaders were in part a reflection of Watergate. Nixon, of course, was facing the worst crisis of all his colleagues, though he clung to office the longest. A reaffirmation of the moral unity of the West simply could not be led by a President of the United States facing impeachment.

We had intriguing testimony of the influence of Watergate in a dispatch in September reporting the view of Etienne Davignon, political director of the Belgian Foreign Ministry, that Jobert had shown a new interest in concluding the Year of Europe rapidly because he predicted that Watergate would be over by November and thereafter America's bargaining position would improve. There was plenty of other evidence. Early in Nixon's second term, Britain had explored a State visit (meaning the President would come in his capacity as head of state and stay at Buckingham Palace). These discussions languished as soon as the full extent of Watergate became apparent. Willy Brandt technically maintained his invitation but the permanent head of the German Foreign Office was reliably reported to have said that a Presidential visit might give rise to "immoderate events," an elegant expression for public demonstrations. The French invitation was never withdrawn, but no date was ever proposed for it.

Europe's leaders hedged their bets. While Watergate was gaining momentum, they saw to it that every meeting with America ended inconclusively. As a result, an initiative that was intended to culminate fairly rapidly at an allied summit meeting slid into the bureaucracies, which were much more interested in preserving a sacramental liturgy than in reaffirming the values of the democracies. European procrastination was made easier by our domestic vacuum. The President was speaking largely for himself, a fact not lost on our European critics. They could count on a more sympathetic hearing for even their most unworthy complaints about American policy than would have been conceivable in ordinary times. They could be sure that even their pettiest maneuvers were unlikely to be challenged.

When all is said and done, I have to conclude that, though the immediate attempt was doomed, it was right to try. We had posed the correct questions, of which the best proof is that most of them are still with us today under much more difficult circumstances. What finally defeated the effort was the inability of the key countries to mesh their domestic politics with the plain needs of the future — revealing the deepest challenge to modern democracy.

Japanese Perspectives

WE had comparable problems with our key ally in the Pacific, Japan. But Japan was going through no identity crisis; it launched no philosophical challenge. Our disagreements never reached the acrimonious. For Japan's national style was quite different.

When I first came into office, there was no major country I understood less than Japan. Like most Americans, I admired its extraordinary recovery from the devastation of World War II. But I did not grasp Japan's unique character. In the West, feudalism was gradually destroyed by industrialization in a process lasting over a century and a half. Japan modernized by merging feudal values of reciprocal obligation with the new ethos of industrial efficiency in less than a generation. The West developed a system of government based on a concept of authority: the right to issue orders that are accepted because they reflect legal or constitutional norms. Japan relies on consensus. A leader's eminence does not imply a right to impose his will on his peers, but the opportunity to elicit their agreement — or at least give the appearance of doing so. High office in Japan does not entitle the holder to issue orders; it gives the privilege of taking the lead in persuasion.

Almost anywhere else, such a system of government would lead to stagnation. But Japan is not like anywhere else. It has built a great civilization on its constricted islands almost in isolation from all other countries. Receiving a cultural impetus from China, Japan endowed it with its own subtle and special forms, blending it into a heritage that has made Japanese society more like a family than a state. In its complex style, meanings and intangibles are understood the same way, enabling decisions (that anywhere else would be made by the political process) to emerge from a social consensus. Whether Japanese culture was imposed by the requirement of coexistence on crowded islands poor in resources, or whether Japan thrived as a result of its culture, is a subject for the anthropologists.

In any event, there is no doubt that the symbiosis between social values and political structure has produced an extraordinary record of achievement. Like many countries that later were colonized, Japan in the late nineteenth century faced what seemed to be a harsh choice between Western modernization and traditional ways. Japan was "opened up" by force of arms. But this did not elicit submission. On the contrary, the Japanese ruling groups opted for whatever was necessary to maintain control over their national destiny — which meant contemporary science and industry. That Japan managed to do the seemingly im-

possible, that it acquired a universal technology and conventional political institutions and yet remained culturally distinctive, was unforeseeable
at the moment of decision. Japan risked its identity to be able to assure
its independence — an act of extraordinary courage and devotion.

By contrast, Imperial China, facing similar pressures, did not dare to
risk what had seemed to make life worth living; it relied on diplomatic
skill to manipulate foreigners even from a position of impotence. At the
cost of constant humiliation it avoided total colonization by giving the
maximum number of nations a stake in exploiting China and preserved
a margin of autonomy by playing off competing greeds against each
other.

Japan had no such confidence in its cultural preeminence or diplomatic skill. It decided first to become so strong that no foreign nation
would dare to impose its will. In time Japan achieved a position from
which it could impose on other nations what it was determined to resist
for itself: It launched itself on the road of colonization.

All this was achieved in one generation by methods that were to become standard for Japan. After the Meiji Restoration of 1868, study
missions were sent abroad to learn the techniques of the most successful
nations in all fields: military affairs, government, business, education,
the arts. Britain was emulated for its navy and parliamentary institutions, Germany for its army, America increasingly for its technological
know-how. The lessons were assimilated by a leadership group of
amazing cohesiveness, deftly expert at combining the experience of the
West with the essence of Japan.

After the debacle of World War II, Japanese leaders set about with
characteristic tenacity to restore Japan's position. They brought Japan to
superpower status economically and to democracy internally. Until now
they have refrained from claiming a corresponding international role because of the shrewd judgment that an assertive foreign policy would
exceed the world's tolerance for unbridled economic competition and
might jeopardize the inexpensive military protection provided by the
American security guarantee.

The methods by which that advance was achieved were well tested.
The leadership group set carefully considered long-range goals. Consensus did not emerge from a compromise between individual preferences;
it was based on meticulous investigation of major trends at home and
abroad. Japan spent more on research into foreign practices and used it
more effectively than any other major industrial country. Consensus became a method to explore the most effective way of dealing with the
future rather than — as is the temptation elsewhere — a system of ratifying the status quo. Only a country of marvelous morale and cohesiveness could have managed the discipline to set social priorities without making them explicit in formal law; to define national objectives

that involve shifting labor to new technologies and new products without significant social conflict.[9]

Japan's economic resurgence was based on a unique set of institutions: a paternalistic labor-management relationship and social structure in which employees are hired in effect for life and are treated as partners cooperating for the common good; a public opinion that is formed by participation in every aspect of the decision-making through media that philosophically are themselves part of the consensus. (This is why the Japanese government finds it so difficult to keep secrets. Openness is inherent in a style in which government and media think of each other not as adversaries but as participants in the same process.)

The Japanese system has not been easy for Americans to comprehend. It took me a long time to grasp how decisions are made, and even after I had understood some of it intellectually I did not always perceive the application to specific circumstances. For one of the features of the Japanese system is its opaqueness to outsiders. It is not that Japanese leaders mask their intentions, though if they choose — which is not always — they can be exceptionally discreet. It is rather that there are fewer secrets in the Western sense than in the decision-making process of conventional bureaucracies. In the other industrial democracies, a problem is defined; the options are identified; someone chooses between them or compromises among them. Bureaucratic self-will and substantive concerns merge. There is either an identifiable winner and loser or else an amalgam of views reflective of a balance of forces. At every point it is possible to define the state of bureaucratic play.

In Japan, by contrast, everything is geared to avoid confrontation. There is no clear-cut elaboration of a formal position. There is a long process of consultation designed to achieve not compromise but a sense of direction. The art of Japanese decision-making is to avoid commitment in the early stages of the process, to enable a serious deliberation to go forward in which participants have the option of changing their minds and the need for decision is avoided until genuine agreement exists. Thus, even if outsiders could obtain correct information about the internal state of play — no easy matter — it would do them little good because the early stages of the process are amorphous and its subsequent evolution depends on group psychology.

Japan thereby acquires an enormous advantage. There is literally no one capable of making a decision by himself. Only amateurs would seek to pressure an individual Japanese minister; even when he yields out of politeness, he cannot carry out his promise. But when the consensus has formed, for whatever reason, it is implemented with speed, determination, and breadth unmatched by any Western country. So many key people have been involved in the decision-making process and they understand the implications of what has been decided so well, that they achieve tremendous momentum. What could be more effective than a society voracious in its collection of information, impervious to pressure, and implacable in execution?

A foreigner underestimates Japanese leaders at his peril. It is true that they are not as conceptually adept as, say, the Chinese, as articulate as most Europeans, or as boisterously open and forthcoming as Americans. They have not been selected for any of these qualities. They gather intelligence about foreigners; they do not seek to persuade them with words. They chart future actions for their society; they do not need to articulate its purposes in rhetoric.

In Japan, the key skill of leadership is the ability to form a consensus not by talking people into what they do not wish to do but by making people wish to do what is in the common interest. Japanese diplomats almost never communicate by the usual process of putting forward a proposition that then becomes the subject of negotiation. This would imply that they have the power of individual decision. It would place them in the embarrassing circumstance of implying that they can change what they did not decide, or of refusing a compromise, or of imposing their will as a last resort — all acts that would offend the legendary courtesy of a country whose social conflicts are resolved without providing a scorecard of winners or losers.

The typical Japanese leader is impelled by his culture to avoid explicitness in dealing with foreign counterparts — at nearly all costs. This creates an almost impenetrable cultural barrier in diplomacy, which in its Western version is geared to a systematic search for the common ground — a practice the Japanese ethos actively discourages. At international conferences the chief Japanese delegate rarely speaks, sometimes seems to doze, while his associates scrupulously write down every word that is being said for later study in Tokyo. The Japanese position generally is put forward once in a carefully drafted statement. Afterward, there is very little give-and-take, but neither is there an assault on the positions of other parties. The views of the other participants will be analyzed in Tokyo. They will evoke a response, but it will emerge from a careful calculation of Japanese imperatives, not from a reaction to the requirements of a conference. It is a dangerous mistake to think of Japanese leaders as unimpressive and to confuse their inarticulateness with lack of perception. In Japan, eminence is reached after a long apprenticeship that ruthlessly weeds out the second-rate. But it rewards the ability to shape Japanese decisions in a Japanese context, not in the ebb and flow of a conference whose procedures seem accidental — indeed, almost arbitrary — to Japanese leaders.

In any event, by the time Japanese leaders appear at international conferences they have usually done far more homework than their counterparts. They reason that an unprepared meeting will force someone to yield or result in a compromise serving nobody's purpose. Japanese leaders therefore tend to make their concessions *before* a diplomatic encounter by preparing negotiations as meticulously as all other decisions. They obtain the necessary information through a flood of unofficial emissaries, many of high status — former Prime Ministers, or present high party officials temporarily without a ministry, for example. These have the advantage of not being able to commit the government. They cannot be blamed for failing to put forward a position because they cannot be expected to have one. But their experience superbly equips them to explore the thinking of their interlocutors, which is then incorporated in the decisions made in Japan that, to do Japanese leaders credit, usually take seriously into account the points of view of other nations.

Japanese diplomats, like other Japanese leaders, seek not victory but consensus; they know that in a society of sovereign states an imposed view offers no guarantee of willing execution. Japanese diplomats bend their efforts toward a disciplined process of conciliation. They will adjust their own position if necessary — preferably before a conference, if necessary afterward, but only most reluctantly during the course of a negotiation since the Japanese system confers on no minister an individual right of decision.

If one wishes one's point of view to be taken into account by the Japanese government, it must be conveyed early before the consensus has had a chance to form and preferably through a technically unofficial but highly respected Japanese. By the same token, when a Japanese diplomat of high rank — and even more, a minister — asks a question, he is rarely seeking enlightenment. He is putting forward the consensus in the most tentative, hence the least demanding, manner. At that point, a meeting of minds is expected. If there is a genuine disagreement, it is important to present it gently to permit an adjustment without loss of face. And one must not expect one's Japanese opposite number to be in a position to respond immediately; time must be left for a change of course.

The erosion of distinctions between the official and the unofficial, the oblique manner of presentation, the seeming (and misleading) imperviousness to counterarguments can confer a maddening quality on encounters with Japanese diplomats. It can also lead to grave misunderstandings. In my early years in government I ignored unofficial emissaries, misunderstanding their "official" role. I listened carefully to what Japanese diplomats said but, more often than not, missed the intangibles that they attempted to convey. When we had a problem, I sought out the responsible minister and tried to persuade him to our point of view. Nonplussed by such lack of delicacy, too polite to admit that he had no authority to make a decision on his own, the hapless minister would seek refuge in evasion or, if pressed to the wall, would agree to propositions he did not know how to implement.*

When I visited Japan in November 1973, following my trip to China, all these tendencies were being put to the test. It was a difficult time in Japanese-American relations because the same pressures panicking Europe afflicted Japan, if anything, more. The energy crisis shook Japan to its core. Like the rest of the industrial world, Japan had built its prosperity on cheap energy. It was almost totally dependent on outside sources, importing 90 percent of its requirements. The cutback in Arab oil production, the beginning of price rises (they had been nearly doubled in October), and the pressures to link oil to a pro-Arab stance on the Arab-Israeli conflict confronted Japan with a serious dilemma. Heretofore its foreign policy had been nonassertive. It had tied its security to our military guarantee, and Japanese leaders, unlike some of their European colleagues, understood that one cannot have the advantage of every course of action: If one is protected by a foreign power it is reckless to pretend that there is an unlimited margin for dissociation on key issues. Nor did the Japanese leaders feel the European need to establish their identity by needling the United States.

And yet by November 1973 Japanese leaders, just like their European counterparts, began to feel — with some reluctance — that their national interest might require them to dissociate from American policy in the Middle East. Japanese leaders became convinced that their public required a demonstration from them that they were doing something about the energy crisis — never mind what.

This did not mean that the Japanese leaders personally disagreed with the substance of our Middle East policy. They never stated an explicit view to us and perhaps did not form one, because Japanese leaders waste no capital on matters they cannot influence. What was involved was more fundamental. A corollary to Japan's sense of its impermeable uniqueness is an uncanny adaptability to requirements affecting Japanese survival. Japan abandoned feudalism for militaristic autocracy and the latter for democracy under the impact of shocks from the outside. In each instance, Japan decided — perhaps not even entirely consciously — to accommodate to an external pressure, in ways that would preserve Japan's essence. The issue for Japan's leaders was not the merit of the various points of view — to which they were largely indifferent — but a calculation of pressures that needed tending.

---

*This was at the heart of the impasse in textile negotiations in 1969–1971. Unwilling to refuse Nixon — and to a lesser extent me — to our faces, then Prime Minister Eisaku Sato agreed to schemes for which he knew he had no backing. This led to the bizarre situation that the Japanese Prime Minister asked us to put forward a *tougher* position in the implementing negotiations to give him some maneuvering room to work with in persuading his colleagues and other key decisionmakers. Our bureaucracy, looking for compromise, undercut him by putting forward moderate demands, ruining the already slight chances of a successful outcome.[10]

Japan's initial reaction to the oil embargo and production cutbacks was its rote response of reliance on the United States. Thus Japan did not join the European Community when on November 6 the Europeans publicly affirmed objectives in the Middle East contrary to our stated policy. But by the time I reached Tokyo on November 14, there had been second thoughts. What had been reassessed was not the substance of our strategy but the impact and the likely persistence of the Arab stranglehold over oil production. If the energy crisis reflected a new trend and not an aberration, Japan could not risk being simply an appendage to American diplomacy. This was true whether the step-by-step approach succeeded or failed; Japanese leaders claimed that they were agnostic on that issue and I believed them. If our policy failed, all the frustrations of the Arab world might fall on Japan — as Prime Minister Kakuei Tanaka pointed out to me. But even a successful American policy might cause Japan to appear irrelevant to the oil producers; we would get the credit while Japanese concerns were neglected.

Though formally similar to Europe's, Japanese policy differed radically in spirit. The Europeans genuinely disagreed with us. Several of their leaders were angry because they believed our domestic political constraints had jeopardized their countries' prosperity and their own political future. The Japanese were in no mood of recrimination. They were not disputing a political choice; buffered by all the exquisite Japanese forms, they were scientists coldly assessing the objective requirements of their energy situation. They needed to make a record, not conduct a policy. Unlike the Europeans, Japan would not agitate for its views nor pretend that it could produce a solution. It would adopt a posture it calculated might deflect the pressures from its shores. And if Japanese leaders could not gain our assent to their cause, they would do their utmost to ease the cost of disagreement.

Machiavelli has been invoked for centuries as the incarnation of cynicism. Yet he thought of himself as a moralist. His maxims described the world as he found it, not as he wished it to be. Indeed, he was convinced that only a ruler of strong moral conviction could keep a steady course while engaging in manipulations on which survival regrettably depended. That, in a way, was the attitude of my Japanese interlocutors. They claimed neither justice nor even wisdom for their course of action. It reflected necessity and was thus beyond debate.

The leaders whose task it was to convey this news to me were Prime Minister Kakuei Tanaka and Foreign Minister Masayoshi Ohira. Tanaka was the first Japanese Prime Minister to have broken the traditional mold. He was not a graduate of one of the great universities. He had come from humble origins. He was aggressive in the Western style; he did not obscure his ambition behind the patient indirection of the classic Japanese politician. He was extremely young for a Japanese Prime Minister — in his early fifties. His eminence was due to his ability to organize the largest "faction" within the ruling Liberal Democratic Party — a faction being held together by the exchange of reciprocal favors. In the normal course of events, Tanaka would have had to wait his turn for the better part of a decade while more senior leaders competed for the top post. But either he was too impatient or else he doubted that as an outsider he would be able to hold his faction together against the systematic erosion by traditional politicians who, while more subtle in their manners, were no less ruthless in their designs. (In this he turned out to be wrong. For his faction survived and even thrived amid the many vicissitudes of his career.)

Tanaka gained the Prime Ministership in 1972 by what in Japanese terms amounted to a near-coup. And he paid the price for it. When he faced various charges, he found himself without the support by which the Japanese Establishment usually protects its own.

Tanaka's fate was thus oddly parallel to Nixon's. Like Nixon he had exceptional abilities; like Nixon he was very insecure and, what is even more remarkable for a Japanese, he showed it. He was Prime Minister for only eighteen months. I found him extremely intelligent, unusually direct. He came closest of any Japanese leader to speaking in the idiom of personal power that is conventional among heads of government of other countries. And strangely enough, it deprived his statements of some credibility. They were clearer than those of his colleagues but in a curious way less informative, for one could never be quite sure whether his assertions reflected the true Japanese consensus or only a personal preference. Thus in a subtle way the Japanese method, which is almost aesthetic in nature, of having the point emerge from a context, won its victory over the rational form of discourse favored by the West.

Tanaka in his rapid-fire, staccato delivery presented Japan's problem without allusion or evasion. He cited the statistics of oil imports; he explained the impact on Japanese production and life-style of a reduction in energy consumption. He could not be perceived by the Japanese public as simply letting matters drift, he said; to do nothing would look as if Japan were acquiescing in being strangled. Some sort of declaration of sympathy for the Arab cause was necessary, according to Tanaka, even granting that it would not change American policy. Nor, he emphasized, was it really Japan's purpose to influence American policy.

I went through the exegesis of our strategy. I asked what it had benefited the Europeans to dissociate from us. It made no sense to wish us success in our efforts and then to undertake actions that were at best irrelevant, or at worst could undermine our policy by making it harder for Arab moderates to accept less than the program our allies were endorsing. If Japan followed the line of the European Community, we would be able to do no better than be silent; if forced to comment, we would have to be critical.

But when a Japanese Prime Minister puts forward a proposition, he is not asking advice. He is announcing a decision. And therefore, both of us having stated our views, the matter was left in abeyance with Tanaka's statement that he and his colleagues would study what I had said — which meant that they would proceed.

Masayoshi Ohira was in the classic Japanese mold, which, it is fair to say, is not automatically compatible with my more assertive temperament. It would be difficult to find two more different personalities than the subtle, indirect Japanese Foreign Minister and the analytical Secretary of State whose policy at that moment invoked the visibly dramatic. I had first met Ohira when I visited Japan in June 1972. Our Embassy organized a dinner for me with several former Japanese foreign ministers. Unfortunately, a successor to Prime Minister Eisaku Sato was being selected at that moment and Ohira would be a key figure. He was not about to reveal his thinking to an American he did not know and whose record on matters Japanese had revealed the absence of a certain delicacy. We spent an evening together. Ohira impressed me by the extraordinary feat of saying little and yet conveying in his marvelously polite way an attitude of great goodwill.

As time went on, a friendship grew up based on genuine affection. Ohira taught me patiently about things Japanese. He expanded my understanding of nuance. He masked his great ability in a modest bearing; he always delivered more than he promised. He demonstrated the wisdom of the adage that friendship can reside in what is unspoken even more than in what is being said.

In his memoirs Ohira has described the cordiality of our relationship, as well as the internal discussions in Japan when I arrived in November 1973.[11] The overwhelming majority of the Japanese cabinet favored some dissociation from the United States. Ohira stood alone in arguing for solidarity with America. In his memoirs he quotes with approval my statement that obsequiousness would serve only to earn Japan the contempt, not the goodwill, of Arab leaders.

Yet he exhibited none of the internal Japanese stresses in his meeting with me. Indeed, in many ways his approach, precisely because it was so elliptical, conveyed an even greater sense of determination than Tanaka's blunt assertions. Characteristically, Ohira began our conversation with an indirection that revealed Japanese thinking without laying down a frontal challenge. Before there had even been one exchange of substance, he submitted a draft memorandum on the basis of which he proposed to brief the press after our talk. Its essence was that pressure had to be brought on Israel to be flexible in the peace negotiations. This served several purposes. It put me on notice as to Japanese thinking while permitting a retreat without loss of face; clearly, Ohira could not announce a joint agreement if I demurred. When I predictably objected,

744	*Years of Upheaval*

Ohira immediately withdrew his proposal — setting up the possibility of briefing Arab capitals that Japan's preference had been thwarted by American pressure.

The rest of the conversation — twice as long as my session with Tanaka — was an application of a maxim in Ohira's autobiography:

[I]n diplomacy, even when an agreement cannot be reached, it is essential that each party have an understanding of the other's position. The fostering of understanding and trust, in fact, is just as important as the actual reaching of agreement. Between Japan and the United States, in particular, it is of the utmost importance.[12]

Ohira subjected me to a patient, gentle cross-examination on Mideast policy that was at once tentative and inexorable, understanding and pliantly firm. What time scale did I envision? What objective did we have — a local or a comprehensive settlement? Why did we object to a Japanese declaration in favor of the Arabs now that the Europeans had already made one? What possible damage could a Japanese statement do, especially if Japan did not press its case? Throughout, Ohira, without ever saying so, made it very clear that Japan could not face the energy crisis without stating a position divergent from ours but also that it would do its utmost to preserve the friendship with the United States.

My own analysis was essentially irrelevant to this clinical approach, which moreover was presented in a manner permitting neither acceptance nor rejection. I argued that the Arab states had three options: reliance on Soviet pressures; reliance on European and Japanese pressures; reliance on the United States. We were determined to block the first option; we had no interest in giving credence to the second — its practical consequence might be to cause us to stop our peace diplomacy altogether. Ohira did not fall for this bluff; he knew we had our own reasons for pursuing our strategy. In his gentle manner he summed up my position precisely, as the official record indicates:

MINISTER OHIRA said that he understood what the Secretary has been saying, and reviewed his understanding that the Secretary said that Japan, even if it paid lip service to Arab demands or took specific action, would not get relief from the present Arab oil embargo. However, he wished also to confirm whether the Secretary also was saying that it would make the United States task of working out a peaceful settlement more difficult if Japan should align itself with the Arabs. Consequently, it seemed that the Secretary was saying that Japan, come what may and regardless of Arab pressures, should follow the United States strategy as the best hope of producing an early settlement in the Middle East and consequently relief from the oil embargo.

Ohira's summing up was exactly on the mark; it disproved the adage that consultation can remove misunderstandings. The problem here was that we understood each other very well indeed. Our position as summed up by Ohira was clearly incompatible with what he and Tanaka had stated as the basic premise of Japanese policy that there had to be a definable and different Japanese position. Hence its very formulation implied the impossibility of acceptance while paying me the courtesy of making clear that I had been understood. Our conversation then moved to other topics: the Year of Europe, my China trip, the supply of oil to American forces in Japan. When it was over, it was clear that Japan would go the road charted by Europe. But I knew, too, that it would do so with some reluctance and no great conviction. It would make statements but not interpose its weight against our policy; it was not, like our European allies, challenging us, but pursuing its own necessities. In its silken, soft, insinuating way Japan, largely under Ohira's guidance, had brought us with a minimum of friction to a position that it considered essential to its national interest and domestic stability without threatening the essence of the Japanese-American partnership.

On November 22, 1973, the Japanese government issued a declaration parallel to that of the European Community. It prepared the ground in typical fashion. Shortly after I left, the English-language press of Tokyo was full of stories that there had been disagreements between me and Japanese leaders (the Japanese-language press was silent on the subject). This was technically true but misstated the essential harmony and good feeling that prevailed. But it served the purpose of conveying in the media most likely to be read by diplomats from the Middle East that Japan was champing at the bit. I complained to the Japanese Ambassador. In response, Ohira made a statement to the *Japanese-language* press denying any rift or disagreement. They, of course, saw no reason to print it, not having reported a disagreement in the first place. With all the complicated maneuvers, I had great confidence in Masayoshi Ohira. I instructed the State Department spokesman to comment that while we did not agree with Japan's decision, we understood the circumstances that impelled it.

By the end of 1973, for whatever reason, the unity of the industrial democracies to which we had dedicated so much effort had eluded us. And yet, despite all crises and disagreements, the seeds of our effort did not fall on stony ground. There was some vindication in events — at least for a while. Within two years the dialogue we had sought to start in 1973 was brought about by reality. The energy crisis of late 1973 forced the creation of a grouping, however tentative, of the oil-consuming nations. By late 1974 the International Energy Agency had been formed to promote consumer cooperation on new sources of energy, conservation, and resistance to new embargoes. Economic summits among the key leaders of the democracies proved necessary to seek common objectives imposed by the interdependence of nations; they emerged as a European, indeed a French, initiative.* And they were soon broadened into political discussions and institutionalized on an annual basis. By the end of 1976, from a variety of pressures and persuasions, relations among the industrial democracies were on a solid basis, fulfilling many of the hopes with which we had ushered in the Year of Europe.

Since then, divisions have reappeared. As before, substance, not procedure, lies at their heart. The fact that debates have persisted through three successor administrations to Nixon's, and have in fact become sharper, indicates that something deeper was involved than clashing tactical approaches. Events have dramatized particularly the perils of allowing the Soviets to practice selective détente, playing off some allies against others — a danger we foresaw when we attempted the Year of Europe. The failure to face the changes in technology and military capabilities in the early Seventies has caused the issues to reemerge explosively a decade later, fueling a polarization between pacifists rejecting all arms and weapons experts supporting whatever is feasible. The doctrinal issue remains preeminent, for neither emotion nor technology provides a sense of direction equal to the age in which we live. The same is true in the economic area, where the industrial countries are still groping to reconcile the imperatives of their domestic policies with the realities of interdependence. The risks are plain. Free societies cannot maintain even their domestic cohesion by simply managing the present and hoping for the best. All too frequently a problem evaded is a crisis invited. The future must be shaped or it will impose itself as catastrophe. That remains the key test of democratic statesmanship.

---

*Not least ironically, it was a French President, Pompidou's successor Valéry Giscard d'Estaing, who insisted on keeping the membership of these summits to the smallest number, preferably France, Britain, the Federal Republic, and the United States. Only over French resistance were invitations made to the other members: Japan, Italy, Canada, and a representative of the European Community.

XVII

The Geneva Conference

The Strategy

AT Geneva just before Christmas in 1973, Arabs and Israelis met to
negotiate face to face at a high political level for the first time
in a quarter of a century. Behind and beyond that conference
lay a complex diplomacy. The enthusiasm of the Israelis, who had long
demanded such a meeting, diminished directly in proportion to its imminence. But it was important for the conference to convene as rapidly
as possible to preserve the cease-fire, to symbolize trends toward making peace, and in particular to create a framework for the separation of
forces to which we had committed ourselves.

The original idea, which emerged late in the diplomacy that led to
the cease-fire, was for a conference of Arabs and Israelis under American and Soviet auspices to discuss a comprehensive peace settlement.
No doubt the Soviets sold the October cease-fire to their Arab clients
with the argument that US–Soviet "auspices" would provide the means
by which the Soviets could press the maximum Arab demands — in
other words, that it meant implementation of the comprehensive scheme
Brezhnev had tried to sell to Nixon in the study at San Clemente.

However, our step-by-step strategy prevailed because in the end all
sides — even radical Syria and the Soviet Union — each for its own
reasons agreed that the tangled military dispositions inherited from the
war were precarious, dangerous, and intolerable. But to get there we
had to reconcile vastly different national aims. The Geneva Conference
was a way to get all parties into harness for one symbolic act, thereby
to enable each to pursue a separate course, at least for a while. It was
as complicated to assemble the great meeting as it was to keep it quiescent afterward while diplomacy returned to bilateral channels.

Sadat had the clearest grasp of his objectives. He was determined to
reverse Egypt's alliance with the Soviet Union and establish a close
association with the United States. This was a delicate and risky maneuver; at any given intermediate point he ran the risk of being too far from
the Soviet Union to enjoy its diplomatic support yet not sufficiently
close to the United States for us to act as Egypt's advocate. He faced a

similar dilemma in his relations with his Arab brethren. Sadat could never reach his objective if he permitted Syria a veto over his policy; yet until his own peace process was well in train, Sadat needed the threat of renewed military action as a bargaining chip, a threat that had no credibility without his alliance with Syria. Suspended between the superpowers, wary of Syria yet dependent on it in a showdown, Sadat saw the Geneva Conference as a safety net, a forum to which he could appeal if all else failed.

Syria's ambivalence was exactly the opposite of Sadat's. The governing political party in Damascus — the radical Baath — had based its program on rejection of the State of Israel. But participating in a peace conference with Israel inevitably implied a degree of acceptance of the Jewish state — for with what other entity was one negotiating? — and therefore incurred domestic political cost without obvious compensating gain. Still, Syria could not function normally while Israeli forces were at the gates of Damascus. Thus Syria's President Hafez al-Asad was driven reluctantly toward a disengagement negotiation.

To Sadat, disengagement was the first step in what he suspected, given Syrian ambivalence, would have to be a separate Egyptian peace; Asad probably rationalized that it was the last phase prior to a renewed confrontation with Israel — at least on the diplomatic level.

Jordan's position was perhaps the most complex. Each Arab state proclaimed its devotion to the Palestinian cause, partly out of conviction, partly to curry favor with the radical trend in the area. Avowal of Palestinian goals was helpful even to states falling in with the step-by-step approach; the inevitable compromises could be presented as stages toward a solution of the Palestinian problem. Every Arab leader was in a position to play this game except our friend King Hussein. A Palestinian state could be formed only at the expense of Jordan's previous position in Palestine (Jordan had governed the West Bank from 1948 to 1967) and indeed its genesis would mark the opening of a struggle over the very existence of the Hashemite state *east* of the Jordan River. Leaders of the PLO had avowed frequently enough that the blood feud with Hussein was even deeper than that with Israel. And Hussein could count on little support from his fellow Arabs.

Jordan, moreover, was in no position to threaten resumption of military operations. But while Hussein had little direct stake in the disengagement schemes being discussed, he favored the Geneva Conference because his participation in it would aid *his* claim to speak for the Palestinians. And any disengagement accords that emerged could serve to establish a precedent for bringing Jordan back onto the West Bank. We wanted Hussein to attend the Geneva Conference for the same reasons.

Israel, too, had an interest in a Geneva Conference leading to step-by-step diplomacy. While it was willing enough to stay where it was for a while, it would need several divisions to hold the territory across the Suez Canal, preventing demobilization. And Israel would never recover its prisoners of war in Syria unless it evacuated the environs of Damascus.

As for the two superpowers, their perspectives differed according to their objectives. The Soviet Union was stymied by its basic dilemma as it had been throughout my period in office. So long as it would not separate itself from the comprehensive Arab program, it could not contribute to the diplomacy; the program was unrealizable even by American pressure. Moscow could not bring about Arab terms by supplying arms to its clients, as had been shown in the just-concluded war. Nor was it ready for a direct military confrontation, as had been demonstrated during the alert. Doomed to impotence by the ponderousness and clumsiness of its diplomacy, the Kremlin sought the Geneva Conference as a means to reduce our freedom of action, to receive joint credit for any progress by riding on our coattails, and, in the more likely eventuality of a deadlock, to shift the onus for it onto our shoulders.

Our position was as promising as it was complicated. We alone had a program that could be implemented. Egypt and ultimately Syria *insisted* on our participation. They valued (and probably exaggerated) our influence over Israel; it was also easier for them to accept American negotiating proposals than to meet Israeli demands. If by our step-by-step approach we achieved some significant breakthrough, radical rhetoric would perforce be muted; moderate Arab states would be encouraged to persevere; Soviet influence would wane. To bring about a negotiated withdrawal via a disengagement would not be irrelevant, as some of our allies claimed; it was the psychological prerequisite for more far-reaching steps. After all, it would represent the first time Israel had been induced by a negotiation to retire from territory it had occupied for any length of time.

The United States's policy therefore proceeded on several levels simultaneously. We helped to organize the Geneva Conference as a symbol of our commitment to overall peace, as a means of keeping in touch with the Soviet Union during the delicate phase while the cease-fire hung in the balance, and as a fallback position if alternative routes failed. Our task was eased because the Soviet Union after the October alert and the November six-point plan found itself powerless to effect the disengagement of forces demanded by both Cairo and Damascus. Moscow knew that Egypt, especially, could not permit its Third Army to remain cut off in the Sinai through the months and perhaps years of a conference on a comprehensive peace. To sabotage disengagement in the Sinai therefore would have had the practical consequence of producing either a war as the Third Army sought to break out or, more likely, an explicitly separate arrangement without even the cover of Geneva. Thus Moscow fell in with making disengagement the first phase of the Geneva Conference — and thus with a strategy designed to reduce its own influence.

The industrial democracies of Western Europe and Japan were reluctant spectators. They sought diplomatic progress in order to end the oil embargo and production cutbacks that threatened to wreck their economies. But they were decidedly unenthusiastic about the US–Soviet "auspices" for negotiations from which they were excluded, even though their own policies had contributed to this situation. They opposed the kind of agreement that was in prospect because they had consistently pressed for a comprehensive approach. Our allies were thus cool to the forum we had chosen and hostile to what we foresaw as the only realistic outcome — not a brilliant state of affairs.

By now we had left no doubt that, Watergate or not, we would resist Soviet, radical, and European pressures in the Middle East. I explained the strategy at an informal luncheon meeting with Jim Schlesinger, Bill Colby, Tom Moorer, and Ken Rush on November 29:

> Our strategy had to be that when the Soviet Union, the British and French press, we stall — so all of them know only we can deliver. That will help Sadat and the moderate Arabs. All the Arabs are coming to us. We will commence on the 16th. That is closer to the Israeli elections.* Then we have to move for a disengagement.

> Diplomacy depends above all on available assets. We had the stronger hand; we played it.

The Kilometer 101 Talks and the Beginning of Disengagement

WHILE our design was unfolding, we had somehow to cope with real life: An Egyptian army was cut off in the desert, its agony bound to increase with every passing week. Even if Sadat was content to wait for our strategy, some of his subordinates, anxious to loosen the Israeli noose around the Third Army, would be tempted to speed up the process without waiting for the complicated minuet leading to Geneva to be completed. Their vehicle was the Egyptian-Israeli military talks at Kilometer 101 on the Cairo-Suez road, where guidelines to implement the November six-point program were being worked out by General Aharon Yariv of Israel and General Abdel Ghany el-Gamasy of Egypt. At first, the meetings dealt primarily with such issues as exchange of prisoners, supplies to Suez and the Third Army, and the establishment

---

*We did not think Israel could make any concessions before its general elections scheduled for December 31. The Geneva Conference was first set for December 16, then December 18, and finally opened on December 21.

of checkpoints — in other words, the last four of the six points.* (The first exchange of Egyptian and Israeli prisoners took place on November 15.) The first two points — maintenance of the cease-fire, and especially the "question of the return to the October 22 positions in the framework of agreement on the disengagement and separation of forces under the auspices of the UN" — were still to be discussed. My understanding with Sadat had been that we would turn to disengagement only *after* the Geneva Conference was assembled.

But Sadat's subordinates were less patient. They wanted progress made toward disengagement *prior* to the Geneva Conference, either by negotiating a complete scheme or by forcing an immediate Israeli withdrawal to the October 22 line — wherever that might be. The adamant refusal to consider this was, of course, the stuff of the crisis of the previous months, including the alert.** In any event, Gamasy injected a certain dynamism into the Kilometer 101 talks by pushing along the discussion with Yariv faster than I had expected on the basis of my talks with Sadat.

There were also elements in Israel tempted by the idea of a rapid disengagement even before Geneva assembled. The Kilometer 101 talks were a means for Israel to free itself from American tutelage. They provided an opportunity to test whether Israel's favorite scheme of a mutual withdrawal from the Suez Canal was as much of a nonstarter as I had alleged. Nor was Golda reluctant to show her electorate as she was campaigning for reelection that *something* was going on at Kilometer 101. The problem was, however, that the Israeli government was not fully agreed as to exactly what should take place at Kilometer 101, nor as to what kind of disengagement to seek with Egypt. General Yariv, a former chief of intelligence and a brilliant strategist, proved most ingenious at developing alternative schemes for resettling Israeli, Egyptian, and UN troops at various lines in the Sinai. His creativity led to a flood of Israeli proposals tested on Gamasy and spelling out in increasing detail an Israeli military conception of disengagement. Gamasy compounded the confusion by matching Yariv's proposals with his counterproposals. Unfortunately, neither negotiator spoke fully for his government. Yariv's plans did not always have cabinet blessing and Sadat wanted to involve, not exclude, us. The talks moved to stalemate.

The whole process tested our patience. For one thing, we never knew exactly what was happening at Kilometer 101. We got different reports

---

*For the six points, see Chapter XIII, p. 641.
**The Israeli attitude was not without justification from a military point of view. Even the Egyptian War Minister, General Ahmed Ismail Ali, told an American diplomat in mid-November that withdrawal to the October 22 line would place the Israeli forces on the west bank of the Canal into a very constricted and vulnerable position; the only scheme that made any sense was a broader disengagement of the two forces.

from the Israelis, the Egyptians, and the UN as to what was going on in the tent where these extraordinary meetings were taking place. Their only common feature was being at least forty-eight hours behind events. Frequently we had three versions of a deadlock to choose from — often four. And deadlock over disengagement was the last thing we wanted, since the separation of forces in the Sinai was the centerpiece of our strategy. On the other hand, we were not, to be frank, too eager for a breakthrough at Kilometer 101 before the Geneva Conference. As I cautioned Ambassador Dinitz on December 3: "Suppose Yariv comes out a great hero on disengagement, what do you discuss on December 18 [at Geneva]?" Our strategy required first that we assemble the conference to defuse the situation and symbolize progress but then that we use its auspices to establish our central role. If disengagement disappeared from the agenda, we would be forced into endless skirmishing over broader issues on which I knew we would not be able to deliver quickly, if at all.

The real problem at Kilometer 101 was not likely to be breakthrough, however, but deadlock. For one thing, I was given strong reason to believe that Golda preferred to have matters not actually come to a head before the Israeli election (and therefore not before the Geneva Conference) and that her cabinet shared her view. For another, Egypt was not really ready either. To be sure, Yariv put forward several principles that were later incorporated in the disengagement scheme — zones of limited armaments on both sides with a UN presence in between. But his ideas as to what armaments these zones could contain were too restrictive to be accepted by even the most moderate Egyptian leader. In any event, it soon was evident that Sadat could not accept any limitation on his own forces on Egyptian soil if it was put forward by Israel. American mediation became essential. On November 29, Egypt solved the problem: It broke off the Kilometer 101 talks, allegedly because Yariv had suddenly begun backtracking, refusing to spell out in detail what force levels or depth of zones he had in mind. Disengagement would now have to be dealt with after Geneva was assembled — much as we had planned.

Throughout, Soviet conduct belied the theory that Moscow always operated on a master plan devised by strategists of diabolical insight. It was so obsessed with getting a piece of the action that it, too, preferred delaying disengagement to the Geneva Conference. On November 26, I told Soviet Ambassador Dobrynin to calm down his colleague in Cairo, Sergei Vinogradov, who was pushing Fahmy's line that some disengagement must precede the Geneva Conference. The next day Dobrynin replied that Vinogradov had only been repeating Egyptian complaints; he was not associating himself with them. On November 30 I discussed the collapse of the Kilometer 101 talks with Dobrynin as if our objectives were parallel instead of the prelude to encouraging Egypt to move away from Moscow. "I really think we are on a good course now," I said, with the road to our preferred strategy now open — though why I thought Dobrynin might share this judgment the record does not reveal and my recollection does not indicate. Dobrynin replied equably: "We may not like the situation, not withdrawing, but realistically we agree with you." I told Dobrynin that while I could not guarantee a specific date for the separation of forces, I could give early January as the starting date for a major American effort to bring it about: "It will be a matter of weeks after that."

Unable to avoid the temptation of scoring a petty point (even at the risk of undermining confidence), the egregious Vinogradov reported this schedule to Fahmy as if it had been exacted by Soviet diplomacy (and as if we were so amateurish as to give a schedule to Moscow that had not been discussed with Sadat). Vinogradov's ploy earned him only cynical comments from Fahmy.

The practical result of the exchanges with Dobrynin was to discourage the Soviets from joining Egyptian pressures for rapid progress on disengagement prior to the Geneva Conference, and thus to keep the pace of disengagement negotiations under our control. While many factors entered into Moscow's decision — including a miscalculation of its ability to increase its influence in the Middle East at Geneva — its restraint was seriously influenced by a desire to preserve the relationship with the United States. On November 10 Brezhnev had written to Nixon that "we want to be sure . . . we shall not only overcome the present Middle East crisis but we shall also move even further ahead in strengthening relations between our countries."

Soviet diplomacy — for all its tendency to grab for loose change — continued in that spirit throughout November, working with us on assembling the Geneva Conference and sidestepping Egyptian pressure for a prepayment. The Soviets may not have had brilliant options, but they pursued those that gave us the least trouble. Détente did not prevent us from seeking to reduce the Soviet role in the Middle East nor the Soviets from scoring points with the Arabs now and then. But fairness compels the recognition that Moscow never launched an all-out campaign against us. And we took pains not to humiliate the Soviet Union overtly even while weakening its influence. Détente is the mitigation of conflict among adversaries, not the cultivation of friendship.

Right after the breakup of the Kilometer 101 talks, Egyptian impatience seemed to mount. (I say "seemed to" because I am not sure it was not largely Fahmy's device to keep our feet to the fire.) Fahmy complained bitterly to Hermann Eilts, our new Ambassador to Egypt, about the lack of progress. According to Fahmy, even Sadat now insisted on some movement toward disengagement as a prerequisite to

Egyptian participation at Geneva. And there were hints that Egypt might ask the United States and the Soviet Union to break the impasse, or alternatively that Egypt might appeal to the UN Security Council. Eilts's reminder that Sadat and I had earlier agreed that disengagement should be the first agenda item of a peace conference brought a sharp retort from Fahmy that the peace conference could always take up a *second* phase of disengagement. But he must have understood the impossibility of this idea. Israel would never make two major withdrawals in the space of one month. And an Egyptian appeal to the Soviet and American governments to break the stalemate would have repeated the crisis of the previous month with the same inconclusive outcome.

What started as a Fahmy pressure play threatened, as so often in the Middle East, to turn into the real thing as the parties listened to their own rhetoric and liked what they heard. We began to receive reports that Egypt was considering resuming military action. Clearly, it was essential to restore some perspective. On December 1, we sent a firm letter from Nixon to Sadat in tandem with one from me to Fahmy warning against any Egyptian appeal to the superpowers:

[W]ith all due respect, asking the United States and the Soviet Union to come into the area to guarantee the implementation of the Security Council Resolution would be an ever more grave step, a step which would not serve either the interests of your country or of world peace generally.

Having made clear that we would resist Soviet pressure in December as we had in October, Nixon's letter reiterated what I also stressed to Fahmy — that a resumption of hostilities would destroy all the achievements of recent months: "A breakdown of the cease-fire would regrettably again force us into a situation of confrontation and that opportunity could be irretrievably destroyed."

Our warnings — which I suspect were not all that unwelcome to Sadat for use with his hotheads — were balanced by our optimistic description of the diplomatic prospects. The objective conditions for progress were better than ever, both letters stated. Nixon's committed the United States to a major effort once Geneva was assembled: "It is at the peace conference that the United States will be in a position to exercise our constructive influence towards peace based on Security Council Resolution 242." And to concert a common strategy, which had almost surely been the purpose of Egyptian complaints, Nixon volunteered me for another trip through the Middle East, which would bring me to Cairo on December 13.

In reply, there was some grumbling for the record by Sadat, some more volatile expressions of exasperation from Fahmy, and some back-and-forth on whether to resume the Kilometer 101 talks and under what conditions. But time worked in favor of what we were trying to achieve.

By bringing us closer to the target date of the conference (December 18) and to the Israeli elections (December 31), every exchange left less opportunity for further prolonged disputation. In the absence of other agreed-upon schemes, disengagement would have to be the first item on the agenda; the road to American mediation and the step-by-step approach was opening.

The Road to Geneva

THE prospect of a peace conference was forcing us to maneuver within a seeming contradiction. We strove to assemble a multilateral conference, but our purpose was to use it as a framework for an essentially bilateral diplomacy. Soviet cooperation was necessary to convene Geneva; afterward, we would seek to reduce its role to a minimum. The peace conference could soothe Moscow's nerves as a prelude to a phase that would no doubt test our relations.

I had seen Dobrynin in Washington on November 17, fresh from my November around-the-world trip. His masters could not have been ecstatic about my forays to Arab capitals, much less about the six-point agreement achieved without Soviet participation or even prior knowledge. Nor was my visit to Peking the sort of exercise that calmed tempers in the Kremlin. It seemed best to turn to less contentious matters. After chatting with Dobrynin briefly and unilluminatingly about my travels, I changed the subject. We were prepared to proceed to assemble the Geneva Conference, I said. I suggested a joint US–Soviet letter to the Secretary-General of the United Nations, who could then issue the formal invitations to the parties, which I listed as Egypt, Syria, Jordan, and Israel. (I made no reference to the Palestinians.) I told Dobrynin we would give him a draft of such a letter shortly for comment. In other words, let us not waste time on recriminations over the past but get on with the business at hand.

Nothing so warms the heart of a professional diplomat as the imminence of a major conference. It provides a testing ground for all the arcane knowledge acquired in a lifetime of study about procedures, about abstruse points of protocol, about "auspices" and "chairmanship." All these were involved in assembling Geneva.

Four days later, on November 21, I sent Dobrynin our draft letter to Waldheim; it stated simply that the United States and the Soviet Union, having canvassed the principal parties, requested the UN Secretary-General to invite Jordan, Israel, Egypt, and Syria to a conference in Geneva beginning on December 17 or 18. The conference would be under the "co-chairmanship" of the United States and the Soviet Union. The rest dealt with technical arrangements.

Moscow's sense of urgency was reflected in the speed of its reply, which arrived the very next day, an unprecedentedly rapid turnaround time. Dobrynin told me the proposed dates for Geneva were convenient; Foreign Minister Andrei Gromyko would be happy to attend. He would appreciate the maximum amount of time I could give to the conference. I promised two days and I offered to dine with Gromyko the evening before the conference opened.

One day later (November 23), Dobrynin handed me a redraft. It was highly revealing about Soviet suspicions that Geneva might prove still-born. It added a clause our draft had ignored: that the conference would take place under the "auspices" of the United States and the Soviet Union. It stressed that the conference, opened at the foreign minister level, should then be continued by "specially appointed representatives with the ambassadorial rank." The fact that the Soviet Union was so eager to have its special status at the conference certified and to have a commitment to some form of permanent machinery at a senior level reflected its fears — in fact quite justified — that we might seek to downgrade the conference. The trouble from Moscow's point of view was that if all the other parties agreed with what it suspected was our strategy, no procedural gimmick could prevent our implementing it. The rank of the plenipotentiaries would be nearly irrelevant if the focus of diplomacy shifted into bilateral forums. Gromyko had analyzed his problem correctly; his difficulty was that there was no solution to it.

At the same time, the eagerness of the Soviets to convene the conference was reflected in the fact that Gromyko's redraft fell in with our omission of any explicit mention of the Palestinians. (It confined the invitation to Syria, Egypt, Jordan, and Israel "without prejudice to possible additional participants at a subsequent stage.")

In the midst of these efforts to assemble a conference, one of whose principal subjects would be just how much territory Israel would relinquish, the Arab leaders felt the need for a summit meeting. In the past they had been able to reconcile their diverse points of view only by an exalted rhetoric certain to inflame passions; the Algiers summit proved no exception. The Arab foreign ministers met on November 24; the heads of government assembled from November 26 to November 28. The purposes were as varied and contradictory as the exuberant personalities that composed the conference. The two extremes of the Arab spectrum — Libya and Iraq on the radical side, Jordan on the moderate side — essentially boycotted the meeting, the radicals because they objected to any peace process, King Hussein for various reasons, among them that he feared (correctly) resolutions weighted in favor of the PLO. Egypt attended because it wanted retroactive Arab approval for its policy since the cease-fire; it was not yet sure enough of the new American connection or sufficiently confident of the peace process to go it alone. Syria sought an expression of Arab solidarity to curb Egyptian temptations for a separate peace. Saudi Arabia worked for a consensus that would avoid the need to choose between radicals and moderates. The remainder were torn between the counsels of prudence, which were on the side of Sadat, and the compulsion for the flamboyant rhetoric of Arab unity, which tilted this, like all other Arab summit meetings, in the direction of militance.

The outcome was that everyone gained a little of what he wanted. Egypt obtained conditional approval for acts already accomplished. There was at least a tepid endorsement of the peace process. But the program for it was no different from what had produced a stalemate for six years: immediate Israeli evacuation of all occupied Arab territories, including Jerusalem, and "the reestablishment of the full national rights for the Palestinian people."[1] The first condition carefully did not define "occupied Arab territories," but since PLO leader Yasir Arafat attended and approved, the reason may have been to leave open the possibility of going even beyond the standard insistence on the 1967 borders to more far-reaching demands such as the UN partition plan of 1947. What the gathering understood by "the full national rights" of the Palestinians .was no more spelled out; that they would not be satisfied by Jordanian rule on the West Bank was underlined by the summit's recognition of the PLO as the "sole" representative of the Palestinians.

The impact of the summit was to sour the attitudes of Israel and Jordan — targets of the Algiers meeting — toward the Geneva Conference. On December 1, Ambassador Dean Brown was told by Jordanian Prime Minister Zaid Rifai that the Algiers resolutions amounted to asking Jordan to try to negotiate with Israel for the return of the West Bank and Arab Jerusalem, assume responsibility (and eventually all the blame) for whatever territorial concessions might be necessary, and then turn over what had been achieved to the PLO. Jordan would not play such a role. However, Rifai reiterated that Jordan was willing "in principle" to attend Geneva; it took seriously our argument that if it did not appear it would risk playing into the hands of its opponents by seeming to abandon its claim to the West Bank.

Getting Israel's agreement to go to Geneva was also made more difficult. Israel was determined to resist the demands that Algiers espoused. The Algiers summit therefore injected new tensions into a diplomacy that soon found all the parties quibbling over the draft letter of invitation. Israel demanded an explicit provision in the invitation stating that the original composition of the conference could not be expanded except by unanimity — so that the PLO would be formally barred and its later participation subject to an Israeli veto. Israel was also highly suspicious of the United Nations and did not want anything more than a ceremonial UN role. Meanwhile, after Algiers, Egypt's Fahmy predictably went in the opposite direction, insisting on explicit reference in the letter to Palestinian participation at a later stage of the conference. He proposed the formula that "the *timing* of the participation of the Palestinians" would be discussed during the first stage of the conference — which implied, of course, that the *fact* of Palestinian participation was already settled. While he was at it, Fahmy also subjected our draft letter to other criticism. He wanted to dilute Soviet influence; hence he objected to Soviet-American "auspices" and wanted a greater UN role. Syria enveloped itself in silence.

However hairsplitting these objections, each had to be conveyed to the other parties; every proposed compromise formulation had to be marketed around the entire circuit. The conference was threatening to drown in paper. The problem was all the greater for me because I left on Saturday, December 8, for a NATO meeting in Brussels, to be followed by my excursion through the Middle East, so that after being received in Washington each revision had to be retransmitted to me wherever I was and then my reaction had to go via Washington to all the parties. The overworked communicators on my airplane performed heroically.

On December 5, we came up with a new version of the letter of invitation that attempted to enable each participant to claim that some of its views had been incorporated. By the same token, of course, each side could complain that it had not achieved all of its ends. The record shows that they were more assiduous in voicing their complaints than their satisfaction.

Our draft finessed the issue of UN auspices by language that could be interpreted as confining the United Nations to convening the conference, not running it; the Secretary-General's participation was expressly limited to the opening phase. As for the Palestinians, we put forward the formulation that "the question" (not "the timing") of their participation would be discussed during the first stage of the conference — implying that the issue was unresolved. To us it seemed not much of a concession, for it permitted only what each participant had the right to raise in any event: whether additional parties should join the conference. But it proved far too much for Golda, who resisted any reference to Palestinians no matter how hedged and qualified.

Then the fun started. The Soviet Union insisted on US–Soviet auspices; Egypt was equally adamant on UN auspices. The Soviet Union and Egypt maintained that the earlier phrase about "timing" of Palestinian participation was sacrosanct. Lest we become overconfident, Israel rejected UN auspices and added a new condition that even if the final text proved acceptable, it would not meet with the Syrians until they released all Israeli prisoners of war. And the proposed opening of the conference was only eleven days away.

A blizzard of telegrams from me resulted. By December 11, all the parties but one had backed off and informally accepted our December 5 draft. Israel, moving closer to elections, remained adamant. As Dayan had told me on a flying visit to Washington on December 7, "Golda cannot go into elections if there is any doubt about the Palestinians going to the conference."

But beyond the electoral situation, Golda Meir in her elemental way had hold of a crucial point that in the passion of the moment had not been so self-evident. Our reference to Palestinians was innocuous enough, but the Arab insistence on referring to them hid a substantive, not a procedural, intent; it singled out one agenda item for special attention in a letter of invitation. For Golda therefore the issue was psychological, not technical; she knew that the peace conference was bound to escalate procedure into hateful and terrifying substance.

Once dug in, Golda was not to be budged. She remained unmoved even by a direct intervention from Nixon. On December 13 the President learned from his morning briefing of the negative attitude of the Israeli government. He appended the following note: "K, tell Eban et al. — if this demand on their part brings another war, they go it alone." In my absence, Brent Scowcroft passed Nixon's message to Dinitz — I suspect in slightly attenuated form. When he roused from the torpor of Watergate, Nixon's combative instincts would come to the fore. He sent a personal letter to Golda, which concluded with the ominous warning of withdrawing American backing:

I want to say to you in all solemnity that if Israel now fails to take a favorable decision to participate in the conference on the basis of the letter that we have worked out, this will not be understood either in the United States or in the world and I will not be able to justify the support which I have consistently rendered in our mutual interests to your government.

Following her usual tactic, Golda ignored Nixon's letter, saying she would reply personally to me in Jerusalem (she never did). As for Scowcroft, he was given the simple comment that the Prime Minister was not persuaded.

On December 13, I was heading from Europe to the Middle East. The opening of the Geneva Conference was set for five days away and there was still no agreement on the language of the invitation.

Algiers

EVERY trip to the Middle East required its own choreography. We were operating simultaneously in three dimensions: the US–Soviet relationship, the struggle for influence between Arab moderates and radicals, and the Arab–Israeli crisis. These were partly overlapping, partly autonomous. Every venture into the Middle East thus had the attributes of a three-ring circus, the principal difference being that as one entered one ring the actors in the other two would stop whatever they were doing and adjust their own actions in the light of what they saw or — more disconcertingly — what they thought they saw.

Experience had taught me that despite the oft-proclaimed Arab solidarity, the intensive inter-Arab rivalries and jealousies were an imponderable element, all the harder to predict because most of them were intensely personal. For example, as I have mentioned, my dinner remark to King Faisal in Riyadh about Sadat's leadership of the Arab world had met with an unenthusiastic reaction (see Chapter XIII). Later I was to hear through other Arab sources that Saudi Arabia was quite sensitive on this point. We were advised not to take it for granted that King Faisal would fall into line with whatever Sadat had agreed; Saudi Arabia would insist on its own views.

I had also found that news traveled with wondrous rapidity through the Arab world, somewhat skewed at each stop, but in its total impact presenting an account that was on the mark psychologically if not factually. And since most political calculations occur in the minds of men, the psychological element is often decisive. The extraordinary volubility of Arab leaders is a device by which they fine-tune their actions and establish the moral terrain. Since key leaders rely on the rumor mill, often giving it more credence than direct reports, it is usually the better part of wisdom to prepare the ground by making sure that some other Arab leader has been exposed to one's arguments. Even if they discount part of what their brother Arab tells them — an almost obligatory test of manhood — they are apt to credit secondhand information as a tribute to their status as insiders and to believe that it gives them an edge over their rivals. One must take care, however, to reserve some important piece of information for one's principal interlocutor. Much as he appreciates indirection, he prizes exclusivity even more.

One aim of the Geneva Conference was to prevent the peace process from becoming engulfed in the polarization between radicals and moderates in the Arab world. From this point of view, Damascus was to be the crucial stop on this my second journey to the Middle East, as Cairo had been on the first. If Syria participated or even acquiesced in the Geneva Conference — and as yet we had heard not a word from it directly — and agreed to disengagement as the first agenda item, our basic strategy would be safe. Otherwise there would be a bitter struggle at each stage. There was reason for hope. Ever since the end of the war, Syria had been edging toward contact with the United States. I had had a meeting in Washington on November 2 with Syrian Deputy Foreign Minister Mohammad Zakariya Ismail, who was in America to attend the UN General Assembly. He had no instructions of any sort; the fact of a first visit to Washington in many years by a relatively senior Syrian official seemed to be as much as the Damascus political situation could take. In Saudi Arabia on November 8 I had been told that Syria's President Hafez al-Asad wanted direct talks with us. Thereafter, I met on November 21 with Syria's UN representative Haytham Kaylani, as a prelude to my visit to Damascus scheduled for December 15.

No leader was better suited to prepare the ground in Damascus than President Houari Boumedienne of Algeria, fiercely independent and a radical with special ties to Syria. During the October war he had paid a flying visit to Moscow to request Soviet military support for the Arab cause. According to Cairo scuttlebutt, he had returned disillusioned. I did not expect Boumedienne publicly to support an American diplomacy; for that he had given too many hostages to ideology. But if he spoke favorably of it in private to Syria, or even if he refrained from opposing it, Asad would have a pretext for cooperation and radical pressures on Saudi Arabia would be eased.

We landed in Algiers on Thursday, December 13, in a steady drizzle that accentuated the aloof welcome. The voluble Abdelaziz Bouteflika, who had been one of the delegation of Arab foreign ministers that had called on Nixon and me during the war (see Chapter XI), could not quite bring himself to match the austere bearing of his associates. Young, vital, fashionably dressed, usually wearing a grand flowing cape and puffing a huge cigar, Bouteflika had no intention of wasting a free opportunity to get on television. Greeting me, he spoke more warmly of my visit than the official line as yet indicated.

As we sped off to Boumedienne's residence in the hills overlooking the Mediterranean, I found myself reflecting on a meeting I had had twenty years earlier with the great French writer Albert Camus in his small office at the Gallimard publishing house in Paris. I was a graduate student and editor of a small journal called *Confluence,* which presented European and American writers on various topics in the hope of encouraging Atlantic understanding. We had reprinted an article by Camus, and I called on him to pay my respects. He showed no surprise at my youth (I was then thirty); nor did he indicate that my quarterly was probably the least significant publication in which his writings had appeared. Unexpectedly — almost as if he were talking to himself and I was simply a convenient pretext for his reflections — Camus started to speak about Algeria, his place of birth, then a French province. He spoke gently of Algeria's embodiment of conciliation and understanding, a product of its Mediterranean sun, stern traditions, and benevolent commingling of different cultures. Here, if anywhere, mankind might aspire to an ideal of brotherhood. Yet Camus already feared for his homeland's future. He hoped that nationalism would not destroy its civilizing mission. He could not bear the thought that the passions of our age might engulf Algeria and separate him from it; its quest for identity should never take the form of separation from France. Much of it was inexplicable to me then, for the rumblings of the Algerian revolution were only beginning. Now, as I traveled to meet the victorious leader of Algerian nationalism, the French had been gone for over a decade. Whatever else could be said for modern Algeria, conciliation, brotherhood, and understanding among different peoples did not seem likely to mark its contribution to history. The product of a bitter war, it had carried over into diplomacy the uncompromising philosophy that had achieved its cohesion and the Marxist rhetoric that enabled its leaders to maintain control without the inconvenience of periodic elections.

When we arrived at Boumedienne's residence, a wing of the palace of the former French Governor General, a colorful guard of honor was at attention in the courtyard. The meeting room was long and cavernous. At the far end, ramrod-straight, stood Boumedienne, wearing a heavy black cape and holding in his hand a cigar. It seemed to be the Algerian uniform. Later on, I learned that Boumedienne tended to time meetings by the number of cigars he consumed: There were one- or two- or, rarely, three-cigar meetings. Not knowing this detail, I did not count the number of cigars I was allotted; at any rate, Boumedienne seemed to have plenty of time.

Almost at once, Boumedienne made a point of telling me his cigar was Cuban. He had the ascetic face and the piercing eyes of a fanatic, but his manner was elegant and his tone courteous. He acted like a man who would not be satisfied with having been the military leader of a cruel struggle for independence. Like many self-taught military men, Boumedienne did not prize the martial art as much as another field less familiar to him and therefore endowed with mystery: that of political philosophy. He was of the generation to which the pop liturgy of Third World rhetoric had become second nature. America was "imperialistic"; Marxism was "progressive"; the Third World was "exploited" and inherently "peace-loving." Like Camus he would insist on the universal significance of Algeria's actions. But unlike the gentle Frenchman he sought Algeria's vindication not in values of conciliation but in puritanical revolutionary insistence; in strident confrontation, not in becoming part of a universal culture he despised. And so the conversation between the President of revolutionary Algeria and the Secretary of State of capitalist America concerned mostly our conflicting philosophies of international relations, as if two professors of political science were debating the nature of their discipline.

Boumedienne began with a courtesy that was at once a reassurance: "It is good to have you in the Middle East." If radical Algeria welcomed my efforts, our strategy was halfway toward its goal. Boumedienne may have sensed that he had gone a shade too far, so he added a warning: "It is a region of passion. Great problems and great passions." Without giving me a chance to comment, Boumedienne went straight to his main point in what he called "the Algerian style of action":

> In recent years, you made a great overture to China, and you made a great initiative on your trip to the Soviet Union. You made a settlement in Indochina. The question is posed, is this a reconversion of the policy of the United States? Is the world still divided into two or three camps?
>
> I am an Arab of the generation that has been subject to two kinds of humiliations: The humiliation of colonialism, British or French, and the colonialism that one calls Israel — a country of 3 million that because of a certain massive support is the gendarme of the region. . . .
>
> In this context, objectively, there are three possibilities: An Arab peace, even one negotiated with Israel. Me, I negotiated with France. But that cannot be done by force. That's our great desire. Given that the world is as it is, and given that the United States and Russia exist, the other possibility is a Russian-American peace. It is they who arranged the cease-fire. It is the United States which plays the primary role in this negotiation.
>
> I cannot be convinced that if it is an American peace it can be just. On one side [of the ledger] is the Vietnam peace, but also there is Israel. On one side was Pakistan, but on the other side was Chile.*

The logic of this presentation was a quest for reassurance. Boumedienne indicated a willingness to negotiate "even" with Israel — a major change for an Arab leader priding himself on his radicalism. And he emphasized the central role of the United States. What he wanted was some intellectual solace that America, the Marxist bugbear of his political schooling, would not live up to his own estimate of it. He respected the America that had opened to China and negotiated with Hanoi and stood by its friends in Pakistan. But he was less enchanted by other steps we had taken in defense of our interests and values. He seemed to want to pick and choose; even more, to convert us to his brand of radical socialism. Failing that, he wanted to convince himself that it was possible to trust us — though why in the light of his own Marxist beliefs about materialism and capitalism my protestations should be persuasive, he left unexplained.

Of the three possibilities he had presented, Boumedienne seemed *least* desirous of a US–Soviet arrangement over the Middle East; his distrust of the Soviet Union despite his own Marxist proclivities became evident in a brief exchange:

BOUMEDIENNE: Do you think the Soviet Union would fight for the Arabs?
KISSINGER: No.
BOUMEDIENNE: I don't think so.

---

*It was interesting that Boumedienne considered our tilt toward Pakistan in 1971 as "progressive."

Boumedienne having set the tone, there was no point wasting time in briefing him on the arcane subtleties of our draft letter of invitation to the Geneva Conference. His confidence would not be won by our demonstrating skill in ambiguous formulation; whatever understanding was possible depended on Boumedienne's comprehension, if not acceptance, of our purposes. The prerequisite for dealing with erstwhile or potential adversaries — as Algeria certainly had been and might well become again — is to establish philosophical premises that can sustain the inevitable wear and tear imposed by practical necessities. So I spent most of the meeting outlining the concepts underlying our policy, particularly seeking to counter Boumedienne's obsession with the danger of superpower domination. I explained:

[O]ur fundamental view of international affairs . . . is that an attempt at physical dominance is incompatible with the objective tendencies and conditions of this period. Therefore, what we have attempted to do is encourage tendencies towards true independence, and to disengage America from — I don't like the word "imperialism" — but from the objective necessity of making decisions for every part of the world. Therefore, we welcome European unity and don't resist it, and we don't object if it occasionally attacks us. Because if it has a real spirit of independence, sooner or later it will defend itself against its real dangers. It needs the support of its people if it is to do this.

We don't do this out of charity but because any other course would exhaust us physically and psychologically.

Therefore Algeria's relations with America, I argued, should not be determined by fashionable slogans like imperialism or colonialism. Instead, the test should be our ability to harmonize clearly understood national interests:

Our objective is to deal with the truly independent Arab states. If in your foreign policy you do things of which we violently disapprove, we will react. If we do things of which you violently disapprove, you will react, as we see often in the United Nations. But if this relationship isn't frozen in permanent hostility, we can live with it. And I told your Foreign Minister in Washington during the war that as soon as the war was over we would make a major effort. And I told him in the presence of more conservative Foreign Ministers of our respect for the revolutionary aspects of Algeria.

So what we seek in this is not an American solution but the possibility for Arab nations to free themselves of their obsession with Israel, and let the natural tendencies of the Arab world assert themselves.

Boumedienne would not abandon his stereotype of superpower perfidy this easily. If there was to be no Soviet-American condominium, there had to be rivalry, and in that case he wanted to know where I proposed to draw the line between the two spheres and what we would do to win over the "gray areas" — simultaneously fearing great-power competition and testing the opportunities for maneuver that it afforded to smaller countries. This allowed me another sally at condominium: "We recognize no Soviet sphere and do not want an American sphere." Our rivalry with the Soviet Union would not be at the Middle East's expense. At the same time I did not want to encourage the idea that small countries could play us off against each other: "Mr. President, serious people cannot be won. We are not going to win you. . . . You will act on your interests. So there will never be permanent victories. The question for us is whether your views and our views can be parallel."

Like many leaders of nonaligned nations, Boumedienne was ambivalent about superpower competition. He professed to dislike being its object; he did not mind exploring whether it lent itself to being a bazaar. He clearly did not like the Soviets. He did not object when I said: "But there is an important question of principle for us, which you must understand. If the Soviet Union in Geneva makes a very dramatic gesture, we will resist. We cannot be pressured."

When we discussed Middle East diplomacy concretely, Boumedienne turned out to be eminently practical. Fresh from the Arab summit held in his own capital, Boumedienne accepted the proposition that in its first phase the Geneva Conference should concentrate on disengagement. This had to mean that Asad had endorsed it or had even asked him to raise it; Boumedienne would never have expressed himself on so sensitive an issue on his own — a conclusion immediately confirmed when he added that he wanted to be certain Syria was not excluded from our diplomacy. I reassured him on that score. I told him that the Arab world was too complicated for me to invent a different story for each stop; he was free to report to Damascus what I had said to him — not much of a concession, since a main reason for seeing him was to get advance word of my attitude to Syria (another was, of course, to learn as much as possible of Asad's thinking before I got to Syria). In any event, Boumedienne was certain to communicate with Asad, whatever my preference. I told him that the same principles of disengagement would be applied on the Golan Heights as in the Sinai. But I rejected the suggestion that we complete the Sinai phase before the opening of the Geneva Conference, especially as this would (he said) ease our oil problem.

I replied sharply to the last point. Oil was a question of principle for us. We could not accept being threatened by those who were at the same time asking for our help. We could not promise the unfulfillable; we would stick to the schedule I had outlined to Sadat at our first meeting: We would adjourn the Geneva Conference after the first session and resume it around January 10. After that we would make a major effort to complete a Sinai disengagement. We would next turn to a Syrian disengagement, probably in February — but only if the embargo was lifted in the meantime.

In line with my strategy of emphasizing the attainable, I avoided a question on the 1967 borders. And with reference to the expected controversies over the letter of invitation, I warned that raising the Palesti:. ian issue at this time would destroy all chances for progress. Boumedienne did not insist, perhaps salving his conscience with the knowledge of General Walters's Rabat meeting with the PLO, on which he had been briefed.

We ended the meeting on a cordial note. Boumedienne agreed in principle that Washington and Algiers would reestablish diplomatic relations, although he thought the present moment premature; the heads of our respective Interests Sections in Algiers and Washington would, however, be immediately raised in rank. It was much the same formula worked out with Egypt four weeks earlier. We decided to characterize the two hours of conversations with the phrases "frank" (meaning we had disagreements) but "very constructive" (meaning that a large area of common view emerged and a good atmosphere had been created).

At the airport, Bouteflika proclaimed to the assembled journalists that my visit had marked a turning point in Algerian-American relations and that Algeria supported the American peacemaking efforts in the Middle East. It meant that Algeria would be helpful in Damascus and not obstructive about the Geneva Conference.

The amity of Algiers was limited: it amounted to tactical cooperation for a brief period and thereafter a tacit understanding not to exacerbate the inevitable differences in our approaches to world affairs. However, during the most fragile beginning phase of our Mideast diplomacy we enjoyed a degree of Algerian support that, given Algeria's revolutionary stature in the Third World, was a not insignificant factor in enabling us to move matters forward.

Cairo Again

I ARRIVED at Cairo airport Thursday evening, December 13, from Algiers. It was still blacked out; the front line was after all only some fifty miles distant. Foreign Minister Fahmy was at the airport, grumpily affectionate as always, masking his skillful and constructive conduct over the previous two weeks in belligerent noises about the limits of Egyptian endurance. I had not yet learned of Golda's rejection of the draft invitation to Geneva. I was pleased that Egypt had accepted our language on the Palestinians (that is, "the question of . . ."). Fahmy had also cleared our draft as a combined "Syrian-Egyptian" position at a joint meeting with the American and Soviet ambassadors. Transmitting our own proposal as an Egyptian demand reduced the temptation for Soviet second thoughts. Clearing it in advance with Syria prevented Soviet or radical attempts to keep raising the ante.

But there were also signs that Egypt's flexibility had its limits. The very day of my arrival the leading Cairo daily, *Al-Ahram,* had warned that the lifting of the oil embargo depended on Israeli withdrawals from Arab territory. And it added: "The solution does not lie in clever diplomatic formulas couched in double meanings which each party can interpret in its own way to suit its purposes." As a reference to our efforts to assemble the Geneva Conference, that was only too true, but if it was aimed at the substance of our Mideast diplomacy it quite missed the point. "It would be stupid Machiavellianism to tell different stories to different parties," I told the reporters on my plane.[2] I hoped they would carry the message to their Egyptian colleagues.

Fahmy and I drove in Nasser's old Mercedes straight to the Barrages, another of Sadat's residences. Once again, Sadat, if anyone, would determine whether the peace process would go forward at the conference — now only five days away — or whether we were going to waste our capital in an endless debate over draft invitations and clever formulas that should never have been raised in the first place. The debate over the letter of invitation could produce only deadlock, not progress. However the letter was phrased, it could not substitute for the actual negotiations. The deadlock had to be broken once and for all or our diplomacy would move from the stylized to the explosive.

How the Geneva Conference was organized was no small matter. Just as in chess, the formal opening moves could determine the outcome. I was anxious to split the conference into subgroups — Egyptian-Israeli, Syrian-Israeli, and Jordanian-Israeli — which would make it impossible for the Soviet Union to use radical Arabs as pawns to block progress at the plenary sessions. The Soviets had swiftly agreed to the subgroups, however, probably because of the eagerness of Egypt and Syria for disengagement. But Moscow had postponed to Geneva itself acquiescence in my follow-up proposal that Soviet and American representatives not participate in the subgroups, where the real work would be done, except at the invitation of the parties. I wanted to promote direct negotiations and retain flexibility to move rapidly behind the scenes without a Soviet veto. If Sadat went along with our preference, there would be little the Soviet Union could do to block it.

The Barrages is an elegant building north of Cairo built for the use of British engineers in the last century. It is located in a verdant part of the Nile valley in the midst of spacious gardens near a canal that has been used for irrigation since time immemorial. We drove through a beautiful garden of jasmine shrubs and banyan trees to a graceful flight of stairs leading to a large villa. To the left of the entrance was a large reception room where Sadat was waiting, wearing a military uniform.

When the press and the security men had left, Sadat began the conversation, seated on a low sofa along the far wall, and then continued at dinner when a table was wheeled in. Without referring to the perplexities of Geneva, he outlined his view of the future. He profoundly distrusted the Soviet Union, he said. On each visit to Moscow he had been humiliated by Soviet crudeness and condescension. The Soviets had only wanted to use Egypt for their own selfish designs. They had broken Nasser's heart in the literal sense of the word; he had returned from his last visit to Moscow a few weeks before his death determined to cut loose from an embrace that threatened to suffocate. Now that he had restored Egyptian self-respect, Sadat intended to carry out this aim. He would gradually eliminate the last vestiges of the Soviet presence: the four MiG-25 Foxbat supersonic jets flying reconnaissance missions from Cairo West airport and the Soviet naval squadron in Alexandria would be sent home. He would let the Soviet-Egyptian Friendship Treaty slide into desuetude or cancel it —he had not yet decided which. But he could not do any of this until the peace process was further advanced. He candidly avowed his dependence on Soviet military supplies. He would prefer to shift to American weapons, but he saw no immediate prospect. Nor could he totally abandon Soviet diplomatic support before he could point to a concrete achievement of another course. And if a negotiating deadlock developed, he would again be driven to war. But he was now looking to the United States: "You hold all the cards here," he said, using what soon became a standard slogan.

It was, to say the least, an unusual presentation. The normal procedure is straight blackmail — to threaten to strengthen ties with one's adversary unless there is progress in the desired direction. Sadat was making no threats, even implied ones. He clearly wanted to free himself of his Soviet connection. All we had to do to induce him to cut his ties to our principal adversary was to proceed on a course on which we had already decided for our own reasons. As often with Sadat, shrewdness masqueraded as naiveté. He had concluded that reliance on the Soviets guaranteed stalemate. He therefore saw no sense in threatening us with what thwarted his own designs. Better to offer the inevitable as a concession, establish a claim for reciprocity, and above all lay the basis for the mutual confidence that was the key to his strategy.

Sadat added that I had been right four weeks earlier in stressing that peace was primarily a psychological problem, but the barriers were not only on the Israeli side. The Arabs were proud; they had been humiliated. They had difficulty knowing how to go from the impasse in which they found themselves to the peace that most of them wanted. He, Sadat, would try to chart a course — if necessary alone, but he hoped not so far ahead of his brothers that they would not follow ultimately. But Israel had to give him some help. I could tell Golda Meir that he genuinely wanted peace but not at the price of "my" territory. He asked whether I thought Golda was strong enough to make peace — a good question, since he knew peace would not be made by an affable Israeli leader but by a strong one. I said that if strength was the prime requirement, Golda was his man.

Of course, none of these philosophical musings advanced a solution to the immediate problem, characterized by the irony that a draft letter of invitation threatened the convening of the conference to which everyone had agreed. Solving *this* conundrum Sadat generously left to me.

By now I was convinced that arguing about the text of the draft letter was an assignment for a theologian, not a diplomat. We would never get an agreement by an exegesis of its clauses. My major contribution would be to clarify first principles. With all respect, I said, I did not think there was a realistic military option. If the war started again — as Sadat had hinted — the objective circumstance of October would repeat itself. The Egyptian army would still be equipped with Soviet weapons, still dependent on Soviet resupply; he would be driven back to the Soviet Union. We would retain our geopolitical interest in demonstrating that the issue could not be settled by Soviet arms. The result would be another stalemate, at a higher level of violence, and the same dilemmas that were being faced now. Only then he would be a prisoner of Moscow unable to shift back to us.

As for the letter of invitation, I argued, it was essential to break out of the irrelevancies by which each party was trying to use the drafting exercise to foreordain the outcome before the conference was even assembled. Peace in the Middle East would not emerge from dependent clauses. Perhaps we should scrap the long draft letter in favor of a simple one-paragraph invitation, and let the conference settle all the procedural nitpicks. If we were serious about disengagement first on the Egyptian and then on the Syrian front, the prime task was to assemble Geneva, using whatever letter was easiest, break up into subgroups as rapidly as possible (preferably without Soviet participation), and get on with the serious negotiation. Any reference to the Palestinians was bound to touch an Israeli raw nerve. It was too much to ask Israel to face the issue in this manner immediately prior to an election and after a war that overturned so many of the premises of its previous policy. A short letter of invitation could skirt the whole dilemma.

Sadat listened in his characteristic pose with slightly narrowed eyes. And he reacted as he had a month earlier. Without argument he accepted the main lines of my presentation. Egypt would attend Geneva, he said, even if Syria stayed away. It could not be beyond the wit of man to draft a letter that met everyone's needs. He would go along with a short letter of invitation, though it might delay matters because a totally new draft ran the risk of starting the whole clearance process over again. I used this opening to offer yet another compromise watering down the language on Palestinians. If we stayed with the long letter, I told Sadat, it might be best if we agreed on a neutral formulation about other participants that made no explicit reference to the Palestinians at all — such as that "the question of *additional participants*" would be discussed during the first stage of the conference. The Arabs could say that they would urge Palestinian participation at that point; Israel could say it would refuse — but all this would happen after the conference had opened and the issue would never be settled unless it did.

Sadat said he would make his decision about this formula after my visit to Damascus; he left little doubt that it would almost certainly be favorable. To ease Israeli anxieties he offered a more fundamental assurance to Israel. Regardless of the phraseology of the letter, he would not raise the issue of the Palestinians during the disengagement part of the negotiations — in other words, not for many months.

As for my procedural concerns, Sadat agreed that the conference should split up as rapidly as possible into subgroups — it was, in fact, the only way there could be a rapid Sinai disengagement since Syria would surely block a separate move in plenary sessions. For a similar reason — this time to prevent a Soviet veto — he went along with the proposition that the Soviet Union and the United States should not participate in the subgroups. But he had two caveats: The United States had to remain active in the negotiations; as a token he wanted me to return to the Middle East in early January to work with him on the principles of a disengagement plan so that when the Geneva Conference resumed on January 10 (as planned) it would not degenerate into a stalemate.

It was now after midnight. Sadat suggested that we reserve a detailed discussion of disengagement for the next morning. But the day that had begun in Brussels and taken me from Algiers to Cairo was not over. I left Sadat to meet in Cairo with Soviet Ambassador Vinogradov at 1:30 A.M. I briefed him on the contingency plan for a very short letter of invitation. Without instructions he could do no more than report to Moscow.

All this while, I was constantly reminded of Watergate and the fragility of our domestic base. By his previous evasions, Nixon had lost the power to dominate events. He had become a prisoner of his versions of what had transpired in Watergate and — I remained convinced — of his very real ignorance of what was actually on the tape recordings. He was caught up in December with the furor over an eighteen-and-a-half-minute gap discovered on one of the tapes and over media accusations of irregularities in his income tax returns.

Nixon would have been superhuman if he had always been able to contain his resentment over his Secretary of State's being praised for a foreign policy that his own steadfastness had sustained. This was particularly the case whenever some dramatic event generated publicity — the lifeblood of politicians. His pent-up frustration would then burst forth. I fear my reaction to it is more understanding in retrospect than it was at the time.

The truth was, as usual, complex. Nixon clearly did not receive the credit that was his due. The attention paid to the exploits of his subordinate was in part disproportionate, but my notoriety reflected Nixon's dilemma; it did not cause it. Once Watergate had gone beyond a certain point — at the latest after the discovery of the tapes — it had its own momentum.

But the same tenacity that made Nixon persist through his travail made it hard for him to abandon the hope that some spectacular achievement might magically end the ordeal. Thus the extensive media coverage of my December 12 speech to the Society of Pilgrims in London inflamed him (see Chapter XVI). I had told Nixon about the planned speech on several occasions. I had cleared the text with the key agencies; General Scowcroft had given him a draft. I do not know whether Nixon read it; it would have been unlikely, given his preoccupations. His objection in any event was not to the substance but to the unexpected publicity — especially as it concerned energy, where he harbored the hope of being able to emerge with some spectacular breakthrough.

Thus, on December 13, when I arrived in the Middle East, Nixon retaliated by suddenly calling in Soviet Ambassador Dobrynin for a private meeting — an extraordinary event. Scowcroft sent me this news:

> The President a few minutes ago directed that Ambassador Dobrynin come in to meet with him — alone. He indicated in general that he wished to talk about the Middle East but was not more specific than that. Dobrynin came in, met with the President for about 30 minutes, and has just left. I asked Dobrynin how the meeting went and he said it went very well — one of the most satisfactory meetings he has ever had with the President.
>
> This is obviously a response to the Pilgrim Speech. I will see if Haig can find out what was discussed and will, of course, pass it immediately to you. While I know this is an upsetting development, it could have been worse.

The last sentence was a tribute to Scowcroft's subtlety and finesse. I did not view the meeting quite so objectively — especially since the press was given the grand explanation that it had been a "general review" of the "overall relationships between the United States and the USSR." It was no laughing matter to have the White House announce what could only be construed as a Presidential move to strengthen our Soviet ties on the same day that Sadat had informed me that he planned to end the Soviet-Egyptian Friendship Treaty. Preoccupied with the serious business at hand in the Middle East, in the wee hours of the morning I sent a string of cables to Scowcroft and Haig demanding to be briefed on what was discussed between the President and the Soviet Ambassador. I warned that the negotiations over the Geneva Conference were at a tenuous stage; I would shortly see Gromyko there and I could not know less of the President's conversation than Gromyko did; Sadat was extremely leery of US–Soviet collusion.

Neither Haig nor Scowcroft was able to elicit from Nixon precisely what had been discussed; his point, after all, was to demonstrate that he was in charge. On the other hand, it probably was general; no reference to the Presidential conversation ever showed up in any Soviet communication to us. The unflappable Scowcroft, in whom the psychiatric profession lost a potentially distinguished member when he entered the US Military Academy, tried to calm me by explaining why it could have been worse: "We [Haig and Scowcroft] were at least successful in turning off a visit by the Saudi Ambassador which had also been directed." Haig warned me to make certain that the State Department press spokesman not permit any impression of distance to arise between me and the White House. And he concluded wisely:

It would be foolish to expect that the present difficulties would disappear and we will, I am sure, have to continue to cope with them and be sensitive to the issues surrounding them. However, nothing would be more self-defeating than to let these concerns dominate the conduct of affairs of overriding importance. Adequate sensitivity to this issue is all that is needed in both the short and long-term, and we have always managed to handle this problem in stride.

And so it turned out — even though the sun dawned over Cairo before I subsided.

At 10:00 A.M. Friday, December 14, I was back at the Barrages with Sadat. We turned to disengagement. Sadat asked for our "plan"; he was loath to relinquish the idea that there just had to be some "Kissinger plan." I told him that it would be a mistake to lay down a hard-and-fast program. It was bound to leak; inability to achieve its precise terms would then be a token of failure overriding the very real accomplishment inherent in any significant Israeli withdrawal and the separation of Egyptian and Israeli forces. I suggested we review the general principles that should guide the negotiations.

When we did so, the Kilometer 101 negotiations proved to have been helpful after all — especially some of the Israeli ideas that Yariv had tried out on Gamasy. Building on the Yariv-Gamasy conversations, I put forward the concept that a thinned-out Egyptian force would remain east of the Canal, Israel would pull back to the area of the Mitla Pass about twenty miles from the Canal, and a UN force would be placed in between. Sadat and I made no effort to draw lines or to define the limitations of arms applicable to each zone. That was to be left for a later trip and for what we still expected would be the subsequent negotiations in Geneva.

After lunch with Sadat, we both met the press. I used the occasion to nail down the agenda of the proposed Geneva Conference: "We agreed that disengagement of forces — separation of forces — should be the principal subject of the first phase of the peace conference and I will go to other countries to discuss with them their views on how to proceed." Sadat took over and put his stamp of approval on what I had said publicly and, even more, on the procedure I intended to propose privately to other leaders: "I am really satisfied after the long, fruitful discussions we have had."

There was an odd exchange about the timing of the disengagement. A reporter who misjudged the significance of that holiday for a devout Moslem asked if Sadat still hoped for a disengagement agreement before Christmas. Sadat said he did. He knew very well that we had agreed that nothing would happen before my next visit early in January. He had not yet learned to cope with the obstreperous American press — a skill he later mastered brilliantly.

As I left Cairo, I felt that the pieces were at last beginning to fall into place: Egypt was almost certain to attend Geneva; Jordan would not stay away lest it leave the field to the PLO. We had agreed with Cairo on a timetable and the general outline of a disengagement scheme. Sadat had also promised to recommend the lifting of the oil embargo in January after disengagement was achieved. The principal question mark was still Syria, but my talk with Boumedienne was encouraging on that score as well. My mood was buoyant. Mocking my 1972 press conference announcing the Vietnam breakthrough, I told the journalists: "It is my judgment that a conference is at hand."

Return to Riyadh

THE city of Riyadh, thrown onto a barren plateau as if by accident, reflected a deliberate decision to move the working capital of the Kingdom from hot, humid Jiddah to the higher elevation, drier air, and relatively more benign temperatures of the desert — though the stress must be on the term "relatively." Riyadh thus incarnated the somewhat mysterious quality of the state. Though the King resided there with his ministers at least eight months of the year, it had no official status. Foreign embassies were in Jiddah with the officials of the Foreign Ministry, whose head, Omar Saqqaf, spent most of his time near the King in Riyadh.

It was a system marvelously designed to limit opportunity for foreign importuning or pressure. Until the late 1970s, hotel space in Riyadh was both scarce and inconvenient. Ambassadors who appeared unbidden might not find accommodation and would certainly have difficulty arranging an interview. Diplomats were summoned or had to request an appointment some time ahead. The American Ambassador was inconvenienced by this arrangement only if, like Hermann Eilts (when he was Ambassador to Saudi Arabia), he disliked flying and drove ten hours to Riyadh whenever a high-level meeting was needed. Appointments were granted to our diplomats to all practical purposes automatically; relations were cordial and friendly.

My arrival on December 14 — my second visit to Saudi Arabia — reflected this amity. Omar Saqqaf, dressed in formal robes, was again at the foot of the stairs with his ubiquitous string of worry beads. As before, he took me by the hand and led me between the two rows of white-robed troops to the marble royal reception hall. We were served bitter Saudi coffee while television filmed the reception and the journalists accompanying me sought to ask questions.

In Saudi Arabia the reporters traveling with me always seemed to me to lack the bite and sassiness they displayed at most other stops. They were being treated with the greatest courtesy as guests of whom a reciprocal courtesy was expected. I will leave it to my companions on many a long trip to respond that courtesy was second nature to them. They would deny that they were intimidated; perhaps their restraint was due to the fact that we usually arrived in Riyadh at the end of exhausting journeys and they were looking forward to a rest that might at any moment be put in jeopardy if a clerk in what was then the only hotel in town mislaid their reservations.

I was again lodged in the spacious state guest house whose vast size was not yet matched by elegance and comfort (though these shortcomings were more than overcome during later visits). After a quick meal, Saqqaf picked me up to take me to the King. I was received in the Royal Diwan, or private study, set up as during my previous audience with two chairs in the center, mine on the King's right and the interpreter facing us. Advisers sat in two rows on opposite sides of the room barely close enough for them to hear, too far away to inject themselves into the conversation. The King looked somber while pictures were being taken. I knew that Boumedienne would already have sent a messenger; at the airport I had seen an Egyptian VIP plane that I suspected had brought Ashraf Marwan, Sadat's confidant, to give Faisal Cairo's version of our encounter.

His Majesty began by expressing his high regard for Nixon. He had known the President for twenty years; it was a friendship independent of office. In his elliptical way he was saying that no conceivable Watergate revelation could affect his esteem. When we turned to substance, Faisal modified what he had said a month earlier. Then, his proposed solution had touched the extreme PLO position: he had urged a secular state in Palestine comprising both Jews and Moslems — a euphemism for the abolition of Israel. Now, he pressed only for the return of Israel to its 1967 borders, including yielding the Old City of Jerusalem. On my previous visit Faisal had insisted that all Palestinians should have the right to return to their homes (in effect destroying Israel by flooding it with new Arabs) or else receive compensation. This time Faisal was less insistent, focusing only on the compensation, and showing that he, too, was trying to be flexible. Characteristically, he advanced the modifications of his previous positions as if they were received truth, indicating by no flicker of expression that, however hesitantly and grudgingly, the Kingdom was for the first time relating itself to the peace process. That was the significance of Faisal's remarks, which remained far from a basis for compromise. It was an attitude, not a program, and it meant that Saudi Arabia would not be an obstacle to the peace efforts of others.

In this atmosphere, I reviewed our plans for assembling the Geneva Conference, the proposed subgroups, and the agenda: disengagement first on the Egyptian, next on the Syrian front. Faisal endorsed our approach in his guardedly elliptical manner. This too was an encouraging sign that Syria was well disposed. Faisal would never have risked Syrian displeasure by going so far out on a limb — especially as one of his closest advisers was Rashad Pharaon, a Syrian.

Then, returning to the guest house, I found a message that threatened to blow up everything: The Israeli cabinet had deferred a decision on attending the Geneva Conference; the draft letter of invitation as it then stood, even as revised, was unsatisfactory. No reference to Palestinians, no matter how conditional, would be accepted. Since I would not visit Israel until Sunday, December 16, the opening date for Geneva of December 18 was now too close. I had no choice but to postpone it three days, to December 21, and as a last resort to proceed if necessary on the basis of the short letter discussed with Sadat. I sent messages to Sadat and Gromyko proposing that course. (It was a measure of their eagerness to get the conference started that this second postponement elicited no objection.) At the same time, another stern Presidential message — drafted by me — went to Golda Meir telling her of the proposed postponement but warning that the United States would attend the opening conference whatever Israel decided. Israel would have to make up its mind when I visited there forty-eight hours hence.

Saturday morning, wise old Omar Saqqaf called on me at the state guest house. I say "old" because though he was in his early fifties, he had the weatherbeaten, somewhat ravaged look of a man much older; he had clearly been living a full life. He came, as he had four weeks earlier, for an exegesis of his King's complicated meanings:

The King personally can't do something he doesn't believe. He has lived this personally since 1936. He believes in this Arab cause. He is a King. The King of Thailand he feels closer to than to President Pompidou. He has this way of thinking of things. That is why he is for the cause and cannot change without seeing something. Of course you saw that he was positive in a real sense. I am convinced he has said more than any time before.

I had not, I regretted to admit, understood him quite so clearly. In fact, if pressed against the wall I would not have been sure exactly what Faisal had said — which was, of course, precisely what the wily King wanted. His intentions were clearly benign; their execution would depend on circumstance, including pressures from the other Arab states and progress in the negotiations. And therefore the theme of Saqqaf's optimistic presentation was that America's position in the rest of the Arab world had been improving; hence Saudi Arabia's freedom of action was increasing. He explained to me the evolving views of the various Arab countries in a fashion only slightly less elliptical than his master's, producing a dialogue that sounded like a desperate imitation of the early Hemingway. "He is very intelligent," said Saqqaf of Boumedienne:

He has changed. Before he was like Iraq or Libya. He offered us his planes and weapons if we needed them. So to that extent his policy hasn't changed. But he's not the same. He's offering you a choice.

KISSINGER: Exactly.

SAQQAF: To fight or have a settlement. There came a time when everyone was not fighting so much for the cause as for the dignity of the Arab man. . . . Is he a man who can use sophisticated weapons? Or does he just go out to die?

KISSINGER: I never believed the theory that the Arabs couldn't fight, because I know history.

SAQQAF: Yes, yes, you know history.

KISSINGER: Some in Israel thought that. But there were hundreds of years when people were afraid the Arabs would never forget to fight.

SAQQAF: Hafez al-Asad said to me he wasn't sure himself. But we had a bad 30 years. And a terrible ten years.

He assured me: "The meeting with the King went well, I think." Saqqaf then asked to speak to me and our Ambassador, James E. Akins, alone. He formally promised that Saudi Arabia would not only lift the embargo and increase its production but would urge the other Arab oil producers to follow suit. Since he gave no precise date, the statement had more dramatic than operational content. But when Saqqaf bade me farewell at the airport, he said the same thing publicly: "We think we are able to remove every stumbling block in our relations."

Saqqaf added another touch: "I appreciated this meeting with my friend Dr. Kissinger, whom I call Henry." This made him the first Arab leader to call me by my first name. It started a trend. It was pleasing not only for its human warmth; it was bound to be helpful in Syria, which was my next stop.

First Visit to Damascus

SYRIA's image was so forbidding that reality could not possibly match what I had been told before our arrival. Syria had distinguished itself as one of the most intransigent of Arab regimes. It was surely the most militant of the so-called confrontation states — those nations bordering Israel that had until now adamantly rejected negotiations with it. Since independence in 1946, Syria's history had been one of violence, radical changes, and a succession of coups d'état reflecting the tensions within Syrian society and the pressures of Arab politics and ideologies. The current (and at this writing still incumbent) President, Hafez al-Asad, had forced his more radical predecessor out of office in November 1970 after Syria's disastrous gamble in the Jordan crisis. Asad, Defense Minister then, had seen the penalties of recklessness and learned his lesson well. Now in office for more than eleven years, he has set the modern record for longevity of a Syrian leader.

Until 1973 Syria had refused any talk of peace. Syria considered the State of Israel an illegal creation and, dedicated to its destruction, had not much cared where the borders of that state were located. After 1967, Damascus had broken diplomatic relations with Washington, not even permitting a small Interests Section such as we had maintained in Cairo as a channel of communication. In international forums, like the United Nations, Syria was known to us as a friend of the Soviet Union and one of the leaders of the radical group. I was paying the first visit by an American Secretary of State to Syria in twenty years.

Arriving on Saturday, December 15, 1973, I was greeted at the airport by the man technically my host, Abd al-Halim Khaddam, Deputy Prime Minister and Minister of Foreign Affairs. The drive into the capital from the airport took about a half hour, the first twenty minutes or so speeding along a straight road, then making a jarring half-circuit of a traffic circle and plunging into the boulevards of modern Damascus. The speed of the ride may have had something to do with the fact that Palestinian refugee camps were in the area near the airport. I was surrounded by the most conspicuous display of security forces I had yet seen anywhere — truckloads of armed men before and behind; innumerable plainclothesmen in the many other cars; and armed soldiers spaced every twenty feet along the airport road. It was less reassuring than it might have been, for I remembered uneasily that a Mideast expert had warned me: "If anything happens to you in Syria, it will come from the security forces."

Khaddam was the distillation of Syria's ambivalences. Compact, dynamic, with a slightly ferocious air that went incongruously with his mirthful laugh and remarkable blue eyes (a legacy of the Crusader period?), he embodied Syria's proud nationalism and its aspirations for an international role. He could not quite make up his mind which was worse: to be left out of the negotiating process or to participate in it. Khaddam told me that, on the one hand, he would not become the first Syrian to sign a document with Israel; on the other hand, I was in Damascus at the explicit request of Syria. Since my visit could have no other purpose than to help Syria participate in the negotiations in some manner, the extraordinary effort being made revealed — whatever Khaddam's protestation to the contrary — that Syria wanted something. Syrian rhetoric might be intransigent but Syrian actions encouraged and to some extent relied on the peace process. I did not attempt to mislead Syria as to the approach that American diplomacy was about to pursue. During a brief courtesy call at the Syrian Foreign Office, I told Khaddam in front of several of his colleagues:

For 25 years we have debated proclamations, declarations, and propositions, and I must tell you frankly that you'll get better declarations from the Europeans than from me. But on the other hand you will get more results from the United States. I tell you candidly that the only way for us to proceed, given our domestic situation, is not to speak of a final settlement but to go step-by-step. We are not children. No solution is possible without your consent. No one who has dealt with you has the illusion you will give up your principles. But we must take this first step or we will never take the final step. Every effort which started with ringing declarations only started explosions.

Before there was time for the inevitable bellicose rejoinder, I was summoned to the Presidency.

What Syrians called, with typical bravado, the Presidential Palace was in fact a small, modern building, formerly a private residence, standing on a narrow tree-lined street amid other undistinguished villas of medium size. It must have belonged once to a merchant of modest means. Only the two candy-striped guard posts outside the entrance revealed its official character. One proceeded through the glass front doors to a staircase leading upstairs to a narrow landing facing the door of the room where the President was always to receive me. The room was small by the usual standards of heads of state, furnished with easy chairs and sofas thrown randomly against the walls. Heavy velvet curtains were always drawn, probably for security reasons; otherwise those in the house across the street could probably keep a diary of what was going on. As my meetings with Asad multiplied — especially during the Syrian shuttle in May 1974 — this generated a somewhat claustrophobic atmosphere.

Asad was of medium height. Flashing dark eyes and a mustache dominated an expressive face. The rear of his head seemed to rise straight from his neck, creating the impression that the Syrian President was always slightly leaning forward ready to pounce on an unwary interlocutor. We invariably sat side by side on a brown sofa so that we both looked left on a painting depicting the conquest of the last Crusader strongholds by Arab armies. The symbolism was plain enough; Asad frequently pointed out that Israel, sooner or later, would suffer the same fate. He spoke in a quiet but firm voice, with a kind of rough shyness; he was as intense as Sadat was remote, as literal-minded as Sadat was reflective — the two men were similar only in their passions.

Asad was the President of a country with a long tradition and a short history. Damascus is at one and the same time the fount of modern Arab nationalism and the exhibit of its frustrations. Ruled for centuries by a succession of conquerors, the most recent being Turkish and French, the Syrian state has never lived up to the dreams of its founders. In its present borders Syria does not have the long history of self-government that gives Egypt historical perspective; nor the size or continuity that enables Egyptian Presidents to operate with the self-assurance deriving from the conviction that, whatever happens, their country will be the focal point of Middle East events. Syrian history alternates achievement with catastrophe, with the accent on the latter. The injustice of foreigners is burned deep into the Syrian soul. Asad said to me that Syria had been betrayed before World War I by Turkey, after it by Britain and France, and more recently by the United States, which had created the State of Israel.

When a people is convinced that all its troubles come from abroad, morbid suspicion becomes a national style. Syria has neither Egypt's faith in its own civilizing tendencies nor Saudi Arabia's wealth and haughty aloofness. Its leaders live by confrontation without the self-confidence to sustain it. They aspire to leadership of the Arab world without the strength to claim it. So they cling defiantly to the purity of their cause, while sullenly recognizing the practicalities of implementing it.

For they sense — even when they do not fully admit it to themselves — that Syria's capacity is no match for its aspirations and that its aspirations are controversial even within Syria. Syria is not a homogeneous nation; it is divided between Sunni Moslems, who represent some 63 percent of the population, and other Moslem sects, including the Alawites (12 percent of the population); and a not insignificant Christian population (13 percent). There are close to 200,000 Palestinians to complete the mosaic. The dominant political party, the Baath, holds itself up as the quintessence of Arab nationalism, a claim contested by its Iraqi branch. Since the Baath stands for the uncompromising defense of Arabism, the mere acceptance of the legitimacy of Israel was a traumatic event for Syrian leaders even before one reached the issue of the precise terms of a peace settlement. Conviction was reinforced by domestic politics; Syrian leaders had to be careful lest the hated Iraqi party outflank it on the side of intransigence. Only the military seemed to understand the consequences of confrontation.

The government was dominated by Alawites — of which Asad was one — who through most of history had been a despised rural-based minority relegated to menial employment. But like many such less privileged groups, they came to be disproportionately represented in the armed forces, which, as elsewhere, offered careers to the talented. Drawn to the Syrian Baath Party and especially to its military wing, the Alawites became preeminent once the Baath seized power in Damascus in 1963. Like other dominant minorities they have since based their rule domestically on their own cohesion and control of key positions, out of proportion to their numbers, and internationally on the uncompromising assertion of Syrian nationalism. And well they might. Syria's military leaders are obliged constantly to look over their shoulders as the radical civilian politicians are tempted to use rabid nationalism as the vehicle to return to power. Syria is one of the few countries where the civilian leaders are more bellicose than the military.

When rhetoric is too greatly at variance with reality, schizophrenia is inevitable. In 1973, the ineluctable reality was that the "rejectionist" course produced only a deadlock; it deposited the Israeli army twenty miles from Damascus and left Syria isolated in its defiance. Asad would have liked to destroy the Jewish state, but he recognized that neither Egypt nor in the final analysis Saudi Arabia would join him in that enterprise and that the cost of attempting it alone would hazard Syria's domestic structure, perhaps even its existence. He had managed to stay in office far longer than any of his predecessors because unlike them he was as prudent as he was passionate, as realistic as he was ideological.

When I met him, Asad had concluded that Syria was not sufficiently strong to unite the Arab nation, and needed to regain its own territory before it could pursue larger ambitions. So Asad had come grudgingly to the same conclusion that Sadat had embraced spontaneously. He would let the peace process proceed. He would strive for a disengagement agreement on the Golan Heights as a first step. How he would act afterward, I doubt that even he knew.

But to achieve even his first goal presented Asad with a complicated tactical problem. From the beginning, it was clear that he did not possess the personal authority exercised by Sadat. I do not recall that Sadat ever mentioned domestic obstacles to his policies. Even if they existed, he absorbed them in his own position; he acted in his own name, which is another way of saying that he assumed the responsibility for Egypt. (And in the end he paid for this bravura with his life.)

Asad at no point claimed this authority. He began many crucial meetings, particularly once negotiations started, alone with me and only my interpreter — probably wanting to leave no trace of his exploratory probing. His tactic was to open with a statement of the most extreme position to test what the traffic would bear. He might then allow himself to be driven back to the attainable, fighting a dogged rearguard action that made clear that concessions could be exacted only at a heavy price and that discouraged excessive expectations of them. (His negotiating style was in this respect not so different from the Israelis', much as both of them would hate the comparison.) Once he knew the lay of the land, he would call in his closest associates, who included senior military people and of course Syrian interpreters. Then we would go through the whole process again, trying to duplicate our previous dialogue as much as possible. By then, Asad and I were acting as if in rehearsal for a play. Time-consuming, nerve-racking, and bizarre as the procedure was, it had the great advantage from Asad's point of view that he never had to argue for a concession himself, at least in the first instance. That onus was on me. His colleagues were part of the negotiations; they had a chance to object; they almost never did so. Whatever arguments persuaded Asad would also have persuaded his colleagues. It was effective domestic politics at the expense of many sleepless nights for me. For during the Syrian shuttle, when I got through with Asad I generally had to return to Israel and report to a negotiating team that took pride in being no easier than Syria's.

Withal, I developed a high regard for Asad. In the Syrian context he was moderate indeed. He leaned toward the Soviets as the source of his military equipment. But he was far being from a Soviet stooge. He had a first-class mind allied to a wicked sense of humor. I believe that I was the first Western leader with whom he had dealt consistently. He grasped the opportunity for some free tutorials on Western political systems. During the Syrian shuttle, almost every bargaining session began with an hour or so of perceptive questioning on the institutions and personalities of the Western democracies. Since Asad was learning English at the same time, these long talks may have left at least one enduring mark. I teased him that he would be the only Arab leader who spoke English with a German accent.

Asad never lost his aplomb. He negotiated daringly and tenaciously like a riverboat gambler to make sure that he had exacted the last sliver of available concessions. I once told him that I had seen negotiators who deliberately moved themselves to the edge of a precipice to show that they had no further margin of maneuver. I had even known negotiators who put one foot over the edge, in effect threatening their own suicide. He was the only one who would actually jump off the precipice, hoping that on his way down he could break his fall by grabbing a tree he knew to be there. Asad beamed.

At this first meeting on December 15, we were both on our best behavior, trying to take each other's measure rather than come to conclusions. Asad opened by saying that he had heard from his Arab brothers, specifically Sadat and Boumedienne, about my conversations with them. Translated, this meant that I had better not try any funny business, but also that what he had heard was at least worth exploring. As it happened, I had told each of them to make sure Asad was informed of our talks; besides, if Geneva was ever going to take place, it was essential that everyone sing from the same music. In response to Asad's query, I outlined the main elements of our strategy along lines well rehearsed with Boumedienne, Sadat, and King Faisal.

Asad left little doubt that he would not die unfulfilled if the Geneva Conference never assembled. He was not "dreaming about going to the conference," he said. What he really wanted was its fruits without contaminating himself by its process. But before he made a final decision, he wanted to know how the United States and the Soviet Union saw the situation. It was a subtle hint: Asad would brook no superpower condominium. He also wanted to suggest that he was not a Soviet puppet; otherwise he would have had no need to ask me about Soviet views. I decided to use the opening:

> We'd rather make an agreement with you rather than the USSR make it with you. . . . They have made specific proposals and a plan for a peace settlement — I've avoided them. Because if it is a viable proposal, we can make it directly to the Arabs. Lots of people give us advice. We have to do some work with the Israelis and [the] Soviet Union can't help us there. They have no influence with Israel. There is only one agreement — a conference, and we'll stay in touch with one another. There is no agreement on substance on any issue. If you are told anything else, then it isn't true. I told Boumedienne that we do not recognize any sphere of influence in the Middle East. What will happen at the conference will depend on you and us. You can talk to the Soviets, we don't want to influence Syrian-Soviet relations.

This was less than the whole truth, of course; it was a statement of reality. We wanted to influence Syrian-Soviet relations: We preferred them to be less close than they were. But Asad would loosen his ties with the Soviets for his reasons, nor ours, and we could affect Syrian-Soviet relations best by giving Damascus a stake in closer ties with the United States.

When I turned to the letter of invitation, I was in for a big surprise. I laboriously went through the text of the letter and the various formulas on the Palestinians, winding up with my recommendation that any explicit reference to them be dropped. Asad accepted *all* of the changes. I told him that the opening of the conference would probably have to be postponed by three days. That gave him no pain either. I thought for a fleeting moment that the Arab President with the fiercest reputation was turning out, amazingly, to be the most tractable.

It was illusory. When I asked him whether there was anything else in the letter to which he objected, he replied that in fact he had one specific reservation: He was happy enough to let me make the modifications in the draft letter concerning what would take place at the conference, but he could not agree with the sentence that all the parties mentioned — Syria, Egypt, Israel, Jordan — had agreed to go to the Geneva Conference. For Syria had no intention of attending! Therefore it made no difference whether he failed to show up on the eighteenth or failed to show up on the twenty-first, or indeed what the letter of invitation said about the Palestinians or the United Nations.

At first I was stunned. But then I realized that Asad was in fact being helpful. He was rejecting only the opening plenary session of the conference, not the concept of the negotiation. He did not seek to block the conference and therefore gave it a sort of left-handed blessing. He did not object to the letter but simply regarded it — correctly — as irrelevant.

What Asad really wanted to know was not the procedures for the conference but its outcome. That would determine Syria's ultimate participation, and in the meantime, in his prickly manner, he would keep his options open. He wanted an answer to three questions: Did the United States agree with Syria that Syria could not give up any of its territory? Did we agree that there could not be a solution without the Palestinian people? Were we going to Geneva for an objective consistent with the first two points, or "only to think and take a long time without reaching a radical solution"?

The questions were as penetrating as they were unanswerable. Any attempt to respond precisely would abort the peace process before it had barely started. At this stage, constructive ambiguity was essential; this is another way of saying that the outcome would have to be left to negotiations, not be determined in advance. That these negotiations would be no joyride was shown in Asad's attitude toward Israel's claim to "secure" borders. He argued that the 1967 border was farther from Tel Aviv than from Damascus. He therefore had a better claim to advance the 1967 frontier into Israel than Israel had to keep the Golan Heights.

As it turned out, once he had made a record, Asad was not eager to press his point. What was really on his mind was disengagement. The Egyptians, to make him more tractable on Geneva, had obviously implied to Asad that the Sinai disengagement agreement was all wrapped up and that one on the Golan could not be far behind. He therefore thought it only proper to use the occasion of my visit to negotiate his own. He told me that he agreed with Sadat that the Geneva Conference should be only a framework and that a Syrian-Israeli disengagement should be negotiated through me. He wanted the outcome settled beforehand.

Matters were unfortunately not quite that simple. We were far from agreement on the Egyptian disengagement, I said. But in Egypt's case there was a history of discussion going back to 1971; there had been the Kilometer 101 talks and other exchanges since the cease-fire. We understood the outlines of a possible Sinai negotiation. There was no such background for a negotiation about the Golan Heights. I would not know what to propose. I had no idea of Israeli thinking. (Indeed, knowing Israeli suspicions of Syria, I was painfully aware that even starting the negotiations would be a horrendous exertion.) I could not promise anything at this stage beyond a serious effort to follow an Egyptian disengagement with a Syrian one.

Undeterred, Asad brought out a map of the Golan to show me what would be involved in disengagement. The practical effect of it would have been for Israel to give up all the territory it captured in the 1973 war and virtually all the territory it captured in 1967. (Asad called this a concession, since by his reasoning the disengagement line should be along the 1967 frontier.) Such a scheme was patently impossible to negotiate; it was even dangerous to present it since it might lead to an Israeli refusal to talk at all. So I brought the discussion of it to a close:

> The best we can do is our best effort. We have not given any promise we can't keep. I'm in no position to make an agreement. . . . It would be irresponsible for me to start drawing lines. I have not studied the matter. You wouldn't respect me if I did this. I am a serious man.

Asad was adamant. "Beginning talks are a loss to us," he argued, pointing to the heart of his political problem. He needed to show some achievement in order to attend Geneva. Syria would go to a peace conference only after a disengagement agreement had already been concluded. On the other hand, he repeated, he would not oppose others' going to Geneva.

The seemingly perverse reaction hid a major breakthrough. In his convoluted way, Asad was in fact blessing the peace process and our strategy. If Syria did not object to the peace conference and was indifferent to the content of the letter of invitation, all roadblocks would disappear. We could finesse the Palestinians by simply placing them among "other participants" in the draft letter. Israel's insistence on the release of its POWs as a precondition for participating with Syria in the peace conference now became academic.

What the exchange with Asad did, among other things, was raise serious questions about Soviet diplomacy. The Soviets and we had agreed that in the preparations for Geneva, Moscow would use its influence in Damascus and we in Israel. In the past four weeks, Moscow had at no time so much as hinted that Syrian participation at the conference was in question, or that Syria had objections, much less prior conditions. Did it not know? Or did it deceive us? And, if so, why? If it had known about Asad's objections and failed to overcome them, its influence with Damascus was less than we had thought. If it had deceived us, it was difficult to understand the motive. Probably the Soviet Ambassador in Damascus was not particularly well connected — later on, the Syrians frequently made disparaging remarks about him. Soviet psychology is not well attuned to the Arab mind, and the Soviets have an uncanny knack for alienating their own best clients by their heavy-handed conduct.

And the Syrian failure coincided with other mixed signals from Moscow. On December 15 Vinogradov told Eilts in Cairo that my alternative of a very short letter of invitation was acceptable. But late that evening, Dobrynin told Scowcroft in Washington that Moscow would go along only if I could convince the other parties. (By then it proved no longer necessary.)

The fact was that Syrian participation at the opening plenary session was in no way essential — indeed, not to put too fine a point on it, we were better off without Syria. (Perhaps Asad knew this as well as anyone.) Nevertheless, to maintain Syrian interest in the peace process, I thought it important to let Asad take the responsibility for refusing, and that required us to make him feel welcome should he change his mind. And as on many other occasions, there was the problem of reconciling perception and reality. It was undesirable to have the meeting end in a seeming impasse. It would make a bad public impression; I would not be able to explain candidly why it was ideal if Syria stayed away from the plenary session. Therefore, to maintain the appearance of momentum, I told Asad that after my visit to Israel the next day, we would send an official to brief him on my talks with Golda and to bring him the final version of the letter of invitation so that at least he knew what he was rejecting. Since he had a stake in not seeming to be excluded, Asad fell in happily with this procedure. And to ease communications between us, I proposed the establishment of Interests Sections in each other's capital. Once again, Asad agreed. He suggested I describe our talks to the press as "frank and useful."

We had achieved somewhat more than what we had hoped for. Syria would not obstruct the peace process; it would probably participate later in the disengagement negotiations that were at the core of our strategy. We had begun the arduous diplomacy of tempting fiercely independent Syria into a more constructive role in the drama of peace.

Respite in Amman

THE meeting with Asad had started at approximately 4:00 P.M.; the plan was for me to leave Damascus for the short flight to Amman around 7:30 P.M. and to dine with King Hussein. In fact, my meeting with Asad lasted until 10:30 P.M. — six and a half hours. Journalists were speculating: Had I been kidnapped? Was I the one hundred and twenty-eighth prisoner of war? Was I meeting secretly with Yasir Arafat? Finally, at 11:00 P.M., they heard the sirens of my motorcade. One weary reporter remarked: "Either he's finally coming, or they're finally coming for us." [3]

By now I felt like an orchestra conductor who had to elicit a harmonious sound from varied and potentially discordant instruments. We wanted Hussein to play a role at Geneva and I owed Hussein a report on the trip. The tardiness of my arrival did not diminish his goodwill. He served a cordial late supper — after midnight — and I had breakfast the next morning with him and his brother, Crown Prince Hassan, to continue our consultations.

At that time, it was soothing to arrive in Amman. Jordan was unconditionally a friend of the United States. It did not threaten us with dire consequences if we failed to adopt its recommendations. It was in no position to invoke the oil weapon. Its participation in the 1973 war had combined respect for the need for Arab solidarity with an understanding that the cause of peace would be served by restraint. And it must be admitted that Hussein paid for it, because now no one was very interested in advancing Jordan's claim to the West Bank.

When I arrived in Amman on December 15, Hussein turned out to be the one Arab ruler to whom his "brothers" had sent no word of my peregrinations or conversations. I therefore had to go through the state of play in some detail with respect to both the Geneva Conference and our general strategy. Jordan's objectives at Geneva paralleled our own. Hussein was no more eager to have Palestinian participation; if their presence was unavoidable, he wanted them as part of the Jordanian delegation. All Jordanian leaders had grave doubts about the intentions of the other Arab states. "I am concerned," said the Prime Minister, Zaid Rifai, "that Egypt will make its own agreement and abandon Jordan." The Crown Prince always suspected Syria of scheming to annex Jordan. For all these reasons the King would have preferred a single Arab delegation at Geneva, to discourage separate arrangements or the introduction of new participants. If that proved unattainable — and it was in fact contrary to our strategy — he would not oppose separate negotiations so long as each formed part of a "package settlement."

We saw an opportunity for an Israeli-Jordanian negotiation after the Syrian disengagement. Rifai urged me, when I visited Israel, to suggest that Israel undertake a modest pullback so as to turn over to Jordan the city of Jericho with its exclusively Arab population and its location close to the Jordan River. It would symbolize Jordan's claim to the West Bank and establish King Hussein as Israel's interlocutor on West Bank negotiations. I promised to do so, and I did. But Israel could not handle simultaneously a Geneva Conference, a parliamentary election, a Sinai disengagement, and a move in Jericho.

So it was not to be. By the time we had completed the Egyptian and Syrian disengagements in mid-1974, Nixon's Presidency was approaching its end. Before the new President could start another initiative the other Arab states, in a fit of emotional myopia, deprived Hussein of his negotiating role on the West Bank and designated the PLO, the one group Israel was least likely to accept, as interlocutor. Thereby the Arabs contributed their share in stalling any Israeli withdrawal from the West Bank.

This explains some of Hussein's later actions — when he chose the risky course of seeking radical backing first from Syria and then from Iraq. He began a more open flirtation with the Soviet Union. He sought greater distance from the United States, in the process moving demonstratively away from some old personal friends and admirers.

Lebanon

ON Sunday, December 16, I flew into Lebanon. In those far-off days, Lebanon was always cited as a model of cooperation between the religious faiths in the Middle East. Theoretically, there was a narrow Christian majority; the high offices of state were apportioned roughly that way. The President of Lebanon was always a Christian, the Prime Minister invariably Moslem. The demographic reality was probably the reverse, but facing it would have rent Lebanon's delicate fabric. It was avoided by simply not taking a census for thirty years.

The two religious communities coexisted; Lebanon prospered; Beirut became a thriving, cosmopolitan metropolis. This happy state of affairs might have continued indefinitely had the Palestinian leadership not decided, upon being expelled from Jordan in 1970, to make Lebanon its main base of operations.

This had two consequences: It drew Lebanon into the Arab-Israeli confrontation in a way that could not conceivably correspond to its national interest, for the frontier between Lebanon and Israel had never been disputed. And it illustrated also the dynamics of the Palestinian liberation movement. It would seem that any country that plays host to organized Palestinian paramilitary forces risks its own sovereignty. Their principal purpose is to conduct raids into Israel, using the host country as sanctuary; this draws the inevitable Israeli retaliation, engulfing the host country in a war it did not seek. (Hussein forbade such raids into Israel, which was one cause of his battle with the Palestinians in 1970. Lebanon was not strong enough to do so.) If allowed to implant themselves and build up their military power, the Palestinians can become a state within a state, first ignoring the writ of the central government in areas they control and then seeking to impose their own will. Again, what Hussein had prevented by force in 1970, backed by the loyal Bedouins of the Jordanian army, Lebanon with its jerry-built governmental structure and weak, divided army proved unable to overcome.

Already in 1973, the danger while nascent was already visible. The Palestinians were beginning to be a disruptive element in Lebanon. The result was that the Lebanese government, one of the most moderate in the Middle East, was the most passionate advocate of a Palestinian homeland: It was a way to get the Palestinians out of Lebanon!

That was indeed the theme of the conversations I had with the Lebanese leaders at Rayak Air Base thirty-eight miles from Beirut. We met there for security reasons. The presence of two Palestinian refugee camps directly in the approach path of airplanes arriving at Beirut airport seemed to my security officers too much of a risk to take in the age of Soviet-made shoulder-carried surface-to-air missiles; general concern was given a concrete content by a report that there was in fact a plan to shoot down my plane; there were also mobs demonstrating in Beirut. Thus the military elegance of the Officers' Club at the air base was the venue for my conversations first with Foreign Minister Fu'ad Naffa' and his staff, and then with President Suleiman Frangieh and Prime Minister Taqi al-Din al-Sulh and their associates. The Foreign Minister had a list of a dozen questions similar in import to those put by Asad. I gave substantially the same answer: Discussion of final frontiers was premature and Palestinian aspirations had to be taken into account in a final settlement. As in Damascus, I refused to go into detail about the meaning of these propositions. I explained the procedures for the Geneva Conference, the subgroups, and the first phase of disengagement. Our hosts could not have been more understanding or appreciative. They welcomed America's interest in the peace process; they had no concrete proposals. Their major concern was that the Soviet role in the Middle East be diminished and, above all, that we help solve the Palestinian problem, finding them a home anywhere other than in Lebanon.

I did not have the heart to tell President Frangieh that, from what I had heard in the Middle East, he was unlikely to obtain relief from his devouring guests. In the judgment of all the other Arab leaders I had met — with the possible exception of those in Saudi Arabia — very few Palestinians would want to return to the West Bank whoever ruled there. Moreover, since Israel would surely insist that any part of the West Bank returned to Arab control be demilitarized, and since it was inconceivable that the Palestinians were going to disarm themselves everywhere, Lebanon was not likely soon to be spared the presence of armed Palestinians.

I think with sadness of these civilized men who in a turbulent part of the world had fashioned a democratic society based on genuine mutual respect of the religions. Their achievement did not survive. The passions sweeping the area were too powerful to be contained by subtle constitutional arrangements. As it had attempted in Jordan, the Palestinian movement wrecked the delicate balance of Lebanon's stability. Before the peace process could run its course, Lebanon was torn apart. Over its prostrate body at this writing all the factions and forces of the Middle East still chase their eternal dreams and act out their perennial nightmares.

Israel

A T last on Sunday evening, December 16, I reached Israel, the third country on that day, the seventh in the four-day Middle East journey. I had come to persuade Israel to go to Geneva on the basis of a bland letter that left all issues open. But I had no illusions. With elections two weeks away, no Israeli leader would risk his or her position for a conference that none of them was overwhelmingly eager to see take place.

But election politics were only the surface manifestation of a deeper anxiety. Israel's tenacious rearguard action reflected not arrogance, as many Arabs imagined: Rather, it was founded on a premonition of potential disaster. The nitpicking legalistic method of negotiation stemmed from the knowledge that a people of three million amidst a hostile population of over a hundred million is historically weak whatever the relative state of armaments at any given point. Deep down, the children of the ghetto knew, railed against, and perversely contributed to their own nightmare: that they had created a state which once again had become a ghetto — ostracized by its neighbors, thrown upon itself, dependent on the support of a faraway country with many other priorities.

Even the complex strategy I was proposing could only ease their dilemmas, not end them. I defended the step-by-step approach as a means of preventing the formation of a global coalition against Israel. Golda was not convinced:

When, in March or April, the world begins pressing again, we'll be X kilometers from the Canal. We'll fight at a great disadvantage. And the world will not say, "a plague on both your houses"; the world will say, "a plague on the House of Israel."

And Golda was close to the mark: Our strategy offered no surcease from anguishing retreat, only mitigation of its impact. Golda was tough enough to look at the real situation, no matter how painful, without flinching. "If we are realistic and honest with ourselves, we Israelis," she said about disengagement, "it really means we have come out of this war, which was as it was, by pulling back. That's what it really is, if you call it by its right name. Just pulling back, that's what it is."

Golda was right and Sadat was the only Arab who understood that she was right. It is a measure of her stature that she traveled that road nevertheless, trading territory for time and geography for acceptance. But it was too much to ask her to do so joyfully or even graciously. Sadat was a great man because he understood the importance of intangibles. Golda had to cling to what she had; circumstance did not permit her to be artful. Yet when the accounts are finally balanced, it must be recorded that she was as indispensable to the process of peace as the Egyptian President and that she performed her duty with courage, occasional snarls of defiance, and constant dignity.

All our sympathy for Israel's historic plight and affection for Golda were soon needed to endure the teeth-grinding, exhausting ordeal by exegesis that confronted us when we met with the Israeli negotiating team. We went through the letter of invitation line by line. In fact, we had won most of the battle when Sadat agreed and Asad acquiesced in omitting the explicit reference to Palestinians; the empty formulation in our new final version stated only that the "question" of "other participants from the Middle East area will be discussed during the first stage of the Conference." (The specific reference to "the Middle East" was in fact Asad's indirect contribution; he had pointed out that if we did not mention the region, *any* country could ask to participate.)

Having prevailed on the Palestinian point, the Israeli negotiating team tried its luck on the other issues. Deeply suspicious of the United Nations, they showed infinite ingenuity in suggesting alternative formulations to weaken the convening authority of that organization and the role of its Secretary-General. Luckily, it was mostly for the record; it was not pressed with the usual persistence, thus ensuring us a few hours' sleep. The solution of the Palestinian point took the steam out of my interlocutors — although even unaroused Israelis can never be described as easy.

After we had substantially agreed on the letter, we went line by line through an accompanying Memorandum of Understanding that the Israelis wanted. At one point I said in exasperation:

I'm trying to bring a sense of reality to this discussion. The mood in America is such that if Israel is increasingly seen as the obstacle to the negotiations and the cause of the oil pressure, you'll have tremendous difficulty. Memorandum or no memorandum.

"I know that," Golda replied wearily. She had her own domestic problems — a belligerent and united right wing and an insecure public. What we were about was not foreign policy but psychology. She had to show that she had raised Israel's concerns and that we had heard them. Our acting on them would belong to another historical period.

Finally at 12:42 A.M. early Monday, after five hours of nonstop negotiation, we were finished with all the documents, including a new draft letter.* It omitted any reference to Palestinians and confined the authority of the United Nations to convening the conference, not supervising it. It was only a minor victory for Israel, since nothing could prevent the Palestinian issue from being raised at the conference. Still, while driving us to the edge of nervous exhaustion, Israel had committed itself to a negotiating process that it knew would have to be fueled with its withdrawals. At 1:00 A.M. the cabinet met and gave its approval. My weary staff had to draft messages to the White House, all other Mideast participants, and the Soviet Union to make certain we had their final acceptance of the suggested changes.

The Israeli cabinet has — or at least had then — a seemingly endless capacity for self-flagellation: If it could not alter the course of events, it would instead reassure itself again and again that nothing slipped by it through inadvertence. The two negotiating teams were back together for another four-hour session on Monday morning, December 17. This time the subject was disengagement. We went through the history of the Kilometer 101 talks, examining the various schemes that had been presented there. I reviewed Sadat's latest thinking; I outlined my own ideas and listened to Israel's preliminary views. Detailed discussion would not come until January. Nonetheless, I now felt convinced that Egypt and Israel had a reasonable chance to complete the make-or-break diplomacy on which we had hazarded our Middle East position.

Just before leaving Jerusalem, I visisted Yad Vashem, the memorial to the six million Jews who had died at the hand of the Nazis. I barred the press from accompanying me. It was a moment of solitary reflection upon my own past, the pitilessness of history, and the human stakes in the exertions of statesmen. And it was intended as a reassurance to the people of Israel that I understood and would respect their fears in a process of peacemaking that was simultaneously inescapable, full of hope, and wrenchingly painful.

As I departed Israel on the afternoon of December 17, I was confident that our strategy was about to unfold much as we had intended. The Geneva Conference was almost certain to assemble in three days' time. A disengagement agreement between Israel and Egypt seemed within reach. I sent messages to Sadat, Hussein, Asad, Faisal, Boumedienne, and the Shah informing them of my discussions of recent days. Our

---

*The final text of the letter of invitation is in the backnotes.[4]

diplomacy depended on confidence, which made it necessary that all of the area's leaders knew what was being said and done. (And because communications from the United States were precious in the Middle East rumor mill, we made certain that the messages were substantially similar — but not identical. Sending the same message word for word would have devalued the communication as it made the rounds of Arab capitals. It would have looked too much like a circular dispatch.) Our NATO allies were informed as well. On December 18, with some other small changes, Israel, Egypt, Jordan, and the Soviet Union accepted the letter of invitation. We made a final check of Asad as promised, on December 18, sending our Ambassador in Beirut, William Buffum, to Damascus with the new text of the letter of invitation. But as expected, Asad reiterated that Syria would not attend the peace conference. Thus, at the last moment the letter to Waldheim was adjusted to delete specific names of countries in favor of saying the "parties concerned" would attend Geneva.

There was one last squall in Washington, where Nixon, still smoldering from Israel's obstinacy the week before, wanted to hold up one-quarter of the $2.2 billion postwar supplemental aid request for Israel as insurance of Israel's good behavior. I opposed it, convinced that desperation would make Israel more defiant. And there were really no outstanding issues to warrant such a step. After some exchanges between me and Scowcroft, the idea was dropped. On December 19, I sent a long report to Nixon outlining the prospects for Geneva and after. (It is included in the backnotes.)[5]

We were at last at the starting gate. It remained to be seen whether we knew how to run the race.

The Geneva Conference

BEFORE reaching Geneva, I stopped in Lisbon, Madrid, and Paris. I owed the Portuguese government a show of support for its assistance during the airlift. We were in the midst of negotiations with Spain over US bases there. I was in Paris for my last meeting with my old North Vietnamese sparring partner, Le Duc Tho, who was growing more unbearably insolent as America's domestic divisions gradually opened up new and decisive strategic opportunities for Hanoi. In the French capital I also briefed President Georges Pompidou on our plans and strategy for the Geneva Conference. In his illness, he had to strain to the utmost to maintain his customary calm and courtesy in the face of the exclusion of France from the proceedings. I understood this proud man's attitude. On the other hand, there was not a single controversial Mideast issue — and precious few in other areas — on which France had taken our side in recent months. So long as France saw its future in the Middle East in one-sided support of the radical Arab program, the consequence of its participation would have been to isolate us in our encouragement of more moderate and limited and, in our view, more attainable goals.

Before I left Paris, Algerian Foreign Minister Abdelaziz Bouteflika, whom I had seen only a week earlier in Algiers, accepted an invitation to call on me at the residence of the American Ambassador for a personal briefing on my tour of the Mideast. I summarized the various conversations I had had; I assured him I understood the reasons for Syria's reluctance to attend the conference. I reiterated our determination to promote a disengagement in the Golan after concluding the one in the Sinai. Bouteflika the revolutionary espoused the cause of his fellow radicals, the Palestinians, in the usual sacramental language, but Bouteflika the man of the world understood that Palestinian disunity and the ulterior motives of Arab governments hindered a resolution of the issue. He frankly acknowledged to me that the problem of the Palestinians was complicated by the fact that each country of the region supported its own group of Palestinians. The upshot was that Algeria no more than Syria would oppose the procedure or the strategy.

Late Thursday afternoon, December 20, my peregrinations of two weeks at last culminated in my arrival in Geneva. While the conference itself had been designed for modest achievement, I hoped with all my heart that it would mark the beginning of a process worthy of the suffering that had led to it and justifying the arduous exertion of the months just past. And in this buoyant mood I spoke to the media at the airport:

The fate of Arabs and Jews has been inextricably linked throughout their history, rising and falling together. In recent centuries both had been reduced to an equally cruel state — the one dispersed and persecuted throughout the world, the other deprived of autonomy and freedom in its own former empire. But over the past quarter century both have stood on the verge of overcoming their past, no longer restrained by outside forces but by their struggle with one another. Thus in the land of Arabs and Jews, where the reality of mistrust and hate so tragically contradicts the spiritual message which originates there, it is essential for the voice of reconciliation to be heard.

A warm and generous backchannel message from Nixon awaited me:

On the eve of the convening of the historic conference on the Middle East, I wanted to express to you my respect and the gratitude of the American people for your crucial role in this great enterprise. Without your diplomatic skill, perseverance, and dedication to the cause of peace, this Conference would not be taking place. While this is but the first step on the road to a just and durable peace in the Middle East, it is a vitally important step, and the American people are proud that it was their Secretary of State who brought it about. Needless to say, you have my full support as we work together in this vital pursuit. Warm regards.

It was probably too much to hope that those gathering at Geneva would display a conspicuous spirit of reconciliation. Each of the contending parties could sustain its experiment with peace only by proving its constant vigilance to the hard-liners back home. And all of the key actors understood that the sole achievement of the conference would be its opening; the progress that was foreseeable would take place in other forums.

That realization had at last dawned on Andrei Gromyko, with whom I dined Thursday night, before the plenary session on Friday. The conference had been assembled by the efforts of the United States, with the Soviet Union playing a subsidiary role if any. Gromyko had forgotten that he had assigned the task to me in order to saddle me with the onus for failure or at least for exacting changes in the letter from reluctant Arab participants. Throughout, the behavior of Soviet diplomats had been either incompetent or duplicitous — probably a combination of both. But far from reducing the influence of the United States, the exertions needed to arrange the conference — and the final success — emphasized our indispensability to all the Arab states, even the radicals.

When Gromyko grumbled that the Soviet Union would not let itself be excluded from the peace process, his frustration must have been all the greater because he must have known that the Soviets' dilemmas were both self-inflicted and insoluble. So long as the Soviet Union had no ties with Israel, we were the only superpower conducting a dialogue with both sides. So long as the Soviets simply repeated the radical Arab program, we were — as I had said to Asad — always better off dealing directly with the Arab states and getting credit for any achievement. Gromyko sought to combine the advantage of close association with our peace effort with unconditional backing of every Arab demand. We refused to play this game. But it was primarily the flat-footedness of Soviet diplomacy, not our maneuvering, that doomed Moscow to increasing irrelevance. We were systematically creating the framework for bilateral diplomacy between the parties through our mediation *after* the conference. The absence of a Soviet alternative caused even its clients, like Syria, to fall in with a procedure that was the only hope for progress.

The upshot of the dinner was a procedural gimmick designed to save Soviet face. Earlier, the Soviet Union and United States had agreed to designate permanent representatives to the Geneva Conference, of ambassadorial rank. Gromyko proposed that these ambassadors remain in Geneva to stay in contact with each other after the ceremonial opening session. They should also be available to meet with the subgroups should the parties so desire — a contingency my trip had ensured was unlikely to arise. Gromyko pressed for this as a way of complicating separate bilateral moves outside the conference. I agreed because I did not think that at this stage the unfolding of our design could be stopped by procedural gimmicks. I designated Ellsworth Bunker, one of the great men of American diplomacy, sure enough of himself so that he would not harass us into a pace incompatible with our plans. Gromyko appointed Vinogradov, who having outworn his welcome in Cairo was available for reassignment. He was to prove the wisdom of a remark by Metternich about a Russian diplomat of Tsarist times: "No one is easier to defeat than a diplomat who fancies himself shrewd. Only the totally honest are difficult to vanquish." Bunker and Vinogradov met sporadically in January. Afterward, Bunker started devoting more and more time to the Panama Canal negotiations, which I had also assigned to him. By June we had completed two agreements elsewhere than in Geneva. Vinogradov had left town. The conference never convened again.

On Friday morning, December 21, 1973, the problem was to assemble all the participants at the Palais des Nations for the formal laying on of hands. But after weeks of effort that one might have thought would cover all imaginable trivia and some beyond previous imagination, an unexpected scrap arose. It concerned the seating arrangements. Gromyko proposed to Waldheim a seating plan that was as transparent as it was unacceptable. He suggested that the USSR, Egypt, and Syria* be placed on the right of the Secretary-General, with the United States, Israel, and Jordan on the left. This would have neatly placed Jordan outside the Arab fold by grouping it with Israel and the United States, while displaying the Soviet Union as the champion of the supposedly genuine Arab cause — defined by a previous history of reliance on Soviet help. From what I knew of Sadat's thinking, the symbolism would appeal no more to him than to the parties Gromyko had assigned to our side of the table.

Since Gromyko's proposal made no rational sense and accorded with no known diplomatic usage, Waldheim rejected it — showing that Waldheim knew who held the stronger diplomatic hand. He proposed instead the UN procedure of seating the Middle East delegations in alphabetical order. Unhappily, this created a new problem because it would have placed Egypt between Israel and the Soviet Union, a position Fahmy thought it prudent to avoid. His counterproposal would have placed Jordan, but not Egypt, next to Israel, but Jordan would have none of that symbolism.

Just when I thought that all was lost — indeed, when the time sched-

---

*An empty seat was left for Syria in the symbolic hope that it would attend at a later time.

uled for the opening of the conference had passed — a Solomonic solution emerged from the nimble brain of Ephraim (Eppie) Evron, then
Deputy Director General of the Israeli Foreign Ministry. The United
States would sit between Egypt and Jordan, the Soviet Union would
wind up between Israel and the empty Syrian seat at a seven-sided table.
There was no more rationale for this seating arrangement than any other
but it did the trick. Having started with a transparent ploy, Gromyko
concluded with a show of goodwill. And he continued it by agreeing to
meet with Israeli Foreign Minister Abba Eban. Moscow had broken diplomatic relations with Israel but I agreed with Eban that Israel's request
for a meeting was reasonable. Gromyko accepted, explaining coolly that
it is normal procedure for a participant in an international conference to
pay a courtesy call on a co-chairman.

At last, the Geneva Conference was under way. As planned, it consisted of a battery of public speeches through which each of the participants sought to protect himself against the accusations that could do
him the most damage at home. For Egypt, this was the Syrian charge
that Cairo was toying with a separate settlement; for Jordan, that it was
less Arab than its brothers. Israel had to navigate between being accused
of softness by its right-wing opposition at home and being blamed for
any deadlock by Europeans and Americans. The Soviet Union wanted
to stake a claim to a continued role; we, to underline our indispensability to the entire process.

Gromyko opened with what was, by Soviet standards, a restrained
presentation. He repeated standard criticisms of Israeli "aggression"
and called for a return to the 1967 frontiers. But he also emphasized
that the Arabs needed to accept Israel's sovereignty and its right to national existence. It was conventional Soviet fare put forward nonconten-
tiously. It offered no perspectives; it did nothing to exacerbate the situation.

I spoke next and made four principal points: the importance of maintaining the cease-fire; the need for some realistic appreciation of what
could be accomplished in a short period of time; the imperative of early
disengagement of forces as a first step; and the necessity of realistic
negotiations between the parties themselves, who would have to live
with the results. At least no one could say afterward that I had not given
public notice of our strategy. I also amused the assembled dignitaries by
attempting to quote a proverb in Arabic. As with a similar display of
bravado in China, my audience did not discern what I was doing until
hearing the official translation into the same language that I was purporting to speak.

Fahmy was next. With an eye to Damascus, he gave an oration uncompromising on substance. It demanded the total withdrawal of Israeli
forces to the 1967 borders; it asked self-determination for the Palestin-

ians. But it also granted every state — and therefore by implication Israel — the right of territorial inviolability and political independence. With impeccable principles firmly established, Egypt was thus free to turn to the problem of disengagement — a subject that Fahmy happened to omit from his speech.

The most hard-line rhetoric came from Jordanian Prime Minister Zaid Rifai, whose actual views were, in fact, the most moderate. His catalogue of Israeli transgressions was considerably longer than Fahmy's, his references to a peaceful settlement far fewer. But then his negotiating position was far more precarious. Jordan was the most suspect in the Arab world for its friendship with the United States and willingness to settle with Israel. Afterward, Rifai admitted to me privately that his tone reflected the necessities of Arab politics. It was a bizarre peace conference — though surely not the only one in history — at which the public positions of the contending parties had on the whole to be seen as a counterpoint to what they were actually doing. The belligerence of the oratory was in direct relation to the conciliatoriness of the policy.

Israel's Foreign Minister Abba Eban spoke at the end. He had requested to be the last speaker, perhaps to reflect on some points made in the morning session, probably to set off his eloquence by having it stand alone — an unnecessary embellishment. In a statement punctuated by the oratorical flourishes for which he had become renowned, Eban gave the longest and clearly the best speech of the conference. Moderate in tone, firm in substance, it stressed the importance of legal obligations of peace, rejected the concept of a Palestinian state, and asked for patience in what was bound to be a prolonged effort. Fahmy found it necessary to rebut; then the formal session of the Geneva Conference was at an end.

I had private meetings with Fahmy, Rifai, Eban, and Gromyko to go over the procedures once again. Fahmy thought it desirable that the conference remain juridically and procedurally in session to provide a framework for the disengagement talks I had promised for January. He was so distrustful of Israeli motives and so eager to prove to his brethren that "something" was going on that he requested the immediate presence in Geneva of an Israeli military officer so that military talks — a continuation of Kilometer 101 — could be seen taking place in the interval. I arranged this with Eban despite my premonitions of what that officer would produce. An Israeli officer promptly appeared for talks starting on December 26 and was to cause no little havoc.

All the tactical maneuvering was the surface manifestation of a fundamental change. The Geneva Conference, whatever its bizarre aspects, was not an inconsiderable achievement in itself. For the first time two Arab states — Egypt and Jordan — sent high-level representatives to sit around the same table with Israel. While all three made speeches de-

signed for their domestic audiences, each carefully avoided setting preconditions or taking positions that would close the door to future negotiations. No one walked out. And all present agreed to the American
step-by-step approach.

Equally significant was the attitude of Syria. True, it did not attend
the conference. But that its absence was largely tactical was reflected in
Damascus's acquiescence in keeping a place at the table for it with its
nameplate. Syria was thus a charter member of the conference, with the
option of joining either the plenary session or a subgroup.

So Geneva was a major step forward in the strategy that we had
tenaciously pursued since the October war. During that war, our nightmare had been a triumph of Soviet arms, growing Soviet influence in
the Middle East, Israeli panic, the rallying of Arab nations behind a
radical program in hostility to the United States, and a coalition of Europe and Japan dissociating from us and backing radical pressures out
of fear of losing oil supplies. In such conditions, no constructive diplomacy could have followed the war.

We had begun a peace process, and had done this in the midst of
Watergate. America's executive authority was draining away daily. My
best explanation for this paradox is that the Arab states could not admit
to themselves the impotence of their deus ex machina nor the Israelis
the potential weakness of their protector. They helped us sustain a mirage of American decisiveness and purposefulness, which, like so many
acts of faith in the Middle East's turbulent history, created its own reality.

Thus, the Geneva Conference of 1973 opened the door to peace
through which later Egypt and Israel walked, and through which it is to
be hoped that other nations of the Middle East will walk in the fullness
of time.

XVIII

The First Shuttle:
Egyptian-Israeli Disengagement

The Origin of Shuttle Diplomacy

SHUTTLE diplomacy" has become the catch phrase for my negotiations in the Middle East — as if commuting between capitals had been invented for that special purpose. In fact, the term was coined by the indefatigable Joe Sisco as we found ourselves flying back and forth between Aswan and Jerusalem during the second week of January 1974. And the idea of completing the Sinai disengagement negotiation in one continuous assault came from Anwar Sadat, who suggested that my January trip — conceived as an effort to define principles of disengagement — be turned into the occasion for a definitive agreement.

In truth, the seeds of the "breakthrough" of January 1974 had been sown at least three months earlier. It was the culmination of the strategy we had imposed on the October war: to thwart a victory of Soviet arms; to prevent the humiliation of the Arabs, especially on the Egyptian front; to convene a peace conference in which subgroups would negotiate detail away from the rhetoric of plenary sessions; to seek results step by step rather than in one comprehensive negotiation; and to cement ties with Egypt, which was courageously willing to show the way.

A rapid separation of forces along the Suez Canal was the key. I was sure it would bring Syria in its wake, almost certainly result in an end to the oil embargo, and enable us to pursue the peace process with less danger of a blowup.

Sadat had been pondering disengagement ever since we had agreed, during my November trip, that it would be the first item on the agenda of the Geneva Conference. He had put forward general ideas then and in December, with the sweetener for Israel that after disengagement he would clear and reopen the Suez Canal (blocked since the June 1967 war). Israeli and Egyptian military officers had discussed disengagement at Kilometer 101, where the Israeli representative, General Yariv, had outlined an Israeli "concept." While the talks had ended in an impasse, they had served a very useful purpose in educating both sides about the outer limits of what was possible.

After the Geneva Conference opened on December 21–22, Egypt was so eager to show progress toward disengagement that it pressed for a meeting of the Egyptian-Israeli military working group at Geneva on December 26 — in essence an extension of Kilometer 101 — even though everyone recognized that nothing could happen until after the Israeli elections on December 31. Separately, I had secured the Israeli government's promise to submit a formal disengagement proposal immediately after the elections. In the complex world of Israeli domestic politics, this was not a simple matter. In Israel's history no party has ever won a majority; every government has been a coalition of competing parties in turn split into factions more cohesive than the party organization. Cabinet unity is all the more tenuous in the aftermath of an election — especially one with ambiguous results. As it turned out, in the December 31, 1973, balloting, the governing Labour Party lost 5 percent of its strength, which translated into a loss of seven seats in the 120-member Parliament (to 49 seats, down from 56). The setback was incurred largely because its prestige had been tarnished by the October war. It could still muster a majority with its traditional coalition partner, the National Religious Party, but the influence of that party, dedicated to annexing the West Bank, would be much greater. Golda could remain as Prime Minister if her party wanted her; but her standing, too, had been diminished by the war's outcome.

Volatile as Israeli cabinets are, however, they are paradoxically at their most stable in the run-up to elections or while coalition negotiations are taking place. By a quirk of the constitution, ministers are not *permitted* to resign during that period; the composition of a caretaker government is, in fact, frozen.

It was at such a time — as coalition negotiations were just starting — that Defense Minister Moshe Dayan appeared in Washington at the beginning of January 1974. He brought with him the first feasible disengagement plan approved by the cabinet. Dayan's new plan put meat on the bones of the "concept" offered by General Yariv at the Kilometer 101 talks. In characteristic Israeli negotiating style, he presented the scheme as one without flexibility; the cabinet insisted that there would be little margin left for negotiation.

Dayan envisaged allowing Egypt to keep the territory it had won, to a line roughly six to ten kilometers forward on the east bank of the Suez Canal, and withdrawing Israeli forces to a new line about twenty kilometers east of the Canal. This meant that Israel was relinquishing its bridgehead on the west bank — in what Golda liked to call "Africa" — by which Israel had cut off the Egyptian Third Army in the southern portion of the front.

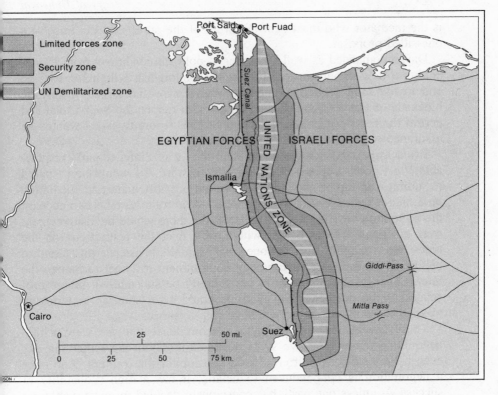

Egyptian-Israeli Disengagement: Dayan's Plan, January 4, 1974

At the same time, Dayan proposed a "thinning-out" of military forces on both sides of the Canal. Specifically, he put forward five separate zones of arms restrictions extending over a total of ninety kilometers. In the Sinai the two sides would be separated by a United Nations buffer zone of a width of six to ten kilometers. On either side the military forces would be thinned out in a "light security zone" of six to ten kilometers; and beyond it on each side would be a further zone of arms limitations to a distance of thirty kilometers. Israel's main forward line would be just to the west of the two Sinai passes.

The practical consequence of Dayan's scheme was to require the withdrawal of all the Egyptian forces that had crossed the Suez Canal during the war except for a mere two or three battalions (or 1,800 men). Two Egyptian field armies, numbering 70,000 men, 720 tanks, and 994 pieces of artillery, would have to leave the Sinai. Dayan was especially adamant that no Egyptian tanks remain on the east bank of the Canal. Behind this belt, in Egypt's zone of limited armaments (the thirty kilometers west of the Canal), Dayan wanted a ceiling of 300 tanks and a pullback of artillery and antiaircraft defenses so that they could not reach the Israeli line. Clearly, Dayan was taking advantage of the fact that it is the mediator who must bear the brunt of the other side's outrage at a one-sided proposal.

Dayan demanded as well a number of political conditions from Egypt, adding a new dimension not previously explored at Kilometer 101: an end to the state of belligerency between Egypt and Israel, lifting the blockade of Bab el-Mandeb, and a pledge to reopen the Suez Canal and permit the transit of Israeli ships and cargoes. From us Israel wanted an assurance of long-term arms supply.

I told Dayan that his disengagement plan was "intellectually respectable," a "good proposal," a "big step forward." I would be prepared to submit it to Egypt, though we could not possibly undertake mediation on a take-it-or-leave-it basis. There had to be room to take into account the Egyptian point of view. I predicted that there would be disagreement over the depth of the Israeli withdrawal; over the restrictions on the types of arms in the various zones; over Israel's insistence on an end to belligerency; and over an Egyptian commitment to Israel to reopen the Suez Canal. Some of the objections would be substantive, others procedural. I did not believe that Egypt would give Israel an undertaking of what it would do on its own sovereign territory.

These caveats did not dampen my confidence that we were within negotiating range. The two sides were talking about the same concepts even if they still gave different practical application to them. And once a negotiation is thus reduced to details, it has a high probability of success — unless one party has consciously decided to make a show of flexibility simply to put itself in a better light for a deliberate breakup of the talks. Egypt was precluded from such a course by the plight of the Third Army, Israel by the fear of diplomatic isolation. The odds favored success, even though major differences remained.

I therefore discussed with Dayan how to give the negotiations maximum momentum. Three possibilities suggested themselves: Israel might introduce its new plan at the Egyptian-Israeli working group at Geneva. The United States could have its Ambassador in Cairo present it to the Egyptian government, preferably to Sadat himself. Or I could travel to the Middle East to work out general principles that would then be turned over to the Geneva working group for implementation. The difficulty with starting at Geneva was that the Soviets would be able to stall progress by putting forward unfulfillable suggestions and embarrassing Egypt if it sought to be flexible. Also, the proposal would have to run the obstacle course of the Egyptian bureaucracy, which would play safe, pointing out the shortcomings and leaving it to Sadat to overrule them. Sadat might be prepared to do that; but it would make life unnecessarily complicated for him. If we asked our Ambassador, Hermann Eilts, to present the Israeli plan we could be sure that Sadat would see it first. But Eilts had no authority to negotiate and no access to Israeli deliberations. The approach did not lend itself to Sadat's propensity for the sudden stroke.

All this drew Dayan and me to the idea that I should present the Israeli proposal to Sadat personally — all the more so as I had promised Sadat that I would involve myself directly as soon as the Israeli elections were over. No doubt there was an element of vanity involved on my side as well, and a touch of flattery and domestic politics on Dayan's. He favored an agreement; but he needed help in putting his ideas through the Israeli Parliament.

What came to be seen as a dramatic, surprising coup was thus in fact carefully prepared. In my view, the Secretary of State should not, as a general rule, go abroad on a serious negotiation unless the odds are heavily in his favor. Since in diplomacy the margins of decisions are narrow, the psychological element can be of great consequence. A reputation for success tends to be self-fulfilling. Equally, failure feeds on itself: A Secretary of State who undertakes too many journeys that lead nowhere depreciates his coin. And it is dangerous to rely on personality or negotiating skill to break deadlocks; they cannot redeem the shortcomings of an ill-considered strategy. By early January 1974, however, the ground was as well prepared as it was ever going to be. We had been working on the problem for two months. The positions of the two sides were approaching each other; both feared the penalties of failure.

As Dayan and I were considering how to proceed, the Israeli proposal surfaced disconcertingly in another channel. Difficult as it is to extract a negotiating position from the Israeli government, it is next to impossible to keep it secret once it has been formulated. Each minister is tempted to raise his own visibility by claiming credit; each negotiator wants to be perceived as the author of the breakthrough. There is rarely a penalty for even a gross breach of discipline. Yet it was essential to keep this Israeli concept secret for several reasons: Egypt would find it easier to accept if it appeared to result from American influence, rather than to be an Israeli demand. It would become a public benchmark, making it harder for either side to yield in the subsequent bargaining. Publicity would tempt other parties, including the Soviets, to enter the process.

My colleagues and I were therefore horror-struck when a telegram from Geneva was brought into my meeting with Dayan on January 5, according to which the Israeli representative on the Geneva working group, General Mordechai Gur, had presented two hypothetical "models," one of which was suspiciously close to what Dayan was putting forward in Washington. Dayan professed to be equally stunned. The American position became especially difficult. We could hardly claim, I told Dayan, that the proposal had been worked on jointly by Israel and the United States when it was being presented in Geneva while he was meeting with me. The Egyptians would not be able to distinguish between a "model" and a formal proposal, not to mention the psychological difficulty for Egypt in accepting something that Israel proposed, however reasonable. Furthermore, the Soviets were bound to involve themselves — as indeed they did a few days later when Dobrynin phoned in some reflections on the Gur "model." The difficulty was overcome when General Gur withdrew his "model" a few days after it was presented, claiming unconvincingly that it had been put forward only as an "illustration."

I doubt that the charade fooled Sadat; after all, similar ideas were all over the Israeli press. He went along with it because it served his strategic purpose to present the disengagement agreement as having resulted from an American initiative. At that point it would be too dangerous for him to treat directly with Israel. We continued therefore to plan for a trip by me to Cairo. I sent Sadat a message that I would be prepared to go to Egypt to obtain his views as to appropriate principles of disengagement. Meanwhile, Dayan would take my suggestions to the Israeli cabinet. On January 8 Sadat urged me to come immediately; he would await me in Aswan.

By this time, Watergate pressures were producing some anxious moments. Nixon, who had extended his stay in San Clemente, was chafing at my growing prominence; his reaction to the Pilgrims speech was not an isolated case. During his retreat he rarely spoke to me; chief of staff Al Haig was my point of contact. He reported that Nixon was tense and distraught. The President had not given up the idea that some spectacular success could demonstrate his indispensability and thereby end his torment. His recurrent dream was an initiative to end the oil embargo. For example, on January 7 Haig told me that a California oil executive had just introduced Nixon to an Arab emissary who promised to be helpful in doing just that. I never learned his name nor what was discussed; it was a replay of the Dobrynin audience of three weeks before. There was no way the oil embargo could be ended through a personal tour de force or through such a channel. But the secretiveness showed that Watergate might soon claim the confidence between President and Secretary of State essential for a functioning foreign policy in the best of times — not to speak of the crisis of institutions through which we were passing.

On January 8 I informed Haig of my conviction that Sadat wanted "to settle fast," yet "with all this fancy footwork going on, if we don't wrap this thing up fast, it will never happen." Haig did not know what Nixon's reaction would be; he still seemed preoccupied with the mysterious emissary. Our fear that Nixon might drag his feet proved groundless. We know from his own diary that he was making notes for himself at this time on how he might run the campaign of his life against impeachment (January 5: "[A]ct like a President"); [1] he certainly acted like one when late in the day he approved my trip.

There were only a few loose ends left. If at all possible, I wanted to keep the Soviets calm while I pushed disengagement. I told Dobrynin that the purpose of my trip was to transform Israeli "models" into a concrete proposal. Ellsworth Bunker, our permanent representative to the Geneva talks, would be with me; the results could then be fed into Geneva for detailed negotiations. That suited Dobrynin fine; he knew the Soviets had no capacity to promote a disengagement scheme and they would get a crack at the "principles" in Geneva. (It was not intended as a trick though it worked out that way; it was precisely the procedure we intended to follow until Sadat speeded matters up *after* I reached Aswan.) Dobrynin wished me the "very best" for the trip — implying that the Soviets would stay quiescent.

I gave UN Secretary-General Waldheim the same briefing. Waldheim could be useful if the negotiations returned to Geneva and would give what he was told wide distribution to those — mostly among the non-aligned — more willing to rely on information from a third party than from us.

With these preliminaries out of the way, I left Andrews Air Force Base shortly after midnight on the morning of Friday, January 11, 1974, for what turned into the first "shuttle."

Watergate Again

WATERGATE was a hydra-headed monster. There was no way of knowing when a new sensation would seize public attention. In the miasma of doubt and suspicion, every revelation — no matter how trivial or how unrelated to others — fed the seemingly inexhaustible obsession with scandal. Anything that appeared to deviate from previous accounts raised the specter of a "credibility gap" for the Administration, and for me the nightmare of dissipating the last vestiges of executive authority for the conduct of foreign policy.

On the very day I left for the Middle East, a bizarre event from the year 1971 became public for the first time. The facts were these: Since October 1962, around the time of the Cuban missile crisis, a representative of the Joint Chiefs of Staff had been assigned to the National Security Council staff as a liaison officer, to improve communication between the Pentagon and the White House. Duties of a liaison office are somewhat ambiguous. Theoretically, the White House is entitled to all the information it needs or requests, and, in turn, it has an interest in seeing that key agencies are adequately informed.

Reality is not so simple. The White House often does not know what papers exist in the bureaucracy; the agencies do not always understand what is wanted; even when they do they are loath to bare their internal disputes. If in doubt, they are tempted to put themselves in the most favorable light — to suppress, not to put too fine a point on it, unfavorable or embarrassing information or views contrary to their final recommendations. The same holds true, of course, for White House dissemination of its own information.

A skillful liaison officer with an alert staff can help the White House and the agencies understand each other better. He functions in some ways like a military attaché overseas. He treads a delicate line between serving the common interest in obtaining what has not been distributed out of ignorance or oversight, and seeking to ferret out what has consciously been kept in restricted channels. When the latter is done by a department or agency against the White House, it approaches spying on the Chief Executive by his subordinates. However they may deplore a President's administrative practices, officials of subordinate agencies should not circumvent them by stealth.

Late in 1971 I became aware that some of the personnel of the NSC liaison office of the Joint Chiefs of Staff may have crossed the line between liaison and abuse of trust. During the India-Pakistan war a passionate controversy broke out in America over whether the Administration was unduly "tilting" toward Pakistan. As part of the bitter bureaucratic battle, a number of highly classified documents were leaked to columnist Jack Anderson; some concerned US naval deployments in the Bay of Bengal. To his enormous credit Rear Admiral Robert O. Welander, head of the JCS liaison office at the time, told Haig, then my deputy, that internal evidence suggested that his office might be the origin of the leaks. Haig told me and, on my instruction, Presidential Assistant John Ehrlichman, who had been assigned by Nixon to investigate the Anderson leaks.

A Navy yeoman on Welander's staff turned out to be a principal suspect; if he gave classified documents to Anderson (which is still disputed), it was the culmination of a remarkable career of systematic reporting on his White House superiors. The young yeoman had the advantage that he was considered so insignificant that no one thought of taking precautions against him. He often served as a trusted messenger carrying important documents between my office and the Executive Office Building across the street, where most of my staff were located. He was an indefatigable worker. General Haig had taken him along on occasional trips to Southeast Asia; on Haig's recommendation he had accompanied me on my around-the-world trip in the summer of 1971. He used the occasion to make himself generally useful, in the process — as he later testified — going through my briefcase, reading or duplicating whatever papers he could get his hands on, and sometimes retaining discarded carbon copies of sensitive documents that were intended to be disposed of in the "burn bag." He delivered a huge quantity of documents to the head of the JCS liaison office, who passed them on to the Chairman of the Joint Chiefs. In this manner the Chairman may have learned of my secret visit to Peking all of two days before it was announced. (The yeoman did not go into China with me nor was he told about it. But he seems to have acquired a copy of trip reports to Nixon and other sensitive messages, which were drafted and typed on the plane ride home.)

The expanding practice of the liaison function apparently started early in my tenure as national security adviser. Whether the then Chairman, General Earle Wheeler, knew how the documents were acquired or whether he simply accepted them as the assiduous work of the liaison officer, I cannot judge. I considered Wheeler (who has since died) a man of extraordinary decency. It was continued under Admiral Thomas Moorer, who became Chairman in 1970. Moorer has insisted that he was not told how the documents were obtained nor did he pay particular attention to them since he had already been told their substance by me. I have no reason to question the word of an officer with whom I worked closely and whom I greatly respected.

In the immediate aftermath of the disclosures I felt less charitable. I learned what I have described here from John Ehrlichman. He permitted me to listen to part of a taped interview with Admiral Welander summing up what I have recounted. On the basis of this, I thought I knew enough in December 1971 to be deeply hurt. At the time, Nixon told me that if I wished he was prepared to take disciplinary action against Welander and not to reappoint Moorer as Chairman when his term expired six months hence. But I should consider, he said, the impact on the military services and the country of washing such dirty linen in public in the midst of the Vietnam war and the pitiless assault on the military establishment. Should we add grist to the peace movement's mill? I accepted Nixon's arguments. In December 1971 I closed the JCS liaison office and requested the transfer of all its personnel within twenty-four hours. I took no other action. Neither did Nixon.

Welander served in other posts and later retired; the yeoman also was transferred elsewhere. As these facts continued leaking out while I was in the Middle East in January 1974, they were turned not against those individuals whom one might have thought guilty of trespass, but against Nixon and his Administration; the media pursued me also. What kind of government was this in which military personnel colluded in the misappropriation of documents and suspects were interviewed on tape? And had I lied in May 1973 when I said I had not been aware of the "Plumbers unit," since the questioning of the Admiral was by "Plumber" David Young? I have already described the degree of my knowledge of the "Plumbers" in Chapter IV. I did, of course, know that investigating security leaks was Ehrlichman's responsibility. My impression was that such investigations as he conducted were ad hoc; the reality seems to be that his aides (Egil Krogh and David Young) had no other responsibilities. The nuance was lost in the sensational stories now unfolding. There was no way of my deducing from listening to the tape of a single interview that Young had no additional responsibilities, nor would I have thought it strange if that had been told me. The fact was that I gave the matter little thought one way or another.

That one interview was all I ever learned of the investigation of the yeoman. Ehrlichman submitted a formal report, which he never showed me. Secretary of Defense Melvin Laird also requested an investigation from his general counsel, Fred Buzhardt; that, too, was never shown to me. This was not unusual in the Nixon White House. The flow of information was strictly compartmentalized and internal security was considered outside my province.

The question might, of course, have been approached differently by the media. If it was true that military secrets were being leaked to the press for political purposes even by uniformed personnel, what the media had been pleased to call Nixon's paranoia might turn out to have some basis in fact. While this would not excuse the transgressions constituting the body of Watergate, it might partially explain their origin and thus mitigate the judgment.

But by then Watergate had its own logic. The quarry would not be permitted to plead extenuating circumstances. The blame for the military spying would be placed on the victim, not the perpetrator. Three lines of argument developed. One was that Nixon's decision-making process was so secretive that the Joint Chiefs had been forced to take matters into their own hands. Another was that since the liaison office existed to speed the flow of information from the Pentagon to the White House, turnabout was fair play: The military had every right to impose reciprocity on the Commander-in-Chief, extracting what information they desired by whatever methods served that purpose. The whole affair, so ran the third line of argument, was a petulant White House reaction to leaking — in other words, the episode proved the original charge of paranoia.

My reaction was summed up in a recommendation I sent from Aswan on January 14 to Scowcroft:

The facts of the case, which I believe should be taken into account in developing any reply, are as follows:

— The activities of the JCS which the [news]papers term "spying" began in 1969, not as a result of initiatives taken in 1971.

— These actions went on during my first secret diplomatic initiative and therefore could hardly have been caused by it.

— No intelligence information of any kind has ever been withheld from any member of the National Security Council. Since the Joint Chiefs were represented on the WSAG, it is insane to say that "transcripts of deliberations" of the WSAG were targets of the intelligence effort.

— The only matters handled on a restricted basis were three secret negotiations. But even here, the substance was reviewed by the various interdepartmental bodies, although the purpose was not always known.

The JCS Liaison Office was established for the precise purpose of giving the military access to the activities of the National Security Council and the NSC staff. This fact also belies the charges now appearing in the press.

It would be useful to challenge those who are making these charges to be specific as to what documents were ever kept from the Chiefs. I know of none.

My analysis was better than my advice. There was no sense in debating whether there could ever be justification for a subordinate agency to purloin documents from the White House without authority. Such actions cannot be condoned, whatever secrecy the White House deems necessary and however it organizes its policymaking. The only sensible course was the one followed by Moorer. He denied that he had any need to spy on the White House since he had a close relationship with me; the whole enterprise was the work of overeager subordinates. I had, in fact, made a similar comment to Senator John Stennis, Chairman of the Senate Armed Services Committee, on January 10, hours before leaving for the Middle East. I had urged him to take jurisdiction as quickly as possible before less responsible groups drew the uniformed military into the maelstrom of Watergate.

Senator Stennis conducted hearings in February 1974.[2] The Armed Services Committee published a report clearing Admiral Moorer and putting the issue into context. The incident is recounted here because it is luridly symptomatic of the Watergate atmosphere that, while our Middle East policy hung in the balance, during the entire week of the first shuttle the media were bemused by pursuing lines of inquiry whose practical consequence could only be to undermine the authority of the negotiator. In fairness to the media, it must be noted that no such harm in fact developed. Still, it all certainly added to the mental and physical burdens of a fateful and frenetic week.

Aswan: January 11–12

THE itinerary for my trip — first to Egypt, then to Israel, and back again to Egypt — had been choreographed with an eye to the psychological necessities and the margins for maneuver available to each side. I did not want to arrive in Egypt with an "Israeli plan," for that would make me appear as if I were Israel's spokesman. General Gur's premature presentation of the "model" at Geneva and its subsequent withdrawal could even be turned to advantage by making it appear as if cabinet divisions had been overcome by our intercession. Sadat correctly understood the Israeli situation — I had, after all, promised him a concrete plan for January — but it served his domestic purpose to exalt the American role. And because the actual scope for negotiation was likely to be limited, it was important to present the initial Israeli plan as something influenced by us and already taking account of Egyptian views (which had the added virtue of being true).

After a brief refueling stop in Spain, we landed around 8:30 P.M. on Friday, January 11, on a blacked-out military airfield in the desert near Aswan. It was my first time in Upper Egypt. Despite the evening hour, one could see concrete shelters, antiaircraft weapons, tanks, armored personnel carriers, and troop concentrations. Aswan was an area of extraordinary sensitivity for Egypt; destruction of the High Dam could ruin the country's economy for a long time to come. My own concerns were more self-centered. We knew that a squadron of North Korean fighter planes was stationed at Aswan. I wondered in what language the Egyptians communicated with their allies and whether the knowledge that the American Secretary of State was approaching would act as a deterrent or a spur to the Korean air force.

Foreign Minister Fahmy greeted me with the by-now traditional kiss and embrace in the dark in front of the dingy terminal. I expected to begin the talks in the morning. Whenever possible I scheduled my overseas trips so that I would arrive too late for serious discussions; this gave me a night's sleep to recover from jet lag. (In fact, I was never consciously aware of any disequilibrium, though those who had to deal with me might differ.) But Fahmy told me that Sadat was waiting, leaving me no choice.

Aswan is a resort town, some 400 miles south of Cairo, whose mild climate drew Sadat to move his office there for several weeks in the winter months. At the first cataract of the Nile, it marks the limit of the Upper Egypt of Pharaonic times; beyond it lie Nubia and present-day Sudan. It is an oasis of serenity alongside that ribbon of water that brings life and hope to men and flood and nourishment to the countryside. The cultivation on both sides of the river is a narrow strip much less extensive than that in Lower Egypt, the fertile Nile Delta; occasionally it disappears altogether.

Driving in from the airport, one traverses the original Aswan Dam, built by British engineers around the turn of the century. It is far less ambitious than the Soviet-constructed High Dam and less effective in controlling floods; on balance it is ecologically far less damaging, for it does not interfere with the life-giving silt that the High Dam has cut off, forcing Egypt to import large quantities of fertilizer and destroying fishing off Alexandria. Dhows can be seen on the river as it winds through the narrow strip of green. On both sides huge sand dunes stretch to a far horizon. The desert here creates a sameness that causes a wanderer without compass soon to lose all sense of direction. Not a sound can be heard, and in the stillness one feels strangely detached, as if transported to some distant, desolate planet.

Sadat's villa was an unprepossessing stone government rest house. One entered a small vestibule. Directly ahead was a study overlooking the Nile; the furniture was placed so that one faced the door and not the view. Sadat and I would usually sit on opposite ends of a sofa, parallel to the windows; there were some other easy chairs scattered about. (On this shuttle we usually met alone; in later negotiations, then–Vice President Hosni Mubarak was almost always present.) To the right of the study was a conference room; to the left a dining room.

Sadat, wearing his military uniform, greeted me with a booming "Welcome" and drew me into the study. As was his wont, he went straight to the heart of the problem. He saw no sense, he said, in developing "principles" that would then be filled in at Geneva. Such a procedure provided too many opportunities for radical Arab opposition and Soviet mischief. And the effort to produce agreed principles could not be much less than that to finish the job. The laborious diplomacy since the October war had to be brought to some conclusion; the time had come to sum up all the exchanges, agreements in principle, and vague hints in a final document. Sadat therefore asked that I stay in the Middle East until the negotiations had either succeeded or failed. He would cooperate to the utmost. A disengagement agreement, in his view, was essential to turn a new page in Arab-American relations and give momentum to the peace process with Israel.

To demonstrate his sincerity, Sadat gave himself a deadline. He had scheduled a trip around the Arab world starting the following weekend (January 18). He hoped to complete the agreement before then. In that case he would urge an end to the oil embargo as he made the rounds of various capitals. And Sadat offered to promote the lifting of the embargo in any manner that would publicly give Nixon the credit — showing that our domestic difficulties had not gone unnoticed in Egypt.

The carrot he held out to us was in fact much less significant than the deadline he gave himself. Normally, a negotiator who sets a time limit weakens his own position, unless the mediator in turn is convinced that the failure of the negotiation is more dangerous to his own country than to the parties — a highly unusual state of affairs. This was far from the case in the disengagement talks. So Sadat's deadline guaranteed that he would go to the limit of possible concessions. We agreed that we would review the substance of the proposals over lunch the next day.

At 11:00 P.M. I finally arrived at my lodging, the New Cataract Hotel, a high-rise modern structure located at a picturesque bend in the Nile. Nestled beside it was the old Cataract Hotel, a superb sandstone relic of a vanished time, with huge fans rotating from high ceilings; shuttered windows made the musty atmosphere appear slightly mysterious. It looked like the setting for an Agatha Christie novel — as indeed it had been — but it had now gone to seed along with the colonial pretensions of Great Britain, the aristocratic taste of whose ruling class it reflected. The New Cataract Hotel bespoke the values of a newer imperialism — that of the Soviet Union. Its only concession to aesthetics was the unavoidable view across the older namesake toward the Nile and beyond it the white marble mausoleum of the Aga Khan. Inside the hotel all is functional and shoddy, as if a concession to personal comfort would acknowledge an individualism that the Communist system is determined to transcend. Fahmy was keen to test our endurance by inviting my party and me to a late supper in the deserted dining room.

On Saturday morning the Egyptians made a gesture to humaneness. They arranged some sight-seeing before I went back to negotiating. I saw at last the monumental High Dam in Aswan, violating one of my cardinal principles of sight-seeing when on official travel: Never visit in a foreign country what you would refuse to see in your own. This rule had enabled me to avoid steel mills, oil refineries, and other wonders of modern technology all with the common feature that their mechanism is as obscure as their architecture is uninteresting. But the Egyptians seemed to want to make some subtle political point by taking me there — whether to needle the United States or the Soviet Union was not clear. So I attempted to look fascinated as engineers explained the operation of the huge turbines and was in fact engrossed by the tremendous manmade lake forming behind the dam's sullen gray walls.

Next we visited a place I would have gone to see anywhere. We took boats to the spectacular Philae temples that were in the process of being rescued from the rising waters of Lake Nasser (as the area inundated by the barrier of the High Dam was called). We saw this engineering feat at an early stage. Two tremendous pylons that marked the entrance stood out from the swirling waters — defying the elements as until now they had withstood time. "Before we are through here," I joked to an accompanying newsman, "we will see it all." I was not far off the mark. During the negotiations of 1975, I paid another visit to Philae. A cofferdam was holding back the waters from the site, by then fully drained of water and dry in the summer sun. We toured the magnificent structures on the lake bottom before the process of moving them to higher ground had begun. Five years later the temples stood fully rebuilt and resplendent on a nearby island.

At 11:00 A.M. I was back at Sadat's villa. Over lunch we reviewed the state of the negotiations. Three sets of issues confronted us: the

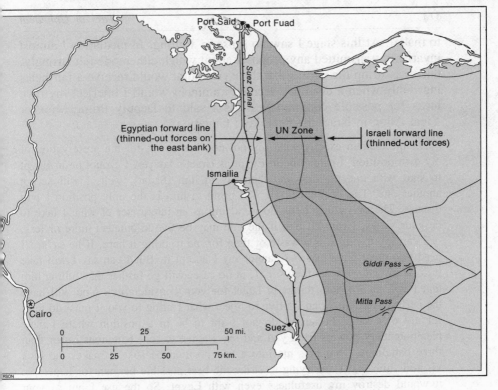

Port Said　Port Fuad

Suez Canal

Egyptian forward line
(thinned-out forces on
the east bank)

UN Zone

Israeli forward line
(thinned-out forces)

Ismailia

Giddi Pass

Mitla Pass

Cairo

Suez

| 0 | | 25 | | 50 mi. |
| 0 | 25 | | 50 | 75 km. |

Egyptian-Israeli Disengagement: Sadat's Concept,
December 1973 (approximation)

location of the forward lines of the two armies; the extent of the zones
of limited armaments and the nature of the limitations; and assurances
on such issues as Israeli passage through the straits of Bab el-Mandeb
and Tiran as well as through the Suez Canal. There was also the Israeli
shopping list of which Sadat was as yet mercifully ignorant, about an
end to the state of belligerency, reopening the Canal, and rebuilding the
Canal cities. (I held this for later; if we got hung up on the principal
issue, these requests would only confuse matters. If we scored a breakthrough, it would ease the disposition of these problems.)

Sadat had long since abandoned his scheme of a deep Israeli withdrawal two-thirds of the way across the Sinai. Still, he maintained his
December position that Israel should vacate the strategic Mitla and Giddi
passes. As for arms limitation, he now reduced the number of troops he
wanted to retain on the east bank of the Canal from three divisions to
an absolute "minimum" of one and a half divisions; he rejected the
stringent restrictions on types of weapons that Israel proposed.

I knew that none of this would be accepted by Israel (and so probably
did Sadat, if his staff had given him summaries of the Israeli press in
full cry since the leaking of the Dayan plan — but he, too, had a record

to make). At this stage I saw no sense in arguing. In mediation I almost invariably transmitted any proposal about which either side felt strongly, thus reassuring the parties that their viewpoint would receive a fair hearing. Only when a deadlock seemed imminent would I interject my own ideas for possible compromises. As I said to Deputy Prime Minister Yigal Allon in Israel the next day (January 13):

> Let me explain exactly what my position has to be, for the preservation of my own position. I cannot be in Egypt as Israel's lawyer. I cannot be in Egypt to start with one position and then say to him [Sadat], well, I will accept another one. The position that I will bring to him is the only position I will discuss. The only thing I can do is, acting as an interpreter of what I take to be your views, I can tell him if the line may be five kilometers more or less, or I can say to him it is a waste of time for me to bring it here. If he says, "I need two more battalions," I cannot say I accept it. But I can say I will take it to Israel and see what they say. I, in no case, will go further than telling him that I will take certain things to Israel for your consideration. You will have the perfect freedom when I arrive to reject what I bring to you. I must do that, for my own sake, because I do not want to be in a position where I have plenipotentiary powers from you and say I agree to four battalions rather than three battalions. That puts me into a bad position because it makes me look vis-à-vis him that I am trying to strike the best possible bargain for Israel. So it would destroy my usefulness even with Egypt. So the use I am as your intermediary is to give him my interpretation of your thinking and steer him away from some things altogether; others I bring here and you can still reject them.

The same principles applied, of course, when I brought Egyptian proposals to Israel. Meticulousness did not necessarily ease my task. Mediation tempts the parties to advance extreme proposals and to blame the mediator for insufficient effort if they are rejected or to use him as an excuse for their failure to put forward what they know cannot be achieved. The Israeli cabinet was especially skillful in using outside mediation as a foil for its own decision-making.

While Sadat's tone was firm, his insistence on a rapid settlement left little doubt that his ideas were not put forward on a peremptory basis. He affirmed that upon disengagement the blockade of Bab el-Mandeb would be lifted and cargoes bound to or from Israel would be able to transit the Suez Canal. He knew, said Sadat with a twinkle in his eyes, that Israel was demanding passage for its own ships, but after all, Dayan's son-in-law, Colonel Dov Sion, had publicly stated that Israel would settle for cargoes. (Another opening position abandoned for a one-day publicity stunt, I thought with melancholy.) More helpfully, Sadat promised not to raise the Palestinian issue during the disengagement phase —including the Syrian one.

Sadat grew so enthusiastic about our prospects that he began to speculate on the modalities of signing. For fear of some Soviet maneuver, he did not want even the signing in Geneva. He proposed Kilometer 101. And proudly he came up with an idea that would have the rare merit of driving both Nixon and the Soviets up the wall: that I attend the signing ceremony. As yet we were far from that point. But I had no intention of infuriating Nixon with another dramatic burst of publicity or humiliating Gromyko by a symbolic demonstration of what had become the reality: that the much-touted, much-debated "US–Soviet auspices" had turned into a unilateral American initiative.

All this left Syria out of the process. Sadat was convinced that unless Egypt proceeded alone, President Hafez al-Asad would always find some pretext for delay or put forward impossible demands. A Sinai agreement would thus, in Sadat's view, help Syria face its realities. Since Syria was reluctant to go to Geneva, Sadat offered to have Syrian officers join the Egyptian military delegation to create a forum for its disengagement talks. I was not sure that relations between the two allies would allow this or that Asad would accept a procedure for Syria different from that followed with Egypt. But these were technical matters almost irrelevant to the key issue. Sadat posed its essence as the choice of either stalemate for everybody, or initial progress for Egypt that would unlock the door for Syria and eventually to a general peace. And in that assessment he was right.

The meeting with Sadat had lasted three and a half hours. At 4:00 P.M. on Saturday, January 12, I left Aswan for the two-hour flight to Israel to receive the final formulation of the Israeli plan.

Jerusalem: January 12–13

EN route, I learned that Golda would be unable to participate in the talks. She had come down with shingles, a nerve disease. (In Israel it was said that Golda suffered from so many illnesses that any Israeli medical student fortunate enough to examine her automatically received a medical degree.) If the negotiations failed, would Sadat ever believe that her illness had been genuine?

Still, I did not really believe the negotiations would fail. Israel needed an agreement for its own reasons. It could not hold its enclave on the west bank of the Suez Canal without remaining mobilized, which meant a difficult burden for its economy. And it would face near-certain isolation in the alternative forum of Geneva. This became clear when I visited Golda in her small private home on a narrow Jerusalem street around 8:00 P.M., shortly after arriving. In America its modest-sized living room, tiny study, and small dining room would have been lower middle-class; here it housed the Prime Minister. Golda was weak and in pain but in fine sardonic form. She expressed her distrust of Sadat, her abiding suspicion of all things Egyptian and of any scheme involving Israeli withdrawals. But it was good-humored; it was to put me on notice not to get overconfident. It lacked a confrontational charge; we were clearly not in for one of the nerve-racking, legalistic, nitpicking sessions.

Not that Israeli negotiators are ever easy. There was to be no sightseeing yet in Israel. Even at less than an all-out pace, there would be a schedule to demonstrate to the cabinet that the Israeli negotiating team had not failed to test my endurance. My call on Golda was followed by a three-hour working dinner on Saturday evening with the negotiating team, ably led by Deputy Prime Minister Yigal Allon, an old and cherished friend since the 1950s when he had been my student at Harvard. Afterward, there was an hour's meeting with Defense Minister Dayan to go over the Israeli plan in detail. On Sunday, January 13, I had breakfast with Allon; a working lunch with Foreign Minister Eban and the negotiating team; a meeting with the families of Israeli prisoners of war held in Syria; yet another review of the political provisions with Eban; and a reception at Dayan's house near Tel Aviv, over an hour's drive away.

Through it all, the negotiators exuded the relaxed manner that in Israel denotes that the internal controversy has been temporarily shelved: For the first time there was a full cabinet decision in favor of disengagement. The Israelis had achieved this by resolving all controversial items in their favor — leaving it to me to persuade Sadat to accept them.

The cabinet had shown considerable ingenuity in response to my argument that I could not go to Sadat with the Dayan plan on a take-it-or-leave-it basis and therefore needed a fallback position. So it broadened my horizon of negotiating methods by simply turning the Dayan plan into the fallback position, giving me an even tougher new position with which to open the bidding. I knew that Sadat would not be taken in; there had been too many leaks of the Dayan plan in the Israeli press. Some bitter sessions were clearly ahead in both Aswan and Jerusalem.

Israel's proposed line of withdrawal in the Sinai was still west of the strategic passes, in the foothills of the mountain range traversing the Sinai from north to south. As for the Egyptian line in the Sinai, the new formal position turned some areas occupied by the Egyptian Third Army over to the United Nations. (The more generous fallback position — the Dayan plan — gave Egypt an unbroken line some six to ten kilometers to the east of the Canal.) The force limitations were unchanged: no more than two or three battalions across the Canal, no tanks, and no artillery. No Egyptian surface-to-air missiles could be established on the west bank within thirty kilometers of the Suez Canal (or forty kilometers west of the Egyptian forward line), nor any artillery capable of reaching Israeli positions. (For this purpose the Israelis had drawn different lines for different calibers of guns. This would involve the backward movement of another 100 Egyptian artillery pieces and several surface-to-air installations.) Tanks even in the thirty-kilometer zone *west* of the Canal would be limited to 300. "I can hardly wait to break this news to Gamasy," I said half-jocularly to the Israeli team.

The Israeli answer was that if Sadat did not intend to go to war, he would not need forward forces. This was true enough, but it overlooked the issue of principle in accepting severe arms limitations deep inside territory that was indisputably Egyptian and accepting withdrawals of major forces from positions held even *before* the recent war.

In addition, Israel toughened its political conditions. It demanded explicit assurances that Sadat would clear the Canal, rebuild the Canal cities, permit Israeli shipping through the Canal, and declare an end to the state of belligerency. I did not debate these terms, concentrating on clarifying the Israeli position and asking factual questions. I pointed out that Sadat's reaction was likely to be complex but I saw no point in seeking to modify the Israeli proposal until I had his view:

We are running into the danger of talking slogans. If he rejects it, from my judgment of what I have seen, it is because of his own domestic position. Just as you have a domestic position, he has one. And you are asking him to give the army, which he has finally got under control, a lot of orders that will be extraordinarily unpalatable to them. I do not know whether he can do it or not. I have no question in my mind, having spent these many hours with him, that he genuinely wants a settlement and that he almost certainly wants peace in the Canal zone. Whether his domestic situation permits him to do what you think you require for your domestic situation, that I don't know, and we will now find out within the next 36 hours. No sense debating it. But it is not as simple as "does he want peace" or "does he not want peace."

And yet there was, despite the seemingly harsh terms, a sense that this was not Israel's last word; that we were seeing a show of bravado for domestic Israeli consumption. In the expressive body language of diplomacy, we were heading for a breakthrough, and in the final analysis, for all the tough talk, Israel would make a significant contribution to it.

The sessions with the Israeli negotiating team had been relatively easygoing; no one spoke of deadlock. That was the mood, too, during the Sunday evening reception in Dayan's simple residence in Tel Aviv; it turned into a festive occasion. The house itself was like a suburban American dwelling; but its garden was a museum of Dayan's archaeological treasures, reflecting the obsession of so many Israelis with reestablishing ties to their distant past or at least with defining the ancient identity of their country — as if to banish the nagging sense of insecurity by a tangible demonstration of historical continuity. Dayan and Chief of Staff General David Elazar took me into a small study to show me two maps: the tough "new" line, which was less forthcoming than what Gur had shown the Egyptians at Geneva; and the one Dayan had submitted in Washington (the same as Gur's) — now the fallback position. We all knew that I would spend little time on the new line; all the Israelis were rather mischievously proud of their ingenuity over the "new" position. When we came out, a crowd of newsmen caught the mood of expectancy. "The reason the Israelis don't get better treatment," I said, "is that Eban doesn't kiss me."

Before leaving for Aswan, I instructed Scowcroft to brief Dobrynin. We were anxious to avoid Soviet interference while negotiations were approaching a climax. If Moscow thought we were destined to fail, it might stake out a tough position to pick up the pieces. If it understood that we were heading not simply toward "principles" but toward a completed agreement, the Kremlin might seek to abort the process and force us back to Geneva. The briefing was factually correct if not a masterpiece of precision and lucidity. It simply informed Dobrynin that I had reviewed the situation with both sides, had made some progress (without defining toward what), and would pass on further information as we went along.

At 8:15 P.M. that Sunday evening, we were airborne again for Aswan. Joe Sisco, efficient, superenergetic, sometimes supplying more answers than there were questions, announced to our press contingent: "Welcome aboard the Egyptian-Israeli shuttle!" Thus was shuttle diplomacy named.

The Flying State Department

THE shuttling command post was a US Air Force Boeing 707 called *SAM 86970*. (SAM stood for the Special Air Missions unit of the Military Airlift Command; 86970 was the tail number.) It had been used on occasion as *Air Force One* by Presidents Eisenhower and Kennedy; it was used as *Air Force Two* by Lyndon Johnson as Vice President.[3] By 1974 it was the third-ranking plane in the Presidential fleet. Like a once-rich family that had seen better days, it obscured its reduced eminence by the pride of its superb crew and the spick-and-span appearance of an upholstery that was not refurbished in the years I used the plane. Its Air Force personnel took loving care of it; they and my team became good friends.

The first object to strike one's eye as one entered the plane from the front was a large electronic console served by two sergeants. It was the hub of a communications network that connected *SAM 86970* with every part of the world in a matter of minutes by coded teletype and — if necessary — telephone, though I used the latter very infrequently. While airborne I received through this machinery all necessary telegrams from the State Department or White House; I sent out over it all instructions to the Department, or backchannel messages to the White House Situation Room. In some capitals where we had no embassies — or where I wanted to keep the exchange with Washington from the local embassy — we used it as a communications center even on the ground. Since I chose to remain in charge of State Department business even while traveling, an enormous volume of cable traffic poured in, handled by the aircraft's skilled communications personnel, annotated by my own staff, digested by me and my colleagues, and sent out again over the same system. This small, rather exposed area was in effect the heart of the entire enterprise. Without it shuttle diplomacy would have been impossible.

Farther back, the passenger area was divided into four compartments. The first, on the starboard side, paralleling a passageway, contained two sofas along the side wall that made up into beds; opposite them were a foldout table and two easy chairs. This was my personal compartment, work area, and retreat. Here I read the briefing books, met with colleagues, and took an occasional nap (rarely on the way to a negotiation, when I devoted my time to reading briefing papers).

The next section was a conference room occupying the width of the plane. Its distinguishing feature was a kidney-shaped table bordered on three sides by sofas in undistinguished but restful bluish-green. The fourth side was an outsized chair built to accommodate Lyndon Johnson. An electric switch controlled its movements in any conceivable direction and some I had heretofore considered inconceivable. The table had a hydraulic movement of its own; owing to the nature of the species it was less versatile than the chair; occasionally an unwary neophyte found himself trapped between a rising chair and a lowering table. The conference area was supposed to be kept clear for the purpose its name suggested. In fact, it usually seated a number of staff aides; it was piled high with bookbags and briefcases and an occasional trunk. When I was closeted in my cabin, exhausted staff members stretched out on the sofas and even the floor. The conference area served a multitude of other purposes. There, I briefed the journalists accompanying me, conducted occasional staff meetings, and frequently took meals with my associates.

The next compartment was a working area for the senior staff, with two tables, one on each side of the aisle, seating eight altogether. In addition, there was a small table with an electric typewriter; another typewriter could be set up on one of the larger tables if needed. Nearby was a small photocopying machine. Here — on Mideast shuttles — Sisco reigned. The senior staff sorted out the incoming cables and occasionally tested me by slipping in a phony message running directly counter to some instruction of mine and standing by for the fireworks. (They were, of course, even more delighted when I missed it.) They prepared briefing papers for the next stop — usually a memorandum comparing the positions of the two sides, our estimate of their flexibilities, and a checklist of what remained to be accomplished.

All this was done in a frenzied haste against the inexorable time limit of the next landing. My staff preferred the Aswan shuttle to the later Syrian shuttle because the flights to and from Egypt provided an extra seventy-five minutes of flying time. Once or twice we circled an airport, to the bafflement of our waiting hosts, while we completed our preparations. Man stood the pace better than machine; the photocopier would undertake periodic acts of rebellion. Sometimes it would simply eat a page, refusing to give up either copy or original; on occasion it would burn a page and with billowing smoke threaten to set the plane on fire. Once it broke loose from its moorings and threatened to devour Joe Sisco. Sisco was saved, and Winston Lord observed with relief that if the machine had not been stopped in time, countless copies of Joe might have been distributed throughout the Middle East — a truly mind-boggling prospect that neither we nor the Middle East was ready to face.

The fourth section was the most fun. In about ten rows of first-class seats were the rest of the staff, security personnel, and communicators, and in the rear, the fourteen or fifteen journalists who generally accompanied me.* The custom of journalists traveling with the Secretary of State had begun, I believe, with Dean Rusk. They were selected by their organizations; the major American newspapers, television networks, wire services, and newsmagazines were almost always represented; the remaining places were rotated among other news organizations. My relationship with that tempestuous bunch was, of course, of a complexity commensurate with our respective functions. The media yearn for access to senior officials and yet are afraid to be taken into camp by them; hence they often err on the side of skepticism or the facile pursuit of credibility gaps. The officials need the media to explain their point of view and are alternately tempted to give them a one-sided account or to pressure them. With all these drawbacks I think back to my association

---

*The journalists who accompanied me on most of my travels included Richard Valeriani of NBC; Marvin Kalb or Bernard Kalb of CBS; Ted Koppel or Barrie Dunsmore of ABC; Jerrold Schecter of *Time;* Bruce van Voorst of *Newsweek;* Barry Schweid of AP; Jim Anderson of Group W News; Richard Growald or Wilbur Landrey of UPI; Lars-Erik Nelson of Reuters; Bernard Gwertzman of the *New York Times;* Marilyn Berger or Murrey Marder of the *Washington Post;* Jeremiah O'Leary of the *Washington Star;* Stan Carter of the *New York Daily News;* John Wallach of the Hearst newspapers; John MacLean of the *Chicago Tribune;* Darius Jhabvala of the *Boston Globe;* Oswald Johnston of the *Los Angeles Times;* Robert Keatley of the *Wall Street Journal;* Charlotte Saikowski or Dana Adams Schmidt of the *Christian Science Monitor;* and Marie Koenig or William Sprague of USIA.[4]

with the men and women in the back of the plane with affection only occasionally tinged with exasperation.

The journalists on the shuttle had a grueling assignment. They had to follow my schedule; they could never be sure when a meeting would end or a newsbreak might occur. After I retired, usually well past midnight, they had to write and file their reports. They had to be up well before me; they had to get to the airport in time to permit their luggage to be x-rayed for security and for the plane to take off as soon as I arrived. Their accommodations were much less comfortable than mine both on the plane and on the ground. Through all these vicissitudes the reporting from my trips was fair and often penetrating. The aircraft was spared the maliciousness and bitterness of Washington during the Watergate period.

I did my best to help by briefing the journalists on every shuttle on a "background" basis — meaning I could be identified only as a "senior official." Usually I invited them up to the conference area soon after we took off from one location for another. I rarely gave details of the actual negotiations, but I strove hard to explain accurately the issues involved and the prospects as I saw them. The regulars on the shuttle grew adept at piecing together what I was saying, so much so that they took delight in trying to get Sadat, especially, to confirm what I was eager to keep confused until all the parties were in agreement. Occasionally he obliged, to my acute dismay; yet he probably understood the politics involved better than I supposed, for his revelations never did the damage I feared.

I hope the media representatives will not think I am letting them down if I record my conviction that as the shuttles went on, my journalistic companions developed a vested interest in a successful outcome, which faced me with a terrible prospect if the end failed to live up to their expectations. Some of this may have sprung from a wish to give purpose to the physical discomfort of the shuttle, or from the reality that our success would give a reporter more exposure and prestige. Whether these hard-bitten professionals would admit it or not, I also believe that among their reasons was a hope that in the midst of Watergate their country could accomplish something of which they could be proud. And though this is not their job, they gave me moral support —not in their reporting but in their attitudes — at several crucial moments.

Such was the caravan that rode *SAM 86970* back to Aswan, carrying with it the formal Israeli proposals.

Aswan Again: January 13–14

WE arrived at 10:30 P.M. in the blackout. Mercifully, Fahmy asked for no debriefing beyond my statement that I had maps now and an official Israeli plan. Sadat was content to wait until morning to see me.

The President greeted me at 10:00 A.M. on Monday, January 14, in the gazebo of his spacious garden outside the villa, on a glorious clear day with the temperature in the seventies. He still wore his heavy military uniform; he showed no impatience while we engaged in small talk for the benefit of the photographers. Finally after half an hour he took me inside. I had aides bring in the two maps given to me by Israel. Since I knew that the so-called fallback position was the only real Israeli line, I went lightly over the first one for fear that Sadat would be offended by it. I said that we would save a lot of time if we started from the premise that Israel would not withdraw farther than to the *west* side of the passes as part of the disengagement scheme. Sadat commented only about the proposal that Egyptian forces to the south withdraw a few kilometers westward in favor of UN forces. That was a moral issue; he insisted Egyptian forces could not be asked to withdraw from their own territory. I outlined the Israeli proposal on deployments and began listing the political demands when Sadat interrupted: "My associates should hear this with me." It was the only time in negotiating that Sadat implied the need for the concurrence of subordinates. It showed how prickly the issue was that Sadat on that one occasion used me to help build a consensus on the Egyptian side.

Consensus was not, however, what emerged at first. We adjourned to the conference room, where for one of the few times in my dealings with Egyptians we faced each other in the classic negotiator's pose. On one side of the table sat the American delegation: I, flanked by Joe Sisco and Ellsworth Bunker (in his capacity as Ambassador to the Geneva Conference), with Peter Rodman as note-taker. Sadat, who was accompanied by Gamasy and Fahmy, did not bow to diplomatic custom all the way — he did not bother to call in a note-taker.

The meeting began with a joke. I said the next few hours would tell whether what I brought was going to be known as the "Kissinger plan" (that is, succeed) or the "Sisco plan" (that is, fail). Fahmy quipped if it turned out to be a Sisco plan, they would preserve his body in the Valley of the Queens. But the jocular mood disappeared quickly when I went through the Israeli disengagement scheme, covering its military aspects in great detail. Sadat said little, puffing on his pipe and interjecting occasional crisp, clarifying questions. When I started listing Israel's other conditions the mood grew frosty. With respect to the obligation to open the Suez Canal, he blurted out: "These are political issues!" When I read out a new Israeli idea that all foreign troops and volunteers leave Egyptian soil, he snapped: "Ridiculous."

General Gamasy was less restrained. He considered the Israeli ideas on arms limitation outrageous; stripping the east bank of the Canal of

any tanks and thinning out the thirty-kilometer zone on the west bank
would leave Egyptian forces there weaker than before the war. The plan,
affirmed Gamasy, was designed to improve Israel's security and weaken
Egypt's. It had so many political components, moreover, that as a military man he would not be the appropriate person to sign it nor would
Kilometer 101 be the right place since it was dedicated to military
matters.

Gamasy, in short, came close to dissociating the Egyptian military
from the negotiations. Disciplined, dependable, the architect of the Suez
Canal crossing, with none of the ebullient passion characteristic of some
of his colleagues, he could not be dismissed as emotional. A man of
absolute reliability and with no visible personal ambitions, Gamasy was
clearly the key to the armed forces' support of the agreement.

Sadat listened sphinxlike with slightly narrowed eyes. Then he asked:
"Can we form a working committee from both sides here?"

"Certainly," I replied, and to give him a chance to work out the
Egyptian position with his associates I added: "Would you like us to
leave you alone now?"

Sadat puffed on his pipe. "No, because we first have to agree, you
and I, on the principles on which they will work." And with this he
asked me to go with him into the study.

Sadat sat pensively in the corner of his sofa. "Do they mean it?" he
asked. I said that I thought the Israeli negotiating team would not change
the Israeli forward line because it was two hundred yards from the only
north-south road on the west side of the strategic passes. If they withdrew beyond it, there would be no logical stopping point except inside
the passes; this in my judgment would never be accepted by the Israeli
Parliament as part of the first phase of disengagement. As for the arms
limitations in the various zones, there might be some flexibility though
I had not heard anything to that effect in Jerusalem. The principal question Sadat had to decide was at what speed he wished to move. Some
of the terms could no doubt be improved but it would take a prolonged
negotiation. He would have to judge what might happen in the interval
in the Arab world. The Soviets would surely maneuver to thwart the
whole negotiation. Disengagement could become engulfed in the haggling over the formation of a new Israeli cabinet, which would start
when the new Parliament assembled in a week's time. And the differences between what might ultimately be attained and what might yet be
negotiated this week might not prove all that significant.

Sadat knew, of course, that he could not let the Third Army sit in the
desert for months more; also, a diplomatic confrontation involving us
would run counter to the change of alignment that was the essence of
his strategy.

Sadat reflected silently for several more minutes that, with our diplomacy hanging in the balance, seemed endless. "Fools," he mused almost to himself, and it was not clear immediately that he was talking of the Israeli cabinet. "Why do they seek to humiliate Gamasy so? If I want to attack, I can put hundreds of tanks across the Canal overnight; if I don't want to attack, it makes no difference how many tanks there are." I replied that the Israelis meant these conditions not as a humiliation but as a sop to conscience; it was to prove that something was gained for what, however dressed up, would amount to a unilateral retreat into the Sinai; it was to calm Israeli hard-liners; and above all it was to still the nagging sense of insecurity I had described earlier.

Sadat continued to brood. And then, stunningly, he made the decision that ensured the success of the negotiation. He agreed that the Israelis could remain at a line at the west end of the passes. But he would not give up the three kilometers in the southern sector to the UN as Israel had wanted; Israel would have to withdraw the extra distance there. Israel could not have its way everywhere. It was vintage Sadat, brave and calculating, at once trusting and devious. The demand reflected Israeli domestic pressures more than military analysis; he pulled its teeth without giving up anything essential. And in the process he committed America to the outcome.

As for limitations on deployment, Sadat said he could not permit anyone to tell Egypt what its main line of defense was to be on its own territory. Nor could he go along with the Israeli plan for forward zones and zones of limited armaments. The various restrictions on armaments were too complicated. To simplify matters he proposed that only *two* lines be defined: the forward Israeli line (just west of the passes) and the forward Egyptian line (six to ten kilometers east of the Canal). The territory in between would be the UN zone. Limits on deployments should then be expressed in kilometers behind each side's forward line. Sadat accepted the principle that neither surface-to-air missiles nor artillery be placed where it could reach the other side's forward line; he tentatively decided that the appropriate distance for surface-to-air missiles was thirty kilometers behind Egypt's forward line (or ten kilometers less than Israel was proposing, since Israel was measuring distances from the Canal). But he wanted to let Gamasy express his views. It would go down hard with his Chief of Staff and I should do my best to improve these distances.*

As for the specific limitations, the two or three Egyptian battalions that Israel would permit across the Canal were too few. He would prefer ten battalions; but he would accept the maximum number that I could extract from Israel so long as it approached that figure. Furthermore, he could not tolerate a total prohibition of tanks on Egyptian territory. His

---

*Sadat's concept was largely reflected in the final disengagement map. See p. 839.

infantry units had trained with them; without tanks they would feel defenseless. He would leave it to me to define a number Israel could accept on the east bank. This was needed for Egyptian self-respect. The same applied to artillery. In consultation with Gamasy, I should find some calibers and units that were compatible with the principle of not reaching beyond the forward line. I warned that the Israelis had given me no maneuvering room with respect to either tanks or artillery. I doubted that they would go along with more than fifty tanks across the Canal. Thirty would be safer, I suggested, and I might fail altogether. Sadat replied that he would settle for any number so long as the principle was assured that Egyptian forces were not barred from Egyptian territory.

None of these obligations could be expressed directly to Israel, however, Sadat added. Why did I not step in with an *American* plan that specified the limitations? It could then be signed by him and Golda Meir. As for the political conditions, he was prepared to express his intentions in letters to President Nixon. We were free to communicate those to whomever we chose. He could not accept a formal obligation to clear and reopen the Suez Canal. But he could tell me that if he could do so as his own decision — if Israel would only stop demanding it — he would begin clearance operations as soon as both armies had reached the lines foreseen in the disengagement agreement. A formal end of the state of belligerency was out of the question; it would lead to an explosion in the Arab world. But he could accept a solemn obligation to observe the cease-fire.

He asked for my comments. There was quite literally nothing to say. Just as in November, Sadat had accomplished the spectacular by winnowing the essential from the tactical. The key points were Sadat's agreement that the Israelis could retain the strategic passes for the time being and his ingenious idea for arms limitations. The rest was mostly cosmetic. He and Golda both understood that the significant event would be the first major voluntary Israeli withdrawal in nearly twenty years. The details that aroused so much passion were essentially secondary; if the peace process continued, the precise location of forces at the end of the first stage would become irrelevant; if it did not, a new and tense situation would arise. The disengagement agreement, above all, would mark Egypt's passage from reliance on the Soviet Union to partnership (in Sadat's phrase) with the United States; and it would give us a major stake in the peace process that would be further magnified by having it be seen to emerge from an American proposal.

The task now was to reduce the general agreement to practical form. Before we rejoined our associates, Sadat called in Gamasy and said: "Dr. Kissinger and I have agreed on how to proceed to an agreement. You, Gamasy, will sign it" — thus quelling any thought of resistance before Gamasy had even heard the proposal. In this manner he performed the one function that a leader cannot delegate: He took on his shoulders the full responsibility.

As we took our seats in the conference room, once more facing each other across the table, I asked Sadat: "Should I sum up our understanding of our conversation?" The subsequent exchange explains the mood of the moment of breakthrough better than any description could:

SADAT: Please, you're much cleverer.

KISSINGER: But not as wise. The President and I had discussions not only of the technical provisions but also of the pros and cons of moving quickly against moving slowly at Geneva. The technical provisions might be better if done at Geneva, but we assessed the advantages of moving quickly.

That is our assessment.

The Egyptian line defends Egypt; the Israeli line doesn't defend Israel. So for the Egyptians to move back their own defense line on Egyptian territory is politically unacceptable. I must say I find this a very persuasive argument.

So I am prepared to go back to Israel with something I had never heard — to abandon all these distinctions between zones. The Israeli forces will move back to this line, and the Egyptian forces will move back to this line, and the Egyptian line is defined here — so there is no Egyptian withdrawal required. So we'll describe any limits not in terms of withdrawal but in terms of distance between the Egyptian line and the Canal and the Israeli line.

The second point President Sadat said is that it is very difficult for Egypt to sign in a document limitations of forces on their own territory.

SADAT: Quite right.

KISSINGER: So we thought of various possibilities, such as letters to the Presidents, etc. Then the President had an idea that should be explored — that we should write a letter to both President Sadat and the Israeli Prime Minister proposing certain limitations. So it is not an obligation to each other.

SADAT: It's an American proposal.

KISSINGER: And there is no suggestion of who imposed what upon whom.

The working group should prepare two documents — an agreement to be signed at [Kilometer] 101 and an American proposal to the two sides which would spell out some of the limitations. With the proviso that I have no idea what the Israeli reaction will be. It can say in the Egyptian-Israeli document that there will be limitations — which are not spelled out — in the two zones, and that all other limitations can be described in terms of distances to and from the Egyptian line.

On limitations, the President thought the number of forces on the East Bank should be increased substantially from what the Israelis suggested. It should be left blank in the documents; I know what he has in mind but I know I won't make the decision. He is not now prepared to accept no tanks.

SADAT: Quite right.

KISSINGER: Then the President and I agreed on the proposition that in these zones, which are described geographically, neither should deploy weapons that can reach the other's line. Up to thirty kilometers from the Egyptian line and thirty kilometers from the Israeli line, there should be no artillery and no surface-to-air missiles. . . .

I warned the President that to my certain knowledge this proposal would almost certainly be published.

SADAT: Not from the American side.

KISSINGER: I don't want to put Egypt in an embarrassing position. But there is no way Israel will not publish it somehow, in their Parliament, etc. . . . Then I told the President that of the Israeli demands —

SADAT: Political ones.

KISSINGER: Political ones. We drop the one on foreign troops and volunteers. We drop the one on passage of Israeli ships through the Canal, and we drop the one on civil flights. On Bab el-Mandeb, we agreed that the President will write me a letter as to the actions of Egyptian forces.

There were further technical discussions on troop deployments. I also informed Sadat that I was deferring my projected trips to Damascus and Amman until after the negotiations were concluded. It seemed to bring him great relief. We were now confident enough to plan the procedure for concluding the talks:

KISSINGER: May I make a practical suggestion?

SADAT: Yes.

KISSINGER: That I meet now with my colleagues and we do two documents, then present them to you at 4:30, and then plan to leave here at 8:30, and that I notify Israel now that I plan to arrive at 10:45 and return here tomorrow night.

They will probably need more than a day to consider it; they will need a Cabinet meeting. So I will probably be back Wednesday. There is no day that is inconvenient for you?

SADAT: No, no.

KISSINGER: Probably I will have to go back once more to Israel, and once more here will do it. Because the tank issue and the line issue will be unresolved.

SISCO: What do we say to the press?

KISSINGER: I don't think we should say anything now. But we agreed that at some point we should say: "It is a complex issue, a difficult negotiation. I have an Egyptian map that I am now taking to Israel. Nevertheless good progress was made today, and I am optimistic that progress will be achieved." So those who oppose the agreement won't think it is on the verge of breaking down. My worry is that the General here hasn't solved the problem of communicating with the North Koreans who are here, and they will shoot me down. [Laughter]

SADAT: They are very near. [Laughter]

KISSINGER: In what language do you communicate?
GAMASY: Korean. [Laughter]
SADAT: I have an idea. We will send Sisco as a test. [Laughter]

That the four-hour session had ended — as it had begun — with a joke about Joe Sisco was a tribute to the affection both sides felt for the ever-optimistic Under Secretary of State whose skill and experience had contributed greatly to bringing us this far.

Just after 5:00 P.M. that afternoon, the Egyptian and American working groups met in a curtained-off corner of the cavernous dining room of the New Cataract Hotel. The Egyptians were not happy with Sadat's decision. Fahmy said so volubly; Gamasy showed his unhappiness in icy reserve. But they were both superb professionals. Now that Sadat had made the decision, matters moved rapidly. Gamasy had discovered a type of artillery that could be placed on the east bank without being able to reach Israeli lines. They were 122-mm howitzers with a range of twelve kilometers. I promised to take it up in Jerusalem. Gamasy was especially bitter about the backward movement of the surface-to-air missiles on the west bank; as a military man, he said, he would go no further than to draw a plan for a withdrawal of twenty-five kilometers, or fifteen kilometers less than Israel demanded. If Israel remained adamant, Sadat would have to make yet another decision. Sisco and I had prepared a draft for the basic Egyptian-Israeli agreement as well as for the "United States proposal" on arms limitations that both sides would be asked to accept. We went through both documents line by line. Gamasy and Fahmy excused themselves at 6:40 P.M. to submit the drafts to Sadat. Sadat would give me his reaction later when I stopped at his residence on the way to the airport.

At 7:15 P.M., I was once again alone with the President in the study of the rest house. He wasted no time on the documents worked out with Gamasy and Fahmy. I should do my best; I now knew Egypt's requirements; he would do his utmost to come to an agreement this week. He had reflected about what I had said about Israeli leaks of the terms, particularly on the proposed arms limits. If leaks occurred before signature, he would not be able to proceed; if they occurred after he had completed his tour of Arab capitals, he would bear up under them; if the leaks came from a secret session of the Israeli Parliament, he would understand. He would make it as easy as possible for Israel psychologically. He would permit American reconnaissance overflights of the disengagement area every two weeks provided both sides received the pictures. He had come up with an ingenious solution to Israel's request that he promise to repopulate the Canal zone (Israel saw this as insurance of his peaceful intentions). He could undertake no guarantee to any foreign government, even the United States, about a matter so clearly in his domestic jurisdiction as rebuilding Egyptian cities near the Canal. But he would get around it by asking us to obtain from Israel an assurance that it would not attack the population centers in the area — a pledge that made sense only in the context of a decision to return the Canal area to normal life.

Sadat was anxious to convey to me again the depth of his desire to dissociate from the Soviet Union. He repeated that he intended to remove the Soviet reconnaissance planes from Egyptian soil and to end the Friendship Treaty with the Soviet Union in 1975. He sought a secure communication link with the United States; he wanted to begin exchanging ideas for future cooperation.

All this was consistent, of course, with a strategy of luring America into pressing Israel for concessions. That Sadat acted for Egyptian reasons was inherent in his position as President. That he understood that Egypt's goals were best served by reconciliation with the United States and peace with Israel marked him as a man of vision.

The Shuttle Concludes

WE arrived at Ben-Gurion Airport in Tel Aviv on Monday, January 14, at 11:00 P.M., a little more than twenty-four hours after having left. It had started to rain on our departure and the driving storm had increased in violence. Thus we could not use the military helicopter that the Israelis proposed to speed the trip to Jerusalem. I was not enamored of riding in helicopters in any event. In those days, before a new road had been completed, the car ride between Ben-Gurion Airport and Jerusalem took well over an hour. It gave Eban and me a chance to review the state of play, though tonight we reserved some key points for Jerusalem, where we would be joined by Dinitz, who was not only Ambassador to Washington but Golda's trusted confidant.

In my suite on the sixth floor of the King David Hotel, the three of us reviewed where we stood. Dinitz and Eban, violating the fundamental Israeli principle of treating every concession as if it were only Israel's due, confessed their astonishment that so much progress had been made in so limited a time. Products of a freewheeling democracy, they had as yet no framework for grasping the sweeping gestures possible in a more authoritarian system, which were characteristic of Sadat and which were to startle them again and again. When I mentioned the figure of thirty tanks across the Canal, Dinitz asked revealingly: "You mean he did not start by asking for 300?" Sadat generally did not haggle; like Zhou Enlai, with whom he otherwise had little in common, he started with his real position and rarely moved from it. I did not stress this aspect of Sadat's tactics in Jerusalem lest my interlocutors — to whom Sadat was still like a being from another planet — accuse me of insufficient vigilance in reducing Sadat's opening position. It was left that the Israeli negotiating team would discuss my report overnight and let me have their reaction in the morning. I might be able to return to Aswan the following evening.

After nearly fifteen hours of nonstop negotiations in two countries, I sent off a report to President Nixon. I also sent another briefing message to Dobrynin via Scowcroft. I told Dobrynin that progress was being made, though once again I left it open toward what. That point was not specified as well in briefing messages to the foreign ministers of Britain, France, and the Federal Republic of Germany. I did not want to court a repetition of earlier European initiatives that might cut across the agreement now so tantalizingly near.

I awakened Tuesday morning to a message from Scowcroft, who urged, on the basis of the report I had sent Nixon the previous night, that I not conclude an agreement without demonstrating Presidential involvement. This required — in Scowcroft's view and in Haig's — that I return to Washington, receive some publicized Presidential instruction, and then complete the negotiation. But that was out of the question. If I left the area for three days — the minimum necessary — the fragile compromises emerging might well break apart. The new Israeli Parliament would assemble in five days' time and probably extract from the government a statement of the limitations on deployments the premature publication of which Sadat had said would prevent him from signing. Sadat would either have to postpone his trip through the Arab world, which would be construed as a confession of failure, or he would have to hedge against stalemate by a rhetoric that preserved his options. In Israel, the whole negotiation would become submerged in the laborious process of forming a new cabinet, which would start then. Publicly, my departure from the area might be interpreted as evidence of a deadlock. In short, leaving the area risked too much.

I delayed a reply until I had heard the response of the Israeli government. That Tuesday morning Dinitz came by for breakfast with good news: The Israeli attitude was basically favorable. I should keep this in mind because the Israeli negotiating team would undoubtedly give me their characteristic going-over. It was a helpful warning, for when I met our Israeli counterparts in the conference room of the Prime Minister's office an hour later, one would not have known that anything unusual had happened at Aswan. As Dinitz had predicted, our Israeli opposite numbers submitted us to a merciless cross-examination on every technical aspect of the problem.* The few kilometers for which Sadat asked

---

*The Israeli negotiating team was usually headed by Prime Minister Golda Meir, though on this occasion she was home recuperating and Deputy Prime Minister Yigal Allon presided. He was accompanied by Foreign Minister Abba Eban, Defense Minister Moshe Dayan, Ambassador Simcha Dinitz, Chief of Staff General David Elazar, Director General of the Prime Minister's Office Mordechai Gazit, Director General of the Foreign Ministry Avraham Kidron, Deputy Director

in the south suddenly became magnified into a device by which Egypt would be able to outflank the Israeli forces in the Mitla Pass (about sixty kilometers northeast) by means of a road nine-tenths of which would remain under Israeli control. But it was plain — or maybe Dinitz had put me at ease — that the tension and near-hysteria of previous meetings were missing. Indeed, the Israeli negotiators were asking questions not to harass me but to receive answers for skeptical cabinet colleagues and a hostile opposition in Parliament. They were looking for pretexts to approve the agreement, not to scuttle it.

At 11:30 A.M. the Israeli negotiators began private deliberations and met with Golda; I went to the Israel Museum on a nearby hill. At 2:00 P.M. we reassembled for lunch in the Foreign Minister's residence. Israeli negotiators consider any time spent on social amenities a violation of their trust. So it was not surprising that Allon opened the meeting by announcing: "Gentlemen, since the soup is very hot we can start business." The reason for the impatience was the eagerness to announce that the Israeli team had approved a breakthrough:

ALLON: By and large we must say you achieved great progress in your visits in Jerusalem and Aswan. We will give you some changes which we think you will consider logical. And we see no reason why there cannot be a signing at Kilometer 101 Friday. What we accept is, we accept the geographic concept. [Laughter]

KISSINGER: It is a great victory, to get Israel to accept its own proposal. [Laughter]

ALLON: But on the southern zone, our Chief of Staff is considering, and we will try to be forthcoming.

KISSINGER: Good.

DINITZ: But not southcoming. [Laughter]

DAYAN: Suppose we do move on the main line southward — which I think we will do — but the area evacuated by us should be kept by the UN, not by them, and they will maintain all the area they have.

DINITZ: They will also move.

KISSINGER: No.

DAYAN: They will stay where they are — which is the change in our map. If we didn't move back there would be no room for the UN.

KISSINGER: Given their mentality, first of all, this will help. Psychologically, if there is one kilometer you can give them, it will help.

ALLON: Our General Elazar went to headquarters and he is studying it.

KISSINGER: Good.

General of the Foreign Ministry Ephraim Evron, and Dayan's aide Colonel Aryeh Bar-On. On the American side I was assisted by Under Secretary of State–designate Joseph J. Sisco, Ambassador at Large Ellsworth Bunker, State Department Legal Adviser Carlyle E. Maw, US Ambassador to Israel Kenneth Keating, Deputy Assistant Secretary of State Alfred L. Atherton, Jr., NSC Senior Staff member Harold H. Saunders, and NSC staff member Peter W. Rodman.

ALLON: On the number of battalions, we had an argument among ourselves, because when we said two–three battalions, we meant it. If you can settle it on five or six, you will be awarded the Ben-Gurion prize.

KISSINGER: Six is impossible.

ALLON: If they stick to ten and we stick to six, maybe eight.

KISSINGER: Maybe. Well, maybe nine.

ALLON: No.

DINITZ: Yigal was not supposed to say that [eight battalions].

KISSINGER: We can't do it, because if it takes too long, his advisers will turn against it.

With this, everything fell into place. We agreed to seek a limit of eight battalions and 7,000 men. My interlocutors urged me to try a lower figure with Sadat first; but I thought I knew my man; it would backfire if we started haggling. Dayan pushed through agreement to permit Cairo thirty tanks east of the Canal conditional on Egypt's finally accepting a limit of thirty kilometers from the forward line for the sur-face-to-air missiles (which meant that Israel was conceding ten kilome-ters of its original proposal). For the rest, the Israelis accepted Sadat's concept of fewer zones and the overall framework of a basic agreement with a separate "United States proposal" on force limits and side letters on other issues. Israel gave up its demand for an end to belligerency; it would settle for the proscription of "hostile" acts. (That was watered down further as the negotiations progressed.)

There was some attempt to link completion of the agreement to the release of Israeli prisoners held in Syria. I stressed that this would be playing Asad's game; since he did not really want a separate Egyptian disengagement agreement, he would be given an incentive not to release the prisoners. He would then raise the ante, able to blackmail both Egypt and Israel. And Sadat, having been linked to Syria by Israeli (and American) actions, would have no choice except to give all-out support to a program likely to become increasingly radical under Syrian influ-ence. The best way to obtain the release of Israeli prisoners in Syria was to complete the current negotiations rapidly. Syria's eagerness to follow suit could then be used as a lever for the prisoners. The proposal was withdrawn.

At 4:00 P.M. I called on Golda at her residence and went over the text of the agreement and its implications. I had already done this twice that day with her colleagues. But she was worried and she was ill; it was, after all, the first Israeli withdrawal since 1956.

Once that meeting was over, the drudgery began. At 5:30 P.M. the Israeli cabinet met to consider its negotiating team's new positions. Back at the King David Hotel, my team and I had to redraft the agreement and the "United States proposal" in the light of the day's discussions.

There was the ubiquitous Memorandum of Understanding by which we confirmed to Israel our definition of specific provisions. By now we were confident enough of success to begin drafting the assurances that Nixon would transmit to each side on behalf of the other. Though the assurances were technically unilateral statements, they had to be checked in both capitals to make sure they would satisfy what was needed. At 11:00 P.M. Dayan, Elazar, Dinitz, and later Evron came by to review the military provisions, and to report the cabinet's basically positive stance, although final approval would await my next visit to Israel. At 2:45 A.M., Wednesday, January 16, we ended a nineteen-hour negotiating marathon.

There remained only to send a message to Washington that for me to return now might unravel the whole delicate fabric. The parties would surely interpret it as some ominous snag on the American side. If the true reason were given, and then leaked (by either of them, to protect their position), my return home would defeat its purpose. Unless receiving explicit orders to the contrary I would stay — giving me a chance to go one more round of shuttle before interrupting the talks. If the agreement were to be completed, Nixon could, of course, announce it from the White House. Nothing was heard again from Washington about my returning home early.

At 7:30 A.M., Wednesday, my colleagues and I reviewed the documents for the umpteenth time. At 8:30 we went over them with the Israeli negotiating team. At 10:30 we left Jerusalem for Ben-Gurion Airport, again by car as the heavy rainstorm continued. Luckily for me, Eban was a stimulating companion; otherwise the long drives to the airport would have been hard to endure. At 11:40 A.M., just before takeoff, Dayan brought to my plane the revised map of the southern front, outlining an additional Israeli withdrawal that I would offer Sadat. On the aircraft I proudly showed Eban and Dayan my traveling office. We chatted with the journalists in the back of the plane. I joked that Eban's definition of objectivity was 100 percent agreement with the Israeli point of view. By that standard I had failed miserably; I had been supportive only 95 percent of the time. Eban spoke wistfully of staying on the plane for the flight to Aswan; after all, he and his wife had spent part of their honeymoon at the old Cataract Hotel in 1945. Now Egypt seemed impossibly far away. And as Eban left the plane I thought of a conversation with his beautiful and charming wife, Suzy, who at some dinner or other had told me that she had lived in more countries than she could remember. "And which people did you like best?" I had asked her. It was at the height of some crisis with Egypt under Nasser. "The Egyptian," she had said, to my amazement, for then Egypt was considered Israel's principal enemy. She had been born and had grown up in Ismailia.

That is what the exertions of the last days and weeks were ultimately about: to see whether out of two decades of war a human bond could reemerge at last. I expressed the thought in my departure statement:

We all hope, of course, that the process in which we are engaged will lead to an agreement that could mark a turning point in affairs in the Middle East. But as the party that has been travelling back and forth between Egypt and Israel, I may be perhaps permitted to make a personal observation. It is that to me one of the most hopeful signs is the spirit of fairness and justice that has characterized both sides and the constructive and positive manner in which both sides have sought to come to an understanding on the very important issue of the separation of forces. And if this spirit can be maintained then there may be hope that this area which has suffered so much may at last find peace.

So in the chilly rain we left for what would have to be the last negotiating session in Egypt if the signing was to take place on Friday, January 18. For it was already noon on Wednesday. I would have to conclude matters on this round or come so close to it that the remainder could be done by telegram.

At 2:15 P.M. we landed in Aswan. The sand reflected the brilliant sunshine; from Sadat's gazebo, which we reached fifteen minutes later, the dunes lay beneath the translucent sky on the Nile as if painted. Sadat and I repaired immediately to the study. Fahmy and Sisco waited outside in the garden and joined us from time to time to consult on points of drafting. I went through the documents as they stood.

I began by offering six Egyptian battalions and 4,500 men across the Canal, as Dayan had asked me to do, but I did not invest much capital in a marginal point since I knew that the Israeli negotiators were willing to accept eight battalions and 7,000 men. I put my main emphasis on the real Israeli concern, which was the distance that Egypt would have to pull back its surface-to-air missiles from the forward line — the point on which Gamasy was likely to prove most recalcitrant. Gamasy had wanted only a twenty-five–kilometer limit; Israel would go no lower than thirty (down from forty). I told Sadat that in my view this was Israel's real — not merely a bargaining — position. Sadat finally confided that he would eventually accept the figure; but as Gamasy was as overwrought as he had ever seen him, I should make one more try at the shorter distance; if Israel refused I should cable him; it would not hold up the agreement. The utility of a mediator is that if trusted by both sides he can soften the edges of controversy and provide a mechanism for adjustment on issues of prestige.

Reviewing the various assurances was more time-consuming than difficult. Sadat was reluctant to give assurances on what he considered Egypt's internal affairs, such as rebuilding the Canal area, but he accepted a proposal I had drafted, picking up on his suggestion of forty-eight hours earlier and taking it a step further: Nixon would send a letter to Sadat saying he "understood" that it was Egypt's intention to clear the Canal and that he looked forward to "the resumption of normal economic activities" in the area. For its part, the United States would "do its utmost to discourage" Israel from attacking population centers. Sadat asked that this passage be changed to "gives you its assurance" that Israel would refrain from doing so. I agreed to remove the implied threat.

The other assurances also passed muster, though not without some quibbles from Fahmy. Sadat agreed that the United States would fly reconnaissance missions over the UN zones randomly, instead of every two weeks as he had first proposed; there would be no predictable time-table, making evasion more difficult. He promised not to interfere with Israeli civilian flights down the Red Sea — a matter of concern to Jerusalem, since that was its only civil air route to Africa. With respect to clearing the Suez Canal, Sadat indicated that he would consider our strategic preferences in determining whether it should be done quickly or not.*

The meeting broke up at 4:45 P.M. At 6:00 Gamasy, Fahmy, and three aides for the Egyptian side met with Bunker, Sisco, Maw, Rodman, and me in the dining room of the New Cataract Hotel. Once again we reviewed all texts, seeking to put them into final form. The process went down hard with Gamasy. At one point he walked out, complaining that this was becoming a political, not a military, agreement; he soon thought better of it and returned. But he continued to fight bitterly for only a twenty-five–kilometer limit for the surface-to-air missiles because he would have to explain to the army why its missile defense had to be withdrawn after a successful war. As Gamasy lamented to my team, he could explain it to the Egyptian civilian population, "but not to our armed forces." He pointed out that Egypt had five reinforced divisions across the Canal at that moment, but "tomorrow [there will be] only seven thousand soldiers." Worse, Egypt's air defense on the west bank would have to be moved: "Psychologically, it is bad for our armed forces."

But Gamasy was a gentleman as well as a patriot. I offered to give a written assurance that Israel would open the supply routes to the Third Army unconditionally within forty-eight hours of concluding the agreement. Gamasy replied: "I don't need a letter. You give your word." He insisted on the right to deploy several batteries of howitzers and mortars on the east bank. I knew Israel would accept this, but I held the

---

*There was some debate in America about whether reopening the Suez Canal was more to the advantage of the Soviet Union, given its otherwise circuitous routes to the Indian Ocean. The consensus in the US government was that this was far outweighed by the strategic setback to the Soviets in Egypt's turn toward peace and toward the West.

concession back on this round to trade it for the surface-to-air missile limitations, with respect to which I knew Israel would be adamant.

At 8:00 P.M. Fahmy accompanied me to see Sadat. The President took me into the study alone. He was philosophical, having learned of Gamasy's outburst. "My army!" he mused. "First I had trouble convincing them to go to war. Now I have trouble persuading them to make peace." He was determined to go ahead; the difference between the various deployment schemes was now down to a quibble. I should do the best I could based on my knowledge of the two sides' sensitivities. He had thought about my frequent references to Israel's insecurity, he said. As a sign of his goodwill I could inform Golda Meir that he would not exercise his right to keep thirty tanks across the Canal. The principle that Egypt had the right to maintain its major weapons on its own soil was fundamental; now that it had been established, he would not use it. Then, dramatically, he asked me to take a personal message to Golda. He dictated it on the spot; it was the first direct message in twenty-six years from an Egyptian head of government to his counterpart in Israel. It stated:

You must take my word seriously. When I made my initiative in 1971, I meant it. When I threatened war, I meant it. When I talk of peace now, I mean it.

We never have had contact before. We now have the services of Dr. Kissinger. Let us use him and talk to each other through him.

And with this we parted. I would not see him again until the negotiations had succeeded or at the last second had failed. For we were now on the home stretch. Egypt had to agree to withdraw its surface-to-air missiles an additional five kilometers; Israel needed to accept a few Egyptian howitzers and antitank guns on the east bank of the Canal. Nothing else stood in the way of an agreement.

Arriving back in Israel to torrential rains late Wednesday night, January 16, I met with Eban, Dinitz, and Evron for a briefing from midnight to 2:00 A.M. My staff and I spent some hours collating all the documents. And we drafted a statement for Nixon to make announcing the successful completion of the negotiation. Afterward — early Thursday morning — I called Haig and gave him the hopeful news that Nixon might be able to go on television by the end of the day.

After four hours of sleep, we awoke to snow. The temperature had fallen sharply; the storm had turned into the first blizzard in Jerusalem in several decades. All movement in Jerusalem stopped. I could gaze out the window of my sixth-floor suite in the King David Hotel and see the stone buildings and wall of the Old City of Jerusalem with the Mount of Olives behind in an eerie white blanket against a gray horizon. It was a spectacular scene, one of utter peace.

My reveries were interrupted by reality. My appointment with Golda had to be canceled because there was no way to get to her residence. I hated to think how Aswan, which had never seen a blizzard, would react to a delay allegedly caused by inability to move about in Israel's seat of government. Dayan came to the rescue. He produced jeeps and personnel carriers to bring the Israeli negotiating team to my suite at the hotel, where we met at 9:30 A.M. As always in the final phase of a negotiation, issues that earlier would not have taken five minutes had to carry the weight of the final calibration. By noon we had in effect agreed that I would ask Sadat by telegram to accept the thirty-kilometer limit for surface-to-air missiles (which I knew he would do). The Israeli negotiating team meanwhile would put before the cabinet for final approval the Egyptian requirement that thirty tanks and six batteries of howitzers remain on the east bank of the Canal. Dayan came up with an imaginative idea to meet Sadat's concern that the arms limits not leak before signature and that any leak afterward should preferably come from a secret session of the Israeli Parliament. Secret sessions of the Parliament being unknown, it was agreed that the terms be conveyed to a secret session of the Defense and Foreign Affairs Committee. (They leaked anyway. Why Sadat preferred this procedure he did not divulge to me. Perhaps he felt the fact of a secret session would demonstrate that Israel was aware of the sensibilities of Egypt's armed forces.) At noon we were finished. "It is a good agreement," I said.

"It is not a bad agreement," said Allon.

" 'Not bad' is Hebrew for 'good,' " explained Eban the diplomat.

At 12:35 P.M. I left for the Prime Minister's residence in an Israeli army vehicle, slithering through the twelve-inch snowfall. She needed to hear from me personally what I had told the negotiating team, because I had learned that despite her illness she would personally chair the cabinet meeting called to approve the agreement. It was reassuring news. I was confident that this guaranteed success; she would be as fierce in fighting for the agreement as she had been steadfast in defending her country's interests. I read her Sadat's personal message. "It is a good thing," she said laconically. "Why is he doing this?" After a generation of conflict it was not easy to believe in the sincerity of the adversary — especially one who had initiated the process in which we were engaged with a surprise attack.

There was now nothing to do but wait. With Golda in the chair, the principal uncertainty was that her colleagues might be jockeying for a position in the new cabinet that was expected to be formed after the Parliament met in four days. Despite what we knew rationally, my colleagues and I were jumpy and afraid of some unforeseeable snag. I telephoned Fahmy — via Washington — that Israel needed another cabinet session but that I hoped to have a positive answer by 5:00 P.M.

local time. In this mood of tense expectancy, I paid a courtesy call on Israel's President Ephraim Katzir, a distinguished scientist.

Then at 3:55 P.M. Eban, Dinitz, and Evron came to my hotel suite with good news:

EBAN: The Cabinet has approved the agreement. We will make a statement.

KISSINGER: You will say that you approve the stage of negotiations as they are now, subject to technical clarifications.

EVRON: They have issued a statement that the government unanimously authorized the Prime Minister to notify the Secretary of State of its decision, but there are a few technical points. I hope they don't get too nervous in Cairo.

KISSINGER: They will get very nervous!

But the technical points were all solvable or indeed already solved. Dinitz ordered champagne and Eban toasted the agreement in the wistful Israeli fashion, coupling mutual congratulations with a plea for assurance:

EBAN: We should toast the agreement. And to a peace agreement.

KISSINGER: This at least opens the possibility of a new relationship with Egypt.

EBAN: You said it could be a turning point.

KISSINGER: Yes, it could be.

Ambassador Eilts and Hal Saunders, who had stayed behind in Egypt, had meanwhile collated the final documents for Sadat. At 7:00 P.M. we learned that Sadat had initialed the "United States proposal" on force limits. ("Initialed" is a technical diplomatic term indicating that the text of the agreement is frozen pending signature. It says in effect: "If I sign anything, it will be this text.") Sisco and I had another glass of champagne.

At 9:00 P.M. Jerusalem time (3:00 P.M. in Washington), a proud President Nixon stepped before the press corps with the following announcement, the text of which had been previously approved by Egypt and Israel:

In accordance with the decision of the Geneva Conference, the Governments of Egypt and Israel, with the assistance of the Government of the United States, have reached agreement on the disengagement and separation of their military forces. The agreement is scheduled to be signed by the Chiefs of Staff of Egypt and Israel at noon Egypt-Israel time, Friday, January 18, at Kilometer 101 on the Cairo-Suez Road. The Commander of the United Nations Emergency Force, General Siilasvuo, has been asked by the parties to witness the signing.

The Final Phase

THE elation accompanying the end of the negotiation was quickly overwhelmed by the minutiae required for its consummation. The

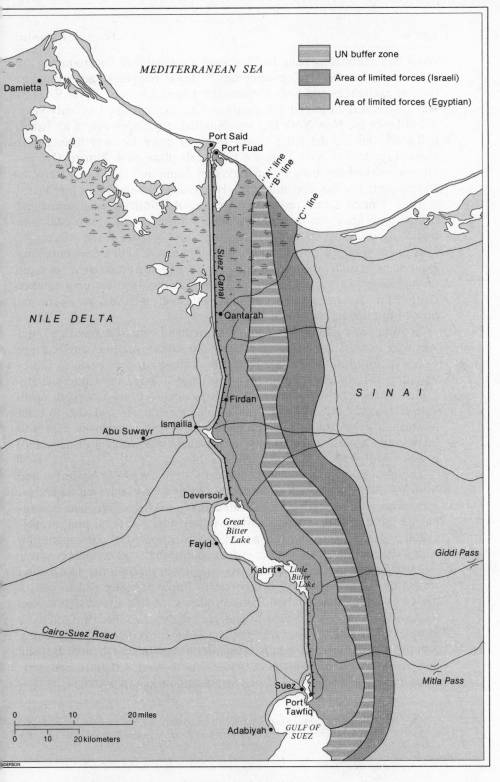

Legend:

UN buffer zone	
Area of limited forces (Israeli)	
Area of limited forces (Egyptian)	

MEDITERRANEAN SEA

Damietta

Port Said
Port Fuad

"A" line
"B" line
"C" line

Suez Canal

NILE DELTA

Qantarah

Firdan

Abu Suwayr   Ismailia

S I N A I

Deversoir

Great
Bitter
Lake

Fayid

Giddi Pass

Kabrit   Little
Bitter
Lake

Cairo-Suez Road

Mitla Pass

Suez

Port
Tawfiq

Adabiyah   GULF OF
SUEZ

0   10   20 miles
0   10   20 kilometers

ANDERSON

Egyptian-Israeli Disengagement Agreement, January 18, 1974
(see text of the Agreement, pages 1250–1251)

American negotiating team had assumed responsibility for producing the
official text for the signing ceremony.* It was retyped to accommodate
the last exchanges and State Department Legal Adviser Carlyle E. Maw
was dispatched to attend the signing. This distinguished seventy-year-
old pillar of the New York Bar was bundled in the open cab of an Israeli
half-track outside the King David Hotel to make his way through the
snowstorm to Tel Aviv, whence an Israeli plane took him to Cyprus.
He was picked up there by an Egyptian plane and taken to Kilometer
101 by staff car the next morning. Hal Saunders would join him there.

The "United States proposal" defining the limitations of armament
behind both lines was included in letters from Nixon to Golda Meir and
Sadat; signature of the proposal constituted acceptance of the scheme.**
Then there were a number of Presidential letters to both sides containing
assurances or statements of intention regarding such matters as passage
through waterways and rebuilding of the Canal cities. Instructions were
drafted for our ambassadors, Keating in Israel and Eilts in Egypt, on
how to put the agreements into effect.

Nothing can culminate in Washington without extensive briefings. And
when the news is good there is nothing the Administration is more eager
to do. It forced my exhausted staff into drafting another batch of cables
with detailed guidance. Brent Scowcroft was to brief key Congressional
leaders before the announcement; he was also to bring Dobrynin up to
date and hand him a text of the basic agreement. He had also to brief
our principal NATO allies and the Chinese. There were many papers to
be drafted, against a short time limit. But the tension had disappeared;
it was joyful work.

There were congratulatory phone calls from President Nixon — and
from Vice President Ford. (The elated Nixon also telephoned Sadat and
Mrs. Meir.) Near midnight I briefed the journalists who had accompanied me in an atmosphere buoyant on all sides. With all their professional cynicism, they derived no little satisfaction from participating in
what they considered an historic event that reflected well on their country.

Early Friday morning I journeyed once more through the snowbound
streets of Jerusalem to call on the ailing Prime Minister and to collect
her signature on the "United States proposal." I had always felt a deep
tenderness toward her. She had held her country together in dire crisis,
at times defied its only friend. She had been converted only reluctantly
to a negotiating process against which all her instincts rebelled. But she
had known when to conclude an agreement with a dignity and self-
confidence that demonstrated that Israel remained in control of its des-

---

*The text of the basic disengagement agreement is in the backnotes.[5]
**The "United States proposal" signed by President Sadat and Prime Minister Meir is in the
backnotes.[6]

tiny in peace as in war. Before cameras Golda signed the document on force limitations. Privately, she gave me a friendly written reply to Sadat's message of two days earlier. The relief, even exaltation, of the moment was reflected in the statements made to the press corps nearly suffocating in Golda's small living room. For me it was one of those occasions that made the exhausting labors of diplomacy worthwhile. After months of sometimes tense controversies Golda exuded relief; the prickly exterior for a moment gave way and revealed her people's longing for, indeed obsession with, peace:

Mr. Secretary, I think that not only those of us who are here take cognizance of this day as a great date, a day which I am hopeful is the beginning, and in its wake will come the day when there will be peace in the Middle East, peace for Israel and its neighbors, and I hope that this is the beginning of a process which will lead to permanent peace between Egypt and Israel.

I don't think it will make news if I would say that you, Mr. Secretary, had something to do with it. We don't like to use words which may sound like only words. But I sincerely and honestly believe that you have made history this week. I know you didn't begin it this week but there's no doubt in my mind. I want to tell you, on behalf of the people of Israel, how much we appreciate it.

I want to tell the President of the United States that his policy of understanding the problems in the Middle East, understanding the problems of Israel, and its neighbors, has certainly led to this day. And our appreciation of what he has done, of his attitude and his efforts, are remembered by Israel and its people.

There will be many, many mothers and young wives and children in Israel in the next few days, when they will see their dear ones, who for many months have been on the front watching over the security and safety of Israel and they will be very happy. We hope to see the day, and I honestly and sincerely believe, the day when armies will become something of the past.

And I want to express my thanks for your patience. Wisdom is something either given to one or not; you're either born with it or not, and for that you deserve no special credit. But for your patience, your work, your patience with both sides. We were easy [laughter] but maybe you had problems with the other side.

Public words of approbation from an Israeli leader were a precious rarity, dealt out sparingly, like a nation's highest decoration. I replied:

No people have suffered more for the past generation than the people of Israel. No people have more cause to wish for peace than the people of Israel. And therefore this day, which we hope will be important for all the peoples of the world, must be a particularly poignant day for this country, which in all of its history has never known what other nations take for granted, a period of acceptance and period of peace.

All of us who have had the privilege of working with you, Madame Prime Minister, and with your colleagues, will try to go on from here to make sure that what happens today is not going to be an interlude but will be remembered as the date that peace came to an area from which so many great things have come to the world, so that the talents and energy of all of its peoples can be devoted to paths of construction. We leave you here today and hope to work with you in what we know will remain a common effort.

My problem now was to get to Aswan to collect Sadat's signature on the same American proposal. The official signing of the basic agreement was set for midday at Kilometer 101. If I arrived in Aswan too late, it would be, as I said to Eban, a "not uninteresting situation," with the basic disengagement agreement signed — in effect beyond recall — but not the American force-limits proposal containing all the relevant details.

Getting to Aswan, or at least leaving Jerusalem, proved to be far from simple. The snow blocking the road to the airport, our resourceful hosts came up with the idea of going by train. (Mercifully, they did not subject me to a wintry helicopter ride.) I had not known that a railway existed between Jerusalem and Tel Aviv; it proved to be knowledge not worth having. The railway cars dated back to Turkish times, or so the erudite Eban claimed. If they were of more recent vintage, they had been strenuously used. But as we were bounding through the snow-covered Judean hills, it seemed an appropriately surrealistic ending to three months of frantic diplomacy.

History is a tale of battles; of victories and defeats; of the triumph of will — all suggesting that one side's celebration is the other side's despair. Rare are the moments of triumph in which there are no losers. So Eban and I talked, over the rattle of the train in the otherwise totally still landscape that had seen so much of man's cruelty as well as of his transcendent aspirations. What impact would peace have on the soul of a country that had wrested its identity from a struggle? Would the Arab nations ever genuinely accept the reality of peace with Israel? Could either side overcome its memories and fears? They were the key questions for the Foreign Minister of a country in which Jews mingled with Arabs, and which yet needed a visitor from 6,000 miles away to explain the psychology of Arab nations that, as far as Israel was concerned, might as well have been located on the far side of the moon. Was Sadat pursuing a devious tactic to accomplish traditional aims, or an historic turn? I thought the latter, but no one could be sure and the Egyptian President could not bind his successors. Was Israel gaining acceptance by its retreat, or starting a process of progressively weakening itself? None of the current actors would be around when the answer became evident. The fact was that Israel had no choice; it could not risk *not* making the experiment, for the Jewish state would consume its moral substance if it sought to rest its existence on naked force.

That morning, at any rate, second thoughts were submerged in hope. The *Jerusalem Post* had printed a cartoon of me as an angel of peace. It was a reflection more of the dreams of a people that had never known a day of formal peace than of my merit. For the length of the train ride, Eban and I abandoned ourselves to happy reminiscence of what deep down we knew would be later remembered — if we were lucky — as the easiest step of a long journey.

And so we boarded the shuttle to Aswan for the last time at 10:30 A.M. on Friday, January 18. However, what we were learning of Soviet conduct was well calculated to quell any euphoria. All week long we had heard that the Soviets were bitter, especially toward Cairo, for being shut out of the diplomacy; that they believed we had paralyzed the Geneva Conference in order to promote our unilateral role. There were indications that they were spreading the word that a role for Moscow in the talks would have strengthened Cairo's position and they were denigrating disengagement as a victory for Israel. There was the implication that Moscow would not moderate Syria's position as long as the USSR was excluded from negotiations.

In parallel, according to Brent Scowcroft, Brezhnev had sent a message to Nixon complaining that the understanding

on active participation of Soviet and American representatives in the discussion in Geneva together with Arab and Israeli delegates of the key issues of the Middle East settlement is actually not being implemented. The question is, in particular, of participation of representatives of the USSR and the US in the consideration of disengagement of troops.

Brezhnev proposed a meeting between Gromyko and me on February 7–8 in Geneva to analyze

everything that has happened since the cease-fire in the Middle East from the point of view of our agreement with you to coordinate the efforts of both countries towards peaceful settlement in this region.

The Soviet complaints to Egypt and the Brezhnev letter starkly brought home to us what would have happened had we gone the Geneva route. Moscow would have taken extreme positions beyond what we could support, pressuring Arab governments that could not afford to seem less Arab than their Soviet spokesman and attempting to force Sadat to dissociate from us. Therefore I had no intention of jeopardizing the disengagement process by raising the specter of a Soviet-American condominium while Egyptian and Israeli armies were moving to new lines and Syria was considering whether or not to join in. One of the arts of diplomacy is to clothe a rejection in the form of an acceptance in principle. In this case I acceded to Soviet wishes by agreeing to a meeting but at a level not suited to political exploitation. I instructed Scowcroft to tell Dobrynin

that the President will want to discuss the Brezhnev messages with me person-ally upon my return. I will then be in touch with Dobrynin.

You should also tell him that, in the meantime, Ambassador Bunker will be arriving in Geneva on Monday where he will meet with Vinogradov for a preliminary review of the situation and my trip through the Middle East.

Bunker was instructed to avoid dramatics, which meant that he had only to act naturally. His occasional and empty meetings with Sergei Vino-gradov, his Soviet counterpart as permanent representative to Geneva, were all that was left of the Geneva Conference.

I arrived in Aswan at 12:45 P.M. and sped to Sadat's rest house. "Welcome, Henry," he greeted me by the gazebo in the garden so that the photographers could take pictures; his use of my first name was new. He took me to his study where he signed the "United States pro-posal" on arms limits without another word. I then handed him Golda's private letter, which read:

I am deeply conscious of the significance of a message received by the Prime Minister of Israel from the President of Egypt.

It is indeed a source of great satisfaction to me and I sincerely hope that these contacts between us through Dr. Kissinger will continue, and prove to be an important turning point in our relations.

I, for my part, will do my best to establish trust and understanding be-tween us.

Both our peoples need and deserve peace. It is my strongest conviction that peace is the goal toward which we must direct all our energies.

Let me reiterate what you said in your message: "When I talk of permanent peace, between us, I mean it."

It is indeed extremely fortunate that we have Dr. Kissinger whom we both trust and who is prepared to give of his wisdom and talents in the cause of peace. I know that he will continue to extend this untiring service to the pro-motion of our common interest.

There followed a scene out of a sentimental motion picture. Sadat had finished reading the letter, folded it, and taken off his glasses when his assistant Ashraf Marwan came into the room and whispered some-thing in his ear. Sadat rose and walked over to me and kissed me on both cheeks: "They have just signed the agreement at Kilometer 101," he said. And then he added: "I am today taking off my military uni-form — I never expect to wear it again except for ceremonial occasions. Tell her [Golda] that is the answer to her letter."

And with that, we resumed our conversation in a matter-of-fact way as if nothing unusual had happened. He would leave for Syria shortly to explain the agreement and to be able to "guarantee" good Syrian behavior if it participated in the next phase of disengagement talks. He also expected the oil embargo to be lifted within the next week. Alas, Sadat's judgment of the reaction of his Arab colleagues was not as acute as his perception of American psychology and the road to peace. Both predictions, as we shall see, proved overoptimistic.

Sadat proceeded to carry out his promise that there would be no pressure for additional Israeli withdrawals while this disengagement was being implemented. To avoid any Soviet temptations to make trouble by putting forward unacceptable schemes, he would pull the Egyptian Ambassador out of the Geneva Conference during the next week. We could inform Israel that he expected to carry out a substantial demobilization by the end of February. (Israel would soon reciprocate.) He had arranged for me to spend the night in Luxor, so I could enjoy some rest before what he knew would be a difficult visit for me in Syria. And with this Sadat escorted me to my limousine. He placed his hands on my shoulders and said in his deep voice, in front of the press corps: "Mr. Secretary, you are not only my friend; you are also my brother." And then the President of Egypt kissed me on both cheeks — this time for the television cameras.

Luxor in ancient times had been Thebes, capital of Upper Egypt and monument to its glory. "Thebes," the French Egyptologist Jean François Champollion, gazing awestruck at its spectacular ruins, is reported to have said, "is the greatest word in any language." In the afternoon we toured the ruins of the Temple of Luxor, on the banks of the Nile, out-of-scale testimony to man's quest for immortality, into a corner of which the largest cathedral would fit and whose central axis seems to stretch into infinity to symbolize the Egyptian sense of eternity. Wherever we walked, cheering crowds expressed the relief of the Egyptian people that the war had ended. It was an earnest of Egypt's dedication to peace, like the courage and eloquence of its President.

After night fell we were driven through the still blacked-out streets to a spot in utter darkness. Suddenly a light switch was thrown; Sadat had ended the blackout on the night of the disengagement agreement as he had always said he would. Before us was the avenue of the ram-headed sphinxes leading to the huge pylons that marked the entrance of the Temple of Karnak — the spectacular city of the "king of gods," Amon, where 80,000 priests had worshipped the deities of ancient Egypt until the sands of time ran out on even that most enduring of civilizations. A literary, perhaps slightly melodramatic, "sound and light" presentation illuminated the monumental statues, columns, gateways, and obelisks over an area so vast that they could not be encompassed in a single view; they required four different vistas for even a partial comprehension. At one point, while a single obelisk was illuminated, there was read a papyrus from an Egyptian queen who lived nearly four thousand years ago. She had wanted to erect a golden obelisk to perpetuate her memory; but her advisers had thwarted her. She had to content herself with stone. Whether the story was apocryphal or true, it was a poignant illustration of the relativity of the concept of glory. The queen achieved permanence because her quest for the spectacular and the personal had been frustrated; a golden obelisk would long since have fallen prey to the greed of one of the conquerors who swept over the ancient capital in the course of the millennia. What had prevented the long-dead queen from gratifying her ego had guaranteed her immortality. What would be left of our work in a decade? And would we be better judges than that ancient queen of what was permanent and what ephemeral?

Aqaba, Damascus, and Tel Aviv

AFTER a week of dramatic exertions, all that followed was bound to be anticlimax. But though we were emotionally exhausted we needed to stop in Jordan to demonstrate that King Hussein, that moderate ruler and old friend, would not suffer for his refusal to pressure us. In the short term, it was even more imperative to engage Syria. If Sadat was to be preserved as a moderating force in the Arab world, his disengagement agreement must not stand alone, hence vulnerable. Everybody, including Israel, had an interest in encouraging Asad to proceed; it would open the prospect for a more hopeful future.

Hussein had invited me to visit him in Aqaba, a resort on Jordan's access to the Red Sea. There are few places that more vividly display the ironies of the Middle East. A shoreline no more than eight miles wide is embedded between the stark mountains of the Saudi coast to the south and the Israeli port of Eilat and the Egyptian Sinai to the west. To the north the desert sweeps to the horizon, interrupted irregularly by jagged hills that recall to mind the carefully contrived boulders in formal Japanese sand gardens. The brief, flat Red Sea shore is shared by the two coastal towns, Israeli Eilat and Jordanian Aqaba, nestling together and nearly merging as if part of the same community. Yet they share no services; their citizens never meet. Water-skiers and scuba divers offshore run the risk of straying inadvertently into the territorial waters of another country that is technically at war with their own. Planes approaching the respective airports must carefully avoid the airspace of the other, forcing one to land in a steep descent with either a Saudi or an Egyptian mountain range uncomfortably close by.

This normal hazard was compounded at Aqaba because King Hussein, a passionate pilot, would occasionally take it into his head to fly out to greet visitors to whom he wished to pay special respect. On this occasion it pleased His Majesty to come out in a helicopter and perform aerobatics in the narrow space between the right wing of *SAM 86970* and the Saudi mountains. Had there been a Jordanian official aboard our plane, he could have easily got us to sign any document as the price of getting his monarch to return to earth.

On Saturday afternoon, January 19, we met in Hussein's bungalow by the sea, less than a hundred yards from the barbed-wire fence that denoted the frontier with Israel. Hussein, his brother Crown Prince Hassan, Prime Minister Zaid Rifai, and Chief of Staff General Zaid Bin Shakir received us as friends. The Jordanians were warm in their praise of the disengagement agreement. "Both chiefs of staff were extremely angry with me," I joked. "It is a tremendous achievement," replied Hussein.

But it also filled our Jordanian hosts with foreboding. They recognized that Syria had to be next; this was important so that radical Syria could not interfere with any move on the Jordanian front. But they wanted to be sure that their turn would come soon after, and if that was possible they would bend every effort to speed the process. In the meantime and as rapidly as possible, they wanted some discussions to begin at the working level on some form of initial Israeli withdrawal from the occupied West Bank of the Jordan River, emulating the procedures in the Egyptian case. Jordan's nightmare was that its Arab brethren would deprive it of the right to recover the territory it had lost to Israel in 1967. Jordan, in fact, had two nightmares about the West Bank: either indefinite Israeli occupation or a PLO state whose first target would be the Hashemite Kingdom.

I was sympathetic. I shared Hussein's strategic assessment:

> Israel has two choices: Either it can deal with Arafat or it can deal with Your Majesty. If I were an Israeli Prime Minister . . . I would rush into negotiations with Your Majesty because that is the best guarantee against Arafat.

But here was a case where stating the alternatives did not advance matters, because in fact Israel wanted neither of them. So our discussions and their aftermath were a replay of what had occurred on my previous visit in December. On that occasion I had presented to Israeli leaders Rifai's suggestion of a very modest "disengagement" in the Jordan valley, involving principally withdrawal from Jericho on the Jordan River. It had been rejected as inconsistent with the Allon plan, according to which Israel was to keep the Jordan valley as a military security line. I suggested that since Allon was in the room, there was nothing to keep the author from modifying his plan. This was treated as a joke and partially it was. But when I then asked whether some disengagement scheme based on the Allon plan could be put forward, I ran into a Catch-22: The Allon plan could not be the basis of disengagement on the Jordanian front because the coalition partner, the National Religious Party, opposed giving up *any* West Bank territory at all. Thus Israel would reject a proposal inconsistent with the Allon plan but would refuse also to negotiate the Allon plan because it could not get the full cabinet behind it.

Undeterred, the Jordanians on this visit put forward a disengagement plan in which Jordan and Israel would each pull back eight kilometers from the river to the foothills of the mountain ranges that mark the Jordan valley. Jordanian civil administration would be established in the area vacated by Israel, especially in the town of Jericho. No Jordanian armed forces would cross the river or come closer than eight kilometers. A working group should be formed as rapidly as possible to ensure Jordan's claim to represent the Palestinians. I told the King I would discuss his ideas with the Israelis in coming weeks.

Hussein's approach was moderate and statesmanlike. But it was futile while a new Israeli coalition was being formed, including a party that opposed any territorial change on the West Bank. Indeed, that state of affairs precluded even the formation of a working group. By the end of the year, doctrinaire fanaticism in the Arab world would soon turn this missed opportunity into strategic disaster. And the consequence was to block progress on the West Bank to the day of this writing.

I spent the night in Hussein's seaside retreat, then flew to Syria on Sunday morning, January 20.

Damascus was even more tense than on my first visit in December. Sadat's courtesy call apparently had not gone well. The Syrian leaders had refused to let him enter the city and insisted on meeting with him at the airport hotel. Damascus had earlier demanded that the Egyptian disengagement be held up until that with Syria was completed. But Sadat had not been prepared to keep his Third Army cut off in the desert while Syria acted out its own ambivalences in a protracted negotiation. Nor could I bring Asad the assurance that Israel would even be willing to discuss disengagement. Golda had been afraid to overload her cabinet with too many painful decisions. Yet she understood that the prospect of a Syrian disengagement might cause Asad to moderate his opposition to Sadat's course. Her solution was Solomonic. Dayan, who in 1967 had been opposed to occupying the Golan Heights in the first place, was authorized to give me some "personal" ideas on a Syrian disengagement. I could convey these to Asad but I could not guarantee that Israel would stick by them if he accepted.

This was too devious even for me. And as it turned out, the occasion for it never arose. For in my five hours with the Syrian leader, he proved much more eager to catalogue his grievances against Sadat and press his own demands than to find out Israel's suggestions. I, in turn, was not eager to present Israeli ideas that were unofficial and so hedged that they were certain to multiply Syrian suspicions. Before my arrival, the head of our Interests Section in Damascus, Thomas Scotes, had sent me his analysis that Asad wanted to negotiate but would have to overcome a congenital hatred of Israel that ran deep in Syria and that if not slowly banked might even jeopardize his domestic position.

The conduct of the Syrian leaders confirmed this. They treated me with great courtesy, partly to show that they did not hold me responsible for Egypt's actions; partly because Sadat's gamble had in fact worked — which may have been the main reason they were so angry. The Syrians were eager to reduce the Israeli bulge toward Damascus and, given their refusal to meet with Israelis, they needed me as a mediator. They no longer put forth preconditions. Unlike four weeks earlier, they did not insist on being handed the outline of an agreement only the technical implementation of which they would discuss. They were clearly willing to negotiate, indeed afraid to be left out.

Abd al-Halim Khaddam, the ferocious Deputy Prime Minister and Minister of Foreign Affairs, led into the new phase in his characteristically needling way by coyly complaining that Jordan seemed to have pride of place in the disengagement process. Would that it were so, I thought. But what I said was: "Israel is giving preferential treatment to Syria based on the long history of affection that exists."

"The affection is reciprocal," replied Khaddam with a grin. He seemed to be seeking reassurance: "Always the right is on the side of the strong," he said sarcastically, referring to Israel, "because he is strong."

I had learned that Khaddam had respect only for those who stood up to him. Therefore I said: "Not all the weak are necessarily innocent."

But Khaddam was not interested in winning philosophical points. He wanted to make sure I would engage myself on the Syrian front as I had on the Egyptian: "All we were asking for is justice. We are certain that your effort will yield positive results. The essential thing is that you have put yourself inside the problem. This is the essential thing."

For Khaddam, fiercely nationalistic, proudly radical, to admit that American cooperation was essential was revolutionary. To express faith in our purposes must have been a wrench. (Khaddam's attitude toward the United States was shown in an exchange with our Ambassador, Richard Murphy, months later. As my plane was coming in to land, Murphy said, not without ambivalence himself: "I think the airplane is God's punishment to mankind." "No," replied Khaddam simply; "America is.") In this mood we repaired to the Presidency, where President Asad treated me to an hour and a half's disquisition on Sadat's duplicity, its controlled fury all the more impressive for his eerily cold, seemingly unemotional demeanor. Asad then encouraged me to give him a tutorial on current international affairs, interspersed with his sardonic comments. Since I suspected he might convey at least part of the conversation to Moscow, I gave him a boilerplate reassurance: "Our policy is not anti-Soviet; we recognize that the USSR has major interests in the Middle East. We are not combating them." Asad might be without experience of the outside world but he understood reality: "You are about to force them out of the peace negotiations and you are not combating them?" he responded without acrimony, even with a tinge of respect.

He then had another little joke. Having heard from all his brethren of my principle that Soviet arms could not be permitted to defeat American arms, he proposed to equip the Syrian army with American weapons! This exchange occurred:

KISSINGER: You should be grateful. Every time I come to Damascus, you get another shipment of tanks [from the Soviet Union].

ASAD: You are going on an errand that might make us not need more tanks. We have asked our Arab brothers who are not on the confrontation line to buy us American weapons.

KISSINGER: What weapons are you interested in?

ASAD: Any kind of weapons — tanks, rockets, anything — just so there will be no more talk about American weapons versus Soviet weapons. The problem should be pictured as Arab against Israel, not as the US versus the USSR. I was told by other Arabs that you would not allow American arms to be defeated by Soviet arms. So, I would propose that we develop a situation where US arms are against US arms.

KISSINGER: The President's next move will be to encourage Israel to buy Soviet arms.

But when the banter was over, Asad accepted in principle the start of a disengagement negotiation for Syria under American auspices. He even had a plan, somewhat scaled down from the version of a month before when he proposed to put the disengagement line along the 1967 border. In Syria, "scaled down" is a relative term. Asad's opening position now was that in the name of disengagement Israel give up all of its gains from the October war plus half of the Golan Heights taken in 1967. I mused about the fireworks that would come when Golda heard this proposition.

Still, Asad had done some homework. He even proposed a scheme for a zone of limited armaments, though it was very modest, extending only five kilometers on either side of a dividing line. This was not much, but then the Golan Heights did not have the depth of Sinai — the whole area is less than twenty miles wide. I did not waste time in debate; there was no sense discussing terms when Israel had not yet accepted even the principle of negotiations. I told Asad I would stop in Israel to leave his ideas there. (I was eager to create an impression of some progress in Damascus to ease the threat of Sadat's isolation.) Asad came close to promising a list of Israeli prisoners of war — the minimum Israeli condition for negotiations: "Once efforts have progressed a little, we will agree with you on giving a suitable number." He added the crucial reassurance that no Israeli prisoners had died.

Asad, finally, agreed that I could brief the press that the talks had been "constructive"— another big boost in the Arab world for the Egyptian agreement. On the way to the airport I summed up to Khaddam what I would say to the media:

I will express my thanks for your hospitality. I will say that I talked with President Asad for over four hours. We reviewed both bilateral relations and above all the prospects for peace in the Middle East. With respect to the Middle East, we discussed disengagement as well as a lasting settlement, which must be our ultimate goal and to which the US has promised to give support. The talks were very useful, very constructive and in my judgment contributed to Syrian–US relations and to peace in the Middle East. President Asad gave me his ideas on the problem of disengagement as well as on the problem of a lasting peace, and we will study them carefully as we continue our efforts.

Khaddam replied: "If asked, I will say I have nothing to add. Which means I support what you have said."

Which also meant that I had a Syrian go-ahead for a step-by-step approach on the Golan Heights.

Unfortunately, I had no such go-ahead from Israel. Late on Sunday I flew to Israel to ease pressures on Sadat by hinting at our readiness to undertake a Syrian shuttle. In a lounge at Ben-Gurion Airport I explained our ideas to Allon and other members of the Israeli negotiating team (minus Dayan, who could not be raised on short notice or, more likely, had enough domestic criticism without involving himself in Syrian negotiations.) The Israelis, still exhausted from the grueling labor of finishing the Egyptian agreement, were not eager to begin wrestling with the much more difficult and emotional Golan problem. They noted Asad's proposals, but without cabinet approval they were not even in a position to quibble, since that implied a negotiation was going on. They pressed for the list of the POWs, with respect to which in turn I could not go beyond what Asad had told me. We settled for a Delphic announcement implying that negotiations were in progress while enabling my Israeli counterparts to avoid a firm commitment:

I brought some ideas on disengagement from Syria to the Israeli Government. The Israeli Government will now study these ideas and after consideration by the Cabinet, will give us its views and we will then see what follows.

With respect to Jordan, the Israeli negotiators were even more opaque. They listened attentively to my summary of Hussein's proposals; they asked perceptive questions. But none of my interlocutors was prepared to mortgage his prospects in the new cabinet by risking the veto of the National Religious Party that was the certain penalty for agreeing to discuss any withdrawal, however trivial, from any part of the West Bank, even from Jericho.

Finally at 8:30 P.M. on Sunday, January 20, after ten dramatic days in the Middle East, we headed home. The evening departure provoked a near-rebellion among the traveling press, who had visited three countries in one day, had had to file from each, and now faced a fourteen-hour plane trip unrelieved, as in my case, by a bed to stretch out on. But I had no choice. An impatient President was waiting for me, eager to begin Congressional briefings and to savor the rare experience of a positive event.

Washington at Last

A T 4:30 A.M. Monday, January 21, we were back in Washington after a short stop at Heathrow Airport to brief Sir Alec Douglas-Home. From the plane I had sent messages to the key Arab leaders and several NATO allies. I gave each a summary of the various stops I had made since leaving Egypt. Asad and Hussein were, of course, especially interested in Israel's reaction to their proposals. I told Hussein that I had passed along his "interest in establishing a Jordanian-Israeli working group in the Geneva framework" and had "let them know that I will want to go into this in some detail with them later this week." To Asad I wrote:

[D]uring my stop in Israel enroute back to Washington Sunday evening, I transmitted your proposal on the disengagement of forces to the Israeli Government. The Israelis told me they would be working on a reply, and, as soon as I hear from them, I will be in further touch with you.

It was not much, but it kept up contacts and it eased the pressure on Sadat.

I found Nixon elated; he had had little enough to encourage him in recent weeks. He was extraordinarily proud that even in the midst of domestic crisis his Administration had managed to play the decisive role in turning the Middle East toward peace. He gave an incisive briefing to the Congressional leaders, whose obsession was to probe for some "secret commitments" — as if American involvement could result only from some hidden document, not from strategic realities, and as if our failure to involve ourselves would not have had far more serious consequences. Buoyed by the widespread public acclaim, the Congressional leaders, at least, dropped almost entirely the sour tone of their Watergate discussions with the President, even if they could not in the end bring themselves — except, ironically enough, J. William Fulbright — to express the unconditional approbation that Nixon sought and, in my view, deserved.

The next day, January 22, I held a news conference covering familiar ground: the terms of the agreement, the assurances passed between the parties. Once more I had to address the issue of "secret" American commitments. A significant part of the news conference was consumed by the affair of the yeoman in my office under whose shadow the trip had started. I had had no time to study the subtleties of the case or prepare for the inquisitional assault of the media, now battle-tested by Watergate. Had I known that an investigation of the Anderson leaks was going on? Was I aware of the investigation being conducted by David Young, one of the "Plumbers," who had once been an assistant of mine? The drift of the questions was becoming clear. The insinuation was that if I knew that much, I had to be implicated in most of the "Plumbers" activities — rather a non sequitur. There were a few more questions of a similar nature. They were not intended maliciously; this is what made them so pernicious. What they showed was the narrowness of the ledge on which all of us were walking. Authority was clearly diminishing; no success could for long reverse the trend; we were in a poor position to endure prolonged international crises.

But this was no more than to confirm the familiar. America in the winter of 1973–1974 was not a happy place. It was ridden with suspicion, bitterness, cynicism. A taste for sensational revelations had developed, much of it unhappily too justified, some of it pursued almost for its own sake. And it was not hard to understand why this should be so. Confidence is a precious commodity. Once plundered, it must grow again organically; it cannot be restored simply by an act of will or on the claim of national security.

And yet if we had built well, the course of events would demonstrate that we had turned a corner in the Middle East. With luck, a peace process would move forward in defiance of all obstacles. Something in this sad period might be remembered with pride. We might not be the leaders who made the final peace; but we would always take satisfaction if someday it could be truly said, it all started here.

XIX

The Energy Crisis

The Years of Complacency

I RETURNED to Washington in exultation. But rare are the crises that lend themselves to dramatic revolutions. Usually change appears in the guise of the commonplace, not as a catharsis but as a series of technical decisions. So it was with the energy crisis, which now reclaimed us.

It began dramatically enough in 1973, and altered irrevocably the world as it had grown up in the postwar period. The seemingly inexorable rise in prosperity was abruptly reversed. Simultaneously, inflation ran like a forest fire through the industrialized countries and recession left millions unemployed. The poorer countries without oil plunged into deeper depression and unredeemable debt, while the oil producers suddenly had more money than they could possibly spend. Their vast, mobile cash balances played havoc with currencies as they moved among capitals for reasons economic or political. Transcending even the economic revolution was the emergence of oil as a weapon of political blackmail. The industrial democracies saw imposed on them not only an economic upheaval but fundamental changes in their social cohesion and political life.

But the remedy proved prolonged; the effects of these convulsions continue to this day. Our economic system has not yet recovered; the political and social consequences are still playing themselves out.

How could a transformation of such a profound and far-reaching nature come so suddenly upon us? Much of it is clearer in retrospect, for the seeds and the signals of dramatic change were there. The oil revolution was of a pattern with many historical revolutions. They were inevitable but their inevitability is obvious only after the fact. It is almost impossible for historians to understand how in advance of some of history's great revolutions it was often not even realized that a change was about to take place. Lulled by the illusion of permanence, the soon-to-be victims treated as fleeting aberrations warnings that posterity now sees as self-evident. And therefore dikes that could have been strengthened to hold back the flood were left unattended until they suddenly burst and the torrents engulfed those who had never suspected danger.

Richard Nixon came into office in a world economy that treated cheap oil as natural and excess production capacity as the main economic problem. If we worried at all about the political dimension, it was how to satisfy insistent oil-producing countries who competed for the favor of access to our market and offered foreign policy benefits in exchange. At the end of the Sixties the United States imported only around 20 percent of its oil needs. We coasted on the assumption that we had large untapped domestic reserves. New discoveries on the North Slope of Alaska promised vast supplies. We possessed oil shale in abundance, which we thought could be quickly exploited if shortages should cause the price to rise.* The so-called Texas Railroad Commission, which decided the level of American production, set output well below capacity in order to maintain a domestic price of $3.30 a barrel — more than one dollar a barrel above the world price — to encourage domestic exploration and drilling. Oil imports were regulated through a system established by President Eisenhower in 1959, setting strict quotas for imports.

In this way, the United States had a decisive influence over the world price of oil. If the price of foreign oil went up beyond what we thought desirable, we could increase our production, restrict our imports, and force our foreign suppliers onto world markets. Or, if we really wanted to make a point, produce more American oil and sell it abroad. The Mideast oil producers therefore had an incentive to keep prices low. The Organization of Petroleum Exporting Countries (OPEC), formed in 1960,** was not perceived as a serious cartel. Conventional wisdom was that the oil producers could not force the price up by restricting production because the necessary cutback would have to be so steep as to bankrupt them before it would affect the industrial democracies. The fiasco of the Arab oil embargo of 1967, which collapsed in the face of uninterrupted Iranian, increased American, and other Western Hemisphere production, seemed to confirm this.

Nothing was further from Nixon's mind than an energy crisis when on March 25, 1969, he created a Cabinet Task Force on Oil Import Control to review the quota system. The Task Force was chaired by the Secretary of Labor, George P. Shultz, and included the Secretaries of State, Defense, Treasury, Interior, and Commerce, the Director of the Office of Emergency Preparedness, and other officials as observers. White House responsibility was vested in Assistant to the President Pe-

---

*When the price of oil was at $3.00 a barrel, it was thought that shale oil would be economical at $5.00. It remained above the world oil price through most of the period.

**OPEC's members consisted of Saudi Arabia, Iraq, Kuwait, Iran, Venezuela, Algeria, Libya, Qatar, the United Arab Emirates, Nigeria, Gabon, Indonesia, and Ecuador.

ter M. Flanigan, a financial expert. My office had no operational role; at most, it maintained a watching brief on any significant national security aspect that might emerge — considered an unlikely contingency.

The Task Force deliberated for a year, took 10,000 pages of testimony, and in February 1970 came up with a 400-page report whose principal recommendation was to replace the import quotas by a system of tariffs. Foreign producers would be free to compete in our market subject only to the customs duty. By letting the market operate, the effect of the tariff system would be some downward pressure on the domestic price of oil; the government would get out of the business of allocating imports. But the tariffs could always be raised if imports became excessive; the level of our imports was treated as essentially a domestic American decision with respect to which we had great flexibility.

The never-never land of national policymaking of 1970 is shown by the report's estimates that even at prevailing prices the United States would be importing only 27 percent of its oil requirements by 1980 and that no substantial rise in the world price was foreseeable over the next decade.[1] (In fact, by the late 1970s we were importing nearly 50 percent of our oil and the world price had increased more than tenfold.) The Task Force's bow to national security consisted of urging that preference continue to be given to Western Hemisphere oil so that dependence on Middle East supplies could be limited to 10 percent of our total imports. (By 1979 it was in fact over 40 percent.)

The domestic agencies of our government, which had responsibility for our oil policy, objected to more foreign competition. The Secretaries of Interior and Commerce and the Chairman of the Federal Power Commission filed a minority report asserting that the proposed tariff program would drive the domestic price of oil down to around $2.50 per barrel, undermine incentives for domestic production, and thereby create an undue dependence on imported oil within ten years. (The minority also rejected the idea of emergency storage as "not economically sensible.") As it turned out, Nixon — for political reasons — sided with the minority and retained the oil import quota system, thereby opting for lower imports and slightly higher prices. With some adjustments the quota system continued for three more years, amid debates that at this reading seem as ancient as the dinosaur.

My office did not participate in these debates. It was neither consulted nor even informed about the key decisions. I am not suggesting that the decisions would have been better had I been involved; I had no expertise on the subject. I mention the fact only to demonstrate to what extent energy was considered a domestic, not a foreign, issue. What foreign policy arguments over oil took place during those first Nixon years concerned allocations *within* the American import ceiling. The producers, not the consumers, appeared as the supplicants, as OPEC countries jockeyed for a favored position in our market. Our relations with Iran were a case in point. Later on, it was sometimes claimed that the Nixon Administration's policy toward the Shah was influenced by our desire to increase his revenues so that he could buy additional military hardware. This is a reversal of the truth. The Shah's perennial complaint was that we were not buying enough Iranian oil. When he visited Washington to attend President Eisenhower's funeral in March 1969, I paid a courtesy call on him at the Iranian Embassy. He used the occasion to offer to help us establish a petroleum stockpile by filling our salt domes, thus protecting against interruption of oil supplies in a major war. To this end he would sell us one million barrels a day for ten years at the amazing bargain price of $1.00 a barrel.

I turned the Shah's suggestion over to our government's oil experts, who rejected it out of hand. An increase in Iran's quota was possible only at the expense of Saudi Arabia and other friendly Persian Gulf countries. There was also the insurmountable problem that the United States government was not in the business of purchasing oil except for military needs, many of which were met from Saudi Arabia. The rest of the oil was purchased by private companies; strong governmental intervention would have been required to force a shift from traditional suppliers. The companies would have had to reduce liftings somewhere else to satisfy the Shah — unless we were prepared to risk a drop in prices by adding imports from Iran to the existing quotas. I was selected to convey the bad news to His Imperial Majesty. (As oil prices later shot up and demand grew with no apparent limits, the Shah, despite his reputation as a secular ruler, must have thanked Providence for our rejection of an arrangement so breathtakingly advantageous to us.)

In October 1969 the Shah again came to the United States, this time on an official visit, and pursued the subject of American oil purchases directly with Nixon. The Shah considered that he was short $155 million in his development program — a sum oil producers would now consider a pittance. Nixon promised that he would do his utmost to increase oil purchases from Iran. This event merely served to teach Nixon how negligible was the influence of the President of the United States over oil import allocations. While the US government set the import quotas, the basic decisions as to where to purchase and produce were made by a consortium of the seven largest oil companies — the so-called majors. The quota established a ceiling but did not require that the ceiling actually be met; for actual sales each country had to deal with the majors.

The companies operated under concessions in the various producing countries, owning the production facilities as well as the refineries and paying the host countries an agreed sum per barrel. The majors — not

governments — made the basic pricing, production, and marketing decisions. They had had trouble enough finding a new share of the market
for Libya, where oil had been discovered in the late Fifties, without
complicating their problem by increasing Iran's share.* When Nixon's
request was put before them, the American partners of the consortium
refused to cooperate even with shifting some Defense Department purchases to Iran because the American share of the Iranian output was
much smaller than in, say, Saudi Arabia. As Flanigan pointed out in a
memorandum to me of January 10, 1970, "a substantial portion of the
profits from these purchases would go to non-American companies if
Iranian oil were sought." On July 30, 1970 — nine months after having
made a promise to be helpful on oil purchases — Nixon was obliged to
write to the Shah in effect that he could not deliver.

Nothing illustrates better the misperceptions that can precede a great
upheaval. The industrial democracies, the companies, and the producing
countries alike were blinded by a kaleidoscope of illusions: by the supposed surplus capacity in the United States, by the fear of a glut of oil
that might lead to a massive break in prices, by the apparent eagerness
of the various producing countries to increase their output, and by an
assumption that individual producers would always be willing to undercut prices to increase their revenues at the expense of the rest — all
notions that were exactly the opposite of the reality that was gradually
emerging. Its full impact was obscured for a while because the oil companies had effectively made all pricing and marketing decisions for over
a generation; the United States government was by habit reluctant to
interfere with the operation of a market that seemed both efficient and
consonant with our long-term interests.

The Gathering Storm: 1970–1973

As the new decade began, all this began to change. World conditions
of supply and demand shifted inexorably against the consumers.
Demand grew, most of all in the United States. Soon we no longer
possessed surplus capacity. In early 1972 the Texas Railroad Commission for the first time took off all restrictions on American production;
by the end of the year the United States was producing at full capacity — with no further margin for discretionary expansion. It was a fate-

---

*Their dilemma has been described by an American scholar:

[A]s Libyan output continued to rise, the majors became increasingly concerned over whether
the Persian Gulf countries would tolerate the necessary compensating reductions in their output
and income. And since the majors' production in the Middle East was some twenty times
their output in Libya, what they might lose in the former area was far greater than any possible
gains in the latter. Yet if they ceased production in Libya, their concessions would probably
be turned over to the independents, who would only increase the volume of uncontrolled
output. . . .[2]

ful turn of events. Domestic and world demand continued to grow, as the global economy headed for the end of its third decade of nearly uninterrupted boom. For America, oil imports turned from a convenience into a necessity: In 1947, the United States imported 8.1 percent of its oil consumption; in 1973, 36.1 percent.[3] No longer able to dampen the world price by spurring our own production further or even to protect ourselves against supply cutoffs, we rapidly lost leverage. The balance of power on energy was shifting from the Texas Gulf to the Persian Gulf. The OPEC producers were moving into the driver's seat. It was only a matter of time before they took advantage of it.

The dimensions of the change were not immediately apparent. Because for a while longer prices were still established through negotiations between the private oil companies and the host countries, the illusion persisted that one was watching commercial bargaining and not a revolutionary upheaval. And because the symptoms, the price increases in the early 1970s, were extremely modest, no issue even of domestic economic policy — not to speak of national security — seemed to be involved.

The proximate cause was the overthrow in September 1969 of the pro-Western King Idris of Libya by the radical Colonel Muammar Qaddafi. (It must be stressed that the price explosion was not a personal decision; one way or another, market conditions would have produced a price explosion, though perhaps over a longer period of time.) Until then the dominant role among the oil-producing countries was played by essentially conservative governments whose interest in increasing their oil revenues was balanced by their dependence on the industrial democracies for protection against external (and perhaps even internal) threats. Qaddafi was free of such inhibitions. An avowed radical, he set out to extirpate Western influence. He did not care if in the process he weakened the global economy. The working level of our government, especially in the State Department, operated on the romantic view that Third World radicalism was really frustrated Western liberalism. Third World leaders, they believed, had become extremist because the West had backed conservative regimes, because we did not understand their reformist aspirations, because their societies were backward and eager for change[4] — for every reason, in fact, other than the most likely: ideological commitment to the implacable anti-Western doctrines they were espousing.

For reasons I have explained earlier, I did not in Nixon's first term take an initiating role in Middle Eastern policy. There were desultory discussions in the Washington Special Actions Group (WSAG) on what attitude to take toward the new Libyan regime. In a meeting of November 24, 1969, I raised the question whether to have the 40 Committee*

* See p. 382n.

canvass the possibility of covert action. A study was prepared of economic and political pressure points on Libya; but the agencies did not have their heart in it. All options involving action were rejected, causing me to exclaim that I was averse to submitting to the President a paper that left us with the proposition that we could do nothing. My reluctance did not change a consensus along precisely those lines. According to the dominant view, the real danger of radicalization resided in our *opposition* to Qaddafi. The huge Wheelus Air Base — which Qaddafi asked us to vacate — was alleged to be of marginal significance. We would protect our oil interests best, it was said, by separating them from military matters. As perceived by the interagency paper prepared for the WSAG meeting, energy supplies were in jeopardy only if we did something to antagonize the new Libyan revolutionary regime:

> We see no immediate threat to these [oil] interests, although such could result if the regime is threatened, or becomes increasingly unstable, or if there were a real confrontation over Wheelus, or in the event of renewed hostilities in the Middle East.

According to the bureaucratic consensus, it followed necessarily that our only choice was to try to get along with Qaddafi:

> Our present strategy is to seek to establish satisfactory relations with the new regime. The return to our balance of payments and the security of U.S. investments in oil are considered our primary interests. We seek to retain our military facilities, but not at the expense of threatening our economic return. We also wish to protect European dependence on Libyan oil; it is literally the only "irreplaceable" oil in the world, from the point of view both of quality and geographic location.

Whereas America was deciding on passivity, Western Europe chose actively to curry favor with Libya's radical ruler. Europe had, of course, made itself far more dependent on imported oil, much of it Libyan. In 1950, 75 percent of Europe's energy needs had been met by coal. By 1970, faith in permanently cheap and plentiful oil, backed up by government incentives, had produced a 60 percent dependence on oil — almost all of it imported. And 25 percent of Europe's energy requirements was supplied by Libya. The result was that within four months of Qaddafi's coming to power, France had negotiated the sale of 100 advanced jet aircraft to Libya. France assuaged its conscience with an inherently absurd and unenforceable Libyan promise that the planes would not be transferred to the states bordering Israel. Since Libya had few pilots trained for jet aircraft, the only possible purpose could be to make the planes available, one way or the other, to brother Arab states. Other European countries followed the same policy of conciliation; an especially friendly relationship developed between Libya and the Federal Republic of Germany.

As is often the case, decisions that seemed prudent and restrained when they were made have come to appear reckless to posterity. In the cause of short-term economic prudence the West accepted Qaddafi's revolution — and this, as it turned out, was bound to affect also the West's political relations with the conservative oil producers. Libya taught these rulers a fateful lesson: The industrial democracies would not protect friendly governments so long as their radical, avowedly hostile successors did not challenge the democracies' access to oil. Hence, there was no point in seeking to buy Western goodwill by restraint on oil prices or anything else. For a year or two, the occasion to apply this insight did not arise. But as market conditions changed, it subtly affected the attitudes of even the moderate governments.

Thus did the political balance also shift, just as market conditions were transforming the economic equilibrium. Radical Libya then triggered a process by which the host governments gradually discovered, and began to exercise, their dominant power over the world oil market. There were three discernible stages in the revolution about to unfold: first, a creeping increase in prices; then the host governments' gradual, de facto takeover of ownership and operational control from the oil companies; and finally the resulting ability of the producer governments to link the sale of oil to political conditions, especially the Arab-Israeli conflict.

At the beginning of 1970, Libya demanded larger oil revenues from the companies operating on its soil. It had a special bargaining advantage in that the majors did not have the stranglehold on Libyan production that they enjoyed in the Persian Gulf. Because of Libya's relatively late entry into the ranks of oil producers, and because of the majors' reluctance to shift their purchases from traditional suppliers, the "independents" came to assume a special prominence in Libya. And they were much more vulnerable than their larger competitors. They could not substitute increased production in the Persian Gulf for cutbacks in Libyan oil or hold out against Libyan threats to shut down their facilities. On January 29, 1970, matters came to a head when the Libyan government demanded an increase of 40 cents a barrel — or 20 percent — in the price of its oil. While tiny in terms of later oil price rises, this represented the largest single jump in the history of oil negotiations. The companies initially resisted the increase and the Libyans thereupon resorted to unprecedented methods of intimidation.

Libya picked on the most vulnerable link in the chain, the independent company Occidental Petroleum, and imposed production cutbacks on it more severe than those on its competitors. On June 12, 1970, Occidental's production was slashed from 800,000 barrels a day to

500,000 and on August 19 it was cut again to 440,000, thus lowering Occidental's output by 45 percent. It was the first time a producing country had implemented what amounted to an embargo. The majors in turn demonstrated their short sightedness by letting an inconvenient competitor twist slowly, slowly in the wind, to use a phrase of a later era, rejecting any measures of support to compensate Occidental for the costs of the cutback. Isolated and vulnerable, Occidental yielded to Libyan blackmail on September 4, 1970, agreeing to an immediate increase of 30 cents a barrel, rising to 40 cents over five years. The other companies soon followed suit.[5]

At this stage, the economic impact of these settlements was less significant than the political implications. Heretofore the oil companies, bargaining as a unit, had imposed a unified price. Now the united front of the companies had been split, shattering one of the buffers between the producing and consuming countries. This set up a "leapfrogging" system between the Mediterranean suppliers and those of the Persian Gulf. Libya justified its higher price on the basis that the transportation costs from Libya were lower than those from the Gulf, that its oil was of a higher quality, and that it was dealing with independents. The Persian Gulf producers did not accept a theory that gave a larger income to a competitor and insisted on receiving matching increases. As soon as they prevailed, Libya would then invoke the loss of its premium to make new demands, triggering additional requests in the Persian Gulf, starting the cycle all over again. No true stopping point emerged; the international petroleum market structure of a generation was collapsing.

It was a clear warning that something was wrong but it was not so perceived. The price increases, while substantial in percentage terms, started from a very low base. The price remained under $3.00 a barrel, which was still below the American domestic price. The increases did not seem to affect the basic premise of cheap and plentiful oil on which the economies of the industrial democracies were based. And therefore Western governments stayed out of the leapfrog negotiations between the producing governments and the oil companies. When Nixon on his European trip stopped at Chequers on October 3, 1970, British Foreign Secretary Sir Alec Douglas-Home informed Secretary of State William Rogers that the British companies in Libya had been told to be guided by "their commercial judgment" — in other words, since no security interests were involved, they would be left to their own devices.

In December 1970 OPEC, emulating the Libyan precedent, convened in Caracas and formally requested new price negotiations between the majors and all the petroleum-exporting nations. In effect, the oil producers were beginning to take full control of their oil. Too late the companies bestirred themselves. In January 1971 they agreed to what they had failed to do four months earlier: to bargain collectively and to

resist selective blackmail by sharing oil. Ironically, to prevent leapfrogging tactics they also demanded that OPEC negotiate as a unit. In time
OPEC accepted the proposal with a vengeance, forging an efficient cartel willing to reduce its production contrary to the historical practice of
almost all its members.

At last the United States government began to take an interest. It was
urged on by the oil companies, which followed their time-honored pattern of asking for assistance only at the last moment, and then only ad
hoc, not for a long-term strategy — which they feared would lead to
government control. They asked for, and received, dispensation from
the Department of Justice so that a united front of the companies would
not be treated as a violation of antitrust laws. At the urgent request of
the companies, Under Secretary of State John N. Irwin II was dispatched to the Mideast on January 16, 1971, to urge moderation on the
oil-producing nations.

Unfortunately, our government would have been hard put to define
what it meant by "moderation." The tactical need to meet the deadlines
imposed by OPEC for new negotiations obscured the necessity for a
more fundamental review. On January 14 my able staff members C. Fred
Bergsten and Harold Saunders, monitoring the fast-moving company negotiations, had recommended a more serious study of the advantages
and disadvantages of United States government involvement. They presented several arguments in favor of staying out of the dispute between
the producers and the companies: The rise in the price of energy would
affect primarily Europe and Japan and probably improve America's
competitive position. To sustain a confrontation would require us to be
prepared to ration oil at home to support the European economies — a
difficult enterprise in a country racked by Vietnam. To improve their
bargaining position with the oil producers the oil companies might bring
pressure on the government to intervene in the Arab-Israeli conflict,
which was contrary to our strategy of demonstrating the limits of Soviet
influence. Confrontation, it was also suggested, could weaken America's relations with the Arab world.

My staff also put the arguments in favor of deeper government involvement, not the least of which was the need to head off a cycle of
escalating producer demands shading into the political field. There was
also the danger of supply disruptions that would seriously affect our
own security as well as that of our allies. Though I leaned to the arguments for a more active governmental role, I concluded that I was in no
position to make a recommendation. Therefore I took the official's time-
honored way out: On January 15, 1971, I ordered a study of the national
security implications of the problem.

Well before the study was fairly launched, the arguments for nonin-
tervention carried the day in keeping with long-established national pol-

icy. The United States government did not as a general practice involve itself in commercial disputes. We would step in to resist the expropriation of American companies when there was no fair compensation; we had not to my knowledge engaged ourselves in price negotiations.

On January 18, while Irwin was in the Middle East, I sent Nixon a memorandum (drafted with the help of Bergsten and Saunders) summing up the status of the negotiations between OPEC and the oil companies. If we were going to encourage the companies to stand up to the producers, I argued, six questions would have to be answered:

> Will the companies stick together and hold the line against the Libyan demands? . . . Will Libya stick to its extreme demands and stop the flow of Libyan oil if they are not met? . . . Will the other Arabs then stick with Libya and shut down their production as well? . . . Will the European governments panic at the potential shortages and attempt to strike their own government-to-government deals with Libya, circumventing the companies? . . . Or will the Europeans join forces to staunchly resist the Arabs? . . . Will we then ration oil domestically to help the Europeans withstand the Arabs, and/or bring new pressures on Israel to buy off the Arabs politically?

My memorandum concluded with the following warning: "However, all of the activity so far is completely tactical and reactive. I have therefore called for a quick study of our basic objectives in the situation, and an analysis of what role we should be playing in trying to help solve it."

Before the questions could be answered or the studies completed, the negotiations had run their course. Irwin had been sent off after a talk between Nixon and Secretary of State William Rogers in which I did not participate. I do not know if any specific instructions were given to him; the probability is that they were general. In the absence of a political directive to force a showdown, the first instinct of American negotiators is to reassure their opposite numbers about our intentions on the theory that a show of goodwill improves the general atmosphere. Not surprisingly, Irwin proudly reported to the President on January 25 that in the three countries he had visited (Iran, Saudi Arabia, and Kuwait), he had stressed that we would follow our tradition of not becoming involved in the details of commercial negotiations — neatly removing the one fear that might have moderated producer demands: the threat of United States governmental intervention. If confrontation was to be avoided and if our government would not involve itself in the details, the preordained outcome was that the companies must yield.

In these circumstances, the leaders receiving Irwin turned the tables on him. They argued that the insistence on OPEC–wide negotiations was a maneuver by the companies to play the producers off against each other. Against all recent experience, they maintained that separate negotiations by the Persian Gulf and the Mediterranean producers were the most effective road to moderation. The Persian Gulf producers wanted to proceed on their own, they said, because if they were part of the same delegation as the Libyans, Qaddafi would veto their proposals. They argued (quite correctly) that the real price of oil had fallen over a five-year period — that is, discounting for inflation — while the cost of goods they imported had risen.

It was a negotiating tactic that the next decade would see refined into an art form: Whatever group within OPEC happened to be doing the talking blamed the oil price rise on someone else. There were elaborate Saudi theories putting the entire responsibility on the Shah and equally complicated Iranian arguments proving that the Arab Gulf producers, notably the Saudis, were the driving force. One could not help wondering how any group of leaders could ever have produced a result so contrary to their professed preferences. The truth was, of course, that *all* producers favored higher prices; none was prepared to break the cartel. In practice, they were all supporting a strategy that would have only one outcome: a sharp rise in prices sustained over a decade.

Irwin's conclusion was that the companies would have to seek the best possible terms. In his report to the President, he stated:

> They [the OPEC countries] stress readiness to stand up to the oil companies in the negotiations, even to the extent of reducing or halting production. Consequently, although I believe my trip gained a little time and impressed on the three governments a certain perspective heretofore lacking, I am not at all sanguine as to their final action unless the company negotiators can convince the producing countries that they are negotiating seriously and within the terms of reference and time frame of OPEC's Caracas resolutions.

Our hands-off policy ordained the result; the companies yielded. They accepted "separate" but "concurrent" negotiations, an elegant phrase for falling in with the leapfrog tactics of the producers. The upshot was the Tehran agreement of February 14, 1971, which amounted to an increase of around 40 cents a barrel for the Persian Gulf; and the Tripoli agreement of April 2, which not unexpectedly led to an even larger price rise for Libya. Both producing groups agreed to maintain this level for five years — a solemn promise that must hold a world record in the scale and speed of its violation.

For a few months, stability seemed to have returned to the oil market. King Faisal visited Washington in May 1971. Oil appears not to have been mentioned. The Mideast price rises had still not begun to have any serious effect on the economies of the industrial democracies, least of all the United States. It is therefore a measure of Nixon's instinct for anticipating looming problems and seeking to shape events that on June 4, 1971, he sent a message to Congress urging an expansion of alternative energy sources. In his oral briefings, Nixon proudly emphasized that "this is the first time that a message on energy of a comprehensive nature has been sent to the Congress by a President." Preparation of the message had been in the hands of domestic agencies. I was not involved. There was no sense of urgency, much less of international crisis. Extended interruptions of supply were still considered inconceivable. Nixon's program addressed a problem of the more or less distant future.

The OPEC Governments Take Control

THE future had, in fact, arrived. The fundamental change in bargaining positions was underlined by the speed and insistence with which OPEC returned to the fray. Only a few months after the February and April 1971 agreements that were supposed to stabilize prices for five years, an OPEC meeting in Beirut in September came forward with new demands. Rather disingenuously, it asked for compensation for the devaluation of the dollar during the summer. This resulted in another increase in oil prices of nearly 9 percent, plus the prospect of quarterly adjustments. More important, OPEC put forth a demand for "equity participation" in the companies. This was creeping nationalization, and it had, of course, the practical effect of increasing the revenues of the host countries further. The companies had the choice of raising prices or absorbing the decline in their earnings resulting from the partial government ownership.

Negotiations on "participation" began in March 1972 between the companies and an OPEC team headed by Sheikh Ahmed Zaki Yamani of Saudi Arabia.* OPEC's initial demand was for 20 percent equity; under heavy Saudi pressure, the companies agreed. Immediately, the terms went up. The Saudis would accept 20 percent as the initial figure but (like the radical states and perhaps driven by them) they wanted 51 percent after a fixed period of time. This galloping nationalization would reduce the major oil companies to marketing and management organizations; the oil price in these circumstances would no longer be negotiated but established by the producer governments.

Quickly, the negotiations on participation turned into a mirror image of the talks on price. An initial concession produced not agreement but escalating demands. The market seemed to provide no ceiling to producer exactions.

In the summer of 1972, negotiations between Yamani and the companies reached an impasse over the issue of financial compensation to

---

*The OPEC front amounted in effect to Saudi Arabia and the smaller Gulf states. Iran did not participate, claiming its oil structure did not lend itself to the participation schemes at issue; Libya pursued a separate path as, in varying degrees, did Iraq and Algeria.

the companies, amidst OPEC threats of unilateral action. For the first time the Saudis felt strong enough to request direct United States government intervention *against* the companies, invoking Faisal's friendship with Nixon. The oil companies also appealed to the White House; they cited the established principle of governmental help in cases of expropriation without adequate compensation. The Saudi offer for compensation in fact grossly underestimated the value of the property.

As it happened, Prince Saud Faisal, then Deputy Oil Minister of Saudi Arabia, was visiting Washington in early August 1972. I had not been involved in the negotiation but at the request of the companies I had a long talk with him (as did, separately, Flanigan and senior State Department officials). I was more concerned about the principle of takeover than the level of compensation. What the Saudis sought ran the risk of turning American companies into instruments of foreign countries while escalating every disagreement into a government-to-government confrontation. With Saud, I followed the line that while it was against our policy to intervene in negotiations involving private companies, in this case the low compensation offered and the high equity participation sought raised the specter of expropriation. Our relations with Saudi Arabia were not based on purely commercial considerations. However, if we were driven against the wall on economic issues, it could affect political relations as well.

Saud, a man of intelligence and subtlety, could not have listened with greater courtesy and understanding. Saudi Arabia did not seek conflict with the United States, he said. It would do its utmost to reach an equitable solution. It was open-minded on compensation. It would be interested in hearing our views on participation. For their guidance the Saudis would appreciate some indication of what terms the United States government considered fair with respect to both issues.

I thought we were well on the way to a compromise. But when I reported Saud's reaction to the companies, a surprise was waiting for me. They had been eager enough to invoke the United States government for general pressure. But they did not want us to conduct the negotiations on their behalf; they refused my offer to pass on, with governmental endorsement, suggestions on fair compensation or participation. They were clearly much more interested in raising the compensation than in diminishing Saudi participation. Compensation would show up in the balance sheet; reducing Saudi participation may have seemed to the companies as simply delaying the inevitable. They may also have been gun-shy after their experience with the Irwin mission. They could never be sure when what had started as government pressure on their behalf would switch to the other side.

The upshot was that over the next few months Saudi Arabia proved forthcoming on compensation. The companies in turn agreed to Saudi participation starting at 25 percent and rising to 51 percent by 1982. The one intercession of the United States government had improved the immediate financial return to the companies. But the companies — in my opinion shortsightedly, at least from the national point of view — had yielded on what turned out to be the key issue. With the producer countries owning 51 percent of the equity, the companies would become instruments of nations whose interests did not necessarily parallel our own.

So long as supplies were ample and costs relatively low, the companies had effectively performed their role of exploration, technological development, and marketing, fueling generations of global economic growth. But nothing in the organization or philosophy of the companies equipped them to address the issues raised by ever more expensive oil, whose price and production would be controlled by a cartel of governments. The companies dreaded confrontation with the producers because they believed — from their perspective, quite accurately — that they would lose in goodwill what they might gain in any showdown. They had specialized in getting along with the countries in the area; they were emotionally unprepared for a siege. The day was rapidly approaching when the supply and price of oil would be determined by the unilateral decisions of producer governments, and no longer needed to be negotiated with the companies.

But established categories of thought have a way of lingering on. This was reflected in the American attitude when Nixon visited Iran in May 1972. Far from seeking to turn Iran into a major alternative source of supply as a hedge against excessive demands from the Arab members of OPEC, the recommendation was to vindicate existing policy. Peter Flanigan followed the orthodox view in a memorandum for the President that, as I summed up for Nixon, urged that

the Shah, during your discussions in Tehran, not be encouraged in his desire for access to the US market for Iranian oil. His [Flanigan's] point is that such access would make our relations with other Persian Gulf countries as well as with Venezuela extraordinarily difficult and would make impossible the already difficult task of managing the mandatory oil import program.

In transmitting Flanigan's view to Nixon, I noted that I agreed in the short run but that I was concerned with a long-range problem: how to make our import program less dependent on potentially hostile suppliers:

The one general issue that this raises in my mind, however, is that of the criteria we should use for deciding from which countries we import oil and other energy products as our needs for imported energy increase over the next decade. It would be possible, for instance, to establish criteria which would make it possible to select friendly countries and to import from them rather than from less friendly ones.

Nixon ignored the analysis. He and the Shah barely discussed oil. The Shah made a brief and prescient comment that since the industrial countries would be importing ever more of their energy needs, the strategic importance of the Middle East was growing. But neither leader explored the practical consequences of their theoretical propositions.

A few weeks after Nixon's visit, the Shah acted to translate his improving bargaining position into increasing revenues. As noted, Iran had not involved itself in the participation negotiations because its industry had a different structure from that of the Arab countries in the Persian Gulf. Instead, the Shah now insisted on his proposal of two years earlier. He imposed on the consortium a variety of measures to step up Iran's oil production, to boost Iran's overall oil income, and to increase Iran's direct involvement in petroleum operations. In return, the companies' role in Iran was to be extended for another fifteen years beyond 1979. The agreement was treated by our government as if it could somehow stand alone; the leapfrogging tactics of the producers had not yet been adequately analyzed. Thus Nixon, on the recommendation of the interested agencies, sent a telegram to the Shah congratulating him on his moderation.

The message was premature. The oil negotiations seemed destined never to achieve equilibrium. Saudi Arabia, having obtained agreement to 51 percent participation, soon began explicitly to link its oil policy to progress toward a solution of the Arab-Israeli conflict. And the Shah, once he understood the extent of participation conceded to Saudi Arabia, thought better of his recently proposed fifteen-year agreement. He decided that his domestic position did not permit him to be outnegotiated by Yamani. In early 1973 he reopened the bidding, in effect reneging on the agreement of the previous year. He put forward a scheme that pressed the implication of the OPEC negotiation to its ultimate conclusion: In effect, it insisted on transforming the companies into sales agents for Iran. The immediate impact on the oil price was negligible. But implicit in this, as in Yamani's formula, was a revolution permitting OPEC governments to establish prices unilaterally.

By late 1972 the price and ownership talks produced a growing awareness that the surge in American oil imports was creating a long-term vulnerability. There were hearings on Capitol Hill, and a proliferation of energy committees in the United States government. In early 1973 Nixon asked John Ehrlichman (soon to depart the scene), George Shultz, and me to study the relationship between energy policies and foreign and security concerns. Before the study could be completed, events supplied the answer.

I was increasingly alarmed by the escalating demands of the producers. And I did not think the United States alone could solve the problem. Cooperation with other consuming nations was essential. On January 16, 1973, I spoke in this sense to Sir Burke Trend, British Cabinet Secretary:

I could see an interruption to the oil supply. Certainly if the consumer nations stay as divided as they are. A comprehensive approach to the energy problem we should discuss. . . . The first thing to define is what we are trying to accomplish; what the needs are, what the sources are, and how to prevent the producer nations from playing off the consumer nations against each other. How does one do this? Alternate sources of supply for some countries, or a united stance, or both.

On March 8 I conveyed to the agencies that the President "has directed a study of the national security implications of world energy supply and distribution." On April 18, 1973, Nixon sent a major energy proposal to the Congress with initiatives to conserve energy, expand domestic production, and reorganize the government for dealing with the problem. The quota system was replaced by a simpler system of licensing (with fees charged for imports higher than the 1973 level); rationing was ruled out. The message frankly acknowledged that in the meantime "it will be necessary for us to increase fuel imports." Nixon followed up with another energy message, including further reorganization, on June 29. The Governor of Colorado, John A. Love, was appointed director of an expanded Energy Policy Office in the Executive Office of the President.

On April 19 I cited our own efforts in an appeal to Burke Trend once again for cooperation among the consumers:

If all the oil consuming nations are going to wait for the debacle of one of the others, so they can jump in and increase their own reserves, then sooner or later we have a prescription for breaking whatever exists in [the] industrial nations. We need some idea on how to cooperate to avoid these dangers. We are prepared to do it.

On April 23, in the Year of Europe address, I urged a concerted response by the industrial democracies to the growing energy problem. Later in the summer, in an interagency discussion of policy toward Libya, I stressed once more the imperative of consumer cooperation:

I know the mythology is that any attempt by the consumer countries to get together will produce a confrontation with the producer countries. That's a shibboleth and we should consider whether it is really true.

Another school of thought considered consumer solidarity a lower priority. Its view was that the oil issue was essentially a bilateral problem with Saudi Arabia; therefore we should strengthen our political and defense ties with the Kingdom. Deputy Defense Secretary William Clements urged that we strengthen defense cooperation; Deputy Treasury Secretary William Simon (soon to be named administrator of the Federal Energy Office) wanted an economic partnership. More and more experts were arguing that the level of Saudi oil production would be heavily influenced by our attitude toward Israel.[6]

I strongly favored expanding our bilateral ties with Saudi Arabia; within the year we had made major progress in the direction advocated by Clements and Simon. As for linking oil policy to the Arab-Israeli conflict, I thought it unwise for us and dangerous for Saudi Arabia. The Kingdom's already delicate position would be even more complicated if it had to take responsibility for Arab-Israeli negotiations. Either it risked being drawn into confrontation with Arab radicals or, if it supported them, it risked conflict with us and demonstration of its inability to produce progress. For there was no possibility, even if we desired it, that we could "deliver what the Saudis require" — as the saying went — in the weakened state of the Presidency.

These differences over tactics were quickly overtaken by events. For three years, a new infrastructure had been elaborated by the oil-producing nations built on the weakness and irresolution of the consumers. Free-market theology had kept the consumer governments, and especially the United States, out of negotiations as the companies were rendered defenseless. Political demands had become mingled with economics. When Western Hemisphere oil could no longer replace imports from the Arab world, the threat of a production cutoff by OPEC suddenly turned into a crucial weapon. The October war put a triumphal arch over this structure. Amazingly, the full implications of it had not yet been absorbed when the war was started. It was probably just as well, for otherwise we might not have mustered the unity or determination to stick to a course that our geopolitical imperatives demanded.

The October War and Energy: The First Oil Shock

WHEN the war began, there was vague talk in our government about a possible oil embargo. Remembering the experience of 1967, few believed that it could have any lasting impact. Deputy Assistant Secretary of State Roy Atherton, however, predicted an embargo as early as the first WSAG meeting on the morning of October 6, and Deputy Secretary Kenneth Rush worried that we had no contingency plans for it. So starting that evening, I called for contingency plans at each WSAG meeting, with no clear idea of what that request implied. Bill Simon, Governor Love, and Charles DiBona (energy consultant to the President) did yeoman work. Still, events moved faster than our capacity to plan. Gasoline rationing was discussed, but all agencies thought it premature. I was advocating a common front of consumer nations, including plans for emergency sharing in case of an embargo, yet none of our allies was prepared even to discuss such a plan.

This became clear on October 11, when French Foreign Minister Michel Jobert called on me for the first time in my new role of Secretary of State. Jobert warned that the producers were about to double the price of oil. Would we accept this? Of course we could not, but resistance by America alone would be ineffective and Jobert opposed consumer solidarity. I told Jobert that the pressure on price was not primarily the result of the war; the OPEC meeting, which began in Vienna on October 8, had been scheduled well before the outbreak of hostilities. As for dealing with a price rise, there were two problems. Heretofore the negotiations had been conducted by the oil companies, which had excluded the governments from their discussions and had passed on the price rises to the consumers. But if governments were now to attempt to break this spiral, all the consumers had to cooperate. I said:

We do not have a strategy. . . . There really is a kind of madness. You are nationalized in Algeria, and then our companies go in to take your place. We might be nationalized somewhere else, and we are replaced by others. We should discuss all of this with the consuming nations. . . .

It is an illusion to think that, once the war is settled, then there would be no problem about oil. However, the present method of dealing with the question is suicidal. First, we must get our own house in order. We are prepared to talk with you about this on a very confidential basis. If you wish to send someone over to see us, we will welcome that.

Jobert did not take up the offer of confidential talks; he remained cool to consumer cooperation. An American proposal to mobilize a common strategy among the consuming nations had been on the table since my Year of Europe speech six months earlier. It had been repeated several times since. It had been ignored because France, in particular, wanted to retain a free hand in energy matters; it sought to use the crisis to make advantageous bilateral deals with the producing nations.

On October 16 OPEC abandoned the creeping increase of oil prices in favor of a dramatic rise. In a stunning and unprecedented move, and without any discussion with the consumers, six Gulf states unilaterally raised the posted price of oil by 70 percent — from $3.01 to $5.12. The Arab members of OPEC, meeting in Kuwait, agreed the next day to cut their oil production by 5 percent and to continue reducing it by 5 additional percent every month until Israel was induced to withdraw from all occupied Arab territories. On October 18 Saudi Arabia announced that it would exceed the agreed quota by cutting its production by 10 percent until Arab Mideast terms were satisfied. These production cuts, whatever their political rationale, in fact sustained the higher price and laid the basis for even more dramatic increases.

Matters soon became even more critical. On October 19 Nixon asked the Congress for a $2.2 billion package of assistance to Israel to pay for the military equipment sent by the airlift. The request was put forward as a routine, largely budgetary, decision. There was no existing appropriation to cover our emergency airlift to Israel. The Defense Department was afraid that it would have to absorb the costs by reducing other programs. Legislative experts argued that it would be easier to obtain a supplementary appropriation while the war was going on than afterward. The decision to submit the request was thus made on technical grounds. I can find no record that anyone warned of an Arab reaction. Those fears had been real enough in the days before our airlift was launched. Now, nearly a week later, the worst was thought to be over.

The timing of the aid request could not have been more unfortunate. Until that point, we had maneuvered so that our airlift appeared as a response to the Soviet buildup and the failure of our cease-fire initiative. In the United Nations we had fended off resolutions we might have had to veto, and thus avoided sparking Arab resentments. But now during the last weekend of the war, while Egypt's army was in difficulty and Israeli forces were close to Damascus, the announcement of our $2.2 billion aid package set up a target for mounting Arab frustrations. We would have been much better advised to defer the formal request until after the cease-fire had been agreed. We could have then explained it as our contribution to bringing the war to an end.

The Arab reaction was swift. The day after our announcement — the day I left for Moscow to negotiate a cease-fire — Saudi Arabia declared a total embargo on oil exports to the United States. Later the Arab members of OPEC extended the embargo to the Netherlands, the European government that expressed most support for our policy. The October 16 OPEC decision on price, the October 17 Kuwait decision on Arab production cutbacks, and the October 20 Arab embargo together revolutionized the world oil market.

The structure of the oil market was so little understood that the embargo became the principal focus of concern. Lifting it turned almost into an obsession for the next five months, partly because Nixon thought that it lent itself to a spectacular that would overcome Watergate. In fact, the Arab embargo was a symbolic gesture of limited practical impact. To be sure, Saudi and other Arab oil was not shipped to the United States. But since the oil companies were operating a common pool, they simply substituted nonembargoed non-Arab oil for embargoed Arab oil and shifted other allocations accordingly. The true impact of the embargo was psychological. The fear that it might be extended — that Arab production might shut down further — triggered a wave of panic buying by Europe and Japan, which constricted supplies and drove prices up even more.

It was, in fact, the production cutbacks that really transformed the market, sharply accelerating the tilt in the balance between supply and demand and demonstrating the extraordinary leverage of the producing countries. The hesitant reaction of the consuming nations compounded their difficulties. Their reluctance to cooperate with one another perpetuated their vulnerability, virtually guaranteeing a permanent crisis.

At a State Department staff meeting on October 18 I objected to the proposition that the companies had no choice but to agree to the new price hike:

What do we want to do? . . . [T]he next year they go to $10.00. Will they then have to accept that too? . . . Then they go to $20.00. Is there some point at which they have to resist? . . . My instinct would be that since the situation is going to get worse, it's better to have a confrontation early.

The figures I had mentioned sarcastically to demonstrate the absurd lengths to which the abdication of the consumers could drive the oil market began to become a reality within six weeks. I was right in my perception, but so was Under Secretary of State for Economic Affairs William J. Casey in his rejoinder: "Well, what does confrontation mean? Nobody in this government has come up with any way to deal with these demands." The beginning of wisdom for an oil strategy should have been solidarity among all major consumer nations. That was prevented by six months of transatlantic tensions now magnified by the panic triggered by the price rises, production cutbacks, and embargo. No European government took up our offer of private exchanges on energy cooperation. They missed no opportunity to dissociate from our Mideast diplomacy — as described in Chapter XVI. Indeed, the European nations refused to share oil supplies even with their embargoed partner, the Netherlands, for fear that the producers might in retaliation extend the embargo to them.

In these circumstances, the United States was forced to implement a strategy unilaterally. This had three components: a national energy program that would attempt to restore some balance in the world energy market; a Middle East diplomacy that would not be deflected by pressures, however painful, whether from allies or producers; and, having established these premises, a return to the effort to mobilize consumer solidarity.

On November 7, 1973, Nixon proclaimed Project Independence, which committed the United States to free itself of the need to import energy by 1980 through conservation and the development of alternative sources. On one level, it was a vainglorious pronouncement, since all indicators showed that our dependence was likely to increase, not diminish, by 1980. On the other hand, while Nixon underestimated the time required for the task, he pointed the country in the right direction. In international affairs, when faced with a problem, Nixon sought the means with which to root it out, not to palliate it. America would have to be less profligate in its use of energy and more inventive and determined in developing alternative resources. If we could reduce our dependence on imported oil, the bargaining position of *all* consumers would improve dramatically. And that is how it turned out, if over a longer period of time than Nixon envisaged.

The long-range strategy did not, of course, solve the immediate problem of our policy differences with our allies.

A corollary of Project Independence was a demonstration by us that pressure could not affect the pace or the content of our diplomacy. We insisted on sticking to the diplomacy we had charted in the early days of the war despite the pressures of many of our allies who sought to placate the producers by embracing their political demands. Painful as we found it, we thought we served our allies best by stressing their inability to affect our decisions, therefore removing an incentive for producer pressures against them.

It took many months for this strategy to take effect, and it could not be achieved without cost, especially to allied relations. Once the process of dissociation — which we had not started — was under way, a vicious circle resulted. For proud nations that until recently had dominated the Middle East, it was not a little humiliating to be shown to be irrelevant to Mideast peace diplomacy. They in turn lost no opportunity to exacerbate the problem. By December 1973, we were being told that some of our allies were asking for preferential treatment from the Arabs for having disavowed our policy. The United States, so the alleged argument ran, must not be rewarded even should our diplomacy make progress. The embargo against us should be kept in force for several months or else the European and Japanese dissociation from our policy would be seen to have been pointless. We could never confirm all these allegations but they were too numerous not to have a foundation. It was not one of the finer moments of allied relations.

As for pressures by the producers, we thought it in the best interests of the moderates among them to shield them from assuming responsibility for what was bound to be a complex and bitter negotiation on Arab-Israeli peace. To involve Saudi Arabia in the details of the negotiations seemed to us to expose a valued friend to unnecessary pressures from all sides. The moderate Arab producers faced a complex enough situation as it was. Having resorted to the oil weapon in a moment of high emotion, they found it hard to end it. The requirement of Arab unity in effect gave the radicals a veto.

Sadat had been instrumental in urging use of the oil weapon during the war. In our early contacts with him he, like his brethren, used the formula that the embargo had been a multilateral decision and could not be lifted except by joint action. Thus he needed to be able to point to some progress in peace talks before he could recommend alleviating the oil pressures. So long as he did not seek to push us beyond what we had decided before the embargo — and what was needed quickly to prevent another blowup — we were prepared to acquiesce. But we insisted all along that we would not carry our diplomacy beyond Egyptian-Israeli disengagement unless the embargo was ended — in effect we turned the oil weapon against the producers. Recognizing this, Sadat from late in November on urged a progressive lifting of restrictions, to coincide with the completion of the first disengagement agreement. But even for Sadat it proved easier to brandish the oil weapon than to sheath it.

King Faisal told me that he could not end the embargo unilaterally or even at the recommendation of a solitary Arab leader like Sadat, and I believe he was telling the truth. Without an Arab consensus, lifting the embargo would prompt a backlash against him; the easing in relations with the United States would be offset by menace from his radical colleagues. As it turned out, Faisal did not want to risk this without some progress on the Syrian front. We could not wait that long. A Syrian disengagement would take months. And if we permitted the producers to erect one set of hurdles after another, there would be no end to the race. Each success would produce only a demand for yet another diplomatic exertion; the oil pressures would become permanent. On the other hand, to the extent that the producers were eager for a Syrian disengagement — and most of them were — our refusal to proceed would make the oil weapon a wasting asset. It left them with the problem of how to disengage from their own handiwork.

The Arab leader most widely identified in the West with oil diplomacy was the Saudi Oil Minister, Sheikh Ahmed Zaki Yamani. I had met him several times before the crisis made him an awesome figure fawned over in his global travels by eager votaries and journalists hanging on his every word. I had found him extraordinarily intelligent and well read; he could speak penetratingly on many subjects, including sociology and psychology. His watchful eyes and little Van Dyke beard made him look like a priggish young don playing at oil policy but not really meaning the apocalyptic message he was bringing, especially as it was put forward with a gentle voice and a self-deprecatory smile at variance with the implications of his actions.

In a different society or at a different time, Yamani might have become a scholar or the leader of one of the tiny political parties on the moderate right or left whose influence depended not on size but on the intellectual integrity of the membership — for example, the Republican

Party in Italy, which prides itself that its small numbers reflect its rigorous standards. But in his country at that time, barred by birth from the political leadership reserved for princes and by talent from an ordinary existence, he emerged in a position as essential as it was peripheral to the exercise of real political power within the Kingdom. He became the technician par excellence, nearly indispensable for the industry central to his country's and ultimately the world's economy. Nothing was possible without him; but the ultimate decisions were made by others, on the basis of calculations to which his contribution was technical and in response to pressures he had no possibility of affecting (and perhaps evaluated in his own way).

There was thus an inevitable gap between Yamani's influence in the world at large and inside Saudi Arabia. Globally, Yamani was celebrated, often feared. He appeared as the authentic voice of the Kingdom, occasionally even of the Arab world. But inside Saudi Arabia his position was much more ambiguous. Not a member of the royal family or of aristocratic rank, he had made his way in a traditional society by his uncommon ability. But he was far from the inner circle. He attended few of my meetings with the leading princes. When he did participate, he was seated in protocol order among the lesser officials in the room, and he never spoke. I have often wondered whether Yamani's occasionally strident pronouncements did not reflect his insecurity in his own political hierarchy and his need to establish himself with key groups around the Arab world rather than the considered opinions of the Kingdom.

In that sense, Yamani embodied the perplexities with which his specialty saddled his country. The passage from feudalism to modernity has always been traumatic. Saudi Arabia's dilemma is that the very oil income that makes it so pivotal in the world economy can also accelerate the process of internal modernization at a rate no society at a comparable state of political evolution has ever had to face. The pace toward such a future must be ambivalently perceived by Saudi leaders. Feudal societies operate by traditional, reciprocal, largely personal obligations. The modern state seeks predictability through legal or bureaucratic norms. A feudal state stresses status; a modern state emphasizes achievement. Yamani represented a meritocracy whose influence would grow as fast as the oil income he was generating. Economic and social development challenges the traditional modes and sources of power; modernization trains thousands in foreign countries, inculcating values not easy to reconcile with those of an inward-looking, authoritarian state based on Bedouin loyalties. One Yamani was an invaluable asset. But what would happen when there were ten thousand? How would new status for such groups be reconciled with the claims of a hereditary ruling class? How would past and future successfully meld?

The artificial-seeming cities in Saudi Arabia that I have described in earlier chapters symbolized the transition from the Bedouin to the new life-style. They would be the homes not only of the new meritocracy but also of a depersonalized, detribalized proletariat all the more restless because it was not poor and was thus freed from the struggle for daily sustenance. America's relationship had been on the whole with the world of the princes; they were good friends of our country; I saw no alternative to their rule that would not be worse for us. I wished them every success in their efforts to adapt themselves to the new challenges invoked by their own oil decisions, which accelerated the process of change and hastened an unpredictable future.

Yamani never so much as hinted at any of these dilemmas; he incarnated them even while probably rejecting them. Yamani performed his assignment brilliantly. But history may yet record that in helping to revolutionize the world economy he conjured up for his own society a monumental challenge of political evolution.

The immediate aftermath of the embargo found Saudi Arabia in a most uncomfortable position. It prized its friendship with the United States for emotional and practical reasons. It feared the tide of radicalism. Yet Arab solidarity corresponded to its moral convictions and to the security needs of the Kingdom. It could not afford isolation in the Arab world; it dreaded being an outcast, stigmatized as reactionary or accused of insufficient dedication to the Arab cause. The oil weapon had sharpened its dilemmas.

The result was a series of Saudi communications that, reflecting the various pulls on Saudi emotions, seemed to cancel each other out. On November 11, Yamani sent me a message expressly hedged by being described as "not official in nature." (On the other hand, Saudi ministers do not send private messages to a Secretary of State unless they believe they have been authorized to do so.) It stated that "something" could be done about the embargo but only if the United States made a "statement regarding implementation of United Nations Security Council Resolution 242, and specifically, withdrawal from occupied Arab territories." What Yamani wanted was a commitment to push Israel back to the 1967 borders; this the United States was in no position to give. On November 12 at a press conference in Peking, responding to a question about guarantees, I gave a much more general (and standard) answer, which accepted the principle of withdrawals but left the final lines to be determined by negotiation:

We have not yet given any particular guarantees. However, I would assume that if the peace negotiations succeed, there will be a very serious problem, especially for Israel, of how its security can be assured under conditions when the final borders will certainly be different from the cease-fire lines and when withdrawals are involved as Security Council Resolution 242 provides. . . .

In my reply to Yamani, making virtue out of necessity, I called his attention to these remarks.

On November 17 I received a somewhat different analysis: King Faisal was said to be unwilling to lift the embargo for only a few miles of Sinai desert. He insisted that a settlement include a denial of Israeli sovereignty over Jerusalem. Furthermore, any modification of the embargo would have to have the approval of Syria, Kuwait, Egypt, and Algeria. Concurrently, we were told that Yamani was being sent to visit other Arab capitals to test the waters, though he did not vouchsafe to us for what.

The next day, an aide to one of the senior princes conveyed yet another shade of Saudi intentions. Faisal's insistence on Israel's 1967 borders represented Saudi Arabia's ultimate aims, we were told; it would not necessarily dictate Saudi oil policies. A modification of the embargo could take place as soon as there were "effective and tangible" moves toward peace, for example, a *beginning* of Israeli withdrawal from existing lines. The aide was not precise about whether that meant Egypt and Syria or Egypt alone.

That same day, November 18, the Arab oil ministers meeting in Vienna reiterated the linkage of oil to Mideast diplomacy. They announced that, in "appreciation" for the European Community stance on the Middle East, they were canceling the 5 percent production cutback scheduled for December. The Arab ministers thus "rewarded" the European Community only by maintaining a most difficult status quo; they did nothing to alleviate the two previous cuts that had caused the raging crisis. Moreover, the embargo against the Netherlands was continued and, what was more significant, accepted by the other states.

On November 19 Yamani informed us of the result of his inter-Arab consultations. He reverted to the hard-line position of linking the end of the embargo with Israeli agreement to "a timetable" for withdrawal from "all" occupied territories. It pleased Yamani to present this decision as a favor to the United States. It would give us "a stronger voice" in dealing with the Israelis to speed up their acceptance of a peace conference and withdrawal. We could never accept this. We had great sympathy for the difficulties of our friends in Saudi Arabia. But once we committed ourselves to impose political terms specified by others in return for oil, we would be on a slippery slope. Saudi Arabia would not be able to rest on its laurels. The radical states would press it to increase its demands. Sooner or later we would have to draw a line. The monarchy, in seeking to ease the pull of conflicting forces on it, would wind up trapped at some point between radical pressures and American resistance. It was better for us to resist before matters got out of hand. This was the essence of a message I sent to Prince Fahd on November 21 inviting him to Washington. I warned that it would be "very difficult for us to be as helpful as we would like in the negotiations ahead if we remain under the threat of a continuing oil boycott." It was not the "act of friends"; it could lead to a confrontation incompatible with the "posture that we shall have to adopt if the negotiations are to have any chance of succeeding."

To convince one's opposite number of one's determination in a test of nerves, it is sometimes useful to adopt a public position from which retreat would involve a loss of prestige. Therefore that same day I repeated in a press conference what we had so far told only the oil producers privately:

Those countries who are engaging in economic pressures against the United States should consider whether it is appropriate to engage in such steps while peace negotiations are being prepared, and, even more, while negotiations are being conducted. I would like to state for the United States Government that our course will not be influenced by such pressures, that we have stated our policy, that we have expressed our commitments, and that we will adhere to those and will not be pushed beyond this point by any pressures. . . .

Moreover, the United States would not simply passively endure blackmail. At a given point, retaliation was probable:

It is clear that if pressures continue unreasonably and indefinitely, then the United States will have to consider what countermeasures it may have to take. We would do this with enormous reluctance, and we are still hopeful that matters will not reach this point.

These were not empty threats. I ordered a number of studies from the key departments on countermeasures against Arab members of OPEC if the embargo continued. By the end of the month, several contingency studies had been completed.

Yamani reacted immediately. Showing that he had been stung, he gave an uncharacteristically intemperate television interview in Copenhagen on November 22. He threatened to cut oil production by 80 percent if the United States, Europe, or Japan retaliated. He warned that any American military action would be "suicide" because Arabs would blow up the oil fields. Noting that the United States was less dependent on Arab oil, he warned Europeans against joining in any American retaliatory policy since "your [Europe's] whole economy will definitely collapse all of a sudden." [7] Carrying this theme around Europe, he and his traveling partner, Algerian Oil Minister Belaid Abdessalam, continued to leave open the possibility that Europe (except the Netherlands) and Japan would receive preferential treatment should they separate from the United States and adopt policies favorable to the Arab cause.

In Riyadh that day our new Ambassador — the oil expert James Akins — met with Minister of State for Foreign Affairs Omar Saqqaf to urge a lifting of the embargo. Saqqaf repeated Yamani's earlier line that the production cuts and embargoes were really designed to strengthen America's hand in urging concessions on Israel; they were meant as a favor to us. Akins suggested that we might be mollified if oil deliveries to our Sixth Fleet were resumed and the next 5 percent production cut abandoned. By cable, I reminded Akins that our oil strategy was not based on "seeking partial relief":

> Our strategy is to make clear to Arabs that if they want our involvement in peace settlement efforts, they must first lift restrictions they have imposed rather than holding off on lifting restrictions until there is progress on settlement front. We want an end to interference with oil supplies for our Fleet, but beyond that we want a return to situation that existed before production cutbacks and embargoes were imposed, not just a suspension of further cuts and restrictions.

On November 25, Nixon delivered another major address outlining a detailed program of energy conservation. At the same time I learned through Haig that he was leaning toward the idea of sending a personal emissary to Riyadh to urge a lifting of the embargo and give assurances as to our conduct at the upcoming Geneva Conference. I was strongly opposed. Part of the reason, I suppose, was the normal reaction of a negotiator to an invasion of what he considers to be his area of responsibility. But it also clashed with our strategy. Sending a special emissary to trade concessions at Geneva for oil was hardly the best way to convey imperviousness to pressure, which was essential to the success of our policy. We would be looking like supplicants, while exposing Saudi Arabia to all the booby traps of the Arab-Israeli negotiations. I managed to dissuade the President. I explained my reasoning to my WSAG colleagues on November 29:

> If we yield to the embargo in the sense of bargaining with the Saudis on the specific terms for the conference, we will get ourselves on a hopeless wicket. It would take too long. It would make the Saudis responsible for every point and they would be driven by their radicals. The British and French would be given an incentive to leapfrog. . . . They may have a monopoly on oil but we have a monopoly on political progress.

To make this equation stick was difficult enough within our government; our allies would have none of it. They continued on their course of dissociation. On November 22 Japan adopted a position similar to Europe's of November 6. On November 28 an Arab summit in Algiers rewarded Japan by extending to it the same concession (canceling the next production cut) as the European Community had received on November 18. And in London, according to press accounts, Yamani assured Britain (and by implication others) that its pro-Arab stance would guarantee it oil supplies at the prewar level.

Meanwhile, the careful minuet with Saudi Arabia went on. It wanted to ease the embargo but do so with radical concurrence. This being impossible in the immediate future, Saudi Arabia struggled to reconcile the incompatible. And while the process was sometimes maddening to us, it was in fact conducted with considerable skill. Saudi Arabia navigated the shoals without catastrophe and eventually lifted the embargo without radical upheaval.

To set the stage the Kingdom sought to gain time. We were told on December 3 that Prince Fahd accepted the invitation to Washington. His goal would be to agree on the modalities for lifting the embargo and restoring the production cuts, to be announced during my visit to Riyadh scheduled for December 14. The only conditions would be prior assent from Sadat, Asad, and Boumedienne and implementation of the November six-point agreement in advance of the Geneva Conference. (This latter condition was already being met.) That same day I cabled Fahd that I was certain it would be possible to work something out, while Nixon sent a friendly letter to King Faisal stressing our two basic themes: If the embargo and production cutbacks were not suspended, American public opinion

will not permit us to play the sustained role which you and we agree is our responsibility. . . . An atmosphere of growing confrontation would only work to our mutual disadvantage and to the benefit of those who wish to maintain the status quo.

Nixon added a handwritten note pledging his total personal commitment to work for the full implementation of Security Council Resolutions 242 and 338.

But the next day, December 4, the Saudi Council of Ministers reversed the decision communicated to us only twenty-four hours earlier. Fahd would not come to America; the Kingdom did not wish to have the end of the embargo appear as a bilateral US–Saudi decision. The natural forum for implementing the program of December 3 — which was reaffirmed — would be at a meeting of Arab oil ministers in Kuwait on December 8. Prince Fahd would serve the common interest better by staying in the Middle East and working there for an end of the embargo and production cuts within the agreed framework.

December 5 brought yet another apparent hardening of the Arab position. Yamani and Abdessalam, the traveling oil ministers of Saudi Arabia and Algeria, called on me in Washington as part of their world tour of industrialized countries. Yamani reverted to the tough line. He said the embargo could be lifted and production restored to prewar levels only "according to a timetable which corresponds to the timetable of Israeli withdrawal." In other words, the hint of December 3 — that the embargo would be lifted in connection with the Geneva Conference — no longer applied. This I rejected:

This is a question of principle. We have given our word to your King and other Arab leaders of our intention. Now, should we be blackmailed while we are in good faith trying to meet Arab aspirations?

A day later Yamani compounded the confusion. Seeing me alone, without the radical Algerian, he indicated that the formal position would be interpreted with great flexibility in practice. The embargo would be lifted if we achieved an Egyptian-Israeli disengagement in January as we planned.

This plethora of statements — tying oil decisions now to an Israeli pledge of total withdrawal, now to completion of one phase of disengagement, now to observance of the six-point plan, now to Syrian disengagement as well — was ended by the meeting of the Arab oil ministers in Kuwait on December 8. They came up with a communiqué that proved no one was willing to take on the radicals. The ministers linked the end of the embargo to Israeli acceptance of a "time schedule" for total withdrawal (including from Jerusalem) and the beginning of the actual relinquishment of territory. This was a clear nonstarter and the ministers knew it. They added yet another item of blackmail: The 5 percent production cuts deferred from December would be reimposed on nations who "don't provide concrete evidence of friendliness such as by showing that they are putting pressure on the United States or Israel."

We were determined not to accept specific conditions for a peace negotiation that had not yet even started, thus legitimizing continued Arab exactions if we failed to deliver rapidly enough. The Arab producers had put forward no other option. By the middle of December we were heading for a stalemate.

The Second Oil Shock: Tehran and Kuwait

THE Arab oil ministers had chosen their ground shrewdly. They emphasized the foreign policy issues most likely to exacerbate our differences with our allies. We insisted on moving at a pace reflecting our judgment of what was possible without crisis. Our allies had come to depend so much on uninterrupted economic growth that they were unwilling to run risks and they calculated those risks by the belligerent rhetoric of the radical Arabs. Still, whatever our disappointments with our allies, we continued to believe that the key to a long-term strategy was solidarity among the oil-consuming nations. This alone offered hope of transforming market conditions and restoring the balance of economic power. We also thought it essential to the political health of the demo-

cracies, racked by economic and social crisis, that they recapture control
over their own destinies.

The European Community used the occasion of its Copenhagen summit on December 14–15, however, to reiterate and strengthen its November 6 declaration on Mideast policy — now in public opposition to
the main thrust of our diplomacy. It was also decided to explore the
possibility of a regular "European-Arab dialogue," the practical consequence of which could only be to institutionalize the Atlantic differences. The next months were characterized by our allies' oscillation
between cooperation with and dissociation from us and by their attempt
to avoid the choice by pursuing both courses simultaneously.

We could slow down Europe's rush to accommodation only by stressing our own imperviousness to pressure. I did my best to cultivate this
impression during my trip to the Mideast in December to prepare for
the Geneva Conference (see Chapter XVII). Everywhere I stressed the
inadmissibility of continuing oil blackmail against the only country in a
position to make progress toward peace and engaged in a major effort
to do so. I warned my hosts not to count on our being swayed by European entreaties. Algerian President Boumedienne professed sympathy
for the proposition that no self-respecting country could allow itself to
be pressured; he said that he favored resuming full oil production in any
event because of Algeria's need for foreign exchange. Sadat promised
that he would work for the removal of the oil embargo as soon as a
disengagement accord on the Egyptian front was achieved. When I visited Riyadh on December 14, King Faisal seemed to agree to Sadat's
scenario and implied that production restrictions would be ended when
the embargo was lifted.

Saudi signals were once more positive. On December 19 Saqqaf assured Ambassador Akins that the Arabs had made their point; the oil
embargo must be lifted. Faisal's view would be conveyed to the Arab
oil ministers meeting shortly after the Geneva Conference, on December 25. Yamani was reported as expressing a similar opinion.

All the while, the economic consequences of the energy crisis wors-
ened. Neither European appeasement of the Arabs nor my wanderings
eased the economic impact of the production cutback or the psychological shock of the embargo. And then, within days of the hopeful encounter in Riyadh, an event occurred as unexpected as it was devastating: yet another doubling of the oil prices.

The oil producers had scheduled two important meetings: The Persian
Gulf members of OPEC were to assemble in Tehran on December 22–
23 to consider oil prices, after which the Arab members of OPEC were
convening in Kuwait on December 24–25 to consider the embargo and
production restrictions. On December 21, just as Yamani was leaving
for Tehran, he told Akins that Faisal and his ministers had reassessed

the situation. They had been too ebullient in recent days. A complete end of the embargo would risk the opposition of all radical Arabs and perhaps even of Sadat. Saudi Arabia could therefore work only for an easing of the embargo and a limited restoration of production.

More astonishing, Yamani suddenly — the day before the Tehran meeting — raised the prospect of another rise in oil prices, though claiming that Saudi Arabia did not favor it. No one had mentioned this prospect previously; when I had visited Riyadh the week before, all our discussions had concerned the lifting of the embargo. Yamani claimed that Saudi Arabia was an innocent bystander, that the Shah of Iran was the villain. Akins urged that we use our influence for moderation with all the OPEC nations. I received Akins's reporting telegram while in Geneva on December 21. The very next day I dispatched messages to Iran and to all other OPEC governments warning strongly against another rise in prices. What is more, I appealed to the governments of all the industrial nations in the West and Japan to weigh in with OPEC against a price increase. There is no record that they did so, certainly not with any emphasis.

Our effort proved useless, if indeed anything could have been done at this late stage. The OPEC ministers in Tehran on December 22–23 boosted the oil price from $5.12 a barrel to $11.65 a barrel — a hike of 128 percent, on top of the 70 percent increase in October, amounting to a 387 percent increase in the price of oil in the space of two months.

It is now obvious that this decision was one of the pivotal events in the history of this century. The statistics were staggering enough. Within forty-eight hours the oil bill for the United States, Canada, Western Europe, and Japan had increased by $40 billion a year; it was a colossal blow to their balance of payments, economic growth, employment, price stability, and social cohesion. The Tehran decision also cost the developing countries more than the entire foreign aid programs extended to them by the industrial democracies, re-creating the desperate conditions that foreign assistance was supposed to cure. But the long-term impact was more grave still. *All* the countries involved, even the producers themselves, faced seismic changes in their domestic structures.

The relatively benign domestic politics of the industrial democracies had been nurtured by two decades of nearly uninterrupted growth. Welfare programs had been financed from a steadily increasing Gross National Product. It was possible to benefit one group without depriving another; the civil rights revolution in America, for example, both reflected the growing economic strength of black Americans since 1945 and spurred it further. The happy idea developed that all social groups would be able to gain simultaneously and indefinitely. And indeed it was largely true. To be sure, student unrest in almost all industrial countries in the Sixties had been a warning that materialism was not enough to sustain a society, that economic growth would not provide emotional sustenance automatically to a new generation searching for a deeper meaning to life. But there was reason to hope that once recognized, these problems would find their solution.

The economic crisis that started in the Seventies — and continues in the Eighties — has devastated these prospects. Conflict rather than cohesion has been fostered within countries and between them. The oil price exactions were price-inflationary but demand-deflationary. The purchasing power removed from the world's economies — represented in the billions of unspent OPEC dollars — could not be replaced by governments trying to overcome inflation as the oil price explosions reverberated through their economies and workers tried to keep pace through wage increases. Restrictive monetary policies and trade protectionism were the order of the day — and still are. The middle classes everywhere, whose savings had helped to sustain growth and whose moderation had laid the basis for reconciliation in politics, were squeezed and squeezed again. The bitterness of social conflict in the middle and late 1970s in some European countries — Britain, Italy, Spain, Portugal, France, even West Germany — was the legacy of the oil price explosion.

Even now, the domestic political implications are still working themselves out. The political dilemma of democracy is that the time span needed for solutions to contemporary economic problems is far longer than the electoral cycle by which leaders' performance is judged at the polls. How many politicians dare to risk their offices in proclaiming that the good times are over? Who is willing to tell his constituents that a wise policy will bring with it a decline in the standard of living, at least for a while? And what happens in the inevitable period of disillusion when young men and women leave school and college to find their skills rejected and join the millions thrown out of work since the oil crisis? The way is open for demagoguery, political polarization, and violence.

As for the developing nations, if it was ever true that economic aid was necessary to prevent the division of our planet into the few who were rich and the many who were poor, if the maintenance of peace required us to try to close the gap, then the oil price rise worked marvelously to defeat these objectives. Most developing countries are wholly dependent on imported oil for industrial or agricultural development, and all depend on expanding world trade and investment as well as development aid. Their hopes for progress were shattered by the oil price explosion. They entered a new dark age of debt and deprivation — which posed the added horror that their financial default could even undermine the banking system of the advanced countries that has extended them credit for decades. One's compassion is perhaps tempered with impatience at the quiescence with which they accepted the exactions of the oil producers and railed instead against their fellow victims in the West. This reflects either helplessness or decrepit ideology. The truth is, as I pointed out in a UN address in September 1975, that "the most devastating blow to economic development in this decade came not from 'imperialist rapacity' but from an arbitrary, monopolistic price increase by the cartel of oil exporters." Nevertheless, the poor countries yielded up sympathetic noises from time to time for the political purposes of the radical oil states. This subservience, of course, did them very little good: a crumb here and a crumb there, aid funds promised and rarely delivered.

Never before in history has a group of such relatively weak nations been able to impose with so little protest such a dramatic change in the way of life of the overwhelming majority of the rest of mankind. The poetic justice, if such it is, is that this "achievement" threatens their own stability, a perception that may be gradually dawning. Few political structures can sustain the accelerated rate of growth made possible by such an enormous transfer of wealth. Dislocations are bound to occur, which even more established political systems and traditions would find it difficult to handle. The institutions in most oil countries are not in that category.

The upheaval in Iran in the late 1970s was at once a caricature and a warning. The overheated economic development made possible by the price increases provoked an elemental reaction that rejected the very materialistic values that gave rise to the rapid growth; the end result was, ironically, the systematic impoverishment of the country. Nor is internal convulsion the only threat to producing nations. The economic enfeeblement of the industrial democracies may yet cause much of the oil states' material acquisitions to evaporate like a mirage. For a financial crisis in the West would destroy also the producers' investments in those countries. Or if the West proves economically unable to sustain the role of military protector in the Persian Gulf — or loses its incentive to do so on behalf of nations systematically undermining the world economy — then many of the oil producers may become easy pickings for foreign predators.

Thus the producers' dilemma approaches a joke played by history on those who would seek to force its pace. If they spend their exactions too rapidly, they risk domestic upheaval; if they hoard them, they court a weakening of the international economic system to a point where they too become victims.

Everybody lost from the oil crisis. And an event of such historic proportions merits more serious analysis than the self-serving excuses of some oil producers or demagogic scapegoating by others. The most absurd example, perhaps, is the widely circulated claim that we were repeatedly warned of the danger of higher prices and turned it aside because Washington welcomed high oil revenues to finance Iranian rearmament.[8] The record sketched in these pages leaves no doubt that neither we nor our industrial allies were informed of the plan for a colossal price increase until it was nearly upon us — too late to affect it — and that we then resisted strenuously. The United States never saw the price rises as anything but a disaster, and no one welcomed them as a means to finance Iranian military purchases or for any other purpose. The record on this particular canard is clear. On December 29, 1973, I sent a message in Nixon's name to the Shah protesting in the strongest terms:

The President is greatly concerned over the destabilizing impact that the price increases agreed to at Tehran for Persian Gulf crudes will have on the world's economy and the catastrophic problems it could pose for the international monetary system. Not only will it result in raising the prices of manufactured products, but it will have [a] severe repressive effect on the economies of oil consumers which could cause a worldwide recession and which eventually would benefit no one including oil exporters.

We believe this drastic price increase is particularly unreasonable coming as it does when oil supplies are being artificially restrained. . . . We strongly urge that (1) the recent decisions made in Tehran be reconsidered; (2) steps be initiated to hold the kind of consultations that we believe most consumer and producer countries endorse; and (3) the oil producer countries seriously examine the deleterious effect of these increases on the balance of payments positions of practically all nations in the free world and the effect this will have on world trade in general and on the international monetary system in particular.

While the argument that Washington encouraged or colluded in the price rise is demagogic ignorance, it is less easy to fix the responsibility among the members of OPEC. Over the three previous years of first gradual and then rapidly escalating exactions, OPEC had developed to a fine art the shifting of responsibility from one member to the other. Iran and Saudi Arabia, the two great rivals for Persian Gulf preeminence, were specially dexterous. Whoever we approached made a convincing case that the other one was the culprit. If one listened to our interlocutors, one was left wondering how prices could ever rise in the face of so much reluctance. The truth was that higher prices were supported by *all* key members of OPEC. The Shah had the more elaborate bureaucratic machinery and staff to formulate a sophisticated, Western-style rationale relating oil prices to the marginal cost of alternative fuels. But he never sought to influence the market by cutting production. Among other reasons, Iran's capacity was too small and its domestic needs too great to permit a reduction that would affect the world price of oil.

Advancing complex theories is not the Saudi style. The Kingdom simply announced production decisions with major price implications that were left to others to make explicit. Metaphysicians can argue forever which was more influential, theory without action or action without theory. Both were necessary conditions for what followed.

Serious analysts agree that Iran threw its weight behind the December price rise not because of collusion with the United States but because at an auction for Iranian oil in mid-December — on the so-called spot, or free, market — bids had reached an unprecedented $16-to-$17 a barrel.[9] The Shah concluded that this proved the official fixed price — then $5.12 — was too low. He suggested that OPEC elevate its price to $11.65 — and all his OPEC partners readily agreed. The Shah's sudden activism was itself surprising; he had not in the past taken a leading role in pricing decisions.[10] Indeed, his production was not large enough to put him in a position to do so. Iran had not participated in either the Arab embargo or production cutbacks in October that were the real foundation of the price rises. When the Arabs imposed these measures, the Shah in fact stressed that he was producing oil at Iran's maximum capacity in order to help mitigate the shortages. He did this not as a favor to us but to increase his own revenues; nevertheless, the impact was to help stabilize the market. The Shah surely sought to maximize his income; he was relentless in seeking what the traffic would bear. But he did not create the conditions he was exploiting. Those came about through the expansion of world demand, the end of American surplus capacity, and the Arab production cuts.

The Shah wound up as the villain of the piece partly because of the prominent role he played in announcing the price rise, which was in fact a unanimous OPEC decision. Ego was surely a factor. Possibly he was tempted into the lead role because at the Tehran meeting he was technically the host. Perhaps he wanted to earn nationalist spurs at home. Very likely he welcomed an opportunity to show solidarity with his Arab neighbors after separating from them during the Mideast war by supplying oil to Israel, fueling our fleet, and denouncing the embargo and production cuts as late as the very day before the Tehran conference opened. Whatever his motives, the Shah later had to suffer the opprobrium of public identification with the oil price explosion that changed economic and political history, though his role in creating the conditions for it was smaller than that of many others and though there is no evidence that any of his colleagues seriously objected (except in secret whispers to their victims). The Shah paid a high price for the vanity of a moment in the limelight.

All the OPEC nations quickly demonstrated that they had learned how to take advantage of the political disunity of the industrial democracies. Partly to deter a united consumers' front, partly to reward those who had broken ranks with the United States, the Arab oil ministers met in Kuwait on December 24–25 to consider the embargo and production cutbacks. The results were strikingly different from what we had been led to expect. The embargo against the United States was neither lifted nor eased. By contrast, oil curbs on Europe (except the Netherlands) and Japan were mitigated; the 5 percent production cutback scheduled for January was canceled in favor of a 10 percent increase. Yamani announced the decision. He justified the discrimination against us on the basis of "a very apparent distinction between those who stand beside the Arabs and those who stand beside the enemy and those who are in between." While "gradual changes" were noted in the American position, the ministers had nonetheless decided to continue the embargo on America until, as Yamani said, more "fruitful results" were obtained.

We reacted to these decisions with less than the controlled rationality that textbooks ascribe to statesmen. We felt misled by weeks of exchanges with various Arab leaders. The huge rise in prices was made doubly wounding by being so totally unexpected and accompanied by a reaffirmation of the discriminatory practices against the United States.

In fact, the subtle Yamani and his complicated government had not been as unhelpful as the rhetoric implied. The expansion in oil production, ostensibly confined to the rest of the world, increased total supplies in the world market. The companies allocating the various quantities among consumers had more oil in the common pool; scarcity was eased. In these circumstances, the continuation of the embargo was an inconvenience and an insult; it did not hurt us significantly. But it did not appear that way at the moment. The symbolism of continued discrimination against the country that was carrying the burden of the peace effort was hard to take. Nor were there any extenuating circumstances to ease the devastating economic impact of the price rise.

Yamani, in conversations with Akins, predictably blamed Kuwait, Abu Dhabi, and Iraq for this debacle, as he had blamed Iran for the previous one, but it made no difference. On December 28 Nixon sent an unusually stiff message to Faisal, warning that these actions were risking the entire American relationship:

> You know the great stress I place on close relations with the Arab world and with Saudi Arabia in particular. However, the clearly discriminatory action of the oil producers can vitiate totally the effective contribution the United States is determined to make in the days ahead. Therefore, I must tell you in candor that it is absolutely essential that the oil embargo and oil production restrictions against the United States be ended immediately.

That day I wrote in the same vein to Saqqaf, protesting as well the "drastic and unjustifiable price increases" announced in Tehran: "I want your Government to know that their predictable and disastrously destabilizing effect on the free world's economic and monetary system is of the deepest concern to us." We used the same double-barreled approach in Egypt. Nixon and I wrote letters to Sadat on December 28 stressing that the United States insisted on an end to the embargo and production restrictions "at once" and warning that the United States would not continue its peace role under embargo conditions. And I have quoted earlier our message to the Shah of December 29, vigorously protesting the price increase.

The price explosion was further proof that disunity among the consuming nations was leaving us all vulnerable. Consumer solidarity was essential. On December 29 I appealed to Sir Alec Douglas-Home:

The decisions were taken, of course, unilaterally, without even the semblance of negotiation with the international companies or consumer nations. Moreover, a further round of substantial increases seems probable next spring unless we move promptly to attempt to bring the whole process into a more rational framework.

It was the probability of just the scenario that is unfolding which prompted my suggestion for the formation of an Energy Action Group. We are in the process of developing a suggested program for implementing such a group, but before coming back to you with a plan, I did want to indicate my deep concern with the recent producer country actions. It seems inconceivable that the consumer nations would be paralyzed in the face of such situations.

But paralysis was exactly the European reaction. Home's reply endorsed consumer cooperation in principle but expressed doubts about a permanent organization to achieve it. Several of our allies saw in the Kuwait decision a vindication of their course; dissociation from the United States had resulted in clearly preferential treatment.

Ending the Embargo

A^T year's end, then, the United States was virtually alone in demanding an immediate end of the embargo. Both Egypt and Saudi Arabia avoided a clear-cut answer. Both countries claimed that the embargo would be lifted as soon as an Arab consensus could be formed. Saqqaf on December 29 expressed amazement at the violence of our reaction. Sadat promised to go to Riyadh and personally urge the lifting of the embargo as soon as Sinai disengagement was achieved. Saqqaf promised on December 31 and again on January 3, 1974, that the embargo would end after an Egyptian disengagement, but he implied there might be additional conditions.

We made clear that we were not supplicants. At a press conference on January 2, 1974, I insisted that continuation of the embargo was less and less appropriate. When asked about possible American countermeasures, I confined myself to saying that no "specific measures" were planned "at this moment" — a moderately threatening formulation. On January 7, Defense Secretary Schlesinger publicly warned of the possibility of reprisals against oil producers. It produced a storm in the Arab world, where some seemed to espouse the doctrine that an assault on the economic jugular of the United States (and other industrial democracies) had to be endured in stoicism and passivity. I had not known of Schlesinger's statement in advance; he and I met frequently to discuss strategy but had not concerted tactics on this occasion. Nevertheless, his comment was salutary, and so at my press conference of January 10 I let the threat stand, though expressing the hope that circumstances would not make its implementation necessary:

Well, as I understand Secretary Schlesinger, he was explaining theoretical situations that might arise if the squeeze became excessive. If I understand him correctly, he also pointed out that this point had not yet been reached.

After midnight, on January 11, I left for the shuttle that culminated in the Egyptian-Israeli disengagement accord. Over the next days and weeks we were treated to a flurry of bewildering messages. Midway through the negotiations, on January 13, I received an ominous signal. The latest Saudi position was that a Sinai disengagement alone would not be enough. It would in fact improve Israel's military position by placing a demilitarized belt between it and Arab forces. "Tangible evidence" was needed that Israel would commit itself to further substantial withdrawals "without delay" and that Palestinian rights were taken into account in a settlement. We were not sure what this report represented beyond the intense pressures operating on the Saudis. For Sadat remained optimistic. In Aswan on January 14, he repeated his promise to visit Riyadh as soon as the Sinai disengagement was achieved. He was confident that he could have the embargo ended no later than January 28. I warned him that any disengagement accord would not be implemented unless the embargo was lifted.

The White House, meanwhile, was agog about the rapid progress being made on Egyptian-Israeli disengagement. My daily reports to Nixon, which mentioned Sadat's promise to bring about an early end of the embargo, stimulated Nixon's drive for a quick White House announcement. Thus Scowcroft warned me by cable on January 19 that Nixon wanted to announce the end of the embargo personally in Washington, in his televised State of the Union address to the Congress on January 30. Given the already powerful tergiversations of Saudi Arabia in the face of radical pressures, it was unlikely that Riyadh would permit the United States to announce what it had always insisted was an Arab decision. From Syria I cabled intemperately to Scowcroft on January 20:

There is no possible way to arrange the lifting of the oil embargo in such a way as to permit the President to make the announcement of its lifting. It should come as no surprise that we are dealing with 10 Arab countries, 6 of whom are radical.

But the event that was the subject of all this jockeying did not arise as rapidly as we had expected. Faisal had effectively given a veto to states with unsatisfied claims who had no interest in helping the United States. One such was Syria. On January 21 Hafez al-Asad demanded the use of the oil weapon on his behalf as it had been available to Egypt: The embargo should be maintained until at least a Syrian disengagement was completed.

Saudi Arabia did not wish to antagonize the United States; yet it was too vulnerable to risk isolating itself in the Arab world. Its vacillations therefore repeated themselves in ever-shorter cycles. For example, on January 20 Saqqaf informed Akins that Saudi Arabia would lift its embargo regardless of the actions of other producers; it would be announced right after a meeting of Arab oil ministers in Cairo on January 22. Yet on January 23 the King himself assured Akins that he was still seeking an Arab consensus. In the interim, Sadat sent me a pained message following his tour around the Arab world. While Cairo was trying hard, it was evident that his "brothers" were increasingly linking the end of the embargo to tangible results on Syrian disengagement. The Saudis continued to hedge. On January 27 Saqqaf still expressed the hope of a favorable reply before Nixon's State of the Union address.

But January 30 came and went. Hints in the American media predicting a definitive announcement in Nixon's State of the Union speech went unfulfilled. All that Nixon was able to say on television was that he understood the Arabs would soon meet to "discuss" the lifting of the embargo — not necessarily to end it. By February 3 Faisal confessed failure; the Arab consensus seemed to make progress on the Syrian front a prerequisite for an end to the embargo. We learned that Boumedienne was leaning toward an end to the embargo but Asad had remained obdurate.

We were determined not to play this game any longer. Our credibility was at risk. We insisted on the promises that had been made. And we conveyed this decision in no uncertain terms.

Nixon sent a sharp letter to Faisal asserting in effect that we had been misled. We would not accept the imposition of new conditions; we would not proceed with a Syrian disengagement if the embargo remained in effect. We even hinted that we might publish the earlier Saudi promises. This provoked Saqqaf's cool (and not incorrect) response that he would then make it known that our request had as often been geared to Nixon's domestic necessities as to the American national interest — underlining the humiliating position in which Watergate had placed us.

I sent harsh messages to Sadat, Asad, and Boumedienne. If the Arab producers took us seriously and if they believed what they professed — that we were indispensable to obtaining Israeli withdrawals — the shoe was now on the other foot: They, not we, had to find a way to end the embargo.

Our communications soon led to a subtle change in the tone of Arab messages. For months the Arab producers had been meeting, laying down ever more peremptory terms, secure in the knowledge that there would be no penalty. But an aroused United States caused second thoughts. There was no longer any talk of further production cutbacks — until recently the recurrent threat. If oil production was kept steady, the impact of the embargo was calculable; its major significance was to demonstrate a capability for unilateral pressure, which we were determined to resist. From this point also, no serious new political conditions were put forward. Almost all Arab communications now concerned tactics for removing the embargo.

On February 6 Faisal reiterated to Akins that he was seeking Arab (in practice Syrian) agreement to end the embargo. Next day Saqqaf was sent to Syria to propose an Arab mini-summit of Faisal, Sadat, Boumedienne, and Asad to take place in Aswan on February 12–13. Asad reluctantly agreed to a meeting but refused to go to Egypt. Whatever the venue, he could hardly have had any doubt about what would await him. His brethren would urge his acquiescence in lifting the embargo; he would be able to delay but he could not hold out indefinitely. The oil weapon would not be available to Syria in its disengagement talks.

On February 9 Asad replied to my message, stating ambiguously that the oil question had a pan-Arab character. He complained that Syria had not yet achieved any practical results that would enable it to change its attitude. It seemed an invitation — almost a plea — for us to bring Syria into the negotiating process and to give it some pretext for changing ground. We had many reasons to want to do the same. The balance in the Arab world was subtly tilting in the direction of the moderate course.

On February 11 Sadat proposed to move the mini-summit to Algiers. It was a shrewd move. Boumedienne, in the midst of reestablishing relations with the United States, was less likely to insist on maintaining the boycott in his own capital than anywhere else. And Boumedienne, a fellow "radical," was Syria's closest supporter. On February 12 Boumedienne sent me a message confirming this judgment: He would work for lifting the embargo; he hoped the United States would avoid any move or statement that might disturb the atmosphere.

The Arab mini-summit came up with the face-saving formula that I should take an exploratory trip through the area in February to pave the way for a Syrian disengagement. This was easy to agree to. A month later the oil embargo was lifted. (I shall describe that trip in Chapter XXI.)

We had come through a difficult period without succumbing to pressure. With the imminent end of the embargo, we had demonstrated that we could resist the vaunted oil weapon. The panic of our allies might now subside.

But we could have no illusions; the achievement was only temporary, the success primarily tactical. The underlying market conditions remained. The economic crisis in the democracies was only beginning. The political and social consequences were only barely discernible. Still before us was the question of whether, and how, the industrial democracies could take charge again of their common destiny. This was the task to which we turned.

XX

Energy and the Democracies

An Energy Strategy

A LONG-RANGE energy strategy required above all a united front of the industrial democracies. We were aware that our allies were reluctant to establish a common negotiating position toward the producers. Still, even strengthening those efforts that the consumers could make among themselves would greatly improve their bargaining position. Cooperation in conservation, development of alternative sources, and emergency sharing would alter market conditions and thereby the negotiating balance.

Because of all the democracies the United States was least dependent on imported oil and had the strongest economy, we thought that we were in the best position to take the lead and to advance proposals for the common good. We hoped that the reality of the present crisis would spare us the equivocations and evasions that had marked the more abstract exercise of the Year of Europe.

Despite the rebuff of previous efforts, we made yet another attempt in my Pilgrims speech delivered on December 12, 1973, in London (described in Chapter XVI). Energy cooperation, I asserted, was not a favor our allies did for us; the United States was in the best position among the industrial democracies to go it alone. Nevertheless, solitary national efforts were bound to be self-defeating. I therefore proposed an Energy Action Group of the industrial democracies — in effect, a consumer grouping to promote alternative energy sources and conservation and to negotiate with the producers:

We must bear in mind the deeper causes of the energy crisis: It is not simply a product of the Arab-Israel war; it is the inevitable consequences of the explosive growth of worldwide demand outrunning the incentives for supply. The Middle East war made a chronic crisis acute, but a crisis was coming in any event. Even when prewar production levels are resumed, the problem of matching the level of oil that the world produces to the level which it consumes will remain.

The only long-term solution is a massive effort to provide producers an incentive to increase their supply, to encourage consumers to use existing supplies more rationally, and to develop alternative energy sources.

This is a challenge which the United States could solve alone with great difficulty and that Europe cannot solve in isolation at all. We strongly prefer, and Europe requires, a common enterprise.

To this end, the United States proposes that the nations of Europe, North America, and Japan establish an Energy Action group of senior and prestigious individuals with a mandate to develop within three months an initial action program for collaboration in all areas of the energy problem. We would leave it to the members of the Nine whether they prefer to participate as the European Community.

European reaction was ambivalent. Editorial comment about the speech was largely favorable. But forthcoming noises from governments stopped well short of commitment to action. The reason was that most of them believed in energy cooperation only in a limited tactical sense: to enlist American technology to develop alternative sources of energy and in an emergency to share in our increasingly stretched supplies. But they had no stomach for a concerted diplomacy, believing that the attempt to join forces would "provoke" the producers into retaliation. Nothing could have better illustrated the demoralization — verging on abdication — of the democracies. A producers' cartel was deemed acceptable; a consumers' grouping was considered too risky. Producers with a combined population of some fifty million in underdeveloped economies were in effect blackmailing advanced industrial societies with a combined population of a billion, dictating not only the terms of trade but the framework of political relations.

On December 20 in Paris, French President Georges Pompidou made this explicit. France, Pompidou told me, would not run the slightest risk of an oil cutoff; it would participate in no group or policy involving any prospect of confrontation:

If we are talking about a dialogue between consumers and producers, we can discuss the modalities of such a dialogue without any problem. I could not concur, however, in establishing a consortium of consumers that would seek to impose a solution on the producers. You only rely on the Arabs for about a tenth of your consumption. We are entirely dependent upon them. We can't afford the luxury of three or four years of worry and misery waiting for the Arabs to understand the problem. I won't be able to accept, no matter what conditions are established, a situation which requires us to forgo Arab oil, for even a year.

But a party to a negotiation that is unable to risk its failure — the mildest form of confrontation — is reduced to choosing among varieties of appeasement. Fundamentally, most of our allies were convinced that their oil supplies were better assured by adaptation to Arab political demands than by forming a united front to resist pressures.

The only concrete action was not a response to the Pilgrims speech but another propitiation of the producers. There was the odd affair of the European Community summit meeting in Copenhagen on December 14–15, where a group of Arab foreign ministers showed up allegedly "unexpectedly" to lobby for pressure on Israel. If the accounts given to us were to be believed, it must have been the first time in history that a delegation of foreign ministers appeared uninvited at the summit meeting of a continent to which they did not belong. We did not know who had engineered the "surprise" visit; we suspected Jobert, but clearly it could not have taken place without the acquiescence of most of his colleagues.

Fundamentally, our proposal for energy cooperation ran at once into the same obstacles that had thwarted our earlier effort at Atlantic cohesion. Jobert, and probably Pompidou, wanted no part of any grouping within which American influence might be decisive and whose purpose was to discourage solitary initiatives. Philosophy was reinforced by expediency. France was in the forefront of those of our allies who were exploiting the embargo to line up bilateral deals with the producers — mostly arms for oil. And it was France that acted as spearhead of the so-called European-Arab dialogue, the European alternative to our Middle East diplomacy, whose rationale — never made explicit — could only be dissociation from the United States.

Jobert wrote me on December 28, after the OPEC decision of December 17. He accepted the principle of consumer cooperation but defined it in terms that prevented any bargaining unity. And no wonder, since he was at that very moment actively promoting bilateral French oil deals with Mideast producers. Addressing me as "Mr. Secretary and dear friend," Jobert sought playfully to pull the teeth of the Pilgrims speech: His suggestions would perhaps complicate the plan I had drawn up, he said, but might, he believed, facilitate its implementation. "Complicate" was not the right word: "scuttle" would have fitted better.

What Jobert proposed was a multistage scheme. Europe, the United States, Canada, and Japan should each elaborate its own autonomous energy policy and conduct separately its relations with the oil-producing countries. On a second level, they could cooperate on high-technology projects such as deep-water drilling and gasification of coal. Third, all industrial democracies could cooperate on conservation and similar efforts within the framework of the Organization for Economic Cooperation and Development (OECD) — a loose grouping of the key industrial nations, descended from the Marshall Plan organization, not known for decisive or rapid action. Finally, the consumer countries would not face the producers as a unit but would deal essentially bilaterally at a world conference devoted to energy matters in preparation for an even more sweeping conference dealing with raw materials in general.

Jobert's scheme was clever but too transparent. He sought access to American advanced technology while throwing all other issues into a forum so unwieldy that each consuming nation would be free — indeed, forced — to act on its own. Moreover, the unorganized consumers would be encountering not individual producers but OPEC. It seemed to us that the French proposal would institutionalize the weakness of the industrial democracies rather than overcome it.

Together with other leaders who favored the European-Arab dialogue, the French strenuously denied any political objective or exclusionary motives. But the secrecy with which the proposed initiative was prepared, the refusal to brief us about its contents, argued otherwise. Gradually we did learn of its scope and implications — usually through diplomats of friendly countries who informed us without the knowledge of other allied partners and occasionally without the knowledge of their own superiors. For example, at a meeting of the political directors (senior foreign office officials) of the European Community in Bonn on January 10–11, France put forward a proposal to begin the European-Arab dialogue at an experts' level and to culminate it at a foreign ministers' conference — in itself proof that the purpose could not be the purely technical and cultural exchange that was advertised to us. On January 30, I ordered instructions sent to our European posts stressing that

consultation is a two way street and before the member states launch a major initiative in the Middle East, we would expect every effort be made to arrange consultations between us in advance and to avoid the possibility of divergent policies. . . .

On February 1, the Middle East experts of the European Community met. When the question of briefing the United States was raised, the West German representative chairing the meeting said that the United States was already informed of general proposals and principles. This statement was true in the sense that unauthorized leaks had alerted us; they hardly provided a basis for serious discussion. It was also demeaning.

On February 6–7, the political directors met again and substantially adopted the French recommendation that the European-Arab dialogue lead to a conference at the foreign minister level. We were never told of this decision officially; in fact, a proposal that I be briefed by German Foreign Minister Walter Scheel in his capacity as President of the Council of Ministers was blocked by France.

Our objection was not to a European-Arab dialogue as such; that was as natural as it was inevitable. We were uneasy about aspects of both procedure and substance. Our allies did not hesitate to use NATO consultative procedures to inform themselves on American policies; at the same time they avoided discussing Community decisions with us until they were irrevocable, by shunting them off into tortuous new procedures requiring the prior approval of all allies. So long as this process was confined to Atlantic relations it was irritating, but its damage was limited to frustrating new departures. In the cauldron of the Middle East, however, the European initiative of a foreign ministers' conference threatened to sabotage our carefully elaborated strategy. We were proceeding step by step; the European Community had committed itself publicly to a comprehensive solution. We dealt with each of the principal Mideast parties separately; the Europeans were aiming at a conclave assembling all Arab countries, a forum that I was convinced would give the whip hand to the radicals. As I said to British Foreign Secretary Sir Alec Douglas-Home in early February:

I just wanted you to know that any getting together of all the Arab states — moderates and radicals — would have most unfortunate consequences. It is bound to lead the radicals to make extreme statements which will be very difficult for the moderates to resist. This will immediately lead to pressures on the European leaders to endorse every point on the Arab radicals' program. Second, they will link all the issues together and this is bound to have a negative effect on our political negotiations. Sadat has told us that the only way to deal with this situation is piece by piece. . . . If you go ahead with this EC initiative it is bound to upset things and then we will have to go in and pick up the pieces.

The dialogue with the Arabs, moreover, was being urged by France explicitly as an alternative to a unified consumer challenge to the oil producers. Even those European leaders who did not share the French hostility to our approach sought relief from the conflicting pressures by adopting portions of each position. The result was institutionalized ambivalence. Few European nations agreed completely with France, yet — as in the Year of Europe — none was prepared for confrontation. Nor did any wish to court our ill will. Therefore, most acknowledged the principle of consumer cooperation but sought to define it so as not to preclude the autonomous policy favored by France. Every move toward one pole evoked a compensating gyration to the other. Early in January many European leaders — though not the French — began to edge toward some kind of energy cooperation. At the same time the European Commission cautioned against approaches to energy that would weaken the "political solidarity the Community intends to demonstrate as evidence of its existence and significance" — clearly a dig at us.

We could see looming before us the same interminable procedural nightmare that had thwarted the Year of Europe, this time on an issue that did not simply mortgage the future but menaced the present. It was for this reason that we decided to bring matters to a head by extending, on January 9, 1974, a formal Presidential invitation to an energy conference in Washington to be held in early February. Federal Energy Administrator William Simon and I held a joint press conference on January 10 to announce the gathering. We stressed the urgent need for the consumers to achieve a common analysis of the situation and a joint strategy. I said:

[A]s far as the consuming nations are concerned, the energy situation, and what it portends for the future, will be a test of the whole approach towards the international system that we . . . have pursued . . . towards developing nations for the last 25 years.

It is a test of the proposition that the world has become truly interdependent, and that isolation and selfish approaches must be destructive for all concerned.

To head off the endless procedural maneuvers over who would speak for Europe, we issued individual invitations to the major energy-consuming nations in the democratic world — initially those represented on the energy committee of the OECD. The European Community was invited to attend in its own right and to decide the level of its participation.* We would now see whether we would again be faced with the insistence that the European countries would speak to us only through a single instructed representative or whether the importance of the subject would produce a more natural pattern of consultation.

None of our allies was eager for a consumer conference, and attitudes ranged from resignation to reluctance. But it was one thing to dissociate from us on Mideast diplomacy with statements known to have little impact; it was another to advertise isolation on energy matters from a partner who, if it went the bilateral route, would have by far the stronger bargaining position and who would be needed as a supplier of last resort if there should be a major oil cutoff. As I said to a staff meeting at State on January 8:

The Europeans have to understand that we believe it to be in the common interest to have a multilateral solution which is of no special benefit to any one group or region, because we believe that beggaring your neighbor is going to hurt us all. So that we are prepared to work with them on a truly cooperative scheme, even though we will probably put more into it than they for the sake of world stability. But they must also understand that under no circumstances

---

*The countries invited were Canada, France, the Federal Republic of Germany, Italy, Japan, the Netherlands, Norway, and the United Kingdom. The invitation to the European Community was in the letter to West German Chancellor Willy Brandt, whose turn it was to serve as President of the Community. Also invited was Jonkheer Emile van Lennep, the Secretary General of the OECD.

will we give them a free field for bilateral deals. And if they will not work multilaterally, we will force them by going bilateral ourselves. If we go bilateral, we can preempt them, I think, in most areas. We will under no circumstances turn over the field to them bilaterally.

All during January we dealt with emissaries — from Britain, the Federal Republic, and smaller states — who sought to do the impossible; they wanted to give us enough of what we proposed for the sake of Atlantic unity, meet French concerns for the articulation of European identity, and court producer goodwill by dissociating from us for the sake of uninterrupted energy supplies. The Japanese also made clear their ambivalence — on the one hand recognizing the need for effective consumer cooperation, on the other hand fearing confrontation with the oil producers. The Prime Ministers of Japan and Britain and the Chancellor of West Germany replied in a week accepting Nixon's invitation. They indicated great reluctance to create a permanent consumer grouping, which they saw as "provocative" — though the oil producers had never consulted the consumers when forming OPEC and prided themselves on acting as a unit. Each leader made clear that he was looking for an early way to bring the producers into the work of the consumer conference — which was almost a contradiction in terms. All kinds of subterfuges were devised to avoid the only solution that would make any sense: a permanent organization of consumer solidarity. The British — in the vanguard of those cooperating with us — went no further than to propose a "contact group" of ambassadors in Washington to coordinate work going on in existing institutions. No other ally risked that degree of specificity. But a group of ambassadors was a soporific, not a remedy. They would need instructions from meeting to meeting; they would lack a staff for serious work. After a few sessions such an institution would fall into desuetude. I told Alec Home (on February 11) that the issue was both moral and political:

We ought to be establishing some kind of machinery which will enable us to prepare common positions among the consumers. We need this. Second, thirty million producers seem to have gotten together and established their own position. They have a cartel. Why should they be able to order around the eight hundred million consumers? Why should we assume that the consumers shouldn't talk together? The important countries in the area are Iran and Saudi Arabia. Both of them are completely dependent on American political support. Why shouldn't Europe want to use this American political power in the energy field? What we have here is an opportunity for a moral demonstration of what the West can do when it wants to get together and that it cannot be pushed around. We have to have a perception that it is a common problem and that we must work for common solutions.

In the meantime, where energy was concerned, the European nations were *not* prepared to entrust their future to a single instructed representative acting for a united Europe. The European Community would participate in some form but so would the foreign ministers of individual countries that had been invited. And the four energy-poor countries of the Community that had not been invited insisted on sending their foreign ministers as well.* In short, on energy, unlike the Alliance itself, we were enabled to deal with allied governments as well as with the Community in the same forum.

There was one ally who suffered no ambivalence. On January 18, Michel Jobert wrote me one of his "dear friend" letters. He objected to a meeting in Washington, to a conference of foreign ministers, to an association of consumers, to the invitation to Japan, and to the manner of inviting the European Community. It was statistically improbable that one document of a serious government could contain as many errors as he ascribed to our letter of invitation. Nevertheless, he graciously put forward an alternative proposal: France wished to see a United Nations conference on energy problems assembled as quickly as possible, on the theory that this might moderate the positions of producers, consumers, and developing countries. What Jobert omitted was that in a UN conference of 150 nations, OPEC would be united, the consumers divided. The developing countries would undoubtedly be led to side with the producers, either having been bought off with vague promises of concessional prices and economic aid or out of a stubborn sense of "Third World" loyalty. The Communist countries would have a field day viewing and exploiting the West's discomfiture. The United States would be isolated. Jobert concluded his letter with another of his paradoxes, assuring me of French concern over energy, of his surprise at our invitation to the February conference, but also, and "most important," of his "very solid friendship."

Our Embassy in Paris reported on January 21 that the French viewed our proposal for an energy conference "with a lack of enthusiasm bordering on hostility." On January 24 Pompidou declared:

> We must talk; producers and consumers must understand one another. Therefore, they must meet, and we are ready to meet bilaterally at the European level with a group of Arab producers, for example, and at a global level between rich and poor consumers — for there are important consumers which are poor and are already suffering severely from the situation. . . .[1]

France, in short, would talk with anyone, except with the United States in any forum involving our allies. Nevertheless, one by one they ac-

---

*The thirteen countries finally attending were Belgium, Canada, Denmark, France, the Federal Republic of Germany, Ireland, Italy, Japan, Luxembourg, the Netherlands, Norway, the United Kingdom, and the United States.

cepted Nixon's invitation. France's answer was for Jobert to travel to Syria, Saudi Arabia, Kuwait, and Iraq and mount a direct challenge to American policy. There he sought barter deals for oil on a national basis, thus acquiescing in the price gouge. And he egged on the Arab radicals to oppose the American mediation. In Baghdad he warned against "interim settlements" — and therefore by implication the just-concluded Egyptian-Israeli disengagement. "Why does the hand that holds the key turn it so slowly?" he jibed at American policy. While at it, he condemned the Washington Energy Conference as a "political" ploy aimed at the Arabs; it would not be another Congress of Vienna, he said — both a crack at my scholarly work and a promise that the Washington Energy Conference would have no lasting results (an outcome that Jobert was in a good position to bring about). While still in Baghdad he pursued the same theme with a Syrian journalist, adding a compliment for the skill with which the Syrians were "consolidating your military position on the front to deal with every eventuality" — hardly a counsel of moderation at the beginning of our disengagement efforts on the Golan Heights. We might be forgiven if we considered such tactics not only inimical to our own interests but also in the long run destructive of the well-being of the other industrial democracies — because if taken seriously in the Arab world they might drive the Middle East to a crisis that France would have no means to contain.

France enveloped itself in silence until five days before the opening session of the conference. Then on February 6, after a meeting of the French cabinet, a spokesman announced that Jobert would attend:

The participation of our country at this meeting responds, in addition to considerations of courtesy, to the desire to permit Europe to take a common position. While France is disposed to participate in an exchange of views on the different aspects of energy problems, it would not be able to give its adherence to the establishment of an organization of oil consuming industrial countries, independent from other consuming countries particularly developing countries, as well as producing countries.

The formal statement of the cabinet decision was forwarded to the White House in a curt telegram from Pompidou *after* having been publicly announced — an unprecedented procedure and a special indignity toward a close ally. The cable contained not one personal explanatory word from the French President.

But not only the procedure was extraordinary. The announcement made explicit France's opposition to the very concept of the conference. Jobert, it was said, was being sent out of "courtesy"; he would not be able to agree to any consumer organization; his sole charter was to exchange views on "different aspects of energy problems" — as if the conference were a scientific colloquium and not a forum for making decisions. The stated purpose of France's attendance was not to achieve any particular goal but to "permit Europe to take a common position" — which, given French views, meant that Paris intended to exercise its veto within the European Community and thereby over the results of the conference.

The direction in which France would seek to push its European partners, and the extent to which French views were beginning to prevail, emerged from a decision of the European Community Council of Ministers in Brussels on February 5, the day before the French cabinet decision (it was perhaps the condition Jobert extracted for attending). The nine foreign ministers designated as the Community's representatives West German Foreign Minister Walter Scheel, in his capacity of President of the Council of Ministers, and Commission President François-Xavier Ortoli. Their instructions were to forswear confrontation with the oil producers; to oppose new permanent organizations of the consumers; to encourage a prompt dialogue with the producers; and to assign all work on energy to existing international institutions.

This was not the purpose of the conference as we conceived it. The omens were hardly encouraging.

The Ministers Convene

THE Washington Energy Conference was a strange event. It was a meeting of allies, but it had something of the character of a clash of adversaries. Its purpose was to develop solidarity among the consumers, yet it meandered into the liturgical byways that had sidetracked the Atlantic dialogue for a year. Once again we found ourselves forced into a confrontation we did not seek. We would have been more than willing to deal with a united Europe in a spirit of give-and-take; there was certainly a margin for divergence. But the challenge laid down by Jobert went far beyond this. He wanted to use energy — as he had the Year of Europe — to create an identity for Europe, under French leadership, in opposition to the United States. The French described our initiative as an American attempt to exploit the energy crisis to increase our influence in the Atlantic area and they fought it doggedly on those grounds. They professed to see evidence of this, oddly, in our invitation to Japan, which seemed to them to resurrect the idea of the Atlantic declarations against which they had fought such a fierce rearguard action.

No doubt the premise that the industrial democracies shared certain problems was at the base of both initiatives. But where the Year of Europe sought a moral rededication in order to face issues that had not yet arisen, the energy conference was designed to combat a clear and immediate danger. It was one thing to argue about methods of consultation when the subject was an abstract declaration; there was some justification for anxiety that Europe's identity might be swallowed in the institutionalization of Atlantic unity — although even then Jobert was carrying a valid theoretical point to extraordinary lengths. But the energy crisis did not lend itself to regional subdivisions. To deal with it through consumer solidarity was not a theoretical preference; it was the only feasible strategy for restoring the balance of the world energy market, and was probably more vital to Europe's (and France's) real interests than even to ours.

I reiterated our objective in remarks on February 6 before the Harvard, Yale, and Princeton clubs of Washington:

> [W]e thought it essential that those nations that consume and import 85 percent of the world's energy meet first, because they have a common problem of a very large size, that is manageable by cooperative effort only; and that will surely lead to the ruin of everybody if it is attempted to be settled on a unilateral basis. . . .
>
> [I]f every nation adopts a policy of beggaring its neighbors a collapse of the world economy will be inevitable and the whole structure of cooperative world relationships that has developed since the war will be in jeopardy.

That was the theme of our talks with the various foreign ministers who began to arrive for the energy conference over the weekend of February 9. I had spent the nearly three weeks since the end of the Egyptian shuttle in continual preparations with a core group of colleagues consisting of Treasury Secretary George P. Shultz, Federal Reserve Board Chairman Arthur Burns, Federal Energy Administrator William Simon, and Under Secretary of State for Security Assistance William Donaldson.* We had drawn up a program for energy cooperation listing seven tasks: conservation; alternative energy sources; research and development; emergency sharing; international financial cooperation; help for the poorer developing countries; and consumer-producer relations. We intended to offer the consumers the outline of an integrated, well-considered strategy, to give them confidence that they could take charge of their future if they all worked together. At a planning session in January I had said:

> What we need to do is to take the mystery out of the energy situation. This means we must give the Europeans and Japanese the facts. If we can show them the situation is manageable and not all bad, that they need not rush after bilateral deals, that our course of cooperation is in their best interest, we will succeed in this endeavor.

---

*Ambassador David Bruce also participated during the conference. A working group, headed by Helmut Sonnenfeldt and Winston Lord and including Bill Donaldson, Arthur Hartman (Assistant Secretary of State for European Affairs), and Charles Cooper as the NSC staff's representative, prepared the working documents, did the first drafts of speeches, and in general buttressed the conference.

This outline had been discussed in the various capitals prior to the conference by a mission headed by Donaldson; we put a fleshed-out version before the key ministers on Sunday, February 10, in a series of bilateral meetings.

I started the day with breakfast with Walter Scheel, attending in his dual capacity as West German Foreign Minister and President of the European Community Council of Ministers. I told him that for us the conference was a test of the possibility of a cooperative world order. Here we would not be a party to a confusing outcome in which rhetoric obscured failure. We would rather announce disagreement and draw the political consequences — a thinly veiled threat that this time intransigence would not be free. Scheel made no attempt to defend the substance of the foreign ministers' decisions at Brussels. He placed the responsibility exclusively on the shoulders of Jobert; France had to be given "something" to stay in the Community:

We look at the situation in Europe and we find ourselves in a difficult situation. The French always seem to proceed in their own worst interests. You have examples of it in their isolated floating and now in their attempts to seek economic benefits on their own. We know that in the end this sort of thing is going to lead to chaos and that's what we are trying to prevent. There are politicians in all of our governments who are anxious to try to keep the French from moving out of the Community.

Scheel wondered whether we could leave open the outcome of the conference until the European foreign ministers met again a few days later. They could then adopt an agreed position and make it appear that Europe had taken the initiative; this would save French prestige. I said this was acceptable provided there was an ironclad assurance that the Community would indeed adopt the consensus of the conference. Scheel sadly confessed his inability to give such an assurance. In these circumstances I could not agree to postponing a decision.

The next problem was whether a permanent consumer energy organization should be created. Scheel warned that any such attempt would meet the bitter opposition of France. I replied that I did not care about the label under which consumer cooperation took place; we would not argue about whether any committees emerging from the conference were called ad hoc or permanent; some of the seven tasks we had outlined could be assigned to existing institutions. This was certainly the case with, for example, international financial cooperation and the plight of the poorer developing countries. Other issues — being new — would require special working groups and some coordinating mechanism; if it would help salve French pride, we could put these groups under the aegis of the OECD, of which France was already a member, though he and I knew this would not change the substance. Scheel gave the impression that he would not leave Washington heartbroken if I forgot about the entire project. At the same time there was little doubt that he saw, if not the force of our arguments, then the realities of the situation. Europe was in no position to refuse consumer solidarity, for in the process it would leave itself totally naked if there should be another emergency. In the end Germany could not afford the precedent of isolated action in a crisis; hence it would side with us. The conversation was significant above all because it revealed that the mandate agreed to a few days earlier at Brussels, under French influence, did not have the enthusiastic support of the other Europeans at the conference. The head of the Council of Ministers of the European Community revealed that his colleagues were seeking an interpretation of their instructions at variance with their literal meaning; later on they would seek to backpedal and compensate France for doing what was right.

Following Scheel, I saw Mitchell Sharp, Canadian Secretary of State for External Affairs; had lunch with Japanese Foreign Minister Masayoshi Ohira; met with European Commission President Ortoli; and breakfasted with Alec Home the next morning. They confirmed my judgment that we were on firm ground; in a showdown it would not be we who would be isolated. The cooperative spirit did, to be sure, stop considerably short of what we thought was needed. Every minister I consulted was still terrified of possible confrontation with the producers. From the tone of their remarks, one would never have known that the producers had just quadrupled oil prices, slashed production, and imposed a selective embargo as a political weapon. If that was not a confrontation forced on us, we would need a new vocabulary.

At least some of the practical measures we were proposing — emergency sharing, conservation, and joint development of alternative energy sources — involved no risks; whatever posture the consumers adopted toward the producers, craven or courageous, these steps would strengthen their bargaining position. It was recognized that we were not defending the American interest in any narrow sense; this was Jobert's Achilles' heel. Of all the participants in the conference, we were in the best position to go it alone. But a world in which all kindred nations were reduced to scavengers or supplicants did not accord with our idea of progress or justice.

There were two more key conversations before the formal opening of the conference on the morning of February 11. The first was around 7:00 P.M. on Sunday evening, February 10, with my old and cherished friend Helmut Schmidt, then German Finance Minister. Schmidt and I had met twenty years earlier when on a visit of mine to the Federal Republic he had been introduced to me as a promising young man. He struck me then as brash, forceful, and intelligent. We stayed in touch over the years. Gradually it dawned on me that the somewhat overbearing manner was the defense mechanism of a gentle, even sentimental, man who had to stress his intellect and analytical power lest his emotions run away with him. Our friendship soon transcended the tasks that destiny imposed on us. We both knew that we served our countries not by imposing our views but by seeking solutions both of us could believe in. I will deal with my evaluation of Schmidt as Chancellor in another place. That evening, as the dusk settled over Washington, we ruminated in my cavernous office at the State Department overlooking the Lincoln Memorial. I told Schmidt of my fear that the crisis of authority in America might become so obvious that no diplomatic tour de force could rescue us from disaster. Nor did I see other countries able to step in to play the role we risked vacating. The West was beginning to act like the old Greek city-states; by exalting self-will it dissipated its inspiration. The conference about to start would become a symbol of our decline or, with luck, a turning point.

Schmidt had his own political crisis at home, for Chancellor Willy Brandt was beginning to lose his own grip on events. But Schmidt never referred to it. He was tired of politics, he affirmed. He had been battling for twenty years, in the cockpit for five. He saw no sense in going on. Later on that year he would probably retire. I had heard him muse like this before; it seemed that this pugnaciously gentle man could keep himself going only by announcing periodically that he would abandon the sole profession that really interested him. I appealed to him with an argument that I knew Schmidt prized above all others: human reliability. I said that everyone had to judge for himself when the wear and tear of high office became too much. I only wanted him to know that it was a great solace to have such an absolutely trustworthy person in high office in the Western world.

Schmidt did not debate the point. Because he did not care whether he stayed or went, he said, he had nothing to lose. He shared our general assessment of the energy crisis and the need for the kind of program we had outlined. He would do his utmost to fight for it. And since Foreign Minister Scheel had to serve as President of the European Community Council of Ministers, Schmidt would in effect present the *German* point of view. He would not participate in the attempt to turn Europe against America on an issue insoluble except by common efforts. He would affirm a program parallel to ours.

With Germany, Japan, and Britain essentially supporting our approach, we held the stronger hand at the conference. But my preference was to bring Jobert into the consensus rather than to outvote him. He had arrived, almost directly from the Middle East, in the early evening of February 10. I called on him at the French Embassy shortly after, around 9:30 P.M. He was the only foreign minister whom I did not ask to come to my office (my schedule would have been unmanageable had

I tried to call on all of them). This was intended as a sign of goodwill.
Despite Jobert's taunts during his recent trip to the Middle East, I was
too committed to Franco-American friendship to court a clash that could
benefit no one. And I liked him personally very much. I had sharply
criticized the Kennedy and Johnson administrations for pushing for a
showdown with France and thereby polarizing European politics. I was
persuaded that there were no winners in such contests; therefore, I wanted
to make a final effort to find a solution and, failing that, prove to myself
that conflict was unavoidable.

Later Jobert wrote dramatic descriptions of the encounter. I had been
making frightful scenes to terrorize the other Europeans, he claimed. He
tamed me by warning me not to use such tactics on him; this allegedly
left me speechless and neither of us spoke for a long period while tempers cooled.[2] It is a tale in keeping with Jobert's romantic streak. Perhaps in a meeting with no witnesses it is impossible later to capture the
historical truth objectively. Philosophers may argue that there are many
truths and that they reside exclusively in the perception of the participants, as in the Japanese film *Rashomon*.

Be that as it may, my recollection of the meeting is quite otherwise.
When I asked Jobert what disturbed him about the energy conference,
he replied quite simply, "American leadership." I appealed to him for
a turn away from a collision course that would be a disaster for all free
peoples. The United States had called the conference, I said, not to
establish our dominance over the Atlantic community; rather, the world's
petroleum crisis permitted no other course. If the dispute was one of
form, I would do my utmost to ease matters for France psychologically.
For example, as I had told Scheel, I would be prepared to see an energy
action group placed under the aegis of OECD if this overcame the French
objection to new institutions. But the substance was valid; we would all
doom ourselves if every consumer nation was left to its own devices.

Jobert, as I remember the encounter, was sardonic. He would happily
support seizing OECD with energy but only in existing committees
(which, as he knew, did not cover all the tasks that we had outlined).
France would welcome a continuation of the Washington conference in
OECD's Paris headquarters but would not pledge itself in advance to an
agreed outcome (meaning it reserved the right to exercise its veto). In
other words, Jobert was giving me an opportunity — and offered his
cooperation — to scuttle our own energy design. Adjournment in Washington without an agreed outcome would guarantee failure in Paris, if
indeed OECD ever met on the subject. Sighing, Jobert hinted once again
that his life was hard: He was caught between the realities of a conference and the pressures of his sick President, with whom he did not fully
agree. I could sympathize with Jobert on this point. But I could not help
him resolve his own domestic political dilemma by sacrificing the pur-

poses of the conference. So we were at least able to agree as to the outcome of the meeting: A showdown was now inevitable.

The Washington Energy Conference

TACTICALLY, the United States was in a good position; the principal participants were not going to support French intransigence. But it was not yet clear whether they would be lined up behind a meaningful, positive program; our danger was not failure but half-measures. After the opening session on February 11, I told Al Haig:

The French are isolated but we are not getting what should be happening — a response of united action. They are all looking for ways of getting into talks with the Arab producers before they know what they want. The basic theory [of consumer unity] they are not willing to buy. We will get enough to make it look respectable. There is no strategic conception there.

The ministers and delegates assembled in what is now called the Loy Henderson Conference Room of the State Department, a vast hall on the ground floor. A large rectangular table had been set up around which the delegates sat by country in alphabetical order. Ministers were at the table, assistants just behind them. Yet another row or more of interested parties was lined in a third echelon. The American contingent was, as customary, especially large — every interested federal agency insisted on being represented in some manner and it was hard to think of an agency, other than the US Postal Service, that did not claim to have a stake in the conference. As a host I sat at the head of the table together with Walter Scheel. Each nation was represented by at least two ministers — usually foreign and finance (the Japanese had sent their foreign minister and minister for science and technology). Only Jobert was alone. Pompidou had disapproved the attendance of Finance Minister Valéry Giscard d'Estaing; he wanted to downgrade the conference as much as possible and he had always been waspish about his brilliant Finance Minister — perhaps because they were both experts in the same field and Giscard made it clear that he hoped to succeed his ailing chief.

I opened the conference with an exposition of the energy problem that my colleagues had leaked in bits and pieces before. I quoted from my great predecessor, Dean Acheson, to the effect that usually failure lies "in meeting big, bold, demanding problems with half measures, timorous and cramped." I asserted that the United States had called the conference before everybody's position hardened, for one central purpose:

to move urgently to resolve the energy problem on the basis of cooperation among *all* nations. Failure to do so would threaten the world with a vicious cycle of competition, autarky, rivalry, and depression such as led to the collapse of world order in the thirties. Fortunately, the problem is still manageable multilaterally: National policies are still evolving, practical solutions to the energy problem are technically achievable, and cooperation with the producing countries is still politically open to us.

I then put forth the seven-point program for consumer cooperation outlined above. I made my bow to the dialogue with producers that all my colleagues were advocating. But I stressed that in our view it would have to grow out of consumer solidarity, not be a substitute for it:

A well-conceived producer-consumer meeting in which the consumers do not seek selfish advantages either as a group or individually, far from leading to confrontation, could instead lay the basis of a new cooperative relationship. But it will do so only if it is well prepared — and if the consumers have first constructed a solid basis of cooperation among themselves.

My speech was buttressed by a presentation by energy czar William Simon. Simon sought to take the terror out of the energy crisis by analyzing its causes and remedies. He showed that the situation, while serious, was manageable over a period of time provided the consuming countries cooperated in the sharing of information, development of new energy sources, and conservation. Simon pressed his favorite theme that it would be in the interest even of producers to reduce prices from the current level of more than $11 per barrel — an argument always more persuasive to him than to any other audience. Treasury Secretary George Shultz suggested measures of joint action to overcome the financial dislocations caused by high oil prices. The American theme, in short, was one of optimism: The consuming nations, while buffeted by crisis, still held their future in their own hands. The energy cataclysm was not the result of sinister forces but of remediable conditions. The way to deal with them was not by submission to the dictates of the producers, but by remedying the economic circumstances that had created the crisis.

It would be too much to say that the ministers assembled shared this perspective. On the whole, they would have far preferred to have had no meeting, or, failing that, to navigate through one without either decision or a blowup. But confronted with a specific program, they were obliged to take a position. Walter Scheel spoke for the European Community in his usual elegant style. It was anything but a clarion call to action. He was torn between a Community mandate that seemed to prohibit any institutionalized consumer cooperation and the reality that most of the ministers gathered in Washington agreed with our approach and were not prepared to thwart American proposals in our capital. Scheel's personal views corresponded to those of the other foreign ministers. He therefore took up my hint in our private conversation that we should avoid the issue of how to define permanence with respect to any new institutions that might emerge. Since the problem was new, ad hoc groups were needed to deal with it; how long they operated would depend on the continued requirement for them, not on their bylaws. However watered down, what Scheel said amounted to acceptance of our basic approach to consumer solidarity. Helmut Schmidt spoke for the Federal Republic of Germany, making Scheel's hints explicit and giving concreteness to his foreign minister's allusions.

Sir Alec Douglas-Home came closest to giving us all-out support. Masayoshi Ohira spoke elliptically, endorsing consumer cooperation and a consumer-producer conference. In classic Japanese fashion he made his point so indirectly that I slipped a note to Simon with the query: "Bill: Do you understand the main point Ohira is making?" Simon, who was attending his first international conference as a principal, scratched his reply: "I am not sure. Being inexperienced in this I take his remarks as being very forthcoming and encouraging as far as cooperation, *but* they intend to pursue bilateral deals with *great vigah.*"

This degree of support for the American position was enough to set off the fireworks. One of the unwritten rules of diplomacy is to separate personal relations from official disagreements. The diplomat is presumed to reflect the interests of his country, not personal predilections. He is assumed to quarrel not out of preference but for reasons of state. This pretense is, of course, far too absolute. In reality, the subjective element cannot be so easily eliminated; still, the myth is useful. It maintains civility even in the midst of controversy. It permits compromise, even yielding, without involving the ego and thus smooths the way to a solution. Jobert was incapable of this distinction. He could be charming and insinuating; his mordant wit was as entertaining as it was perceptive. But once engaged — especially before an audience — Jobert did not seem able to maintain self-control. Sarcastically, he accused Scheel of violating Community instructions and therefore speaking without authority. He implied that Schmidt was committing treason — presumably against Europe — and acting as an American mouthpiece. He had come, he said, to save the unity of Europe because his colleagues had accepted their invitations without reference to France. He presented himself as the watchdog of the Community mandate. The fears that had brought him to Washington, he claimed, had been warranted.

Jobert was no gentler with the United States. He accused us of having assembled an ill-prepared, ill-conceived conference designed to achieve American predominance rather than to settle the energy problem. He quoted Democratic Senator Edmund Muskie in criticism of Administration policy. He offered no proposal of any kind, neither an alternative to what we had put forward nor a supplement. He wanted no common energy policy in any guise. He was out to torpedo the conference. Plainly, France was ready to gamble on fulfilling its energy needs through bilateral deals; it would seek a preferred position through political support to radical regimes, particularly Iraq. It would attempt to drag Europe in its wake by means of the European-Arab dialogue.

The silence of his colleagues around the table should have made clear to Jobert that this time he had overplayed his hand.

After the plenary sessions end, the real work of conferences begins, and that usually turns on a draft document purporting to reflect the consensus. Almost always one issue emerges that symbolizes the conflicting views and permits a test of the contending positions. The manner in which it is resolved will determine the course of the conference; afterward, matters generally fall into place. In this case, the issue was whether some follow-up machinery (never mind its label) should be established to take up the tasks we had listed.

Before that issue could move to the confrontation stage, the European Community had to sort out its internal position. It had to decide whether to stick with Jobert's interpretation of its mandate, or Scheel's. Ministers had the option, too, of not acting as a Community at all but making their decisions as individual sovereign nations. That process would take the better part of Tuesday, February 12, the day the conference was supposed to end. It was therefore agreed to extend the conference by one more day — even though this presented some difficulties for the British delegation, eager to return home for the general election that was then only two weeks off.

Before these deliberations could start, there was the obligatory dinner given by the Chief of State of the host country, in this case Nixon. The tormenting year had taken its toll. Watergate had drained him. Most of his news conferences were consumed in relentless badgering over this or that new revelation. On January 30, less than two weeks before the opening of the conference, he had interpolated seemingly extemporaneous remarks — almost surely carefully prepared — at the end of his State of the Union address, asking for a quick resolution of the proceedings to impeach him so that the normal processes of government could resume. It was an idle hope, unfulfillable procedurally, inconsistent with the psychological need of many of his opponents to prolong his humiliation, thwarted finally by his own inability to put the tawdry collection of events that constituted the body of Watergate into a definitive revelation that might have ended his ordeal.

The energy conference was in these circumstances more of a nuisance to Nixon than a source of exhilaration, which normally would have been his attitude. I reported to him twice a day on our sessions. His comments were perceptive; he backed the strategy. But there was an uncharacteristic detachment, almost as if he had become an observer of his own Presidency. In this atmosphere the State dinner was a depressing prospect. Nixon sought to escape it; at a minimum he wanted not to have to give the obligatory toast. As late as 5:30 P.M., two hours before the start of the dinner, I was still pleading with Nixon, Haig, and Scow-croft for some Presidential remarks.

In truth, there was no point in the dinner without some comment from Nixon. Social gatherings of participants at an international conference tend to be dreary affairs. The same people who have been boring one another or wrangling with one another all day meet again in the evening, seated in the same protocol order. It would be astonishing if they had anything new to say. The principal significance of the assemblage is as a gesture of respect by the host, reinforced by whatever message he wishes to convey to them. At last Nixon agreed to say something; he was insistent, however, that it should not culminate in a toast — the reason he gave was that Alec Home was the only foreign minister present he liked; if protocol forbade his toasting Home, he would toast nobody. I urged him to recognize Scheel in his capacity as President of the European Council; Nixon was noncommittal. When Nixon rose to speak, I had no idea of either what he would say or how he would conclude.

As it turned out, Nixon's speech at the dinner — improvised, reluctantly delivered — caused the greatest stir of the conference. Only a few of us knew the absurdity of Jobert's — and in truth many other ministers' — conviction that it was part of a carefully calculated pressure play. It was in fact vintage Nixon, spontaneous and all the more noteworthy because he was truly its sole author. My only contribution to it had been to warn Nixon against being confrontational; I had thought the tactical situation favored our approach and that we would prevail to the extent that we could avoid the appearance of American pressure. Nixon said that he agreed. But he also liked to live dangerously. Even in his salad days, he had amused himself by showing how close he could come to transgressing against the "points to avoid" that he himself had insisted be part of the briefing memoranda for each meeting. Time and again he had skirted so close to the precipice I had defined as perilous that it was hard to tell whether the briefing memorandum served as a warning or as a challenge. Given Nixon's nature, probably a combination of both.

Nixon ran true to form this evening. He did not issue threats; on the contrary, he explicitly disavowed them. Nothing was further from his mind, he said innocently, than to link the fields of energy and security. It was not his fault — he was only describing reality when he portrayed the pressures in the Congress urging him to withdraw forces from all over the world, including Europe:

[T]here has been growing in recent years — and perhaps it has been accelerated to a certain extent by our very difficult experience in Vietnam — a growing sense of isolationism, not just about security — those, for example, who believe that the United States unilaterally should withdraw forces from

Europe and, for that matter, withdraw its forces from all over the world and make our treaty commitments to other nations in the Far East and in Europe meaningless — but also with regard to trade where those who completely oppose the initiatives we have undertaken in the trade area and who oppose even some of the initiatives in the international monetary area that you are all familiar with.

He of course avowed that he would resist the lure of isolationism as long as possible, but he nevertheless owed it to his guests to warn them that these forces in America might be strengthened by European unilateralism in energy and might yet overwhelm him:

[I]t is possibly good short-term politics, but disastrous long-term statesmanship for this reason, because if each of the nations in effect goes off on its own or, as I have put it, goes into business for himself, the inevitable effect will be this: It will drive the prices of energy up, it will drive our economies down, and it will drive all of us apart. . . .

I believe that the, let me put it, the "enlightened selfish interest" of each nation here is better served by cooperation in security, by cooperation in trade, and by cooperation in developing our sources of energy and in acquiring the energy we need to keep the great industrial complex of the free world moving ahead to ever and ever higher plateaus.

Summing up, Nixon — in a sort of "to hell with it" mood — affirmed what he had just denied, that he was linking security and energy policy after all: "Security and economic considerations are inevitably linked and energy cannot be separated from either." And to end my private suspense, Nixon did make the toast to Walter Scheel I had recommended — though he arrived there by a circuitous route. He pointed out that he had contemplated toasting foreign ministers who had been Prime Ministers (his bow to his friend Alec Home) but finally gave pride of place to the only Foreign Minister who also carried the title of President (of the Council of Ministers of the Community) — for Nixon cognoscenti a neat way of separating the toast from any attribution of personal merit to the German Foreign Minister.

The speech was a remarkable performance. And it had the desired effect. All media reported the linkage that Nixon had both denied and affirmed — some, especially in Britain, approvingly; others, almost exclusively in France, citing it as an example of the American quest for domination that had to be resisted. And the speech made clear to the participants that what had been put forward at the conference was the considered view of the American President, not the personal idiosyncrasy of his lieutenants.

Even then, compromise would have been easy for Jobert, and indeed such a course could have scuttled our strategy more effectively than intransigence. Most foreign ministers would have leaped at any available face-saving formula even at the risk of depriving the conference of operational significance. But Jobert chose to fight to the finish. He resisted any consumer institutions. (His real purpose was shown a few weeks later when he proposed — unsuccessfully — a European energy grouping whose principal virtue in his eyes must have been that we were excluded.) He was adamant against any follow-up to the Washington Energy Conference in whatever form.

Tuesday, February 12, the second day of the conference, thus turned into a showdown. The plenary sessions were frequently interrupted for consultations, the most important of which were the caucuses of the members of the European Community. The United States adopted a low profile; we went to great lengths not to spark the Franco-American duel that might have enabled Jobert to rally his colleagues in the name of European solidarity.

At 11:45 A.M., Home came to my office to announce the tentative outcome of European deliberations. The eight would resist French efforts to prevent consumer institutions. Their biggest worry was that while they stood firm, we would compromise bilaterally with France. It was an ironic relic of the period when Jobert had shrewdly lured us into bilateral talks on the Atlantic dialogue excluding the European Community. I assured Home that no talks were taking place; we would inform him of any approaches; we would conclude nothing without the agreement of the allies who stood with us. I also suggested that if the deadlock persisted into the closing plenary session, the best procedure might be to have Japan put forward the proposal for follow-up machinery. It would be less challenging for France, more compatible with the cohesion of the European Community, if the Europeans did not themselves put forth a scheme objectionable to Paris or derived from an American proposal. Home said he would have a word with Ohira.

At one o'clock I gave a lunch for all the foreign ministers. To show conciliation I placed Jobert out of protocol order, to my right. The gesture was only partially successful. Jobert arrived late but then suggested a private meeting between us — a suggestion that, even if overheard by only a few of our colleagues (as he had ensured that it would be), would spread like wildfire among the others. Jobert clearly hoped to upset the deliberations of the Europeans. I had a word with Home to tell him that our understanding stood. He informed me that Ohira was willing to introduce a resolution calling for follow-up machinery.

At 4:00 P.M. Jobert and I met for forty minutes. As so often before, he said that he hoped I understood his belligerence was based on instructions; he himself professed to hold more flexible views. He agreed with me that an open rupture would hurt everyone. He would be prepared to put a compromise to Pompidou based on our conversation of the previous Sunday night. I reported Jobert's proposal to Nixon as follows:

They don't want this conference to set up machinery that is semi-permanent because they don't want Washington to get the credit for having done it. . . . [T]hey have now proposed to me that there be a conference held in a month in Paris under OECD which would set up the machinery and they would be willing to have a few machineries of a temporary nature set up between now and then.

The implication was that France would not exercise its veto at the OECD but rather work to support follow-up machinery; as a sign of good faith it would even support some interim machinery prior to the OECD conference.

It was a tempting proposal, but it also had the makings of a booby trap. For one thing, the OECD was an unwieldy institution that the French, if they were being mischievous, could use to wage guerrilla warfare against our proposals. The interim measures might be permitted to lapse. In a month's time, the existing unanimity (minus France) might dissolve into second thoughts. The key was whether France and we were agreed on the substance. Another time we might have tried it, but we had lost all confidence; we had, after all, gone this route before. If we now settled directly with France, we might never get the other European nations to hold firm again.

I told Jobert that I would have to check his proposal with Nixon and with the other participants. We would be able to consider it only if he would support the establishment of interim machinery along the lines apparently backed by the consensus of the conference; if Pompidou promised a positive French vote at the conference; if, in short, the OECD in Paris was primarily a ratification and elaboration of decisions taken in Washington.

To my amazement, Jobert said that he would submit these propositions to Pompidou. In turn I informed Home of the conversation, reiterating my promise to take no separate step with Jobert that the other members of the European Community had not approved (a neat reversal of the procedures on the Atlantic Declaration).

There was another brief plenary session at 5:00 P.M. with everyone still marking time waiting for Jobert.

Around 6:30 P.M. I went to a private party for the ninetieth birthday of Mrs. Alice Roosevelt Longworth, Theodore Roosevelt's daughter, whose life spanned our century. Nixon attended too, being a great admirer of that astringent, waspish lady with the wicked sense of humor. He had introduced her to me as my "date" at a small family dinner during his first week in the White House. On that occasion I was still an obscure member of the White House staff and, having just left academic life, slightly overwhelmed by the propinquity to power and not at all sure how I would fare. "You will be a great success," she had said then. "You have that twinkle in the eye."

Mrs. Longworth was one of the few members of the old Eastern Establishment from whom Nixon felt no threat or condescension. She was now beyond ambition and she was wise. She remembered a Washington where the President could go riding every afternoon in Rock Creek Park and spend months at a time in Oyster Bay. She had seen too much of human foibles and of Washington skulduggery to be impressed by the self-important. She had experienced the perishability of fame; she knew the meaning of character. At the height of my power she had told me once that the day would inevitably come when I left office and then my test would be how I reacted to my successors — not publicly but in the recesses of my soul. Would I have compassion for their discomfitures or secretly relish them? She confessed that she and her father had failed that test miserably during the Administration of President Taft.

I met Alice Longworth regularly at the home of various friends; once or twice she invited me to dinner. She held court now in her musty old house on Massachusetts Avenue. A frail old lady with wispy gray hair, she nevertheless seemed more up-to-date and more relevant than most of the colleagues with whom I had just spent the day. We had all talked glibly of revolutionary change and the need to rise to our challenge. But as I thought of current leaders, I saw none who would age as gracefully as Alice Longworth. Lacking the inward assurance, they would be afraid to risk themselves. How many world leaders would be impressive separate from the power they exercised? How many could stand failure or loss of office without losing confidence in themselves? And if they were afraid to fail, how could they succeed? How would they dare to transcend the conventional — the requirement for truly dealing with revolutionary events — when they were emotionally anchored in it?

Within minutes of my return to my office, the humdrum reclaimed us. Sir Alec Douglas-Home — the minister who came closest to Alice Longworth's qualities — called to report the result of the European caucus. All the Europeans, he said, were absolutely firm with the French that there had to be a follow-up to this conference. They simply could not tolerate failure. Jobert was dead set against follow-up machinery of any kind, but his colleagues were willing to proceed in the plenary session to declare that they all agreed to appoint officials to a follow-up meeting; France could either join or reserve its position.

Home added that Jobert had cabled back to Paris for instructions. He warned that we must not wind up with a "washy formula, a papered over thing." Aware of my Gaullist leanings, he urged me to hold firm with Jobert. I repeated once more that I would not move beyond agreed positions and that I would consult with him before doing anything.

The occasion that Home both feared and hoped for never arose. Jobert's instructions were reaffirmed — or so he told us. Pompidou rejected the compromise discussed between Jobert and me. He would not permit Jobert to go along with the follow-up machinery proposed by the Europeans. There was nothing, now, except to break the deadlock at the plenary session.

The Consumers Unite

THE conference reassembled at 9:50 A.M., Wednesday, February 13. A working group had prepared a draft communiqué affirming that the energy crisis was a global problem from which no nation could hope to insulate itself. The draft affirmed "the need for a comprehensive action program to deal with all facets of the world energy situation by cooperative measures." It then listed for special attention the seven areas I had outlined in my opening speech. To this end, it established a group headed by senior officials with a full-time staff to coordinate implementation.

I decided to hold two plenary sessions in the morning. The first would deal with principles underlying the communiqué, the second with approval of the actual text. This procedure would avoid the impression of American imposition; it would also prevent delaying tactics in the form of haggling over communiqué phrases. Also, if some new, unforeseen resistance were to develop, there would be an opportunity for adjustment in the second session.

I had arranged for the conceptual part of the communiqué to be introduced by Foreign Minister Knut Frydenlund of Norway, an old and trusted friend of many years. He had the advantage of representing a country that was not a member of the European Community, thus sidestepping the issue of Community instructions. Ohira of Japan had already agreed to introduce the proposal on follow-on institutions. To buffer the collision further, every foreign minister would be given an opportunity to speak — though all of them knew what the key speeches would say. I went around the table starting on my left, which had the advantage that Jobert would get the floor only after Frydenlund and Ohira had already spoken. A chairman who has all except one minister on his side can afford such "conferencemanship."

At the beginning, the affair went as planned. Frydenlund could not have been more effective, obscuring his sharp mind with a facade of ponderous bonhomie. It was not until we reached Ohira that things started getting out of hand. The Japanese Foreign Minister made a lengthy statement. The only trouble was that its meaning was impenetrable. He was too elegantly Japanese to make a clear-cut point in a confrontational situation; instead, he presented his view in the Japanese manner, sketching both points of view with just a slight weight in favor of the direction we favored. It was masterfully subtle but not suitable for a showdown because to the uninitiated it sounded as if there was considerable merit in the French position as well as in ours. It was hard to distill a votable proposition out of so much indirection, a fact reflected in the baffled expressions around the table, especially among those who had been led to expect a breakthrough.

Alec Home saved the day. With the classy effrontery that can be acquired only from several centuries of aristocratic forebears, he took the floor as soon as Ohira had finished. "If I understand the distinguished foreign minister of Japan correctly," Home began, and then summed up the previously agreed position in a manner vaguely reminiscent of some things Ohira had implied but of nothing that he had actually said. Beaming at the one civilized colleague among a group of clumsy barbarians, Ohira announced that he had indeed been clearly understood. He could be satisfied because in its skillful Japanese way his speech had broken the deadlock after all.

The conference had to endure another vitriolic attack by Jobert aimed equally at his European partners, especially Schmidt, and at the United States. By 11:40 A.M., the principles were agreed.

At 12:36 P.M., the second plenary session assembled to consider the communiqué. It was adopted as drafted; only France dissented from the operational parts outlining specific tasks for consumer cooperation and creating follow-up machinery.

We had achieved much of what we had set out to accomplish. A consumers' organization would now emerge. To be sure, it had not been given an heroic mission; it was much easier to achieve cooperation on issues involving no risk of confrontation, such as conservation, emergency sharing, development of new energy sources. But the sum total of these efforts would be to strengthen the bargaining position of the consumers vis-à-vis the producers. Some participants would deny that this was the purpose and even believe it in their fear of the moment. But reality transcends what people say about it, and the reality of what came to be known as the International Energy Agency (formally established later in the year) was to promote the cohesion of the industrial democracies in the field of energy, which in turn made a major contribution to improving the bargaining position of the consumers.

In buoyant spirits, I called all the members of the American delegation to thank them for their contributions. It had been almost a textbook case of meticulous preparation and disciplined execution. The steering committee of Shultz, Burns, Simon, Bruce, and me had operated free of normal bureaucratic backbiting. This group had established the conceptual framework of the conference, refining tactics almost daily. The working group mentioned earlier had done the actual drafting. These dedicated officials ensured that the American side was by far the best prepared and that the conference — contrary to Jobert's petulant remarks — was one of the most productive and effective in memory.

A century earlier, that would have been the end of it. But in our time there is a referee for international events awarding the palm of victory: The media follow their own necessities and they pronounce on the significance of the outcome. The diplomat is considered biased; the journalists act as judge and jury and they decide what the public will hear or read. By nature they are more finely attuned to the drama of the moment than to the trends of the future, which they discount with a skeptical, even cynical, eye. No international gathering is really over, in other words, until it has been explained in the media. Therefore each of the chief protagonists of the Washington conference was compelled to mount the stage, act out his part in the drama, and promote his own perceptions, seeking to influence future events by shaping the interpretation of current ones. And thus the news conferences by Jobert and me during the course of the afternoon must be seen as the last stage of the Washington conference. (Of course, other delegations also briefed their own press but they neither received the attention nor did they seek it, since it was in their interest to play down controversy and to hedge their bets.)

I let Jobert go on first, not simply as a matter of courtesy but so that I could adjust my remarks to his. He would, I judged, stress the struggle of the moment; this would only lend emphasis to my proposed theme of the necessity of cooperation. Jobert knew my purpose well enough but he had in fact no choice, because with Europe six hours ahead of Washington he had to make his case quickly or not at all. Jobert was at his most acerbic. He rejected the proposition that the Washington Energy Conference had accomplished anything of consequence. It was all a clever American ruse to dominate Europe:

I believe that quite wrongly, the headlines used in this affair were too large. After all, from our viewpoint this conference has been a minor one, slightly slap-dash in its preparation and even a little slap-dash in the way it was conceived, because when it was convened all these important lines were not yet apparent. A lot of papers had to be received later. . . . [It seems to have been] a slightly political operation probably for the benefit of the United States — consciously or unconsciously, I do not know — and . . . energy was largely an excuse.

He repeated his Baghdad wisecrack that the Washington conference was not like the Congress of Vienna; in other words, it was not destined to leave any permanent mark. He reiterated that he had never wanted to come in the first place; he had yielded reluctantly to the entreaties of his European partners and with goodwill toward them (not, by implication, toward the United States); he had come on the basis of a previously agreed position:

> But since they wanted me to go with them aware as they were of the French Government's objections to this conference, I agreed to accompany them as soon as they were good enough to sign an agreement with me which apparently satisfied everyone.

This was a not too subtle way of asserting that his European colleagues had betrayed him by violating the Community's mandate. He did not explain how a vote of eight to one against him could violate the intentions of the European Community. Nor did he consider the vote as final: "Some people spoke from emotion rather than reason. Maybe once they are home they will see the difference between emotion and reason."

Jobert held Helmut Schmidt personally responsible, denouncing him for choosing America over Europe — as if these were inherently antagonistic concepts. While he was engaged in personalities, he took a personal swipe at me. He objected to a newspaper article that had drawn parallels between his life and mine because we had both been born abroad — he in Morocco — and had both come to the countries we now represented as adolescents. Jobert would accept no such comparison; he was French, but I not quite American: "You see how Americans see things. I think our listeners know quite simply that I was born in Morocco in fact and that I have always been French."

Forbearance is not usually my forte. In this instance, anything less would have defeated our purpose. What we had secured would have to be carried out in a cooperative spirit over many years and would one day, we hoped, include France. It was in Jobert's interest to downplay the conference, it was in ours to downplay the controversy. His strategy required an emphasis on the present; ours, a steady vision of the future. Therefore I opened my press conference on a conciliatory note:

> [T]his conference . . . was based on the assumption, on our conviction, that the world was facing a problem that had come upon it — at least in the dimensions in which we faced it — somewhat unexpectedly. And in a situation of seeming supply shortages there was a tendency to react with panic, produced in part by lack of information, and with a sense that perhaps the control over our destiny had escaped us.
>
> To this supply shortage was added at the end of December the serious problem of the rapid escalation of prices.
>
> The United States holds the view that the problem that has been produced by these two phenomena — the demand, at least for a while, outrunning supply and the rapid increase of prices — can be solved only on a global basis and by multilateral action.
>
> We hold this view not to vindicate any particular theory of the organization

of the world. We have not advocated institutions simply to create institutions. We were convinced, and remain convinced, that it is a problem of global nature incapable of isolated solution and indeed a problem *par excellence* in which the general interest is identical with the individual interest. . . .

I refused to take Jobert's bait. Disagreements with France were temporary; Atlantic unity was not in danger:

The United States considers the Atlantic relationship the pivot of its foreign policy. Our efforts during the last year have been directed toward strengthening that relationship.

The fact that there are some differences of view between us and France on how this Atlantic relationship should be strengthened should not obscure the central importance we attach to it nor our recognition that friendship with all European countries, including France, is essential for the security of all of the nations of the Atlantic alliance. . . .

The industrial democracies, in my view, would not be able to maintain even their domestic cohesion, much less their relationship with one another, unless they acted in a manner perceived by their publics as mastering the new economic challenge. A policy of jockeying for national advantage in the hope of riding out the immediate crisis was bound to fail — weakening confidence in democratic institutions, demoralizing governments, and eroding political ties on which Western security depended. Next to this stake, the quarrels between France and the United States were petty and indeed unworthy. And I thought it our duty to end them at the earliest opportunity.

The Washington Energy Conference contributed to this ultimate goal. At the beginning of my conversation with Ohira, Japanese Ambassador Takeshi Yasukawa had commented that if the conference turned out not to be a failure it would have to be judged a success. I disagreed: If it was not a success, I said, it should be considered a failure. Like many a play on words, it reflected an attitude. Failure was easy to determine; success was bound to be fragile. On the tactical level we had done well. We saw a conference of thirteen nations through to a conclusion that the other participants had initially hesitated to embrace out of fear of annoying the oil producers. Over the next years the democracies systematically put the key elements of our proposed strategy into place: conservation, financial safety nets, technical cooperation, emergency sharing plans, help for developing countries. Despite many misgivings, the conference had created an organization of consumer unity and given it tasks that over time were bound to strengthen the consumers. The International Energy Agency has thrived, and it remains to this writing the principal vehicle of solidarity among the industrial democracies on energy.

Over the years ahead the energy situation improved considerably, partly due to growing consumer solidarity. The world oil market stabilized. For five years after the shock of 1973, there were no further dramatic increases in the price of oil. From 1974 through 1978 the price rose less than world inflation; the real price of oil in fact *declined* by some 25 percent over that period.[3] It took the upheaval in Iran in 1978–1979, with the loss of four million barrels of Iranian oil a day, to trigger another price spiral, which seems to have been arrested at this writing partly by an intensification of the measures of conservation and substitution we put forward in 1974.

Another Blowup

THE immediate aftermath of the conference, however, was dominated by the legacies of the controversies just surmounted, not a sense of direction. Before we achieved our goal, we had yet to endure the explosion that we had avoided in Washington. Normally, a diplomat expects an occasional disappointment; he knows that if everything is sacrificed to vindicating the point of view of one party on every issue, all trust is destroyed. Jobert did not accept such restraints. He was determined to thwart the emergence of America as leader of the industrial democracies — the Gaullist nightmare. He could not undo the decisions of the energy conference, but he could press within the European Community for decisions that he knew would generate conflict with the United States. And his colleagues were tempted to conciliate him to compensate for their uncharacteristic resolution at the energy conference.

In the weeks after the energy conference, therefore, Jobert's assault was unremitting. In a briefing of the foreign affairs committee of the French National Assembly on February 21 he defended his conduct, claiming that he had never raised his voice though he had been insulted and brutalized. He complained elsewhere that the United States had insisted that France had no right to make any bilateral arrangement with oil-producing Arab countries. (In fact, we had emphasized the self-defeating nature of bilateral deals in general.) That same day a well-placed Quai d'Orsay official told our Embassy that the heart of the current French analysis of European-American relations was that the United States was attempting to "resume the direction of operations in Atlantic affairs." He mocked my planned stopover in London to brief the British on my Mideast diplomacy, saying it "embarrassed" my hosts (who had specifically requested the visit).

The image of Atlantic relations as an endless contest between the United States and France for dominance of the Alliance was as far as possible from our conception — and even more, our execution. Indeed, our biggest mistake had been too eager an effort to collaborate with

France in 1973, carried to lengths that had alienated the other Europeans, especially the smaller members of the Community. The combination of obsession and misrepresentation came to a peak in a long background interview that Jobert gave to the influential French journal *Le Point*. Jobert made three points: first, that the US–Soviet Agreement on the Prevention of Nuclear War was a watershed, establishing a special relationship between the superpowers amounting to condominium; second, that November 6, 1973, was another watershed, because Europe in formulating its own Mideast policy had issued a sort of declaration of independence from the United States; and third, that Jobert had finally realized that I did not really favor European unity, as supposedly shown by my repeated proposals to deal with only the three major countries in Europe.

What was true in these arguments — the second point — was the heart of the problem; the remaining two assertions were false and demogogic. Matters had reached a pretty pass when Europe had to prove its independence by thwarting the sole peace process taking place in the Middle East. Whatever one's view about the wisdom of the Agreement on the Prevention of Nuclear War (and I do not think it was one of our greatest triumphs) Jobert knew very well — we had told him repeatedly — that it was our way of putting an embarrassing Soviet proposal on ice and elaborating a legal obstacle to an attack on China, not a new direction of policy. As for our alleged preference for negotiating only with the major countries in Europe, it was the opposite of the truth and breathtakingly cynical. It was Jobert who had made cooperation in the Year of Europe dependent on dealing only with the major countries and only bilaterally. That France opposed our course was understandable; the bitterness of the assault was dangerous and explicable only on the theory that American protection required no reciprocity whatever.

Nor was Jobert's assault confined to Europe. From February 20 to February 23 I attended an important meeting of Western Hemisphere foreign ministers in Mexico City to start a new dialogue between the United States and its neighbors — of no conceivable direct interest to France. In at least one major South American capital, on the day before the Foreign Minister's departure for Mexico City (as the minister told me) the French Ambassador had left him a copy of the Agreement on the Prevention of Nuclear War with a warning against a US–Soviet condominium. And there continued to be allegations, too frequent to be ignored, that some French diplomats in the Middle East were talking in a manner that their excitable hosts construed as advice not to rush headlong into lifting the oil embargo against the United States.[4]

Jobert went further and pursued a European-Arab political dialogue in a manner most calculated to clash with the American peace diplomacy. Even with the best of intentions, a gathering of all Arab foreign ministers would inevitably place the moderates under pressure from the radicals and the Europeans would end up endorsing a radical-leaning program at odds with what we considered realistic. I had made this point emphatically to several allied foreign ministers at the Washington Energy Conference, including Home and Scheel. I repeated it to Home in London on February 26, when I was on my way to the Middle East for exploratory talks to begin the Syrian disengagement. I shall describe in the next chapter the diplomacy involved and its relationship to the lifting of the oil embargo. For present purposes it is enough to point out that the situation was still delicately poised.

On my way home I scheduled a trip to Bonn for the evening of Sunday, March 3, as a result of Helmut Schmidt's remark to me in Washington that German leaders were hurt because I seemed to use only Paris or London for overnight rest stops. In fact, the reason — at least on the conscious level — was the convenience of the airplane schedulers. But once informed of the symbolic significance Bonn attached to such a visit, I made sure that on my next trip to the Middle East I would stop over in the German capital. And to show our commitment to Atlantic relations I scheduled a briefing of the North Atlantic Council in Brussels for the following afternoon.

These two visits turned into a demonstration of the fallibility of human foresight. For they achieved the exact opposite of our goal, setting the stage for an explosion that finally served as a catharsis.

The foreign ministers of the Community were convening in Brussels early on March 4. It was a sad state of affairs that the Secretary of State of the United States should be at NATO headquarters to brief allied ambassadors while seven foreign ministers were in the same town some fifteen minutes away, not daring to come to my briefing for fear of offending France. But that was the situation and I had decided not to make an issue of it. I even suggested to Scheel, as President of the Council of Ministers, that I could postpone my visit to NATO so as to avoid the appearance of seeking to influence the Europeans. He saw no reason for such punctiliousness, which in truth would have implied that there was some incompatibility between NATO and the European Community.

My conversation with Scheel over dinner on March 3 could not have been more agreeable. He was complimentary about my journey through the Middle East. He discussed Atlantic tension as if it were a French disease to which the Federal Republic was immune. He said he did not understand French policy; Jobert had complexes; his attitude was illogical. "This is why we will never understand what the French objective is."

We were meeting at the Bungalow, the residence built for the German Chancellor along the Rhine in the garden of the nineteenth-century Palais Schaumburg. Konrad Adenauer had moved the Chancellor's office into the Palais when Bonn became West Germany's new capital. (Adenauer selected Bonn because it was near his residence some ten miles away in the village of Rhoendorf. The story went that he had answered a complaint about the selection with the query: "What did you want me to do? Select Rhoendorf?") His successor Ludwig Erhard, not having the benefit of an ancestral home close by, had felt obliged to construct an official residence. What possessed that quintessential middle-class Bavarian to place so modernistic a structure into a traditional setting has never been explained. But the building manages to look heavy, even though one side is glass, and obtrusive, even though it is only one story high. The public rooms are too large, the family rooms amazingly crowded for so elaborate an edifice. Everything seems designed to impress on the occupant that he is only a transient; there is not a hint of anything warm or personal or idiosyncratic. One of the decisions of Willy Brandt that I never questioned was his refusal to live there.

Reflections on architectural style did not interrupt the bonhomie of the evening. Scheel's presentation of Jobert's attitudes was put forward as if it were a common German-American problem to be resolved with patience and the passage of time. In the warm afterglow of the Washington Energy Conference I had no specific complaints; the slow pace of drafting the various Atlantic declarations was nettlesome but essentially irrelevant, for in truth by now the declarations had lost much of their meaning. Scheel announced that a new draft of the Community declaration would be ready in another week's time. We began making plans for a Nixon visit to sign them; the last week of April seemed most suitable.

At the very end of the conversation, Scheel mentioned in passing that when the Community foreign ministers dealt with the European-Arab dialogue the next day (as newspapers had been hinting), they would probably agree to some exchanges in technical fields such as health and science. I saw no problem with that and quickly passed on to other subjects.

The next morning I called on Chancellor Brandt in Venusberg, a hillside suburb of Bonn, at what had originally been the official residence of the Foreign Minister, a post he had occupied in the late 1960s. He had maintained his domicile in this more human house on a mountain overlooking Bonn even after his elevation to Chancellor. Brandt was only two months away from being forced out of office; he had the melancholy, faraway look I had come to know so well from Nixon that seemed to augur the imminent loss of something cherished. There were pauses in our conversation, but no tension. I covered many of the same topics as with Scheel the night before. I explained again the risk that any gathering of European and Arab foreign ministers would reinforce the Arab radicals; on too many occasions I had seen how individual Arab ministers were moderate when alone with me but were forced to take more extreme positions when thrown together with their brethren. We were not against European unity, I told him, whatever Jobert's insinuations: "A European identity is not inconsistent with consulting with us on matters that concern us both." There was no hint from Brandt that anything unusual was about to happen in Brussels.

From Brandt's residence I helicoptered to the airport and reached Brussels about 2:00 P.M. Arriving at NATO headquarters, I found a message from Scheel that he would appreciate it if I called on him at the German Embassy in downtown Brussels after finishing my NATO chores. He wanted to brief me about that morning's meeting of the Community ministers. The European Community's psychological separation from NATO had evidently reached the point where the President of its Council of Ministers could no longer go to the headquarters that ensured the common defense to talk to Europe's principal ally — even though he knew that NATO headquarters was right next to the airport and I had a long transatlantic flight ahead of me.

I explained to the NATO ambassadors our overall Middle East strategy as well as the diplomacy we intended to pursue over the coming months — in somewhat general terms but specific enough so that the Middle East parties would recognize the outline of what had been agreed when the briefing would be played back to them, as I was certain it would be. Afterward, NATO Secretary General Joseph Luns and I met the press in an optimistic atmosphere. I gave my impression that

around the table in the NATO Council there was a considerable unity of views as to the objectives and considerable understanding as to the method. I do not recall that any contrary views were expressed. Am I unfair, Mr. Secretary General?

Luns exuberantly stressed that I had been too modest. There had been more than unity:

There was on the part of all the countries of the Alliance great appreciation for what the United States in the person of its Secretary of State has been doing in the Middle East since November last when the first talks started. We have been somewhat encouraged by the prospect of going step by step further in the direction of a peace which will be in the interest of all the members.

The happy atmosphere disappeared with a thunderbolt. Was I aware, a journalist wanted to know, that the nine ministers of the European Community had just announced in the person of Walter Scheel their decision to open a European-Arab dialogue in many fields culminating in a foreign ministers' meeting? I replied stiffly that it would be improper to comment on something of which I had not yet been officially informed. I looked forward to my meeting with Scheel at the German Embassy.

There was little doubt of what had happened. Despite the absence of a British foreign secretary — Edward Heath had just lost the general election — Jobert had forced a decision; his colleagues had been unable to resist, or perhaps had compensated for having deserted him at the Washington Energy Conference. I had warned the Community for months that a decision like the one now apparently taken would cause us to dissociate ourselves openly. I was not about to back off now, especially when our Middle Eastern policy stood so narrowly poised.

The shock of being presented publicly and without warning with a fait accompli turned the meeting with Scheel chilly despite the fact that less than twenty-four hours earlier we had shared a most pleasant evening. Scheel now outlined a procedure, no aspect of which had ever been discussed with us. It was the French plan for the Euro-Arab dialogue. Scheel could have no doubt that we would be far from pleased. He tried to assuage us by promising a new draft of the declaration of the European Community (see Chapter XVI) within two weeks, as if the rhetorical affirmation of Atlantic unity was a special favor to us for which we would accept unilateral actions belying that unity. And he expressed his willingness to arrange an invitation to Nixon for the second half of April — as if Nixon would swallow anything for the domestic boon a trip to Europe would bring him. I replied sharply:

I note that we are now being informed of a decision after first having read about it in the newspapers and after I have been asked about it at a press conference. This, therefore, underlines our concern about decisions which are prepared without informing us and taken without consultation with us.

Second, the fact that the Community has no interest in undermining peace efforts is largely irrelevant. The Community is not able to guarantee that this will not happen in any event.

Third, I have already told you what our strong views are on bringing the Arabs together in this way.

Fourth, the United States will reserve its freedom of action to take similar steps if we believe them to be in our own national interests, and to report on them to the Community thereafter.

Fifth, I say in all seriousness that the United States will not accept this procedure in the long run without its having a great effect on our relationship.

Scheel, who throughout was cool, composed, and precise, argued that it was all a procedural error. The Community had only carried out its earlier decision made in Copenhagen in December. He would make a public statement that the Community had informed me of the Euro-Arab dialogue; he indicated the Europeans stood ready to invite Nixon to complete the various declarations. But I had had enough of the humiliation of having allies dangle an invitation to our President before us for bargaining purposes:

I would appreciate it if that second part relating to the President's visit were not made public. I will discuss this with the President and let you know his views about the signing of the Declaration. I will let you know whether the new dates for the Political Directors are acceptable, and when the President might come to Europe. . . .

As to Copenhagen, I find it difficult to refer back to that meeting since we were neither informed of that conference or told how the Arabs got there. Yet that Conference led to work about which we were not told, and now to a meeting about which we were not informed. I must say in all formality that this is not a procedure that can last long.

We were determined to draw the line. The new methods of "consultation" between Europe and the United States were being carried beyond the largely theoretical plane of the declarations. We now had divergent policies in areas we considered vital. On my way back from Europe, the soon-to-become-familiar "senior official" on my aircraft briefed the press about the unacceptability of existing procedures and our reaction to the Euro-Arab dialogue. Upon my return on March 6, Nixon sent a sharp letter to Brandt in the latter's capacity as President of the European Community. Nixon recited the familiar objections to both procedure and substance. He canceled for the time being any further American participation in the draft declaration with the European Community pending a review of the situation; the practical consequence was that he was postponing his trip to Europe.

Brandt replied quickly on March 8, urging continuation of work on the declarations, which would "serve to temper discussion on the European-American relationship." He expressed the hope that Nixon might find it possible to come to Brussels in the second half of April. At least we had escaped the demeaning position of appearing as supplicants in a project to invigorate Atlantic ties. However, Brandt defended the European decision to meet with Arabs as a supportive and by no means competitive undertaking.

On March 11, I made an inadvertent contribution to keeping tensions high. Addressing a group of wives of Congressmen — in what I thought was a background session — I said that Europe had never really recovered psychologically from the exhaustion of World War I. The remark was made to explain the reason why a nuclear war would do irreparable damage to all sides; World War I had shown how casualties beyond a certain point could rend the cohesion of societies. Though put forward in the context of US–Soviet relations, the comment was greeted with outrage in some parts of Europe. My own outrage was only slightly less, though it was aimed at my hapless staff, who had failed to inform me that the meeting was open to journalists.

My comment was in any case secondary to the drama that was developing. On March 15 Nixon returned a reply to Brandt. It rejected further efforts to draft a US–European Community declaration and it put on ice the invitation to sign it. It made clear that Nixon placed the national interest above his Watergate problems; he would not come to Europe at any price:

> In our view, a truly consultative relationship would be the most natural and normal manifestation of the partnership which had existed so long between the United States and the Nine within the Atlantic framework. But it seems clear from the experience of the past several months that the Nine have reservations on this score and that therefore the effort to produce formulations that we believe to be essential are bound to lead to continued arguments or even acrimony. On the other hand, to gloss over the obvious difference of view by compromise language would obscure what I believe to be a fundamental issue that must sooner or later be faced on both sides of the Atlantic and could even lead relationships between us to fall into a pattern which we would not want for the future. Consequently, I have concluded that it would be preferable to let the situation mature further in the hope that at a later time events will demonstrate the mutual benefit all of us will derive from the achievement of more organic, consultative arrangements. In these circumstances, the possibility of my participation in the signature of the declaration, which you were kind enough to mention in your letter, should, of course, also be deferred until a later time.

The Nixon letters were largely drafted by my staff and me, but once engaged Nixon took up the cudgels with abandon and with his characteristic instinct for the jugular. On March 15 in a question-and-answer session before the Executives' Club of Chicago, Nixon left little doubt that his patience was at an end:

> Now, the Europeans cannot have it both ways. They cannot have the United States participation and cooperation on the security front and then proceed to have confrontation and even hostility on the economic and political front. And until the Europeans are willing to sit down and cooperate on the economic and political front as well as on the security front, no meeting of heads of government should be scheduled.

On March 19 he repeated the same theme in a question-and-answer session before the National Association of Broadcasters in Houston. By then new forces were at work.

Our hectic Mideast diplomacy was paying off. On March 18 the Arab oil ministers lifted the embargo unconditionally, subject to a review on June 1, which never took place. A day later Saudi Arabia announced it was increasing its oil production by one million barrels a day, helping to stabilize prices. The sense of panic in Europe immediately diminished. European attitudes began to change. In some ways our firm reaction had lanced the boil. If we no longer pressed for an Atlantic Declaration or for a trip by Nixon to Europe, the Europeans could no longer imagine that they had leverage on us. The substantive disagreements were no cause for crises. We favored European unity; we simply did not want its organizing principle to be hostility to the United States. What we asked for in consultation was what the Community did with every other area of the world. The blowup had developed from an unusual mix of events and people. Nixon's Watergate ordeal, the growing weakness of both the Heath and Brandt governments, and Pompidou's fatal illness threw Atlantic policy into unnecessary confusion.

Other events began to alter the political landscape. By the time the explosion occurred, Edward Heath — almost compulsively reluctant to separate from France — had been defeated in the election of February 28. The successor Labour government under Harold Wilson had a more subtle view of the requirements of European unity. When I passed through London a month later, the new Foreign Secretary, James Callaghan, told his subordinates in my presence that he wanted an end put to the mutual needling. On March 16 the German Ambassador in Washington, Berndt von Staden, came up with an idea for new consultative machinery: The Community would no longer delay consultation until the foreign ministers had frozen the various projects in concrete. What did I think of consultations after the political directors had agreed but before an issue had been put before the foreign ministers? I told von Staden that this would probably solve the procedural problem.

On March 24 I stopped in Bonn, at the request of Scheel, on the way to Moscow. Brandt unexpectedly joined the meeting. The German leaders transformed von Staden's ideas into a formal proposal. I accepted it on the spot, having previously discussed it with Nixon. While we were at it, we reviewed a whole host of issues before the Alliance and reached a common position. There was no longer any hint that this was prevented by Community procedures.

A little more than a week later, Georges Pompidou died, and therewith Jobert's tenure drew to a close. In early April I had most conciliatory meetings with Scheel and Gaston Thorn, then Luxembourg Foreign Minister, whose career proved to what extent integrity, intelligence, and goodwill in even a tiny country can be turned into important, sometimes decisive, factors. The British took over the drafting of the NATO declaration. Key elements of the proposed declaration between the United States and the European Community were incorporated into it; the rest were dropped. The new French government under the Presidency of Valéry Giscard d'Estaing, with Jean Sauvagnargues as Foreign Minister, dealt with us in a new spirit. By the next NATO meeting in Ottawa in June, the immediate crisis was over. By then, too, Brandt had been replaced by Helmut Schmidt, who had already made clear his priorities at the energy conference. What emerged at Ottawa was the single Atlantic Declaration we had proposed in the first place.

The close relationship we had sought to achieve with formal declarations came about instead as a result of common necessity, practical arrangements, and a restoration of mutual human confidence. Suddenly, key issues were handled easily; consultations were regular and intimate. Mid-1974 ushered in one of the best periods of Atlantic cooperation in decades.

And yet the free world's problem was deeper than personalities and broader than energy. It remains my conviction that the vitality of democracy in the modern period depends in large part on public confidence that the democratic world is master of its own future. As economic difficulty ate away at the morale, optimism, and social peace of the industrial nations, an emphatic demonstration of an effective collective response seemed to me of profound political and moral importance. Our divisions would only compound the pervasive sense of helplessness, dependency, and vulnerability in the West and encourage those forces in the world that consider the West decadent and doomed. The challenge remains. If we truly value our civilization, we will maintain the unity and common purpose that give it both its meaning and its strength.

XXI

The Road to Damascus:
An Exploratory Shuttle

ETWEEN the energy conference and the explosion with our allies,
I flew to the Middle East for another shuttle, less dramatic in its
results but almost as important in its consequences as the Sinai
negotiation a little more than four weeks earlier.

Our diplomatic strategy for the Middle East hinged, in February 1974,
on reconciling two mortal enemies, Israel and Syria. Everything turned
on the perception of our ability to negotiate between them a disengagement of forces on the Golan Heights. Insofar as Arab leaders thought
that the United States and only the United States could achieve it, there
was credibility to our position that we would not mediate unless the oil
embargo was called off. The linkage was audacious, for we ourselves
wanted to pursue such a negotiation so as to continue to dominate Mideast diplomacy and prevent the isolation of Sadat. But turning the oil
weapon against the producers was more than a tactic. It was at the heart
of our policy to rally the oil-consuming countries who were so worried
about oil supplies that they were in danger of succumbing to political
blackmail. It was a piece of necessary bravado when we told them at
the Washington Energy Conference that we would end the embargo on
our own without anyone's help.

A less auspicious pair for mediation than Israel and Syria would be
hard to imagine. Deeply distrustful of each other as only nations can be
that claim the same soil, they had lived in sullen enmity for a generation, hatred for the other indelible in each country's soul. Syrians considered Palestine part of "Greater Syria" and the Jewish state the obstacle to Arab unification. Israelis recognized that among their immediate
neighbors Syria was the most militant and implacable. Deep down, Egypt
had no Palestinian vocation; it had to overcome nationalist impulses to
dedicate itself to that cause. Indeed, it is a tribute to the power of Arab
ideology that Egypt sacrificed so much for so long for an enterprise
emotionally so distant. Lebanon yearned for peace but was too anxious
for its own fragile cohesion to play an active role in Mideast diplomacy.

It advocated a Palestinian homeland but for a negative reason: to solve the problem of the refugee Palestinian population in Lebanon that threatened to destroy the fabric of the nation, and later carried out the threat. The Hashemite Kingdom of Jordan had been prepared to negotiate at almost every stage. Only Syria had made intransigence a national characteristic. It had steadfastly refused to accept Israel, to talk to Israel in any forum, or to entertain any mediation based on the proposition that Israel had a right to exist.

The persecution of Jews in Syria and its history of hostile instability fused menace with mystery in Israeli eyes. Yet strangely enough — and as much as both Syrians and Israelis will resent me for saying this — they were more similar in attitude and behavior than either was to Egypt, for example. The Egyptian leadership group is suave, jaded, cosmopolitan. Their Syrian counterparts are prickly, proud, quick to take offense. Egypt is accustomed to leadership in the Middle East; there is a certain majesty in its conduct and in its self-assurance. Syria fights for recognition of its merit; it consumes energy in warding off condescension. Israel shares many of Syria's qualities.

The Egyptian President was sure of his authority; he did not need to build a consensus for individual acts, or if he did, he managed masterfully to obscure the process by which he achieved it. Sadat in one form or another had been negotiating since 1971; Hafez al-Asad was entering the negotiating process for the first time. For so controversial a move as a negotiation with Israel, he had to build a consensus daily, maybe even hourly. Even had he been so disposed, he could not dare the great gestures of Sadat, who sacrificed tactical benefit for long-term gain. The Syrian President needed to win every point if he wished to retain his authority; he could yield only to overwhelming *force majeure*. The Israeli leaders, for wholly different reasons, were in the same position.

But had each side understood the domestic difficulties of the other — and of them they were, in fact, woefully ignorant — it would not have helped a great deal. The mirror image of a dilemma is a dilemma. Neither could transcend itself. Even finding a framework for negotiations between them was a struggle.

To begin with, there was no Israeli cabinet decision to proceed with a negotiation with Syria on disengagement; indeed, in a manner of speaking there was no Israeli cabinet. Discussions on forming a new government after the inconclusive general election of December 31, 1973, were still proceeding. The governing Labour Party's loss of seven seats proved fateful in a small Parliament of 120 in which coalitions had to emerge from many groupings. The Likud opposition headed by Menachem Begin was in no position to take over; but neither was Labour able to form a new government on its own without, in Dayan's words, "having to make far-reaching concessions to a few small parties for joining a coalition."[1] As Golda Meir wrote of the election outcome, the entire right wing had now combined into a bloc of its own. A coalition would have to be formed again, and it would clearly be a back-breaking job to form it, since the religious bloc, which was a traditional coalition partner of ours, was itself deeply divided on the question of who should lead it and what its policy should be at this tremendously difficult time.[2]

In the meantime, the old cabinet ministers were frozen in their jobs by the quirk of Israeli law that no member of an interim government is permitted to resign. Stable as is no other Israeli cabinet and yet conscious of its ephemerality, the caretaker government maneuvers amidst perils, temptations, and pressures. It was aware that the Egyptian disengagement might wither if not matched on the Golan Heights and that the prolongation of the oil embargo would then be blamed on Israel. But it also knew that public sentiment in Israel regarded peace with Syria as a delusion. Sporadic artillery duels persisted between Syrian and Israeli units on the Golan Heights throughout this period.

The Golan, moreover, was not the Sinai. The Suez Canal was over two hundred kilometers from Israel's 1967 border, across a useless and unpopulated desert. The depth of the Israeli penetration on the Golan Heights after the 1967 war was about twenty-five kilometers; the Israeli salient toward Damascus after the 1973 war added roughly an equal distance. Everything about the Golan was immeasurably more complicated than the Sinai. Much less territory was available to bargain over; every mile of territory came close to having strategic significance. There were few Israeli settlements in the Sinai, mainly close to Israel's borders. But Israel had established twenty-odd in the crowded Golan, many within a few kilometers of the 1967 armistice line (see the map on page 938). Since Israel had never yet abandoned a settlement in its history and would surely not do so for a mere disengagement accord, the margin for compromise on withdrawal was narrow. And Syria, it was expected, would want to repopulate the towns and villages in the area, flooding them with thousands of civilians and complicating Israel's security problem as well as the task of inspecting agreed arms limitations. Finally, Syria had neighbors — specifically radical, Baathist Iraq — opposed to any negotiations with Israel and in deadly rivalry with its sister party in Damascus.

Against this background, neither side moved with particular grace; each tended to phrase its contributions to the peace process in the form of peremptory demands. But to their credit, both the Israeli cabinet and the Syrian President overcame their misgivings.

The attempt to reconcile the apparently irreconcilable began on Sunday, January 20, 1974. Before returning home after completing the Egyptian-Israeli disengagement agreement, I had stopped in Damascus to symbolize our interest in progress on the Syrian front. Asad had given me his ideas for disengagement. They were not modest. He showed his

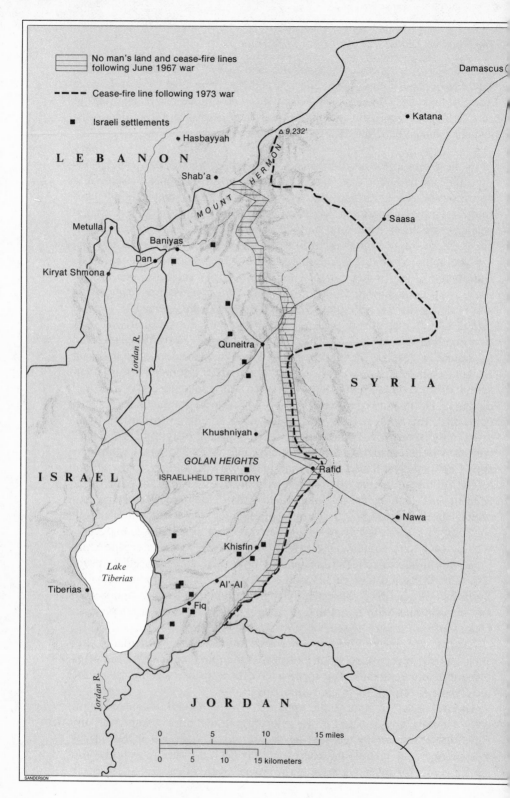

The Golan Front: Cease-Fire Line after the October War

inexperience in negotiation by suggesting three options for Israeli withdrawal — guaranteeing that only the one most favorable to Israel would receive any consideration. But not much consideration. Even his minimum option required that Israel abandon all Syrian territory captured in the 1973 war as well as half of the Golan taken in 1967, in return for a mere cease-fire and separation of forces. But the hard line was less significant than the fact that Syria was willing to negotiate at all. That marked a sea change in Syria's attitude. To give the impression of progress, I stopped in Tel Aviv that same evening and left Asad's ideas with an Israeli negotiating team so reluctant to confront them that it refused even to haggle.

On January 28, now back in Washington, I received Mrs. Meir's formal reply. In order to avoid having to put the issue before her caretaker cabinet, she raised a condition: There could be no negotiation until there was some sign that Israeli prisoners of war held in Syria would be returned. At a minimum, Israel wanted the names of its POWs and Red Cross visits to verify their treatment. By now I was getting more skilled at the exegesis of Israeli formulations. I pointed out to Israeli Ambassador Simcha Dinitz that Golda had carefully avoided saying that she *would* negotiate if these conditions were fulfilled. Dinitz admitted that this was so; the lack of a cabinet decision left no other choice. However, he believed that Syrian compliance with these terms would make the start of negotiations highly probable.

I decided to act on this assumption. On January 29 I informed Asad (and Sadat) that if Syria provided a list of prisoners and permitted Red Cross visits there was a good chance of obtaining an Israeli counterproposal on disengagement. On January 30 Dinitz confirmed this. Over the next few days, in Washington, I worked out a package deal and a schedule and transmitted them to Asad on February 5.

The proposal contained five steps. First, we would convey to Israel the number of prisoners of war that Syria held. Second, Syria would send the list of names of these Israeli prisoners of war to its Interests Section in Washington. Third, Israel would be asked to come up with a concrete proposal on disengagement, which it would make available to me in exchange for the list of prisoners of war. Fourth, after the Red Cross had visited Israeli prisoners in Syria, I would transmit Israel's disengagement proposal to Asad, and simultaneously ask Israel to send a senior official to Washington to discuss possible modifications. Fifth, a negotiating process would begin, in the framework of the already existing Israeli-Egyptian military working group in Geneva.

I emphasized that I would not proceed with the negotiations, however, until the oil embargo had been lifted: "I will only be able to initiate with Israel such efforts to solve the immediate problem of getting Syrian-Israeli disengagement moving after the oil embargo has been lifted." On February 6 I instructed Ambassador Hermann Eilts in Cairo to inform Egyptian Foreign Minister Ismail Fahmy of the proposal, also stressing that the oil embargo should be lifted "promptly."

Asad waited only forty-eight hours to fulfill the first step I had proposed. On February 7 we received word that the Israeli prisoners in Syria numbered sixty-five. The number exceeded Israeli expectations and it put a floor under Israeli concerns. They knew now that Syria could not deliver fewer as part of a disengagement arrangement.

The Soviet Dilemma

IN the meantime, another visitor had added to our complications. Soviet Foreign Minister Andrei Gromyko, who had accompanied Leonid Brezhnev on a visit to Havana, stopped in Washington on February 4 and 5 to chide us for "unilateral" actions in the Middle East. Before he met Nixon, I summed up the problem posed by Soviet Middle East policy in a memorandum to Nixon:

The Soviets were obviously caught by surprise by the rapid pace of US negotiations with Israel and the Arabs, and, of course, chagrined by their virtual exclusion. Initially, at least, they made their displeasure known, particularly to the Egyptians. But in recent days — as reflected in Brezhnev's remarks in Cuba — the Soviets seem to be shifting to accommodate themselves to the concept of disengagement and to the procedure of piecemeal, temporary settlements. . . . [T]hey are using whatever influence they have in Damascus to encourage the Syrians to negotiate their own disengagement, but on the condition that the link to Geneva be firmly established, and that the Soviets have some role.

The major unknown is whether the Soviets will become a disruptive force in the next phase: whether they will . . . block any serious negotiations or complicate them, for example, by pressing the Palestinians into Geneva. In any case, there are a wide variety of tactical moves they could initiate to ensure that the more fundamental issues remain stalemated. The risk for Moscow is that the negotiations will become a confrontation, with a new risk of war. It is for this reason that the Soviets probably support disengagement which complicates the resort to arms by either side, but leaves the basic questions open for Soviet manipulation.

Gromyko was in an especially dour mood when he met Nixon at 4:30 P.M. on February 4. The President and the scowling Soviet diplomat sat in straight-backed easy chairs flanking the fireplace of the Oval Office. State Department Counselor Helmut Sonnenfeldt, Ambassador Walter Stoessel, and I were on the sofa by Nixon's chair. Soviet Ambassador Anatoly Dobrynin and the interpreter Viktor Sukhodrev were on the opposite sofa. Gromyko accused the United States of systematically violating the understanding, reached on my trip to Moscow in October only a few months earlier, that Mideast negotiations would proceed under joint US–Soviet "auspices." The Soviet Union had its own capacity to act unilaterally in the Middle East, he claimed; it could be obstructive if it chose; it had so far avoided doing so. If we had acted jointly, he added, more progress would already have been made.

Gromyko's version of the meaning of US–Soviet "auspices" was bizarre. We had agreed to joint auspices in Moscow in order to make it more palatable for the Arab states to negotiate directly with Israel; even then we had limited American and Soviet participation to the opening phase and other "key" moments. It had never occurred to anyone that "auspices" should be imposed on parties that might prefer a different procedure or that the understanding should be invoked as a brake on negotiations that were making progress. At the time, it was beyond our imagination that countries that we considered Soviet allies would ultimately prefer to proceed without the Soviets. But this is what happened.

Gromyko's claim that Soviet participation would have advanced matters happened to be the opposite of our assessment. If Gromyko became a full participant in negotiations, he was certain to follow the by-now stereotyped, formalistic Soviet methods: He would put forward a detailed program for comprehensive peace starting from general principles and working down into minute detail. He would then slog his way through this agenda, session after weary session, deepening the stalemate with each round. Such tactics were effective in exhausting peace-loving middle-class societies of the West but they would raise tensions unbearably in the volatile Middle East. Moreover, Soviet policy had shown itself to be wedded to a one-sided version of the Arab position, adding rigidity, not flexibility, to the process. Soviet negotiating methods were paralyzing even if one assumed Soviet good faith; in its absence all the dangerous trends would be accelerated. That view was shared by Sadat as well — not to speak of Israel, which, since Moscow's cutoff of diplomatic relations in 1967, had no interest whatever in Soviet participation.

As for Gromyko's threat that Moscow had the capacity to line up other Arab states against the peace process, we considered it a vast exaggeration — at least during the early phase of the negotiations. Algerian President Houari Boumedienne had told me that he favored our strategy; Syria, Moscow's ally, was insisting on an American role on the Sinai model, that is to say, without the USSR. That left the Soviets with such consorts as Iraq and Libya — hardly enough of a base from which to thwart our efforts, especially while Iran was our ally and was keeping Iraq's armed forces occupied on its eastern frontier, far away from Syria.

We were not prepared to change our strategy, therefore, but we also did not want a blowup with the Soviet Union. It had a capacity for mischief; an all-out Soviet assault on our policy would make our own effort more difficult; in the middle of Watergate, we could not be sure of our domestic support. We wanted to play it cool and get through the Gromyko visit with the minimum of strain.

The Oval Office meeting was made to order for Nixon's skills at obfuscation; he was a master of the philosophical explanation that explained nothing but created the impression that he was sharing a confidence with his interlocutor. So Nixon blithely expressed his satisfaction with the diplomatic progress that had been made. The United States had been active because the parties wanted it that way. There was no record that we had discouraged this development, but that did not keep Nixon from avowing his general preference for cooperative endeavors with the USSR. On the other hand, the concrete circumstances differed for each superpower: "Some areas we can get into where you can't. We must consider this." In other words, Nixon favored superpower cooperation in the Middle East except where it did not serve his purpose. Where and how to work jointly, mused Nixon, was a tactical problem to be solved by Gromyko and me — thus neatly getting himself out of the line of fire. All this was presented in Nixon's best country-boy manner, as if there had been some terrible misunderstanding about a subject too trivial for him to focus on. He was all for US–Soviet cooperation in the Middle East and elsewhere, but he could not be expected to bother with the details. Nixon cheerfully concluded the encounter by expressing his confidence that Gromyko and I would figure out a way to solve the problem.

Gromyko was nobody's fool. He realized very well that Nixon had given him nothing tangible; indeed, at the end of his talk with the President he was right back to where he had started. On the other hand, Nixon had thrown out enough tantalizing hints to tempt an old professional like Gromyko to press me for precision. This he did at a private meeting on February 5. My evasive footwork was generally less nimble than Nixon's; in any event, Gromyko would not accept from me the degree of empty generality that protocol permitted a head of state. It served Gromyko's purpose to pretend that Nixon had agreed in principle never to proceed in the Middle East except on the basis of accord between the Soviet Union and the United States. Of course, I knew my wily chief's mind better than he and I doubt that Gromyko seriously held this view. The extremity of the proposition merely masked the extent of the Soviet predicament. Gromyko had no other options. He wanted to join a diplomacy to which he had little to contribute and, what was more significant, was seeking a role that no Arab client of his was advocating.

Our purpose was not to embarrass the Soviet Union but to obtain freedom of maneuver. If Moscow were genuinely interested in stability in the Middle East, our central negotiating role would prick its vanity but not undermine its interests. Syrian disengagement was needed to defuse the Middle East and to keep open the option of peace. Our helping to mediate it would give us few lasting benefits. Nations rarely pay for services already rendered; our long-term influence would depend on what we could contribute afterward. Gromyko nevertheless put me through the paces. I offered a vague assurance that the United States was prepared in principle to exchange information with the Soviet Union and, when appropriate, act in coordination. He pressed me for specificity. I hid behind the parties concerned; I answered that in fairness we had to ask their views. The nub of the problem, of course, was not simply the absence of diplomatic relations between Moscow and Jerusalem but the Soviets' one-sided commitment to an Arab program that experience had shown to be unfulfillable. It was precisely the realization that the Soviets could produce no progress that was driving the Soviets' best friends in the area — like Syria — in our direction, as it had already convinced Sadat to change course.

While Gromyko sought to determine how far we were prepared to go in joint action, I wanted to find out just what flexibility the Soviet Union might help elicit from the Arab side. It soon became apparent that the Soviets saw their principal contribution to the negotiations as a US–Soviet "guarantee" that peace agreements would not be violated. In Gromyko's interpretation this would authorize superpower intervention in the case of perceived violations, jointly if we agreed, and presumably unilaterally if not — just as Moscow had attempted at the time of the October alert. We could not have any interest in such an arrangement. I probed him for specificity: Would the Mideast parties have to agree to it, or request it? What did he have in mind? We did not exclude participation in guarantees if the parties requested it, but we would not be part of an arrangement by which it could be imposed on them against their will. Gromyko commented wryly that he detected "a lack of enthusiasm." In truth, he and I were sparring, both too professional to have any illusions about the implications of our actions yet still too committed to the US–Soviet relationship to court an open break.

Our strategy sought to reduce the Soviet role in the Middle East because our respective interests in the area (and our different diplomatic styles) could not be reconciled, at least as long as the Soviet Union identified itself only with a maximum Arab program and did nothing to induce compromise on the part of its clients. In these circumstances, the best that could be accomplished by US–Soviet diplomacy was to soften the impact of the clashing Mideast approaches by maintaining enough of a Soviet stake in other areas of our relationship. And we succeeded. The Soviets did not dare risk a deterioration in other dimensions of US–Soviet relations. In that sense, then, it was détente that enabled the

United States to bring about a diplomatic revolution in the Middle East. We would not have had such a margin for unopposed action in a period of open, across-the-board confrontation with the Soviet Union. The Mideast is an important refutation of the facile slogan that détente was a "one-way street."

I kept my promise to Gromyko to check with the parties on the Soviet proposal, which I described in a message to the Syrians of February 6:

that in [the] future all our Middle East diplomatic activities should be carried out on a joint U.S.–Soviet basis and that modalities should be joint. They also want all activities to be carried out in Geneva and to have U.S. and Soviet participation in all Geneva meetings between the parties.

The obligation to check with Damascus was reinforced because it was near-certain that Gromyko would convey some version of his Washington conversation to Asad and it seemed likely that the Kremlin would learn from the Syrians what, if anything, we conveyed. The Israeli reaction was predictable; it would never agree to a Soviet veto or Soviet participation in every negotiating session.

The Syrians' response was more interesting and ambiguous. They put two questions: First, had we told Moscow that we were soliciting Asad's views? And second, had we confided to Moscow the substance of my various exchanges with Asad, including our February 5 plan to start negotiations? This had to mean that Moscow and Damascus were not in such close contact as we thought; specifically, the plan on the basis of which we were proceeding appeared not to have been conveyed to Syria's ally. The Syrians were obviously nervous about Moscow's learning from us what they had failed to communicate. Their queries raised the fascinating possibility that they wanted to exclude the Soviets, despite the alliance, and were attempting to assess what they risked. In fact, the queries implied the answer, for if Syria were going to insist on Soviet participation it would welcome our having told Moscow that it was being consulted. On February 8 we returned a careful reply: We had told Gromyko only that we would solicit Syrian views; we had not specified the level. We had not given the Soviets the details of our February 5 plan.

Asad lost no time in acting on our information. On February 9, we received an extremely careful and subtle formal reply directly from Asad. The Syrian President thanked me for informing him of the US–Soviet talks on the Middle East. Syria had no objection to US–Soviet coordination, he said, but did not have enough information to suggest any practical plan for accomplishing it. If that meant anything, it was that Syria would acquiesce in joint US–Soviet mediation if such was our desire; that Syria would not jeopardize its ties with Moscow to thwart it, but also would make no effort to encourage it.

Clearly, Asad was reluctant about Soviet participation; he was at pains to emphasize that Moscow enjoyed no preferential consultative status in Damascus. He would not even comment on the Soviet proposal for coordination that I had communicated to him. Residual doubts were removed when in the same message Asad accepted the procedures in our plan of February 5 — which excluded Moscow and assigned to the United States the function of mediator.

This sequence dramatized how far Syria had come in the three weeks since the Egyptian disengagement agreement. It had disclosed the number of prisoners it held; it had promised to turn over a list of the prisoners to us and to permit Red Cross visits; and it had agreed to a procedure for American mediation. In return, we were now bound to deliver an Israeli reply to Asad's ideas of what a Golan Heights disengagement should look like. But first we had to make clear that the Golan negotiations would not proceed in isolation. The next day, therefore, I expressed my appreciation for Asad's positive attitude but made clear that the negotiations would not move ahead while the oil embargo continued:

> As the Secretary indicated in his February 5 letter to President Asad, as soon as the oil embargo question has been resolved he will initiate with the Israelis the steps outlined in our procedural proposal. . . . Further steps on our part must await a solution of the embargo question.

Similar messages went to Sadat, Boumedienne, and Faisal, who were about to join Asad in an Arab mini-summit meeting in Algiers beginning on February 12. During the Washington Energy Conference we were awaiting the results of this Arab meeting.

Fahmy and Saqqaf Visit Washington

AT the Washington Energy Conference, it was a byword that a confrontation with the oil producers had to be avoided. References to the need for a consumer dialogue with the producers bordered on the liturgical. Suspicion that the United States did not share these objectives with equal fervor was rampant. Yet the Arab oil-producing countries hardly complained to us, the organizers of the conference. The Arab leaders meeting in Algiers took no special note of the Washington conclave. Our threats of withdrawing from negotiation led not to the brandishing of the oil weapon but to a new appeal to the United States to engage itself in a Syrian negotiation.

This was not apparent immediately, because of the way the real preferences of the key leaders were submerged in an Arab consensus whose rhetoric was heavily influenced by the radicals. I was by now convinced that those who went to Algiers — Sadat, Boumedienne, Faisal, and even Asad — considered the embargo an encumbrance. But none of them wanted to risk being accused of insufficient militance. Each was happy enough to agree to a decision of his brethren but — except for Sadat — each was reluctant to be perceived as the instigator. This was a particular problem for Saudi Arabia, whose defense of overall Arab interests both accorded with its convictions and gave it protection against rapacious radical neighbors. The ambivalence was reflected in a bewildering series of developments.

The Algiers meeting was supposed to be followed by a meeting of Arab oil ministers in Tripoli, Libya, on February 14 to consider lifting the embargo. The first news from Algiers was that the Tripoli meeting was canceled, which meant that the four leaders at the mini-summit were unsure of how much backing they had in the rest of the Arab world. This was followed by a communiqué reaffirming with "total unanimity" the requirement of complete Israeli withdrawal and the "guarantee of the rights of the Arab Palestinian people in their territories and their nation."

It was explained that this hard-line response was a reaction to Israeli intransigence. And to be sure, on February 9, Prime Minister Golda Meir had let herself be tempted into making some highly contentious and unwise statements to a group of Israeli settlers on the Golan Heights. She was much too intelligent not to understand the diplomatic risks but she was being assailed by opposition leader Menachem Begin for being too accommodating — mind-boggling to those who had negotiated with her — and urged by potential coalition partners of the religious parties to be tougher. She had declared that she regarded the Golan Heights with its settlements as an inseparable part of Israel and could not conceive of any withdrawal from the 1967 cease-fire lines with Syria, including the town of Quneitra. On February 11 I told Dinitz that Golda's remarks could not have been more untimely. On February 14 we informed Damascus that we had "taken up Mrs. Meir's statement on the Golan with the Israelis through diplomatic channels."

It turned out, however, that the Algiers communiqué was like a conjurer's movement of the hands. While radicals were being diverted by the tough language, Foreign Ministers Omar Saqqaf and Ismail Fahmy, from Saudi Arabia and Egypt, were being dispatched to Washington to tell us the "secret" conclusions. No one bothered to forewarn us of that happy event, forcing me to turn right around from Key Biscayne, where I had just arrived to spend a quiet weekend with the President.

Meanwhile, I was receiving separate reports from various participants at Algiers. Boumedienne's chief aide told us that the embargo would indeed be lifted at another oil ministers' meeting; that the Syrians would soon give us the list of Israeli prisoners to implement the procedure I had laid down on February 5; and that the four leaders thought I should come to the Middle East immediately to get the negotiating process started. But then we heard from Saudi Oil Minister Yamani, who told

Ambassador James Akins that the mini-summit had failed. Asad had been "adamant"; only Israel had been helped by disengagement in the Sinai; we would have to bring about an initial Israeli withdrawal on the Golan Heights *before* the embargo could be lifted. Was Yamani relaying general gossip or inside information? In Akins's report of a subsequent meeting with King Faisal, the King's exposition was as usual ambiguous: Lifting the embargo would be difficult in the absence of some progress on Syria. The King felt I should go to the Middle East personally as an earnest of our good faith.

On February 16 a Syrian official told our chargé d'affaires in Damascus, the extremely able and energetic Thomas Scotes — a junior edition of Joe Sisco — that the decision was to lift the embargo in stages: a partial lifting at the next oil ministers' meeting; a complete lifting when disengagement on the Golan was completed. He blamed the grudging procedure on Golda Meir's recent statement. Asad was said to be facing major opposition within the Syrian government even for discussing disengagement; he would have to prove his manhood if he was to continue the process. In other words, a show of ferocity was needed to make possible a conciliatory position. Such is the Middle East.

What this confusion of partly conflicting, partly overlapping messages amounted to was that there had been a decision involving some sort of linkage. The embargo would be lifted in step with our progress on the Golan. But while the Algiers decision might be a face-saving device to end the embargo, it was bound to lead us into the trap of escalating conditions that we had no choice except to resist. Syria's plan to release the prisoner list (not yet officially communicated to us) was a hopeful sign. Yet it could also prove to be a tactic enabling Syria to continue insisting on the embargo if the Israeli disengagement proposal it elicited was unacceptable or outrageous — a likely prospect, given the Israeli negotiating style and Golda's domestic difficulties. A trip by me to the Middle East might help mitigate the sharp reaction that was inevitable if Syria's leaders had before them only a paper plan with no explanation. On the other hand, a blowup while I was in the Middle East would leave us no further recourse. My presence could become the excuse either for lifting the embargo or for continuing it.

My inclination was to go for broke and to refuse all further activity until the embargo was irrevocably abandoned. Nixon for once, however, was reluctant to force a showdown. In the tenth month of his torment he was still in thrall to the idea that a dramatic lifting of the embargo under his personal leadership was the cure-all for his Watergate agonies. On this his usually sure political judgment deserted him. He knew that the lines at gasoline stations spelled political disaster; what he could not bring himself to face was that ending them would not ensure political salvation. Not even the most spectacular success could arrest the ponderous doomsday machinery now so inexorably grinding him down. Nevertheless, every few weeks there was some new Presidential plan to send some special emissary to King Faisal with an appeal based on personal friendship. I was always opposed to this as demeaning and more likely to generate pressures than to end them. But since I invariably learned of it only from others to whom Nixon broached the idea, I had — as Nixon intended — no opportunity to make a direct objection.

On February 7, at the very height of our pressure to force an unconditional end of the embargo, Nixon launched another such initiative. He used the opportunity of my absence on a one-day trip to Panama to make a personal appeal via the Saudi Ambassador. Nixon received him in the Map Room to emphasize the special nature of the meeting — and called in photographers. The President then gave in effect his personal guarantee that the end of the embargo would lead not only to a settlement on the Golan but to a permanent peace. He was careful not to draw any final borders, but he left little doubt about his leanings: "We will work out a permanent settlement as quickly as possible. The full prestige of my office is dedicated to that. You should know that that means I will catch it from some groups in this country." Nixon expressed an interest in visiting the Middle East himself, as early as the spring.

I was not informed in advance, and having for three weeks insisted on an unconditional end of the embargo, I was not amused when I learned about the sudden meeting. Brent Scowcroft and I therefore went through our usual minuet. Once informed, I wired him from the Panama-bound plane that I considered the meeting "dangerous" and "counterproductive." Scowcroft responded that the visit of the Ambassador was better than other alternatives (such as sending a special Presidential emissary to Saudi Arabia) — Scowcroft's standard bromide certain both to calm and to disquiet me. In the end, the ambassadorial visit passed without visible impact one way or another.

Now after Algiers I urged the President to use the visit of Fahmy and Saqqaf to force a showdown. My recommendation was to tell the two foreign ministers that Nixon would not receive them unless they were prepared to promise an unconditional end of the oil embargo. I would go to the Middle East in any event in fulfillment of the procedure proposed to Asad on February 5; that is, to obtain an Israeli disengagement plan in return for the list of POWs held in Syria. But we should make clear that further progress would depend on Arab oil policy. We would not act under pressure. Nixon was dubious:

You see, my only interest is the embargo. That's the only thing the country is interested in. They don't give a damn what happens to Syria. That is our problem. I think we should see them but I don't know that we want to build up the fact that you are going out there if it cannot be in any way linked to the embargo — you see the problem we've got there.

My reply was: "Well, it can't be linked to the embargo, Mr. President, and I think the more we build up the embargo the less we are going to get it [removed]."

Nixon, as nearly always when choosing between politics and substance in foreign policy, ultimately accepted the strategic necessities. He agreed that we would refuse to discuss the embargo any further; we would reject linkage, or, more precisely, we would turn it against the oil producers. He would not receive the two emissaries unless there was a promise to end the embargo unconditionally. Thus on February 16 I sent new instructions to our diplomats in Cairo, Jiddah, Kuwait, Algiers, and Damascus:

As part of our overall position in the coming days we intend to refrain from saying anything about the embargo. Our position on this matter has been made clear time and again and we intend to make no further pleas either privately or formally on this point. There, therefore, should be no comments either publicly or privately by posts and anything that will be said on this matter will be said in Washington.

Ismail Fahmy and Omar Saqqaf arrived late on February 16, having terminated what would have been the first restful weekend in two months for me. They were a bit bedraggled because during their flight a coffee-making machine had exploded on the airplane, convincing Saqqaf that they were the targets of a Zionist plot. Everybody calmed down soon enough and, their equilibrium restored, they treated me to a classic display of the tension between unity and individualism in the Arab world.

Saqqaf and Fahmy were Arab brothers; they were also rivals for preeminence. This expressed itself in a dozen little ways. I called for them at the airport and took them to the Shoreham Hotel, where each of them had a suite. We met at Saqqaf's suite — he was the senior of the two emissaries in terms of service. This raised a prickly issue with Fahmy, who had the title of Foreign Minister while his Saudi colleague, performing the same functions, had only the title of Minister of State. Once they were settled, I told them that I was prepared to go to the Middle East to carry the Syrian list of prisoners to Israel in return for a concrete Israeli proposal on Golan disengagement. I gave them my estimate that this first Israeli proposal was bound to be unacceptable to Syria; its primary value was the symbolic opening of negotiations. But the United States would accept no linkage between how the Israelis responded and continuation of the oil embargo. If they wanted to see President Nixon, they would have to promise first that the embargo would be lifted whatever happened on my trip.

Fahmy and Saqqaf were experienced diplomats. They knew that it
would be a loss of face for them to leave Washington without being
received by the President; it would cast doubt on the policy of both their
countries. They understood immediately that the party was over, that a
decision was now unavoidable. And being professionals, they did not
argue or recriminate but sought a solution. They would immediately ask
for instructions; they would have an answer within forty-eight hours.

That left the problem of what to do in the interval. When I escorted
Fahmy to his suite, he proposed that he meet the President alone before
the two emissaries delivered their joint message; he would be able to
give him the "real story" of Algiers. The meeting should, of course,
be kept secret. When I bade him goodbye, he insisted on seeing me not
only to the door of his suite but to the front door of the hotel. It was
partly the legendary Egyptian politeness. At the same time the unworthy
thought struck me that it was a neat way to keep me from having a
separate meeting with Saqqaf.

I chose not to risk the Saudi's jealousy. So I entered my limousine
and had it drive around the block and deposit me at a different entrance
from the one I had just left. (Luckily, the Shoreham Hotel was large
enough for such maneuvers.) Reentering the hotel, I called on Saqqaf,
who immediately proved to me that as far as one-upmanship is concerned, Arab minds run along parallel courses. He too would value a
separate secret meeting with Nixon before delivering the joint démarche. He thought he could make an important contribution to the
President's understanding of the real meaning of their message.

I knew my two friends too well to hope that any such meeting could
take place in secret. Half the fun in having it would be to demonstrate
to the world a special relationship to America. I compromised by seeing
Saqqaf and Fahmy separately on Sunday, February 17, to review the
situation for the umpteenth time. I also breakfasted with Simcha Dinitz
to explain our strategy. The Israeli cabinet had meanwhile done its bit
to complicate matters by informing us that it would refuse to discuss
Syrian disengagement in the Egyptian-Israeli military commission in
Geneva, one of the steps in the five-point plan of February 5. (Luckily,
if we followed the procedure of my shuttling, this would be irrelevant.)

I had yet to hear the formal Arab message from Algiers. All that had
been presented were vague allusions to a linkage between lifting the
embargo and Syrian disengagement.

By 11:35 A.M. on Monday, February 18, over thirty-six hours after
their arrival, the two emissaries had at last received new instructions
and they came to see me at the State Department. They said that they
could unlink lifting the embargo from Syrian disengagement; our tactics
had paid off. The list of Israeli prisoners in Syria was on its way to
Washington and it would be handed to me just before I left for the

Middle East, for delivery in Jerusalem. This being settled, Saqqaf said reasonably enough: "Henry, I do not know what we are going to discuss now. You saw me; you saw my friend. I do not know what more there is." But I wanted to be sure I understood the state of play:

KISSINGER: I understand you to say that a decision has been made in principle to lift the embargo.

SAQQAF: At the 1st of March.

KISSINGER: At the next meeting of the oil ministers.

SAQQAF: In two weeks or ten days.

KISSINGER: That is essentially unconditional. The decision is made. Second, you are urging us to do our utmost to bring about disengagement on the Syrian side. Third, the four heads of government would consider it useful if I came to the Middle East. You proposed that I go before the Islamic Conference [in Lahore, February 22–24].

SAQQAF: Before the Mexico trip.

KISSINGER [laughing]: Yes. I cannot, but I will come immediately afterward. This is your understanding? . . .

SAQQAF: Yes.

KISSINGER: I will report this now fully to the President.

The next issue was what to do with the prisoner list coming to Washington. If it remained in the Syrian mission in Washington until just before I left for the Middle East more than a week hence, it would look like blackmail; moreover, the Syrian leadership might change its mind. If we transmitted it to Jerusalem immediately, the Israeli cabinet under the pressure of coalition-making might invent new conditions by the time I got there. More important, if Israel's Golan proposal turned out to be as uncompromising as I suspected, the fact that it had been prepared over a period of ten days was likely to add insult to injury for Damascus.

We finally settled on a compromise of sufficient deviousness to appeal to the complex Arab mind (not to mention mine). Fahmy and Saqqaf would urge the Syrian representative in Washington to turn the list of prisoners over to me in a sealed envelope. I would keep it in a safe until my departure. My first stop in the Middle East would be Damascus. Having carried the envelope with me from America, I would take it from Syria to Israel, which in return would hand over a plan for disengagement on the Golan Heights. Thus, face would be saved on both sides. Syria would not have paid too early; Israel would have achieved its goal; we would be able to say that there had not been enough time to elicit a negotiable proposal. The two emissaries deserve the credit for a scheme of classic Middle Eastern intricacy.

The POW list was handed over to me in Washington in a sealed envelope on February 20. I kept it in my safe. I altered the plan in one detail. In order to ease Golda's anguish, I told her through Dinitz in strictest confidence that the list was in my hands and that I would hand it to her on February 27 when I came to Israel from Damascus. Golda proved to me that the Israeli government could keep a secret when it chose (or maybe she did not tell anyone). No word of the advance information ever leaked.*

At last on February 19, three days after arriving in Washington, the emissaries met the President in the Oval Office. Nixon, rested after four days in Florida, was in fine form. Saqqaf and Fahmy and I had honed our presentations over the last three days of repeating the same point: how to avoid a linkage that reality imposed and diplomacy rejected. Nixon began by asking me to sum up. I repeated the main points of the previous meeting, stressing that the lifting of the oil embargo was unconditional and that all the Arab ministers were asking from us was our "best influence" for a Syrian-Israeli disengagement. Fahmy, who throughout had been extremely helpful, affirmed that my summary was correct. Saqqaf, aware of the fine balance that his kingdom had to strike, demurred mildly by giving a new meaning to the term "unconditional": "It is true there was no condition to the lifting of the embargo but you must bear in mind it will not be lifted for nothing. . . . The embargo is not going to be lifted without something else happening."

I objected strongly. Nixon gave his own ingenious version of our resistance to linkage in the Middle East — much as we favored it in East-West relations. We wanted the lifting of the oil embargo to stand on its own, so that we could be more helpful to the Arabs:

> We will work for peace and assist to the extent that you want us, including the provision of aid. If the embargo is lifted, you will be playing a decisive role towards hastening an agreement; if not, you will make it more difficult for us to play a useful role. The key question is: do you want us to play a major role, to get Israel to be reasonable, to work toward a reasonable peace? That is what is on the line — our help, economically, industrially, culturally. What is important is not the embargo or related conditions but the opportunity to build in the Middle East.

Fahmy professed that what he had just heard was of "historic importance." On the basis of it, "the embargo will be lifted, there will be no linkage." Nixon in return promised to move the disengagement talks to a successful resolution. Though I had been saying the same thing for four weeks, Saqqaf chose to treat it as an important new concession: "This is what we had in mind. We do not want to commit you, Mr. President, but this is what I wanted to hear."

---

*After I had delivered the list to Israel, I told the journalists accompanying me that I had in fact had it before visiting Damascus.

Afterward, we all met the press. Nixon announced that he was sending me to the Middle East again, to promote a Syrian-Israeli disengagement. He vowed to work for a "permanent" peace. Saqqaf, calling Nixon "my friend," allowed that he was extremely relaxed and hopeful that something would happen, and soon, "for the benefit of the United States, of the Middle East, for the world as a whole." Fahmy, making clear that the two emissaries had conveyed important decisions from the four heads of state at Algiers, welcomed both Nixon's commitment to permanent peace and my imminent visit to the region.

Uncharacteristically, I said nothing. My mind reeling from unconditional conditions and unlinked linkages, I was reflecting about my forthcoming journey to the Middle East. It would be a strange trip. I was being sent to extract from Syria a list of prisoners already in my possession and from Israel a negotiating proposal certain to be unacceptable. All the key actors knew this. But in the Middle East, poetry and reality merge; all agreed that only by acting out the script could the embargo be lifted and the war on the Golan Heights be ended. And as in many Middle East fairy tales, the charade became reality when during the course of my journey it transpired that the trip had been essential after all; the script suddenly changed. My task became less to make progress on negotiations than to make stalemate psychologically supportable.

An Eventful Visit to Damascus

THERE was a fretful overture to my fourth visit to the Middle East. I had told Gromyko on February 19 what he could read in the newspaper: that I was leaving in a few days for another trip at the request of Saudi Arabia and Egypt "to produce an appropriate framework for the negotiations acceptable to the parties." There was no response. But on February 24, Syrian Foreign Minister Abd al-Halim Khaddam wired me from Lahore, where he was attending the Islamic summit with Asad: Out of the blue, Gromyko had announced himself on a trip to Damascus, supposedly in order to participate with me in the negotiations on disengagement. Khaddam asked me urgently whether the United States had a prior agreement with the Soviet Union that Gromyko would meet with me in the Syrian capital.

Moscow's attempt to inject itself into the diplomacy was both clumsy and a confession of weakness. And the Syrian reaction implied, stunningly, that Asad would go along with Gromyko's presence only if America insisted on it. I decided to test this assumption by expressing no view as to the desirability of Gromyko's presence in Damascus, simply putting the facts before Khaddam: "The US has no prior agreement with the USSR, and we have no knowledge of such an approach."

Gromyko, it turned out, was not yet in Damascus when I arrived there from London at 9:35 P.M. on Tuesday, February 26, to a warm greeting by Khaddam and the usual hair-raising motorcade past sullen Palestinian refugee camps into the center of town. Damascus lies on a plain stretching toward the east as far as the eye can see, bounded on the west by the Mount Hermon range, which on my many visits was always capped by snow. I must have visited Damascus at least thirty times but I never saw anything of the city except the road from the airport to the state guest house and then from there to the President's office just around the corner. My one attempt to visit the old city was aborted by security considerations, as I shall describe. The part of the city my motorcade traversed showed the French influence — wide, tree-lined avenues bordered by buildings that had clearly seen happier days. Indifference would be the best description for the demeanor of the average Syrian. There was none of the ebullient applause of Cairo, or the mixture of hope for peace and fear of betrayal that one met in Jerusalem. The Syrian was too proud to show interest in an American emissary but too much in the Arab tradition of hospitality to take his lead from the anti-American propaganda that usually filled the Syrian press.

Despite their fearsome reputation, the Syrians were always impeccable hosts, making up in courtesy for the Spartan accommodations in the guest house. Khaddam insisted that I have dinner with him despite the late hour. Tom Scotes, head of the Interests Section, had warned me that a light supper was awaiting me. "Light supper," I later complained to Asad, "does not even translate into Arabic." The lavish meal and Khaddam's uncharacteristic cordiality showed that Syria had staked a great deal on disengagement on the Golan. He told me that Syria appreciated my efforts enormously — an unheard-of compliment from this exemplar of Baathist militance. He was benign also about the Washington Energy Conference. He did not dispute that oil prices were too high, but he blamed the price explosion on Israel; without the war, he insisted, the producers would not have taken such dramatic advantage of market conditions. He could not forgo the opportunity to explain that historically Palestine had been part of Syria — a complex proposition since Syria in its modern form has existed only since 1920 (though a satellite Kingdom of Syria, including all the territory between Turkey and Egypt, had come into being as part of the Ottoman Empire). But Khaddam was also at pains to point out that Syria would not let itself be provoked. This was a promising hint that it would not break off the talks if Israel's first proposal turned out to be unsatisfactory, as I had consistently predicted.

All this was really just filling the time until President Asad had completed a State dinner for visiting Romanian President Nicolae Ceauşescu. At midnight I was summoned to a session with Asad that was to last more than three and a half hours. We met as usual behind drawn velvet curtains in the womblike upstairs sitting room of the grandly named Presidential Palace. Asad and I took our places on straight-backed chairs and our advisers on sofas, the Syrian group again stationing themselves below the inspirational painting showing the destruction of the last Crusader strongholds by Mohammedan armies.

Asad began the conversation by stressing his reliance on our active role:

ASAD: Certain information media and certain of your statements gave the impression that you were just an innocent conveyor of messages here and there.

KISSINGER: That is the public impression.

ASAD: It is very innocent. Even if we wanted this, it is impossible with you.

KISSINGER: You do not think I am innocent, or you do not want me to be innocent?

ASAD: The word "innocent" may have more than one sense. The needed impression may be that Dr. Kissinger does no more than just convey the viewpoint of one side to the other; this suffers from an absence of any dynamism, the impression that you are not doing something effective. This could be called an innocent role, but not [for] Dr. Kissinger.

A word must be said here about the distinguished individual who served as interpreter for my meetings in Damascus and Riyadh. All Arabs paid him lyrical tributes for the accuracy of his translations into Arabic (which not all of them were in a position to judge) and for their literacy and poetic quality (which they were). Isa Sabbagh, Palestinian by birth, was a gray-haired gentleman whose goatee and courtly manner suggested a retired scholar of the turn of the century from a family fallen upon hard times. He was famous in the Arab world from his many years of broadcasting for the BBC and *Voice of America*. I never found out what twist of fate had made Sabbagh an American citizen and pillar of the Foreign Service (his principal job then was special assistant to our Ambassador in Saudi Arabia). It was my good fortune to team up with a man whose background reflected the Middle East's tragedy and passion. I am certain that Sabbagh's heart was with the Palestinians; yet his work for me was in the service of a policy that gave that problem a relatively low priority. His conduct throughout was impeccable, as if he could spur the aspirations of his people best by the scrupulousness and excellence of his performance.

When we turned to the procedure for giving Mrs. Meir the list of Israeli prisoners, Asad agreed with the next key step in my scenario: Red Cross visits could start promptly, and to show his goodwill Asad offered to begin them the next day or as soon as possible thereafter. He used another of his allegorical news stories to stress his desire to cooperate. He had read some news accounts, he said, alleging that I judged his flexibility more limited than Sadat's because of domestic pressures.

(This was indeed my view, though I remembered no story making that claim.) He denied that this was true. There were no groupings hostile to him; he was as "mobile" as any other Arab leader. I took his point, responding in a manner most compatible with his fierce pride:

I think I understand you. Your situation is more complex, you are closer to Palestine, you are not dealing with a desert, and with less territory. Your situation is not like Sinai, and you run risks through the process. That is my judgment. [Asad nods yes.] You have more neighbors than Egypt.

And that was in fact the case. Asad's turn to moderation would be challenged at home as well as by his radical neighbor Iraq; my summing up had rephrased, not denied, that condition.

It rapidly became apparent that Asad had grave misgivings about the negotiating procedure that I had outlined. He had wanted to convey that his hesitations reflected conviction, not weakness. I had proposed on February 5 that Syrian and Israeli officers meet in the Egyptian-Israeli military working group that still technically functioned in Geneva, though it had not met since early January. The idea had come from Sadat, who thought it would relieve Asad of the embarrassment of a separate Syrian-Israeli negotiation, and incidentally provide an assurance of Syrian "good behavior." But the idea carried risks: It would be difficult to exclude the Soviets from any Geneva meetings as Gromyko's insistence made clear; and the effort to assemble a direct Syrian-Israeli meeting anywhere invited a dangerous early deadlock.

Asad saw this sooner than I had. He argued that any Geneva meeting of Syrian and Israeli officers should take place *after* an agreement in principle had been reached. In other words, Asad clearly wanted *me* to handle the principal negotiation as I had done with Egypt:

We could discuss all you have mentioned *when* it is achieved. But with the list and the Red Cross visits, . . . immediately thereafter . . . to send the officers [to Geneva], when the statements are emanating, would be a bit much.

Nor did he want the Soviets to be part of it, as he made clear by telling me proudly and in great detail how he had prevented Gromyko from visiting Damascus while I was there. The Soviet Foreign Minister was scheduled to arrive after my departure and to leave the morning of my next return to Damascus on March 1 — hardly glorious treatment for Syria's principal weapons supplier.

The idea that I would be stuck with the entire Syrian negotiation filled me with horror. "I would have to spend all my time here," I said more presciently than I realized. In fact, there was no alternative. And it also enabled me to avoid the most serious pitfall I saw ahead. If Asad turned down the first Israeli proposal, which I had promised to bring him on my return in forty-eight hours, we would be bogged down both in the disengagement talks and in our efforts to lift the embargo (however we might disclaim any linkage). What I had to do, I realized, was to get through the next few days without a blowup. If worse came to worst, I would have to stall until the embargo was lifted and count on political and economic pressures to keep it from being reimposed.

I therefore repeated my refrain of the preceding weeks. The Israeli plan I would bring when I next came to Damascus would probably not be acceptable to Syria, given the state of Israeli coalition politics. Asad had already told me he could not settle for restoration of the pre–October 6, 1973, line; he needed more Israeli withdrawal than that or else he would have incurred 6,000 dead for nothing. I was sure that the Israeli proposal would be even less favorable than the October 6 line. I therefore stressed to Asad that the major significance of whatever Israeli proposal I brought in two days would be that it committed Israel to negotiate on the Golan. Whatever it contained, I would ask Mrs. Meir to send a senior official to Washington in a few weeks for further discussion and possible modification of the first proposal. After that, a senior Syrian official should visit Washington to continue the talks. Once the issues were sufficiently narrowed, I would return to the Middle East to finish the negotiations. The two visits to Washington would serve as the substitute for the Geneva military working group.

Asad accepted the proposal. He could have given no better proof of his commitment to the disengagement process than agreeing to so vague and noncommittal a procedure that would see us safely through the forthcoming oil ministers' meeting.

Though it was by now close to 3:00 A.M. Wednesday morning and my day had started in London, it ended, as did nearly all my meetings with Asad, with another hour of general conversation. Asad wanted to know when we had first learned of the Egyptian-Syrian plan to attack on October 6. He was inordinately pleased to hear me confirm that we had had only a few hours' warning. We reminisced about the Jordan crisis of 1970, like two old veterans whom fate had placed on opposite sides of nearly forgotten battles but whose conflict created a firmer bond with each other than with those who had never known the passions of the struggle at all. We agreed to meet again in the morning — a few hours hence — largely so that I could use the pretext of an uncompleted meeting to avoid briefing the press. I did not want what little there was to report to reach Israel before I did.

I staggered to bed in the guest house at 4:00 A.M. for a few hours' sleep, only to fall victim to what I considered in my exhausted state an example of Syrian psychological warfare. The state guest house was right next to a mosque. Starting at 4:30 A.M. the muezzin began to call the faithful to prayers, aided by an electronic amplifier that seemed to be placed right next to my bedroom window. I implored my aide Larry

Eagleburger to get the noise stopped. He made the officious moves of a Foreign Service Officer confronted by a demented Secretary of State. Fortunately for me, he had the good sense to make no attempt to interfere with sacred religious observances.

Asad and I met again at 9:40 A.M. on Wednesday, February 27. Though the session had been planned as a formality, it extended over three hours. Asad asked for a day's delay for technical reasons before the start of Red Cross visits to Israeli prisoners. We reviewed the agreed-upon procedures. Asad could not let me leave without taking another run at extracting a guarantee that the final disengagement line would show he had gained territory from the October war (an objective not even the most moderate Israeli could share with him). There was no little bravado in his claim that he would rather keep the existing situation than to end the war with Israel's relinquishing only its newly won territory:

> It is not necessary that we extract our right today; we can get it tomorrow. But for the result of this war to be begging Israel — that is impossible. Neither would I be accepting it, as a person. No. After having said this, I want to say we will leave no opportunity unutilized to achieve peace. But there is a difference between peace and surrender.

The words were defiant, but the actions bespoke a desire for accommodation. He had first given us the number of Israeli prisoners, then the list of names; he had agreed to Red Cross visits; and he had accepted a procedure that for all he knew might be designed primarily to waste time. The leader of the most militant of Israel's neighbors was putting all his chips on the United States. In the Syrian context this was an act of daring comparable to Sadat's change of course some weeks earlier. But, unlike his Egyptian colleague, Asad went no further. Having made his initial move, he acted as if it was now up to the United States to accomplish his goals and solve his dilemmas. He saw no need — or perhaps had no scope — for the acts of grace by which the Egyptian President created the psychological framework that left no alternative to peace.

But on February 27 we considered it achievement enough to have started the process of negotiation. The morning meeting, as it turned out, had lasted too long for a planned sight-seeing visit to the Omayed Mosque, a glorious edifice that had once been a Byzantine church and that now presided grandly over the bustling Damascus bazaar. The postponement may have saved my life. We learned the next day that mines had been buried in the road to the mosque, to be detonated under my car. This was discovered only when the Palestinian terrorists who had planted them sought instructions for my return forty-eight hours hence: Should they try again to blow me up? We took no chances on the answer.

Security became even tighter afterward. We varied the routes of my travel within Damascus; we even once resorted to a dummy motorcade as a decoy while I rode in a separate caravan. Whether this confused the terrorists as much as it confused me, I cannot say. We later received reports that they always knew what motorcade I was in. The Syrians were extremely embarrassed (and angry at the fedayeen), and the terrorists seem never to have organized another attempt. But I never got to visit the Omayed Mosque.

When I left Damascus, I was not aware of any of this. I was heading for Israel hoping that we had nursed the negotiations through the first stage.

Drama in Israel

THE demoralizing aspect of negotiating between Syria and Israel was that what one side considered a huge concession would be taken for granted by the other. For Asad, turning over the list of Israeli prisoners and agreeing to Red Cross visits were a major gesture and a political risk. He would have preferred to deal with the POWs in the North Vietnamese manner: to release neither names nor information about their condition, treating them in effect as hostages. But for Israel, which had been prepared for a mutual exchange of POWs ever since the cease-fire,* the list of names was a paltry minimum and not a concession requiring reciprocity. Likewise for Syria, any negotiation that merely restored the October 6 line — returning only the salient captured by Israel in the 1973 war — put into question why the war had been fought and thus weakened Asad's domestic position. Any other likely new line also had its problems, implying Syrian acquiescence in Israeli occupation of the remainder of the Golan Heights. But Israel perceived that its military interest favored doing nothing; its forces were only thirty-five kilometers from Damascus on a line easier to defend than any other. In short, by the end of February I had nudged these two most fractious horses almost to the starting gate; my problem now was to make them run.

Israel's caretaker cabinet was hardly ideal for such a negotiation. It was a coalition of Labour (Golda's party) and the National Religious Party. But the Religious Party was refusing to continue in coalition with Golda on various pretexts, a major reason perhaps being the precipitate drop in her popularity as a result of the October war. One focal point of attack was Moshe Dayan, who as Defense Minister was an easy target for critics of Israel's unpreparedness for the October war. Every

---

*Israel held 380 Syrian prisoners of war; 140 Israeli soldiers were missing in action on the Syrian front, of whom the 65 survivors were on the Syrian POW list.

public appearance led to demonstrations: the cry of "murderer" frequently greeted the architect of Israel's military victories in 1956 and 1967. But Dayan controlled the important Rafi faction within the Labour Party, so that if he withdrew, it would complicate Golda's task of cabinet-making even more — to the point of unmanageability, in fact.

That is, however, precisely what Dayan did. Just before I left on my shuttle, he dramatically announced that he would not serve in Golda's new cabinet. There were even rumors that he would not meet with me on this trip, that he would be out of the country. The impact on the Syrian negotiations could have been disastrous. Dayan was grudgingly admired in the Arab world as a man of imagination and even flexibility. It was known that the last phase of Egyptian disengagement had been ushered in by Dayan's January visit to Washington; indeed, the Israeli cabinet position was widely considered to have been Dayan's plan. I had been dangling before Asad the prospect of a Dayan visit to Washington as a token of progress. His refusal to participate just as I arrived to elicit an Israeli disengagement proposal would have been widely misconstrued — including by me. I made strenuous appeals for Dayan to reconsider. Ultimately, Golda persuaded him to stand again for the cabinet. But the aftershocks of the controversy were still being felt when I arrived. We did not find Dayan in his most creative mood — sullen and bitter would be more apt descriptions.

In fact, I could not have come to Israel at a worse moment. The new government had yet to be formed and the last thing Golda and her caretaker cabinet needed was another divisive problem. Any new line on the Golan, wherever drawn, would inevitably be closer to Israeli settlements. Golda had just about as much opposition as she could handle. The dominant mood in Israel was for procrastination. While en route to the Middle East, I received a message that Israel would demand the actual *release* of prisoners as the first agenda item of any disengagement talks. This, of course, was a new condition. It was certain to lead to stalemate. I returned a sharp reply that I would stick strictly to the procedure of February 5, which had insisted only on prisoner lists and Red Cross visits. Golda via Dinitz had replied with the attitude that there had been no harm in trying: She had been misunderstood; she wanted the prisoner release as *one* agenda item. That, of course, scarcely needed saying.

My visit to Jerusalem began with one of the moving occasions that ennoble public life. At 4:30 P.M. on February 27, I called on Golda in the Prime Minister's office in the sandstone government building overlooking the western outskirts of Jerusalem. After the usual commotion with photographers, she ushered me into her small, Spartan private office where we seated ourselves in chairs around the coffee table. She was accompanied by Simcha Dinitz, I by Peter Rodman. In Israel every human life is infinitely precious. America had recently known the anguish over prisoners of war or men missing in action in Indochina. But Israel is so small as to constitute in effect one extended family (with the bitter quarrels only families can afford). And the vivid memory of centuries of persecution and attempted extermination is etched so deeply into the individual consciousness that the loss of even one person evokes premonitions of catastrophe. Like many basically sentimental peoples, Israelis sometimes cultivate a surface abrasiveness; it is because they dare not give vent to what they feel lest they be thought weak or prove unable to contain their emotions.

For Golda the list of surviving Israeli prisoners was not a negotiating counter or a political coup; it was a record of the life or death of members of her family, names of young men that would bring joy to their loved ones and despair by omission to others. Her bearing and her careworn face showed the anticipation and then the relief that she felt, though she forced herself to address the mundane technical requirements of the moment:

KISSINGER: Let me get to the immediate problem first. Here is the list. It is in Arabic. [I handed it over and she pored over it intently.]

MEIR: There are 65?

KISSINGER: Yes.

MEIR: They are all alive?

KISSINGER: Yes, it is guaranteed they're all alive. Red Cross visits will start this morning. [They started March 1.] They'll get in touch with us tomorrow.

MEIR [agitated]: We mustn't lose a moment. I've met with the families the night before last. I have had everything set in case Dr. Kissinger had the list. We will take it to Tel Aviv to translate and all the parents will know within two hours.

KISSINGER: The Syrians don't want Israel to be the only one making an announcement.

MEIR: You should do it?

KISSINGER: No, you can do it, but they don't want you to be the only one. Here is what we propose to say.

I handed over a brief American announcement summing up the agreed procedure:

Secretary of State Kissinger has informed the President of the following:

(1) The Secretary of State is authorized by the Government of Syria to transmit to the Government of Israel a list of the total number of Israeli Prisoners of War now held by the Government of Syria. There are 65 (sixty-five) names on the list.

(2) The Government of Syria has agreed that Red Cross visits to the Israeli Prisoners of War it holds shall begin on the morning of March 1.

(3) The Government of Israel will give its ideas on disengagement of Syrian and Israeli forces to the Secretary of State on March 1 for transmittal to the Government of Syria. The Secretary of State will personally take those ideas to Damascus.

I continued:

KISSINGER: You're not bound by these words, but you should say the third paragraph in some form.

When do you propose to speak?

MEIR: Not until we hear the families are notified. Would you mind if Elazar comes in now and takes it?

KISSINGER: No.

I told Golda that I would hold up our announcement until she had made hers. As Dinitz got up to call in the Chief of Staff, he paused by the door and turned to me in a quiet voice: "It's very exciting, Mr. Secretary."

Chief of Staff David Elazar was one of the truly noble men I have met, who by now knew he would become — unjustly — the sacrificial victim for Israel's frustrations in the October war and yet bore his fate in silence and dignity. He came into the room, took the list from the Prime Minister, read it, and turned away so that I would not see that he was crying. Then he faced me and spoke hoarsely: "Dr. Kissinger, we are very grateful." Golda and I discussed the notification of families and set a time for the announcement, which I made sure would be confirmed from the White House shortly after Golda had spoken. Then Elazar rushed out to dispatch the list to the Defense Ministry in Tel Aviv.

We turned immediately to the business at hand, in which my main task was to ensure Golda's understanding of the new procedure to which I had obtained Asad's concurrence. I informed her that Asad had said he would break off the talks if Israel offered only a return to the October 6 line; I suspected that Israel would offer nothing better (a wildly optimistic estimate). The problem was, I said, to gain time and prevent the whole enterprise from blowing up at this sensitive juncture: "We can't have it blow up before Pompidou goes to Russia . . . and while Gromyko is in the area. You would then get everybody into the act — everybody who is now mesmerized by success." And I would see Faisal after my next visit in Israel. The best solution would be to keep the talks going; I would like to confirm to Asad that, whatever he thought of Israel's proposed disengagement plan, Dayan would come to Washington in two weeks' time for further discussion.

Golda could be maddeningly stubborn, but not when she was handed on a silver platter an opportunity for a delay that would get her through the period of the formation of her cabinet. She accepted my proposal with alacrity. She would send Dayan or whoever was appointed defense minister.

With that, at 6:00 P.M. we joined the negotiating teams, the veterans of the Egyptian disengagement talks that had ended in so warm a glow that one nearly forgot the many teeth-grinding sessions that had preceded it. But not quite. Seeing them all assembled gave me a sinking feeling nearly equal to my personal affection for them. Golda began by thanking me in front of her colleagues for the prisoner list. In her gruffly delicate way she paid me the highest compliment of suggesting that I had acted out of humanity, not reasons of state:

I think without words the Secretary realizes what he has done, what it has meant for us to get this list. Maybe in some places people don't get excited about 60 names, 65 names, but you people understand, and to us it means more than we can say, and we really — I don't want to say "thank you" because I know you did it because you understood what this is about, but I want you to know how our people feel. You will feel it, I am sure, in the streets and everywhere. This is a great thing that you have done.

The warmth of the opening in no way softened the fundamental Israeli position, which became clear immediately. Dayan, who acted as spokesman, summed it up in the proposition that disengagement on the Syrian front was a unilateral Israeli concession; unlike the Sinai disengagement, it brought no corresponding benefits to Israel. "We shall get absolutely nothing in return," said Dayan, who had spearheaded the Sinai disengagement plan, had opposed occupying the Golan in 1967, but by now was already psychologically out of government and in opposition. Part of it was tough negotiating tactics. If you start out by rejecting the very concept underlying the negotiation, you can avoid pressure on substance; any small movement after that (including the very presentation of a plan) is endowed with symbolic significance for which a price can be exacted. But part of it was a reflection of the primeval Israeli hatred and fear and suspicion of all things Syrian — an exact mirror image of what I had found on the other side.

Whether by design or instinct, the practical result was that we spent a great deal of time not on Israel's plan for disengagement, for which I had come, but on why there should be negotiations at all — an exercise I had thought settled weeks earlier. I made a lengthy argument to the effect that disengagement on the Golan Heights was a political imperative. It was the key to a moderate political evolution in the whole region:

What Israel gets out of the Syrian negotiation is to have a radical Arab state sign a document with Israel. It is to remove the pressures on Egypt, which really only Syria can generate. . . . . It gives the moderate Arabs . . . an opportunity to legitimize their course. And from then on every argument with the Syrians will not be a question of principle but a question of tactics. And finally, with Syria having been drawn into this negotiation, the frantic Soviet effort to get itself involved will be thwarted for at least — since we are living here in a crisis, any six month period I consider an asset.

An additional advantage, I argued, was that it would prevent the coalescence of Soviet, European, and Japanese pressures. But the overwhelming reason was positive; it was the best, perhaps the only, route to peace:

> I have to tell you honestly: my judgment is that Egypt is genuinely willing to make peace with Israel, and that I have never discussed. It is not inconceivable to me that Sadat would be as balanced about an overall settlement, so long as the sovereignty issue can somehow be avoided, as he was in the disengagement agreement. . . .

My Israeli interlocutors, never having met Sadat or Asad, thought this farfetched. They suspected a trick with Sadat; they were sure of it with Asad. Still, Golda accepted the rest of my arguments with far less belligerence than she had displayed in the early phases of the Egyptian negotiation, so soon after the war. This hardly meant she was prepared to strike a deal. On the other hand, she was ready — contrary to much of her cabinet — to begin the process of negotiation. Therefore she was happy enough to have her colleagues exposed to a geopolitical analysis that might overcome their resistance to entering into negotiations. Unfortunately, it was not sufficiently persuasive to tempt my Israeli interlocutors into putting forward a proposal that offered even the remotest basis for compromise. Dayan and Elazar did the briefing; what they presented turned out to be not a formal disengagement proposal but a "schematic presentation" — a coy formula probably meaning that the entire cabinet had not yet seen it and would therefore have an escape hatch should Asad inconceivably accept it.

Fundamentally, the "schematic presentation" was similar to the complex plans or "models" over which the Kilometer 101 talks had foundered. It envisaged a UN buffer zone of a few kilometers' width, on each side of which would be a zone ten kilometers wide of (unspecified) force limitations; a twenty-kilometer belt free of artillery; and a thirty-to-forty-kilometer belt free of surface-to-air missiles. This would require a mathematician to unravel: seven zones on the crowded Golan Heights — an area at most twenty-five kilometers deep — and extending to well behind Damascus. Even that might be manageable, or could be simplified in negotiation, provided the final line to which the Israelis withdrew had some attraction for Asad.

That, however, proved to be the biggest stumbling block. Asad, I have said, had told me that he would not negotiate on the basis of an Israeli pullback only to the October 6 (prewar) line; he had to regain some territory beyond that, some land that Israel had captured in 1967, or he would not be able to justify the negotiation domestically. The "schematic" outline would spare him even that embarrassment: It would have moved the old Israeli line *forward*. Specifically, it involved only the Israeli salient newly captured in the October war divided into three parts: The easternmost section — practically the environs of Damascus — would be returned to Syria; the central portion would become a UN zone; the western part would remain under Israeli occupation, thereby permanently advancing the Israeli line east into Syria from the October 6 line. Since the arms limitation would be counted from the forward *Syrian* line, the practical result would be to push the Syrian air defense to behind Damascus and even the artillery into the outskirts of the capital.

There was no point exploring these propositions. Put forward without the customary Israeli bravado — even a little sheepishly — they reflected the absence of a government rather than a considered position. The schematic presentation was so preposterous as to be actually reassuring. I was sure that it would not be maintained after a new government was formed. So there was not the intense debate that would surely have followed had I taken the plan seriously. I said briefly that in my estimate the final disengagement line would have to involve pulling back some two to four kilometers *west* of the prewar line and would have to return the town of Quneitra (held since 1967) to Syria. Normally, I went at least one round before putting forth my own ideas. But the Israeli plan was so impossible of achievement that I thought it best to bring my Israeli friends down to earth. I did not press the point, nor did they debate it — a basically hopeful sign.

My much more serious difficulty was what would happen in Damascus when on March 1 I returned with the famous, long-awaited Israeli plan for the sake of which so many messages had flown back and forth across the ocean. Asad had promised me that he would send an emissary to Washington for further talks in a few weeks, but that was before he knew how preposterous the Israeli scheme was. If he was serious about his warning that he would reject the prewar line out of hand, he would surely send me packing with this offer. Our Mideast mediation would then fall apart at the worst possible moment — with Gromyko still in the area, Pompidou heading for Moscow, our allies about to launch a Euro-Arab dialogue, and the Arab oil ministers still to meet on the embargo.

So I decided to vary the script in favor of the unexpected. The objective now was to avoid the demonstration of failure, and that could be achieved only by showing Asad *no* Israeli plan at all on this trip, despite the commitment that had induced Asad to release the POW list. I would argue that at this stage I preferred to sketch only broad ideas, not a plan; details would be discussed better by Syrian and Israeli emissaries when they came to Washington. I told the Israeli negotiating team:

The position I will take [with Asad] is that we discussed the plan; that since this was the first time you ever discussed it with me, since you never had the list, it opened up so many complexities that I didn't feel I could present it, but, on the other hand, to show your goodwill, you offered to send a senior minister to Washington in two weeks. I am sure I can get Sadat's support for it, because Sadat cannot want this mission to blow up. Any other approach is too dangerous.

Relieved of the anxiety of being blamed for a breakdown of the talks, incapable of adopting a formal position until a new government was in place, the Israeli negotiating team cheerfully accepted my suggestion, uncharacteristically without a single demurrer. I would play out the scenario — visit Cairo, stop in Jerusalem again to pick up the nonexistent plan, and then hope to get through an evening in Damascus without having everything unravel.

Back to Cairo

I WAS confident Sadat would give his support to my playing for time. He shared with us the desire to avoid a blowup, for that would force him to strike a militant pose contrary to his overall strategy and would prolong the oil embargo, which he knew would cost him dearly in anti-Arab sentiment in the United States. Nor did I think he would be impatient at the deliberateness of my scenario. If Syrian disengagement happened too easily, he ran the risk of being told he should have stalled on Sinai to achieve a joint Syrian-Egyptian agreement, or that he wasted too much time on negotiation. It would be human, too, if subconsciously at least he preferred Asad's achievement to be slightly less than his own.

Beyond these tactical motives, Sadat and I shared similar philosophies about the conduct of diplomacy. We were both sure that passivity is the worst posture. Inevitably, other parties step in to define the terms of reference and one's energies are absorbed in responding to initiatives one has not designed. Gradually one loses the ability to shape events. A sense of direction is lost; one comes to define success as calamity avoided. Much better to talk from one's own agenda, or failing this, to prevail with a procedure that husbands the maximum degree of control.

Nourished by these reflections, I arrived in Egypt on Thursday morning, February 28, and met Sadat at the Presidential rest house at Giza. The sight of the eternal Pyramids, subtly shifting contours with the changing light, eased taut nerves. I explained to Sadat the complexities of the Israeli domestic situation, the Israeli proposal so extreme that it could not be serious, and the new procedure I proposed to adopt. The precise geography of the Golan being somewhat hazy in his mind, he had his Chief of Staff, General Gamasy, bring in a large map which, like a jigsaw puzzle, had to be fitted together on the floor. I noted that it showed the proposed disengagement lines that Asad had handed to me on January 20 and had obviously also transmitted to Cairo. With his shrewd sense of public relations, Sadat called in the photographers for a picture of a group of senior advisers earnestly poring over situation maps — tangible proof that something serious was going on. My pleasure at the stratagem was subdued by the fear that some published photo might show the lines proposed by Syria, producing an explosion in Israel.

When we were alone again, Sadat ordered General Gamasy to leave immediately for Damascus. He was sending Gamasy, Sadat said with a twinkle in his eye, in his capacity as commander-in-chief of the joint Arab armies, which from my knowledge of Syrian perceptions seemed to me to be rubbing salt into their wounds. Gamasy's assignment, based on his experience as negotiator at Kilometer 101, was to educate Asad on Israeli negotiating tactics and to convince the Syrian leader that even in the absence of a formal Israeli proposal the procedure I had outlined was the one most likely to succeed.

Sadat and I then retired to lunch alone. As during our earlier talks in Aswan, he asked for an honest assessment and, as then, I gave it to him. After the Israeli cabinet was formed, I told him, it would probably be possible with tremendous effort to induce Israel to withdraw to the October 6 line, which Asad had already declared was insufficient. With another burst of effort a few kilometers beyond that line might be conceded, to be put under Syrian civil administration as a UN–controlled area. To achieve these objectives, many weeks would be required. The Syrians with their confrontational negotiating tactics would be able to achieve nothing on their own; it would be difficult to imagine two parties less able to come to an agreement by themselves even if both of them wanted it.

Sadat agreed with the analysis. However, he raised two considerations implying contradictory pulls on Egyptian diplomacy. He was determined to move toward peace and away from the Soviet Union at an accelerating pace. But he was honor bound to Syria, at least until it had recovered the prewar line. If Israel returned less than the newly conquered territories and Syria went to war, he would support his ally even though it would wreck the design of his entire policy. If Asad did achieve a full Israeli withdrawal to the prewar line, Sadat was prepared to tell the other Arab states that this was a major accomplishment. Even if no more than that was gained, he would praise American efforts — though he could not blame Asad for rejecting it; he would have to back Asad in that case. If, however, Israel was prepared to pull back a few more kilometers west, *beyond* the October 6 line, Asad's achievement would be in a sense the equivalent of his own in the Sinai. Should Syria refuse such an offer, Sadat would be prepared publicly to blame Asad for breaking up the talks. And he would not join Syria in a war fought over such an issue.

Unfortunately, Sadat was not my Arab interlocutor in these negotiations. He could not move matters forward on the Golan with one of his bold strokes. All he was able to do was to put his prestige behind my efforts and thereby place obstacles in the way of any Syrian temptations to wreck the negotiations. Sending Gamasy ostentatiously to Damascus after my briefing signified that Sadat had heard enough to convince him that the peace process on the Golan Heights should continue. The corollary, of course, was that Asad would be in the wrong were he to break off the talks after my next visit to Damascus, even if I did not bring the Israeli plan that I had promised him. After lunch, Sadat preempted with another supportive move. He went public with his views even before I left Cairo. Meeting with the press on the veranda, Sadat called attention to the fact that he was wearing civilian clothes; it was a symbolic confirmation of the new era of peace. Aside from that, he expressed public appreciation for my efforts. Asked what advice he had for Asad, he said: "Trust Henry."

Sadat went further; he publicly endorsed our strategy. Syria would have to go through stages similar to his experience with the Sinai agreement, he said. Lest Gromyko — who was arriving the next afternoon — get too insistent, Sadat cleverly gave the Soviets, too, a stake in a rapid conclusion of the Syrian disengagement talks. The second stage of a Geneva Conference, the President proclaimed, would have to wait for the completion of the Syrian-Israeli disengagement. Thus was the approaching Gromyko put on notice that any interference with the disengagement process meant the end as well of the Geneva Conference, the Soviets' principal — indeed, only — forum for participation in Mideast diplomacy.

That evening at ten o'clock, Fahmy took my party to the Sheraton Hotel for a late dinner — but mainly to see Nagwa Fuad, the famed belly dancer. Looking like a somewhat ripe younger Rita Hayworth, she put on an awesome display justifying her reputation as the top dancer in the Middle East. Despite the late hour and their perennial complaints of exhaustion, my staff showed vigor and indeed ruthless dedication in elbowing their way to the edge of the dance floor. The journalists accompanying me for once found a subject worthy of their intellectual and cultural interests. Richard Valeriani of NBC wrote a detailed pool report describing in lavish and expressive prose Miss Fuad's movements as well as the nervously dignified reactions of my staff.[3]

Our hosts were achieving several purposes in addition to the simple goal of showing their guests a good time. The appearance of the Egyptian Foreign Minister at a nightclub signified that there was no crisis, the peace process was on course. Even more deliciously, it lent itself to a little dig at Gromyko. He had been so incautious as to demand ahead of time the same treatment accorded to me. He would soon be invited to the top floor of the Sheraton Hotel along the Nile, just as I had, to see the undulating Miss Fuad. How he would explain such an excursion in his puritanical capital or to some of his equally puritanical radical friends in the Arab world was left to him. (I do not know if he went.)

For the next morning, Friday, March 1, his Egyptian hosts had prepared for the arriving Soviet diplomat another demonstration that their priorities had changed. Sadat had decided that there was no better day for the announcement of the restoration of full diplomatic relations with the United States. He was so pleased that he jumped the gun of the agreed announcement by nearly two hours.

It was not a world-shaking event because practically speaking we had had normal relations — indeed, extraordinarily cordial and productive diplomatic links — ever since my first visit in November. Legally Hermann Eilts in Cairo still headed a US Interests Section attached to the Spanish Embassy and likewise Ashraf Ghorbal in Washington. But symbolically it meant a great deal, and my colleagues and I were deeply moved that Friday morning as the Stars and Stripes rose on the flagpole in front of our Embassy for the first time in nearly seven years. Fahmy and I made friendly little speeches at the flag-raising ceremony, which enabled the Egyptian media to eclipse Gromyko's arrival with the report. Sadat could hardly have made his new course clearer.

One could almost feel sorry for Gromyko traveling around capitals that a few short months earlier had been bulwarks of Soviet influence. He had been shunted about in Damascus to fit my schedule. Now he was greeted in Cairo with a studied rebuff. These were Arab decisions, not American. "It is not in our interest to humiliate Gromyko," I told Golda during a six-hour stop at the Guest House near Tel Aviv, where on Friday afternoon I briefed her and her colleagues on my visit in Cairo. It was true. We tried to reduce the Soviet strategic position in the Middle East but we had no interest in making its impotence obvious. In foreign affairs one usually must choose between posture and policy; the stronger one's real position, the less one need rub in the other side's discomfiture. It is rarely wise to inflame a setback with an insult. An important aspect of the art of diplomacy consists of doing what is necessary without producing extraneous motives for retaliation, leaving open the option of later cooperation on other issues.

The Israeli negotiating team was not concerned with such philosophical questions; it was still obsessed with cabinet-making. Golda hoped to present her new government to the Parliament in three days; if necessary she would organize a minority government. In the meantime, the Israeli negotiators wished me godspeed to Damascus. My assignment: to keep negotiations going without an Israeli plan to talk about.

Damascus Again: Asad Stays Cool

E N route to Damascus early Friday evening, I learned that the Watergate avalanche was moving relentlessly on. Scowcroft sent me a flash cable reporting that a federal grand jury had indicted Nixon Administration officials H. R. Haldeman, John Ehrlichman, John Mitchell, Charles Colson, Robert Mardian, Gordon Strachan, and Washington attorney Kenneth Parkinson. I had never had much sympathy for Colson. I barely knew Mardian and was not conscious of having met Strachan and Parkinson. But I was moved by the enormity of the disaster that had befallen Haldeman, Ehrlichman, and Mitchell. They had been colleagues in a difficult period, working sometimes competitively, more frequently cooperatively, for the success of an Administration in which they believed and for the good of their country. I could not bring myself to think of them as criminals then — nor for that matter now — though I had no doubt that there were sordid elements in the White House that undoubtedly engulfed them. Knowing their families, I could never share the contemporary outrage at them, which occasionally struck me as pharisaical in its hypocrisy.

Their tragedy underlined the fact that the Administration quite literally could not afford to add a single foreign setback to its domestic debacles. This was not because it would weaken Nixon further — by then I saw no way he would be able to restore his authority. Rather, once our credibility in foreign policy was destroyed, the gossamer illusion by which he had maintained authority abroad in the absence of it at home would be fatally rent, tempting challenges and inviting crises that we would be in a poor condition to overcome.

My meeting with Hafez al-Asad on the evening of March 1 therefore was one of those encounters whose failure could do enormous damage even though its success would not be measurable; indeed, the definition of success would be the absence of failure, the admission ticket to a negotiation guaranteed to be long and nerve-racking. By 7:30 P.M. I found myself alone again with Asad in his heavily curtained sitting room. This time each of us had only one aide (mine was Roy Atherton, though Isa Sabbagh, as always, acted as interpreter). We met for four hours, following the pattern that had become almost a ritual. Despite the stakes involved, we generally spent the first hour on subjects having nothing to do with the issue at hand but helpful in enabling each of us to gauge the other's cast of mind. We began with banter about the suffering of staff members working for me, the relative effectiveness of prepared as against extemporaneous speeches, and the relationship between what arguments appeal to a crowd and what makes a good State document. We graduated from there to a discussion of Franklin Roosevelt's foreign policy; I explained my view that Roosevelt was a great leader whose grasp of geopolitical realities was less sure than his feel for the idealistic values of America. FDR had not understood, I said, that one of his problems was to conduct the war so as to have the best possible bargaining position vis-à-vis the Soviet Union afterward. Asad wanted to know whether I was rectifying that error in the conduct of our Mideast diplomacy. I was evasive. We were not anti-Soviet in the Middle East, I said (remembering that he must report something to his ally); we sought no clients (to ease his fears and Boumedienne's about American "imperialism"); our hope was that Arab states would pursue a policy independent of the Soviet Union (which, of course, as far as Syria was concerned, would be a major step toward us). Asad affirmed that this was his goal as well; there were no obstacles to improved relations with the United States unless the United States was adamant in its support of Israeli occupation of Syrian territory.

It was the first time in an hour that disengagement came to be raised: "When the disengagement agreement is signed," said Asad simply, "we could raise the level of our representatives. . . ." It was impossible not to notice that he had said "when" and not "if."

Still, the Syrian President was in no hurry to plunge into substance. He talked about Gromyko. Gromyko had been in the Syrian capital, he said, for nearly twenty-four hours before Asad had received him. (The longest I had had to wait was a few hours and then only because Asad was at a State dinner.) In foreign policy, small gestures often define important priorities.

If Asad's account of the meeting was accurate, Gromyko had received thin gruel during his visit. Asad had told Gromyko little that could not be read in the newspapers. He had said nothing about a disengagement line, because he did not want to be committed in the eyes of the Soviets to a posture of intransigence that might blow up the negotiation. Later on in our conversation, he urged me to be sure not to tell the Soviets what my ideas were on that delicate subject. Apparently he wanted no premature pressure. And what, I asked, would happen when Gromyko reappeared in Damascus on his trip back from Cairo, as had just been announced? Asad saw no problem: He and Gromyko had also discussed bilateral issues, including economic relations; when Gromyko returned, the Soviet Foreign Minister would take up these matters with other Syrian officials. Asad also assured me he would find a way to prevent Gromyko from being present in Damascus when I came back for the final phase of negotiations.

Shuttle diplomacy works only if the diplomat undertaking it has an

object that all parties want and cannot get without him. Gromyko was
far from being in that position. He could contribute nothing to what was
most on the minds of his Arab allies. His trip was for Soviet prestige
and amour propre — rarely a negotiable currency in international affairs. It was a symptom of Soviet insecurity, not a demonstration of
mastery over events.

The Soviet Union had placed itself into that unpromising position by
its own heavy-handedness. It had had a free run in the key countries of
the Arab world ever since 1967. Even we had been forced to accept its
presumed special influence with its clients, appealing to it for support
at crucial moments such as the crisis of 1970 and the October war. It
must have been galling for Gromyko to be relegated so visibly to a
secondary role, but the steps he took to remedy it made his situation
worse. For if the Soviet Union had been willing to contribute to a solution, or if it had been less concerned with appearances, it would have
understood that our current preeminence was tactical. But the Soviets'
insecurity is such that they could not bear even the appearance of declining influence, and in railing against the inevitable weakened their
position beyond necessity.

After more time spent on such musings, and about an hour and a half
into the discussions, with my nerves becoming slightly frayed, I finally
suggested, "if the President is willing, perhaps we can discuss disengagement."

Asad was willing to go no further than to note that he had received a
personal briefing about my visit to Cairo from General Gamasy. Whether
he was engaging in psychological warfare or wanted to prolong the conversation to impress outsiders, he thought he needed to reciprocate
my tutorial on geopolitics with a lecture on the structure of the Palestine Liberation Organization. He stressed that Fatah, the group headed
by Yasir Arafat, was only one faction; the Syrian-dominated Saiqa was
of equal importance. Though smaller in numbers it was better trained;
we should establish contact with it. This led naturally to further remi-
niscences of the Jordan crisis of 1970.

Finally, after another twenty minutes of chitchat, Asad deigned to
turn to the subject of my visit. Of course, neither the media nor other
outside observers knew this. They were left to assume of our lengthy
meetings that we were either locked in mortal struggle or making major
progress. Asad said that Gamasy's visit to Damascus had been disturbing — though it was not easy to tell whether it was the presence of an
Egyptian official or the substance of the communication that was upset-
ting him. At any rate, the Egyptian message had clearly served the minimum purpose of preparing the ground psychologically. Asad did not
blow up at the feared moment when I told him that I had not found the
Israeli ideas worth presenting and had brought no plan with me. Rather
than submit a proposal that could not serve as a basis for discussion, I

urged, we should start the process with a visit of an Israeli negotiator to Washington. A Syrian emissary should come next, provided, I needled, that Asad had enough confidence in someone to entrust him with his mission. In other words, I was saying that no plan was better than the Israeli plan. Asad sputtered about Israeli unreasonableness fostered by American support. He would fight for Syrian territory, if necessary alone. But when the long harangue — delivered without emotion, clearly for the record — was over, he accepted my proposal. He may have been relieved not to have to take a position on an Israeli plan right on the spot. This would enable him to avoid briefing Gromyko and give him more time to build his own consensus.

The next hour was consumed by the new wrinkle Asad managed to add to every procedural discussion. Most statesmen enter a negotiation in order to crystallize a solution; Asad sought a guarantee of the result before he would begin negotiating. He now wanted to make a side-deal on the line to which Israeli forces would retreat. Having just experienced Israeli hesitations to put forward any line at all, it would have been foolhardy to encourage Asad's ambitious one. But Asad was as persistent as his idea — reflecting his domestic risks — was unfulfillable. At one point I exclaimed: "You are such a tenacious negotiator that our nerves could not stand having you as an opponent all the time." The exchange gave me an opportunity to make clear to Asad that even the minimum line he had previously given me (returning half of the Golan Heights) was not attainable; Israel would not move any of its settlements for a mere disengagement scheme. The maximum that was attainable was a bit beyond the prewar line but short of the settlements. When Asad agreed to continue the process I had outlined, the parameters of the disengagement negotiation were in effect established — though I knew that even this change would require bruising negotiations.

It remained only to tidy up the public presentation. Asad wanted it said that he, not I, had rejected Israel's "ideas" — a point helpful to both of us domestically. We settled on the following press line:

A. [The] Secretary brought Israeli ideas to Damascus for discussion with President Asad. Syria did not accept [the] Israeli ideas and provided some ideas of its own. The discussions will continue in Washington.

B. Israel has agreed to send a senior representative to Washington in the next two weeks or so for further discussions there. Thereafter, Syria is prepared to send senior representatives to Washington if necessary to continue discussion with the Secretary.

C. We are hopeful about the evolution of the process we are engaged in and will make every effort to bring the discussions to a successful conclusion.

We had achieved our immediate objective. Negotiations between Syria and Israel were started according to a procedure that we dominated and that would not continue unless the oil embargo was lifted. Syria agreed to the public expression of "hope" about the prospects. I informed Jerusalem and Cairo. I would take care of briefings in Riyadh and Amman personally.

Riyadh

RIYADH on Saturday, March 2, was relaxed as it had not been during my previous two visits. I had decided to stick to the pose of taking it for granted that the oil embargo would be lifted at the next meeting of the oil ministers; therefore, the subject required no lengthy discussion. Nor was it necessary to debate a great deal about the Golan disengagement. A procedure accepted in Damascus would not be challenged in Riyadh; it was totally against Saudi policy to object to a decision for peace made by one of the radical Arab countries.

As for us, we had decided to institutionalize the US–Saudi dialogue and to move it away from the embargo to positive goals. (We also did not want to be isolated by the Euro-Arab dialogue.) For several months I had assigned task forces the responsibility of working out forms of cooperation that would give the Kingdom a tangible stake in the well-being of the United States and concrete benefits from such association provided the embargo was lifted. This would reduce Saudi readiness to take new measures hurtful to our economy. Ambassador Akins and a study group of State, Treasury, and NSC staff officials had sketched out programs in technical assistance and economic development; the Defense Department had many long-standing ideas on US–Saudi military cooperation. I thought that the best way to coordinate all of these subjects was to create Saudi-American joint commissions in the various fields; these would be permanent forums for discussion even in the absence of immediate needs.

I had three meetings in a space of six hours. First, I briefed Omar Saqqaf on the status of disengagement. As I had expected, Saudi Arabia's main desire was that some process acceptable to Syria be visible. Like every other Arab leader, Saqqaf had heard of Asad's allergy to the October 6 line. But he was too wise to make an issue of this before negotiations had even started. I told him that I would talk with Prince Fahd and the King mainly on long-range US–Saudi relationships, not on oil and disengagement. Saqqaf was pleased; he said that the King liked to talk about such things and that the Saudis were particularly interested in economic relations. I said we were prepared to pursue these on a substantial scale after the embargo was lifted.

By the time I arrived at Prince Fahd's palace, word of my conversation with Saqqaf had already reached the Prince, the second man in the Kingdom. His reaction vindicated our strategy, which had among other goals to demonstrate to Europe that the United States could win any competition in bilateral approaches to the Arabs if the more desirable route of consumer solidarity was rejected. The bilateral relationship with the United States had the top priority of the Saudis, Prince Fahd volunteered as the meeting opened. Many European countries had offered long-term projects, Fahd pointed out, but these offers had been declined because the Kingdom wanted a close relationship with the United States. I outlined the various joint programs we were envisaging. We were also willing, I said, to coordinate our policy with the Kingdom in the Arabian peninsula — to assuage the growing Saudi uneasiness about being squeezed in a radical pincer movement between Iraq in the north and South Yemen in the south. I told him that we considered the enemies of Saudi Arabia our own enemies. I added a word about the embargo only as the meeting was ending. It was a blight on our relations; another delay in lifting it would produce a very serious crisis of confidence. Fahd gave it as his impression that the King was very interested in "repumping" the oil — a hint that the even more harmful production cuts would be eased, together with the embargo.

The King himself was too wily to make an unambiguous commitment. He greeted me cordially, peering benevolently from around his headgear as I sat by his side, and offering prayers for the success of my mission. One did the Kingdom no favor by asking it to state a formal view on contentious issues. I briefed the King; I did not ask him to commit himself. And time and again I found that his protestations of friendship had concrete content, revealing itself in many signs of support for our diplomacy, never more importantly than in influencing Syria to pursue the disengagement process.

Most of our conversation was devoted to his standard recital of the evils of Communism and Zionism, separately and especially in combination. Faisal did not consider the demonstrated enmity of Moscow to the Jewish state nearly so significant as the fact that many leaders of Israel had been born in Russia and that Russia was now letting more Jews emigrate to Israel. But that strange tale, like a cloud of dust in the desert, served marvelously to soften all dividing lines. Compared to that epic conflict between good and evil, what did the day-to-day issues matter? And when the cloud had passed, what was left was Faisal's blessing of our approach to Syrian-Israeli disengagement. Without placing him in the direct line of fire, the King's affirmation that he would pray for our success left little doubt of Saudi support. To foreshadow the approaching end of the embargo, the King in my presence ordered his ministers to join us immediately in talks on technological, economic, and military cooperation. The King could not have imagined that he could forge closer ties while wielding the oil weapon. He must have wondered at my obtuseness when I raised the subject of oil explicitly at the end of our talks. Faisal cautiously confined himself to saying that he would do his utmost to lift the embargo. It was probably as far as he could go if the decision had to reflect an Arab consensus. But I believed him. His evident eagerness for US–Saudi technical and economic cooperation showed that the leverage was not so one-sided.

Omar Saqqaf, who suspected that I probably never grasped Saudi complexities, sought on the way to the airport to put my mind totally at ease. He said that it was clear from the conversation that the King would lift the embargo. Faisal had gone to great lengths to avoid saying anything of the sort. "That was," said Saqqaf wearily in the face of such invincible dullness, "so that you would not be able to give it away in talking to the press at the airport; we cannot have the decision announced in Saudi Arabia." In the Kingdom my alleged obsession with secrecy had not reached the legendary status it enjoyed in America. At any rate, Saqqaf's prediction came true in two weeks' time.

The Jordanian Option

I T had become customary on these journeys for Jordan to be the last port of call. This was partly because it was then the friendliest stop, a perfect place to unwind among associates of many crises. But I fear another reason was that for the time being Jordan was also the country least involved in our diplomatic exertions. Deep down it was a sad visit, the occasion for a feeling of guilt all the more nagging because it was finally irresolvable. In the short term everyone, including the doughty King of Jordan, agreed that Syrian disengagement had to come first. It was needed to give Sadat's policy a radical anchor, however temporary. Jordan preferred to follow Syria rather than precede it, in order to avoid a repetition of the Syrian-Jordanian enmity of 1970.

The Jordanian case was a classic demonstration that correct analysis does not always produce correct policy. At the risk of enhancing my hard-earned reputation for lack of humility, I must state that I understood the dynamics of the situation quite accurately. I repeatedly warned Israel that it had the choice of settling with Hussein or with Arafat; it had to be one or the other. For example, I told a group of American Jewish leaders before the shuttle on February 8:

I predict that if the Israelis don't make some sort of arrangement with Hussein on the West Bank in six months, Arafat will become internationally recognized and the world will be in a chaos. . . . If I were an adviser to the Israeli Government, I would tell the Prime Minister: "For God's sake do something with Hussein while he is still one of the players."

I made the same point to Israeli Ambassador Dinitz on February 9: If Israel did not negotiate some sort of arrangement with Hussein, "within a year, Arafat will be the spokesman for the West Bank."

But in this period Israeli domestic politics were even less hospitable to any discussion of West Bank issues than before — while a new government coalition was still being formed, in which the National Religious Party was again needed as a partner. On March 1, as I was leaving for Damascus, Riyadh, and Amman, Golda and her colleagues had implored me not to mention publicly that the West Bank had even been discussed.

My overnight stop in Amman March 2–3 thus had an air of melancholy about it despite its surface of friendship and cordiality. The meetings with King Hussein, Crown Prince Hassan, and Prime Minister Zaid Rifai were bound in these circumstances to lead to substantial agreement in concept and a shared frustration about execution — all the more so since Israel had recently rejected the modest Jordanian disengagement plan given to me in Aqaba on January 19 right after the Sinai disengagement (see Chapter XVIII).

I urged Hussein to raise the issue once again after a new government was formed in Israel. Hussein had heard rumors to the effect that the United States welcomed a Palestinian state or would go along with the formation of a government in exile by the PLO, as some other Arabs were advocating. I emphatically rejected these schemes. (I did not doubt, though I did not say so, that these views may have been fairly widespread at working levels of the State Department.) I said:

> Your Majesty has our total support. Whatever rumors you hear have no basis unless we confirm them. If we have a message to communicate to you, we tell you directly; there is no need for rumors or other means. . . . There will be no dealing behind your back with the PLO. . . . In fact we cannot see any possible acceptable solution unless Your Majesty is the spokesman for the West Bank. This is our policy.

But no amount of reassurance could remove Hussein's basic dilemma. He summed it up as the choice of either continuing "to exercise full responsibility for securing Israeli withdrawal from the West Bank" or else informing his brother Arabs that "we are unable to get a solution on those lines and they would have to consult with the Palestinians to try other means." We had little choice except to give Syria pride of place. Israel's domestic structure made it impossible to negotiate more than one issue at a time; everyone — including Hussein — agreed that we needed a Syrian disengagement to start a momentum toward peace.

This shuttle in the Middle East, the most relaxed of any of my period in office, ended with a spectacular entertainment that morning as the royal family and my staff and I were treated to the Jordanian marching bands' performance of the British ceremony of "beating the retreat." For our part, we thought we had made important progress on this trip. We had achieved more than we had set out to do. The Syrian-Israeli negotiations were in train. The oil embargo was all but lifted — a fact Saqqaf confirmed a few days later to Akins. And we thought the door was not yet closed on an Israeli–Jordanian negotiation to settle the West Bank and with it the so-called Palestinian problem.

On March 18, the Arab oil ministers lifted the oil embargo unconditionally, subject to a review meeting on June 1 (which took no action). Saudi Arabia announced that it was increasing its oil production by one million barrels a day — helping to stabilize prices (and indeed to reduce them in real terms in the years to come). The hectic diplomacy of the past month had paid off. We had maneuvering room for our Mideast diplomacy, energy policy, and allied relations.

XXII

The Decline of Détente:
A Turning Point

Détente under Attack

WE were making progress, if slowly and painfully, toward peace in the Middle East. But we could not forget that our ultimate task was to strengthen peace in the world. The American people expected it from their leaders; the nuclear age imposed it as a moral and practical necessity. The Vietnam trauma had taught a fateful lesson: The American people's faith in their leaders' dedication to peace was a precious asset without which no foreign policy could be sustained. Similarly, our allies' confidence that peace was the goal of our foreign policy was the prerequisite of the cohesion of our alliances. We could resist aggressive policies best from a platform of peace; men and women of goodwill and decency could be enlisted only in support of a policy of positive aspirations.

But the responsibility of leaders is not simply to affirm an objective. It is above all to endow it with a meaning compatible with the values of their society. If peace is equated simply with the absence of war, if the yearning for peace is not allied with a sense of justice, it can become an abject pacifism that turns the world over to the most ruthless. To build peace on reciprocal restraint; to suffuse our concept of order with our country's commitment to freedom; to strive for peace without abdication and for order without unnecessary confrontation — therein resides the ultimate test of American statesmanship.

The discipline and sense of proportion necessary for such a course fell prey to the passions of the Watergate era. Somewhat unexpectedly, the quest for regional peace proved easier than its global corollary. Regional peace, especially in the Middle East, often emerges from the resolution of crises. And against my original expectations, of all aspects of foreign policy Watergate affected crisis management the least. Until the day he left office, Nixon retained an international reputation for being willing to stake American power and prestige swiftly and ruthlessly. Adversaries did not dare to test, under the pressure of short crisis deadlines, to what extent his authority had been impaired. No country took us on frontally until the Soviets prompted our alert at the end of the Middle East war, when one of its clients found itself in desperate straits. And even then the Soviets subsided as soon as we showed our teeth. We were thus able to use the crisis to shape events and reverse alliances in the Middle East in defiance of the pressures of our allies, the preferences of the Soviets, and the rhetoric of Arab radicals.

But in the overarching policy of East-West relations, we were less fortunate. Even as we were moving from success to success in the Middle East, the structure of our East-West policy was being systematically dismantled. We were like an acrobat on a tightrope who, having made it to the middle, sees his safety net taken away and new weights added to his balancing pole; onlookers imagine that since he got this far the task cannot have been so difficult and can be made more complex without risks, tempting them to shout from below that there were better ways to get there in the first place.

In the light of America's historical experience, relations with the Soviets were a difficult challenge in the best of circumstances. The American perception of international affairs has traditionally been Manichean: Relations among states are either peaceful or warlike — there is no comfortable position in between. Periods of peace call for goodwill, negotiation, arbitration, or any other method that tends to equate relations among nations with human relations. In war the attitude must be one of unremitting hostility. Conflict is perceived as "unnatural"; it is caused by evil men or motives and can thus be ended only by the extirpation of the offenders.

Americans traditionally have seen foreign policy less as a seamless web than as a series of episodic events or discrete self-contained problems each of which could be dealt with by the application of common sense and the commitment of resources. The image has been of an essentially benign world whose harmony was interrupted occasionally by crises that were aberrations from the norm. This belief derived in part from our geographic remoteness from the center of world affairs, which enabled us to shift to other countries the burden of maintaining the global balance of power. The perception would thus have become impossible to sustain in any event when the growth of Soviet power ended our invulnerability and forced us to abandon isolationism. But what might have been a slow philosophical evolution was turned into a trauma by the special characteristics of the postwar period.

The Soviet Union is a tyranny and an ideological adversary, thus fulfilling our traditional image of irreconcilable conflict between good and evil. But Soviet ideological hostility translates itself into geopolitical rivalry in the manner of a traditional great power, seeking gains any one of which might be marginal but whose accumulation will upset the global equilibrium. Emotionally committed to facing an overall moral challenge in an apocalyptic confrontation, we thus run the risk of floundering vis-à-vis more ambiguous Soviet attempts to nibble away at the balance of power. At the same time, the postwar world was nuclear; statesmen now no longer risked their armies but their societies and all of mankind. Our adversary thereby became in a sense a partner in the avoidance of nuclear war — a moral, political, and strategic imperative.

No society has ever faced such a manifold task; few could have been less prepared for it. The only kind of threat to the equilibrium for which history and experience had prepared us — an all-out military assault on the Hitlerian model — was the least likely contingency in an age of proxy conflicts, guerrilla subversion, political and ideological warfare. The modern challenges were ambiguous in terms of our expectations, were resisted hesitantly if at all, and — from Korea through Vietnam to Angola — caused profound division within our society. And the proposition that to some extent we had to collaborate with our adversary while resisting him found a constituency only with great difficulty; the emotional bias was with the simpler verities of an earlier age. Liberals objected to the premise of irreconcilable conflict and to the necessities of defense; conservatives would not accept that an adversary relation in the nuclear age could contain elements of cooperation. Both rebelled against the concept of permanent exertion to maintain the global balance.

The most important task of the second Nixon Administration was therefore psychological: to educate the American public in the complexity of the world we would have to manage. The United States as the leader of the democracies had a responsibility to defend global security even against ambiguous and seemingly marginal assaults. We would have to do this while simultaneously exploring the limits of coexistence with a morally repugnant ideology. We would have to learn that there would be no final answers. I was convinced then — and remain so — that we cannot find our goals either in an apocalyptic showdown or in a final reconciliation. Rather, we must nurture the fortitude to meet the Soviet challenge over an historical epoch at times by resistance, at times by negotiation. Inevitably, this means that at any point in time the process will be incomplete and the solutions imperfect, hence vulnerable to domestic attack.

The Nixon Administration strove to end America's traditional oscillation between overcommitment and isolationism, between crusading and escapism. We sought to ground American policy in a realistic sense of national interest and the requirements of the balance of power; American idealism would furnish the staying power needed for a long-term struggle that had no clearly definable turning point. Such a policy could in the end be carried out only with public confidence and a shared sense of proportion. These qualities were never more needed — nor more elusive — than when so much of the nations's energy was consumed in our Watergate purgatory.

Historians will forever debate whether without Watergate Nixon could have achieved this goal. Serious men and women whom I respect consider our approach incompatible with the American psyche much as I consider their alternative of a crusade *à outrance* incompatible with contemporary realities.* We obviously believed that we had set an attainable objective; no other conviction could have sustained us through the turmoil of the period. We were deeply aware of the ideological and geopolitical conflict — after all, we had persisted in Vietnam in a commitment made by our predecessors, over the bitterest domestic opposition since the Civil War, precisely to maintain the faith of free peoples in our credibility. But we recognized as well our responsibilities to the survival of mankind. And we could never forget the anguish our society had been undergoing for a decade. We sought no avoidable confrontations; we husbanded the hard-won faith of the public in our dedication to peace, considering it crucial for either of two possibilities: that despite our best efforts Soviet expansionism might propel us into confrontation, or that somewhere along the line what both sides began for tactical reasons might turn into genuine coexistence.

Détente was thus built on the twin pillars of resistance to Soviet expansionism and a willingness to negotiate on concrete issues, on the concept of deterrence and a readiness to explore the principles of coexistence. In Jordan and Cienfuegos in 1970; in the India-Pakistan war of 1971; most recently in the alert at the end of the October 1973 war, the Nixon Administration had vigorously opposed geopolitical challenges by the Soviet Union and its allies. We fought for a strong defense policy over bitter Congressional opposition. Simultaneously, beginning with the Berlin agreement of 1971, we also explored the prospects of negotiation. By the Moscow summit of 1972 our strategy was clearly visible; by early spring 1973 a number of agreements in arms control and technical cooperation had been achieved and others were on the horizon. None of them caused us to imagine that tensions with our adversary had ended; those who made that the test of our policy misconceived its design or misrepresented its purpose. We slackened neither our determination to maintain the military balance nor to resist Soviet expansionism. What we were prepared to do was to reduce the risks of competition and to elaborate criteria for coexistence. We had learned that in a democracy, the prerequisite for effective prolonged struggle is the continued demonstration of the willingness to end it. And we were convinced,

---

*See Chapter VII, p. 242.

finally, that the corrosive effect of a long period of peace on the cohesion of the Soviet system would be much greater than on ours.

A chief executive with the prestige that Nixon had earned with the foreign policy successes of his first term might have brought off this pedagogical effort. The realities of the nuclear age and the imperatives of protracted competition could have been presented in a patient, serious, open public dialogue such as transformed American isolationism in the aftermath of World War II. But the bitter divisions of Vietnam and the ugly suspicions of Watergate produced a domestic climate ill suited for any thoughtful discussion.

As a result, conservatives who hated Communists and liberals who hated Nixon came together in a rare convergence, like an eclipse of the sun. Conservatives were uneasy with the number of agreements being signed with a declared adversary. They did not believe America could remain vigilant while seeming "progress" was being made under the aegis of détente. They were convinced that American preparedness could be honed only by ideological militance. They wanted uncompromising verbal hostility; they sometimes seemed to prize rhetorical intransigence more than toughness in substance.

The liberal case was more complex. The Nixon Administration was pursuing arms control, East-West trade, and other negotiations that liberals had been urging for decades. But the blood feud with Nixon ran too deep. If Nixon was for détente, so the subconscious thinking seemed to run, perhaps the Cold War wasn't all bad! At the same time many liberals who had fought bitterly against American overseas involvement — especially in Indochina — discovered during the Middle East war the peril to free nations if the United States abdicated its concern for regional balances of power against countries armed by the Soviets. Like many converts, they propagated their new insight with the same passion and sometimes the same absence of discrimination with which they had held their earlier, opposite, beliefs.

And both liberals and conservatives felt safe in their attack on our East-West policy partly because of its apparent successes. Had the Cold War been in full force, Nixon would surely have been blamed and there would have been a great clamor for a more conciliatory policy. But as time went on and there appeared to be no immediate danger on the Soviet front, it seemed safe to challenge our policy and tempting to turn the tables on the erstwhile Red-baiter — especially over human rights, which had the advantage of charging Nixon with moral insensitivity without any military or demonstrable political risks.

The result was intellectual chaos. For years Nixon had been decried as a Cold Warrior, as needlessly prolonging an anti-Communist war in Indochina. I received my share of brickbats for the insistence on ending the Vietnam war on honorable terms. Suddenly there was a new myth:

that we were both being taken in by the Soviet Union. Human rights advocates affected outrage that détente was not being used to change the Soviet domestic structure by legislated ultimatums. Our arms control efforts were denounced as going too far by one side of the strange liberal-conservative coalition, and not far enough by the other. Doctrinaire defense experts demanded that arms control negotiations bring about what unilateral Defense Department programs had not sought and what the Congress would have proscribed had it been put forward: an exact numerical equivalence in all categories of strategic power. Liberals took the relaxation of tensions for granted while conservatives assailed it as if, in the midst of a national trauma, a failing President could court a crisis with a superpower. Whatever their disagreements with each other, both groups of critics combined, in the economic and arms control fields, to dismantle our policy by public attacks and legislative restrictions — without having a coherent strategy of their own to put in its place.

All this might have remained inchoate sniping but for the emergence of a formidable leader able to unite the two strands of opposition and direct them to concrete issues that lent themselves to legislative intervention in foreign policy. Senator Henry M. Jackson of the state of Washington was a mainstream Democrat, popular with the labor movement for his progressive views on domestic policy; he had earned his spurs on the conservative side because of his staunch advocacy of a strong defense and his courageous support of two administrations in the Vietnam war. He had the unsought advantage that the Nixon Administration did not perceive him as an opponent. We admired him; we could not believe that he was assaulting our basic assumptions; we thought the disagreements were tactical or based on misunderstanding and could be removed by patient explanation and ultimately by some negotiation between Jackson and the Administration.

We began to realize that the attack was fundamental. Jackson sought to destroy our policy, not to ameliorate it. Stolid, thoughtful, stubborn, as could be expected from the combination of Scandinavian origin and Lutheran theology, Jackson mastered problems not with flashy rhetoric or brilliant maneuvers but with relentless application and undeflectable persistence. He had carefully studied Soviet strategy and tactics; he was convinced that their goal was to undermine the free world, that any agreement was to the Soviets only a tactical maneuver to bring about our downfall more surely. This was a true enough reading of Soviet intentions. Where we differed was in Jackson's corollary that therefore all negotiation was futile and his implication that the struggle with the Soviets had only a confrontational mode.

In my view, we had to find a policy appropriate to both international circumstances and our domestic condition. Jackson was an absolutist; he saw issues in black and white. We were gradualists, seeking a policy that could be sustained over an historical period. Jackson objected to almost any agreement that afforded some benefits to the Soviet Union. We took it for granted that the Soviets would sign no agreement from which they did not promise themselves *some* gain; our test was whether we were, on balance, better off with an accord than without. We did not accept the counsel of despair that we were bound to be outmaneuvered; our experience in the Middle East and elsewhere had convinced us of the opposite.

Jackson was not a man to welcome debate over firmly held convictions; he proceeded to implement his by erecting a series of legislative hurdles that gradually paralyzed our East-West policy. He was aided by one of the ablest — and most ruthless — staffs that I encountered in Washington. They systematically narrowed whatever scope for discussion existed between the Administration and the Senator by giving the most invidious interpretations to Administration motives; they were masterful in the use of press leaks. The impact of the assault was all the greater because it caught us philosophically and emotionally quite unprepared. Neither Nixon nor I had expected that the end of the war in Vietnam would see the demand for peace at any price replaced by a clamor for a course whose practical consequence was to elevate confrontation into a principle of policy — in the middle of our worst domestic crisis in a century and with the most hobbled Chief Executive of the postwar period.

The détente controversy was one in which passions ran deep. There will be differing perceptions of these events, including on the part of individuals for whom I have great respect and who on other issues were allies rather than adversaries. That was part of the tragedy. Nonetheless, I must endeavor to explain how the conflict appeared to those of us responsible for policy in a turbulent time. We suddenly found ourselves in the midst of assaults difficult to combat because symbolism dominated substance and specific objections were surrogates for a philosophical disagreement.

The Jackson-Vanik Amendment

ONE target of the campaign against détente was East-West trade; the triggering issue was Jewish emigration from the Soviet Union.

It was a strange turn of affairs. As noted in Chapter VII, when Nixon came into office he was greeted by insistent pressures to increase East-West trade by granting Most Favored Nation (MFN) status to the Soviets — even though the Soviet invasion of Czechoslovakia was less than six months old. We resisted, on the ground that the Soviet Union should first demonstrate a commitment to restrained international conduct and willingness to help settle concrete issues, including Vietnam and Berlin.

That attitude — dubbed ''linkage'' — was decried as an unworkable relic of the Cold War, as a misguided device that would generalize all conflicts and fritter away opportunities for settlement of specific problems. We stuck to our position. When the Soviets reduced pressures in areas of vital concern, such as Berlin, the Middle East, or SALT, and stood aside while we pressed Hanoi, we went ahead in 1972 with a trade agreement whose terms included the settlement of wartime Lend-Lease debts in return for granting MFN status to the Soviet Union. Neither the terms of that agreement nor its context were challenged at that time.

We did not believe — as was later alleged — that trade by itself could moderate Soviet conduct. Our basic reliance was on resisting Soviet adventures and on maintaining the global balance of power; economic incentives could not substitute for equilibrium. We believed, however, that Soviet restraint would be more solidly based if reinforced by positive inducements, including East-West trade. And as I have explained, Most Favored Nation status is a misnomer; it gives the recipient only what over a hundred other nations are already granted; this status of equality, rather than economic boon, was indeed the principal reason for Soviet interest in it.

Suddenly, in Nixon's second term the previous detractors of linkage adopted the theory with a vengeance. But they went us one better. We applied it to international conduct, to which foreign nations have historically and legally addressed themselves; our critics sought to use linkage to bring about changes in the Soviet domestic system — a much more problematical and sensitive area. Neither Senator Jackson nor other leaders of the campaign for Soviet Jewish emigration had expressed any critical opinion on the subject during Nixon's first term. Our diplomatic efforts had achieved almost a hundredfold increase in the numbers allowed to leave — from 400 a year in 1968 to nearly 35,000 in 1973. We were convinced that we owed the achievement to quiet diplomacy; we never publicized it or made formal demands; our approaches were invariably in the confidential Presidential Channel. Even in the heat of the 1972 election campaign Nixon forbore to claim credit, preferring the continuation of his policy to scoring electoral points. Similarly, when Aleksandr Solzhenitsyn expressed fears for his life, I repeatedly raised the matter with Dobrynin in the Presidential Channel, promising that if Solzhenitsyn were permitted to leave the Soviet Union we would not exploit his presence in the West for political purposes.

I have already described in Chapter VII how Senator Jackson seized on Jewish emigration in 1972, holding our pledge of MFN for the Soviet Union hostage to the abolition of a newly imposed exit tax on emigrants. Initially, we saw merit in his efforts, which in fact proved highly successful. In April 1973 the Soviets agreed to suspend the tax; we thought the road was now clear to implement the agreed program. Unfortunately, his success confirmed Jackson in the correctness of his assessment of Soviet tactics. He saw it as proof of his thesis that the Soviets would ultimately always yield to pressure. After the Soviets had in effect abandoned the exit tax, he raised his demands, seeking to turn a tactical success into a reversal of an established national policy. He continued to insist on his amendment, which barred MFN status to any nonmarket (that is, Communist) country that restricted emigration. (Its text is in the backnotes.)[1]

We were convinced that Jackson was acting like a man who, having won once at roulette, organizes his yearly budget in anticipation of a recurrence. Inevitably, his approach would backfire sooner or later. It was one thing for the Soviet Union to give ground with respect to a single administrative act, quite another to permit a foreign nation to impose policies on matters that international law clearly placed in the domestic jurisdiction of a sovereign state — and, to compound the injury, to do so publicly. Soviet policy on emigration would clearly depend on the overall state of US–Soviet relations. If Jackson succeeded in souring the relationship, he was almost certain to reduce rather than increase emigration. (The Jackson-Vanik amendment did, in fact, exactly that.) And suddenly to raise a new set of conditions after an agreement was concluded — conditions that had never been part of either our diplomacy or our domestic debate — seemed to us to involve serious questions about our reliability as a negotiating partner. I said in a press conference on June 25, 1973:

> [I]t would cast serious doubt on our ability to perform our side of understandings and agreements if in each case that part of an agreement that is carried out later by one side or the other is then made the subject of additional conditions that were not part of the original negotiation.

But we did not believe that Jackson was going to drive matters to such an extreme. We respected him and admired his integrity. We thought that we could settle with him on terms that might extend our definition of what was possible without destroying the premises of our policy.

So we waited for Jackson, convinced that after building up some credit with Jewish constituencies he would eventually agree to a compromise. I told Jewish leaders repeatedly that we would cooperate in giving Jackson the major credit for any additional easing of Soviet emigration practices: I was prepared to grant that, if kept within limits, his pressures were helpful. Too slowly did it dawn on us that Jackson's whole crusade depended on proving that our sense of what was attainable was flawed; he did not want a compromise, at least on terms deserving of that name. And the summer of 1973, with Watergate revelations cascading in a steady stream, was not the easiest time for the Administration to make its case against what Jackson presented as a moral challenge.

The Soviets complicated our problem with a series of characteristically heavy-handed blunders: In the summer of 1973, the historian Andrei Amalrik was sentenced to two years in prison. The distinguished physicist Andrei Sakharov was summoned by the police and warned about his political activities. Harassment of Solzhenitsyn was stepped up. Two other dissidents were put on trial.

Under the impact of these events, liberal groups who had heretofore favored détente and stigmatized Jackson's views on Vietnam and defense began to support his amendment. The Americans for Democratic Action and the Federation of American Scientists came out for it. The *New York Times,* which in 1969 had argued that trade restrictions were self-defeating relics of the Cold War,[2] began to reverse course. Nixon's continuation of trade talks in the face of these human rights violations, the *Times* complained snidely on September 3, 1973, seemed to be reciprocated by the sparse treatment of Watergate in the Soviet press, creating "a de facto Nixon-Brezhnev alliance against dissent in each other's country." On September 18, the *Times* (while saying it still supported MFN) stressed its relationship to the human rights issue — thus strengthening the hand of MFN's opponents:

> The Soviet leadership would do well to recognize that American moral indignation over the fate of the Russian dissenters is a fact of political consequence. We would like to see this concern also expressed openly and at the highest levels of the United States Government. The recent trip to Moscow of H.E.W. Secretary [Caspar] Weinberger and the scheduled visit of Secretary of the Treasury [George] Shultz suggest, on the contrary, that the Administration is so intent on trade and detente that it is willing to shunt aside the equally important concern of the American people for human rights everywhere.

By then, the United States Congress had received a public letter from Academician Sakharov supporting the Jackson amendment.[3] Sakharov had come to prominence in the West in 1968 with an eloquent essay urging increased economic and scientific exchanges between East and West because they would ameliorate the Soviet system.[4] Sakharov's striking reversal of position opened the floodgates. Arthur M. Schlesinger, Jr. — heretofore another strong defender of East-West trade —wrote in the *Wall Street Journal* on September 27, 1973: "Always trust the man on the firing line."

Unfortunately, the issue was not so simple. I greatly admired Sakharov's heroic journey from the coddled, privileged status of a nuclear scientist working on Soviet military technology to the chilly isolation and harassment that the Soviet state inflicts on its dissidents. I had been helpful to friends at MIT who had sought exit permits so that Sakharov's children could study in the United States. During my confirmation hearings, I had said on September 7, 1973:

> I have been very moved as an individual by Academician Sakharov, who wrote 5 or 6 years ago a very lengthy declaration of his conception of human liberty and of the progress that at that time he felt was being made in the Soviet Union toward that goal. I am disappointed, as a member of the intellectual profession, that this progress has not continued, and I am certainly dismayed by the conditions that Academician Sakharov reports.

Yet for a Secretary of State, moral issues become transmuted into operational ones: in this case, to what extent these conditions could be changed by overt American pressure. We agreed with Jackson about the desirability of improving the rights of individuals within the Soviet Union as well as emigration procedures; we were working toward these ends by methods our experience had taught us were the only ones that would work. But the single-minded dedication of the dissidents did not reflect selfish motives; they were not interested in improving the conditions of their own existence. Had that been their purpose, they would not have run the risks of opposition in the first place. What they sought, with extraordinary courage and fortitude, was to change the political and moral character of the Soviet system. The rigorous standards that had impelled them to court suffering and harassment made them resentful of the gradualism inherent in diplomatic methods.

And this is why the "men on the firing line" were not the best witnesses to design American strategy. Diplomacy may be, in Clausewitz's terms, the continuation of war by other means, but it has its own appropriate tactics. It acknowledges that in the relations between sovereign states, even the noblest ends can generally be achieved only in imperfect stages. Prophets are needed to raise sights; yet the statesman cannot always live by their maxims. An attempt to transform the Soviet system — not by starting an historical process of erosion, the means we favored, but by insisting on instant conversion — was certain to be fiercely resisted by the Soviet Politburo. What are Bolsheviks if not experts in the seizure and holding of power? It would make an across-the-board confrontation inevitable — as the Carter Administration was later to find out. And if America then proved unready or unwilling to stay the course, we stood to lose in two ways: in the further deterioration of human rights in the USSR and in the weakening of the credibility of our foreign policy.

Upon Congress's return from summer recess in September 1973, Jackson inserted Sakharov's letter into the *Congressional Record*. The same day, AFL–CIO chief George Meany sent a telegram to the House Ways and Means Committee urging passage of the Jackson amendment.

Still, the Administration continued to seek a compromise with Jackson. Our first move was to gain time through a parliamentary maneuver: to eliminate all reference to MFN in the trade bill then before the House so as to eliminate the Jackson amendment with it. The idea was to force a conference between the Senate, which was expected to pass Jackson's amendment, and the House; in the conference we would then work out a compromise. It was a clever ploy thought up by our legislative liaison experts. It stood no chance. In fact, it demonstrated to what indirections our inability to fight the issue head-on had reduced us. The Administration, which wanted MFN, wound up in the absurd tactical position of seeking to delay it; while Jackson, who sought to defeat it, urged a vote on it so that he could encumber it with his amendment.

The public could not be expected to understand such intricacies. No Congressman wanted to be recorded as opposed to what was presented as a chance to increase Soviet emigration. Jewish groups either supported Jackson or did not know how to dissociate from him. Nixon-haters were set to oppose whatever the President favored. Conservatives were only too happy to vote against the Soviet Union. Watergate had deprived the President of moral or political leverage. The trade bill with the Jackson-Vanik amendment in it passed the House Ways and Means Committee on September 26, 1973 — hardly an auspicious prelude to Soviet Foreign Minister Andrei Gromyko's annual global review with Nixon scheduled for two days hence. Gromyko and Nixon talked vaguely about the amendment; the Soviets still believed Nixon's assurance that in the end he would be able to handle matters.

The Mideast war and its aftermath imposed a hiatus in Congressional maneuvering that worked in favor of the Jackson forces. The shorter the time available for a decision before the Congressional recess, the harder it would be for the Administration to corral the necessary votes. Jackson did not mind if the trade bill languished until the next Congressional session, calculating — correctly — that in the end its proponents would not permit a dispute over MFN for the Soviet Union to stand in the way of a general liberalization of trade.

The debate over the Jackson amendment soon spread to other aspects of our foreign policy. Normally, Jackson would have supported our policy, which was, after all, a tough, occasionally ruthless strategy of assisting our ally Israel while reducing Soviet influence in the Arab world. (In fact, he supported us over the alert.) But to prevail with his amendment, he could not let stand the proposition that détente had enabled us to limit Soviet pressures in the Middle East, resist them effectively, and finally outmaneuver Moscow. (The Chinese — careful students of international politics — understood this very well.) Jackson and his supporters had an incentive to portray the Administration as insufficiently resolute. The way the issue was posed, the Administration could not win, for even Soviet restraint was used against us. A sympathetic Jewish leader working for a compromise described Jackson's arguments to me in April 1974: "The Soviets must be getting something to be good boys; what is it? QED, it is not in the American interest." Jackson posed a Catch-22 situation for us: If the Soviets were restrained they had to have been given some pay-off, which, if it was not apparent, was likely to be even more insidious because it was secret. If they were uncooperative, they must be punished by the withholding of already agreed-to commitments. Either way, the amendment would go forward, for Jackson was risking nothing. He relied on the contradictory arguments that détente was both fraudulent and impervious to his maneuver. According to one chronicler of the period, Jackson briefed his supporters with the reassuring argument that "if you believe détente will unravel, then you're foolish."[5]

While Jackson marshaled his forces, I was far away in the Middle East and China. Finally, early in December 1973, Nixon wrote to House Speaker Carl Albert putting the President's prestige behind a straight choice: defeat the Jackson-Vanik amendment or delete MFN from the trade bill. But by that time, the President had little prestige left. On December 11 — while I was once again on my way to the Middle East — the Jackson-Vanik amendment passed the House by 319 to 80. An amendment to delete MFN from the trade bill was defeated by 298 to 106.

The battle over the trade bill now moved to the Senate, an even more difficult forum for the Administration. I was still seeking an agreement with Jackson. On February 8, 1974, just before the Washington Energy Conference, I told a group of Jewish leaders that I was eager to work things out with Jackson:

KISSINGER: I know we can settle it amicably and in a way that he gets credit. If he is interested.

PARTICIPANT: Would it be helpful that he be made aware that if he settles it in a compromise, he won't get flak?

KISSINGER: Even more, that his standing in the Jewish Community would be enhanced. I am afraid that if I approach him prematurely, it will be an issue between him and me. . . .

PARTICIPANT: Jackson sincerely thinks he has succeeded with his amendment and his policy, and he is right.

On March 6, 1974, two days after returning from the Middle East trip that started up the Syrian-Israeli negotiation, I finally met with Jackson to resolve the issue. It was the beginning of a dialogue that made me long for the relative tranquillity of the Middle East. In preparation for the meeting, Dobrynin had given me in writing, at my request, statistics on emigration. The previous year the Soviets had promised us that emigration would not be reduced, in effect guaranteeing a level of about 35,000 a year. That promise was kept but because there had been a decline of 28 percent in the last quarter of 1973 (compared with the same period in 1972) the Soviets felt they owed us an explanation. It was that "the recent events in the Middle East" made Soviet citizens reluctant to emigrate there — a not-illogical proposition in the middle of a war. More significant than the explanation itself was the fact that the Soviets volunteered any explanation at all for what was, after all, legally a domestic matter. The explanation implied, moreover, that but for the Mideast war there would have been a greater rise in emigration. Another breakthrough was that for the first time the Soviets responded formally to compassionate appeals about "hardship cases" — individuals dismissed from their jobs or in prison — both from the Congress and the executive branch. I had brought a list of 738 hardship cases to Dobrynin's attention; we were now told that 268 had received or were about to obtain exit permits; 177 allegedly had not applied; 149 had been refused visas but their cases were being reviewed. It was an unprecedented gesture for the Soviet Union to account for specific individuals to a foreign government. Was it Jackson's pressure or our quiet diplomacy that brought this about? Almost certainly a combination of both. The former provided an incentive, the latter a mechanism, for easing the fate of those prisoners of conscience. I was quite prepared to acknowledge Jackson's role and I considered we were starting our dialogue on a firm foundation. I had much to learn.

Jackson was a fierce negotiator. He quickly tied me up in another Catch-22 proposition: If the Soviets stonewalled, it proved that his amendment was essential. If we warned about the dangers of his course, he inveighed against the insufficient commitment of the Administration to human rights. If the Soviets made a concession, it showed that the ante could be raised at will. Jackson affably pocketed the Soviet note as of little consequence but as an augury of what could be achieved if we pressed his tactics.

I realized soon enough that I was up against a master psychological warrior. Jackson and his staff tried to make it appear that it was my reluctance to ask the Soviets to increase the rate of emigration that was the obstacle to a solution. The real problem was my conviction — which turned out to be correct — that there was a limit beyond which the Soviets would not let themselves be pushed. When that was reached they would turn, reduce emigration, and perhaps damage the design of our foreign policy — especially in the midst of delicate Mideast negotiations that the Soviets had at least some capacity to complicate.

As bad luck would have it, the morning after my first meeting with Jackson I fulfilled a commitment of many weeks' standing to testify before the Senate Finance Committee, which was considering the trade bill. I had proposed a compromise to Jackson whereby the Senate, after granting MFN, could review Soviet emigration practices at agreed intervals — say, every two years — and thereby exercise some leverage on Soviet actions. Jackson had rejected it; nothing less than a written Soviet guarantee of a greatly increased number of emigrants would be acceptable. Invariably, my prepared statement, drafted days before my meeting with Jackson, repeated my familiar arguments against Jackson's amendment. His staff later characterized this as pressure. In fact, in my testimony I leaned over backward to be conciliatory and to avoid even the appearance of seeking a showdown:

I have hesitated putting forward a compromise proposal because I did not want to turn it into a contest between an administration proposal and that of the sponsors of these amendments because I am very hopeful that we can come up with something that everyone will agree to.

Senator Gaylord Nelson, a Democrat from Wisconsin and no supporter of the Administration, took this as an invitation to put forward his own idea of a compromise. It turned out to be along the lines Jackson had rejected the night before. So far as I knew, Nelson was unaware of the fact that I had even met with Jackson, much less of what I had proposed to him. On the other hand, I could not evade a direct question; I spoke sympathetically of Nelson's ideas. Jackson's staff (and, for all I knew, Jackson) claimed to be offended; they leaked to the press that I was trying an end-run via the Finance Committee — a curious idea since the Secretary of State had a duty to give his honest views to the committee dealing with the bill. To leave me no escape hatch, Jackson on March 8 put out a statement rejecting the compromise. Our dialogue was beginning to resemble negotiations between sovereign countries.

On March 15, 1974, still hoping to ease the tension, I met with Jackson and Abraham Ribicoff, another Senator close to the Jewish community and a man of exemplary decency and fairness who later became a close friend. Jackson suggested that a written Soviet guarantee of 100,000 exit visas — or three times the existing number — would cause him to take another look at his amendment. Ribicoff was clearly uncomfortable.

It was out of the question for the Soviets to agree to such a number, Senatorial pressures or no. On the other hand, unwilling to accept an adversary relationship with Jackson, I treated Jackson's 100,000 figure as a bargaining device — to "toughen me up and not absolutely your last word," as I said to the Senator. He made no reply, perhaps out of pity for my obtuseness. The next thing I knew was that the figure had leaked and Jackson was castigating me for the disclosure. The probability was that his staff had done so; they had everything to gain from it. Obviously, the State Department had no conceivable interest in leaking a figure that we knew to be unfulfillable, that at the same time nailed

Jackson to a position from which he would find it difficult to retreat, and that might convince the Soviets that no conceivable concession could end the impasse.

Just to keep things suspenseful, Jackson reserved his position for the improbable contingency that the Soviets would meet the figure of 100,000 exit visas. That was an admission price, he implied, to "consider" the "possibility" of a compromise. The negotiation began to remind me of my encounters with the North Vietnamese, whose tactic also consisted of inviting proposals they then "graded" by criteria they never vouch-safed to me.

Jackson's tactics forced me to put forward my own idea of a compromise, fully aware that the odds were that it would be refused by the Senator. It was symptomatic of the developing adversary relationship that I tried it out first on Gromyko, judging him to be the easier party. I later summed up the compromise to the Senate Finance Committee:

I would attempt to obtain clarifications of Soviet domestic practices from Soviet leaders. These explanations could then be transmitted to them [to the Soviet leaders] in the form of a letter behind which our government would stand.

The theory behind the proposal was to get around the Soviet refusal to submit its internal practices to another country's review. The Kremlin might conceivably acquiesce in a statement of the United States government's understanding of Soviet domestic practices, so long as it did not have to confirm them as a formal international obligation implying an American right of intervention.

The occasion to put the proposal to Gromyko was a trip to Moscow from March 24 to March 28, 1974. Its purpose was to prepare Nixon's third summit with Brezhnev, scheduled for late June. It was not a pro-pitious time. Nixon's plight became more apparent with every day. The Soviets were being squeezed to the sidelines in the Syrian disengage-ment negotiations; obstacles to US–Soviet trade were multiplying from the most unexpected quarters. On March 8 the General Accounting Of-fice, an arm of the Congress, had raised questions about whether the Administration had followed the required procedures for extending cred-its to the Soviet Union. Accordingly, the Export-Import Bank stopped working on loan applications for the Soviet Union between March 11 and 23. (The Attorney General then overruled the GAO.) With Water-gate raging, MFN deadlocked, détente and SALT becoming increas-ingly controversial, it was not a glorious moment to negotiate with the Soviet leaders. Nevertheless, Gromyko did not reject the proposal; he was opaque. I took this as a green light to proceed with Jackson.

Upon my return from Moscow, in early April I put the compromise to Senators Jackson, Ribicoff, and Javits. But the Senators had no incentive to give ground. I was there to be blamed for any failure to achieve their demands. Ribicoff — never at ease with Jackson's methods — presciently remarked that "nothing we got would satisfy the Senator." Jackson again mentioned his figure of 100,000 as a "target" — a slight amelioration. Javits said there was no sign of any Soviet "movement." Jackson, perhaps thinking that he had given me too easy an assignment, came up with a new refinement. Exit visas, he claimed, were being given preferentially to Jews living in the provinces and hence of a lower educational and cultural level than residents of Moscow. That, in Jackson's view, amounted to harassment; it would have to be rectified if the Soviets wanted MFN. Javits summed up the consensus: "The idea is that the Secretary go back and talk some more." I was being asked to triple Jewish emigration from the Soviet Union (on top of the hundredfold increase we had already achieved before Jackson entered the lists) and to specify from what region emigrants should be drawn — all in return for giving the Soviets the same trade treatment already enjoyed by over one hundred other nations.

It was maddening to see a policy that our Administration had originated and nursed to success become part of a political tug-of-war — and just when we needed all our assets for the effort to tranquilize the Soviet Union for the Syrian-Israeli shuttle about to begin. To keep the Soviets from harassing that negotiation, I met Gromyko in Geneva on April 28 and 29. To keep faith with the Senators, I felt honor bound to raise the emigration issue again — a subject hardly calculated to calm Gromyko. I found myself in the position of a matador trying to deflect a bull with complicated capework while, behind his back, someone waves a red flag focusing the animal's attention on the bullfighter. I reminded Gromyko that both he and Brezhnev had told me that there was no legal bar to emigration except for those holding security clearances; that there would be no harassment. Why could I not express these assurances, which had been volunteered by Soviet leaders? The complex of these assurances, if implemented in the right spirit, I added, was certain to yield some increase in emigration. Could I transmit them to the Senators upon my return, together with a target figure of 40,000 to 45,000 emigrants (an increase of nearly 15 to 30 percent over the previous figures)?

Gromyko's reply was grudging but generally positive. I could transmit the criteria for emigration to the Senators. The figure of up to 45,000 could be conveyed "approximately as a trend," though not as a Soviet commitment since the Soviets could not know how many applications there would be. The Soviet leadership, deadpanned Gromyko, did not want to put itself into the position where it had to recruit citizens to emigrate to fulfill a moral obligation to the United States.

I decided to press my luck and raised the issue of geographic distribution of emigrants. Gromyko managed to keep his temper though the temperature became chilly. He would check with Moscow, he said icily. Our ingenuity in coming up with new demands seemed inexhaustible.

Normally, an increase of emigration to 45,000 would have been treated as a major concession. And, in fairness, Jackson deserved a great deal of credit for his role in pushing matters to this point. But the controversies of the previous months had drawn heavily on the stock of mutual confidence between the Senator and the Administration. I did not dare to cable to Washington what Gromyko had told me because I was fearful that Jackson would declare it inadequate while I was on the shuttle and unable to respond, complicating our Mideast peace efforts, already hanging by a thread. I therefore decided to brief the Senators personally after the shuttle, which I expected to last ten days at most. Instead, it went on for a maddening thirty-four days, during which Jackson mobilized his forces against any compromise.

After I had returned to Washington, on June 4, Dobrynin confirmed the figure of 45,000 orally and conveyed to me in writing that only 1.6 percent of those applying for exit permits had been turned down. He supplied a month-by-month breakdown of the disposition of applications over a period of six months — another unprecedented gesture. Now, if ever, was the moment to settle. Jackson unfortunately wanted an issue, not a solution.

That issue was détente. In this Jackson differed from Javits and Ribicoff. At my next meeting with the three Senators, they agreed to consider a draft letter regarding Soviet practices as I had suggested to the Finance Committee. On June 8 Jackson made what from him was a conciliatory statement: "We are not asking for everyone to be let out of the Soviet Union at once."

Soon it appeared that Jackson wanted to put himself into a position to ask for just that. What was being given with one hand was being withdrawn by the other. For the Jackson forces had been organizing for two months to put a *double* lock on East-West trade. They arranged that whatever happened to MFN in the trade bill, US–Soviet commerce could be throttled by turning off credits from the Export-Import Bank.

In a big government it is impossible to give equal attention to all issues simultaneously. Hence, a skillful adversary can occasionally transform what has heretofore been a routine decision into a major crisis. On June 30, 1974, the President's authority to use the facilities of the Export-Import Bank came up for renewal in the Congress, as it had biannually for decades without controversy. But this time a preoccupied Administration was caught flat-footed by opponents who espied a double opportunity in restricting credits: either as a fallback position should the Jackson amendment be defeated or else as another, supplementary lever against East-West trade.

As a result, in the name of reasserting Congressional control over the conduct of foreign policy, a package of amendments was put forward by Senators Adlai Stevenson and Henry Jackson and supported by eighteen other Senators. It provided for Congressional authority to review any Eximbank loan in excess of $50 million, and it put a flat ceiling of $300 million on *all* loans to the Soviet Union. Stevenson left no doubt about the motive: "This amendment reflects [Jackson's] concerns as well as a prodigious commitment of his time and effort."

Though it would take weeks before final Congressional action, the implications were clear immediately. The Jackson forces would have a vehicle for raising obstacles to every loan even of medium size, on any ground whatever. They would thus be able to generate new conditions at will even if Soviet assurances on emigration led to a compromise of MFN. And the credit ceiling would prohibit substantial financing in any event. The result was a vicious circle: The assault on credits reduced Soviet readiness to spell out the assurances on emigration; failure to feed the seemingly insatiable appetite for additional assurances provided an excuse for foot-dragging on a compromise.

Implicit in all this maneuvering — contributing to its success — was the fear that Nixon might seek to use the forthcoming summit in Moscow to escape Watergate. Normally, the imminence of a summit produces a bipartisan closing of ranks. In the summer of 1974 many were worried that Nixon might be planning some spectacular in Moscow to cheat his pursuers. It was a misreading of Nixon, so conscious that his place in history now more than ever would depend on lasting foreign policy accomplishments, not public relations gimmicks. But it had a certain plausibility if one knew Nixon only through the media or his public persona. Jackson and others in the anti-détente lobby were determined that Nixon should have no negotiating chips in Moscow. To this end, they sought — successfully — to drag out the "compromise" discussions until after Nixon's return from Moscow and with luck beyond the date that his fate would be decided. On June 24 — two days before Nixon left for Moscow — Jackson announced that he was going to put forward new, unspecified conditions, thereby interrupting all negotiations *and* preventing Nixon from discussing the emigration issue meaningfully in Moscow. Jackson admitted that some progress had been made but he declared it insufficient; in his view it was possible to achieve more concessions "if we remain steadfast. . . . Why give them concessions and ask for nothing back?" He did not specify what concessions we had been making, or why what the Soviets had proposed on emigration was "nothing." He was not concerned, he added, about risking the summit since he felt that it should not be held in the first place.

By now the opponents of détente had achieved one part of their objective. They had turned what we had conceived as a safety valve into a contentious issue both domestically and vis-à-vis the Soviets. Our pol-

icy toward the Soviets was based on a balance between the carrot and
the stick. But we had failed to produce MFN; we seemed to be unable
to organize the financial mechanisms for even such trade as there was —
and all this despite Soviet concessions on Jewish emigration that would
have been considered inconceivable a few years earlier. By the summer
of 1974, the carrot had for all practical purposes ceased to exist.*

Defense Dilemmas

W E were not, however, given a bigger stick, either. The rhetoric of
confrontation did not lead to a willingness to support an increased
defense effort. Liberals might favor an ideological showdown over human rights; they saw no connection between that and increased military
preparedness. Indeed, for another two years defense budgets continued
to be under assault in the Congress. Our critics were thus tempting crises
that at the same time they were denying us the means of managing.

Some took refuge in arguing that it was détente which was sapping
our defense effort. This was standing history on its head. In Nixon's
first term, before détente had been heard from, $40 billion had been cut
by Congress from our defense budget with the argument that only in
this manner could the Administration be forced into conciliatory policies. For the first term Nixon had to fight a desperate continuing battle
against Congressional cuts, assaults on new weapons, and a concerted
effort to withdraw our overseas forces even from Western Europe.[6] The
cumulative impact of these stringencies and of changes in military technology had, by the beginning of Nixon's second term, brought about
worrisome deficiencies in our military posture.

We never believed détente would ease our defense burden. On the
contrary, soon after the 1972 Moscow summit, Nixon proposed a rise
in defense expenditures of $4.5 billion. It was ironic, but not accidental,
that after years of trying, vainly, to preempt critics with a trimmed-
down budget, we were able after the conclusion of the SALT agreements to submit formal increases. Nixon with my encouragement consistently picked the highest budget option presented by the Defense Department. No weapons system recommended by the Joint Chiefs and the
Defense Department was ever disapproved in the White House. We
sought, in fact, to increase our military options, to build a credible force
to meet foreseeable levels of aggression.

The challenge turned out to be defense direction even more than defense spending. Vietnam war expenditures had tilted the defense budget
toward consumables for military operations, leaving many gaps in our
force structure, and the Congress had resisted almost all the programs

---

*The trade bill passed — with the Jackson amendment — at the end of 1974. Emigration from
the Soviet Union fell to 13,200 in 1975, down more than 20,000 from the peak of 1973.

we recommended to adapt to new military realities. We had lived for over a decade through a revolution in technology. After their humiliation in the Cuban missile crisis of 1962, as I have pointed out, the Soviets started a relentless building program to catch up with us in strategic forces. This was bound in time to challenge the basis of our strategy since 1945: the reliance on superior American strategic nuclear power to compensate for the Soviets' advantage in conventional forces and geographic proximity to key strategic areas, such as Western Europe and the Middle East. By the beginning of Nixon's second term, the Soviets had achieved parity in numbers of strategic delivery vehicles and superiority in throwweight (the total aggregate weight of warheads). Thus, resort to strategic nuclear war as the principal instrument of defense became less and less credible. The prohibitive price of a nuclear exchange — rising to over a hundred million casualties in a matter of days — was as likely to inhibit resistance as to discourage aggression. Our capacity to resist would be questioned, especially in crises in the vital so-called gray areas not protected by alliances, such as the Middle East. And in the democracies, pacifism was bound to be nurtured by the stark alternatives of nuclear warfare: surrender or cataclysm. "Better red than dead" turned from a parody into a program.

The paradox of contemporary military strength is that a momentous increase in the element of power has eroded the traditional relationship of power to policy. Until the end of World War II, it would never have occurred to a leader that there might be an upper limit to useful military power. Since the technological choices were limited, strength was largely defined in quantitative terms. Today, the problem is to ensure that our strength is relevant to our foreign policy objectives. Under current conditions, no matter how we or our adversaries improve the size or quality of our strategic arsenals, one overriding fact remains: An all-out strategic nuclear exchange would risk civilized life as we know it.

Had the democracies focused on their necessities, they would have drawn two conclusions from the new state of affairs. First, it was in their interest to maintain for as long as possible a counterforce capability, that is, a capacity to threaten the Soviet land-based missiles — the backbone of Soviet strategic forces. So long as the Soviets had to fear a counterforce attack in response to local aggression, their inhibition against such adventures would be considerable.*

Secondly — and contrarily — even major efforts to modernize our

---

*The counterargument is that they would be tempted into a preemptive strike against us. So long as we retain the proper mix among various categories of strategic forces, that danger can be reduced. As it is, less than 40 percent of our throwweight is in land-based missiles, while more than 85 percent of the Soviets' is — creating an asymmetry in our favor. If the Soviets can attack or pressure neighbors only by simultaneously attacking the United States, deterrence will be greatly enhanced. They will think twice if they must fear the destruction of their retaliatory force. If they have to choose between an attack on a neighbor coupled with an attack on the United States or doing nothing, they will probably do nothing.

strategic forces could only delay, not forever prevent, a decline in the reliance we could place on them. No nuclear weapon has ever been used in modern wartime conditions or against an opponent possessing means of retaliation. Indeed, neither side has even tested the launching of more than a few missiles at a time; neither side has ever fired them in a north-south direction as they would have to do in wartime. Yet initiation of an all-out surprise attack would depend on substantial confidence that thousands of reentry vehicles launched in carefully coordinated attacks — from land, sea, and air — would knock out all their targets thousands of miles away with a timing and reliability exactly as predicted, before the other side launched any forces to preempt or retaliate, and with such effectiveness that retaliation would not produce unacceptable damage. Any miscalculation or technical failure would mean national catastrophe.

For these reasons, the strategic arsenals of the two sides find their principal purpose in matching and deterring the forces of the opponent and in making certain that third countries perceive no inequality. In no postwar crisis has an American President come close to considering the use of strategic nuclear weapons. There was, in short, no more urgent task for American defense policy than to increase substantially the capacity for local resistance. American defense policy had announced this goal since the early 1960s, but the necessary strengthening of conventional and tactical nuclear forces had been prevented by the Vietnam war and the resulting antimilitary mood.

By 1973, a strong President serving for a full term was needed to impose a reexamination of doctrine and weapons systems, and the expenditures for a new strategy. Nixon's heart was in the right place but the authority of the Presidency was declining. Congress was much more preoccupied with multiplying restrictions on the discretion of the Chief Executive than with building up American strength. Opposition to the war in Vietnam had been transmuted into an attack on military preparedness across the board. A buildup of strategic forces was resisted as being provocative and unnecessary; a buildup of conventional forces was decried as dangerous because it would tempt distant adventures. This rationale twice enabled Senate Majority Leader Mike Mansfield to defeat a Nixon Administration proposal for rapid-deployment logistical ships — an idea revived years later to protect the Persian Gulf. Conservatives were uncomfortable with Mansfield's line of reasoning but they knew that public opinion was inhospitable to the massive increases in military spending that a real change in the composition of our forces would have required.

After the Vietnam cease-fire, we managed to increase the defense budget by some 5 percent. The programs were mostly attempts to offset growing Soviet strategic power: the B-1 strategic bomber; the Trident

With Nancy on a shuttle.

Verification Panel meeting in the Situation Room, 1974. Left to right: Admiral Thomas Moorer, Helmut Sonnenfeldt, Brent Scowcroft, Joseph Sisco, HAK, Paul Nitze.

ABOVE: *Chatting with Senator Henry M. Jackson before delivering testimony to Jackson's Armed Services subcommittee, June 24, 1974.* LEFT: *With Brezhnev in Moscow, March 1974. His "MIRVed" cigarette case is on the table to his right.*

THE JUNE 1974 NIXON-BREZHNEV SUMMIT:

ABOVE: *At Brezhnev's villa in Oreanda.*

RIGHT, ABOVE: *Getting ready for a cruise on the Black Sea*

RIGHT, BELOW: *At Oreanda, by Brezhnev's swimming pool, waiting for Nixon and Brezhnev to emerge from their tête-à-tête in the grotto. Left to right: Andrei Gromyko, HAK, Anatoly Dobrynin, Alexander Haig, Helmut Sonnenfeldt.(See Chapter XXIV.)*

Nixon's visit to Egypt, June 1974. Facing camera, left to right: HAK, Nixon, Sadat, Mrs. Nixon, Mrs. Sadat.

...n's tumultuous reception in Egypt, June 1974.

Nixon departing the White House, August 9, 1974.

submarine and missile; the cruise missile; and a new, heavier, land-based intercontinental missile named the MX. The reorientation toward regional defense was started but did not gain momentum until after the change in Congressional attitudes.

Even this relatively modest change ran up against the lingering inhibitions of Vietnam, compounded by Watergate. After the end of the Vietnam war some of the more extreme arguments — that America was bellicose and congenitally interventionist — lost some of their currency; the line of attack shifted to less emotional themes equally inhospitable to increased defense spending. Every new strategic weapons system had to run the gauntlet of objections not always consistent with each other: that it was unnecessary because we already had an "overkill" capability; that it was dangerous because it would compel offsetting Soviet moves, spurring an arms race; that it would jeopardize SALT negotiations. As time went on, new variants appeared: that a new system would even weaken us in a strange way because it might preclude newer and even better weapons some ten years down the road. Even if opponents failed to kill a weapons system, they could delay it by bringing about endless studies — of the mode of deployment; of its environmental impact; of its implications for arms control.

Since the middle Sixties, every new strategic weapons system in whatever administration has been attacked on some or all of those grounds, and the casualty list — either in delay, atrophy, or cancellation — is an impressive tribute to the combined impact of the various antidefense lobbies: The B-70 bomber, the ABM, the B-1, MX, the Trident II missile have all been canceled or delayed for years — sometimes for a decade — by constant reexamination. The principal target is whatever weapon is under consideration at the moment.

On September 30, 1973, the *Chicago Tribune* commented accurately:

> The critics attack important new weapons programs, not by the frontal assault of calling these programs totally wrong but by subtle hints that we are going too fast or too far or in the wrong way or at too great an expenditure of money. They seek restrictive changes which may not actually kill a useful weapon but will castrate it.

In 1973, the targets were the Trident nuclear submarine and missile and the B-1 strategic bomber. The B-1 was designed to replace the B-52 bomber, by then over twenty years old. The Trident would increase the range of our submarine-based missiles (as well as their payload), reducing their vulnerability by providing a larger operating area in the oceans.

The arguments against these weapons followed the new stereotype. In the early Seventies, the Brookings Institution, a Washington-based think tank, began publishing an annual report entitled *Setting National Priorities,* which tended to reflect the view of the Democratic majority of the Congress and of some Republicans as well. With respect to Trident, it argued in 1973 not that the system was unnecessary but that its objectives could be accomplished "at a more moderate pace and at a significantly lower cost over the balance of this decade without jeopardizing U.S. security."[7] It proposed either slowing down the program or deferring it until a new, more accurate missile — the Trident II — was ready in the early Eighties. (By the late Seventies, of course, the Nixon Administration having proceeded with the Trident I missile, opponents of new strategic programs criticized the Trident II missile as unnecessary and succeeded in postponing it further.)

As for the B-1 bomber, the Brookings study — again reflecting widespread Congressional sentiment — expressed fear that in 1975, the date of the scheduled procurement decision, "the B-1 will be chosen simply because it is the only option available." It suggested postponing a decision on any new bomber until SALT II discussions "shed more light on future requirements." Another alternative was to "postpone a decision for two or three years and invest now in the parallel development of a different kind of strategic aircraft: a standoff bomber carrying long-range cruise missiles."[8] (That view, too, eventually prevailed with our successors in the Carter Administration.)

The impact of these assaults could not be measured in victory and defeat on specific votes. A vicious circle was produced in which the Pentagon, to ease the harassment and to protect key programs, tried to preempt Congressional criticism by curtailing its research and its programs. Generally, only one type of weapon was pursued lest the Congress select from among various projects those which in the Pentagon's view least advanced its purposes. For example, I have already noted in Chapter VII the Pentagon's reluctance to proceed with the cruise missile, fearing it would be used as an excuse to kill the B-1 bomber. These premonitions were in fact borne out by events. Similarly, after Nixon approved funds for research and development on the MX ICBM in 1973, the military abandoned a project for increasing the number of warheads on Minuteman III, fearing that this might reduce the incentive to proceed with the newer missile. The result was that for the better part of a decade we had neither an improvement of Minuteman III nor a new ICBM.

The Trident lived on precariously. On September 27, 1973, the Senate by just two votes (47 to 49) rejected a proposal that would have emasculated the entire program. The victory took its toll. During the fall of 1973 the Pentagon, in the budget planned for submission in January 1974, was proposing to reduce the rate of procurement of Trident submarines from three a year to one a year. It took major White House pressure to reverse that decision — and then only partially.

My own attitude toward the controversial Trident and B-1 programs was heavily affected by our domestic debate. Ideally, I would have favored a systematic reexamination of our strategic doctrine in the light of changes brought about by the massive Soviet defense effort, the declining significance of our strategic forces, and the increased importance of conventional defense. But I was painfully conscious of the fact that any reexamination would lend itself to procrastination as easily as to clarification; in the existing climate of opinion, probably more so. If every new American weapons system was gutted while the Soviets were known to be developing four new missile types, we would sooner or later fall behind, whatever the airy calculation of systems analysts. Over a foreseeable period Soviet missiles would become more accurate and ours would grow more vulnerable; our refusal to participate in the competition would amount to unilateral disarmament.

The MX found itself immediately embroiled in the contradictory crosscurrents of the defense debate. The argument for it — Minuteman's vulnerability — was rebutted with the proposition that our triad of land- and sea-based missiles backed up by bombers made a Soviet first strike too dangerous for them — all the more so as there was no operational experience with so massive an attack. The deprecation of a Soviet first strike did not prevent some of the same groups from opposing the MX because it might be so threatening to the Soviets as to tempt a first strike after all (despite the triad). How the Minuteman could be safe and the MX vulnerable was rarely explained; one result was the elaboration of basing modes of a complexity and cost certain to undermine Congressional and public support. My own view was that the Soviets were more vulnerable to a first strike than we since most of their strategic force was land-based and fixed. An American counterforce capability gave us some insurance, and the Soviets additional reasons for restraint. But it did not obviate or even diminish the need for a major reorientation of our defense policy toward regional defense.

As for the Trident submarine, I did not think much of the concept. I thought it a mistake to put twenty-four missiles on a large vessel instead of the sixteen on the smaller Polaris and Poseidon submarines. Each Trident risked a larger percentage of our sea-launched missile force than did its predecessors, and since some improvement in antisubmarine technology was nearly inevitable, it was my view that we should have moved in the opposite direction — fewer missiles on more boats. Defense Secretary James Schlesinger shared this view and in fact had ordered research on a smaller submarine. Yet I also feared that if we changed designs every time we were ready to go into production, we would play into the hands of those who really wanted to freeze all our programs; no weapons would ever be built. I therefore appealed the preliminary Defense Department decision to reduce the rate of Trident production in a memorandum to Nixon at the beginning of January 1974:

I share Schlesinger's concern regarding the size and cost of the Trident boats and fully support his efforts both to develop a smaller, cheaper boat and to speed-up the Trident I missile deployment. Nevertheless, we will have to procure at least 6 Trident boats if we wish to have an operational force of practical size. Given this requirement for at least 6 boats, funding the three per year rate for another year would not foreclose the option to deploy a cheaper, smaller boat in place of further Tridents when it becomes available.

In the event, the smaller boat proved impractical; a combination of factors slowed down the rate of Trident production. While the Trident I missile went forward, the Trident II missile was deferred. Neither of these delaying decisions originated in the White House.

The concern that the attainable was being blocked by a quest for the ideal was also my immediate reason for supporting the B-1. Whether its particular design was optimum is for weapons experts to decide; it seemed inarguable to me then that the United States could not indefinitely rely on an airplane older than many of its pilots (the B-52). We had to break the cycle by which new weapons were defeated by appealing to the virtues of an obsolescent system or to the glories of designs barely on the drawing boards. (At this writing, the prospect of future "stealth" radar-evading technology is being invoked in the classic manner as another argument for not building the B-1.)

Philip Odeen, then responsible for defense matters on the NSC staff, had warned me in a memorandum of August 10, 1973:

We are entering the late 1970s relying on two high-risk modernization programs (Trident and B-1) to guarantee the future survivability of our bombers and SLBMs. Our flexibility is limited by the lack of hedge programs such as mobile ICBMs and a viable cruise missile program. *Moreover, we are working ourselves into an increasingly untenable position to respond to a failure of SALT II.* [Emphasis in original.]

I shared his uneasiness and I pushed not only the cruise missile but research on an airborne ICBM to reduce the vulnerability of our land-based force. At a minimum, if a weapons system was to be given up, I favored doing so not as a unilateral budgetary decision but as part of SALT — thereby exacting some Soviet concession.

The vehicle I chose for making these points was the review of the upcoming defense budget in the Defense Program Review Committee. On October 3, 1973, in my capacity as chairman, I issued a directive asking that the Defense Department urgently study a strategic cruise missile program.

That memorandum caused me to run afoul of the redoubtable Secretary of Defense. Schlesinger had one of the most brilliant analytical minds I have encountered in government. He was at that moment engaged in a heroic effort to overcome many of the dilemmas I have re-counted here, being thwarted occasionally by insufficient resources, never by lack of insight. Our views on strategy were nearly identical. But no academic likes to cede pride of place to another; no Secretary of Defense willingly accepts directives from the Secretary of State.

Moreover, Schlesinger's vanity matched my own; he would not tolerate having what he considered Defense Department prerogatives challenged by the chairman of an interdepartmental committee. On October 29, I learned indirectly that Schlesinger had ordered all copies of my directive impounded. Beyond issues of jurisdiction, Schlesinger undoubtedly calculated that he had his hands full with Trident and the B-1 without taking on a fractious Congress with new weapons systems. October 29 was the height of the Mideast crisis; it was urgent that State and Defense cooperate. Nixon was preoccupied with Watergate. I chose not to make an issue of the challenge and did not take the case to the President.

I mention this not to settle a bureaucratic score at the remove of eight years but to illustrate the cross-currents eroding defense policy at the very moment we were being urged into confrontation with the Soviets. We had to defend, at one and the same time, our commitments both to upgrading our national defenses and to negotiating with the Soviet Union; the allies of one battle became the adversaries of the other. The military services were defending what they had; they did not dare propose a revision of defense doctrine lest they lose existing forces. Even Cabinet members with comparable views — like Schlesinger and me — found it difficult to settle differences in the absence of a White House capable of enforcing discipline.

The impasse was even more serious with respect to conventional forces, in which the always existing gap continued to widen against us despite the increase in our defense budget. The bulk of budget cuts had fallen on forces for regional defense. Since its peak during the Vietnam war, the Army had been reduced by five divisions; it desperately needed modernization. The Air Force had absorbed budgetary cuts by the hallowed method of maintaining its force structure but reducing its readiness. By 1973 this had gone as far is it could. As a result, the Defense Department program for Fiscal Year 1974 cut five wings from the previously planned fighter force, a reduction of slightly over 20 percent. The Navy was one lap behind the Air Force. It was still paying for modernization by skimping on maintenance. My staff estimated that 50 percent of Navy ships were at best only marginally ready.

Despite this, the Congressional pressures for troop reductions abroad had not diminished since the battles over the Mansfield amendment of 1971. On September 27, 1973, the Senate by a vote of 49 to 46 legislated a 40 percent reduction in the number of American troops overseas.

After strenuous Administration effort, the amendment was defeated (by 51 to 44), to be replaced by another version proposing a reduction of 110,000 men (a 23 percent reduction). When that too, was overcome, the Senate voted a cut in troops stationed in any country that did not in fact pay for them. We headed off these measures but in 1973 it seemed only a question of time until one of these crippling amendments would pass.

The same tendency to reduce our capacity for foreign intervention caused the Congress to prohibit the construction of permanent installations or the basing of B-52s at our newly established facility of Diego Garcia in the Indian Ocean.

The details of the annual budget battles are best consigned to the oblivion their intellectual merit deserves. Their significance is that we were being urged to confront the Soviet Union on issues of peripheral importance while defense policy was stalemated by the Congress and the authority of the President was reduced by Watergate and by a host of restrictive legislation. Revisionist historians tend to suppress the fact that the Administration was fighting on two fronts: against those who accused it of being insufficiently confrontational and against those who wanted to deprive it of the military means to meet even the foreseeable challenges. The confrontational stance of many of our critics neither reflected the public mood nor was it backed by the realities of Congressional attitudes on defense. Rhetorical toughness allied with neither strategic concept nor public support creates not a policy but an anomaly; that is where our domestic debate was driving us.

SALT Again

WHAT gave the national debate its nightmarish quality was that each issue seemed to produce its own constituency with no obvious logical relationship to any other. The majority for the Jackson amendment did not necessarily back a strong defense. But perversely the antidefense majority would not rally behind the negotiations on strategic arms limitations, which became even more controversial than the effort to strengthen our defenses. Like the Jackson amendment, SALT increasingly turned into a symbol; its opponents sought to defeat it independently of the merit of its particular provisions or of the alternatives that were left to us if it failed.

If Soviet domestic policies had provided the liberals with a target to thwart East-West trade, SALT performed a similar function for the conservatives. Senator Jackson merged the two groups. Once again, a single Senator demonstrated what a determined, able man of strong convictions could achieve in the vacuum of a disintegrating Presidency. Even more than with respect to MFN, Jackson was in a position to affect the prospects of SALT. As the second-ranking Democrat on the Senate Armed Services Committee, he was a force for the Pentagon to reckon with. He could punish by withholding funds; merely withdrawing to the sidelines, he could tilt the scales toward the antimilitary lobby. The Joint Chiefs of Staff and the senior officials of the Defense Department faced an impossible choice: between their convictions, or at least loyalty to the Administration, and the imperative that they needed Jackson's support on key issues, programs, and personnel choices.

SALT differed from East-West trade also in that it cannot be demonstrated that a more united America would have been able to improve the outcome. The Soviets never put forward a proposal that *any* of the parties to our domestic debate considered accepting. Technically, our government's positions reflected a unanimous viewpoint. In that sense, our internal controversies were shadowboxing; they never concerned an actual decision, only fears over what *might* happen. At the same time, there is no doubt that our unified positions as often as not represented an uneasy compromise rather than a conceptual thrust. And this fact created a vacuum in the negotiation.

Experience has shown that the Soviet bureaucracy may be structurally incapable of originating a creative SALT position. If Dobrynin was to be believed, each Soviet department was confined to issues in its jurisdiction. Thus the Foreign Ministry was not entitled to a view of strategic programs, which were within the competence of the Defense Ministry. Allegedly, the Defense Ministry could not comment on diplomatic proposals — though I had difficulty believing this when its head, first Andrei Grechko and then Dmitri Ustinov, was serving on the Politburo. In this view overall goals emerge from the Politburo or perhaps the General Secretary's personal office. This, Dobrynin claimed, was easier to do in response to an American proposal than as a Soviet initiative; the Soviet bureaucracy is apparently no exception to the rule that no one likes to volunteer for the role of having proposed a concession. Thus, Soviet proposals tend to be formalistic and outrageously one-sided. I know no instance in which a breakthrough did not result from an American initiative. And as other elements of détente systematically disintegrated, there were fewer and fewer nonmilitary incentives for the Soviets to respond to our increasingly feeble attempts to break the deadlock.

I have described in Chapter VII the debate generated by the SALT I agreement, in which force levels unilaterally established by the United States for over ten years by administrations of both parties — without opposition — suddenly were declared "dangerous" when embodied in an agreement. In fact, *both sides'* force levels reflected deliberate decisions taken long before the acronym "SALT" had been coined or there were serious talks on arms control. In total numbers of strategic systems — land- and sea-based missiles, and bombers — the United States was slightly behind, if one counted the 150 overage Soviet strategic bombers as serious weapons. On the other hand, the United States was far ahead in the technology, accuracy, and numbers of multiple warheads for its missiles and these were after all what reached targets.

The significance of the trends therefore depended on the time frame selected. If both sides continued their existing programs without restraint, then during the better part of the decade of the Seventies, the United States would be ahead in the number, quality, and accuracy of deliverable weapons, that is, missile warheads and bombs. On the other hand, sooner or later the Soviets would be able to translate the heavier throwweight of its missiles into more individual warheads. Sometime in the Eighties our land-based missiles would be vulnerable to a Soviet first strike unless either we built up or the Soviets slowed down. We would still retain a large force of submarine-launched missiles and of heavy bombers; these were useful as retaliatory weapons and as means of destroying cities, but they were not considered accurate or secure enough to be used against Soviet land-based missiles in underground silos.

The debate concerned what role arms limitations could play in the effort to overcome the vulnerability of our retaliatory force. It was part of a larger controversy over whether arms control enhanced our security or damaged it. Arms control by the Seventies had had a complicated history. In the earliest days of the nuclear age, some concerned scientists had argued that unilateral restraint would induce the Soviets to follow suit. For example, in the early Fifties a significant body of opinion led by J. Robert Oppenheimer urged us to forgo development of the hydrogen bomb on the ground that this would prompt the Soviets to show similar restraint. The notion reappeared in the debate over the antiballistic missile defense;[9] it was later a contributing factor in President Carter's decision to cancel the B-1 bomber. There was not the slightest proof that the Soviets operated by such a maxim, and overwhelming evidence to the contrary. Soviet weapons programs do *not* seem driven by our decisions. Secretary of Defense Harold Brown said later in the Carter Administration: "We have found that when we build weapons, they build; when we stop, they nevertheless continue to build. . . ."[10]

By the Sixties, another theory had emerged. Instead of unilateral restraint, it asserted a shared interest in strategic stability to be achieved by invulnerable strategic forces on both sides. Arms control negotiations were to seek a situation in which neither side could benefit from a first strike or avoid cataclysmic destruction in retaliation. With the elimination of the fear of surprise attack, there would disappear as well the danger of hairtrigger decisions that might escalate a crisis into conflagration.

Nuclear strategy is abstract and theoretical because there does not exist — fortunately for mankind — any experience on which to draw. In the hands of academicians it was barely noticed that even *mutual* restraint had unprecedented strategic consequences. Never had a major power considered the invulnerability of the forces of its principal opponent, or the vulnerability of its own population, a contribution to stability. And it involved a corollary that not all of its proponents were willing to accept. If mutual invulnerability of strategic forces was to be the objective — or even the tendency of technology — our strategic power would no longer compensate for the Soviet superiority in conventional strength or the Soviet capacity for regional intervention. Under conditions of strategic parity, whether resulting from arms control or technology or both, the democracies would have to build up their conventional strength if they wanted to avoid political blackmail.

Regrettably, the fewest advocates of arms control were prepared to face these consequences; in general, the groups favoring control of strategic weapons opposed increases in other categories of military power. This produced the anomaly that opponents of SALT generally sought to redress the strategic balance by restoring our traditional nuclear superiority, which in view of the large numbers of warheads on both sides was largely chimerical. On the other hand, proponents of SALT were reluctant to draw the consequences for local defense from the strategic parity they were both advocating and accelerating. Both schools of thought for different reasons therefore tended to neglect the need for a strengthening of regional or conventional forces.

By the time Nixon came into office, arms control doctrine was well established among opinion leaders; it had also been given institutional expression in the creation of the Arms Control and Disarmament Agency (ACDA), charged with developing policies and negotiating agreements. The Kennedy and Johnson administrations had started negotiations with the Soviet Union on the subject. Kennedy had concluded an atmospheric test ban; Johnson had signed a nonproliferation treaty. SALT had been on the agenda of a projected meeting between President Johnson and Soviet leaders in 1968 that was canceled because of the Soviet invasion of Czechoslovakia.

The Nixon Administration at first sought to link SALT to Soviet geopolitical conduct. But while never abandoning the theory, it found itself under mounting pressures to begin arms control talks — in effect unconditionally.[11] Finally, the Defense Department, hitherto institutionally leery of the enterprise, seized on SALT as a means to close the gap that Congressional budget cuts were opening up between Soviet and American strategic forces; the Pentagon urged us to put a numerical ceiling on Soviet offensive missile deployments through arms control negotiations. A memorandum from Deputy Secretary of Defense David Packard in

1970 urged that our SALT delegation be given new instructions "with which we can attempt to achieve an agreement at Vienna by mid-October or, at the latest, November." An early, though limited, agreement, he believed, was important because the coming "squeeze on the national budget," which was "likely" to result in "large reductions in defense programs, including strategic forces," would have "significant effect on the timing of our SALT tactics." The cuts dictated by the budget would be more acceptable in the United States and a "sign of good intentions" to the USSR if there had been progress at SALT but would "decrease our bargaining leverage" if there had not.[12]

All these strands had come together to produce SALT I. They were present as well in the formal negotiations for SALT II that got under way in 1973. There were many arguments, at once theoretical and highly technical, about the nature of the agreement to be sought (see Chapter VII). But the major division was the one I have already noted, between the psychiatric and the theological approaches to foreign policy. The "psychiatrists" saw in SALT a major step toward a relaxation of tension and a world from which the specter of nuclear war was being lifted. The "theologians" were suspicious of any agreement with the Soviet Union, which was evil incarnate; anything the Kremlin was willing to sign could not be in our interests. They sought to defeat SALT because they objected not to its terms but to the principle of it.

In this debate I was in a lonely position. I was a hawk on defense and a dove on SALT, earning opponents on both sides. I was opposed to the "assured destruction" theory of emphasizing civilian casualties in a nuclear war, and I was convinced we had to strengthen conventional forces. But I also saw an important role for SALT in a well-defined national security policy. I did not believe that arms control could by itself alleviate tensions. Indeed, if not linked to some restraint of the geopolitical competition, strategic arms control might become a safety valve for Soviet expansionist designs — a vehicle for Soviet peace offensives to mask or compensate for some new act of aggression. Every time there was a Soviet aggressive move, there would be appeals that the new tensions now made arms control talks even more important. This is why I favored linkage.

But I parted company with some conservative critics in my conviction that nuclear weapons added a new dimension of horror to warfare and a new dimension of responsibility for national leaders. Technology tended toward parity in any case; arms control could thus stabilize the strategic race and free resources for building up our conventional and regional forces, where clear and present imbalances existed.

Large sections of American and allied opinion insisted on an effort to curb the arms race. The worst posture was to be dragged kicking and screaming into a negotiation by outside pressures; a statesman should always seek to dominate what he cannot avoid. And we also faced a highly practical problem in the strategic field: If the Soviets MIRVed all of their land-based missiles with accurate warheads, our land-based missiles would be at risk by the early part of the Eighties. SALT II seemed to me to provide an opportunity to postpone this danger for a significant period of time.

Soviet technological progress indicated that there was some urgency about the task. By 1973 we had become aware that the Soviets were developing four new missiles — which it pleased them to call "modernization" of existing models. SALT I did not prohibit "modernized" ICBMs provided the dimensions of the silo were not increased by more than 15 percent. But clearly what the Soviets were doing was hardly arms restraint; these weapons were new by any rational definition. Emerging so soon after the signature of SALT I, they left little doubt that the Soviet perception of stability was not the same as that of our arms controllers. Two new MIRVed Soviet ICBMs were identified in the process of testing by the summer of 1973: the new "light" ICBM, the SS-17, which would replace the SS-11 and carry three to four warheads; and the huge SS-18, to be the replacement for the SS-9 and to carry an estimated nine MIRV warheads (in the end, eight). Both of these missiles were launched by a new technique called "cold launching" — that is, "popping up" the missiles out of the silo with an auxiliary engine, after which the rocket engine would ignite and start the missile on its flight path. This technique saved fuel, and increased throwweight and therefore the number of warheads that could be carried; it also allowed the silos to be reused. Later in 1973 yet another missile appeared — the SS-19 — which used the old "hot" launching technique but turned out to be the most formidable of the new weapons. It was technically a medium-sized missile if measured against the monster SS-18. But by any other calculation it approached in effectiveness the "heavy" missile limited in number to 308 by SALT I. The Soviets were using the quantitative freeze to engage in a qualitative race. It was now mathematically predictable that by the middle Eighties at the latest, our Minuteman land-based missile force would be vulnerable to a Soviet strike.

But opinions on how to deal with this danger diverged radically. Our critics fundamentally wanted to destroy the SALT process; their specific objections were less significant than their passionate desire to defeat SALT to put an end to détente. Insofar as they gave their attack a concrete content, it was under the banner of "equal aggregates." In 1972 Jackson had added another one of his amendments to the Senate approval of SALT I, requiring equality in the follow-up negotiations and thereby implying that the existing agreement had fallen short. The Defense Department interpreted it as meaning numerical equivalence in every category of weapons. It was an interesting example of the precedence of political emotion over cool calculation. Even should the hotly contested Trident and B-1 programs pass the Congress, we would still be short of the numerical equivalence in delivery vehicles that the Joint Chiefs of Staff nevertheless insisted was the precondition for their support of SALT. They had put forward no building program to reach numerical equivalence, yet they were asking me to negotiate that result with the Soviet Union. If that meant anything, we were going to demand that the Soviets reduce to *our* level in an agreement; unfortunately, the penalty we threatened if they refused was to concede them numerical superiority in the absence of agreement! The Soviets were thus better off without arms control than with it — a curious way of standing a theory on its head.

In my judgment, the issue was more complex: Numerical equivalence of delivery vehicles was only one criterion, and not the most important one. I sought to use SALT negotiations to push the vulnerability of our land-based strategic forces as far into the future as possible; that required slowing down the rate at which the Soviets placed multiple warheads on their missiles. Any other goal, in my view, was simply playing with numbers. No one challenged the desirability of the objective. The debate concerned what we would be willing pay for it. And the truth was that no one was willing to pay much. Our last formal proposal, in May 1973, had simply ducked the issue. It proposed equal aggregates and a freeze on the MIRVing of all land-based missiles (see Chapter VII). Since we had already deployed 350 MIRVed Minuteman IIIs (out of a total planned deployment of 550) and the Soviets had deployed none, there was no likelihood that the Soviets would let us take them so neatly out of the MIRV field. The Soviets saw no benefit in a scheme where we would give up 400 warheads* for potentially 7,000 Soviet ones. The proposal was put forward despite its implausibility because it was a good way to stifle our domestic debate. No one could be accused of softness if we asked for a number of delivery vehicles beyond our intention to build while restricting the Soviets to levels of MIRVs far below their capacity. It was fairy-tale diplomacy: If one wished hard enough, one could achieve all one's aims without having to pay any price.

Once the numbers game had started, even equal aggregates became controversial — in spite of the fact that we were far from achieving them. Our missiles were smaller, hence they carried fewer warheads. Pentagon analysts thus came up with a new definition of equivalence: equal throwweight. (All this was in the absence of any American pro-

---

*We would give up 600 MIRV warheads (three for each of 200 Minuteman IIIs) and substitute 200 single warheads; hence the figure of 400.

gram to correct the deficiencies.) Throwweight, too, was a largely theoretical measurement depending, for its impact, entirely on where it was set. If the throwweight ceiling was at our level, the Soviets would either have to reduce their existing strategic force to something like a fifth of ours or else tear it down and rebuild it in our image — a highly improbable outcome of SALT. If it was set at the higher, Soviet, level, it would be meaningful only if we dismantled our force and rebuilt it in the Soviet image. Or else we could double the number of our Minutemen, achieving something like a two-to-one advantage. Neither course was ever put forward or enjoyed any prospect of support in the Congress.

I did not differ with the goal of reducing the Soviet throwweight. My disagreement arose over the attempt to assign to SALT the burden it was being asked to carry; over whether negotiations could achieve what our unilateral building programs did not seek. Some of our critics seemed to think so. Since the schemes were advanced by highly intelligent men, the impression is unavoidable that they were more afraid of the lash of Senator Jackson than of aborting the negotiations on SALT. Indeed, by 1973 the Joint Chiefs were so insistent on "strategic equivalence" that they were willing to pay the price of abandoning *all* MIRV limitations for exact equivalence in launchers — thereby giving the Soviets a huge potential edge in warheads in return for a nonexercised right to build a few hundred additional launchers. Moreover, if each side was free to MIRV its entire force, numerical ceilings on delivery vehicles — equal or not — would become nearly meaningless; each side's land-based missiles would become vulnerable as the number of warheads increased enormously while the number of targets remained fixed.

I asked incredulously at a Verification Panel meeting of August 15, 1973: "So you would drop all MIRV restrictions, go to equal aggregates with freedom to mix, maybe reductions — never mind [Soviet] MIRV superiority as long as we have the right to become a mirror image of the Soviet force?" Which, I might have added, the Defense Department had never shown an interest in doing.

Schlesinger understood at least as well as I the strategic vulnerability we faced if the Soviets MIRVed most of their land-based missiles. But he had Jackson to deal with and the Joint Chiefs of Staff to placate. Under his urging, the Pentagon put forward as a "compromise" a new variant — equal MIRVed throwweight — to be added to the Joint Chiefs' proposal of an equal aggregate ceiling of 2,350 delivery vehicles. It landed us right back at the dilemmas of the earlier schemes. Since the Soviets' throwweight per missile was much larger than ours, this would mean that they would be able to MIRV many fewer missiles than we — the precise number would depend on which type of missile they would elect to MIRV. It was an ingenious proposal whose sole drawback was its lack of reality; under it we would give up nothing, and if the Soviets refused it we had no program to reach equality unilaterally.

By the summer of 1973 the equal aggregates doctrine had led to an inherently inconsistent position. The agencies were prepared to live with the inferior numbers of launchers and the inferior throwweight they had decided to build (and maintained through every succeeding Administration, including Reagan's). They were not willing to see these numbers specified in an agreement, even though in doing so we might collect the prize of limiting total Soviet warheads to a number considerably inferior to our own. The negotiators were being pressed to produce a theoretical equality in every category — but they were given nothing to trade.

It is against this background that the internal debate on SALT must be considered. A month after Brezhnev's visit to America — on July 26, 1973 — I reviewed SALT with Dobrynin. Our proposal to stop Soviet land-based deployment, he said, had been taken very badly by Brezhnev; land-based ICBMs were, after all, the "principal weapon" in the Soviet strategic arsenal. The Soviets would be willing to consider limits on both land-based and submarine-based MIRVs according to the principle of "equal security." The next day the Soviets submitted an "oral note" elaborating on these propositions. Lest we get the illusion that détente had altered its pettifogging style, the Kremlin asked as a matter of right for a superiority in numbers all across the board. Moscow arrived at this conclusion by including American forward-based nuclear weapons in our totals (aircraft in Europe or on carriers) — the bugbear of Europeans afraid that in the guise of SALT we would bargain away their security in their absence. (This would have added 600 launchers to Soviet totals.) And the Soviets asked for additional "compensation" for having to prepare against China in addition to preparing for a war in Europe. Modesty is not an attribute of Soviet opening positions; the Soviets asked for a numerical advantage in strategic weapons as "compensation" for the number of enemies they had made through a diplomacy of pressure and threat.

In a memorandum of August 1, my staff pointed out that the Soviet proposal contained the "usual shabby verbal tricks." The willingness to include MIRVed submarine-launched ballistic missiles meant little since the USSR would not be ready to deploy that kind of weapon for five years and it might thus use up its entire quota of permitted MIRVs on the land-based systems we were most eager to limit. On the other hand, the Soviet message defined the issue: The Soviets would not give up land-based MIRVs, certainly not for what we had heretofore offered (stopping our own deployment of Minuteman III only after it was 60 percent completed) and almost surely not for any other terms. We were thus left with the question of how to define limits for MIRVs that made strategic sense and were verifiable.

On August 9, I met Dobrynin to discuss the Soviet "oral note" of July 27. I said that I did not know what the Soviets meant by "equal security" as applied to MIRVs. If they wanted equal numbers of missiles, we would insist on equal numbers of warheads. Another way of approaching the problem, I added, putting forward Jim Schlesinger's point, would be to proceed on the basis of equal throwweight. (I did not explain that this meant far fewer Soviet missiles could be MIRVed.)

Dobrynin's reply was startling. Instead of going into all this technical detail, he said, the United States and the Soviet Union should take a "big step" and agree not to deploy *any* new missiles for ten years. In reply to my question Dobrynin suggested that this, of course, applied to Trident. Carried away, he threw the Soviet SS-17 and SS-19 into the pot as well. By our next meeting he was back in line: Our weapons were all "new," hence proscribed; the Soviet missiles were only "modernized," therefore did not fall under the ban. This piece of effrontery ended the only apparently innovative Soviet SALT proposal of my public life.

On August 15, 1973, I assembled the Verification Panel to prepare for the resumption of formal SALT talks in Geneva in the second half of September. Bureaucratic positions had not changed. No agency was willing to face the root fact that in the absence of an agreement the Soviets would exceed us in the number of MIRVed missiles in the early part of the Eighties and would have many more warheads than we. In the climate of the times, there was next to no prospect that the Congress would vote to increase strategic forces beyond the already disputed Trident and B-1. Even if we built up our strategic forces beyond what was planned — amidst the foreseeable public outcry — the funds would surely come out of the general purpose forces for strengthening regional defense that were our most urgent military priority.

Nevertheless, the Joint Chiefs of Staff continued to insist adamantly on equal aggregates (that is, equal overall totals of delivery vehicles); in return, they remained prepared to drop any attempt to limit MIRVs, thus substituting a Soviet edge in warheads for an advantage in delivery vehicles. The Chiefs maintained this position throughout the fall; at one point their representative, Lieutenant General Edward Rowny, on November 23 argued that the Chiefs did not see "anything they would pay for an MLBM [heavy missile] MIRV testing agreement that would be worth it." In other words, the doctrine of equal aggregates — for which we had no program — had become so sacrosanct that we were willing in its name to permit the Soviets to MIRV their heavy missiles even though that would speed the day of the total vulnerability of our entire Minuteman force and turn the achievement of equal aggregates into a strategic absurdity. And in such a world, what was the significance of numerical ceilings?

In truth, it was difficult to come up with an intellectually satisfying answer. Equal aggregates would not ease the vulnerability of our land-based missiles. Reductions — passionately advocated by some conservative opponents of SALT — were likely to make things worse, not better, at least in an interim period, until very low levels of MIRVed vehicles were achieved. Otherwise, since each missile by definition carried many weapons, a lower number would not alter the ratio between warheads and launchers; it would reduce the number of targets and thereby simplify a surprise attack.

So the fall of 1973 went by without major initiatives by either side. We maintained our position of May, proscribing Soviet land-based MIRVs even as a rapid Soviet testing program made it clear that SALT would not be able to achieve that objective. The Soviets formally put forward the proposal suggested to me by Dobrynin, to ban the introduction of new systems for ten years. But since it was based on the eccentric Soviet definition of what was new — including all American and no Soviet missiles — it offered no basis for exploration. Gromyko came and went for his annual fall visit without producing more than the promise to study the problem again. Gromyko had me at a slight disadvantage because we had never responded to the last Soviet offer. The gap between our two positions was so wide it was not worth the bureaucratic bloodletting to modify our existing proposal, however intellectually unsatisfying it might prove to be.

The Middle East war and its aftermath preoccupied leaders of both sides through the end of the year. It was not until January 1974 that SALT deliberations gained momentum again. At a National Security Council meeting on January 24, I presented the issues to the President in purely strategic terms: "[W]e want essential equivalence. But we have to be careful that we do not accept essential inequivalence in an arms race because we could not get what we thought was equivalence in SALT." And later in the meeting I made the same point again: "Many people have insisted on absolute equivalence in throwweight. I wish the same vigor were applied to our military programs as is applied to our SALT position."

My own view was that limiting Soviet MIRVs was paramount and that there could be no harm in accepting by agreement the ceilings that the Pentagon had established in its own *published* five-year projections and had no plans to exceed (and indeed, given the Congressional mood, would be lucky to reach). This meant in practice that I favored extending the 1972 Interim Agreement for a few years — with its disparity in numbers of total missile launchers — *provided* the Soviets accepted a reciprocal inequality in numbers of land-based ICBMs with MIRVs. Depending on how one counted, this inequality would be roughly 300 MIRVed missiles in our favor. Thus, the existing Soviet edge in overall numbers of delivery vehicles would be more than offset by an American advantage in the crucial category of MIRVed ICBMs, which would give us an advantage in warheads and reduce the vulnerability of our launchers. Counterbalancing asymmetries, if you will.

The problem was how to translate the theory into operational terms, which meant that before we could negotiate it with the Soviets we had to make it palatable to our bureaucracy. By then our agencies had learned from the Soviets; they were not to be bested in putting forward one-sided propositions. Ambassador U. Alexis Johnson, the head of our SALT delegation, advanced an aggregate ceiling of 2,350 launchers (some 150 above our unilateral program and 200 below the Soviets') *plus* equal ceilings on aggregate throwweight and on MIRVed throwweight. On January 11, 1974, the Pentagon at last spelled out the precise throwweight level it preferred. A joint memorandum from the Deputy Secretary of Defense and the Chairman of the Joint Chiefs ingeniously permitted us to fulfill all possible American programs while curtailing every Soviet one. It would allow us to increase our planned MIRV program by 450 to reach 1,000 Minuteman IIIs as well as to carry out the entire submarine-launched missile program (including 240 Trident missiles). The Soviets were given several options; under each of them they would have to abandon MIRVing their 308 heavy missiles as well as at least one of the new medium-range missiles, the SS-17 or SS-19. If the Soviets chose to deploy the heavier throwweight SS-19, they could MIRV only a hundred of them and would have to give up *all* other land-based MIRV programs.

How such a bargain was to be consummated was left to the negotiator. Since ultimately this was assumed to be me, no agency ran a great risk in putting forward a one-sided proposal. If I failed to achieve it, it could be ascribed to lack of negotiating skill or lack of firmness, as Jackson's aides constantly implied to the media. It was the bureaucracy's revenge for my freewheeling diplomacy in Nixon's first term.

There was, of course, no possibility of persuading the Soviets that they should reduce in every category while we would be free to build up in each. At the NSC meeting there was some desultory talk about increases in our defenses if SALT failed. Schlesinger suggested that for $2 billion a year more, we could undertake "significant new programs." Chief of Naval Operations Admiral Elmo Zumwalt, with understandable service bias, translated this into two more submarines — or forty-eight missiles — a year (never mind that at that point the Navy was in fact reducing the program). At that rate, it would take us nearly ten years to achieve equal aggregates by unilateral efforts, assuming the Soviets would do nothing to counteract what we did — an unlikely proposition.

No one was ready for the internal disputes involved in generating a more realistic approach. Nixon was wrapped up in Watergate. I was just back from the Sinai shuttle and was getting ready for the Washington Energy Conference. The Pentagon did not mind a deadlock. And I, too, judged that my preferred approach could issue only from a stalemate. We first had to prove that what had become conventional wisdom would not work, and that it was not really in our interest.

So we came up with a position that gave everybody what he wanted — usually the best proof that consensus was replacing a coherent strategy. The Chiefs' prize was equal aggregates; Ambassador Johnson got his ceiling of 2,350; Schlesinger prevailed with his theory of equal MIRV throwweight. No specific figure was agreed to, though Johnson was told that we were unlikely to accept a level for land-based MIRVs larger than the throwweight of our entire Minuteman force. Reducing the Soviets to our throwweight level meant limiting their MIRVs to about 200. In the meantime Senator Jackson had weighed in with a letter to the President indicating that his communication lines to the Joint Chiefs were in good working order. He put himself squarely behind the concepts in the Defense Department paper and took them a step further by linking them to reductions of launchers to 1,760 and commensurate reductions in MIRVs (based on a throwweight equivalence). He saw the "preoccupation" with MIRV limits as a "diversion." Having seen what Jackson could accomplish in blocking legislation that did not have to go through any of the Congressional committees of which he was a member, I had no doubt about what he could do to a SALT agreement from his senior position on the Armed Services Committee.

Quick deadlock was inevitable when American and Soviet SALT delegations resumed their deliberations in Geneva on February 19, 1974. The only new wrinkle was a hint from the Soviet delegation that it might drop its insistence on counting American forward-based systems, at the very end of the process after all other issues were resolved. In practice this meant that the next opportunity to break the deadlock would occur when I visited Moscow at the end of March to prepare the summit scheduled for June.

What we really needed was concept, not new arithmetic. SALT might have many uses but it could not reduce Soviet capabilities while increasing ours unless we had a massive building program. Therefore I came up with a scheme for an extension of the Interim Agreement for up to three years provided the Soviets accepted an inferiority in MIRVed land-based ICBMs comparable to its advantage in the overall number of launchers. The Soviets would therefore have 280 fewer land-based MIRVed missiles — the numerical advantage they enjoyed in delivery vehicles. The 550 Minuteman IIIs of our program were to be the baseline. I thought the agencies that were insistent on equal overall aggregates for a permanent agreement might go along with an interim arrangement. It offered us, even in the immediate trade, a gain of over

1,400 warheads.* We would also deprive the Soviets of several thousand warheads on missiles that could not be MIRVed under the agreement.

I did not really expect the Soviets to accept the numbers we would be proposing. There was no realistic prospect that they would confine themselves to 270 land-based MIRVed ICBMs. But if the principle of unequal aggregates for MIRVs was accepted, I hoped to shape an outcome that would delay the Soviets' achievement of a first-strike capability.

An NSC meeting on the subject took place on the afternoon of March 21. I summed up the case for extending the Interim Agreement coupled with MIRV limitation. (To make my point I assumed that we would MIRV all 1,000 of our Minuteman missiles though no such program existed, only a reference in a January 11 Defense Department memorandum that SALT limits on throwweight should permit us to MIRV them all.)

We have to decide whether we want a MIRV agreement in the Interim Agreement or to push forward to a permanent agreement; if we do the latter, we have to decide how much time we will take and set a deadline for ourselves. We can either slow down their rate or increase ours. To do nothing will produce a bigger gap, given the state of their deployments.

If the Soviet proposition is unacceptable, our practical choice will be to set an internal time limit and kick off development of Jim's program. But I must note our disparity — with Minuteman III we could have 3,000 weapons, or maybe 7,000 if we put seven MIRVs on it. They've got 1,500 weapons, with six to eight MIRVs each. The disparity will increase. With SALT II, we may be able to slow down the rate, and use Jim's new systems for leverage; or we can set a cutoff point and hold out for a permanent agreement. *The worst possible situation is to continue negotiating a permanent agreement and continue with our present programs.* [Emphasis added.]

Which, it must be said, is exactly what our domestic debate imposed on us.

Schlesinger gave a qualified approval to this approach:

I think it would be tragic if we cannot get a SALT agreement that ultimately leads to comprehensive equality. But we endorse a MIRV agreement, but more as a way-station on the road to permanent agreement providing essential equivalence. Adding a MIRV agreement to an interim agreement may be beneficial. In the long run, throwweight is important, but in the short run, it's not so important since they cannot exploit it. There is no risk before 1980 that the Soviet Union could obtain a measurable advantage.

---

*Depriving the Soviets of 280 medium-range missiles with six warheads, minus the 280 single warheads they would be permitted.

The Joint Chiefs would not oppose the Secretary of Defense; our SALT negotiator was relieved to have something to negotiate. So Nixon approved the proposal at the end of the meeting. I put it into an oral note that Dobrynin could send ahead of my scheduled arrival on March 24 to permit time for the Soviets to study our approach. Nixon in a personal letter to Brezhnev indicated that I had latitude to respond to Soviet counterproposals.

There is always the danger of confusing bureaucratic progress with substantive achievement. And so it was in this instance, as I set off for Moscow with more optimism than the situation warranted.

Another Visit to Moscow

ANYONE appointed to a senior position should engrave into his consciousness these fundamental principles of Washington public relations: One, never predict a result you are not 100 percent certain of achieving. And two, even then you are better off understating the probable outcome. The media never let you forget a failed forecast. They deal in deadlines and certitudes; they have little scope for nuance or probabilities. If the policymaker fails to call attention to imponderables, the media will rarely discover them on their own; even if he mentions them, they may be slighted because reporting lends itself better to simplifications than to qualifications. In the best of circumstances the promise of an achievement can never live up to its reality; the prediction will always be challenged when it is made and the achievement will be taken for granted afterward precisely because it has been foreshadowed.

I violated all these principles in a press conference on March 21 just prior to my departure for Moscow. Carried away by having brought our internal SALT position into the realm of intellectual respectability, I permitted myself to speculate that a similar achievement might await me in Moscow. In response to a question I gave a little lecture on the history of SALT that, while true enough, lacked a sure psychological touch:

All the SALT negotiations and, indeed, all the disarmament negotiations have gone through three phases. There is an initial phase of an exchange of technical information which usually takes place during a stalemate in the negotiating process; that is to say, the negotiating positions do not approach each other, but the technical comprehension of the issues is clarified.

Then — this is essentially what has been going on in Geneva up to now — then a point is reached where there has to be a conceptual breakthrough; that is to say, where the two sides have to agree on what it is they are trying to accomplish. And after that there has to be the hard negotiation on giving concrete content to this conceptual breakthrough.

As political theory for a seminar in international relations, this was great material. Unfortunately, the media looked for phrases that lent themselves to encapsuling an outcome, not understanding a process. They focused on the slogan "conceptual breakthrough," not on the explanation underlying it. And in predicting a "breakthrough," conceptual or otherwise, I created a yardstick against which my trip three days hence could be measured. I overlooked that no negotiating position prevails this rapidly with the Soviets; there was no precedent for achieving a breakthrough in SALT with a single message to Brezhnev. And in this case, the Soviets had no particular reason to be accommodating on SALT in order to maintain the momentum of other relationships which were in fact atrophying. So the "conceptual breakthrough" took its place with my "peace is at hand" press conference eighteen months earlier. One final rule for aspirants to high office: If you cannot resist the urge to make a prediction, use turgid and impenetrable prose; you will never escape your mistakes if you have a talent for aphorisms.

I was not in Moscow for long before I realized that things were not destined to go swimmingly. A faint chill became evident when the venue was shifted from the informality of the Politburo hunting preserve in Zavidovo (where Gromyko had told me in February the meetings were scheduled) to the more protocol-conscious Moscow. Not that Soviet hospitality lacked anything in exuberance. The reception was cordial. Brezhnev was buoyant and cheerful. He had some new toys. Before him there was a dome-shaped brass object. When the top was lifted, it revealed six brass cartridgelike objects pointing skyward. I asked whether it was a model of a Soviet MIRV, and whether I could report that each Soviet MIRV had six warheads (I had seen estimates based on less concrete evidence). Brezhnev, hugely amused, removed the cover from one of the cartridges, revealing six cigarettes. Two other new toys were a French-made wristwatch, all of whose works were visible, and a mariner's clock that Brezhnev set to chime on occasions he considered significant, such as when he slightly modified his original SALT proposal.

Brezhnev began the session by stressing that despite "complications" (he rejected my use of the word "disappointments"), his commitment to détente remained unimpaired. He said that without going into the "various details" of what was taking place in the United States — and he was hearing and reading a lot about it — President Nixon seemed to be displaying firmness and resolve to move ahead toward the further "deepening" of relations between the Soviet Union and the United States. He felt obliged to point out that in order to move further ahead we had to overcome a few "difficulties and obstacles" that were integrally linked to improving not only US–Soviet relations but also the atmosphere in the world. He felt sure, nevertheless, that the experience of the past would help us find correct solutions without violating the principles we had agreed upon.

I replied in kind, but protestations of goodwill cannot sustain relations among superpowers that are ideological adversaries. And the fact was that each of the subjects on the agenda bred controversy. On MFN, as I have already described, I brought additional demands rather than progress. I had the unenviable task of telling the General Secretary of a totalitarian state not only that we insisted on increased emigration but that we proposed to dictate the geographic areas within his country from which these emigrants should be drawn. We avoided a blowup on that issue and indeed obtained some Soviet concessions later in the month. But there are no free lunches in international relations. What we might gain on Jewish emigration was bound to reduce Soviet responsiveness in other areas.

It was on the Middle East that we had our most difficult talks. Brezhnev bristled. As had Gromyko six weeks earlier in Washington, he accused us of violating the understanding on joint auspices, first with respect to Egypt and now with Syria. As then, I replied that the "appropriate auspices" had been intended to facilitate negotiations between the parties, not to prevent them from talking in the most convenient forum. I offered to meet Gromyko or other Soviet representatives for regular discussions on the Middle East. Brezhnev growled — not inaccurately — that I was talking procedure; he was concerned with substance. I was offering information; he wanted participation. After listening to a half-hour quibble between Gromyko and me about methods of our consultations, Brezhnev got to the heart of the matter, in the process demonstrating the Soviet adaptability to reality. He broke his silence to say that he had been listening "attentively" to the colloquy between Gromyko and me, and felt it only pointed up the correctness of his original complaint: Never before, Brezhnev avowed, had he heard such an open statement of the American intention to exclude Soviet participation. The two sides having stated their views on this question, he concluded darkly, it left "hands free to act at one's own discretion."

I said somewhat irrelevantly that five kilometers one way or another on the Golan Heights were less important than US–Soviet relations. Brezhnev professed his own dedication to the relationship, which meant that he would not let the Middle East impair it.

But it also gave him no reason to hasten any progress on SALT, the discussion of which framed the other subjects. We took it up during our first two sessions on March 25 and during our last session on March 27. At the first session Brezhnev put forward a proposal to extend the Interim Agreement through 1980 and add to it an equal limitation of 1,000 MIRVs for each side. The United States and the Soviet Union would be free to decide on the composition of their forces; in technical terms there would be "freedom to mix" between the land-based or sea-based missiles. Strangely enough — except for keeping the unequal aggregates left over from SALT I — this proposal came closer to the real preferences of the Joint Chiefs of Staff than what I had brought with me to Moscow. But it did not really meet our needs, for reasons that I gave to Brezhnev in the evening session on March 25:

Let me explain our difficulties, and let me explain how it will present itself in the United States. You will remember from my public testimony when Senator Jackson attacked the first agreement, we defended it on the grounds that MIRV made up for the imbalance in numbers in the first phase. If we now extend that agreement, and add to it a provision of 1,000 MIRVed missiles, there will be two criticisms made, at least: One, that the numerical advantage now will become effective because of the number of warheads. Second, because the Soviet Union has more MIRVs on each launcher than we do, you will have a numerical advantage not only in the number of missiles but in the number of warheads. Thirdly, because the Soviet warheads are heavier than ours, it means the land-based force of the Soviet Union will be able to acquire a first-strike capability against ours. And therefore if there is not some ceiling on land-based missiles that takes account of the different numbers of warheads on each of these missiles, the position will become very complicated. In addition, we have the problem that at the level of 1,000, we would have to stop deploying MIRVs soon, while you would be starting yours. We would have no way of knowing if you are stopping. You will reach 1,000 at the very end of this process. So if you put, say, 500–800 on your land-based missiles — I give you the arguments quite honestly as they will be put to us — and if our calculation is correct that you have six on each, you would have 3,000–5,000 warheads, and you would be able to destroy our Minuteman.

I don't want to give you ideas, but these are the arguments that will be made. I just wanted to give you the reasoning of our people.

Brezhnev, of course, strenuously denied that the Soviet leadership could have in mind anything so gross as an attack on our Minuteman force. And he rejected the proposition that SALT I was unequal. He produced a map showing areas of the Soviet Union that could be reached from our forward-based systems in Europe or in the Mediterranean. It was reasonably accurate if one assumed one-way missions for our fighter bombers, which Soviet planners — applying their own version of the "worst case" scenario — are bound to do. Our proposal to confine Soviet land-based deployments to 270 ICBMs was impossible for the Soviet Union. Said Brezhnev: "If I agree to this, this will be my last meeting with Dr. Kissinger, because I will be destroyed." After reviewing all kinds of technical matters, we agreed to allow time for further study before another discussion.

This took place on my last day in Moscow, March 27. On that occasion a kind of conceptual breakthrough did in fact occur, though it was not treated as such by a skeptical press corps or for that matter by all elements of our government. A six-hour Politburo session delayed our meeting with Brezhnev; characteristically, we were given no explanation until afterward. Our morning meeting was canceled; we waited in our guest house in the Lenin Hills for the summons that did not come until about 5:00 P.M. I had told a protocol officer sarcastically that I had always wanted to spend a winter vacation in Moscow. But then the meeting convened — not, I am sure, because of my comment but because the Politburo meeting had ended. After opening pleasantries Brezhnev announced that the Soviet Union was now prepared to accept the *principle* of unequal MIRV aggregates. Brezhnev proposed 1,100 MIRVed vehicles for the United States, 1,000 for the Soviet Union.

It was a major step forward, advanced in a characteristically grudging manner. The Soviets always leave room for bargaining; I knew no instance where a Soviet opening position was anywhere close to the final outcome. Once the principle of unequal MIRV aggregates in our favor had been conceded, the gap would almost certainly be subject to improvement through negotiations.

Brezhnev presented his proposal with considerable ingenuity. The figure for total aggregates was fair, he argued, because the Soviets were scrapping 210 missiles as part of SALT I and they did not count the 90 missiles in the British and French strategic forces. In other words, the Kremlin out of the goodness of its heart was giving up precisely the 300 missiles we claimed constituted their advantage. (That turned out to be wrong; even after scrapping 210 missiles the Soviets would retain a numerical advantage.) And now to carry generosity almost to extremes, in Brezhnev's version, they were throwing another 100 missiles into the bargain. This gave Brezhnev even simpler arithmetic. He could have argued that by agreeing to an advantage of 100 MIRVed missiles for us he was giving us 500 extra warheads, thus closing the gap. Equal aggregates would then have been achieved.

Brezhnev implied but never made these arguments explicitly — perhaps because his arms controllers had not yet reached the abstruse level of sophistication of ours. In any event, these arguments would not have been conclusive. The breakthrough was as yet conceptual; the numbers remained inadequate. Given the Soviet advantage in throwweight, the total of 1,000 Soviet MIRVed missiles was far too high, the gap in our favor far too small. We doubted whether the Soviet Union would be able to deploy more than 1,000 MIRVed missiles before the end of 1980 when the proposed agreement would expire; we would thus be doing little more than ratifying each side's program. (There would, of course, be a presumption that the limits might be extended upon expiration of the interim period.) More worrisome, Brezhnev's proposal was consistent with an attempt to freeze our deployment while the Soviet Union was catching up in MIRVs — especially because we would have fulfilled our program by 1977 (except for Trident) while the Soviets were still building. Thus the Soviets could theoretically build their permitted MIRVs on land and switch to sea-based MIRVs only after 1980 when the agreement would have expired.

This is why I insisted that any ceiling on MIRVs must contain a sublimit on land-based missiles. But Brezhnev adamantly refused to make any such commitment. He was prepared, he said, to promise an informal understanding to notify us each year of planned submarine-launched missile deployments; he would not accept a formal limit. Such notification was meaningless. If there were no agreed limits we would have no basis for objecting; and a yearly report would be too late to affect our decisions and would not add much, if anything, to what we knew from our own intelligence reports.

We thus were in a position not unfamiliar from previous negotiations: The concept of an inequality of MIRVs in our favor was extremely important. The particular application of it was preposterous; I turned it down without even checking with Washington. I stressed that the prospect of converting Brezhnev's "breakthrough" into an agreement would depend on two factors: whether the gap in MIRVs between the two forces could be increased; and whether the Soviets would accept a ceiling on the total number of MIRVed land-based missiles. Without these two conditions, a SALT agreement would be largely optical. We left it that both sides would reexamine their positions and continue their exchanges.

This outcome, when it became known, led to many lugubrious comments in our media about the failure of the Moscow trip, reflecting substantial ignorance of Soviet negotiating tactics. At the end of the talks in Moscow we were not, in fact, in a bad tactical position: A new proposal had been put forward by the Soviets in the most ungenerous manner possible, raising the prospect of strenuous bargaining to achieve the final result. We had been through that particular wringer before. It is not possible to prove whether the approach of differential MIRV limits would have ultimately succeeded. One *can* say that we were basically heading in the right direction. Agreement would depend on many factors: pressures on the Soviet system, trade-offs for gains that the Soviets might seek in other areas, single-mindedness and unity in the American negotiating position, and the Soviets' assessment of Nixon's staying power.

Regrettably, the single-mindedness and unity of our bargaining position were far from evident. One of the gravest problems was the galloping weakness of the President. By April 1974, the Judiciary Committee of the House of Representatives was clearly heading for impeachment. The omens were so apparent that Gromyko in April inquired into the procedures of our government in that contingency. The likelihood that the Nixon Presidency was coming to an early end must certainly have affected the Politburo's calculations about how many more concessions were sensible in this round of negotiations.

Previous experience had shown that if one wanted progress, one had to keep up the pressure on an agreed concept, exploring the many variations and permutations until the Soviets could convince themselves concessions were imperative if they wanted to avoid a blowup. A functioning Nixon could have imposed this on a bureaucracy that had acquiesced in the new approach but did not have its heart in it. But under Watergate conditions, internal divisions became self-perpetuating. Clearly, the agencies preferred an agreement enshrining a numerical equality in launchers across the board — even though this would eventually lead to far more Soviet warheads than my preferred scheme (and even the unacceptable Soviet scheme). One of the principal reasons for this seemingly perverse attitude was the calumny to which officials would be exposed in testifying before the Congress.

Whatever the reason, a Verification Panel meeting of April 27 made clear that there was little enthusiasm for our official position. I was scheduled for talks with Gromyko in Geneva on April 28–29; our major purpose was to deal with Syria but we were certain to review SALT as well. At the Verification Panel I favored a counterproposal to the Soviets limiting Soviet MIRVed missiles to no more than 850 by 1980. My staff and I — backed by intelligence reports — calculated that the Soviets were likely to deploy some 200 submarine-based MIRVed missiles in that period; the practical effect would therefore be to reduce Soviet land-based MIRVed ICBMs to around 600. I now heard the astonishing proposition that this figure — which reduced the Soviet potential by several thousand warheads — was insignificant because even 600 ICBMs could threaten our Minuteman force. The corollary was that it made no difference how many warheads the Soviets had beyond a certain number. In that case, of course, it was hard to understand why there was such an uproar about the unequal aggregates in launchers of the SALT I agreement — amounting to a Soviet edge of only 300 single warheads, counterbalanced by our large superiority in bombers. There was merit in the proposition that even 600 MIRVed missiles could threaten our Minuteman force. What was less clear was how our critics proposed to improve the situation by torpedoing an agreement and why the saving of a few thousand warheads was without significance (which, if true, raised profound questions about our own defense program).

By now our domestic debate had turned liturgical. Slogans had become the weapons in a philosophical dispute over the nature of East-

West relations. We encountered a dilemma already familiar from our experience in Vietnam: Philosophical opponents were even more afraid of the success of a negotiation than of its failure. Whenever we seemed to make even marginal progress, they surfaced new objections: demands for equal aggregates for which we had no unilateral program; complaints about throwweight totals that we had imposed upon ourselves and never tried to alter; now a denial of the significance of any MIRV limits. After all, we could have mitigated the throwweight gap by equipping Minuteman with six or seven warheads and the disparity in numbers by pushing cruise missiles. Nor was a new missile precluded by any of the SALT proposals on the table. SALT was both resented and given unrealistic tasks. In exasperation I said at the April 27 meeting:

What's all this I read about the throwweight problem? I want to know why it is that we are always talking ourselves into a lather. If we want a bigger missile, why aren't we building one? Who's stopping us? I've certainly never heard of a proposal for a new ICBM since I've been here. . . .

Nothing in the Interim Agreement stops you from deploying a new missile. No one is stopping [you] from deploying this; and I assure you the White House will not stop you. All we've got now is Trident under the Interim Agreement. In an extended Interim Agreement we could start a new missile. . .

No one ever made the case that SALT would stop their programs. You can't blame the Interim Agreement for that. Those are their decisions. Our program is the result of our decisions. SALT does not stop any of our programs.

At the end I was authorized to "explore" my scheme; but I had little conviction that a united bureaucracy would sustain me if the Soviets were to accept it, even less once Jackson launched his predictable assault. Indeed, there was a strong probability that many of my associates would disavow the scheme in the end. It was not the most uplifting way to leave for a meeting with Gromyko.

Predictably, the SALT portion of my talks with Gromyko on April 28–29 ended inconclusively. There were simply too many uncertainties on both sides to permit an all-out effort. Gromyko had other fish to fry; I had no latitude to explore variations. Gromyko asked the key question from the Soviet point of view: "What's in it for us?" And in truth, there was little incentive for the Soviets to constrain their programs while we fulfilled ours. I painted a lurid prospect of what we would do in the absence of an agreement: MIRV all our Minutemen; continue building Tridents. But Gromyko knew our five-year projections because we were helpfully publishing them each year. And he must have doubted that the mortally wounded President would be able to get such programs through a rebellious Congress.

By the time I returned from the Syrian shuttle a month later, our bureaucratic pattern had frozen. Nixon's Presidency was in its terminal phase. Many serious senior officials were concerned that a SALT agreement achieved under these conditions would be badly flawed whatever its intrinsic merit; it would look like a Nixon ploy to escape his fate. And whatever the terms, they were bound to wonder whether a successor President might not improve on them.

Such reasoning must have been behind Schlesinger's decision to go into open opposition to what was still our official position, which he had approved a month earlier. Reversing his earlier support of the concept of unequal MIRVs offsetting unequal aggregates, he dramatically affirmed the concept of equal aggregates all across the board and in the process embraced drastic reductions as well. The occasion was a reply to a letter from Jackson to Schlesinger on April 22 asking the Secretary to comment on his reductions proposal, which had also advocated equal aggregates. Schlesinger took his time but on June 3 he praised Jackson's approach:

> Your proposal, generally, satisfies most criteria currently being used as guidelines for SALT, and also has other inherently attractive features, as discussed in the enclosed assessment.

In practice this meant the end of the scheme we were negotiating. The Soviets, having seen what Jackson could do to block East-West trade, could have no doubt what he could accomplish when backed by Nixon's own Secretary of Defense. In any event, ratification of an agreement not wholeheartedly supported by the Pentagon was unlikely, probably even undesirable. SALT II was reviewed again by our government in preparation for the summit, and Nixon and Brezhnev had a long discussion about it when we were in the USSR (see Chapter XXIV). But at least in retrospect, it is clear that serious prospects for SALT in the Nixon Presidency ended by early June 1974 with the Schlesinger letter.

Conclusion

E<small>VEN</small> with the perspective of nearly a decade, I believe that the approach we put forward in the spring of 1974 offered a better chance to constrain the buildup of Soviet MIRVs than any imposed on us afterward by domestic pressures. The equal aggregates that were the rallying cry of so many opponents turned out to be more symbol than substance. The Soviets agreed to equal aggregates at Vladivostok in November 1974. But none of the succeeding administrations (including Reagan's) ever made any effort to build up to the permitted level; each has lived voluntarily with a numerical gap in delivery vehicles that it would not accept as part of the agreement. And in the meantime, Soviet MIRV deployment has reached a level far higher than what was envisaged in the run-up to the summit and then rejected by SALT opponents as too dangerous. They have thousands more warheads than they would have had if in 1974 we had succeeded in negotiating the schemes we pursued. And we have no more delivery vehicles.

One can argue that the differential in our favor of several thousand warheads makes no strategic difference; one cannot maintain at the same time that the Administration was ''soft'' in being willing to achieve it at the price of 300 single warhead launchers. Nor did it ever make any sense to ask SALT negotiators to reduce Soviet forces by diplomacy to a nonthreatening level when we had no building program to produce an incentive for it. But even a building program would have had to answer the query: If an advantage of 1,500 warheads in SALT was meaningless, what edge could a building program achieve that was strategically significant? In other words, as I said in a much-maligned press conference in Moscow at the end of the summit: ''What in the name of God is strategic superiority?'' Until we answer that question, arms control will be threatened by demagoguery and the strategic buildup by the absence of a rationale.

To be sure, the Soviets' offers were almost invariably preposterous. But this is par for the course. I cannot prove what would have happened had negotiations evolved in normal circumstances with a strong and functioning President and a united American government. I am convinced that in the spring of 1974, SALT became the whipping boy in a more fundamental philosophical contest over East-West relations. For its votaries, SALT turned into an end in itself; for its opponents, it was a danger to be combatted at any cost. SALT was no longer a part of a broader, coherent security policy or an overall strategy. Thrust upon itself, it became an orphan and a victim, ground down between a liberal idealism unrelated to a concept of power and a conservative dogmatism unleavened by a sense of proportion or strategy. And it was doomed above all by the inability of the President to supply consistent leadership during his Watergate travail.

Missed opportunities unfortunately can never be proven. What gave the period discussed here its melancholy cast was that the United States weakened its capacity both to resist Soviet aggression and to build a better world by domestic disputes that turned honest disagreements into a species of civil war. Shortly after Golda Meir tendered her resignation, I said to her in a somber mood:

The world may be heading for a war because the totalitarian countries are too bureaucratic and the democracies too demagogic. Frankly, I may have to consider in the next six months the same decision you made. I can't keep fighting against labor, the Congress, the liberals, the intellectuals. It has nothing to do with your problem. Six months of Cold War and we will be back to "peace at any cost." The people who demoralized us for years about Vietnam are responsible. If I explained in detail what I am doing, I would win Meany but lose the Russians. I am carrying out the toughest policy that can be sustained over a long period.

This is not to suggest that we "provoked" the Soviets into the acts of aggression that followed. Nations do not have the right to send proxy troops around the world because they have been denied MFN. Nor is it proper for a country to shift to its interlocutor the intellectual burden of breaking every deadlock as has been the Soviet attitude in SALT. There is no excuse for the Soviet-Cuban expeditionary forces in Angola and Ethiopia, the Soviet encroachment in South Yemen and invasion of Afghanistan, the Kremlin's encouragement of North Vietnam's takeover of first South Vietnam and Laos and then Cambodia, and the brutal pressures on Poland. Other nations have suffered disappointment without assaulting the international order in response. Though we made our share of mistakes, the fundamental assault on détente came from Moscow, not Washington.

Still, I reflect with melancholy on the way America consumed its unity in 1973–1974. One would have thought that an America racked by Watergate, with the Vietnam cease-fire in a precarious state, and a Middle East and energy crisis on its agenda, would be surfeited with confrontation. Instead, we found that the area of policy we had quieted down — East-West relations — became increasingly controversial. We reckoned it a considerable achievement to have kept Moscow from taking advantage of our crisis of authority, just as we earlier had used détente to isolate Hanoi and extricate ourselves from Vietnam. We were in the process of dramatically reducing Soviet influence in the Middle East. None of this prevented first rumblings about détente and then open season on it — as if a mortally wounded President had that much choice about the risks to which he could expose his country.

There is no question in my mind that one of the casualties of the period was a balanced, careful, thoughtful approach to East-West relations. The sober teaching of the 1973–1974 period is that idealism did not, in the end, enhance the human rights of Jews in the Soviet Union (the emigration figure for 1975 was less than 40 percent of that for 1973); that the undermining of SALT did not improve our military posture; and that where the crusade against détente was successful it produced perverse consequences. The approach being legislated did not deter Soviet expansion. That increased, and the same domestic divisions that had spawned the confrontation prevented an effective response. The Soviet Union was not induced to behave in a more reasonable manner. The Administration had no illusions about Soviet purposes, but the domestic debate confused, instead of illuminated, the nation's understanding of the complexity of our challenge. Thereby it diminished, rather than enhanced, our nation's ability either to block Soviet adventures or to explore the possibilities of coexistence.

The fact was that our critics had a better philosophical case than the technical obstacles that they were so ingeniously throwing into the path of our policy. It was a serious issue whether the American people could sustain a long drawn-out contest on grounds other than a moral crusade. Our policy did involve the risk of lowering vigilance through the fact of constant negotiations — this surely was the Soviet strategy. On the other hand, our critics refused to face the reality that the alternative they advocated involved the danger of isolating us from our allies and alienating us from our own people. We believed that our policy of seeking to dominate the peace issue would better prepare us for the long struggle in which we agreed with our conservative critics we were involved. It was a national tragedy that those who shared a similar strategic analysis should conduct a civil war over tactics.

For our security and well-being in the nuclear age and to give hope to the world, our foreign policy must have a sense of positive purpose and design. That, in turn, requires a united people and a sense of continuity. Our goals in the world must not again be subordinated to our differences; foreign policy cannot be segmented into a series of domestic skirmishes. A divided America deprives the world of all hope; only a united country has a chance to help preserve international security and to help shape a better future for the peoples of this planet.

XXIII

The Syrian Shuttle

I N the spring of 1974, it was clear on any calculation that the Syrian negotiation required priority. It was the capstone of the Middle East peace process. Its achievement would enable Sadat to proceed without being accused of betraying his ally; it would prevent pressures for the restoration of the oil embargo; and it would seal our domination of Middle East diplomacy. But the world does not stand still so that one may gather one's wits. While a diplomat is often flatteringly viewed as moving in an orderly manner from one chess puzzle to another, in practice that cocoon of urbane concentration is not often or easily reached. I returned from the travels that established the negotiating procedures for the Syrian disengagement on March 4. Immediately afterward, we had the blowup with our European allies toward which both sides had been building for the better part of a year. Less than two weeks later I was in Moscow. Then the Sixth Special Session of the General Assembly of the United Nations, focusing on problems of economic development, brought a seemingly unending stream of distinguished visitors to Washington.

And on March 30, in an act transcending all else in its effect on my life, Nancy Maginnes and I were married.

In all, it was almost two months before I resumed my Middle East travels. Not until the end of April did I embark on the Syrian shuttle, the exhausting negotiation that finally led to the disengagement of the Israeli and Syrian armies on the Golan Heights. I invited my new bride to join me and I told her to pack lightly. Little did I realize when I set out what a prolonged effort and drama lay ahead. For thirty-four weary days, I was to shuttle back and forth between Damascus and Jerusalem, greeted by hostile demonstrations against me in Israel and sullen stares in the streets of Damascus. How well I came to know the roads to the airports in these two capitals less than 150 miles apart and yet so totally uncomprehending of each other, the stark Judean hills and the flat plain of Damascus with snow-covered Mount Hermon framing the horizon! I interpreted each side to the other, came up with proposals to break the recurring deadlocks, and spent many a long night grappling with arcane issues whose intrinsic insignificance was transmuted into historic causes by the passions and traumas of the Middle East.

And yet that was not the essence of the story. What made the Syrian-Israeli shuttle as moving as it was tortuous was that in the process each side caught at least a glimpse of the truth that the only hope for their future lay in coexistence. And in traveling that road they did more than achieve an agreement; they discovered something about themselves.

Caging the Bear

BEFORE any of this could begin, the most important preliminary task was to prevent the Soviets from intruding into the negotiation in a manner that would have made it futile. Détente assisted in this process; so did the design of the negotiation. But success here was more than anything a reflection of the strategic reality our policy had fostered — that we were the only power capable of talking effectively to all parties.

One result of my February shuttle was that Israel and Syria had agreed to send emissaries to Washington to discuss disengagement separately with me. This plan had been devised to get around the difficulty that the Israeli plan for disengagement was so grudging that I could not conceivably put it to Asad; indeed, it was less a plan than a stopgap device to permit Israel to resolve its cabinet crisis before turning to serious negotiation. I set the visit by Moshe Dayan to follow my trip to Moscow in March so that I would not have to brief the Soviet leaders on what he brought, which I anticipated to be still less than satisfactory. The visit of the Syrian emissary was scheduled so that it followed the start of a visit by President Asad to Moscow in mid-April; this would forestall any temptation for Syria to add Soviet pressures to its own.

None of these stratagems would have worked if Asad and Sadat had not had a clear understanding that their own interests were best served by American mediation. I was reasonably certain of Sadat but Asad had not yet really been put to the test. An opportunity soon arose. When I visited Moscow on March 24–28, both Brezhnev and Gromyko demanded that the Syrian disengagement be negotiated in Geneva in the presence of Soviet representatives. My judgment about the futility of this course had not changed since I had turned it down in February. As then, I used the Soviets' Arab friends as an excuse; from Moscow I sent cables to obtain the reaction of both Sadat and Asad.

On Sadat's behalf, Fahmy asked me not to "budge" even if Asad yielded. I expected this because Sadat — even more than we — needed a demonstration that only the United States could deliver in the Middle East.

Heroic as Sadat's posture was, I have no idea how we could have insisted on an exclusively American mediation had Asad chosen otherwise. Nothing so much demonstrated the weakness of the Soviet position than the fact that Asad did not. Within hours of receipt of my query, Asad replied that he stuck to the agreed procedure. He favored a movement to Geneva only *after* I had worked out the main features of an agreement "in the area"; Geneva could then tie up loose details. There had been nothing, we were told, to require a change in the procedures settled upon in early March. The President of Syria, remarkably, preferred to negotiate *without* his principal ally.

The Soviets did not, of course, give up. A transparent example of Soviet disinformation followed. Reports began circulating in the Middle East that while in Moscow I had told the Soviets that Israel would never withdraw from the Golan Heights. On March 30, in a message to Asad, I sharply denied this story. Asad replied on April 2, accepting my version and characterizing the reports as malicious and specious. Asad specifically assured me that he did not believe the rumors.

Next, there was a double squeeze, with Gromyko confronting Nixon in Washington at the same time that Brezhnev was attempting to suborn Asad in Moscow. Gromyko, taking time out on April 12 from the special UN General Assembly session in New York, assailed Nixon with acerbic complaints. He called our actions "separatist"; he would not be satisfied with a form of consultation that did no more than keep him informed. Joint action was the Soviet desire, though Gromyko was at a loss how to give it concrete meaning. Prior to the meeting I had warned Nixon by memorandum:

> Any direct Soviet participation in Middle East negotiations would inevitably greatly reduce the chances of success in bringing peace to the area. For one thing, Sadat and Asad as well as Israel want to keep them out. For another, they want to lump all the issues together in one big negotiation at Geneva, and we believe the whole process will stall unless we can continue to segment the negotiation into politically manageable units. Thus, we must continue to exclude the Soviets, while at the same time publicly minimizing their exclusion and privately reassuring them of our intention to keep them informed at every step of the negotiations. We are prepared to discuss the Syrian-Israeli disengagement in a general way or to discuss in theory the future role of the Geneva Conference, but we do not want to get into such detail as to enable the Soviets to build resistance to specific proposals.

Nixon threaded his way through that maze with admirable ambiguity. Nothing was further from his mind, he told Gromyko, than to exclude Moscow. Indeed, our whole strategy was designed to enable the Soviets to play a significant role — which was nearly as much news to me as to Gromyko. The United States was simply dealing with those parts of the problem where it was better placed to produce progress. If Gromyko wanted to exchange roles and deliver the Israelis to a Golan agreement, he was surely welcome to try. In that case, we would be glad to take on the Syrians as clients. (Of course, even that definition of the problem would always leave the Soviets on the outside since there was no fore-seeable issue on which they would be able to exercise a major influence on Israel.) But Nixon affected the pose of being above such trivia as the modalities of an agreed negotiation; as in February, he turned the solution of this technical problem over to foreign ministers, whose mis-sion prevented them from sharing his lofty vision: "I hope you and Dr. Kissinger can work out some understanding so we can proceed to our goal, the peace settlement which we both pursue. I leave it to both of you and Dobrynin can be the referee."

In my own discussion with Gromyko I proposed a meeting with him in Geneva on my way to the Syrian shuttle in late April. Gromyko countered with Damascus as a venue. But it takes two to meet, and I would not import the implication of US–Soviet condominium into a Middle Eastern capital.

Asad, of course, held the key. He could have ended our diplomacy at any time he chose. As a reflection of his crucial position, he was wooed with a lavish reception on his visit to Moscow; at the Kremlin dinner in Asad's honor, Brezhnev warned that "ersatz plans" for dis-engagement would mean "replacing an overall settlement with partial agreements of a different kind." Rather pathetically, he went on to thank Syria for recognizing "the importance of the Soviet Union's participa-tion" in any peace settlement. What that meant was unclear. It surely did not extend to the current negotiation.

The joint Soviet-Syrian communiqué issued on April 16 asserted that any disengagement "must be part and parcel" of an overall Middle East peace settlement. The two sides had "discussed and outlined steps for further strengthening" Syria's military capacity. Mischievously throw-ing a match into a vat of oil, the Soviets affirmed Syria's "inalienable right to use all effective means for liberation of her occupied lands."[1]

Asad, a supreme nationalist, pocketed the Soviet arms aid but did not adopt the Soviet program. On April 18 he wrote me that while in Mos-cow he had conducted a "general review" of activities concerning dis-engagement. However — and that was the important part — he main-tained that no agreement was reached which would contradict the procedure he and I had already agreed on. In other words, lavish recep-tion in Moscow or not, Asad would stick with the plan that excluded the Soviets. As for Gromyko's desire to meet with me in Damascus, Asad went as far as he dared to dissociate himself; the Soviets had not raised the subject, he pointed out. Syria would agree provided it repre-sented "a joint desire" by the two superpowers. In other words, Asad would not request such a meeting nor would he seek to undo my oppo-sition to it; he would not, however, be the fall guy — that honor he reserved for me. Later in the day a Syrian Presidential aide, fearing that his chief had not been explicit enough, spelled it all out for our chargé, Tom Scotes. The aide made clear that if both sides desired the meeting, Syria would agree, but Damascus would not agree if Washington did not agree. I got the point.

A meeting between Gromyko and me in Geneva was much less than what the Soviets wanted; it turned out to be more than Egypt favored. On April 18 — the day Sadat publicly declared the end of an era of Egypt's exclusive reliance on Soviet military aid — Foreign Minister Ismail Fahmy called on Nixon. He was in the United States in connection with a UN Security Council session on Lebanon. Fahmy underlined what he had already conveyed to us from Cairo, that any visible Soviet role in the Middle East would undermine American influence and Sadat's freedom of maneuver; Egypt sought American political support, he said, and a "red light" to the Soviets. Some helpful European allies had allegedly told him that we had committed ourselves to joint action with the Soviet Union in the Middle East. There was no problem in reassuring Fahmy about our strategy, though we did not have the same interest in humiliating Moscow and flaunting its impotence as Egypt had in seeking to justify its switch from reliance on the Soviet Union to close cooperation with the United States.

The Arab World

THE exclusion of the Soviets gave the United States a relatively free hand, for there was already a consensus among Arab leaders on the priority of a prompt Syrian negotiation. Radical Asad and Boumedienne agreed on this, as did moderate Faisal and Hussein. So even did Yasir Arafat of the PLO.

The PLO was heard from again in early 1974. We had as little desire to involve Arafat as we had to share the table with Gromyko, for we viewed the PLO as a potentially disruptive force.

It is important to recall how the PLO appeared at that time. Not yet recognized even by most Arab states as the sole spokesman for the Palestinians, it presented itself to us largely as a terrorist group. The PLO program still called for the destruction of Israel under the slogan of creating a secular state in Palestine. Its determination to destroy the Hashemite Kingdom of Jordan had been personally expressed to us in our sole high-level contact with the PLO.

I have described in Chapter XIII the meeting between a senior PLO leader and General Vernon Walters, then Deputy Director of the CIA, in November 1973. This had been to encourage PLO quiescence in the delicate postwar phase when we were assembling the Geneva Conference and preparing for Egyptian-Israeli disengagement. We were at a comparably critical juncture now.

Since we had briefed the Arabs (and the Israelis), it was not surprising that there was some follow-up, though as long as the PLO did not disavow its terrorist aims or recognize Israel, our position on its unacceptability as a negotiating partner remained unchanged. A few days after the end of the January 1974 shuttle, Sadat briefed Ambassador Hermann Eilts on Arab attitudes in the wake of disengagement. Sadat mentioned that he had talked with Arafat and King Hassan of Morocco; a meeting for me with the head of the PLO could be arranged at any time I wished. I evaded the proposal.

On February 10 Fahmy proposed that Eilts establish contact with PLO representatives in Cairo. We were anything but eager to link Egyptian policies to those of the PLO or to involve Egyptian prestige in messy West Bank negotiations. So when on February 12 we were approached through Morocco for another meeting with Walters, it seemed to solve several problems at once. It defused the Cairo pressures; it would ease the decision of various OPEC fence-sitters with respect to the oil embargo; most important, it could calm the atmosphere for the planned Syrian shuttle. Therefore, on February 16 we agreed to another meeting between Walters and a PLO representative in Morocco.

The meeting was actually held on March 7. Once again Walters had only a listening brief. He played for time, as was our plan, by telling the PLO leader that we were not ready for further contacts until after a Syrian disengagement. The PLO representative had nothing to add to his previous presentation, either. He tried to pressure us by stressing that the PLO had the option of dealing with the Soviet Union, not to mention the huge oil revenues now available to it. He took credit for aborting an attack on my airplane when I had planned to visit Beirut in December (see Chapter XVII). Walters in turn pointed out that I had not been overjoyed by the threat on my life in Damascus in February (see Chapter XXI). Walters warned, as in the previous meeting, against acts of terrorism directed at the United States. Neither Walters nor the PLO representative touched on the issues of a peace settlement.

On April 20 an associate of Arafat's approached an American Embassy officer in Beirut asking for clarification of the American attitude toward future PLO participation in Geneva. On May 1, after the start of the Syrian shuttle, we returned a bland reply. Aside from some low-level technical contacts during the 1976 Lebanon crisis, we engaged in no further exchange with the PLO during my tenure in office.

But one trend was clear. The longer the delay of negotiations to relieve Israeli occupation of the West Bank, the more inexorable the growth of the political status and weight of the PLO. Stalemate on the West Bank spelled humiliation for King Hussein; it undercut his claim that his moderate course would return Palestinian lands to Arab control.

Hussein was understandably in a somber mood when he visited Washington on March 12. After our talk in Aqaba in January, the King had followed my advice and put his modest scheme for disengagement along the Jordan River directly to the Israelis. The timing reflected Hussein's growing impatience, for it was clearly premature to raise the West Bank issue formally while a new cabinet was being formed in Israel. Not surprisingly, Hussein's proposal was flatly rejected. The Israelis countered with their old scheme of inviting Jordan to take over civil administration in the West Bank while Israeli military occupation continued.* This Jordan could not accept; it was, in fact, an amazing reflection of how little the Israelis understood Arab psychology that the proposal was continually put forward; not even the most moderate Arab head of government could accept administering the West Bank under Israeli occupation.

Hussein was depressed; he recognized that it was impossible to ask the Israeli cabinet to deal simultaneously with the Golan Heights and the West Bank. And he agreed that the explosive military dispositions on the Golan and the insistence of all Arab states made it imperative to give Syria pride of place. But Hussein was beginning to wonder whether the same constellation of forces might not thwart him later on as well; he was seriously considering withdrawing from the negotiations altogether. This, however, would make the PLO Israel's only valid negotiating partner and Hussein continued to be convinced that its hostility toward him and his dynasty was implacable.

I shared Hussein's frustration. During his call on Nixon on March 12, I said: "Israel hasn't faced what their real alternatives are. They have to deal either with King Hussein or with Arafat. They can't deal with neither." But I also knew that there was no choice about priorities. We had to wait for the Syrian negotiation to be completed before turning to the West Bank. We did not want the full fury of Arab radicalism turned on Jordan, or Asad in frustration blaming Sadat for the impasse on his front. Given the tenuousness of the Israeli domestic situation as well as our own, I was not sure whether we were pursuing an intellectual theory or an operational plan. I felt like the character in the nightmare who finds himself tied to a railway track and struggles for release as the express train thunders toward him. With respect to the West Bank we did not quite make it.

Prelude to the Shuttle

A T this stage, we had no cause to be sanguine, either, about the Syrian negotiation. Bringing off agreement between two nations so bitterly

---

*At the time, the opposition Likud Party, led by Menachem Begin, opposed even this. Later, in office, Begin adopted the earlier Labour position and renamed it "autonomy."

suspicious of each other had never been a warming prospect. Daily artillery duels on the Golan Heights continued. But other clouds hovered.

The predominant one was Israel's prolonged cabinet crisis. The negotiations for a new government proved bitter and inconclusive. There were extreme demands by all sides, including by the National Religious Party — Labour's indispensable coalition partner — over the price for joining a new Meir government. But much of the turmoil raged around the figure of Moshe Dayan. As Defense Minister he continued to be assigned a major part of the blame for the success of the Arab surprise attack in October. On February 25, as noted in Chapter XXI, he dramatically announced his unavailability for the new cabinet. His colleague and disciple Shimon Peres followed suit. But this deprived Golda of the eight seats of their faction and strengthened the Religious Party's determination to stay out of the government. By March 4, after Golda herself threatened dramatically to resign, Dayan had been induced to change his mind. Artillery duels with Syria on the Golan Heights had intensified — which enabled Golda to give him the pretext of a threat of war for doing so. On March 10 Golda was able to announce the formation of a new government with Dayan and Peres back in their old positions.

But the storm surrounding Mrs. Meir's new government did not abate. On April 2, the Agranat Commission, set up in November to investigate responsibility for the October intelligence failures, issued its first report. Casualties of that report — which focused on individual "direct responsibility" for the failure to anticipate the Arab attack — included Chief of Staff General David Elazar, who had to resign immediately. It is a rule of politics, which I have never seen broken, that when a political crisis passes a certain point, the offering of sacrifices whets appetites rather than slakes them. With Elazar as victim, his superior Dayan became an even more logical target; it was hard to maintain the position that the Defense Minister was not responsible for the performance of the Chief of Staff.

After that, it was only a question of time until the tide inundated Golda. Recognizing this, on April 10 Golda told her party leadership that she had had enough. On April 11 she announced her resignation formally to the Parliament. She immediately became head of a caretaker government while a successor was chosen. The nominee was my old friend Yitzhak Rabin, former war hero, Chief of Staff, and Ambassador in Washington. It was then Rabin's turn to negotiate with Israel's fractious factions to put together a coalition. Thus the Syrian-Israeli negotiation overlapped the Israeli coalition negotiations — complicating our already difficult prospects.

At the end of March 1974, what roused Israeli passions in foreign policy was not the prospect of a new disengagement with Syria but implementation of the existing one with Egypt. The disengagement of forces in the Sinai was completed on March 5. Inspection of the new force deployments by the UN and by American reconnaissance flights began shortly afterward. By March 10 it was discovered that three sites capable of receiving surface-to-air missiles had been built by Egypt in the thirty-kilometer zone where the missiles were prohibited. The UN inspectors considered it an open question whether sites without launchers or missiles were technically a violation; they certainly were against the spirit of the agreement, for they would enable Egypt to deploy a forward air defense literally overnight. It was also discovered that Egypt had double the number of 122-mm howitzers we had thought were permitted in the zone of limited armaments (seventy-two as against thirty-six). There were also six more tanks than allowed.

The violations confronted us with a problem. I was certain what Israel's reaction would be. Having ceded territory in return for security arrangements, Israel had to be adamant in insisting on the letter of the agreement; if it stood still for a gradual erosion of the security provisions, the negotiating process would turn into unilateral unconditional retreat. But I was convinced that Sadat would not knowingly jeopardize his strategy for such trivial benefits. It was not unlikely that the violations reflected either a misunderstanding of the terms of the agreement or lower-level actions of which Sadat was ignorant. And for our part, we needed Sadat's support for the Syrian negotiation.

It seemed to me, therefore, unnecessary and unwise to turn the issue immediately into a public confrontation with Sadat. A formal charge of violation might involve Egyptian prestige in a test of wills or humiliate Sadat by forcing him to back down publicly. So I sent an intelligence expert to brief both Sadat and the Israelis on what our reconnaissance had found. Sadat was to be seen first. I instructed the briefer to tell him that the next overflight would take place a week hence. Sadat was thus given an opportunity to bring Egypt into conformity with the agreement in the meantime without admitting a violation. To make the arrangements to dispatch the expert took several days after we had the reconnaissance pictures. The Israeli cabinet would be briefed two days after Sadat by the same intelligence expert.

The briefing of Sadat went well enough. Sadat immediately ordered the removal of *all* tanks from across the Canal, fulfilling the promise he had made to me during the disengagement talks. Sadat explained the excess artillery on technical grounds: The agreement permitted six batteries of howitzers in the zones of limited armament. The Israelis (and we) had assumed that an Egyptian battery contained six guns, whereas it had twelve. Nevertheless, in the presence of Ambassador Eilts he ordered the Egyptian War Minister to comply with our understanding of the agreement.

But it was expecting too much to assume that a caretaker Israeli government would handle the matter quietly. Word began leaking to the press that Israel was charging Egypt with "violations," particularly excess artillery — just what we had been trying to avoid. I complained to Dinitz on March 21: "Please keep the debate down with Egypt. Egypt cannot act for you in Syria if you keep attacking Egypt." On March 22, afraid that the Egyptian military would drag their feet in carrying out Sadat's orders, I warned Fahmy that in January it had taken me enormous effort to persuade the Israeli government to accept the existing limits. I therefore had "a personal responsibility for the number of guns to be limited to a total of 36. I hope this misunderstanding can be worked out without further difficulties."

Fahmy grudgingly agreed to speed up the withdrawal but pointed out that removing the extra artillery pieces required a modification in Egyptian military organization and could therefore not be accomplished in time for the next reconnaissance mission on March 25. To save Egyptian face, I arranged a delay for another few days. This launched me in short order into a fracas with Golda. Tormented by her domestic critics for negligence before the October war, even then accused (amazingly) of being too soft, she sent me an ultimatum on March 23, just before I was leaving for Moscow: If the excess artillery pieces were not removed by March 27, Dayan would cancel his March 29 visit to Washington that was to begin the Syrian negotiation.

If there was anything I needed less than a public showdown with Sadat, it was the collapse of the Syrian negotiation a little more than a week after the oil embargo had been lifted. Asad had gone along with what he knew was a charade to give Israel an opportunity to get through its domestic crisis. But a cancellation of the Dayan trip — the one tangible "achievement" of my previous shuttle — would force him back into confrontation and reliance on Soviet support, especially since Asad was due to visit Moscow shortly. Linking Syrian disengagement to Egyptian controversies, moreover, would generalize the Mideast crisis after we had spent months trying to split it into its components. And all this for the timing of the removal of thirty-six howitzers that Sadat had already agreed to withdraw.

I therefore made a blistering complaint to Dinitz: "It cannot be in your interest to have a public confrontation with Sadat. . . . You cannot want to emphasize violations while I am in Moscow, for God's sake." I threatened that if Dayan did not appear on the agreed date I would withdraw from the negotiations — though in retrospect it is not clear to me why an American abdication would have improved our position or why I thought Israel would be heartbroken at the prospect. A tantrum would normally not have moved Golda unless it coincided with her preferences. Having shown her toughness to her opposition, she withdrew her ultimatum. On April 3 we were informed by Cairo that the offending guns had been removed; photo reconnaissance on April 6 confirmed it. During the delicate phase ahead of us, the Egyptian front settled down with no further dispute.

Dayan Visits Again

A T last on March 29, the day after my return from Moscow — and on the eve of my wedding — the real Syrian negotiation began with Dayan's long-awaited trip to Washington. Under the best of circumstances no single diplomatic visit could have carried the weight assigned to this one. For two months we had used it as a pretext for repeated postponements of concrete proposals. Nor did Dayan come close to moving matters forward. He was showing the strain of the abusive, humiliating, and grossly unfair attacks on him at home. And he was unable to rise above his tormentors, for he was acutely sensitive. Self-centered, poetic, aloof, a brilliant manipulator of people and yet emotionally dependent on them, Dayan at his best had the most fertile and creative mind of Israel's leaders. When he felt rejected he would withdraw and turn bitter. In the present circumstances, even had Dayan been less vulnerable politically or emotionally, he would have had a hard time initiating a breakthrough on the Golan Heights. For the Israeli cabinet, fighting for its life, was being asked to pull out of land captured at tremendous human cost from a hated enemy, and it saw few corresponding benefits.

What we were about to explore, it will be recalled, was how far Israel would go, and for what price, in giving up not only the territory freshly gained in the October 1973 war — started by Syria — but also some symbolic piece of territory, even if it were only a sliver, of what Israel had taken in the 1967 war. The 1973 fighting had ended with minor Israeli advances on the southern end of the Syrian front, but in the north, Israel had carved out a big bulge running from west to east into Syria to a point only twenty miles from Damascus and backed up by Mount Hermon overlooking the Damascus plain. Disengagement would establish a new dividing line between Israel and Syria, running north and south, with a demilitarized buffer zone to be patrolled by a United Nations force, and zones of limited armaments on either side of the central line. During my previous shuttle, Israel had argued that any territory conquered in the last war from which it withdrew should be turned over to the United Nations; Syrian civilians should not be permitted to return there.

Dayan's new plan marked a considerable step forward. It conceded that Syrian forces could return to about a third of the salient, which would become a zone of limited armaments; it waived the objection to civilian repopulation of the UN area, thereby agreeing that civilians could return to two-thirds of the salient. The Israeli forward line, or line of separation, was, however, still drawn *east* of the prewar line (toward Damascus). This meant Israel proposed to end the war by acquiring about a third of the salient. The Israeli concessions were important, but every Arab leader, radical or moderate, had told me that Asad could not even settle on restoration of the October 6 line; he had to keep pace with Egypt, which had recovered a slice of the Sinai; some symbolic comparable Syrian gain of lands taken by Israel in 1967 was imperative.

The trouble was that some twenty Israeli settlements had been established on the Golan Heights after the 1967 war — some as close as five kilometers to the line before the October war (see the map on page 938). The issue of the negotiation was whether in the name of disengagement we could draw some line in that narrow belt that yet did not touch Israel's settlements so that Syria could show some gain comparable to Egypt's. I told Dayan:

From abstract logic, you are reasonable. The civilians returning is reasonable. But these lines are impossible. We can present it only on the basis that something else can be done. . . . I have told your Ambassador, some slice of the Golan Heights, including Quneitra, will have to be part of this arrangement. I know you're not authorized to discuss it here. You don't have to discuss it. But one reason I am going in so leisurely a pace is to let Israel reflect on it.

I assumed from Dayan's silence that we had not yet heard Israel's last word — only that he did not want to be the minister to put it forward.

My next task was to keep Asad aboard. My usual report to all interested parties — a procedure designed to minimize the danger of suspicions fed by rumors — would be pretty skimpy this time. I had already exchanged several cables with Asad. I had resisted an attempt by him on March 7 to commit me in advance to a Syrian disengagement line that implied abandoning some Israeli settlements. I had repeatedly stressed to all the Arab leaders that Israel would not give up a single settlement for disengagement and I had told Israeli leaders I would not press them to do so. On the other hand, I had made the most of an unofficial talk with Foreign Minister Abba Eban, who dropped in on me in Washington on March 15, and his subsequent public statements stressing Israel's desire for a Golan disengagement. Now on March 30 I reported on Dayan's visit to President Asad, listing with some straining its positive elements — including redefinition of the zones of limited armament and the return of civilians. I pointed out that I had told Dayan that "in the light of [my] knowledge of President Asad's position," the latest Israeli proposals were not likely to be sufficient. I took care as well to brief Sadat, Hussein, Fahmy, and Saqqaf.

On April 3 I wrote to Prime Minister Meir that a new Israeli proposal was needed along the lines of my presentation to Dayan. On April 9 she responded that the plan Dayan brought remained the official position of her government — in the light of Israel's constitutional procedures, she could not do otherwise than to back the cabinet's position. But she hinted at some flexibility by agreeing to discuss during my visit "any ideas you may wish to offer." The next day she announced her resignation to her party and the day after to the Parliament — so that during the negotiations that followed, she was a lame duck. Ironically, once relieved of her burden she was freed of the day-to-day political pressures, and the lioness rallied herself for one more heroic effort to bring about an agreement with the hated Syrians for which she had no heart but which she recognized was essential for the security of her country.

The Syrian Emissary

ON April 13 the Syrian negotiator arrived at last. It was the first time in twenty years that a senior Syrian emissary had been dispatched to Washington. He, like us, was uncertain of the significance of Golda's resignation. We wondered whether it would abort the negotiations or at least delay them. We decided to proceed as if nothing had happened.

President Asad had selected Brigadier General Hikmat al-Shihabi, Chief of Staff for Intelligence of the Syrian army. A good friend of Asad's, he was well suited for his assignment; he seemed sincerely interested in improving relations with the United States. He reflected as well the dilemma of his country — fiercely proud and at the same time a little insecure, challenging and yet deep down eager for acceptance. Syria was not strong enough to insist on its views, but it was also too unsure of itself (hence the braggadocio) and too distrustful to rely on the help of others. It could not prevail by force but neither was it able to impose itself by moral assurance. And yet — like Israel — it was making a major effort to transcend its preconceptions and its premonitions. Asad had sent me a letter on April 1 establishing that Shihabi was not coming in a confrontational mood. Everybody would be waiting to see what I could deliver.

Like Dayan, Shihabi brought concessions that were far-reaching in the Syrian context though I knew they would not go nearly far enough for Israel. In our meeting on the morning of April 13, he accepted the idea of reciprocal force limits on both sides of the dividing line — heretofore rejected as incompatible with Syrian sovereignty. He favored a UN buffer zone, though given the presence of thousands of Syrian civilians he wanted the inspectors to have a nonmilitary character. He urged a simplification of the zones of limited armament (which, from the Egyptian experience, I guessed was attainable). Shihabi would not consider the line of separation that Dayan had put forward; instead, he brought with him a slightly modified version of Asad's original idea of an Israeli withdrawal deep into the Golan. I told Shihabi what I had said also to Dayan: "I have always told your President that I do not think I can achieve the line he proposed. But I will achieve the maximum line that is possible."

Carried away by my eloquence I summed up where we stood:

> So the . . . components will be: a movement forward of Syrian forces, a withdrawal of Israeli forces, a thinning out of Israeli forces beyond the line of withdrawal, and return of Syrian civilians to the vacated territories. Those are the positive elements that have already been achieved. What has not yet been satisfactorily achieved is the line. . . . Therefore what remains to be done when I come to the Middle East is to move the line. And to agree on the disposition of forces. On both sides.

It was like saying Switzerland would be a flat country if someone would move the Alps. Shihabi, who did not have to deliver the prescription, assented happily enough. When I airily told him that only two issues were left — the line and the limitation of forces — I was influenced too headily by the memory of the Sinai negotiations.

It is relatively easy to learn from failure. But the nemesis of success is the refusal to believe that there is anything to learn. The temptation is overwhelming to seek to repeat earlier achievements. But while the rhythm of history may echo itself, concrete conditions can rarely be replicated. The wise statesman will avoid acting by rote; he will analyze carefully the actual circumstances as well as the distinguishing and unique characteristics that had made for past success. The Sinai disengagement had worked rapidly because both sides were eager for an accord. Israel's pocket across the Suez was over 100 miles from Israel, sustainable only by continued substantial mobilization. Israel needed to reduce the danger of the resumption of hostilities; Golda was eager to have the negotiation completed before her new Parliament engulfed her in the foreseeable struggle to form a cabinet. Sadat was anxious to free his Third Army and above all to make a sharp change in the direction of Egyptian policy. He did not wish to risk the unraveling of his patiently nursed design as a result of military actions that were nearly inevitable if the status quo continued. Israel without faith and with much hope, Egypt with much faith but less hope, were both feeling their way toward a state of peace. And Sadat was available to help sort out the trivial from the crucial by one of his dramatic moves.

Neither the compulsions nor the convictions existed on the Syrian front. Both Syria and Israel — certainly Israel — considered the military situation quite tolerable. Neither believed that it was starting a new, much less an irreversible, process. For all the plight of the Third Army Egypt did have five divisions across the Suez Canal, along the line that marked the new boundary after disengagement. There were no Syrian troops anywhere near the line deep in the Golan claimed by Asad or even near any more modest line beyond the prewar frontier. Asad was claiming in the negotiation what he had not achieved on the battlefield. To the Israelis, a Golan disengagement looked suspiciously like a unilateral withdrawal to enable Asad to proclaim that Syria had not fought in vain — not a compelling goal for the victim of surprise attack.

The Egyptian disengagement left Israel still holding most of the Sinai as a bargaining chip for the later peace conference. But in Syria, if Israel accepted the judgment that it would have to make a token withdrawal westward beyond the 1967 line — if only for the sake of Syrian equivalence with Egypt — its cupboard would be bare for Geneva (since Golda quite literally could not imagine giving up Israeli settlements on the Golan).

But Syria, too, had to alter deeply held convictions. For it, the willingness to break with a generation of nonrecognition and to negotiate with the hated adversary was a traumatic event. To draw a line on the Golan for even an interim disengagement agreement almost unthinkably granted Israel some right to be there. To define this line, even tacitly, by the existence of Israeli settlements was an agonizing concession deeply wrenching for any Syrian leader. Even the limitation of forces was a psychological problem. Given the distances involved, any zone of limited armaments would come perilously close to including Damascus. And it would involve a retreat of the Syrian forces from some of their prewar positions.

For both Israel and Syria, in short, the negotiation was an anguishing experience. Doubt, frustration, and at times impotent fury assailed both sides. Once during the shuttle when I pointed out the strategic stakes, Golda responded emotionally that she was not prepared to pay for even very important American objectives in Israeli coin:

As I said over and over and over again, we have no oil, we have no nuisance value. We can't say to the United States, "You won't do this for us, so we will invite Gromyko to come." He won't come, and we have no oil to stop pumping. We have nothing, except one thing: a determination to live and not to have our people killed. . . . But the only one thing that I can't agree to — maybe it is not nice — is that Israel has to pay the price for all these things.

What Golda considered "her" price Asad regarded as "his" territory. He was too fierce to engage in Golda's biblical soliloquies, but late in the shuttle he ventilated the parallel view that disengagement might not be in the interests of the Arabs: "The disengagement concept itself, as seen from the Arab point of view, has been like deflating various balloons, taking away the certainty of the preparedness, the readiness, the unison of the Arabs." Unfortunately, psychological travail did not ensure acceptable proposals. On the contrary, both sides needed so much psychic energy to generate any proposal at all that they were tempted to consider its mere existence as transcending any substance.

This made it tough on the mediator, who functioned at once as alibi and deus ex machina. Syria entered the negotiations to begin the process of pushing Israel off the Golan Heights; those Israelis who favored disengagement on the Golan — a bare majority — saw in the negotiations a means to cement Israel's hold there. This gap was unbridgeable in preliminary talks. Whatever compromise was possible would have to be made at the highest level.

And yet everybody needed the appearance that progress was being made: the moderate Arabs, to justify the lifting of the oil embargo; Syria, to keep open the possibility of regaining at least the territory lost in the October war; Israel, to liberate its prisoners; the United States, to preserve its dominant role in the peace process and its growing influence in the Arab world. Disparate, sometimes incompatible motives produced a de facto collusion in a complicated make-believe without which, however, the real negotiation could never have taken place.

Even before the shuttle started there were many twists and turns. On April 27, on the eve of my departure, came another ominous sign. Asad suddenly claimed there had been a misunderstanding. Having let Shihabi agree to a UN buffer zone, Asad now informed me it was unnecessary to have zones of limited armaments as well — to which Shihabi had also agreed. But it was inconceivable that Israel would tolerate having the main force of the Syrian army follow it into territories evacuated as a result of the agreement. I was thus faced with two conditions certain to blow up the negotiations: If Israel maintained its view about the location of the line of separation, the negotiation would collapse in Damascus. If Asad insisted on his second thoughts about zones of limited armaments, the shuttle would come to a halt in Jerusalem.

That was not the way it turned out, however. For as each leader voiced doubts, each also was careful to leave some room for hopes. Asad and Golda, for all their distrust of each other, were engaged in an extraordinary battle with their preconceptions and those of their colleagues. In the main meetings, Golda was always surrounded by key members of her cabinet. Asad would first listen to me alone and then make me repeat the same arguments to his principal advisers — probably to avoid the charge that he had been taken in. Gradually, they closed a gap that yawned as a chasm when they started. When it was all over, with anguish, doubt, and many small compromises the two leaders, so distrustful of each, wrote another chapter in the Middle East's history of faith.

Lebanese Interlude

THE built-in hesitations and complexes of the parties were sufficient problems in themselves. But circumstances continually threatened the fragile imagery of progress. On April 11 Palestinian guerrillas infiltrated from Lebanon attacked the northern Israeli town of Kiryat Shmona, killing eighteen inhabitants, all civilians. Israel retaliated with air attacks against villages in southern Lebanon that it suspected of harboring terrorists. Events after that were a classic case history of modern United Nations practice. That radical guerrillas attack a sovereign state from sanctuaries in a neighboring country seems to be regarded as normal by a growing number of members of the world organization; the implication is that the nation being attacked is somehow outside international law. Acts of retaliation by the victim are condemned. The double standard requires unusual reserves of hypocrisy when the victim is, like Israel, a member of the United Nations. But the world organization has always risen undaunted to the occasion and voted its prejudices.

By now, UN practice for the cycle of terrorism and retaliation was well established: The Lebanese government felt compelled (in part by radical pressures) to call for a Security Council meeting wherein everyone demanded a resolution condemning *only* Israel's response, not the original attack. We would then veto it. In this instance, the scenario was routine, but the surrounding circumstances were not, for I was about to launch the Syrian shuttle. I had every reason not to antagonize Israel, which would have to make the larger concession in the negotiations. At the same time, I needed — or thought I needed — the support of other Arab states to induce Syria to abandon its own extreme demands. The moderate Arabs argued that an American veto would seriously impair their ability to urge restraint. And the Lebanese Foreign Minister, a decent and harassed representative of a government caught in the meat grinder between uninvited guerrillas and determined neighbors, prophetically implored us to find a way to affirm Lebanon's territorial integrity lest his country's independence be taken too lightly.

As a general proposition, it is best in such a situation to cut through the rhetoric to the heart of the matter. Oddly enough, to do the right thing is the wisest in practical terms. Once one begins to maneuver among conflicting pressures, one in fact encourages extremes as each side digs in to pull the "middle ground" as close to its own preference as possible. And the right course here was to condemn either both sides or neither. Once one obscures the simple verities with manipulation, the fundamental is lost in the expedient. This is especially true in the never-never land of UN voting procedures. There, soothing inanities tempt one to lose track of the reality that progress must have other criteria than amending the outrageous to the preposterous.

That wisdom most certainly eluded us on this occasion. A "nonaligned" draft resolution circulated; it contained seven operative paragraphs, five of which strongly condemned Israel's attacks on Lebanon; none mentioned the terrorist attack on Kiryat Shmona. The United States circulated a counterdraft "deploring" both the attack on Kiryat Shmona and Israel's retaliation. It found not a single supporter. A European "compromise" condemned all "acts of violence" but singled out the Israeli retaliatory attack on Lebanon for specific mention. It seemed at the time a safe middle ground between the various pressures on us, all the more so as it enabled us to make a unilateral public statement insisting that the attack on Kiryat Shmona was one of the "acts of violence" being condemned.

Eager to accumulate capital in the Arab world for the imminent shuttle, we voted for this resolution. It was an evasion. No matter how artfully drafted, it made a moral distinction between the assault on an Israeli village and Israel's retaliation. It criticized the former only by vague implication, the latter explicitly. Israel was outraged and with good reason. Yet its votaries overdid their protests. They had witnessed an unwise tactical move, not, as they clamored, a shift in our policy — but a move that heightened the sense of beleaguerment and insecurity in Israel.

The Shuttle Begins: The Line of Separation

THE shuttle began in a warm glow. It was the first diplomatic trip abroad on which Nancy came with me, easing the lives of everybody with her serenity and goodwill and her mellowing effect on me. What she absorbed of my strain, despite the courtesies of our hosts, is exemplified by her acquisition of two ulcers, which put her in the hospital for weeks at the end of the trip.

I traveled with my usual team of Mideast aides: Joe Sisco, Roy Atherton, Hal Saunders, and Peter Rodman. Robert McCloskey accompanied me as adviser and senior press spokesman, along with Department press secretary Robert Anderson. Ellsworth Bunker, who had been a stalwart Ambassador in Saigon and had journeyed with me through the hostile labyrinth of the Vietnamese peace negotiations, came along on the Syrian shuttle in his capacity as American "permanent representative" to the quiescent Geneva Conference. Present throughout was a party of fourteen hardy journalists who were on my plane on all the hops between Damascus and Jerusalem and around the Middle East. Even had I sought solitude, it is unimaginable that the press would have left a Secretary of State unmonitored for days — in the end weeks — certainly not least during the Watergate paroxysms.

The first few stages were a triumphal tour. I met Gromyko in Geneva on the weekend of April 28–29. We went through our usual shadow-boxing. The Soviet Union wanted to participate in a negotiation to which it had nothing to contribute and in which none of the parties wanted it. Gromyko continued on a course that seemed to me more humiliating than beneficial to the Soviet Union. He pressed once again for a symbolic meeting between us in Damascus; he implied strongly that he would show up there whatever my preferences. I evaded the proposal. Afterward, I notified Asad of Gromyko's plans, adding the obvious: that I could not object to the visit of a Soviet foreign minister to the capital of a friendly country — provided his plans did not imply a meeting with me.

I was confident to the point of cockiness. I told Gromyko that I hoped to complete the agreement by May 9 or 10. He did not dispute it. Nor did he argue over my formulation that the main problem was to obtain an Israeli withdrawal to the prewar line with perhaps a few kilometers of 1967 land added. Gromyko seemed somewhat ambivalent about where Soviet interests lay. For both Egypt and we had made the reopening of the Geneva Conference firmly dependent on the conclusion of the Syrian disengagement.

It all wound up in a communiqué that met the first test of any successful US–Soviet colloquy on the Middle East: It was too little for the Soviets and at the borderline of being too much for Israel and Egypt (Syria expressed no opinion):

> The Minister and the Secretary exchanged views on the current status of the negotiations of a Middle East settlement and on the next phase of these negotiations. The two sides agreed to exercise their influence toward a positive outcome and to remain in close touch with each other so as to strive to coordinate their efforts for a peaceful settlement in the area. Both sides expressed themselves in favor of the resumption of the work of the Geneva Peace Conference on the Middle East at an early date.

On Monday, April 29, I stopped overnight in Algiers, hoping to enlist Boumedienne's influence with Asad. I had seen him a little more than two weeks earlier when he had called on Nixon in Washington. As then, he favored a Golan disengagement even while insisting on the conventional argument that it could only be a first step toward Syrian recovery of the pre-1967 borders. He would act in support of our efforts, he said. This gave us hope that he might urge Syria toward compromise.

Boumedienne, though thinking of himself as a radical, had little use for the Soviets. He had heard that Gromyko was coming to the Mideast. I said that I would not meet him in an Arab capital: "I won't do it because I don't want to leave the impression that he and we are dictating to Arab countries." Boumedienne agreed that it would leave a poor impression and not be helpful to the Syrians. He claimed that even Asad was embarrassed at Gromyko's insistence on meeting me in Damascus. The meeting in Geneva had been sufficient, Boumedienne thought. In reply to his query I gave him my honest appraisal of the Soviets:

I will speak frankly with you, Mr. President. I give you first my estimate. You've met them; you have your own opinion. They are not very far-sighted. They are very bureaucratic, very much affected by their internal maneuvering. They are prepared to pay a very high price for appearances instead of reality. They rely on intimidation but are not willing to run great risks. Therefore, when intimidation doesn't succeed, they pull back immediately. That is my general evaluation. . . .

On the other hand, in case of a war, they are afraid of a Syrian defeat because that might force them to make decisions they are not prepared to make and bring them into conflicts they do not wish. So their policy is confused. They don't really want me to succeed, but they are also afraid of my failure.

Boumedienne had his own, similar experiences:

The Soviets are complicated. We have long-time relations with them going back to 1963. In spite of this, I do agree their positions are always character-ized by this aspect of hesitation. . . .

For instance, Sadat was demanding weapons, emphasizing this before the October War. They sent weapons, but not in the quantities which were re-quested nor of the kinds that were requested. During the war, they were obliged to send Sadat the weapons he was demanding.

But in general, they have a limit which I call the red line. They will not go beyond the red line. It is the line drawn between them and the United States.

Boumedienne's analysis reflected the Soviet dilemma in the Middle East. They were willing enough to fish in troubled waters but they were loath to run major risks. They wanted the fruits of success without its exertions or complexities. Their strength was not a master plan but the exploitation of the confusion of their adversary. They wanted no show-down with the United States. There was thus a limit to expansionism provided we were determined and an opportunity for coexistence if we were farsighted.

After Algiers I did not head directly for the capitals of the two prin-cipals in the negotiation. I went instead to Alexandria to concert strategy with the Egyptian President. Sadat had pulled out all the stops. Safa Palace along the waterfront had been put at our disposal. Colorful honor guards accompanied us everywhere. We visited the excavation of a Ro-man amphitheater around whose periphery Egyptian lancers on horses formed a most dramatic backdrop. Sadat and Fahmy were insistent that I complete the Syrian disengagement on this shuttle. If I returned to America without it, Syria might appeal to the Security Council, restor-ing the Soviets to a principal role in the negotiations. After that, matters would move to an Arab summit and rapidly get out of control. Our Egyptian hosts were ebullient; they foresaw no need for any of these expedients. They promised to support any scheme that could be presented as comparable to Egypt's, yielding Syria both the salient taken in 1973 and a few kilometers of Israel's 1967 conquests, including the town of Quneitra. The only thing the Egyptians failed to tell me was how to get Israel to accept this proposition.

For the next few weeks, Quneitra haunted every waking hour and probably our dreams (or rather nightmares) as well. Before the 1967 war it had been the provincial capital of the Golan region, a dusty little town of under 20,000 shopkeepers, peasants, and clerks nestling under the Golan hills. It now became for a month the focal point of Mideast diplomacy. It qualified for the role because it was situated three kilometers inside the line of the Israeli conquests in 1967 (see the maps on page 938 and facing). It had been heavily damaged first in the 1967 war, then in the 1973 war, and then further by Israeli bulldozers for no apparent reason after the 1973 war.

It fulfilled all prerequisites for its symbolic role. Israelis had never settled there; the nearest Israeli settlement was on the far slope of a hill, another four kilometers to the west. However, some of the farmlands connected with the nearby Israeli settlements approached a few hundred meters from the edge of town. And various hills a few kilometers to the west of town provided vantage points (and strategic positions) that complicated the task of drawing a dividing line through this bitterly fought-over terrain. Quneitra was not a strategic asset but a prize, a trophy, a symbol for both sides, all the more contested for that; its disposition would determine the outcome of the negotiations.

More than is usually the case depended on the stamina of the negotiator. For at that moment my ultimate recourse, the President, was approaching the climax of Watergate. On April 30 in Washington, the White House released a huge compilation of the transcripts of taped Oval Office conversations relating to Watergate. This extraordinary gesture of self-abasement was meant to show that the President had nothing to hide and that the tapes showed no wrongdoing. It was also designed to forestall even more sweeping requests for tapes from the Special Prosecutor or the House Judiciary Committee. It backfired. The blunt, hard-boiled, occasionally tawdry conversations were shocking to the public both for their content and for their crude language. Senator Hugh Scott of Pennsylvania, the Republican Minority Leader of the Senate, called them ''disgusting.'' The media dealt with little else. I was negotiating without an authoritative President behind me.

I arrived on Thursday, May 2, in an Israel in turmoil. In January I had been hailed as a messenger of peace. Three months later signs spelling my name in Arabic — as if I were an Arab representative — wel-

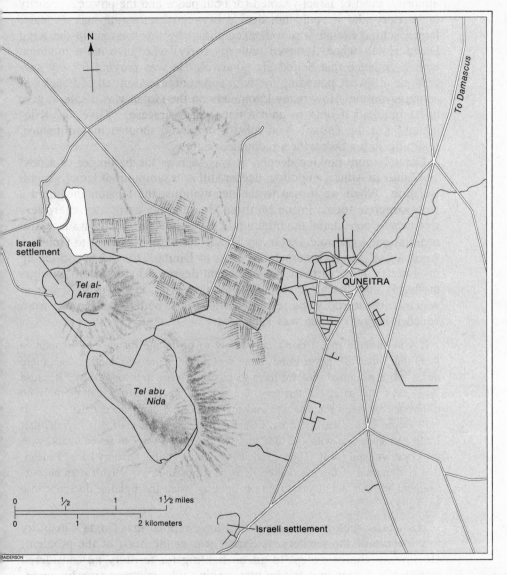

N

To Damascus

Israeli
settlement

Tel al-
Aram

Tel abu
Nida

QUNEITRA

0   ½   1   1½ miles

0   1   2 kilometers

ANDERSON

Israeli settlement

Quneitra and Environs

comed me. Begin's Likud Party organized street demonstrations; they blocked the street on which Golda Meir's house was located, so we usually met in the Prime Ministerial office. The abuse came from a minority; most of Israel yearned for both peace and the physical security of territory and it could not decide between its longing and its fears. Israeli schizophrenia was well exemplified by the masseur in the King David Hotel (where I stayed with my party) who gave me a rubdown with a violence that belied his goodwill. He was praying for my success, he allowed, pounding me with apparent affection; all of Israel was counting on me. How many kilometers on the Golan was it safe to give up? I inquired if only to gain a temporary surcease. "Give up? Kilometers? On the Golan? You must be crazy!" shouted my tormentor, returning to his task with a redoubled vigor.

Our UN vote rankled deeply. It was seen as the harbinger of a possible shift in American policy; deeper still as a symptom of Israel's moral isolation. When we turned to the negotiations, the tensions acquired a more concrete focus. Prime Minister Meir and her associates knew very well what I considered the minimum concessions needed for a successful negotiation. I had told Dayan on March 29; I had written it to Golda in April; I had said so innumerable times to Dinitz. This did not soften up my Israeli counterparts to any significant degree. Their concern was less the terms than the principle. Why should Syria, after starting a war in which it lost territory, be rewarded with a line better than the one from which it started? Golda was vehement:

> If you strangle me, I don't know how to go to the people and explain to them that, after all, never mind, there was a war, there was another war, more dead, more wounded, but we have to give up Syrian territory. Why? Because Asad says that it is his territory. . . . I can never accept that there is no difference between the attacker and the attacked; I can't accept that. . . . It isn't Begin that scares us; it isn't Sharon that scares me, but it is myself, that I can't make peace with the idea that [we had] two wars in seven years, with the price we paid for it. Then Asad says he must get his territory back. I mean, that is chutzpah of the nth degree. How is it possible? . . . Isn't it an encouragement for our neighbors to go on fighting when the fighting does not lose anything?

Had Asad been present, he would have replied that Golda's inability to conceive of the territory as Syrian was at the heart of the problem. He saw no choice except to go on fighting for territory he considered historically Syrian and felt he was making a huge concession by agreeing to even a temporary cease-fire line.

But my role as mediator was not to repeat each side's debating points. Israel's long-term outlook was in truth one of almost metaphysical gravity. It had only one ally; it was alone as no other sovereign nation. It would have to bear the world's opprobrium even when it was the victim of paramilitary attack. Its neighbors might at any point raise more demands and, as Golda never tired of insisting, the same reasoning that had led to current requests for concessions would then generate new pressures. Few nations could have stood the psychological strain. Israel's case was better than its posture of nitpicking defiance. It touched the eternal premonition of the Jewish people that at the end of the day it would be the victim of all its environment's frustrations.

I had deep sympathy for Golda's views; I understood her premonition. And yet my duty was to conduct the best policy that I could distill from sober analysis. Neither despair nor a sense of injustice could serve as a guide. My responsibility was to describe to Israel its geopolitical necessities. Israel's heart might be heavy but it needed a clear head and cool judgment. And so my meetings in Israel were a series of presentations more appropriate to a seminar on the philosophy of international relations than a diplomatic negotiation.

My theme was that Israel's position was serious no matter what it did. But it was not hopeless. With discipline and conviction it could rescue a margin of maneuver. The most certain way to disaster was to maintain the status quo.

Later on it was alleged that my negotiating tactic was to tell each party what it wanted to hear. This is a superficial way of looking at diplomacy; it was emphatically not my method. The only safe assumption in a negotiation is that one's counterpart is of comparable intelligence. It will not be possible to trick him (or her) for any extended period; he is bound to discover the truth eventually. If he has been misled, the basis of trust has disappeared forever. And since in foreign policy one meets the same people over and over again, the loss of trust can become an insuperable handicap.

The allegation also erroneously implied that I had fallen into one of the worst errors a negotiator can make: to assume that the nations with which he deals do not exchange ideas, particularly in the Arab world. Even the officials of states that do not have diplomatic relations monitor one another's public statements and media and seek to penetrate one another's decisions through intelligence means. It is not possible to keep different sets of books and retain confidence. Once lost, confidence is irretrievable — and without confidence every negotiation becomes a brutal test of strength.

When acting as mediator, I tried to understand the real goals of the two sides as thoroughly as possible, since the formal positions often reflected domestic or bureaucratic necessities rather than conviction. I would invariably tell the goal I sought to achieve to *both* parties early in the process in nearly identical terms. It was as much a practical as a moral decision, because how else was I going to get them to the ultimate destination? This did not, of course, preclude my using different arguments to explain to each party why the final goal was in its interest. But that reflected reality. After all, there would never have been a controversy if the purposes of the parties were not different, and even to some extent incompatible. An agreement will emerge only if both sides can promise themselves *some* benefit to their own interests as they perceive them, and these benefits will differ with the interests. Only amateurs believe that it is possible to achieve unilateral advantages for one side; even if it were possible, such an agreement would never be maintained. A mediator who encouraged it would soon forfeit the trust of one of the parties and hence the precondition for his effectiveness. The challenge in mediation is to find why an agreed goal can be in the *common* interest for *different* purposes.

This is why I spent most of my time in Israel, especially in the early days of the shuttle, explaining the international environment; only in that context would the specific solutions make any sense. The following are excerpts from various presentations I made in Israel through the course of the month:

If this negotiation fails, I think we have to assume that the dominant American role in the peace effort is at an end, if we cannot produce an acceptable solution in a disengagement scheme. . . . [T]he argument that we have made [to the Arabs] is that we promise less but at least it leads to a little progress that is better than no progress. That, in my judgment, will be at an end.

. . . I think it is essential that the gravity of a failure of negotiation be understood in relation to what happens diplomatically, what happens militarily and what happens in the United States. (May 2)

In America right now you have an odd combination of circumstances in that the anti-Nixonites, the Jackson people, the anti-detente people, conservatives, they can all combine. So for about six months you may get an illusion of something in America, so long as it doesn't cost anything or risk anything. I have managed enough crises in America to know. . . . And the tough boys don't know how to manage; all they know is how to posture, and they aren't so tough when it is more than words. This is my nightmare. (May 4)

Now, then the next question is: Is what we are now discussing more likely to help Israel or more likely to hurt Israel? Is a disengagement agreement better for Israel, even involving all the dangers which Rabin and Peres mentioned, or is it not? I believe that even though every consequence that was mentioned is correct, on balance it helps Israel. Because it keeps the United States in the forefront of the diplomacy, because it makes it easier to decouple things from Geneva, because it quiets down the Syrian front and continues the Egyptian line. . . .

The nature of the situation is, can the United States effectively back up an

Israeli position over an extended period of time? I don't believe we can back up a negotiation that breaks down on issues that the American public doesn't understand, leading to an oil embargo, leading to a constant series of crises and maybe to war. We will be under great pressure from the Jewish community to do so. But I call your attention to the difference between crisis management and speeches. One can make great speeches and still manage crises in such a way that step by step you lose everything. And speech-makers can continue their rhetoric and even be tough and still be ineffective. (May 5)

[I]t cannot be beyond the wit of man, when we are committed to your defense and you are determined to survive, for us to make an assessment of the essential factors — the role of the Soviet Union; the role of the Arabs; the role of the Europeans; the problem of the arms race in the area and what is to be expected, how the U.S. can use its political, economic and military strength in such a way that it isn't just muscle-bound; how crises are to be managed. To improvise these things, to wait for something to blow up, is totally irresponsible. (May 14)

On May 2, my first day in Israel, I met Golda and her colleagues in varying combinations with only brief interruptions from 12:15 P.M. until 1:30 A.M. Formally, the Israelis maintained the position of the Dayan plan. But I could sense that they were reviewing it. It was not that I convinced the Israeli negotiating team of an unfamiliar point of view. Rather, I provided a pretext to modify a proposal imposed by internal politics; many on the Israeli negotiating team knew their plan would not work even if they were not yet ready to embrace my ideas. Late at night, Dayan came up with a "personal" concept: Maybe the Israeli line of separation could be pulled west a bit (by broadening the UN buffer zone) so that the eastern part of Quneitra could be given to Syria; Israel would keep the western part. Syria would never accept a divided Quneitra, and it made no sense even from Israel's point of view, except for domestic politics. But that was not the point. Dayan's "personal" idea showed that Israel had crossed the psychological Rubicon; it was at least considering pulling back from the prewar line.

Clearly, Israel's journey toward the negotiable would be painful and prolonged. And exasperating as Israeli negotiating tactics could be, it was not in our interest to seek subservience. For, as I have said, once it was proved that we could make Israel do *anything,* Arab demands would escalate. Then we would be blamed for Israel's failure to meet Arab terms, which would be raised with the ease of their accomplishment. Our strategy depended on being the only country capable of eliciting Israeli concessions, but also on our doing it within a context where this was perceived to be a difficult task. There is no doubt that the Israelis dedicated themselves to the second part of that proposition with more intensity than to the first.

So I decided to return to the tactics of the previous journey. I would go to Damascus without a firm proposal, exploring subsidiary issues to give Israel more time for reassessment. I would have a merry initial reception in the Syrian capital, but I was convinced that if we embarked on the road of imposing terms, we would transform an Arab-Israeli conflict into an Arab-American one. From Damascus I would go to Alexandria to mobilize whatever Arab support was possible behind my strategy and then return to Israel. I was now into the sixth day of the shuttle. At a comparable period in the Egyptian case we had made our breakthrough and were cleaning up technical points. Here at the beginning of my long-awaited Syrian shuttle, I had not even presented an opening position in Damascus.

It was a strange situation. So far, the negotiations had been between me and Israel. For weeks a series of Israeli propositions had been made — all unacceptable, as not only Asad but all other Arabs had told me. I had conveyed them to Syria, sometimes through other Arabs, not as plans but as "illustrations" of Israeli thinking, as examples of the difficulty of the problem, as models; as anything, in short, other than a formal proposal. Asad had thus not been given an opportunity to reject any specific scheme; his prestige was not yet involved. I thought it best to reserve that for when the two positions were closer to each other. By the same token, in Israel I never put forward the original Syrian line as anything but an illustration of Asad's thinking. Strictly speaking, I was less a mediator on this trip than a consultant on what the traffic would bear, a philosopher of the structure of international order, a political and psychological adviser about a neighbor who was as mysterious as a visitor from outer space.

Asad had turned over the list of Israeli prisoners to me more than two months earlier because of my promise that I would bring an Israeli proposal in return. Now, at the beginning of the shuttle, I was still seeking to avoid the decisive issue of the location of the line of separation; I wanted first to explore subsidiary issues in the hope that Syrian flexibility on them would make it easier for Israel to pull back the line.

The gap between the two sides was brought home on the car ride into Damascus from the airport when at last on Friday, May 3, I went to Syria to begin negotiating. If Golda considered the relinquishing of any territory a threat to Israel's security and a reward for an aggressor, Syrian Foreign Minister Khaddam, who escorted me into Damascus, felt with equal fervor that for Syria to regain what it considered its own territory was not a boon but a right or else a duty:

KHADDAM: Wouldn't it be also true that the Israeli people, so beleaguered for 25 years and living under the pall of uncertainty, would want peace?

KISSINGER: In the long run. But they were beleaguered so long that it is very hard for them to accept the idea of peace. And especially they have a complex about Syria. They have the impression you are very tough. I tell them the opposite — that you are very gentle, easy to deal with, conciliatory. [Laughter.]

KHADDAM: Do they seriously believe we could be lenient when they are on our own territory?

Damascus had no lavish facility for entertaining foreign guests. Khaddam had therefore arranged a lunch for me in the Orient Club — a restaurant and social club frequented by prominent Syrians — to meet other Syrian ministers; it was a gesture not without meaning. The proud Syrians would not have risked their domestic position by associating themselves with what they thought was a doomed enterprise or one whose outcome would prove unpopular.

The lunch went off amiably enough. But the atmosphere in Asad's conference room soon afterward turned less friendly — though neither then nor later did Asad abandon his personal courtesy. Luckily, Gromyko gave us an opening subject. He had announced himself in Damascus for two days hence (May 5), to the discomfort of his Syrian hosts, who knew it would interrupt the shuttle. Simultaneously, Dobrynin had approached Scowcroft to arrange a meeting with me in Damascus. I rejected Damascus once again and proposed Cyprus. I picked May 7 to give the Israeli cabinet more time to deliberate; indeed, it gave me another pretext for slowing things down because I was not eager to have Gromyko dissect the opening positions. I now informed Asad that I would not return to Damascus until May 8 or after Gromyko had left the area — giving the Syrians an incentive to cut the visit short. Thus real negotiating would only *start* on the eleventh day of the shuttle — assuming we had by then brought the two sides close enough so that we could present their positions as formal proposals.

Historians studying the record will no doubt conclude that despite this long hiatus Asad and I did everything possible that afternoon to avoid getting to the point. Asad had a genius for creating the impression that he could go on talking about irrelevancies forever. We bantered about Gromyko. Asad told me of a visit of a group of business leaders sponsored by *Time*. I gave him my usual tutorial in response to his acute questions, this time about Israeli domestic politics. But all this was atmospherics; it conveyed goodwill; it implied the probability of progress. That attitude was severely strained when I lifted the veil on the Dayan plan — not as a proposal but as a project the Israeli cabinet was in the process of reconsidering. (I did it in part, as I told Sadat later, because the Dayan plan was so far off the mark that it would make any later Israeli modification look good.)

My gloss did little to assuage Asad's feelings. The plan was "insulting"; it made him "nervous and irritable"; it proved that Israel preferred conquest to peace. Showing that in a contest of intransigence the Syrians were no amateurs, Asad reaffirmed the plan Shihabi had brought to Washington, requiring Israel to withdraw from over half of the pre-war Golan area: "If my line is unacceptable, we won't reach an agreement. . . . There is no room for bargaining on our line. . . . I am not going to accept one meter less than the line we have set down." That was no more probable than that Israel would insist on the so-called Dayan plan. Both sides had gone too far not to make a serious effort to bridge their differences.

I discreetly decided to turn to secondary issues. We did better here. Asad agreed to reduce artillery fire against the Israeli pocket and to stop probing raids altogether while I was in the area. He accepted the principle of a demilitarized buffer zone under UN supervision, modeled on the Egyptian agreement. He agreed to a prisoner exchange. With respect to zones of limited armament, Asad did not commit himself. Demilitarization was a more difficult problem on the Golan than in the Sinai because it was envisaged that Syrian civilians could return to the entire area evacuated by Israel including the UN zone; Syria did not relish leaving them undefended. I raised the issue again with Khaddam on the way to the airport early Saturday, May 4. That afternoon Asad sent a message to me in Alexandria conveying Syria's "non-approval" of the idea of arms limitations. The term "non-approval" was clearly something less than rejection but neither was it approval.

One of Asad's aides told Tom Scotes that I had brought "nothing" from Israel; he was not far wrong. The Syrian leaders, he added, were "disappointed, surprised and discouraged." It had taken a six-hour meeting to get this far. Clearly, it would be a long negotiation.

I decided to mobilize Arab support for a compromise plan whose chief attribute at this point was that none of the parties had seen or approved it. Back in Alexandria on May 4, I reviewed with Sadat what Egypt could support. Sadat defined the issue acutely: Could Asad recover a few kilometers beyond the October 6 line to save face? I had Hal Saunders explain the topography — the hills three kilometers west, the two hills just to the north and south, all of which the Israelis prized as valuable defensive positions. Sadat replied:

A very difficult problem, but it should be approached from a political aspect and not only from the military aspect. It is to their benefit, and ours too, that this fire should be ceased. Both sides are suffering casualties. And at the same time we have the Soviet Union which is maneuvering for extreme positions. For Israel's internal problems, they need quiet, a breathing space, to sort out their house. I, myself, want breathing space to prepare everything for the next step. Can't they understand this? Asad is raising hell for me in the Arab world. They should have an understanding of this. It is in their benefit, 100%. We are not trying to get their settlements, but we are saying that psychologically they [the Syrians] must have something beyond October 6. What it is, we can discuss. It must include Quneitra. I can sell it to the whole Arab world, and save face for Hafez Asad.

And again Sadat added:

Let's give the Syrians the whole pocket first and any distance we can have with the Israelis, including Quneitra, beyond the October 6 line. It is purely psychological. Anything like that I can support 100%, even in the Arab world.

The trouble was, of course, that Israel had agreed to none of it — not even, yet, to withdraw completely from the "pocket." We were assembling Arab pressures on Syria on behalf of an as-yet nonexistent Israeli proposal that Asad was likely to reject. Nevertheless, Sadat proposed that his confidential aide Ashraf Marwan accompany Saunders immediately to Saudi Arabia and Algeria to enlist their support.

Marwan and Saunders were received by King Faisal within an hour after their arrival late on May 4. This was unusual given their protocol level; even more so was the King's readiness to listen to a joint US–Egyptian position. I had instructed Saunders to brief Faisal but to ask for nothing specific; the King would know himself what to do — if indeed he felt disposed to act. Faisal was his ambiguous, uninformative, and oddly supportive self. He did not object to the compromise scheme; nor did he clearly endorse it. We could count on his assistance for Egypt and Syria, whenever it was needed, he said in his Delphic fashion.

The next day Saqqaf followed the usual procedure of spelling out the meaning of the King's allusions. What gave particular force to Saqqaf's remarks was that he was accompanied by Rashad Pharaon, who was perhaps Faisal's closest adviser — and a Syrian. He might not be in touch with Damascus, though I suspected he was. But he would surely be sensitive to what the traffic would bear there. If the Israelis would leave Quneitra and if Quneitra came under Syrian administration, Pharaon said it would be a good agreement that Saudi Arabia and, he thought, Algeria would support. By now I had learned enough of Saudi methods to grasp that a Saudi royal adviser "thought" only what he knew.

Saunders and Marwan went on to Algeria. Boumedienne was cautious. Israel's quibbling over a kilometer or two raised serious questions about its ultimate intentions, he said. However, he could state as a general principle that Asad had to achieve something comparable to what Sadat had obtained — in other words, some slice of territory beyond the prewar lines. He wished me luck; he would do nothing to complicate my task. He told Marwan privately that his reaction was positive. Marwan went on alone to Kuwait, whose reaction too was positive.

We had assembled as much Arab support as possible. It was, in fact, remarkable that so many Arab leaders would commit themselves to a plan not yet approved by Syria. This Arab hegira also served the purpose of getting my ideas to Asad. I could be sure that every Arab leader consulted was reporting — not giving himself the worst of it —to Damascus.

But we still lacked an Israeli proposal. From Egypt I returned to an Israel torn by demonstrations. In long sessions (on Saturday, May 4, from 8:15 P.M. to 1:15 A.M. and on Sunday from 10:15 A.M. to 1:30 P.M.), I reviewed where we stood. I reported the various Arab reactions, emphasizing that the first Israeli proposal would never be accepted. Even should Asad want to do so, he could not ignore the opinion of every other Arab leader. Dayan's "personal" proposal that Quneitra be divided between Israel and Syria would be even more dangerous. It would inflame injury with insult:

The problem we have is, I repeat, as follows: One, to get an agreement. Two, if we cannot get an agreement to have it break down on any issue other than the line — zones of limitation, status of UNEF, anything of a technical nature that does not lead to an issue of absolute principle. Three, if it breaks down on the issue of a line, to have it break down in such a way that it does not elicit the united opposition of all of the Arab states, the Soviet Union and Western Europe.

Golda was adamant; she would not recommend withdrawal from Quneitra; the Syrians had no right to gain territory after losing a war. "So what we are [really] bringing to the cabinet is *not* giving up Quneitra to the Syrians." The cabinet would go no further than to make Dayan's proposal official: the eastern third of Quneitra to Syria, the western two-thirds to Israel. We were down to haggling. Having agreed to divide that city, however, the Israelis had breached the prewar line; it made no sense to risk the whole step-by-step process over a few streets in Quneitra. There was a good chance that Golda was putting me through these paces to prove to her cabinet (perhaps to herself) that the proposal would not fly. So I formally requested a reconsideration. To give the cabinet a chance to reflect, I left for Amman. After over a week of the shuttle I had been in Damascus exactly once.

Hussein did me the greatest kindness imaginable during my overnight visit on May 5: He brought no pressure. Like his Arab brothers, he agreed with our general strategy; unlike them, he knew that he carried little weight in Damascus. Hussein thought that in the end Asad would almost surely accept what I was seeking, in effect a minor rectification of the prewar line plus Quneitra. If the agreement succeeded, it would make it possible for Asad to change Syria's radical course. As for Jordanian disengagement, I promised to turn to West Bank problems after

Syrian disengagement and after the impeachment issue was settled, which I hoped would be during the summer.

When I returned to Jerusalem on Monday evening, May 6, I found that the cabinet had made new modifications. The grudging Israeli procedures, the interminable working sessions, the innuendos about duress, the Talmudic precision, the obvious anguish of our interlocutors, created an atmosphere compounded of petty irritation and a strange kind of exaltation at witnessing a people baring its soul so nakedly. It obscured the fact that crabwise, in a manner least calculated to get it credit, the Israeli cabinet was extending itself to overcome its nightmares and grasp its future. In the new plan, Israel's retreat from east Quneitra now became the official government position. More important, the Israeli defense line would be moved behind the October 6 line to the west of Quneitra. But Israeli domestic politics prohibit any sweeping and generous gesture. Married to this scheme was a complicated proposal according to which Quneitra would still be divided: Syria could administer the eastern part of Quneitra, a mixed UN–Israeli group the central part, while Israeli settlers would be permitted in the western outskirts. (The reason for this plan — Israeli domestic politics apart — must have been to prevent Syria from resettling the town so close to Israeli farmlands.) It was a preposterous concept, especially for so small a town. What had tormented a cosmopolitan city like Berlin — a wall in its center — was bound to be even less tolerable in a small provincial city. On the other hand, the new Israeli position seemed to me a stage by which Israel's leaders slowly convinced themselves that time could be an ally and was worth a few kilometers on the Golan. That the Israeli cabinet had understood the problem was shown by some helpful changes it was considering in the prewar line in the south.

So I thought things were moving in the right direction. But I asked the Israelis to take another look because I was meeting Gromyko the next day in Cyprus and wanted to be able to tell him that no formal Israeli position existed. I did not believe that the plan as it stood was acceptable, but in diplomacy the first advance is crucial. Once de Gaulle had granted independence to France's black African colonies, independence for Algeria was only a question of time. Once the Israeli cabinet had moved its defense line west of Quneitra, it was clear that the negotiations would not break down over a lesser issue, such as Israel's right to settle the outskirts of a city to which settlers had never moved when it was permitted — and from which, under Israel's own scheme, the Israeli army would be barred. The Israeli cabinet was in no hurry to proceed; it was only too happy to send me off to see Gromyko uninstructed.

My meeting with Gromyko in Nicosia on Tuesday, May 7, had its bizarre aspects. It took place under the avuncular aegis of the President of Cyprus, Archbishop Makarios, who was clearly having the time of his life. For once, issues were being discussed on his island of a scope equal to his view of his talents. He received Gromyko and me separately and he joined the two delegations for a formal welcome; his aplomb and knowing countenance suggested that fate had done him a dirty trick in saddling him with the provincial problems of an obscure island. He seemed fascinated by our complexities; one had the impression that it would not have required much persuasion to induce him to join the Mideast shuttle. As Gromyko and I withdrew for our private meeting in the Presidential Palace, it was with regret that His Eminence tore himself loose from the contemplation of problems to which he could have brought a wiliness and indirection inaccessible to those without the traditions of a millennium of Byzantine statecraft behind them.

It was a suitable opening for the encounter that followed. To establish the appearance of Soviet participation, Gromyko had invited himself to the Middle East for a time that he judged — on the basis of what I had told him in Geneva — would see the climax of the negotiation. The many delays in the negotiation now deprived his journey of any purpose except perhaps to prove that a sober analysis of national interest is not the sole motivation of the actions of statesmen.

Wounded pride at being at the periphery where Soviet policy had been dominant no doubt played a role. Perhaps Gromyko's clumsy persistence reflected Soviet internal strains. Some of our Sovietologists believed that within the Politburo Gromyko was being blamed for Soviet setbacks in the Middle East and that he sought to recoup Moscow's position by frenetic, if pointless, activity. Whatever the reason, he had miscalculated the speed of our progress just as we had; we could do little more than rehearse the arguments of the previous week in Geneva.

Gromyko, telling us what we already knew, affirmed that Quneitra was the key as far as Damascus was then concerned. He repeated the Soviet objection to partial agreements in principle, but then conceded that some good might come out of them if they were linked in some undefined way to a general settlement and if they involved a large enough return of territory to bespeak good faith. These propositions were general enough to enable me to indicate vague agreement. Gromyko, much too experienced and intelligent to misunderstand what was going on, contented himself with what he was in no position to change. As I reported to Nixon:

His presentation confirmed our own judgment that the principal issue for the Syrians is Quneitra and that if they get it, the negotiation with Syria has a chance of succeeding. I made the point firmly to him several times that the U.S. and USSR would inflame the situation if we tried to compete with each other in backing the maximum demands of the two sides. He assured me the Soviet Union did not want the area in a state of tension.

In short, while I believe we probably cannot expect the Soviets to be particularly helpful on the Syrian negotiations, I do not see serious signs that they are determined — or able — to disrupt the negotiations at this point.

Makarios interrupted our meeting to serve a luncheon of Wiener schnitzel (in my honor, I gathered) and then Gromyko and I went our separate ways. The meeting had in fact been briefer than we had anticipated because Gromyko had to return to Moscow to greet some foreign dignitary. One casualty of our early departure was a distinguished journalist in our entourage, Marilyn Berger of the *Washington Post,* who was left behind sunning herself on a beach. My aircraft was about to take off — the ramp of stairs had already been removed — when someone remembered her passport and threw it out the door to an Embassy staffer so Marilyn could catch up with us on her own. Luckily, Cyprus was then a convenient transfer point between the Arab world and Israel with frequent flights in both directions. Marilyn rejoined us in Jerusalem the next day.

When I returned to Israel Tuesday night, I learned of a welcome show of Congressional support. Senator Mike Mansfield, the Majority Leader and a Democrat, had that morning made the following statement:

I take this occasion to rise only to indicate that the Senate is taking note of Dr. Kissinger's travels, that we support him fully and completely in his efforts to find a road to peace in the Middle East, a road which now seems to lead to Damascus.

It could not have come at a better time. The Israeli cabinet had approved a number of further modifications on which I was briefed by the new Chief of Staff, General Mordechai Gur. The first few times I met him I resented his gruff manner, which I took to be arrogant and condescending, until I understood that it was his way of dissociating from what he considered political pettifogging. As with many native-born Israelis, the rough edges were the cover by which he protected an innate gentleness against a hostile world. In his spare time, Gur was the author of books of fables for children. He was gregarious, self-assured, and honest.* Having been commander in the north, Gur was familiar with the Syrian front. He obviously would not give his country the worst of any argument. But neither would he deceive me. He now presented a modified Israeli line. He confirmed the retreat of the defense line to the west of Quneitra. In addition, Israel was willing to pull back farther on Mount Hermon in the north, to withdraw in the south from a small town called Rafid and from three strongpoints near the prewar line, and to extend the proposed buffer zone around some villages so that more Syrian ci-

---

*In 1981, retired from the military, he was elected to the Parliament and began a promising political career.

vilians could return. There was no change with respect to the civil administration of Quneitra.

I cabled Sadat, Boumedienne, and Faisal that we were making progress. The next morning I told Golda that in Damascus I would present only the Quneitra part of the plan. Since Asad was almost certain to reject it, I did not want the other Israeli concessions to fall by the wayside with it; I would use them later either to overcome a deadlock or as sweeteners should there be an unexpected breakthrough. There is no record of an Israeli leader's ever objecting to concessions being doled out in the smallest possible segments. Golda did not break with tradition this time; she was, not to put too fine a point on it, delighted. After all, if Asad blew up the negotiations over the civil administration of Quneitra, it would put a stop to these endless night sessions with the insistent American ally who argued that safety consisted of maneuver rather than defiance, followed by even more maddening sessions with a cabinet that shifted to the Prime Minister the burden for the flexibility required to keep their country from being engulfed by hostile or uncomprehending forces all around it.

By Wednesday, May 8, the eleventh day of the shuttle, its difference from the Egyptian model was searingly self-evident. In Aswan we dealt with one Arab leader with a gift for the essential. In Syria we could make progress only by involving most of the Arab world. This gave us a safety net if we failed; it also made for extraordinary rigidity because it provided a checklist against which to measure progress. In the Sinai, Israel had started with close to its best offer; on the Golan, the best offer had to be extracted almost street by street in a series of long, anguishing all-night sessions.

On that day, May 8, I paid my second visit to Damascus. (My equanimity might have been shaken had I known I was, in all, to make no fewer than thirteen of these journeys to Damascus on this shuttle alone.) I knew that the problem of the line of separation could no longer be evaded. I was greeted as usual by Khaddam, who used the ride in from the airport to convey continuing Syrian goodwill — a hopeful sign, since by now the Syrians had undoubtedly heard about our ideas from every Arab leader we had visited: "Any time whether there be disengagement talks or not, you are always welcome," said the man considered by many a scourge of the West. I said a word about the psychological travail in Israel. Khaddam's reply summed up what made the problem so intractable: "If they find it difficult to withdraw from other people's territory, how do they expect it to be easy for the other people to give it up?"

Nothing ever seemed able to deflect Asad from beginning with small talk. This time it concerned the characteristics of the American F-111 bomber, which fascinated him as a former air force commander. By a route the record leaves mercifully vague, this led us to some banter about decision-making at Arab summits. Only after we had then tried our latest one-liners on each other did we turn to the subject at hand, which did not, regrettably, lend itself to humor. Since I knew that my message would be unpalatable, I began by explaining the context. Whereas in Israel I sketched the international environment to convince the cabinet that it had to offer more than it wanted, in Syria I presented an analysis of why Asad had to settle for less than he sought:

My assessment is as follows: First, the Syrian negotiation is much more difficult than the Egyptian negotiation for many reasons. For one thing, the territory involved is much smaller. Also, there is a civilian population. The territory is much closer to the security centers of each country. It raises an emotional and psychological response in Israel.

And the military situation is different: The "pocket" that Israel had across the Canal had a narrow supply route in a corridor 15–20 kilometers wide. It was pinched by two Egyptian armies. It was in flat country at the end of a very long supply line. They had a great sense of vulnerability. In the Syrian pocket, they don't feel as vulnerable. I am just assessing the situation, not defending it. They have a line of hills behind it and Mount Hermon beside it. They are not eager to give it up.

If you study the Egyptian agreement, they [the Israelis] didn't withdraw from any place where there were not Egyptian troops. There were five Egyptian divisions across the Canal. In Egypt, we established a line on the existing line of control and the withdrawal of the pocket. There was a UN zone in a flat place with no population.

In Syria, we are doing separate things: One, to restore Syrian civilian administration. And secondly, we are talking about Israeli withdrawal from newly-acquired territories. In Egypt, they withdraw from no new territories.

I added that the ultimate issue was not military but political and psychological.

Asad responded with what in the Syrian context was extraordinary moderation, showing that he had understood the intangibles involved very well:

ASAD: The Syrian difficulty is that people here who have been nurtured over 26 years on hatred, can't be swayed overnight by our changing our courses. We would never take one step except in the interests of our own people. We are all human — we all have our impulsive reaction to things. But in leadership, we have to restrain ourselves and analyze and take steps in our own interest. A just peace is in the interest of our people.

KISSINGER: And of Israel and of all people in this area.

But philosophical musing could not delay forever the moment when I had to present the Israeli proposal and with it take the risk of a Syrian explosion. I proceeded as I had told Golda I would, placing emphasis on Israel's movement of its defense line west of Quneitra, mentioning a few of Gur's rectifications to show the general direction but holding back the concessions on Mount Hermon in the north and at Rafid in the south.

Asad did not explode, nor did he harangue. Coolly and analytically, he dissected what I had presented:

So I make these observations: Observation #1: There is no return behind the October 6 line. Observation #2: There is no straight parallel line. This complicates the situation. Observation #3: They keep points they occupied after October 22. For example, on Mount Hermon, where they had no positions. The only observer post they had was on the October 6 line. Observation #4: There is no significant area of land from which they are withdrawing. There is no withdrawal of any substance.

I pointed out that Israel was, after all, giving up the salient captured in 1973 as well as Quneitra. Asad did not miss a trick. He must have been reading the Israeli press, which sometimes was more rapidly informed of the cabinet's deliberations than the American delegation. "They are not giving back Quneitra," said Asad. "They have just split Quneitra."

In a complicated negotiation, nuances are decisive. Asad had certainly not been hospitable to what I had brought. But he had not flatly rejected it, either. He seemed to imply that what bothered him at Quneitra was less the depth of Israeli withdrawal than the administrative division of the city. Even more important, he did not insist any longer on the extensive withdrawals of the "Shihabi plan." He now asked for a line "near" the one he had indicated. "Near" in the constricted area of the Golan is a relative term. Weirdly, across a militant oratory, indeed by means of it, the two sides were almost imperceptibly moving toward each other. And it came to expression, too, in the fact that Asad encouraged me to tell the press that there had been no rupture. The implication was that progress was being made.

After I had talked to the media at the airport and while our own press contingent was boarding the plane, Shihabi drew me aside into a small reception room. He said that he was an old friend of Asad's. He could assure me that Asad and his closest associates wanted an agreement but it had to be one they could defend domestically against bitter radical opposition. The meaning of regaining Quneitra would be lost if its people could not be resettled there. Current Israeli proposals made that totally impossible both because of the partition of the city and because the Israeli lines were too close to it. If we could bring some adjustments, such as further Israeli retreat from the hills around Quneitra, Asad would make a major effort to come to an agreement.

So we were back on the treadmill. Israel thought it had made major concessions — which was true in terms of its starting position. Syria believed that it was gaining little — which was equally true in terms of its ultimate aspirations. Israel's leaders were outraged that what had caused them so much pain was not considered sufficient. In Damascus, Israeli haggling over streets in a Syrian city was considered an affront. There was no escape from these irreconcilable perspectives, goals, emotions, fears, histories. My task was to hold patiently before both parties the dire consequences if they failed over the issues that now so inflamed them, and the hopeful opportunities before them if they managed to overcome their powerful inhibitions.

Back in Jerusalem the night of May 8, I told Golda that a review of the Israeli position should wait until I had visited King Faisal and Sadat. Decisions should not be made in a vacuum. I learned for the first time that one of the obstacles to further Israeli withdrawal from the edge of Quneitra was the existence of three cultivated fields belonging to an Israeli settlement a few kilometers distant. Israel, never having given up cultivated land, could not bring itself to do so as part of a disengagement of forces. It was agonizing to see the peace process in the Middle East hinge on such a narrow issue. I reported to Nixon:

I will, of course, make a major effort with Asad. If the above Israeli position proves insufficient, the Israelis will then face a critical choice: to permit the negotiations to reach an impasse and thereby face the probability of an escalated attritional resumption of hostilities on the Golan Heights, or to face up to giving up another kilometer or so of territory which would not affect their security adversely but would require giving up some of the cultivated fields attached to settlements they established near Quneitra in 1968. . . . At the same time, Asad, who seems to want a disengagement agreement, also has internal pressures which concern him. He stressed repeatedly that he must have the kind of disengagement agreement which he can explain to his people after 26 years of struggle and not provide the opponents of his regime an opportunity to upset him.

King Faisal on May 9 was ambiguously helpful. He repeated his hopes for the success of our diplomacy. He told me that, from his knowledge, the Syrians would be reasonable provided the Israelis were reasonable. It was clear that he had been in close touch with Damascus. The King supported Asad's position: Syria wanted the hills around Quneitra as well as the town and some further withdrawal all along the front. But no more than with Asad the day before was there any discussion of Asad's earlier maps — the Shihabi plan. At the airport before the media, Saqqaf repeated the King's wishes for my success. The cautious Saudis would never have done this had they not agreed with our approach and, more significant, had not their information convinced them that it had a good chance to succeed.

I arrived in Cairo late the same night. After I met briefly with Sadat at 10:00 P.M., Ismail Fahmy conceived the idea that Nancy's knowledge of the Middle East would be incomplete without exposure to Nagwa Fuad, the renowned belly dancer whom I had seen perform on the last shuttle. So he and my entire party repaired once again to the Sheraton Hotel — the only hitch being that Nagwa Fuad was at that moment in Alexandria, about three hours away. Fahmy was nonplussed. Some telephone calls were made; Nagwa Fuad drove all the way back herself, changed into more appropriate costume, and treated us all to another show at two o'clock in the morning. Miss Fuad proved her professionalism by sublimating her resentment in spectacular gyrations. Fahmy beamed proudly, puffing on his Cuban cigar. He must have calculated that for us to get to bed one night before 3:00 A.M. would have had the same risk as decompression for a deep-sea diver. But if he thought it unwise to break the nocturnal routine that diplomacy had imposed, at least he made it more tolerable. We owe Fahmy (and the talented Nagwa Fuad) the most relaxed evening of our thirty-four-day odyssey.

During a four-hour meeting the next morning with Sadat at his Giza residence, we went over a hill-by-hill analysis of the line of separation between Israeli and Syrian forces. I told Sadat about the Israeli concessions on Mount Hermon in the north and in the Rafid area in the south that I had not yet presented in Damascus. But Israel's defense line around Quneitra would be difficult to change, I said. The idea of an Israeli civilian presence in the western outskirts of an unsettled city, however, I judged was not a serious proposal.

Sadat felt that we were close to our objective. Asad needed Quneitra to symbolize a tangible gain and to maintain equal standing with Egypt. Enough had been achieved to make a settlement possible. Asad enjoyed haggling too much to forgo any prospect of it, Sadat said, but I should move rapidly from now on. Sadat repeated his warning of the previous week: If the negotiations failed, an Arab summit meeting heavily influenced by radicals would convene and make decisions binding on all participants, including Egypt. The peace process would be endangered. The Soviet role would grow. Sooner or later there would be another explosion. Sadat said that he was prepared to support our position publicly, especially if we obtained some more breathing space for Quneitra. If necessary, he would send his War Minister, Marshal Ahmed Ismail Ali, or his Chief of Staff, General Gamasy, to Damascus to recommend to Asad that it was now time to settle. I should let him know when these visits would be most effective.

It was comforting to have Saudi goodwill and Egyptian support. But as I flew toward Israel on Friday, May 10, I knew that I should not count too heavily on this under stress. Not that our Arab friends were insincere. But if there were a final rupture, the issue would be dealt with emotionally, not analytically, and the leaders would then perhaps be swept along by sentiments difficult to foresee or to contain. Indeed, a few days later, Asad cautioned me not to take his Arab brethren's moderate statements too seriously. If instead of disengagement he insisted on reclaiming all his territory, none of them would be able to stand aside.

That was one aspect of our dilemma. The other was that Israel did not want these negotiations to set a precedent for further demands on the Golan; it was afraid that generous concessions created an appetite for still more. In this deadlock I would have to keep Asad from launching himself into a holy war and Israel from turning the negotiations into a test of manhood.

I was in effect alone. Nixon read my daily reports carefully; in many ways they were his remaining psychological purchase on the Presidency. He never wavered in his support. But the publication of the tapes had ushered in the terminal phase of his Presidency. The *Chicago Tribune*, hitherto a stalwart supporter, on May 9 came out for impeachment or resignation. House Minority Leader John Rhodes made a hint along similar lines; Vice President Gerald Ford warned of "a crisis in confidence" produced by Watergate and welcomed a "cleansing process" that would uphold the law and establish the truth.

Nixon was willing to take an active part in the negotiations. He wrote a number of strong, even threatening, letters to Israeli leaders backing my various compromise proposals. But they had only a marginal impact since the Israeli cabinet was too familiar with his weakened condition to believe that he could risk a showdown. (In this they were wrong. Nixon was never more formidable than when wounded.) At any rate, on May 10 it was senseless to ask for further changes in the Israeli position until I had shown the other concessions on Mount Hermon and at Rafid to Asad on May 12 and until Asad had had an opportunity to react to the reports he was certain to receive from Riyadh and Cairo.

I had even conceived a scheme worthy of the Levantine practices of the area: I planned to present Israel's additional changes in the northern and southern portions of the line, which I had held back on the last visit, as responses to Sadat's and Faisal's appeals. Asad probably would not have believed that it happened quite that way, but I had seen myths thrive in the area based on much less evidence. Israeli politics, regrettably, do not lend themselves to filigreed work. By the time I returned to Jerusalem from Cairo on May 10, the Israeli position was in all the newspapers; it had leaked from the Knesset Foreign Affairs Committee to which Dayan had presented it. What I intended to offer in Damascus as "new" Israeli concessions would now appear — as I complained to the Israeli negotiating team — as if "Sadat and Faisal cooperated with me to sell Asad a lousy deal." Consequently, the sessions with the

Israeli negotiating team were less serene than they might have been; no change was made in the conclusion that we would postpone new decisions until after my next visit to Damascus.

May 11 was Ellsworth Bunker's eightieth birthday. He had defended American honor and interests nobly and unselfishly in Saigon for five years during the most searing period of the Vietnam war. He had served in the face of public calumny, governmental hesitations, and ungrateful allies, reporting the facts as he saw them, living strictly by the maxims of duty and service that had inspired his career. Bunker had come to diplomacy relatively late in life; he had nothing to prove to himself; he knew that when the passions were spent, the country would be left and that we would be judged not by how well we registered the emotions of the moment but by how steadfastly we upheld the principles of the United States. A lanky, taciturn New Englander, he would have been embarrassed at such grandiloquent interpretations. He did better; he incarnated them. I gave him controversial assignments like the Panama negotiations because he was unafraid of defending his beliefs; critics could challenge his conclusions, but it was impossible to question his patriotism or integrity. And he had an instinct for fundamentals. I had appointed him our representative to the Geneva talks because I wanted an emissary of high prestige who would not bridle at the irrelevance to which our strategy condemned that forum. I valued his presence on these Mideast trips. He was a steadying influence; his observations were acute. He withstood the exhausting thirty-four-day ordeal as well as, if not better than, staffers fifty years younger.

Now in the midst of the tensions, discouragements, and beginning doubts of the shuttle, he united us all at a surprise party that Ambassador Keating gave him at the King David Hotel. Israeli and American negotiators and staff met in a rare display of unanimity to pay tribute to our colleague. I proposed a toast, to the effect that Bunker represented what was best and most permanent in America; he epitomized "where we stand as a people and a society." So sensitive was our domestic situation that some of the press reported it as a Watergate comment — an implied contrast with Nixon. It was not — at least not on the conscious level. Rather, it was an attempt to give us all courage for the exertion still ahead and to remind ourselves that we were, with all our frustrations, privileged to be on such a mission of hope and peace. Soon enough, the shuttle reclaimed us, for next morning, Sunday, May 12, we headed back to Damascus.

The visits to each capital had by now become stylized. I would arrive by plane with my frazzled aides and the wild-eyed press contingent. In Damascus, Khaddam would greet me at the airport, slightly ill at ease with a fate that brought him into such frequent contact with the representative of imperialist America, sardonic, yet invariably with words of appreciation for my efforts. During the fast motorcade from the airport he would assure me of Syria's eagerness for an agreement and for better relations with the United States. He would convey a mood, but no specifics. He did not mind hearing my impressions about Israel but he was not anxious for details. These as well as any policy pronouncements he reserved for his President (or perhaps as a loyal Baathist he did not wish to assume the responsibility for negotiating with Israel). After a brief stop at the guest house, we would assemble in Asad's conference room for an hour of banter before my report, whereupon Asad's affability would turn to icy sarcasm at the thought that Israel was bargaining with what he considered "his" territory. Often, he would call in his key associates to make me go through the entire exposition again. Afterward, I had to say something to the press — usually a brief statement at Damascus airport conveying an attitude, supplemented by a background briefing on the plane back to Israel. Invariably, Asad insisted that my comments be upbeat; he did not want to foreclose his options by fostering pessimism.

At Tel Aviv's Ben-Gurion Airport, Abba Eban, urbane, witty, cordial, would be waiting. Simcha Dinitz would be there, eager, joking, anxious. They felt no compulsion to save my report for their Prime Minister. Nor would they risk enhancing my self-confidence by excessive praise. Without wasting a moment, Eban and Dinitz would press me on the hour's drive to Jerusalem for a detailed account of what had occurred in Damascus — grading me, so to speak, on how well I had fulfilled their expectations, which were rarely modest. I would then have to repeat the performance with the Israeli negotiating team, followed at crucial moments by a yet larger group. The basic Israeli theme was not the merit of individual proposals — fundamentally, they did not like the entire concept — but the iniquity of the Syrians, their total unreliability, and the near-certainty of another war. The Syrian reaction was ominous in its controlled fury; the Israelis', desperate in its sense of vulnerability. Syrian negotiators, with their armies pushed back into the environs of their capital, exuded the sense that history was on their side; militarily predominant Israel acted as if one wrong step would spell its destruction. And so there was in the negotiation a curious reversal between victor and defeated, with the stronger asking for guarantees and the weaker demanding territorial advance. Syria commanded respect in its self-discipline; Israel, compassion in its foreboding.

Damascus did not vary the script on May 12. Khaddam greeted me with "thank God for your safe return." He said he was very desirous of an agreement. To give Asad something to think about in the half hour set aside for me to freshen up at the guest house, I asked Khaddam to look at the proposals I was bringing, not simply in terms of a kilometer here and there but of this fundamental reality:

The problem is to meet needs on both sides and start a process. The fact of a retreat on the Syrian front is more significant psychologically in Israel than the Suez withdrawal. An important difference: The Syrian army will actually be going forward; the Egyptian army went backwards under the agreement.

I knew that a favorable comparison with the Egyptian agreement would do much for Syrian self-respect.

It was far from enough to gain Asad's assent, however. During the course of our five-hour meeting beginning at 1:30 P.M., we were joined by Minister of Defense General Mustafa Tlas and Air Force Chief of Staff General Najd Jamil, as well as by Shihabi and Khaddam. The discussion was about the Israeli proposals I had brought a few days earlier. Asad said that he could not send civilians back to Quneitra so long as the Israelis held all surrounding hills and indeed still reserved part of the town for the United Nations, to separate Syrians from Israelis working in fields at the edge of town. He proposed that Israel withdraw one and a half kilometers to the far side of the western hills and draw a straight line south from there so the city would not seem encircled. I had been over this ground many times with the Israeli negotiating team. I knew that in Israeli thinking, security had become identified with the range of hills adjoining Quneitra, but I was convinced, too, that some adjustments were still possible and that the proposed Israeli lines around Quneitra did, in fact, look more like a humiliation than an achievement for the Arabs.

We were, I thought, reaching the limit of what was compatible with a serious mediation. It was absurd to stake America's credibility over the sort of retail rug-merchanting now going on. After all, if the talks broke down, Syria stood to lose the resulting war; Israel would forfeit the opportunity for peace. We had saved Israel from total isolation and shown Syria a way to regain without risk the pocket Israel had conquered. So I decided that the time had come to bring matters to a head. I would ask both sides for their final positions on the line of separation and recess the negotiation if the gap could not be bridged. In other words, I was using the heaviest sanction available to me: the fact that both sides knew they would not by themselves be able to break the deadlock resulting from the end of our mediation.

The suggestion that Israel reconsider its position evoked an explosion from Golda. "He can't have what he wants," she stormed on Monday, May 13. "He is not entitled to everything he wants." Considering Asad's starting point, there was no danger that he would get anything close to what he wanted. I replied with some heat:

It was always understood, indeed it was always believed by us that it was desired by you, that the war would end with some form of direct negotiations. We have managed to cushion the impact of these negotiations on Israel, and we have the issue narrowed down to such considerations that we are now being constantly put in the position of defending Asad when we are talking about half a kilometer at a line a kilometer from the old dividing line, when you could easily be in an international forum where every day you get beaten [up] on the '67 line, where every day the U.S. will be asked to take a position on the '67 line. . . . In the process, we broke the oil embargo, we made the Russians ridiculous in the Middle East. Now if you had to face all of this, under Russian pressure, with the oil embargo on, you wouldn't be talking about the Druze village in the northern sector. You would be talking about a hell of a lot worse things.

I warned the negotiating team, as I had the day before warned Asad, not to become obsessed with marginal changes. The real issue was

whether you are willing to run the risk of liquidation of the whole strategy that has pretty well insulated you from the total impact of the consequences of the war, after the war, or whether we are going to pursue a different strategy.

My presentation proved no more conclusive to the Israelis than to Asad. Precariously poised governments tend to have little margin for the long-range. All my arguments were in effect judgments about the future; the domestic penalty for taking my advice was immediate, the benefits speculative. After three sessions, the Israeli negotiating team finally agreed to a modest concession, which I had suspected was its fallback position all along: that Syria could take over civilian control in *all* of Quneitra and that Syrian civilians could return there.

However, the Israeli cabinet still insisted that the land surrounding Quneitra on three sides remain Israeli, including all the hills; that Israeli forces remain in control to the edge of the city to protect Israeli settlers cultivating their fields; and that barbed wire close off all streets. If that was Israel's final offer, we had reached a dead end.

As a last desperate maneuver, I informed Sadat that now was the critical moment to send an emissary to Damascus. General Gamasy left immediately to confer with Asad.

Asad's reaction on Tuesday, May 14, when I visited, was as I had predicted. He saw no way of repopulating Quneitra under these circumstances and no utility in acquiring Quneitra unless he could do that. He made a counterproposal: to *divide* the hills west of Quneitra between Israel (on the western slopes) and Syria (on the eastern slopes), with the ridge under UN control. Amazingly, Asad said he would not challenge the existence of Israeli settlements in the disengagement process; what he wanted was breathing room for his own settlements. Given Syrian passions about who owned the Golan Heights, this was an extraordinary concession, showing how eager — despite his protestations to the contrary — Asad was to liquidate the Israeli salient in front of Damascus.

I had originally planned to break off the talks after this round. On the evening of May 14 — the seventeenth day of the shuttle — a major subject of my conversation with Golda was the manner of recessing the negotiations. Two things changed my mind. First, Asad had asked me to make one more effort. Gamasy returned to Egypt from Damascus reporting Asad's serious commitment to a successful outcome and the Syrian media were still expressing optimism.

Finally, on the morning of May 15, we awoke to news of a staggering event: a Palestinian terrorist attack on the northern Israeli town of Ma'alot. The guerrillas began with the murders of three members of one family; they then seized the Ma'alot school and took four teachers and more than ninety schoolchildren hostage while demanding the release of twenty fedayeen in Israeli prisons. They designated the ambassadors of France and Romania as intermediaries.

An unearthly silence settled over Jerusalem. Israel's premonition of living in a hostile and friendless world determined on the nation's destruction was fulfilling itself. Israeli children were in mortal danger even while peace negotiations were going on. And yet in its crisis, Israel was calm and composed. The prospect of relatively minor withdrawal from territory never historically part of Palestine had evoked nearly hysterical demonstrations in the streets and outraged passion in the cabinet. Yet now that its deeply ingrained nightmare seemed to be coming true, Israel behaved with the stoic endurance that went far to explain how the Jewish people have survived the trials of millennia. The demonstrators who had dogged my footsteps disappeared; the cabinet went into businesslike session. The leaders who had seized on any action that could be twisted into an example of Arab duplicity forbore from using the calamity as an example of what they had been talking about.

On the contrary, Golda sent Simcha Dinitz to my suite at the King David Hotel to explain apologetically that the cabinet grappling with the Ma'alot crisis could not keep the day's appointment with me. This surely went without saying. But she who had bitterly fought every concession asked Dinitz to reaffirm her deep commitment to the success of the negotiations. She knew that I was frustrated by the endless Talmudic quibbling by which the Syrian recovery of Quneitra was being established in increments of 100 meters. Perhaps Dinitz could explain why the concern over the hills around Quneitra was not simply a psychological aberration. Golda's gesture of thinking of peace while she was anguishing about the fate of the children was more meaningful to me than all the rhetoric of the previous weeks.

And she could have selected no better emissary. Dinitz and I had gone through a lot together. He had won my trust and we had become good friends. He would defend Israel's position tenaciously, but he would also find the human dimensions and he would not deceive me.

Now Dinitz told me that the real Israeli concerns had never been put forward. Israel clung to the prewar line not out of a sense of strength but out of insecurity. Israel did not have the manpower to man a continuous fortified line as the Syrians did on their side. The Israeli defense line depended on a series of fortified strongpoints and was thus unusually dependent on topography. Indeed, the demarcation line on the Golan had been established where it was in 1967 precisely because it was the most easily defensible position — in some spots the sole defensible one. This is why the cabinet had been so obdurate about moving the line south of Quneitra; there simply was no other comparable position in that area. Therefore, too, the hills behind Quneitra were essential both for psychological and for military reasons. It was not a question of haggling over a few meters; it was that Israel could not give up its entire defensive position for a separation-of-forces agreement.

I replied that we would have saved ourselves a lot of tension had somebody explained matters that clearly earlier. Dinitz said that the reason the argument had not been put forward previously was because it implied that Israel would make no further withdrawal on the Golan and the cabinet was worried about how I would react. Moreover, Israeli cabinet politics did not permit a conceptual approach. The cabinet could make only a series of individual decisions, each of which had to be presented with no latitude for maneuver. And the process of reaching a decision was so difficult that it left no emotional resources for understanding, much less adjusting to, the psychological needs of others. Only in its hour of anguish did Israel open its heart to the sensitivities of the other parties and thus the agony of Ma'alot was the chrysalis of the eventual breakthrough.

I told Dinitz that if and when the negotiations resumed, Israel had to show more understanding of Syrian pride. It had to widen the Syrian territory around Quneitra; it must, within the limits of its security, attempt an act of grace. I in turn would try to head off Asad's demand that Israel move off the western hills. For now, I certainly recognized Israel's need to concentrate on Ma'alot.

I did not want it to appear that an act of terrorism caused the end of my mission lest this become a precedent tempting further such acts. As soon as Dinitz had left, I sent messages to Asad, Sadat, Hussein, Saqqaf, and Boumedienne urging their intercession on behalf of the hostage children. The cable to Asad pointed out:

> Anything that the President can do to dissociate Syria in the public mind from this incident would help the cause of the Arabs and of Syrian-American relations in the United States more than anything else [I] can think of.

I also issued a public statement in which the United States invited all responsible governments to condemn the outrage and appealed to those holding the hostages to release them: "[V]iolence such as this will serve no cause but to undermine the prospects for peace."

During the morning of May 15, the Israeli cabinet in emergency session took the unprecedented step of agreeing to negotiate over the terrorist demands. Golda explained: "Everyone in the country knows the problems involved in releasing terrorists, but the Cabinet decided that we do not wage war on the backs of children."

Of the Arab leaders only Sadat replied to my message. He regretted the incident; he urged Israel to persevere on the course of disengagement; he was willing to discuss how such incidents could be prevented in the future. As for Syria, Asad's aides complained to Tom Scotes that Lebanese and Syrian civilians had been killed by Israeli raids around Mount Hermon without American protests. But later in the day, one of Asad's aides told Scotes that the incident should not be allowed to interfere with the negotiations; as far as Syria was concerned, it knew nothing about the operation and did not consider itself responsible. In a strange sense, the hostage children reminded everyone of fundamentals. After nearly three weeks of frustrating haggling, neither side, in the face of the threat of bloodshed, was prepared to abandon a negotiation all had been on the verge of recessing twenty-four hours earlier.

As for Washington, a cable suggested that the Watergate strain of recent weeks had taken its toll. Nixon's press secretary, Ron Ziegler, complained to Brent Scowcroft that my public statement about Ma'alot had not mentioned the President (who had in any case already publicly expressed his concern and outrage). Scowcroft reported to me: "I got him [Ziegler] calmed down." But even the usually imperturbable Scowcroft was beginning to be alarmed and annoyed by what he called "these outbursts on trivia."

That was only a pinprick. More worrying was an intervention by the President himself. He had been following my daily reports closely. On a number of occasions I had asked him to intercede with the Israeli cabinet in urging a modification of the Israeli position. That undoubtedly reinforced his already strong propensity to hold Israel responsible for the deadlock. Now the prospect of a diplomatic failure inflamed his fears that his strongest suit in the Watergate crisis, his ability to conduct an effective foreign policy, was evaporating. It was too much. In the middle of the night — before he had learned of Ma'alot — he phoned Scowcroft twice to order him to cut off all aid to Israel unless it changed its position by the next morning. He did not specify what precisely he wanted.

Ma'alot made such a directive particularly inappropriate. In a cable to Scowcroft I opposed it on many grounds. Such a course would transform our strategy and unleash unpredictable forces in the Middle East. We had achieved our pivotal position because it was perceived that we alone could move Israel — but also that this was a Herculean task. If it once appeared that we were prepared to break the back of our ally, every later deadlock would be ascribed to lack of American determination. Israel might lash out in desperation. The Soviet Union would see a clear field for aggressive meddling. This was not the time for a public dissociation from Israel.

Before Nixon could reply, the Israelis ended the Ma'alot crisis by force. The negotiations had dragged on — or maybe they had been intended to lull the terrorists all along. At the end of the day, Israeli commandos stormed the schoolhouse and killed the three terrorists. But sixteen schoolchildren died and sixty-eight were wounded — all by Palestinian hand grenades.[2]

Israel was stunned by the losses but astonishingly disciplined. Nancy and I called on Golda; now that the demonstrators had disappeared, it was possible for us to enter her residence. I have always considered words of consolation in the face of tragedy an insult to the bereaved. Probably the best that one human being can do for another in such circumstances is to convey that one understands the anguish, and that should not require many phrases. Golda said that ultimately she had to assume responsibility; that was the meaning of being a national leader. Being victim seemed to be the destiny of Jews, but the killing of children was too much. It was said without pathos, analytically, as a scientist deals with a fact. In the same almost resigned manner, Golda said that we all had better get back to making peace; she would call a cabinet meeting tonight to see whether any modification of the proposal was possible. We could meet with the negotiating team the next morning; perhaps the time had come when I should put an American proposal to them.

The "United States Proposal"

WHATEVER the spiritual impact of Ma'alot on Golda, it surely had not increased the cabinet's willingness to run risks. We met at 9:45 A.M. on Thursday, May 16. The last days had taken their toll; Golda had fallen ill; Deputy Prime Minister Yigal Allon was in the chair. I said that I was prepared to make one more effort. But we should have no illusions. A recess would last a month to six weeks and during it each side would state its positions publicly, dig in, and seek to mobilize support. Concessions that might have broken the deadlock as part of a continuing negotiation would almost surely be inadequate to revive it. There was a high probability that an Arab summit meeting would formulate demands that would bind Asad as well as Sadat; the Soviet Union would become more active; the United States would lose control over events.

The Israeli negotiating team questioned none of these propositions. They simply had neither the conviction nor the domestic structure to generate a new proposal. If they could be sure that the next set of proposals was indeed the final one, Allon said, they might muster the energy to do it. But they could not keep putting forward modifications — however marginal they seemed to me — that would then be rebuffed in Damascus. I thought (but did not say) how much better it would have been and how much further we would have advanced if all concessions had been lumped into one offer at the beginning — as the Chinese had taught me. It would have saved everyone much anguish and, where so much depended on intangibles, might have gained more moral terrain. It was now too late for that.

From Allon's wistful remarks refusing to make changes but inviting a final offer, I concluded that the time had come for me to pick up Golda's idea and make an "American proposal" to both sides. I had done this in the Egyptian negotiation in January — but then it had been largely a face-saving label on terms that both sides were ready to agree on in any event. This time the two sides were still far apart, psychologically if not substantively. It would be up to me to estimate what represented a fair compromise. I ran the risk that if the two sides could not bring themselves to make the leap, both would reject the compromise. But I also saw the benefits. I said to the negotiating team:

If we make it a U.S. proposal to the Israelis, I think this would have a tactical advantage, (a) because it would in his [Asad's] mind look as if we would have made you do it. It is not a polite way to say it. It would be an injection of the United States into it. And it would then be *my* judgment that this is the limit and not *your* assertion that that is the limit. So it isn't that he is yielding to an Israeli demand but to my judgment of what the limit is. [Emphasis added.]

And a little later:

You have told me as much as you can tell me. . . . The image I have of your Cabinet is to fight for every hundred yards, to prove that a tremendous fight was put up, and maybe gradually — having proved that they contested every inch — to wind up at a line like what I described, or maybe not. But at any rate, not easily. And they want to see the effort and they want to prove to themselves that the effort was made. . . .

The best chance I have — I like the U.S. proposal idea — is to say, "Look, this is my judgment of the absolute maximum that can be attained. There is no sense for you to argue any more. There is no sense to haggle. This is what we can do with a bloody discussion in the Israeli Cabinet. More than this, no, and this I can do only if you say, yes." But then it has to look somewhat significant. And then I can't have stories all over the United States and Israel that I betrayed Israel in my eagerness to get an agreement because I wanted to help the President, that in my eagerness to help the President in the Watergate crisis, I raped Israel. Let's be honest with each other. . . .

So I want you to know this. You don't have to tell me any more, but if we are going to proceed this way, we have to proceed with some compassion for each other. I am assuming the mere fact that you are letting me make a U.S. proposal, or encouraging it, indicates that you are prepared for a reconsideration or we wouldn't be here. Otherwise, I could break it up.

The Israeli negotiating team accepted that approach. Not that it had enough faith in me — nor should it have had — to give me a blank check. I was told that the cultivated fields at the edge of Quneitra were not negotiable. The Chief of Staff gave me a general lecture on the security criteria he would apply when the cabinet asked him to comment on my proposal. I had a pretty good idea of what the traffic would bear. But I wanted to have it confirmed — or refined — by Golda, who would have to put it through the cabinet if I got Asad to accept. So I called on her once again at her residence.

Strangely, Golda, destined to leave the government as soon as the negotiation was completed, remained the dominant figure. Yitzhak Rabin, who would take over, attended meetings but played a marginal role partly by his choice, largely because Golda, freed of any further political considerations, now towered over everyone. She had fought passionately, shrewdly, and obstinately for every square yard. But she also recognized the appropriate time to settle. She said she knew that many of her colleagues spoke for the record; she would take it upon herself to put an American proposal through the cabinet.

Based on the earlier meeting with the cabinet and Golda's observations, I told her that the "United States proposal" would have the following three elements:

• The line around Quneitra would move about 200 meters west, with the area between this line and the western hills (about one and a half kilometers) demilitarized under UN supervision.

• The hills themselves would be under Israeli control but the armaments on them would be strictly limited. The United States would guarantee this bilaterally to Syria.

• The Israeli line of control would be moved one kilometer back to the north and south of Quneitra so as to meet Asad's concern about returning civilian population to a city surrounded on three sides by Israeli forces. It also gave Asad something like the straight north-south line he had been asking for.

Alone, Golda saw no need for formal speeches. She understood very well that by going along with the "American proposal" she secured her moral terrain: at a minimum, the assurance that Israel would not be blamed if the talks broke up. And also American agreement that Israel had reached the limit of territorial concessions in the current round of talks and would not be asked for more.

Feelings ran deeply on the Syrian side as well. As in Israel, the danger of the collapse of the negotiations seemed to bring home their importance. Sixteen dead Israeli children had achieved what had eluded diplomats in three weeks of testy exchanges: that when all was said and done, peace was important because its alternative would be paid for by the suffering of the innocent.

Khaddam on the way in from the airport Thursday afternoon, May 16, spoke of certain powers in the area trying to move matters in the opposite direction from peace. He did not contradict me when I guessed that these were the Soviet Union, Iraq, and the Palestinians.

This was the prelude to a grueling eight-hour meeting with Asad that lasted from 6:00 P.M. to 2:00 A.M. The first part of the discussion concerned Ma'alot, about which Asad was icily aloof. He did not defend the Palestinian attack; he avoided the usual justification that the Palestinians were seeking no more than to liberate their own territory. Rather, he raised a practical question: "Why wouldn't Israel give up twenty prisoners and save its children?" But he understood very well the question of principle involved; there was even an element of grudging admiration. He was less moderate about Lebanon.* The Israeli retaliation there might sooner or later draw in Syria, he said. Even now it created fifty new guerrillas for every Palestinian killed.

But all this was preliminary to turning to disengagement. Once again, we gazed at the gulf in which concessions that seemed to the Israelis to come out of their very flesh appeared to the Syrians as almost insolent intransigence.

Asad said:

> What is it that the Israelis want? I already agreed that we won't touch any settlements. I have already agreed that I will take into account hills. All I want is a straight line some distance from the old line for reasons of my population, and then they can build any defense line they want behind that distance as close to that distance as they want.

Of course, the Israeli leaders claimed that there was no other defense line available; that Asad's proposal was a trick. Both sides were probably sincere. In terms of Israeli military doctrine, the Syrian demand amounted to unilateral disarmament. In terms of Syrian national consciousness, the very concept of an Israeli defense line on the Golan Heights was an affront. The Israelis could not grasp the Syrians' pri-

---

*The Israeli Air Force had attacked Palestinian targets in Lebanon on May 16 as retaliation for the Ma'alot attack. A limited ground assault followed the next day.

meval sense of honor; the Syrians did not understand that Israeli assertiveness was an amalgam of fear and insecurity.

And for that reason, too, Asad's next question was destined to be
irrelevant:

The basic thing the Israelis ought to understand is that if we get a satisfactory
settlement in disengagement, then we can have a long stamina there [*sic*], then
we can stay there and settle and reconstruct. If we are forced to accept an
unsatisfactory settlement, even if we accept it, we will be constantly pressing
to go on. Why don't they understand that?

Since Israel had little intention of making any further territorial concessions, Asad's state of mind made no difference to its leaders. It was a
pity, for I believe that in the summer of 1974 both sides caught at least
a glimmer of the possibility of living in peace.

There being no further point in abstract explorations, I put forward
the "United States proposal." Asad stopped me at this point and called
for his Defense Minister and Chief of Staff. Clearly he did not wish to
take sole responsibility for major steps. And he wanted to be sure that
his colleagues (and potential rivals) could not claim later that he had
been taken in. To this end it was not enough for him to repeat what I
had said; they had to be persuaded by the same arguments. It proved,
at any rate, that matters were reaching a point of decision.

While waiting for the generals, I teased him: "You are trying to intimidate me." Asad made the revealing reply that I should be intimidated by the Foreign Minister; the generals were the peace-loving element and they liked the Russians as much as I did. Indeed, in Syria it
was the politicians who were ideologues and the military who understood the risks and costs of continued war with Israel.

Asad and the others listened to my proposal. Israeli control of the
hills was the sticking point. Asad still insisted that Israel move off the
crests and keep only the western slopes. The United Nations should be
on top and even on the eastern slopes, where he no longer insisted on a
Syrian presence. If the Israelis were on top of the hills, they would be
able to observe the peaceful life he hoped to start in Quneitra. He asked
for UN — or even American — control there.

I replied that we were beyond argument. I could not very well begin
renegotiating an *American* proposal in Jerusalem, and one, moreover,
that had not yet been accepted there. I suggested drafting an announcement recessing the talks. Asad was a cool negotiator. Without any show
of emotion, he fell in with my suggestion. We produced a statement
recessing the talks and implying that they would be resumed in a few
weeks' time. It was cordial with mutual expressions of respect.

When we had completed the draft, Asad said that it pained him to end it. Could I make one more round trip? I replied that I could go no further than my own proposal:

The only effort I can make is to propose my scheme to the Israelis. I can recommend my scheme to them and I can transmit your scheme to them, but it would be clear that my recommendation stops at the limit of my scheme and beyond that it is your proposal which I tell you now is, in my judgment, going to be rejected.

Asad urged: "Please do it anyway, and come back to Damascus, and then we can recess the talks after having made one more effort."

So the "United States proposal" amounted to an admission ticket to another round of the shuttle. We returned to Israel at 2:30 A.M. on Friday, May 17. Nancy, who had remained in Jerusalem for the last few rounds because she was not feeling well, found that one of the joys of being married to me was to be awakened in Israel in the middle of the night for an hour's ride to the airport to meet me and then an hour's ride to accompany me back to our hotel in Jerusalem, along with Eban and Dinitz, who would not give up their desire of being the first to be briefed.

I met with Mrs. Meir for an hour on Friday morning at her residence, and with the entire negotiating team for three hours on Friday afternoon. There was no possibility of Israel's accepting Asad's proposal to place the top of the hills into neutral or third-party hands. The Israeli negotiators did show flexibility, however, by agreeing to station no weapons there that could fire into Quneitra. I elaborated this into a special zone of limited armaments for the crest of the hills, with respect to which the United States would send a formal letter to Asad. None of this had yet been authorized officially by the cabinet; nor would it be until Asad accepted it.

I was convinced that Asad would not yield and the talks would have to be recessed. I drafted a statement to that effect with the Israeli negotiating team, to be published side by side with its counterpart already approved in Damascus. I was so sure that Asad would reject the proposal that I made plans to fly from Damascus to Ben-Gurion Airport for a quick farewell meeting with the Israeli negotiating team and from there to Alexandria. I would return to Washington the next day.

Thus it was that on Saturday, May 18 — the twenty-first day of my Mideast excursion — I left again for Damascus on what I thought would be the last stop on a failed shuttle.

Yigal Allon accompanied me to the airport — a low-key affair because of the Sabbath. Allon was the Israeli minister I had known the longest; he had been a student of mine at Harvard in 1957; we were good friends. He was one of the founders of the Israeli army and one of the heroes of the war of independence. He was the most warmhearted if perhaps one of the least analytical of the second generation of leaders. When not in Jerusalem, he resided at his beloved kibbutz at the foot of the Golan Heights that I had once visited in the early Sixties. Normally among the most conciliatory of the Israelis, he was passionate on the subject of the Golan. Too many of his friends had been killed by gunfire from there; his kibbutz had needed to build too many shelters against Syrian artillery for him to be hospitable to the proposition that a new relationship with Syria might emerge from a generous Israeli proposal. Unprepared to rely on Syrian goodwill, he sought tangible guarantees. Yet precisely because of his warmth and decency, he exhibited the Israeli dilemma in dramatic form. He longed for peace with an intensity and even naiveté possible only in relation to what one has never possessed. I used to chide him that for most people in most periods of history, peace had been a precarious state and not the millennial disappearance of all tension that so many Israelis envisaged. And yet he also wanted absolute security, which in practice meant reducing Israel's neighbors to impotence or acquiring as a security belt what they considered their territory. It was a difficult, perhaps impossible, balance to strike.

Now as we drove through the Judean hills out of Jerusalem, Yigal spoke to me wistfully of his longing for peace. The tough Israeli pioneer struck the same mood as the fierce Syrian nationalist Khaddam when we raced across the plain toward Damascus. Neither knew how to give operational content to his yearning; both tended to expect me to come up with some magical formula to dissolve the impasse. On this occasion Allon did not even expect a new formula; he had participated in all the discussions; he knew we had run out the string. In extremity, the Jewish recourse is to prophetic intervention. "You will pull it out," he told me. "I know you will be back tonight." What a pity, I thought, that miracles seem to happen only to those who do not count on them.

Dayan was waiting for me on the plane. (The Defense Ministry is in Tel Aviv, much closer to the airport.) Badly bruised by the assaults on him, he had played a role in the discussions that ranged from the sullen to the sardonic. He would not be included in the next cabinet; he suspected that he had reached the end of his public career. I was certain that in his private capacity he supported a settlement; he had, after all, opposed occupying the Golan in 1967. But in the deliberations in the cabinet room, he was determined to make a record of vigilance; he pointed out the flaws of whatever was being put forward without offering a remedy. One reason that Golda had asked me to come up with an American proposal was to avoid a conflict with Dayan over whether Israel should modify its position once again.

Once a decision had been made — and others had assumed the responsibility — Dayan was constructive, imaginative, and helpful as ever.

On Friday night it had suddenly occurred to me that we did not have an accurate map for the "United States proposal." I needed the help of Israel's accomplished military cartographers but it also happened to be the Sabbath. Around 1:00 A.M., I called Dayan, who was at his home near Tel Aviv. By then good manners had collapsed in the general exhaustion. When I awakened him, I wasted no time on preliminaries. "Why not bring some maps of the 'US proposal' to my airplane in the morning?" I said. "Why not?" replied Dayan and hung up. Saturday morning he was there, with the maps under his arm. (In the event, I studied them but left them on the plane in Damascus; walking into the Presidential Palace with Israeli maps would make our proposal look like an Israeli ultimatum, defeating its purpose.)

By now, all passengers on my plane had been caught up in the strange mood composed of equal parts of exaltation, total exhaustion, and despair. Whatever their assignments — diplomats, staff, journalists, airplane crew, security personnel, communicators — they seemed all to share the sense of being part of a common enterprise. I had warned those of the Jewish faith that a few more shuttles would qualify them as Israeli citizens under the Law of Return and see them drafted into the Israeli army.

The journalist captives of my mission had taken to wearing display buttons with the legend, "Free the Kissinger 14."* These champions of the First Amendment, watchdogs of the public weal, thought of themselves as detached, skeptical, personally uninvolved. It is to their credit that they were not. All seemed to absorb by osmosis the hope and fear in Israel and the grudging experimentation with new departures in Syria. They knew that while success did not guarantee peace, failure would make war all but inevitable. They were glum as we boarded the plane for what all of us thought would be the last visit to Damascus. Normally eager to visit Egypt, they did not look forward to the overnight stop in Alexandria; it would be the symbol of failure. Marvin Kalb, one of the most sensitive and scholarly of the reporters, came into my little cabin on the short hop to Damascus: "Hang in there, Mr. Secretary," he said. "We believe in you; you can make it." Few events

---

*The hardy survivors of the Syrian shuttle were Richard Valeriani of NBC, Marvin Kalb of CBS, Barrie Dunsmore of ABC, Marilyn Berger of the *Washington Post*, Bernard Gwertzman of the *New York Times*, Barry Schweid of AP, Wilbur Landrey of UPI, Jim Anderson of Group W News, Bruce van Voorst of *Newsweek*, Jeremiah O'Leary of the *Washington Star*, John Mulliken of *Time* magazine, Marie Koenig of USIA, Darius Jhabvala of the *Boston Globe*, and Charlotte Saikowski of the *Christian Science Monitor*. The rivalry between the *Washington Post* and *Star* — Marilyn Berger and Jerry O'Leary — reached a particular degree of intensity on the Syrian shuttle. One result was some frenetic jockeying for position at the background briefings I gave in the lounge compartment of the aircraft. A formal rotation system had to be devised for the seating arrangements, which came to be known as the "Berger-O'Leary separation of forces agreement" — almost as difficult to negotiate as the Syrian-Israeli disengagement.

in those nerve-racking weeks sustained me so much as that brief conversation.

Kalb as well as Allon gave me too much credit. The issue no longer had anything to do with my ingenuity. Whatever contribution I could make at the moment was to ensure that each side clearly understood the position of the other, to explain why an impasse threatened the real interests of both sides, and, most important of all, to keep alive the glimpse of the common humanity that strangely enough all of them had instinctively felt during the hiatus when the children were hostages.

Khaddam greeted me at the airport Saturday afternoon. Normally, he would not dream of preempting his President's opportunity to be the first to hear a full report. This time he broke his restraint so far as to ask whether the Israelis had accepted Asad's latest proposal. I replied that there had been some modification, though not going nearly as far as his President had proposed. Khaddam insisted that even if the talks broke up, a major effort should be made to strengthen Syrian-American relations. It depended, I said, on whether Syria would turn a recess of the talks into a superpower confrontation. Khaddam insisted on Syrian independence. Whatever happened, he said, the Golan was an issue of Syrian national interest and would not be delegated to a superpower. But he and I knew that if the shuttle failed, neither of us would be in a position to control the ultimate outcome by vainglorious pronouncements; in large degree the real purpose of the disengagement agreement was precisely that: to preserve the ability to continue to shape events.

There are many occasions in diplomacy when dedication is measured by the ability to pretend indifference when every fiber strains for getting to the point. It pleased Khaddam to entertain us at another lunch at the Orient Club with key members of the Syrian cabinet. Whether it was a show of Arab hospitality or a method of psychological warfare it was hard to tell, but certainly an outsider would not have been able to detect from the pleasant, friendly, jocular atmosphere that the afternoon was climactic. Or that anyone was in a hurry to find out what the decision would be.

At last at 4:05 P.M., President Asad received me. Even then, we did not deviate from the ritual of trading one-liners for a while. I told Asad that Vinogradov, the Soviet emissary to the dormant Geneva Conference, had asked for a meeting with our representative, Ellsworth Bunker, who had not been in Geneva in three months: Vinogradov refused to be alone in doing nothing, I quipped. Asad allowed that Vinogradov wanted someone else to share his heavy burden. We joked in this manner about a rumor that had reached me of a possible Brezhnev visit to Damascus: Asad claimed he knew of it only from the press and he showed no great eagerness for it. I gave a brief tutorial on the negotiating methods of the Vietnamese, North and South, and on Israel's internal political crisis. The Syrians showed their concern not by any display of impatience but by cutting the irrelevant from the customary two hours to thirty minutes.

I then presented the latest refinement of the "United States proposal" in a matter-of-fact way. At this point it included the following:

• All of Quneitra would be under Syrian administration.

• A line would be drawn 200 meters west of Quneitra measured from the line of buildings on the west side of the western road. This line would be marked by a physical barrier.

• The area to the west of this line would be demilitarized. The UN would assure compliance. Israeli civilians would be permitted to cultivate the fields in this area.

• The Israeli military line would be at the eastern base of the two key hills, but no weapons would be allowed on the crest of the hills that could fire on Quneitra in a straight line. This assurance would be contained in a letter from President Nixon to President Asad.

• The line to the north and south of Quneitra would be straightened out so Quneitra would not be encircled by Israeli positions.

Asad had obviously made his decision. He did not haggle; nor did he ask for further explanations. He astounded me by accepting it:

> Dr. Kissinger is expending this serious effort on behalf of the United States and many do not want his mission to succeed; and if this is not realized, the opportunities will be lost. Therefore we want to be on record with the United States that we are more positive. We want you to know who is standing in the way of peace. On this basis, we will forgo the question of the hills. . . .
>
> We are doing this not for Israel, not out of fear of Israel — the result of war would be on our side — but because we want to leave as wide a field as possible for a just peace. A just peace must mean complete total withdrawal and restoration of Palestinian rights. We are doing this in order to create favorable circumstances for the United States' efforts for peace. We appreciate the internal U.S. condition also. We know if this did not succeed, it would be used to upset you in the United States.

It was a proud statement that could not have been easy to make. With all my vaunted self-esteem, I did not believe for a moment that Asad was yielding to protect my personal position. Asad accepted a fraction of his original demands, from an adversary bargaining with territory historically Syrian, because a statesman ultimately must come to grips with realities. And the reality was that while the Syrians had the capacity to throw the Middle East into chaos, they could not by their own efforts recover the territory gained by Israel in the October war nor the modest improvements beyond it that I offered them. Israel's concessions were grudging; its negotiating methods frequently maddening; but the outcome represented a Syrian gain over what a strict calculation of the existing balance of forces would have warranted. That differential was the result of the influence of the United States, which convinced Israel to make a down payment — without much conviction — on the peace process. It was a measure of Asad's statesmanship that he was willing to face facts that every previous Syrian leader had evaded.

On the way to the airport, Khaddam and I felt the relief of having avoided what we both dreaded and yet had seen no means to prevent: "When we entered the room I was convinced the decision would be the other way." I was telling the truth when I replied: "So was I."

The Limitation of Forces

WE left Damascus elated. The trip to Egypt was postponed, the Israeli negotiating team was informed of our return. The King David Hotel in Jerusalem would annoy many tourists who lost their confirmed reservations to the returning American caravan. But Israel's hospitality to us and its hopes for peace would not have it any other way. I informed Sadat, Boumedienne, Hussein, and Faisal of the apparent breakthrough, laying stress on the "United States proposal" and — certain that my message would find its way back to Damascus — praising Asad's statesmanship.

I thought that final agreement on detail would now be relatively easy. Asad and I spoke of concluding the text by Thursday, May 23. The agreed plan was to delineate, as in the Egyptian agreement, zones of limited armaments behind the forward positions of the two sides.

I turned out to be wildly overoptimistic. There were, to begin with, the same differences between the Sinai and the Golan that had befouled the issue of the line of separation. The Sinai disengagement agreement took place relatively far from Egypt's capital, in a desert. Even then it had been hard to convince Gamasy of the virtue of zones of limited armaments extending thirty kilometers on either side; in fact, it had taken a direct order by Sadat to do so. And General Gamasy was calmer, had a more comprehensive view, and was less emotional about Israel than any of the Syrian generals, including Asad. But if transposed, a zone of such a size would reach to the outskirts of Damascus. Even the Israelis suggested reducing the extent of the zone to twenty-five kilometers. Syria countered with the hardly magnanimous proposal of five kilometers. Moreover, the Sinai disengagement took place in an essentially unpopulated area. In Syria, over 20,000 civilians were expected to return to the "pocket," an undetermined number to Quneitra and Rafid. There would have to be Syrian civil administrators and Syrian police — raising a problem of verification to prevent violations of limits on numbers and weapons in the guise of internal security forces.

At the same time, precisely because of the presence of Syrian civilians, Asad strenuously resisted the idea of a UN military force. He proposed instead a slight expansion of a group of UN observers who had been stationed on the Golan to supervise the line of separation established after the 1967 war. Israel asked for organized UN military units of no fewer than 3,000 men; Asad wanted only a few hundred individual observers.

Then there was the problem of fashioning a UN buffer zone separating the two sides. In the Sinai, the UN zone took up between six and ten kilometers in the desert and, more important, it was entirely located on territory previously occupied by the Israelis. It therefore reduced by that amount the Israeli area of control. On the Golan the Israeli forces withdrew behind the prewar line in only two places and then but a few kilometers. Therefore, to create a UN buffer would require an eastward withdrawal of Syria's prewar forward military positions — even as Syrian civil administration moved in the opposite direction into the UN zone. The line of separation in the west to which Israel was retreating had been designated the "blue line" for purposes of negotiation. On the other side of the UN buffer zone, the new line of Syrian military deployment was called the "red line" (see the final map on page 1100). As the realization sank in on Asad that the red line was in fact a retreat from the prewar line, it produced arguments as bitter and complex as the original line of separation (the blue line). Israel sought to push the red line as far into Syria as possible (they wanted it six to eight kilometers to the east of the prewar line) so that in fact the Syrian military would be further back than before the war. Painful disputes arose over Israel's insistence that some villages heretofore *behind* the Syrian lines be incorporated into the UN zone, where they would not have their accustomed protection by the Syrian army.

Mount Hermon presented yet another problem. It is really a mountain range paralleling the frontier with Lebanon and overlooking the Syrian plain, including Damascus. Since the outbreak of the October war, Israel had occupied five positions near its summit. Syria first insisted on having them returned to its control; at most, Israel would give them only to the UN. It was not a trivial issue, for it involved with respect to Damascus the same issues as the western hills about Quneitra. Israel from there would be able to observe the entire Damascus plain. At the same time, in Syrian hands they would permit surveillance of all the Israeli-occupied Golan.

The most intractable issue, however, proved to be Israeli insistence that Asad promise to prevent Palestinian terrorist raids across the line of separation. Ironically, unlike so much of the contention, this issue was more theoretical than practical. Asad had never encouraged, or for that matter permitted, guerrilla raids from Syrian territory. It was not in the Syrian character to permit others to involve them in risky ventures they could not control. But giving an assurance to that effect was something else again. Sadat had had no problem with it because there were no fedayeen in Egypt and because the disengagement line was over 100 miles from Israel's borders. But the drive into Damascus from the airport past Palestinian refugee camps made vivid the importance of the issue in Syrian political life. No Syrian leader could afford publicly to disavow the Palestinians' cause even as he sought to restrict their impact on Syrian politics and to influence PLO policy through Saiqa, the Palestinian element that Damascus controlled. Nor was the Israeli position without its elements of contradiction. Refusing an agreement would not end the guerrilla threat but compound it with the prospect of a military confrontation.

In solving these various remaining issues I would get little help from other Arab leaders. They had been willing to encourage a compromise over the line of separation because they recognized that it involved a major, otherwise unattainable, retreat of Israeli forces from the salient. But except for Sadat, they would find the limitation of forces too technical and the Palestinian issue too deadly; their response was bound to be to side with Asad. So while I kept the key Arab leaders generally briefed, I did not ask for their support. Nor was there enough time left for a side trip even to Cairo to explain the various deadlocks.

And the situation in Washington was deteriorating. As early as May 17, James Reston in the *New York Times* had ascribed the prolonged shuttle to my desire to stay out of the Watergate battles at home:

> Mr. Kissinger is the key figure in this Cabinet question. He is staying out of the Watergate and impeachment battles. One suspects he may even be prolonging his shuttle diplomacy in order to avoid the even more complicated and poisonous controversies of Washington.

It was untrue, but by May 22 this had become a general theme taken up by both the CBS and NBC television correspondents on my shuttle.

If some of the media were eager to get me home — or to criticize my prolonged absence — the White House suddenly decided that it had to keep me in the Middle East as a way of demonstrating its control of the negotiations. On May 18, the day of the breakthrough on the line of separation, the White House press office let it be known that the President had asked me to stay in the area as long as necessary. This was a near-disaster. My most effective means of putting pressure on both Israel and Syria was to threaten that I would leave. On May 21, after I had in fact given both sides an ultimatum that negotiations had to be completed by Friday, May 24, Nixon's press aides, with him in Key Biscayne, mindlessly repeated the original statement. It was not even intended to contradict me; it was simply the most convenient way to show Presidential direction of the negotiations. I cabled an urgent warning to Scowcroft:

Please get the press people under tighter control. I have told both parties here that I am leaving on Friday in order to put heat on the negotiations. . . . It seems to me that if the President wants to issue me instructions, there are far better ways to do it than through the press.

In any event, I am leaving this weekend having reached, I am convinced, the limit of what can be done on this trip. We will succeed or fail in the next 48 hours.

Another sign of Washington restlessness was the obsession with planning a Presidential trip to the Middle East. I received innumerable White House instructions to explore such a prospect with my hosts. I did so at some cost, because it convinced the parties that the United States desperately needed a settlement, tempting them to stall. Such a trip clearly presupposed a successful shuttle; failure would have the President in the area with our mediation disintegrating and tensions rising. As the shuttle dragged on, the planned date for the Presidential journey necessarily kept being postponed, only to multiply the number of insistent White House directives urging me to stay on to finish the job.

All this time, I had as well to conduct the other business of the Department of State. Luckily it was a quiescent period. In the Federal Republic of Germany, France, and Britain, new governments were in the process of taking over and they welcomed a respite in order to get their bearings. China was wishing our diplomacy well; it would not deliberately distract us from our main challenge. The Soviet Union, while unhappy about my solo efforts, did not choose to risk détente by being visibly obstructive — especially with the imminence of another Presidential visit to Moscow. And the developing countries had temporarily sated their yearning for center stage by an orgy of rhetoric at the Sixth Special Session of the UN General Assembly in April.

Still, a calm period for a Secretary of State is a relative term. Every day, reams of cables descended on my traveling caravan requiring some sort of action. My diligent State Department staff, on the plane and in Washington, kept the paper flowing in both directions. I made key decisions on a myriad of issues. The Atlantic Declaration was at last being finished; I had already had two important gatherings with Latin American foreign ministers to start a valued new dialogue with our hemispheric neighbors. There was a point beyond which it would not be possible to conduct my office out of my briefcase.

In these hectic conditions I resumed my role as itinerant psychiatrist. Dayan's suggestion, drawn from the Sinai negotiations — that the heavy weapons of each side should be placed where they could not reach the frontline of the opponent — made unexceptionable military sense. It was less persuasive to the President of Syria, who saw it as a means to protect Israeli settlements on Syrian soil and who had visions of being asked to move his air defense behind Damascus. Asad was eloquent in expounding the requirements of Syrian sovereignty and dignity. But the alternative he faced was not fully armed Syrian forces in front of Damascus but the collapse of the agreement, leaving an unrestricted number of Israeli forces a short distance from his capital.

And so with anguish and chagrin, and without grace, the two adversaries began to grapple with harsh detail. My mediation consisted of explaining each side's thinking to the other, occasionally coming forward with a formula to break a deadlock.

In the final days, a regular schedule developed. I would meet with the Israeli negotiating team in the morning in Jerusalem. Around noon my motorcade would depart for Ben-Gurion Airport an hour away. Early in the afternoon I would arrive in Damascus. After a meeting with Asad — usually lasting several hours — I returned to Israel, where I would generally meet again with the Israeli negotiating team. Between May 20 and May 25 alone, I logged some twenty hours in conversations with the Israelis; some thirty hours in talks with the Syrians. There was no night when I retired before 3:00 A.M. And my associates worked even longer hours. Somehow by Saturday evening, May 25, we were again close to an agreement — so close, in fact, that I said: "If it fails now, nobody will be able to explain how it happened."

Except through psychological exhaustion. Both sides had stripped themselves to the bone. They had agreed on the numbers of troops and types of equipment in a first zone of limited armaments ten kilometers from each side's forward position. A "United States proposal" signed by both sides would spell these out. Asad was reluctant to commit himself in an agreement with Israel to limit his ground forces in front of Damascus in a second zone ten to twenty kilometers in depth, but he was willing to have me write a letter of his intentions, provided we could agree on what they were. The "United States proposal" would also spell out the arms limitations in the ten- to twenty-kilometer belt: No artillery with a range of more than twenty kilometers would be introduced there and no surface-to-air missiles would be deployed closer than twenty-five kilometers to the forward line.

What remained to be settled was the exact location of the line from which all these distances would be measured. Asad remained adamantly opposed to pulling back the forward Syrian military line (the red line) so as to leave exposed villages that had previously enjoyed Syrian military protection; Israel would not consider any other possibility. With respect to the UN presence, a concept was emerging that combined the structure of the UN Emergency Force in Egypt with the nomenclature that had been traditional on the Golan since 1967. Asad did not want a "force" but was willing to accept "observers." Golda rejected observers and insisted on a force. What could be more natural than to create a hybrid called the United Nations Disengagement Observer Force whose function or charter no one could possibly deduce from its title? Asad was still haggling about replacing the word "force" with "organization," but I did not think he would collapse the negotiation over it. The number of UN personnel was still seriously disputed. And the Syrians remained unwilling to give any formal assurances about paramilitary Palestinian activity.

Meanwhile, too, the Soviets had become active again. Whether because he thought an agreement was imminent or because he anticipated failure, or perhaps because he wanted to deal with either contingency, Gromyko had again announced himself for Damascus. I gave Asad this reaction:

One, I will not see Gromyko in Damascus; two, I will not come to Damascus if Gromyko is in Damascus; three, except for that, you are a sovereign country and I will not tell you what to do so long as my other two points are understood. What you do with Gromyko is up to you.

By May 26 it was becoming clearly incompatible with my position as Secretary of State to remain absent from the United States any longer. As it was, no Secretary of State had ever been abroad for such an uninterrupted period. Gromyko was now scheduled to arrive in Damascus on May 27 — my birthday. I could have wished myself a better present. My next visit to Damascus would really have to be my last trip.

The Final Phase: Damascus, Another Crisis

O N Sunday, May 26, the twenty-ninth day of the shuttle, both parties were once again at a point they dreaded but did not know how to transcend. They knew that relatively minor concessions now would clinch the final agreement. Yet every move had been wrung from reluctant souls. They had come this far because someone — now the Israelis, now the Syrians — recoiled at the specter of a world without an agreement and yet neither side had been able to rise to a genuine vision of peace. The American negotiators, themselves spent physically or emotionally, were being asked by both leaders for irreconcilable private assurances so as to provide a pretext for a final concession. And time would not ease the problem. If we failed when so close, much more difficult decisions would be required to resume, and the whole area was more likely to drift to explosion rather than to reconciliation. If someone jumps across an abyss, he falls as surely if he misses by an inch as by a yard.

Before my departure for Damascus, Golda scheduled a ceremonial lunch on Sunday honoring me in the appropriately named Blue Room at the King David Hotel. The start had to be delayed several times because my talks with the Israeli negotiating team ran on; it finally took place at 3:00 P.M. We hungrily gulped down our food because there was not much time left before we had to rush to the airport to make our scheduled arrival in Damascus. There was an atmosphere of near-despair that we would probably fail so close to our goal and yet of hope that all the sacrifices that had been made must not prove futile when success was almost palpable. Golda delivered a very moving speech about how my shuttle had helped Israel's understanding of the Arabs, which was, after all, the key intangible:

I think he has given us a lesson: that it is not enough to be right and to be convinced that one is right; that we know. But in order to reach a point where we can really sit together with the people in our area, we must also have some understanding not to accept things that are not right but to at least understand them. I think he's gotten to know us; he's shown an awful lot of patience with us — hours and hours and hours. . . . No matter what happens, you and all of you who will leave this area will know there is nothing that is more desirable to every Israeli, to every man, woman, and child in this country; that is the simple thing of peace. Getting up in the morning and being sure that nobody died because he was attacked by somebody across the border. We don't want them to die; we don't want them to kill; we don't want them to shoot at anybody else. When we get peace in this area, Dr. Kissinger, without any exaggeration, I think you will be first on the list, after the Israelis, that will have made this possible because you understood, because you wanted peace, because you know that is the thing that we want. We hope it will come. I am sure someday it will come. But if you can possibly make it come while I'm still around, I'll be doubly thankful to you.

I replied:

As we have embarked on this effort, sometimes thinking that it would fail, sometimes making progress, we have all been determined that whether we succeed on this particular effort or not, the course on which we embark must succeed, that peace must be brought to this area, and that all of us will make the greatest effort to realize what we have started. . . . Madame Prime Minister, you represent this generation that came to this country when it was only a dream, and you have done what is given to very few — to bring a people to a country, to make the country a state, and to turn the state into a home. All of us who have had the privilege of working with you have been inspired by your greatness as a human being as well as by your leadership of your country. . . . We join you in your hope for a peace that will last, in which children can guard their innocence and all the men can turn to tasks of construction.

If emotion could fuel diplomacy, we would have left at 4:30 for the climactic meeting in Damascus certain of a breakthrough. But emotion can supply only the endurance to persist through the tedium by which diplomacy inches forward, adjusting nuances along the way. I had sent Asad a letter from Israel warning that this would be irrevocably my last visit to Damascus.

When I arrived, the Syrian President showed that he was not to be bluffed. He informed me that since I had announced my departure for the next morning, he had accepted Gromyko's visit starting at noon. But he also showed the limits of the Syrian-Soviet relationship. Told that this seemed to cut matters rather closely, he turned to an aide and coolly delayed the arrival of the Foreign Minister of his principal armorer until ten o'clock in the evening. Still, that left us a little more than twenty-four hours to finish.

Two sessions with Asad followed that Sunday night, May 26, one from 9:00 P.M. to midnight with a larger group of advisers, including on his side the Defense Minister, the Air Force Chief of Staff, Shihabi, and Khaddam; then from 12:15 to 2:30 A.M., as I entered the day of my birth, Asad and I dined alone with only an aide present while Khaddam and Joe Sisco reviewed the texts of the various documents. But the result was the same in both meetings. Asad was implacable, haggling endlessly about the Syrian forward line (the red line), the force limits, the size of the UN contingent, and the Palestinians. Asad also sought to extract a written assurance to the effect that the United States would support Israel's ultimate return to the 1967 borders. I could go no further than to promise continued American involvement in the peace process. Simultaneously, Sisco in his meeting with Khaddam encountered a stone wall.

I met with Sisco and my other associates between 3:00 and 4:00 A.M. in the state guest house. Somberly, feeling drained, we concluded that the shuttle had failed. I would turn the meeting scheduled with Asad in the morning into a courtesy farewell call.

My associates were kind enough to see that my birthday was marked by something less bleak than this. Tom Scotes gave me a surprise birthday party in the morning with a cake of epic proportions. The press contingent presented me with a poster parodying an airline advertisement: "I am Henry, Fly Me to Damascus."

My staff, by this time a bit demented from fatigue, had come up with a birthday present of its own. I had jocularly criticized them a month earlier when Ron Ziegler claimed that a letter referring to Nixon had been washed up in a bottle on an island in the Bahamas where he had spent a weekend. "Why can't you do something like this for me?" I asked Robert McCloskey, who acted as supervisor of press relations, Congressional relations, and any other subject requiring wise and unflappable counsel. He had taken my yearning to heart and had induced some Israelis skillful in faking antiquities to produce a smallish flat brown rock bearing the carved inscription in Hebrew: "HAK was here — 5683* — Quneitra." The theory was that I was a reincarnation of an early ruler of the area; only this could explain my obsession with every street, hill, and rock of the provincial capital of the Golan. An accompanying press release spelled all this out. At the last moment McCloskey's nerve failed him, or on my birthday he thought — wisely — the mood was not right. He handed the rock to me with great flourish in a ceremony on the aircraft three days later on the way back home.

I was gratified by the birthday cake but contemplated my impending departure with some sense of letdown. It was therefore a mellow and melancholy occasion when shortly before 10:00 A.M. I met Asad with only one aide each (mine was Peter Rodman) and Isa Sabbagh as interpreter, to say our farewells. We chatted in a desultory manner about various turning points in the negotiation, as if we had been spectators at a natural event that we had been unable to influence. Conscious of White House pressures, I raised again Nixon's desire to visit the area. Asad thought that it would not be consistent with the dignity of the President of the United States to come to the Middle East after a failure of American diplomacy. Should Nixon come to a different conclusion, perhaps on the advice of other Arab leaders (he said tactfully), Asad would be delighted to receive him in Damascus. We drafted yet another statement announcing a breakup; there was some dispute about a phrase suggested by me that Asad would send someone to Washington to continue the talks. Asad said resignedly: "We could say we could send someone to Washington for any other purpose. If we here couldn't do it, one person in Washington couldn't do it." We settled on announcing a Syrian emissary to develop Syrian-American relations, not to promote disengagement on the Golan.

Through a month of negotiation I had grown to like Asad. He was proud, tough, shrewd, cordial. He had given us many a difficult moment. But I had witnessed how he had gone through the searing process of coming to grips with the problem of Arab-Israeli coexistence. He rebelled against the idea and yet had come close to accepting it. Like Golda from the other end of the telescope, he had caught a glimpse of the reality of peace. And all the concessions and bartering had been in part tactical, in part a spiritual odyssey. I rose with some sadness to say goodbye. He too stood up, and as we began to move toward the door Asad suddenly said:

After having established this nice human personal contact, then out of loyalty, out of fondness, when we look at the imperative of Syrian-American relations, I'm particularly looking at the need not to harm you. In your view,

---

*On the Hebrew calendar, 5683 was the equivalent of 1923, the year of my birth — a memorable year in Fürth if not in Quneitra.

how far could the red line [the Syrian forward line] be moved? When it can be moved. Let's speak openly.

It was a stunning performance. Asad had played out the string to absolutely the last possible millimeter, and now opened the way to another, conclusive, effort to get an agreement. I had told him in December that he reminded me of someone who negotiated at the edge of a precipice and who in order to increase his bargaining position jumped into the abyss hoping that on the way down something would break his fall. That "something" was now I. Clearly, no Syrian leader would conclude an agreement with Israel out of fondness for an American Secretary of State; but it was best to fall in with the pretense, which could have plausibility only in the Arab world. There personal relations are never trivial; they are the solvent for the passions of peoples:

I don't want to do anything that would hurt President Asad. If the President accepted something that was extremely difficult for him and caused complications later for him, we would have defeated an important American purpose. So I don't want to be responsible for having made the President — through persuasiveness — do something that will later on hurt him. Because that would be a tactical success but a strategic defeat.

Asad was now over the hump. If he wanted to commit suicide out of uncontrollable passion for me, as he seemed to imply, it was his business. The truth must have been that the Syrian leadership had decided to settle the night before but wanted to be absolutely sure it had squeezed the last drop of blood out of the stone. I presented — as my personal idea — another one-kilometer move forward of the red line, which the Israeli negotiating team had allowed me to offer but which I had held back the night before because it would simply have been swallowed up in the general controversy. I also added as my suggestion a solution to the problem of Syrian villages that were in limbo outside the new Syrian line: that the red line loop around them in a sausage-shaped bulge and that the Syrians accept the same restrictions there as the Israelis on the hills west of Quneitra — that is, no weapons able to shoot directly into the Israeli area.

We sparred for a few minutes about the fedayeen. Asad said that he could not agree to any legal obligation to prohibit Palestinian actions; it was an unmanageable political problem and an issue of principle. I proposed an American statement asserting that in our view the cease-fire in the Golan Heights covered guerrilla actions; if any took place, the United States would support Israel politically if it retaliated. Asad allowed that American statements were our problem; he would see no reason for Syria to object publicly. A solution seemed once more in sight.

But we had been burned too often. I told Asad that I would be prepared to make one more effort provided he assure me that he would stop haggling; we should complete a document, requiring only Israeli approval, that I could take back to Jerusalem. There could be no further negotiating; we were meeting for a drafting session. Asad should consult with his colleagues; I would review matters with mine. He and I should meet in an hour and agree whether it was feasible. I would not resume otherwise. We parted at 11:30 A.M.

At 12:35 P.M. we met again and pledged to each other that we would undertake a drafting effort, not a bargaining session. We allocated a maximum of three hours. I informed the Israeli cabinet to expect me back at 6:00 P.M.

Asad and I met with our advisers starting at 2:20 P.M. But to tell a Syrian not to haggle is like ordering a fish not to swim. Within minutes we found ourselves again in one of those nightmarish tests of will mitigated only slightly by Asad's sardonic humor and the exquisite forms of Arab hospitality (which in the excitement of the concluding phase of a negotiation did not on this occasion extend to feeding us). By 10:00 P.M., seven and a half hours later, we had ended up roughly where Asad and I had been at the end of the morning's conversation — except that Asad had proved to himself and to his colleagues once again that no more could be accomplished by intensive bargaining. We fixed the red line — subject to Israeli approval — where Asad and I had agreed (see the map on page 1100). We settled on the number of UN personnel at 1,250 and finalized the name of the organization as the United Nations Disengagement Observer Force (UNDOF). Asad won his point that he could not limit his tanks and personnel in front of Damascus beyond the ten-kilometer zone by agreement, but he assured me that he would deploy there no more than nine brigades, of which no more than three would be armored. I would convey these limitations in a letter to the Israelis. He accepted a ceiling on artillery of 162 guns of a range not exceeding twenty kilometers in the ten-to-twenty-kilometer zone; artillery with a longer range would be kept beyond twenty kilometers; surface-to-air missiles would be no closer than twenty-five kilometers to the Syrian forward line. All force limitations — as in the Sinai disengagement — would be part of a Syrian and Israeli response to a "United States proposal." We left it that Sisco would bring back the Israeli answer by noon the next day. This was to imply that there would be no further negotiation; Sisco would be empowered only to transmit completed documents.

Gromyko remained to be dealt with. His plane had arrived over Damascus around 9:00 P.M., while Asad and I were still in deep negotiation. I commented that to speed Israeli acceptance it was important to avoid any implication that Gromyko had had a decisive role. This was no problem, allowed the Chief of Staff of the Air Force; Gromyko's

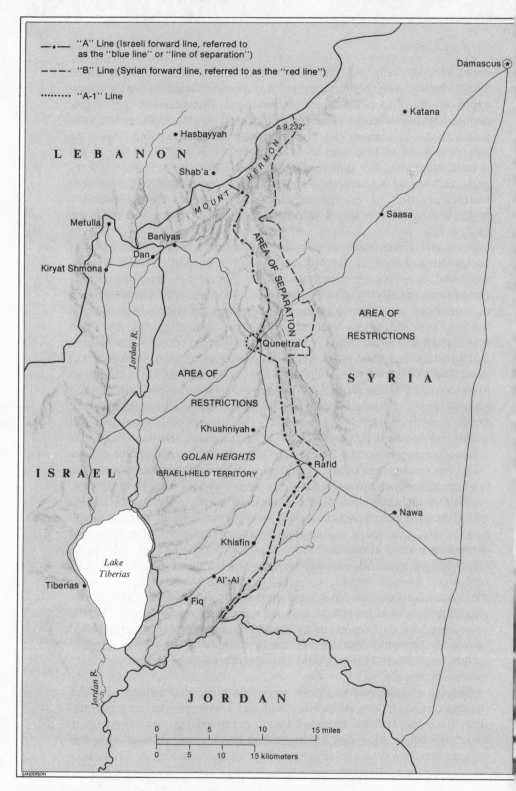

Syrian-Israeli Disengagement Agreement, May 31, 1974
(see text of the Agreement, pages 1253–1254)

airplane could circle for a while. By 9:45 P.M., Gromyko's plane was running out of fuel. I graciously agreed that it might land, provided it was not parked next to mine — I did not want press photographs implying joint action. So Gromyko's plane was moved to a dark corner of the airfield where the Soviet Foreign Minister was greeted by Syria's Deputy Foreign Minister — all senior leaders being involved in negotiations with me. Asad, for good measure, promised not to meet with Gromyko until he had received Sisco with Israel's answer.

I was accompanied to the airport by Shihabi and Khaddam. Gromyko's motorcade passed us in the opposite direction. It was a pregnant moment more symbolic of the recent revolution in Middle East diplomacy than all the arcane points that we had been debating all that month.

I had received the best birthday present of my life: if not peace in the Middle East, then at least the absence of war for long enough to give diplomacy a chance.

I knew that I did not yet have Israel's final approval, but every instinct told me that it was impossible to come this close and fail.

The Final Phase: Israel

O N the way to the airport I had warned Khaddam that every solution we had found in Damascus would be a problem in Jerusalem. There might be a long all-night session with the negotiating team; it could go into the day with the cabinet. I would send back Sisco with the answer the next day; there could not be another negotiation. Syria would have to be ready to say yes or no.

Though we had just finished drafting documents incorporating almost all of Israel's ideas, I had a painful recollection of the occasion in November 1973 when I naively assumed that we had an agreement because Sadat had agreed to almost all the points raised by Golda. Then I had sent Sisco to obtain final Israeli approval — and for my pains was accused of proceeding by ultimatum. It was important for Israel's self-respect not to have the final phase of the negotiation appear as if dictated from Damascus. Therefore I spoke with extraordinary restraint to the press at Damascus airport:

We have narrowed the differences to a very few and I am now returning to Israel to meet with the Israeli negotiating team tonight to see what their view is about how these differences might be bridged. Tomorrow Mr. Sisco of my group is going to return to Damascus to bring these considerations to President Asad and to the Foreign Minister.

I added that I would not return to Syria on this trip.

For once the subtle, tough, and experienced journalists on my plane missed a nuance. Exhaustion no doubt played its role. But they misunderstood the significance of Sisco's returning. It could, in fact, have only one of two meanings: that an agreement was all but wrapped up or that it was out of reach. Nearly five weeks of near-misses made the second interpretation the more plausible. As a result, on the very day that success seemed inescapable, many thoughtful journalists speculated on the causes and consequences of failure. It was done in sorrow and with goodwill. It did no damage except to the equanimity of the White House.

Golda, assembling her team at 1:00 A.M. early Tuesday, May 28, suffered no such doubts. She knew immediately that a breakthrough had been achieved. I went over the discussions of the previous twenty-four hours in great detail. We reviewed once again the location of the Syrian line, Mount Hermon, the Palestinians, the composition of UNDOF. I said that I nearly set the number of UNDOF at the nonsensical figure of 1,286 to drive the Israeli cabinet into a frenzy to determine the reasoning behind it!

We talked for two hours. I was hoarse, barely able to speak, tired. It was nearly 3:00 A.M. Finally, Golda had heard enough. She was going to call a cabinet meeting for 8:00 A.M., five hours away. The time for decision was nearly at hand. "You young people go to bed," said Golda with a smile, and adjourned the meeting.

And I knew that she would fight for the agreement with the same intensity with which she had heretofore insisted on Israel's requirements. After all the weeks of sometimes stormy and frequently abstruse debate, we were now reduced to fundamentals; there was no sense in pressure. So I summed up:

You've gone a long way. If you decide against it, no one on the American side will feel you were unreasonable, so that shouldn't enter into it. What should enter into it is the basic merits of the consequences of an agreement against the consequences of no agreement, with a country whose basic reliability is uncertain but whose reliability is no more certain without the agreement.

The American team retired around 3:30 A.M. and slept until about 9:00 A.M. By then Golda had assembled her cabinet. I had expected the decision to be made quickly and had told Asad that Sisco would be bringing him Israel's last word by noon. His promise not to receive Gromyko before seeing Sisco demonstrated Syria's priorities.

After weeks of frantic nonstop effort, my colleagues and I had nothing left to do. We sat in my suite at the King David Hotel overlooking the Old City of Jerusalem. The golden Dome of the Rock, one of Islam's holiest mosques, gleamed in the mellow sunlight of spring. What passion had other, less beautiful hills evoked these past weeks! Dinitz called periodically to inform us that the cabinet was still meeting. My nervousness was shown by the fact that I called him three times. At last, at 1:15 P.M. Dinitz told me the news: The cabinet was well disposed, but another meeting with me was needed. At 2:00 P.M., I met with Golda, Dayan, Eban, Dinitz, Gur, and the Director of the Prime Minister's office, Mordechai Gazit. I was accompanied by Sisco and Rodman.

Golda wasted no time in getting to the point. "Look, from 8:30 to fifteen minutes ago — it is a tragic meeting, because everybody agrees we must have an agreement — but everybody agrees that without something tangible as far as the terrorists are concerned —''

We were back to the most intractable issue. It was impossible to tell Israel after Ma'alot that terrorism could be left out of the agreement. It was equally impossible to ask the passionate nationalists in Damascus to dissociate themselves publicly from the Palestinians. At the same time, it was a fact that the Golan Heights had been virtually free of terrorist incidents all these years; anyone familiar with the Syrian style of government knew that Damascus was unlikely to let a paramilitary organization it did not control operate from its territory. It was the last thing Asad wanted, I said:

The real problem is, as I see the situation, your domestic situation requires you to call attention to it [terrorism] and his domestic situation requires him to deny it. While the practical matter is as I said. . . . The more formal you want it, the less likely you'll get it.

But the Israelis wanted something — what, they did not quite know. What they were insisting on was that I should go back to Damascus yet again and come back with some reassurance. A tall order. They were well aware that the collapse of an agreement over this issue would not ease the terrorist danger; it would almost surely make it worse. They sought legal protection for what was a political and psychological problem. They needed above all something to tell the Knesset, to which they had rashly promised to submit any agreement before signing it.

To ease my task, the Israeli team accepted the existing texts, after making some halfhearted attempts to modify the language here and there. They agreed to advance the Syrian forward line as I had proposed, except at one location. Around 3:15 P.M., Golda took me to her small office. She would be stepping down from her post in three days, she said; this agreement was her way of drawing a line under the last war. She could then say that she had finished her task. She wanted me, rather than Sisco, to go to Damascus so that if it failed at the last moment she could live with herself. I could get more out of Asad than anyone else, and if not she would at least know that nothing more could have been done. I reluctantly agreed. I did warn her that in Damascus I would have to pay a brief courtesy call on Gromyko; it was too insulting to be with him in the same city and to refuse.

So we notified Damascus that I would leave Israel at 5:30 P.M. and that I hoped to see Asad as soon thereafter as possible — a symptom of how our relations had changed. Four months earlier it would have been inconceivable that the prickly Syrians would have let an American set a time for the meeting with their President.

Thus, less than twenty-four hours after I had announced my final departure from Damascus, I was back in the Syrian capital. Khaddam was at the airport that Tuesday evening to resume our friendly conversation. "Welcome," he said warmly. "I think not even the Foreign Minister can ruin this agreement," I replied. On the way to the guest house, Khaddam told me that when Sisco's mission kept being postponed, Asad had seen no way of keeping his promise not to receive Gromyko. It had been a courtesy call lasting half an hour; the Syrians had given very little information about the state of the negotiations. I had seen enough of my secretive and proud interlocutors to believe him.

At 8:15 P.M., I met Asad alone, accompanied only by Isa Sabbagh. It had finally come down to a human problem and my role was to explain motivations, not to find formulas. I explained with some emotion the Israeli sense of insecurity especially in the week of Ma'alot. Asad, I believe, understood, though he had his own imperatives. He spoke softly but passionately of the travail of a people that had no home, no identity, and above all no hope. He had no right to diminish what little faith in the future the Palestinians had left by seeming to side with their enemies. At the same time, the absence of guerrilla activity in the past had been no accident; nor was that state of affairs likely to change in the future. The Golan would not be guerrilla country because of Syria's chosen policy, not because of Israeli threats or nonbinding Syrian promises. I gained some increased understanding of the reasons why guerrilla actions on the Golan would be unlikely. After we had spent five weeks tying down every little detail, I would have to take responsibility for conveying to the Israeli cabinet my judgment that guerrilla action was highly improbable. Israel, I felt, should settle for an American assurance that if my judgment proved wrong and Israel responded to guerrilla attacks on the Golan it would have our support as not being in violation of the cease-fire.

It was now 10:45 P.M. I was prepared — nay eager — to leave. I knew that Golda and indeed the entire negotiating team were waiting for me. Asad would hear none of it. I could not depart without having dinner with him and his closest collaborators, Defense Minister General Tlas, who wrote poetry; Army Chief of Intelligence General Shihabi; Air Force Chief Jamil; and Deputy Prime Minister and Foreign Minister Khaddam. They had been invited to a dinner with Gromyko; they were getting hungry. I protested that Gromyko was waiting for me. "It is all right," said Asad coolly; "you are eating his dinner."

So we repaired to Asad's small dining room, which had the same cocoonlike quality as his other chambers. The mood was relaxed and genial as never before. I mentioned that Gromyko had told me of a Siberian bird he hunted which had to be lured by imitating its mating call. I asked whether Gromyko had ever given him the privilege of hearing it. "He only sings it in your presence," cracked Asad. I suggested that Gromyko might do it in lieu of a departure statement.

Asad twitted me about being afraid to let Sisco come alone to Damascus. It was not his failure that I feared, I rejoined, but his success. I then sarcastically paid tribute to the inspiration of the UN force:

KISSINGER: It's an epic poem. [Laughter.] He got it from the Defense Minister. As long as this group lives, it will know it has done something that has not been done in 6,000 years of recorded history: There has never been an organization called UNDOF. [Laughter.]

ASAD: These were my sentiments yesterday.

KISSINGER: I've never heard the Defense Minister's poetry.

SHIHABI: I have; the difference in comprehension is the same. [Laughter.]

Whereupon the Defense Minister recited a long poem in nonsense Arabic that amused our Syrian hosts hugely.

After an hour of this we returned to the conference room to check the maps yet once more. The Army Chief of Staff had joined us as we went one last time through all the hills and streets that had so possessed us for nearly five weeks. Finally, we agreed on a procedure for announcing the agreement — which we hoped to do by 7:00 P.M. Syrian time the next day. Signature was to take place on Friday (May 31).

At midnight, I finally called on Andrei Gromyko in a state guest house unfamiliar to me. It was a demeaning position for the Soviet Foreign Minister, but he carried it off with aplomb. Unless Gromyko was a better actor than I thought possible, he knew next to nothing about the disengagement negotiations, which we discussed for less than ten minutes. The only subject he seemed vaguely informed on was Syria's refusal to undertake formal obligations to restrain the guerrillas. Predictably, Gromyko supported the Syrian view, but without any passion. He acted more like a professor analyzing a diplomatic event far removed in time than like the foreign minister of a superpower. There were some boilerplate exchanges about the European Security Conference and SALT, and after barely half an hour Khaddam collected me to take me to the airport.

In the car Khaddam promised once again that there would be no Syrian reaction to a unilateral American statement of our attitude toward guerrilla attacks. Despite Gromyko's presence in Damascus, Khaddam preferred that the formal notification of Moscow about the agreement be made from Washington. The reason seemed inscrutable to me unless it reflected perversity. He hoped the announcement of the accord could be moved up to 5:00 P.M.

In Israel, my return very early Wednesday morning, May 29, was the start of another all-night session — beginning immediately, at 2:10 A.M. Golda informed me that Rabin had succeeded in forming a cabinet. He would present it to the Parliament on Sunday, June 2; Friday, May 31, would be her last day in office. She showed no emotion at the end of her public career. I thought I detected a sense of relief that she would be the Prime Minister who brought back the last Israeli prisoners from a war for which she would never cease blaming herself, and that she could preside over a cease-fire on the Golan Heights.

But neither the imminence of leaving office nor the yearning to end her career on a high note induced any flagging of vigilance. In the quiet of the early morning hours, I met with her alone and reviewed the discussions I had had with Asad. We agreed that Golda could make a statement to her Parliament on the subject of guerrilla attacks, which after several drafts emerged in the Knesset debate in this form:

As for the prevention of terrorist activities, the United States has informed us of its position on that first paragraph of the agreement, and this is: "Raids by armed groups or individuals across the demarcation line are contrary to the cease-fire. Israel, in its exercise of its right of self-defense, may act to prevent such actions by all available means. The United States would not consider such actions by Israel as violations of the cease-fire, and will support them politically."

I assume that the United States would not have made such a declaration to us had it not had a solid foundation for doing so, and I make this statement public with the knowledge of the United States.

There was no Syrian response.

Golda Meir, who had fought bitterly for every square inch and had scanned every escape clause, was resting her case on an act of faith. It was symbolic that in the end both of these leaders, so suspicious of each other, would end up by affirming the reality of intangibles.

From 2:45 A.M. to 4:00 A.M., I met with the full Israeli negotiating team. A short while later, the cabinet met again and approved the agreement.

There was no time for a letdown. We had to work frantically to complete all documents, send them to Damascus (not an easy matter as they had to be routed through Washington), and set up the arrangements for the various procedures such as announcement and signing. There was a last-minute hitch when the Syrians suddenly asked for a five-hour delay of the announcement and a delay of the signing from May 31 to June 2 — which would put it past the end of Mrs. Meir's term of office and require another approval by the new cabinet. I suspected Gromyko's fine hand at work. In the event, after a series of rather strong messages, Asad returned to the original schedule.

Finally, at 1:00 P.M. Washington time that Wednesday, May 29 (7:00 P.M. in Jerusalem, 8:00 P.M. in Damascus), President Nixon read the following statement in the White House briefing room:

The discussions conducted by United States Secretary of State Dr. Henry Kissinger with Syria and Israel have led to an agreement on the disengagement of Syrian and Israeli forces. The agreement will be signed by Syrian and Israeli military representatives in the Egyptian-Israeli Military Working Group of the Geneva Conference on Friday — this Friday — May 31.*

That evening Golda gave a reception in the Spartan conference room of her office. All the cabinet was there, as well as leaders of the Parliament. Exhaustion was etched on all the faces, and an immense relief. Were these tired men and women the same people who had bargained so obstinately and had seemed so ready to risk everything? Did the relief indicate that they had really dreaded the consequences of the tension that they seemed so ready to court? Probably both questions must be answered in the affirmative. Israel's leaders were at the end of their psychic resources after eight months of nearly unending crises. They did not give in to their fears and they did not dare to trust in their hopes, and so they had moved crabwise, carefully, not excessively generously, but when all was said and done unequivocally toward agreement.

Golda was almost too tired to speak, but what she said was imbued with the great dream of a people that had only known war:

There is no doubt that this is a great evening, an evening that spells great efforts, a lot of soul-searching, and searching possibilities that maybe some time ago seemed to be impossible.

This is a day that we hope will be a day that will not only bring immediate quiet on our northern borders and that Syrian mothers, Israeli mothers, Syrian young wives, Israeli young wives, children on both sides of the border can go to sleep at night without terror, dreams of who knows — if their dear one is alive today, will he be alive again on the next day? This is what we hope for our people and for our neighbors, and we hope that this goes well. We pray that it should, that this is a beginning for a real and lasting peace with all our neighbors and all our borders. Again, for the sake of the people on both sides of the border.

Israel had come a long way when its Prime Minister could speak feelingly of the hopes and dreams of the people of Syria as well as those of the people of Israel.

---

*The agreement was signed on schedule. Its text and that of the "United States proposal" are in the backnotes.[3]

I uttered a few banalities, to the effect that we would never forget the experience of the past month and the mood of its culmination. And then I kissed Golda on the cheek. But Golda would not tolerate sentimentality for long. Mindful — and slightly resentful — of my embraces of Arab leaders, she said: "I have been afraid you only kissed men."

The next day, Abba Eban brought me to the airport and spoke nostalgically:

The Secretary will not be coming back tonight. Now that is something that I'm capable of grasping intellectually, but not emotionally. The experience of the daily meetings had become almost part of our lives.

And then he summed up the psychological significance of the past five weeks: We had gone to the point of despair and then beyond it through an act of will and faith in peace.

There was a brief stop in Cairo to call on the father of disengagement, Anwar Sadat. We met at the President's residence in the Giza section of Cairo, first alone, then with advisers. Sadat was immensely relieved. For nearly six months he had endured Arab taunts because he had made a separate disengagement agreement in January. But without his courage, stalemate would have been certain on both fronts. The thirty-four-day ordeal of the Syrian shuttle showed what would have happened if the Sinai and Golan negotiations had been attempted simultaneously. Deadlock would have been inevitable, another explosion highly probable. The Third Army could not have sat in the desert all that time without efforts to free it. Asad would have had great difficulty obtaining domestic support for his step toward peace. Sadat had made possible the first withdrawal of Israeli forces in which Arab diplomacy played an important role.

But he was already thinking of the future. The road was now open to larger steps toward peace and to acceleration of the shift of his diplomacy toward Washington. He was looking forward to Nixon's imminent visit to symbolize Egypt's confidence in America. We decided to announce the formation of a joint commission of economic, scientific, and cultural cooperation. And we spoke in the confidence and affection that had grown up between us of next steps that might be taken on the various Arab fronts. Sadat asked whether Rabin had Golda's guts; I complimented him on asking the significant question, not the superficial one of whether he was a hawk or a dove. Sadat wanted Rabin to have enough time to get "on his legs"; he was wise enough to understand that only patience would get Israel over its psychological hurdles and thus paradoxically speed the peace process. And Sadat needed the time, too, to build "a new image for America" in the Arab world. He called me a "magician"; I said he had made me a magician. Which was true. He had changed reality; I had only helped the two sides to begin walking down the path that he had opened.

If the Syrian shuttle was a grueling experience, it also represented a process of maturing. Sinai disengagement had been all innocence: huge obstacles overcome; a great man to keep the focus on essentials; a rapid conclusion; an almost perfect symmetry between aspiration and achievement. But it was not the real world, at least of the Middle East with its clash of profound passions and principles. On the Golan Heights, there was no room for the acts of grace by which Sadat ennobled the peace process and made appear inconsequential the abstruse debates that for decades had substituted for real dialogue. Neither side had that scope; concession had to be wrested from their very souls. The negotiation took the form of an endless series of haggles but these were all way stations on a journey through spiritual necessities. At every critical point, the two sides went to the edge of the abyss that bespoke renewed conflict. And then they drew back; they could not bring themselves to give up their first chance for peace. So the long shuttle produced an accord that, with all its inherent complexity, fragility, and mistrust, has endured without significant challenge for nearly a decade. There have been no serious complaints of violations; through crises in Lebanon there has been no moment when the accord on the Golan seemed in jeopardy. In the eight years since the agreement was signed, no event has occurred to mar the judgment I made about guerrilla action late at night in Asad's somber sitting room. So the acts of faith that culminated it proved justified.*

The significance of the Golan disengagement was not all or even primarily psychological. On the political plane, it marked a major breakthrough. If radical Syria could sign an agreement with Israel, there were no ideological obstacles to peace talks with any other Arab state. During the summer, a procession of foreign ministers from all over the Middle East descended on Washington to divine our policies, symbolizing — not by accident — the shrinking of the Soviet role in the area. Our plan was to take at least two more partial steps before attempting more comprehensive goals: We would seek to bring Jordan and Israel together in a serious negotiation over the West Bank. And we knew further steps were possible in the Sinai, trading additional Israeli withdrawals for political steps toward peace. At the end of the Syrian shuttle we had not yet decided which course to follow first; but the Syrian disengagement was a prerequisite for either. Somewhere along the line we would be in a position to move forward on several fronts simultaneously. Even Syria was counting on us to continue the negotiating process. After a step

---

*This was written before the Israeli annexation of the Golan Heights in December 1981.

with Jordan and another Egyptian accord, we intended to explore the conditions for an end to the state of belligerency on all fronts.

Thus, the Syrian shuttle seemed to us the watershed between the world of crisis ushered in by the October war and the world of peace toward which we were striving. How much a country racked by constitutional crisis could attempt and achieve was unclear; but we did not feel we were at the end of the road. On the contrary. We planned to proceed — and we did. And in the process, we fervently hoped, a moment would be reached when all the nations of the area would take that step toward reconciliation to which their sacrifices have long since entitled them.

XXIV

The Last Hurrah

The Salzburg Press Conference

As the Syrian shuttle went on and on, we sustained ourselves by visions of the return home, which took on the quality of an oasis for a wanderer in the desert. The longer the working days, the tauter the nerves, the more idyllic the end of the shuttle appeared to us. We would not have believed that the vision would turn into a mirage.

The Syrian-Israeli disengagement proved to be the last major achievement of the Nixon Administration. To a great extent, the heart of our foreign policy had seemed to be insulated from the most corrosive domestic effects of Watergate, as if by a tacit national recognition of the needs of survival. It could not continue. When the fabric of a society is sufficiently rent, all restraints give way sooner or later. Shortly after the Syrian agreement was completed, foreign policy was subjected to a direct assault. The cocoon that seemed to protect me from personal attack was abruptly torn asunder.

I arrived at Andrews Air Force Base at 1:50 A.M. on May 31 at the conclusion of the thirty-four-day shuttle to what may have been the high point of public acclaim ever accorded to a Secretary of State. *Newsweek*'s cover showed me in a Superman suit. *Time*'s cover was less heady but its praise nearly as excessive. Commentators described the shuttle as one of the greatest diplomatic achievements in history; there is no record indicating that I resisted the hyperbole. The (apocryphal?) story made the rounds that I responded to someone at a dinner party who thanked me for saving the world with the smug reply, "You are welcome."

In fact, my mood was more complex. I was physically exhausted and emotionally drained. I was experiencing the letdown that always followed great exertions. And better than most, I knew how narrow had been the dividing line between success and failure. Had Asad not called me back a few days earlier — on my birthday — as I was walking out of his room, the whole agreement would have aborted. Many now applauding would have been castigating the investment of so much prestige in a prolonged personal negotiation. A foretaste of these ashes had been provided when the talks seemed to stalemate three days before the signing, as in this report filed by the fair-minded CBS correspondent Marvin Kalb on May 28:

This is the 31st day of the Kissinger journey to a disengagement agreement between Syria and Israel. There have been 16 visits to Israel, 12 to Damascus, 18,200 miles from Washington and back and forth between Jerusalem and Damascus — an extraordinary expenditure of energy and personal influence on the Secretary's part. He wanted an agreement. That he failed to achieve it, it seems, [was] no failure of effort or commitment. . . .

Mistakes and misjudgments have been made. Perhaps Kissinger should not have come here at all. Perhaps he should have sent Sisco to do the basic diplomatic spade work and come here only when the differences had narrowed sufficiently for him to use his influence and crack the deadlock. Perhaps after two weeks he should have gone home and not wait[ed here] for the chance to conclude a final agreement. . . .

He invested so much and he did not get his deal. It is unlikely that he will ever invest so much again on a single negotiation. He will return to Washington probably tomorrow and then he will have to answer the many questions that will be raised about the negotiation, about his judgment, about the future of the Middle East. Kissinger has always been fatalistic about negotiations — there are things that can be done, there are things that cannot be done. The worst thing for him is not to have tried. He will not be guilty of that.

But if I had succeeded in the shuttle, I knew also it was only a beginning, in the manner of an Alpine climber who pauses for a brief respite at the top of a hilly meadow and sees the distant peaks as far away as ever. We had gained maneuvering room but I had learned the price of it. The period for apparent miracles was over. To build upon the two agreements a durable peace in the Middle East, which was our firm resolve, would dwarf in complexity the disengagements that had required such massive labors; and it would in its course evoke passions far more elemental than those that had already driven all of us, as Abba Eban said on my departure, more than once beyond the point of despair.

In these first days back in Washington, I wondered how we could begin such an odyssey while poised over the widening fissure of Watergate. By now I considered Nixon's impeachment inevitable. The release of even his version of the taped conversations in the Oval Office had removed the last inhibitions. Almost no major figure was prepared to speak out on his behalf. His public support had dwindled to a hard core of about 25 percent. The disintegration of the Presidency was painful to observe. Nixon's self-discipline was extraordinary, but it only masked his vulnerability and he was drained now of a sense of proportion. One could not work with a man for over five years as I had without being touched by the sinking of a spirit that had so often borne us up.

It was in this mood, suspended between awe and dread, and seeking to regain my balance amidst adulation and disintegration, that with stunning unexpectedness I found myself drawn into the pit.

By now the lust for revelation had developed its own logic. What had started out as a means to break through official obfuscation of wrongdoing had become an insatiable demand for a "truth" that often was itself a distortion. Each inquiry was treated as if it stood entirely by itself; any official document was handled as if it were the revealed truth and as if no one had ever heard of the self-serving papering of files, of memoranda written to cover the author's tracks. There is no question that the Watergate investigations dramatized the indispensable principle that not even the highest in the land are above the law. By the summer of 1974, however, Watergate turned into a kind of national masochism that threatened to consume our substance in an obsession with our failings. Suddenly it was my turn.

The occasion was yet another regurgitation of the twin issues of wiretapping and the "Plumbers." The first rumblings had been apparent during the Syrian shuttle. John Ehrlichman was due to go on trial later in the summer for offenses related to the activities of the "Plumbers," including the burglary of Daniel Ellsberg's psychiatrist's office. Seeking to justify his actions on grounds of national security, Ehrlichman filed a court affidavit on May 1 asserting that the "Plumbers" unit had been formed at three meetings in 1971, one of which I had attended. Charles Colson, indicted for other offenses, on April 29 had filed an affidavit for the Ehrlichman trial making the same point.* Both these events made headlines. The implication was that I had known about the "Plumbers" and their illegal activities all along and that my denials had been untrue. It was a replay of issues that had surfaced in my confirmation hearings in September 1973 and that had then been rehashed in the January 1974 investigation of the Navy yeoman who had rifled my briefcase (see Chapters X and XVIII). Repetition did not make the accusations any more valid.

In July 1971, while I was on my secret trip to China, Ehrlichman had asked David Young, then an aide of mine, to join his staff. On my return on July 13, I protested to Ehrlichman that he should not have done this in my absence. Two days later, Nixon invited a number of his

---

*Colson's assertions were flatly contradicted by an unsolicited letter he had sent me on June 11, 1973, in which he said:

At no time in the interview [with the US Attorney] did I suggest that you caused the Plumbers to be formed, although I did say that the concerns of all at that period of time were very grave.

I specifically told the prosecutors that I was not privy to the formulation of the Plumbers, that I was not present at meetings when it was decided the Plumbers be formed.

senior staff, including Ehrlichman and me, to dine with him in Los Angeles to celebrate his television appearance in which he announced my secret trip. After a convivial evening with Nixon basking in one of the rare moments of general public approbation, Ehrlichman and I shared a forty-minute helicopter ride back to San Clemente and fell into another bicker about David Young. Ehrlichman boasted that he was better able to use talent than I was, as demonstrated by his ability to attract Young; I put it down to jealousy over the attention paid to my China exploit. If Ehrlichman mentioned "Plumbers" or that Young was intended for such a group, it passed me by. My perception was that Young had been assigned to a project involving declassification of documents. As I have said earlier, I would not have seen anything wrong with a small unit in Ehrlichman's office charged with investigating security leaks. And nobody ever claimed that I knew of the "Plumbers'" later illegal activities.

No matter; in May 1974 following Ehrlichman's and Colson's affidavits, we were back to the nightmarish speculation on whether I should have deduced Young's other duties from the interview of an Admiral who reported a security violation in December 1971 or on how I recalled a July 1971 helicopter ride at the end of an emotion-filled day entirely devoted to the China breakthrough. On May 11, Morton Halperin, a former NSC staff aide whose telephone had been wiretapped and who was making a career out of pursuing me in the courts and in the media, told a conference of journalists in Boston that I was guilty of perjury. The *Boston Globe* reported this on May 12, while I was in the Middle East.

A week later, newspapers of the Knight newspaper chain published revelations about a White House tape recording leaked by the House Judiciary Committee. On a garbled tape of an Oval Office conversation with John Dean on February 28, 1973, Nixon said something that sounded as if he was recalling a request by me for a wiretap on my former aide Anthony Lake after he had gone to work for Presidential candidate Edmund Muskie.[1] Such a request by me would have contradicted my testimony before the Senate Foreign Relations Committee that I had only followed security criteria established by Nixon in submitting names for the investigation. Joining the staff of a Presidential candidate was obviously not one of those criteria. It was also untrue. The President's taped recollections three years after the event were clearly erroneous. (The tapping of Lake had begun in May 1970, while he was still in the government, long before he went to work for Muskie — and around the time that, at Nixon's orders, wiretap reports from the FBI ceased being sent to me.) What Nixon's comment quoted out of context might have meant was never cleared up. The key words were practically inaudible. Nixon's meaning — and what he might have been trying to accomplish by telling such a story to Dean — would depend largely on the context, however. Nobody familiar with Nixon would treat an isolated sentence as being anything other than part of a design.

But the media, riding high on the Watergate wave, were more interested in publishing secret documents than in subjecting them to any critical scrutiny. On May 21 — still on the shuttle — I was sent an article appearing in the left-wing magazine *New Times,* which was rather revealing of the mood developing among some journalists:

The honeymoon is over for Henry Kissinger. There are signs that the media is [*sic*] going after him for the first time. . . . And a Washington editor told me: "There's a strong feeling that Kissinger may get indicted for perjury for telling the Senate he didn't know about those wiretaps. We're going to look dumb if we don't get off our asses before a grand jury does."

The rumblings turned into an avalanche just as I returned from the shuttle. In early June, as part of the impeachment proceedings, the House Judiciary Committee began reviewing the FBI records on the wiretaps. This material, too, was leaked.

Whoever on the Judiciary Committee (or committee staff) was leaking these documents to the press was unaware that the same material had been examined in September 1973 by Senators John Sparkman and Clifford Case, who had been charged by the Senate Foreign Relations Committee to review that aspect of my record in executive session during my confirmation hearings. As I have discussed in earlier chapters, my recollection of events contradicted some of the memoranda in the internal files of the FBI; J. Edgar Hoover had invariably listed some official outside the FBI hierarchy as "requesting" each wiretap even in cases where I had heard Hoover himself specifically recommend them to Nixon. As former Secretary of State Dean Rusk later testified before the Senate Foreign Relations Committee when it looked into the subject, Hoover was a very experienced and astute bureaucrat who understood the importance of protecting his flanks and his rear.[2]

In 1973 I had reviewed each wiretap and the FBI documents with Senators Sparkman and Case and explained my recollection. Elliot Richardson, then Attorney General, and William Ruckelshaus, then Deputy Attorney General and Acting Director of the FBI, supported my testimony. Afterward, in executive session with the Senate Committee, I had gone over each case of which I had personal knowledge. None of this was known to the House Judiciary Committee when it started reviewing the records. Eager staffers, sensing a fresh victim, leaked what they considered "new evidence" that my earlier public testimony was untrue. The air was heavy with hints of perjury. The *Washington Post,* loath to fall behind in the pursuit of evildoers, rehashed the earlier stories in its edition of June 6.

That day — barely six days after my Mideast shuttle — I held my first press conference since my return. For nearly five weeks I had been far away, geographically and mentally, from the fevered atmosphere of Washington. I had been preoccupied every waking moment with matters very distant from the semantic hairsplitting over who had "initiated" or "requested" wiretaps five years earlier. Nothing was further from my mind than the possibility that I was about to be cross-examined about Watergate. I was soon brought to earth.

Bizarrely, none of the first six questions touched upon the Golan disengagement. The first question concerned the imminence of the signing of the Atlantic Declaration; the second inquired whether we still sought to "expel" the Soviets from the Middle East, as I had hinted some four years earlier in San Clemente. After that, it was open season. A journalist inquired about the "Plumbers" and the Ehrlichman and Colson affidavits. Then a question was asked about "evidence" before the House Judiciary Committee that I had been one of those who had "initiated" the wiretaps. After a few more perfunctory questions on the Middle East, the press returned to the charge. I was asked once again to reconcile my claimed ignorance of the "Plumbers" with awareness of Young's investigation of the Navy yeoman. The next question transformed requests for elucidation into thinly veiled accusation: Had I retained counsel for a possible perjury indictment? That prospect had never occurred to me. By now I was rattled and I replied querulously:

I have not retained counsel, and I am not conducting my office as if it were a conspiracy. I stand on the statements that I have made and I will answer no further questions on this topic.

There is no more provocative posture in a press conference than a flat refusal to answer questions on a particular subject. And it showed how much I had lost control. My insecurity had the same effect on the reporters present as the thrashing of a wounded fish has on a shark. Up jumped Clark Mollenhoff, long known as the scourge of evasive officials, shouting in a stentorian voice:

Mr. Secretary, on that question — what you have engaged in here, it's been a matter of evasion and failure to recollect and some other patterns that we've seen over a period of weeks through the Watergate period. I wonder why you cannot answer the direct question if you had any role in initiating the wiretaps on your subordinates.

When I referred to my testimony before the Senate Foreign Relations Committee, he shouted me down with four follow-up questions each of which got me deeper into the morass of how one defined "initiate," until I said rather plaintively: "I think this is a press conference, not a cross-examination."

I was learning that in the Watergate atmosphere, an official was suspect if he did not have at his fingertips all the data required to respond on matters that might have occupied him for only a few minutes four or five years previously. And the slightest hesitation — even if caused by consternation — attracted to the story other journalists who were afraid that failure to pursue the wounded quarry would reflect on their professional reputations.

The June 6 press conference opened the floodgates. There was next to no coverage of the foreign policy questions and answers. The *New York Times* over the next three days devoted four news stories to the wiretap issue under such headlines as: "Kissinger Again Denies Initiating Taps" (June 7); "Data on Politicians Traced to Wiretaps on 'Security'" (June 7); "Kissinger Rebuts Nixon on Wiretap" (June 8); "Kissinger Linked to Order to F.B.I. Ending Wiretaps" (June 9).

The *Washington Post* and other leading newspapers followed more or less the same pattern — picking up stories from one another, so that (though there was essentially no new material) a sense of momentum was maintained. The *Washington Post* took up the charge: "What about Kissinger?" read its lead editorial on June 7, recommending a new investigation by the Senate Foreign Relations Committee. "Dissembling Intelligence," read the *New York Times* editorial of June 11, hinting at the need for prosecution:

We regretfully observe that Secretary Kissinger seems to be vulnerable to the charge of dissembling about his role in this distasteful affair. If there are to be more serious charges, that is up to the Congress and the courts to decide.

The weekly news magazines followed suit. *Time* headed its story: "A Kissinger Connection?" *Newsweek*'s lead was: "An Ugly Blot on Mr. Clean?"

I was shattered. I had tumbled in one week from the exaltation of the Mideast breakthrough into the squalor of Watergate. What had sustained me through the bitter years of Vietnam and the pain of Watergate was the belief that I was repaying the country that had rescued my family from tyranny by upholding its honor and values in a time of crisis. I had been involved in many difficult decisions leading to strong and often forceful actions. But I persevered, convinced — perhaps arrogantly — that when the final balance sheet was drawn, to have helped sustain the world position and creative engagement of the United States of America during an era of turbulence was a contribution to freedom everywhere. Statesmen, after all, are not entitled to insist on serving only in simple periods. If the moral basis of my service were lost, public life would have no meaning for me. I am aware that high officials often find it hard to distinguish between the general welfare and their own role, but my concern was not totally a matter of personal vanity. Almost miraculously, our country was surviving the trauma of a disintegrating Presidency without a mortal foreign challenge. Our risks would multiply if a President in danger of impeachment were saddled with a tainted Secretary of State.

By Tuesday, June 11, the leading news media of the United States — the *New York Times, Washington Post, Time* and *Newsweek,* the *Washington Star-News,* the *Chicago Sun-Times,* and many others — had taken the position that serious new evidence had raised suspicion of perjury requiring a new investigation. Given the symbiotic relationship between Congress and the press, and the usual workings of the news cycle, I reasoned that if I did nothing, the next stage would see members of Congress take up the same theme. In the normal course — particularly since no one except me was in a position to rebut it — Congressmen and Senators would feel obliged to appear on television seconding the call for a new investigation. The legislators' charges would be the subject of further news coverage and news commentary, creating the impression of a torrent of revelations. The tide would be against me; I would have to stay on the defensive while touring the Middle East with Nixon and in no position to offer a sustained defense.

It was essential to bring matters to a head quickly and either clear my name or turn my office over to some less controversial figure. No doubt I was deeply distressed. But I also made a cold analysis of the situation. I knew the FBI material that was before the House Judiciary Committee, having gone through it with the Senate Foreign Relations Committee the previous September. I judged that if the documents were leaked out one at a time, there would be an endless series of questions and denials all about essentially the same body of fact. By the time Nixon and I returned from the Middle East, my reputation would be so tarnished that it might be irrelevant whether I stayed or left. Against the advice of all my close associates (Larry Eagleburger excepted), I decided to hold a press conference staking everything on one throw of the dice. I would lump all the arguments against me into one coherent account; I would then refute the charges. I would insist on complete exoneration or I would resign. It was strong medicine. But it would force a rapid showdown and end the slow hemorrhaging of the past few weeks. My colleagues — including Al Haig — thought that holding a press conference would attract attention to a story we should prefer to let peter out. I was convinced that the story would not peter out unless we went on the attack.

That was the background to the extraordinary news conference I held in Salzburg on Tuesday, June 11, 1974. Nixon was on the way to the Middle East and had stopped in Salzburg for two nights and a full day to get used to the change in time zones before going on to Cairo. It was also an exercise in nostalgia. He had stopped there in May 1972 before his triumphal visit to Moscow following the mining and bombing of North Vietnam. He wanted to recapture the moment when he had defied his critics and some of his advisers and risked his career defending his conception of the national honor in the face of a cynical North Vietnamese invasion of South Vietnam. Now, in June 1974, he was besieged and in great pain from phlebitis. Disconcertingly, a journey that he hoped would demonstrate his foreign policy achievements seemed about to be swallowed up by a scandal involving me. The last thing he wanted was headlines that deflected attention from the substance of his Middle East trip. On the plane I did not discuss my travail with him. He did not raise it — in itself an interesting commentary on our relationship. But Haig made clear enough either what the President's preferences were or what his chief of staff would recommend to him: that I endure the assault, just as he had, until the story had spent itself.

I did not believe such a course of action possible. Passivity would see the destruction of our foreign policy, together with me, in daily sensations. Nixon would not be permitted a triumphal Middle East tour focusing only on substance. Once the assault on me had started, it would not stop by itself; indeed, the media would feel obliged to continue it to justify having begun it in the first place. Our choice, I thought, was either to force a showdown or to be gradually worn down by techniques refined over a year and a half of aggressive journalism.

Haig, Eagleburger, Scowcroft, and I discussed the matter at anguishing length on the plane to Salzburg. I had tried to regain the initiative by writing on June 10 to Senator Fulbright, Chairman of the Foreign Relations Committee, asking his committee to review the allegations:

You will remember that my testimony concerning the national security wiretaps ordered by the President and carried out by the FBI under the authority of the Attorney General was in three parts: public testimony, an extensive executive session, and a session with Senators Sparkman and Case in which we went over relevant FBI files. The meeting with Senators Sparkman and Case was conducted in the presence of the then Attorney General Richardson and the then Deputy Attorney General Ruckelshaus.

I emphasize this because no new material has appeared since my testimony except a brief excerpt from a Presidential tape, a large part of which is described as unintelligible. The documents now being leaked were, to the best of my knowledge, available to me before my testimony; they were given to Senators Sparkman and Case prior to my meeting with them. In a few cases my recollection differed in emphasis from the documents; in those cases I pointed out apparent discrepancies and explained them at the time. The innuendos which now imply that new evidence contradicting my testimony has come to light are without foundation. All the available evidence is to the best of my knowledge contained in the public and closed hearings which preceded my confirmation.

What tipped the scale in favor of a full-dress press conference was the *New York Times* editorial on June 11, quoted above, implying that legal proceedings against me might be indicated. By the time the plane reached Austria, I had decided to reject my colleagues' advice; Haig remained reluctant but acquiesced. It was unclear to me whether he had consulted Nixon. I had not.

And so it was that I stepped before the hastily assembled White House press corps on June 11 at the Kavalier Haus on the grounds of the state guest house, Schloss Klessheim, in picturesque Salzburg, the home of Mozart. The Kavalier Haus was a "training hotel," used for the staffs of guests staying at Klessheim and in general for schooling hotel personnel to high Austrian standards. The large room where the press conference was set up had enormous, beautiful tapestries on the walls. The television lights were hot, the atmosphere highly charged.

I led off by reading aloud my letter to Senator Fulbright calling for a reopening of the investigation to lay the innuendos to rest once and for all. I reviewed the circumstances of the origins of the wiretapping, my role, the FBI memoranda, the Foreign Relations Committee's awareness of all the above, and various specific issues that had come up in the press. I then addressed the matter of the "Plumbers" and my relationship to David Young. I defended my public honor, and pledged to repeat the same explanations under oath before the appropriate Congressional committee:

[O]ur national debate has now reached a point where it is possible for documents that have already been submitted to one committee to be selectively leaked by another committee without the benefit of any explanation, where public officials are required to submit their most secret documents to public scrutiny, but unnamed sources can attack the credibility and the honor of senior officials of the Government without even being asked to identify themselves.

At the end of my opening presentation, I hinted — and in response to questions I stated flatly — that I could not continue to perform my duties unless I was exonerated:

QUESTION: Mr. Secretary, you seem to imply here that if this campaign is not stopped, you are going to resign. Is that a fair assumption from what you said?

KISSINGER: I am not concerned with the campaign. I am concerned with the truth. I do not believe that it is possible to conduct the foreign policy of the United States under these circumstances when the character and credibility of the Secretary of State is at issue. And if it is not cleared up, I will resign.

The White House reaction was churlish. Nixon would not speak to me. Even Ron Ziegler would not speak to me. Haig in background comments to the press implied that I had been overwrought and cranky from the prolonged Mideast negotiations. At the end of the day, Ziegler issued an artful statement in Nixon's name recognizing my "desire" to defend my honor, but asserting that "those in the United States and in the world who seek peace and are familiar with Secretary Kissinger's contributions to international trust and understanding share his [the President's] view that the Secretary's honor needs no defense." (In other words, my press conference had been gratuitous.)

In Washington, the Salzburg press conference was a bombshell. Congressional comment was overwhelmingly favorable, and on a bipartisan basis. Senators Muskie, Mansfield, Fulbright, Humphrey, Cranston, Javits, and Percy made strong statements of support. Representative Robert Drinan, a virulent Administration critic serving on the Judiciary Committee, stated that he would be happy to be able to report that I was directly responsible for the wiretap program but he could not do so. By the end of the day on Thursday, June 13, a resolution introduced into the Senate by conservative Senator James B. Allen of Alabama, expressing support for me, had picked up fifty-one cosponsors. It did not deal with the wiretap issue directly; its main thrust was praise for my diplomatic achievements coupled with an expression of the Senate's "complete confidence" and conviction that my "integrity and veracity" were above reproach. The sponsors ran the gamut from conservative Senators Barry Goldwater and Henry Jackson — and Sam Ervin — to liberals John Tunney and Thomas Eagleton. William Ruckelshaus, Acting FBI Director during the previous investigation — and now one of the heroes of the "Saturday night massacre" — stated on "Face the Nation" on June 16, 1974: "I think his role, as best I've been able to determine, is pretty much as he's described it."

Under that counterassault, the media soon began to retreat. The dominant theme was that I had overreacted; I was tired from overwork, oversensitive, and too thin-skinned for the rough and tumble of politics. My old friend Hubert Humphrey struck that chord:

> We obviously do not want Dr. Kissinger to resign. I want to say to him as a friend "stay with it — cool it." I think he's tired. He's working too hard. He's not an elected official. He's not accustomed to some of the body blows that some of us in politics are used to. Just cool it.

Other secretaries of state had taken their lumps, so another argument ran, without threatening to resign. The main criticism soon shifted from allegations of perjury to my proneness to temper tantrums.

Nothing could have proved more convincingly that I was right to force a showdown and that there was no alternative to the press conference. For the four days before Salzburg, the air had been full of ominous insinuations of new malfeasances; afterward, the implicit charge was that I had been oversensitive to accusations that were all good clean political fun, hence not all that serious. Being the butt of various jokes about being thin-skinned was far preferable to being inundated by a mounting tide of charges of having lied to a Senate Committee under oath. It may have been true, as some critics argued, that Secretary of State Dean Acheson had endured serious calumny without threatening to resign. But it is one thing to be attacked on questions of policy and judgment, quite another — in the middle of a constitutional crisis — to be accused of perjury. It was my view that I had to bring matters to a head. I could do so only by threatening to resign; any other course would have appeared too plaintive. I did not see how a country whose Vice President had resigned in disgrace and whose President was near to being impeached could afford a Secretary of State under a moral cloud. I meant it when I said at the press conference:

> I have believed that I should do what I could to heal division in this country. I believed that I should do what I could to maintain the dignity of American values and to give Americans some pride in the conduct of their affairs.
>
> I can do this only if my honor is not at issue and the public deserves to have confidence. If that cannot be maintained, I cannot perform the duties that I have exercised, and in that case, I shall turn them over immediately to individuals less subject to public attack.

Had the reaction been otherwise, I would have carried out that intention.

As it was, I paid a heavy price for the press conference. No one gets away with an attack on the media. And I had concentrated my criticism on its use of unnamed sources. I continue to believe that anonymous accusers give journalists a power no branch of government possesses and expose public officials to much scurrilous abuse by individuals whose motives — and veracity — escape examination. But a news conference was not the ideal place to make these points, even if necessity gave me no other choice. My relations with the media never fully recovered. While there was no systematic assault, I was thereafter exposed to much more criticism than before. And my threat of resignation made it legitimate to speculate on my decline thereafter.

The impact on my relationship with Nixon was more serious still, if of necessity short-lived. Though he never said anything to me directly, it was clear from his aloof manner that he was extremely displeased. Why he should have been quite so upset is difficult to fathom. To be sure, I stole — if that is the right word — the limelight for one day. But this should have been weighed, and would have been by a calmer President, against the steady seepage that would have occurred otherwise. Or was it that I succeeded in lancing the boil by the full disclosure which in retrospect he knew he too should have made and for which it was now too late? Had Watergate not soon overwhelmed him, I doubt whether I could have maintained my position in his Administration.

The Salzburg press conference achieved its immediate objective; it broke the wave of anonymous accusations. It forced a consideration of the documentary evidence. No doubt some of the Nixon-haters eased up on me because they concluded that opening a new line of inquiry might complicate or delay the pursuit of their principal quarry. The Senate Foreign Relations Committee started another set of hearings on July 10. On July 12, President Nixon sent a letter to Senator Fulbright, reciting his version of events. Fulbright had asked Nixon particularly about his public statement of May 22, 1973, in which the President had taken responsibility for the wiretapping: "I authorized this entire program. Each individual tap was undertaken in accordance with procedures legal at the time and in accord with longstanding precedent." Nixon's letter of July 12, 1974, reaffirmed his earlier statement and also his judgment that the wiretapping was justified and legal. He said that my account of his role was "entirely correct," and he (Nixon) took full responsibility.* Attorney General William Saxbe, FBI Director Clarence Kelley, and other FBI officials gave evidence that sustained my version of events and made the interesting point that the average number of national security wiretaps had not varied significantly among the Eisenhower, Kennedy, Johnson, and Nixon administrations. Dean Rusk appeared, as noted earlier, and described J. Edgar Hoover's bureaucratic methods and imperious style: Giving orders to Hoover would be like giving orders to General de Gaulle, he observed. I testified on July 23, going over the same ground as before and reviewing each tap with which I was familiar. All the hearings were in executive session, but the transcripts were later released with only minor deletions.[4]

On August 6 the committee published its report. Unanimously it held that the record "should lay to rest the major questions raised about Secretary Kissinger's role." The dispute was in a large sense semantic; "there are no significant discrepancies between the new information developed and Dr. Kissinger's testimony before the Committee during the confirmation hearings last year." The committee therefore reaffirmed its conclusion as stated the year before: that my role in the wiretapping "did not constitute grounds to bar his confirmation as Secretary of State." The August 6 report effectively ended the controversy over my role in wiretapping for the remainder of my term of office. It was quickly engulfed by the cataclysm of Nixon's resignation three days later.

Nixon's Middle East Trip

Nixon's journey through the Middle East was both a triumph and a nightmare, a climax and an augury of the end. For several months,

---

*The full text of the Nixon letter is in the backnotes.[3]

Nixon had indicated a growing eagerness to undertake the trip, and in May he had intensified the pressure on me to arrange it. I believe that by then he was beyond hoping that it might deflect his critics from Watergate. Deep down, he must have realized that matters were out of control, that his political fate would be settled by accidents or the actions of others. I was on the Syrian shuttle while the Nixon trip was being planned and was therefore not privy to his inner thoughts. My own view was that a Presidential visit was important to symbolize America's new role in the Middle East and our commitment to the peace process — provided we succeeded with disengagement on the Golan.

Visits of a head of state serve many purposes. Not the least significant is to give tangible expression to a new departure. In that sense the drama of Nixon's visit to China in 1972 was even more important than the talks he held there, useful as they were. Nixon in Peking conveyed to the world that the period of Sino-American hostility was over — indeed, that the two great nations were moving toward cooperation on fundamentals of foreign policy. The same was true of Nixon's journey through the Middle East in 1974. In all the capitals Nixon's would be the first visit ever by an American President, except for Cairo, where Franklin Roosevelt had gone for a wartime conference in 1943.

Anyone would have been considered mad who predicted a year earlier that an American President would be greeted by millions of delirious Egyptians in Cairo, Alexandria, and every village in between. Or that radical Syria would extend an invitation and warmly welcome an American President to Damascus. Or that in nations as bitterly opposed as Israel and Saudi Arabia, leaders would extol the central role of the American President, however wounded he might be. And that all this would be happening eight months after a Mideast war that saw America as the armorer of Israel, the Arabs imposing an oil embargo on us, the Soviets threatening to intervene, and the Europeans desperate to put as much distance between themselves and the United States as possible.

These pages recounting my own personal experiences may well leave an impression that the reins of this diplomacy were in my hands alone. This was not the case. I certainly managed the tactics. But no Secretary of State, however influential, can make strategy by himself. Only a President could have imposed the complex and tough policy that got us this far and sustained it against a hesitant bureaucracy, vacillating allies, a nervous Soviet Union, and the passionate combatants of the Middle East. The applause Nixon was harvesting reflected the faith of the peoples of the Middle East in an America that had shown firmness, strength, and the vision of a more hopeful future; it was also a personal tribute.

Even in the midst of Watergate, the media seemed to recognize this. Editorial writers, while noting the public relations benefits of the trip, were on the whole sympathetic. Some now worried in fact that, far from proving irrelevant, the President's tour might succeed so well as to exacerbate US–Soviet relations. (This was the editorial line of the *New York Times* on June 10, the *Baltimore Sun* on June 11, and columnist Joseph Kraft the same day.) But other papers — the *Los Angeles Times* (May 31), the *Christian Science Monitor* (June 5), the *Wall Street Journal* (June 10), and the *Chicago Tribune* (June 11) — all published editorials supportive of the trip.

What even the most understanding editorialist could not penetrate was the personal tragedy of the journey. Nixon was being feted but the noisy celebrations, the elaborate machinery of State visits, alternately buoyed and depressed him. As the various leaders unburdened themselves about their hopes for the future, one could sense the relief with which Nixon engaged in the discussions. This was the subject that interested him and about which he had thought a great deal. Yet within moments the relief and elation gave way to despondency. The conversations illuminated what Nixon's policy had accomplished; they also faced him with the stark truth that he would not be part of the future he had made possible. His visit was celebrating an achievement that was as yet only a longed-for opportunity. More and more often as the trip progressed, his face took on the waxen appearance and his eyes the glazed distant look of a man parting from his true — perhaps his only — vocation; it was excruciatingly painful to watch. In Washington he had been inundated by the sordid details and desperate struggles of Watergate, yet ironically it was on his triumphant Middle East travels that the true dimension of his personal disaster was being brought home to him: He was being vouchsafed a glimpse of the Promised Land that he would never be able to enter. Afterward, Golda Meir made the penetrating comment to me: "We still have never had a visit from an American President. Nixon was here but his thoughts were far away."

And all this time he suffered from phlebitis. He was often in great pain — a fact none of his close associates was at first aware of. In truth, when he overruled his doctors by going, he risked serious danger to his life if the blood clot in the veins of his leg broke loose and traveled toward the heart.

For a few days the anguish was submerged in the exuberant joy of our reception in Cairo. We arrived on Wednesday, June 12. From the moment Nixon stepped on Egyptian soil, it was apparent that all had been designed to hail his role as the key factor in the peace process. Having been spoiled as the recipient of abundant flattery and attention on previous trips, I found it — not to my credit — somewhat disconcerting, even painful, to be relegated to what in the context of a Presidential trip was quite properly a subsidiary role. The press, freed from previous restraints by my Salzburg press conference, gleefully reported both the fact that I received "little attention" and that I seemed "glum."

As for Nixon, he was uplifted by Sadat's welcoming remarks, which paid tribute to America's central contribution "under the leadership of President Nixon" in promoting peace.

The words were cordial enough but they paled before Nixon's triumphal progress from Cairo Airport to his residence at Qubbah Palace. Perhaps a million cheering Egyptians lined the street as Nixon and Sadat rode by in an open-top limousine (to the chagrin of the Secret Service, which, since the Kennedy assassination, has preferred the President to ride in a closed vehicle). Obviously the demonstrations had been carefully organized; it was unlikely that tens of thousands of Egyptians would have kept pictures of Nixon in their drawers during all the years that Egypt and the United States had had no diplomatic relations. A sound truck blaring "Long live Nixon; long live Sadat" in English hardly appeared by happenstance any more than did the signs: "Peace for the land of peace," "We trust Nixon." Several White House staffers at the tail end of the motorcade also claimed that they had seen trucks picking up crowds after the Presidents had passed by to move them further up the parade route, thus generating a double dose of delirium.

Still, whether the crowds all appeared spontaneously or were in part organized, there was no mistaking the enthusiasm and friendliness that could not have been organized. At a minimum, it meant that Sadat was using Nixon's trip to underline the irreversibility of the policy on which he was embarked — in itself a significant event. But one reason he chose so demonstrative a method must have been the happiness of the mass of the Egyptian people with a new course that meant an end to war and the beginning of peace. The crowds were in a holiday mood. Many had red flowers in their hands; others waved banners. The Presidents seemed to be propelled to Qubbah Palace by the noise from frenzied multitudes threatening to break through police cordons and jamming balconies to the point that they seemed about to hurtle from bursting buildings.

Qubbah Palace is a vast, ornate edifice erected by one of the nineteenth-century kings of Egypt as a bow to British royal tradition. It has innumerable rooms, though its overall impact inside is rather that of a slightly rundown luxury hotel in some Eastern European Communist country. Amid splendid gardens, its spectacular facade made an imposing backdrop for the formal arrival ceremony, which was held on its veranda. Sadat celebrated Nixon as a "man of peace." Nixon saw in his visit an opportunity to "cement the foundations of a new relationship between two great peoples who will dedicate themselves in the future to working together for great causes." For once on a State visit, the arrival statements reflected a reality: The leaders of both countries were determined to make peace and the people of Egypt seemed rapturous at the thought of it.

Nixon and Sadat met later that day for talks in Tahra Palace, where I had had my first encounter with the Egyptian President. Sadat used the opportunity to present directly to Nixon his analysis of the Middle East situation, his view of the superpower relationship, and his ideas on the next steps. Much of it was familiar to me, though it was important for the President to hear Sadat's own passionate presentation — or it would have been had Nixon been in a position to advance the policy he had begun so conspicuously. Sadat put forward the standard Arab program: total Israeli return to the 1967 borders and satisfaction of Palestinian rights. He placed special emphasis on the demand for Egypt's 1967 borders. As for assembling the Geneva Conference, Sadat favored delay; he was not eager to bring the Soviets back into the act. His device for procrastination was launching prior bilateral talks between the parties — a procedure that we had learned in the Year of Europe is marvelously designed to produce activity without movement.

Nixon's response followed his standard pattern. He was acute in his own analysis of the international situation. He was thoughtful about the Middle East. Sadat's approach to the Geneva Conference was complex enough to appeal to Nixon's convoluted sense of tactics and there was easy agreement on that. But no more in Cairo than in Washington was Nixon prepared to debate a concrete proposal with which he disagreed. On the question of Israeli withdrawal my briefing papers had given him advice that was as opaque as it was necessary: Since this was an issue for negotiation, he should avoid either endorsing or refusing to endorse the 1967 borders. The deliberate nebulousness of our position would have tested the mettle of even a healthy Nixon not preoccupied with Watergate. Nixon handled it as well as its ambiguity permitted. He resorted to his all-purpose approach of implying that he agreed with his interlocutor's goals and that tactical problems should be handled by others. He hinted that he was heading in the direction desired by Sadat if by a slower, perhaps more indirect route; the final destination would emerge from the process. Sadat behind his affable exterior was not that easily put off. He persisted tactfully but firmly. Nixon gradually gave ground, making a series of elliptical statements that Sadat could well have construed as fully agreeing with the Egyptian point of view. Nixon cognoscenti would have recognized Nixon's statements as a means to evade pressure that was becoming uncomfortably specific, as a way to end a difficult subject, not as a national commitment. What Sadat may have thought has gone unrecorded; he seemed happy enough. In all probability, he was not looking for an affirmation that would give him a legal claim on Nixon; his purpose was served by studying Nixon's reactions to pressure for the 1967 borders.

That evening Sadat gave a splendid dinner in the garden of Qubbah Palace that, for the edification of Americans who had heard their colleagues' tales of high life in Cairo, included a spectacular performance by Nagwa Fuad. Sadat delivered an eloquent toast, paying his dues to the Palestinians:

Mr. President, let me be candid with you lest in the future there would be a misunderstanding or false reading of the turn of events in our region. The political solution and the respect of the national aspirations of the Palestinians are the crux of the whole problem. . . . [T]here is no other solution and no other road for a durable peace without a political solution to the Palestinian problem.

He offered no concrete proposal to achieve it.

The next day Sadat took Nixon through the villages of the Nile Delta to Alexandria on a train trip amidst a delirium that dwarfed even the Cairo spectacular. The two leaders rode in an opulent Victorian car with open sides. When they passed through a village, they would show themselves to the crowds, holding on to an overhead rail. A sudden lurch might well have deprived one or both of the countries of its leadership. Signs in English extolling peace were everywhere; the fact that the crowds almost certainly could not read the signs they were carrying in no way dampened their frenzy. They knew that they wanted peace; no governmental directive could produce such universal and wild enthusiasm unless there was deep longing for it and genuine affection for Sadat. The two leaders held a brief press conference on the train, raising again the danger that the jostling press might propel both leaders through the open side of the car, thereby solving the problem of what would be the lead story on the evening news. Nixon reaffirmed the step-by-step approach "not because we want to go slow but because we want to get there." While he was at it, Nixon suggested that we would proceed country by country — "first with Egypt" — which, given the distrust among Arab brethren, could hardly have been music to the ears of the rulers of Syria and Jordan. Sadat looked on with avuncular approval, calling attention to the banners that proclaimed: "We trust Nixon." Nixon must have been musing about how unfortunate it was that Egyptians were not represented on the House Judiciary Committee when Sadat declared:

Since October 6 and since the change that took place in American policy, peace is now available in the area and President Nixon never gave a word and didn't fulfill it. . . . He has fulfilled every word he gave. So, if this momentum continues, I think we can achieve peace.

And Sadat added two pregnant words that were perhaps the most significant uttered by either leader during the day. A reporter asked, in reference to the bilateral talks planned prior to reassembling the Geneva Conference, whether Egypt would talk with Israel. "Not yet," said Sadat, puffing on his pipe.

Each reception in Egypt seemed to exceed the one preceding. Alexandria was wild with jubilation. More than a million cheering Egyptians lined the motorcade route from the train station along the coast to the fairy-tale Ras el-Tin Palace — a monumental conceit of Farouk's father thrown onto a peninsula in the harbor of Alexandria in imitation of Versailles. I calculated that it took ten minutes to walk, even at a brisk pace, from the front portal to my assigned room — if I did not get lost on the way.

At Ras el-Tin the two leaders reviewed documents that had been prepared for their signature the next day in Cairo. One, grandiloquently entitled "Principles of Relations and Cooperation between Egypt and the United States," called for sweeping cooperation in scientific, technical, economic, and cultural areas, following a pattern we had already established with Saudi Arabia. We were creating new institutions of bilateral cooperation with Arab countries in many fields for the purpose of cementing political ties. It would take some time for all of these projects to go into high gear. But they represented a network giving various Arab nations a stake in our well-being and creating an obstacle to the political misuse of the oil weapon. (They also gave us a hedge against European bilateralism.)

Included in this document was a statement on the Middle East whose reference to the Palestinians was virtually identical to that in the 1973 Nixon-Brezhnev summit communiqué. A just settlement, it affirmed, "should take into due account the legitimate interest of all the peoples in the Mideast including the Palestinian people, and the right to existence of all states in the area." Jerusalem would be unenthusiastic about the first part, pleased with the second. For some reason lost in the mists of time, we also promised to reconstruct the Cairo Opera House burned down some decades earlier. It was the first time a Western nation sought to woo a Middle East state by promising to support an art form having no roots in the area at all. Someday *Aïda* may be heard there once again, perhaps in honor of a State visit by a President of Ethiopia.

The most controversial item was an accord not destined for rapid implementation. The two nations pledged to negotiate on cooperation in the field of nuclear energy under agreed safeguards. Our motive was to preempt European maneuvers to use nuclear power as an entering wedge, as France had done in Iraq. We also thought that we could achieve better safeguards against diversion to military uses and had a higher incentive to do so than any other potential supplier. All this was reasonable enough; but the nuclear issue turned out to be too explosive, politically if not literally. Israel protested, its deeper fears masked under the complaint of lack of consultation (we offered Israel a similar accord, but there was disagreement over the inspection provisions). Congress proved leery, the ubiquitous Henry Jackson leading the charge. Not until seven years later was an implementing agreement with Egypt signed.[5]

The Nixons hosted a return dinner in Ras el-Tin Palace in a convivial atmosphere inhibited only by the curse inflicted by protocol on State visits that forces one to sit next to the same people at every meal. Inevitably, by the end of the second day one has exhausted all reasonable subjects of conversation and is reduced to the surrealistic or the banal.

A helicopter trip to Sadat's rest house overlooking the Pyramids and another ecstatic entry into Cairo, this time from the direction of Giza, concluded the journey. Altogether it was estimated that at least seven million Egyptians had turned out to greet Nixon. By this time the camaraderie between the two leaders had developed to the point that when Sadat expressed admiration for the Presidential helicopter, Nixon made him a gift of it on the spot.

From ebullient, cosmopolitan Cairo we went to puritanical, aloof, secretive Jiddah, the administrative center of Saudi Arabia, on Friday evening, June 14. Saudi Arabia does not prize abandon in any of its manifestations; it does not believe in making policy in fits of enthusiasm. His Majesty King Faisal, dour of countenance, regal in bearing, was at the airport to escort Nixon to the huge state guest house. The motorcade reflected the Saudi sense of the fitness of things. It might have seemed impolite to have no crowds in the street; it would have been indecorous and totally against Saudi tradition to encourage demonstrative emotions. So we passed what the media would call "respectable" crowds clapping in unison as the closed cars of the leaders rolled by.

In the large reception hall of the guest house, King Faisal, Nixon, and some aides chatted inconclusively while no doubt Faisal reflected on how the usually impeccable Saudi protocol department had slipped up to permit Mrs. Nixon into his presence. Normally in Saudi Arabia, women are strictly segregated. (On my visits, Nancy had usually disappeared at the airport, not to be seen again until departure, when she rejoined me at the plane with marvelous tales of extraordinary hospitality by the ladies of the Kingdom, whom in turn I never met.) Or maybe the subtle King had arranged the whole thing so that he could pay his respects to the mores of our country and the personality of the First Lady. Whatever the reason, Faisal's grave mien seemed a shade more doleful on this occasion. Afterward, Saudi custom prevailed. No male member of the American party, except the President, saw Mrs. Nixon until she rejoined us at the airport.

The Kingdom followed its accustomed pattern. The King at an all-male dinner offered an eloquent toast applauding our role in the Middle East negotiations and adding the obligatory moralism of the need for a Palestinian solution. Nixon in reply reviewed his foreign policy achievements, and in the exuberance of the moment dwelt heavily on his breakthroughs with China and the Soviet Union — on whose dastardly and evil designs, especially of the latter, Faisal discoursed at length during the next day.

Saudi Arabia, not being a direct party to the Middle East negotiations, was mainly concerned with the direction of American policy rather than the tactical ramifications. Faisal remained true to his method of not exposing himself by needlessly explicit statements. He was receptive to Nixon's argument that there should be no rush to Geneva; he welcomed the advance notice of our intention to announce resumption of diplomatic relations with Syria during our visit there; he seemed pleased when Nixon described a strong Saudi Arabia as important to the security of the Gulf. The King did not respond to Nixon's theme that the West Bank negotiations would advance more rapidly if Jordan were Israel's interlocutor, rather than the PLO. On oil, Faisal indicated a general propensity to lower oil prices, provided the other oil-producing countries heeded his counsel (an unlikely contingency).

Two impressions emerged from the conversation: Nixon had at last met his match in indirection; I knew by now that the King was more likely to act than to affirm. Still, there was no mistaking the fact that Faisal genuinely admired Nixon. And the King's farewell statement marked a sharp departure from custom. In addition to a commitment to joint policies in the Middle East, it also contained an explicit reference to American domestic politics:

> What is very important is that our friends in the United States of America be themselves wise enough to stand behind you, to rally around you, Mr. President, in your noble efforts, almost unprecedented in the history of mankind, the efforts aiming at securing peace and justice in the world. . . .
>
> And anybody who stands against you, Mr. President, in the United States of America, or outside the United States of America, or stands against us, your friends, in this part of the world, obviously has one aim in mind: namely, that of causing the splintering of the world, the wrong polarization of the world, the bringing about of mischief, which would not be conducive to tranquility and peace in the world.

As a general rule, chiefs of state do not visit capitals with which no diplomatic relations exist, for the simple reason that the absence of embassies is usually a good indication of the state of political relations. The rule did not seem to apply to Nixon. He broke it twice by scheduling State visits designed not to celebrate friendly relations but to inaugurate them. He had visited Peking in 1972 even though Taipei was still recognized by us as the legitimate government of all of China. And the incongruity of his visit to Damascus was only slightly less. It had been barely six months since we had established communications. But during the May shuttle, Asad had made clear that he wanted Nixon to

visit; Asad wanted no second-class status with the country he accepted
as the key to peace. But he had surely had major domestic obstacles to
overcome. Around the Arab world I had been reliably told that there
had been powerful opposition within Syria to the disengagement agreement. I was confident that Nixon would get a good reception; there was
no sense for Asad to extend an invitation just to humiliate him. One
does not gratuitously make an enemy of the strongest nation in the world.

The Syrians seemed about to do just that or worse, despite their best
intentions, as we approached Damascus on June 15. Syrian protocol
prescribes that heads of state be escorted over Syrian air space by a kind
of honor guard of Syrian military airplanes. American protocol accepts
no such provision; our security people are too afraid of a collision between pilots using different languages. Our preferences had been communicated to the Syrians; they either had been overruled or had not
filtered down to lower levels.

The splendid Presidential pilot, Colonel Ralph Albertazzie, had just
let down *Air Force One* to 15,000 feet when he saw four Soviet-built
MiGs approaching, two on each side of the aircraft. One does not become pilot of *Air Force One* without a healthy dose of self-confidence
in one's flying ability. He decided not to find out whether they were an
honor guard or some rogue radical air force unit. Putting his heavy
plane into a steep bank, he maneuvered to throw off the escort — an
improbability for a Boeing 707 to execute against modern fighter planes.
Unfortunately, it also threw the passengers on *Air Force One* about a
bit. So imbued were the civilians on the plane with the notion that *Air
Force One* was invulnerable, however, that no excessive attention was
paid. But one look at Brent Scowcroft — a Lieutenant General of the
US Air Force — taught me otherwise. He was clearly shaken; hence we
were obviously in danger. Larry Eagleburger showed the impenetrable
sangfroid of the Foreign Service. He had been writing me a note about
protocol details when Scowcroft's pallor caused him to add a word of
caution. He had got as far as to write: "You will get off the plane right
behind Mrs. Nixon." He simply added the two words "I hope" and
silently handed me the note.

In the event, the Syrian pilots must have decided that the stunt-flying
of *Air Force One* was some demented American reciprocal honor. They
doggedly kept up with us. Never was an American delegation happier
to reach Damascus than on this occasion.

Asad had arranged an all-military arrival ceremony of dignified aloofness. There were no crowds at the airport, whose distance from the city
does not in any event lend itself to mass demonstrations. But there were
large and friendly crowds as Nixon and Asad rode through the streets
of Damascus at a speed designed to discourage both assassins and demonstrations. As an added security measure, the route of the motorcade

had not been published, though I suspect the population knew that the available options were severely limited. Given these inhibitions, the public response in Syria was remarkably warm. The long period of estrangement between the two countries seemed to be over. Foreign Minister Khaddam and I rode together chatting about our adventures during the shuttle. Although he would have resented the comparison, he made almost the same joke as Eban had when I left Israel two weeks earlier: "After you left, it was like a vacuum in our lives, because it seemed like there was nothing to do!"

Asad had set the stage well. In the previous issue of *Newsweek,* Asad had given an interview to Arnaud de Borchgrave.[6] By Syrian standards it was conciliatory. It paid tribute to my contribution to the disengagement negotiations ("It could not have been done without him"). It affirmed Syria's desire for a "real peace in the Middle East," in the interest of "every country" of the area, in the context of Security Council Resolutions 242 and 338, which Syria had only recently recognized. While implying that there were still differences with the United States about what the resolutions meant, Asad seemed to give us the central role in achieving peace; significantly, he did not mention either Gromyko or the Soviet Union. He refused to commit himself to the idea of a Palestinian state, leaving the decision up to the PLO. De Borchgrave saw the opportunity to put Asad on the spot: "Even if the decision is to dismantle the state of Israel?" Asad's response was significant: "I would imagine that what the PLO decides will not exceed the spirit of UN resolutions. And these do not call for the dismantling of Israel." It was a deft way for Syria to declare its acceptance of the State of Israel and to inform the PLO that its demand for the destruction of Israel was incompatible with the negotiating process as well as with UN resolutions that Syria recently accepted.

This took no little courage. Syria's government seemed to have decided to explore the peace process even though its public had been fed for decades on a rhetoric of intransigence and many political groups within Syria, from the left wing of the Baath party to radical Palestinians, were violently opposed to negotiation with Israel and rapprochement with the United States. My experience during the shuttle had convinced me that Asad's relatively conciliatory course would have to be wrung, day after day, from a reluctant leadership — especially on the civilian side. There seemed to be a pervasive fear that in the end Syria would be betrayed by Arab allies making separate arrangements or by superpowers getting tired of their exertions.

For these reasons, Asad in talking with Nixon on Sunday morning, June 16, was not content with a general philosophical framework as Sadat had been, or with an atmosphere of personal goodwill as had been the case with Faisal. He needed both reinsurance against his radical critics and reassurance about his Arab allies. He was far too Syrian to accept bromides and far too intelligent not to understand evasions. So his meeting with Nixon turned into a cross-examination of our interpretation of appropriate UN resolutions and a probing for the precise goals of our policy — a policy that sustained itself precisely by avoiding precision as to ultimate goals.

During the May shuttle, Asad had repeatedly asked me for a written assurance that we would support Syrian demands to regain all the Golan Heights. I had evaded it. Asad now returned to the charge with Nixon, who was emotionally never comfortable with a style that sought to close off intellectual escape routes.

Nixon started in his usual elliptical way, implying that he agreed with Asad's objectives but that it would be self-defeating to avow them. At the same time he affirmed his commitment to the survival of Israel. He chose an unfortunate metaphor:

> It would be pleasing if I engaged in rhetoric about what will be achieved. But this would start an international debate about the ultimate steps, and no more important steps would be possible. Let me give an example. If you want to push a man off a cliff, you say to him take just one step backward, then another and another. If he knew where he was going, he would take no steps. . . .
> If I say what is in the back of my mind, this will destroy the chances and the result will be a return to a military approach which has not worked in 25 years. This is the only reason we want to keep the language of our statements general.

Normally these generalities, delivered with the air of a man imparting a profound confidence, worked. Either Nixon's interlocutor would be embarrassed to admit that he did not fully understand what the President was talking about, especially as he was being invited to share a deep mystery, or he would think it inappropriate to press the American Chief Executive. Some statesmen probably understood the game that was being played very well and decided on discretion as the better part of valor. Asad did not fit into any of these categories. His domestic position was too precarious to enable him to be polite and his rapprochement with the United States was too recent to serve as a restraint.

At first, things went well enough. Asad fell in with the polite and philosophical chitchat; it turned out to be largely a device to maintain a cordial atmosphere for the appearance of the two Presidents at 12:45 P.M., before a pool of journalists assembled on the steps of the Presidential Palace to announce the resumption of relations between Syria and the United States.

But after they had made the announcement, the two Presidents returned to Asad's study where Asad made an all-out effort to put meat on the bones of Nixon's generalities. Before the meeting with the press he had professed himself satisfied with our approach to détente, revealing at the same time that the subject inspired contradictory feelings in the nonaligned whatever their protestations to the contrary: While détente lessened the risk of confrontation, Asad said, it should not be pursued at the expense of small countries. He also did not dispute that the step-by-step approach should be continued. What he wanted to know with some precision was at what stage and how it would include Syria. This led him to raise a whole series of penetrating questions about our future negotiating strategy: Even if a compromise move was difficult all at once, was the United States nevertheless prepared to see Resolution 338 carried out in full? Did the United States object to Syria's pursuing all the elements of Resolution 338? Did our step-by-step approach mean pursuing only one subject at a time? Would we focus on all borders at once, or one at a time? Did we envisage that Israel would vacate the Golan Heights when it vacated the Sinai? And finally — permitting no evasion — how did the United States see the future, final borders of Israel?

There was nothing Nixon hated more than this type of cross-examination. I tried to gain him some time — fortunately, we had to leave by 2:30 to make our scheduled arrival in Israel — by explaining what was bothering Asad: "President Asad believes we have already reached agreement with Egypt [on final borders]. That is not true. . . . We have had only general talks with Sadat on this question." But fundamentally, Nixon was on his own in the sort of direct confrontation that he abhorred. Nixon equivocated as much as possible; he put his refusal to be explicit as much on tactical grounds as he could. But in the end he edged ever closer to endorsing Asad's position on frontiers. Asad, unfamiliar with my chief's method of operation, would not have been far off the mark if he distilled from the conversation the idea that Nixon, in his own elliptical way, was agreeing to total Israeli withdrawal from the Golan.

I did not think it was in anybody's interest to leave illusions about what had been agreed. On the way to the airport Khaddam allowed that the negotiations had been, if anything, too easy. I warned:

You are sophisticated. You will not draw too sweeping conclusions. Seriously, Mr. Foreign Minister. Today we can promise anything. I don't want to promise anything we can't deliver. In the final stage, when the difference is very small, then we can talk realistically about what final borders are possible.

And on the rest of our journey to the airport, the prickly nationalist Khaddam and I mused about the personal ties that had been established between us and the confidence that was developing between our leaderships.

Much has happened since to throw our two countries into opposition to each other, and to some Syria appears once again as a Soviet satellite. I have my doubts. It was not my impression then when I dealt with the Syrians almost daily. Whether there is a solution to their conflict with Israel can be tested only in the crucible of an actual negotiation. This seems unlikely as I write. But no one would have thought a negotiation possible at the beginning of the disengagement process in 1973. I hope that the lines of communication may open up again between America and that proud, difficult, fiercely nationalistic people.

The welcome in Israel on the afternoon of June 16 had a different texture from those at all other stops. Israel was our friend and ally; we had stood together through grave crises; yet it was the first visit of an American President to that country, so anguished by its ostracism, so reluctant to admit it. It was an emotional experience for both sides. For there was a noticeable undercurrent of uneasiness in the rather too strident insistence on our historic and permanent friendship. Everywhere else the leaders wanted to commit America to maintain, and if possible to accelerate, the peace process. In Israel, a new government sought a respite above all. It was anxious about where the current course would lead, how peace would be defined, and perhaps even more about the domestic controversies it would encounter on the way. Israel's leaders were insecure about the diplomatic revolution that had lured Nixon into the area in the first place. If truth serum had been administered and the distinguished Israeli assemblage had bared their subconscious, they would probably have preferred to forgo the Presidential visit if it had been possible to undo the sequence of events that brought it about. Nixon in turn was determined that negotiations must continue, and he found himself in the only country of his journey where the peace process seemed to require justification. The atmosphere of potential strain — which neither side was willing to admit, much less to face up to — translated itself into a reception that Nixon correctly described in his autobiography: "Our reception in Israel, although warm by ordinary standards, was the most restrained of the trip."[7]

That is why, too, the official toasts had more hidden meanings and the meetings more substance than those on any other part of the trip. On State occasions the President, Ephraim Katzir — speaking on behalf of the cabinet — consistently affirmed the indissoluble bond between Israel and the United States and our hosts' deep gratitude for Nixon's role in arranging for aid to Israel. The implication was that the traditional pattern was its own justification, needing no modification. Nixon took precisely the opposite line. He stressed his willingness to continue long-term economic and military aid. But he added a muted warning that in return he expected Israeli flexibility at the conference table. At the arrival ceremony, he expressed his appreciation for the understanding shown by the people of Israel for the purpose of his visit to their traditional adversaries — which came close to rubbing it in. At the State dinner — also extemporaneously — he expanded on the theme of the need for Israeli diplomatic flexibility.

Yitzhak Rabin had just taken over as head of government. Nixon had known him as Ambassador to Washington and thought very highly of him. He now dilated on the new Prime Minister's qualities, praising his background as a military leader and then offering the advice that there were two roads open to him: that of the politician taking no chances or that of the statesman prepared to run risks for peace. Nixon left no doubt that he was urging the latter approach, which he defined as follows:

> It is a way that recognizes that continuous war in this area is not a solution for Israel's survival and, above all, it is not right — that every possible avenue be explored to avoid it in the interest of the future of those children we saw by the hundreds and thousands on the streets of Jerusalem today.

And Nixon made the same point even more emphatically in his meeting with Rabin and his principal colleagues, Foreign Minister Yigal Allon, Defense Minister Shimon Peres, and Ambassador Simcha Dinitz:

> We really feel that the days when Israel felt very comfortable with a relationship with the United States, where we supported Israel, we were going to be Israel's best friend and where your immediate, more warlike neighbors, Syria and Egypt, were considered to be the enemies of the United States; those days — some might say in this country and many of our very good friends in the Jewish community in the United States say it now: Let's go back to the old days. Just give us the arms and we can lick all of our enemies and all of the rest.
>
> I don't think that's a policy. I don't think it is viable for the future . . . time will run out.

Fundamentally, there was no dispute about the desirability of peace. But so soon after the two disengagement accords, we emphasized momentum, while Israel feared losing control to a negotiating process that threatened to become its own purpose. Rabin outlined Israel's approach: Peace had to be related to security; the peace process would take time because to be meaningful it must involve a change in attitudes; it could not consist simply of a series of Israeli withdrawals; there had to be reciprocity; Israel would not tolerate terrorist attacks; it was essential that Israel's strength be maintained; he hoped the United States would improve its ties to the Arabs at a "moderate" pace and emphasize economic, not military, assistance.

These points were unexceptionable, but in fact laid bare the diplomatic bedrock, which was that we lacked an agreed US–Israeli answer to the kind of questions Asad had posed to us in Damascus: What concrete steps should be taken? How were they going to be accomplished?

Four broad strategic options presented themselves. We could stay with the status quo that had emerged from the two disengagement agreements; we could return to Geneva for a comprehensive solution; we could make another move with Egypt; or we could take an initial step with Jordan on the West Bank.

The option of staying put did not really exist. It would undermine the American position in all Arab countries and lead in time to another blowup. The comprehensive approach was in our view still premature. It would bring the Soviets back into the area; it would raise a whole host of issues where no solution was even vaguely perceived; it would risk an explosion while Nixon was heading for impeachment and a new government with only a single-vote margin had come into office in Israel; moreover, Egypt was reluctant to go to Geneva. In any event, it would lead to an early impasse and a braking if not a reversal of the diplomatic process.

The real choice was between taking another step in the Sinai and pursuing a disengagement agreement with Jordan. Sadat had urged us to give priority to the Egyptian front. He was eager to press on toward the peace treaty that he alone of the participants in the process thought attainable.

My own view was that we should make the next move with Jordan. In many ways, the decision in the summer of 1974 to delay Jordan and the West Bank issue until after our domestic crisis was resolved turned out to be crucial; it affected profoundly the evolution of the entire area. It was an amalgam of American, Israeli, and Arab domestic politics and inhibitions in which each party for different reasons took the path of least resistance and brought about the worst possible outcome.

I had thought that everybody's interest would be served best by establishing as rapidly as possible a Jordanian presence on the West Bank. This would make moderate Jordan the negotiator for the Palestinian phase of the peace process. More and more bystanders — European governments, American intellectuals — were putting forward the PLO as the fashionable key to unlock the West Bank. I was sure that it would bolt the door to a settlement. Simply to get Israel into a conference room with a group that had sworn its destruction and conducted a decade-long terrorist campaign against it would be a monumental assignment, consuming energy, emotion, and enormous amounts of time during which all future progress would be frozen. I did not think it was achievable without demonstrating to Israel brutally and irrevocably its total dependence on American support. In my view, this would break Israel's back psychologically and destroy the essence of the state. It would also be against America's interest — not least of all because a demoralized Israel would be simultaneously more in need of American protection and less receptive to our advice. We would be involved as guarantor in every border skirmish, in the long run mortgaging our relations with every state in the area. And even if my judgment was wrong and a psychologically undamaged Israel could be brought into the conference room with the PLO, it would be the beginning of a negotiating nightmare, not the end of it.

No, if there was to be immediate progress on the West Bank, it had to be through Jordan. If the PLO were indeed becoming more moderate — which was far from clear — it could prove this in its subsequent dealings with Jordan as well as other Arab countries that had a stake in the Palestinian question. In this manner, the PLO would become an Arab, not an American problem.

I repeated this theme on many occasions during the fateful summer of 1974. On May 31 I had told an executive session of the Senate Foreign Relations Committee:

> The sensible next step, speaking frankly to this committee, would be Jordan, for two reasons: one, because it is the most moderate of the Arab governments. It has been the one that is friendly to the United States.
>
> And secondly, because the best way to deal with the Palestinian question would be to draw the Jordanians [into] the West Bank and thereby turn the debate of the Palestinians into one between the Jordanians and the Palestinians rather than between the Palestinians and Israelis.
>
> On the other hand, Israeli domestic politics does not permit a disengagement on the Jordan River right now because they need the National Religious Party in order to support the government.

On June 5 I told a group of American Jewish leaders: "I've said to them [the Israeli leadership] they should next take up Jordan, but the Israeli domestic situation makes this impossible." On June 8 I said to Moshe Dayan, who was visisting the United States after leaving the government a few days earlier: "There are two possible strategies — to bring the Jordanians into the West Bank, or to stonewall with Jordan and sooner or later all hell will break loose with the Palestinians." On June 17, during Nixon's visit in Israel, I made the same point to Prime Minister Rabin and repeated it at a press conference that day:

> Of course, the most efficient way for the Palestinians to be brought into the process is through a Jordanian negotiation, in which there is the historical background and for which Israel has always declared its readiness in principle.

But the conditions did not exist for such a step. The Israeli cabinet faced two insuperable difficulties. Its one-vote majority in the Parliament was too narrow a base to sustain a negotiation as divisive as disengagement on the West Bank. A large body of Israeli opinion was opposed to the reestablishment of *any* autonomous Arab political authority on the West Bank; others resisted relinquishing the smallest slice of land they believed had been given to the Jews in the Old Testament. The National Religious Party would surely bring down the government at the first sign of a West Bank negotiation. All this had caused Golda Meir — and this was the second obstacle — to promise that there would be a new election *before* any agreement concerning the disposition of the West Bank was concluded. Rabin and his colleagues were understandably reluctant to call for new elections within weeks of having achieved office.

Our inhibitions were equally great. If we insisted on a Jordan negotiation, we had to calculate on new elections in Israel, which from starting day usually took a minimum of six months to produce a new government. We would be stalemated at the precise moment that as a result of the Golan disengagement our influence was at its highest. Moreover, a President facing impeachment was not in a brilliant position to insist on a negotiation that — if Israel resisted, as was nearly certain — would multiply his domestic opponents.

Then there was the problem of Egypt. We admired Sadat; we saw him as the indispensable driving force toward Middle East peace. Without his cooperation the Middle East was certain to slide again into impotent frustration. And Sadat was opposed to what was later called the Jordanian option; at any rate, he did not want to defer his own claim to another slice of the Sinai for the better part of a year through the Israeli election process and the uncertain number of months it would take to negotiate. Sadat's visceral distrust of Hussein reinforced his cool calculation that the process of Jordanian disengagement involved too many pitfalls to stake on it the Middle East peace process he had so painfully nursed along to this point. He must have reasoned that a Jordanian disengagement could never be an isolated act. It would open the Palestinian drama, reverberating throughout the area by a logic not amenable to the timetables of others.

Nor was Syria eager for a Jordanian move. During the shuttle I had talked to Asad about the desirability of assigning to Hussein the principal responsibility for West Bank negotiations. He had not rejected it; he had replied noncommittally that a great deal of thinking would be needed to find a proper approach to the Palestinian problem. But at a minimum it meant that Syria's attitude toward the PLO had also been aloof. Syria staunchly supported what it called the rights of the Palestinian people; at the same time it sought to control the PLO in fulfillment of an age-old dream that sees Palestine as part of Greater Syria. A few years later it resisted a PLO takeover of Lebanon, temporarily allying itself with the hated Christians to prevent Palestinian domination of a neighboring country. In 1974 Syria advanced no concrete plan in behalf of the Palestinian cause; it appeared reserved about the PLO; it was more aware of the complexities of the Jordanian option than its possibilities. No senior Syrian official ever mentioned West Bank disengagement, with whatever partner, as a serious prospect.

Torn between our analysis and objective conditions, I played for time, keeping both the Egyptian and Jordanian options open — finally committing to neither — hoping that circumstance might resolve our perplexities. It is a course I have rarely adopted and usually resist intellectually. Circumstance is neutral; by itself it imprisons more frequently than it helps. A statesman who cannot shape events will soon be engulfed by them; he will be thrown on the defensive, wrestling with tactics instead of advancing his purpose.

And that is exactly what happened on the Palestinian question. When on October 28, 1974, an Arab summit in Rabat designated the PLO as the sole Arab representative and spokesman for the West Bank and removed Jordan from the diplomacy, the Israeli dilemma and the Palestinian negotiating stalemate that I predicted — and did not head off — both became inevitable. They have not been resolved to this day.

During Nixon's visit to Israel, all this was still in the future. Rabin and Nixon discussed the next steps in a general, almost random way. Rabin was eager to link further diplomacy to an arms package for Israel, Nixon to a general commitment to negotiate. Each got what he wanted. The result did little to resolve the choice before us. But it suited the necessities of both sides at that moment to submerge the strategic questions in a process of consultation. It was agreed that Yigal Allon, the new Foreign Minister, would visit Washington later in the summer and Rabin soon after. In the meantime we would also invite the foreign ministers of Egypt and Syria as well as the King and Prime Minister of Jordan. Out of these exchanges we hoped to crystallize a strategy by the early fall.

On the face of it, this was a sensible course. With the Syrian disengagement agreement barely two weeks old and a new government in office in Jerusalem, a period for consultation and reflection was in everybody's interest. It was what we had told all the Arab countries we would seek. What we had not counted on was the Rabat decision, though even without it the trend was probably against the Jordanian option.

Jordan's thankless situation was symbolized by two facts: that it was the last stop on Nixon's journey, and that I was unable to accompany him there. The reason for the former was the same as what had placed our Hashemite friends close to the end of every shuttle: No decisions were required in Amman; we knew what needed doing; to get it done depended on events elsewhere. Amman was a good place for summing up and seeking perspective in a friendly environment. The cause of my absence was the semiannual meeting of NATO foreign ministers in Ottawa, of which I had already missed the first day. Since the meeting was to agree at last to the Atlantic Declaration that I had personally proposed fourteen months earlier, it would have been a callous affront to my Atlantic colleagues not to be present at the consummation of our own enterprise. And since the Mideast trip had to be squeezed in before the Moscow summit and one could not arrive in Israel on the Sabbath, there was no flexibility there, either.

But this was little consolation to the Jordanians, who must have felt that the absence of Nixon's principal negotiator symbolized their relegation to a secondary role. Nixon's visit on June 17 and 18, as I could gather from Scowcroft's reports to me, went as well as circumstances permitted. Nixon repeated his by-now standard theme that the methods that had opened relations with China and pacified the Soviet Union would also work in the Middle East. In a toast he used a rather effective line that he had tried out at every occasion on the trip: "I do not tell you where this journey will end. I cannot tell you when it will end. The important thing is that it has begun." The trouble with Jordan was unfortunately that its journey had not even begun. Nevertheless, Hussein sent off his distinguished guest warmly with the spectacular parade ceremony of "beating the retreat" I had witnessed earlier, performed by four British-trained Bedouin bands marching in perfect precision.

So ended Nixon's foray into the Middle East. For his associates it was an anguishing experience. We sensed in the exaggerated solicitude of our hosts the pity that is the one sentiment a head of state can never afford to evoke. The pretense that they were dealing with a functioning President was possible for some leaders only because they were not familiar enough with American domestic affairs, for others because they knew no other mode of treating a visiting head of state, and for still others because their whole policy had been based on belief in American mastery of events. But the members of the Nixon party were beyond illusion and we knew too much. We were torn up inwardly by the difference between what might have been and what deep down we all realized there now must be. Of course, we could not yet predict the precise modality that would spell the end of the Presidency, one of whose major achievements was being celebrated daily in the motorcades and banquets of the Middle East.

Despair manifested itself in much petty bickering. Ron Ziegler protected his notion of Presidential preeminence in news stories with the ferocity of a police dog. There were disputes about the assignment of quarters and seats on the Cairo-Alexandria train. But these were the symptoms of the frustration all of us felt over what was the grim, unspoken backdrop of the journey.

We witnessed with some wonder the tumultuous receptions in capitals with which relations had been established only in recent months. We were proud that our country was playing a central role in making peace not just for itself but between nations that without us would have found neither the language nor the method of reconciliation. All heads of state were seeking from us a road map for the future. Nixon acquitted himself well while suffering excruciating physical and emotional pain. He provided sensible comments; he responded to the needs of his interlocutors with firmness and perception. The only thing he could not provide was what was most needed: a reliable guide to the long-term thrust of American foreign policy. For it would not be long now before he would become an observer of the forces he had helped shape.

More Accusations

BY now our domestic struggle was malarial. The fever chart would rise and the patient would approach delirium for a few days. Suddenly the fever would break, leaving no trace save the increased weakness of the victim. The only difference was that normally a malaria patient recovers.

I had returned from the Syrian shuttle to the assault over wiretaps; we came back from Nixon's Mideast journey to another charge so absurd and technical that it was hard to know where to begin to refute it: Senator Henry Jackson's accusation that Nixon and I had made a secret deal with the Soviets enabling them to exceed the limits of the first SALT agreement by up to 124 missiles. Where the uproar over the wiretaps had reflected some hypocritical confusions, the charges of secret deals were pure domestic political warfare.

By the summer of 1974, Nixon seemed so close to the end of the line that whatever tenuous restraints had until then inhibited wholesale domestic attacks on our international position fell away. Indeed, the incipient collapse of the Presidency encouraged rather than stifled dissent; a school of opinion developed that handcuffing the mortally wounded Nixon was in the national interest lest the President at the imminent summit with Brezhnev make improvident concessions.

Nixon was scheduled to arrive in Moscow on June 27, 1974, for his third summit with the Soviet leaders. How little deference he paid to Soviet sensibilities even at this late stage of his Presidency was shown by the fact that he had postponed his Moscow visit by three days to give him an opportunity to journey to the Middle East and to stop over in Brussels on the way to Moscow to sign the just-completed Atlantic Declaration — neither action calculated to endear him to the Kremlin. Nevertheless, Jackson considered that he was performing a national service if he constricted the Administration's freedom to negotiate by undermining its credibility. For all I know, he may have actually believed what his staff told him about the fantasy of a secret deal.

Jackson, whatever the accuracy of his charges, was redoubtable. He knew a great deal about defense, which enabled him to speak with technical knowledge. As the second-ranking member of the Senate Armed Services Committee, he had many friends in the Pentagon supplying him with their version of inside information. When I testified before Jackson, I often found myself in the anomalous position of being confronted with secret documents from the Joint Chiefs of Staff that had never been seen in the White House. And Jackson had as allies many groups who were supporting his other causes, such as Jewish emigration from the Soviet Union. While they had no special animosity toward me, they also did not want Jackson's credibility eroded — thus in effect giving him moral support.

In a normal period, the absurdity of his charges would have made them fall of their own weight. What could possibly induce a President and his chief aide to concede gratuitously and secretly to the Soviets 124 more missiles than those provided in an agreement? It was implausible even in the absence of detailed knowledge. But in the final weeks of the Nixon Administration, no accusation was too preposterous to receive a hearing; and in fairness, many seemingly incredible allegations had turned out to be true. What made Jackson's accusations more effective than they deserved to be was that they concerned highly technical provisions of the SALT agreement nearly incomprehensible to the layman. Indeed, the effort to rebut them involved so many complexities that the uninitiated were likely to believe that, where that much explanation was needed, something was bound to be wrong. Conceivably, my account in these pages will contribute to this impression.

Under the 1972 Interim Agreement on limitations of strategic offensive weapons, the Soviet Union was permitted 950 modern ballistic missiles on sixty-two nuclear submarines. To reach that figure and stay within the agreed overall ceiling, the Soviets were obliged to dismantle 210 older ICBMs. The debate between American and Soviet negotiators at the 1972 summit in Moscow concerned what older missiles the Soviets should replace.[8] It was in the Soviets' interest to "trade in" their oldest, most obsolete weapons, preferably missiles of less than intercontinental range that they would have retired anyway. Our aim was precisely the opposite: to bring about a dismantling of missiles most dangerous to us. In the course of the final negotiations in Moscow, my staff and I, on the basis of consultations with the Joint Chiefs of Staff, had worked out the following priorities among the Soviet missiles available for retirement. The missile we were most eager to get rid of was the land-based ICBM designated as the SS-7. This had a range of over 6,000 miles and a warhead of six megatons; seventy of these heavy throwweight weapons were in hardened underground silos and thus were reasonably invulnerable. Next in priority were 134 SS-7 and SS-8 intercontinental missiles on vulnerable above-ground launching pads (the SS-8 was a variation of the SS-7); they were useful for a first strike or for retaliation against an American nuclear attack that had spared Soviet strategic forces. Our third priority was thirty missiles on an older Soviet nuclear submarine that we designated as the H-class. Each of these missiles had a range of only 900 miles and a relatively small warhead, but the submarine was capable of sustained operation. The lowest priority was assigned to sixty or seventy missiles on even older submarines we designated as the G-class. These vessels were diesel-powered, noisy, and of limited endurance. The range of their missiles was 300 to 700 miles; nine of these submarines (carrying twenty-seven of the shorter-range missiles) had to surface before they could fire.

We did not consider the G-class submarines a strategic threat. None had been operating off our Atlantic coast since 1966 or off our Pacific coast since 1969. In truth, it made no sense to imagine that the Soviet Union would cart seventy relatively low-yield weapons to within a few hundred miles of our shores on obsolescent submarines while it already had over 1,000 intercontinental missiles and was building to 1,500 ICBMs and 950 submarine-based missiles with a range of 1,500 miles and over. We therefore did not want the Soviets to use these obsolete weapons for a 'trade-in.''

As it turned out, the SALT agreement reflected our priorities precisely: The H-class submarines were defined as ''modern''; if the Soviets wanted to build 950 of the newest sea-based missiles, the H-class submarines would have to be retired; otherwise their thirty missiles would count in the total. The 210 SS-7s and SS-8s would have to be dismantled. We had achieved our objective, we thought, of preventing the Soviet Union from trading in a weapon that would in any case have to be retired, for a modern weapon. To close every loophole, we insisted that if for some unfathomable reason the Soviets placed modern missiles on the obsolescent G-class submarine, they too would count against the total of 950. We were rather proud of the negotiating accomplishment.

The night the agreement was signed, on May 26, 1972, I briefed the press after midnight in a Moscow nightclub converted into a press center. When asked about the G-class submarine, I replied:

If they are modernized, they are counted against the 950. . . . They don't have to retire them. They do have to retire the H-class submarines if they want to go up to 950. They do not have to retire the G-class submarines, but if they modernize them, they are counted against the 950.

The replacement provisions were therefore hardly secret. On June 5, on our return home, we briefed the relevant departments and agencies in the same sense and sent guidance instructing them to use this interpretation "in preparing testimony and in responding to questions."

On June 14 the Soviet Union sent us an oral note containing a typical Soviet ploy reflecting its second thoughts, neatly reversing the position it had taken in Moscow. We had initially insisted that the missiles on G-class boats be counted in the permitted total of 950. The Soviets had strenuously resisted with the argument that neither the missiles nor the submarines were "modern" by any rational definition of the term. We had settled on the replacement provision, which actually turned out to be more favorable to us than our original proposal. The Soviet note of June 14 in effect welshed on the "compromise"; it accepted our first proposal. The practical consequence would have been that the Soviets could trade in the seventy missiles on G-class boats; when the replacement process was completed, the Soviets could be left with the seventy SS-7 intercontinental missiles in hardened silos — precisely the weapon we were most eager to get rid of.

Not surprisingly, our reply of mid-June insisted on what we knew the negotiating record unambiguously sustained. The Soviets, having failed to put one over on us, took the attitude that there had been no harm in trying. They accepted our interpretation. I briefed a bipartisan leadership meeting in that sense. In July Gerard Smith, the principal SALT negotiator, testified before Congress as to our interpretation with no objection from the Soviet Union.

There the matter would have rested had I not decided to tidy up all loose ends. Even in the heady glow of détente I was not prepared to rely on oral understandings with the Soviets; I asked them to sign a document incorporating the agreed interpretation. Uncharacteristically conciliatory, the Soviets agreed. On July 24, 1972, Dobrynin and I signed a one-page document pedantically entitled "Clarification of Interpretation of the Protocol to the Interim Agreement." It repeated once again our understanding of the replacement provisions together with some other odds and ends. In an excess of meticulousness we defined a "modern" missile as "a missile of the type which is deployed on nuclear-powered submarines commissioned in the USSR since 1965." Exchanges in the Presidential Channel were generally not distributed to the bureaucracy. The paper was handled in the normal way and kept in the White House. It was a triumph of routine over substance. It made no difference, we thought, since nothing had changed. The relevant departments had already been notified in writing more than five weeks earlier of the official interpretation precisely along the lines of the signed document.

It turned out to be a mistake, however innocent. The Soviets, having no reason to believe that there was anything confidential about the document, referred to it in the Geneva SALT session in June 1973. Queried, the White House thereupon circulated the text to the appropriate agencies. The wrath of officials who feel themselves bypassed can be wondrous; their method of combat is to argue that they would have done much better had they been consulted and to find retroactively some flaw that would never have passed their eagle eyes. In this case, some jailhouse lawyer pounced on our definition of modern missiles with the hairsplitting argument that the phrase "a missile of the type which is deployed on nuclear-powered submarines commissioned in the USSR since 1965" enabled the Soviets to deploy an entirely new missile just for the diesel-powered G-class so long as it did not appear on any nuclear-powered submarine.

The genius who came up with this interpretation did not explain what could possibly induce the Soviets to develop an entirely new missile for an obsolete submarine that had not been off our coast for five years and use it nowhere else. He was not deflected by the fact that such an outrageous gimmick would have augmented the Soviet total by exactly seventy missiles. The Soviets — never ones to give up a slight benefit — made no such claim. Nor would we have permitted such a distortion of the negotiating record. As I said in a press conference on June 24, 1974:

> [W]hile perhaps this hair-splitting interpretation is possible, it is totally inconsistent with the negotiating record — it is totally inconsistent with all the exchanges that took place previously. It would be absolutely rejected by the United States.

Of course the Soviets were not developing any such new missile, and never did.

Whatever my judgment of the motive that had produced the bureaucracy's complaints, I thought it prudent to make sure that the imaginary loophole was closed off. On October 15, 1973, I instructed the American representative to the US–Soviet Standing Consultative Commission monitoring the SALT agreement to put forward another clarification. The astonished Soviets, finding us discovering loopholes for them that they had never claimed, agreed to the new clarification after some back-and-forthing. The text had already been agreed when Jackson went public; it was to be signed together with a host of subsidiary agreements when Nixon visited Moscow. Jackson must have known this — or with his sources of information would have had no difficulty in finding out.

When he surfaced what he called "rather startling" new information that the Soviets had been permitted to exceed the ceilings established by SALT I, Jackson had quite literally no subject matter. But he confused the issue further by raising yet another charge of even less merit than the first, if that was possible. This had to do with the replacement of older ICBMs by sea-launched missiles. When the Soviets were given the right to trade in their older ICBMs, we insisted on a comparable right. The only older missiles we had available to trade in were fifty-four Titan II ICBMs. That they still existed was due largely to the fact that the White House, at my urging, had overruled several attempts by the Pentagon to cut costs by dismantling them unilaterally (as it finally decided to do in 1981). The only difficulty was that we would have nothing to trade them in for until after the expiration of the Interim Agreement; the new Trident submarine and missile were not planned to go into operation until 1978 (they have since slipped even further). At the end of the 1972 summit, Nixon engaged in the sort of prestidigitation by which negotiations are often concluded: He gave Brezhnev a letter affirming what he intended to do anyway: that we would not exercise the right to trade in Titans before the expiration of the Interim Agreement in 1977. Indeed, we could not, since the new boats would not exist. While the letter itself was secret, the intention was not. In my briefing of the bipartisan Congressional leadership on June 15, 1972, I said:

> [T]he Interim Agreement . . . will not prohibit the United States from continuing current and planned strategic offensive programs, since neither the multiple-warhead conversion nor the B-1 is within the purview of the freeze and since the ULMS [that is, what is now called the Trident] submarine system is not, or never was planned for deployment until after 1977.

And the Defense Department's posture statement published a five-year projection with the same figures as Nixon's letter to Brezhnev. In other words, there was nothing "secret" about this understanding, either.

Jackson's charge that our "secret" agreement had given the Soviets an advantage of 124 additional missiles was therefore made up, preposterously, by adding our own fifty-four older Titan missiles (which we had "promised" not to trade in for more advanced Trident submarine missiles before 1977) and the seventy Soviet SLBMs on their obsolete G-class submarines (which counted against their total allowance only if they were ever modernized).

The Soviets never attempted to "modernize" the missiles on the G-class submarines, which at this writing (1981) have not been seen off our shores for over twelve years. They could have done so in any event only by violating the negotiating record and risking the entire East-West relationship; if they were willing to run that risk, they would have surely broken the agreement in much more significant ways. As for the replacement provision, it has since become moot. But even in June 1974, when Jackson raised the issue, the fact was that not a single missile beyond the SALT limits had been conceded to the Soviets. There was no secret deal, the Soviets were given no new rights, and there was no Soviet advantage.

But at this point in June 1974, the Watergate atmosphere ensured a headstart to any charges, however ill-founded. So, within forty-eight hours of my return from Nixon's Middle East trip, the domestic nightmare began all over again. All television networks reported matter-of-factly the accusation that there had been secret agreements and that these had given the Soviets an edge. Leading newspapers had banner headlines on the subject. It was an interesting case history of the morphology of politics as permanent scandal. When the first news stories appeared on Thursday, June 20, I quite literally did not know what Jackson was talking about. I spent the next two days determining what the charge was while Henry Jackson appeared on every evening television news program skillfully playing the role of the honest country boy trying to shed light on arcane secrecy. He made no specific charges but implied strongly that something dangerous was afoot. The ubiquitous unnamed sources kept the accusations going and Jackson gave them credibility by speaking darkly about what his investigation might reveal. There was no brief statement I could make that could possibly explain the issue and in any event I needed to study the record, much of which was vague in my mind. So I announced a news conference for Monday, after the weekend, which in turn left the impression that where there was so much smoke that there had to be fire.*

Over the weekend, speculation raged whether another "scandal" had been unearthed. On Monday, June 24 — the day before I was to leave for Brussels and Moscow with Nixon — I summed up the facts at my news conference:

[T]he totals for the Soviet side which were submitted to the Congress, and which were publicly stated, have not been changed by any agreement, understanding, or clarification — public or private. The totals for the United States that were submitted to the Congress and stated publicly have not been altered by any agreement or understanding — public or private. The figures are exactly those that have been represented — exactly those that have been agreed to —

---

*These excerpts from the CBS evening news on Saturday, June 22, give the flavor. (I want to stress that correspondent Dan Rather was fair; he was a victim of what the newscycle produced for him):

RATHER: Washington sources say that the 1972 Strategic Arms Limitation Agreement that Congress approved provides that the Soviets are to have 950 of the missiles, but that a later agreement, apparently a secret one, raised the Soviet total to 1020. And these sources say, the original figure of 710 US sea-based missiles was cut to 656. . . .

JACKSON: I can answer that better after he's testified on Monday. I don't know whether these agreements, understandings, interpretations involve Dr. Kissinger and the Russians, or whether it involves just the President and the Russians. This we'll have to find out. . . .

RATHER: But in Washington, the State Department denied that there are any secret agreements of any kind with the Soviets on missile totals. A spokesman said Kissinger will go into the matter at a news conference on Monday, the same day Kissinger appears before Jackson's committee.

and all of the disputes arise over esoteric aspects of replacement provisions, and not about the substance of the agreement.

Jackson, sticking to the letter of his charge, claimed he had proof of the secret agreements — which was true, if one took a novelist's license with the terms "agreement" and "secret." And the subject was so complicated, the rebuttal so complex, while the charges were so simple that the media had a terrible time establishing a balance (though they were on the whole sympathetic, especially those journalists who had studied the subject).

That afternoon I testified before Jackson's subcommittee of the Senate Armed Services Committee. Jackson made me swear to tell the truth — implying that only the threat of perjury charges could elicit honesty from the Secretary of State. It was technically an executive session, which meant that the media were barred. Jackson got around this inconvenience by leaving the hearing at frequent intervals to brief the waiting press about the "revelations" he had extracted from me, at one point getting into a heated exchange with my Assistant Secretary of State for Congressional Relations, former Virginia Governor Linwood Holton, who rightly complained about the procedures.

The stakes were high. On June 25 the *Washington Post,* giving me a clean bill, commented editorially: "Secretary Kissinger, whose credibility is also under challenge in the matter of wiretaps, could scarcely have gone on if his word on missiles had been shown to be untrue."

But I was only an incidental target; my personal career was hardly the issue. The victim of the assault was any negotiating flexibility on SALT II at the forthcoming Moscow summit. All members of the bureaucracy were put on notice of the grilling that would await them before the Armed Services Committee; their safest course was to stick rigidly to the least controversial options. The Soviets knew that any proposal put forward by the already gravely damaged President would be submitted to the most brutal scrutiny upon his return. Whatever limited incentive the Soviets might have had to attempt a serious negotiation of outstanding issues, especially of SALT, was reduced even further.

The absurd charges against me soon petered out. I had to respond at one more press conference while we were already enroute, in Brussels on June 26, on the esoteric point of what was meant by "missiles of the type" — in any case, superseded by the new clarification. After that, the issue was dropped; it did not resurface after our return from Moscow. Once I had put the facts on the record, they were fairly covered and the media soon turned to other, juicier subjects. But the episode was another nail in the coffin of East-West relations. Probably never has a President left for a negotiation with the Soviet Union in more difficult and hard-pressed circumstances or with as little scope for diplomatic initiative. I hope none ever does again.

The Moscow Summit, 1974

SALT was not the only subject on the Moscow agenda embroiled in our domestic turmoil. The impression having been fostered that Nixon was planning to save himself by pulling some rabbit out of a hat at the Moscow summit, opponents sought systematically to close off *all* avenues of negotiation. I have already described in Chapter XXII how Jackson on June 24, the day before Nixon's departure for Moscow, announced that he planned to put forward new unspecified conditions on the issue of trade and emigration, effectively removing the subject from the summit agenda. Concurrently, restrictions on credit had been added to limitations on trade in the trade bill before the Senate. While we had assured the Soviets that we would resist these, similar promises with respect to the Jackson-Vanik amendment had proved unfulfillable. Nor did the Soviets see any great prospect elsewhere for joint action for the sake of which they might have made concessions on subjects of interest to us. There was certainly precious little joint effort in the Middle East. And SALT options were being systematically foreclosed as well.

Liberal and conservative opponents of Nixon could unite on the proposition that he must not be permitted to save his Presidency by deals in Moscow. What "concessions" Nixon was supposed to be planning were never clear. This made the innuendo all the more ominous. Our internal preparations for the summit thus labored under the mutual suspicion of some of the agencies (especially the Pentagon) and the White House, inflamed by the bureaucracy's fear of Congressional retribution if they offended the broad coalition closing in on the President.

On June 14, innuendo was given concreteness when Paul Nitze resigned as Defense Department representative on the SALT delegation. (He had apparently attempted to do so as early as May 28 but had been dissuaded by Schlesinger.) Nitze was one of our nation's most distinguished public servants and ablest theorists on national defense. He had served as Director of the State Department's Policy Planning Staff under Truman and Acheson; as Secretary of the Navy under Kennedy; as Deputy Secretary of Defense under Johnson. He had studied issues of national strategy all of his adult life; he had been one of the small group of dedicated and thoughtful men and women whose bipartisan support and occasional criticism had enabled American foreign policy to steer a steady course in the postwar period. He and I had had occasional disagreements, as is inevitable among serious men, but I had, and continue to have, the highest regard for him. In 1969, on my recommendation, Nixon nearly appointed him as ambassador to Bonn. He thought better of it when his Congressional experts told him that Nitze's nomination would run into conservative opposition in the Senate.

The reason for the conservative distrust of Nitze has never been clear to me; he must have done something to offend in the late Forties or early Fifties, for he was vetoed by Republican Senator Robert A. Taft for the position of Assistant Secretary of Defense in the Eisenhower Administration. Whatever it was, it testifies to the liturgical implacability of the conservatives. For Nitze's record over the subsequent twenty years was staunchly firm on almost every issue. Melvin Laird appointed him, with strong White House approval, as Defense Department representative on the SALT negotiating team in 1970. In March 1974, James Schlesinger once again proposed him for a position requiring Senate confirmation: it was the same slot of Assistant Secretary that had aborted twenty years earlier. It was a tribute to Nitze's patriotism that he was willing to serve in the Nixon Administration and at a lower rank than he had held under Johnson. I supported the nomination and urged it upon an unenthusiastic Senator John Stennis, Chairman of the Senate Armed Services Committee. Once again conservative opposition, this time led by Senator Barry Goldwater, aborted the project; the nomination was never forwarded by the White House. Nitze remained on the SALT delegation until he abruptly resigned on June 14 with a blistering public attack on Nixon:

> In my view it would be illusory to attempt to ignore or wish away the depressing reality of the traumatic events now unfolding in our nation's capital and of the implications of those events in the international arena.
>
> Until the office of the presidency has been restored to its principal function of upholding the Constitution and taking care of the fair execution of the laws, and thus be able to function effectively at home and abroad, I see no real prospect for reversing certain unfortunate trends in the evolving situation.

In other words, Nitze was saying that he could no longer serve a President — from whom he had been willing to accept a senior appointment three months earlier — because he thought Nixon's Watergate-related infirmities precluded the effective conduct of foreign policy. He also had substantive disagreements. It was an amazing attack so short a time before Nixon's trip to Moscow. But it made dramatically clear that Nixon had no domestic base for any significant agreement in Moscow regardless of its content.

That is almost certainly how the Soviets read it. It had been noticeable for months that in their encounters even with Nixon the allusions to Watergate multiplied. On April 11, on a visit to Washington, Gromyko had said to Nixon:

> We in the Soviet leadership are most satisfied that you hold true to the line you have taken despite certain known difficulties — which I don't want to go into — and we admire you for it on the human plane.

That same day, by coincidence, our Ambassador in Moscow, Walter Stoessel, had been received by Brezhnev. The General Secretary wondered whether and to what extent American "domestic problems" could hinder the course of events. Brezhnev answered his own question by saying this would become clearer in the near future — showing that he was following Watergate closely. But the finer points of constitutional government still eluded him. He expressed, in Stoessel's words, "amazement that the United States had reached the point that the President would be bothered about his taxes. . . . He respected the President for fighting back." On April 28 in Geneva, Gromyko had asked me in detail about the impeachment process. Since Dobrynin was no doubt reporting at length about events in Washington, one reason for the extraordinary query may have been to bring home to us the growing Soviet doubts about our bargaining position.

Whether it was Watergate that caused Moscow to put East-West negotiations into low gear in the spring of 1974; whether it was the general trend of our domestic debate; or whether both of these were used as a cover for decisions that Moscow made for its own reasons cannot be established from American documents alone. The fact is that during April 1974, Soviet conduct changed. Usually preparations for a summit as well as the SALT talks followed a familiar pattern: An outrageous Soviet opening position would be followed by a period of prolonged haggling. After the Soviets had decided that they had squeezed all they could from intransigence, there would be a breakthrough. Although its initial formulation would still be unacceptable it would give the congenital haggling some concrete basis. If then we stuck to our basic concept, the gaps would gradually narrow until some outside event — usually a summit — would supply the incentive for the final push.

This seemed to be true of the SALT negotiations in the spring of 1974. For well over a year both sides had been making proposals for the record. Then in March, all agencies in our government had converged on a scheme of "counterbalancing asymmetries": a Soviet edge in total delivery vehicles (reflecting the existing program of both sides) counterbalanced — in our view, more than counterbalanced — by an American advantage in numbers of MIRVed missiles. When I visited Moscow in March, Brezhnev seemed to accept this principle. He proposed an extension of the 1972 Interim Agreement, which would continue the Soviets' existing advantage in delivery vehicles, but he conceded us an advantage of 100 MIRVed missiles over the extended term of the agreement. For reasons I have explained in Chapter XXII, we considered the 100-missile gap in our favor inadequate, even derisory. But if past practice were any guide, the negotiations that Gromyko and I would pursue would soon see more realistic figures.

It did not happen that way. Instead, negotiations stalemated. The Soviets rejected various schemes to lower their MIRV ceiling; they refused to set separate limits for the land-based ICBMs that were our gravest concern. The curious aspect of our domestic debate was that *nobody* in our government favored accepting what the Soviets had put forward. There was no basis whatever for the often expressed fear that Nixon might make a disadvantageous deal to preserve his Presidency. What the White House sought was a realistic elaboration of our March proposals, which all agencies had approved: some consensus on what counterbalancing asymmetries might be in the American interest should the door to a breakthrough open. And it followed extremely careful procedures — much less freewheeling than in earlier periods — to elaborate this consensus.

But suddenly battle lines were drawn, for reasons that I still find difficult to explain in retrospect. The leader of the revolt within the Administration was Nixon's own Secretary of Defense, James Schlesinger. I have already described my high regard for Schlesinger's analytic skill and overall ability. He had done a remarkable job in strengthening our military capabilities despite a largely hostile Congress; in the process he had revised our defense doctrine in important and healthy directions with respect to both strategic and tactical forces. In this, one of Schlesinger's staunchest allies had been Senator Jackson. What may have started as a marriage of convenience soon turned into a symbiotic relationship. The two men became fast friends, sharing similar assessments. This gradually edged Schlesinger into open opposition to his President.

Undoubtedly, there was an element of personal rivalry as well. As I have already pointed out, Schlesinger saw no intellectual reason for conceding my preeminence as Presidential counselor. He resented the not always tactful methods — to put it mildly — by which I operated. For example, until late in my term of office I handled the SALT negotiations using my own staff and excluding representatives from the Department of Defense. This was both tactless and unwise; participation would have been educational for the Defense Department representative; he would have learned to calibrate Pentagon rhetoric against negotiating realities (as indeed occurred when SALT expert James P. Wade joined my team in the Ford Administration); it would have made it easier to gain Defense Department support in NSC deliberations. On the other hand, Schlesinger was no shrinking violet, either; he gave as good as he received. After a while, Schlesinger missed few opportunities to score points against me, even though our strategic assessments were substantially similar. He found it convenient to cast himself in the role of being more vigilant and wary on SALT matters than I was — as one would expect from a Secretary of Defense. On the other hand, I was usually more ready to resist what I considered geopolitical encroachments. At any rate, the differences between Schlesinger and me, though partly rooted in the different perceptions and missions of the departments we headed, were more personal than intellectual. It was a pity; for he was one of our ablest public servants and the country needed our cooperation. In more normal times we probably would have had much less difficulty working in tandem. (Of course, in normal circumstances neither of us would have been in the cabinet in the first place.)

Be that as it may, Schlesinger, by early June, seems to have come to much the same conclusions as Nitze. He no longer wanted progress on SALT; he thought there was not enough moral capital left in the Administration to sustain a debate on a controversial agreement. He therefore began to block the diplomacy openly. And if he was at least my equal in intelligence, I conceded him pride of place in arrogance. In any normal administration this would have led to his immediate dismissal — a course that a Watergate-haunted Nixon could not even consider.

The previous December, Jackson had made a public proposal of a SALT agreement calling for reductions and equal aggregates, and describing the concern with MIRV limits — the heart of our SALT position — as "exaggerated." In April, Jackson wrote Schlesinger asking for his comment. On June 3, 1974, by what must have been prearrangement, Schlesinger sent a reply praising Jackson's proposal — in other words, dissociating himself from the American negotiating position now before the Soviets (see Chapter XXII). The practical consequence was to undercut the various schemes that were still on the table, all of which were attempts to balance asymmetries, that is to say, to offset one set of *un*equal aggregates against another. Schlesinger's letter enabled Jackson to claim that the Defense Department supported his position, in effect that it opposed its Commander-in-Chief.

Schlesinger's June 3 letter paralleled one by Paul Nitze to the President. Nitze, whose resignation was still some ten days away, argued that any agreement that permitted the Soviets more than 200–300 MIRVed ICBMs was strategically intolerable because a larger number would put America's land-based strategic forces at risk. It was the fallacy of many SALT opponents to ask arms control negotiations not simply to stabilize the arms race but to solve all our strategic dilemmas as well. The absence of a SALT agreement would not keep MIRVed Soviet missiles to below 300, nor would it ease the potential vulnerability of our land-based force; in fact, by all projections it would lead to larger Soviet MIRVed forces and an increased or at least earlier threat to our land-based ICBMs. A useful debate would have been whether these projections were reasonable; whether the absence of an agreement eased the Soviet threat; and whether a SALT agreement could alleviate our vulnerability. After all, it was not as if the Congress in the era of Vietnam and Watergate was eager to undertake a really large-scale building program, or even the relatively paltry $2 billion a year Schlesinger was talking about.

All this, it must be reiterated, occurred in the absence of any particular bureaucratic provocation. I was only just back from the Syrian shuttle. When Schlesinger dropped his bombshell, there had been no new move on SALT toward the Soviets. It was a maneuver to preempt a non-maneuver, for Nixon was not planning any fancy footwork in Moscow.

Nixon reacted to Schlesinger's letter to Jackson by calling the Defense Secretary to the Oval Office on June 6; he obviously suspected that there had been collusion with Jackson. And in truth in a normal Administration no Cabinet member who valued his position would publicly dissociate from a Presidential policy. It was a symbol of how far his Presidency had disintegrated that Nixon found himself obliged to deal with his Secretary of Defense as if the latter were a sovereign equal; it was a tribute to his tenacity that, overcoming his fear of personal confrontations, he managed to analyze the basic problem very well:

Let me tell you how I see the players. It is amusing that Defense, State, and everyone now see Communism is bad and you can't trust the Soviet Union, I knew both of those things all along. Nitze's view is that we should stonewall the Soviet Union on everything — SALT, MIRV, TTB,* ABM. I understand. There are differences in objectives within the bureaucracy. State would like it to blow up because they didn't dream it up — the same with CIA. In the DOD — not you — they would like to stonewall so we get a bigger budget — more ships, etc. That is not totally selfish. They honestly believe no agreement is to our advantage. It's like in SALT I — although we didn't give anything up. Frankly, as Secretary you have to lead the Department. You must express your views. It has been the practice of recent secretaries to send over letters to get on record — with something that can't be accepted or refused, so it can go either way. I am disappointed to see you go this route.

Schlesinger was opaque but firm. He insisted that he was in favor of MIRV limits but agreed that above the figure of 360–450 Soviet MIRVed ICBMs the limitations were meaningless; no more than Nitze did he explain how the absence of an agreement would keep the Soviets to that limit. He implied that he favored a ceiling of equal total aggregates at around 2,500 delivery vehicles — which happened to be at least 350 above any planned American program and about 100 below Soviet totals. The difficulty was that Nixon had no alternative scheme. What he wanted from Schlesinger was general flexibility and moral support, not endorsement of any particular new proposal since none existed. In that situation, Nixon's almost plaintive plea was uttered in a vacuum:

We need your help. Help Kissinger to devise a way around this. I will take on Brezhnev. I made the speech about the U.S. being second to none. The American people in their simplistic way are not on a peace-at-any-price kick,

---

*This was the threshold test ban, discussed below in this chapter.

but they want peace. Many of my friends are horrified at our even talking to the Soviet Union. But are we going to leave the world running away with an arms race, or will we get a handle on it?

In this weird situation, stonewalled by the Soviets, assailed by subordinates, Nixon assembled the National Security Council on June 20, five days before leaving for Moscow. There was no decision to make; it was a deliberation to examine the contingency that the Soviets might make an offer while we were in Moscow. At Nixon's request, I outlined where we stood:

With no added U.S. forces, the Soviet Union will pass the U.S. in number of MIRVed missiles by the 1980's, perhaps by 1980, maybe by 1982. This depends on the rate of building. At the maximum rate they have gone in the past, the gap would become quite dramatic. Our real choice is either to achieve constraints on their programs, or have a build-up of our own. The worst case is to have no constraints on their program and no build-up of our own.

Nixon intervened to indicate that this was exactly what might occur: "If there were no constraints, we could raise hell to try to drum up Congressional support and that might happen. But I am mainly concerned that it might not happen either."

I then summed up the strategic issue:

[T]he status of the negotiations is as follows. The current scheme we were talking about would be an extension of the Interim Agreement numbers to perhaps 1979 or '80 — the date is important here because Trident comes in in the 1977–78 period. In return for this, we would expect to achieve limits on the total number of MIRVed missiles. They have offered us 1100 versus a thousand for them. We have told them that this is not adequate. It would stop us essentially in the next year or so, and allow the Soviet build-up to continue. I know of no one in the government that recommends accepting this approach. But they may offer a better differential. . . . Right now, Mr. President, you have no decisions to make. We have an offer, but only an unsatisfactory offer. But suppose they should increase the gap — would we then be prepared to extend the Interim Agreement to 1979 or 1980, and bring some larger missiles into our deployments? . . . You may face such decisions. I have no indication that you will, and in fact my prediction is that you will not have to face it, because they won't offer an increase in the differential.

It must be noted that what I put forward was a request to explore the margins of our own proposal. We were seeking contingency guidance should the Soviets respond more flexibly than we anticipated to what we had put before them in March with the approval of *all* agencies represented at this meeting. Schlesinger responded with an elaboration of what he had said to Nixon on June 6, an entirely new scheme that, a week before a scheduled summit meeting, simply wiped out the negotiating record of the previous six months, dismissing as irrelevant the only proposal currently under discussion. He proposed equal total aggregates of 2,500; a limit on MIRVed ICBMs of 660 Minutemen for us and 360 for the Soviet Union; no limitation on submarine-based MIRVs; and extension of the Interim Agreement to 1979.

The trouble was that this proposal had essentially been rejected by the Soviets in March and for understandable reasons: It constrained no American program; it would reduce the only major Soviet MIRV program. The ceiling for the Minutemen was *above* what had been published as our plan in the Defense Secretary's annual posture statement projecting our forces five years into the future. The Soviets, on the other hand, had — according to our own estimates — the capability to deploy at least 500 more MIRVed ICBMs than the Pentagon plan would concede them over the life of the agreement. Our only proposed counter was to build 150 Minuteman IIIs with three warheads each as against six on the best Soviet missile. Thus we were trying to stop a possible 3,000 Soviet warheads by threatening to build 450 of our own. Nobody, regardless of how strident his anti-Communist rhetoric, could have made this sound menacing enough to induce Soviet agreement. Brezhnev had told me in March, when I presented it the first time, that he would not be in office long if he accepted it.

Schlesinger would hear none of it. The fact that the Soviets had already turned his proposal down was not conclusive; they had so far only dealt with me; at the summit they would confront the master:

Mr. Brezhnev has a very high respect for you, Mr. President. You can be very persuasive — you have great forensic skills. I believe if you can persuade them to slow down to 85 per year versus 200 per year, you will have achieved a major breakthrough.

"Major breakthrough" was an understatement. Forensic skill could not achieve it; the task would have defeated Demosthenes or Daniel Webster.* It would require a downright miracle.

Only a conviction that Nixon was finished could have produced so condescending a presentation by a cabinet officer to his President. Nixon recorded in his diary that it was "really an insult to everybody's intelligence and particularly to mine."[9] And in a calmer period, it would have been seen that there was no possible justification for the self-righteous dogmatism with which our domestic opponents conducted the assault on East-West policy. For the issue was perfectly susceptible to rational analysis. Both Schlesinger and I agreed that a ceiling of 1,000 on Soviet MIRVs was too high; in fact, it was no ceiling at all. We agreed that a limit of 360 for Soviet missiles was desirable; we differed

---

*Even though Daniel Webster was a Secretary of State — twice.

only about its attainability. Assuming my judgment was right and the Soviets rejected the scheme despite Nixon's forensic skill, the issue came down quite simply to this question: Was there any limit on Soviet MIRVs higher than 360 and lower than 1,000 that would constitute an improvement in our position? Common sense would suggest that there had to be.

Schlesinger had indicated that his counterproposal, if we failed to agree that summer, would be to recommend augmenting our Minuteman III program by 150 (or 450 warheads). Holding the Soviets to 800–850 MIRVed missiles, a level that I considered (perhaps wrongly) as attainable, would have deprived the Soviets of an additional 900–1,200 warheads compared with Brezhnev's proposal and 3,000 warheads compared with current levels. If that was considered insignificant, it is hard to know what the shouting over a Soviet edge of 300 single-warhead missiles in SALT I was about.

As it turned out, we never built the additional Minuteman IIIs, largely because the Pentagon never put such a program forward. The absence of an agreement soon turned the ceiling of 360 proposed for Soviet MIRVed ICBMs into fantasy. The Soviets have since exceeded the limit of 1,000 we thought intolerable in 1974. The current SALT II ceiling is 1,200, two hundred above Brezhnev's offer. Three administrations later, the total aggregate of our strategic forces is slightly lower than was foreseen in the five-year plan of 1974. None of the successor administrations to Nixon's put forward the aggregates the Pentagon asked SALT to produce in 1974. They were content to stick with our existing programs even in the absence of an agreement. So much for the argument that SALT is responsible for the strategic dilemmas we face today.

In any other period a campaign to paint the "warmongers" of 1972 as the "peace-at-any-price appeasers" of 1974 would have been ludicrous. In the fevered atmosphere of Nixon's last weeks, it was treated as the most natural accusation in the world. And the NSC meeting was followed the next day by the charges of a secret missile deal described earlier.

What made the whole argument even more futile was that there was probably no chance of getting an agreement on terms compatible with our national honor, and Nixon would make no other. It was not our SALT divisions that prevented an agreement; this was foreclosed by a Soviet policy decision not to proceed — for whatever reason — during the summer of the visible disintegration of the Nixon Administration. But the squabbling did deprive the President of dignity on his last foreign journey as Chief Executive.

If the summit took place under unfortunate circumstances within the United States, its international context was no more favorable. In 1972, the Soviets maintained the summit invitation despite the blockade and bombing of North Vietnam; this was the clearest indication that the Soviets expected to do important business; it was indeed their commitment to it. The Soviets did not want to fall behind the pace of the rapidly evolving Chinese-American relationship. In 1973, the Soviets wanted to conclude the Agreement on the Prevention of Nuclear War and Brezhnev was most eager to discuss the Middle East. But by late June 1974 none of these factors, except the desire to isolate China, could overcome the reality that Nixon's authority was disappearing almost by the week.

The Soviet position was not particularly brilliant. In the abstract, the years of détente had been kinder to us than to our adversaries — the strident claims of our critics to the contrary notwithstanding. As I wrote in a briefing memorandum to Nixon for the summit:

> Sensitive as they are to shifts in the power balance, the Soviets leaders cannot fail to recognize that America's diplomatic position has not, in fact, been weakened since you last saw Brezhnev, while the Soviet position in some respects has undergone a decline: in the Middle East, to some extent in Europe, and in the Far East. Indeed, Soviet setbacks and disappointment have probably raised some question in Moscow about the validity of pursuing a detente with the West and with the United States. Brezhnev's commitment to this general line, however, is such that he cannot easily abandon it, without jeopardizing his own personal power position.

The assessment turned out to be right. Brezhnev proved most reluctant to give up his attempt to ease East-West relations. What he abandoned — as the full extent of our domestic debacle sank in — was any major commitment to expand the existing framework. For that he needed what the French call an *interlocuteur valable* — an opposite number who could deliver. And that is exactly what Nixon more and more had lost the power to do. A second-term President is under a serious handicap in any event; every passing month brings him closer to retirement and political irrelevancy. In Nixon's case Watergate multiplied this occupational hazard hugely. In the perception of almost all observers, he was approaching the end of his period in office in the second year of his second term.

A statesman's tools are insight and authority. Nothing can substitute for the intuition of what events are interrelated and basic, and which are surface manifestations, what factors are relevant and which are diversions. That quality of insight Nixon maintained, even honed, until the bitter end. But a statesman's labor becomes an academic exercise if he cannot convince his opposite numbers that he is able to implement his perception. The stuff of diplomacy is to trade in promises of future performance; that capacity Nixon was losing with alarming rapidity. Inevitably, he became less and less interesting to the Soviets as a negotiating partner. They treated him politely, even respectfully, to the last. But by the summer of 1974 they were no longer prepared to make long-term commitments to Nixon or to pay a price for his goodwill. The trouble with the 1974 Moscow summit was not the danger of secret deals unfavorable to the American national interest; it was rather the opposite — an encounter doomed to irrelevance.

Nixon stopped first in Brussels, where the heads of government of the North Atlantic Alliance met to celebrate their signature of the Atlantic Declaration over a year late. It was NATO's twenty-fifth anniversary, but the mood was not joyful. The principals in the major allied countries — Germany, France, Britain, Italy — and the participants in the passionate debate of the previous year had all changed. The words of the Declaration were substantially what we had sought for a new Atlantic Charter. But an affirmation of unity requiring no concrete action that nevertheless takes fourteen months to negotiate is hardly a sign of moral rededication.

Nixon's reputation in Europe was high; most Europeans affected to regard Watergate more as a political coup by Nixon's opponents than as a disregard of legality by the Administration. The Western leaders treated Nixon with the respect they felt for him and the solicitude shown to terminally ill patients. In a way, the reiteration of unity against potential Soviet aggression — among other things — while the President was on his way to what was turning into an annual summit with the Soviet leaders could be taken as an indication that the twin pillars of our East-West policy, containment and coexistence, were both in working order. Yet by the same token the symbolism lost dramatic impact because the meeting was taking on more the character of a farewell appearance than of a political event.

Given these limitations, our Soviet hosts were uncharacteristically sensitive to Nixon's human predicament. Brezhnev greeted him at Moscow's Vnukovo II airport on June 27 as he had not done during his last visit. Brezhnev's only position then was General Secretary of the Communist Party and he rarely went to greet foreign visitors at the airport unless they were also high Communist Party functionaries. He escorted Nixon to the same luxurious Tsars' Apartments in the Kremlin that the President had occupied in May 1972. Soon after, there was a private meeting between the two leaders attended only by the Soviet interpreter Viktor Sukhodrev, which delayed the start of the welcoming dinner for half an hour and caused the usual anxiety among those excluded. Nixon did not tell me what was discussed; the Soviets never referred to it. Nixon resigned soon after, so it had no operational consequences. It was like a solitary cry on the North Pole, a noise without sound disappearing into the void.

But there were limits beyond which the Soviets would not permit personal goodwill to be pushed. When Nixon responded to Brezhnev's toast, he extrapolated a mood into a general principle, as he often did when speaking extemporaneously. Praising the accomplishments of the past two years of US–Soviet relations, Nixon asserted:

They were possible because of a personal relationship that was established between the General Secretary and the President of the United States. And that personal relationship extends to the top officials in both of our governments.

It has been said that any agreement is only as good as the will of the parties to keep it. Because of our personal relationship, there is no question about our will to keep these agreements and to make more where they are in our mutual interests.

It would have been difficult in the best of times for Soviet leaders to accept the proposition that their policy was based on personalities. Communist philosophy, after all, is nothing if not materialist. Even in their private comments, Soviet leaders like to preen themselves on the belief that their policy is based on objective factors, not on accident or sentiment. But with Nixon all but doomed, Brezhnev had an interest beyond vindicating Marxist philosophy in unlinking his policy from Nixon's fate. What TASS reported to the Soviet people, therefore, was a somewhat free translation of Nixon's remarks. It dropped the word "personal" and edited Nixon's remarks so that they would be taken as describing the relationship between two countries, rather than two men. Soviet solicitude toward Nixon clearly did not extend to associating the Kremlin with the proposition that détente depended on him alone.

Our press caught the discrepancy at once. Leonid M. Zamyatin, Director General of TASS, who participated with Ron Ziegler in daily joint briefings for the media, explained smoothly that the Soviet translation was accurate and that news reports to the contrary reflected the journalists' ignorance of the Russian language. Sukhodrev told us the omission was inadvertent — a statement events soon proved to be more tactful than accurate. Ziegler, carried away with his assignment of emphasizing Nixon's personal indispensability, ascribed the whole contretemps to the fact that *Pravda,* the party newspaper published in the mornings, went to press on a short deadline. "I expect to see 'personal relationship' in tonight's *Izvestia,*" said Ziegler, referring to the government daily, published in the evening. He soon learned that the Soviets' devotion to accurate journalism is so intense that nothing appears in the Soviet media under the pressure of deadlines. *Izvestia* repeated the version of *Pravda.* TASS also made another modification of the toast. Nixon had referred to Brezhnev's return visit to the United States as being scheduled for "next year" — following the pattern of annual summit meetings. The Soviets refused to commit themselves to a definite schedule: TASS reported the reference to a return visit but omitted a target date. No explanation was offered. None was necessary. The Soviets were cutting their losses.

The Moscow summit of 1974 thus suffered from the same incongruity as the Mideast journey. Nixon's paladins, now reduced in effect to Ziegler, stressed his personal role. But the Soviets had an interest in not tying a major policy to the fate of an individual. That, in fact, was also the American national interest and the only way we could rescue our international position from Watergate: to demonstrate that well-founded policies could survive our domestic debacles because they reflected long-term national objectives.

In this mood of tension, anguish, and premonition, the petty squabbles among staff that had blighted the Mideast journey reappeared even more sharply and in sometimes absurd form. There was an unworthy dispute between Al Haig and me about whose suite in the Kremlin palace would be closest to Nixon's — a status symbol of somewhat debatable value in the circumstances. Haig won the battle. It was like fighting over seats at the captain's table on the *Titanic* after it had struck the iceberg.

My personal relations with Nixon were unusually distant at this point. I could not tell whether he continued to resent my Salzburg press conference, or whether, as suggested by the columnist William Safire — considered close to several of Nixon's associates — Nixon used my own difficulties to reestablish his authority.[10] If the latter, it was a vain effort; Nixon retained enough power to diminish my standing; there was nothing he could do to restore his own. The most logical explanation is that he counted the thirty-four votes he needed in the Senate to defeat impeachment and found most of them on the conservative side. On this thesis, since I was under fire for détente, the Safire column was one of Nixon's attempts to dissociate from me and an effort to reestablish his credentials with his erstwhile constituency.

Whatever, contacts between the President and me were stiffer than before. The media had not forgiven me for the Salzburg press conference. They never let me forget the threat of resignation. They looked for every shred of evidence of seeming estrangement from Nixon, diminution of my authority, or tenseness on my part. The fact that Gromyko and I walked ten feet behind Brezhnev and Nixon on a stroll in the gardens at Brezhnev's seaside resort in the Crimea was headline news: I was either sulking, or being relegated to a secondary role, or both.

The truth was simpler. To be sure, I was exhausted from over two months of uninterrupted travel. But the President, in acute pain from phlebitis, was going through a much more traumatic experience than shuffling the members of his entourage. Nixon was much too serious a student of foreign policy and government not to understand that the biggest obstacle to serious negotiation was the Soviet conviction that if he survived politically he would lack authority but that in all likelihood he would not survive. Nixon must have found it hard to bear that I — with all the difficulties I faced — was certain to survive the debacle he could not bring himself to accept and yet which he now must have sensed was inevitable. And this on top of a long history in which the media had emphasized my role as peace negotiator and his almost as the "mad bomber."

No wonder that the physical effort required to keep functioning seemed to consume more and more of Nixon's energy. Doubtless he was preoccupied and withdrawn — only incidentally from displeasure with me, above all because he was in the process of parting from what heretofore had given his life meaning, the obsession that had made possible the almost inhuman self-discipline and the public persona at odds with his basically shyer and gentler nature. And while surrounded by the appurtenances of the Presidency he had to steel himself for the days of exile when the bands would stop playing and his lifelong dream had evaporated.

The procedures this time followed those of the Moscow summit of 1972.[11] There was a welcoming dinner in the marvelous fifteenth-century Granovit Hall in the Grand Kremlin Palace with its vaulted ceilings covered with religious paintings. There were generally two plenary sessions a day in St. Catherine's Hall, a gilded, ornate salon. Gromyko and I met in the lacunae of the formal sessions to negotiate outstanding issues in the various documents slated for signature. Brezhnev took our whole party to the Crimea from Saturday afternoon, June 29, to Monday morning, July 1.

On the Soviet side, the troika of Brezhnev, Kosygin, and Podgorny was still much in evidence though Brezhnev seemed to have less of a need to defer to the forms of collective leadership than he had two years earlier. He now dominated the discussions and was well briefed and acute, especially on military matters. One of the poignant features of the summit was in fact the disproportion between the protocol pomp and circumstance and what Nixon's plight permitted to be realized. For as it had become apparent that no major breakthrough was in the cards, tension eased and indeed the appearance of harmony became its own objective. The atmosphere was congenial. Miraculously, meetings started on time. There was none of the attempted browbeating that characterized the first two summits, in 1972 on Vietnam and in 1973 on the Middle East. The reason was not all that flattering to us. Precisely because they did not want to risk too much on Nixon's continuation in office, the Soviet leaders had scaled down their expectations. They recited their objectives but in what was for them a low-key manner. There was a discussion of the European Security Conference; by now so many West European leaders had agreed to culminate the conference at a summit gathering that there was no longer any purpose in America's holding out on this point. (This was to be the Helsinki conference of 1975, which Gerald Ford was attacked at home for attending.) And the remaining issues in what later became the Helsinki Final Act were too abstruse — they were mostly pedantic drafting problems in a collective document — to lend themselves to top-level solutions, though they were discussed inconclusively at considerable length.

There was some sparring on the Middle East. Brezhnev inquired as to the goal of our policy and stressed the need for joint US–Soviet action, though without the fire of his March meeting with me. The Soviets had learned from recent experience. Since it never hurts for a diplomat to give the impression that the inevitable has been affected by his policy decisions, Brezhnev made a point of noting the propriety of unilateral efforts where these were most efficient. Gromyko in a separate meeting with me allowed that our policy in the Middle East was more complicated than at first glance. It was said without rancor. The Soviets seemed at last to have drawn the correct conclusion from their embarrassments in the spring. Importuning for a formal role only highlighted their impotence; they would have to wait for a mistake on our part or a collapse of our current strategy.

The Soviets finessed controversial items by scheduling many meetings between the leaders on subjects that normally would have been left to the foreign ministers: arcane technical discussions on agreements that had been prepared for signature at the summit. Of these, three were of some importance: an agreement to explore the possibilities of banning environmental warfare; an agreement to forgo the option of the second ABM site allowed by the 1972 treaty limiting defensive weapons; and a draft treaty to prohibit underground nuclear tests over a certain "threshold" of explosive power.

The agreement to negotiate a ban on environmental warfare — for example, weather modification for military purposes — was the sort of marginally useful accord that ingenious bureaucrats devise under the pressure of the necessity to make their leaders look good. It was a bow to humane sentiments; it was not controversial because it was not easy to know what its subject matter would be and because few were bold enough to advocate environmental warfare publicly. A completed international convention on the subject was later signed by the United States, the USSR, and thirty other countries in Geneva in May 1977.

The protocol on ABM systems had its origin in the treaty signed in 1972 limiting antiballistic missile defense sites to two in each country separated by no less than 1,300 kilometers. Each side was given the right to defend its national capital and one field of ICBMs. As it turned out, neither country had taken full advantage of its rights under the treaty. The Soviet Union already had an ABM system around Moscow;

we had built one defense site protecting a missile field near Grand Forks, North Dakota. Neither country had proceeded with a second site. At the summit in 1974 it was agreed to formalize practice and to confine each country to one antimissile defense site. The agreement was slightly more advantageous to us than to the Soviet Union since there was no possibility that the Congress would ever appropriate money for the second permitted site, while the Soviets labored under no such inhibitions.

This amendment pushed to its logical conclusion the reasoning underlying the original ABM agreement. If deterrence was enhanced by leaving each side's population vulnerable to attack, it was better that there be one site than two; in fact, it made little sense to have any. What all this left unexamined was the validity of the reasoning that led to the treaty in the first place, and this silence is an interesting reflection of the impact of conventional wisdom. After 1972, the numbers of offensive weapons permitted in the first SALT agreement became controversial though in fact they did little more than ratify what both sides were planning anyway. What went nearly unremarked was the extraordinary doctrine that based a nation's security on the vulnerability of its population and of its missile fields. In retrospect it is less clear to me than it seemed then, as I went along with the consensus, why protection of the missile fields would not have added to strategic stability especially after the MIRV threat emerged. Leaving fixed ICBM silos totally undefended reduces an attack on them into a mere engineering problem; as accuracy improves and the number of attacking warheads expands, it is not irrational to consider ABM defense of missile fields as a possible protection if the requisite technology is available. Be that as it may, the ABM agreement of 1974 was another modest step forward on a route to which there was literally no opposition.

The most interesting agreement was the "threshold" nuclear test ban. A staple of Soviet disarmament schemes had been the proposal for a complete ban on nuclear testing. (The 1963 test ban, negotiated by the United States, Britain, and the USSR, prohibited nuclear tests in the atmosphere, in space, or under water, but permitted underground testing to continue.) In the usual Soviet version, *all* testing would be banned and other nations would be asked to accede. If they did not, the signatories would have the right to renounce the treaty. The Soviet proposal had been consistently rejected by American administrations of both parties. The Defense Department and its scientific advisers argued persuasively that our weapons arsenal could not be improved without testing and that it was difficult to detect clandestine underground tests. The State Department objected to the pressure against other nuclear powers — for example, China or France — implicit in the withdrawal clause. In early February 1974, Dobrynin, true to the Soviet maxim that you can never know whether a door has been unlocked until you try it, trotted out the by-now venerable Soviet scheme for a comprehensive test ban. We turned it down. On February 4, Gromyko tried to find out whether our cold-shouldering Dobrynin's overture might be a question of rank; so he, a member of the Politburo, repeated it to the President. The answer was again in the negative. The Soviets retreated to the idea of a quota ban — that is, limiting both sides to an agreed number of tests per year. That was less dangerous than the comprehensive ban but presented significant verification problems.

During my visit to Moscow in March, I raised the verification problems and refused any agreement involving — even tacitly — pressure on third countries. Brezhnev countered with a proposal of a "threshold" test ban — that is, banning underground tests of nuclear weapons above a certain yield. This I was prepared to discuss. Soviet strategy was more dependent on high-yield weapons than ours; limiting tests to the lower ranges should therefore on balance favor us. The major verification problems, moreover, were in the lower-yield explosions. And such an agreement would cause less offense to allies like France and friendly countries like China; it involved no implied pressure on them because it was independent of their actions. In the months prior to the 1974 summit, we refined the concept of a threshold ban both within our government and in talks with the Soviets. The original concept of defining the threshold by the seismic shock of the explosion was replaced by the simpler idea of setting the ceiling at 150 kilotons.

Though the arms control utility of a threshold test ban was marginal, it opened up discussions on verification that represented a major advance. If we were to verify that nuclear tests were below the 150-kiloton threshold, the Soviet Union would have to reveal its test sites, agree to test at no other site, and supply information about the geological formations at each site to permit us to calibrate our equipment. This — surprisingly — the Soviet Union agreed to do. The question of "peaceful nuclear explosions" then arose — that is, the theoretical use of nuclear devices to build canals or divert waterways. Neither side wanted to close off this possibility, but the United States especially did not want to permit the loophole of masking a military device as a peaceful explosive. Since the locale of peaceful explosions would be impossible to specify by international agreement in advance, we asked for on-site inspection. After prolonged wrangling, the Soviet Union agreed, for the first time in its history, to the principle. The details were to be worked out, according to a protocol attached to the agreement, before the threshold test ban would go into effect in 1976.

All concerned with the verification problem — as must be all serious students of arms control — should have welcomed the threshold test ban as a potentially important pilot project. Never before had the Soviets agreed to on-site inspection; never had they been willing to give so much information about a military testing program. And since not even those most rabidly suspicious of Soviet motives thought the threshold test ban worked to our military disadvantage, the Soviet conciliatoriness with respect to it must have been to maintain some momentum in the flagging détente.

But by then détente had been engulfed in controversy in America and growing doubt in Moscow. As a result, the threshold test ban did little to enliven the summit or to raise its level of discourse. Its subject matter was too technical to attract the undivided attention of the leaders, or for that matter to concentrate their minds on just what was being talked about. When it came up, on Friday, June 28, Kosygin must have forgotten his script or was so used to the old dispensation that he returned constantly to the familiar litany, in effect attacking the threshold test ban as inferior to a comprehensive one. Gromyko and I were supposed to report on the progress of the negotiations. But Kosygin had other ideas. As soon as he heard what the subject was, he launched himself into a passionate advocacy of a complete end of nuclear testing. He shrugged off any counterargument, including that of Nixon, who also seemed oblivious to the fact that we were assembled to laud a completed agreement, not to pursue one laid aside. Nixon resorted to his standard rebuttal to the effect that he really agreed with Kosygin but was reaching the same goal by a different route, which was news to me. Kosygin was arguing against an agreement his own government was about to sign and Nixon accepted as an objective what he had turned down four months earlier. After creating total confusion for about an hour, the principals subsided and the subject was remanded to the foreign ministers.

At home, the threshold test ban failed not by attracting bitter animosity, as was the case with the SALT agreement, but by indifference. It simply had no constituency, except possibly for a small group of professional arms controllers interested in the principle of on-site inspection. Most liberals preferred a comprehensive test ban; thus they mocked the 150-kiloton ceiling, fought against the agreement, and thereby killed the first breakthrough toward on-site inspection. It was a classic case of the best being the enemy of the good. Conservatives did not oppose the threshold test ban. But they surely would not fight for causes abandoned by the liberals who had generated them. A coalition formed between those who wanted to do more and others who were not willing to press for it. The Carter Administration abandoned it. The treaty still awaits Senate ratification nearly eight years after its signature. And once it became apparent that the treaty was going nowhere in America, the Soviets lost interest in it and returned to their campaign for a complete test ban. Nothing could better symbolize the fact that the policy of détente and arms control was losing its domestic base in the United States.

SALT remained the most difficult issue. The problems were partly self-inflicted. It was, after all, only the second year of the 1972 five-year Interim Agreement, which would not run out until 1977. The hurry toward a new agreement was internal. The Nixon Administration had come up with a surprise at each previous summit: in 1972, the fact that it took place at all, coupled with the rapid conclusion of SALT and the principles of international conduct; in 1973, the Agreement on the Prevention of Nuclear War. Regardless of Watergate, it would have been in our interest in 1974 to make clear that if summits were becoming annual events they could not possibly produce a major announcement each time. Relations between two nations cannot be geared to a schedule of spectaculars; even less, relations between ideological and geopolitical adversaries. There simply were not that many controversies susceptible to yearly solution. Indeed, once East-West summits became institutionalized, their utility lay in the opportunity they afforded each leader to explore the other's mind and to understand the limits of pressure as well as the possibilities of agreement. In that sense, the 1974 summit was a "normal" summit and the others unusual.

But in the tumultuous summer of 1974, that insight was not widespread. The public, the media, and, to some extent, the Administration had become hooked on the dramatic like a dope addict on his fix. Any meeting with the Soviets at the Presidential or Secretary of State level that did not lead to a breakthrough was dismissed by the media as a failure even if its other accomplishments were not negligible. The imminence of any meeting at a high level triggered a bitter bureaucratic debate in the United States. Even when all agencies should have known that no major breakthrough was possible, they were not sure that something might not be going on in backchannels and they sought to block an outcome with which they disagreed.

By the summer of 1974, SALT had become too politicized; as I have said, it was a whipping boy in a deeper struggle over the entire nature of US–Soviet relations and even over Nixon's fitness to govern. In retrospect, it would have been wiser to announce ahead of time — surely after the disastrous NSC meeting of June 20 — that no basis for a breakthrough existed and that the leaders would defer their consideration of SALT until more progress had been made at a lower level. Such a sensible course was never considered, partly because of my preoccupation with the Middle East; partly because it would have been blamed on Watergate and would have fueled pressures to remove Nixon from office; partly because it would have been used by opponents of SALT to show that the basic thrust of Nixon's East-West policies was failing.

So we wound up with the worst of all worlds. A bitter domestic controversy prevented us from pursuing the coherent, persistent strategy without which no negotiation with the Soviets can succeed. After the

Soviets had conceded the principle of inequality in MIRVs in March, Dobrynin had told me privately that it would be possible to widen the MIRV differential as we favored. But the United States never managed to put forward and stick to a consistent scheme; Nixon and I constantly had to protect our flanks against sniping from those who specialized in showing the weakness of any position by comparing it with some ideal world, but who felt no similar compulsion to analyze what would happen in the absence of an agreement.

What had emerged as the Defense Department position at the NSC meeting of June 20 guaranteed a deadlock. No forensic skill could produce an agreement that simultaneously raised our total aggregates and lowered the Soviet MIRV program in return for absolutely nothing.

And it did not. Even the setting symbolized our difficulties. The main town near where we met in the Crimea on June 30 was Yalta. Nixon was not eager to revive memories of the controversy over Franklin Roosevelt's 1945 conference there with Stalin, long a target of conservative criticism. Therefore, the White House insisted on referring to the site of Nixon's meetings as the suburb of Oreanda, where the Politburo villas in fact were located and the meetings took place. Unfortunately, the press center was set up in a hotel in downtown Yalta and all news reports to America went out under the dreaded dateline "Yalta" after all.

We were meeting in the garden of Brezhnev's residence, an elaborate beach complex set into the steep hills that dropped down to the Black Sea. Brezhnev took Nixon into what was aptly called the grotto, a cave-like structure cut into the limestone at the foot of a cliff — a romantic, nineteenth-century conceit somewhat incongruous for the leader of a country avowing a materialistic interpretation of history. While they talked alone, Gromyko and I sat with our aides near the huge Olympic-size swimming pool surrounded by glass walls that could be opened or closed electrically. This time the pool area was open to the surrounding breezes on a beautiful, clear, sunny day. Nixon and Brezhnev were secluded for over three hours. As in Moscow, I did not learn right away what they discussed — nor did the Soviets ever refer to it or claim that Nixon made any commitment. Eventually we were invited to join the principals.

The subject clearly had not been SALT. The two leaders had apparently waited for the arrival of Gromyko and me to get into the topic. Nixon, who had not mastered all the statistics, asked me to lead the SALT discussions for our side. He was seconded by Brezhnev:

I was telling the President that we appreciate him sending Dr. Kissinger to Moscow. He took a tough line with us in March, and we candidly told him our view. We told him our limits. The truth is there somewhere, so he should tell us where we should start to reach agreement.

It was an invitation to propose a compromise, put forward in a manner that was by Soviet standards conciliatory, suggesting that he would not insist on the original Soviet position. I presented a variant of the Defense Department's plan; this found no favor and in fact got us off into a futile and acrimonious debate. Brezhnev would not consider any of its aspects. He pointed out that our proposal would give us 4,000 more warheads than the Soviet Union, which was roughly true. He had discovered, almost surely from published accounts, that the limits we proposed for ourselves substantially coincided with our planned program: "It is important to reach an agreement but it should be one that restrains the race, slows it down. Under the proposal Dr. Kissinger is making, the US does not do far less than they would do without an agreement." I replied that in fact under our scheme our MIRV buildup would move at a slower rate than the Soviet Union's. But Brezhnev understood that this was because we were close to completing our program. He said he did not regard it as much of a concession; we were far ahead and we should not pretend otherwise.

Despite these exchanges, the mood in the Crimea was mellow. The Soviets were not eager to embarrass Nixon. Indeed, all the American participants were convinced that the Soviets did not relish a deadlock. Brezhnev and his colleagues kept inviting new proposals within the context of counterbalancing asymmetries. But our domestic situation gave us no flexibility and it provided the Soviets with no incentive to be generous — never their forte in the best of circumstances. Brezhnev, backed up by two generals, produced maps that showed how the Soviets calculated our own first-strike potential, taking into account our overseas bases — the same presentation I had been given in March. To be sure, Brezhnev did not give himself the worst of the analysis; at the same time, the argument was not preposterous; it was the classic worst-case scenario of military planning, the nightmare of the strategist in which everything goes wrong simultaneously. It is as unlikely to occur as it is necessary to prepare for it. The difficulty is how to negotiate restraints when two worst-case scenarios confront each other.

The grotto meeting ended inconclusively. But neither side was eager to admit failure. It was decided that I would not accompany Nixon on the ceremonial visit to Minsk the next day but would return with Brezhnev to Moscow to see whether some progress could be made. But Brezhnev was not eager, either, to give the impression that he could be persuaded in a face-to-face encounter with the American Secretary of State. We talked little about SALT on the plane. At the airport we were greeted by Dmitri Ustinov, at this writing Soviet Minister of Defense and then a Politburo member with responsibility for defense industries. In the VIP lounge of the airport, Brezhnev made me repeat my basic proposition on counterbalancing asymmetries, together with the numbers I had put forward in the Crimea. In my presence he ordered a

Politburo meeting for that afternoon. Afterward, Gromyko and I should meet for one more review.

Gromyko and I discussed SALT again later that evening. The American numbers provided no basis for a solution, Gromyko stated; the constraints were too heavy and the time period (to 1979) too short. I suggested that the problem was to relate time to quality and quantity. We had been talking about extremes: either a permanent agreement that sounded forbidding and caused everyone to protect against every conceivable contingency, or a two- to three-year extension that led to an endless debate about equities for too short a period of time. Perhaps we should aim for a new agreement that would supersede the Interim Agreement and run for a longer period, say ten years, from 1975 to 1985. I put forward the idea to give ourselves the choice of either pursuing "equal aggregates" or "counterbalancing asymmetries" within a time frame relevant to military planning. It would enable the Soviets to change the numbers in the Interim Agreement without loss of face; it gave us another opportunity to review the MIRV problem. Gromyko accepted this, and the negotiations were placed in a different framework. Nixon and Brezhnev agreed to meet during the winter to implement the new approach. That gave the Soviets a chance to assess the prospects of Nixon's survival without breaking off the SALT process.

The new framework for SALT was no minor achievement and might have been regarded in its true light except by media and a bureaucracy geared toward spectaculars. It opened the way to the Vladivostok accord and a serious negotiation on SALT II. Nevertheless, its reception at home was another clear sign that SALT had lost its conceptual grounding. Instead of a thoughtful analysis of different strategies, our domestic debate continued to be consumed in symbolism. Some opponents of détente came to see in the defeat of SALT the key to their preferred policy — as if (in the absence of other measures) the defeat of a treaty would improve America's strategic position. Some of the defenders of a policy of relaxation of tensions began to treat SALT almost as an end in itself — as if the US–Soviet relationship did not also depend on a military balance and on responsible Soviet geopolitical conduct. The concept of equal aggregates dominated the SALT debate just when multiple warheads made the number of delivery vehicles a less and less reliable criterion of strategic equivalence. It was difficult to imagine any scheme that could survive the relentless ideological and sophisticated technical assault to which it would surely be subjected. We were edging ourselves into the worst possible position: with no SALT agreement to limit Soviet weapons and no support yet in the Congress for the necessary expansion of our own strategic programs.

That we were within reach of agreement in the Crimea was proved not quite five months later, in late November, when another President

signed an accord in Vladivostok that fulfilled both the framework established at the summit of 1974 and the schedule set by the summit of
1973. The Vladivostok agreement enshrined the principle of equal aggregates. The counterbalancing asymmetries approach, which I had favored, by then had been shown to have no bureaucratic or domestic
support. In the process it was barely recognized that to achieve a paper
equality in overall totals we let the Soviets have an additional 2,400 or
more warheads they would not otherwise have had.* It was a triumph
of theology over analysis.

Brezhnev may not have wanted to risk a SALT agreement with a
mortally wounded President. But no occasion was too unpromising for
him to pursue his obsession with China. My former associate, William
G. Hyland, has since suggested that a fundamental motive of Brezhnev's détente policy was to isolate China: thus the many overtures to us
attempting to lure us into arrangements whereby we would acquiesce in
China's destruction. When it became clear that we would not go along
with this, Hyland suggests, Brezhnev's interest in détente may have
flagged as well.[12] How much cooperation Brezhnev genuinely expected
from us, or could have expected from us, in his designs on China is not
clear, nor was it clear to either Hyland or me then. But there were
surely enough signs that it was never far from Brezhnev's mind. In
1970, before détente really got under way, there had been an approach
to one of our SALT negotiators seeking American acquiescence in a
Soviet preemptive move against China.[13] In 1972, there were broad
hints during my April trip and at the Moscow summit, though no explicit proposals. In 1973, Moscow did not conceal that its version of the
Agreement on the Prevention of Nuclear War was designed to prohibit
an American nuclear response to a Soviet attack on China. Also in 1973,
Brezhnev had sounded me out in Zavidovo and had warned Nixon in
San Clemente that our arming of China would mean war. In April 1974,
Podgorny, meeting with Nixon in Paris on the occasion of Pompidou's
funeral, had suggested that China should be *forced* into the disarmament
process if it did not join voluntarily. We had rebuffed or ignored all
these overtures.

Now the Soviets returned to the charge. Brezhnev's tête-à-tête discussion with Nixon in the grotto turned out to be on the subject of an
unconditional treaty of nonaggression between the United States and the
Soviet Union. Nixon told me about it cryptically in Oreanda and suggested that we explore the proposition. Perhaps, he said, it could be put

---

*The Soviets in the summer of 1974 offered us a ceiling of 1,000 MIRVed missiles, which I
believe hard bargaining could have reduced to the 800 range. The SALT II treaty of 1979 granted
both sides 1,200 MIRVed ICBMs and SLBMs. If one assumes six warheads per Soviet missile,
one reaches the figure of 2,400 additional Soviet warheads.

on the agenda of the mini-summit together with SALT later in the year. Gromyko apparently warned Nixon that China was a threat to peace when they chatted during the reciprocal dinner that the President offered to the Soviet leadership on the evening of July 2.[14] Nixon called me over and, in the hearing of Sukhodrev, the Soviet interpreter, summarized Brezhnev's proposition and instructed me to pursue the nonaggression idea in the Channel for inclusion on the mini-summit agenda — much as he had told me privately in the Crimea.

A year earlier I would not have given the exchange a second thought. I would have assumed that Nixon was engaged in one of his complex maneuvers to gain time and was using the prospect of the nonaggression treaty as an inducement for Brezhnev to concede on more immediate matters. Based on the unhappy experience with the Agreement on the Prevention of Nuclear War, I would probably have judged the strategy too risky, but I would have been confident that I could convince Nixon that it was too dangerous to flirt thus with condominium: It had the clear implication that the United States was giving the Soviet Union a free hand to attack China.

Now as I watched the tormented, physically suffering President discipline every ounce of his strength to get through the week, I was not so sure that Nixon would be able to handle the forces he was unleashing. He seemed to me to be risking either our Soviet or our Chinese anchor or both for a marginal tactical success. I told Scowcroft that I would not carry out this order and I would resign if Nixon insisted on it. Nixon never returned to the subject and the Soviets never raised it again because I told Dobrynin that it was not a useful line to pursue.

I do not mean to suggest that Nixon meant to go through with the scheme; given his record, his acuity, and his convictions, he would surely have stopped well short even if he had toyed with it briefly. But it was symptomatic of the disintegration of the Nixon Administration that this degree of suspicion could arise between two men who, whatever our difference in personality, had worked together for five and a half turbulent years to elaborate and to a great extent implement a new design for our foreign policy — a key element of which was, after all, the Chinese connection.

This was the atmosphere in which I met with the press in Moscow on July 3. Much had changed since those innocent days of two years earlier when I had briefed the media on SALT I and genuinely thought that the chessboard of diplomacy revealed unusual, even historic prospects. Now the atmosphere was redolent with skepticism and suspicion. I had been abroad, with but two brief interruptions, for more than two months: first the Syrian shuttle, then Nixon's Middle Eastern trip, finally the Soviet summit. The two interludes in Washington (for ten days and six days respectively) had been more taxing than the journeys. The first was consumed defending myself on the wiretap issue, the second on the charge of "secret deals" on SALT, and both with frenetic preparations for the Presidential trips. Before and during the Soviet trip we had been subjected to broad innuendos — in public statements and hints by Senator Jackson, by Paul Nitze, by retiring Chief of Naval Operations Elmo Zumwalt, and in press commentary — warning against excessive concessions. It seemed to me also that the delicate structure of East-West relations was being undermined at the very moment of upheaval in our institutions, risking international crises we might not be able to surmount. It led to two utterances at the press conference that could be read as gaffes but were *cris de coeur,* expressions of despair over trends that risked a structure so painfully built up and especially over the nihilism of our domestic dialogue. In response to a question about why the arms limits were not broader, I replied:

[B]oth sides have to convince their military establishments of the benefits of restraint and that is not a thought that comes naturally to military people on either side.

Later in the press conference I was asked what would happen by 1985 if we failed to conclude a new SALT agreement before 1977. I responded with passion:

If we have not reached an agreement well before 1977, then I believe you will see an explosion of technology and an explosion of numbers at the end of which we will be lucky if we have the present stability, in which it will be impossible to describe what strategic superiority means. And one of the questions which we have to ask ourselves as a country is: What in the name of God is strategic superiority? What is the significance of it, politically, militarily, operationally, at these levels of numbers? What do you do with it?

The first comment was a statement of fact, perhaps not too tactful but based on much experience. Military men cannot be expected to think creatively about restraining the arms race; nor is it desirable that they do so. Their duty is to keep the nation strong; their assignment must be to prevail should all else fail. Military men who become arms controllers are likely to neglect their primary mission. It is the political leadership that must strike the balance on which restraint may be based. Truisms as my remarks were, they were less than prudent when uttered in the Soviet capital.

As for my observations on superiority, they fairly accurately predicted what has in fact happened. But they lent themselves to the oversimplification that strategic superiority had lost all significance, which was not really my view.[15] I had been haunted by the loss of our strategic superiority for nearly twenty years. I had been preaching, both as an academic and as a policymaker, that we were entering a new era in which greater attention had to be paid to regional defenses, especially of the conventional kind. I had been a strong advocate of programs necessary to maintain the strategic balance, from ABMs and MIRVs to new SLBMs and cruise missiles. But I was beginning to despair of the rote tendency to measure the strategic balance by numbers of delivery vehicles in a period when the numbers of warheads on both sides were much more worrisome and when any analysis showed that no building program could avoid casualties likely to paralyze statesmen and frighten peoples toward pacifism. Whatever we did, it would be impossible to recapture the overwhelming superiority that we had enjoyed until the early 1960s and it was sheer escapism to yearn for a past that technology proscribed.

The issue of the significance of superiority was much more complicated than our domestic debate allowed. We had gone through several phases: Until the early Fifties we had an atomic monopoly enabling us to substitute strategic power for conventional inferiority without fear of retaliation. Until the Sixties we were in a position of such superiority that in a first strike we could probably have destroyed the Soviet retaliatory force, and the Soviets had no comparable capability. In any event the Soviets, calculating the worst-case scenario, would not risk it. Until the early Seventies, in fact, the worst-case scenario analysis of the Soviets was bound to be a significant restraint on adventurism. Thereafter, our loss of strategic superiority was a strategic revolution even if the Soviets did not achieve a superiority of their own. For that, to some extent, freed the Soviet capacity for regional intervention. The Soviets would still not lightly tempt a war with the United States because they feared our mobilization potential and they could never be totally certain that we might not use strategic nuclear weapons against all calculation. But by the time of the 1974 summit we could no longer avoid, as I pointed out earlier, a fundamental strategic reassessment.

And that was precisely what our domestic debate was inhibiting. Two simpleminded schools of thought seemed to me to be drowning out all rational discussion. One sought to base strategy on the horrors of nuclear war and calculated the minimum number of nuclear weapons required to inflict some horrendous civilian slaughter. The other side of the debate was counting every numerical advantage as strategically significant unrelated to circumstance or risk. I always favored maintaining a substantial counterforce capacity as insurance and to absorb Soviet calculations in worst-case assessments. But in my mind it was a palliative; there was no way to escape the necessity of greater efforts in regional and conventional defense. My nightmare was that our internal squabbles were focusing on symbolic issues. My call for an analysis of what constituted strategic superiority did deal with the heart of our security problem, even if my formulation of it turned out to be too epigrammatic to explain the range of my meaning and yet sufficiently aphoristic to lend itself to being exploited in our domestic debate. My real fear was made clear in the sentences immediately following my comments on superiority:

[W]e will be living in a world which will be extraordinarily complex, in which opportunities for nuclear warfare exist that were unimaginable 15 years ago at the beginning of the nuclear age, and that is what is driving our concern, not the disputes that one reads in the day-to-day [debate].

But Washington in July 1974 was not hospitable to such reflections. While we were still in Moscow, Defense Secretary Schlesinger held a press conference at the Pentagon expressing his confidence in the military devotion to arms control and challenging my views on strategic superiority without exactly explaining what they were. To a disintegrating Presidency was now added a public disagreement between the Secretary of State and the Secretary of Defense.

The strange thing was that by all normal criteria, the summit had been a success. Significant agreements had been signed — not so earthshaking as on previous occasions but the sort of accords that showed that the two superpowers took progress in their relationship seriously. Even in SALT we had come much closer to an understanding of each other's position than was generally realized; otherwise it would not have been possible for a new President to conclude the negotiations within four months of entering office as Ford did at Vladivostok. Furthermore, it remains desirable, as I have said, to shift summits away from the obsession with spectacular signing ceremonies to an emphasis on a serious review of the international situation. And that was what Nixon and his opposite numbers accomplished in June 1974 with less strain than at any previous meetings. In that sort of *tour d'horizon,* Nixon was at his best; he managed to overcome the agony more and more devouring him for one last exhibition of his conceptual prowess.

The gentle Soviet treatment of the mortally wounded President was indeed one of the best testimonials to the impact of his policies. The Soviet system has no categories for those who lose political power for whatever reason. It must have been tempting to make Nixon — the old Communist-baiter — feel his decline. He could have been harassed in the manner at which the Politburo are masters. Instead, he was treated with respect and courtesy, a tribute to his predictability, which Soviet leaders prize more than sentimentality, and to his firmness and sober calculation, to which the Kremlin pays more attention than to professions of goodwill.

That is not the way it appeared to our media. The *New York Times* lamented the "fragility of détente." The *Washington Post* referred to the summit as a "great disappointment." *Newsweek* spoke of a "summit that never peaked.'' All in all, the end of the 1974 summit brought home to me that we had reached the end of the line. If authority was not soon restored, a debacle was certain — not because the summit had failed but because preparing for it had made clear that the President was losing control of his Administration.

By the middle of July, I had become convinced that Watergate had to be brought to an end and that this almost certainly required Nixon's resignation. Until then I had sought to banish the hitherto unthinkable idea. I understood that Nixon's power was draining away. At the latest in May, after the publication of the tapes, his fate was sealed. But I had seen it as my duty to ward off crises by prolonging the illusion of authority and continuity for as long as possible, to the point that I did not permit myself to speculate on how the end might come. And I was arrogant enough to believe that I would be able to keep foreign policy going no matter how badly damaged the President was.

The events surrounding Nixon's journeys destroyed that illusion. They proved that no Secretary of State can by himself manage the foreign policy of our nation. The ebbing of Presidential authority encouraged a creeping irresponsibility within the government, in the Congress, and in the media that would ultimately undermine our security. It did not matter who was right in the various controversies raging within the Washington bureaucracy. The impossibility of resolving them would sooner or later deprive our policy of strength and direction and our strategy of credibility. What had been a nightmare began to appear a necessity: that it might in fact be better for the nation if Nixon's Presidency came to an end. I remained convinced that he had been judged with extraordinary severity; that hypocrisy as well as justice animated his tormentors. I admired his endurance and self-control; despite all our disagreements I felt more warmly toward my doomed chief than at any previous time. Nor did I do anything to give effect to my views. Whatever happened and whoever else deserted, I had determined to stick by the President, who had appointed me to high office, to vindicate the continuity of government. But in the recesses of my soul, I began to feel what I am told is sometimes the attitude of survivors toward the terminally ill. I hoped that since the end was unavoidable, it would — for the sake of our country — be quick, and that if it had to happen it would — for the sake of the President — be merciful.

XXV

The End of the Administration

The Long Voyage Home

THE televised welcoming ceremony for the President's return from
the Moscow summit on July 3, 1974, was arranged for Loring Air
Force Base in Maine. It was held at an air base at the farthest
feasible remove from Washington because it would not have been a
simple matter to organize a reception in the nation's capital that was
representative. Vice President Ford was there to praise Nixon for yet
another contribution to the structure of peace in the world, and for a
better foreign policy "than we have had in our lifetime and perhaps in
the history of our country." With the assistance of base personnel and
a few local residents, a typically enthusiastic Presidential homecoming
was arranged. Only its location testified to Nixon's ordeals.

I had stayed on in Europe to fulfill the commitment of the Atlantic
Declaration to brief our allies about our talks with Brezhnev. I stopped
at NATO headquarters in Brussels, then Paris, Rome, Munich, London,
and Madrid. It was not entirely an accident that I met the German leaders in Munich, where they had assembled for the finals of the quadrennial World Cup championship soccer match. I told the press at the airport that I would let no sporting event stand in the way of my obligation
to our allies. Knowing that I am a passionate soccer fan, the German
government made sure that my briefing of them did not keep me from
the Olympic Stadium for the final. It was a relaxed weekend. Hans-
Dietrich Genscher, the new West German Foreign Minister in Helmut
Schmidt's coalition cabinet, helicoptered me into the foothills of the
Alps on Saturday afternoon, July 6, for a long exchange of views. In
the evening he threw a huge party, including many key figures from
politics, the media, and the entertainment world. The next day Germany
won the final in a game that confirmed a theory I had long held about
the relationship of national character and tradition to the style of soccer
played. Germany used the methods of the Schlieffen plan, of complicated maneuver with intricately plotted designs, almost irresistible when
everything worked as planned and with the psychological impetus of a
friendly crowd. One could not be sure how the German team would

react if its careful design were thwarted and it had to improvise. The Dutch lost, despite an even more cerebral style of soccer that was beautiful to watch but lacked the final will to prevail. (And so it was with other teams: England, once preeminent, now relying on condition and reputation to sustain its slightly old-fashioned, somewhat pedantic style, and therefore long since eliminated from the World Cup tournament. And Brazil, unsurpassed in daring virtuosity, but at that moment undecided whether to rely on its traditional spontaneity or to follow the more methodical European style. In 1974 it finished fourth, which is close to the Brazilian definition of national catastrophe.)

Washington was calm. Scowcroft reported that "activity here, as far as I can determine, is nil. Everyone seems busily engaged in relaxing. Talking with Al [Haig] the mood seems to be relaxed."

It was the quiet before the final convulsion. I returned to Washington on July 9 to a city awaiting the catharsis of the Watergate obsession. No one knew when the climax would come; but there was no longer any doubt of its imminence or inevitability. On June 15 the Supreme Court had agreed to review whether the Watergate grand jury had the right to name President Nixon as an unindicted co-conspirator in the cover-up of the Watergate break-in. The Supreme Court had agreed, about two weeks earlier, to rule on whether Special Prosecutor Leon Jaworski could subpoena tapes of sixty-four White House conversations. On June 21 the House Judiciary Committee completed six weeks of closed hearings on the impeachment evidence. On June 26 former White House aide John Ehrlichman went on trial for complicity in the break-in at the office of Daniel Ellsberg's psychiatrist and for making false statements under oath.

The year before, the Senate Watergate hearings had descended on Nixon the very day his summit with Brezhnev ended. In 1974, the July 4 weekend intervened. But from then on, the impending denouement of Watergate dominated the national life.

On July 8 the question whether Nixon should be forced to hand over the tapes of sixty-four conversations in the Oval Office was argued before the Supreme Court. On July 12 Ehrlichman, among others, was found guilty. The next day, the Senate Watergate Committee released its unanimous three-volume, 2,000-page report on the Watergate cover-up and financing irregularities in Nixon's 1972 campaign. The Senators avoided stating whether the President had participated in the cover-up, but on July 19 the majority and minority counsels of the House Judiciary Committee joined in urging a Senate trial on one or more of five central impeachment charges, including obstruction of justice, abuse of Presidential power in dealing with government agencies, and contempt of Congress and the courts. "Reasonable men acting reasonably," they maintained, "would find the President guilty."

These were the way stations on the road to the destruction of a President and I observed them with dismay. By now Nixon was in San Clemente awaiting the unfolding of events he could no longer control or even greatly influence. I stayed in Washington but flew to California for two brief stretches — July 19–20 and July 25–26 — to be with the President. He rarely spoke about Watergate; when he did, it was not about the substance but about the arithmetic of the impeachment vote, first in the House, then in the Senate. He was a man awake during his own nightmare. His vaunted self-discipline had not prevented the debacle and may even have caused it. For he had suppressed all the instincts that would normally have alerted him to his peril; he had been sustained on the fatal course by associates who subordinated policy to procedure and who were at a loss as to how to react when the procedures miscarried.

Those of us who had worked with Nixon for five and a half years found it impossible to join in the wave of outrage sweeping through the media. We did not condone the shabby practices revealed by Watergate; we were as appalled as anyone. Nor did we have any illusions about the evasions and untruths unearthed. We had seen some of these tendencies at first hand. But we had a different perspective. We could see how they had helped to turn a serious error into a national disaster. We knew better than most that Nixon not so much lied as convinced himself of an expedient account. At various times we had been manipulated and set one against the other by the President. We were all too familiar with Nixon's congenital inability ever to confide totally in anyone. Even his closest associates rarely were sure that they knew all the ramifications of his thinking and therefore did not know how to help him.

Nixon had no truly close friends. Even his intimates lived with the consciousness that they might be abandoned or dropped if it served some inscrutable purpose. The atmosphere was summed up in a remark I made to the late John Osborne, one of the wisest of columnists, who manned the "White House Watch" for *The New Republic*. In 1971, shortly after my secret trip to China had made me a public figure, John asked me how it felt to be the director of the play. I replied truthfully: "John, I don't know whether I am the director of this play or an actor in some other play whose plot they have not told me."

No modern President could have been less equipped by nature for political life. Painfully shy, Nixon dreaded meeting new people; only the anonymity of large, approving crowds could make him feel secure. Fearful of rejection, he constructed his relationships so that a rebuff, if it came, would seem to have originated with him. Fiercely proud, he could neither admit his emotional dependence on approbation nor transcend it. Deeply insecure, he first acted as if a cruel fate had singled him out for rejection and then he contrived to make sure that his premonition came to pass. It is a truism that none of us really knew the inner man. More significant, each member of his entourage was acquainted with a slightly different Nixon subtly adjusted to the President's judgment of the aide or to his assessment of his interlocutor's background.

When the transcripts of the Oval Office conversations on Watergate were first published, I was astounded at the muscular language sometimes bordering on jive talk. Unless his more colorful expressions had become so much a part of the landscape that I took them for granted — which I doubt — the Nixon who talked with me on foreign policy did so rather with the prissy pedantry of his public personality. Moreover, as I have said many times, those closest to him had learned to discount much of what he said and to filter out many assertions made under stress. We were expected, we believed, to delay implementing more exuberant directives, giving our President the opportunity to live out his fantasies and yet to act, through us, with the calculation that his other image of himself prescribed.

One of the Walter Mitty dimensions of his personality, and one of the causes, I am convinced, of Watergate, was Nixon's love-hate relationship with the Kennedy family. He and John and Robert Kennedy had been bitter opponents in the 1960 campaign and after. Nixon was thought to be at the opposite end of the political spectrum from his martyred rivals. Actually, it is probable that the Kennedys were (or at least started out to be) more conservative or more skeptical than many of their followers, while Nixon was far more moderate and sophisticated than his conservative constituency.

Nixon, much like Lyndon Johnson before him, would have given anything to achieve the adulation that had come to John Kennedy. Nixon ascribed the successes of the Kennedy family to technique, not conviction, and he spent hours each week ruminating about the ruthless political tactics and public relations gimmicks that he thought had made the Kennedys so formidable. Nixon was convinced that wiretapping had been a key weapon in the Kennedy arsenal during the campaign of 1960, a view doubtless shared by others around him. He never offered any evidence to that effect. Though there is nothing to show that Nixon ordered the wiretapping of the Democratic National Committee headquarters, the event might have had its origin in that obsession. When one asks oneself why the Nixon team in 1972 would run the risk of wiretapping an opponent in a campaign that was already won, a possible answer is that a victory was not enough unless it emulated the hated, feared, and at the same time admired Kennedys. It was an act of retaliation for perhaps imagined injuries, not a step to achieve a specific purpose. (Nixon used to hint darkly that his and Agnew's planes had had listening devices installed in the 1968 campaign — though how this could be blamed on the Kennedys, even if true, was less clear in the telling.)[1]

Most men mature around a central core; Nixon had several. This is why he was never at peace with himself. Any attempt to sum up his complex character in one attribute is bound to be misleading. The detractors' view that Nixon was the incarnation of evil is as wrong as the adulation of his more fervent admirers. On closer acquaintance one realized that what gave Nixon his driven quality was the titanic struggle among the various personalities within him. And it was a struggle that never ended; there was never a permanent victor between the dark and the sensitive sides of his nature. Now one, now another personality predominated, creating an overall impression of menace, of torment, of unpredictability, and, in the final analysis, of enormous vulnerability.

This is why at the end of the day those of us who worked closely with Nixon developed, despite the exasperations, the indirections, and the bizarre qualities, a grudging respect and something akin to tender protectiveness for him. We had witnessed how his maddening aberrations grew out of a desperate conflict of discordant elements so that he was in truth the first victim of his own unharmonious nature. We saw a Nixon who could be gentle and thoughtful; indeed, some of his most devious methods were mechanisms to avoid hurting people face-to-face. He was highly analytical; he had an acute ability to get to the heart of a problem, especially in foreign policy. He was a great patriot; he deeply believed in America's mission to protect the world's security and freedom. He did not blame the Vietnam war on his Democratic predecessors as he might have; he thought he owed it to the families of servicemen killed in Vietnam to affirm that their cause had been just. And he did believe that the cause was just. With all his tough-guy pretensions, what he really wanted to be remembered for was his idealism. On his first day as President he had called for Woodrow Wilson's desk and he used it while he was in the Oval Office; a portrait of Wilson graced the Cabinet room. He spoke often of his mother, and the quality that he recounted most about her was her gentleness; he seems to have missed her dreadfully when she left him when he was quite young to take care of an older brother dying of tuberculosis.

Of course, more than most, his close associates were familiar with the absence of any sense of proportion. His self-image of coolness in crisis was distorted by the dogged desperation with which he attacked his problems — born out of the fatalism that in the end, nothing ever worked as it was intended. His courage was all the more remarkable because it was not tied to a faith in ultimate success that distinguished leaders like de Gaulle or Churchill or Roosevelt.

My own feelings toward Nixon were commensurably complex. I recoiled at some of his crudities. I resented being constantly manipulated. I would have felt more comfortable had his words been less ambiguous or his methods more explicit. Yet I was deeply grateful for the opportunity he had given me to serve my country, first as national security adviser, then as Secretary of State. Where outsiders saw a snarl, I saw the fear of rejection. What often appeared as deviousness I understood as a means to preserve his options in the face of inner doubt about his own judgment. Few men so needed to be loved and were so shy about the grammar of love. Complexity was his defense, a sense of inadequacy his secret shame, until they became second nature and produced what he feared most. I had seen the lonely process of decision-making: the struggle with self-doubt and the frequently brave outcome. In *White House Years,* I summed up my feelings about Nixon the night he announced the Vietnam cease-fire, and eighteen months later as the end of the Nixon Presidency approached I felt the words even more deeply:

What extraordinary vehicles destiny selects to accomplish its design. This man, so lonely in his hour of triumph, so ungenerous in some of his motivations, had navigated our nation through one of the most anguishing periods in its history. Not by nature courageous, he had steeled himself to conspicuous acts of rare courage. Not normally outgoing, he had forced himself to rally his people to its challenge. He had striven for a revolution in American foreign policy so that it would overcome the disastrous oscillations between overcommitment and isolation. Despised by the Establishment, ambiguous in his human perceptions, he had yet held fast to a sense of national honor and responsibility, determined to prove that the strongest free country had no right to abdicate. What would have happened had the Establishment about which he was so ambivalent shown him some love? Would he have withdrawn deeper into the wilderness of his resentments, or would an act of grace have liberated him? By now it no longer mattered. Enveloped in an intractable solitude, at the end of a period of bitter division, he nevertheless saw before him a vista of promise to which few statesmen have been blessed to aspire. He could envisage a new international order that would reduce lingering enmities, strengthen friendships, and give new hope to emerging nations. It was a worthy goal for America and mankind. He was alone in his moment of triumph on a pinnacle, that was soon to turn into a precipice. And yet with all his insecurities and flaws he had brought us by a tremendous act of will to an extraordinary moment when dreams and possibilities conjoined.[2]

In the months of Nixon's final torment I often reflected on a journey through his youth that he and I took in the summer of 1970. The incursion into Cambodia was behind us but its scars had not yet healed. Nixon was in San Clemente recovering from the ordeal of defending his decision — in his view essential if we were to extricate ourselves from Indochina honorably — against an extraordinary outburst of domestic violence and abuse. On a Saturday afternoon I had stopped off at the hotel in Laguna Beach that served as the press center when the ubiquitous White House switchboard operator reached me. Would I like to drive with the President and Bebe Rebozo to Los Angeles? We could have dinner at Chasen's restaurant. The operator knew no precedent of an assistant's refusing a Presidential invitation of this kind. She informed me that the President had already left and would pick me up shortly; I should be waiting on the sidewalk in front of the shops and restaurants opposite the hotel.

It turned out that the President did not wish to go directly to Los Angeles. He had his heart set on showing Rebozo and me his birthplace in Yorba Linda. So we set off in a brownish unmarked Lincoln, driven by a Secret Service agent, to the unprepossessing house where Nixon was born. Until we reached it, it was like any other sentimental journey. For Nixon's companions, the significance of the trip was the honor of being invited; we could not possibly share the emotion that obviously gripped him. We walked around the outside of the house when suddenly Nixon noticed that two cars had followed us; one was filled with Secret Service agents, the other contained the obligatory press pool.

All of this — Secret Service and press — was standard procedure anytime the President moved; it was indeed a minimum Presidential entourage. But Nixon lost his composure as I had never seen him do before or after. He insisted that all follow-up cars leave immediately; he would not move so long as the Secret Service car and the journalists were in his motorcade. He did not want company. He was President and he was ordering privacy for himself. The orders were delivered at the top of his voice — itself an event so unprecedented that the Secret Service car broke every regulation in the book and departed, followed by the press pool.

Then, for a unique moment in his Presidency, Nixon was alone outside the Presidential compound with a friend, an associate, and one single Secret Service driver. I am sure that the mouths of many terrorists would have watered had they known what easy targets were available to them that Saturday afternoon. The President of the United States and his national security adviser, between them possessing almost all the national security secrets of the country worth having, were cruising around Southern California with only a single bodyguard who had to double in brass as a chauffeur.

When we were alone again Nixon became more relaxed than I have ever seen him. He and I sat in the rear of the car, Rebozo in front, as we headed toward the town of Whittier. Nixon pointed out the gasoline station his family had run and had sold just before oil was discovered on their former property. He showed us the hotel where a discouraged Republican party had canvassed volunteers to run for the United States Congress against the presumably unbeatable incumbent Democrat of the district — itself an almost unprecedented procedure. Nixon had applied because he had nothing better to do. To his surprise, he had been selected, and he won an election that even his associates had conceded to his opponent.

We drove around Whittier College, where he recalled the teachers who had been an inspiration to him. For once, I did not think that there was any *arrière pensée*. The Nixon in the backseat was not the convoluted, guarded, driven politician I knew from the Oval Office, but a gentler man, simpler in expression, warmer in demeanor.

And as he was talking softly and openly for the first time in our acquaintance, it suddenly struck me that the guiding theme of his discourse was how it had all been accidental. There was no moral to the tale except how easily it could have been otherwise — a theme much more apparent to Nixon than to me. For the lesson I had been drawing from what I heard was that only a man of unusual discipline and resilience could have marched the path from candidate in a hopeless Congressional race to the Presidency of the United States. Clearly, this was not the way it seemed to Nixon, who, that afternoon in Whittier, acted as if he belonged among his simple origins in a way he never did in any of the Presidential settings.

I have always thought of this car ride through Southern California as one clue to the Nixon enigma. "Give me a place to stand and I shall move the earth," said Archimedes. Nixon sought to move the world but he lacked a firm foothold. That, I suppose, is why he always turned out to be slightly out of focus. His very real gentleness, verging on sentimentality, ran the risk of sliding into mawkishness. And his cult of the tough guy was both exaggerated and made irrelevant because it had to be wrung from essentially resistant material. Nixon accomplished much but he never was certain that he had earned it.

As we headed for Los Angeles, Nixon suddenly conceived the idea that Rebozo and I should see not only his origin but how far he had come. He wanted to drive by the residence where he had lived for two years and recovered his sense of direction after losing the Presidential election of 1960. He would direct the driver; it would take us only a few minutes out of the way.

It soon emerged that Nixon had no precise idea of the location of that residence. He remembered it was in a big development in some canyon near the Beverly Hills Hotel. We explored every canyon and the streets leading off them. We searched for well over an hour. But try as we might, we could not find the house. And in the process of looking, the relaxed, almost affable, Nixon gave way to the agitated, nervous Nixon with whom I was familiar. He was at ease with his youth; he could recount his struggles; he could not find the locus of his achievements.

Nixon had set himself a goal beyond human capacity: to make himself over entirely; to create a new personality as if alone among all of mankind he could overcome his destiny. But the gods exacted a fearful price for this presumption. Nixon paid, first, the price of congenital insecurity. And ultimately he learned what the Greeks had known: that the worst punishment can be having one's wishes fulfilled too completely. Nixon had three goals: to win by the biggest electoral landslide in history; to be remembered as a peacemaker; and to be accepted by the "Establishment" as an equal. He achieved all these objectives at the end of 1972 and the beginning of 1973. And he lost them all two months later — partly because he had turned a dream into an obsession. On his way to success he had traveled on many roads, but he had found no place to stand, no haven, no solace, no inner peace. He never learned where his home was.

One More Crisis

BY July, we were all trapped in the wait for the court cases, the investigations, and the impeachment proceedings that, each following its own momentum, seemed to be coming to a head simultaneously as if guided by an invisible hand. Even international relations slowed down. At home, we had to fight off criticisms that the summit had failed and détente was in jeopardy because we had not concluded a SALT agreement. But had we succeeded, the charge would have been that we had concluded agreements on unfavorable terms to save the President. It would have been an exacerbation of the process that had drained us for over a year. Since no agreement is possible that does not involve a balance of concessions, the group arguing that better terms were available would always have the better of the debate. Who could not claim that more might have been accomplished — especially in a Presidency whose credibility had collapsed? By July 1974 only 13 percent of the public still thought that Nixon was doing a good job as President — the lowest figure since polls were taken.

The controversy over SALT was symbolized by the supposed conflict between Schlesinger and me. We both denied major substantive disagreements, which was true, and implied that there was no dispute, which was not. It was an old-fashioned struggle for turf, made insoluble by the absence of a functioning Presidency. It is not necessary for present purposes to rehearse the debate. The fact is that it should never have occurred. But it illustrated the precariousness of America's position in the world in the summer of 1974. Our system requires a strong President to establish coherence; as Presidential authority disintegrates, so does the ability to settle disputes. The prospects for the Administration were frightening if impeachment proceedings were to be added to the existing malaise.

Foreign countries were watching with awe and confusion the growing paralysis of one of the key supports of the international system. They could not believe what was happening; except for a few especially sophisticated leaders, all thought that the harassment of Nixon might subside at any moment. And even when during the course of July the unthinkable became more and more obvious, our adversaries showed amazing restraint — in what was perhaps the greatest tribute to the foreign policy of the Nixon Administration.

We, especially Nixon, had been talking about a "structure of peace" for years, perhaps to a point where critics were gagging at the phrase. No doubt Nixon did not moderate his customary hyperbole as he grew more and more desperate. And yet when he was reduced to impotence, when every minor-league American bureaucrat dared to challenge him with impunity, foreign leaders almost without exception remained silent and respectful. Some did so because they expected him to recover, but for the vast majority it was because they had been drawn into the orbit of our design. Almost all thought that they were better off with the international system as it existed than with any alternative that they could imagine. The Soviets wanted to preserve the option of détente as a counterweight to China; the Chinese needed us as a counterweight to the Soviets; the industrial democracies harassed us when it was safe but their new leadership relied on us for security and progress; the nations of the Middle East had no alternative to the peace process under our aegis. We had built better than we perhaps knew; the greatest tribute Nixon received was the quiescence of the nations of the world while he lay mortally wounded.

Only in the Aegean, where the primeval hatreds of Greeks and Turks flared again on Cyprus, did we have to endure an international crisis in those last weeks of Nixon's office, and it was not that they took advantage of Nixon's plight or even calculated it in their decisions. It was an eruption of old frustrations and oppressions; but nonetheless it laid bare the vulnerabilities of a divided Administration with a President in no position to impose coherence. I must leave a full discussion of the Cyprus episode to another occasion, for it stretched into the Ford Presidency and its legacy exists unresolved today. I touch on it here only to the extent that it illuminated the fragility of our policymaking process and because it showed that foreign policy claimed our energies even as we were steeling ourselves for the final act of Nixon's tragedy.

Greeks and Turks first came into contact when the Turks burst out of Asia and systematically reduced the Byzantine Empire, finally occupying Constantinople in the year 1453 and later coming to rule Cyprus in 1571. From then on, the fates of the two peoples had been intertwined, generating hatreds out of reciprocal cruelties made more bitter by their inability to escape their interdependence. For a while, major offices of state in the Ottoman Empire were held by Greeks who were then better educated and more experienced; their conquerors relieved their frustrations by frequent pogroms until the Greek population in Turkey was to all practical purposes eliminated by massacre and expulsion in the early 1920s. The two nations continued to coexist (if that is the word), the

Greeks remembering Turkey's military predominance, the Turks obsessed by their fear of Greek intellectual subtlety — each convinced that in the end the other was out to rob it of its birthright; each seeing itself the victim and prepared to preempt fate by wreaking vengeance on its neighbor. The Greek-Turkish conflict has belonged to the blood feuds of history.

After World War II, the old enemies Greece and Turkey were allies in NATO with a common stake in the security of the eastern Mediterranean. But their atavistic bitternesses found a focus in the island of Cyprus, forty-four miles from mainland Turkey, with a population 80 percent Greek and about 20 percent Turk — a lethal cocktail.

As in many other nations of mixed nationalities, a tenuous civil peace had been possible while the island was under foreign rule. But when the British granted independence to the island in 1960, with Britain, Greece, and Turkey as guarantors of its internal arrangements, the subtle Greek Orthodox Archbishop Makarios III, leader of the Greek Cypriot community and of the campaign against British rule, found himself obliged to concede a degree of self-government to the Turkish minority, offensive to all his notions of government or nationality. He did not have his heart in it, and with independence he systematically reneged on what he had promised, seeking to create in effect a unitary state in which the Turkish minority would always be outvoted. The history of independent Cyprus was thus plagued by communal strife, and in 1967 Turkey's threat to intervene militarily was aborted only at the last moment by a strong warning from President Johnson. It had become since an article of faith in Turkish politics that this submission to American preferences had been unwise and would never be repeated. I had always taken it for granted that the next communal crisis in Cyprus would provoke Turkish intervention.

Makarios nevertheless continued to play with fire. In 1972 he introduced Czech arms on the island for the apparent purpose of creating a private paramilitary unit to counterbalance those set up by the constitution. In 1974 he again took on the Greek-dominated National Guard in an effort to bring them under his control. Greece was then governed by a military junta, violently anti-Communist, deeply suspicious of Makarios's flirtation with radical Third World countries, which it took to be a sign of his pro-Communist sympathies. It therefore encouraged plans to overthrow him and install in Cyprus a regime more in sympathy with Greece, oblivious to the fact that an overthrow of the constitutional arrangements on Cyprus would free Turkey of previous restraints. Ankara was, to be sure, at least as disquieted by the trend of Makarios's policy as Athens, but to the Turks the preferred solution was a federal state amounting to de facto partition. Uniting Cyprus with Greece would in Turkish eyes doom the Turkish community and jeopardize Turkish security interests on the island. No reassurance was possible. After all, the Turks remembered how they had handled a similar problem five decades earlier by exterminating the minority.

On July 15 — six days after my return from the Soviet Union and Europe — Makarios was overthrown in a coup d'état just as he returned from a weekend in the mountains; he was nearly assassinated. He was replaced by an unsavory adventurer, Nikos Sampson, known as a strong supporter of union with Greece. A crisis was now inevitable.

There was nothing we needed less than a crisis — especially one that would involve two NATO allies. Whomever we supported and whatever the outcome, the eastern flank of the Mediterranean would be in jeopardy. And our government was neither cohesive enough, nor did the President have sufficient authority, to sustain a prolonged period of tension.

The issue immediately became entangled in our domestic politics. Greece was a military dictatorship; hence, all groups critical of our approach to human rights urged us to turn on it as the instigator of the upheaval; failure in Cyprus would, it was hoped, produce the overthrow of the hated Greek colonels. This view was held passionately not only among traditional opponents of Nixon; it was the dominant conviction in the State Department; the Secretary of Defense moved toward it increasingly as the week progressed.

To me the issue was more complicated. I thought it most unlikely that Turkey would tolerate the union of Cyprus with Greece. That Turkey was driving toward a showdown was obvious — at least to me. A good test of whether a country is seeking a pretext for military action or a basis for a compromise is whether it can live with its own proposals. If they are inconsistent with its real interests and with its previous stands, one can be pretty certain that a *casus belli* is being prepared. That was the case with the Turkish position in the first week of Makarios's overthrow. It would be difficult to imagine a foreign leader more unpopular in Turkey than Makarios. He had been blamed, with considerable justice, for the plight of the Turkish minority on Cyprus. During previous crises Turkey had insisted on his removal. Suddenly Ankara put forward the demand that Makarios be returned to office. The motivation had to be that Ankara calculated Athens was even more reluctant to see Makarios restored; Ankara presumably was counting on using the Greek refusal as a pretext to move its army into Cyprus. (There was also the slight technical problem that for about a day no one knew whether Makarios was alive and if so where he could be found.)

Turkey's demands left little doubt that it was planning to intervene. Explicit condemnation of the Greek junta by the United States would have turned a likelihood into a certainty. A Greek debacle was in my view probable; only a regime that had lost touch with reality would take on both Makarios and Turkey over the Cyprus question. My view, as I was to explain to a WSAG meeting of July 21, was that the Greek government was unlikely to survive its follies. That made it all the more necessary that the United States not be seen in Greece as the agent of its humiliation. At the same time, we could not without cost resist a Turkish invasion because that would be considered as objectively supporting the Greek junta. In any case, only the threat of American military action could have prevented a Turkish landing on the island; this was an impossibility. My consultations with Congressional leaders produced the unanimous advice that we should not get involved at all. We could not avoid diplomatic engagement in a NATO crisis, but in the last three weeks of Nixon's Presidency we were in no position to make credible threats or credible promises — the instrumentalities of diplomacy.

During the week of July 15 I therefore dispatched Joe Sisco to London, Ankara, and Athens. Britain, as one of the guarantor powers, was seeking to mediate between the parties. Sisco's mission was to help Britain start a negotiating process that might delay a Turkish invasion and enable the structure under Sampson in Cyprus to fall of its own weight. But Turkey was not interested in a negotiated solution; it was determined to settle old scores. On July 19 it invaded Cyprus, meeting unexpectedly strong resistance.

We faced a strategic dilemma. We wanted to keep both Greece and Turkey in the Alliance; we sought to prevent unbridgeable fissures. The dominant view of the bureaucracy during the first week was expressed at the WSAG meeting of July 21. Two days after the Turkish invasion of Cyprus had started, Schlesinger urged a conspicuous dissociation from the Greek government, a withdrawal of American nuclear weapons from Greece, and an end to home-porting arrangements in Greece for the US Sixth Fleet. To force my hand the proposal was helpfully leaked to the *Washington Post*. For my part, I was convinced that the junta in Athens would not last out the week but I was certain that if we were perceived as the cause of Greece's debacle we would pay for it for years to come. Whatever one's view of the wisdom of our previous policy toward the Greek junta, a Greek-Turkish war was not the moment to dissociate ourselves. Our immediate task was to stop the war; to remove nuclear weapons from *Greece* while Turkey invaded Cyprus would eliminate all restraints on Turkish military action. I also feared that if we once withdrew nuclear weapons we might never be able to return them — setting a dangerous precedent.

Nixon was in San Clemente and, while I briefed him regularly, he was in no position to concentrate or decide between my basic view and Schlesinger's, especially not in a rapidly changing situation. The preoccupation with Watergate had reached a point where we were losing even the ability to transmit papers bearing on vital foreign policy matters instantaneously between the President and the White House. So many documents relating to Watergate were being moved over the circuits to San Clemente that on July 19 I had had to ask for special priority for cables bearing on the Cyprus crisis.

During the night of July 21–22, we forced a cease-fire by threatening Turkey that we would move nuclear weapons from forward positions — especially where they might be involved in a war with Greece. It stopped Turkish military operations while Turkey was occupying only a small enclave on the island; this created conditions for new negotiations slated to start two days hence, with the Turkish minority obviously in an improved bargaining position and with some hope of achieving more equitable internal arrangements.

On July 22, the junta in Athens was overthrown and replaced by a democratic government under the distinguished conservative leader Constantine Karamanlis. Within days, the mood in America changed. The very groups that had castigated us for our reluctance to assault Greece now wanted us to go into all-out opposition to Turkey. We were being asked to turn against Turkey over a crisis started by Greece, to gear our policies to the domestic structures of the governments in Athens and Ankara regardless of the origins or merits of the dispute on Cyprus, to take a one-sided position regardless of our interest in easing the conflict between two strategic allies in the eastern Mediterranean, and to do all this in the very weeks that the United States government was on the verge of collapse. For two weeks we maintained our tightrope act, but during the weekend following Nixon's resignation the crisis erupted again, culminating in a second Turkish invasion of the island. While Ford struggled to restore executive authority over the next months, a freewheeling Congress destroyed the equilibrium between the parties we had precariously maintained; it legislated a heavy-handed arms embargo against Turkey that destroyed all possibility of American mediation — at a cost from which we have not recovered to this day.

But even in the third week of July it was clear that we were losing control over events. Foreign policy, as I have repeatedly stated, is the mastery of nuance; it requires the ability to relate disparate elements into a pattern. That coherence was rapidly disintegrating.

Our internal disputes were no longer geared to substance; they had become a struggle for preeminence. Schlesinger and I battled over turf continually; every issue, whether it was SALT or human rights or Cyprus, became a source of tension between us. The bureaucratic struggle reduced my dominance only to create a deadlock; for it could not be resolved by a President *in extremis* three thousand miles away. The merit of our respective positions is now irrelevant. I made the key point to Haig on the morning of July 21: It was impossible to keep going through crises with the procedures we were now following; sooner or later something would get out of hand. The unspoken corollary was that our own constitutional crisis had to be brought to an end if the nation was to avoid catastrophe.

The End of the Road

THE climax finally announced itself. It was heralded by the United States Supreme Court. On July 24 it ruled by a vote of 8 to 0 that executive privilege, though a valid doctrine grounded in our constitutional history, could not prevail over the impartial administration of justice. The President must turn over to Judge John Sirica the sixty-four tapes subpoenaed for the cover-up trial of the six former White House aides. Nixon's lawyer announced his compliance at once. But for those of us who knew Nixon's way of talking, the ruling spelled the end; if the tapes did not prove legally fatal, they would be politically.

Yet Nixon, still in San Clemente, would not discuss Watergate during our frequent daily conversations, or at least did not refer to the substance of the issues. We went over the day's foreign policy events in a routine fashion. Now and then he would mention one or another Congressman — usually a conservative Democrat from the South — to whom it would be useful to pay attention; the vote in the House on impeachment was expected to be that close.

I began a discreet investigation into the mechanics of impeachment. According to the Constitution, the House of Representatives by a majority vote may impeach, or accuse, the President of specific charges — acting much like a grand jury in our judicial system. The Senate then sits as trial judge and jury presided over by the Chief Justice of the United States; a two-thirds vote is necessary to convict, that is, to remove the President from office.

Nixon's fate thus resolved itself into arithmetic: whether there was a majority in the House for impeachment and whether one-third plus one could be mobilized in the Senate to oppose. Senator Jacob Javits told me that he did not expect the Senate trial to start before November; the outcome would not be certain until late January. It was a horrendous prospect. In the light of what we had just been through, a further five-month period with even weaker executive authority was unthinkable. Worse, Javits predicted that Nixon would be forced to be "in court" for the greater part of the trial.

I therefore intended to ask Nixon to institute a small group to act in his place when he was not available, with his authority and subject always to his review. The group I had in mind was Ford, Schlesinger, Simon (now Treasury Secretary), Haig, and me. I intended to suggest that the bipartisan Congressional leadership — Senate Democratic leader

Mike Mansfield and Republican leader Hugh Scott, Speaker of the House Carl Albert and House Republican leader John Rhodes — be invited to meet with this group twice a week to be briefed on major policy issues. Such a system could at best keep matters reasonably under control although it was quite unsuited for crisis management or serious planning. Luckily, it never had to be created.

Meanwhile, foreign policy claimed its routine. And I report its manifestations here because they in fact took more of my time than the denouement of the Nixon Presidency. The day after the Supreme Court ruling, West German Foreign Minister Hans-Dietrich Genscher paid his first official visit to America. Naturally he wanted to meet the President. Genscher and I had met for the first time on June 11, the day of my Salzburg press conference. He had invited me to nearby Bad Reichenhall on German soil to begin the process of improving German-American relations frayed by the Year of Europe and the vacillations of the end of the Brandt period. Genscher was then a novice in foreign policy, without either prior experience or independent study. Still, I was impressed by his strong, self-confident manner and perceptive questions. It was not the ideal day for a calm discussion. He did not bring up my press conference; I did not raise it. Only as I was leaving did I say that I had had to lance the boil; I did not think the new investigation I had requested would end in my resignation; if I had thought that, it would not have been worth staying in the first place. I had also briefed him in early July, as I have noted, on my way back from the Moscow summit.

Genscher turned out to be the rare phenomenon of a man who, coming to diplomacy late in life, shows an extraordinary talent for it. He understood that Germany's exposed position permitted no complicated maneuvers. He made his impact by steadiness, good judgment, shrewdness, decency, and the ability to evoke confidence. Through my term in office and that of my successors, he became known as a leader to take with the utmost seriousness; one whose views were reassuring when supportive and a welcome warning on the few occasions we disagreed. For me, our personal friendship has been one of the rewards of my public life.

On this occasion I took him, on July 25, to San Clemente to meet Nixon. On the way west, we stopped in North Dakota to inspect a field of Minuteman missiles and the one ABM installation remaining (since closed for budgetary reasons). It was the first time I had seen either. (The principal reason for my visit was to help out Senator Milton Young of North Dakota, ranking member of the Senate Appropriations Committee, who was in a fight for reelection and had been a staunch supporter.)

There is always something abstract and esoteric in the contemplation of nuclear strategy. The visit made it more tangible and at the same time, paradoxically, more abstract. It is an awesome sight. Flying over fields of missiles capable of destroying humanity on the basis of a single decision by an individual of normal fallibility, whatever the safeguards, evokes a latent uneasiness about the human condition. Here are weapons in a state of readiness for which there is no precedent in history, yet for whose use and consequence no practical experience is possible. The abstract relationship of decision-makers to the weapons on which their strategy depends is shown by the attitude toward testing them. No Minuteman has ever been test-fired from an operational silo even without a warhead — no Secretary of Defense has wanted to run the slight risk that some malfunction might cause a burning rocket to fall on American territory; all test-firings have been from a special silo at Vandenberg Air Force Base on the Pacific coast. No more than one Minuteman at a time has ever been tested, despite the fact that our strategy depends on multiple launches in an extremity. (Of course the Soviets must have similar problems.) All this suggests the inherent fragility of fashionable theories of hair-trigger response or reliance on general nuclear war.

Moreover, the abstractness of these weapons has another dimension: Their vulnerability requires that they be kept in a state of readiness so high that it cannot be increased; hence, they are almost useless for diplomatic purposes. In a crisis one cannot raise their alert status — as, for example, with bombers — to warn that things are getting serious. In the Middle East alert of October 1973, one component of our forces whose readiness was not enhanced and that therefore curiously did not contribute to this diplomatic pressure was the backbone of America's military power, the 1,054 intercontinental ballistic missiles in our arsenal.

No previous generation of statesmen has had to conduct policy in so unknown an environment at the border line of Armageddon. Very few top leaders (Nixon being a notable exception) have had as many hours to study the issues of nuclear strategy as the experts have had years. They risk becoming the victims of the simplifiers — mindless pacifism on the left and on the right the equally mindless insistence on treating the new technology as conventional. Will we, I wondered, forever maintain the sense of proportion that does not stake the fate of mankind on a single judgment — and the fortitude to shun the pacifist temptation that will abandon the world to the most ruthless? Genscher and I toured the facilities impressed by the professionalism and dedication of the personnel and by the technical marvel of both weapons and warning installations. But they did not relieve the unease at the fact that the survival of our civilization must be entrusted to a technology so out of scale with our experience and with our capacity to grasp its implications.

I introduced Genscher to Nixon on July 26, two days after the Supreme Court decision. I was shocked by the ravages just a week had wrought on Nixon's appearance. His coloring was pallid. Though he seemed composed, it clearly took every ounce of his energy to conduct a serious conversation. He sat on the sofa in his office looking over the Pacific, his gaze and thought focused on some distant prospect eclipsing the issues we were bringing before him. He permitted himself no comment about his plight. He spoke rationally, mechanically, almost wistfully. What he said was intelligent enough and yet it was put forth as if it no longer mattered: an utterance rather than an argument. The night before, he had addressed the nation on television about inflation — another incongruity in the effort to maintain some semblance of normality twenty-four hours after the devastating Supreme Court decision. Genscher congratulated Nixon on his remarks; the President looked at him with grateful melancholy, more like a professor being praised for an academic paper than a chief of government about to implement a program.

After Genscher and I met the press — and he replied noncommittally to a question about a possible Presidential trip to Germany — we walked along the edge of the cliff overlooking the Pacific. "How long can this go on?" asked Genscher suddenly. It was the key question. What would happen to our allies if the Presidency remained paralyzed? Genscher wanted to know. What about the structure of peace, so banal in its rhetoric, so fateful in its reality? I made reassuring noises that there was bound to be an early resolution, that we were prepared to act decisively as we had in the October alert. It was all make-believe. The question, once having been asked, hung in the air. In a way it supplied its own answer.

That afternoon I broke an unspoken rule between Haig and myself. We had both shied away from ever mentioning the possibility of Nixon's resignation; it had become an implicit agreement that it would not do to show doubt even to each other; it was our duty to keep the government going. But things had gone too far; a catastrophe was clearly imminent. So in his little office overlooking the Pacific, right next to the President's, I asked Haig Genscher's question: "How long can this go on?" Haig seemed tired. He did not know how it would end, he said. He was unfamiliar with the tapes being turned over; they were being reviewed. But, like me, he was convinced that a "smoking gun" would emerge sooner or later, if not from this batch then from some other. Nixon said too many things that he did not really mean to be able to withstand this kind of scrutiny. What did I think Haig's duty was? I had worked with Haig long enough to be sure that he had thought deeply about it and had pretty much decided on a course of action. The question was more designed to gather intelligence than to seek guidance.

I said that since the end of Nixon's Presidency was now inevitable, it was in the national interest that it occur as rapidly as possible. Haig and I had a special responsibility to end the agony if that was in our power and to bring about a smooth transition. And yet we were in a difficult position. An impeachment trial had to be avoided at nearly any cost. But Nixon's fall must not occur as the result of a push by his closest associates. If at all possible, he had to resign because his own judgment of the national interest dictated it. Or else he should be brought to this realization by elected officials. We who owed our governmental positions to Nixon had a duty to sustain him in his ordeal; perhaps this would give him the strength for what must be done — after all, he had never failed at a moment of decision. We should not discuss the plight of the President with those able to affect his fate or lend ourselves to the impression that his closest aides were wavering. Our service would consist of loyalty to the President. The end — for the sake of everyone's perception of our country — could not be the destruction of the President by his own appointees.

Haig said he agreed completely; he surely had come to the same conclusion independently. When the critical point arrived, he added, he would almost certainly know this before I did. He would then get in touch with me. He counted on me to stand shoulder to shoulder with him as we had so often in the past.

Only those who lived through the fervid atmosphere of those months can fully appreciate the debt the nation owes Al Haig. By sheer willpower, dedication, and self-discipline, he held the government together. He more than anyone succeeded in conveying the impression of a functioning White House. He saw to it that decisions emerged from predictable processes. He served his President loyally but he never forgot his duty to his country. To be sure, only a man of colossal self-confidence could have sustained such a role. His methods were sometimes rough; his insistence on formal status could be grating. But the role assigned to Haig was not one that could be filled by choirboys. He had to preserve the sinews of America for its indispensable mission of being the last resort of the free, the hope of the oppressed, and the one country that with all its turbulent vitality could be relied upon to walk the paths of mercy. It is not necessary that in an hour of crisis America's representatives embody all of these qualities so long as they enable our country to do so.

Haig performed unique services before and after the fateful last month of the Nixon Presidency. He will never deserve better of the Republic than during that tragic and frenetic period when he sustained the President while moving him toward the resignation that Nixon dreaded, resisted, and yet knew increasingly to be inevitable. Haig kept the faith with his President and he kept it with the institutions of this country. Without him, I doubt that a catastrophe could have been avoided.

By now the juggernaut bearing down on Nixon was unstoppable. The very next day, July 27, a Saturday, the House Judiciary Committee passed its first impeachment article by a vote of 27 to 11, with six Republicans joining all the Democrats. The charge was obstruction of justice. I watched the proceedings on television for a few minutes and I was sick about our country and about the personal horror that had befallen the President with whom I had worked for five and a half years. I could not bear the righteous moralizing of the commentators or the self-serving comments of some of the Congressmen even as I realized — and perhaps because of it — that had I been on that committee my duty would have been to vote with the majority. On July 29, the Committee approved its second article of impeachment, charging the President — by a vote of 28 to 10 — with abuse of power. That day the formation of a committee called Conservatives for the Removal of the President was announced. All the old bastions were crumbling. The Senate was getting ready for the impeachment trial by asking its Rules Committee to review relevant rules and precedents. On July 30, the House Committee voted a third article of impeachment — by a vote of 21 to 17 — charging the President with unconstitutionally defying its subpoenas. On July 31, John Ehrlichman was sentenced to twenty months to five years for conspiracy and perjury. The personal tragedies were mounting. In destroying himself, Nixon had wrecked the lives of almost all who had come into contact with him.

The President had returned to Washington on July 28. On July 31, Haig called me for an urgent appointment. It was one of the rare occasions he came to the State Department. Usually we met in his office at the White House after some interdepartmental meeting I had attended in the Situation Room. He wasted no time. The "smoking gun" had been found; one of the tapes turned over the day before to the Special Prosecutor — an Oval Office conversation between Nixon and Haldeman on June 23, 1972, less than a week after the Watergate break-in — left no doubt that Nixon was familiar with the cover-up; he may in fact have ordered it. Impeachment was now certain, conviction highly probable. We needed to coordinate our efforts. Should he inform defenders of Nixon not to go too far out on a limb? I said that the tape was bound to become public. Either the Special Prosecutor or the House Judiciary Committee was certain to leak it; the White House might consider preempting this by publishing the tape itself with whatever explanatory comment might be possible. Approaching any of Nixon's defenders was not Haig's job, I counseled; in the longer term it would make him the villain. Haig's role now — and to the extent possible mine — was to ease Nixon's decision to resign. The most important task before him — which no one else could carry out — was to give Nixon the psychological support to do the necessary.

Haig was in touch with me every day thereafter. Usually I started my day at the White House in a brief meeting with him. On Thursday,

August 1, he said matters were heading toward resignation though the Nixon family was violently opposed. On Friday, August 2, he told me that Nixon was digging in his heels; it might be necessary to put the 82nd Airborne Division around the White House to protect the President. This I said was nonsense; a Presidency could not be conducted from a White House ringed with bayonets. Haig said he agreed completely; as a military man it made him heartsick to think of the Army in that role; he simply wanted me to have a feel for the kinds of ideas being canvassed. A big meeting was taking place over the weekend at Camp David, including Nixon's closest confidants (which clearly did not include me) to chart the course. Whatever the decision, the damaging tape would be released on Monday, August 5, to give the White House an opportunity to put it into perspective. Nixon would not make his final decision until he could judge the public reaction. I wondered then, was the tape more marginal than Haig had at first believed? Haig did not show me a transcript, saying it was just then being prepared. I was somewhat at a loss to judge whether months of harassment had caused Haig to overreact or whether we really were at the end of the line.

We were heading for some kind of catharsis in substantial ignorance of its nature. I knew that those who had been working on Watergate matters full time were by now inured to the public impact; they had seen so many climaxes that they could not believe any one revelation could be the final one. And there is a momentum to power and to the office of the Presidency that makes it hard to face the fact — even when one knows it intellectually — that a term in office is drawing to a close. The routine of decision creates the illusion that authority is undiminished even when it has nearly evaporated. That inability to come to grips emotionally with the end of one's power — so noticeable when a Presidential term draws to a close in the normal way — was even stronger as the Nixon Presidency was collapsing.

I suspected that Haig's judgment of the impact of the tapes was cor- rect. Still, I spent the weekend in my office not preparing for the transfer of power but getting ready for testimony before the Senate Foreign Relations Committee scheduled for the following Thursday —August 8 — on the subject of détente. The Committee's Chairman, Senator Fulbright, had called the hearings weeks before to permit a balanced, philosophical exploration of East-West relations. Our opponents from both sides of the spectrum jumped at the opportunity to assault Nixon's foreign policy. Former servants of liberal administrations as well as hardliners were queuing up for the chance to testify — presumably not in defense of the Administration's approach.

On Sunday afternoon, August 4, Ron Ziegler's assistant Diane Sawyer stopped by to check some public relations items before going to

Camp David to confer with Ziegler. I asked her whether any of it made any sense in light of the tape about to be released. Beautiful, clever Diane was nonplussed. She had not read the tape but she was beginning to think that there would never be a climax, simply an endless hemorrhaging. "As likely as not," she said, "the tape will be drowned out in the political uproar."

By now we were living in a surrealistic world. Its victims had coexisted with a nightmare for so long that it had come to seem the natural state of affairs. They had reduced their peril to a banality and therefore could not believe in its culmination. On Monday morning, August 5, I talked to Nixon. He complimented me on the monthly meetings I had arranged with the leadership of the House of Representatives. Still, he warned, I had to remember most of the Democrats were enemies. The Democrats worth cultivating were the Southerners; I should invite them to a briefing. Vice President Ford, he was sure, would be happy to arrange it. Not a word about Watergate or the imminent release of the tape.

I called Ford as the President had requested. I have never asked Ford what he thought I was doing — probably that I was trying to bring myself to his attention prior to the imminent transfer of power. But he played it straight. Yes, he would be glad to arrange such a meeting with his old friends in the House of Representatives. No, he did not think it would do much good. In his view the battle in the House, while still close, was going to be lost. Yes, we should stay in touch; perhaps I should come by for one of my regular briefings soon.

Early in the afternoon, Ziegler called. He thought I should have a preview of a portion of the tape that would be released around 4:00 P.M. But the advance indication Ziegler brought to my attention did not concern Watergate. It was an exchange between Nixon and Haldeman on whether Rogers had to be included in a meeting in which I would brief Nixon upon my return from China or whether a photograph with Nixon would be enough. Ziegler thought I would be amused. I was appalled; there had to be more to the tape than this. If there was not, Haig had lost his sense of proportion; if there was, Ziegler had abandoned his grip on reality.

I had to wait until 4:00 P.M. to find out, like everyone else, when the tape transcript was released from the White House. Haig, it turned out, had a good sense of proportion. The transcript consisted of three conversations the President had had with Haldeman on June 23, 1972, a week after the break-in, in which he tried to order a halt to the FBI investigation at least partly because he wanted to protect people connected with his reelection committee. The transcript was released together with an extremely defensive Presidential statement admitting that the cover-up had political as well as national security implications, and that in concealing this conversation from his lawyers the President was responsible for a serious act of omission. But the President went on to say that despite these mistakes the basic truth remained, that when all the facts were brought to his attention he insisted on a full investigation and prosecution of those guilty: "I am firmly convinced that the record, in its entirety, does not justify the extreme step of impeachment and removal of a President. I trust that as the Constitutional process goes forward, this perspective will prevail."

It was much too late for that. The tape proved to be the last straw; it provided the pretext for all waverers to commit themselves to impeachment; it gave others a pretext to abandon Nixon. By now there had been too many shocks; everybody wanted to get it over with.

I was flooded with phone calls asking for my comments. I refused them. There were hints that I should condemn Nixon and thus force his resignation. I rejected them. I had charted my course. I would not turn on Nixon. Privately I would steer him gently — if that was possible — toward resignation.

At almost every crucial turning point in the Watergate saga, there seemed to be, incongruously, a dinner in my honor by the Chinese Liaison Office in Washington. On April 30, 1973, the Chinese had toasted the end of the Watergate affair when Nixon had dismissed Haldeman and Ehrlichman. On October 19, the evening before the "Saturday night massacre," they had been pleased at the thought that the Stennis compromise would be the end of the whole inscrutable business. Now on Monday evening, August 5, much of the Washington Establishment was assembled at the Chinese Liaison Office to honor me. But clearly Watergate — or at least the Nixon portion of it — was drawing to a close. There was no mood of celebration. Many of the dinner guests had worked to destroy Nixon; a few were even then gloating while piously protesting their dismay at the turn of events. But the dominant feeling was one of awe — beyond righteousness, transcending the hatreds of a lifetime. For a fleeting moment there was a sense that we might all be in danger, that the public spectacle of the destruction of a President was more than a society should be asked to endure.

Our Chinese hosts inquired whether there would be any change of policy if Nixon left office — the first time they entertained that possibility in speaking to me. They asked whether I would stay on; obviously, continuity was important to them. In my toast I assured them that the relationship between our two countries was based on permanent factors, but I was careful to use no language that the journalists present could interpret as taking the President's departure, by resignation or by impeachment, for granted.

By the end of the dinner the reaction on which Haig told me the President's decision would depend had become plain for all to see. Four

Republicans who had voted against impeachment on the Judiciary Committee said that they would vote for it when it reached the House floor. The Senate Republican Whip, Senator Robert Griffin, asked for Nixon's resignation. Vice President Ford dissociated himself in a statement saying that

the public interest is no longer served by repetition of my previously expressed belief that, on the basis of all the evidence known to me and the American people, the President is not guilty of an impeachable offense.

By now, I was approached by many concerned people urging me to bring matters to a head by threatening to resign unless Nixon did so; a few even suggested I invoke the Twenty-fifth Amendment to the Constitution and declare the President incapacitated. It was unthinkable. It was not only that a Presidential appointee had no moral right to force his President to resign; it would also be an unbearable historical burden for a foreign-born to do so. Though Haig told me that Nixon was still hesitating, I was convinced that in the end he would do the right thing and that it was important for the nation that he be perceived as having come to this conclusion on his own.

The next morning, Tuesday, August 6, a Cabinet meeting had been scheduled for some time for 10:00 A.M. It was shifted to 11:00 when the President was late reaching the Oval Office. When I entered the Cabinet Room it was obvious that as far as the Cabinet was concerned, Nixon was on his way out. Ford stood behind the Vice Presidential chair talking affably to the Cabinet members crowding around him — not, to put it mildly, the usual scene in Cabinet meetings with functioning Presidents, where the Vice President is treated politely but as a supernumerary. I was sitting in my place to the right of the Presidential chair when Nixon walked in, setting off a scramble for the seats. It was impossible not to feel sorry for this tormented man. I had spent too many hours with him not to sense his panic; I knew the bravado was only skin-deep.

Nixon began the meeting by saying that he wanted to talk about the most important subject before our nation; it was — bizarrely — inflation. He commented on how he had vetoed $35 billion of appropriations even during Watergate. The time ahead would be even tougher.

Abruptly he switched to the subject on everybody's mind. He thanked the Cabinet for having supported him through all difficulties. He was aware what a blow the tape of June 23, 1972, was to his case. He asked for nothing from his Cabinet officers they might find personally embarrassing or contrary to their convictions. They could serve their country and the President by running their departments well in the trying months ahead. As for him, he was aware that there was sentiment for his resignation. He had gone through difficult times before; he also had some achievements to his credit. He would have to consider not only his personal preferences but the office of the Presidency. If he resigned under pressure, he might turn our Presidential system into a parliamentary one in which a President could stay in office only so long as he could win a vote of confidence from the legislative branch.

That was, of course, hardly the issue. Impeaching a President was not the same as a parliamentary vote of no-confidence. I was convinced that Nixon was not delivering a political science lecture. What he sought in his oblique manner was a vote of confidence from his Cabinet, some expression of sympathy for his plight, a show of willingness to continue the fight, some statement that the battle to maintain his Presidency was in the national interest.

But all he encountered was an embarrassed silence. Papers were being shuffled amidst much fidgeting when Ford at last ended the impasse: "Mr. President, with your indulgence I have something to say." Nixon nodded, and Ford continued:

Everyone here recognizes the difficult position I'm in. No one regrets more than I do this whole tragic episode. I have deep personal sympathy for you, Mr. President, and your fine family. But I wish to emphasize that had I known what has been disclosed in reference to Watergate in the last twenty-four hours, I would not have made a number of the statements I made either as Minority leader or as Vice President. I came to a decision yesterday and you may be aware that I informed the press that because of commitments to Congress and the public, I'll have no further comment on the issue because I'm a party in interest. I'm sure there will be impeachment in the House. I can't predict the Senate outcome. I will make no comment concerning this. You have given us the finest foreign policy this country has ever had. A super job, and the people appreciate it. Let me assure you that I expect to continue to support the Administration's foreign policy and the fight against inflation.[3]

Nixon seemed to hear only the comment about inflation. He told Ford that his position was correct but it was not exactly clear that he was referring to Watergate. For he picked up a proposal Ford had floated publicly a few days earlier of an economic summit of business and labor leaders to overcome the inflation problem. There was some desultory talk on that subject as well as about the new agricultural appropriation bill. Attorney General William Saxbe interrupted: "Mr. President, I don't think we ought to have a summit conference. We ought to be sure you have the ability to govern." George Bush, then Chairman of the Republican National Committee, took up the theme. The Republican party, he said, was in a shambles; the forthcoming Congressional election threatened disaster. Watergate had to be brought to an end expeditiously. He did not say so but everyone in the room knew the corollary: The only way Watergate could end quickly was for Nixon to resign immediately.

It was cruel. And it was necessary. For Nixon's own appointees to turn on him was not the best way to end a Presidency. Yet he had left them no other choice. If he had genuinely sought the opinion of his Cabinet, he should have asked a few of the senior members to the Oval Office, perhaps individually. It would have been a much better gauge of the mood of his associates than this performance by desperate men impelled by the presence of their colleagues to make a record, unsure of what it was for which their support was being solicited. It was vintage Nixon. Fearing individual rejection, he had assembled the largest possible forum; hoping for a group vote of confidence, he sought to confront them with a fait accompli and thereby triggered their near-rebellion.

There is no body less likely to rebel than a President's Cabinet. Every member owes his appointment to the President and derives his authority from him. I have seen meetings between Presidents and senior Cabinet advisers since the days of John Kennedy; their normal tendency is deference, occasionally bordering on obsequiousness. If Nixon's Cabinet officers felt impelled to say what they did, they must have felt that they had been deceived on Watergate; if they felt free to say it, their judgment must have been that Nixon's days were numbered. But it was too unfeeling toward Nixon to allow this to continue, and it would also have deprived his resignation of one important message: that our institutions remained vital, our procedures democratic, our future infused by the national spirit of optimism of which Watergate threatened to rob us. More than enough had been said. The Cabinet owed it to the President not to deprive him of self-respect or his almost certain departure of dignity. So I took the floor as the senior Cabinet officer:

> We are not here to offer excuses for what we cannot do. We are here to do the nation's business. This is a very difficult time for our country. Our duty is to show confidence. We must demonstrate that the country can go through its constitutional processes. For the sake of foreign policy we must act with assurance and total unity. If we can do that, we can vindicate the structure of peace.[4]

Afterward, I went out to the driveway in front of the West Wing of the White House. Several Cabinet members were making statements as they were leaving. I stepped before the television cameras and sought to offer some reassurance to the American public and to convey steadiness to foreign governments:

> [T]he foreign policy of the United States is always and continues to be conducted on a bipartisan basis in the national interest and in the interest of world peace. When questions of peace or war are considered, no foreign government should have any doubts about the way in which foreign policy will be conducted.[5]

Around 12:45 P.M., I returned to the Oval Office unannounced. Alone with the President, I told Nixon of my comments to the media. Neither they nor my remarks to the Cabinet were the full story, I said. Having worked closely with the President for five and a half years, I owed it to him to say that his best service to the country now would be to resign. It was one thing to show fortitude in the face of political attack as he always had. But, I continued, an impeachment trial would preoccupy him for months, obsess the nation, and paralyze our foreign policy. It was too dangerous for our country and too demeaning to the Presidency. In my view, he should leave in a manner that appeared as an act of his choice. No matter what his decision, I concluded, I would not repeat these views outside the Oval Office.

Through all the tormented deliberations of the past week, Nixon had never sought my views. Nor did he do so now. He said he appreciated what I said. He would take it seriously. He would be in touch.

Then there was silence. Haig told me later in the day that Nixon was again tilting toward resignation; he was thinking about doing so late in the week and had asked speechwriter Ray Price to begin work on a resignation speech. But it would be a close call; in the evening his family might change his mind again. During the course of the afternoon I faced many opportunities to dissociate from the President publicly, thereby precipitating a crisis. I refused.

Later that evening, around 7:00 P.M., I received a phone call from Nixon that made no reference to what had occurred earlier in the day and was convulsing the nation. He had just — as a matter of a bureaucratic routine that followed its own drummer — received an Israeli request for long-term military assistance. He would disapprove it, he said. In fact, he would cut off all military deliveries to Israel until it agreed to a comprehensive peace. He regretted not having done so earlier; he would make up for it now. His successor would thank him for it. I should prepare the necessary papers.

Was it retaliation for our conversation of a few hours ago — on Nixon's assumption that my faith made me unusually sensitive to pressures on Israel? Or was it the expression of a long-held belief? Almost certainly both. I told Haig about the conversation. Nixon did not return to the subject; the relevant papers were prepared but never signed.

The next day, Wednesday, August 7, I began with two hours at my White House office so as to be available for talks with Haig and with the President. Nixon did not call for me, but I learned from Haig that he (Haig) was making "progress." He was encouraging old friends of the President who stood by him in difficult times to tell him frankly about the prospects in Congress. There would be a meeting that afternoon between the President and a delegation of key Republican leaders of the Congress: Senator Hugh Scott, Congressman John Rhodes, and

the respected conservative Senator Barry Goldwater. That might well
prove decisive.

Despite the mounting tension, I spent the day conducting foreign policy, partly to maintain the appearance of normality. I asked Brent Scowcroft and Larry Eagleburger — on a strictly personal basis — to prepare
what in bureaucratese is called a "scenario" for the eventuality of resignation: how to notify foreign governments and in what order; who
would get letters and what they would say; what foreign ambassadors,
if any, the new President should receive. I would submit this to Ford
for his approval once the decision was made.

I met with State Department staffers working on my détente statement
for the Senate Foreign Relations Committee; I had a meeting on the
Cyprus crisis; I lunched with Deputy Secretary of State Robert Ingersoll;
I had meetings with Jordanian Prime Minister Rifai and Moroccan Foreign Minister Dr. Ahmed Laraki. The consultations on next steps in the
Middle East could hardly have taken place under more preoccupying
circumstances.

At 5:58 P.M. Haig called me, interrupting a staff meeting on the Middle East with Sisco, Saunders, and Atherton. Could I come right over
to the White House? He did not tell me the reason. It was not necessary;
the decision had obviously been made. When I entered the Oval Office,
I found Nixon alone with his back to the room, gazing at the Rose
Garden through the bay windows. I knew the feeling from the time
when as a boy I had left the places where I had been brought up to
emigrate to a foreign land: attempting to say goodbye to something familiar and beloved, to absorb it, so to speak, so that one can never be
separated from it. In the process, sadly, one loses it imperceptibly because the self-consciousness of the effort destroys what can only be
possessed spontaneously. I knew the way each minute would now seem
infinitely precious and inexorably terminal; I felt his torment of seeking
both to prolong the moment by an act of will and to get it over with.
And I understood above all that there was absolutely nothing I could do
or say to ease the solitary pain he was experiencing.

Nixon turned when he heard me. He seemed very composed, almost
at ease. He had decided to resign, he said. The Republican leaders had
reinforced his instinct that there was not enough support left in the Congress to justify a struggle. The country needed some repose. He could
save our foreign policy only by avoiding a constitutional crisis. He would
speak to the nation the very next evening, Thursday, August 8; he would
resign effective at noon Friday, August 9. He hoped I would stay on to
help the new President continue the foreign policy of which he was so
proud.

The effort seemed to drain him and I feared for his composure. "History," I said, "will treat you more kindly than your contemporaries

have.'' What I remember is that at that moment I put my arm around him, bridging at the end the distance that had separated us on the human level all these years. Nixon does not report it in his memoirs. So perhaps it did not happen and I only felt like doing it. Or perhaps when writing his book Nixon did not want to admit that he needed solace, an emotion that he considered weak but that was in fact the most human reaction possible. It makes no real difference. At the moment of his fall, I felt for Nixon a great tenderness — for the tremendous struggle he had fought within his complex personality, for his anguish, his vulnerability, and for his great aspirations defeated in the end by weaknesses of character that became destructive because he had never come to grips with them. And if I did not in fact embrace him, I felt as if I had.

I was at home having dinner that same evening with Nancy, my children, and my dear friend the columnist Joseph Alsop when near 9:00 P.M. the phone rang. It was Nixon, alone in the Lincoln Sitting Room. Could I come over right away? There had been many calls like this on happier occasions, for example, the evening in 1971 when we knew that the China breakthrough had become a reality. This, however, was the end, not the beginning, of an adventure. And nothing could be more poignant than that at the close of his political career Nixon was left with the one associate about whom he was the most ambivalent, who made him uneasy even while counting on him to embody the continuity of his achievements.

I found Nixon sitting in a characteristic pose, slouched in the brown-covered chair, his legs on the settee, a yellow pad on his lap — a last crutch at the moment of despair. A reading lamp threw a thin beam on his chair; the rest of the room was in shadows broken only by the distant lights from the White House grounds. Other memories crowded in: I had called on the President there when the White House was besieged by passionate and vocal Vietnam protesters in the tens of thousands. Often I had sensed in that room the tangible aura of concentrated power. Now all was silence and solitude.

There are several accounts of our encounter that night. Nixon has me summoned from my office for an hour-long, relatively businesslike meeting. There is also extant an unfeeling account of an out-of-control President beating his fist on the carpet and railing against a cruel fate.[6] Neither fits with what I remember. There is no doubt that the meeting lasted nearly three hours. Nixon was not calm or businesslike. Nor was he out of control. He was shattered and he would not be worthy of further reflection had it been otherwise. But he was also in control of himself. There was no doubt he was deeply distraught; but I found his visible agony more natural than the almost inhuman self-containment that I had known so well. To have striven so hard, to have molded a public personality out of so amorphous an identity, to have sustained that superhuman effort only to end with every weakness disclosed and every error compounding the downfall — that was a fate of biblical proportions. Evidently the Deity would not tolerate the presumption that all can be manipulated; an object lesson of the limits of human presumption was necessary.

It was only natural, in a way, that Nixon should spend his last solitary evening in the White House seeking to distill some positive meaning from all those years of exertion. What would history say of him? That he made a difference? Was the world a safer place? Could we go over some of what we had done together? He kept pouring out questions, seeking some succor in his loneliness without either being able to believe what he was told or daring to reject it.

What is the meaning of a political life? How does one assess a trend in international politics? Even in the best of times, no judgment is more tenuous than an assessment of the significance of a statesman's actions. History is infinite compared to the human lifespan and the human perspective is even more foreshortened. Conventional wisdom often runs counter to the necessities of history, especially in times of great upheaval. The statesman has built truly only if he perceives the trend of events and puts it into the service of his purposes. For that task his scope is not unlimited. If he confines himself to riding with the trend, he will soon become irrelevant; if he goes beyond the capacity of his people, he will suffer shipwreck. If politics is the art of the possible, stature depends on going to the very limits of the possible. Great statesmen set themselves high goals yet assess unemotionally the quality of the material, human and physical, with which they have to work; ordinary leaders are satisfied with removing frictions or embarrassments. Statesmen create; ordinary leaders consume. The ordinary leader is satisfied with ameliorating the environment, not transforming it; a statesman must be a visionary and an educator. Blessed are the people whose leaders can look destiny in the eye without flinching but also without attempting to play God.

In his way, in the field of foreign policy Nixon met the test of his encounter with destiny. He understood what was at stake in the world. In the midst of unbridled emotions, he held fast to the truth that America's credibility must not be squandered, especially by its leaders. He fought for America's honor in distant jungles into which his predecessors had committed our troops, convinced that we had no right to abandon those who had depended on us and that tens of millions would curse the abdication his critics wished to impose on us. Against the rhetoric of a lifetime, he bravely affirmed the impossibility of an international order that excluded China, a quarter of the human race. Contrary to the simpler categories of an earlier period, he perceived that resistance to

Communist aggression requires a psychological foundation that positions America as the defender of a structure of peace open even to our adversaries should their ambitions yield to the imperatives of coexistence. He identified the need of the industrial democracies for a moral rededication to common purposes. He broke through the congealed hatreds of the Middle East and at the very height of his agony showed a road toward peace where all had been frustration. And he was beginning to educate the American people to the permanent challenge of responsible American involvement in the world so that they might avoid their historical oscillation between extremes of crusading and of abdication, between impetuosity and naiveté.

To be sure, Nixon had failed in the task of educator. He had been too unsure of himself to inspire his society not simply by technical virtuosity but by nobility of purpose. He had not met the moral challenge. And he was now paying the price for at a minimum neglecting that aspect of his trust.

Nixon in the final analysis had provoked a revolution. He had been reelected by a landslide in 1972 in a contest as close to being fought on ideological issues as is possible in America. Neither Nixon nor George McGovern was a charismatic figure, to put it mildly. The American people for once had chosen on philosophical grounds, not on personality. Overwhelmingly, they had chosen the moderate conservative course rather than the radical liberal. For reasons unrelated to the issues and unforeseeable by the people who voted for what Nixon represented, this choice was now being annulled — with as-yet unpredictable consequences.

So the verdict of history would be mixed. But I did not recite my caveats that evening; he would hear enough of that in the lonely months ahead — most tellingly from himself. I spoke less philosophically and more anecdotally than I write here but to the same effect. Occasionally Nixon interrupted to ask me to drink some brandy with him as we had done in happier days after some accomplishment. It was evident that he could hardly bear the thought of the indignity of a criminal trial for a former President. And neither, in truth, could I. If this came to pass, I told him, I would retire from office. And I believe I would have.

I kept returning to the theme that the judgment of history would be less severe, that it would remember his major achievements. But Nixon was not easily consoled. ''It depends who writes the history,'' he kept saying. He did not do justice to himself in these desperate hours. He had built better than he knew: Nearly a decade later, the basic categories of our public discourse on international affairs — China, the Mideast, SALT and the strategic balance, energy policy, new initiatives with allies — are still those established during the years of upheaval now coming to an end.

To professional Nixon-haters, all this may seem a maudlin rendition of a self-inflicted denouement that was entirely justified. I was too close to events to be able to see it that way. That night of August 7, in any event, I was nearly shattered by the human tragedy of the President seeking a solace beyond anybody's capacity to furnish.

Near midnight, after about two hours in the Lincoln Room, I prepared to leave. Nixon started escorting me to the elevator through the long hallway that bisects the Presidential residence. He stopped at the door of the Lincoln Bedroom. And he suggested that he and I pray there together. There was no good way to end that evening or to put a period to such a tempestuous career. And I am not sure that this was not as meaningful as any other and more appropriate than most.

Nixon's recollection is that he invited me to kneel with him and that I did so. My own recollection is less clear on whether I actually knelt. It is a trivial distinction. In whatever posture, I was filled with a deep sense of awe which seemed its own meaning so that I did not know exactly what to pray for. A passage from Aeschylus kept running through my mind — the verse that, as it happened, was a favorite of one of Nixon's obsessions, Robert Kennedy:

> *Pain that cannot forget*
> *falls drop by drop*
> *upon the heart*
> *until in our despair*
> *there comes wisdom*
> *through the awful*
> *grace of God.*

Shortly after midnight — after about a half hour in the Lincoln Bedroom — I returned to my White House office. Scowcroft and Eagleburger were waiting for me; Eagleburger had come over from the State Department to be on hand if I needed him. Within a few minutes, Nixon called. I must not remember our encounter that evening as a sign of weakness, he said. He hoped that I would keep in mind the times when he had been strong. How strange is the illusion by which men sustain themselves! There were many occasions that Nixon identified with strength that had made me uncomfortable. This evening when he had bared his soul I saw a man of tenacity and resilience. And so I told the stricken President that if I ever spoke of the evening, it would be with respect. He had honored me by permitting me to share with him his last free night in the White House where so many memories united us. And he had conducted himself humanly and worthily.

The next morning, Thursday, August 8, resignation was transmuted from the tragic to the routine. During my sojourn at my White House office, Haig told me that Nixon would see Ford at 11:00 A.M. to tell him formally of his plan to resign the next day. I worked on draft letters for the new President to send to key heads of government. I also went over a plan for the new President to meet all of the ambassadors accredited in Washington in regional groups. It was important to demonstrate that a firm hand was taking over. There were many interruptions. Some Cabinet members called asking whether they should publicly announce their readiness to continue in office. I counseled against it; they should not seem to try to deprive the new President of options. Friends offered advice on how to resist assaults on my position after the change of administration. I was not in the mood for it. I had seen the beginnings of two Presidential terms. I knew that whatever decisions the new President might make now about formal assignments would not determine the ultimate hierarchy. Months of jockeying for position were ahead of us. I had no stomach for going through it all again. Yet there would be no choice; all that would come soon enough. This day we had to keep to fundamentals.

At 12:30 P.M. Vice President Ford called. He was calm and steady. He had just left the President, he said. He wanted to waste no time in urging me to stay on and to "stand with me in these difficult times." These occasions always seemed to bring out the banal in me, or perhaps it is the incongruity between the immensity of the occasion and the nature of language. I said he could count on me: "You know the whole world depends on you, Mr. Vice President."

Nixon was still President. I owed it to him to inform him of my conversation with Ford. I reviewed with Nixon how I would suggest to Ford to take the helm and reassure foreign governments. Nixon was appreciative of the call though apathetic. He offered no comments on substance.

At 3:00 P.M. I called on the President-designate in his office at the Executive Office Building. I had known Gerald Ford for many years. Over a decade earlier he had been a guest lecturer to my National Security Policy Seminar at Harvard. Since coming to Washington I had briefed him regularly, first as Republican leader of the House, for the past nine months as Vice President. We have since become such close friends that it is difficult to reconstruct my feelings at the time. I liked him immensely. Even then I knew he was a good and decent man. I had no idea how he would perform as President and almost certainly neither did he. But he seemed at ease, neither overawed nor falsely boastful. He urged me again to stay on and referred to the fact that we had always gotten along well. I pointed out that it was not his job to get along with me; it was my job to get along with him. We reviewed the scenario for informing foreign governments and demonstrating that the new President was firmly in control. Ford agreed to meet all the foreign ambassadors during his first twenty-four hours in office. He changed some of the letters to world leaders so that they sounded more like language he might use.

When I left his office after an hour and a half, I suddenly realized that for the first time in years after a Presidential meeting I was free of tension. It was impossible to talk to Nixon without wondering afterward what other game he might be engaged in at the moment. Of one thing you could be sure: No single conversation with Nixon ever encapsuled the totality of his purposes. It was exciting but also draining, even slightly menacing. With Ford, one knew that there were no hidden designs, no morbid suspicions, no complexes. And I reflected again on the wisdom of Providence. Gerald Ford was clearly not Nixon's first choice as successor; John Connally was. But for that moment of near-despair I could think of no public figure better able to lead us in national renewal than this man so quintessentially American, of unquestioned integrity, at peace with himself, thoughtful and knowledgeable of national affairs and international responsibilities, calm and unafraid.

That night Nixon announced his resignation in a simple speech that was well delivered, without pathos. It stopped short of confessing guilt but it admitted mistakes — not an easy matter for one so proud. I watched the last minute of his speech in the Oval Office from behind the television cameras. When he was finished, Nixon stood for a moment or two ordering his papers and then he placed his hand on the top of Wilson's desk before turning his back for the last time on the Oval Office. I caught up with him in the passageway next to the Rose Garden. I said: "Mr. President, after most of your major speeches in this office we have walked together back to your house. I would be honored to walk with you again tonight."

So we walked along the corridor to the residence for the final time. By now we had uttered all the words possible. I repeated that history would treat him more kindly. And he repeated that this would depend on who wrote it. At the door of the residence, Julie Nixon Eisenhower was waiting. She wordlessly embraced her father and escorted him the rest of the way.

James St. Clair, Nixon's lawyer, was in my office when I returned. I do not know what brought him there. He and I had exchanged only a few words during the preceding months. Now he obviously needed someone to talk to. He reviewed matter-of-factly the various stages of his experience: Nixon's reluctance to inform even his own lawyer of what he was facing, making St. Clair's job with his client similar to the Special Prosecutor's. He was obviously bothered about whether he could have done better, whether something had been overlooked. "It was not a legal case," I told him. "It was a Greek tragedy. Nixon was fulfilling his own nature. Once it started it could not end otherwise."

The next morning Nixon's Cabinet and White House staff were assembled for the last time, packed into the East Room. Many of us could remember the exuberance of two inaugural celebrations and the high hopes of being sworn in there. At 9:30 A.M., the military aide announced President and Mrs. Nixon, followed by the strains of "Hail to the Chief." The poignancy was nearly unbearable. And then Nixon delivered a speech that was as rambling as the previous night's had been disciplined, as emotional as the previous night's had been controlled. It was too much. It was as if having kept himself in check all these years he had to put on display all the demons and dreams that had driven him to this point. He even wore glasses in public for the first time, symbolically forswearing the vanity and image-making of his career. It was horrifying and heartbreaking; and it was unavoidable. Nixon could not leave as the automaton that had been his public personality. I was at the same time moved to tears and outraged at being put through the wringer once again, so that even in his last public act Nixon managed to project his ambivalence onto those around him. When he was praising his mother, I wondered irrationally why he had omitted his wife, Pat, who without his capacity for make-believe must have suffered the most grievously of all.

And then that mood passed, too, as the anguish on the platform engulfed us all. In defeat and disgrace Nixon had at last prevailed; he had stripped us of our reserve; we were naked before these elemental feelings and our hearts in the end went out to this man who transcended his extremity by refusing to act as if he were defeated.

A few minutes later I stood on the South Portico of the White House, from which Nixon had always waved with foreign guests to the crowds that assembled for arrival ceremonies. Down below on the South Lawn, incongruously a red carpet stretched toward the waiting helicopter and an honor guard presented arms for the last time to the President and Mrs. Nixon accompanied by the Fords. The President-designate said a few inaudible words to President and Mrs. Nixon at the foot of the helicopter's stairs. As he was about to board, Nixon turned to his colleagues for the last time with a wave of his arms that was intended to be jaunty but that conveyed more than anything that he had reached the end of his physical and emotional resources.

Soon the helicopter was just a tiny dot beside the Washington Monument and then it disappeared on the way to Andrews Air Force Base. Ford, President-designate for another ninety minutes, turned and strode firmly toward the White House, his arm around his wife's shoulders. They were virtually alone; there was as yet no retinue of aides or visible security; Ford appeared subdued and yet confident.

I felt an immense relief. We had traversed a constitutional crisis without catastrophe. Whatever was ahead of us could not match in peril the

period of the collapse of our executive authority. Somehow we had preserved a vital foreign policy in the debacle. Yet I reflected also that one
cannot engage with impunity in a flirtation with the nihilistic. No one
had taken over the Presidency in more challenging circumstances; great
crises were surely ahead. And the prayer that had eluded me two nights
earlier came to me as I watched Gerald Ford enter the White House: for
the sake of all of us, that fate would be kind to this good man, that his
heart would be stout, and that America under his leadership would find
again its faith.

Appendix

The 1973 Bombing Campaign in Cambodia

Memorandum for the Historian of the State Department from Emory C. Swank, U.S. Ambassador to the Khmer Republic, 1970–73, and Thomas O. Enders, Deputy Chief of Mission, Phnom Penh, 1970–74, and dated October 10, 1979.

(Following this memorandum are Tab A: State Department Instruction 015050, January 26, 1973; Tab B: Letter from William N. Harben, Chief of the Political Section, Phnom Penh, 1972–1973; and Tab C: Letter from John W. Vogt, General USAF, Ret., Commander of the US Seventh Air Force and of the United States Support Activities Group, 1973.)

The 1973 Bombing Campaign in Cambodia

IN a book published earlier this year (*Sideshow: Kissinger, Nixon and the Destruction of Cambodia*, Simon and Schuster, New York, 1979) William Shawcross makes assertions and inferences which misrepresent the conduct and consequences of the 1973 bombing campaign in Cambodia and the roles each of us played in it. Although they are by no means the only errors of fact and interpretation contained in Mr. Shawcross's book, these are of particular importance historically, because they appear to be the main basis for his conclusions concerning the "destruction of Cambodia."

According to Mr. Shawcross,

— Embassy Phnom Penh "approved and controlled" the bombing;
— It was instructed to do so by Assistant to the President for National Security Affairs Kissinger without the knowledge of the Secretary of State;
— Bombing was "indiscriminate" because out-of-date maps were used rather than photography;
— Control of bombing was shifted to the Cambodian armed forces after a Congressional sub-committee investigation in April 1973;
— The bombing resulted in massive civilian casualties.

None of these statements is correct.

1. *Assertion:* That from early February 1973 on, Embassy Phnom Penh was no longer to be merely "a conduit, passing Cambodian requests for bombing strikes on to the Seventh Air Force," but "was to be actively involved in the entire bombing process, selecting, examining, approving and controlling the bombing."[1] Mr. Shawcross cites no source for this statement.

Clarification: The Embassy did not approve or control air strikes; only Military Assistance Command Vietnam (MACV) and its successor command — the United States Support Activities Group (USSAG) — had that authority. The role of the Embassy was to receive FANK requests for air support, validate them "consistent with means and time available" and forward them to MACV for decision. The operative part of the Embassy's instructions, as sent to Swank in State Department cable 15050, dated January 26, 1973 and classified Secret/NODIS, reads:

"At the time when the FANK [Forces Armées Nationales Khmeres] suspend offensive military operation all U.S. TACAIR and B-52 strikes in Cambodia will cease. RECCE, airlift, medevac and other U.S. air operations that are not ordnance delivery associated are permitted.

"U.S. TACAIR and B-52 forces will be prepared to strike designated targets in Cambodia in order to assist FANK forces when the situation so dictates. To this

---

[1]*Sideshow*, p. 265.

end a simple, rapid request-validation-execute procedure will be set up between US Ambassador Cambodia and MACV. In essence, US Ambassador will be responsible for receiving requests for air support from GKR [Government of the Khmer Republic] and validating requests consistent with his means and time available. The Ambassador will pass the requests to MACV who has the authority to validate and direct air strikes by US TACAIR or B-52's as the situation dictates. All air strikes executed under this guidance are to counter specific hostile acts against GKR/FANK. Escort of Mekong convoys is authorized.''[2]

As explained to Swank on February 8, 1973, by then Assistant to the President for National Security Affairs Kissinger, the purpose of these arrangements was to back up the unilateral U.S. statement on Cambodia made at the last session of the Paris Peace Talks on January 23, 1973. The U.S. had been unsuccessful in engaging the Khmer Rouge in the talks either directly or indirectly. In the absence of any agreement, the U.S. offered to suspend hostilities in Cambodia, if reciprocated. If the Khmer Rouge attacked, government forces and the Seventh Air Force would respond. The role of the Embassy, Dr. Kissinger told Swank, was to make sure the response to any such attacks was no more than required to back up the unilateral statement.

In implementing this instruction, the Embassy, according to the report prepared for Senator Stuart Symington of the Senate Foreign Relations Committee by Staff Members James G. Lowenstein and Richard M. Moose, performed three functions, none of which included the approval or control of air strikes:[3]

"A. *As a communications relay point*
We were shown the radio-telephone relay system, known as 'Area Control' located in the Air Attache's Office in the Embassy which is manned by an augmented staff of U.S. military personnel temporarily assigned to the Defense Attache's Office. It provides a communications link between the Cambodian General Staff, Seventh Air Force, the Airborne Battlefield Command and Control Center plane and the U.S. Forward Air Control planes.

"B. *As an on-the-spot coordinator of forward air control planes and strike aircraft*
U.S. Forward Air Control planes which are assigned daily to the control of the Air Attache and which regularly refuel at Phnom Penh airport are shifted by Area Control from place to place in response to requests from the Cambodian General Staff or in response to tactical emergencies; and

"C. *As a screener of Cambodian or Seventh Air Force requests for strikes except in eastern Cambodia*
A panel of Embassy officers, both civilian and military, validates each request for B-52 and F-111 strikes, and the Defense Attache screens tactical air requests.

The degree and nature of the Embassy's involvement varies depending on the location of air activity and on whether strategic or tactical air is involved. The Embassy has relatively little to do with air activity in the eastern third of Cambodia where there is no Cambodian Government presence. (This area is designated for air operations purposes as 'Freedom Deal.') Its role in both strategic and tactical air operations is much greater in the remainder of Cambodia where Cambodian Government forces are engaged with an enemy which is now composed almost entirely of Khmer Communist insurgents and North Vietnamese.''

The first two functions — communications with and coordination of the U.S. For-

[2]Text at Tab A.

[3]*U.S. Air Operations in Cambodia: April 1973,* a staff report prepared for the use of the Subcommittee on U.S. Security Agreements and Commitments Abroad of the Committee on Foreign Relations, p. 5.

ward Air Controllers operating in light planes over Cambodia, who validated and authorized TACAIR strikes — were performed by the Embassy only pending construction of a Direct Air Support Center (DASC) in FANK headquarters. When the DASC was completed in late April, they were transferred from the Embassy to it.

The third function — screening of B-52 and F-111 bombing requests — was exercised by the Embassy throughout the bombing campaign. These steps were involved:[4]

"The Embassy validates all B-52 and F-111 strikes outside the 'Freedom Deal' area. When the Cambodian General Staff submits a request, it does so on a form which contains information regarding the nature of the target, its justification, and a certification that friendly forces, villages, hamlets, houses, monuments, temples, pagodas or holy places are not within certain specified distances of the target area.

"The Embassy Air Attache's Office then plots the target and the bombing 'box,' the area in which the bombs will fall, on a one-to-fifty thousand map which is supposed to show the exact location of all permanent houses and buildings. The Air Attache told us that the maps being used by the Embassy were several years old and that the Embassy did not have current photography on proposed target areas which would permit the identification of new or relocated villages.

"The original Cambodian request and the map are then considered by an Embassy bombing panel which meets daily. The panel is chaired by the Deputy Chief of Mission. Its other members are the Defense Attache who is an Army Colonel, the Chief of the Military Equipment Delivery team who is an Army Brigadier General, the Counselor for Political-Military Affairs and the Embassy intelligence chief.

"The panel discusses the target in terms of consistency with the Rules of Engagement, the probable utility of the target, air safety and political factors. The final decision rests, according to the rules of the panel, with the Deputy Chief of Mission. According to him, decisions are, as a practical matter, made unanimously and approximately 40 percent of the requests are turned down. The Ambassador does not sit on the panel but is informed of decisions as they are made, and, according to the rules of the panel, before any particularly sensitive decision. [Note: Swank joined the panel in May 1973; Enders remained a member.] The panel then sends its recommendation to Seventh Air Force through Embassy communications facilities in the form of a message from the Ambassador to the Seventh Air Force Commander. Targets are again reviewed at Seventh Air Force for consistency with the Rules of Engagement. The Embassy is then informed by message from Seventh Air Force of targets scheduled for attack, and, subsequently, of the results. The Embassy then relays this information to Cambodian General Staff Headquarters."

2. *Assertion:* That instructions for making the Embassy into "the command post for the new aerial war in Cambodia" were given in Bangkok to Swank directly by Dr. Kissinger on February 8, 1973. "Although the general instructions were laid out in a cable from the State Department," Secretary of State Rogers "was not told how fully his subordinates in Phnom Penh were now involved in the bombing."[5] No source is cited by Mr. Shawcross.

Clarification: We cannot say for certain that Secretary Rogers knew of the instruction to the Embassy cited above, which laid out succinctly what the Embassy was to do. According to the file copy, two of his senior associates were involved in its preparation (Assistant Secretary of State for East Asian and Pacific Affairs Marshall Green as drafter, and Undersecretary of State for Political Affairs U. Alexis Johnson as authorizer), and two copies were distributed to the Secretary. The cable is dated January 23, 1973, two weeks before Dr. Kissinger met with Swank in Bangkok.

---

[4] *U.S. Air Operations in Cambodia: April 1973,* pp. 5–6.
[5] *Sideshow,* p. 265.

3. *Assertion:* That the bombing was not done "carefully"[6] by the Embassy and was "indiscriminate,"[7] because recent photography was not available and targets were plotted on large-scale, out-of-date maps that did not "show the location of new settlements in the massive forced migrations that the Khmer Rouge were now imposing on the areas they controlled."[8] Mr. Shawcross cites as the source for his comment on maps and photography the Lowenstein and Moose report.[9]

Clarification: All B-52 strikes were subject to detailed Rules of Engagement and executed on the basis of pre-strike photography. As noted above the Embassy never had a substantive role in tactical air operations.

Rules of Engagement prohibited use of B-52 ordnance closer than one kilometer to friendly forces, villages, hamlets, houses, monuments, temples, pagodas or holy places.[10]

General John W. Vogt, who as commander of the United States Support Activities Group and the Seventh Air Force had responsibility for the bombing, states:[11]

> "The choice of targets was made by my headquarters, the United States Support Activities Group in Thailand. The personnel in the headquarters were skilled professionals from all of the Services (Army, Navy, Marines and Air Force). Many of them had been with me in Vietnam when I conducted the Linebacker operation of 1972. By 1973 we had developed targeting techniques based heavily on reconnaissance and employing sophisticated sensors such as infra-red (IR) and precision radar (SLAR). We had up-to-the-minute photography on all areas of Cambodia in which the bombing was conducted. LORAN coordinates were obtained on all B-52 targets and were completely independent of map accuracy. We bombed in all cases with B-52s by reference to this sensor or photographic information. In all cases the targets were covered by reconnaissances both pre-strike and post-strike. On a number of occasions we turned down FANK requests for targets because our recon showed risks to civilian population we were unwilling to take."

Mr. Shawcross appears to have been misled by the fact that the *Embassy* did not have available to it such photography. But it did not have to, since any FANK target the Embassy validated was re-validated or rejected by *USSAG* on the basis of photography. Messrs. Lowenstein and Moose did visit USSAG headquarters in April 1973. It is not known whether they were told of use of photography in USSAG target validation. In any case, they do not mention it in their report, and that omission appears to be the basis for Mr. Shawcross's charges. General Vogt is categorical on the question: "The B-52s bombed without the need for maps at all."[12]

4. *Assertion:* That "after the Moose and Lowenstein investigation in April [1973], control of the bombing was shifted to FANK."[13] Mr. Shawcross gives no source.

Clarification: At no point did FANK control B-52, F-111 or U.S. TACAIR strikes; only USSAG did.[14]

The only change in the arrangements made after April 1973 was the establishment of a direct communications link with FANK headquarters (DASC), by-passing the Embassy on TACAIR (see Point 1 above). Processing of B-52 and F-111 strikes was not involved. Throughout the war, control of U.S. TACAIR was in the hands of U.S. Forward Air Controllers, not the FANK.

---

[6][*Sideshow,*] p. 271.

[7]P. 396.

[8]P. 271.

[9]*U.S. Air Operations in Cambodia: April 1973,* p. 6.

[10]Seventh Air Force OPORD 71-17.

[11]Vogt to Enders letter, July 8, 1979, p. 2, Tab C [p. 1228 below].

[12]Vogt to Enders letter, p. 3 [p. 1229 below].

[13]P. 295n.

[14]*U.S. Air Operations in Cambodia: April 1973,* report on visit to Seventh Air Force Headquarters, p. 1.

5. *Inference:* That the bombing resulted in massive civilian casualties. Mr. Shaw-cross does not make an explicit statement to this effect, but he implies it in the map/photography misinterpretation cited above and in the three (and three only) pieces of evidence he cites on civilian casualties. First he quotes Embassy political officer William Harben as saying "I began to get reports of wholesale carnage. One night a mass of peasants from a village near Saang went out on a funeral procession. They walked straight into a 'box.' Hundreds were slaughtered.' "[15] Second, he cites the bombing of Neak Luong on August 7, 1973 (the town was held at that time by Khmer Republic forces) due to bombardier error, and writes: "The accident inevitably raised the question of how often such errors occurred in parts of the country where reporters could never penetrate."[16] Finally Cambodian generals "took a casual view of the risks to civilians." "As one air attache, Mark Berent, recalls, 'They never plotted anything. We could have given the coordinates of the palace and they would have said yes.' "[17]

Clarification: There is no evidence of massive civilian casualties. Two major B-52 accidents are known, one at Sa'ang and the other at Neak Luong; both were reported by the Embassy as well as cited by Mr. Shawcross. The former could not have been prevented (the target, in conformance to the Rules of Engagement, was well away from an inhabited area); the latter was Seventh Air Force responsibility. No doubt there were other civilian casualties, although on a smaller scale.

Mr. Harben, who is often portrayed in *Sideshow* as a bitter critic of U.S. (and Embassy) policy, makes these comments on casualties:[18]

"In retrospect I think it likely that accidents involving TACAIR, particularly Khmer Air Force, may have been confused with B-52's in the retelling during the heightened public awareness of the latter. . . . In the case of the Sa'ang tragedy, . . . it is clear that the rules of engagement were respected . . . (as regards my statement that) 'I began to get reports of wholesale carnage . . .' [Mr. Shawcross] garbled it slightly: In referring to the Sa'ang raid, I used the expression used by my informant on that raid: 'c'etait un veritable carnage.' Shawcross seems to have written this down in such a way as to give the impression that such a description applied to all the raids about which I had heard. The context was simply a narration of events."

Mr. Harben concludes:

"So civilian casualties were unavoidable, but far fewer, I am sure, than Shawcross and others claim. Had they been so great, the reports I received would not have been so vague. It is curious also that, although thousands of Khmers who were living in enemy-held areas at that time have fled to Thailand, and some have even gone to Europe, Shawcross seems to have made no effort to question them, although he made the effect of bombing upon them a major theme of his book. He did not even speak to So Satto, ex-chief of the Khmer Air Force, as I suggested. Nor did he contact In Tam, who was speaking to dozens of peasants every day recently arrived from the other side — and to enemy emissaries discussing defection."

General Vogt makes this comment about the possibility of other offset bombing errors like that at Neak Luong:[19]

"Every accident my headquarters was aware of was made known immediately, the worst being the off-set bombing error by B-52s against Neak Luong. To set the

---

[15] P. 272.
[16] P. 294.
[17] P. 271.
[18] Harben to Enders letter, June 22, 1979, Tab B.
[19] Vogt to Enders letter, p. 1, Tab C [pp. 1227–1228 below].

record straight, B-52s employed this off-set technique on only a handful of missions. The beacons were there primarily for F-111 use. The latter used them successfully throughout 1973 without a single incident. Their equipment, of course, was much better as they were much later generation airplanes. After Neak Luong the B-52s stopped using this practice . . . Virtually all of the B-52 bombing was precisely controlled by Seventh Air Force control systems. They were led in by F-4 LORAN-equipped pathfinders. These lead planes had a demonstrated accuracy by photo-recon confirmation of less than 400 feet miss distance.''

Finally, since at no time did FANK control B-52 strikes (or for that matter F-111 or TACAIR strikes), Mr. Shawcross's third and last piece of evidence — an air attache's comment on FANK's own concern for civilians — does not apply.

It is worth noting that all B-52 strikes were photographed afterwards, as well as before. Not only was there available to General Vogt immediate evidence of any accident, but such evidence is preserved in Air Force archives. Seventh Air Force post-strike photography on Cambodia could be examined by a photo-reconnaissance specialist to confirm the conclusions on casualties reported here.

> [*signed*] Emory C. Swank 10/10/79
> U.S. Ambassador to the
> Khmer Republic, 1970–73

> [*signed*] Thomas O. Enders 10/10/79
> Deputy Chief of Mission
> Phnom Penh, 1970–74

Tab A

IMMEDIATE PHNOM PENH

PRIORITY SAIGON, BANGKOK PRIORITY, VIENTIANE PRIORITY, FRANCE PRIORITY

STATE 015050

260022Z JAN 73

FOR AMBASSADOR SWANK

SUBJECT: USAF ACTIVITIES IN CAMBODIA FOLLOWING A CEASEFIRE IN VIETNAM

REF: PHNOM PENH 634

1. USAF activities in Cambodia will be related to Lon Nol's proposed announcement of unilateral suspension by FANK of offensive military actions while reserving the right of self-defense. Thus, we propose from the time Lon Nol takes this action that USAF will stand down TACAIR and B-52 strikes. If a FANK unit is in trouble due to enemy action, we can react locally to provide appropriate air support clearly commensurate with the defensive requirements of the units under attack. You may inform Lon Nol that USAF activities in Cambodia will be related to his proposed declaration but that US air support will be provided, as necessary, in accordance with the JCS instructions below:

2. Chief JCS has just sent CINCPAC, info COMUSMACV, following guidance:

3. Quote: At the time when the FANK suspend offensive military operation all US TACAIR and B-52 strikes in Cambodia will cease. RECCE, airlift, MEDEVAC and other U.S. air operations that are not ordnance delivery associated are permitted.

4. Quote: U.S. TACAIR and B-52 forces will be prepared to strike designated targets in Cambodia in order to assist FANK forces when the situation so dictates. To this end a simple, rapid request-validation-execute procedure will be set up between U.S. Ambassador Cambodia and MACV. In essence, US Ambassador will be responsible for receiving requests for air support from GKR and validating requests consistent with his means and time available. The Ambassador will pass the requests to MACV who has the authority to validate and direct air strikes by US TACAIR or B-52's as the situation dictates. All air strikes executed under this guidance are to counter specific hostile acts against GKR/FANK. Escort of Mekong convoys is authorized. Unquote

5. MACV requested to set up procedures as outlined above as soon as possible and to inform Chief JCS of details agreed upon.

ROGERS

Tab B

Ambassador Thomas O. Enders   June 22, 1979
American Embassy
Ottawa, Canada

Dear Tom:

Recently I had an opportunity to read the Shawcross book. Your questions assume that I knew much more than I did. I knew hardly more than any literate Cambodian about the bombing — nothing, for example, of the rules of engagement, or the fact that there was an Embassy targeting committee which you chaired.

(i) Is the account of the bombing campaign given in Mr. Shawcross' book on pages 270–272 accurate?

Answer: I know too little, even now, to assess his accuracy. The assertion that only maps of 1:50,000 were used is absurd on the face of it, but beyond that I cannot comment.

(ii) What accidents causing civilian casualties did you learn of?

Answer: As the B-52 raids began to hit near Phnom Penh foreign journalists told me they had heard of many civilian casualties. One quoted a woman refugee who said her husband had been killed "with blood coming from his eyes and ears" in what sounded from her description like a B-52 attack. Another was said to have been near Kompong Speu, and still another mentioned by a Khmer Red Cross official to a journalist. Then In Tam summoned me and said that many civilians had been killed by "B-52's" near Skoun. You checked and said it must have been Tacair. In retrospect I think it likely that accidents involving Tacair, particularly Khmer Air Force, may have been confused with B-52's in the retelling during the heightened public awareness of the latter. Perhaps some of the reports mentioned above applied to the same raid. About this time an airgram from one of our border posts in Vietnam quoted Cambodian refugees as saying that hundreds of peasants conscripted for work in enemy camps had been killed by B-52's. I had this in mind when I told Shawcross that most civilian casualties were certainly due to the Communists drafting peasants for use as porters and laborers in legitimate target areas. He chose to omit this comment. Another incident was reported to me by a Democratic Party official who was a mathematics professor at the university. He said his uncle, mayor of Sa'ang, near Phnom Penh, had sent word that some hundreds of peasants had walked into a B-52 box while on a nocturnal procession some kilometers from that village to bury or burn a deceased favorite bonze. They did not go by day fearing that such a column would invite Tacair attack, he said. I reported it to you, and a few days later it was mentioned in the Khmer press.

About this time also the only remaining Khmer newspaper which had not been banned — the Army organ — published an editorial condemning the B-52 bombing and saying that it would be more appropriate for us to bomb North Vietnam, and not our Cambodian ally. I believe this editorial mentioned some civilian casualties or implied that there had been some.

About this time I met Liz Trotta, a rather bold NBC television reporter, with whom one day I watched Tacair bombing a retreating enemy unit on the east bank of the Mekong from the Chrui Changwar peninsula. Refugees with sampans loaded with bedding, furniture, bicycles, and even farm animals were streaming toward us from the far bank, fleeing either the bombing or the enemy or both.

Liz insisted on going to the other side when a Khmer soldier told us it was safe for about a kilometer back of the riverbank, and I accompanied her and her TV crew. We followed Khmer troops of the rearguard in their leisurely pursuit southward, and stopped to question some peasants through a French-speaking schoolteacher. Miss Trotta, having heard the uproar about civilian casualties, asked them if they could cite specific instances of civilian deaths. After some palaver they cited three in that area from all bombings: a farmer who had gone too close in order to rescue his strayed cattle, a bonze, and another villager. Miss Trotta thought this rather a small and unavoidable toll, and did not bother to report it. When she asked the peasants if they opposed the bombing, they said they did not mind as long as it was not on *their* village. Liz was so surprised that she thought the teacher was giving us a bit of government propaganda, but when I questioned him he quite freely said he had no use for Lon Nol or any of the other politicians either.

(iii) Were they caused by B-52 or Tacair strikes?

Answer: I have no other information other than that given above.

(iv) If B-52, were the rules of engagement respected (i.e. no strikes closer than one kilometer to inhabited areas)?

Answer: It was not until I received this question that I knew what the rules of engagement were. In any case I did not seek or obtain enough detail on the raids to determine this. In the case of the Sa'ang tragedy, however, it is clear that the rules of engagement *were* respected.

(v) Were these accidents caused or made more likely by use of maps several years old, or by lack of care by the Embassy or the Seventh Air Force?

Answer: I do not think the accidents were due to old maps or lack of care. I believe they were due to factors I will explain in answer to your question (vii) below. You refer only to B-52 attacks, but I feel that in order to be complete I should say what I knew of the rules of engagement in Tacair strikes, about which I knew more, since they were more easily observed.

Conversations in the staff meetings convinced me that we were exercising great care to avoid civilian casualties in Tacair bombing, and I assumed that the same care was exercised with respect to B-52 raids. On one occasion Gen. Cleland complained that the enemy were so confident that we would not bomb villages that they had set up their guns in villages on the banks of the Mekong to shoot at our convoys. I recall that I suggested that smoke bombs be dropped upwind of these positions to blind them. He replied that that had been considered by the "High Command" and rejected as impractical since it would obstruct navigation. Although that might be true only for certain azimuths I did not pursue it, but on the way down the stairs I met the Naval Attache coming up. I told him that "someone" had suggested smoke bombs. He said it was a good idea — it ought to be tried. I then said that "someone" had objected that it would blind the navigators. He scoffed at that and pointed out that they had brought a convoy up in the middle of a moonless night a few nights earlier. I mentioned to Shawcross that the enemy put guns in villages confident that they would not be attacked, but he chose to omit this also.

Rules of engagement were mentioned on one other occasion in my presence. A Jesuit priest, a speechwriter in the White House, arrived and was shunted to me. He was quite interested in the bombing, and I asked one of the Assistant Air Attaches over for a drink, since I could not enlighten him. The priest questioned him quite closely as to whether the rules of engagement were being observed, and even pretended to be a "firebreather" — claiming that there are no neutrals in total war — in order to provoke the Ass't Air Attache into admitting some departure from the rules. The latter insisted, however, that deliberate violations were rare and minor. He would go no further than to say that a pilot receiving fire from a cluster of huts slightly over the maximum attackable size might stretch a point. The priest asked what the size of the cluster was, and the Ass't Air Attache declined to give it to him, saying that it was information which could be of great use to the enemy.

(vi) Is the quotation attributed to you accurate? If so, to whom did you make it, when, and in what context?

Answer: There are several, but I assume you mean that in which I said "I began to get reports of wholesale carnage . . ." etc. This was said to Shawcross in my house in 1977, I believe. I think he garbled it slightly. In referring to the Sa'ang raid, I used the expression used by my informant on that raid: "c'etait un veritable carnage". Shawcross seems to have written this down in such a way as to give the impression that such a description applied to all the raids about which I had heard. The context was simply a narration of events. Shawcross is inaccurate in a number of other quotations: When I said that Lon Nol, when Washington was distracted elsewhere, resumed his dictatorship with the usual army backing, Shawcross inserted in brackets "United States" in front of "army", although I meant *Khmer* Army. If I had meant United States Army I would have used the word "acquiescence", although some might think that Gen. Cleland's threats of terminating U.S. aid made to officers who were discussing a coup against Lon Nol might amount to more than that. Shawcross also says that my proposals were rejected "contemptuously". I did not use such a word and did not feel that you or Coby were ever contemptuous toward me. The General was another matter. Shawcross also states that officers in the Political Section "like Bill Harben" were unhappy over your allegedly more vigorous prosecution of the "Nixon Doctrine". I am not sure what he means by that. I do not recall such sentiments in my section. If anything, I found your more vigorous approach a refreshing change.

(vii) Did you cut out a B-52 box, apply it to Central Cambodia, and conclude that nowhere could bombing be carried out without civilian casualties? Is that your view now?

Answer: I did. I did not attend the Air Attache's briefings, but journalists told me that the Embassy claimed that there were *no* civilian casualties, and jeered at the idea. Convinced, for reasons given below, that it was impossible to conduct such bombing without inflicting *some* civilian casualties, I felt the Embassy might once again be creating a "credibility gap". On the spur of the moment I decided to demonstrate to myself how easily hostile outsiders might make us appear to be cruel and foolish. I tried to orient the B-52 "box", cut to scale, on my office map and covered a village in Central Cambodia in all positions.

I felt I should apprise someone of this, but had clashed with Gen. Cleland whenever I reported Khmer Army corruption. He had even insisted I burn a memo of Carney's on front-line bribes for delivery of US munitions, though I felt it might even be a violation of federal law for the Political Section to conceal such information which had come to its attention. So I shunned the military and wrote a memorandum to Paul Gardner, since the title of his "Political Military" Section seemed to indicate some responsibility.

But it was not just this exercise with the map which convinced me that some civilian casualties were unavoidable. Most of my career had been spent on international Communist matters, and I thought that if a public scandal about civilian casualties would hurt our war effort, they would see to it that we did kill civilians, despite our caution. Furthermore I had knocked about rural Java a good deal in the early 60's, and had encountered mysterious religious processions at night far out in the countryside. While climbing mountains I had come upon small villages hidden under palms not shown on my maps. They were so remote from the national life that they did not know what money was, and dropped it on the ground when I paid them for coconuts. Such villages would have been wiped out in any "carpet bombing" of "uninhabited" areas. In war the problem is worse. People whose draft animals have been commandeered or whose rice has been confiscated go foraging in the jungle for food. They hide in unusual places at night to avoid enemy conscription. Often they are fleeing by night to the safety of the government lines. Some of our reports from the other side spoke of the Communists marching villagers to bases at night to harangue them with political speeches. No air force can know where such people are at any given moment.

So civilian casualties were unavoidable, but far fewer, I am sure, than Shawcross and the others claim. Had they been so great, the reports I received would not have been so vague. It is curious also that, although thousands of Khmers who were living in enemy-held areas at that time have now fled to Thailand, and some have even gone to Europe, Shawcross seems to have made no effort to question them, although he made the effect of bombing upon them a major theme of this book. He did not even speak to So Satto, ex-chief of the Khmer Air Force, as I suggested. Nor did he contact In Tam, who was speaking to dozens of peasants every day recently arrived from the other side — and to enemy emissaries discussing defection. (Actually I suspect that Shawcross' French is too poor to have done a complete job).

Shawcross quotes me as "appalled" at the time. I was not appalled by the casualties to civilians, which I think were minor and unavoidable, but by the fact that they were in vain in the absence of vigorous measures to stamp out Khmer Army corruption, build an efficient fighting force, ensure the coming to power of the honest and much more capable In Tam, whose popularity as demonstrated in his election victory and his contacts with disaffected enemy held out a prospect of victory. When he described to me his plan of buying off the Khmer Rumdoh piecemeal with FANK ranks and wages, gradually thus reducing the Communists to a minority and isolating them back in the Cardamoms, I thought it workable, but asked him where he would get the money. He replied: "Your own figures, announced in Washington, say that Lon Nol and his officers are stealing the wages of enough men to buy off the whole insurgent army — that is where I intend to get the money." That would have required strong support from us — and I did not think Congress could raise protests on behalf of embezzlers of US funds and equipment.

The B-52 bombing even made corruption worse. When Cheng Heng pleaded with Lon Nol to act against corrupt officers, Nol told him to calm down, since "the American B-52's are killing a thousand enemy every day and the war will soon be over."

With regard to the morality of killing any civilians at all, I feel it was justified in the attempt to save them from a much greater slaughter at the hands of the Communists, who in every country have liquidated far more people than may have been accidentally killed in Cambodia. The bombing of German extermination camps is now debated in retrospect. We are criticized for failing to do so. Would Shawcross object to such bombing on the grounds that "hundreds" of non-combatants would have been killed? In the invasion of Normandy we killed many French civilians. In Sicily we even bombed our own troops. In World War II Mr Shawcross' country devised a policy of deliberately aiming at civilians, and made the author of that policy a peer of the realm, whereas our country is probably the only one in recent decades in which strict rules of engagement were imposed to avoid or reduce civilian deaths.

There will be a next time, and when that time comes I think we should be more attentive to the problem of public relations and history. We might, for example, shower enemy-occupied areas with leaflets announcing our intention in a general way and urging civilians to avoid enemy military concentrations at night, etc. Still there will be civilian casualties, but we will have visible evidence of concern for their safety.

In retrospect I do not envy you the role you were asked to play, which I am sure you exercised as humanely as possible. Our commissions read that we serve "at the pleasure of the president". If the press or the public regards some of the results of our obedience as unfortunate, then they should devote their attention to the faults of the system which "program" such occurrences, instead of to the pursuit of villains. Any embassy, under the circumstances, would have come up with about the same cast of characters, doing, or not doing, the same things.

Sincerely

[*signed*] *Bill*

W. N. Harben

Tab C

The Honorable Thomas Ostrom Enders   July 8, 1979
Ambassador of the USA
100 Wellington Street
Ottawa, Ontario K1P 5T1

Dear Tom,

I delayed this response until I finished reading Shawcross' book which you kindly sent me. My comments on his charges and answers to your questions follow.

First let me say that his description of the 1973 bombing as "indiscriminate" is completely contrary to fact. As one who led his squadron over the beaches of Normandy in World War II and later operated against targets in support of Allied troops on the Western front, I can assure you I have some basis for judging the nature of bombing activities. I state flatly that the precision, degree of control, validity of targets attacked and professionalism of the crews involved in the 1973 Cambodian campaign were as high or perhaps even higher than all of World War II bombing, the 1965–68 Rolling Thunder campaign, or the Linebacker campaigns in 1972 in North and South Vietnam.

There were some accidents, but surprisingly few considering the weight of effort involved (which as the author points out was far higher than World War II).

Every accident my headquarters was aware of was made known immediately, the worst being the off-set bombing error by B-52s against Neak Luong. To set the record straight, B-52s employed this off-set technique on only a handful of missions. The beacons were there primarily for F-111 use. The latter used them successfully throughout 1973 without a single incident. Their equipment, of course, was much better as they were much later generation airplanes. After Neak Luong the B-52s stopped using this practice so the author's statement ''The accident inevitably raised the question of how often such errors occurred in parts of the country where reporters could never penetrate'', is groundless speculation like so much of his description of the 1973 bombing campaign.

Virtually all of the B-52 bombing was precisely controlled by 7th Air Force control systems. They were led in by F-4 LORAN-equipped pathfinders. These lead planes had a demonstrated accuracy by photo-recon confirmation of less than 400 feet miss distance.

The choice of targets was made by my headquarters, The United States Support Activities Group in Thailand. The personnel in the headquarters were skilled professionals from all of the Services (Army, Navy, Marines and Air Force). Many of them had been with me in Vietnam when I conducted the Linebacker operations of 1972. By 1973 we had developed targeting techniques based heavily on reconnaissance and employing sophisticated sensors such as infra-red (IR) and precision radar (SLAR). We had up-to-the-minute photography on all areas of Cambodia in which the bombing was conducted. LORAN coordinates were obtained on all B-52 targets and were completely independent of map accuracy. We bombed in all cases with B-52s by reference to this sensor or photographic information. In all cases the targets were covered by reconnaisances both pre-strike and post-strike. On a number of occasions we turned down FANK requests for targets because our recon showed risks to civilian population we were unwilling to take.

As you will recall, charges were constantly being made in 1973 that we were hitting Cambodian villages. Except for the very few accidents, in not one single case were we able to substantiate such charges. A prime example occurred in June or July '73 when the Assistant Secretary of Defense for Public Affairs, Jerry Friedheim, sent me a message including the full text of an East Coast newspaper article which stated B-52s had destroyed or heavily damaged 10 Cambodian villages causing the villagers to flee. The reporter stated he had personally interviewed many of these villagers. He named each village supposedly involved. Friedheim wanted an immediate answer to the charges. I dispatched recon aircraft to each village and took low altitude photography of excellent quality. *In no case* could we find any evidence of B-52 bomb drops (the pattern of craters is unmistakable). The majority of the villages were relatively untouched by war damage of any kind. A few near the Vietnam border showed some damage from artillery fire or 250 lb. bombs (dropped only by the South Vietnamese Air Force; we did not use them at all). Even in these cases the amount of damage was relatively small and usually was found at the edges of the towns. This hard photographic evidence was immediately dispatched to Washington with a full explanatory text. It was never used by OSD to refute the story because (I was told later) ''the whole incident had died down in the Press and they didn't want to rekindle it''. I am afraid the author's charges are based largely on such unsubstantiated evidence.

Now to your specific questions: — In what cases was photography used prior to target adoption? Ans. In the case of B-52 operations it was used in *all* cases. Tac Air which was under FAC control (forward air controllers) did not require such pre-strike recon but the combat areas were photographed each day for precise location of enemy and friendly positions and was available to the FACs.

— How often was it used? Ans. Answered in the first question.

— Is there evidence that in those where photography was not used accidents occurred or the risk of accidents was significantly greater? Ans. As I indicated above photography on the precise target was not required in the case of Tactical aircraft only. The precise nature of FAC control virtually precluded accidents. I can recall no accidents occurring with TAC air all during 1973.

— Were your photo surveillance assets adequate to your needs or were you constrained? Ans. Fully adequate. I retained within 7th Air Force following the Vietnam settlement RF-4 assets which gave me proportionately far better coverage than I had when we were operating throughout all of S.E. Asia.

— What is your view of the adequacy of available mapping? Could up-to-date maps have been prepared? How long would it have taken? Ans. As I indicated above, we were relying far more on up-to-the-minute photography, LORAN precision coordinates gained from that photography or, in the case of F-111 operations, highly precise off-set radar beacon techniques than on the maps themselves. The B-52s bombed without the need for maps at all. In the case of TAC air good maps are an asset to help the FAC find the target quickly, but from that point on, the pilot's eyeballs plus the photography available to him fixed the actual target. All FACs had strict orders to avoid villages and did so with remarkable professionalism. So while up-to-date maps would have helped the FACs find the target more quickly they were not a factor in the actual bomb delivery. The Defense Mapping Agency was fully responsive to my mapping needs and sent us the latest available to them. They were constantly updating from our photography. Nevertheless there was a lag in some areas like Cambodia, but I doubt very much the involved process of map making could have been speeded up much more than it was.

A few general comments: I suspect Shawcross had determined his theme before he gathered the evidence and wrote the book. For example, much of what I have said above I told to Shawcross when I discussed the bombing campaign with him in February of 1977. He chose to use none of this information. Even if he didn't believe what I said an objective presentation would have required that he include it. After all I was the commander running the bombing operations and had access to far more hard data than his hear-say reporters.

There is ample documentary evidence of the 1972 Cambodian air operations. My own oral report to the Air Force Historical Research Center at Air University at Maxwell AFB, Alabama, for example, contains a full statement of the 10 village incident I mentioned above. Unfortunately the report is classified secret but parts of it I am sure could be declassified if the effort were made.

Shawcross does quote my statement to him that the 1973 bombing "saved Phnom Penh by killing 16,000 enemy". There is an interesting sidelight to this. After the Washington announcement to stop all bombing by August 15, 1973 the enemy launched a series of all-out attacks to capture the city even though they knew the job would be much easier after 15 August. Why? We found out later. Captured intelligence revealed the Khmer Rouge had issued direct orders to their forward commanders to take the city before August 1973 so they could prove to the world that they could humble the U.S. In callous disregard for human life they threw in their troops in repeated attacks and since they were no longer able to use jungle cover, they suffered huge losses to air attack. This should have given us some clue as to how this regime would treat its own people after they seized control. They so decimated their elite forces that after the bombing stopped they took until April 1975 to finally take the city. Had we remained steadfast in support of the Cambodian government and provided air support as needed the country would be in non-communist hands today instead of North Vietnam's. I am not proud of my country's bug-out in either Vietnam or Cambodia. After losing more than 50,000 American lives we quit even though we had turned back the Easter offensive in Vietnam. Air power had applied great pressure on Hanoi itself causing them to accept terms which would have kept South Vietnam free if enforced by a meaningful threat of the resumption of that bombing. We turned our backs on our friends when they called on us to back up our promises made in January 1973. Likewise in Cambodia we had broken the back of the Khmer Rouge forces in 1973 and then let them regain their strength to reattack a year and a half later while denying our friends ammunition. The pervasive effects of Watergate had set in.

One final comment: Shawcross has gone to great lengths to disparage the leadership in Cambodia. I knew all the key Cambodian generals through close personal contact. Having worked with the military in South Vietnam and Laos, I think I had a valid basis for comparison. Considering their limited means and experience (because of Sihanouk's policy of making them no more than a palace guard) they displayed remarkable qualities. They had to go from the role of company commanders to that of division and larger in just a few months. They had the ability to defeat the enemy and would have done so if we had not pulled the rug out from under them.

In Lon Nol, whom I met and talked to on a number of occasions, I found a man truly dedicated to preventing his country from falling to the communists. I hope future historians will present the case of Cambodian leaders' ability and patriotism in a better light than Shawcross has done.

Please feel free to use any or all of the above as you find necessary to set the record straight. The distortion of the true state of events in Cambodia which has occurred in the liberal press, of which Shawcross is obviously a part, needs to be set straight.

With all best wishes
[signed] John
John W. Vogt, General USAF (Ret.)

Chapter Notes

Henry Kissinger, *White House Years* (Boston: Little, Brown and Co., 1979), is referred to throughout the notes as *White House Years*. Public statements by the President, the Secretary of State, and the Assistant to the President for National Security Affairs can, unless otherwise indicated, be found in the *Public Papers of the Presidents of the United States,* the *Weekly Compilation of Presidential Documents,* and/or the *Department of State Bulletin.*

I
A MOMENT OF HOPE

1. See H. R. Haldeman with Joseph DiMona, *The Ends of Power* (New York: New York Times Books, 1978), pp. 175–180. See also Chapter X below.
2. See *White House Years,* pp. 917–918, 1185–1186, 1455–1456. William Safire has subtly described the way the White House dealt with its "Kissinger problem" in *Before the Fall: An Inside View of the Pre-Watergate White House* (Garden City, N.Y.: Doubleday & Co., 1975), Part III, Chapter 5.
3. Safire, *Before the Fall,* p. 170.

II
A VISIT TO HANOI

1. In a message of October 20, 1972, I recited back to Le Duc Tho several of the assurances he had given me in our secret meetings:

   — "The questions of the war in Vietnam and Cambodia are closely linked; when the war is settled in Vietnam, there is no reason for the war to continue in Cambodia" (September 27);

   — "Once the Vietnam problem is settled, the question of Cambodia certainly will be settled; and the end of the Vietnamese war will create a very great impact that will end the war in Cambodia perhaps immediately" (October 8);

   — "It is an understanding between us that the DRV [Democratic Republic of Vietnam] will abide by the principle that all foreign forces, including its own, must put an end to their military activities in Cambodia and be withdrawn from Cambodia and not be reintroduced" (September 26);

   — "The DRV will follow the same principles in Cambodia that it will follow in South Vietnam and Laos, that is, it will refrain from introducing troops, armament, and war material into Cambodia" (October 11); and

   — "As Article 18 [later 23] states, the obligations of this agreement come into force on the day of its signing" (October 11).

2. See *White House Years,* pp. 1432–1435.
3. The relevant portion of Article 20 of the Paris Agreement reads as follows:

   (a) The parties participating in the Paris Conference on Vietnam shall strictly respect the 1954 Geneva Agreements on Cambodia and the 1962 Geneva Agreements on Laos, which recognized the Cambodian and the Lao peoples' fundamental national rights, i.e., the independence, sovereignty, unity, and territorial integrity of these countries. The parties shall respect the neutrality of Cambodia and Laos. The parties participating in the

Paris Conference on Vietnam undertake to refrain from using the territory of Cambodia and the territory of Laos to encroach on the sovereignty and security of one another and of other countries.

(*b*) Foreign countries shall put an end to all military activities in Cambodia and Laos, totally withdraw from and refrain from reintroducing into these two countries troops, military advisers and military personnel, armaments, munitions and war material.

4. In early 1973 the North Vietnamese were providing the Khmer Rouge with military advisers, some combat help (particularly the manning of heavy artillery and rocket launchers), rear-service administrative support, transport and other logistical assistance, and military equipment and supplies. Testimony of Dennis J. Doolin, Deputy Assistant Secretary of Defense for International Security Affairs, June 6, 1973, in US Congress, House, Committee on Foreign Affairs, *U.S. Policy and Programs in Cambodia,* Hearings before the Subcommittee on Asian and Pacific Affairs, 93d Cong., 1st sess., 1973, p. 85. This Defense Department testimony was ridiculed by other witnesses who doubted the degree of North Vietnamese assistance to the Khmer Rouge. Prince Sihanouk's recent memoirs confirm beyond doubt that the Defense Department assessment was correct. See Prince Norodom Sihanouk, *War and Hope: The Case for Cambodia* (New York: Pantheon Books, 1980), pp. 14–15, 20, 24–27, 71–72.

5. See *White House Years,* pp. 1414–1415.

6. Ibid., pp. 1169–1174.

7. See the sources collected in Martin F. Herz, *The Prestige Press and the Christmas Bombing, 1972: Images and Reality in Vietnam* (Washington: Ethics and Public Policy Center, 1980), pp. 54–60; and in Guenter Lewy, *America in Vietnam* (New York: Oxford University Press, 1978), pp. 413–414. See also *White House Years,* pp. 1454–1455.

8. Harrison E. Salisbury, "Hanoi Premier Tells View; Some in U.S. Detect a Shift," *New York Times,* January 4, 1967. See also Harrison E. Salisbury, *Behind the Lines: Hanoi* (New York: Harper & Row, 1967), Chapter XVIII.

9. See *White House Years,* pp. 1109, 1381.

10. See note 3 above.

11. Sihanouk, *War and Hope,* pp. 21–23, 64–65. It is confirmed also by a Khmer Rouge document of 1978, Democratic Kampuchea, *The Black Book: Facts and Proofs of Vietnam's Acts of Aggression and Annexation against Kampuchea* (Phnom Penh: September 1978), Chapter V, section 2 (b).

III
China: Another Step Forward

1. *White House Years,* pp. 750, 1089–1090.

2. Ross Terrill, *Mao: A Biography* (New York: Harper & Row, 1980), p. 372.

IV
The Gathering Impact of Watergate

1. Henry A. Kissinger, "The Viet Nam Negotiations," *Foreign Affairs* 47, no. 2 (January 1969): 211–234.

2. See *White House Years,* pp. 254–256.

3. See, e.g., William Safire, *Before the Fall: An Inside View of the Pre-Watergate White House* (Garden City, N.Y.: Doubleday & Co., 1975), Part III, Chapter 5.

4. On President Johnson's taping system, see Bill Gulley with Mary Ellen Reese, *Breaking Cover* (New York: Simon & Schuster, 1980), pp. 77–85. On President Kennedy's, see William F. Buckley, Jr., "Observations on Presidential Tapes," *Washington Star-News,* July 26, 1973; Richard Nixon, *RN: The Memoirs of Richard Nixon* (New York: Grosset & Dunlap, 1978), p. 501; Victor Lasky, *It Didn't Start with Watergate* (New York: Dial Press, 1977), p. 357.

5. H. R. Haldeman with Joseph DiMona, *The Ends of Power* (New York: New York Times Books, 1978), Book VI.

6. See, e.g., the planning of the Laos operation of 1971. *White House Years,* pp. 994–1001.

7. Ibid., pp. 1185–1186.

8. Ibid., pp. 252–253.

9. See Robert Dallek, *Franklin D. Roosevelt and American Foreign Policy, 1932–1945* (New York: Oxford University Press, 1979), pp. 224–226, 289–290, 313, 334–336; Safire, *Before the Fall,* p. 166n; Lasky, *It Didn't Start with Watergate,* pp. 161–172, 195–221, and sources listed in backnotes; US Congress, Senate, Select Committee to Study Governmental Opera-

tions with Respect to Intelligence Activities, *Final Report, Book III: Supplementary Detailed Staff Reports on Intelligence Activities and the Rights of Americans,* 94th Cong., 2d sess., April 23, 1976, "Warrantless FBI Electronic Surveillance," pp. 271–351.

10. See the testimony of Attorney General William B. Saxbe before the Senate Foreign Relations Committee, July 10, 1974, in US Congress, Senate, Committee on Foreign Relations, *Hearings on the Role of Dr. Henry A. Kissinger in the Wiretapping of Certain Government Officials and Newsmen,* 93d Cong., 2d sess., September 1974, pp. 58–59.
11. See especially the testimony of former Secretary of State Dean Rusk before the Senate Foreign Relations Committee on July 23, 1974, ibid., pp. 224–241.
12. See *White House Years,* p. 253.
13. Safire, *Before the Fall,* p. 364.
14. Chalmers M. Roberts, "Foreign Policy under a Paralyzed Presidency," *Foreign Affairs* 52, no. 4 (July 1974): 675.

V
THE YEAR OF EUROPE

1. James Reston, "Pompidou Favors U.S.–Europe Talks," *New York Times,* December 14, 1972.
2. *White House Years,* pp. 938–949.
3. See, e.g., "Dr. Kissinger and Europe," editorial in the *Washington Post,* April 25, 1973.
4. Ibid. Compare the editorials in the *New York Times,* April 25, 1973; *Christian Science Monitor,* April 26, 1973; and *Washington Star-News,* April 27, 1973.
5. *White House Years,* pp. 949–962.

VI
THE MIDDLE EAST IN FERMENT

1. Nixon interview with Garnett D. Horner, November 5, 1972, *Washington Star,* November 9, 1972; Rogers interview with Henry Trewhitt, November 5, 1972.
2. Evans and Novak in the *Washington Post,* February 1, 1973; *New York Times* editorial, February 3, 1973; *Baltimore Sun* editorial, February 6, 1973; *Washington Post* editorial, February 8, 1973.
3. See *White House Years,* Chapter XXX.
4. See William Safire, *Before the Fall: An Inside View of the Pre-Watergate White House* (Garden City, N.Y.: Doubleday & Co., 1975), Part VIII, Chapter 3, "Nixon and the Jews," for a thoughtful treatment of the subject.
5. See Anwar el-Sadat, *In Search of Identity: An Autobiography* (New York: Harper & Row, 1977), pp. 220 ff.
6. See *White House Years,* pp. 1246–1248, and notes 3 and 4 on pp. 1493–1494.
7. See Sadat, *In Search of Identity,* pp. 228–231; *White House Years,* pp. 1295–1297.
8. See *New York Times,* January 29, 30, and February 1, 1973.
9. I had tried this notion on the Israelis in 1972. See *White House Years,* p. 1290.
10. See William Beecher, "Israelis Will Buy More Jets in U.S., Total Put at 48," *New York Times,* March 14, 1973.
11. "The Battle is Now Inevitable," Sadat interview with Arnaud de Borchgrave, *Newsweek,* April 9, 1973, pp. 44–46.

VII
DÉTENTE: ZAVIDOVO TO SAN CLEMENTE

1. See Maurice J. Goldbloom, "Nixon So Far," *Commentary* (March 1970): 30–31; Norman Podhoretz, "A Note on Vietnamization," *Commentary* (May 1971): 9.
2. See, e.g., Norman Podhoretz, "The Present Danger," *Commentary* (March 1980): 31–32.
3. See Norman Podhoretz, "The Future Danger," *Commentary* (April 1981): 32.
4. See *White House Years,* e.g., pp. 59–70, 128–130, 1252–1257.
5. See, e.g., James Burnham, *The Struggle for the World* (Cornwall, N.Y.: John Day Co., 1947); Daniel P. Moynihan, "The Politics of Human Rights," *Commentary* (August 1977); Podhoretz, "The Future Danger."
6. For a brilliant analysis see Raymond Aron, *In Defense of Decadent Europe* (South Bend, Ind.: Regnery/Gateway, 1979); originally published as "My Defence of Our Decadent Europe" in *Encounter* 49, nos. 3 and 4, September and October 1977.
7. See *White House Years,* pp. 150–155.

8. Ibid., pp. 1269–1271.
9. US Congress, House, Committee on Foreign Affairs, *Tension and Detente: Congressional Perspectives on Soviet-American Relations: Report of a Study Mission to the Soviet Union,* 93d Cong., 1st sess., April 1973, p. 11.
10. The Soviet statement on the exit tax, as approved by Dobrynin on April 16, 1973, was as follows:

OFFICIAL COMMUNICATION
OF THE SOVIET GOVERNMENT

Applications of Soviet citizens who wish to leave the USSR for permanent residence in other countries are considered, and decisions concerning such applications are made on an individual basis, taking account of concrete circumstances. As a rule these requests are granted. For example, with regard to persons who in 1972 expressed the desire to go to Israel permission was received by 95.5% of those who applied. A similar approach will be maintained in the future. (It may be noted that more than 2000 persons who received permission to leave for Israel in 1972 did not in fact make use of that permission.)

As regards the refunding of state educational expenses by Soviet citizens leaving for permanent residence abroad, the decree of the Presidium of the USSR Supreme Soviet of August 3, 1972, and a decision taken in accordance with it by the USSR Council of Ministers, provide that Soviet citizens who receive permission to emigrate can be exempted fully from refunding the expenses mentioned above. Accordingly, Soviet authorities, in considering the applications of Soviet citizens wishing to emigrate, have the right to decide that only state duties normal in such cases be collected from such persons. The authorities are now being guided by this right. Consequently, only such normal and insignificant duties — which were also collected before the decree of August 3, 1972 — are being collected, and will be collected, from those persons who are leaving the Soviet Union for permanent residence in other countries.

It goes without saying that as is true with other states, there are cases in the USSR, and there may be such cases in the future, where citizens are denied permission to go abroad for reasons of state security.

In reply to certain supplementary questions, the Soviet government provided the following information:

a. The above statement should be regarded as an official one.

b. The phrase in the statement that "only such normal duties — which were also collected before the decree of August 3, 1972 — are being collected and will be collected" has no time limit attached to it, and any interpretation implying the existence of a time limit would not correspond to the position of the Soviet Government.

c. The exemption from the requirement to refund state educational expenses is being granted on the basis of the terms of the decree of August 3, 1972, itself and of a subsequent decision taken in accordance with that decree by the USSR Council of Ministers. In the Soviet view, this situation obviates the need for suspending or repealing the decree of August 3, 1972.

d. The President and members of the Administration are free to transmit the contents of the official Soviet statement and these additional explanatory points to the Congress.

11. For a detailed discussion of these and other aspects of SALT I, see *White House Years,* especially Chapter XXVIII.
12. Ibid., pp. 1130–1131.
13. Compare the McNamara Posture Statement of February 24, 1965, with Secretary Clark Clifford's Posture Statement of January 22, 1968, p. 94.
14. See *White House Years,* pp. 1152, 1251.
15. The final text signed in Washington on June 22, 1973, read as follows:

AGREEMENT BETWEEN THE UNITED STATES OF AMERICA
AND THE UNION OF SOVIET SOCIALIST REPUBLICS
ON THE PREVENTION OF NUCLEAR WAR

The United States of America and the Union of Soviet Socialist Republics, hereinafter referred to as the Parties,

Guided by the objectives of strengthening world peace and international security,

Conscious that nuclear war would have devastating consequences for mankind,

Proceeding from the desire to bring about conditions in which the danger of an outbreak of nuclear war anywhere in the world would be reduced and ultimately eliminated,

Proceeding from their obligations under the Charter of the United Nations regarding the maintenance of peace, refraining from the threat or use of force, and the avoidance of war, and in conformity with the agreements to which either Party has subscribed,

Proceeding from the Basic Principles of Relations between the United States of America and the Union of Soviet Socialist Republics signed in Moscow on May 29, 1972,

Reaffirming that the development of relations between the United States of America and the Union of Soviet Socialist Republics is not directed against other countries and their interests,

Have agreed as follows:

ARTICLE I

The United States and the Soviet Union agree that an objective of their policies is to remove the danger of nuclear war and of the use of nuclear weapons.

Accordingly, the Parties agree that they will act in such a manner as to prevent the development of situations capable of causing a dangerous exacerbation of their relations, as to avoid military confrontations, and as to exclude the outbreak of nuclear war between them and between either of the Parties and other countries.

ARTICLE II

The Parties agree, in accordance with Article I and to realize the objective stated in that Article, to proceed from the premise that each Party will refrain from the threat or use of force against the other Party, against the allies of the other Party and against other countries, in circumstances which may endanger international peace and security. The Parties agree that they will be guided by these considerations in the formulation of their foreign policies and in their actions in the field of international relations.

ARTICLE III

The Parties undertake to develop their relations with each other and with other countries in a way consistent with the purposes of this Agreement.

ARTICLE IV

If at any time relations between the Parties or between either Party and other countries appear to involve the risk of a nuclear conflict, or if relations between countries not parties to this Agreement appear to involve the risk of nuclear war between the United States of America and the Union of Soviet Socialist Republics or between either Party and other countries, the United States and the Soviet Union, acting in accordance with the provisions of this Agreement, shall immediately enter into urgent consultations with each other and make every effort to avert this risk.

ARTICLE V

Each Party shall be free to inform the Security Council of the United Nations, the Secretary General of the United Nations and the Governments of allied or other countries of the progress and outcome of consultations initiated in accordance with Article IV of this Agreement.

ARTICLE VI

Nothing in this Agreement shall affect or impair:

(a) the inherent right of individual or collective self-defense as envisaged by Article 51 of the Charter of the United Nations,

(b) the provisions of the Charter of the United Nations, including those relating to the maintenance or restoration of international peace and security, and

(c) the obligations undertaken by either Party towards its allies or other countries in treaties, agreements, and other appropriate documents.

ARTICLE VII

This Agreement shall be of unlimited duration.

ARTICLE VIII

This Agreement shall enter into force upon signature.

DONE at Washington on June 22, 1973, in two copies, each in the English and Russian languages, both texts being equally authentic.

FOR THE UNITED STATES OF AMERICA:
[signed] Richard Nixon
    President of the
    United States of America

FOR THE UNION OF SOVIET
SOCIALIST REPUBLICS:
[signed] L. Brezhnev
    General Secretary of the
    Central Committee, CPSU

16. See *White House Years,* pp. 1222–1229; Richard Nixon, *RN: The Memoirs of Richard Nixon* (New York: Grosset & Dunlap, 1978), pp. 613–614.
17. The Middle East section of the US–Soviet summit communiqué of June 24, 1973, read as follows:

> The parties expressed their deep concern with the situation in the Middle East and exchanged opinions regarding ways of reaching a Middle East settlement.
>
> Each of the parties set forth its position on this problem.
>
> Both parties agreed to continue to exert their efforts to promote the quickest possible settlement in the Middle East. This settlement should be in accordance with the interests of all states in the area, be consistent with their independence and sovereignty and should take into due account the legitimate interests of the Palestinian people.

VIII
INDOCHINA: THE BEGINNING OF THE END

1. See Chapter II, note 11.
2. See Chapter II, note 4.
3. See Spencer Rich, "No Legal Bar Is Found To Resuming Warfare," *Washington Post,* April 9, 1973. Secretary Rogers's memorandum on the legality of air operations is at note 21 below.
4. See, e.g., McGeorge Bundy, "Vietnam, Watergate and Presidential Powers," *Foreign Affairs* 58, no. 2 (Winter 1979–1980): 397–407.
5. President Kennedy's private assurances to the President of Pakistan are listed in *White House Years,* p. 895 and note 7 on p. 1488. In 1963, messages from President Kennedy to Crown Prince Faisal of Saudi Arabia pledged to send American military forces to aid Saudi Arabia against threats from Nasser's Egypt during the Yemen crisis. See Christopher J. McMullen, *Resolution of the Yemen Crisis, 1963: A Case Study in Mediation* (Washington: Institute for the Study of Diplomacy, Georgetown University, 1980), pp. 9–10, 13, 20.
6. Among the many public statements pledging US enforcement of the Paris Agreement were the following:

President Nixon's Address to the Nation, January 23, 1973:

> [T]he terms of the agreement must be scrupulously adhered to. We shall do everything the agreement requires of us, and we shall expect the other parties to do everything it requires of them. We shall also expect other interested nations to help insure that the agreement is carried out and peace is maintained.

Dr. Kissinger's Press Conference, January 24, 1973:

> QUESTION: If a peace treaty is violated and if the ICC proves ineffective, will the United States ever again send troops into Vietnam?
>
> KISSINGER: I don't want to speculate on hypothetical situations that we don't expect to arise. . . .

Deputy Assistant Secretary William Sullivan on NBC–TV's Meet the Press, January 28, 1973:

> QUESTION: There's also reports from Saigon today, Mr. Ambassador, that the United States has given official but private assurances to Saigon that we would intervene militarily again if Hanoi commits serious violations. Just what is our commitment? What would we do if a cease-fire breaks down?

SULLIVAN: I am not going to speculate on that, Mr. Rosenfeld. I think you have seen Dr. Kissinger's statement concerning the method in which the agreement has stipulated the requirements for carrying out this accord. There are no inhibitions upon us, but we are not going to discuss any hypothetical questions at this time about what the future prospects may bring.

Dr. Kissinger's Interview on CBS News with Marvin Kalb, February 1, 1973:

KALB: Dr. Kissinger, I think what I was trying to get at is what happens — and I suppose this question must be asked. In the best of all possible worlds the cease-fire is going to hold. In the world that we live in it may not. President Thieu said in an interview tonight on CBS that he would never call upon American air power to go back. And Ambassador Sullivan said only last Sunday that there are no inhibitions — I believe were his words — on the use of this air power. Is that correct?

KISSINGER: That is legally correct.

KALB: Politically and diplomatically?

KISSINGER: We have the right to do this. The question is very difficult to answer in the abstract. It depends on the extent of the challenge, on the nature of the threat, on the circumstances in which it arises; and it would be extremely unwise for a responsible American official at this stage, when the peace is in the process of being established, to give a checklist about what the United States will or will not do in every circumstance that is likely to arise.

For the future that we can foresee, the North Vietnamese are not in a position to launch an overwhelming attack on the South, even if they violate the agreement. What happens after a year or two has to be seen in the circumstances which then exist.

Most of the violations that one can now foresee should be handled by the South Vietnamese.

KALB: So that for the next year or two, if I understand you right, there would be no need for a reinvolvement of American military power?

KISSINGER: Marvin, we did not end this war in order to look for an excuse to reenter it, but it would be irresponsible for us at this moment to give a precise checklist to potential aggressors as to what they can or cannot safely do.

President Nixon's News Conference, March 15, 1973:

I will only suggest this: that we have informed the North Vietnamese of our concern about this infiltration and of what we believe it to be, a violation of the cease-fire, the cease-fire and the peace agreement. Our concern has also been expressed to other interested parties. And I would only suggest that based on my actions over the past four years, that the North Vietnamese should not lightly disregard such expressions of concern when they are made with regard to a violation. That is all I will say about it.

Under Secretary for Political Affairs William Porter, speech in Grand Rapids, March 21, 1973:

President Nixon has made clear our concern at North Vietnamese infiltration of large amounts of equipment into South Vietnam. If it continued, this infiltration could lead to serious consequences. The North Vietnamese should not lightly disregard our expressions of concern.

President Nixon's Address to the Nation, March 29, 1973:

There are still some problem areas. The provisions of the agreement requiring an accounting for all missing in action in Indochina, the provisions with regard to Laos and Cambodia, the provisions prohibiting infiltration from North Vietnam into South Vietnam have not been complied with. We have and will continue to comply with the agreement. We shall insist that North Vietnam comply with the agreement. And the leaders of North Vietnam should have no doubt as to the consequences if they fail to comply with the agreement.

Defense Secretary Richardson on NBC-TV's Meet the Press, *April 1, 1973:*

RON NESSEN: Mr. Secretary, can you say that the United States will never under any circumstances send military forces back to Indochina?

RICHARDSON: No, I cannot give any categorical assurance, Mr. Nessen. Obviously the future holds possible developments that are unforeseeable now. But certainly we very much hope that this will not be necessary.

NESSEN: And if I ask you the same question about, can you say whether the United States will never bomb again in North or South Vietnam, your answer would be the same?

RICHARDSON: Yes, but of course our hope and expectation is that the cease-fire agreements will be observed.

NESSEN: President Nixon has warned several times North Vietnam that it should have no doubt about the consequences if it violates the cease-fire. What does he mean, what are the consequences?

RICHARDSON: This is obviously something that cannot be spelled out in advance, Mr. Nessen. . . .

They have, I think, had some reason, looking back over the past, to know that the President has been willing to do what has been necessary in order to bring about a negotiated solution and to bring an end to the war.

Defense Secretary Richardson to the Senate Armed Services Committee, April 2, 1973:

QUESTION: There are reports out of South Vietnam today that President Thieu of South Vietnam says that the United States and the South Vietnamese Government have an agreement that if there is an offensive, that if the North Vietnamese do come in, that the United States will come back with its airplanes and with its air support? Do we have such a commitment?

RICHARDSON: This is a question simply of very possible contingencies. I wouldn't want to try to amplify on anything he said or to subtract from it. . . .

We, of course, continue to adhere to the proposition that the cease-fire agreements not only have been signed but are in the interest of all the parties and our objective is to assure so far as is possible that they are carried out. . . .

Our job is to reinforce the considerations that will, we trust, lead them to carry out the agreement. . . .

If he [the President] had the constitutional power to carry on the war while winding it down, we think it's a natural extension of this to say that he has the constitutional power to take whatever incidental steps that are now required in order to assure that the cease-fire agreements are carried out.

US–GVN Communiqué (San Clemente), April 3, 1973:

Both Presidents, while acknowledging that progress was being made toward military and political settlements in South Vietnam, nevertheless viewed with great concern infiltrations of men and weapons in sizeable numbers from North Vietnam into South Vietnam in violation of the Agreement on Ending the War, and considered that actions which would threaten the basis of the agreement would call for appropriately vigorous reactions. They expressed their conviction that all the provisions of the Agreement, including in particular those concerning military forces and military supplies, must be faithfully implemented if the cease-fire is to be preserved and the prospects for a peaceful settlement are to be assured. President Nixon stated in this connection that the United States views violations of any provision of the Agreement with great and continuing concern. . . .

Defense Secretary Elliot Richardson, interviewed by newsmen prior to his appearance before the House Appropriations Subcommittee on Defense, April 3, 1973:

QUESTION: Mr. Secretary, under what conditions might we have to begin bombing in support of the South Vietnamese?

RICHARDSON: It would be one of those questions that it's impossible to answer in general terms. We can only see what develops, and hopefully, what will develop is the full and complete implementation of the cease-fire agreements.

QUESTION: But is it possible that we will have to bomb either North Vietnam or in support of the South Vietnamese army again?

RICHARDSON: It's certainly something we cannot rule out at this time.

Dr. Kissinger's Press Conference, May 2, 1973:

QUESTION: You say if North Vietnam does not obey the call for an honorable cease-fire, it would risk revived confrontation with us. Could you spell out a little bit more clearly what you mean there [in the Foreign Policy Report]?

KISSINGER: . . . Now, on the confrontation, we have made clear that we mean to have the agreement observed. We are now engaged in an effort to discuss with the North Vietnamese what is required to bring about the strict implementation of the agreement. We have every intention and every incentive to make certain that our side of the agreement is maintained, and to use our influence wherever we can to bring about the strict implementation of the agreement.

But the United States cannot sign a solemn agreement and within weeks have major provisions violated without our making an attempt to indicate it. Now, the particular measures: Some of them are, of course, obvious and we would prefer, as we state in the report and as we have stated publicly many times, to move our relationship with the North Vietnamese toward normalization, and to start a process which would accelerate, such as other processes normally have.

So the general thrust of this paragraph is that the tension existing between us certainly cannot ease as rapidly as we want if the agreement is not observed.

President's Foreign Policy Report, May 3, 1973:

We hope that the contending factions will now prefer to pursue their objectives through peaceful means and political competition rather than through the brutal and costly methods of the past. This choice is up to them. We shall be vigilant concerning violations of the Agreement. . . .

Hanoi has two basic choices. The first is to exploit the Vietnam Agreement and press its objectives in Indochina. In this case it would continue to infiltrate men and materiel into South Vietnam, keep its forces in Laos and Cambodia, and through pressures or outright attack renew its aggression against our friends. Such a course would endanger the hard won gains for peace in Indochina. It would risk revived confrontation with us. . . . The second course is for North Vietnam to pursue its objectives peacefully, allowing the historical trends of the region to assert themselves. . . .

The Republic of Vietnam will find us a steady friend. We will continue to deal with its government as the legitimate representative of the South Vietnamese people, while supporting efforts by the South Vietnamese parties to achieve reconciliation and shape their political future. We will provide replacement military assistance within the terms of the Agreement. We expect our friends to observe the Agreement just as we will not tolerate violations by the North Vietnamese or its allies. . . .

We have told Hanoi, privately and publicly, that we will not tolerate violations of the Agreement.

Dr. Kissinger's Press Conference, June 13, 1973:

QUESTION: Do you feel now that with the signing of the document you have more or less ended your work in the Indochina area or that you will still have a lot of difficulties, especially concerning Cambodia?

KISSINGER: The remaining issues in Indochina will still require significant diplomatic efforts, and we expect to continue them. Of course, we remain committed to the strict implementation of the agreement, and we will maintain our interest in it.

President Nixon's Message to the House of Representatives, June 27, 1973, opposing the Indochina bombing halt:

A total halt would virtually remove Communist incentive to negotiate and would thus seriously undercut ongoing diplomatic efforts to achieve a cease-fire in Cambodia. It would effectively reverse the momentum toward lasting peace in Indochina set in motion last January and renewed in the four-party communiqué signed in Paris on June 13. . . .

A Communist victory in Cambodia, in turn, would threaten the fragile balance of negotiated agreements, political alignments and military capabilities upon which the overall peace in Southeast Asia depends and on which my assessment of the acceptability of the Vietnam agreements was based.

Finally, and with even more serious global implications, the legislatively imposed acceptance of the United States to Communist violations of the Paris agreements and the conquest of Cambodia by Communist forces would call into question our national commitment not only to the Vietnam settlement but to many other settlements or agreements we have reached or seek to reach with other nations. A serious blow to America's international credibility would have been struck — a blow that would be felt far beyond Indochina.

Secretary Kissinger's Letter to Senator Kennedy, March 25, 1974:

As a signator of the Paris Agreement, the United States committed itself to strengthening the conditions which made the cease-fire possible and to the goal of the South Vietnamese people's right to self-determination. With these commitments in mind, we continue to provide to the Republic of Vietnam the means necessary for its self-defense and for its economic viability. . . .

We have . . . committed ourselves very substantially, both politically and morally.

Interview with Tran Van Lam, former South Vietnamese Foreign Minister, April 14, 1975, Saigon (Press Report):

> Foreign Minister Lam stated that President Nixon promised to "react immediately and vigorously" to any large-scale North Vietnamese offensive. But, he added, "no secret agreement was signed."

It is interesting that the Bundy article only paraphrases, but does not quote in full, the warnings by Secretary of Defense Richardson. And he paraphrases them misleadingly, claiming — obviously incorrectly — that they referred to the existing bombing in Cambodia and not to possible reintervention in Vietnam in response to renewed North Vietnamese attacks. See Bundy, "Vietnam, Watergate and Presidential Powers," pp. 400–401.

7. Godfrey Hodgson, *America in Our Time: From World War II to Nixon* (Garden City, N.Y.: Doubleday & Co., 1976), p. 397.

8. See, e.g., Michael Ledeen and William Lewis, *Debacle: The American Failure in Iran* (New York: Alfred A. Knopf, 1981).

9. Stephen T. Hosmer, Konrad Kellen, and Brian M. Jenkins, *The Fall of South Vietnam: Statements by Vietnamese Military and Civilian Leaders* (Santa Monica: The Rand Corporation, R–2208–OSD [HIST], December 1978), pp. 10–15.

10. On the 1969 EC-121 incident, see *White House Years,* pp. 313–321.

11. Ibid., pp. 1030–1031.

12. This is the thesis of William Shawcross, *Sideshow: Kissinger, Nixon and the Destruction of Cambodia* (New York: Simon & Schuster, 1979). For an analysis of the book's errors, sleight of hand, and deceptive documentation, see Peter W. Rodman, "Sideswipe: Kissinger, Shawcross and the Responsibility for Cambodia," *The American Spectator* 14, no. 3 (March 1981), and the exchange between Rodman and Shawcross in *The American Spectator* 14, no. 7 (July 1981).

13. See Kenneth M. Quinn, "Political Change in Wartime: The Khmer Krahom Revolution in Southern Cambodia, 1970–1974," *Naval War College Review* (Spring 1976): 8–9.

14. See, e.g., Shawcross, *Sideshow,* p. 389 and *passim.*

15. Ibid., p. 265, for example.

16. Democratic Kampuchea, *The Black Book: Facts and Proofs of Vietnam's Acts of Aggression and Annexation against Kampuchea* (Phnom Penh: September 1978), Chapter V, Section 2 (c).

17. François Ponchaud, *Cambodia: Year Zero* (New York; Holt, Rinehart & Winston, 1978), pp. 21, 192. See also pp. xvi, 135–136.

18. Quinn, "Political Change in Wartime," pp. 8–19. Shawcross cites Ponchaud and Quinn, but never these passages that directly contradict his thesis that American actions caused Khmer Rouge brutality.

19. "Sihanouk: The Man We May Have to Settle for in Cambodia," *New York Times,* Aug. 12, 1973.

20. Versions of this remark by Congressman O'Neill appear in several sources: e.g., remarks by Congressman Robert Giaimo on *The CBS-TV Evening News,* June 25, 1973; Shawcross, *Sideshow,* p. 285. Members of Congress have the privilege of amending or rewriting their statements before publication in the *Congressional Record,* and this remark does not appear there.

21. The President's legal authority to continue air operations in Cambodia after the Paris Agreement was spelled out in detail in a memorandum that Secretary Rogers submitted to the Senate Foreign Relations Committee on April 30, 1973 (footnotes omitted):

PRESIDENTIAL AUTHORITY TO CONTINUE U.S. AIR COMBAT OPERATIONS IN CAMBODIA

The purpose of this memorandum is to discuss the President's legal authority to continue United States air combat operations in Cambodia since the conclusion of the Agreement on Ending the War and Restoring Peace in Vietnam on January 27, 1973 and the completion on March 28, 1973 of the withdrawal of United States armed forces from Vietnam and the return of American citizens held prisoner in Indochina. The memorandum also discusses the background of the Agreement of January 27 and the purposes of various United States actions in order to clarify the legal issues.

For many years the United States has pursued a combination of diplomatic and military efforts to bring about a just peace in Vietnam. These efforts were successful in strengthening the self-defense capabilities of the armed forces of the Republic of Vietnam and in bringing about serious negotiations which culminated in the Agreement on Ending the War and Restoring Peace in Vietnam, signed at Paris on January 27, 1973. This Agreement provided for a cease-fire in Vietnam, the return of prisoners, and the withdrawal of United States and allied armed forces from South Vietnam within sixty days. The Agreement (in Article 20) also required the withdrawal of all foreign armed forces from Laos and Cambodia and obligated the parties to refrain from using the territory of Cambodia and Laos to encroach on the sovereignty and security of other countries, to respect the neutrality of Cambodia and Laos, and to avoid any interference in the internal affairs of those two countries. This Article is of central importance as it has long been apparent that the conflicts in Laos and Cambodia are closely related to the conflict in Vietnam and, in fact, are so inter-related as to be considered parts of a single conflict.

At the time the Vietnam Agreement was concluded, the United States made clear to the North Vietnamese that the armed forces of the Khmer Government would suspend all offensive operations and that the United States aircraft supporting them would do likewise. We stated that, if the other side reciprocated, a *de facto* cease-fire would thereby be brought into force in Cambodia. However, we also stated that, if the communist forces carried out attacks, government forces and United States air forces would have to take necessary counter measures and that, in the event, we would continue to carry out air strikes in Cambodia as necessary until such time as a cease-fire could be brought into effect. These statements were based on our conviction that it was essential for Hanoi to understand that continuance of the hostilities in Cambodia and Laos would not be in its interest or in our interest and that compliance with Article 20 of the Agreement would have to be reciprocal.

It has recently been suggested that the withdrawal of all U.S. armed forces from South Vietnam and the return of all U.S. prisoners has created a fundamentally new situation in which new authority must be sought by the President from the Congress to carry out air strikes in Cambodia. The issue more accurately stated is whether the constitutional authority of the President to continue doing in Cambodia what the United States has lawfully been doing there expires with the withdrawal of U.S. armed forces from Vietnam and the return of American prisoners despite the fact that a cease-fire has not been achieved in Cambodia and North Vietnamese troops remain in Cambodia contrary to clear provisions of the Agreement. In other words, the issue is not whether the President may do something new, but rather whether what he has been doing must automatically stop, without regard to the consequences even though the Agreement is not being implemented by the other side.

The purposes of the United States in Southeast Asia have always included seeking a settlement to the Vietnamese war that would permit the people of South Vietnam to exercise their right to self-determination. The President has made this clear on many occasions. For example, on May 8, 1972, when he made the proposals that formed the basis for the ultimately successful negotiations with North Vietnam, he said there were three purposes to our military actions against Vietnam: first, to prevent the forceful imposition of a communist government in South Vietnam; second, to protect our remaining forces in South Vietnam; and third, to obtain the release of our prisoners. The joint communique issued by the President and Mr. Brezhnev in Moscow on May 29, 1972 in which the view of the United States was expressed said that negotiations on the basis of the President's May 8 proposals would be the quickest and most effective way to obtain the objectives of bringing the military conflict to an end as soon as possible and ensuring that the political future of South Vietnam should be left for the South Vietnamese people to decide for themselves, free from outside interference. The recent opinion of the United States Court of Appeals for the District of Columbia Circuit in *Mitchell* v. *Laird* makes it clear that the President has the constitutional power to pursue all of these purposes. In the words of Judge Wyzanski the President properly acted "with a profound concern for the durable interests of the nation — its defense, its honor, its morality."

The Agreement signed on January 27, 1973 represented a settlement consistent with these objectives. An important element in that Agreement is Article 20 which recognizes the underlying connections among the hostilities in all the countries of Indochina and required the cessation of foreign armed intervention in Laos and Cambodia. The importance of this article cannot be overestimated, because the continuation of hostilities in

Laos and Cambodia and the presence there of North Vietnamese troops threatens the right of self-determination of the South Vietnamese people, which is guaranteed by the Agreement.

The United States is gratified that a cease-fire agreement has been reached in Laos. It must be respected by all the parties and result in the prompt withdrawal of foreign forces. In Cambodia it has not yet been possible to bring about a cease-fire, and North Vietnamese forces have not withdrawn from that country. Under present circumstances, United States air support and material assistance are needed to support the armed forces of the Khmer Republic and thereby to render more likely the early conclusion of a cease-fire and implementation of Article 20 of the Agreement. Thus, U.S. air strikes in Cambodia do not represent a commitment by the United States to the defense of Cambodia as such but instead represent a meaningful interim action to bring about compliance with this critical provision in the Vietnam Agreement.

To stop these air strikes automatically at a fixed date would be as self-defeating as it would have been for the United States to withdraw its armed forces prematurely from South Vietnam while it was still trying to negotiate an agreement with North Vietnam. Had that been done in Vietnam, the Agreement of January 27 would never have been achieved; if it were done in Cambodia, there is no reason to believe that a cease-fire could be brought about in Cambodia or that the withdrawal of North Vietnamese forces from Cambodia could be obtained. It can be seen from this analysis that unilateral cessation of our United States air combat activity in Cambodia without the removal of North Vietnamese forces from the country would undermine the central achievement of the January Agreement as surely as would have a failure by the United States to insist on the inclusion in the Agreement of Article 20 requiring North Vietnamese withdrawal from Laos and Cambodia. The President's powers under Article II of the Constitution are adequate to prevent such a self-defeating result. It is worth noting that in reaching a similar conclusion, the report entitled "Congress and the Termination of the Vietnam War" recently prepared for your Committee by the Foreign Affairs Division of the Congressional Research Service, arrived at the same general conclusion as to the President's Constitutional power.

One must recognize that the scope and application of the President's powers under Article II of the Constitution are rarely free from dispute. Under the Constitution, the war powers are shared between the Executive and Legislative branches of the Government. The Congress is granted the powers "to provide for the common defense", "to declare war, grant letters of marque and reprisal, and make rules concerning captures on land and water", "to raise and support armies", "to provide and maintain a navy", "to make rules for the government and regulation of the land and naval forces", and "to make all laws which shall be necessary and proper for carrying into execution the foregoing powers. . . ." On the other hand, the Constitution provides that "the executive power shall be vested in a President," that he "shall be Commander-in-Chief of the army and navy of the United States," and that "he shall take care that the laws be faithfully executed." The President is also given the authority to make treaties with the advice and consent of two thirds of the Senate, to appoint ambassadors with the advice and consent of the Senate, and to receive ambassadors and other public ministers.

The proceedings of the Federal Constitutional Convention in 1787 suggest that the ambiguities of this division of power between the President and the Congress were deliberately left unresolved with the understanding that they were to be defined by practice. There may be those who wish the framers of the Constitution would have been more precise, but it is submitted that there was great wisdom in realizing the impossibility of foreseeing all contingencies and in leaving considerable flexibility for the future play of political forces. The Constitution is a framework for democratic decision and action, not a source of ready-made answers to all questions, and that is one of its great strengths.

There is no question but that Congress should play an important role in decisions involving the use of armed forces abroad. With respect to the continuation of U.S. air combat activity in Cambodia, what is that role? The Congress has cooperated with the President in establishing the policy of firmness coupled with an openness to negotiation which has succeeded in bringing about the Agreement of January 27 and which can succeed in securing its implementation. This cooperation has been shown through consultations and through the authorization and appropriation process. The Congress has

consistently rejected proposals by some members to withdraw this congressional participation and authority by cutting off appropriations for necessary military expenditures and
foreign assistance. The Congress has also enacted several provisions with specific reference to Cambodia. The President's policy in Cambodia has been and continues to be fully
consistent with these provisions.

It was, of course, hoped that the Agreement signed at Paris on January 27 would be
strictly implemented according to its terms, including the prompt conclusion of cease-
fires in Laos and Cambodia and the withdrawal of foreign troops from those two countries. What has happened instead is that, in Laos, the cease-fire has been followed by
continuing communist stalling in forming the new government and, in Cambodia, the
communists responded to the efforts of the Khmer Government to bring about a *de facto*
cease-fire with a fierce, general offensive. North Vietnamese forces remain in Laos and
Cambodia and continue to infiltrate men and war material through these countries to the
Republic of Vietnam. North Vietnamese forces in Cambodia continue to participate in
and to support Communist offensive operations.

United States air strikes in Laos were an important element in the decision by North
Vietnam and its Laotian allies to negotiate a cease-fire in Laos. If United States air strikes
were stopped in Cambodia despite the communist offensive, there would be little, if any,
incentive for the communists to seek a cease-fire in that country, and the temptation
would doubtless be great for North Vietnam to leave its troops and supply lines indefinitely in Laos and Cambodia. Such a situation would be the opposite of that prescribed
by Article 20 of the Vietnam Agreement and would so threaten the viability of the
settlement in Vietnam and the right to self-determination of the South Vietnamese people
as to be totally unacceptable to the Republic of Vietnam and to the United States. In light
of these facts, it seems clear that the argument that the Constitution requires immediate
cessation of U.S. air strikes in Cambodia because of the Paris Agreement is, in reality,
an argument that the Constitution which has permitted the United States to negotiate a
peace agreement — a peace that guarantees the right of self-determination to the South
Vietnamese people as well as the return of United States prisoners and withdrawal of
United States armed forces from Vietnam — is a Constitution that contains an automatic
self-destruct mechanism designed to destroy what has been so painfully achieved. We are
now in the process of having further discussions with the North Vietnamese with regard
to the implementation of the Paris Agreement. We hope these discussions will be successful and will lead to a cease-fire in Cambodia.

See also the excellent constitutional analysis and testimony submitted by Senator Barry M.
Goldwater on May 10, 1973, to the House Foreign Affairs Committee. US Congress, House,
Committee on Foreign Affairs, *U.S. Policy and Programs in Cambodia,* Hearings before the
Subcommittee on Asian and Pacific Affairs, 93d Cong., 1st sess., 1973, pp. 41–52 and 82.

22. "Mr. Nixon's War Veto," *Washington Post,* June 29, 1973. Similar comments appeared in
    the *Baltimore Sun* of June 18; the *New York Post,* June 26; the *St. Louis Post-Dispatch,*
    August 7; and the *Baltimore Sun,* August 14, 1973.
23. See, e.g., Michael Parks, "Soviet Trying to End Feud with Sihanouk," *Baltimore Sun,* July
    8, 1973.
24. James Pringle, "Sihanouk Adapts to 'Austere Life,' " *Washington Post,* July 18, 1973.
25. My letter to Mrs. Aase Lionaes of the Nobel Peace Prize Committee on April 30, 1975, read
    as follows:
    Dear Mrs. Lionaes:
       The award to me in 1973 of the Nobel Peace Prize was one of the proudest moments
    of my life. Together with millions of others, I hoped that the Paris Agreements would
    finally bring peace in Indochina. But that was not to be; the peace we sought through
    negotiations has been overturned by force.
       While I am deeply conscious of the honor done me by the Nobel Foundation, I feel
    honor bound to return the prize. I, therefore, enclose the Nobel Gold Medal and the Nobel
    Diploma so graciously presented to me in 1973.
       As you know, rather than accept the financial award which accompanied the prize, I
    used the money to endow a fund to provide scholarship assistance to children of American
    servicemen killed or lost in Indochina. Others have since made additional contributions
    to the fund, and the first scholarship grants will be announced shortly.

Nevertheless, I feel I must reimburse the Nobel Foundation, or, should the Foundation prefer, make a contribution of like amount to a charity acceptable to the Foundation. I ask that you let me know the wishes of the Foundation in this regard, so that I may comply with them immediately.

I regret, more profoundly than I can ever express, the necessity for this letter. But the anguish and tragedy that have been inflicted upon millions who sought nothing more than the chance to live their own lives leave me no alternative.

Sincerely,

[signed] Henry A. Kissinger

IX

CHILE: THE FALL OF SALVADOR ALLENDE

1. US Congress, Senate, Select Committee to Study Governmental Operations with Respect to Intelligence Activities, *Covert Action in Chile: 1963–1973,* Staff Report, 94th Cong., 1st sess., 1975, pp. 2, 28.
2. *White House Years,* pp. 654–655.
3. Régis Debray, *The Chilean Revolution: Conversations with Allende* (New York: Random House, Pantheon Books, 1971), pp. 119, 118, 82.
4. See *White House Years,* Chapter XVI.
5. Ibid., Chapter XVII.
6. Nathaniel Davis in "US Covert Actions in Chile 1971–73," in two issues of *Foreign Service Journal,* November and December 1978. The quotations here are from p. 11 of the December article.
7. See Davis, "US Covert Actions in Chile," November 1978, pp. 12–13; William Colby and Peter Forbath, *Honorable Men: My Life in the CIA* (New York: Simon & Schuster, 1978), pp. 379–382.
8. Davis, "US Covert Actions in Chile," December 1978, p. 11.
9. *New York Times,* June 13, 1972.
10. Paul E. Sigmund, *The Overthrow of Allende and the Politics of Chile, 1964–1976* (Pittsburgh: University of Pittsburgh Press, 1977), p. 171.
11. Ibid., p. 186.
12. See US Congress, Senate, *Covert Action in Chile: 1963–1973,* p. 31.
13. Sigmund, *The Overthrow of Allende and the Politics of Chile,* p. 215.
14. The following is the Chile portion of my conversation with Ambassador Nathaniel Davis on September 8, 1973:

KISSINGER: Tell me how things are going in Chile.

DAVIS: Well, I certainly haven't improved the situation. The economy continues to go downhill; polarization of the political forces continues; and each of the three armed forces has at one point or another faced an internal crisis. As a result, the Anti-Allende forces are stronger in each of the three services. As you know, General Prats has resigned.

KISSINGER: Why did he leave?

DAVIS: Well, partly because of the wives of Prats' officers, including the wives of many of his Generals, who demanded his resignation. Partly because Prats has fallen in with and become something of a tool of the Allende forces in the Government.

KISSINGER: Will there be a coup?

DAVIS: In Chile you can never count on anything, but the odds are in favor of a coup, though I can't give you any time frame.

KISSINGER: We are going to stay out of that, I assume.

DAVIS: Yes. My firm instructions to everybody on the staff are that we are not to involve ourselves in any way.

KISSINGER: Do the Chileans ever ask us for our view?

DAVIS: Yes, on occasion they'll sidle up and ask what we think about the situation. But as I said, my strong instructions to the staff are that they are not to get drawn into any conversations on the subject.

KISSINGER: Can Allende last out his term?

DAVIS: His chances of doing so are decreasing with every week.

KISSINGER: Well, what happens in those circumstances? Has there ever been a President who resigned?

DAVIS: Yes. In 1891 there was a case like this. In fact the situation was somewhat similar to the circumstances today.

KISSINGER: Well, if Allende leaves, what happens? Is there a new election?

DAVIS: If he resigns, then the President of the Senate becomes Chief of State. That's Frei, but I don't think you should count on that [as a] likely possibility. If the Army should take over, I doubt very much that they will be prepared to give up power in a hurry.

KISSINGER: Then Chile would go the way of Brazil?

DAVIS: Yes, or Peru.

KISSINGER: What would the military government be like? Would it be like Peru or Brazil?

DAVIS: It would be very pro-American. We have good contacts with the Chilean military. But Chile has a radical history and the military will not want to look as if it is running away from that history and returning to the old conservative status quo.

KISSINGER: Yes, but Chile under those circumstances would not be a center for revolutionary activity in Latin America, would it?

DAVIS: No.

KISSINGER: What should we do there?

DAVIS: Things are moving fast enough. Our biggest problem is to keep from getting caught in the middle. We must leave the Chileans to decide their future for themselves.

KISSINGER: What's your bet on an Allende overthrow?

DAVIS: I would think that Allende has about a 25 percent chance of finishing out his term in 1976. I think there's a 35 to 40 percent chance that there will be a *golpe*. I think there is perhaps a 20 to 25 percent chance that the military will enter the government but in such a role that it really runs the government. I think there is a very small percentage chance that Chile will become a Cuba-type situation.

KISSINGER: Well, if it were to become one, from what base would it develop?

DAVIS: It would develop from a failure of nerve on the part of the military. I have to admit that the Chilean military's nerve has failed it before.

KISSINGER: What about the carabineros?

DAVIS: They are moving closer to the military point of view these days. The top leaders, however, still want to stay out of the middle.

15. Sigmund, *The Overthrow of Allende and the Politics of Chile,* pp. 4–5, 244–247, assesses the conflicting accounts and comes to the conclusion that "the weight of the evidence seems to point toward suicide."

16. Interview with Madrid newspaper *ABC,* October 10, 1973, quoted in *Facts on File Yearbook 1973,* vol. XXXIII, p. 872.

X
BECOMING SECRETARY OF STATE

1. See *White House Years,* especially pp. 26–32.

2. See, e.g., H. R. Haldeman with Joseph DiMona, *The Ends of Power* (New York: New York Times Books, 1978), pp. 94–97; Bill Gulley with Mary Ellen Reese, *Breaking Cover* (New York: Simon & Schuster, 1980), pp. 133, 251.

3. Fred Greenstein and Robert Wright, "Reagan . . . Another Ike?" *Public Opinion* 3, no. 6 (December–January 1981): 52–53. See also Greenstein and Wright, "The Political Savvy of Dwight Eisenhower," *Wall Street Journal,* January 28, 1981.

4. Haldeman, *The Ends of Power,* pp. 176–177. Herb Klein reports overhearing me, in late 1972 after the election, asking Haldeman when I would be named as Rogers's replacement. But Haldeman's account, referring to the same period, makes clear that at that stage Kenneth Rush was to be Rogers's replacement. See Herbert G. Klein, *Making It Perfectly Clear* (Garden City, N.Y.: Doubleday & Co., 180), pp. 309–310.

5. I realize that Nixon gave a different account to David Frost. See David Frost, *"I Gave Them a Sword": Behind the Scenes of the Nixon Interviews* (New York: William Morrow, 1978), pp. 166–167.

6. See, e.g., "The Talk of the Town," *The New Yorker,* September 17, 1973; William Safire, "Advise and Condone," *New York Times,* September 13, 1973.

7. Testimony of Attorney General Elliot Richardson before the Senate Foreign Relations Com-

mittee, September 10, 1973. See note 8 below. See also the comment of William Ruckelshaus, former Acting Director of the FBI, on CBS-TV's *Face the Nation,* June 16, 1974: "It wasn't his [Kissinger's] idea to tap; he simply complained about the leaks."

8. US Congress, Senate, Committee on Foreign Relations, *Hearings on the Role of Dr. Henry A. Kissinger in the Wiretapping of Certain Government Officials and Newsmen,* 93d Cong., 2d sess., published September 29, 1974, includes my testimony in both public and executive session in both 1973 and 1974.

9. Muskie is cited in "U.S. Split on Defense Costs, Muskie told Soviet Premier," *Washington Star,* January 26, 1971.

10. See *White House Years,* pp. 38–48.

XI
THE MIDDLE EAST WAR

1. See Abba Eban, *An Autobiography* (New York: Random House, 1977), p. 502. Menachem Begin, then opposition leader and now Prime Minister of Israel, later charged inaccurately that I accepted Zayyat's version of events that morning and that I automatically "assumed" that Israel had started the war with the alleged naval attack. This is simply not true. See interview with Prime Minister Menachem Begin of Israel, by Robert Siegel, *Communiqué: The Weekly Report on World Affairs from National Public Radio* (NPR), June 18, 1981.

2. Roberta Wohlstetter, *Pearl Harbor: Warning and Decision* (Stanford: Stanford University Press, 1962).

3. Barton Whaley, *Codeword BARBAROSSA* (Cambridge, Mass.: The MIT Press, 1973).

4. Sun Tzu, *The Art of War,* translated and with an introduction by Samuel B. Griffith (Oxford: Oxford University Press, 1963), p. 66.

5. See, e.g., Commission of Inquiry — Yom Kippur War (The Agranat Commission), *Partial Report,* 2 April 1974 (State of Israel, Government Press Office, Press Bulletin), paras. 9–12; Lt. Gen. Haim Bar Lev, "Surprise and the Yom Kippur War," paper delivered to the International Symposium on the Military Aspects of the Israeli-Arab Conflict, Jerusalem, October 1975, in Louis Williams, ed., *Military Aspects of the Israeli-Arab Conflict* (Tel Aviv: University Publishing Projects, 1975), pp. 259–265.

6. Eban, *An Autobiography,* p. 496.

7. See Ray S. Cline, "Policy Without Intelligence," *Foreign Policy,* no. 17 (Winter 1974–1975), especially pp. 131–133.

8. Anwar el-Sadat, *In Search of Identity: An Autobiography* (New York: Harper & Row, 1977), p. 246.

9. Ibid., pp. 247, 249, 252–254.

10. See *New York Times,* September 29, 1973, p. 1. See also Claire Sterling, *The Terror Network* (New York: Holt, Rinehart & Winston, 1981), pp. 144–145.

11. See Golda Meir, *My Life* (New York: G. P. Putnam's Sons, 1975), pp. 426–427; Moshe Dayan, *Story of My Life* (New York: William Morrow, 1976), pp. 460–461; "Israel Knew Attack Was Coming, Envoy to the U.S. Asserts," *New York Times,* October 11, 1973, p. 18; Edward N. Luttwak, "Strategy for a War," *Washington Star-News,* October 14, 1973.

12. Dayan, *Story of My Life,* p. 460; Eban, *An Autobiography,* pp. 508–509.

13. Sadat, *In Search of Identity,* pp. 252–254.

14. See, e.g., Edward N. Luttwak and Walter Laqueur, "Kissinger and the Yom Kippur War," *Commentary* (September 1974).

15. See the *Washington Post,* October 15, 16, and 18, 1973.

XII
MOSCOW, THE CEASE-FIRE, AND THE ALERT

1. UN Security Council Resolution 338 of October 22, 1973, the text of which was worked out in Moscow, read as follows:

> *The Security Council*
>
> 1. *Calls upon* all parties to the present fighting to cease all firing and terminate all military activity immediately, no later than 12 hours after the moment of the adoption of this decision, in the positions they now occupy;
>
> 2. *Calls upon* the parties concerned to start immediately after the cease-fire the implementation of Security Council resolution 242 (1967) in all of its parts;

3. *Decides* that, immediately and concurrently with the cease-fire, negotiations start between the parties concerned under appropriate auspices aimed at establishing a just and durable peace in the Middle East.

2. *White House Years,* p. 1155. The aircraft pilot regarded it as a computer malfunction. J. F. terHorst and Colonel Ralph Albertazzie, *The Flying White House: The Story of Air Force One* (New York: Coward, McCann & Geoghegan, 1979), Chapter 9.
3. Resolution 339, adopted October 23, read as follows:

> *The Security Council*
> *Referring to* its resolution 338 (1973) of 22 October 1973,
>   1. *Confirms* its decision on an immediate cessation of all kinds of firing and of all military action, and urges that the forces of the two sides be returned to the positions they occupied at the moment the cease-fire became effective;
>   2. *Requests* the Secretary-General to take measures for immediate dispatch of United Nations observers to supervise the observance of the cease-fire between the forces of Israel and the Arab Republic of Egypt, using for this purpose the personnel of the United Nations now in the Middle East and first of all the personnel now in Cairo.

4. Richard Nixon, *RN: The Memoirs of Richard Nixon* (New York: Grosset & Dunlap, 1978), p. 938.
5. See *White House Years,* pp. 614–630.
6. See US Congress, House, Committee on Foreign Affairs, *Inquiring into the Military Alert Invoked on October 24, 1973,* Report No. 93–970 to Accompany H. Res. 1002, 93d Cong., 2d sess., 1974, which described the briefings in general terms and agreed with the Administration that sufficient public disclosure had been made.
7. Resolution 340, adopted on October 25, was as follows:

> *The Security Council*
> *Recalling* its resolutions 338 (1973) of 22 October and 339 (1973) of 23 October 1973,
> *Noting with regret* the reported repeated violations of the cease-fire in non-compliance with resolutions 338 (1973) and 339 (1973),
> *Noting with concern* from the Secretary-General's report that the United Nations military observers have not yet been enabled to place themselves on both sides of the cease-fire line,
>   1. *Demands* that immediate and complete cease-fire be observed and that the parties return to the positions occupied by them at 1650 hours GMT on 22 October 1973;
>   2. *Requests* the Secretary-General, as an immediate step, to increase the number of United Nations military observers on both sides;
>   3. *Decides* to set up immediately under its authority a United Nations Emergency Force to be composed of personnel drawn from States Members of the United Nations except the permanent members of the Security Council, and requests the Secretary-General to report within 24 hours on the steps taken to this effect;
>   4. *Requests* the Secretary-General to report to the Council on an urgent and continuing basis on the state of implementation of the present resolution, as well as resolutions 338 (1973) and 339 (1973);
>   5. *Requests* all Member States to extend their full co-operation to the United Nations in the implementation of the present resolution, as well as resolutions 338 (1973) and 339 (1973).

XIII
First Middle East Breakthrough

1. See William B. Quandt, *Decade of Decisions: American Policy Toward the Arab-Israeli Conflict, 1967–1976* (Berkeley: University of California Press, 1977), pp. 251–252; Edward R. F. Sheehan, *The Arabs, Israelis, and Kissinger: A Secret History of American Diplomacy in the Middle East* (New York: Reader's Digest Press, 1976), *passim.*
2. See *White House Years,* pp. 1246–1248 and Chapter XXVIII, notes 3 and 4, pp. 1493–1494.
3. See Richard Valeriani, *Travels with Henry* (Boston: Houghton Mifflin Co., 1979), pp. 249–251; Marvin Kalb and Bernard Kalb, *Kissinger* (Boston: Little, Brown & Co., 1974), pp. 505–506; John P. Wallach, "Mr. K as tourist . . . diplomat . . . negotiator," *Boston Sunday Herald Advertiser,* November 16, 1973, p. A24.

4. Miles Copeland, *The Game of Nations* (New York: Simon & Schuster, 1969), p. 177.
5. See Anwar el-Sadat, *In Search of Identity An Autobiography* (New York: Harper & Row, 1977), pp. 228–231; *White House Years*, pp. 1295–1297.
6. Kalb and Kalb, *Kissinger*, p. 509.
7. See Sheehan, *The Arabs, Israelis, and Kissinger*, pp. 51–61.

XIV
PERSIAN GULF INTERLUDE

1. See Norman Podhoretz, "AWACS: The Ghost of Presidents Past," *Washington Post,* April 26, 1981, p. C7.
2. See, e.g., Nixon's foreign policy report, *U.S. Foreign Policy for the 1970's: Building for Peace,* February 25, 1971, Part I, "The Nixon Doctrine."

XVI
TROUBLES WITH ALLIES

1. See the *Christian Science Monitor,* October 26, 1973.
2. Ibid., October 11 and October 30, 1973.
3. See the *New York Times,* October 15, 1973, p. 16.
4. *Christian Science Monitor,* October 29, 1973.
5. Paul Kemezis, "Common Market Said to Resist U.S. on Joint Statement," *New York Times,* November 9, 1973.
6. See Nan Robertson, "French Criticize U.S.–Soviet Role," *New York Times,* November 13, 1973.
7. Quoted in David Binder, "U.S. and 3 Allies Try to Heal Rift," *New York Times,* November 3, 1973.
8. Zbigniew Brzezinski, "The Mideast: Who Won?" *Washington Post,* November 21, 1973.
9. See Ezra Vogel, *Japan as Number One* (Cambridge, Mass.: Harvard University Press, 1979). See also Chie Nakane, *Japanese Society* (London: Weidenfeld and Nicolson, 1970).
10. See *White House Years*, pp. 336–340.
11. Masayoshi Ohira, *Brush Strokes: Moments from My Life* (Tokyo: Foreign Press Center, 1979), pp. 119–120.
12. Ibid., p. 118.

XVII
THE GENEVA CONFERENCE

1. The text of the Algiers Arab summit communiqué of November 28, 1973, may be found in the *New York Times,* November 29, 1973.
2. Marvin Kalb and Bernard Kalb, *Kissinger* (Boston: Little, Brown & Co., 1974), p. 520.
3. Ibid., p. 524.
4. Letter of invitation to UN Secretary-General Kurt Waldheim from the Foreign Ministers of the United States and the USSR, December 18, 1973:

> Dear Mr. Secretary-General:
> On 22 October 1973, the Security Council adopted Resolution 338 jointly sponsored by the Soviet Union and the United States which calls for negotiations to start between the parties concerned under appropriate auspices, aimed at establishing a just and durable peace in the Middle East. The Soviet Union and the United States have now been informed by the parties concerned of their readiness to participate in the peace conference which will begin in Geneva on 21 December. The conference should be convened under the auspices of the United Nations.
> The parties have agreed that the conference should be under the co-chairmanship of the Soviet Union and United States. The parties have also agreed that the question of other participants from the Middle East area will be discussed during the first stage of the conference.
> It is our hope that you will find it possible to participate in the opening phase of the conference, at which it is expected that the governments concerned will be represented by their respective foreign ministers and later by their specially appointed representatives with ambassadorial rank. We also hope that you can make available a representative who would keep you fully informed as the conference proceeds. Finally, we would also ap-

preciate it if the United Nations could make appropriate arrangements for the necessary conference facilities.

If as we hope you find it possible to participate, as co-chairmen the Soviet Union and the United States would appreciate it if you would agree to serve as convener of the conference and preside in the opening phase.

We request that you circulate this letter to members of the Security Council for their information. We believe it would be appropriate for the President of the Security Council to consult informally with the membership with a view to secure a favorable consensus of the Council.

Sincerely, . . .

5. MEMORANDUM FOR THE PRESIDENT   December 19, 1973
   FROM: Secretary Kissinger

As we look towards the opening of the Conference on the Mid East in Geneva of Friday, I thought you might want to have some perspectives of where we are and where we want to go. The strategy we developed in the wake of the Arab-Israeli war is unfolding largely as planned. We have built on the ceasefire and negotiating formula worked out during my October 20–22 trip to Moscow to stabilize the ceasefire on the Israeli-Egyptian front and to launch the negotiating process which will begin in Geneva. This is a historical development, the first time the Arabs and the Israelis will negotiate face to face in a quarter of a century. We have done this while enhancing our influence in the Arab world and reducing that of the USSR.

Egypt, Jordan, and Israel will participate. Syria, historically the great spoiler of the Mid East, has decided for the time being to stay away. Waldheim will be there in a limited role, taking some of the European and non-aligned pressure off our back while satisfying Israeli concern.

The Syrian non participation decision is very satisfactory for us — a blessing in disguise. We narrowly averted a situation in which all three Arab states would go to Geneva while Israel, in the midst of an election campaign, would decide not to participate because of Syrian intransigence in refusing to give prisoner lists.

But Asad, under pressure from the Baath Party, adhered rigidly to the position that there must be prior agreement on Syrian-Israeli disengagement before he attends the Conference. If he had dropped this condition, Israel would not have participated unless Syria first made available the list of POWs and allowed Red Cross visits. This was unlikely. If it was Israel that was seen balking, our whole effort and hard won renewal of confidence in the Arab world would have been set back; the likelihood of renewal of war increased; any chance of easing the *oil* embargo would have disappeared and further restrictions applied; and the possibilities for a Russian resurgence in the area enhanced.

In present circumstances: (1) we can now concentrate on agreement between Egypt, Jordan, and Israel; (2) the fact that there is a Geneva Conference will help achieve disengagement of forces in the next six weeks; (3) the Geneva Conference provides some, though not a decisive deterrent to a renewal of hostilities; (4) it provides Faisal an excuse to lift the *embargo,* hopefully sometime in January.

For these reasons, *we should let Asad stew in his own juice* for a while and let moderate Arab pressures and possibly some Soviet pressure build on him as he watchfully, with suspicion and mistrust, awaits developments at Geneva. We shall have to watch him carefully and *make clear to the Soviets* that they are contributing to another war in the Middle East by the substantial supplying of Syria, and that another war would have a serious effect on our relations. Intelligence indicators are beginning to point to a *possible renewal of fighting* on the Syrian-Israeli front, and we should make clear to the Russians they must pull out all the stops with their Syrian ally to prevent this. If it were to occur, Sadat could not stay out, and Hussein would be under even greater pressure than in the past to participate in a meaningful way, and once again the specter of a Soviet-American confrontation could face us.

As I look ahead, *I believe there is a real chance of an Egyptian-Israeli agreement on disengagement.* Sadat has bought our concept of a step by step phased approach. He has been consistent throughout — he decided he was going to Geneva no matter what.

The prospects between Jordan and Israel are also hopeful since they share a mutual interest in keeping out the Palestinian radicals from the West Bank. Both seem ready to explore ideas that will strengthen Hussein's authority in the West Bank as an insulation against radical inroads.

As to Syria, its participation later may prove possible if progress can be made behind the scenes with our help to resolve the POW issue and get agreement on the outlines of Syrian-Israeli disengagement. We thus in a way have the best of both worlds. Regardless of their non participation, their unwillingness to talk separately to the Israelis, and their distaste for partial solutions, our relations with Syria have improved. As a result of my talk with President Asad, we shall soon be establishing an Interests Section in Damascus. This should lead to a better dialogue and enable us to play a more effective role between Israel and Syria.

The Russian role will be tested anew. I do not believe they will be obstructive; neither will they be particularly helpful. We must meet the strong Arab desire that they deal with us directly; they want agreements to come largely as a result of US efforts. At the same time, we will have to keep the Russians in the picture and coordinate our efforts with them as much as possible.

As for Israel, the reality of their situation is beginning to sink in. If Mrs. Meir's Labor Party wins sufficient support, at least the door is open. Israel finds itself unable to afford another attritional war, and at the same time unable to score an overwhelmingly decisive victory. They are beginning to see this very unpleasant fact. Anguishingly, they seem to be moving towards serious negotiations. In this connection, *our continuing sea pipeline of arms is absolutely essential.* But a rightist victory could be seriously complicating to our peace efforts; we will know soon.

XVIII
THE FIRST SHUTTLE: EGYPTIAN-ISRAELI DISENGAGEMENT

1. Richard Nixon, *RN: The Memoirs of Richard Nixon* (New York: Grosset & Dunlap, 1978), p. 971.
2. See US Congress, Senate, Committee on Armed Services, *Transmittal of Documents from the National Security Council to the Chairman of the Joint Chiefs of Staff, Hearings,* 93d Cong., 2d sess., Part 1 (February 6, 1974) and Part 2 (February 20, 21, 1974).
3. J. F. terHorst and Colonel Ralph Albertazzie, *The Flying White House: The Story of Air Force One* (New York: Coward, McCann & Geoghegan, 1979).
4. On the adventures of the traveling press, see Richard Valeriani, *Travels with Henry* (Boston: Houghton Mifflin Co., 1979).
5. The Egyptian-Israeli Agreement on Disengagement of Forces in Pursuance of the Geneva Peace Conference, signed on January 18, 1974, at Kilometer 101 by the Chiefs of Staff of Egypt (Gamasy) and Israel (Elazar) and witnessed by UNEF Commander Siilasvuo, read as follows:

A. Egypt and Israel will scrupulously observe the ceasefire on land, sea, and air called for by the UN Security Council and will refrain from the time of the signing of this document from all military or paramilitary actions against each other.

B. The military forces of Egypt and Israel will be separated in accordance with the following principles:

1. All Egyptian forces on the east side of the Canal will be deployed west of the line designated as Line A on the attached map [see the map on p. 839]. All Israeli forces, including those west of the Suez Canal and the Bitter Lakes, will be deployed east of the line designated as Line B on the attached map.

2. The area between the Egyptian and Israeli lines will be a zone of disengagement in which the United Nations Emergency Force (UNEF) will be stationed. The UNEF will continue to consist of units from countries that are not permanent members of the Security Council.

3. The area between the Egyptian line and the Suez Canal will be limited in armament and forces.

4. The area between the Israeli line (Line B on the attached map) and the line designated as Line C on the attached map, which runs along the western base of the mountains where the Gidi and Mitla Passes are located, will be limited in armament and forces.

5. The limitations referred to in paragraphs 3 and 4 will be inspected by UNEF.

Existing procedures of the UNEF, including the attaching of Egyptian and Israeli liaison officers to UNEF, will be continued.

    6. Air forces of the two sides will be permitted to operate up to their respective lines without interference from the other side.

    C. The detailed implementation of the disengagement of forces will be worked out by military representatives of Egypt and Israel, who will agree on the stages of this process. These representatives will meet no later than 48 hours after the signature of this agreement at Kilometer 101 under the aegis of the United Nations for this purpose. They will complete this task within five days. Disengagement will begin within 48 hours after the completion of the work of the military representatives and in no event later than seven days after the signature of this agreement. The process of disengagement will be completed not later than 40 days after it begins.

    D. This agreement is not regarded by Egypt and Israel as a final peace agreement. It constitutes a first step toward a final, just and durable peace according to the provisions of Security Council Resolution 338 and within the framework of the Geneva Conference.

> For Egypt: [signed] Mohammad Abdel Ghani Al-Gamasi, Major General
> Chief of Staff of the Egyptian Armed Forces

> For Israel: [signed] David Elazar, Lieutenant General
> Chief of Staff of the Israel Defence Forces

Witness:

[signed] Ensio P. H. Siilasvuo, Lieutenant General
    Commander of the United Nations Emergency Force

6. The "United States proposal" on force limitations, signed by President Sadat and Golda Meir, read as follows:

    In order to facilitate agreement between Egypt and Israel and as part of that agreement, and to assist in maintaining scrupulous observance of the ceasefire on land, air, and sea the United States proposes the following:

    1. That within the areas of limited armaments and forces described in the agreement, there will be: (a) no more than eight reinforced battalions of armed forces and 30 tanks; (b) no artillery except anti-tank guns, anti-tank missiles, mortars and six batteries of howitzers of a caliber up to 122 mm. (M-3) with a range not to exceed 12 kilometers; (c) no weapons capable of interfering with the other party's flights over its own forces; (d) no permanent, fixed installations for missile sites. The entire force of each party shall not exceed 7,000 men.

    2. That to a distance 30 kilometers west of the Egyptian line and east of the Israeli line, there will be no weapons in areas from which they can reach the other line.

    3. That to a distance 30 kilometers west of the Egyptian line and east of the Israeli line, there will be no surface-to-air missiles.

    4. That the above limitations will apply as from the time the agreement on disengagement between Egypt and Israel is signed by the parties and will be implemented in accordance with the schedule of implementation of the basic agreement.

XIX
THE ENERGY CRISIS

1. US Cabinet Task Force on Import Control, *The Oil Import Question: A Report on the Relationship of Oil Imports to the National Security,* February 1970, pp. 124–125.
2. John M. Blair, *The Control of Oil* (New York: Vintage Books, 1978), p. 215.
3. Craufurd D. Goodwin, ed., *Energy Policy in Perspective: Today's Problems, Yesterday's Solutions* (Washington, D.C.: The Brookings Institution, 1981), Table A-4, p. 694.
4. See, e.g., David D. Newsom, "Our Arsenal Must Include Our Values," *Washington Star,* April 2, 1981. Newsom was the Assistant Secretary of State responsible for relations with Libya at the time of Qaddafi's takeover.
5. Blair, *The Control of Oil,* pp. 221 ff.

6. For example, at least twice in 1973 (once during the October war), James E. Akins, White House energy expert and subsequently Ambassador to Saudi Arabia, advised the oil companies to urge Saudi Arabia to link oil policy to a "satisfactory" change of American policy in the Arab-Israeli dispute. US Congress, Senate, Committee on Foreign Relations, *Multinational Oil Corporations and US Foreign Policy, Report by the Subcommittee on Multinational Corporations,* 93d Cong., 2d sess., January 2, 1975, p. 143.

7. See *New York Times,* November 23, 1973.

8. This was the sophomoric thesis of a segment of CBS television's news program *60 Minutes* — "The Kissinger-Shah Connection?" — broadcast on May 4, 1980, as well as of numerous columns by Jack Anderson in the *Washington Post,* e.g., December 5, 10, and 26, 1979. See also the even more spurious account in Jean-Jacques Servan-Schreiber, *The World Challenge* (New York: Simon & Schuster, 1981), pp. 51–56, 65–70.

9. US Senate, *Multinational Oil Corporations and US Foreign Policy,* p. 150; Edith Penrose, "The Development of Crisis," in Raymond Vernon, et al., "The Oil Crisis: In Perspective," *Daedalus* 104, no. 4 (Fall 1975): 51. See also Mohammed Reza Pahlavi, *Answer to History* (New York: Stein & Day, 1980), p. 97.

10. Blair, *The Control of Oil,* p. 264.

XX
ENERGY AND THE DEMOCRACIES

1. Quoted in Daniel Colard, "De la crise de l'énergie au dialogue 'Nord-Sud,' " *Studia Diplomatica* (Brussels), 28 (1975): 647; Richard P. Stebbins and Elaine P. Adam, eds., *American Foreign Relations 1974: A Documentary Record* (New York: New York University Press for the Council on Foreign Relations, 1977), p. 34.

2. Michel Jobert, *Mémoires d'avenir* (Paris: Bernard Grasset, 1974), p. 287; Michel Jobert, *L'Autre regard* (Paris: Bernard Grasset, 1976), p. 379.

3. William M. Brown and Herman Kahn, "Why OPEC is Vulnerable," *Fortune,* July 14, 1980: The decline was 25 percent measured in US dollars; in deutsche marks the real price of oil fell 40 percent; in yen 50 percent. "Moreover, during much of that five year period, almost every OPEC country offered substantial discounts from the official prices in order to increase its own exports."

4. See, e.g., the column by Rowland Evans and Robert Novak in the *Washington Post,* March 23, 1974. The French Ambassador denied the charge in a letter to the editor, *Washington Post,* March 26, 1974.

XXI
THE ROAD TO DAMASCUS: AN EXPLORATORY SHUTTLE

1. Moshe Dayan, *Story of My Life* (New York: William Morrow, 1976), p. 599.

2. Golda Meir, *My Life* (New York: G. P. Putnam's Sons, 1975), p. 455.

3. See Richard Valeriani, *Travels with Henry* (Boston: Houghton Mifflin Co., 1979), pp. 267–269.

XXII
THE DECLINE OF DÉTENTE: A TURNING POINT

1. As finally passed in the Trade Act, P.L. 93–618 of January 3, 1975, the key paragraph of the Jackson amendment read as follows:

SEC. 402. FREEDOM OF EMIGRATION IN EAST-WEST TRADE

(a) To assure the continued dedication of the United States to fundamental human rights, and notwithstanding any other provision of law, on or after the date of the enactment of this Act products from any nonmarket economy country shall not be eligible to receive non-discriminatory treatment (most-favored-nation treatment), such country shall not participate in any program of the Government of the United States which extends credits or credit guarantees or investment guarantees, directly or indirectly, and the President of the United States shall not conclude any commercial agreement with any such country, during the period beginning with the date on which the President determines that such country —

(1) denies its citizens the right or opportunity to emigrate;

(2) imposes more than a normal tax on emigration or on the visas or other documents required for emigration, for any purpose or cause whatsoever; or

(3) imposes more than nominal tax, levy, fine, fee, or other charge on any citizen as a consequence of the desire of such citizen to emigrate to the country of his choice,

and ending on the date on which the President determines that such country is no longer in violation of paragraph (1), (2), or (3).

2. See, e.g., "Clear It with Everett," *New York Times* editorial, June 3, 1969; and *White House Years,* pp. 150–155.
3. See Andrei D. Sakharov, *Sakharov Speaks* (New York: Vintage Books, 1974), pp. 211–215.
4. Andrei D. Sakharov, *Progress, Coexistence and Intellectual Freedom* (New York: New York Times Books, 1968).
5. Paula Stern, *Water's Edge: Domestic Politics and the Making of American Foreign Policy* (Westport, Conn.: Greenwood Press, 1979), p. 99.
6. See *White House Years,* pp. 199–215, 938–949.
7. Edward R. Fried, Alice M. Rivlin, Charles L. Schultze, and Nancy H. Teeters, *Setting National Priorities: The 1974 Budget* (Washington: The Brookings Institution, 1973), p. 339. Similar arguments were made by George W. Rathjens and Jack Ruina in "Trident: A Major Weapons Decision," *Washington Post,* September 22, 1973.
8. Fried, et al., *Setting National Priorities: The 1974 Budget,* p. 341.
9. *White House Years,* pp. 204–210.
10. Statement of Secretary of Defense Harold Brown before the Senate Foreign Relations Committee, July 9, 1979, in US Congress, Senate, *Hearings on the SALT II Treaty before the Committee on Foreign Relations,* 96th Cong., 1st sess., Part 1, p. 111.
11. *White House Years,* pp. 130–138.
12. Ibid., Chapter XIII, note 4, p. 1486.

XXIII
The Syrian Shuttle

1. See the *New York Times,* April 12 and 17, 1974.
2. Moshe Dayan, *Story of My Life* (New York: William Morrow, 1976), pp. 583–589.
3. The Agreement on Disengagement between Israeli and Syrian Forces, signed in Geneva on May 31, 1974, and the "United States proposal" on force limits, read as follows:

A. Israel and Syria will scrupulously observe the ceasefire on land, sea and air and will refrain from all military actions against each other, from the time of the signing of this document, in implementation of United Nations Security Council Resolution 338 dated October 22, 1973.

B. The military forces of Israel and Syria will be separated in accordance with the following principles:

1. All Israeli military forces will be west of the line designated as Line A on the map attached hereto, except in the Quneitra area, where they will be west of Line A-1 [see the map on p. 1100].

2. All territory east of Line A will be under Syrian administration, and Syrian civilians will return to this territory.

3. The area between Line A and the line designated as Line B on the attached map will be an area of separation. In this area will be stationed the United Nations Disengagement Observer Force established in accordance with the accompanying protocol.

4. All Syrian military forces will be east of the line designated as Line B on the attached map.

5. There will be two equal areas of limitation in armament and forces, one west of Line A and one east of Line B as agreed upon.

6. Air forces of the two sides will be permitted to operate up to their respective lines without interference from the other side.

C. In the area between Line A and Line A-1 on the attached map there shall be no military forces.

D. This agreement and the attached map will be signed by the military representatives of Israel and Syria in Geneva not later than May 31, 1974, in the Egyptian-Israeli Military Working Group of the Geneva Peace Conference under the aegis of the United Nations, after that group has been joined by a Syrian military representative, and with the participation of representatives of the United States and the Soviet Union. The precise delineation of a detailed map and a plan for the implementation of the disengagement of forces will be worked out by military representatives of Israel and Syria in the Egyptian-Israeli Military Working Group who will agree on the stages of this process. The Military Working Group described above will start their work for this purpose in Geneva under the aegis of the United Nations within 24 hours after the signing of this agreement. They will complete this task within five days. Disengagement will begin within 24 hours after the completion of the task of the Military Working Group. The process of disengagement will be completed not later than twenty days after it begins.

E. The provisions of paragraphs A, B and C shall be inspected by personnel of the United Nations comprising the United Nations Disengagement Observer Force under this agreement.

F. Within 24 hours after the signing of this agreement in Geneva all wounded prisoners of war which each side holds of the other as certified by the ICRC will be repatriated. The morning after the completion of the task of the Military Working Group, all remaining prisoners of war will be repatriated.

G. The bodies of all dead soldiers held by either side will be returned for burial in their respective countries within ten days after the signing of this agreement.

H. This agreement is not a peace agreement. It is a step toward a just and durable peace on the basis of Security Council Resolution 338 dated October 22, 1973.

For Israel: [signed] Major General Herzl Shafir

For Syria: [signed] Brig. General Hikmat al-Shihabi

Witness for the United Nations: [signed] Ensio Siilasvuo

United States Proposal

In order to facilitate agreement between Israel and Syria and in implementation of that agreement, and to assist in maintaining scrupulous observance of the ceasefire on land, air and sea, the United States proposes the following provisions:

(1) That the area of limitation in armament and forces west of Line A and east of Line B will be 10 kilometers in width. In each area, respectively, the following are permitted: (a) two brigades of armed forces, including 75 tanks and 36 pieces of short-range 122 mm artillery; and (b) the entire force of each party shall not exceed 6,000 men. The United Nations Disengagement Observer Force will inspect these provisions in the 10 kilometer zone.

(2) That in the area between 10 and 20 kilometers west of Line A and east of Line B: (a) there will be no artillery pieces whose range exceeds 20 kilometers; and (b) the total number of artillery pieces permitted is 162 with a range of not exceeding 20 kilometers; and (c) surface-to-air missiles will be stationed no closer than 25 kilometers west of Line A and east of Line B.

(3) Inspection of the provisions in paragraph 2 above will be performed by the U.S. aerial reconnaissance and the results will be provided to both sides.

(4) The area of separation between Lines A and B will not have any military forces. In the towns and villages in the area there will be stationed police forces of a size and character similar to those stationed in other Syrian towns and villages of comparable size.

(5) The United Nations Disengagement Observer Force will take over the positions in the area of separation on Mount Hermon. No military observation of any kind may be conducted in that area.

XXIV
The Last Hurrah

1. See the *Baltimore Sun*, May 18, 1974; the *Miami Herald*, May 19, 1974; the *Detroit Free Press*, May 19, 1974. The authors were James McCartney and Saul Friedman.

2. US Congress, Senate, Committee on Foreign Relations, *Hearings on the Role of Dr. Henry A. Kissinger in the Wiretapping of Certain Government Officials and Newsmen*, 93d Cong., 2d sess., 1974 (executive session of July 23, 1974, made public September 29, 1974), p. 227.

3. Nixon's letter to Fulbright, dated July 12, 1974, read as follows:

Dear Mr. Chairman:

Your letter of June 25 has been brought to my attention, and I welcome this opportunity to affirm my public statement of May 22, 1973, as quoted in your letter, and to add the following comments.

You appreciate, I am sure, the crucial importance of secrecy in negotiations with foreign countries. Without secret negotiations and essential confidentiality, the United States could not have secured a ceasefire in South Vietnam, opened relations with the People's Republic of China, or realized progress in our relations on the SALT negotiations with the Soviet Union.

The circumstances that led to my decision to direct the initiation of an investigative program in 1969 are described in detail in the May 22 statement. I ordered the use of the most effective investigative procedures possible, including wiretaps, to deal with certain critically important national security problems. Where supporting evidence was available, I personally directed the surveillance, including wiretapping, of certain specific individuals.

I am familiar with the testimony given by Secretary Kissinger before your Committee to the effect that he performed the function, at my request, of furnishing information about individuals within investigative categories that I established so that an appropriate and effective investigation could be conducted in each case. This testimony is entirely correct; and I wish to affirm categorically that Secretary Kissinger and others involved in various aspects of this investigation were operating under my specific authority and were carrying out my express orders.

Sincerely,

[signed] Richard Nixon

4. See note 2 above.
5. A US–Egyptian agreement on cooperation in the peaceful uses of nuclear energy was signed in Washington on June 29, 1981, and submitted to the Congress. See Barbara Crossette, "U. S. Nuclear Pact with Egypt Gains," *New York Times,* September 13, 1981.
6. Asad interview with Arnaud de Borchgrave, *Newsweek,* June 10, 1974.
7. Richard Nixon, *RN: The Memoirs of Richard Nixon* (New York: Grosset & Dunlap, 1978), p. 1015.
8. *White House Years,* pp. 1216–1222, 1229–1242.
9. Nixon, *RN,* p. 1024.
10. William Safire, "Under the Summit," *New York Times,* June 27, 1974.
11. *White House Years,* Chapter XXVIII.
12. William G. Hyland, *Soviet-American Relations: A New Cold War?* (Santa Monica: The Rand Corporation, Series in International Security and Arms Control, R–2763–FF/RC, May 1981), pp. 26–28.
13. *White House Years,* p. 548.
14. Nixon, *RN,* p. 1030.
15. See also my testimony on the SALT II treaty before the Senate Foreign Relations Committee, July 31, 1979, in US Congress, Senate, *Hearings on the SALT II Treaty before the Committee on Foreign Relations,* 96th Cong., 1st sess., Part 3, p. 169.

XXV
THE END OF THE ADMINISTRATION

1. On assertions that the Kennedys may have resorted to wiretapping in the 1960 campaign see Victor Lasky, *It Didn't Start with Watergate* (New York: Dial Press, 1977), pp. 38–45 and sources cited on p. 418. On the possible wiretapping of Nixon's campaign plane in 1968, see Nixon interview with James J. Kilpatrick in the *Washington Star News,* May 16, 1974, quoted, ibid., p. 215. Nixon was apparently told this by J. Edgar Hoover.
2. *White House Years,* pp. 1475–1476.
3. Gerald R. Ford, *A Time to Heal* (New York: Harper & Row, 1979), p. 21.
4. Other participants have slightly different recollections of the statement though they agree in substance. See Ford, *A Time to Heal,* pp. 21–22; Richard Nixon, *RN: The Memoirs of Richard Nixon* (New York: Grosset & Dunlap, 1978), p. 1066.
5. Carroll Kilpatrick, "Nixon Says He Won't Resign," *Washington Post,* August 7, 1974.
6. Nixon, *RN,* pp. 1076–1077; Bob Woodward and Carl Bernstein, *The Final Days* (New York: Simon & Schuster, 1976), pp. 422–424.

Index